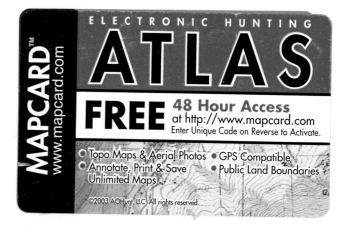

Colt Model 1911
Semi-Automatic Pistol

Adopted by the U.S. Ordnance Department in 1911, the Colt semi-automatic pistol was originally manufactured by Colt and the government's Springfield Armory. In 1917, with the US entry into World War I, the government contracted with Colt for one million pistols and contracts were signed for the production of a total of two million more pistols with Remington-UMC, North American Arms, Savage, Winchester, National Cash Register Co., Burroughs Adding Machine, Lamston Monotype, and Caron Bros. A total of 629,000 pistols were completed by the war's end in 1918. Production was resumed in 1924 with a series of design modifications introduced during the inter-war period resulting in the Model 1911 A1. From the onset of World War II until its end in 1945 Colt, Remington UMC, Remington-Rand, Ithaca, Singer, and Union Switch and Signal Company manufactured nearly 2 million M1911A1s.

NRA Perfect Condition is 100 percent original condition. This Colt 1911 has all original parts and commands the same price with or without the box. The frame and receiver are in perfect condition with no wear or damage. The checkering on the grip is in "as new" condition and the wood shows no wear, scratches, or stains.

NRA Good Condition ranges from 60 to 80 percent original condition. There are no replacement parts. This 1911 has worn, rounded edges on the frame with slight pitting and scratches. The bluing is thinning on the working surfaces and stampings show minor wear in areas. The checkering on the grips is slightly rounded with minor nicks. The wood is in good condition, not cracked or stained. A good condition pistol must be in safe working condition.

NRA Fair Condition ranges from 20 to 60 percent original condition. This Model 1911 is in well-worn condition with the frame retaining only 40 percent of its original finish. Some major and minor parts have been replaced and scratches and pitting from rust and corrosion are evident on the frame and slide. Serial numbers and other markings are shallow and difficult to identify. While the grips on this pistol are not badly scratched or soiled, they show worn checkering and several large and small dents. The gun must function and shoot properly.

Winchester Model 94

Winchester produced approximately 2,550,000 Model 94 lever action rifles between 1894 and 1962. The Model 94 was manufactured in both rifle and carbine versions with several configurations that included pistol- and straight-grip stocks, various grades of wood, and several different barrel lengths and magazine capacities. Crescent and shotgun style buttstocks and takedown barrels were also offered. The Model 94 was produced in 25-35, 30, 30-30, 32-40 and 38-55 calibers.

NRA Perfect Condition ranges from 95 to 100 percent original condition. This Model 94 shows very little use and looks in new condition with 96 percent of its original finish remaining. All parts are original and in excellent condition. There is no noticeable wear with the wood and metal showing no stains, scratches or nicks. The bluing is in near-perfect condition. The action functions smoothly and the rifle is in perfect working condition.

NRA Good Condition ranges from 60 to 80 percent original condition. There are no replacement parts. The gun has all original parts and shows no corrosive rusting or pitting. The edges of the action are slightly rounded and the bluing is beginning to wear thin on the working surfaces. The stampings show minor wear in areas. There are no broken parts and the stock fits smoothly to the metal with only minor nicking. The gun must be in safe working condition.

NRA Fair Condition ranges from 20 to 60 percent original condition. This Model 94 is in well-worn condition with some minor parts replaced or requiring restoration or adjustment. The serial numbers and descriptive stampings are shallow and hard to read. The wood is badly scratched and dented with evident repairs. There is corrosive pitting and scratches but the gun remains in safe firing condition.

Winchester Model 12

When introduced in 1912, the hammerless Model 12 slide-action shotgun was offered only in 20-guage with a 2½-inch chamber. In 1914 12- and 16-guage versions were introduced followed by a 28-guage in 1937. The Model 12 was available with various chokes and with walnut, straight or pistol grip stock and forearm. Winchester sold more than 1,900,000 Model 1912s during the shotgun's 51-year history.

NRA Perfect Condition is 100 percent original condition. This Model12 is in NIB condition and has not been previously sold at retail. The shotgun shows no signs of use and retains 100 percent of its original finish. All parts are original and in new condition.

NRA Good Condition ranges from 60 to 80 percent original condition. This gun has all original parts in good condition. There is no corrosive pitting or rusting and the action displays only slightly rounded edges. The gun retains 70 percent of its original finish with bluing beginning to wear on the working surfaces. The stock fits smoothly to the metal and has only minor nicking. The shotgun must be in good working order.

NRA Fair Condition ranges from 20 to 60 percent original condition. Showing a well-worn condition, this gun may require minor parts to be replaced or adjusted. The serial numbers and descriptive stamping are shallow and difficult to read. The wood is badly scratched and dented with evident repairs. Corrosive pitting and scratches in the metal, while considerable, do not render the gun unsafe.

Twenty-Sixth Edition
Completely Revised And Updated

Gun Trader's Guide

STOEGER PUBLISHING COMPANY
Accokeek, Maryland

Stoeger Publishing.
Great Outdoor Books Since 1925

**STOEGER PUBLISHING COMPANY
is a division of Benelli U.S.A.**
Benelli U.S.A.
Vice President and General Manager: Stephen Otway
Director of Brand Marketing and Communications:
Stephen McKelvain
Vice President of Sales/Strategic Marketing:
Jack Muety

Stoeger Publishing Company
President: Jeffrey K. Reh
Publisher: Jay Langston
Managing Editor: Harris J. Andrews
Design and Production Director: Cynthia T. Richardson
Photography Director: Alex Bowers
Imaging Specialist: William Graves
Editorial Assistant: Christine Lawton
Editor / Gun Trader's Guide: Stephen D. Carpenteri

© 1953, 1957, 1962, 1964, 1968, 1973, 1975, 1978, 1981,
1983, 1984, 1986, 1987, 1990, 1992, 1993, 1994, 1995,
1996, 1997, 1998, 1999, 2000, 2001, 2002, 2003
by Stoeger Publishing Company. All rights reserved.

ISBN:0-88317-245-3   BK0302
Library of Congress Control number: 2002110063

Manufactured in the United States of America

*Distributed to the book trade and to the sporting goods
trade by:*
Stoeger Industries, Stoeger Publishing Company
17603 Indian Head Highway, Suite 200
Accokeek, Maryland 20607-2501

Front cover: This edition's front cover features a selection of
popular collectible firearms: the U.S. Springfield Model 1903
rifle (top), a French-made Walther P-38 pistol (center), and the
Ruger Mark I Target autoloading pistol (at bottom). The classic
Springfield Model 1903 rifle was the U.S. Army's standard issue
rifle from 1903 until its replacement by the M-1 Garand during
WWII. The M1903, noted for accuracy and dependability, featured a Mauser-type bolt action firing the U.S. caliber .30-06
Springfield cartridge. The rifle pictured here was manufactured
in 1909 and features a case-hardened receiver and early pattern sight and handguard. Assembled from wartime German
parts at the French occupied Mauser-Werke in Oberndorf,
Germany, this "SVW" marked P-38 9mm automatic pistol has
roughly finished parts, pressed steel grips and a dark gray phosphate finish. Beginning in May 1945, some 50,000 of these P-
38s were assembled at Oberndorf over a two-year period and
many saw service in Algeria and Indochina. Manufactured by
Sturm, Ruger and Co., Inc., beginning in 1951, the Ruger Mark
I Target autoloading pistol became an instant classic and
launched the successful career of firearms designer William B.
Ruger. The Mark I Target fires .22 LR ammunition and features
a 10-shot magazine. The pistol shown here is fitted with a 6.88-
inch heavy tapered barrel and sold originally for $57.50.

Contributing Revisers:
C. Rodney James
Wayne Lehman

Introduction

The 25th edition of the *Gun Trader's Guide* provides the gun enthusiast with more specifications and photographs of collectible firearms than ever before. In the past 50 years, the *Gun Trader's Guide* has grown tremendously and now lists more than 6,000 firearms and variations.

The first edition of the *Gun Trader's Guide* contained some 1,360 listings accompanied by 100 illustrations. Now, after 25 revisions, the book has evolved into a complete catalog of the rifles, shotguns and handguns of the 20th century.

The current edition of the *Gun Trader's Guide* has been expanded to include more listings than ever before, with nearly 2,750 illustrations. Hundreds of thousands of gun buffs have made the *Gun Trader's Guide* their primary reference for identification and comparison of sporting, military and law enforcement firearms, including rare and unusual collectibles and commemoratives.

SIMPLIFIED STRUCTURE
Production Data Includes:
- *Specifications*
- *Variations of different models*
- *Dates of manufacture*
- *Current values*
- *Tabbed sections for user friendly reference*
- *Complete index of all firearms*

The format of the *Gun Trader's Guide* is simple and straightforward, listing thousands of firearms manufactured since 1900 in the United States and abroad. Most entries include complete specifications: Model number and name, caliber/gauge, barrel length, overall length, weight, distinguishing features, variations and the dates of manufacture (when they can be accurately determined). Many illustrative photos accompany the text to help the reader with identifications and comparisons.

The *Gun Trader's Guide* is revised annually to ensure that its wealth of information is both current and detailed. The principal features that contribute to the unique nature of this firearms reference guide include the extensive pictorial format and accompanying comprehensive specifications. It provides a convenient procedure for identifying vintage firearms while simultaneously determining and verifying their current value.

Values shown are based on national averages obtained by conferring with hundreds of different gun dealers and auctioneers, not by applying an arbitrary mathematical formula that could produce unrealistic figures. The values listed accurately reflect the prices being charged nationwide at the time of publication.

In some rare cases, however, like the Winchester Model 1873 "One of One Thousand" rifle or the Parker AA1 Special shotgun in 28 gauge, where very little (if any) trading took place, active gun collectors were consulted to obtain current market values.

ORGANIZATION OF LISTINGS

In the early editions of the *Gun Trader's Guide*, firearms were frequently organized chronologically by date of production within manufacturers' listings because firearms aficionados know that many gunmaking companies used the date that a particular model was introduced as the model number. For example, the Colt U.S. Model 1911 semiautomatic pistol was introduced in 1911; the French Model 1936 military rifle was introduced in 1936; and the Remington Model 32 shotgun debuted in 1932. However, during the first quarter of the 20th century, gunmakers began assigning names and numbers that did not relate to the year that gun was introduced. As these recent models and their variations multiplied through the years, it became increasingly difficult to track them by date especially for less-experienced collectors

Some Winchester and Remington firearms are grouped differently in this edition. For example, The Winchester Model 1894, in its many variations, has been produced since 1894 and is still being manufactured under "Model 94" by U.S. Repeating Arms Co. In general, Winchester used the year of introduction to name its firearms; that is, Model 1890, 1892, 1894, 1895, etc. Shortly after World War I, Winchester dropped the first two digits and listed the models as 90, 92, 94, 95 etc. Later, guns were given model numbers that had no relation to the date of manufacture. Marlin and several other manufacturers used a similar approach in handling model designations.

Consequently, Winchester rifles are grouped alphanumerically in two different groups: Early Winchesters, manufactured before 1920 under the 4-digit model/date designations; and those manufactured after 1920 with their revised model format designations. If any difficulty is encountered in locating a particular model, the different models and their variations are cross-referenced in the index.

Past readers have reported difficulty in finding certain Remington rifles. In this edition, Remington rifles have been grouped according to action type: That is, single-shot rifles, slide actions, autoloaders, etc. Our surveys revealed this to be the easiest way to locate a particular firearm. Again, use the index if difficulty in finding a specific model is encountered.

In researching data for this edition, we found that not all

manufacturers' records were available and some information was unobtainable. For example, many early firearms production records were destroyed in a fire that ravaged the Winchester plant. Some manufacturers' records have simply been lost, or were just not maintained accurately. These circumstances resulted in some minor deviations in the presentation format of certain model listings. For example, production dates may not be listed when manufacturing records are unavailable. As an alternative, approximate dates of manufacture may be listed to reflect the "availability" of guns from the manufacture or distributor. These figures may represent disposition dates indicating when that particular model was shipped to a distributor or importer. Frequently, especially with foreign manufacturers, production records are unavailable. Therefore, availability information is often based on importation records, that reflect domestic distribution only.

This is simply to advise the reader of the procedure and policy used regarding these published dates and further establish the distinction between "production dates," which are based on manufacturers' records and "availability dates," which are based on distribution records in the absence of recorded production data.

To further ensure that we have the most accurate information available, we encourage and solicit the users of the

Gun Trader's Guide to communicate with our research staff at the Stoeger offices and forward any verifiable information they may have, especially in relation to older, out-of-production models.

CAUTION TO READERS

To comply with new Federal regulations, all manufacturers who produce firearms intended for disposition to the general public and designed to accept large capacity ammunition feeding devices are required to redesign those models to limit their capacities to 10 rounds or less, or discontinue production or importation. This amendment to the Gun Control Act of 1968 prohibits the manufacture, transfer or possession of all such devices manufactured after October 13, 1994. The grandfather clause of this amendment exempts all such devices lawfully possessed at the time the legislation became law. These pre-ban arms (manufactured before October 13, 1994) may therefore be bought, sold or traded without any additional restrictions imposed by this law.

All post-ban feeding devices must meet the new requirements. For the purposes of this book models previously designed to accept high capacity feeding devices will be listed at their original specifications and capacities if only the feeding device was modified to reduce that capacity.

Regarding shotguns, the reader should be aware that shotgun barrels must be 18 inches or longer except when used by military or law enforcement personnel. A special permit from the Bureau of Alcohol, Tobacco and Firearms is required for all others.

ACKNOWLEDGEMENTS

The publisher wishes to express special thanks to the many collectors, dealers, manufacturers, shooting editors and other industry professionals who provide product information and willingly shared their knowledge in making this the best *Gun Trader's Guide* ever.

Also, our appreciation is extended to the firearm firms and distributors' public relations and production personnel, and all the research personnel who we work with throughout the year. We are especially grateful to everyone for their assistance and cooperation in compiling information for the *Gun Trader's Guide* and for allowing us to reproduce photographs and illustrations of their firearms.

Finally, our thanks to all the dedicated readers who take the time to write us with comments, suggestions and queries about various firearms. We appreciate your input and encourage you to continue.

Send your comments or suggestions to: Editor, Gun Trader's Guide, Stoeger publishing Company, 17603 Indian Head Highway, Suite 200, Accokeek, MD 20607-2501.

Stoeger Publishing

NEW FOR 2003

SHOOTER'S BIBLE 2004

BASSING BIBLE 2004

CONSERVING WILD AMERICA

CONSERVING WILD AMERICA

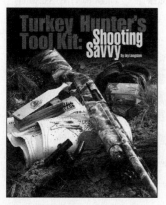
TURKEY HUNTER'S TOOL KIT: SHOOTING SAVVY

ULTIMATE BASS BOATS

HUNTING WHITETAILS EAST & WEST

WILD ABOUT GAME BIRDS
WILD ABOUT FRESH WATER FISH

GUN TRADER'S GUIDE

MORE BOOKS FROM STOEGER PUBLISHING!

ARCHER'S BIBLE 2004

ARCHER'S BIBLE PRESENTS:
THE BOWHUNTING GUIDE

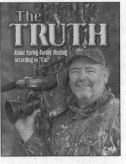
THE TRUTH ABOUT SPRING
TURKEY HUNTING
ACCORDING TO "CUZ"

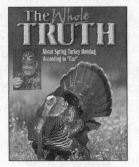
THE WHOLE TRUTH ABOUT
SPRING TURKEY HUNTING
ACCORDING TO "CUZ"

HECKLER & KOCH:
ARMORERS OF THE
FREE WORLD

MODERN BERETTA
FIREARMS

P-38 AUTOMATIC PISTOL

COWBOY ACTION
SHOOTING

SPORTING COLLECTIBLES

THE ULTIMATE IN
RIFLE ACCURACY

THE WALTHER
HANDGUN STORY

ANTIQUE GUNS

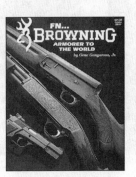
COMPLETE GUIDE TO
CLASSIC RIFLES

FN BROWNING ARMORER
TO THE WORLD

EXPLODED VIEWS
FIREARMS DISASSEMBLY
WITH EXPLODED VIEWS

GUNSMITHING AT HOME

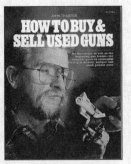
HOW TO BUY &
SELL USED GUNS

COMPLETE GUIDE TO
MODERN RIFLES

COMPLETE GUIDE TO
SERVICE HANDGUNS

SPANISH HANDGUNS

6

How To Use This Guide

Are you buying or selling a used gun? Perhaps you want to establish the value of a favorite gun in your collection. The gun enthusiast inevitably turns to the *Gun Trader's Guide* to determine specifications, date of manufacture and the value of a specific firearm. Opening the book, he silently asks two questions: "How much will I be able to get (or expect to pay) for a particular gun?" and, "How was that price determined?"

Prices contained in this book are "retail;" that is, the price the consumer may expect to pay for a similar item. However, many variables must be considered when buying or selling any used gun. Scarcity, demand, geographical location, the buyer's position and the gun's condition govern the selling price of a particular gun. Sentiment often affects the value of an individual's gun, but can be neither logically cataloged nor effectively marketed.

To illustrate how the price of a particular gun may fluctuate, let us consider the popular Winchester Model 94 and see what its value might be.

The Model 1894 (94) is a lever-action, solid-frame repeater. Round or octagon barrels of 26 inches were standard when the rifle was first introduced in 1894. However, half-octagon barrels were available for a slight increase in price. Various magazine lengths were also available.

Fancy-grade versions in all Model 94 calibers were available with 26-inch round, octagon or half-octagon nickel steel barrels. This grade used a checkered fancy walnut pistol grip stock and forearm, and was available with either shotgun, or rifle-type butt plates.

In addition, Winchester produced this model in carbine-style with a saddle ring on the left side of the receiver. The carbine had a 20-inch round barrel and full or half magazine. Some carbines were supplied with standard-grade barrels while others were made of nickel steel. Trapper models were also available with shortened 14-, 16- and 18-inch barrels.

In later years, the Rifle and Trapper models were discontinued and only the carbine remained. Eventually, the saddle ring was eliminated from this model and the carbine butt-stock was replaced with a shotgun-type butt stock and shortened forend.

After World War II, the finish on Winchester Model 94 carbines changed to strictly hot caustic bluing; thus, prewar models usually demand a pre-mium over postwar models.

Then in 1964, beginning with serial number 2,700,000, the action on Winchester Model 94s was redesigned for easier manufacturing. Many collectors and firearm enthusiasts considered this design change to be inferior to former models.

Whether this evaluation is correct or not is not the issue; the justification for a price increase of pre-1964 models was that they were no longer available. This diminished availability placed them immediately in the "scarce" class and made them increasingly more desirable to collectors.

Shortly after the 1964 transition, Winchester started producing Model 94 commemoratives in virtually endless numbers, further adding to the confusion of the concept of "limited production." Increased availability adversely affected the annual appreciation and price stability of these commemorative models. The negative response generated by this marketing practice was further stimulated when the Winchester Company was sold in the 1980s and the long-established name of this firearms manufacturer was changed to U.S. Repeating Arms Co. This firm still manufactured the Model 94 in both standard

Carbine and Big Bore models, and later introduced its Angle-Eject model to allow for the mounting of telescopic sights directly over the action.

With the above facts in mind, let's explore the the the *Gun Trader's Guide* to establish the approximate value of your particular Winchester Model 94. We will assume that you recently inherited a rifle that has the inscription *Winchester Model 94* on the barrel. Turn to the Rifle Section and look under the Ws until you find Winchester. The Contents Section will also indicate where the Winchester Rifle Section begins. The index (in the back of the book) is another possible means of locating your rifle.

The listings in the *Gun Trader's Guide* are arranged within each manufacturer's entry, first by model numbers in consecutive numerical order followed by model names in alphabetical order.

At first glance, you realize there are two model designations that may apply — the original designation (Model 1894), or the revised shorter designation, Model 94. Which of these designations applies to your recently acquired Winchester?

The first step is to try to match the appearance of your model with an illustration in the book. They may all look similar at first, but close evaluation and careful attention to detail will enable you to eliminate the models that are not applicable. Further examination of your gun might reveal a curved or crescent-shaped butt plate. By careful observation of your gun's char-

acteristics and close visual comparison of the photographic examples, you may logically conclude that your gun is the Winchester Model 94 Lever Action Rifle.

You have now tentatively determined your model, but, to be sure, you should read through the specifications and further establish that the barrel on the pictured rifle is 26 inches long, round, octagonal, or

---

When the dealer offers you about half of what you expected, you are shocked!

---

half-octagonal. Upon measuring, you find that your rifle barrel is approximately 26 inches long, maybe a trifle under, and it is obviously round. *(Please note that the guns in the Gun Trader's Guide are not always shown in proportion to one another; that is, a carbine barrel might not appear shorter than a rifle.)*

Additionally, your rifle is marked .38-55 (the caliber designation). The caliber offerings in the listed specifications include .38-55, so you are further convinced that this is your gun. You may read on to determine that this rifle was manufactured from 1894 to 1937. After that date, only the shorter-barreled carbine was offered by Winchester, and then only in calibers .25-35, .30-30, and .32 Special.

At this point you know you have a Winchester Model 94 rifle manufactured before World War II. You read the value as $1550 and decide to take the rifle to your local dealer

to initiate the sale.

Here are some of the scenarios you may encounter:

SCENARIO I

If the rifle is truly in excellent condition — that is, if it retains at least 95 percent of its original finish on both the metal and wood and has a perfect bore — then the gun does have a retail value of $1550. However, the dealer is in business to make some profit. If he pays you $1550 for the gun, he will have to charge more than this when he sells it in order to realize a reasonable profit. If more than the fair market value is charged, then either the gun will not sell, or someone will pay more than the gun is worth. Therefore expect a reputable dealer to offer you less than the published retail price for the gun. However, the exact amount will vary. For example, if this dealer already has a dozen or so of the same model on his shelf and they do not sell well, his offer will probably be considerably lower. On the other hand, if the dealer does not have any of this model in stock and knows several collectors who want it, chances are his offer will be considerably higher.

SCENARIO II

Perhaps you overlooked the rifle's condition. Suppose the gun apparently functions flawlessly but not much of the original bluing is left. There are several shiny bare-metal spots mixed with a brown patina over the remaining metal. Also, much of the original varnish on the wood has been worn off from extended use. Consequently,

While any gun's exterior condition is a big factor in determining its value, internal parts also play an important role in pricing. Photograph courtesy of Browning Firearms, 2000

your rifle is not truly in "excellent" condition and you will have to settle for a lesser value than shown in this book.

SCENARIO III

Your Winchester Model 94 rifle looks nearly new, as if it were just out of the box, and the rifle works perfectly. Therefore, you are convinced that the dealer is going to pay you full value (less a reasonable profit of between 25 percent and 35 percent). When the dealer offers you about half of what you expected, you are shocked!

Although the rifle looks new to you, the experienced dealer has detected that the gun has been refinished. Perhaps you did not notice the rounding of the formerly sharp edges on the receiver, or the slight funneling of some screw holes — all of which are a dead giveaway that the rifle has been refinished. If so, your rifle is not in excellent condition as you originally assumed, and is, therefore,

worth less than "book" value.

A knowledgeable gun dealer will check the rifle to determine that it functions properly, and the condition of interior parts may also be a factor in determining the value of any firearm.

Now, if you are somewhat of an expert and know for certain that your rifle has never been refinished or otherwise tampered with, there is still at least 95 percent of its original finish left, and you believe you have a firearm that is worth full book value, understand that a dealer will *still* offer you from 25 percent to 50 percent less if he is overstocked with this model.

One alternative is to advertise your gun in a local newspaper and sell the firearm directly to a private individual. However, this approach may prove both frustrating and expensive. In addition, there may be federal and local restrictions on the sale of firearms in your area.

If you experience such complications, chances are the next

time you have a firearm to sell you will be more than happy to take it to a dealer and let him make his fair share of profit.

CONDITION

The condition of a firearm is an important factor in determining its value. In some rare and unusual models, a variation in condition from "Excellent" to "Very Good" can mean a value difference of several thousand dollars. Therefore, you must be able to determine the gun's condition before you can accurately evaluate the value of the firearm.

Several sets of standards are available, but the National Rifle Association Standards of Condition of Modern Firearms are probably the most popular. In recent years, condition has been established by the percentage of original finish remaining on the wood and metal of the firearm. Let's see how these standards stack up against each other.

EXCELLENT

When a collectible firearm has been expertly refinished to "Excellent" condition, a rule of thumb is to deduct 50 percent from the value indicated in this book. If poorly done, deduct 80 percent.

For the purpose of assigning comparative values as a basis for trading, firearms listed in this book are assumed to be in "excellent" condition if they have 95 percent or more remaining original finish, no noticeable marring of wood or metal and bores with no pits or rust.

To the novice, this means a

practically new gun, almost as though you had removed it from the factory carton. The trained eye, however, will see the difference between "new" or "mint" condition, and "excellent."

VERY GOOD

Any other defects, regardless of how minor, will lower the value of the subject firearm below those listed in this book. For example, if more than 5 percent of the original finish is gone and there are minor surface dents or scratches — regardless of how small — the gun is no longer in "excellent" condition. Rather, it is considered to be in "very good" condition, provided the gun is in perfect working order. In this state, and despite the minor defects, the gun will still look relatively new to the uninitiated gun buyer.

GOOD

If the gun is in perfect working condition and functions properly but has minor wear on working surfaces, (perhaps some bad scratches on the wood or metal, etc.), the gun takes on the condition of "good," one grade below "very good," according to the NRA standards. Again, the price in this book for that particular firearm must be lowered more to reflect its true value.

The two remaining NRA conditions fall under the headings of "fair" and "poor," respectively.

Previous editions of Gun Trader's Guide gave multiplication factors to use for firearms in other than "excellent" condition. These factors are listed below, but please be aware that they are not infallible. They are only one rough means of establishing a value or a gun.

For guns in other than "excellent" condition, multiply the price in this book for the model in question by the following appropriate factors:

Multiplication Factors For Guns Not In Excellent Condition

Condition	X Factor
Mint or New (NiB)	1.25
Excellent (Ex)	1.00
Very Good	.85
Good (Gd)	.68
Fair	.35
Poor	.15

Remember, the word "guide" in Gun Trader's Guide should be taken literally. This book is meant to be a reference only and is not the gospel of the collectible gun trade. We sincerely hope, however, that you find this publication helpful when you decide to buy or sell a used or collectible firearm.

Also, keep in mind that gun values vary from region to region. For this reason, we recommend that you attend gun shows and actions near you to develop a better understanding of gun values and pricing in your part of the country

NATIONAL RIFLE ASSOCIATION STANDARDS OF CONDITION

- **New:** *Not previously sold at retail. In same condition as current factory production.*

- **New, discontinued:** *Same as New, but a discontinued model.*

- **Perfect:** *In new condition in every respect, sometimes referred to as mint.*

- **Excellent:** *New condition. Used very little, no noticeable marring of wood or metal, bluing perfect (except at muzzle or sharp edges).*

- **Very Good:** *In perfect working condition, no appreciable wear on working surfaces, no corrosion or pitting, only minor surface dents or scratches.*

- **Good:** *In safe working condition, minor wear on working surfaces. No broken parts, no corrosion or pitting that will interfere with proper functioning.*

- **Fair:** *In safe working condition but well worn, perhaps requiring replacement of minor parts or other adjustments that should be reported by the seller. No rust, but may have corrosion pits that do not render the gun unsafe or inoperable.*

- **Poor:** *Badly worn, rusty and battered, perhaps requiring major adjustment or repairs to return to operating condition.*

Contents

Colt Model 1911

Winchester Model 94 Traditional

Winchester Model 12 Standard

Twenty-Sixth Edition
GUN TRADER'S GUIDE

Handguns

NOTE: *The following abbreviations are used throughout the Handgun section: DA = Double Action; SA = Single Action; LR = LR; WMR = Winchester Magnum Rimfire; adj. = Adjustable; avail. = Available; bbl., = Barrel; disc. = Discontinued; TT = Target Trigger; TH = Target Hammer*

Accu-Tek Model AT-.380

Accu-Tek Model BL-9

AA ARMS — Monroe, North Carolina

AP-9 SERIES
Semiautomatic recoil-operated pistol w/polymer integral grip/frame design. Fires from a closed bolt. Caliber: 9mm Parabellum. 10- or 20*-shot magazine, 3- , 5- or 11-inch bbl., 11.8 inches overall w/5-inch bbl., Weight: 3.5 lbs. Fixed blade, protected post front sight adjustable for elevation, winged square notched rear. Matte phosphate/blue or nickel finish. Checkered polymer grip/frame. Made 1988 to date.

AP9 model
(pre-94 w/ventilated bbl., shroud . . **NiB $425 Ex $325 Gd $210**
AP9 Mini model
(post-94 w/o bbl., shroud) . . . . **NiB $220 Ex $200 Gd $125**
AP9 Target model
(pre-94 w/11-inch bbl.) . . . . **NiB $420 Ex $350 Gd $240**
Nickel finish, add. $25

ACCU-TEK — Chino, California

MODEL AT-9 AUTO PISTOL
Caliber: 9mm Para. 8-shot magazine, Double action only. 3.2-inch bbl., 6.25 inches overall. Weight: 28 oz. Fixed blade front sight, adj. rear w/3-dot system. Firing pin block with no external safety. Stainless or black over stainless finish. Checkered black nylon grips. Announced 1992, but made1995 to date.
Satin stainless model . . . . **NiB $260 Ex $200 Gd $125**
Matte black stainless . . . . **NiB $231 Ex $185 Gd $126**

MODEL AT-25 AUTO PISTOL
Similar to Model AT380 except chambered .25 ACP w/7-shot magazine, Made 1992-96.
Lightweight w/aluminum frame . . . . . **NiB $150 Ex $125 Gd $75**
Bright stainless (disc. 1991) . . . . **NiB $163 Ex $131 Gd $89**
Satin stainless model . . . . **NiB $157 Ex $126 Gd $86**
Matte black stainless . . . . **NiB $151 Ex $120 Gd $81**

MODEL AT-32 AUTO PISTOL
Similar to Model AT-.380 except chambered .32 ACP. Made 1990 to date.
Lightweight w/aluminum
Frame (disc. 1991) . . . . **NiB $125 Ex $100 Gd $68**
Satin stainless model . . . . **NiB $175 Ex $150 Gd $100**
Matte black stainless . . . . **NiB $175 Ex $150 Gd $100**

MODEL AT-40 DA AUTO PISTOL
Caliber: .40 S&W. Seven-shot magazine, 3.2-inch bbl., 6.25 inches overall. Weight: 28 oz. Fixed blade front sight, adj. rear w/3-dot system. Firing pin block with no external safety. Stainless or black over stainless finish. Checkered black nylon grips. Announced 1992, but made 1995-96.
Satin stainless model . . . . **NiB $260 Ex $195 Gd $135**
Matte black stainless . . . . **NiB $260 Ex $195 Gd $135**

MODEL AT-380 AUTO PISTOL
Caliber: .380 ACP. Five-shot magazine, 2.75-inch bbl., 5.6 inches overall. Weight: 20 oz. External hammer w/slide safety. Grooved black composition grips. Alloy or stainless frame w/steel slide. Black, satin aluminum or stainless finish. Made 1992 to date.
Standard alloy frame (disc. 1992) . . . **NiB $156 Ex $125 Gd $85**
Satin stainless model . . . . **NiB $249 Ex $200 Gd $140**
Matte black stainless . . . . **NiB $249 Ex $200 Gd $140**

Accu-Tek HC-380SS

MODELS BL-9, BL 380 . . . . **NiB $175 Ex $140 Gd $95**
Ultra compact DAO semiautomatic pistols. Calibers: .380 ACP, 9mm Para. 5-shot magazine, 3-inch bbl., 5.6 inches overall. Weight: 24 oz. Fixed sights. Carbon steel frame and slide w/black finish. Polymer grips. Made 1997 to date.

MODELS CP-9, CP-40, CP-45
Compact, double action only, semiautomatic pistols. Calibers: 9mm Parabellum, .40 S&W, .45 ACP, 8-, 7- or 6-shot magazine, 3.2-inch bbl., 6.25 inches overall. Weight: 28 oz. Fixed blade front sight, adj. rear w/3-dot system. Firing-pin block with no external safety. Stainless or black over stainless finish. Checkered black nylon grips. Made 1997 to date.
Black stainless model . . . . **NiB $220 Ex $165 Gd $115**
Satin stainless model . . . . **NiB $220 Ex $165 Gd $115**

MODEL HC-380SS AUTO PISTOL . . . . **NiB $250 Ex $200 Gd $150**
Caliber: .380 ACP. 13-shot magazine, 2.75-inch bbl., 6 inches overall. Weight: 28 oz. External hammer w/slide safety. Checkered black composition grips. Stainless finish. Made 1993 to date.

ACTION ARMS — Philadelphia, Pennsylvania
See also listings under CZ pistols. Action Arms stopped importing firearms in 1994.

AT-84 DA AUTOMATIC PISTOL . . . **NiB $545 Ex $475 Gd $425**
Caliber: 9mm Para. 15-shot magazine, 4.75-inch bbl., 8 inches overall. Weight: 35 oz. Fixed front sight, drift-adj. rear. Checkered walnut grips. Blued finish. Made in Switzerland 1987-89.

AT-84P DA AUTO PISTOL . . . . **(SRP) NiB $660 Ex $525 Gd $340**
Compact version of the Model AT-84. Only a few prototypes were manufactured in 1985. No resale value established.

AT-88P DA AUTO PISTOL . . . . **(SRP) NiB $623 Ex $498 Gd $339**
Compact version of the AT-88S w/3.7-inch bbl. Only a few prototypes of this model were manufactured in 1985. No resale value established. Note: The AT-88 pistol series was later manufactured by Sphinx-Muller as the AT-2000 series.

AT-88S DA AUTOMATIC PISTOL . . . **NiB $550 Ex $450 Gd $295**
Calibers: 9mm Para. or .41 Action Express, 10-shot magazine, 4.6-inch bbl., 8.1 inches overall. Weight: 35.3 oz. Fixed blade front sight, adj. rear. Checkered walnut grips. Imported 1989-91.

ADVANTAGE ARMS — St. Paul, Minnesota

MODEL 422 . . . . **NiB $170 Ex $130 Gd $80**
Hammerless, top-break, 4-bbl., derringer w/rotating firing pin. Calibers: .22 LR and .22 Mag., 4-cartridge capacity, 2.5 inch bbl., 4.5 inches overall. Weight: 15 oz. Fixed sights. Walnut grips. Blued, nickel or PDQ matte black finish. Made 1985-87.

S. A. ALKARTASUNA FABRICA DE ARMAS — Guernica, Spain

"RUBY" AUTOMATIC PISTOL. . . . . **NiB $270 Ex $250 Gd $150**
Caliber: .32 Automatic (7.65mm). Nine-shot magazine, 3.63-inch bbl., 6.38 inches overall. Weight: About 34 oz. Fixed sights. Blued finish. Checkered wood or hard rubber grips. Made 1917-22. Note: Mfd. by a number of Spanish firms, the Ruby was a secondary standard service pistol of the French Army in World Wars I and II. Specimens made by Alkartasuna bear the "Alkar" trademark.

Action Arms AT-84 with Prototype of Model AT-84P in background

AMERICAN ARMS — Kansas City, Missouri

BISLEY SA REVOLVER . . . . **NiB $425 Ex $340 Gd $250**
Umberti reproduction of Colt's Bisley. Caliber: .45 LC. Six-shot cylinder, 4.75-, 5.5- or 7.7-inch bbl., Case-hardened steel frame. Fixed blade front sight, grooved top strap rear. Hammer block safety. Imported 1997 to date.

CX-22 DA AUTOMATIC PISTOL
Similar to Model PX-.22 except w/8-shot magazine, 3.33-inch bbl., 6.5 inches overall. Weight: 22 oz. Made 1990 to 1995.
Standard w/chrome
Slide (disc. 1990). . . . . **NiB $200 Ex $155 Gd $100**
Classic model . . . . **NiB $181 Ex $145 Gd $99**

EP-380 DA AUTOMATIC PISTOL . . . . **NiB $450 Ex $425 Gd $390**
Caliber: .380 Automatic. Seven-shot magazine, 3.5-inch bbl., 6.5 inches overall. Weight: 25 oz. Fixed front sight, square notch adj. rear. Stainless finish. Checkered wood grips. Made 1989-91.

ESCORT DA AUTO PISTOL . . . . **NiB $270 Ex $200 Gd $110**
Caliber: .380 ACP. 7-shot magazine, 3.38-inch bbl., 6.13 inches overall. Weight: 19 ounces. Fixed, low-profile sights. Stainless steel frame, slide, and trigger. Nickel-steel bbl., Soft polymer grips. Loaded chamber indicator. Made 1995-97 .

MATEBA AUTO REVOLVER
Unique combination action design allows both slide and cylinder to recoil together causing cylinder to rotate. Single or double action. Caliber: .357 Mag. Six-shot cylinder, 4- or 6-inch bbl., 8.77 inches overall w/4-inch bbl., Weight: 2.75 lbs. Steel/alloy frame. Ramped blade front sight, adjustable rear. Blue finish. Smooth walnut grips. Imported 1997 to date.
Mateba model (w/4-inch bbl.) . . . . **NiB $1031 Ex $825 Gd $561**
Mateba model (w/6-inch bbl.) . . . . **NiB $1094 Ex $875 Gd $595**

P-98 DA AUTOMATIC PISTOL . . . . **NiB $170 Ex $140 Gd $100**
Caliber: .22 LR. Eight-shot magazine, 5-inch bbl., 8.25 inches overall. Weight: 25 oz. Fixed front sight, square notch adj. rear. Blued finish. Serrated black polymer grips. Made 1989-96.

**American Arms
Regulator Deluxe Model**

**American Derringer
Model 1**

**American Derringer
Model 3**

PK-22 DA AUTOMATIC PISTOL . . . NiB $165 Ex $140 Gd $115
Caliber: .22 LR. Eight-shot magazine, 3.33-inch bbl., 6.33 inches
overall. Weight: 22 oz. Fixed front sight, V-notch rear. Blued finish.
Checkered black polymer grips. Made 1989-96.

PX-22 DA AUTOMATIC PISTOL . . . NiB $165 Ex $140 Gd $115
Caliber: .22 LR. Seven-shot magazine, 2.75-inch bbl., 5.33 inches
overall. Weight: 15 oz. Fixed front sight, V-notch rear. Blued finish.
Checkered black polymer grips. Made 1989-96.

PX-25 DA AUTOMATIC PISTOL . . . NiB $175 Ex $140 Gd $125
Same general specifications as the Model PX-22 except chambered
for .25 ACP. Made 1991-92.

REGULATOR SA REVOLVER
Similar in appearance to the Colt Single-Action Army. Calibers: .357
Mag., .44-.40, .45 Long Colt. Six-shot cylinder, 4.75- or 7.5-inch bbl.,
blade front sight, fixed rear. Brass trigger guard/backstrap on Standard
model. Casehardened steel on Deluxe model. Made 1992 to date.
Standard model . . . . NiB $320 Ex $250 Gd $155
Standard combo set

(cont'd.) REGULATOR SA REVOLVER
(45 LC/.45 ACP & .44-.40/.44 Spec.) . . . . NiB $345 Ex $270 Gd $190
Deluxe model . . . . .NiB $313 Ex $250 Gd $170
Deluxe combo set (.45 LC/.45
ACP & .44-40/.44 Spec.) . . . . NiB $365 Ex $315 Gd $175
Stainless steel . . . . NiB $344 Ex $275 Gd $187

BUCKHORN SA REVOLVER
Similar to Regulator model except chambered .44 Mag. w/4.75-, 6-
or 7.7-inch bbl., Fixed or adjustable sights. Hammer block safety.
Imported 1993-96.
Buckhorn model (standard sights) . . NiB $325 Ex $255 Gd $175
W/adjustable sights, add $15

SABRE DA AUTOMATIC PISTOL
Calibers: 9mm Para., .40 S&W. Eight-shot magazine (9mm), 9-shot
(.40 S&W), 3.75-inch bbl., 6.9 inches overall. Weight: 26 oz. Fixed
blade front sight, square, notch adj. rear. Black polymer grips. Blued
or stainless finish. Advertised 1991 but not imported.
Blued finish . . . . NiB $386 Ex $309 Gd $210
Stainless steel . . . . NiB $424 Ex $339 Gd $231

SPECTRE DA AUTO PISTOL
Blowback action, fires closed bolt. Calibers: 9mm Para., .40 S&W,
.45 ACP. 30-shot magazine, 6-inch bbl., 13.75 inches overall.
Weight: 4 lbs. 8 oz. Adj. post front sight, fixed U-notch rear. Black
nylon grips. Matte black finish. Imported 1990-94.
9mm Para. . . . . NiB $500 Ex $425 Gd $380
.40 S&W (disc. 1991) . . . . NiB $400 Ex $320 Gd $218
.45 ACP . . . . NiB $456 Ex $370 Gd $260

WOODMASTER SA AUTO PISTOL . . . . NiB $219 Ex $175 Gd $119
Caliber: .22 LR. 10-shot magazine, 5.88-inch bbl., 10.5 inches
overall. Weight: 31 oz. Fixed front sight, square-notch adj. rear.
Blued finish. Checkered wood grips. Disc. 1989.

454 SSA REVOLVER . . . . NiB $875 Ex $690 Gd $500
Umberti SSA chambered 454. Six-shot cylinder, 6-inch solid raised
rib or 7.7-inch top-ported bbl., satin nickel finish. Hammer block
safety. Imported 1996-97.

AMERICAN DERRINGER CORPORATION —
Waco, Texas

MODEL 1, STAINLESS
Single-action pocket pistol similar to the Remington O/U derringer. Two-
shot capacity. More than 60 calibers from .22 LR to .45-70. Three- inch
bbl., 4.82 inches overall, weight: 15 oz. Automatic bbl., selection. Satin
or high-polished stainless steel. Rosewood grips. Made 1980 to date.
.45 Colt, .44-40 Win., .44
Special, .410 . . . . NiB $385 Ex $341 Gd $275
.45-70, .44 Mag., 41 Mag.,
.30-30 Win., .223 Rem. . . . . NiB $470 Ex $454 Gd $350
.357 Max., .357 Mag., .45 Win.
Mag., 9mm Para. . . . . NiB $335 Ex $312 Gd $225
.38 Special, .38 Super, .32 Mag.,
.22 LR, .22 WRM. . . . . NiB $320 Ex $293 Gd $175

MODEL 2 STEEL "PEN" PISTOL
Calibers: .22 LR, .25 Auto, .32 Auto (7.65mm). single-shot. Two-
inch bbl., 5.6 inches overall (4.2 inches in pistol format). Weight: 5 oz.
Stainless finish. Made 1993-94.
.22 LR . . . . NiB $170 Ex $135 Gd $95
.25 Auto . . . . NiB $175 Ex $140 Gd $100
.32 Auto . . . . NiB $200 Ex $150 Gd $110

MODEL 3 STAINLESS STEEL . . . . NiB $95 Ex $75 Gd $50
Single-shot. Calibers: .32 Mag. or .38 Special. 2.5-inch bbl., 4.9
inches overall. Weight: 8.5 oz. Rosewood grips. Made 1984-95.

MODEL 4 DOUBLE DERRINGER
Calibers: .357 Mag., .357 Max., .44 Mag., .45 LC, .45 ACP (upper
bbl., and 3-inch .410 shotshell (lower bbl). 4.1-inch bbl, 6 inches
overall. Weight: 16.5 oz. Stainless steel. Staghorn grips. Made 1984 to
date.
.357 Mag., .357 Max . . . . NiB $425 Ex $370 Gd $250
.44 Mag., .45 LC, .45 ACP . . . . NiB $515 Ex $457 Gd $300
Engraved, add $1125

MODEL 6
Caliber: .22 Mag., .357 Mag., .45 LC, .45 ACP or .45 LC/.410 or .45
Colt. Bbl.: 6 inches, 8.2 inches overall. Weight: .22 oz. Satin or
high-polished stainless steel w/rosewood grips. Made 1986 to date.
.22 Magnum . . . . NiB $440 Ex $335 Gd $270
.357, .45 ACP, .45 LC . . . . NiB $440 Ex $335 Gd $280
.45/LC/.410 O/U . . . . NiB $450 Ex $340 Gd $300
Engraved, add $1295

MODEL 7
Same general specifications as the Model 1 except high-strength air-
craft aluminum is used to replace some of the stainless steel parts,
which reduces its weight to 7.5 oz. Made 1986 to date.
.22 LR, .22 WMR. . . . . NiB $290 Ex $150 Gd $100
Calibers .32, .38 and .44 . . . . NiB $500 Ex $450 Gd $390

MODEL 10
Same general specifications as the Model 7 except chambered for
.38 Special, .45 ACP or .45 Long Colt.
.38 Special or .45 ACP . . . . NiB $330 Ex $275 Gd $225
.45 Long Colt . . . . NiB $380 Ex $275 Gd $225
Model 11 . . . . NiB $194 Ex $155 Gd $105
Same general specifications as Model 7 except with a matte gray finish only, weight: 11 oz. Made 1980 to date.

25 AUTOMATIC PISTOL
Calibers: .25 ACP or .250 Mag. Bbl.: 2.1 inches, 4.4 inches overall.
Weight: 15.5 oz. Smooth rosewood grips. Limited production.
.25 ACP blued
(est. production 50) . . . . NiB $550 Ex $400 Gd $300
.25 ACP stainless
(est. production 400) . . . . NiB $400 Ex $300 Gd $250
.250 Mag. stainless
(est. production 100) . . . . NiB $560 Ex $500 Gd $385

MODEL 38 DA DERRINGER
Hammerless, double action, double bbl (o/u). Calibers: .22 LR, .38
Special, 9mm Para., .357 Mag., .40 S&W. Three-inch bbl., weight:
14.5 oz. Made 1990 to date.
.22 LR or .38 Special . . . . NiB $435 Ex $399 Gd $350
9mm Para. NiB $236 Ex $190 Gd $128
.357 Mag. . . . . NiB $475 Ex $435 Gd $380
.40 S&W . . . . NiB $281 Ex $225 Gd $153

ALASKAN SURVIVAL MODEL . . . . . NiB $475 Ex $434 Gd $300
Same general specifications as the Model 4 except upper bbl., chambered for .45-70 or 3-inch .410 and .45 Colt lower bbl. Also available in
.45 Auto, .45 Colt, .44 Special, .357 Mag. and .357 Max. Made 1985 to
date.

COP DA DERRINGER . . . . NiB $250 Ex $220 Gd $190
Hammerless, double-action, four-bbl., derringer. Caliber: .357 Mag.
3.15-inch bbl., 5.5 inches overall. Weight: 16 oz. Blade front sight,

American Derringer
Model .38 DA

American Derringer
Lady Derringer

open notched rear. Rosewood grips. Intro. 1990 but only limited
production occurred. No resale value established.

LADY DERRINGER
Same general specifications as Model 1 except w/custom-tuned
action fitted w/scrimshawed synthetic ivory grips. Calibers: .32 H&R
Mag., .32 Special, .38 Special (additional calibers on request).
Deluxe Grade engraved and highly polished w/French fitted jewel-
ry box. Made 1991 to date.
Lady Derringer . . . . NiB $360 Ex $330 Gd $290
Deluxe . . . . NiB $375 Ex $345 Gd $305
Engraved . . . . NiB $920 Ex $850 Gd $800

MINI-COP DA DERRINGER . . . . . . NiB $260 Ex $200 Gd $140
Same general specifications as the American Derringer Cop except
chambered for .22 Magnum. Made 1990-95.

SEMMERLING LM-4
Manually operated repeater. Calibers: .45 ACP or 9mm. Five-
shot (.45 ACP) or 7-shot magazine (9mm)., 3.6-inch bbl., 5.2
inches overall. Weight: 24 oz. Made 1997 to date. Limited
availability.
Blued finish . . . . NiB $2494 Ex $1995 Gd $1357
Stainless steel . . . . (SRP) NiB $3313 Ex $2650 Gd $1802

TEXAS COMMEMORATIVE
Same general specifications as Model 1 except w/solid brass
frame, stainless bbls. and rosewood grips. Calibers: .22 LR,
.32 Mag., .38 Special, .44-40 Win. or .45 Colt. Made 1991 to
date.
.38 Special . . . . NiB $365 Ex $325 Gd $250
.44-40 or .45 Colt . . . . NiB $450 Ex $400 Gd $375

AMT
.45 ACP Backup

AMT
.45 ACP Hardballer

AMT
.45 ACP Hardballer Long Slide

AMERICAN FIREARMS MFG. CO., INC. — San Antonio, Texas

25 AUTO PISTOL
Caliber: .25 Auto. 8-shot magazine, 2.1-inch bbl., 4.4 inches overall. Weight: 14.5 oz. Fixed sights. Stainless or blued ordnance steel. Smooth walnut grips. Made 1966-74.
Stainless steel model . . . . **NiB $219 Ex $180 Gd $125**
Blued steel model . . . . **NiB $165 Ex $140 Gd $105**

380 AUTO PISTOL. . . . . **NiB $700 Ex $650 Gd $575**
Caliber: .380 Auto. 8-shot magazine, 3.5-inch bbl., 5.5 inches overall. Weight: 20 oz. Stainless steel. Smooth walnut grips. Made 1972-74.

AMT (ARCADIA MACHINE & TOOL) — Irwindale, California (Previously Irwindale Arms, Inc.)

NOTE: *The AMT Backup II automatic pistol was introduced in 1993 as a continuation of the original .380 backup with the traditional double action function and a redesigned double safety.*

45 ACP HARDBALLER
Caliber: .45 ACP. Seven-shot magazine, 5-inch bbl., 8.5 inches overall. Weight: 39 oz. Adj. or fixed sights. Serrated matte slide rib w/loaded chamber indicator. Extended combat safety, adj. trigger and long grip safety. Wraparound Neoprene grips. Stainless steel. Made 1978 to date.
.45 ACP Hardballer . . . . **NiB $450 Ex $300 Gd $180**
Long slide conversion kit
(disc. 1997), add **$300**

45 ACP HARDBALLER LONG SLIDE
Similar to the standard AMT Hardballer except w/2-inch-longer bbl. and slide. Also chambered for .400 Cor-Bon. Made 1980 to date.
.45 ACP long slide . . . . **NiB $425 Ex $350 Gd $225**
.400 Cor-Bon long slide
(Intro.1998) . . . . **NiB $406 Ex $325 Gd $221**
5-inch conversion kit
(disc. 1997), add **$300**

1911 GOVERNMENT MODEL
AUTO PISTOL . . . . **NiB $325 Ex $275 Gd $200**
Caliber: .45 ACP. Seven-shot magazine, 5-inch bbl., 8.5 inches overall. Weight: 38 ounces. Fixed sights. Wraparound Neoprene grip. Made 1979 to date.

AUTOMAG II
AUTOMATIC PISTOL . . . . **NiB $400 Ex $280 Gd $170**
Caliber: .22 Mag. Seven- or 9-shot magazine, bbl., lengths: 3.38-4.5-, 6-inch. Weight: 32 oz. Fully adj. Millett sights. Stainless finish. Smooth black composition grips. Made 1986 to date.

AUTOMAG III
AUTOMATIC PISTOL . . . . **NiB $525 Ex $450 Gd $350**
Calibers: .30 M1 and 9mm Win. Mag. Eight-shot magazine., 6.38-inch bbl., 10.5 inches overall. Weight: 43 ounces. Millet adj. sights. Stainless finish. Carbon fiber grips. Made 1989 to date.

AUTOMAG IV
AUTOMATIC PISTOL . . . . **NiB $530 Ex $445 Gd $350**
Calibers: 10mm Mag., .45 Win. Mag. 8- or 7-shot magazine, 6.5- or 8.63-inch bbl., 10.5 inches overall. Weight: 46 oz. Millet adj. sights. Stainless finish. Carbon fiber grips. Made 1990 to date.

AUTOMAG V
AUTOMATIC PISTOL . . . . **NiB $850 Ex $725 Gd $650**
Caliber: .50 A.E. Five-shot magazine, 7-inch bbl., 10.5 inches overall. Weight: 46 oz. Custom adj. sights. Stainless finish. Carbon fiber grips. Made 1994-95.

BACKUP AUTOMATIC PISTOL
Caliber: .22LR, .380 ACP. Eight-shot (.22LR) or 5-shot (.380 ACP) magazine, 2.5-inch bbl., 5 inches overall. Weight: 18 oz. Open sights. Carbon fiber or walnut grips. Stainless steel finish. Made 1990 to date.
.22 LR (disc. 1987) . . . . **NiB $300 Ex $185 Gd $130**
.380 ACP (disc. 1993) . . . . **NiB $250 Ex $175 Gd $120**

BACKUP II

AUTOMATIC PISTOL . . . . **NiB $260 Ex $190 Gd $150**
Caliber: .380 ACP, 5-shot magazine, 2.5-inch bbl., 5 inches overall. Weight: 18 oz. Open sights. Stainless steel finish. Carbon-fiber grips. Made 1993 to date.

BACKUP DAO AUTO PISTOL

Calibers: .380 ACP, .38 Super, 9mm Para., .40 Cor-Bon, .40 S&W, .45 ACP. Six-shot (.380, .38 Super 9mm) or 5-shot (.40 Cor-Bon, .40 S&W, .45 ACP) magazine, 2.5-inch bbl., 5.75-inches overall. Weight: 18 oz. (.380 ACP) or 23 oz. Open fixed sights. Stainless steel finish. Carbon fiber grips. Made 1992 to date.

.380 ACP . . . . **NiB $225 Ex $175 Gd $135**
.38 Super, 9mm . . . . **NiB $250 Ex $190 Gd $120**
.40 Cor-Bon, .40 S&W,
.45 ACP . . . . **NiB $244 Ex $195 Gd $133**

BULL'S EYE

TARGET MODEL . . . . **NiB $400 Ex $340 Gd $295**
Caliber: .40 S&W. Eight-shot magazine, 5-inch bbl., 8.5 inches overall. Weight: 38 oz. Millet adjustable sights. Wide adj. trigger. Wraparound Neoprene grips. Made 1990-92.

JAVELINA . . . . **NiB $560 Ex $460 Gd $350**
Caliber: 10mm. Eight-shot magazine, 7-inch bbl., 10.5 inches overall. Weight: 48 oz. Long grip safety, beveled magazine well, wide adj. trigger. Millet adj. sights. Wraparound Neoprene grips. Stainless finish. Made 1991-93.

LIGHTNING AUTO PISTOL

Caliber: .22 LR. 10-shot magazine, 5-, 6.5-, 8.5-, 10-inch bbl., 10.75 inches overall (6.5-inch bbl.). Weight: 45 oz. (6.5-inch bbl.). Millett adj. sights. Checkered rubber grips. Stainless finish. Made 1984-87.
Standard model . . . . **NiB $350 Ex $200 Gd $150**
Bull's-Eye model . . . . **NiB $425 Ex $350 Gd $285**

ON DUTY DA PISTOL

Calibers: .40 S&W, 9mm Para., .45 ACP. 15-shot (9mm), 13-shot (.40 S&W) or 9-shot (.45 ACP) magazine, 4.5-inch bbl., 7.75 inches overall. Weight: 32 oz. Hard anodized aluminum frame. Stainless steel slide and bbl., Carbon fiber grips. Made 1991-94.
9mm or .40 S&W . . . . **NiB $385 Ex $295 Gd $250**
.45 ACP . . . . **NiB $425 Ex $350 Gd $200**

SKIPPER AUTO PISTOL . . . . **NiB $375 Ex $280 Gd $250**
Calibers: .40 S&W and .45 ACP. Seven-shot magazine, 4.25-inch bbl., 7.5 inches overall. Weight: 33 oz. Millet adj. sights. Walnut grips. Matte finish stainless steel. Made 1990-92.

ANSCHUTZ PISTOLS — Ulm, Germany Mfd. by J.G. Anschutz GmbH Jagd und Sportwaffenfabrik

Currently imported by Accuracy International, Boseman, MT and AcuSport Corporation, Bellefontaine, OH

MODEL 64P

Calibers: .22 LR or .22 Magnum. Five- or 4-shot magazine, 10-inch bbl., 64MS action w/two-stage trigger. Target sights optional. Rynite black synthetic stock. Imported 1998 to date.
.22 LR . . . . **NiB $463 Ex $356 Gd $300**
.22 Mag. . . . . **NiB $494 Ex $480 Gd $425**
W/tangent
sights, add **$80**

AMT Backup

AMT Backup DAO

AMT Bull's Eye Target

AMT Skipper

Anschutz Exemplar

Anschutz Exemplar Hornet

Anschutz Exemplar XIV

Astra Model .44 DA

EXEMPLAR (1416P/1451P) BOLT-ACTION PISTOL
Caliber: .22 LR, single-shot or 5-shot clip. Seven- or 10-inch bbl., 19 inches overall (10-inch bbl.). Weight: 3.33 lbs. Match 64 action. Slide safety. Hooded ramp post front sight, adjustable open notched rear. European walnut contoured grip. Exemplar made 1987-95 and 1400 series made 1997 to date. Note: The .22 WMR chambering was also advertised but never manufactured.

Exemplar w/7- or 10-inch bbl. . . . . NiB $395 Ex $345 Gd $290
Left-hand model (disc. 1997). . . . . . NiB $500 Ex $450 Gd $370
Model 1451P (single-shot). . . . . NiB $406 Ex $325 Gd $221
Model 1416P (5-shot repeater) . . . . NiB $394 Ex $315 Gd $214

EXEMPLAR HORNET. . . . . NiB $835 Ex $685 Gd $550
Based on the Anschutz Match 54 action, tapped and grooved for scope mounting with no open sights. Caliber: .22 Hornet, 5-shot magazine, 10-inch bbl., 20 inches overall. Weight: 4.35 lbs. Checkered European walnut grip. Winged safety. Made 1990 to 1995.

EXEMPLAR XIV . . . . NiB $500 Ex $450 Gd $370
Same general specifications as the standard Exemplar bolt-action pistol except w/14-inch bbl., weight: 4.15 lbs. Made 1989-95.

ARMSCOR (Arms Corp.) — Manila, Philippines
Currently imported by K.B.I., Harrisburg, PA. (Imported 1991-95 by Ruko Products, Inc., Buffalo NY. Previously by Armscor Precision, San Mateo, CA.)

MODEL M1911-A1
AUTOMATIC PISTOL . . . . NiB $390 Ex $350 Gd $210
Caliber: .45 ACP. Eight-shot magazine, 5-inch bbl., 8.75 inches overall. Weight: 38 oz. Blade front sight, drift adjustable rear w/3-dot system. Skeletonized tactical hammer and trigger. Extended slide release and beavertail grip safety. Parker-ized finish. Checkered composition or wood stocks. Imported 1996-97.

MODEL 200DC/TC
DA REVOLVER. . . . . NiB $165 Ex $145 Gd $120
Caliber: .38 Special. Six-shot cylinder, 2.5-, 4-, or 6-inch bbl.; 7.3, 8.8, or 11.3 inches overall. Weight: 22, 28, or 34 oz. Ramp front and fixed rear sights. Checkered mahogany or rubber grips. Imported 1996 to date.

ASAI AG — Advanced Small Arms Industries Solothurn, Switzerland
Currently imported by Magnum Research Inc., Minneapolis, MN.

See listings under Magnum Research Pistols

ASTRA PISTOLS — Guernica, Spain
Manufactured by Unceta y Compania
Currently imported by E.A.A. Corporation, Sharpes, FL.

MODEL 357 DA REVOLVER . . . . . . NiB $250 Ex $215 Gd $180
Caliber: .357 Magnum. Six-shot cylinder. 3-, 4-, 6-, 8.5-inch bbl., 11.25 inches overall (with 6-inch bbl.). Weight: 42 oz. (with 6-inch bbl.). Ramp front sight, adj. rear sight. Blued finish. Checkered wood grips. Imported 1972-88.

MODEL 44 DA REVOLVER
Similar to Astra ..357 except chambered for .44 Magnum. Six- or 8.5-inch bbl., 11.5 inches overall (6-inch bbl.). Weight: 44 oz. (6-inch bbl.). Imported 1980-93.
Blued finish (disc. 1987) . . . . NiB $280 Ex $235 Gd $210
Stainless finish (disc. 1993) . . . . . . NiB $285 Ex $235 Gd $210

MODEL 41 DA REVOLVER . . . . . . .NiB $280 Ex $240 Gd $160
Same general specifications as Model 44 except in .41 Mag. Imported 1980-85.

MODEL 45
DA REVOLVER. . . . . NiB $285 Ex $235 Gd $210
Similar to Astra .357 except chambered for .45 Colt or .45 ACP. Six- or 8.5-inch bbl., 11.5 inches overall (with 6-inch bbl.). Weight: 44 oz. (6-inch bbl.). Imported 1980-87.

MODEL 200 FIRECAT
VEST POCKET AUTO PISTOL . . . . . **NiB $250 Ex $200 Gd $185**
Caliber: .25 Automatic (6.35mm). Six-shot magazine, 2.25-inch bbl., 4.38 inches overall. Weight: 11.75 oz. Fixed sights. Blued finish. Plastic grips. Made 1920 to date. U.S. importation disc. in 1968.

MODEL 202 FIRECAT
VEST POCKET AUTO PISTOL . . . . . **NiB $475 Ex $400 Gd $350**
Same general specifications as the Model 200 except chromed and engraved w/pearl grips. U.S. importation disc. 1968.

MODEL 400 AUTO PISTOL. . . . . . **NiB $400 Ex $360 Gd $150**
Caliber: 9mm Bayard Long (.38 ACP, 9mm Browning Long, 9mm Glisenti, 9mm Para. and 9mm Steyr cartridges may be used interchangeably in this pistol because of its chamber design). Nine-shot magazine., 6-inch bbl., 10 inches overall. Weight: 35 oz. Fixed sights. Blued finish. Plastic grips. Made 1922-45. Note: This pistol, as well as Astra Models 600 and 3000, is a modification of the Browning Model 1912.

MODEL 600 MIL./POLICE-TYPE
AUTO PISTOL . . . . **NiB $395 Ex $320 Gd $190**
Calibers: .32 Automatic (7.65mm), 9mm Para. Magazine: 10-shot (.32 cal.) or 8-shot (9mm)., 5.25-inch bbl., 8 inches overall. Weight: About 33 oz. Fixed sights. Blued finish. Checkered wood or plastic grips. Made 1944-.45.

MODEL 800 CONDOR
MILITARY AUTO PISTOL. . . . . . **NiB $1475 Ex $1100 Gd $725**
Similar to Models 400 and 600 except has an external hammer. Caliber: 9mm Para. Eight-shot magazine, 5.25-inch bbl., 8.25 inches overall. Weight: 32.5 oz. Fixed sights. Blued finish. Plastic grips. Imported 1958-65.

MODEL 2000 CAMPER
AUTOMATIC PISTOL . . . . **NiB $370 Ex $260 Gd $170**
Same as Model 2000 Cub except chambered for .22 Short only, has 4-inch bbl., overall length, 6.25 inches; weight: 11.5 oz. Imported 1955-60.

MODEL 2000 CUB
POCKET AUTO PISTOL. . . . . **NiB $250 Ex $190 Gd $120**
Calibers: .22 Short, .25 Auto. Six-shot magazine, 2.25-inch bbl., 4.5 inches overall. Weight: About 11 oz. Fixed sights. Blued or chromed finish. Plastic grips. Made 1954 to date. U.S. importation disc. 1968.

MODEL 3000
POCKET AUTO PISTOL. . . . . **NiB $500 Ex $480 Gd $225**
Calibers: .22 LR, .32 Automatic (7.65mm), .380 Auto (9mm Short). Ten-shot magazine (.22 cal.), 7-shot (.32 cal.), 6-shot (.380 cal.). Four-inch bbl., 6.38 inches overall. Weight: About 22 oz. Fixed sights. Blued finish. Plastic grips. Made 1947-56.

MODEL 3003
POCKET AUTO PISTOL. . . . . **NiB $1000 Ex $650 Gd $480**
Same general specifications as the Model 3000 except chromed and engraved w/pearl grips. Disc. 1956.

MODEL 4000
ALCON AUTO PISTOL . . . . **NiB $500 Ex $400 Gd $240**
Similar to Model 3000 except has an external hammer. Calibers: .22 LR, .32 Automatic (7.65mm), .380 Auto (9mm Short). Ten-shot magazine (.22 LR), 8-shot (.32 Auto), 7-shot (.380 Auto), 3.66-inch bbl., 6.5-inches overall. Weight: 20 oz. (.22 cal.) or 24.75 oz. (.32 and .380). Fixed sights. Blued finish. Plastic grips. Made 1956-71.

MODEL A-60 DA
AUTOMATIC PISTOL . . . . **NiB $400 Ex $350 Gd $220**
Similar to the Constable except in .380 only, w/13-shot magazine and slide-mounted ambidextrous safety. Blued finish only. Imported 1980-91.

Astra Model
3003 Pocket

Astra Model
4000 Falcon

Astra
Model A-80

MODEL A-70 COMPACT AUTO PISTOL
Calibers: 9mm Para., .40 S&W. Eight-shot (9mm) or 7-shot (.40 S&W) magazine., 3.5-inch bbl., 6.5 inches overall. Blued, nickel or stainless finish. Weight: 29.3 oz. Imported 1992-96.

Blued finish . . . . **NiB $275 Ex $250 Gd $170**
Nickel finish . . . . **NiB $305 Ex $280 Gd $200**
Stainless finish. . . . . **NiB $365 Ex $325 Gd $275**

MODEL A-75 DECOCKER AUTO PISTOL
Similar to the Model 70 except in 9mm, .40 S&W and .45 ACP w/decocking system and contoured pebble-textured grips. Imported 1993-97.

Blued finish, 9mm or .40 S&W . . . . **NiB $280 Ex $250 Gd $185**
Nickel finish, 9mm or .40 S&W. . . . **NiB $295 Ex $250 Gd $170**
Stainless, 9mm or .40 S&W . . . . **NiB $285 Ex $250 Gd $180**
Blued finish, .45 ACP. . . . . **NiB $310 Ex $250 Gd $160**
Nickel finish, .45 ACP . . . . **NiB $333 Ex $270 Gd $160**
Stainless, .45 ACP . . . . **NiB $375 Ex $325 Gd $225**

Astra Cadix DA

Astra Constable DA

**Auto-Ordnance 1927
A-5 w/drum magazine**

MODEL A-75 ULTRALIGHT . . . . . . NiB $300 Ex $255 Gd $170
Similar to the standard Model 75 except 9mm only w/24-oz. alloy
frame. Imported 1994-97.

MODEL A-80 AUTO PISTOL . . . . . . NiB $370 Ex $320 Gd $210
Calibers: 9mm Para., .38 Super, .45 ACP. 15-shot magazine or 9-
shot (.45 ACP). Bbl.: 3.75 inches., 7 inches overall. Weight: 36 oz.
Imported 1982-89. See illustration previous page.

**MODEL A-90 DA
AUTOMATIC PISTOL** . . . . NiB $400 Ex $325 Gd $220
Calibers: 9mm Para., .45 ACP. 15-shot (9mm) or 9-shot (.45 ACP)
magazine, 3.75-inch bbl., 7 inches overall. Weight: about 40 oz.
Fixed sights. Blued finish. Checkered plastic grips. Imported 1985-90.

MODEL A-100 DA AUTO PISTOL
Same general specifications as the Model A-90 except selective double
action chambered for 9mm Para., .40 S&W or .45 ACP. Imported 1991-97.

(cont'd) **MODEL A-100 DA AUTO PISTOL**
Blued finish . . . . NiB $375 Ex $325 Gd $225
Nickel finish . . . . NiB $400 Ex $347 Gd $220
For night sights, add $85

CADIX DA REVOLVER
Calibers: .22 LR, .38 Special. Nine-shot (.22 LR) or 5-shot (.38 cal.)
cylinder. Four- or 6-inch bbl., Weight: About 27 oz. (6-inch bbl.). Ramp
front sight, adj. rear sight. Blued finish. Plastic grips. Imported 1960-68.
Standard model . . . . NiB $195 Ex $165 Gd $100
Lightly engraved model . . . . NiB $313 Ex $250 Gd $170
Heavily engraved model (shown) . . . . . NiB $619 Ex $495 Gd $337

CONSTABLE DA AUTO PISTOL
Calibers: .22 LR, .32 Automatic (7.65mm), .380 Auto (9mm Short).
Magazine capacity: 10-shot (.22 LR), 8-shot (.32), 7-shot (.380). 3.5-
inch bbl., 6.5 inches overall. Weight: about 24 oz. Blade front sight,
windage adj. rear. Blued or chromed finish. Imported 1965-92.
Stainless finish . . . . NiB $344 Ex $275 Gd $187
Blued finish . . . . NiB $294 Ex $235 Gd $160
Chrome finish (disc. 1990) . . . . NiB $313 Ex $250 Gd $170

AUTAUGA ARMS — Prattville, Alabama

**MODEL 32 (MK II)
DAO AUTOMATIC PISTOL** . . . . . . NiB $325 Ex $225 Gd $170
Caliber: .32 ACP. Six-shot magazine, 2-inch bbl., weight: 11.36 oz.. Double
action only. Stainless steel. Black polymer grips. Made 1997 to date.

AUTO-ORDNANCE CORPORATION — West Hurley, New York

1911 A1 GOVERNMENT AUTO PISTOL
Copy of Colt 1911 A1 semiautomatic pistol. Calibers: 9mm Para.,
.38 Super, 10mm, .45 ACP. 9-shot (9mm, .38 Super) or 7-shot
10mm, .45 ACP) magazine. Five-inch bbl., 8.5 inches overall.
Weight: 39 oz. Fixed blade front sight, rear adj. Blued, satin nickel
or Duo-Tone finish. Checkered plastic grips. Made 1983-99.
.45 ACP caliber . . . . NiB $360 Ex $295 Gd $215
9mm, 10mm, .38 Super . . . . NiB $369 Ex $295 Gd $201

1911A1 .40 S&W PISTOL . . . . NiB $360 Ex $295 Gd $215
Similar to the Model 1911 A1 except has 4.5-inch bbl., w/7.75-inch overall
length. Eight-shot magazine, weight: 37 oz. Blade front and adj. rear sights
w/3-dot system. Checkered black rubber wraparound grips. Made 1991-99.

1911 "THE GENERAL" . . . . NiB $380 Ex $320 Gd $200
Caliber: .45 ACP. Seven-shot magazine, 4.5-inch bbl., 7.75 inches
overall. Weight: 37 oz. Blued nonglare finish. Made 1992-99.

1927 A-5 SEMIAUTOMATIC PISTOL
Similar to Thompson Model 1928A submachine gun except has no provision for automatic firing and does not have detachable buttstock. Caliber:
.45 ACP, 5-, 15-, 20- and 30-shot detachable box magazines. 30-shot drum
also available. 13-inch finned bbl., 26 inches overall. Weight: About 6.75
lbs. Adj. rear sight, blade front. Blued finish. Walnut grips. Made 1977-94.
W/box magazine . . . . NiB $869 Ex $695 Gd $473
W/drum magazine (illustrated) . . . . NiB $1188 Ex $950 Gd $646

**ZG-51 PIT BULL
AUTOMATIC PISTOL** . . . . NiB $385 Ex $310 Gd $215
Caliber: .45 ACP. Seven-shot magazine, 3.5-inch bbl., 7 inches
overall. Weight: 32 oz. Fixed front sight, square-notch rear. Blued
finish. Checkered plastic grips. Made 1991-99.

LES BAER — Hillsdale, Illinois

1911 CONCEPT SERIES AUTOMATIC PISTOL

Similar to Government 1911 built on steel or alloy full-size or compact frame. Caliber: .45 ACP. Seven-shot magazine, 4.25- or 5-inch bbl. Weight: 34 to 37 oz. Adjustable low mount combat or BoMar target sights. Blued, matte black, Two-Tone or stainless finish. Checkered wood grips. Made 1996 to date.

Concept models I & II . . . . NiB $1119 Ex $895 Gd $609
Concept models III, IV & VII . . . . . NiB $1231 Ex $985 Gd $670
Concept models V, VI & VIII . . . . NiB $1281 Ex $1025 Gd $697
Concept models IX & X . . . . NiB $1294 Ex $1035 Gd $704

1911 PREMIER SERIES AUTOMATIC PISTOL

Similar to the Concept series except also chambered for .38 Super, 9x23 Win., .400 Cor-Bon and .45 ACP. 5- or 6-inch bbl. Weight: 37 to .40 oz. Made 1996 to date.

Premier II
(9x23 w/5-inch bbl.) . . . . NiB $1369 Ex $1095 Gd $745
Premier II (.400
Cor-Bon w/5-inch bbl.) . . . . NiB $1244 Ex $995 Gd $677
Premier II (.45 ACP
w/5-inch bbl.) . . . . NiB $1156 Ex $925 Gd $629
Premier II (.45 ACP
S/S w/5-inch bbl.) . . . . NiB $1281 Ex $1025 Gd $697
Premier II (.45/.400
combo w/5-inch bbl.) . . . . NiB $1438 Ex $1150 Gd $782
Premier II (.38
Super w/6-inch bbl.) . . . . NiB $1619 Ex $1295 Gd $881
Premier II (.400
Cor-Bon w/6-inch bbl.) . . . . NiB $1456 Ex $1165 Gd $792
Premier II (.45 ACP
w/6-inch bbl.) . . . . NiB $1369 Ex $1095 Gd $745

S.R.P. AUTOMATIC PISTOL

Similar to F.B.I. Contract "Swift Response Pistol" built on a (customer-supplied) Para-Ordance over-sized frame or a 1911 full-size or compact frame. Caliber: .45 ACP. Seven-shot magazine, 5-inch bbl., weight: 37 oz. Ramp front and fixed rear sights, w/Tritium Sight insert.

SRP 1911Government
or Commanche model . . . . NiB $1994 Ex $1595 Gd $1085
SRP P-12 model . . . . NiB $2281 Ex $1825 Gd $1241
SRP P-13 model . . . . NiB $2063 Ex $1650 Gd $1122
SRP P-14 model . . . . NiB $1938 Ex $1550 Gd $1054

1911 ULTIMATE MASTER COMBAT SERIES AUTOMATIC PISTOL

Model 1911 in Combat Competition configuration. Calibers: .38 Super, 9x23 Win., .400 Cor-Bon and .45 ACP. Five- or 6-inch NM bbl., weight: 37 to 40 oz. Made 1996 to date.

Ultimate MC (.38 or 9x23
w/5-inch bbl.) . . . . NiB $2063 Ex $1650 Gd $1122
Ultimate MC (.400 Cor-Bon
w/5-inch bbl.) . . . . NiB $1906 Ex $1525 Gd $1037
Ultimate MC (.45 ACP
w/5-inch bbl.) . . . . NiB $1813 Ex $1450 Gd $986
Ultimate MC (.38 or 9x23
w/6-inch bbl.) . . . . NiB $2119 Ex $1695 Gd $1153
Ultimate MC (.400 Cor-Bon
w/6-inch bbl.) . . . . NiB $1969 Ex $1575 Gd $1071
Ultimate MC (.45 ACP
w/6-inch bbl.) . . . . NiB $1869 Ex $1495 Gd $1017
Ultimate "Steel Special"
(.38 Super Bianchi SPS) . . . . . . NiB $2369 Ex $1895 Gd $1289
Ultimate "PARA" (.38, 9x23
or .45 IPSC comp) . . . . NiB $2406 Ex $1925 Gd $1309
W/Triple-Port Compensator, add $95

Auto-Ordnance
ZG-51 Pit Bull

1911 CUSTOM CARRY SERIES AUTOMATIC PISTOL

Model 1911 in Combat Carry configuration built on steel or alloy full-size or compact frame. 4.5- or 5-inch NM bbl., chambered for .45 ACP. Weight: 34 to 37 oz.

Custom carry (steel frame
w/4.24- or 5-inch bbl.) . . . . NiB $1313 Ex $1050 Gd $714
Custom carry (alloy frame
w/4.24-inch bbl.) . . . . NiB $1531 Ex $1225 Gd $833

BAUER FIREARMS CORPORATION — Fraser, MI

.25 AUTOMATIC PISTOL . . . . NiB $150 Ex $130 Gd $90
Stainless steel. Caliber: .25 Automatic. Six-shot magazine, 2.13-inch bbl., 4 inches overall. Weight: 10 oz. Fixed sights. Checkered walnut or simulated pearl grips. Made 1972-84.

BAYARD PISTOLS — Herstal, Belgium
Mfd. by Anciens Etablissements Pieper

MODEL 1908
POCKET AUTOMATIC PISTOL . . . . NiB $350 Ex $250 Gd $125
Calibers: .25 Automatic (6.35mm). .32 Automatic (7.65mm), .380 Automatic (9mm Short). Six-shot magazine, 2.25-inch bbl., 4.88 inches overall. Weight: About 16 oz. Fixed sights. Blued finish. Hard rubber grips. Intro. 1908. Disc. 1923.

MODEL 1923 POCKET
.25 AUTOMATIC PISTOL . . . . NiB $350 Ex $290 Gd $150
Caliber: .25 Automatic (6.35mm). 2.13-inch bbl., 4.31 inches overall. Weight: 12 oz. Fixed sights. Blued finish. Checkered hard-rubber grips. Intro. 1923. Disc. 1930.

MODEL 1923 POCKET
AUTOMATIC PISTOL . . . . NiB $358 Ex $290 Gd $150
Calibers: .32 Automatic (7.65mm), .380 Automatic (9mm Short). Six-shot magazine, 3.31-inch bbl., 5.5 inches overall. Weight: About 19 oz. Fixed sights. Blued finish. Checkered hard-rubber grips. Intro. 1923. Disc. 1940.

MODEL 1930 POCKET
.25 AUTOMATIC PISTOL . . . . NiB $350 Ex $250 Gd $120
This is a modification of the Model 1923, which it closely resembles.

BEEMAN PRECISION ARMS, INC. — Santa Rosa, CA

P08 AUTOMATIC PISTOL . . . . NiB $395 Ex $330 Gd $170
Caliber: .22 LR. 10-shot magazine, 3.8-inch bbl., 7.8 inches overall. Weight: 25 oz. Fixed sights. Blued finish. Checkered hardwood grips. Imported 1969-91.

Benelli MP90S

Benelli MP95E

Beretta Model 21

MINI P08 AUTOMATIC PISTOL . . . NiB $369 Ex $295 Gd $201
Caliber: Same general specifications as P08 except shorter 3.5-inch bbl., 7.4 inches overall. Weight: 20 oz. Imported 1986-91.

SP METALLIC SILHOUETTE PISTOLS
Caliber: .22 LR. Single-shot. Bbl. lengths: 6-, 8-, 10- or 15-inches. Adj. rear sight. Receiver contoured for scope mount. Walnut target grips w/adj. palm rest. Models SP made 1985-86 and SPX 1993-94.
SP Standard W/8-or 10-inch bbl.. . . NiB $244 Ex $195 Gd $133
SP Standard W/12-inch bbl. . . . . . . NiB $288 Ex $230 Gd $156
SP Standard W/15-inch bbl. . . . . . . NiB $306 Ex $245 Gd $167
SP Deluxe W/8-or 10-inch bbl.. . . . NiB $294 Ex $235 Gd $160
SP Deluxe W/12-inch bbl.. . . . . NiB $313 Ex $250 Gd $170
SP Deluxe W/15-inch bbl.. . . . . NiB $331 Ex $265 Gd $180
SPX Standard W/10-inch bbl. . . . . NiB $619 Ex $495 Gd $337
SPX Deluxe W/10-inch bbl.. . . . . . NiB $844 Ex $675 Gd $459

BEHOLLA PISTOL — Suhl, Germany
Mfd. by both Becker and Holländer and Stenda-Werke GmbH

POCKET AUTOMATIC PISTOL . . . . NiB $225 Ex $180 Gd $110
Caliber: .32 Automatic (7.65mm). Seven-shot magazine, 2.9-inch bbl., 5.5 inches overall. Weight: 22 oz. Fixed sights. Blued finish. Serrated wood or hard rubber grips. Made by Becker and Hollander 1915-1920, by Stenda-Werke circa 1920-25. Note: Essentially the same pistol was manufactured concurrently w/the Stenda version as the "Leonhardt" by H. M. Gering and as the "Menta" by August Menz.

BENELLI PISTOLS — Urbino, Italy
Imported by Benelli USA

MP90S WORLD CUP TARGET PISTOL
Semiautomatic blowback action. Calibers: .22 Short, .22LR, .32 W.C. Five-shot magazine, 4.33-inch fixed bbl. 6.75 inches overall. Weight: 36 oz. Post front sight, adjustable rear. Blue finish. Anatomic shelf-style grip. Imported 1992 to 2001.
MP90S (.22 LR) . . . . NiB $1230 Ex $1050 Gd $550
MP90S (.22 Short, disc. 1995). . . . NiB $1031 Ex $825 Gd $561
MP90S (.32 WC) . . . . NiB $1281 Ex $1025 Gd $697
W/conversion kit, add. $550

MP95E SPORT TARGET PISTOL
Similar to the MP90S except with 5- or 9-shot magazine, 4.25- inch bbl., Blue or chrome finish. Checkered target grip. Imported 1994 to date.
Blue MP95 (.22 LR) . . . . NiB $700 Ex $575 Gd $350
Blue MP95 (.32 WC) . . . . NiB $688 Ex $550 Gd $374
Chrome, add $85

BERETTA USA CORP. — Accokeek, Maryland

Beretta firearms are manufactured by Fabbrica D'Armi Pietro Beretta S. p. A. in the Gardone Val Trompia (Brescia), Italy. This prestigious firm has been in business since 1526. In 1977, Beretta U.S.A. Corp., a manufacturing and importing facility, opened in Accokeek, MD. (Previously imported by Garcia Corp., J.L. Galef & Son, Inc. and Berben Corporation.) Note: Beretta also owns additional firearms manufacturing companies including: Benelli, Franchi, Sako, Stoeger, Tikka and Uberti.

MODEL 20 DOUBLE-
ACTION AUTO PISTOL. . . . . NiB $160 Ex $140 Gd $90
Caliber: .25 ACP. Eight-shot magazine, 2.5-inch bbl., 4.9 inches overall. Weight: 10.9 oz. Plastic or walnut grips. Fixed sights. Made 1984-85.

MODEL 21 DOUBLE-ACTION AUTO PISTOL
Calibers: .22 LR and .25 ACP. Seven-shot (.22 LR) or 8-shot (..25 ACP) magazine, 2.5-inch bbl., 4.9 inches overall. Weight: About 12 oz. Blade front sight, V-notch rear. Walnut grips. Made 1985 to date.
Blued finish . . . . NiB $194 Ex $155 Gd $105
Nickel finish (.22 LR only). . . . . NiB $231 Ex $185 Gd $126
Model 21EL engraved model . . . . . . NiB $306 Ex $245 Gd $167

MODEL 70 AUTOMATIC PISTOL . . NiB $225 Ex $180 Gd $122
Improved version of Model 1935. Steel or lightweight alloy. Calibers: .32 Auto (7.65mm), .380 Auto (9mm Short). Eight-shot (.32) or 7-shot (.380) magazine, 3.5-inch bbl., 6.5 inches overall. Weight: Steel, 22.25 oz.; alloy, 16 oz. Fixed sights. Blued finish. Checkered plastic grips. Made 1959-85. Note: Formerly marketed in U.S. as "Puma" (alloy model in .32) and "Cougar" (steel model in .380). Disc.

MODEL 70S. . . . . **NiB $240 Ex $210 Gd $130**
Similar to Model 70T except chambered for .22 Auto and .380 Auto. Longer bbl. guide and safety lever blocking hammer. Front blade and rear sight fixed on breechblock. Weight: 1 lb., 7 oz. Made 1977-85.

MODEL 70T
AUTOMATIC PISTOL . . . . **NiB $275 Ex $250 Gd $150**
Similar to Model 70. Caliber: .32 Automatic (7.65mm). Nine-shot magazine, 6-inch bbl., 9.5 inches overall. Weight: 19 oz. adj. rear sight, blade front sight. Blued finish. Checkered plastic grips. Intro. in 1959. disc.

MODEL 71
AUTOMATIC PISTOL . . . . **NiB $220 Ex $195 Gd $125**
Same general specifications as alloy Model 70. Caliber: .22 LR. Six-inch bbl., 8-round magazine, Adj. rear sight frame. Single action. Made 1959-89. Note: Formerly marketed in U.S. as the "Jaguar Plinker."

MODEL 72 . . . . **NiB $220 Ex $195 Gd $120**
Same as Model 71 except has 6-inch bbl., weight: 18 oz. Intro. in 1959. Disc. Note: Formerly marketed in U.S as "Jaguar Plinker."

MODEL 76 AUTO TARGET PISTOL
Caliber: .22 LR. 10-shot magazine, 6-inch bbl., 8.8 inches overall. Weight: 33 oz. adj. rear sight, front sight w/interchangeable blades. Blued finish. Checkered plastic or wood grips. Made 1966-85. Note: Formerly marketed in the U.S. as the "Sable."
Model 76 w/plastic grips. . . . . **NiB $369 Ex $295 Gd $201**
Model 76W w/wood grips. . . . . **NiB $431 Ex $345 Gd $235**

MODEL 81 DOUBLE-
ACTION AUTO PISTOL. . . . . **NiB $310 Ex $250 Gd $160**
Caliber: .32 Automatic (7.65mm). 12-shot magazine, 3.8-inch bbl., 6.8 inches overall. Weight: 23.5 oz. Fixed sights. Blued finish. Plastic grips. Made principally for the European market 1975-84, w/similar variations as implemented on the Model 84.

MODEL 82 DOUBLE-
ACTION AUTO PISTOL. . . . . **NiB $294 Ex $235 Gd $160**
Caliber: .32 ACP. Similar to the Model 81 except with a slimmer-profile frame designed to accept a single column 9-shot magazine. Matte black finish. Importation disc. 1984.

MODEL 84 DOUBLE-
ACTION AUTO PISTOL. . . . . **NiB $295 Ex $250 Gd $150**
Same as Model 81 except made in caliber .380 Automatic w/13-shot magazine, 3.82-inch bbl., 6.8 inches overall. Weight: 23 oz. Fixed front and rear sights. Made 1975-82.

MODEL 84B DA AUTO PISTOL . . . **NiB $295 Ex $250 Gd $170**
Improved version of Model 84 w/strengthened frame and slide, and firing-pin block safety added. Ambidextrous reversible magazine release. Blued or nickel finish. Checkered black plastic or wood grips. Other specifications same. Made c. 1982-84.

MODEL 84(BB) DOUBLE-ACTION AUTO PISTOL
Improved version of Model 84B w/further-strengthened slide, frame and recoil spring. Caliber: .380 ACP. 13-shot magazine, 3.82-inch bbl., 6.8 inches overall. Weight: 23 oz. Checkered black plastic or wood grips. Blued or nickel finish. Notched rear and blade front sight. Made c. 1984-94.
Blued w/plastic grips. . . . . **NiB $425 Ex $340 Gd $231**
Blued w/wood grips . . . . **NiB $444 Ex $355 Gd $241**
Nickel finish w/wood grips . . . . **NiB $488 Ex $390 Gd $265**

Beretta Model 71

Beretta Model 72

Beretta Model 84

MODEL 84 CHEETAH SEMI-AUTO PISTOL
Similar to the Model 84 BB except with required design changes as mandated by regulation, including reduced magazine capacity (10-shot magazine) and marked as 9mm short (.380) as a marketing strategy to counter increased availability of 9mm chamberings from other manufacturers. Made 1994 to date. See illustration next page.
Blued w/plastic grips. . . . . **NiB $406 Ex $325 Gd $221**
Blued w/wood grips . . . . **NiB $444 Ex $355 Gd $241**
Nickel finish w/wood grips . . . . **NiB $481 Ex $385 Gd $262**

MODEL 85 DOUBLE-
ACTION AUTO PISTOL. . . . . **NiB $435 Ex $340 Gd $190**
Similar to the Model 84 except designed with a slimmer-profile frame to accept a single column 8-shot magazine, no ambidextrous magazine release. Matte black finish. Weight: 21.8 oz. Introduced in 1977 following the Model 84. See illustration next page.

MODEL 85B DA AUTO PISTOL . . . **NiB $440 Ex $350 Gd $220**
Improved version of the Model 85. Imported 1982-85.

GRADING: **NiB** = New in Box **Ex** = Excellent or NRA 95% **Gd** = Good or NRA 68%

Beretta Model 84
Cheetah (Nickel finish)

Beretta Model 85

Beretta Model 85BB

Beretta Model 86 Cheetah

MODEL 85BB DOUBLE-ACTION PISTOL

Improved version of the Model 85B w/strengthened frame and slide. Caliber: .380 ACP. Eight-shot magazine, 3.82 inch bbl., 6.8 inches overall. Weight: 21.8 oz. Blued or nickel finish. Checkered black plastic or wood grips. Imported 1985-94.

Blued finish
w/plastic grips . . . . NiB $375 Ex $300 Gd $204
Blued finish
w/wood grips . . . . NiB $419 Ex $335 Gd $228
Nickel finish
w/wood grips . . . . NiB $469 Ex $375 Gd $255

MODEL 85 CHEETAH SEMI-AUTO PISTOL

Similar to the Model 85 BB except with required design changes as mandated by regulation and marked as 9mm short (.380) as a marketing strategy to counter increased availability of 9mm chamberings from other manufacturers. Made 1994 to date.

Blued w/plastic grips . . . . NiB $375 Ex $300 Gd $192
Blued w/wood grips . . . . NiB $426 Ex $345 Gd $241
Nickel w/wood grips . . . . NiB $474 Ex $385 Gd $271

MODEL 85F DOUBLE-ACTION PISTOL

Similar to the Model 85BB except has re-contoured trigger guard and manual ambidextrous safety w/decocking device. Bruniton finish. Imported in 1990.

Matte black Bruniton
finish w/plastic grips . . . . NiB $375 Ex $300 Gd $190
Matte black Bruniton
finish w/wood grips. . . . . NiB $439 Ex $355 Gd $248

MODEL 86 CHEETAH

DA AUTO PISTOL . . . . NiB $485 Ex $380 Gd $190
Caliber: .380 auto. Eight-shot magazine, 4.4- inch bbl., 7.3 inches overall. Weight: 23.3 oz. Bruniton finish w/wood grips. Made 1986-89. (Reintroduced 1990 in the Cheetah series.)

MODEL 87 CHEETAH AUTO PISTOL

Similar to the Model 85 except in .22 LR w/8- or 10- shot magazine (Target) and optional extended 6-inch bbl. (Target in single action). Overall length: 6.8 to 8.8 inches. Weight: 20.1 oz. to 29.4 oz (Target). Checkered wood grips. Made 1987 to date.

Blued finish
(double-action) . . . . NiB $485 Ex $380 Gd $190
Target Model
(single action) . . . . NiB $441 Ex $355 Gd $245

MODEL 89

GOLD STANDARD TARGET
AUTOMATIC PISTOL . . . . NiB $630 Ex $510 Gd $325
Caliber: .22 LR. Eight-shot magazine, 6-inch bbl., 9.5 inches overall. Weight: 41 oz. Adj. target sights. Blued finish. Target-style walnut grips. Made 1988 to date.

MODEL 90

DA AUTO PISTOL . . . . NiB $275 Ex $198 Gd $130
Caliber: .32 Auto (7.65mm). Eight-shot magazine, 3.63-inch bbl., 6.63 inches overall. Weight: 19.5 oz. Fixed sights. Blued finish. Checkered plastic grips. Made 1969-83.

MODEL 92 DA AUTO

PISTOL (1ST SERIES) . . . . NiB $650 Ex $550 Gd $275
Caliber: 9mm Para. 15-shot magazine, 4.9-inch bbl., 8.5 inches overall. Weight: 33.5 oz. Fixed sights. Blued finish. Plastic grips. Initial production of 5,000 made in 1976.

MODEL 92D DA AUTO PISTOL
Same general specifications as Model 92F except DA only w/bobbed hammer and 3-dot sight. Made 1992 to date.
Model 92D . . . . NiB $460 Ex $360 Gd $275
With Tritium
sight system add $80

MODEL 92F COMPACT
DA AUTOMATIC PISTOL . . . . NiB $570 Ex $460 Gd $190
Caliber: 9mm Para. 12-shot magazine, 4.3-inch bbl., 7.8 inches overall. Weight: 31.5 oz. Wood grips. Square-notched rear sight, blade front integral w/slide. Made 1986-93.

MODEL 92F COMPACT L TYPE M DA AUTOMATIC PISTOL
Same general specifications as the original 92F Compact except 8-shot magazine, Weight: 30.9 oz. Bruniton matte finish. Made 1998 to date.
Model 92F
Compact L Type M. . . . . NiB $570 Ex $460 Gd $190
Model 92F
Compact L Type M Inox. . . . . NiB $570 Ex $460 Gd $190
W/Tritium
sight system, add $80

MODEL 92F DA AUTOMATIC PISTOL
Same general specifications as Model 92 except w/slide-mounted safety and repositioned magazine release. Replaced Model 92SB. Blued or stainless finish. Made 1985 to date.
Blued finish . . . . NiB $570 Ex $460 Gd $200
Stainless finish . . . . NiB $570 Ex $460 Gd $200
Model 92F-EL gold. . . . . NiB $699 Ex $575 Gd $417

MODEL 92FS DA AUTOMATIC PISTOL
Calibers: 9mm, 9mmx19 and .40 S&W. 15- shot magazine, 4.9- inch bbl., 8.5 inches overall. Weight: 34.4 to 35.3 oz. Ambidextrous safety/decock lever. Chrome-lined bore w/combat trigger guard. Bruniton finish w/plastic grips or Inox finish w/rubber grips. Made 1991 to date.
Model 92FS . . . . NiB $620 Ex $490 Gd $275
Model 92FS, Inox . . . . NiB $645 Ex $545 Gd $275
Model 92FS — Brigadier
(Made 1999 to date) . . . . NiB $531 Ex $425 Gd $289
Model 92FS —
Brigadier Inox . . . . NiB $645 Ex $545 Gd $280
Model 92FS — Centurion
(Made 1992 to date) . . . . NiB $645 Ex $545 Gd $280
Model 92FS — 470th Anniver.
(Made 1999) . . . . NiB $2090 Ex $1850 Gd $1075

MODEL 92S DA AUTO
PISTOL (2ND SERIES) . . . . NiB $650 Ex $550 Gd $250
Revised version of Model 92 w/ambidextrous slide-mounted safety modification intended for both commercial and military production. Evolved to Model 92S-1 for U.S. Military trials. Made 1980-85.

MODEL 92SB DA
AUTO PISTOL (3RD SERIES) . . . . . . NiB $670 Ex $580 Gd $290
Same general specifications as standard Model 92 except has slide-mounted safety and repositioned magazine release. Made 1981-85.

MODEL 92 SB-F
DA AUTO PISTOL . . . . NiB $650 Ex $550 Gd $250
Caliber: 9mm Para. 15-shot magazine, bbl.: 4.9 inches, 8.5 inches overall. Weight: 34 oz. Plastic or Beretta Model 92 SB-F DA Auto Pistol wood grips. Square-notched rear sight, blade front sight integral w/slide. This model, also called Model 92S-1, is the standard-issue sidearm for the U.S. Armed Forces. Made 1985 to date.

Beretta Model 90

Beretta Model 92F

Beretta Model 92
Compact L Type M

Beretta Model 92FS
Brigadier Inox

Beretta Model 96

**Beretta Model 949
Olimpionico**

**Beretta Model 950BS
Jetfire**

MODEL 96 DOUBLE-ACTION AUTO PISTOL
Same general specifications as Model 92F except in .40 S&W. 10-shot magazine (9-shot in Compact model). Made 1992 to date.
Model 96 D (DA only) . . . . NiB $413 Ex $330 Gd $224
Model 96 Centurion (compact) . . . . NiB $460 Ex $360 Gd $225
W/Tritium sights, add $80
W/Tritium sights system, add $95

MODEL 101 . . . . NiB $250 Ex $220 Gd $125
Same as Model 70T except caliber .22 LR, has 10-shot magazine, Intro. in 1959. Disc.

MODEL 318
(1934) AUTO PISTOL . . . . NiB $275 Ex $240 Gd $130
Caliber: .25 Automatic (6.35mm). Eight-shot magazine, 2.5-inch bbl., 4.5 inches overall. Weight: 14 oz. Fixed sights. Blued finish. Plastic grips. Made 1934 to c. 1939.

MODEL 949
OLIMPIONICO AUTO PISTOL . . . . NiB $660 Ex $550 Gd $200
Calibers: .22 Short, .22 LR. Five-shot magazine, 8.75-inch bbl., 12.5 inches overall. Weight: 38 oz. Target sights. Adj. bbl., weight. Muzzle brake. Checkered walnut grips w/thumbrest. Made 1959-64.

MODEL 950B AUTO PISTOL. . . . . . NiB $158 Ex $120 Gd $70
Same general specifications as Model 950CC except caliber .25 Auto, has 7-shot magazine, Made 1959 to date. Note: Formerly marketed in the U.S. as "Jetfire."

MODEL 950BS JETFIRE SA PISTOL
Calibers: .25 ACP or .22 Short (disc.1992). Seven- or 8- shot magazine, 2.4- or 4- inch bbl., 4.5 to 4.7 inches overall. Weight: 9.9 oz. Fixed blade front and V-notch rear sights. Matte Blue or Inox (Stainless) finish. Checkered black plastic grips. Made 1987 to date.
Blued finish . . . . NiB $156 Ex $125 Gd $85
Nickel finish . . . . NiB $206 Ex $165 Gd $112
Inox finish . . . . NiB $181 Ex $145 Gd $99
W/4-inch bbl.,
(.22 Short) . . . . NiB $188 Ex $150 Gd $102

MODEL 950CC
AUTO PISTOL . . . . NiB $135 Ex $115 Gd $70
Caliber: .22 Short. Six-shot magazine, hinged 2.38-inch bbl., 4.75 inches overall. Weight: 11 oz. Fixed sights. Blued finish. Plastic grips. Made 1959 to date. Note: Formerly marketed in the U.S. as "Minx M2."

MODEL 950CC
SPECIAL AUTO PISTOL . . . . NiB $135 Ex $115 Gd $70
Same general specifications as Model 950CC Auto except has 4-inch bbl. Made 1959 to date. Note: Formerly marketed in the U.S. as "Minx M4."

MODEL 951 (1951)
MILITARY AUTO PISTOL . . . . NiB $285 Ex $235 Gd $160
Caliber: 9mm Para. Eight-shot magazine, 4.5-inch bbl., 8 inches overall. Weight: 31 oz. Fixed sights. Blued finish. Plastic grips. Made 1952 to date. Note: This is the standard pistol of the Italian Armed Forces, also used by Egyptian and Israeli armies and by the police in Nigeria. Egyptian and Israeli models usually command a premium. Formerly marketed in the U.S. as the "Brigadier."

MODEL 1915
AUTO PISTOL . . . . NiB $950 Ex $700 Gd $300
Calibers: 9mm Glisenti and .32 ACP (7.65mm). Eight-shot magazine, 4-inch bbl., 6.7 inches overall (9mm), 5.7 inches (.32 ACP). Weight: 30 oz. (9mm), 20 oz. (.32 ACP). Fixed sights. Blued finish. Wood grips. Made 1915-1922. An improved postwar 1915/1919 version in caliber .32 ACP was later offered for sale in 1922 as the Model 1922.

MODEL 1923
AUTO PISTOL . . . . NiB $1000 Ex $850 Gd $250
Caliber: 9mm Glisenti (Luger). Eight-shot magazine, 4-inch bbl., 6.5 inches overall. Weight: 30 oz. Fixed sights. Blued finish. Plastic grips. Made c. 1923-36.

MODEL 1934 AUTO PISTOL
Caliber: .380 Automatic (9mm Short). Seven-shot magazine, 3.38-inch bbl., 5.88 inches overall. Weight: 24 oz. Fixed sights. Blued finish. Plastic grips. Official pistol of the Italian Armed Forces. Wartime pieces not as well made and finished as commercial models. Made 1934-59.
Commercial model . . . . NiB $375 Ex $325 Gd $190
War model. . . . . NiB $350 Ex $320 Gd $180

MODEL 1935 AUTO PISTOL
Caliber: .32 ACP (7.65mm). Eight-shot magazine, 3.5-inch bbl., 5.75 inches overall. Weight: 24 oz. Fixed sights. Blued finish. Plastic grips. A roughly-finished version of this pistol was produced during WW II. Made 1935-1959.

Commercial model	NiB $350	Ex $315	Gd $175
War model	NiB $300	Ex $250	Gd $150

MODEL 3032 DA SEMIAUTOMATIC TOMCAT
Caliber: .32 ACP. Seven-shot magazine, 2.45-inch bbl., 5 inches overall. Weight: 14.5 oz. Fixed sights. Blued or stainless finish. Made 1996 to date.

Matte blue	NiB $265	Ex $200	Gd $120
Polished blue	NiB $309	Ex $255	Gd $186
Stainless	NiB $333	Ex $270	Gd $190

**Beretta
Model 3032 Tomcat**

MODEL 8000/8040/8045 COUGAR DA PISTOL
Calibers: 9mm, .40 S&W and .45 Auto. Eight- or 10- shot magazine, 3.6 to 3.7- inch bbl., 7- to 7.2 inches overall. Weight: 32 to 32.6 oz. Short recoil action w/rotating barrel. Fixed sights w/3-dot Tritium system. Textured black composition grips. Matte black Bruniton finish w/alloy frame. Made 1994 to date.

8000 Cougar D (9mm DAO)	NiB $600	Ex $545	Gd $300
8000 Cougar F (9mm DA)	NiB $600	Ex $545	Gd $300
8040 Cougar D (.40 S&W DAO)	NiB $600	Ex $545	Gd $300
8040 Cougar F (.40 S&W DA)	NiB $600	Ex $545	Gd $300
8045 Cougar D (.45 Auto DAO)	NiB $620	Ex $550	Gd $310
8045 Cougar F (.45 Auto DA)	NiB $620	Ex $550	Gd $310

**Beretta
Model 8000 Cougar D**

MODEL 8000/8040/8045 MINI COUGAR DA PISTOL
Calibers: 9mm, .40 S&W and .45 Auto. Six- 8- or 10-shot magazine, 3.6- to 3.7- inch bbl., 7 inches overall. Weight: 27.4 to 30.4 oz. Fixed sights w/3-dot Tritium system. Ambidextrous safety/decocker lever. Matte black Bruniton finish w/anodized aluminum alloy frame. Made 1998 to date.

8000 Mini Cougar D (9mm DAO)	NiB $620	Ex $490	Gd $240
8000 Mini Cougar F (9mm DA)	NiB $640	Ex $510	Gd $250
8040 Mini Cougar D (.40 S&W DAO)	NiB $640	Ex $510	Gd $250
8040 Mini Cougar F (.40 S&W DA)	NiB $640	Ex $510	Gd $250
8045 Mini Cougar D (.45 Auto DAO)	NiB $630	Ex $500	Gd $225
8045 Mini Cougar F (.45 Auto DA)	NiB $640	Ex $510	Gd $250

**Beretta
Model 8000 Cougar F**

MODEL 9000S SUBCOMPACT PISTOL SERIES
Calibers: 9mm, .40 S&W. 10-shot magazine, 3.5- inch bbl., 6.6 inches overall. Weight: 25.7 to 27.5 oz. Single/double and double-action only. Front and rear dovetail sights w/3- dot system. Chrome-plated barrel w/Techno-polymer frame. Geometric locking system w/tilt barrel. Made 1999 to date. See illustration next page.

Type D (9mm)	NiB $482	Ex $405	Gd $249
Type D (.40 S&W)	NiB $495	Ex $395	Gd $250
Type F (9mm)	NiB $520	Ex $424	Gd $255
Type F (.40 S&W)	NiB $530	Ex $439	Gd $262

**Beretta
Model 8040 Mini Cougar D**

**Beretta
Model 9000 Type F**

**Bernardelli
Model 60 Pocket**

**Bernardelli
Model 80 Pocket**

VINCENZO BERNARDELLI, S.P.A.
Gardone V. T. (Brescia), Italy

Currently imported by Armsport, Inc., Miami, FL

MODEL 60 POCKET
AUTOMATIC PISTOL . . . . **NiB $220 Ex $195 Gd $130**
Calibers: .22 LR, .32 Auto (7.65mm), .380 Auto (9mm Short). Eight-shot magazine (.22 and .32), 7-shot (.380). 3.5-inch bbl., 6.5

(cont'd) **MODEL 60**
inches ovr-all. Weight: About 25 oz. Fixed sights. Blued finish. Bakelite grips. Made 1959-90.

MODEL 68 AUTOMATIC PISTOL . . . **NiB $140 Ex $120 Gd $80**
Caliber: 6.35. Five- and 8-shot magazine, 2.13-inch bbl., 4.13 inches overall. Weight: 10 oz. Fixed sights. Blued or chrome finish. Bakelite or pearl grips. This model, like its .22-caliber counterpart, was known as the "Baby" Bernardelli. Disc. 1970.

**MODEL 69 AUTOMATIC
TARGET PISTOL** . . . . **NiB $575 Ex $475 Gd $300**
Caliber: .22 LR. 10-shot magazine, 5.9-inch bbl., 9 inches overall. Weight: 2.2 lbs. Fully adj. target sights. Blued finish. Stippled right- or left-hand wraparound walnut grips. Made 1987 to date. Note: This was previously Model 100.

**MODEL 80
AUTOMATIC PISTOL** . . . . **NiB $185 Ex $160 Gd $100**
Calibers: .22 LR, .32 ACP (7.65mm), .380 Auto (9mm Short). Magazine capacity: 10-shot (.22), 8-shot (.32), 7-shot (.380). 3.5-inch bbl., 6.5 inches overall. Weight: 25.6 oz. adj. rear sight, white dot front sight. Blued finish. Plastic thumbrest grips. Note: Model 80 is a modification of Model 60 designed to conform w/U.S. import regulations. Made 1968-88.

**MODEL 90
SPORT TARGET** . . . . **NiB $210 Ex $185 Gd $110**
Same as Model 80 except has 6-inch bbl., 9 inches overall, weight: 26.8 oz. Made 1968-90.

**MODEL 100 TARGET
AUTOMATIC PISTOL** . . . . **NiB $395 Ex $325 Gd $210**
Caliber: .22 LR. 10-shot magazine, 5.9-inch bbl., 9 inches overall. Weight: 37.75 oz. Adj. rear sight, interchangeable front sights. Blued finish. Checkered walnut thumbrest grips. Made 1969-86. Note: Formerly Model 69.

MODEL AMR AUTO PISTOL . . . . . . **NiB $395 Ex $325 Gd $200**
Simlar to Model USA except with 6-inch bbl. and target sights. Imported 1992-94.

"BABY" AUTOMATIC PISTOL . . . . . **NiB $250 Ex $175 Gd $100**
Calibers: .22 Short, .22 Long. Five-shot magazine, 2.13-inch bbl., 4.13 inches overall. Weight: 9 oz. Fixed sights. Blued finish. Bakelite grips. Made 1949-68.

**MODEL P010
AUTOMATIC PISTOL** . . . . **NiB $675 Ex $575 Gd $350**
Caliber: .22 LR. Five- and 10-shot magazine, 5.9-inch bbl. w/7.5-inch sight radius. Weight: 40 oz. Interchangeable front sight, adj. rear. Blued finish. Textured walnut grips. Made 1988-92 and 1995-97.

P018 COMPACT MODEL . . . . **NiB $485 Ex $460 Gd $225**
Slightly smaller version of the Model P018 standard DA automatic except has 14-shot magazine and 4-inch bbl., 7.68 inches overall. Weight: 33 oz. Walnut grips only. Imported 1987-96.

P018 DOUBLE-ACTION AUTOMATIC PISTOL
Caliber: 9mm Para. 16-shot magazine, 4.75-inch bbl., 8.5 inches overall. Weight: 36 oz. Fixed combat sights. Blued finish. Checkered plastic or walnut grips. Imported 1987-96.
W/plastic grips . . . . **NiB $485 Ex $400 Gd $230**
W/walnut grips . . . . **NiB $514 Ex $415 Gd $289**

P. ONE DA AUTO PISTOL

Caliber: 9mm Parabellum or .40 S&W. 10- or 16-shot magazine, 4.8-inch bbl., 8.35 inches overall. Weight: 34 oz. Blade front sight, adjustable rear w/3-dot system. Matte black or chrome finish. Checkered walnut or black plastic grips. Imported 1993-97.

Model P One blue finish . . . . NiB $580 Ex $485 Gd $280
Model P One chrome finish. . . . . . . NiB $611 Ex $495 Gd $346
W/walnut grips, add 35

P. ONE PRACTICAL VB AUTO PISTOL

Similar to Model P One except chambered for 9x21mm w/2-, 4- or 6-port compensating system for IPSC competition. Imported 1993-97.
Model P One
Practical (2 port) . . . . NiB $1000 Ex $925 Gd $660
Model P One
Practical (4 port) . . . . NiB $1123 Ex $910 Gd $638
Model P One
Practical (6 port) . . . . NiB $1508 Ex $1220 Gd $852
W/chrome finish, add $60

SPORTER AUTOMATIC PISTOL . . . . . NiB $305 Ex $275 Gd $175
Caliber .22 LR. Eight-shot magazine, bbl., lengths: 6-, 8- and 10-inch, 13 inches overall (10-inch bbl.). weight: About 30 oz. (10-inch bbl.) Target sights. Blued finish. Walnut grips. Made 1949-68.

MODEL USA AUTO PISTOL

Single-action, blowback. Calibers: .22 LR, .32 ACP, .380 ACP. Seven-shot magazine or 10-shot magazine (.22 LR). 3.5-inch bbl., 6.5 inches overall. Weight: 26.5 oz. Ramped front sight, adjustable rear. Blue or chrome finish. Checkered black bakelite grips w/thumbrest. Imported 1991-97.

Model USA blue finish . . . . NiB $380 Ex $295 Gd $180
Model USA chrome finish . . . . NiB $466 Ex $385 Gd $281

VEST POCKET

AUTOMATIC PISTOL . . . . NiB $250 Ex $195 Gd $125
Caliber: .25 Auto (6.35mm). Five- or 8-shot magazine, 2.13-inch bbl., 4.13 inches overall. Weight: 9 oz. Fixed sights. Blued finish. Bakelite grips. Made 1945-68.

Bernardelli P010

Bernardelli "Baby"

BERSA PISTOLS — Argentina

Currently imported by Eagle Imports, Wanamassa, NJ (Previously by Interarms & Outdoor Sports)

MODEL 83 DOUBLE-ACTION AUTO PISTOL

Similar to the Model 23 except for the following specifications: Caliber: .380 ACP. Seven-shot magazine, 3.5-inch bbl., Front blade sight integral on slide, square-notch rear adj. for windage. Blued or satin nickel finish. Custom wood grips. Imported 1988-94.
Blued finish . . . . NiB $235 Ex $180 Gd $150
Satin nickel . . . . NiB $294 Ex $245 Gd $183

MODEL 85 DOUBLE-ACTION AUTO PISTOL

Same general specifications as Model 83 except 13-shot magazine, Imported 1988-94. See illustration next page.
Blued finish . . . . NiB $285 Ex $245 Gd $140
Satin nickel . . . . NiB $381 Ex $315 Gd $230

MODEL 86 DOUBLE-ACTION AUTO PISTOL

Same general specifications as Model 85 except available in matte blued finish and w/Neoprene grips. Imported 1992-94.
Matte blued finish . . . . NiB $315 Ex $265 Gd $160
Nickel finish . . . . NiB $374 Ex $305 Gd $217

Bernardelli P018

MODEL 95 DA AUTOMATIC PISTOL

Caliber: .380 ACP. Seven-shot magazine, 3.5-inch bbl., weight: 23 oz. Wraparound rubber grips. Blade front and rear notch sights. Imported 1995 to date.
Blued finish . . . . NiB $229 Ex $165 Gd $110
Nickel finish . . . . NiB $252 Ex $187 Gd $132

Bersa Model 85

Bersa Model 383

Bersa Thunder .380

Bersa Thunder .380 Deluxe

MODEL 97
AUTO PISTOL . . . . NiB $325 Ex $280 Gd $170
Caliber: .380 ACP. Seven-shot magazine, 3.3-inch bbl., 6.5 inches overall. Weight: 28 oz. Intro. 1982. Disc.

MODEL 223
Same general specifications as Model 383 except in .22 LR w/10-round magazine capacity. Disc. 1987.
Double action . . . . NiB $200 Ex $170 Gd $110
Single action . . . . NiB $190 Ex $160 Gd $107

MODEL 224
Caliber: .22 LR. 10-shot magazine, 4-inch bbl., weight: 26 oz. Front blade sight, square-notched rear adj. for windage. Blued finish. Checkered nylon or custom wood grips. Made 1984. SA. disc. 1986.
Double-action . . . . NiB $200 Ex $170 Gd $110
Single action . . . . NiB $195 Ex $169 Gd $104

MODEL 226
Same general specifications as Model 224 but w/6-inch bbl. Disc. 1987.
Double action . . . . NiB $200 Ex $170 Gd $110
Single action . . . . NiB $190 Ex $160 Gd $107

MODEL 383 AUTO PISTOL
Caliber: .380 Auto. Seven-shot magazine, 3.5-inch bbl. Front blade sight integral on slide, square-notched rear sight adj. for windage. Custom wood grips on double-action, nylon grips on single action. Blued or satin nickel finish. Made 1984. SA. disc. 1989.
Double action . . . . NiB $120 Ex $95 Gd $50
Single action . . . . NiB $160 Ex $121 Gd $75
Satin nickel . . . . NiB $201 Ex $160 Gd $87

MODEL 622
AUTO PISTOL . . . . NiB $156 Ex $125 Gd $85
Caliber: .22 LR. Seven-shot magazine, 4- or 6-inch bbl., 7 or 9 inches overall. Weight: 2.25 lbs. Blade front sight, square-notch rear adj. for windage. Blued finish. Nylon grips. Made 1982-87.

MODEL 644
AUTO PISTOL . . . . NiB $230 Ex $195 Gd $120
Caliber: .22 LR. 10-shot magazine, 3.5-inch bbl., weight: 26.5 oz. 6.5 inches overall. Adj. rear sight, blade front. Contoured black nylon grips. Made 1980-88.

THUNDER 9
AUTO PISTOL . . . . NiB $235 Ex $195 Gd $120
Caliber: 9mm Para. 15-shot magazine, 4-inch bbl., 7.38 inches overall. Weight: 30 oz. Blade front sight, adj. rear w/3-dot system. Ambidextrous safety and decocking device. Matte blued finish. Checkered black polymer grips. Made 1993-96.

THUNDER .22
AUTO PISTOL (MODEL 23)
Caliber: .22 LR, 10-shot magazine, 3.5-inch bbl., 6.63 inches overall. Weight: 24.5 oz. Notched-bar dovetailed rear, blade integral w/slide front. Black polymer grips. Made 1989 to date.
Blued finish . . . . NiB $230 Ex $195 Gd $110
Nickel finish . . . . NiB $242 Ex $195 Gd $131

THUNDER .380 AUTO PISTOL
Caliber: .380 ACP. Seven-shot magazine, 3.5-inch bbl., 6.63 inches overall. Weight: 25.75 oz. Notched-bar dovetailed rear, blade integral w/slide front. Blued, satin nickel, or Duo-Tone finish. Made 1995 to date.

Blued finish	NiB $225	Ex $240	Gd $115
Satin nickel finish	NiB $264	Ex $215	Gd $153
Duo-Tone finish	NiB $251	Ex $205	Gd $146

THUNDER .380 PLUS AUTO PISTOL
Same general specifications as standard Thunder .380 except has 10-shot magazine and weight: 26 oz. Made 1995-97.

Matte finish	NiB $231	Ex $185	Gd $126
Satin nickel finish	NiB $281	Ex $225	Gd $153
Duo-Tone finish	NiB $263	Ex $210	Gd $143

Browning
Model 25 Automatic

BROLIN ARMS — La Verne, California

"LEGEND SERIES" SA AUTOMATIC PISTOL
Caliber: .45 ACP. Seven-shot magazine, 4- or 5-inch bbl., weight: 32-36 oz. Walnut grips. Single action, full size, compact, or full size frame compact slide. Matte blued finish. Lowered and flared ejection port. Made 1995 to date.

Model L45	NiB $425	Ex $365	Gd $225
Model L45C	NiB $440	Ex $380	Gd $250
Model L45T	NiB $450	Ex $390	Gd $260

"PATRIOT SERIES" SA AUTOMATIC PISTOL
Caliber: .45 ACP. Seven-shot magazine, 3.25- and 4-inch bbl., weight: 33-37 oz. Wood grips. Fixed rear sights. Made 1996 to date.

Model P45	NiB $585	Ex $475	Gd $300
Model P45C (disc. 1997)	NiB $610	Ex $620	Gd $550
Model P45T (disc. 1997)	NiB $620	Ex $500	Gd $280

"PRO-STOCK AND PRO-COMP" SA PISTOL
Caliber: .45 ACP. Eight-shot magazine, 4- or 5-inch bbl., weight: 37 oz. Single action, blued or two-tone finish. Wood grips. Bomar adjustable sights. Made 1996-97.

Model Pro comp	NiB $685	Ex $550	Gd $374
Model Pro stock	NiB $620	Ex $500	Gd $330

TAC SERIES
Caliber: .45 ACP. Eight-shot magazine, 5-inch bbl., 8.5 inches overall. Weight: 37 oz. Low profile combat or Tritium sights. Beavertail grip safety. Matte blue, chrome or two-tone finish. Checkered wood or contoured black rubber grips. Made 1997 to date.

Model TAC 11 service	NiB $610	Ex $495	Gd $300
Model TAC 11 compact	NiB $620	Ex $500	Gd $300
W/Tritium sights, add			$95

BRONCO PISTOL — Eibar, Spain
Manufactured by Echave y Arizmendi

MODEL 1918 POCKET
AUTOMATIC PISTOL .... NiB $175 Ex $150 Gd $75
Caliber: .32 ACP (7.65mm). Six-shot magazine 2.5-inch bbl., 5 inches overall. Weight: 20 oz. Fixed sights. Blued finish. Hard rubber grips. Made c.1918-.25.

SEMIAUTOMATIC PISTOL .... NiB $160 Ex $125 Gd $88
Caliber: .25 ACP, 6-shot magazine, 2.13-inch bbl., 4.13 inches overall. Weight: 11 oz. Fixed sights. Blued finish. Hard rubber grips. Made 1919-35.

BROWNING PISTOLS — Morgan, Utah

The following Browning pistols have been manufactured by Fabrique Nationale d'Armes de Guerre (now Fabrique Nationale Herstal) of Herstal, Belgium, by Arms Technology Inc. of Salt Lake City and by J. P. Sauer & Sohn of Eckernforde, W. Germany. (See also FN Browning and J.P. Sauer & Sohn listings.)

.25 AUTOMATIC PISTOL
Same general specifications as FN Browning Baby (see separate listing). Standard Model, blued finish, hard rubber grips. Light Model, nickel-plated, Nacrolac pearl grips. Renaissance Engraved Model, nickel-plated, Nacrolac pearl grips. Made by FN 1955-69.

Standard model	NiB $500	Ex $440	Gd $200
Lightweight model	NiB $500	Ex $440	Gd $200
Renaissance model	NiB $975	Ex $750	Gd $400

.32 AND .380 AUTOMATIC PISTOL, 1955 TYPE
Same general specifications as FN Browning .32 (7.65mm) and .380 Pocket Auto. Standard Model, Renaissance Engraved Model as furnished in .25 Automatic. Made by FN 1955-69.

Standard model (.32 ACP)	NiB $433	Ex $350	Gd $230
Standard model (.380 ACP)	NiB $365	Ex $300	Gd $200
Renaissance model	NiB $950	Ex $800	Gd $575

.380 AUTOMATIC PISTOL, 1971 TYPE
Same as .380 Automatic, 1955 Type except has longer slide, 4.44-inch bbl., is 7.06 inches overall, weight: 23 oz. Rear sight adj. for windage and elevation, plastic thumbrest grips. Made 1971-75.

Standard model	NiB $395	Ex $300	Gd $200
Renaissance model	NiB $975	Ex $775	Gd $500

BDA DA AUTOMATIC PISTOL
Similar to SIG-Sauer P220. Calibers: 9mm Para., .38 Super Auto, .45 Auto. Nine-shot magazine (9mm and .38), 7-shot (.45 cal), 4.4-inch bbl., 7.8 inches overall. Weight: 29.3 oz. Fixed sights. Blued finish. Plastic grips. Made 1977-79 by J. P. Sauer.

BDA model, 9mm, .45 ACP	NiB $465	Ex $395	Gd $250
BDA model, .38 Super	NiB $475	Ex $380	Gd $290

BDA-.380 DA AUTOMATIC PISTOL
Caliber: .380 Auto. 10- or 13-shot magazine, bbl. length: 3.81 inches., 6.75 inches overall. Weight: 23 oz. Fixed blade front sight, square-notch drift-adj. rear sight. Blued or nickel finish. Smooth walnut grips. Made 1982-97 by Beretta. See illustration next page.

Blued finish	NiB $450	Ex $345	Gd $200
Nickel finish	NiB $436	Ex $355	Gd $251

Browning
BDA .380 Nickel finish

Browning
Buck Mark 22 Field (5.5)

Browning
Buck Mark 22 Bullseye

Browning
Buck Mark 22 Plus

Browning
BDM 9mm DA

BDM SERIES AUTOMATIC PISTOLS
Calibers: 9mm Para., 10-shot magazine, 4.73-inch bbl., 7.85 inches overall. Weight: 31 oz., windage adjustable sights w/3-dot system. Low profile removable blade front sights. Matte blued, Bi-Tone or silver chrome finish. Selectable shooting mode and decocking safety lever. Made 1991 to date.

BDM Standard . . . . NiB $481   Ex $385   Gd $262
BDM Practical . . . . NiB $488   Ex $390   Gd $265
BDM-D Silver Chrome . . . . NiB $494   Ex $395   Gd $269

BUCK MARK .22 AUTOMATIC PISTOL
Caliber: .22 LR. 10-shot magazine, 5.5- inch bbl., 9.5 inches overall. Weight: 32 oz. Black molded grips. Adj. rear sight. Blued or nickel finish. Made 1985 to date.

Blued finish . . . . NiB $215   Ex $175   Gd $100
Nickel finish . . . . NiB $274   Ex $225   Gd $163

BUCK MARK .22 BULLSEYE PISTOL
Same general specifications as the standard Buck Mark 22 except w/7.25-inch fluted barrel, 11.83 inches overall. Weight: 36 oz. Adjustable target trigger. Undercut post front sight, click-adjustable Pro-Target rear. Laminated, Rosewood, black rubber or composite grips. Made 1996 to date.

Standard model
(composite grips) . . . . NiB $325   Ex $265   Gd $180
Target model . . . . NiB $400   Ex $300   Gd $180

BUCK MARK .22
BULLSEYE TARGET . . . . NiB $400   Ex $300   Gd $180
Caliber: .22 LR. 10-shot magazine, 7.25- inch fluted bbl., 11.83 inches overall. Weight: 31 oz. Rosewood wrap-around finger groove grips w/matte blued finish. Made 1996 to date.

BUCK MARK .22 FIELD
(5.5) AUTO PISTOL . . . . NiB $325   Ex $240   Gd $150
Calibers: .22 LR. 10-shot magazine, 5.5- inch bbl., 9.58 inches overall. Weight: 35.5 oz. Standard sights. Matte Blue finish. Made 1991 to date.

BUCK MARK .22 MICRO AUTOMATIC PISTOL
Same general specifications as standard Buck Mark .22 except w/4-inch bbl., 8 inches overall. Weight: 32 oz. Molded composite grips. Ramp front sight, Pro Target rear sight. Made 1992 to date.

Blued finish . . . . NiB $265   Ex $210   Gd $108
Nickel finish . . . . NiB $284   Ex $238   Gd $179

**Browning
Buck Mark .22 Silhouette**

BUCK MARK .22 MICRO PLUS AUTO PISTOL
Same specifications as the Buck Mark .22 Micro except ambidextrous, laminated wood grips. Made 1996 to date.
Blued finish . . . . NiB $265 Ex $210 Gd $110
Nickel finish . . . . NiB $297 Ex $248 Gd $186

BUCK MARK .22 PLUS AUTOMATIC PISTOL
Same general specifications as standard Buck Mark .22 except for black molded, impregnated hardwood grips. Made 1987 to date.
Blued finish . . . . NiB $265 Ex $210 Gd $100
Nickel finish . . . . NiB $303 Ex $253 Gd $189

BUCK MARK .22 TARGET (5.5) AUTO PISTOL
Caliber: .22 LR. 10-shot magazine, 5.5- inch bbl., 9.6 inches overall. Weight: 35.5 oz. Pro target sights. Wrap-around walnut or contoured finger groove grips. Made 1990 to date.
Matte blue finish . . . . NiB $350 Ex $280 Gd $150
Nickel finish (1994 to date) . . . . NiB $422 Ex $348 Gd $254
Gold finish (1991-99) . . . . NiB $463 Ex $385 Gd $286

BUCK MARK .22 SILHOUETTE . . . . NiB $360 Ex $285 Gd $150
Same general specifications as standard Buck Mark .22 except for 9.88-inch bbl. Weight: 53 oz. Target sights mounted on full-length scope base, and laminated hardwood grips and forend. Made 1987 to date.

BUCK MARK .22
UNLIMITED SILHOUETTE . . . . NiB $425 Ex $330 Gd $200
Same general specifications as standard Buck Mark .22 Silhouette except w/14-inch bbl., 18.69 inches overall. Weight: 64 oz. Interchangeable post front sight and Pro Target rear. Nickel finish. Made 1992 to date.

BUCK MARK .22
VARMINT AUTO PISTOL . . . . NiB $315 Ex $255 Gd $160
Same general specifications as standard Buck Mark .22 except for 9.88-inch bbl. Weight: 48 oz. No sights, full-length scope base, and laminated hardwood grips. Made 1987 to date.

CHALLENGER AUTOMATIC PISTOL
Caliber: .22 LR. 10-shot magazine, bbl. lengths: 4.5 and 6.75-inches. 11.44 inches overall (with 6.75-inch bbl.). Weight: 38 oz. (6.75-inch bbl.). Removable blade front sight, screw adj. rear. Standard finish, blued, also furnished gold inlaid (Gold model) and engraved and chrome-plated (Renaissance model). Checkered walnut grips. Finely figured and carved grips on Gold and Renaissance models. Standard made by FN 1962-75, higher grades. Intro. 1971. Disc.
Standard model . . . . NiB $375 Ex $315 Gd $200
Gold model . . . . NiB $1450 Ex $1250 Gd $500
Renaissance model . . . . NiB $1450 Ex $1250 Gd $500

CHALLENGER II
AUTOMATIC PISTOL . . . . NiB $220 Ex $190 Gd $110
Same general specifications as Challenger Standard model w/6.75-inch bbl. except changed grip angle and impregnated hardwood grips. Original Challenger design modified for lower production costs. Made by ATI 1976-83.

**Browning
Buck Mark .22 Target (5.5)**

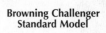

**Browning
Buck Mark .22 Micro**

**Browning Challenger
Standard Model**

**Browning Challenger
Renaissance Model**

Browning
Challenger III Sporter .22

Browning
9mm Hi-Power w/Molded Grips

Browning
9mm Hi-Power Ambidextrous Safety

Browning
Hi-Power Captain

Browning
Hi-Power Mark III

CHALLENGER III

AUTOMATIC PISTOL . . . . NiB $220 Ex $190 Gd $110
Same general description as Challenger II except has 5.5 inch bull bbl., alloy frame and new sight system. Weight: 35 oz. Made 1982-84. Sporter Model w/6.75-inch bbl.. Made 1984-86.

HI-POWER AUTOMATIC PISTOL
Same general specifications as FN Browning Model 1935 except chambered for 9mm Para., .30 Luger and .40 S&W. 10- or 13-shot magazine, 4.63-inch bbl., 7.75 inches overall. Weight: 32 oz. (9mm) or 35 oz. (.40 S&W). Fixed sights, also available w/rear sight adj. for windage and elevation, and ramp front sight. Ambidextrous safety added after 1989. Standard model blued, chrome-plated or Bi-Tone finish. Checkered walnut, contour-molded Polyamide or wraparound rubber grips. Renaissance Engraved model chrome-plated, w/Nacrolac pearl grips. Made by FN from1955 to date.
Standard model,
fixed sights, 9mm . . . . NiB $690 Ex $560 Gd $400
Standard model, fixed sights,
.40 S&W (intro. 1986) . . . . NiB $700 Ex $675 Gd $500
Standard model, .30
Luger (1986-89). . . . . NiB $675 Ex $575 Gd $375
Renaissance model,
fixed sights. . . . . NiB $1350 Ex $1290 Gd $500
W/adjustable
rear sight, add $50
W/ambidextrous
safety, add $95
W/moulded grips,
deduct $40
W/tangent rear sight
(1965-78), add* $295
W/T-Slot grip &
tangent sight
(1965-78), add* $595
*Check FN agent to certify value

HI-POWER
CAPITAN AUTOMATIC . . . . NiB $610 Ex $500 Gd $325
Similar to the standard Hi-Power except fitted w/adj. 500-meter tangent rear sight and rounded serrated hammer. Made 1993 to date.

HI-POWER MARK
III AUTOMATIC PISTOL . . . . NiB $540 Ex $395 Gd $300
Calibers: 9mm and .40 S&W. 10-shot magazine, 4.75-inch bbl., 7.75 inches overall. Weight: 32 oz. Fixed sights with molded grips. Durable non-glare matte blue finish. Made 1985 to date.

**Browning
Hi-Power Practical**

**Browning
Hi-Power Silver Chrome**

HI-POWER PRACTICAL AUTOMATIC PISTOL
Similar to the standard Hi-Power except has silver-chromed frame and blued slide w/Commander-style hammer. Made 1991 to date.
W/fixed sights . . . . NiB $570 Ex $435 Gd $300
W/adj. sights . . . . NiB $602 Ex $493 Gd $354

HI-POWER SILVER CHROME
AUTOMATIC PISTOL . . . . NiB $695 Ex $550 Gd $315
Calibers: 9mm and .40 S&W. 10-shot magazine, 4.75-inch bbl., 7.75 inches overall. Weight: 36 oz. Adjustable sights with Pachmayer grips. Silver-chromed finish. Made 1991 to date.

HI-POWER 9MM CLASSIC
Limited Edition 9mm Hi-Power, w/silver-gray finish, high-grade engraving and finely-checkered walnut grips w/double border. Proposed production of the Classic was 5000 w/less than half that number produced. Gold Classic limited to 500 w/two-thirds proposed production in circulation. Made 1985-86.
Gold classic . . . . NiB $2494 Ex $1995 Gd $1357
Standard classic . . . . NiB $1244 Ex $995 Gd $677

INTERNATIONAL
MEDALIST AUTOMATIC
TARGET PISTOL . . . . NiB $850 Ex $700 Gd $400
Modification of Medalist to conform w/International Shooting Union rules. 5.9-inch bbl., Smaller grip with no forearm. Weight: 42 oz. Made 1970-73.

MEDALIST AUTOMATIC TARGET PISTOL
Caliber: .22 LR. 10-shot magazine, 6.75-inch bbl. w/vent rib, 11.94 inches overall. Weight: 46 oz. Removable blade front sight, click-adj. micrometer rear. Standard finish, blued also furnished gold-inlaid (Gold Model) and engraved and chrome-plated (Renaissance Model). Checkered walnut grips w/thumbrest (for right- or left-handed shooter). Finely figured and carved grips on Gold and Renaissance Models. Made by FN 1962-75. Higher grades. Intro. 1971.
Standard model . . . . NiB $850 Ex $700 Gd $450
Gold model . . . . NiB $1950 Ex $1650 Gd $881
Renaissance model . . . . NiB $2350 Ex $1950 Gd $1221

NOMAD
AUTOMATIC PISTOL . . . . NiB $300 Ex $250 Gd $150
Caliber: .22 LR. 10-shot magazine, bbl. lengths: 4.5 and 6.75-inches, 8.94 inches overall (4.5-inch bbl.). Weight: 34 oz. (with 4.5-inch bbl.). Removable blade front sight, screw adj. rear. Blued finish. Plastic grips. Made by FN 1962-74.

**Browning
Hi-Power 9mm Classic**

**Browning
Medalist International**

**Browning
Medalist Automatic Target Pistol**

Browning
Renaissance

Charter Arms
Bonnie

Charter Arms
Clyde

**RENAISSANCE 9MM, .25 AUTO
AND .380 AUTO (1955) ENGRAVED
MODELS, CASED SET** .... NiB $4494 Ex $3595 Gd $2445
One pistol of each of the three models in a special walnut carrying case, all chrome-plated w/Nacrolac pearl grips. Made by FN 1955-69.

BRYCO ARMS INC. — Irvine, California
Distributed by Jennings Firearms. Inc. Carson City, NV

MODELS J22, J25 AUTO PISTOL
Calibers: .22 LR, .25 ACP. Six-shot magazine, 2.5-inch bbl., about 5 inches overall. Weight: 13 oz. Fixed sights. Chrome, satin nickel or black Teflon finish. Walnut, grooved black Cycolac or resin-impregnated wood grips. Made from 1981 to date.
Model J-22. .... NiB $81 Ex $65 Gd $44
Model J-25 (disc. 1995) .... NiB $65 Ex $55 Gd $40

MODELS M25, M32, M38 AUTO PISTOL
Calibers: .25 ACP, .32 ACP, .380 ACP. Six-shot magazine, 2.81-inch bbl., 5.31 inches overall. Weight: 11oz. to 15 oz. Fixed sights. Chrome, satin nickel or black Teflon finish. Walnut, grooved, black Cycolac or resin-impregnated wood grips. Made from 1988 to date.
Model M25 (disc.) .... NiB $65 Ex $50 Gd $40
Model M32 .... NiB $94 Ex $75 Gd $51
Model M38 .... NiB $106 Ex $85 Gd $58

MODEL M48
AUTO PISTOL .... NiB $85 Ex $75 Gd $50
Calibers: .22 LR, .32 ACP, .380 ACP. Seven-shot magazine, 4-inch bbl., 6.69 inches overall. Weight: 20 oz. Fixed sights. Chrome, satin nickel or black Teflon finish. Smooth wood or black Teflon grips. Made from 1989-95.

MODEL M58
AUTO PISTOL .... NiB $85 Ex $75 Gd $50
Caliber: .380 ACP. 10-shot magazine, 3.75-inch bbl., 5.5 inches overall. Weight: 30 oz. Fixed sights. Chrome, satin nickel, blued or black Teflon finish. Smooth wood or black Teflon grips. Made 1993-95.

MODEL M59
AUTO PISTOL .... NiB $95 Ex $85 Gd $50
Caliber: 9mm Para. 10-shot magazine, 4-inch bbl., 6.5 inches overall. Weight: 33 oz. Fixed sights. Chrome, satin nickel, blued or black Teflon finish. Smooth wood or black Teflon grips. Made 1994-96.

MODEL NINE SA
AUTO PISTOL .... NiB $120 Ex $100 Gd $60
Similar to Bryco/Jennings Model M59 except w/redesigned slide w/loaded chamber indicator and frame mounted ejector. Weight: 30 oz. Made 1997 to date.

MODEL T-.22
TARGET PISTOL .... NiB $113 Ex $90 Gd $61
Similar to Bryco/Jennings Model M48 except chambered for .22 LR only, w/target configuration sights and redesigned slide w/loaded chamber indicator and hold open. Made 1997 to date.

BUDISCHOWSKY PISTOL — Mt. Clemens, Michigan, Mfd. by Norton Armament Corporation

TP-70 DA AUTOMATIC PISTOL
Calibers: .22 LR, .25 Auto. Six-shot magazine, 2.6-inch bbl., 4.65 inches overall. Weight: 12.3 oz. Fixed sights. Stainless steel. Plastic grips. Made 1973-77.
.22 LR .... NiB $330 Ex $275 Gd $200
.25 Auto. .... NiB $313 Ex $250 Gd $170

CALICO LIGHT WEAPONS SYSTEMS — Bakersfield, California

MODEL 110 AUTO PISTOL .... NiB $625 Ex $558 Gd $400
Caliber: .22 LR. 100-shot magazine, 6-inch bbl., 17.9 inches overall. Weight: 3.75 lbs. Adj. post front sight, fixed U-notch rear. Black finish aluminum frame. Molded composition grip. Made 1986-94.

MODEL M-950 AUTO PISTOL .... NiB $450 Ex $375 Gd $258
Caliber 9mm Para. 50- or 100-shot magazine, 7.5-inch bbl., 14 inches overall. Weight: 2.25 lbs. Adj. post front sight, fixed U-notch rear. Glass-filled polymer grip. Made 1989-94.

CHARTER ARMS CORPORATION — Stratford, Connecticut

MODEL 40 AUTOMATIC PISTOL . . . . . NiB $265 Ex $240 Gd $125
Caliber: .22 RF. Eight-shot magazine, 3.3-inch bbl., 6.3 inches over-all. Weight: 21.5 oz. Fixed sights. Checkered walnut grips. Stainless steel finish. Made 1985-86.

MODEL 79K
DA AUTOMATIC PISTOL . . . . NiB $325 Ex $300 Gd $190
Calibers: .380 or .32 Auto. Seven-shot magazine, 3.6-inch bbl., 6.5 inches overall. Weight: 24.5 oz. Fixed sights. Checkered walnut grips. Stainless steel finish. Made 1985-86.

BONNIE AND CLYDE SET . . . . NiB $425 Ex $365 Gd $235
Matching pair of shrouded 2.5-inch bbl., revolvers chambered for .32 Magnum and .38 Special. Blued finish w/scrolled name on bbls.. Made 1989-90.

BULLDOG .44 DA REVOLVER
Caliber: .44 Special. Five-shot cylinder, 2.5- or 3-inch bbl., 7 or 7.5 inches over-all. Weight: 19 or 19.5 oz. Fixed sights. Blued, nickel-plated or stainless finish. Checkered walnut Bulldog or square buttgrips. Made from 1973-96.
Blued finish/
Pocket Hammer (2.5-inch) . . . . NiB $225 Ex $195 Gd $90
Blued finish/
Bulldog grips (3-inch disc. 1988) . . . . NiB $205 Ex $162 Gd $110
Electroless nickel . . . . NiB $231 Ex $185 Gd $126
Stainless steel/
Bulldog grips (disc. 1992) . . . . NiB $195 Ex $155 Gd $100
Neoprene grips/
Pocket Hammer . . . . NiB $200 Ex $160 Gd $109

BULLDOG .357 DA REVOLVER . . . . NiB $185 Ex $150 Gd $90
Caliber: .357 Magnum. Five-shot cylinder, 6-inch bbl., 11 inches overall. Weight: 25 oz. Fixed sights. Blued finish. Square, checkered walnut grips. Intro. 1977-96.

BULLDOG NEW POLICE DA REVOLVER
Same general specifications as Bulldog Police except chambered for .44 Special. Five-shot cylinder, 2.5- or 3.5-inch bbl. Made 1990-92.
Blued finish . . . . NiB $231 Ex $172 Gd $121
Stainless finish (2.5-inch bbl. only) . . . . NiB $175 Ex $140 Gd $90

BULLDOG POLICE DA REVOLVER
Caliber: .38 Special or .32 H&R Magnum. Six-shot cylinder, 4-inch bbl., 8.5 inches overall. Weight: 20.5 oz. Adj. rear sight, ramp front. Blued or stainless finish. Square checkered walnut grips. Made 1976-93. Shroud dropped on new model.
Blued finish . . . . NiB $205 Ex $162 Gd $110
Stainless finish . . . . NiB $195 Ex $157 Gd $99
.32 H&R Magnum (disc.1992) . . . . . NiB $210 Ex $165 Gd $110

BULLDOG PUG DA REVOLVER
Caliber: .44 Special. Five-shot cylinder, 2.5 inch bbl., 7.25 inches overall. Weight: 20 oz. Blued or stainless finish. Fixed ramp front sight, fixed square-notch rear. Checkered Neoprene or walnut grips. Made 1988-93.
Blued finish . . . . NiB $225 Ex $195 Gd $125
Stainless finish . . . . NiB $225 Ex $195 Gd $125

BULLDOG TARGET DA REVOLVER
Calibers: .357 Magnum, .44 Special (latter intro. in 1977). Four-inch bbl., 8.5 inches overall. Weight: 20.5 oz. in .357. Adj. rear sight, ramp front. Blued finish. Square checkered walnut grips. Made 1976-92.
Blued finish (disc.1989) . . . . NiB $190 Ex $149 Gd $100
Stainless steel . . . . NiB $225 Ex $150 Gd $85

Charter Arms
Bulldog Police

Charter Arms
Bulldog Police

Charter Arms
Bulldog Target

Charter Arms
Bulldog Tracker

Charter Arms
Explorer II

Charter Arms Explorer II
Silvertone w/optional barrels

Charter Arms Undercover
.32 S&W Long

Charter Arms
Undercover Stainless

Charter Arms
Pathfinder

Charter Arms Police Undercover
.32 H&R Magnum

BULLDOG TRACKER
DA REVOLVER . . . . NiB $185 Ex $150 Gd $90
Caliber: .357 Mag. Five-shot cylinder, 2.5-, 4- or 6-inch bbl., 11 inches overall (6-inch bbl.). Weight: 21 oz. (2.5-inch bbl.). Adj. rear sight, ramp front. Checkered walnut grips. Blued finish. 4- or 6-inch bbl., Disc.1986. Reintroduced 1989-92. See illustration previous page.

EXPLORER II SEMIAUTO SURVIVAL PISTOL
Caliber: .22 RF. Eight-shot magazine, 6-, 8- or 10-inch bbl., 13.5 inches overall (6-inch bbl.). Weight: 28 oz. finishes: Black, heat cured, semigloss textured enamel or silvertone anticorrosion. Disc.1987.
Standard model . . . . NiB $90 Ex $80 Gd $50
Silvertone (w/optional
6- or 10-inch bbl.) . . . . NiB $112 Ex $99 Gd $60

OFF-DUTY DA REVOLVER
Calibers: .22 LR or .38 Special. Six-shot (.22 LR) or 5-shot (.38 Spec.) cylinder. Two-inch bbl., 6.25 inches overall. Weight: 16 oz. Fixed rear sight, Partridge-type front sight. Plain walnut grips. Matte black, nickel or stainless steel finish. Made 1992-96.
Matte black finish . . . . NiB $170 Ex $145 Gd $85
Nickel finish . . . . NiB $200 Ex $151 Gd $100
Stainless steel . . . . NiB $189 Ex $153 Gd $100

PATHFINDER DA REVOLVER
Calibers: .22 LR, .22 WMR. Six-shot cylinder, bbl. lengths: 2-, 3-, 6-inches, 7.13 inches overall (in 3-inch bbl.), and regular grips. Weight: 18.5 oz. (3-inch bbl.). Adj. rear sight, ramp front. Blued or stainless finish. Plain walnut regular, checkered Bulldog or square buttgrips. Made 1970 to date. Note: Originally designated "Pocket Target," name was changed in 1971 to "Pathfinder." Grips changed in 1984. Disc.1993.
Blued finish . . . . NiB $185 Ex $150 Gd $90
Stainless finish . . . . NiB $185 Ex $150 Gd $90

CHARTER ARMS PIT BULL DA REVOLVER
Calibers: 9mm, .357 Magnum, .38 Special. Five-shot cylinder, 2.5-, 3.5- or 4-inch bbl., 7 inches overall (2.5-inch bbl.). Weight: 21.5 to 25 oz. All stainless steel frame. Fixed ramp front sight, fixed square-notch rear. Checkered Neoprene grips. Blued or stainless finish. Made 1989-93.
Blued finish . . . . NiB $230 Ex $180 Gd $100
Stainless finish . . . . NiB $240 Ex $190 Gd $100

CHARTER ARMS UNDERCOVER DA REVOLVER
Caliber: .38 Special. Five-shot cylinder,. bbl., lengths: 2-, 3-, 4-inches, 6.25 inches overall (2-inch bbl.), and regular grips. Weight: 16 oz. (2-inch bbl.). Fixed sights. Plain walnut, checkered Bulldog or square buttgrips. Made 1965-96.
Blued or nickel-plated finish . . . . NiB $175 Ex $145 Gd $85
Stainless finish . . . . NiB $260 Ex $195 Gd $110

CHARTER ARMS UNDERCOVER
Same general specifications as standard Undercover except chambered for .32 H&R Magnum or .32 S&W Long, has 6-shot cylinder and 2.5-inch bbl.
.32 H&R Magnum (blued) . . . . NiB $175 Ex $145 Gd $85
.32 H&R Magnum
nickel . . . . NiB $175 Ex $145 Gd $85
.32 H&R Magnum (stainless) . . . . . . NiB $260 Ex $195 Gd $150
.32 S&W Long (blued) disc. 1989 . . . . NiB $260 Ex $195 Gd $150

CHARTER ARMS UNDERCOVER POCKET POLICE DA REVOLVER
Same general specifications as standard Undercover except has 6-shot cylinder and pocket-type hammer. Blued or stainless steel finish. Made 1969-81.
Blued finish . . . . NiB $155 Ex $140 Gd $90
Stainless steel . . . . NiB $210 Ex $172 Gd $124

CHARTER ARMS UNDERCOVER POLICE DA REVOLVER
Same general specifications as standard Undercover except has 6-shot cylinder. Made 1984-89. Reintroduced 1993.
Blued, .38 Special . . . . NiB $205 Ex $175 Gd $100
Stainless, .38 Special . . . . NiB $204 Ex $165 Gd $115
.32 H&R Magnum . . . . NiB $185 Ex $150 Gd $105

CHARTER ARMS UNDER-COVERETTE DA REVOLVER . . . . NiB $155 Ex $140 Gd $90
Same as Undercover model w/2-inch bbl. except caliber .32 S&W Long, 6-shot cylinder, blued finish only. Weight: 16.5 oz. Made 1972-83.

CIMARRON F.A. CO. — Fredricksburg, Texas

CIMARRON EL PISTOLERO
SINGLE-ACTION REVOLVER. . . . . . NiB $395 Ex $300 Gd $175
Calibers: .357 Mag., .45 Colt. Six-shot cylinder, 4.75- 5.5- or 7.5-inch bbl., polished brass backstrap and triggerguard. Otherwise, same as Colt Single-Action Army revolver w/parts being interchangeable. Made 1997-98.

COLT MANUFACTURING CO., INC. — Hartford, Connecticut

Previously Colt Industries, Firearms Division. Production of some Colt handguns spans the period before World War II to the postwar years. Values shown for these models are for earlier production. Those manufactured c. 1946 and later generally are less desirable to collectors and values are approximately 30 percent lower.

Cimarron
El Pistolero

NOTE: *For ease in finding a particular firearm, Colt handguns are grouped into three sections: Automatic Pistols, Single-Shot Pistols, Derringers and Revolvers. For a complete listing, please refer to the Index.*

AUTOMATIC PISTOLS

COLT MODEL 1900 .38 AUTOMATIC PISTOL
Caliber: .38 ACP (modern high-velocity cartridges should not be used in this pistol). Seven-shot magazine, 6-inch bbl., 9 inches overall. Weight: 35 oz. Fixed sights. Blued finish. Hard rubber and plain or checkered walnut grips. Sharp-spur hammer. Combination rear sight and safety unique to the Model 1900 (early production). In mid-1901 a solid rear sight was dovetailed into the slide. (SN range 1-4274) Made 1900-03. Note: 250 models were sold to the military (50 Navy and 200 Army).
Early commercial model
(w/sight/safety) . . . . NiB $6500 Ex $4650 Gd $1700
Late commercial model
(W/dovetailed sight) . . . . NiB $4670 Ex $3685 Gd $2505
Army Model w/U.S. inspector
marks (1st Series - SN 90-150
w/inspector mark J.T.T.) . . . . NiB $15,000 Ex $10,000 Gd $7985
(2nd Series - SN 1600-1750
w/inspector mark R.A.C.) . . . . NiB $9375 Ex $7500 Gd $5100
Navy model (Also marked
w/USN-I.D. number) . . . . NiB $16,500 Ex $10,850 Gd $8225

COLT MODEL 1902 MILITARY .38 AUTOMATIC PISTOL
Caliber: .38 ACP (modern high-velocity cartridges should not be used in this pistol). Eight-shot magazine, 6-inch bbl., 9 inches overall. Weight: 37 oz. Fixed sights w/blade front and V-notch rear. Blued finish. Checkered hard rubber grips. Round back hammer, changed to spur type in 1908. No safety but fitted w/standard military swivel. About 18,000 produced with split SN ranges. The government contract series (15,001-15,200) and the commercial sales series (15,000 receding to 11,000) and (30,200-47,266). Made 1902-29.
Early military model (w/front
slide serrations) . . . . NiB $3450 Ex $3200 Gd $3000
Late military model (w/rear
slide serrations) . . . . NiB $2718 Ex $2200 Gd $2000
Marked "U.S. Army" (SN 15,001-
15,200) . . . . NiB $8500 Ex $6500 Gd $4250

COLT MODEL 1902 SPORTING
.38 AUTOMATIC PISTOL. . . . . . NiB $3500 Ex $2250 Gd $900
Caliber: .38 ACP (modern high-velocity cartridges should not be used in this pistol). Seven-shot magazine, 6-inch bbl., 9 inches overall. Weight: 35 oz. Fixed sights w/blade front and V-notch rear. Blued finish. Checkered hard rubber grips. Round back hammer was standard but some spur hammers were installed during late production. No safety and w/o swivel as found on military model. Total production about 7,500 w/split SN ranges (4275-10,999) and (30,000-30,190) Made 1902-08.

Colt
Model 1902 Military

Colt
Model 1903 Pocket Hammer

Colt
Model 1903 Pocket Hammerless

MODEL 1903 POCKET .32 AUTOMATIC PISTOL
FIRST ISSUE - COMMERCIAL SERIES
Caliber: .32 Auto. Eight-shot magazine, 4-inch bbl., 7 inches over-all. Weight: 23 oz. Fixed sights. Blued or nickel finish. Checkered hard rubber grips. Hammerless (concealed hammer). Slide lock and grip safeties. Fitted w/barrel bushing but early models have no magazine safety. Total production of the Model 1903 reached 572,215. The First Issue production occurred 1903-08 (SN range 1-72,000).
Blued finish . . . . NiB $845 Ex $550 Gd $390
Nickel finish . . . . NiB $935 Ex $570 Gd $405

MODEL 1903 POCKET .32 AUTOMATIC PISTOL
SECOND ISSUE - COMMERCIAL SERIES
Same as First Issue but with 3.75-inch bbl. and small extractor. Production occurred 1908-10 (SN range 72,001 -105,050).
Blued finish . . . . NiB $625 Ex $460 Gd $325
Nickel finish . . . . NiB $647 Ex $515 Gd $355

MODEL 1903 POCKET .32 AUTOMATIC PISTOL,
THIRD ISSUE - COMMERCIAL SERIES
Caliber: .32 Auto. Similar to Second Issue w/3.75-inch bbl. except with integral barrel bushing and locking lug at muzzle end of bbl. Production occurred 1910-26 (SN range 105,051-468,096).
Blued finish . . . . NiB $560 Ex $425 Gd $275
Nickel finish . . . . NiB $600 Ex $450 Gd $250

MODEL 1903 POCKET .32 AUTOMATIC PISTOL
FOURTH ISSUE - COMMERCIAL SERIES
Caliber: .32 Auto. Similar to Third Issue except a slide lock safety change was made when a Tansley-style disconnector was added on all pistols above SN 468,097, which prevents firing of cartridge in chamber when the magazine is removed. Blued or nickel finish. Checkered walnut grips. These design changes were initiated 1926-.45 (SN range 105,051-554,446)
Blued finish . . . . NiB $556 Ex $445 Gd $303
Nickel finish . . . . NiB $619 Ex $495 Gd $337

MODEL 1903 POCKET (HAMMER) .38 AUTOMATIC PISTOL
Caliber: .38 ACP (modern high-velocity cartridges should not be used in this pistol). Similar to Model 1902 Sporting .38 but w/shorter frame, slide and 4.5-inch bbl. Overall dimension reduced to 7.5 inches. Weight: 31 oz. Fixed sights w/blade front and V-notch rear. Blued finish. Checkered hard rubber grips. Round back hammer, changed to spur type in 1908. No safety. (SN range 16,001-47,226 with some numbers above 30,200 assigned to 1902 Military). Made 1903-1929.
Early model
(round hammer) . . . . NiB $2175 Ex $1885 Gd $900
Late model
(spur hammer). . . . . NiB $1740 Ex $1150 Gd $650

MODEL 1903 POCKET HAMMERLESS (CONCEALED HAMMER)
.32 AUTOMATIC PISTOL - MILITARY
Caliber: .32 ACP. Eight-shot magazine, Similar to Model 1903 Pocket .32 except concealed hammer and equipped w/magazine safety. Parkerized or blued finish. (SN range with "M" prefix M1-M200,000) Made 1941-.45.
Blued service model (marked
"U.S. Property") . . . . NiB $1435 Ex $950 Gd $650
Parkerized service model (marked
"U.S. Property") . . . . NiB $1425 Ex $460 Gd $600
Blued documented
Officer's model . . . . NiB $3375 Ex $3600 Gd $1500
Parkerized documented
Officer's model . . . . NiB $2325 Ex $2000 Gd $1400

MODEL 1905 .45 AUTOMATIC PISTOL
Caliber: .45 (Rimless) Automatic. Seven-shot magazine, 5-inch bbl., 8 inches overall. Weight: 32.5 oz. Fixed sights w/blade front and V-notch rear. Blued finish. Checkered walnut, hard rubber or pearl grips. Predecessor to Model 1911 Auto Pistol and contributory to the development of the .45 ACP cartridge. (SN range 1-6100) Made 1905-11.
Commercial model . . . . NiB $5500 Ex $3250 Gd $1500
W/slotted backstrap
(500 produced) . . . . NiB $8250 Ex $7500 Gd $6000
W/shoulder stock/holster . . . . $7500 to $10,000

MODEL 1905 .45 (1907)
CONTRACT PISTOL . . . . NiB $12,000 Ex $9500 Gd $6250
Variation of the Model 1905 produced to U.S. Military specifications, including loaded chamber indicator, grip safety and lanyard loop. Only 201 were produced, but 200 were delivered and may be identified by the chief inspector's initials "K.M." (SN range 1-201) Made 1907-08.

MODEL 1908 POCKET .25 HAMMERLESS AUTO PISTOL
Caliber: .25 Auto. Six-shot magazine, 2-inch bbl., 4.5 inches over-all. Weight: 13 oz. Flat-top front, square-notch rear sight in groove. Blued, nickel or Parkerized finish. Checkered hard rubber grips on early models, checkered walnut on later type, special pearl grips illustrated. Both a grip safety and slide lock safety are included on all models. The Tansley-style safety disconnector was added in 1916 at pistol No. 141000. (SN range 1-409,061) Made 1908-41.
Blued finish . . . . NiB $850 Ex $650 Gd $500
Nickel finish . . . . NiB $900 Ex $750 Gd $600
Marked "U.S. Property"
(w/blued finish) . . . . NiB $3095 Ex $1570 Gd $1198
Marked "U.S. Property"
(w/parkerized finish) . . . . NiB $2490 Ex $2000 Gd $1350

MODEL 1908 POCKET .380 AUTOMATIC PISTOL
Similar to Pocket .32 Auto w/3.75-inch bbl. except chambered for .380 Auto w/seven-shot magazine. Weight: 23 oz. Blue, nickel or Parkerized finish. (SN range 1-138,009) Made 1908-45.
First Issue (made 1908-11, w/bbl.,
lock and bushing, w/SN 1-6,250) . . . . . NiB $850 Ex $650 Gd $300
Second Issue (made 1911-28,
w/o bbl., lock and bushing,
w/SN 6,251-92,893) . . . . NiB $800 Ex $500 Gd $250
Third Issue (made 1928-45,
w/safety disconnector,
w/SN 92,894-138,009) . . . . NiB $531 Ex $425 Gd $289
Parkerized service model
(Marked "U.S. Property" made
1942-45, w/SN "M" prefix.) . . . . . NiB $2250 Ex $1650 Gd $1400
Documented officer's model
(service model w/military
assignment papers) . . . . NiB $2688 Ex $2150 Gd $1462

NOTE: *During both World Wars, Colt licensed other firms to make these pistols under government contract, including Ithaca Gun Co., North American Arms Co., Ltd. (Canada), Remington-Rand Co., Remington-UMC, Singer Sewing Machine Co., and Union Switch & Signal Co. M1911 also produced at Springfield Armory.*

MODEL 1911 AUTOMATIC PISTOL
Caliber: .45 Auto. Seven-shot magazine, 5-inch bbl., 8.5 inches overall. Weight: 39 oz. Fixed sights. Blued finish on Commercial model. Parkerized or similar finish on most military pistols. Checkered walnut grips (early production), plastic grips (later production). Checkered, arched mainspring housing and longer grip safety spur adopted in 1923 (on M1911A1).
Model 1911
commercial (C-series) . . . . NiB $1688 Ex $1350 Gd $918
Model 1911A1 commercial
(Pre-WWII) . . . . NiB $3494 Ex $2795 Gd $1901

U.S. GOVERNMENT MODEL 1911
Colt manufacture. . . . . NiB $1295 Ex $1095 Gd $780
North American
manufacture . . . . NiB $23,688 Ex $18,950 Gd $12,886
Remington-UMC manufacture . . . . . NiB $2156 Ex $1725 Gd $1173
Springfield manufacture . . . . . . NiB $2119 Ex $1695 Gd $1153
Navy Model M1911 type . . . . . . NiB $2813 Ex $2250 Gd $1530

U.S. GOVERNMENT MODEL 1911A1
Singer manufacture . . . . . NiB $24,938 Ex $19,950 Gd $13,566
Colt, Ithaca, Remington-
Rand manufacture . . . . NiB $906 Ex $725 Gd $493
Union Switch &
Signal manufacture . . . . NiB $1369 Ex $1095 Gd $745

Colt
Model 1905 Military

Colt
Model 1908 Pocket 25

Colt
Model 1911

Colt
1991 A1

Colt Cadet .22

**Colt All American
Model 2000**

MODEL M1991 A1 SEMIAUTO PISTOL

Reissue of Model 1911A1 (see above) w/a continuation of the original serial number range 1945. Caliber: .45 ACP. Seven-shot magazine, 5-inch bbl., 8.5 inches overall. Weight: 39 oz. Fixed blade front sight, square notch rear. Parkerized finish. Black composition grips. Made 1991 to date. (Commander and Compact variations intro. 1993).

Standard model	NiB $850	Ex $795	Gd $600
Commander w/4.5-inch bbl.,	NiB $600	Ex $540	Gd $300
Compact w/3.5-inch bbl., (six-shot)	NiB $700	Ex $600	Gd $450

.22 CADET AUTOMATIC PISTOL . . . . . NiB $231 Ex $185 Gd $126

Caliber: 22 LR. 10-shot magazine, 4.5-inch vent rib bbl., 8.63 inches overall. Weight: 33.5 oz. Blade front sight, dovetailed rear. Stainless finish. Textured black polymer grips w/Colt medallion. Made 1993-95. Note: The Cadet Model name was disc. under litigation but the manufacturer continued to produce this pistol configuration as the Model "Colt 22". For this reason the "Cadet" model will command slight premiums.

.22 SPORT AUTOMATIC PISTOL . . . . . NiB $395 Ex $295 Gd $150

Same specifications as Cadet Model except renamed Colt .22 w/composition monogrip or wraparound black rubber grip. Made 1995-98.

.22 TARGET PISTOL. . . . . NiB $295 Ex $250 Gd $125

Similar to Colt 22 Sport Model except w/6-inch vent rib bbl., 10.12 inches overall. Weight: 40.5 oz. Partridge style front sight, adjustable white outline rear on full length grooved rib. Made 1995 to date.

ACE AUTOMATIC PISTOL

Caliber: .22 LR (regular or high speed). 10-shot magazine. Built on the same frame as the Government Model .45 Auto w/same safety features, etc. Hand-honed action, target bbl., adj. rear sight. 4.75-inch bbl., 8.25. inches overall. Weight: 38 oz. Made 1930-.40.

Commercial model	NiB $1938	Ex $1550	Gd $1054
Service model (1938-42)	NiB $2744	Ex $2195	Gd $1493

ALL AMERICAN
MODEL 2000 DA PISTOL . . . . NiB $750 Ex $650 Gd $400

Hammerless semiautomatic w/blued slide and polymer or alloy receiver fitted w/roller-bearing trigger. Caliber: 9mm Para. 15-shot magazine, 4.5-inch bbl., 7.5 inches overall. Weight: 29 oz. (Polymer) or 33 oz (Alloy). Fixed blade front sight, square-notch rear w/3-dot system. Matte blued slide w/black polymer or anodized aluminum receiver. Made 1992-94.

AUTOMATIC .25 PISTOL

As a result of the 1968 Firearms Act restricting the importation of the Colt Pocket Junior that was produced in Spain, Firearms International was contracted by Colt to manufacture a similar blowback action with the same exposed hammer configuration. Both the U.S. and Spanish-made .25 automatics were recalled to correct an action malfunction. Returned firearms were fitted with a rebounding firing pin to prevent accidental discharges. Caliber: .25 ACP. Six-shot magazine, 2.25-inch bbl., 4.5 inches overall. Weight: 12.5 oz. Integral blade front, square-notch rear sight groove. Blued finish. Checkered wood grips w/Colt medallion. Made 1970-75.

Model as issued	NiB $300	Ex $250	Gd $100
Model recalled			
& refitted	NiB $300	Ex $250	Gd $100

CHALLENGER
AUTOMATIC PISTOL . . . . NiB $495 Ex $395 Gd $200

Same basic design as Woodsman Target, Third Issue but lacks some of the refinements. Fixed sights. Magazine catch on butt as in old Woodsman. Does not stay open on last shot. Lacks magazine safety. 4.5- or 6-inch bbl., 9 to 10.5 inches overall. Weight: 30 oz. (4.5-inch bbl.) or 31.5 oz. (6-inch bbl.) Blued finish. Checkered plastic grips. Made 1950-55.

COMBAT COMMANDER AUTOMATIC PISTOL

Same as Lightweight Commander except has steel frame w/blued or nickel-plated finish. Weight: 36 oz. Made 1950-76.

9mm Para.	NiB $619	Ex $495	Gd $337
.38 Super, .45 ACP.	NiB $719	Ex $575	Gd $391

COMMANDER LIGHTWEIGHT AUTOMATIC PISTOL

Same basic design as Government Model except w/shorter 4.25-inch bbl., and a special lightweight "Coltalloy" receiver and mainspring housing. Calibers: .45 Auto, .38 Super Auto, 9mm Para. Seven-shot magazine (.45 cal.), nine-shot (.38 Auto and 9mm), 8 inches overall. Weight: 26.5 oz. Fixed sights. Round spur hammer. Improved safety lock. Blued finish. Checkered plastic or walnut grips. Made 1950-76.

9mm Para.	NiB $606	Ex $485	Gd $330
.38 Super, .45 ACP.	NiB $656	Ex $525	Gd $357

CONVERSION
UNIT—.22-.45. . . . . NiB $2688 Ex $2150 Gd $1462

Converts Service Ace .22 to National Match .45 Auto. Unit consists of match-grade slide assembly and bbl., bushing, recoil spring, recoil spring guide and plug, magazine and slide stop. Made 1938-42.

CONVERSION
UNIT — .45-.22 . . . . NiB $469 Ex $375 Gd $255

Converts Government Model .45 Auto to a .22 LR target pistol. Unit consists of slide assembly, bbl., floating chamber (as in Service Ace), bushing, ejector, recoil spring, recoil spring guide and plug, magazine and slide stop. The component parts differ and are not interchangable between post war, series 70, series 80, ACE I and ACE II units. Made 1938 to date.

DELTA ELITE SEMIAUTO PISTOL

Caliber: 10 mm. Five-inch bbl., 8.5 inches overall. Eight-round magazine, Weight: 38 oz. Checkered Neoprene combat grips w/Delta medallion. Three-dot, high-profile front and rear combat sights. Blued or stainless finish. Made 1987-96.

First Edition
(500 Ltd. edition)	NiB $1119	Ex $895	Gd $609
Blued finish	NiB $594	Ex $475	Gd $323
Matte stainless finish	NiB $619	Ex $495	Gd $337
Ultra stainless finish	NiB $719	Ex $575	Gd $391

DELTA GOLD CUP SEMIAUTO PISTOL

Same general specifications as Delta Elite except in match configuration w/Accro adjustable rear sight. Made 1989-93 and 1995-96.
Blued finish (disc. 1991)	NiB $688	Ex $550	Gd $374
Stainless steel finish	NiB $895	Ex $750	Gd $600

GOLD CUP MARK III

NATIONAL MATCH .... NiB $1050 Ex $845 Gd $570

Similar to Gold Cup National Match .45 Auto except chambered for .38 Special Mid Range. Five-shot magazine, Made 1961-74.

GOLD CUP NATIONAL

MATCH .45 AUTO. .... NiB $950 Ex $800 Gd $458

Match version of Government Model .45 Auto w/same general specifications except: match grade bbl., w/new design bushing, flat mainspring housing, long wide trigger w/adj. stop, hand-fitted slide w/improved ejection port, adj. rear sight, target front sight, checkered walnut grips w/gold medallions. Weight: 37 oz. Made 1957-70.

GOVERNMENT MODEL 1911/1911A1

See Colt Model 1911.

HUNTSMAN .... NiB $450 Ex $350 Gd $250

Same specifications as the Challenger. Made 1955-76.

MK I & IL/SERIES '90 DOUBLE

EAGLE COMBAT COMMANDER ..... NiB $569 Ex $455 Gd $309

Calibers: .40 S&W, .45 ACP. Seven-shot magazine, 4.25-inch bbl., 7.75 inches overall. Weight: 36 oz. Fixed blade front sight, square-notch rear. Checkered Xenoy grips. Stainless finish. Made 1992-96.

MK IL/SERIES '90 DOUBLE EAGLE DA SEMIAUTO PISTOL

Calibers: .38 Super, 9mm, .40 S&W, 10mm, .45 ACP. Seven-shot magazine. Five-inch bbl., 8.5 inches overall. Weight: 39 oz. Fixed or Accro adj. sights. Matte stainless finish. Checkered Xenoy grips. Made 1991-96.

.38 Super, 9mm, .40
S&W (fixed sights)	NiB $598	Ex $477	Gd $321
.45 ACP (adjustable sights)	NiB $594	Ex $475	Gd $323
.45 ACP (fixed sights)	NiB $569	Ex $455	Gd $309
10mm (adjustable sights)	NiB $588	Ex $470	Gd $320
10mm (fixed sights)	NiB $563	Ex $450	Gd $306

MK IL/SERIES '90 DOUBLE

EAGLE OFFICER'S ACP .... NiB $594 Ex $475 Gd $323

Same general specifications as Double Eagle Combat Commander except chambered for .45 ACP only, 3.5-inch bbl., 7.25 inches overall. Weight: 35 oz. Also available in lightweight (25 oz.) w/blued finish (same price). Made 1990-93.

MK IV/SERIES '70 COMBAT COMMANDER

Same general specifications as the Lightweight Commander except made 1970-83.
Blued finish	NiB $572	Ex $455	Gd $300
Nickel finish	NiB $637	Ex $421	Gd $329

Colt Delta
Gold Cup

Colt Gold Cup
National Match

Colt MK II/Series '90
Double Eagle Officer's ACP

MK IV/SERIES '70 GOLD CUP

NATIONAL MATCH .45 AUTO .... NiB $950 Ex $780 Gd $600

Match version of MK IV/Series '70 Government Model. Caliber: .45 Auto only. Flat mainspring housing. Accurizor bbl., and bushing. Solid rib, Colt-Elliason adj. rear sight undercut front sight. Adj. trigger, target hammer. 8.75 inches overall. Weight: 38.5 oz. Blued finish. Checkered walnut grips. Made 1970-84.

MK IV/SERIES '70 GOV'T.

AUTO PISTOL .... NiB $800 Ex $600 Gd $350

Calibers: .45 Auto, .38 Super Auto, 9mm Para. Seven-shot magazine in .45, 9-shot in .38 and 9mm. Five-inch bbl., 8.38 inches overall. Weight: 38 oz., (.45); 39 oz. in .38 and 9mm. Fixed rear sight and ramp front sight. Blued or nickel-plated finish. Checkered walnut grips. Made 1970-84.

Colt MK IV/
Series '80 .380

Colt MK IV/Series '80
Combat Commander

Colt MK IV/Series '80
Gold Cup National Match

Colt MK IV/Series '80
Government Model

MK IV/SERIES '80 .380 AUTOMATIC PISTOL

Caliber: .380 ACP, 3.29-inch bbl., 6.15 inches overall. Weight: 21.8 oz. Composition grips. Fixed sights. Made since 1984 to date.

Blued finish
(disc.1997). . . . . NiB $425 Ex $295 Gd $195
Bright nickel
(disc.1995). . . . . NiB $495 Ex $330 Gd $215
Satin nickel
Coltguard (disc.1989) . . . . NiB $475 Ex $325 Gd $210
Stainless finish . . . . NiB $480 Ex $335 Gd $225

MK IV/SERIES '80 COMBAT COMMANDER

Updated version of the MK IV/Series '70 w/same general specifications. Blued, two-tone or stainless steel w/"pebbled" black Neoprene wraparound grips. Made since 1979.

Blued finish
(disc.1996). . . . . NiB $565 Ex $470 Gd $300
Satin nickel
(disc.1987). . . . . NiB $595 Ex $485 Gd $315
Stainless finish . . . . NiB $615 Ex $475 Gd $337
Two-tone finish . . . . NiB $639 Ex $495 Gd $340

MK IV/SERIES '80 COMBAT ELITE

Same general specifications as MK IV/Series '80 Combat Commander except w/Elite enhancements. Calibers: .38 Super, .40 S&W, .45 ACP. Stainless frame w/blued steel slide. Accro adj. sights and beavertail grip safety. Made 1992-96.

.38 Super,
.45 ACP . . . . NiB $730 Ex $620 Gd $330
.40 S&W . . . . NiB $700 Ex $600 Gd $300

MK IV/SERIES '80 GOLD CUP NATIONAL MATCH

Same general specifications as Match '70 version except w/additional finishes and "pebbled" wraparound Neoprene grips. Made 1983-96.

Blued finish . . . . NiB $875 Ex $700 Gd $350
Bright blued
finish . . . . NiB $914 Ex $637 Gd $420
Stainless finish . . . . NiB $720 Ex $580 Gd $360

MK IV/SERIES '80 GOVERNMENT MODEL

Same general specifications as Government Model Series '70 except also chambered in .40 S&W, w/"pebbled" wraparound Neoprene grips, blued or stainless finish. Made since 1983.

Blued finish . . . . NiB $697 Ex $495 Gd $305
Bright blued
finish . . . . NiB $775 Ex $530 Gd $429
Bright stainless
finish . . . . NiB $700 Ex $600 Gd $300
Matte stainless finish . . . . NiB $697 Ex $499 Gd $310

MK IV/SERIES '80 LIGHT-
WEIGHT COMMANDER . . . . NiB $595 Ex $465 Gd $300

Updated version of the MK IV/Series '70 w/same general specifications.

MK IV/SERIES '80 MUSTANG .380 AUTOMATIC

Caliber: .380 ACP. Five- or 6-shot magazine, 2.75-inch bbl., 5.5 inches overall. Weight: 18.5 oz. Blued, nickel or stainless finish. Black composition grips. Made 1986-97.

Blued finish . . . . NiB $415 Ex $320 Gd $225
Nickel finish
(disc.1994). . . . . NiB $469 Ex $319 Gd $232
Satin nickel
Coltguard (disc.1988) . . . . NiB $450 Ex $300 Gd $223
Stainless finish . . . . NiB $469 Ex $319 Gd $232

MK IV/SERIES '80 MUSTANG PLUS II

Caliber: .380 ACP, 7-round magazine, 2.75-inch bbl., 5.5 inches overall. Weight: 20 oz. Blued or stainless finish w/checkered black composition grips. Made 1988-96.

Blued finish . . . . NiB $415 Ex $320 Gd $228
Stainless finish . . . . NiB $469 Ex $319 Gd $232

MK IV/SERIES '80 MUSTANG POCKETLITE

Same general specifications as the Mustang 30 except weight: 12.5 oz. w/aluminum alloy receiver. Blued, chrome or stainless finish. Optional wood grain grips. Made since 1988.

Blued finish . . . . NiB $415 Ex $320 Gd $225
Lady Elite
(two-tone) finish . . . . NiB $439 Ex $395 Gd $260
Stainless finish . . . . NiB $469 Ex $319 Gd $232
Teflon/stainless finish . . . . NiB $495 Ex $315 Gd $220

MK IV/SERIES '80 OFFICER'S ACP AUTOMATIC PISTOL

Calibers: .40 S&W and .45 ACP, 3.63-inch bbl., 7.25 inches overall. Weight: 34 oz. Made 1984-97. .40 S&W, disc.1992.

Blued finish
(disc.1996). . . . . NiB $520 Ex $421 Gd $287
Matte finish . . . . NiB $498 Ex $397 Gd $279
Satin nickel finish . . . . NiB $581 Ex $462 Gd $307
Stainless steel . . . . NiB $544 Ex $435 Gd $296

MK IV/SERIES '80 SA LIGHTWEIGHT CONCEALED

CARRY OFFICER . . . . NiB $589 Ex $472 Gd $314
Caliber: .45 ACP. Seven-shot magazine, 4.25-inch bbl., 7.75 inches overall. Weight: 35 oz. Aluminum alloy receiver w/stainless slide. Dovetailed low-profile sights w/3-dot system. Matte stainless finish w/blued receiver. Wraparound black rubber grip w/finger grooves. Made since 1998.

MK IV/SERIES '90 DEFENDER

SA LIGHTWEIGHT . . . . NiB $580 Ex $461 Gd $299
Caliber: .45 ACP. Seven-shot magazine, 3-inch bbl., 6.75 inches over-all. Weight: 22.5 oz. Aluminum alloy receiver w/stainless slide. Dovetailed low-profile sights w/3-dot system. Matte stainless finish w/Nickel-Teflon receiver. Wraparound black rubber grip w/finger grooves. Made since 1998.

MK IV/SERIES 90

PONY DAO PISTOL . . . . NiB $479 Ex $390 Gd $257
Caliber: .380 ACP. Six-shot magazine, 2.75-inch bbl., 5.5 inches overall. Weight: 19 oz. Ramp front sight, dovetailed rear. Stainless finish. Checkered black composition grips. Made since 1997.

MK IV/SERIES 90

PONY POCKETLITE. . . . . NiB $460 Ex $375 Gd $243
Similar to standard weight Pony Model except w/aluminum frame. Brushed stainless and Teflon finish. Made 1997 to date.

NATIONAL MATCH AUTOMATIC PISTOL

Identical to the Government Model .45 Auto but w/hand-honed action, match-grade bbl., adj. rear and ramp front sights or fixed sights. Made 1932-40.

W/adjustable
sights . . . . NiB $2688 Ex $2150 Gd $1462
W/fixed sights . . . . NiB $1869 Ex $1495 Gd $1017

NRA CENTENNIAL .45 GOLD CUP

NATIONAL MATCH . . . . NiB $1356 Ex $1100 Gd $740
Only 2500 produced in 1971.

Colt MK IV/Series
'80 Mustang Plus II

Colt MK IV/Series '80
Mustang Pocketlite

Colt MK IV/Series
'80 Officer's ACP

POCKET JUNIOR MODEL

AUTOMATIC PISTOL . . . . NiB $350 Ex $260 Gd $150
Made in Spain by Unceta y Cia (Astra). Calibers: .22 Short, .25 Auto. Six-shot magazine, 2.25 inch bbl., 4.75 inches overall. Weight: 12 oz. Fixed sights. Checkered walnut grips. Note: In 1980, this model was subject to recall to correct an action malfunction. Returned firearms were fitted with a rebounding firing pin to prevent accidental discharges. Made 1958-68. See illustration next page.

Colt Pocket Junior

Colt Super Match .38

Colt Targetsman

Colt Woodsman
Match Target First Issue

Colt Woodsman
Match Target Second Issue

SUPER .38 AUTOMATIC PISTOL
Identical to Government Model .45 Auto except for caliber and magazine capacity. Caliber: .38 Automatic. Nine-shot magazine, Made 1928-70.

Pre-war . . . . NiB $2656 Ex $2119 Gd $1540
Post-war. . . . . NiB $986 Ex $781 Gd $542

SUPER MATCH .38 AUTOMATIC PISTOL
Identical to Super .38 Auto but w/hand-honed action, match grade bbl., adjustable rear sight and ramp front sight or fixed sights. Made 1933-46.

W/adjustable sights . . . . NiB $6619 Ex $5295 Gd $3601
W/fixed sights . . . . NiB $4438 Ex $3550 Gd $2414

TARGETSMAN. . . . . NiB $600 Ex $540 Gd $200
Similar to Woodsman Target but has "economy" adj. rear sight, lacks automatic slide stop. Made 1959-76.

WOODSMAN MATCH TARGET
AUTOMATIC PISTOL
FIRST ISSUE. . . . . NiB $1400 Ex $1350 Gd $750
Same basic design as other Woodsman models. Caliber: .22 LR. 10-shot magazine, 6.5-inch bbl., slightly tapered w/flat sides, 11 inches overall. Weight: 36 oz. Adjustable rear sight. Blued finish. Checkered walnut one-piece grip w/extended sides. Made 1938-42.

WOODSMAN MATCH
TARGET AUTO PISTOL,
SECOND ISSUE. . . . . NiB $850 Ex $680 Gd $420
Same basic design as Woodsman Target Third Issue. Caliber: .22 LR (reg. or high speed). 10-shot magazine, Six-inch flat-sided heavy bbl., 10.5 inches overall. Weight: 40 oz. Click adj. rear sight, ramp front. Blued finish. Checkered plastic or walnut grips. Made 1948-76.

WOODSMAN MATCH
TARGET "4 1/2" AUTO-
MATIC PISTOL . . . . NiB $800 Ex $490 Gd $350
Same as Match Target second issue except w/4.5-inch bbl., 9 inches overall. Weight: 36 oz. Made 1950-76.

WOODSMAN SPORT MODEL
AUTOMATIC PISTOL,
FIRST ISSUE. . . . . NiB $875 Ex $700 Gd $450
Caliber: .22 LR (reg. or high speed). Same as Woodsman Target second issue except has 4.5-inch bbl., adjustable rear sight w/fixed or adjustable front sight. Weight: 27 oz., 8.5 inches overall. Made 1933-48.

WOODSMAN SPORT
MODEL AUTOMATIC
PISTOL, SECOND ISSUE . . . . NiB $875 Ex $700 Gd $450
Same as Woodsman Target third Issue but w/4.5-inch bbl., 9 inches overall. Weight: 30 oz. Made 1948-76.

WOODSMAN TARGET MODEL
AUTOMATIC, FIRST ISSUE . . . . NiB $700 Ex $650 Gd $300
Caliber: .22 LR (reg. velocity). 10-shot magazine, 6.5-inch bbl., 10.5 inches overall. Weight: 28 oz. Adjustable sights. Blued finish. Checkered walnut grips. Made 1915-.32. Note: The mainspring housing of this model is not strong enough to permit safe use of high-speed cartridges. Change to a new heat-treated mainspring housing was made at pistol No. 83,790. Many of the old models were converted by installation of new housings. The new housing may be distinguished from the earlier type by the checkering in the curve under the breech. The new housing is grooved straight across, while the old type bears a diagonally-checkered oval.

WOODSMAN TARGET MODEL
AUTOMATIC, SECOND ISSUE . . . . NiB $650 Ex $500 Gd $300
Caliber: .22 LR (reg. or high speed). Same as original model except has heavier bbl., and high-speed mainspring housing. (See note under Woodsman, First Issue). Weight: 29 oz. Made 1932-48.

WOODSMAN TARGET MODEL
AUTOMATIC, THIRD ISSUE . . . . . . NiB $520 Ex $400 Gd $225
Same basic design as previous Woodsman pistols but w/longer grip, magazine catch on left side, larger thumb safety, slide stop, slide stays open on last shot, magazine disconnector thumbrest grips. Caliber: .22 LR (reg. or high speed). 10-shot magazine, 6-inch bbl., 10.5 inches overall. Weight: 32 oz. Click adjustable rear sight, ramp front sight. Blued finish. Checkered plastic or walnut grips. Made 1948-76.

WORLD WAR I 50TH ANNIVERSARY
COMMEMORATIVE SERIES
Limited production replica of Model 1911 .45 Auto engraved w/battle scenes, commemorating Battles at Chateau Thierry, Belleau Wood Second Battle of the Marne, Meuse Argonne. In special presentation display cases. Production: 7,400 Standard model, 75 Deluxe, 25 Special Deluxe grade. Match numbered sets offered. Made in 1967, 68, 69. Values indicated are for commemoratives in new condition.
Standard grade . . . . NiB $906 Ex $725 Gd $493
Deluxe grade . . . . NiB $1869 Ex $1495 Gd $1017
Special Deluxe grade . . . . NiB $3688 Ex $2950 Gd $2006

WORLD WAR II
COMMEMORATIVE
.45 AUTO . . . . NiB $925 Ex $775 Gd $590
Limited production replica of Model 1911A1 .45 Auto engraved w/respective names of locations where historic engagements occurred during WW II, as well as specific issue and theater identification. European model has oak leaf motif on slide, palm leaf design frames the Pacific issue. Cased. 11,500 of each model were produced. Made in 1970. Value listed is for gun in new condition.

WORLD WAR II
50TH ANNIVERSARY
COMMEMORATIVE. . . . . NiB $2145 Ex $1795 Gd $1321
Same general specifications as the Colt World War II Commemorative .45 Auto except slightly different scroll engraving, 24-karat gold-plate trigger, hammer, slide stop, magazine catch, magazine catch lock, safety lock and four grip screws. Made in 1995 only.

WORLD WAR II
D-DAY
INVASION COMMEMORATIVE . . . . NiB $1265 Ex $1195 Gd $829
High-luster and highly decorated version of the Colt Model 1911A1. Caliber: .45 ACP. Same general specifications as the Colt Model 1911 except for 24-karat gold-plated hammer, trigger, slide stop, magazine catch, magazine catch screw, safety lock and four grip screws. Also has scrolls and inscription on slide. Made in 1991 only.

**Colt Woodsman
Sport Model First Issue**

**Colt Woodsman
Sport Model Second Issue**

**Colt Woodsman
Target Model First Issue**

**Colt Woodsman
Target Model Second Issue**

**Colt Woodsman
Target Model Third Issue**

GRADING: **NiB** = New in Box   **Ex** = Excellent or NRA 95%   **Gd** = Good or NRA 68%

Colt
World War II D-Day Invasion Commemorative

Colt
Camp Perry First Issue

Colt
Camp Perry Second Issue

Colt World War II
50th Anniversary Commemorative

Colt
Woodsman Match Target First Issue

**WORLD WAR II GOLDEN ANNIVER-
SARY V-J DAY TRIBUTE .45 AUTO . . . . NiB $2300 Ex $1890 Gd $1340**
Basic Colt Model 1911A1 design w/highly-polished bluing and decorated w/specialized tributes to honor V-J Day. Two 24-karat gold scenes highlight the slide. 24-karat gold-plated hammer. Checkered wood grips w/gold medallion on each side. Made 1995.

NOTE: *For ease in finding a particular firearm, Colt handguns are grouped into three sections: Automatic Pistols (which precedes this one), this section, and Revolvers, which follows. For a complete listing, please refer to the index.*

SINGLE-SHOT PISTOLS & DERRINGERS

CAMP PERRY MODEL SINGLE-
SHOT PISTOL, FIRST ISSUE .... NiB $1619 Ex $1295 Gd $881
Built on Officers' Model frame. Caliber: .22 LR (embedded head chamber for high-speed cartridges after 1930). 10 inch bbl., 13.75 inches overall. Weight: 34.5 oz. Adj. target sights. Hand-finished action. Blued finish. Checkered walnut grips. Made 1926-34.

CAMP PERRY MODEL
SECOND ISSUE.............. NiB $1400 Ex $1150 Gd $800
Same general specifications as First Issue except has shorter hammer fall and 8-inch bbl., 12 inches overall. Weight: 34 oz. Made 1934-41 (about 440 produced).

CIVIL WAR CENTENNIAL MODEL PISTOL
Single-shot replica of Colt Model 1860 Army Revolver. Caliber: .22 Short. Six-inch bbl., weight: 22 oz. Blued finish w/gold-plated frame, grip frame, and trigger guard, walnut grips. Cased. 24,114 were produced. Made in 1961.
Single pistol.................... NiB $244 Ex $195 Gd $133
Pair w/consecutive serial numbers .... NiB $563 Ex $450 Gd $306

DERRINGER NO. 4
Replica of derringer No. 3 (1872 Thuer Model). Single-shot w/side-swing bbl., Caliber: .22 Short, 2.5-inch bbl., 4.9 inches overall. Weight: 7.75 oz. Fixed sights. Gold-plated frame w/blued bbl., and walnut grips or completely nickel- or gold-plated w/simulated ivory or pearl grips. Made 1959-63. 112,000 total production. (SN w/D or N suffix)
Single pistol (gun only) .... NiB $125 Ex $100 Gd $68
Single pistol (cased w/accessories) .... NiB $375 Ex $275 Gd $150

DERRINGER NO. 4 COMMEMORATIVE MODELS
Limited production version of .22 derringers issued, w/appropriate inscription, to commemorate historical events. Additionally, non-firing models (w/unnotched bbls.) were furnished in books, picture frames and encased in plexiglass as singles or in cased pairs..
No. 4 Presentation Derringers
(Non-firing w/accessories) .... NiB $375
Ltd. Ed. Book Series
(W/nickel-plated derringers) .... NiB $350
1st Presentation Series
(Leatherette covered metal case) .... NiB $325
2nd Presentation Series
(Single wooden case) .... NiB $225
2nd Presentation Series
(Paired wooden case) .... NiB $350
1961 Issue Geneseo, Illinois,
125th Anniversary (104 produced)................ NiB $695
1962 Issue Fort McPherson,
Nebraska, Centennial (300 produced) .... NiB $425

LORD AND LADY DERRINGERS (NO. 5)
Same as Derringer No. 4. Lord model with blued bbl., w/gold-plated frame and walnut grips. Lady model is gold-plated w/simulated pearl grips. Furnished in cased pairs. Made 1970-72. (SN w/Der sufix)
Lord derringer, pair in case .... NiB $438 Ex $350 Gd $238
Lady derringer, pair in case .... NiB $450 Ex $360 Gd $245
Lord and Lady derringers,
one each, in case............... NiB $469 Ex $375 Gd $255

ROCK ISLAND ARSENAL
CENTENNIAL PISTOL .... NiB $400 Ex $395 Gd $215
Limited production (550 pieces) version of Civil War Centennial Model single-shot .22 pistol, made exclusively for Cherry's Sporting Goods, Geneseo, Illinois, to commemorate the centennial of the Rock Island Arsenal in Illinois. Cased. Made in 1962.

**Colt Agent
First Issue**

Colt Anaconda

NOTE: *This section of Colt handguns contains only revolvers. For automatic pistols or single-shot pistols and derringers, please see the two sections that precede this. For a complete listing, please refer to the Index.*

REVOLVERS

.38 DS II REVOLVER .... NiB $419 Ex $328 Gd $219
Caliber: .38 Special. Six-shot cylinder, 2-inch bbl., 7 inches overall. Weight: 21 oz. Ramp front sight, fixed notch rear. Satin stainless finish. Black rubber combat grip w/finger grooves. Made 1997 to date.

AGENT DA REVOLVER,
FIRST ISSUE.................. NiB $425 Ex $375 Gd $230
Same as Cobra, first issue except has short-grip frame .38 Special only, weight: 14 oz. Made 1955-72.

AGENT (LW) DA REVOLVER,
SECOND ISSUE................ NiB $395 Ex $365 Gd $200
Same as Colt Agent, first issue except has shrouded ejector rod and alloy frame. Made 1973-86.

ANACONDA DA REVOLVER
Calibers: .44 Mag., .45 Colt., bbl. lengths: 4, 6 or 8 inches; 11.63 inches overall (with 6-inch bbl.). Weight: 53 oz. (6-inch bbl.). Adj. white outline rear sight, red insert ramp-style front. Matte stainless or Realtree gray camo finish. Black Neoprene combat grips w/finger grooves. Made since 1990.
Matte stainless .... NiB $650 Ex $495 Gd $300
Realtree gray camo
finish (disc. 1996) .... NiB $700 Ex $525 Gd $325
Custom model
(.44 Mag. w/ported bbl.)........ NiB $875 Ex $600 Gd $300
First Edition model
(Ltd. Edition 1000).............. NiB $950 Ex $750 Gd $400
Hunter model
(.44 Mag. w/2x scope)......... NiB $1095 Ex $895 Gd $525

Colt Banker's Special

Colt Bisley

Colt Buntline Special .45

Colt Commando Special

ANACONDA TITANIUM DA REVOLVER
Same general specifications as the standard Anaconda except chambered .44 Mag. only w/titanium-plated finish, gold-plated trigger, hammer and cylinder release. Limited edition of 1,000 distributed by American Historical Foundation w/personalized inscription. Made 1996.
One of 1000 . . . . **NiB $2369 Ex $1895 Gd $1289**
Presentation case, add **$200**

ARMY SPECIAL DA REVOLVER . . . . . . **NiB $725 Ex $650 Gd $400**
.41-caliber frame. Calibers: .32-20, .38 Special (.41 Colt). Six-shot cylinder, right revolution. Bbl., lengths: 4-, 4.5, 5-, and 6-inches, 9.25 inches overall (4-inch bbl.). Weight: 32 oz. (4-inch bbl.). Fixed sights. Blued or nickel-plated finish. Hard rubber grips. Made 1908-27. Note: This model has a somewhat heavier frame than the New Navy, which it replaced. Serial numbers begin w/300,000. The heavy .38 Special High Velocity loads should not be used in .38 Special arms of this model.

BANKER'S SPECIAL DA REVOLVER
This is the Police Positive w/a 2-inch bbl., otherwise specifications same as that model, rounded butt intro. in 1933. Calibers: .22 LR (embedded head-cylinder for high speed cartridges intro. 1933), .38 New Police. 6.5 inches overall. Weight: 23 oz. (.22 LR), 19 oz. (.38). Made 1926-.40.
.38 caliber . . . . **NiB $1015 Ex $812 Gd $60**
.22 caliber . . . . **NiB $2005 Ex $1612 Gd $1115**

BISLEY MODEL SA REVOLVER
Variation of the Single-Action Army, developed for target shooting w/modified grips, trigger and hammer. Calibers: General specifications same as SA Army. Target Model made w/flat-topped frame and target sights. Made 1894-1915.
Standard model . . . . **NiB $7869 Ex $6295 Gd $4281**
Target model (flat-top) . . . . . . **NiB $11,563 Ex $9250 Gd $6290**

BUNTLINE SPECIAL .45 . . . . **NiB $1156 Ex $925 Gd $629**
Same as standard SA Army except has 12-inch bbl., caliber .45 Long Colt. Made 1957-75.

COBRA DA REVOLVER,
ROUND BUTT, FIRST ISSUE . . . . . . **NiB $450 Ex $360 Gd $245**
Lightweight Detective Special w/same general specifications as that model except w/Colt-alloy frame. Two-inch bbl., calibers: .38 Special, .38 New Police, .32 New Police. Weight: 15 oz., (.38 cal.). Blued finish. Checkered plastic or walnut grips. Made 1951-73.

COBRA DA REVOLVER,
SECOND ISSUE . . . . **NiB $450 Ex $350 Gd $200**
Lightweight version of Detective Special, Second Issue has aluminum alloy frame. 16.5 oz. Made 1973-81.

COBRA DA REVOLVER
SQUARE BUTT . . . . **NiB $425 Ex $325 Gd $200**
Lightweight Police Positive Special w/same general specifications except has Colt-alloy frame, 4-inch bbl., Calibers: .38 Special, .38 New Police, .32 New Police. Weight: 17 oz. in .38 caliber. Blued finish. Checkered plastic or walnut grips. Made 1951-73.

COMMANDO SPECIAL
DA REVOLVER. . . . . **NiB $425 Ex $325 Gd $225**
Caliber: .38 Special. Six-shot cylinder, 2-inch bbl., 6.88 inches overall. Weight: 21.5 oz. Fixed sights. Low-luster blued finish. Made 1982-86.

DETECTIVE SPECIAL DA REVOLVER, FIRST ISSUE
Similar to Police Positive Special w/2-inch bbl., otherwise specifications same as that model, rounded butt intro. 1933. .38 Special only in pre-war issue. Blued or nickel-plated finish. Weight: 17 oz. 6.75 inches overall. Made 1926-46.
Blued finish . . . . **NiB $450 Ex $350 Gd $250**
Nickel finish . . . . **NiB $820 Ex $665 Gd $490**

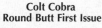

**Colt Cobra
Round Butt First Issue**

**Colt
Detective Special First Issue**

DETECTIVE SPECIAL DA REVOLVER, 2ND ISSUE
Similar to Detective special first issue except w/2- or 3-inch bbl., and also chambered .32 New Police, .38 New Police. Wood, plastic or over-sized grips. Made 1947-72.
Blued finish . . . . NiB $438 Ex $350 Gd $238
Nickel finish . . . . NiB $494 Ex $395 Gd $269
W/three-inch bbl., add $95

DETECTIVE SPECIAL DA REVOLVER, 3RD ISSUE
"D" frame, shrouded ejector rod. Caliber: .38 Special. Six-shot cylinder, 2-inch bbl., 6.88 inches overall. Weight: 21.5 oz. Fixed rear sight, ramp front. Blued or nickel-plated finish. Checkered walnut wraparound grips. Made 1973-84.
Blued finish . . . . NiB $450 Ex $350 Gd $250
Nickel finish . . . . NiB $460 Ex $370 Gd $255
W/three-inch bbl., add $75

**Colt
Detective Special Second Issue**

DETECTIVE SPECIAL DA REVOLVER, 4TH ISSUE
Similar to Detective Special, Third Issue except w/alloy frame. Blued or chrome finish. Wraparound black neoprene grips w/Colt medallion. Made 1993-95.
Blued finish . . . . NiB $425 Ex $395 Gd $250
Chrome finish . . . . NiB $430 Ex $350 Gd $228
DAO model (bobbed hammer) . . . . NiB $460 Ex $370 Gd $255

DIAMONDBACK DA REVOLVER
"D" frame, shrouded ejector rod. Calibers: .22 LR, .22 WRF, .38 Special. Six-shot cylinder, 2.5-, 4- or 6-inch bbl., w/vent rib, 9 inches overall (with 4-inch bbl). Weight: 31.75 oz. (.22 cal., 4-inch bbl.), 28.5 oz. (.38 cal.). Ramp front sight, adj. rear. Blued or nickel finish. Checkered walnut grips. Made 1966-84.
Blued finish . . . . NiB $650 Ex $550 Gd $250
Nickel finish . . . . NiB $584 Ex $445 Gd $295
.22 Mag. model . . . . NiB $615 Ex $475 Gd $309
W/2.5-inch bbl., add $75

DA ARMY (1878) REVOLVER. . . . NiB $5250 Ex $4750 Gd $2500
Also called DA Frontier. Similar in appearance to the smaller Lightning Model but has heavier frame of different shape, round disc on left side of frame, lanyard loop in butt. Calibers: .38-40, .44-40, .45 Colt. Six-shot cylinder, bbl. lengths: 3.5- and 4-inches (w/o ejector), 4.75-, 5.5- and 7.5-inches w/ejector. 12.5 inches overall (7.5-inch bbl.). Weight: 39 oz. (.45 cal., 7.5-inch bbl.). Fixed sights. Hard rubber bird's-head grips. Blued or nickel finish. Made 1878-1905.

**Colt
Diamondback**

Colt Lightning/Thunderer
1877-1912

Idaho Territorial
Centennial 1963 Issue

New Jersey Tercentenary — 1964 issue

General Hood Centennial
1964 issue

FRONTIER SCOUT REVOLVER

SA Army replica, scale. Calibers: .22 Short, Long, LR or .22 WMR (interchangeable cylinder available). Six-shot cylinder, 4.75-inch bbl., 9.9 inches overall. Weight: 24 oz. Fixed sights. Plastic grips. Originally made w/bright alloy frame. Since 1959 w/steel frame and blued finish or all-nickel finish w/composition, wood or Staglite grips. Made 1958-71.

Blued finish, plastic grips.	NiB $379	Ex $305	Gd $205
Nickel finish, wood grips.	NiB $425	Ex $350	Gd $235
Buntline model, add	$60		
Extra interchangeable cylinder, add	$75		

FRONTIER SCOUT REVOLVER COMMEMORATIVE MODELS

Limited production versions of Frontier Scout issued, w/appropriate inscription, to commemorate historical events. Cased. Note: Values indicated are for commemoratives in new condition.

1961 ISSUES
Kansas Statehood Centennial
(6201 produced) . . . . NiB $435
Pony Express Centennial
(1007 produced) . . . . NiB $475

1962 ISSUES
Columbus, Ohio, Sesquicentennial
(200 produced) . . . . NiB $595
Fort Findlay, Ohio, Sesqui-
centennial (130 produced) . . . . NiB $730
Fort Findlay Cased Pair, .22 Long
Rifle and .22 Magnum (20 produced) . . . . NiB $2950
New Mexico Golden Anniversary . . . . NiB $445
West Virginia Statehood
Centennial (3452 produced) . . . . NiB $435

1963 ISSUES
Arizona Territorial Centennial
(5355 produced) . . . . NiB $425
Battle of Gettysburg Centennial
(1019 produced) . . . . NiB $435
Carolina Charter Tercentenary
(300 produced) . . . . NiB $425
Fort Stephenson, Ohio, Sesquicentennial
(200 produced) . . . . NiB $595
General John Hunt Morgan Indiana Raid . . . . NiB $675
Idaho Territorial Centennial (902 produced) . . . . NiB $425

1964 ISSUES
California Gold Rush
(500 produced) . . . . NiB $445
Chamizal Treaty (450 produced) . . . . NiB $450
General Hood Centennial
(1503 produced) . . . . NiB $435
Montana Territorial Centennial
(2300 produced) . . . . NiB $425
Nevada "Battle Born"
(981 produced) . . . . NiB $435
Nevada Statehood Centennial
(3984 produced) . . . . NiB $420
New Jersey Tercentenary
(1001 produced) . . . . NiB $415
St. Louis Bicentennial
(802 produced) . . . . NiB $435
Wyoming Diamond Jubilee
(2357 produced) . . . . NiB $425

1965 ISSUES
Appomattox Centennial
(1001 produced) . . . . NiB $425
Forty-Niner Miner
(500 produced) . . . . NiB $435
General Meade Campaign
(1197 produced) . . . . NiB $435
Kansas Cowtown Series—Wichita
500 produced) . . . . NiB $425
Old Fort Des Moines Reconstruction
(700 produced) . . . . NiB $445
Oregon Trail (1995 produced) . . . . NiB $435
St. Augustine Quadricentennial
(500 produced) . . . . NiB $445

1966 ISSUES
Colorado Gold Rush
(1350 produced) . . . . NiB $445
Dakota Territory (1000 produced) . . . . NiB $425
Indiana Sesquicentennial
(1500 produced) . . . . NiB $420
Kansas Cowtown Series—Abilene
(500 produced) . . . . NiB $425
Kansas Cowtown Series—Dodge City
(500 produced) . . . . NiB $435
Oklahoma Territory (1343 produced) . . . . NiB $425

1967 ISSUES
Alamo (4500 produced) . . . . NiB $435
Kansas Cowtown Series—Coffeyville
(500 produced). . . . . NiB $425
Kansas Trail Series—Chisholm
Trail (500 produced). . . . . NiB $435
Lawman Series—
Bat Masterson (3000 produced) . . . . NiB $445

1968 ISSUES
Kansas Trail Series—Santa Fe Trail
(501 produced). . . . . NiB $425
Kansas Trail Series—Pawnee Trail
(501 produced). . . . . NiB $415
Lawman Series—Pat Garrett
(3000 produced). . . . . NiB $455
Nebraska Centennial
(7001 produced). . . . . NiB $420

1969 ISSUES
Alabama Sesquicentennial
(3001 produced) . . . . NiB $420
Arkansas Territory Sesquicentennial
(3500 produced) . . . . NiB $415
California Bicentennial (5000 produced). . . . . NiB $400
General Nathan Bedford Forrest
(3000 produced) . . . . NiB $425
Golden Spike (11,000 produced) . . . . NiB $445
Kansas Trail Series—Shawnee Trail
(501 produced) . . . . NiB $420
Lawman Series—Wild Bill Hickock
(3000 produced) . . . . NiB $455

1970 ISSUES
Kansas Fort Series—Fort Larned
(500 produced) . . . . NiB $425
Kansas Fort Series—Fort Hays
(500 produced) . . . . NiB $425
Kansas Fort Series—Fort Riley
(500 produced) . . . . NiB $425
Lawman Series—Wyatt Earp
(3000 produced) . . . . NiB $525
Maine Sesquicentennial
(3000 produced). . . . . NiB $415
Missouri Sesquicentennial (3000 produced) . . . . NiB $420

1971 ISSUES
Kansas Fort Series—Fort Scott (500 produced) . . . . NiB $425

1972 ISSUES
Florida Territory Sesquicentennial (2001 produced) . . . NiB $420

1973 ISSUES Azizona ranger
(3001 produced) . . . . NiB $609 Ex $525 Gd $315

Indiana Sesquicentennial
1966 Issue

Golden Spike
Centennial 1969 Issue

Colt King Cobra

COLT KING COBRA REVOLVER
Caliber: .357 Mag., bbl. lengths: 2.5-, 4-, 6- or 8-inches, 9 inches overall (with 4-inch bbl.). Weight: 42 oz., average. Matte stainless steel finish. Black Neoprene combat grips. Made 1986 to date. 2.5-inch bbl. and "Ultimate" bright or blued finish. Made 1988-92.
Matte stainless. . . . . NiB $419 Ex $329 Gd $220
Ultimate bright stainless . . . . NiB $460 Ex $355 Gd $242
Blued. . . . . NiB $400 Ex $350 Gd $200

**LAWMAN MK III
DA REVOLVER**
"J" frame, shrouded ejector rod on 2-inch bbl., only. Caliber: .357 Magnum. Six-shot cylinder, bbl. lengths: 2-, 4-inch. 9.38 inches overall (w/4-inch bbl.), Weight: (with 4-inch bbl.), 35 oz. Fixed rear sight, ramp front. Service trigger and hammer or target trigger and wide-spur hammer. Blued or nickel-plated finish. Checkered walnut service or target grips. Made 1969-1982.
Blued finish . . . . NiB $375 Ex $275 Gd $150
Nickel finish . . . . NiB $395 Ex $300 Gd $165

Colt Lawman
MK V

Colt New Central
Fire Lightning

Colt New Navy

LAWMAN MK V DA REVOLVER
Similar to Trooper MK V. Caliber: .357 Mag. Six-shot cylinder, 2- or 4-inch bbl., 9.38 inches overall (4-inch bbl.). Weight: 35 oz. (4-inch bbl.). Fixed sights. Checkered walnut grips. Made 1983-85.
Blued finish . . . . **NiB $275 Ex $229 Gd $150**
Nickel finish . . . . **NiB $305 Ex $241 Gd $162**

MAGNUM CARRY DA REVOLVER . . . . **NiB $400 Ex $320 Gd $225**
Similar to Model DS II except chambered for .357 Magnum. Made 1998 to date.

MARINE CORPS MODEL (1905) DA REVOLVER
General specifications same as New Navy Second Issue except has round butt, was supplied only in .38 caliber (.38 Short & Long Colt, .38 Special) w/6-inch bbl. (SN range 10,001-10,926) Made 1905-09.
Marine Corps model . . . . **NiB $2800 Ex $2250 Gd $1525**
Marked "USMC" . . . . **NiB $3700 Ex $3100 Gd $2125**

METROPOLITAN MK
III DA REVOLVER . . . . **NiB $425 Ex $330 Gd $229**
Same as Official Police MK III except has 4-inch bbl. w/service or target grips. Weight: 36 oz. Made 1969-72.

NEW DA CENTRAL
FIRE REVOLVER. . . . . **NiB $1744 Ex $1395 Gd $949**
Also called Lightning Model. Calibers: .38 and .41 centerfire. Six-shot cylinder, bbl. lengths: 2.5-, 3.5-, 4.5- and 6-inch without ejector, 4.5- and 6-inch w/ejector, 8.5 inches overall (3.5-inch bbl.). Weight: 23 oz. (.38 cal., with 3.5-inch bbl.) Fixed sights. Blued or nickel finish. Hard rubber bird's-head grips. Made 1877-09.

NEW FRONTIER BUNTLINE SPECIAL
Same as New Frontier SA Army except has 12-inch bbl.,
Second generation (1962-75) . . . . **NiB $1244 Ex $995 Gd $677**
Third generation (1976-92) . . . . . . **NiB $1031 Ex $825 Gd $561**

NEW FRONTIER SA ARMY REVOLVER
Same as SA Army except has flat-top frame, adj. target rear sight, ramp front sight, smooth walnut grips. 5.5- or 7.5-inch bbl., Calibers: .357 Magnum, .44 Special, .45 Colt. Made 1961-92.
Second generation (1961-75) . . . . **NiB $1200 Ex $950 Gd $600**
Third generation (1976-92) . . . . . . **NiB $1000 Ex $800 Gd $550**

NEW FRONTIER SA .22 REVOLVER . . . . . . **NiB $350 Ex $250 Gd $140**
Same as Peacemaker .22 except has flat-top frame, adj. rear sight, ramp front sight. Made 1971-76; reintro. 1982-86.

NEW NAVY (1889) DA, FIRST ISSUE
Also called New Army. Calibers: .38 Short & Long Colt, .41 Short & Long Colt. Six-shot cylinder, left revolution. Bbl. lengths: 3-, 4.5- and 6-inches, 11.25 inches overall (with 6-inch bbl.). Weight: 32 oz. with 6-inch bbl. Fixed sights, knife-blade and V-notch. Blued or nickel-plated finish. Walnut or hard rubber grips. Made 1889-94. Note: This model, which was adopted by both the Army and Navy, was Colt's first revolver of the solid frame, swing-out cylinder type. It lacks the cylinder-locking notches found on later models made on this .41 frame; ratchet on the back of the cylinder is held in place by a double projection on the hand.
First issue. . . . . **NiB $1744 Ex $1395 Gd $949**
First issue w/3-inch bbl. . . . . . . **NiB $2438 Ex $1950 Gd $1326**
Navy contract, marked
"U.S.N.(SN 1-1500). . . . . **NiB $3244 Ex $2595 Gd $1765**

NEW NAVY (1892) DA, SECOND ISSUE
Also called New Army. General specifications same as First Issue except has double cylinder notches and double locking bolt. Calibers: .38 Special added in 1904 and .32-20 in 1905. Made 1892-07. Note: The heavy .38 Special High Velocity loads should not be used in .38 Special arms of this model.
Second issue . . . . **NiB $1494 Ex $1195 Gd $813**
Second issue w/3-inch bbl. . . . . **NiB $2188 Ex $1750 Gd $1190**
Navy contract, marked "U.S.N". . . . . . **NiB $2494 Ex $1995 Gd $1357**

NEW POCKET DA REVOLVER . . . . **NiB $619 Ex $495 Gd $337**
Caliber: .32 Short & Long Colt. Six-shot cylinder. bbl. lengths: 2.5, 3.5- and 6-inches. 7.5 inches overall w/3.5-inch bbl., Weight: 16 oz., with 3.5-inch bbl. Fixed sights, knife-blade and V-notch. Blued or nickel finish. Rubber grips. Made 1893-05.

NEW POLICE DA REVOLVER . . . . . **NiB $525 Ex $465 Gd $300**
Built on New Pocket frame but w/larger grip. Calibers: .32 Colt New Police, .32 Short & Long Colt. Bbl. lengths: 2.5-, 4- and 6-inches, 8.5 inches overall (with 4-inch bbl.). Weight: 17 oz., with 4-inch bbl. Fixed knife-blade front sight, V-notch rear. Blued or nickel finish. Rubber grips. Made 1896-05.

NEW POLICE TARGET DA REVOLVER . . . . **NiB $1350 Ex $1200 Gd $700**
Target version of the New Police w/same general specifications. Target sights. Six-inch bbl., blued finish only. Made 1896-05.

NEW SERVICE DA REVOLVER

Calibers: .38 Special, .357 Magnum (intro. 1936), .38-40, .44-40, .44 Russian, .44 Special, .45 Auto, .45 Colt, .450 Eley, .455 Eley, .476 Eley. Six-shot cylinder, bbl. lengths: 4-, 5- and 6-inch in .38 Special and .357 Magnum, 4.5-, 5.5- and 7.5 inches in other calibers; 9.75 inches overall (with 4.5-inch bbl.). Weight: 39 oz. (.45 cal. with 4.5-inch bbl.). Fixed sights. Blued or nickel finish. Checkered walnut grips. Made 1898-42. Note: More than 500,000 of this model in caliber .45 Auto (designated "Model 1917 Revolver") were purchased by the U.S. Gov't. during WW I. These arms were later sold as surplus to National Rifle Association members through the Director of Civilian Marksmanship. Price was $16.15 plus packing charge. Supply exhausted during the early 1930s.

Commercial model . . . . **NiB $1619 Ex $1295 Gd $881**
Magnum . . . . **NiB $1031 Ex $825 Gd $561**
1917 Army. . . . . **NiB $994 Ex $795 Gd $541**

NEW SERVICE TARGET . . . . NiB $1130 Ex $995 Gd $600

Target version of the New Service. Calibers: Originally chambered for .44 Russian, .450 Eley, .455 Eley and .476 Eley, later models in .44 Special, .45 Colt and .45 Auto. Six- or 7.5-inch bbl., 12.75 inches overall (7.5-inch bbl.). Adj. target sights. Hand-finished action. With blued finish. Checkered walnut grips. Made 1900-40.

OFFICERS' MODEL MATCH . . . . . . NiB $700 Ex $575 Gd $300

Same general design as Officers' Model revolvers. Has tapered heavy bbl., wide hammer spur, Adjustable rear sight ramp front sight, large target grips of checkered walnut. Calibers: .22 LR, .38 Special. Six-inch bbl., 11.25 inches overall. Weight: 43 oz. (in .22 cal.), 39 oz. (.38 cal.). Blued finish. Made 1953-70.

OFFICERS' MODEL SPECIAL . . . . . . NiB $750 Ex $500 Gd $300

Target version of Officers' Model Second Issue w/similar characters except w/heavier, nontapered bbl. redesigned hammer. Ramp front sight, Colt Officers' Model Special "Coltmaster" rear sight adj. for windage and elevation. Calibers: .22 LR, .38 Special. Six-inch bbl. 11.25 inches overall. Weight: 39 oz. (in .38 cal.), 43 oz., (.22 cal.). Blued finish. Checkered plastic grips. Made 1949-53.

OFFICERS' MODEL TARGET DA
REVOLVER, FIRST ISSUE . . . . NiB $1156 Ex $925 Gd $629

Caliber: .38 Special. Six-inch bbl., hand-finished action, adj. target sights. Checkered with walnut grips. General specifications same as New Navy, Second Issue. Made 1904-08.

OFFICERS' MODEL TARGET, SECOND ISSUE

Calibers: .22 LR (intro. 1930, embedded head-cylinder for high-speed cartridges after 1932), .32 Police Positive (made 1932-1942), .38 Special. Six-shot cylinder, bbl. lengths: 4-, 4.5-, 5-, 6- and 7.5-inch (in .38 Special) or 6-inch only (.22 LR and .32 PP), 11.25 inches overall (6-inch bbl. in .38 Special). Adj. target sights. Blued finish. Checkered walnut grips. Hand-finished action. General features same as Army Special and Official Police of same date. Made 1908-49 (w/exceptions noted).

Second issue (.38 caliber) . . . . **NiB $956 Ex $765 Gd $520**
Second issue (.32 caliber) . . . . . . **NiB $1531 Ex $1225 Gd $833**
Second issue (.22 caliber) . . . . . . **NiB $1063 Ex $850 Gd $578**
W/shorter bbls. (4-, 4.5- or 5-inches), add **40%**

OFFICIAL POLICE DA REVOLVER

Calibers: .22 LR (intro. 1930, embedded head-cylinder for high-speed cartridges after 1932), .32-20 (disc. 1942), .38 Special, .41 Long Colt (disc. 1930). Six-shot cylinder, bbl. lengths: 4-, 5-, and 6-inch or 2-inch and 6-inch heavy bbl. in .38 Special only; .22 LR w/4- and 6-inch bbls. only; 11.25 inches overall. Weight: 36

Colt New Service

Colt New Service Target

Colt Officer's Match

Colt
Officers' Target Second Issue

(cont'd) OFFICIAL POLICE DA REVOLVER
oz. (standard 6-inch bbl.) in .38 Special. Fixed sights. Blued or nickel-plated finish. Checkered walnut grips on all revolvers of this model except some of postwar production had checkered plastic grips. Made 1927-69. Note: This model is a refined version of the Army Special, which it replaced in 1928 at about serial number 520,000. The Commando .38 Special was a wartime adaptation of the Official Police made to government specifications. Commando can be identified by its sandblasted blued finish. Serial numbers start w/number 1-50,000 (1942-45). See illustration next page.

Commercial model (pre-war) . . . . . **NiB $500 Ex $400 Gd $272**
Commercial model (post-war). . . . . **NiB $438 Ex $350 Gd $238**
Commando model. . . . . **NiB $531 Ex $425 Gd $289**

Colt Official Police

Colt Peacekeeper

Colt Pocket Positive

Colt Police Positive First Issue

OFFICIAL POLICE MK
III DA REVOLVER . . . . NiB $250 Ex $200 Gd $135
"J" frame, without shrouded ejector rod. Caliber: .38 Special. Six-shot cylinder. bbl., lengths: 4-, 5-, 6-inches, 9.25 inches overall w/4-inch bbl., weight: 34 oz. (4-inch bbl.). Fixed rear sight, ramp front. Service trigger and hammer or target trigger and wide-spur hammer. Blued or nickel-plated finish. Checkered walnut service grips. Made 1969-75.

PEACEKEEPER DA REVOLVER . . . . . NiB $395 Ex $325 Gd $140
Caliber: .357 Mag. Six-shot cylinder, 4- or 6-inch bbl., 11.25 inches overall (6-inch bbl.). Weight: 46 oz. (with 6-inch bbl.). Adj. white outline rear sight, red insert ramp-style front. Non-reflective matte blued finish. Made 1985-89.

PEACEMAKER .22 SECOND AMENDMENT
COMMEMORATIVE. . . . . NiB $550 Ex $450 Gd $200
Caliber: .22, revolver w/7.5-inch bbl., nickel-plated frame, bbl. ejector rod assembly, hammer and trigger, blued cylinder, backstrap and trigger guard. Black pearlite grips. bbl., inscribed "The Right to Keep and Bear Arms." Presentation case. Limited edition of 3000 issued in 1977. Top value is for revolver in new condition.

PEACEMAKER .22 SA REVOLVER . . NiB $350 Ex $250 Gd $200
Calibers: .22 LR and .22 WMR. Furnished w/cylinder for each caliber, 6-shot. Bbl.: 4.38-, 6- or 7.5-inches, 11.25 inches overall (with 6-inch bbl.). Weight: 30.5 oz. (with 6-inch bbl.). Fixed sights. Black composite grips. Made 1971-76.

POCKET POSITIVE
DA REVOLVER. . . . . NiB $525 Ex $465 Gd $300
General specifications same as New Pocket except this model has positive lock feature (see Police Positive). Calibers: .32 Short & Long Colt (disc. 1914), .32 Colt New Police (.32 S&W Short & Long). Fixed sights, flat top and square notch. Blue or nickel finish. Made 1905-40.
Blue finish . . . . NiB $494 Ex $395 Gd $269
Nickel finish . . . . NiB $594 Ex $475 Gd $323

POLICE POSITIVE DA, FIRST ISSUE
Improved version of the New Police w/the "Positive Lock," which prevents the firing pin coming in contact w/the cartridge except when the trigger is pulled. Calibers: .32 Short & Long Colt (disc. 1915), .32 Colt New Police (.32 S&W Short & Long), .38 New Police (.38 S&W). Six-shot cylinder, bbl. lengths: 2.5- (.32 cal. only), 4- 5- and 6-inches; 8.5 inches overall (with 4-inch bbl.). Weight 20 oz. (with 4-inch bbl.). Fixed sights. Blued or nickel finish. Rubber or checkered walnut grips. Made 1905-47.
Blue finish . . . . NiB $438 Ex $350 Gd $238
Nickel finish . . . . NiB $500 Ex $400 Gd $272

POLICE POSITIVE DA, SECOND ISSUE
Same as Detective Special second issue except has 4-inch bbl., 9 inches overall, weight: 26.5 oz. Intro. in 1977. Note: Original Police Positive (First Issue) has a shorter frame, is not chambered for .38 Special.
Blue finish . . . . NiB $425 Ex $340 Gd $231
Nickel finish . . . . NiB $494 Ex $395 Gd $269

POLICE POSITIVE
SPECIAL DA REVOLVER . . . . NiB $494 Ex $395 Gd $269
Based on the Police Positive w/frame lengthened to permit longer cylinder. Calibers: .32-20 (disc. 1942), .38 Special, .32 New Police and .38 New Police (intro. 1946). Six-shot cylinder; bbl. lengths: 4-(only length in current production), 5- and 6-inch; 8.75 inches overall (with 4-inch bbl.). Weight: 23 oz. (with 4-inch bbl. in .38 Special). Fixed sights. Checkered grips of hard rubber, plastic or walnut. Made 1907-73.

COLT POLICE POSITIVE
TARGET DA REVOLVER. . . . . NiB $744 Ex $595 Gd $405
Target version of the Police Positive. Calibers: .22 LR (intro. 1910, embedded-head cylinder for high-speed cartridges after 1932), .22 WRF (1910-35), .32 Short & Long Colt, (1915), .32 New Police (.32 S&W Short & Long). Six-inch bbl., blued finish only, 10.5 inches overall. Weight: 26 oz. in .22 cal. Adj. target sights. Checkered walnut grips. Made 1905-40.

PYTHON DA REVOLVER

"I" frame, shrouded ejector rod. Calibers: .357 Magnum, .38 Special. Six-shot cylinder, 2.5-, 4-, 6- or 8-inch vent rib bbl., 11.25 inches overall (with 6-inch bbl.). Weight: 44 oz. (6-inch bbl.). Adj. rear sight, ramp front. Blued, nickel or stainless finish. Checkered walnut target grips. Made 1955 to date. Ultimate stainless finish made 1985 to date.

Blued finish	NiB $895 Ex $775 Gd $300
Royal blued finish	NiB $611 Ex $500 Gd $358
Nickel finish	NiB $599 Ex $490 Gd $351
Stainless finish	NiB $674 Ex $550 Gd $392
Ultimate stainless finish	NiB $925 Ex $775 Gd $350
Hunter model (w/2x scope)	NiB $1395 Ex $1225 Gd $700
Silhouette model (w/2x scope)	NiB $1450 Ex $1275 Gd $650

SHOOTING MASTER DA REVOLVER

Deluxe target arm based on the New Service model. Calibers: Originally made only in .38 Special, .44 Special, .45 Auto and .45 Colt added in 1933, .357 Magnum in 1936. Six-inch bbl., 11.25 inches overall. Weight: 44 oz., in (.38 cal.), adj. target sights. Hand-finished action. Blued finish. Checkered walnut grips. Rounded butt. Made 1932-41.

Shooting Master .38 Special	NiB $1250 Ex $1100 Gd $700
Shooting Master .357 Mag.	NiB $1295 Ex $1030 Gd $689
Shooting Master .44 Special, .45 ACP, .45LC	NiB $3600 Ex $3300 Gd $1900

SA ARMY REVOLVER

Also called Frontier Six-Shooter and Peacemaker. Available in more than 30 calibers including: .22 Rimfire (Short, Long, LR), .22 WRF, .32 Rimfire, .32 Colt, .32 S&W, .32-20, .38 Colt, .38 S&W, .38 Special, .357 Magnum, .38-40, .41 Colt, .44 Rimfire, .44 Russian, .44 Special, .44-40, .45 Colt, .45 Auto, .450 Boxer, 450 Eley, .455 Eley, .476 Eley. Six-shot cylinder. Bbl. lengths: 4.75, 5 .5 and 7.5 inches w/ejector or 3 and 4 inches w/o ejector. 10.25 inches overall (with 4.75-inch bbl.). Weight: 36 oz. (.45 cal. w/4.75-inch bbl.). Fixed sights. Also made in Target Model w/flat top-strap and target sights. Blued finish w/casehardened frame or nickel-plated. One-piece smooth walnut or checkered black rubber grips. Note: S.A. Army Revolvers w/serial numbers above 165,000 (circa 1896) are adapted to smokeless powder and cylinder pin screw was changed to spring catch at about the same time. The "First Generation" of SA Colts included both blackpowder and smokeless configurations and were manufactured from 1873 to 1940. Production resumed in 1955 w/serial number 1001SA and continued through 1975 to complete the second series, which is referred to as the "Second Generation." In 1976, the "Third Generation" of production began and continues to to date. However, several serial number rollovers occurred at 99,999. For example, in 1978 the "SA" suffix became an "SA" prefix and again in 1993, when the serial number SA99,999 was reached, the serialization format was changed again to include both an "S" prefix and an "A" suffix. Although the term "Fourth Generation" is frequently associated with this rollover, no series change actually occurred, therefore, the current production is still a "Third Generation" series. Current calibers: .357 Magnum, .44 Special, .45 Long Colt.

Pinched frame (1873 only)	NiB $79,438 Ex $63,550 Gd $43,214

Colt SA Army

Colt Police Positive Target

Colt Python

(cont'd.) SA ARMY REVOLVER

Early commercial (1873-77)	NiB $40,938 Ex $32,750 Gd $22,270
Early military (1873-77)	NiB $46,875 Ex $37,500 Gd $25,500
Large bore rimfire (1875-80)	NiB $38,125 Ex $30,500 Gd $20,740
Small bore rimfire (1875-80)	NiB $29,375 Ex $23,500 Gd $15,980
Frontier six-shooter, .44-40 (1878-82)	NiB $44,438 Ex $35,550 Gd $24,174
Storekeeper's model, no ejector (1883-98)	NiB $46,875 Ex $37,500 Gd $25,500
Sheriff's model (1883-98)	NiB $44,375 Ex $35,500 Gd $24,140
Target model, flat top strap, target sights	NiB $24,375 Ex $19,500 Gd $13,260
U.S. Cavalry model, .45 (1873-92)	NiB $43,125 Ex $34,500 Gd $23,460

Colt SA Army — 125th Anniversary

Colt 150th Anniversary Deluxe

Colt 150th Anniversary Engraving Sampler

In the previous section the GTG deviates from the observed practice of listing only the value of firearms produced after 1900. This deliberate departure from the standard format is intended to provide a general reference and establish proper orientation for the reader, because the Colt SSA had its origins in the last quarter of the 19th century. Consequently, antique firearms produced prior to 1898 have been listed as a preface and introduction to the first series of production (what is now recognized as "1st Generation") in order to systematically demonstrate the progressive and sequential development of the multi-generation Colt SAA. Therefore, the previous general values have been provided to establish a point of reference to allow a more comprehensive examination of the evolution of the Colt SAA. However, please note that the following values apply only to original models, not to similar S.A.A. revolvers of more recent manufacture.

Standard model, pre-war
(1st generation) . . . . $12,750 to 65,000
Standard model
(1955-75)
(2nd generation) . . . . NiB $2244 Ex $1795 Gd $1221
Standard model
(1976 to date) . . . . NiB $1063 Ex $850 Gd $578

SA ARMY — 125TH ANNIVERSARY . . . . . NiB $1744 Ex $1395 Gd $949
Limited production deluxe version of SA Army issued in commemoration
of Colt's 125th Anniversary. Caliber: .45 Long Colt., 7.5-inch bbl., cold-
plated frame trigger, hammer, cylinder pin, ejector rod tip, and grip medallion. Presentation case w/anniversary medallion. Serial numbers "50AM."
7368 were made in 1961. See illustration previous page.

SA ARMY COMMEMORATIVE MODELS
Limited production versions of SA Army .45 issued, w/appropriate
inscription to commemorate historical events. Cased. Note: Values
indicated are for commemorative revolvers in new condition.

1963 ISSUES
Arizona Territorial Centennial
(1280 produced) . . . . NiB $1425
West Virginia Statehood
Centennial (600 produced) . . . . NiB $1350

1964 ISSUES
Chamizal Treaty (50 produced) . . . . NiB $1450
Colonel Sam Colt Sesquicentennial
Presentation (4750 produced) . . . . NiB $1425
Deluxe Presentation
(200 produced) . . . . NiB $2650
Special Deluxe Presentation
(50 produced) . . . . NiB $4250
Montana Territorial Centennial
(851 produced) . . . . NiB $1425
Nevada "Battle Born"
(100 produced) . . . . NiB $1495
Nevada Statehood Centennial
(1877 produced) . . . . NiB $1395
New Jersey Tercentenary
(250 produced) . . . . NiB $142
Pony Express Presentation
(1004 produced) . . . . NiB $1495
St. Louis Bicentennial
(450 produced) . . . . NiB $1425
Wyatt Earp Buntline
(150 produced) . . . . NiB $2595

1965 ISSUES
Appomattox Centennial
(500 produced) . . . . NiB $1425
Old Fort Des Moines Recon-
struction (200 produced) . . . . NiB $1350

1966 ISSUES
Abercrombie & Fitch Trailblazer
—Chicago (100 produced) . . . . NiB $1250
Abercrombie & Fitch Trailblazer
—New York (200 produced) . . . . NiB $1225
Abercrombie & Fitch Trailblazer
—San Francisco (100 produced) . . . . NiB $1250
California Gold Rush
(130 produced) . . . . NiB $1425
General Meade (200 produced) . . . . NiB $1425
Pony Express Four Square (4 guns) . . . . NiB $6250

1967 ISSUES
Alamo (1000 produced) . . . . NiB $1425
Lawman Series—Bat Masterson
(500 produced) . . . . NiB $1595

1968 ISSUES
Lawman Series—Pat Garrett (500 produced) . . . . NiB $1425

Colt SA Army Flat Top

1969 ISSUES
Lawman Series—Wild Bill Hickok
(500 produced) . . . . NiB
$1425

1970 ISSUES
Lawman Series—Wyatt Earp
(501 produced) . . . . NiB $2595
Missouri Sesquicentennial (501 produced) . . . . NiB $1425
Texas Ranger (1000 produced) . . . . NiB $2395

1971 ISSUES
NRA Centennial, .357 or .45 (5001 produced) . . . . NiB $1425

1975 ISSUES
Peacemaker Centennial .45
(1501 produced) . . . . NiB $1450
Peacemaker Centennial .44-40
(1501 produced) . . . . NiB $1550
Peacemaker Centennial Cased
Pair (501 produced) . . . . NiB $2995

1979 ISSUES
Ned Buntline .45 (3000 produced) . . . . NiB $1025

1986 ISSUES
Colt 150th Anniversary (standard) . . . . NiB $1695
Colt 150th Anniversay (engraved) . . . . NiB$2695

COLT SA COWBOY REVOLVER . . . . NiB $445
SSA variant designed for "Cowboy Action Shooting." Caliber: .45
Colt. Six-shot cylinder, 5.5-inch bbl., 11 inches overall. Weight: 42
oz. Blade front sight, fixed V-notch rear. Blued finish w/color casehardened frame. Smooth walnut grips. Made 1999 to date.

SA SHERIFF'S MODEL .45
Limited edition replica of Storekeeper's Model in caliber .45 Colt,
made exclusively for Centennial Arms Corp. Chicago, Illinois.
Numbered "1SM." Blued finish w/casehardened frame or nickel-
plated. Walnut grips. Made in 1961.
Blued finish (478 produced) . . . . NiB $2619 Ex $2095 Gd $1425
Nickel finish (25 produced) . . . . . NiB $6369 Ex $5095 Gd $3465

THREE-FIFTY-SEVEN DA REVOLVER
Heavy frame. Caliber: .357 Magnum. Six-shot cylinder, 4 or 6-inch
bbl. Quickdraw ramp front sight, Accro rear sight. Blued finish.
Checkered walnut grips. 9.25 or 11.25 inches overall. Weight: 36
oz. (4-inch bbl.), 39 oz. (6 inch bbl.). Made 1953-61.
W/standard hammer and service grips . . . . . NiB $544 Ex $435 Gd $296
W/wide-spur hammer and target grips . . . . . NiB $581 Ex $465 Gd $316

TROOPER DA REVOLVER
Same specifications as Officers' Model Match except has 4-inch bbl.
w/quick-draw ramp front sight, weight: 34 oz. in .38 caliber. Made 1953-69.
W/standard hammer and service grips . . . . . NiB $419 Ex $335 Gd $228

Colt Trooper

Colt Trooper MK V

Colt U.S. Bicentennial Commemorative Set

TROOPER MK III DA REVOLVER
"J"frame, shrouded ejector rod. Calibers: .22 LR, .22 Magnum, .38 Special, .357 Magnum. Six-shot cylinder. bbl. lengths: 4-, 6-inches. 9.5 inches overall (with 4-inch bbl.). Weight: 39 oz. (4-inch bbl.). Adj. rear sight, ramp front. Target trigger and hammer. Blued or nickel-plated finish. Checkered walnut target grips. Made 1969-78.
Blued finish . . . . NiB $395 Ex $325 Gd $125
Nickel finish. NiB $440 Ex $350 Gd $125

TROOPER MK V REVOLVER
Re-engineered Mark III for smoother, faster action. Caliber: .357 Magnum. Six-shot cylinder, bbl. lengths: 4-, 6-, 8-inch w/vent rib. Adj. rear sight, ramp front, red insert. Checkered walnut grips. Made 1982-86.
Blued finish . . . . NiB $425 Ex $350 Gd $250
Nickel finish. NiB $475 Ex $400 Gd $225

VIPER DA REVOLVER . . . . NiB $425 Ex $375 Gd $250
Same as Cobra, Second Issue except has 4-inch bbl., 9 inches overall, weight: 20 oz. Made 1977-84.

U.S. BICENTENNIAL
COMMEMORATIVE SET . . . . NiB $2250
Replica Colt 3rd Model Dragoon revolver w/accessories, Colt SA Army revolver, and Colt Python revolver. Matching roll-engraved unfluted cylinders, blued finish and rosewood grips w/Great Seal of the United States silver medallion. Dragoon revolver has silver grip frame. Serial numbers 0001 to 1776. All revolvers in set have same number. Deluxe drawer-style presentation case of walnut w/book compartment containing a reproduction of "Armsmear." Issued in 1976. Value is for revolvers in new condition.

COONAN ARMS, INC. — Maplewood, Minnesota (formerly St. Paul, Minnesota)

MODEL .357 MAGNUM AUTO PISTOL
Caliber: .357 Mag. Seven-shot magazine, 5- or 6-inch bbl., 8.3 inches overall (with 5-inch bbl.). Weight: 42 oz. Front ramp interchangeable sight, fixed rear sight, adj. for windage. Black walnut grips. Made 1983-99.
Model A Std. grade w/o grip
safety (disc. 1991) . . . . NiB $781 Ex $625 Gd $425
Model B Std. grade w/5-inch bbl., ... NiB $563 Ex $450 Gd $306
Model B Std. grade w/6-inch bbl., ... NiB $594 Ex $475 Gd $323
Model B w/5-inch
compensated bbl., (Classic). . . . . NiB $1063 Ex $850 Gd $578
Model B w/6-inch
compensated bbl . . . . NiB $844 Ex $675 Gd $459

.357 MAGNUM CADET COMPACT
Similar to the standard .357 Magnum model except w/3.9-inch bbl., on compact frame. Six-shot (Cadet), 7- or 8-shot magazine (Cadet II). Weight: 39 oz., 7.8 inches overall. Made 1993-99.
Cadet model . . . . NiB $669 Ex $535 Gd $364
Cadet II model. . . . . NiB $785 Ex $630 Gd $350

CZ PISTOLS — Uhersky Brod (formerly Strakonice), Czechoslovakia Mfd. by Ceska Zbrojovka-Nardoni Podnik (formerly Bohmische Waffenfabrik A. G.)

Currently imported by CZ USA, Kansas City, KS. Previously by Magnum Research and Action Arms. Vintage importation is by Century International Arms.

MODEL 27 AUTO PISTOL . . . . **NiB $550 Ex $450 Gd $260**
Caliber: .32 Automatic (7.65mm). Eight-shot magazine, 4-inch bbl.,
6 inches overall. Weight: 23.5 oz. Fixed sights. Blued finish. Plastic
grips. Made 1927-51. Note: After the German occupation. (March
1939), Models 27 and .38 were marked w/manufacturer code "fnh."
Designation of Model .38 was changed to "Pistole 39(t)."

MODEL .38 AUTO PISTOL (VZ SERIES)
Caliber: .380 Automatic (9mm). Nine-shot magazine, 3.75-inch
bbl., 7 inches overall. Weight: 26 oz. Fixed sights. Blued finish.
Plastic grips. After 1939 designated as T39. Made 1938-.45.
CZ DAO model . . . . **NiB $387 Ex $312 Gd $215**
CZ SA/DA model . . . . **NiB $1237 Ex $955 Gd $640**

MODEL 50 DA AUTO PISTOL . . . . **NiB $169 Ex $135 Gd $92**
Similar to Walther Model PP except w/frame-mounted safety and trigger guard not hinged. Caliber: .32 ACP (7.65mm), 8-round magazine,
3.13-inch bbl., 6.5 inches overall. Weight: 24.5 oz. Fixed sights. Blued
finished. Intro. in 1950. disc. Note: "VZ50" is the official designation
of this pistol used by the Czech National Police ("New Model .006"
was the export designation but very few were released).

MODEL 52 SA AUTO PISTOL
Roller-locking breech system. Calibers: 7.62mm or 9mm Para. Eight-
shot magazine, 4.7-inch bbl., 8.1 inches overall. Weight: 31 oz. Fixed
sights. Blued finish. Grooved composition grips. Made 1952-56.
7.62mm model . . . . **NiB $180 Ex $150 Gd $85**
9mm model . . . . **NiB $180 Ex $150 Gd $85**

MODEL 70 DA AUTO PISTOL . . . . . . **NiB $406 Ex $325 Gd $221**
Similar to Model 50 but redesigned to improve function and
dependability. Made 1962-83.

MODEL 75 DA/DAO AUTOMATIC PISTOL
Calibers: 9mm Para. or .40 S&W w/selective action mode. 10-, 13-
or 15-shot magazine, 3.9-inch bbl., (Compact) or 4.75-inch bbl.,
(Standard), 8 inches overall (Standard). Weight: 35 oz. Fixed sights.
Blued, nickel, Two-Tone or black polymer finish. Checkered wood
or high-impact plastic grips. Made 1994 to date.
Black polymer finish . . . . **NiB $369 Ex $295 Gd $201**
High-polish blued finish . . . . **NiB $431 Ex $345 Gd $235**
Matte blued finish . . . . **NiB $394 Ex $315 Gd $214**
Nickel finish . . . . **NiB $419 Ex $335 Gd $228**
Two-tone finish . . . . **NiB $406 Ex $325 Gd $221**
W/.22 Kadet conversion, add **$250**
Compact model, add **$35**

82 DA AUTO PISTOL . . . . **NiB $300 Ex $275 Gd $155**
Similar to the standard CZ 83 model except chambered in 9x18
Makarov. This model currently is the Czech military sidearm.

83 DA AUTOMATIC PISTOL
Calibers: .32 ACP, .380 ACP. 15-shot (.32 ACP) or 13-shot (.380 ACP) mag-
azine, 3.75-inch bbl., 6.75 inches overall. Weight: 26.5 oz. Fixed sights.
Blued (standard); chrome and nickel (optional special edition) w/brushed,
matte or polished finish. Checkered black plastic grips. Made 1985 to date.
Standard finish . . . . **NiB $330 Ex $260 Gd $150**
Special edition . . . . **NiB $466 Ex $372 Gd $250**
Engraved . . . . **NiB $1044 Ex $825 Gd $560**

85 AUTOMATIC DA PISTOL
Same as CZ 75 except w/ambidextrous slide release and safety.
Calibers: 9mm Para., 7.65mm. Made 1986 to date.
Black polymer finish . . . . **NiB $426 Ex $340 Gd $232**
High-polish blued finish . . . . **NiB $530 Ex $425 Gd $275**
Matte Blued finish . . . . **NiB $475 Ex $325 Gd $225**

CZ Model 75 Compact

CZ Model 75 Kadet

CZ Model 83

CZ Model 85 Combat

CZ Model 97B

CZ Model 100

Daewoo DH40

85 COMBAT DA AUTOMATIC PISTOL
Similar to the standard CZ 85 model except w/13-shot magazine, combat-style hammer, fully adj. rear sight and walnut grips. Made 1986 to date.
Black polymer
finish . . . . **NiB $455 Ex $395 Gd $225**
High-polished
blued finish . . . . **NiB $494 Ex $395 Gd $269**
Matte blued
finish . . . . **NiB $494 Ex $395 Gd $269**

MODEL 97B DA
AUTOLOADING PISTOL. . . . . **NiB $525 Ex $460 Gd $275**
Similar to the CZ Model 75 except chambered for the .45 ACP cartridge. 10-shot magazine, Frame-mounted thumb safety that allows single-action, cocked-and-locked carry. Made 1997 to date.

MODEL 100 DA
AUTOMATIC PISTOL . . . . **NiB $365 Ex $310 Gd $180**
Caliber: 9mm, .40 S&W. 10-shot magazine, 3.8-inch bbl., Weight: 25 oz. Polymer grips w/fixed low-profile sights. Made 1996 to date.

MODEL 1945 DA
POCKET AUTO PISTOL. . . . . **NiB $231 Ex $185 Gd $126**
Caliber: .25 Auto (6.35mm). Eight-shot magazine, 2.5-inch bbl., 5 inches overall. Weight: 15 oz. Fixed sights. Blued finish. Plastic grips. Intro. 1945. disc.

DUO POCKET
AUTO PISTOL . . . . **NiB $225 Ex $195 Gd $120**
Caliber: .25 Automatic (6.35mm). Six-shot magazine, 2.13 inch bbl., 4.5 inches overall. Weight: 14-.5 oz. Fixed sights. Blued or nickel finish. Plastic grips. Made c.1926-60.

DAEWOO PISTOLS — Seoul, Korea
Mfd. by Daewoo Precision Industries Ltd.

Imported by Daewoo Precision Industries, Southhampton, PA, Previously by Nationwide Sports Distributors and KBI, Inc.

DH40 AUTO PISTOL. . . . . **NiB $385 Ex $328 Gd $200**
Caliber: .40 S&W. 12-shot magazine, 4.25-inch bbl., 7 inches overall. Weight: 28 oz. Blade front sight, dovetailed rear w/3-dot system. Blued finish. Checkered composition grips. DH/DP series feature a patented "fastfire" action w/5-6 lb. trigger pull. Made 1994-96.

DH45 AUTO PISTOL. . . . . **NiB $619 Ex $495 Gd $337**
Caliber: .45 ACP. 13-shot magazine, 5-inch bbl., 8.1 inches overall. Weight: 35 oz. Blade front sight, dovetailed rear w/3-dot system. Blued finish. Checkered composition grips. Announced 1994, but not imported.

DP51 AUTO PISTOL . . . . **NiB $360 Ex $285 Gd $190**
Caliber: 9mm Para. 13-shot magazine, 4.1-inch bbl., 7.5 inches overall. Weight: 28 oz. Blade front and square-notch rear sights. Matte black finish. Checkered composition grips. Made 1991-96.

DP52 AUTO PISTOL . . . . **NiB $320 Ex $275 Gd $160**
Caliber: .22 LR. 10-shot magazine, 3.8-inch bbl., 6.7 inches overall. Weight: 23 oz. Blade front sight, dovetailed rear w/3-dot system. Blued finish. Checkered wood grips. Made 1994-96.

DAKOTA/E.M.F. CO. — Santa Ana, California

MODEL 1873 SA REVOLVER
Calibers: .22 LR, .22 Mag., .357 Mag., .45 Long Colt, .30 M1 carbine, .38-40, .32-20, .44-40. Bbl. lengths: 3.5, 4.75, 5.5, 7.5 inches. Blued or nickel finish. Engraved models avail.
Standard model . . . . NiB $325 Ex $250 Gd $200
W/extra cylinder . . . . NiB $666 Ex $555 Gd $413

MODEL 1875 OUTLAW
SA REVOLVER . . . . NiB $419 Ex $335 Gd $228
Calibers: .45 Long Colt, .357 Mag., .44-40. 7.5-inch bbl. Casehardened frame, blued finish. Walnut grips. This is an exact replica of the Remington Number 3 revolver produced 1875-89.

MODEL 1890 REMINGTON POLICE
Calibers: .357 Mag., .44-40, .45 Long Colt, 5.75-inch bbl., blued or nickel finish. Similar to Outlaw w/lanyard ring and no bbl. web .
Standard model . . . . NiB $444 Ex $355 Gd $241
Nickel model . . . . NiB $531 Ex $425 Gd $289
Engraved model . . . . NiB $619 Ex $495 Gd $337

BISLEY SA REVOLVER
Calibers: .44-40, .45 Long Colt, .357 Mag, 5.5- or 7.5-inch bbl., disc. 1992. Reintroduced 1994.
Standard model . . . . NiB $350 Ex $285 Gd $195
Target model . . . . NiB $395 Ex $315 Gd $200

HARTFORD SA REVOLVER
Calibers: .22 LR, .32-20, .357 Mag., .38-40, .44-40, .44 Special, .45 Long Colt. These are exact replicas of the original Colts w/steel backstraps, trigger guards and forged frames. Blued or nickel finish. Imported 1990 to date.
Standard model . . . . NiB $350 Ex $275 Gd $180
Engraved model . . . . NiB $619 Ex $495 Gd $337
Hartford Artillery,
U.S. Cavalry models . . . . NiB $395 Ex $325 Gd $200

SHERIFF'S MODEL
SA REVOLVER . . . . NiB $385 Ex $300 Gd $200
Calibers: .32-20, .357 Mag., .38-40, .44 Special, .44-40, .45 LC. 3.5-inch bbl. Reintroduced 1994.

TARGET SA REVOLVER . . . . NiB $350 Ex $265 Gd $185
Calibers: .45 Long Colt, .357 Mag., .22 LR; 5.5- or 7.5-inch bbl. Polished, blued finish, casehardened frame. Walnut grips. Ramp front, blade target sight, adj. rear sight.

CHARLES DALY HANGUNS — Manila, Philippines. Currently imported by K.B.I., Harrisburg, PA.

MODEL M1911-A1 FIELD FS AUTOMATIC PISTOL
Caliber: .45 ACP. Eight- or 10-shot magazine (Hi-Cap), 5-inch bbl., 8.75 inches overall. Weight: 38 oz. Blade front sight, drift adjustable rear w/3-dot system. Skeletonized tactical hammer and trigger. Extended slide release and beavertail grip safety. Matte blue, stainless or Duo finish. Checkered composition or wood stocks. Imported 1996 to date.
Matte blue (Field FS) . . . . NiB $435 Ex $375 Gd $225
Stainless (Empire FS) . . . . NiB $595 Ex $475 Gd $300
Duo (Superior FS) . . . . NiB $469 Ex $375 Gd $255
W/.22 conversion kit, add $200

Dakota Hartford

DAVIS INDUSTRIES, INC. — Chino, California

MODEL D DERRINGER
Single-action double derringer. Calibers: .22 LR, .22 Mag., .25 ACP, .32 Auto, .32 H&R Mag., 9mm, .38 Special. Two-shot capacity, 2.4-inch or 2.75-inch bbl., 4 inches overall (2.4-inch bbl.). Weight: 9 to 11.5 oz. Laminated wood grips. Black Teflon or chrome finish. Made 1987 to date.
.22 LR or .25 ACP . . . . NiB $75 Ex $60 Gd $41
.22 Mag., .32 H&R Mag., .38 Spec. . . . . NiB $94 Ex $75 Gd $51
.32 Auto. . . . . NiB $88 Ex $70 Gd $48
9mm Para. . . . . NiB $106 Ex $85 Gd $58

LONG BORE DERRINGER. . . . . NiB $94 Ex $75 Gd $51
Similar to Model D except in calibers .22 Mag., .32 H&R Mag., .38 Special, 9mm Para. 3.75-inch bbl., weight: 16 oz. Made 1995 to date.

MODEL P-.32 . . . . NiB $81 Ex $65 Gd $44
Caliber: .32 Auto. Six-round magazine, 2.8-inch bbl., 5.4 inches overall. Weight: 22 oz. Black Teflon or chrome finish. Laminated wood grips. Made 1987 to date.

MODEL P-.380 . . . . NiB $85 Ex $75 Gd $50
Caliber: .380 Auto. Five-shot magazine, 2.8-inch bbl., 5.4 inches overall. Weight: 22 oz. Black Teflon or chrome finish. Made 1990 to date.

DESERT INDUSTRIES, INC. — Las Vegas, Nevada (Previously Steel City Arms, Inc.)

DOUBLE DEUCE DA PISTOL . . . . . NiB $350 Ex $295 Gd $200
Caliber: .22 LR. Six-shot magazine, 2.5-inch bbl., 5.5 inches overall. Weight: 15 oz. Matte-finish stainless steel. Rosewood grips.

TWO-BIT SPECIAL PISTOL . . . . NiB $350 Ex $295 Gd $190
Similar to the Double Deuce model except chambered in .25 ACP w/5-shot magazine,

(NEW) DETONICS MFG. CORP — Phoenix, Arizona (Previously Detonics Firearms Industries, Bellevue, WA)

COMBAT MASTER
Calibers: .45 ACP, .451 Detonics Mag. Six-round magazine, 3.5-inch bbl., 6.75 inches overall. Combat-type w/fixed or adjustable sights. Checkered walnut grip. Stainless steel construction. Disc. 1992.
MK I matte stainless,
fixed sights, (disc. 1981) . . . . NiB $530 Ex $450 Gd $300
MK II stainless steel
finish, (disc. 1979) . . . . NiB $530 Ex $450 Gd $300

Detonics Combat Master

Detonics Scoremaster

Dreyse Model 1907

(cont'd) COMBAT MASTER
MK III chrome,
(disc. 1980) . . . . NiB $469 Ex $375 Gd $255
MK IV polished blued,
adj. sights, (disc. 1981) . . . . NiB $519 Ex $415 Gd $282
MK V matte stainless,
fixed sights, (disc. 1985) . . . . NiB $663 Ex $530 Gd $360
MK VI polished ptainless, adj.
sights, (disc. 1989). . . . . NiB $719 Ex $575 Gd $391
MK VI in .451 Magnum,
(disc. 1986) . . . . NiB $1063 Ex $850 Gd $578
MK VII matte stainless steel,
no sights, (disc. 1985) . . . . NiB $938 Ex $750 Gd $510
MK VII in .451 Magnum,
(disc. 1980) . . . . NiB $1244 Ex $995 Gd $677

POCKET 9 . . . . NiB $575 Ex $450 Gd $350
Calibers: 9mm Para., .380. Six-round magazine, three-inch bbl.,
5.88 inches overall. Fixed sights. Double- and single-action trigger
mechanism. Disc. 1986.

SCOREMASTER . . . . NiB $995 Ex $850 Gd $700
Calibers: .45 ACP, .451 Detonics Mag. Seven-round magazine. Five- or
6-inch heavyweight match bbl., 8.75 inches overall. Weight: 47 oz.
Stainless steel construction, self-centering bbl., system. Disc. 1992.

SERVICE MASTER . . . . NiB $825 Ex $675 Gd $425
Caliber: .45 ACP. Seven-round magazine, 4.25-inch bbl., weight: 39
oz. Interchangeable front sight, Millett rear sight. Disc. 1986.

SERVICE MASTER II. . . . . NiB $925 Ex $750 Gd $475
Same general specifications as standard Service Master except
comes in polished stainless steel w/self-centering bbl., system. Disc.
1992.

DOWNSIZER CORPORATION — Santee, California

MODEL WSP
DAO PISTOL . . . . NiB $415 Ex $300 Gd $200
Single-shot, tip-up pistol. Calibers: .22 Mag., .32 Mag., .380 ACP.
9mm Parabellum, .357 Mag., .40 S&W, .45 ACP. Six-shot cylinder,
2.10-inch bbl. w/o extractor, 3.25 inches overall. Weight: 11 oz. No
sights. Stainless finish. Synthetic grips. Made 1994 to date.

DREYSE PISTOLS — Sommerda, Germany
Mfd. by Rheinische Metallwaren und Maschinenfabrik ("Rheinmetall")

MODEL 1907
AUTOMATIC PISTOL . . . . NiB $250 Ex $185 Gd $125
Caliber: .32 Auto (7.65mm). Eight-shot magazine, 3.5-inch bbl.,
6.25 inches overall. Weight: About 24 oz. Fixed sights. Blued finish.
Hard rubber grips. Made c. 1907-14.

VEST POCKET
AUTOMATIC PISTOL . . . . NiB $325 Ex $235 Gd $150
Conventional Browning type. Caliber: .25 Auto (6.35mm). Six-shot
magazine, 2-inch bbl., 4.5 inches overall. Weight: About 14 oz.
Fixed sights. Blued finish. Hard rubber grips. Made c. 1909-14.

DWM PISTOL — Berlin, Germany
Mfd. by Deutsche Waffen-und-Munitionsfabriken

POCKET AUTOMATIC PISTOL . . . . NiB $744 Ex $595 Gd $405
Similar to the FN Browning Model 1910. Caliber: .32 Automatic
(7.65mm). 3.5-inch bbl., 6 inches overall. Weight: About 21 oz.
Blued finish. Hard rubber grips. Made c. 1921-31.

ED BROWN — Perry, Montana

"CLASS A LTD" SA
AUTOMATIC PISTOL . . . . NiB $2250 Ex $1900 Gd $850
Caliber: .38 Super, 9mm, 9x23, .45 ACP. Seven-shot magazine,
4.25- or 5-inch bbl., weight: 34-39 oz. Rubber checkered or optional Hogue exotic wood grip. M1911 style single action pistol. Fixed
front and rear Novak Lo-mount or fully adjustable sights.

HANDGUNS

**"CLASSIC CUSTOM" SA
AUTOMATIC PISTOL** . . . . **NiB $2750 Ex $2250 Gd $1100**
Caliber: .45 ACP. Seven-shot magazine, 4.25- or 5-inch bbl.,
weight: 39 oz. Exotic Hogue wood grip w/modified ramp or post
front and rear adjustable sights.

**"SPECIAL FORCES" SA
AUTOMATIC PISTOL** . . . . **NiB $1200 Ex $1015 Gd $675**
Caliber: .45 ACP. Seven-shot magazine, 4.25- or 5-inch bbl.,
weight: 34-39 oz. Rubber checkered, optional exotic wood grips.
Single action M1911 style pistol.

ENFIELD REVOLVER — Enfield Lock, Middlesex, England
Manufactured by Royal Small Arms Factory

**(BRITISH SERVICE) NO. 2
MK 1 REVOLVER** . . . . **NiB $235 Ex $195 Gd $135**
Webley pattern. Hinged frame. Double action. Caliber: .380 British
Service (.38 S&W w/200-grain bullet). Six-shot cylinder, 5-inch bbl.,
10.5 inches overall. Weight: About 27.5 oz. Fixed sights. Blued finish.
Vulcanite grips. First issued in 1932, this was the standard revolver of
the British Army in WW II. Now obsolete. Note: This model also pro-
duced w/spurless hammer as No. 2 Mk 1* and Mk 1**.

ENTREPRISE ARMS — Irwindale, California

**"ELITE" SA AUTO-
MATIC PISTOL** . . . . **NiB $625 Ex $565 Gd $500**
Single action M1911 style pistol. Caliber: .45 ACP. 10-shot magazine, 3.25-, 4.25-, 5-inch bbl., (models P325, P425, P500). Weight:
36-40 oz. Ultraslim checkered grips, Tactical 2 high profile sights
w/3-dot system. Lightweight adjustable trigger. Blued or matte black
oxide finish. Made 1997 to date.

"MEDALIST" SA AUTOMATIC PISTOL
Similar to Elite model except machined to match tolerances and target configuration. Caliber: .45 ACP, .40 S&W. 10-shot magazine, 5-
inch compensated bbl. w/dovetail front and fully adjustable rear Bo-
Mar sights. Weight: 40 oz. Made 1997 to date.
.40 S&W model . . . . **NiB $994 Ex $795 Gd $541**
.45 ACP model . . . . **NiB $869 Ex $695 Gd $473**

"TACTICAL" SA AUTOMATIC PISTOL
Similar to Elite model except in combat carry configuration. De-
horned frame and slide w/ambidextrous safety. Caliber: .45 ACP. 10-
shot magazine, 3.25-, 4.25-, 5-inch bbl., weight: 36-40 oz. Tactical
2 Ghost Ring or Novak Lo-mount sights.
**Tactical 2 ghost
ring sights** . . . . **NiB $925 Ex $825 Gd $500**
Novak Lo-Mount . . . . **NiB $794 Ex $635 Gd $432**
Tactical plus model . . . . **NiB $860 Ex $690 Gd $470**

**BOXER SA AUTO-
MATIC PISTOL** . . . . **NiB $1200 Ex $995 Gd $650**
Similar to Medalist model except w/profiled slide configuration and
fully adjustable target sights. weight: 42 oz. Made 1997 to date.

"TSM" SA AUTOMATIC PISTOL
Similar to Elite model except in IPSC configuration. Caliber: .45
ACP, .40 S&W. 10-shot magazine, 5-inch compensated bbl.,
w/dovetail front and fully adjustable rear Bo-Mar sights. Weight: 40
oz. Made 1997 to date.

**Enfield
(British Service)No. 2 MK 1 Revolver**

**Erma
Model ER-772 Match Revolver**

(cont'd) **"TSM" SA AUTOMATIC PISTOL**
TSM I model . . . . **NiB $2000 Ex $1800 Gd $950**
TSM II model . . . . **NiB $2094 Ex $1675 Gd $1139**
TSM III model . . . . **NiB $2313 Ex $1850 Gd $1258**

ERMA-WERKE — Dachau, Germany

**MODEL ER-772
MATCH REVOLVER** . . . . **NiB $1100 Ex $875 Gd $495**
Caliber: .22 LR. Six-shot cylinder, 6-inch bbl., 12 inches overall.
Weight: 47.25 oz. Adjustable micrometer rear sight and front sight
blade. Adjustable trigger. Interchangeable walnut sporter or match
grips. Polished blued finish. Made 1991-94.

**MODEL ER-773
MATCH REVOLVER** . . . . **NiB $925 Ex $825 Gd $450**
Same general specifications as Model 772 except chambered for .32
S&W. Made 1991-95.

**MODEL ER-777
MATCH REVOLVER** . . . . **NiB $875 Ex $775 Gd $450**
Caliber: .357 Magnum. Six-shot cylinder. 4- or 5.5-inch bbl., 9.7 to
11.3 inches overall. Weight: 43.7 oz. (with 5.5-inch bbl.).
Micrometer adj. rear sight. Checkered walnut sporter or match-style
grip (interchangeable). Made 1991-95.

MODEL ESP-85A COMPETITION PISTOL
Calibers: .22 LR and .32 S&W Wadcutter. Eight- or 5-shot maga-
zine, 6-inch bbl., 10 inches overall. Weight: 40 oz. Adj. rear
sight, blade front sight. Checkered walnut grip w/thumbrest.
Made 1991-97.
Match model . . . . **NiB $1225 Ex $925 Gd $550**
Chrome match . . . . **NiB $1334 Ex $1110 Gd $824**
Sporting model . . . . **NiB $1056 Ex $845 Gd $575**
Conversion unit .22 LR . . . . **NiB $969 Ex $775 Gd $527**
Conversion unit .32 S&W . . . . **NiB $1063 Ex $850 Gd $578**

**European American Armory
Big Bore Bounty Hunter**

**Erma-Werke
Model KGP69**

**Erma Model ESP-85A
Competition Pistol**

MODEL KGP68
AUTOMATIC PISTOL . . . . **NiB $450 Ex $400 Gd $250**
Luger type. Calibers: .32 Auto (7.65mm), .380 Auto (9mm Short). Six-shot magazine (.32 Auto), 5-shot (.380 Auto), 4-inch bbl., 7.38 inches overall. Weight: 22.5 oz. Fixed sights. Blued finish. Checkered walnut grips. Made 1968-93.

MODEL KGP69
AUTOMATIC PISTOL . . . . **NiB $450 Ex $400 Gd $185**
Luger type. Caliber: .22 LR. Eight-shot magazine, 4-inch bbl., 7.75 inches overall. Weight: 29 oz. fixed sights. Blued finish. Checkered walnut grips. Imported 1969-93.

EUROPEAN AMERICAN ARMORY — Hialeah, Florida
See also listings under Astra Pistols.

EUROPEAN MODEL AUTO PISTOL
Calibers: .32 ACP (SA only), .380 ACP (SA or DA), 3.85-inch bbl., 7.38 overall, 7-shot magazine, Weight: 26 oz. Blade front sight, drift-adj. rear. Blued, chrome, blue/chrome, blue/gold, Duo-Tone or Wonder finish. Imported 1991 to date.
Blued .32 caliber (disc. 1995) . . . . . **NiB $156 Ex $125 Gd $85**
Blue/chrome .32 caliber
(disc. 1995) . . . . **NiB $181 Ex $145 Gd $99**
Chrome .32 caliber
(Disc. 1995) . . . . **NiB $188 Ex $150 Gd $102**
Blued .380 caliber . . . . **NiB $163 Ex $130 Gd $88**
Blue/chrome .380 caliber
(disc. 1993) . . . . **NiB $181 Ex $145 Gd $99**
DA .380 caliber (disc. 1994) . . . . . . **NiB $200 Ex $160 Gd $109**
Lady .380 caliber (disc. 1995) . . . . . **NiB $244 Ex $195 Gd $133**
Wonder finish .380 caliber . . . . **NiB $163 Ex $130 Gd $88**

BIG BORE BOUNTY HUNTER SA REVOLVER
Calibers: .357 Mag., .41 Mag., .44-40, .44 Mag., .45 Colt. Bbl. lengths: 4.63, 5.5, 7.5 inches. Blade front and grooved topstrap rear sights. Blued or chrome finish w/color casehardened or gold-plated frame. Smooth walnut grips. Imported 1992 to date.
Blued finish . . . . **NiB $244 Ex $195 Gd $133**
Blued w/color-
casehardened frame . . . . **NiB $315 Ex $255 Gd $150**
Blued w/gold-plated frame . . . . **NiB $294 Ex $235 Gd $160**
Chrome finish . . . . **NiB $330 Ex $270 Gd $193**
Gold-plated frame, add **$100**

BOUNTY HUNTER SA REVOLVER
Calibers: .22 LR, .22 Mag. Bbl. lengths: 4.75, 6 or 9 inches. Blade front and dovetailed rear sights. Blued finish or blued w/gold-plated frame. European hardwood grips. Imported 1991 to date.
Blued finish (4.75-inch bbl.) . . . . NiB $81 Ex $65 Gd $44
Blued .22 LR/.22 WRF combo
(4.75-inch bbl.) . . . . NiB $100 Ex $80 Gd $54
Blued .22 LR/.22 WRF combo
(6-inch bbl.). . . . . NiB $106 Ex $85 Gd $58
Blued .22 LR/.22 WRF combo
(9-inch bbl.). . . . . NiB $113 Ex $90 Gd $61

EA22 TARGET . . . . NiB $356 Ex $285 Gd $194
Caliber: .22 LR. 12-shot magazine, 6-inch bbl., 9.10 inches overall. Weight: 40 oz. Ramp front sight, fully adj. rear. Blued finish. Checkered walnut grips w/thumbrest. Made 1991-94.

FAB 92 AUTO PISTOL
Similar to the Witness model except chambered in 9mm only w/slide-mounted safety and no cock-and-lock provision. Imported 1992-95.
FAB 92 standard . . . . NiB $335 Ex $280 Gd $175
FAB 92 compact . . . . NiB $335 Ex $280 Gd $175

STANDARD GRADE REVOLVER
Calibers: .22 LR, .22 WRF, .32 H&R Mag., .38 Special. Two-, 4- or 6-inch bbl., blade front sight, fixed or adj. rear. Blued finish. European hardwood grips w/finger grooves. Imported 1991 to date.
.22 LR (4-inch bbl.) . . . . NiB $169 Ex $135 Gd $92
.22 LR (6-inch bbl.) . . . . NiB $181 Ex $145 Gd $99
.22 LR combo (4-inch bbl.) . . . . . . NiB $244 Ex $195 Gd $133
.22 LR combo (6-inch bbl.) . . . . . . NiB $281 Ex $225 Gd $153
.32 H&R, .38 Special (2-inch bbl.) . . NiB $175 Ex $140 Gd $95
.38 Special (4-inch bbl.) . . . . NiB $188 Ex $150 Gd $102
.357 Mag . . . . NiB $205 Ex $170 Gd $100

TACTICAL GRADE REVOLVER
Similar to the Standard model except chambered in .38 Special only. Two- or 4-inch bbl., fixed sights. Available w/compensator. Imported 1991-93.
Tactical revolver . . . . NiB $220 Ex $190 Gd $120
Tactical revolver w/compensator . . . . . NiB $319 Ex $255 Gd $173

WINDICATOR TARGET REVOLVER . . . . . . NiB $425 Ex $325 Gd $200
Calibers: .22 LR, .38 Special, .357 Magnum. Eight-shot cylinder in .22 LR, 6-shot in .38 Special and .357 Magnum. Six-inch bbl. w/bbl. weights. 11.8 inches overall. Weight: 50.2 oz. Interchangeable blade front sight, fully adj. rear. Walnut competition-style grips. Imported 1991-93.

WITNESS DA AUTO PISTOL
Similar to the Brno CZ-75 w/a cocked-and-locked system. Double or single action. Calibers: 9mm Para. .38 Super, .40 S&W, 10mm; .41 AE and .45 ACP. 16-shot magazine (9mm), 12 shot (.38 Super/.40 S&W), or 10-shot (10mm/.45 ACP), 4.75-inch bbl., 8.10 inches overall. Weight: 35.33 oz. Blade front sight, rear sight adj. for windage w/3-dot sighting system. Steel or polymer frame. Blued, satin chrome, blue/chrome, stainless or Wonder finish. Checkered rubber grips. EA Series imported 1991 to date.
9mm blue . . . . NiB $350 Ex $280 Gd $190
9mm chrome or blue/chrome. . . . . NiB $363 Ex $290 Gd $197
9mm stainless . . . . NiB $419 Ex $335 Gd $228
9mm Wonder finish. . . . . NiB $375 Ex $300 Gd $204
.38 Super and .40 S&W blued. . . . . NiB $369 Ex $295 Gd $201
.38 Super and .40 S&W chrome
or blue/chrome. . . . . NiB $406 Ex $325 Gd $221
.38 Super and .40 S&W stainless . . . . NiB $431 Ex $345 Gd $235
.38 Super and .40 S&W Wonder finish . . . . NiB $394 Ex $315 Gd $214
10mm, .41 AE and .45 ACP blued. . . . . . . NiB $456 Ex $365 Gd $248

**European American Armory
Windicator Target**

European American Armory Witness

(cont'd) WITNESS DA AUTO PISTOL
10mm, .41 AE and .45 ACP
chrome or blue/chrome . . . . NiB $475 Ex $380 Gd $258
10mm, .41 AE and .45 ACP stainless. . . . . . NiB $531 Ex $425 Gd $289
10mm, .41 AE and
.45 ACP Wonder finish . . . . NiB $481 Ex $385 Gd $262

COMPACT WITNESS DA AUTO PISTOL (L SERIES)
Similar to the standard Witness series except more compact w/ 3.625-inch bbl., and polymer or steel frame. Weight: 30 oz. Matte blued or Wonder finish. EA Compact series imported 1999 to date.
9mm blue . . . . NiB $360 Ex $300 Gd $200
9mm Wonder finish. . . . . NiB $380 Ex $325 Gd $210
.38 Super and .40 S&W blued. . . . . NiB $369 Ex $295 Gd $201
.38 Super and .40 S&W Wonder finish . . . . NiB $394 Ex $315 Gd $214
10mm, .41 AE and .45 ACP blued . . . . NiB $456 Ex $365 Gd $248
10mm, .41 AE and .45 ACP Wonder fin. . . . . NiB $481 Ex $385 Gd $262
W/ported bbl., add $30

WITNESS CARRY COMP
Double/Single action. Calibers: .38 Super, 9mm Parabellum, .40 S&W, 10mm, .45 ACP. 10-, 12- or 16-shot magazine, 4.25-inch bbl., w/1-inch compensator. Weight: 33 oz., 8.10 inches overall. Black rubber grips. Post front sight, drift adjustable rear w/3-dot system. Matte blue, Duo-Tone or Wonder finish. Imported 1992 to date.
9mm, .40 S&W . . . . NiB $425 Ex $360 Gd $200
.38 Super, 10mm, .45 ACP. . . . . NiB $369 Ex $295 Gd $201
W/Duo-Tone finish (disc.), add $25
W/Wonder finish, add $10

Feather Guardian Angel Derringer

FEG Mark II AP-.22

WITNESS LIMITED
CLASS AUTO PISTOL . . . . **NiB $855 Ex $715 Gd $400**
Single action. Calibers: .38 Super, 9mm Parabellum, .40 S&W, .45 ACP. 10-shot magazine, 4.75-inch bbl., Weight: 37 oz. Checkered competition-style walnut grips. Long slide w/post front sight, fully adj. rear. Matte blue finish. Imported 1994 to date.

WITNESS SUBCOMPACT DA AUTO PISTOL
Calibers: 9mm Para., .40 S&W, 41 AK, .45 ACP. 13-shot magazine in 9mm, 9-shot in .40 S&W, 3.66-inch bbl., 7.25 inches overall. Weight: 30 oz. Blade front sight, rear sight adj. for windage. Blued, satin chrome or blue/chrome finish. Imported 1995-97.
9mm blue . . . . **NiB $325 Ex $300 Gd $275**
9mm chrome or blue/chrome . . . . . **NiB $369 Ex $295 Gd $201**
.40 S&W blue . . . . **NiB $369 Ex $295 Gd $201**
.40 S&W chrome or blue/chrome . . **NiB $406 Ex $325 Gd $221**
.41 AE blue . . . . **NiB $438 Ex $350 Gd $238**
.41 AE chrome or blue/chrome . . . . **NiB $469 Ex $375 Gd $255**
.45 ACP blued . . . . **NiB $450 Ex $360 Gd $245**
.45 ACP chrome or blue/chrome . . . **NiB $425 Ex $360 Gd $250**

WITNESS TARGET PISTOLS
Similar to standard Witness model except fitted w/2- or 3-port compensator, competition frame and S/A target trigger. Calibers: 9mm Para., 9x21, .40 S&W, 10mm and .45 ACP, 5.25-inch match bbl., 10.5 inches overall. Weight: 38 oz. Square post front sight, fully adj. rear or drilled and tapped for scope. Blued or hard chrome finish. Low-profile competition grips. Imported 1992 to date.
Silver Team (blued w/2-port
compensator) . . . . **NiB $859 Ex $685 Gd $460**
Gold Team (chrome
w/3-port compensator) . . . . **NiB $1781 Ex $1395 Gd $981**

FAS PISTOLS — Malino, Italy
Currently imported by Nygord Precision Products *(Previously by Beeman Precision Arms and Osborne's, Cheboygan, MI)*

601 SEMIAUTOMATIC MATCH TARGET PISTOL
Caliber: .22 Short. Five-shot top-loading magazine, 5.6-inch ported and ventilated bbl., 11 inches overall. Weight: 41.5 oz. Removable, adj. trigger group. Blade front sight, open-notch fully adj. rear. Stippled walnut wrapaound or adj.target grips.
Right-hand model . . . . **NiB $906 Ex $725 Gd $493**
Left-hand model . . . . **NiB $1025 Ex $875 Gd $500**

602 SEMIAUTOMATIC MATCH TARGET PISTOL
Similar to Model FAS 601 except chambered for .22 LR. Weight: 37 oz.
Right-hand model . . . . **NiB $875 Ex $600 Gd $450**
Left-hand model . . . . **NiB $895 Ex $600 Gd $475**

603 SEMIAUTOMATIC
MATCH TARGET PISTOL . . . . **NiB $975 Ex $875 Gd $500**
Similar to Model FAS 601 except chambered for .32 S&W (wadcutter).

607 SEMIAUTOMATIC
MATCH TARGET PISTOL . . . . **NiB $975 Ex $875 Gd $450**
Similar to Model FAS 601 except chambered for .22 LR, w/removable bbl. weights. Imported 1995 to date.

FEATHER INDUSTRIES, INC. — Boulder, Colorado

GUARDIAN ANGEL DERRINGER
Double-action over/under derringer w/interchangeable drop-in loading blocks. Calibers: .22 LR, .22 WMR, 9mm, .38 Spec. Two-shot capacity, 2-inch bbl., 5 inches overall. weight: 12 oz. Stainless steel. Checkered black grip. Made 1988-95.
.22 LR, .22 WMR . . . . **NiB $180 Ex $80 Gd $50**
9mm, .38 Special (disc. 1989) . . . . . . **NiB $120 Ex $85 Gd $55**

FEG (FEGYVERGYAN) PISTOLS — Budapest, Soroksariut, Hungary *(Currently imported by KBI, Inc. and Century International Arms (Previously by Interarms)*

MARK II AP-.22 DA AUTOMATIC PISTOL . . . . **NiB $235 Ex $200 Gd $120**
Caliber: .22 LR. Eight-shot magazine, 3.4-inch bbl., Weight: 23 oz. Drift-adj. sights. Double action, all-steel pistol. Imported 1997 to date.

MARK II AP-.380 DA AUTOMATIC PISTOL . . . **NiB $235 Ex $200 Gd $130**
Caliber: .380. Seven-shot magazine, 3.9-inch bbl., weight 27 oz. Drift-adj. sights. Double action, all-steel pistol. Imported 1997 to date.

MARK II APK-.380 DA
AUTOMATIC PISTOL . . . . **NiB $235 Ex $200 Gd $130**
Caliber: .380. Seven-shot magazine, 3.4-inch bbl., weight: 25 oz. Drift-adj. sights. Double action, all-steel pistol. Imported 1997 to date.

MODEL GKK-9 (92C) AUTO PISTOL . . . . **NiB $315 Ex $280 Gd $160**
Improved version of the double-action FEG Model MBK. Caliber: 9mm Para. 14-shot magazine, 4-inch bbl., 7.4 inches overall. Weight: 34 oz. Blade front sight, rear sight adj. for windage. Checkered wood grips. Blued finish. Imported 1992-93.

MODEL GKK-.45 AUTO PISTOL

Improved version of the double-action FEG Model MBK. Caliber: .45 ACP. Eight-shot magazine, 4.1-inch bbl., 7.75 inches overall. Weight: 36 oz. Blade front sight, rear sight adj. for windage w/3-dot system. Checkered walnut grips. Blued or chrome finish. Imported 1993-96.

Blued model (disc. 1994) . . . . NiB $306 Ex $245 Gd $167
Chrome model. . . . . NiB $300 Ex $265 Gd $160

MODEL MBK-9HP

AUTO PISTOL . . . . NiB $250 Ex $225 Gd $100
Similar to the double-action Browning Hi-Power. Caliber: 9mm Para. 14-shot magazine, 4.6-inch bbl., 8 inches overall. Weight: 36 oz. Blade front sight, rear sight adj. for windage. Checkered wood grips. Blued finish. Imported 1992-93.

MODEL PJK-9HP AUTO PISTOL

Similar to the single-action Browning Hi-Power. Caliber: 9mm Para. 13-shot magazine, 4.75-inch bbl., 8 inches overall. Weight: 21 oz. Blade front sight, rear sight adj. for windage w/3-dot system. Checkered walnut or rubber grips. Blued or chrome finish. Imported 1992 to date.

Blued model . . . . NiB $244 Ex $195 Gd $133
Chrome model. . . . . NiB $250 Ex $225 Gd $150

MODEL PSP-.25 AUTO PISTOL

Similar to the Browning .25. Caliber: .25 ACP. Six-shot magazine, 2.1-inch bbl., 4.1 inches overall. Weight: 9.5 oz. Fixed sights. Checkered composition grips. Blued or chrome finish.

Blued model . . . . NiB $250 Ex $175 Gd $130
Chrome model. . . . . NiB $250 Ex $175 Gd $130

MODEL SMC-.22 AUTO PISTOL . . . NiB $238 Ex $190 Gd $129

Same general specifications as FEG Model SMC-.380 except in .22 LR. Eight-shot magazine, 3.5-inch bbl., 6.1 inches overall. Weight: 18.5 oz. Blade front sight, rear sight adj. for windage. Checkered composition grips w/thumbrest. Blued finish.

MODEL SMC-.380 AUTO PISTOL . . . NiB $205 Ex $180 Gd $115

Similar to the Walther DA PPK w/alloy frame. Caliber: .380 ACP. Six-shot magazine, 3.5-inch bbl., 6.1 inches overall. Weight: 18.5 oz. Blade front sight, rear sight adj. for windage. Checkered composition grips w/ thumbrest. Blued finish. Imported 1993 to date.

MODEL SMC-918 AUTO PISTOL. . . . NiB $210 Ex $180 Gd $125

Same general specifications as FEG Model SMC-.380 except chambered in 9x18mm Makarov. Imported 1994-97.

FIALA OUTFITTERS, INC. — New York

REPEATING PISTOL. . . . . NiB $475 Ex $400 Gd $200
Despite its appearance, which closely resembles that of the early Colt Woodsman and High-Standard, this arm is not an automatic pistol. It is hand-operated by moving the slide to eject, cock and load. Caliber: .22 LR. 10-shot magazine, bbl. lengths: 3-, 7.5- and 20-inch. 11.25 inches overall (with 7.5-inch bbl.). Weight: 31 oz. (with 7.5-inch bbl.). Target sights. Blued finish. Plain wood grips. Shoulder stock was originally supplied for use w/20-inch bbl. Made 1920-23. Value shown is for pistol w/one bbl. and no shoulder stock.

F.I.E. CORPORATION — Hialeah, Florida
The F.I.E Corporation became QFI (Quality Firearms Corp.) of Opa Locka, Fl., about 1990, when most of F.I.E's models were disc.

FEG Model PJK-9HP

F.I.E. Model A27BW

MODEL A27BW "THE
BEST" SEMIAUTO . . . . NiB $125 Ex $105 Gd $70
Caliber: .25 ACP. Six-round magazine, 2.5-inch bbl., 6.75 inches overall. Weight: 13 oz. Fixed sights. Checkered walnut grip. Disc. 1990.

ARMINIUS DA STANDARD REVOLVER

Calibers: .22 LR, .22 combo w/interchangeable cylinder, .32 S&W, .38 Special, .357 Magnum. Six, 7 or 8 rounds depending on caliber. Swing out cylinder. bbl. lengths: 2-, 3-, 4, 6-inch. Vent rib on calibers other than .22, 11 inches overall (with 6-inch bbl.). Weight: 26 to 30 oz. Fixed or micro-adj. sights. Checkered plastic or walnut grips. Blued finish. Made in Germany. disc. See illustration next page.

.22 LR . . . . NiB $80 Ex $70 Gd $50
.22 Combo. NiB $150 Ex $125 Gd $75
.32 S&W . . . . NiB $160 Ex $119 Gd $78
.38 Special. NiB $112 Ex $133 Gd $89
.357 Magnum . . . . NiB $189 Ex $155 Gd $110

BUFFALO SCOUT SA REVOLVER

Calibers: .22 LR, .22 WRF, .22 combo w/interchangeable cylinder. 4.75-inch bbl., 10 inches overall. Weight: 32 oz. Adjustable sights. Blued or chrome finish. Smooth walnut or black checkered nylon grips. Made in Italy. disc.

Blued standard. . . . . NiB $75 Ex $55 Gd $35
Blued convertible . . . . NiB $94 Ex $75 Gd $51
Chrome standard. . . . . NiB $81 Ex $65 Gd $44
Chrome convertible. . . . . NiB $115 Ex $94 Gd $67

F.I.E. Arminius

F.I.E. Titan Tiger

F.I.E. Titan II

F.I.E. Model TZ75

HOMBRE SA REVOLVER . . . . NiB $220 Ex $180 Gd $110
Calibers: .357 Magnum, .44 Magnum, .45 Colt. Six-shot cylinder. bbl. lengths: 6 or 7.5 inches, 11 inches overall (with 6-inch bbl.). Weight: 45 oz. (6-inch bbl.). Fixed sights. Blued bbl., w/color-casehardened receiver. Smooth walnut grips. Made 1979-90.

SUPER TITAN II
Caliber: .32 ACP or .380 ACP, 3.25-inch bbl., weight: 28 oz. Blued or chrome finish. Disc. 1990.
.32 ACP in blue . . . . NiB $215 Ex $185 Gd $100
.32 ACP in chrome . . . . NiB $194 Ex $155 Gd $105
.380 ACP in blue . . . . NiB $200 Ex $160 Gd $109
.380 ACP in chrome . . . . NiB $219 Ex $175 Gd $119

TEXAS RANGER
SINGLE-ACTION REVOLVER
Calibers: .22 LR, .22 WRF, .22 combo w/interchangeable cylinder. bbl. lengths: 4.75-, 6.5-, 9-inch. 10 inches overall (with 4.75-inch bbl.). Weight: 32 oz. (with 4.75-inch bbl.). Fixed sights. Blued finish. Smooth walnut grips. Made 1983-90.
Standard . . . . NiB $80 Ex $70 Gd $40
Convertible . . . . NiB $136 Ex $113 Gd $84

LITTLE RANGER SA REVOLVER
Same as the Texas Ranger except w/3.25-inch bbl. and bird's-head grips. Made 1986-90.
Standard . . . . NiB $80 Ex $70 Gd $50
Convertible . . . . NiB $142 Ex $118 Gd $88

TITAN TIGER DOUBLE-
ACTION REVOLVER . . . . NiB $130 Ex $110 Gd $70
Caliber: .38 Special. Six-shot cylinder, 2- or 4-inch bbl., 8.25 inches overall (with 4-inch bbl.). Weight: 30 oz. (4-inch bbl.). Fixed sights. Blued finish. Checkered plastic or walnut grips. Made in the U.S. Disc. 1990.

TITAN II SEMIAUTOMATIC
Caiibers: .22 LR, .32 ACP, .380 ACP. 10-round magazine, integral tapered post front sight, windage-adjustable rear sight. European walnut grips. Blued or chrome finish. Disc. 1990.
.22 LR in blue . . . . NiB $130 Ex $105 Gd $55
.32 ACP in blued . . . . NiB $169 Ex $135 Gd $92
.32 ACP in
chrome . . . . NiB $213 Ex $174 Gd $124
.380 ACP in blue . . . . NiB $194 Ex $155 Gd $105
.380 ACP in
chrome . . . . NiB $219 Ex $175 Gd $119

MODEL TZ75 DA SEMIAUTOMATIC
Double action. Caliber: 9mm. 15-round magazine, 4.5-inch bbl., 8.25 inches overall. Weight: 35 oz. Ramp front sight, windage-adjustable rear sight. European walnut or black rubber grips. Imported 1988-90.
Blued finish . . . . NiB $375 Ex $325 Gd $220
Satin chrome . . . . NiB $444 Ex $355 Gd $241

YELLOW ROSE SA REVOLVER
Same general specifications as the Buffalo Scout except in .22 combo w/interchangeable cylinder and plated in 24-karat gold. Limited Edition w/scrimshawed ivory polymer grips and American walnut presentation case. Made 1987-90.
Yellow Rose
.22 combo . . . . NiB $130 Ex $110 Gd $95
Yellow Rose
Limited Edition . . . . NiB $250 Ex $210 Gd $150

FIREARMS INTERNATIONAL CORP. — Washington, D.C.

MODEL D
AUTOMATIC PISTOL . . . . **NiB $231 Ex $185 Gd $126**
Caliber: .380 Automatic. Six-shot magazine, 3.3-inch bbl., 6.13 inches overall. Weight: 19.5 oz. Blade front sight, windage-adjustable rear sight. Blued, chromed, or military finish. Checkered walnut grips. Made 1974-77.

REGENT DA
REVOLVER. **NiB $113 Ex $90 Gd $61**
Calibers: .22 LR, .32 S&W Long. Eight-shot cylinder (.22 LR), or 7-shot (.32 S&W). Bbl. lengths: 3-, 4-, 6-inches (.22 LR) or 2.5-, 4-inches (.32 S&W). Weight: 28 oz.(with 4-inch bbl.). Fixed sights. Blued finish. Plastic grips. Made 1966-72.

FN BROWNING PISTOLS — Liege, Belgium
Mfd. by Fabrique Nationale Herstal

See also Browning Pistols.

6.35MM POCKET AUTO PISTOL
(See FN Browning Baby Auto Pistol)

MODEL 1900 POCKET
AUTO PISTOL . . . . **NiB $500 Ex $405 Gd $200**
Caliber: .32 Automatic (7.65mm). Seven-shot magazine, 4-inch bbl., 6.75 inches overall. Weight: 22 oz. Fixed sights. Blued finish. Hard rubber grips. Made 1899-10.

MODEL 1903 MILITARY AUTO PISTOL
Caliber: 9mm Browning Long. Seven-shot magazine, 5-inch bbl., 8 inches overall. Weight: 32 oz. Fixed sights. Blued finish. Hard rubber grips. Note: Aside from size, this pistol is of the same basic design as the Colt Pocket .32 and .380 Automatic pistols. Made 1903-39.
Model 190
Standard . . . . **NiB $494 Ex $395 Gd $269**
Model 1903
(w/slotted backstrap). . . . . **NiB $744 Ex $595 Gd $405**
Model 1903 (w/slotted
backstrap, shoulder stock
and extended magazine) . . . . . . **NiB $3063 Ex $2450 Gd $1666**

MODEL 1910
POCKET AUTO PISTOL . . . . **NiB $350 Ex $325 Gd $210**
Calibers: .32 Auto (7.65mm), .380 Auto (9mm). Seven-shot magazine (.32 cal.), or 6-shot (.380 cal.), 3.5-inch bbl., 6 inches overall. Weight: 20.5 oz. Fixed sights. Blued finish. Hard rubber grips. Made 1910-54.

MODEL 1922 (10/.22)
POLICE/MILITARY AUTO
Calibers: .32 Auto (7.65mm), .380 Auto (9mm). Nine-shot magazine (.32 cal.), or 8-shot (.380 cal.), 4.5-inch bbl., 7 inches overall. Weight: 25 oz. Fixed sights. Blued finish. Hard rubber grips. Made 1922-59.
Model 1910
commercial . . . . **NiB $400 Ex $325 Gd $200**
Model 191
Military contract . . . . **NiB $494 Ex $395 Gd $269**
Model 1910 (w/Nazi
proofs 1940-44), add **$25%**

Firearms International
Model D

Firearms
International Regent

FN Browning
6.35mm Pocket

FN Browning
1900 Pocket

FN Browning 1910
Pocket

FN Browning 1922
Police/Military

FN Browning 1935
Military Hi-Power

FN Browning
Baby

MODEL 1935 MILITARY HI-POWER PISTOL
Variation of the Browning-Colt .45 Auto design. Caliber: 9mm Para.13-shot magazine, 4.63-inch bbl., 7.75 inches overall. Weight: About 35 oz. Adjustable rear sight and fixed front, or both fixed. Blued finish (Canadian manufacture Parkerized). Checkered walnut or plastic grips. Note: Above specifications in general apply to both the original FN production and the pistols made by John Inglis Company of Canada for the Chinese government. A smaller version, w/shorter bbl. and slide and 10-shot magazine, was made by FN for the Belgian and Rumanian Governments about 1937-1940. Both types were made at the FN plant during the German occupation of Belgium.

Pre-war commercial (w/fixed sights)..... NiB $1000 Ex $800 Gd $600
Pre-war commercial
(w/tangent sight only)............... NiB $1875 Ex $1200 Gd $600
Pre-war commercial
(w/tangent sight, slotted backstrap) ... NiB $2750 Ex $2400 Gd $1250
Pre-war Belgian military contract....... NiB $1063 Ex $850 Gd $578
Pre-war Foreign military contract..... NiB $1994 Ex $1595 Gd $1085
War production (w/fixed sights) .... NiB $744 Ex $595 Gd $405
War production (w/tangent sight only)... NiB $1244 Ex $995 Gd $677
War production
(w/tangent sight and slotted backstrap) ... NiB $3188 Ex $2550 Gd $1734
Post-war/pre-BAC (w/fixed sights) .... NiB $619 Ex $495 Gd $337
Post-war/pre-BAC (w/tangent sight only) .. NiB $688 Ex $550 Gd $374
Post-war/pre-BAC
(w/tangent sight, slotted backstrap) ..... NiB $1244 Ex $995 Gd $677
Inglis manufacture
Canadian military (w/fixed sights) .... NiB $900 Ex $675 Gd $400
Canadian military
(w/fixed sight, slotted) .... NiB $1688 Ex $1350 Gd $918
Canadian military
(w/tangent sight, slotted) .... NiB $1369 Ex $1095 Gd $745
Canadian military
(marked w/Inglis logo) .... NiB $2406 Ex $1925 Gd $1309
Chinese military contract
(w/tangent sight, slotted) .... NiB $3125 Ex $2500 Gd $1700
Canadian military
(w/fixed sight, slotted backstrap) ...... NiB $1688 Ex $1350 Gd $918
Canadian military
(marked w/Inglis logo) .... NiB $2406 Ex $1925 Gd $1309
W/issue wooden holster, add $400

BABY AUTO PISTOL .... NiB $500 Ex $440 Gd $300
Caliber: .25 Automatic (6.35mm). Six-shot magazine, 2.13-inch bbl., 4 inches overall. Weight: 10 oz. Fixed sights. Blued finish. Hard rubber grips. Made 1931-83.

FOREHAND & WADSWORTH — Worcester, Massachusetts

REVOLVERS
See listings of comparable Harrington & Richardson and Iver Johnson revolvers for values.

LE FRANCAIS PISTOLS — St. Etienne, France Produced by Manufacture Francaise d'Armes et Cycles

ARMY MODEL AUTOMATIC PISTOL ... NiB $1500 Ex $1100 Gd $700
Similar in operation to the Le Francais .25 Automatics. Caliber: 9mm Browning Long. Eight-shot magazine, 5-inch bbl., 7.75 inches overall. Weight: About 34 oz. Fixed sights. Blued finish. Checkered walnut grips. Made from 1928-.38.

HANDGUNS

POLICEMAN MODEL
AUTOMATIC PISTOL . . . . **NiB $850 Ex $800 Gd $300**
DA. Hinged bbl., Caliber: .25 Automatic (6.35mm). Seven-shot magazine, 3.5-inch bbl., 6 inches overall. Weight: About 12 oz. Fixed sights. Blued finish. Hard rubber grips. Intro. 1914. disc.

STAFF OFFICER MODEL
AUTOMATIC PISTOL . . . . **NiB $275 Ex $230 Gd $150**
Caliber: .25 Automatic. Similar to the "Policeman" model except does not have cocking-piece head, bbl., is about an inch shorter and weight is an oz. less. Intro. 1914. disc.

FREEDOM ARMS — Freedom, Wyoming

MODEL 1997
PREMIER GRADE SA REVOLVER
Calibers: .357 Mag., .41 Mag. or .45 LC. Five- or 6-shot cylinder, 4.25-, 5-, 5.5-, 6- or 7.5- inch bbl., removable front blade with adjustable or fixed rear sight. Hardwood or black micarta grips. Satin stainless finish. Made 1997 to date.
Premier grade 97 . . . . **NiB $1650 Ex $1225 Gd $700**
For extra cylinder, add. $200
For fixed sights, deduct $75

MODEL FA-.44 (83-44) SA REVOLVER
Similar to Model 454 Casull except chambered in .44 Mag. Made from 1988 to date.
Field grade. . . . . **NiB $1325 Ex $995 Gd $750**
Premier grade . . . . **NiB $1650 Ex $1200 Gd $700**
Silhouette class
(w/10-inch bbl.) . . . . **NiB $1330 Ex $1000 Gd $760**
Silhouette pac
(10-inch bbl., access.) . . . . **NiB $1325 Ex $995 Gd $750**
For fixed sights,
deduct $95

MODEL FA-.45 (83-45) SA REVOLVER
Similar to Model 454 Casull except chambered in .45 Long Colt. Made 1988-90.
Field grade . . . . **NiB $1200 Ex $900 Gd $550**
Premier grade . . . . **NiB $1069 Ex $855 Gd $581**
For fixed sights,
deduct $95

MODEL FA-252 (83-22) SA REVOLVER
Calibers: .22 LR w/optional .22 Mag. cylinder. Bbl. lengths: 5.13 and 7.5 (Varmint Class), 10 inches (Silhouette Class). Adjustable express or competition silhouette sights. Brushed or matte stainless finish. Black Micarta (Silhouette) or black and green laminated hardwood grips (Varmint). Made 1991 to date.
Silhouette class . . . . **NiB $1828 Ex $1525 Gd $600**
Silhouette class
w/extra .22 Mag. cyl . . . . **NiB $1406 Ex $1125 Gd $765**
Varmint class . . . . **NiB $1063 Ex $850 Gd $578**
Varmint class
w/extra .22 Mag. cyl . . . . **NiB $1344 Ex $1075 Gd $731**

MODEL FA-353 (83-357) SA REVOLVER
Caliber: .357 Mag., bbl. lengths: 4.75, 6, 7.5 or 9 inches. Removable blade front sight, adjustable rear. Brushed or matte stainless finish. Pachmayr Presentation or impregnated hardwood grips.
Field grade. . . . . **NiB $938 Ex $750 Gd $510**
Premier grade . . . . **NiB $1528 Ex $1425 Gd $600**
Silhouette class
(w/9-inch bbl.) . . . . **NiB $956 Ex $765 Gd $520**

Freedom Arms
FA-252

Freedom Arms
FA-353

Freedom Arms
FA-454AS

Freedom Arms
FA-454FS

Freedom Arms
FA-555

MODEL FA-454AS (83-454) REVOLVER
Caliber: .454 Casull (w/optional .45 ACP, .45 LC, .45 Win. Mag. cylinders). Five-shot cylinder, bbl. lengths: 4.75, 6, 7.5 or 10 inches. Adjustable express or competition silhouette sights. Pachmayr presentation or impregnated hardwood grips. Brushed or matte stainless steel finish.
Field grade . . . . NiB $1527 Ex $1125 Gd $500
Premier grade . . . . NiB $1976 Ex $1650 Gd $600
Silhouette class
(w/10-inch bbl.) . . . . NiB $969 Ex $775 Gd $527
For extra cylinder, add $250

MODEL FA-454FS REVOLVER
Same general specifications as Model FA-454AS except w/fixed sight.
Field grade . . . . NiB $1556 Ex $1350 Gd $800
Premier grade . . . . NiB $1591 Ex $1375 Gd $800

MODEL FA-454 GAS REVOLVER . . . . . . NiB $1556 Ex $1350 Gd $800
Field Grade version of Model FA-454AS except not made w/12-inch bbl., Matte stainless finish, Pachmayr presentation grips. Adj. Sights or fixed sight on 4.75-inch bbl.,

MODEL FA-555 REVOLVER
Similar to Model .454 Casull except chambered in .50 AK. Made 1994 to date.
Field grade . . . . NiB $1375 Ex $995 Gd $750
Premier grade . . . . NiB $1725 Ex $1250 Gd $900

MODEL FA-BG-22LR
MINI-REVOLVER . . . . NiB $175 Ex $135 Gd $100
Caliber: .22 LR. Three-inch tapered bbl., partial high-gloss stainless steel finish. Disc. 1987.

MODEL FA-BG-22M
MINI-REVOLVER . . . . NiB $200 Ex $150 Gd $110
Same general specifications as model FA-BG-22LR except in caliber .22 WMR. Disc. 1987.

MODEL FA-BG-22P
MINI-REVOLVER . . . . NiB $200 Ex $160 Gd $100
Same general specifications as Model FA-BG-22LR except in .22 percussion. Disc. 1987.

MODEL FA-L-22LR
MINI-REVOLVER . . . . NiB $160 Ex $150 Gd $75
Caliber: .22 LR, 1.75-inch contoured bbl., partial high-gloss stainless steel finish. Bird's-head-type grips. Disc. 1987.

MODEL FA-L-22M
MINI-REVOLVER . . . . NiB $170 Ex $140 Gd $100
Same general specifications as Model FA-L-22LR except in caliber .22 WMR. Disc. 1987.

MODEL FA-L-22P
MINI-REVOLVER . . . . NiB $185 Ex $125 Gd $90
Same general specifications as Model FA-L-22LR except in .22 percussion. Disc. 1987.

MODEL FA-S-22LR
MINI-REVOLVER . . . . NiB $160 Ex $150 Gd $75
Caliber: .22 LR. One-inch contoured bbl., partial high-gloss stainless steel finish. Disc. 1988.

MODEL FA-S-22M
MINI-REVOLVER . . . . NiB $160 Ex $140 Gd $100
Same general specifications as Model FA-S-22LR except in caliber .22 WMR. Disc. 1988.

MODEL FA-S-22P
MINI-REVOLVER . . . . NiB $160 Ex $140 Gd $75
Same general specifications as Model FA-S-22LR except in .22 percussion. Disc. 1988.

FRENCH MILITARY PISTOLS — Cholet, France
Mfd. originally by Société Alsacienne de Constructions Mécaniques (S.A.C.M.). Currently made by Manufacture d'Armes Automatiques, Lotissement Industriel des Pontots, Bayonne

MODEL 1935A AUTOMATIC PISTOL . . . . . . NiB $275 Ex $225 Gd $100
Caliber: 7.65mm Long. Eight-shot magazine, 4.3-inch bbl., 7.6 inches overall. Weight: 26 oz. Two-lug locking system similar to the Colt U.S. M1911A1. Fixed sights. Blued finish. Checkered grips. Made 1935-45. Note: This pistol was used by French troops during WW II and in Indo-China 1945-54.

MODEL 1935S AUTOMATIC PISTOL . . . . . . NiB $325 Ex $295 Gd $150
Similar to Model 1935A except shorter (4.1-inch bbl., and 7.4 inches overall) and heavier (28 oz.). Single-step lug locking system.

MODEL 1950 AUTOMATIC PISTOL . . . . . . NiB $406 Ex $325 Gd $221
Caliber: 9mm Para. Nine-shot magazine, 4.4-inch bbl., 7.6 inches overall. Weight: 30 oz. Fixed sights, tapered post front and U-notched rear. Similar in design and function to the U.S. .45 service automatic except no bbl., bushing.

MODEL MAB F1 AUTOMATIC PISTOL . . . . . NiB $550 Ex $500 Gd $200
Similar to Model MAB P-15 except w/6-inch bbl. and 9.6 inches overall. Adjustable target-style sights. Parkerized finish.

MODEL MAB P-8 AUTOMATIC PISTOL . . . . . NiB $481 Ex $385 Gd $262
Similar to Model MAB P-15 except w/8-shot magazine,

MODEL MAB P-15 AUTOMATIC PISTOL . . . . NiB $550 Ex $500 Gd $300
Caliber: 9mm Para. 15-shot magazine, 4.5-inch bbl., 7.9 inches overall. Weight: 38 oz. Fixed sights, tapered post front and U-notched rear.

FROMMER PISTOLS — Budapest, Hungary
Mfd. by Fémáru-Fegyver-és Gépgyár R.T.

LILLIPUT POCKET
AUTOMATIC PISTOL . . . . NiB $400 Ex $300 Gd $150
Caliber: .25 Automatic (6.35mm). Six-shot magazine, 2.14-inch bbl., 4.33 inches overall. Weight: 10.13 oz. Fixed sights. Blued finish. Hard rubber grips. Made during early 1920s. Note: Although similar in appearance to the Stop and Baby, this pistol is blowback operated.

STOP POCKET
AUTOMATIC PISTOL . . . . NiB $300 Ex $250 Gd $100
Locked-breech action, outside hammer. Calibers: .32 Automatic (7.65mm), .380 Auto (9mm short). Seven-shot (.32 cal.) or 6-shot (.380 cal.) magazine, 3.88-inch bbl., 6.5 inches overall. Weight: About 21 oz. Fixed sights. Blued finish. Hard rubber grips. Made 1912-20.

BABY POCKET
AUTOMATIC PISTOL . . . . NiB $250 Ex $215 Gd $100
Similar to Stop model except has 2-inch bbl., 4.75 inches overall. Weight 17.5 oz. Magazine capacity is one round less than Stop Model. Intro. shortly after WW I.

Galena Industries Inc., — Sturgis, South Dakota

Galena Industries purchased the rights to use the AMT trademark in 1998. Many, but not all, original AMT designs were included in the transaction.

AMT BACKUP
Caliber: .380 (small frame, 2.5-inch bbl. only), .38 Super, .357 Sig, .40 S&W, .400 CorBon, .45 ACP, 9mm; magazine capacity: 5 or 6 rounds. Double action, 3-inch bbl., weight: 18 oz. (in .380), or 23 oz. . . . . **NiB $320 Ex $225 Gd $175**
.38 Super, .357 Sig, .400 CorBon. . . . . **Add $50**

AUTOMAG II SEMI AUTO
Caliber: .22 WMR, 9-shot magazine (except 7-shot in 3.38-inch bbl.); 3.38- 4.5- or 6-inch bbls.; weight: About 32 oz.
. . . . **NiB $425 Ex $300 Gd $225**

AUTOMAG III
Similar to Automag II except chambered for the .30 Carbine cartridge, 6.38-inch bbl., weight: About 43 oz.
Stainless steel finish. . . . . **Nib $525 Ex $400 Gd $300**

AUTOMAG IV
Caliber: .45 Winchester Magnum; 7-round magazine, 6.5-inch bbl., weight: 46 oz.
. . . . **NiB $600 Ex $450 Gd $350**

AUTOMAG .440 CORBON
Semiautomatic, 7.5-inch bbl., 5-round magazine, checkered walnut grips, matte black finish, weight: 46 oz. Intro. 2000.
. . . . **NiB $900 Ex $750 Gd $500**

GALENA HARDBALLER
Based on the Colt Model 1911 frame. Caliber: .45 ACP, .40 S&W, .400 CorBon, 7-round magazine capacity, 5-inch bbl., weight: About 38 oz.
. . . . **NiB $445 Ex $325 Gd $250**

GALENA LONGSLIDE
Similar to Hardballer model except caliber: .45 ACP, 7-inch bbl., 7-round magazine capacity, weight: About 46 ounces.
Stainless steel finish. . . . . **NiB $525 Ex $400 Gd $300**

GALENA ACCELERATOR
Similar to Hardballer model except caliber: .400 CorBon, 7-inch bbl., 7-round magazine capacity, weight: About 46 ounces.
Stainless steel finish. . . . . **NiB $550 Ex $425 Gd $300**

GALENA COMMANDO
Similar to Hardballer model except caliber: .40 S&W, 4-inch bbl., 8-round magazine capacity, weight: About 38 ounces.
Stainless steel finish. . . . . **NiB $425 Ex $300 Gd $225**

GALESI PISTOLS — Collebeato (Brescia), Italy Mfd. by Industria Armi Galesi

MODEL 6
POCKET AUTOMATIC PISTOL
Calibers: .22 Long, .25 Automatic (6.35mm). Six-shot magazine, 2.25-inch bbl., 4.38 inches overall. Weight: About 11 oz. Fixed sights. Blued finish. Plastic grips. Made from 1930 to date.
. . . . **NiB $160 Ex $120 Gd $80**

**Galesi
Model 6 Pocket**

MODEL 9 POCKET
AUTOMATIC PISTOL
Calibers: .22 LR, .32 Auto (7.65mm), .380 Auto (9mm Short). Eight-shot magazine, 3.25-inch bbl., 5.88 inches overall. Weight: About 21 oz. Fixed sights. Blued finish. Plastic grips. Made from 1930 to date. Note: Specifications vary, but those shown for .32 Automatic are commom.
.22 LR or
.380 Auto. . . . . **NiB $190 Ex $150 Gd $100**
.32 Auto. . . . . **NiB $160 Ex $140 Gd $90**

GLISENTI PISTOL — Carcina (Brescia), Italy Mfd. by Societa Siderurgica Glisenti

MODEL 1910 ITALIAN
SERVICE AUTOMATIC
Caliber: 9mm Glisenti. Seven-shot magazine, 4-inch bbl., 8.5 inches overall. Weight: About 32 oz. Fixed sights. Blued finish. Hard rubber or plastic grips. Adopted 1910 and used through WWII. . . . . **NiB $800 Ex $675 Gd $350**

GLOCK, INC. — Smyrna, Georgia

NOTE: *Models: 17, 19, 20, 21, 22, 23, 24, 31, 32, 33, 34 and 35 were fitted with a redesigned grip-frame in 1998. Models: 26, 27, 29, 30 and all "C" guns (compensated models) retained the original frame design.*

MODEL 17 DA AUTOMATIC PISTOL
Caliber: 9mm Parabellum. 10-, 17- or 19-shot magazine, 4.5-inch bbl., 7.2 inches overall. Weight: 22 oz. w/o magazine, Polymer frame, steel bbl., slide and springs. Fixed or adj. rear sights. Matte, nonglare finish. Made of only 35 components, including three internal safety devices. Imported 1983 to date.
Model 17 (w/fixed sights) . . . . **NiB $495 Ex $425 Gd $250**
Model 17C (compensated bbl.) . . . . **NiB $650 Ex $545 Gd $275**
W/adjustable sights, add $30
W/Meprolight sights, add $80
W/Trijicon sights, add $105

MODEL 17L COMPETITION
Same general specifications as Model 17 except weight: 23.35 oz. with 6-inch bbl. 8.85 inches overall. Imported 1988 to date. Imported1983 to date.
Model 1 L7 (w/fixed sights) . . . . **NiB $650 Ex $545 Gd $300**
W/ported bbl., (early production), add $35
W/adjustable sights, add $30

**Glock Model 19
Compact**

**Glock
Model 30**

MODEL 19 COMPACT
Same general specifications as Model 17 except smaller version with 4-inch bbl., 6.85 inches overall and weight: 21 oz. Imported 1988 to date.
Model 19 (w/fixed sights) . . . . NiB $495 Ex $425 Gd $250
Model 19C (compensated bbl.). . . . . NiB $506 Ex $405 Gd $275
W/adjustable sights, add $30
W/Meprolight sights, add $80
W/Trijicon sights, add $105

MODEL 20 DA AUTO PISTOL
Caliber: 10mm. 15-shot, hammerless, 4.6-inch bbl., 7.59 inches overall. Weight: 26.3 oz. Fixed or adj. sights. Matte, nonglare finish. Made from 1991 to date.
Model 20 (w/fixed sights) . . . . NiB $700 Ex $600 Gd $250
Model 19C (compensated bbl.) . . . . NiB $666 Ex $533 Gd $363
W/adjustable sights, add $30
W/Meprolight sights, add $80
W/Trijicon sights, add $105

MODEL 21 AUTOMATIC PISTOL
Same general specifications as Model 17 except chambered in .45 ACP. 13-shot magazine, 7.59 inches overall. Weight: 25.2 oz. Imported 1991 to date.
Model 21 (w/fixed sights) . . . . NiB $608 Ex $485 Gd $300
Model 21C (compensated bbl.) . . . . NiB $660 Ex $528 Gd $358
W/adjustable sights, add $30
W/Meprolight sights, add $80
W/Trijicon sights, add $105

MODEL .22 AUTOMATIC PISTOL
Same general specifications as Model 17 except chambered for .40 S&W. 15-shot magazine, 7.4 inches overall. Imported 1992 to date.
Model .22 (w/fixed sights) . . . . NiB $641 Ex $495 Gd $295
Model 22C
(compensated bbl.) . . . . NiB $591 Ex $473 Gd $321
W/adjustable sights, add $30
W/Meprolight sights, add $80
W/Trijicon sights, add $105

MODEL 23 AUTOMATIC PISTOL
Same general specifications as Model 19 except chambered for .40 S&W. 13-shot magazine, 6.97 inches overall. Imported 1992 to date.
Model 23 (w/fixed sights) . . . . NiB $495 Ex $425 Gd $275
Model 23C (compensated bbl.) . . . . NiB $531 Ex $425 Gd $289
W/adjustable sights, add $30
W/Meprolight sights, add $80
W/Trijicon sights, add $105

MODEL 24 AUTOMATIC PISTOL
Caliber: .40 S&W, 10- and 15-shot magazines (the latter for law enforcement and military use only), 8.85 inches overall. Weight: 26.5 oz. Manual trigger safety; passive firing block and drop safety. Made 1995 to date.
Model 24 (w/fixed sights) . . . . NiB $665 Ex $525 Gd $300
Model 24C (compensated bbl.) . . . . NiB $653 Ex $522 Gd $355
W/adjustable sights, add $30

MODEL 26 DA AUTOMATIC PISTOL
Caliber: 9mm, 10-round magazine, 3.47-inch bbl., 6.3 inches overall. Weight: 19.77 oz. Imported 1995 to date.
Model 26 (w/fixed sights) . . . . NiB $495 Ex $425 Gd $300
Model 26C (compensated bbl.) . . . . NiB $538 Ex $430 Gd $292
W/adjustable sights, add $30

MODEL 27 DA AUTO PISTOL
Similar to the Glock Model .22 except subcompact. Caliber: .40 S&W, 10-shot magazine, 3.5-inch bbl., Weight: 21.7 oz. Polymer stocks, fixed or fully adjustable sights. Imported 1995 to date.
Model 27 (w/fixed sights) . . . . NiB $495 Ex $425 Gd $300
W/adjustable sights, add $30
W/Meprolight sights, add $80
W/Trijicon sights, add $105

MODEL 28 COMPACT (LAW ENFORCEMENT ONLY)
Same general specifications as Model .25 except smaller version. .380 ACP with 3.5-inch bbl., weight: 20 oz. Imported 1999 to date.

MODEL 29 DA AUTO PISTOL
Similar to the Glock Model 20 except subcompact. Caliber: 10mm. 10-shot magazine, 3.8-inch bbl., weight: 27.1 oz. Polymer stocks, fixed or fully adjustable sights. Imported 1997 to date.
Model 29 (w/fixed sights) . . . . NiB $585 Ex $490 Gd $300
W/adjustable sights, add $30
W/Meprolight sights, add $80
W/Trijicon sights, add $100

MODEL 30 DA AUTO PISTOL
Similar to the Glock Model 21 except subcompact. Caliber: .45 ACP. 10-shot magazine, 3.8-inch bbl., weight: 26.5 oz. Polymer stocks, fixed or fully adjustable sights. Imported 1997 to date.
Model 27 (w/fixed sights) . . . . NiB $585 Ex $490 Gd $300
W/adjustable sights, add $30
W/Meprolight sights, add $80
W/Trijicon sights, add $105

MODEL 31 DA AUTOMATIC PISTOL
Caliber: .357 Sig., safe action system. 10- 15- or 17-shot magazine, 4.49-inch bbl., weight: 23.28 oz. Safe Action trigger system w/3 safeties. Imported 1998 to date.
Model 31
(w/fixed sights) . . . . NiB $495 Ex $425 Gd $300
Model 31C
(compensated bbl.) . . . . NiB $553 Ex $449 Gd $316
W/adjustable sights, add $30
W/Meprolight sights, add $80
W/Trijicon sights, add $105

MODEL .32 DA AUTOMATIC PISTOL
Caliber: .357 Sig., safe action system. 10- 13- or 15-shot magazine, 4.02-inch bbl., weight: 21.52 oz. Imported 1998 to date.
Model .32
(w/fixed sights) . . . . NiB $495 Ex $425 Gd $300
Model 32C. . . . . NiB $513 Ex $410 Gd $279
W/adjustable sights, add $30
W/Meprolight sights, add $80
W/Trijicon Sights, add $105

MODEL 33 DA AUTOMATIC PISTOL
Caliber: .357 Sig., safe action system. Nine- or 11-shot magazine, 3.46-inch bbl. Weight: 19.75 oz. Imported 1998 to date.
Model 33
(w/fixed sights) . . . . NiB $495 Ex $425 Gd $300
W/adjustable sights, add $30
W/Meprolight sights, add $80
W/Trijicon sights, add $105

MODEL 34 AUTO PISTOL. . . . . NiB $655 Ex $555 Gd $325
Similar to Model 17 except w/redesigned grip-frame and extended slide-stop lever and magazine release. 10-, 17- or 19-shot magazine, 5.32- inch bbl. Weight: 22.9 oz. Fixed or adjustable sights. Imported 1998 to date.

MODEL 35 AUTO PISTOL. . . . . NiB $655 Ex $585 Gd $325
Similar to Model 34 except .40 S&W. Imported 1998 to date.

MODEL 36 DA AUTOMATIC PISTOL
Caliber: .45 ACP., safe action system. Six-shot magazine, 3.78-inch bbl., weight: 20.11 oz. Safe Action trigger system w/3 safeties. Imported 1999 to date.
Model 36
(w/fixed sights) . . . . NiB $585 Ex $490 Gd $300
W/adjustable sights, add $30
W/Meprolight sights, add $80
W/Trijicon sights, add $105

DESERT STORM
COMMEMORATIVE. . . . . NiB $995 Ex $825 Gd $500
Same specifications as Model 17 except "Operation Desert Storm, January 16-February 27, 1991" engraved on side of slide w/list of coalition forces. Limited issue of 1,000 guns. Made in 1991.

GREAT WESTERN ARMS CO. — North Hollywood, California

NOTE: *Values shown are for improved late model revolvers early Great Westerns are variable in quality and should be evaluated accordingly. It should also be noted that, beginning about July 1956, these revolvers were offered in kit form. Values of guns assembled from these kits will, in general, be of less value than factory-completed weapons.*

Grendel Model P-12

DOUBLE BARREL DERRINGER . . . . NiB $300 Ex $275 Gd $150
Replica of Remington Double Derringer. Caliber: .38 S&W. Double bbls. (superposed), 3-inch bbl. Overall length: 5 inches. Fixed sights. Blued finish. Checkered black plastic grips. Made 1953-62.

SA FRONTIER REVOLVER . . . . NiB $500 Ex $450 Gd $250
Replica of the Colt Single Action Army Revolver. Calibers: .22 LR, .357 Magnum, .38 Special, .44 Special, .44 Magnum .45 Colt. Six-shot cylinder, bbl. lengths: 4.75-, 5.5 and 7.5-inches. Weight: 40 oz. in .22 cal. w/5.5-inch bbl. Overall length: 11.13 inches w/5.5-inch bbl. Fixed sights. Blued finish. Imitation stag grips. Made 1951-1962.

GRENDEL, INC. — Rockledge, Florida

MODEL P-10 AUTOMATIC PISTOL
Hammerless, blow-back action. DAO with no external safety. Caliber: .380 ACP. 10-shot box magazine integrated in grip. Three-inch bbl., 5.3 inches overall. Weight: 15 oz. Matte blue, nickel or green Teflon finish. Made 1988-91.
Blued finish . . . . NiB $140 Ex $125 Gd $85
Nickel finish . . . . NiB $184 Ex $150 Gd $107
Teflon finish . . . . NiB $190 Ex $155 Gd $110
W/compensated bbl., add $45

MODEL P-12 DA AUTOMATIC PISTOL
Caliber: .380 ACP. 11-shot Zytel magazine, 3-inch bbl., 5.3 inches overall. Weight: 13 oz. Fixed sights. Polymer DuPont ST-800 grip. Made 1991-95.
Standard model . . . . NiB $155 Ex $130 Gd $85
Electroless nickel . . . . NiB $201 Ex $165 Gd $119

MODEL P-30 AUTOMATIC PISTOL
Caliber: .22 WMR. 30-shot magazine, 5-or 8-inch bbl., 8.5 inches overall w/5-inch bbl., weight: 21 oz. Blade front sight, fixed rear sight. Made 1991-95.
W/5-inch bbl., ... NiB $240 Ex $200 Gd $175
W/8-inch bbl., ... NiB $240 Ex $200 Gd $175

MODEL P-31
AUTOMATIC PISTOL . . . . NiB $350 Ex $315 Gd $190
Caliber: .22 WMR. 30-shot Zytel magazine, 11-inch bbl., 17.3 inches overall. Weight: 48 oz. Adj. blade front sight, fixed rear. Checkered black polymer DuPont ST-800 grip and forend. Made 1991-95.

Hammerli Model
33MP Free Pistol

Hammerli
Model 101

Hammerli
Model 102 Deluxe

Hammerli
Model 105

GUNSITE — Paulden, Arizona

"ADVANCED TACTICAL" SA AUTO PISTOL
Manuafactured w/Colt 1991 or Springfield 1991 parts. Caliber: .45
ACP. Eight-shot magazine, 3.5-, 4.25-, 5-inch bbl. Weight: 32-38 oz.
Checkered or laser-engraved walnut grips. Fixed or Novak Lo-mount
sights.
Stainless finish . . . . NiB $994 Ex $795 Gd $541
Blued finish . . . . NiB $869 Ex $695 Gd $473

"CUSTOM CARRY" SA AUTO PISTOL
Caliber: .45 ACP. Eight-shot magazine, 3.5-, 4.25-, 5-inch bbl.,
Weight: 32-38 oz. Checkered or laser-engraved walnut grips. Fixed
Novak Lo-mount sights. Single action, manufactured based on
enhanced colt models.
Stainless finish . . . . NiB $1031 Ex $825 Gd $561
Blued finish . . . . NiB $994 Ex $795 Gd $541

H&R 1871, INC. — Gardner, Massachusetts

NOTE: *In 1991, H&R 1871, Inc. was formed from the residual of the
parent company, Harrington & Richardson, and then took over the
New England Firearms facility. H&R 1871 produced firearms under
both their logo and the NEF brand name until 1999, when the
Marlin Firearms Company acquired the assets of H&R 1871. See
listings under Harrington & Richardson, Inc.*

HÄMMERLI AG JAGD-UND SPORTWAFFE FABRIK — Lenzburg, Switzerland

Currently imported by Sigarms, Inc., Exeter, NH. Previously by Hammerli, USA; Beeman Precision Arms & Mandall Shooting Supplies.

MODEL 33MP FREE PISTOL . . . . . . NiB $925 Ex $725 Gd $450
System Martini single-shot action, set trigger. Caliber: .22 LR. 11.5-inch octagon
bbl., 16.5 inches overall. Weight: 46 oz. Micrometer rear sight, interchangeable
front sights. Blued finish. Walnut grips, forearm. Imported 1933-49.

MODEL 100 FREE PISTOL
Same general specifications as Model 33MP. Improved action and
sights, redesigned stock. Standard model has plain grips and forearm,
deluxe model has carved grips and forearm. Imported 1950-56.
Standard model . . . . NiB $800 Ex $660 Gd $450
Deluxe model . . . . NiB $990 Ex $770 Gd $500

MODEL 101 . . . . NiB $880 Ex $660 Gd $500
Similar to Model 100 except has heavy round bbl. w/matte finish,
improved action and sights, adj. grips. Weight: About 49 oz.
Imported 1956-60.

MODEL 102
Same as Model 101 except bbl., has highly polished blued finish.
Deluxe model (illustrated) has carved grips and forearm. Made
1956-60.
Standard model . . . . NiB $880 Ex $660 Gd $500
Deluxe model . . . . NiB $990 Ex $770 Gd $500

MODEL 103 . . . . NiB $935 Ex $775 Gd $450
Same as Model 101 except has lighter octagon bbl. (as in Model
100) w/highly polished blued finish, grips and forearm of select
French walnut. Weight: About 46 oz. Imported 1956-60.

MODEL 104 . . . . NiB $760 Ex $660 Gd $350
Similar to Model 102 except has lighter round bbl., improved action
redesigned grips and forearm. Weight: 46 oz. Imported 1961-65.

MODEL 105 . . . . NiB $935 Ex $715 Gd $400
Similar to Model 103 except has improved action, redesigned grips
and forearm. Imported 1961-65.

MODEL 106 . . . . NiB $910 Ex $690 Gd $380
Similar to Model 104 except has improved trigger and grips. Made
1966-71.

MODEL 107
Similar to Model 105 except has improved trigger and stock. Deluxe
model (illustrated) has engraved receiver and bbl., carved grips and
forearm. Imported 1966-71.
Standard model . . . . NiB $990 Ex $770 Gd $380
Deluxe model . . . . NiB $1320 Ex $990 Gd $450

Hammerli
Model 106

Hammerli
Model 107 Deluxe

MODEL 120 HEAVY BARREL
Same as Models 120-1 and 120-2 except has 5.7-inch heavy bbl., weight: 41 oz. Available w/standard or adj. grips. Imported 1972 to date.
W/standard grips. . . . . NiB $600 Ex $540 Gd $300
W/adj. grips. . . . . NiB $650 Ex $500 Gd $300

MODEL 120-1 SINGLE-
SHOT FREE PISTOL . . . . NiB $600 Ex $540 Gd $300
Side lever-operated bolt action. Adj. single-stage or two-stage trigger. Caliber: .22 LR, 9.9-inch bbl., 14.75 inches overall. Weight: 44 oz. Micrometer rear sight, front sight on high ramp. Blued finish bbl., and receiver, lever and grip frame anodized aluminum. Checkered walnut thumbrest grips. Imported 1972 to date.

MODEL 120-2 . . . . NiB $600 Ex $540 Gd $300
Same as Model 120-1 except has hand-contoured grips w/adj. palm rest (available for right or left hand). Imported 1972 to date.

MODELS 150/151 FREE PISTOLS
Improved Martini-type action w/lateral-action cocking lever. Set trigger adj. for weight, length and angle of pull. Caliber: .22 LR, 11.3-inch round free-floating bbl., 15.4 inches overall. Weight: 43 oz. (w/extra weights, 49.5 oz.). Micrometer rear sight, front sight on high ramp. Blued finish. Select walnut forearm and grips w/adj. palm shelf. Imported 1972-93.
Model 150 (disc. 1989) . . . . NiB $1850 Ex $1495 Gd $850
Model 151 (disc. 1993) . . . . NiB $1850 Ex $1495 Gd $850

MODEL 152 ELECTRONIC PISTOL
Same general specifications as Model 150 except w/electronic trigger. Made 1990-92
Right hand . . . . NiB $1995 Ex $1600 Gd $990
Left hand . . . . NiB $1870 Ex $1507 Gd $1043

MODELS 160/162 FREE PISTOLS
Caliber: .22 LR. Single-shot. 11.31-inch bbl., 17.5 inches overall. Weight: 46.9 oz. Interchangeable front sight blades, fully adj. match rear. Match-style stippled walnut grips w/adj. palm shelf and polycarbon fiber forend. Imported 1993 to date.
Model 160 w/mechanical
Set trigger . . . . NiB $1725 Ex $1475 Gd $800
Model 162 w/ electronic trigger. . . . . . . NiB $1781 Ex $1425 Gd $969

MODEL 208 STANDARD
AUTO PISTOL . . . . NiB $1600 Ex $1300 Gd $800
Caliber: .22 LR. Eight-shot magazine, 5.9-inch bbl., 10 inches overall. Weight: 35 oz. (bbl. weight adds 3 oz.). Micrometer rear sight, ramp front. Blued finish. Checkered walnut grips w/adj. heel plate. Imported 1966-88.

MODEL 208S TARGET PISTOL . . . . . NiB $1750 Ex $1300 Gd $675
Caliber: .22 LR. Eight-shot magazine, 6-inch bbl., 10.2 inches overall. Weight: 37.3 oz. Micrometer rear sight, ramp front sight. Blued finish. Stippled walnut grips w/adj. heel plate. Imported 1990 to date.

MODEL 211 . . . . NiB $1550 Ex $1275 Gd $690
Same as Model 208 except has standard thumbrest grips. Imported 1966-91.

Hammerli
Model 120 Heavy Barrel

Hammerli
Model 120-1

Hammerli
Model 150

Hammerli
Model 160

Hammerli
Model 208

Hammerli
Model 215

Hammerli
Model 206 International

Hammerli
Model 207 International

Hammerli
International Model 210

Hammerli
Model 232 Rapid Fire

MODEL 212
HUNTER'S PISTOL . . . . NiB $1250 Ex $1080 Gd $650
Caliber: .22 LR, 4.88-inch bbl., 8.5 inches overall. Weight: 31 oz. Blade front sight, square-notched fully adj. rear. Blued finish. Checkered walnut grips. Imported 1984-93.

MODEL 215 . . . . NiB $1395 Ex $1050 Gd $575
Similar to the Model 208 except w/heavier bbl. and fewer deluxe features. Imported 1990-93.

MODEL 230-1 RAPID
FIRE AUTO PISTOL . . . . NiB $1395 Ex $1125 Gd $650
Caliber: .22 Short. Five-shot magazine, 6.3-inch bbl., 11.6 inches overall. Weight: 44 oz. Micrometer rear sight, post front. Blued finish. Smooth walnut thumbrest grips. Imported 1970-83.

MODEL 230-2 . . . . NiB $735 Ex $655 Gd $645
Same as Model 230-1 except has checkered walnut grips w/adj. heel plate. Imported 1970-83.

MODEL 232 RAPID FIRE
AUTO PISTOL . . . . NiB $1395 Ex $1125 Gd $650
Caliber: .22 Short. Six-shot magazine, 5.1-inch ported bbl., 10.5 inches overall. Weight: 44 oz. Fully adj. target sights. Blued finish. Stippled walnut wraparound target grips. Imported 1984-93.

INTERNATIONAL MODEL
206 AUTO PISTOL. . . . . NiB $675 Ex $625 Gd $330
Calibers: .22 Short, .22 LR. Six-shot (.22 Short) or 8-shot (.22 LR) magazine, 7.1-inch bbl. w/muzzle brake, 12.5 inches overall. Weight: 33 oz. (.22 Short), 39 oz. (.22 LR) (supplementary weights add 5 and 8 oz.). Micrometer rear sight, ramp front. Blued finish. Standard thumbrest grips. Imported 1962-69.

INTERNATIONAL
MODEL 207 . . . . NiB $725 Ex $650 Gd $375
Same as Model 206 except has grips w/adj. heel plate, weight: 2 oz. more. Made 1962-69.

INTERNATIONAL
MODEL 209
AUTO PISTOL . . . . NiB $800 Ex $690 Gd $485
Caliber: .22 Short. Five-shot mag., 4.75-inch bbl., w/muzzle brake and gas-escape holes, 11 inches overall. Weight: 39 oz. (interchangeable front weight adds 4 oz.). Micrometer rear sight, post front. Blued finish. Standard thumbrest grips of checkered walnut. Imported 1966-70.

INTERNATIONAL
MODEL 210 . . . . NiB $800 Ex $715 Gd $525
Same as Model 209 except has grips w/adj. heel plate, is 0.8-inch longer and weight: 1 ounce more. Made 1966-70.

MODEL 280 TARGET PISTOL

Carbon-reinforced synthetic frame and bbl., housing. Calibers: .22 LR, .32 S&W Long WC. Six-shot (.22 LR) or 5-shot (.32 S&W) magazine, 4.5-inch bbl. w/interchangeable metal or carbon fiber counterweights. 11.88 inches overall. Weight: 39 oz. Micro-adj. match sights w/interchangeable elements. Imported 1988 to date.

.22 LR . . . . NiB $1450 Ex $1125 Gd $575
.32 S&W
Long WC . . . . NiB $1604 Ex $1305 Gd $923
.22/.32
Conversion
kit, add $800

VIRGINIAN SA REVOLVER . . . . NiB $525 Ex $490 Gd $250
Similar to Colt Single-Action Army except has base pin safety system (SWISSAFE). Calibers: .357 Magnum, .45 Colt. Six-shot cylinder. 4.63-, 5.5- or 7.5-inch bbl., 11 inches overall (with 5.5-inch bbl.). Weight: 40 oz. (with 5.5-inch bbl.). Fixed sights. Blued bbl. and cylinder, casehardened frame, chrome-plated grip frame and trigger guard. One-piece smooth walnut stock. Imported 1973-76 by Interarms, Alexandria, Va.

WALTHER

OLYMPIA MODEL 200
AUTOMATIC PISTOL, 1952-TYPE. . . . NiB $660 Ex $605 Gd $385
Similar to 1936 Walther Olympia Funfkampf model. Calibers: .22 Short, .22 LR. Six-shot (.22 Short) or 10-shot (.22 LR) magazine, 7.5-inch bbl., 10.7 inches overall. Weight: 27.7 oz. (.22 Short, light alloy breechblock), 30.3 oz. (.22 LR). Supplementary weights provided. Adj. target sights. Blued finish. Checkered walnut thumbrest grips. Imported 1952-58.

WALTHER

OLYMPIA MODEL 200, 1958-TYPE . . . NiB $715 Ex $605 Gd $415
Same as Model 200 1952 type except has muzzle brake, 8-shot magazine (.22 LR). 11.6 inches overall. Weight: 30 oz. (.22 Short), 33 oz. (.22 LR). Imported 1958-63.

WALTHER

OLYMPIA MODEL 201 . . . . NiB $660 Ex $605 Gd $385
Same as Model 200, 1952 Type except has 9.5-inch bbl. Imported 1955-57.

WALTHER

OLYMPIA MODEL 202 . . . . NiB $715 Ex $605 Gd $450
Same as Model 201 except has grips w/adj. heel plate. Imported 1955-57.

WALTHER

OLYMPIA MODEL 203
Same as corresponding Model 200 (1955 type lacks muzzle brake) except has grips w/adj. heel plate. Imported 1955-63.
1955 type . . . . NiB $715 Ex $605 Gd $450
1958 type . . . . NiB $770 Ex $660 Gd $470

WALTHER

OLYMPIA MODEL 204
American model. Same as corresponding Model 200 (1956-Type lacks muzzle brake) except in .22 LR only, has slide stop and micrometer rear sight. Imported 1956-63.
1956-type . . . . NiB $745 Ex $635 Gd $490
1958-type . . . . NiB $800 Ex $690 Gd $495

WALTHER

OLYMPIA MODEL 205
American model. Same as Model 204 except has grips w/adj. heel plate. Imported 1956-63.
1956-type . . . . NiB $800 Ex $690 Gd $495
1958-type . . . . NiB $855 Ex $745 Gd $525

**Hammerli-Walther
Olympia Model 203 1958-Type**

**Hammerli-Walther
Olympia Model 205**

**SIG-Hammerli
Model P240 Target**

MODEL P240 TARGET AUTO PISTOL

Calibers: .32 S&W Long (wadcutter), .38 Special (wadcutter). Five-shot magazine, 5.9-inch bbl., 10 inches overall. Weight: 41 oz. Micrometer rear sight, post front. Blued finish/smooth walnut thumbrest grips. Accessory .22 LR conversion unit available. Imported 1975-86.
.32 S&W Long . . . . NiB $1475 Ex $1225 Gd $700
.38 Special . . . . NiB $2119 Ex $1695 Gd $1153
.22 LR conversion
unit, add . . . . NiB $550 Ex $495 Gd $330

Harrington & Richardson SL .32

Harrington & Richardson USRA
Model Single-Shot Target Pistol

Harrington & Richardson Model 4

Harrington & Richardson Model 5

HARRINGTON & RICHARDSON, INC. —
Gardner, Massachusetts
Now H&R 1871, Inc., Gardner, Mass.

Formerly Harrington & Richardson Arms Co. of Worcester, Mass. One of the oldest and most distinguished manufacturers of handguns, rifles and shotguns, H&R suspended operations on January 24,1986. In 1987, New England Firearms was established as an independent company producing selected H&R models under the NEF logo. In 1991, H&R 1871, Inc., was formed from the residual of the parent company and then took over the New England Firearms facility. H&R 1871 produced firearms under both its logo and the NEF brand name until 1999, when the Marlin Firearms Company acquired the assets of H&R 1871.

NOTE: *For ease in finding a particular firearm, H&R handguns are grouped into Automatic/Single-Shot Pistols, followed by Revolvers. For a complete listing, please refer to the index.*

AUTOMATIC/SINGLE-SHOT PISTOLS

SL .25 PISTOL . . . . NiB $375 Ex $330 Gd $165
Modified Webley & Scott design. Caliber: .25 Auto. Six-shot magazine, 2-inch bbl., 4.5 inches overall. Weight: 12 oz. Fixed sights. Blued finish. Black hard rubber grips. Made 1912-16.

SL .32 PISTOL . . . . NiB $330 Ex $305 Gd $150
Modified Webley & Scott design. Caliber: .32 Auto. Eight-shot magazine, 3.5-inch bbl., 6.5 inches overall. Weight: About 20 oz. Fixed sights. Blued finish. Black hard rubber grips. Made 1916-24.

USRA MODEL SINGLE-
SHOT TARGET PISTOL . . . . NiB $450 Ex $425 Gd $225
Hinged frame. Caliber: .22 LR, bbl. lengths: 7-, 8- and 10-inch. Weight: 31 oz. w/10-inch bbl., Adj. target sights. Blued finish. Checkered walnut grips. Made 1928-41.

REVOLVERS

MODEL 4
(1904) DA . . . . NiB $95 Ex $85 Gd $35
Solid frame. Calibers: .32 S&W Long, .38 S&W. Six-shot cylinder (.32 cal.), or 5-shot (.38 cal.), bbl. Lengths: 2.5-, 4.5- and 6-inch. Weight: About 16 oz. (in .32 cal.) Fixed sights. Blued or nickel finish. Hard rubber grips. Disc. prior to 1942.

MODEL 5 (1905) DA . . . . NiB $95 Ex $85 Gd $40
Solid frame. Caliber: .32 S&W. Five-shot cylinder, bbl., lengths: 2.5-,4.5- and 6-inch. Weight: About 11 oz. Fixed sights. Blued or nickel finish. Hard rubber grips. Disc. prior to 1942.

MODEL 6 (1906) DA . . . . NiB $95 Ex $85 Gd $40
Solid frame. Caliber: .22 LR. Seven-shot cylinder, bbl. lengths: 2.5, 4.5- and 6-inches. Weight: About 10 oz. Fixed sights. Blued or nickel finish. Hard rubber grips. Disc. prior to 1942.

.22 SPECIAL DA . . . . NiB $165 Ex $140 Gd $70
Heavy hinged frame. Calibers: .22 LR, .22 Mag. Nine-shot cylinder, 6-inch bbl., weight: 23 oz. Fixed sights, front gold-plated. Blued finish. Checkered walnut grips. Recessed safety cylinder on later models for high-speed ammunition. Disc. prior to 1942.

MODEL 199 SPORTSMAN

SA REVOLVER . . . . **NiB $275 Ex $235 Gd $110**
Hinged frame. Caliber: .22 LR. Nine-shot cylinder, 6-inch bbl., 11 inches overall. Weight: 30 oz. Adj. target sights. Blued finish. Checkered walnut grips. Disc. 1951.

MODEL 504 DA . . . . **NiB $165 Ex $145 Gd $100**
Caliber: .32 H&R Magnum. Five-shot cylinder, 4- or 6-inch bbl., (square butt), 3- or 4-inch bbl., round butt. Made 1984-86.

MODEL 532 DA . . . . **NiB $100 Ex $90 Gd $50**
Caliber: .32 H&R Magnum. Five-shot cylinder, 2.5- or 4-inch bbl., weight: Approx. 20 and 25 oz. respectively. Fixed sights. American walnut grips. Lustre blued finish. Made 1984-86.

MODEL 586 DA . . . . **NiB $175 Ex $155 Gd $100**
Caliber: .32 H&R Magnum. Five-shot cylinder. bbl. lengths: 4.5, 5.5, 7.5, 10 inches. Weight: 30 oz. average. Adj. rear sight, blade front. Walnut finished hardwood grips. Made 1984-86.

MODEL 603 TARGET . . . . **NiB $165 Ex $120 Gd $80**
Similar to Model 903 except in .22 WMR. Six-shot capacity w/unfluted cylinder. Made 1980-83.

MODEL 604 TARGET . . . . **NiB $170 Ex $130 Gd $80**
Similar to Model 603 except w/6-inch bull bbl., weight: 38 oz. Made 1980-83.

MODEL 622/623 DA . . . . **NiB $115 Ex $95 Gd $50**
Solid frame. Caliber: .22 Short, Long, LR, 6-shot cylinder. bbl., lengths: 2.5-, 4-, 6-inches. Weight: 26 oz. (with 4-inch bbl.). Fixed sights. Blued finish. Plastic grips. Made 1957-86. Note: Model 623 is same except chrome or nickel finish.

MODEL 632/633

GUARDSMAN DA REVOLVER . . . . . **NiB $104 Ex $80 Gd $45**
Solid Frame. Caliber: .32 S&W Long. Six-shot cylinder, bbl., lengths: 2.5- or 4-inch. Weight: 19 oz. (with 2.5-inch bbl.). Fixed sights. Blued or chrome finish. Checkered Tenite grips (round butt on 2.5-inch, square butt on 4-inch). Made 1953-86. Note: Model 633 is the same except for chrome or nickel finish.

MODEL 649/650 DA . . . . **NiB $140 Ex $120 Gd $80**
Solid frame. Side loading and ejection. Convertible model w/two 6-shot cylinders. Calibers: .22 LR, .22 WMR. 5.5-inch bbl., Weight: 32 oz. Adj. rear sight, blade front. Blued finish. One-piece, Western-style walnut grip. Made 1976-86. Note: Model 650 is same except nickel finish.

MODEL 666 DA . . . . **NiB $100 Ex $90 Gd $35**
Solid frame. Convertible model w/two 6-shot cylinders. Calibers: .22 LR, .22 WMR. Six-inch bbl., weight: 28 oz. Fixed sights. Blued finish. Plastic grips. Made 1976-78.

MODEL 676 DA . . . . **NiB $140 Ex $120 Gd $45**
Solid frame. Side loading and ejection. Convertible model w/two 6-shot cylinders. Calibers: .22 LR, .22 WMR, bbl. lengths: 4.5-, 5.5-, 7.5-, 12-inches. Weight: 32 oz. (with 5.5-inch bbl.). Adj. rear sight, blade front. Blued finish, color-casehardened frame. One-piece, Western-style walnut grip. Made 1976-1980.

Harrington & Richardson
Model 6

Harrington & Richardson
.22 Special

Harrington & Richardson
Model 199 Sportsman

Harrington & Richardson
Model 632

Harrington & Richardson
Model 622

Harrington & Richardson
Model 649

Harrington & Richardson
Model 650

Harrington & Richardson
Model 666

Harrington & Richardson
Model 676

Harrington & Richardson
Model 830

Harrington & Richardson
Model 686

Harrington & Richardson
Model 830

MODEL 686 DA . . . . **NiB $185 Ex $160 Gd $90**
Caliber: .22 LR and .22 WMR. Six-shot magazine, 4.5-, 5.5-, 7.5-,
10- or 12-inch bbl. Adj. rear sight, ramp and blade front. Blued,
color-casehardened frame. Weight: 31 oz. (with 4.5-inch bbl.).
Made 1980-86.

MODEL 732/733 DA . . . . **NiB $127 Ex $100 Gd $55**
Solid frame, swing-out 6-shot cylinder. Calibers: .32 S&W, .32 S&W
Long. bbl., lengths: 2.5-, 4-inch. Weight: 26 oz. (with 4-inch bbl.).
Fixed sights (windage adj. rear on 4-inch bbl. model). Blued finish.
Plastic grips. Made 1958-86. Note: Model 733 is the same except
with nickel finish.

MODEL 826 DA . . . . **NiB $130 Ex $105 Gd $60**
Caliber: .22 WMR. Six-shot magazine, 3-inch bull bbl., ramp and
blade front sight, adj. rear. American walnut grips. Weight: 28 oz.
Made 1981-83.

MODEL 829/830 DA
Same as Model 826 except in .22 LR caliber. Nine-shot capacity.
Made 1981-83.
Model 829, blued . . . . **NiB $130 Ex $110 Gd $65**
Model 830, nickel . . . . **NiB $135 Ex $115 Gd $70**

MODEL 832,1833 DA
Same as Model 826 except in .32 SW Long. Blued or nickel finish.
Made 1981-83.
Model 832, blued . . . . **NiB $148 Ex $125 Gd $70**
Model 833, nickel . . . . **NiB $145 Ex $130 Gd $75**

MODEL 900/901 DA . . . . **NiB $90 Ex $85 Gd $45**
Solid frame, snap-out cylinder. Calibers: .22 Short, Long, LR. Nine-
shot cylinder, bbl. lengths: 2.5-, 4-, 6-inches. Weight: 26 oz. (with
6-inch bbl.). Fixed sights. Blued finish. Cycolac grips. Made 1962-
73. Note: Model 901 (disc. in 1963) is the same except has chrome
finish and white Tenite grips.

MODEL 903 TARGET . . . . **NiB $150 Ex $135 Gd $80**
Caliber: .22 LR. Nine-shot capacity. SA/DA, 6-inch target-weight
flat-side bbl., swing-out cylinder. Weight: 35 oz. Blade front sight,
adj. rear. American walnut grips. Made 1980-83.

MODEL 904 TARGET . . . . **NiB $150 Ex $230 Gd $80**
Similar to Model 903 except 4- or 6-inch bull bbl. Weight: 32 oz.

Harrington & Richardson
Model 900

Harrington & Richardson
Model 925

Harrington & Richardson
Model 903

Harrington & Richardson
Model 905

Harrington & Richardson
Model 922, First Issue

Harrington & Richardson
Model 922, Second Issue

Harrington & Richardson
Model 926

MODEL 905

TARGET . . . . **NiB $179 Ex $140 Gd $98**
Same as Model 904 except w/4-inch bbl. only. Nickel finish. Made 1981-83.

MODEL 922
DA REVOLVER

FIRST ISSUE. . . . . **NiB $207 Ex $160 Gd $110**
Solid frame. Caliber: .22 LR. Nine-shot cylinder, 10-inch octagon bbl., (early model) or 6-inches, round bbl. (later production). Weight: 26 oz. (with 6-inch bbl.). Fixed sights. Blued finish. Checkered walnut grips. Safety cylinder on later models. Disc. prior to 1942.

MODEL 922/923
DA REVOLVER,

SECOND ISSUE . . . . **NiB $94 Ex $75 Gd $51**
Solid frame. Caliber: .22 LR. Nine-shot cylinder, bbl. lengths: 2.5-, 4-, 6-inches. Weight: 24 oz. (with 4-inch bbl.). Fixed sights. Blued finish. Plastic grips. Made 1950-86. Note: Second Issue Model 922 has a different frame from that of the First Issue. Model 923 is same as Model 922, Second Issue except for nickel finish.

MODEL 925

DEFENDER . . . . **NiB $137 Ex $110 Gd $75**
DA. Hinged frame. Caliber: .38 S&W. Five-shot cylinder, 2.5-inch bbl., weight: 22 oz. Adj. rear sight, fixed front. Blued finish. One-piece wraparound grip. Made 1964-78.

MODEL 926 DA . . . . **NiB $137 Ex $110 Gd $75**
Hinged frame. Calibers: .22 LR, .38 S&W. Nine-shot (.22 LR) or 5-shot (.38) cylinder, 4-inch bbl., weight: 31 oz. Adj. rear sight, fixed front. Blued finish. Checkered walnut grips. Made 1968-78.

Harrington & Richardson
Model 939

Harrington & Richardson
Model 929

Harrington & Richardson
Model 949

Harrington & Richardson
Model 950

Harrington & Richardson
Model 999, First Issue

Harrington & Richardson
Model 999, Second Issue

MODEL 929/930
SIDEKICK DA REVOLVER . . . . **NiB $112 Ex $90 Gd $62**
Caliber: .22 LR. Solid frame, swing-out 9-shot cylinder, bbl. lengths: 2.5-, 4-, 6-inches. Weight: 24 oz. (with 4-inch bbl.). Fixed sights. Blued finish. Checkered plastic grips. Made 1956-86. Note: Model 930 is same except with nickel finish.

MODEL 939/940
ULTRA SIDEKICK
DA REVOLVER . . . . **NiB $148 Ex $115 Gd $80**
Solid frame, swing-out 9-shot cylinder. Safety lock. Calibers: .22 Short, Long, LR. Flat-side 6-inch bbl. w/vent rib. Weight: 33 oz. Adj. rear sight, ramp front. Blued finish. Checkered walnut grips. Made 1958-86, reintroduced by H&R 1871 in 1992. Note: Model 940 is same except has round bbl.

MODEL 949/950
FORTY-NINER
DA REVOLVER . . . . **NiB $135 Ex $105 Gd $70**
Solid frame. Side loading and ejection. Calibers: .22 Short, Long, LR. Nine-shot cylinder, 5.5- or 7.5 inch bbl., weight: 31 to 38 oz. Adj. rear sight, blade front. Blued or nickel finish. One-piece, Western-style walnut grip. Made 1960-86, reintroduced by H&R 1871 in 1992-99. Note: Model 950 is same except has nickel finish.

MODEL 976 DA . . . . **NiB $110 Ex $85 Gd $60**
Same as Model 949 except has color-casehardened frame, 7.5-inch bbl. Weight: 36 oz. Intro. 1977. disc.

HARRINGTON & RICHARDSON
MODEL 999 SPORTSMAN
DA REVOLVER, FIRST ISSUE . . . . **NiB $200 Ex $160 Gd $95**
Hinged frame. Calibers: .22 LR, .22 Mag. Same specifications as Model 199 Sportsman Single Action. Disc. before 1942.

MODEL 999 SPORTSMAN
DA REVOLVER
SECOND ISSUE . . . . **NiB $215 Ex $170 Gd $100**
Hinged frame. Caliber: .22 LR. Nine-shot cylinder, 6-inch bbl. w/vent rib. Weight: 30 oz. Adj. sights. Blued finish. Checkered walnut grips. Made 1950-86.

(NEW) MODEL 999
SPORTSMAN
DA REVOLVER . . . . **NiB $213 Ex $170 Gd $116**
Hinged frame. Caliber: .22 Short, Long, LR. Nine-shot cylinder. Six-inch bbl. w/vent rib. Weight: 30 oz. Blade front sight adj. for elevation, square-notched rear adj. for windage. Blued finish. Checkered hardwood grips. Reintroduced by H&R 1871 in 1992.

AMERICAN DA . . . . **NiB $94 Ex $75 Gd $51**
Solid frame. Calibers: .32 S&W Long, .38 S&W. Six-shot (.32 cal.) or 5-shot (.38 cal.) cylinder, bbl. lengths: 2.5-,4.5- and 6-inches. Weight: About 16 oz. Fixed sights. Blued or nickel finish. Hard rubber grips. Disc. prior to 1942.

AUTOMATIC EJECTING DA REVOLVER . . . . . **NiB $170 Ex $135 Gd $90**
Hinged frame. Calibers: .32 S&W Long, .38 S&W. Six-shot (.32 cal.) or 5-shot (.38 cal.) cylinder, bbl. lengths: 3.25-, 4-, 5- and 6-inches. Weight: 16 oz. (.32 cal.), 15 oz. (.38 cal.). Fixed sights. Blued or nickel finish. Black hard rubber grips. Disc. prior to 1942.

BOBBY DA . . . . **NiB $300 Ex $245 Gd $155**
Hinged frame. Calibers: .32 S&W, .38 S&W. Six-shot cylinder (.32 cal.) or 5-shot (.38 cal.). Four-inch bbl., 9 inches overall. Weight: 23 oz. Fixed sights. Blued finish. Checkered walnut grips. Disc. 1946. Note: Originally designed and produced for use by London's bobbies.

DEFENDER .38 DA . . . . **NiB $145 Ex $115 Gd $75**
Hinged frame. Based on the Sportsman design. Caliber: .38 S&W. Bbl. lengths: 4- and 6-inches, 9 inches overall (with 4-inch bbl.). Weight: 25 oz. with 4-inch bbl. Fixed sights. Blued finish. Black plastic grips. Disc. 1946. Note: This model was manufactured during WW II as an arm for plant guards, auxiliary police, etc.

EXPERT MODEL DA . . . . **NiB $188 Ex $150 Gd $102**
Same specifications as .22 Special except has 10-inch bbl., weight: 28 oz. Disc. prior to 1942.

HAMMERLESS DA, LARGE FRAME . . . . **NiB $125 Ex $100 Gd $65**
Hinged frame. Calibers: .32 S&W Long 38 S&W. Six-shot (.32 cal.), or 5-shot (.38 cal.) cylinder, bbl. lengths: 3.25-, 4-, and 6-inches. Weight: About 17 oz. Fixed sights. Blued or nickel finish. Hard rubber grips. Disc. prior to 1942.

HAMMERLESS DA, SMALL FRAME . . . . **NiB $125 Ex $100 Gd $68**
Hinged frame. Calibers: .22 LR, .32 S&W. Seven-shot (.22 cal.) or 5-shot (.32 cal.) cylinder, bbl. lengths: 2-, 3-, 4-, 5- and 6-inches. Weight: About 13 oz. Fixed sights. Blued or nickel finish. Hard rubber grips. Disc. prior to 1942.

HUNTER MODEL DA . . . . **NiB $140 Ex $110 Gd $70**
Solid frame. Caliber: .22 LR. Nine-shot cylinder, 10-inch octagon bbl., weight: 26 oz. Fixed sights. Blued finish. Checkered walnut grips. Safety cylinder on later models. Note: An earlier Hunter Model was built on the smaller 7-shot frame. Disc. prior to 1942.

NEW DEFENDER DA . . . . **NiB $255 Ex $200 Gd $140**
Hinged frame. Caliber: .22 LR. Nine-shot cylinder, 2-inch bbl., 6.25 inches overall. Weight: 23 oz. Adj. sights. Blued finish. Checkered walnut grips, round butt. Note: Basically, this is the Sportsman DA w/a short bbl., Disc. prior to 1942.

PREMIER DA . . . . **NiB $105 Ex $90 Gd $60**
Small hinged frame. Calibers: .22 LR, .32 S&W. Seven-shot (.22 LR) or 5-shot (.32) cylinder. Bbl. Lengths: 2-, 3-, 4-, 5 and 6-inches. Weight: 13 oz. (in .22 LR), 12 oz. (in .32 S&W). Fixed sights. Blued or nickel finish. Black hard rubber grips. Disc. prior to 1942. (See illustration next page.)

MODEL STR 022 BLANK REVOLVER . . . . **NiB $81 Ex $65 Gd $44**
Caliber: .22 RF blanks. Nine-shot cylinder, 2.5-inch bbl. Weight: 19 oz. Satin blued finish.

MODEL STR 032 BLANK REVOLVER . . . . **NiB $94 Ex $75 Gd $51**
Same general specifications as STR 022 except chambered for .32 S&W blank cartridges.

Harrington & Richardson
Automatic Ejecting

Harrington & Richardson Bobby

Harrington & Richardson
Defender .38

Harrington & Richardson
Hammerless, Small Frame

Harrington & Richardson Premier

Harrington & Richardson Vest Pocket

Harrington & Richardson Target

Harrington & Richardson Young American

Harrington & Richardson Trapper

Harrington & Richardson Ultra Sportsmen

TARGET MODEL DA . . . . **NiB $163 Ex $130 Gd $88**
Small hinged frame. Calibers: .22 LR, .22 W.R.F. Seven-shot cylinder, 6-inch bbl., weight: 16 oz. Fixed sights. Blued finish. Checkered walnut grips. Disc. prior to 1942.

TRAPPER MODEL DA . . . . **NiB $150 Ex $120 Gd $80**
Solid frame. Caliber: .22 LR. Seven-shot cylinder, 6-inch octagon bbl., weight: 12.5 oz. Fixed sights. Blued finish. Checkered walnut grips. Safety cylinder on later models. Disc. prior to 1942.

ULTRA SPORTSMAN . . . . **NiB $223 Ex $175 Gd $125**
SA. Hinged frame. Caliber: .22 LR. Nine-shot cylinder, 6-inch bbl., weight: 30 oz. Adj. target sights. Blued finish. Checkered walnut grips. This model has short action, wide hammer spur, cylinder is length of a .22 LR cartridge. Disc. prior to 1942.

VEST POCKET DA . . . . **NiB $94 Ex $75 Gd $51**
Solid frame. Spurless hammer. Calibers: .22 Rimfire, .32 S&W. Seven-shot (.22 cal.) or 5-shot (.32 cal.) cylinder, 1.13-inch bbl., weight: About 9 oz. Blued or nickel finish. Hard rubber grips. Disc. prior to 1942.

YOUNG AMERICA DA . . . . **NiB $94 Ex $75 Gd $51**
Solid frame. Calibers: .22 Long, .32 S&W. Seven-shot (.22 cal.) or 5-shot (.32 cal.) cylinder. Bbl. lengths: 2-, 4.5- and 6-inches. Weight: About 9 oz. Fixed sights. Blued or nickel finish. Hard rubber grips. Disc. prior to 1942.

92

www.StoegerIndustries.com

HARTFORD ARMS & EQUIPMENT CO. — Hartford, Connecticut

Hartford pistols were the forebearer of the original High Standard line. High Standard Mfg. Corp. acquired Hartford Arms & Equipment Co. in 1932. The High Standard Model B is essentially the same as the Hartford Automatic.

AUTOMATIC TARGET PISTOL. . . . . NiB $648 Ex $525 Gd $350
Caliber. .22 LR. 10-shot magazine, 6.75-inch bbl., 10.75 inches overall. Weight: 31 oz. Target sights. Blued finish. Black rubber grips. This gun closely resembles the early Colt Woodsman and High Standard pistols. Made 1929-30.

REPEATING PISTOL. . . . . NiB $494 Ex $395 Gd $269
Same general design as the automatic pistol of this manufacture, but this model is a hand-operated repeating pistol on the order of the Fiala. Made 1929-30.

SINGLE-SHOT TARGET PISTOL. . . . NiB $486 Ex $385 Gd $250
Similar in appearance to the Hartford Automatic. Caliber: .22 LR, 6.75-inch bbl., 10.75 inches overall. Weight: 38 oz. Target sights. Mottled frame and slide, blued bbl., Black rubber or walnut grips. Made 1929-30.

HASKELL MANUFACTURING — Lima, Ohio
See listings under Hi-Point.

HAWES FIREARMS — Van Nuys, California

DEPUTY MARSHAL SA REVOLVER
Calibers: .22 LR, also .22 WMR in two-cylinder combination. Six-shot cylinder, 5.5-inch bbl., 11 inches overall. Weight: 34 oz. Adj. rear sight, blade front. Blued finish. Plastic or walnut grips. Imported from 1973-81.
.22 LR (plastic grips) . . . . NiB $88 Ex $70 Gd $48
Combination, .22 LR/.22 WMR (plastic) . . . . . . NiB $94 Ex $75 Gd $51
Walnut grips, add. $10

DEPUTY DENVER MARSHAL
Same as Deputy Marshal SA except has brass frame. Imported from 1973-81.
.22 LR (plastic grips) . . . . NiB $94 Ex $75 Gd $51
Combination, .22 LR/.22 WMR (plastic) . . . . . . NiB $94 Ex $75 Gd $51
Walnut grips add $10

DEPUTY MONTANA MARSHAL
Same as Deputy Marshal except has brass grip frame. Walnut grips only. Imported from 1973-81.
.22 LR . . . . NiB $125 Ex $100 Gd $70
Combination, .22 LR/.22 WMR . . . . . NiB $150 Ex $120 Gd $82

DEPUTY SILVER CITY MARSHAL
Same as Deputy Marshal except has chrome-plated frame, brass grip frame, blued cylinder and bbl., Imported from 1973-81.
.22 LR (plastic grips) . . . . NiB $100 Ex $80 Gd $50
Combination, .22 LR/.22 WMR (plastic) . . . . NiB $120 Ex $100 Gd $70
Walnut grips add $10

DEPUTY TEXAS MARSHAL
Same as Deputy Marshal except has chrome finish. Imported from 1973-81.
.22 LR (plastic grips) . . . . NiB $105 Ex $90 Gd $60
Combination, .22 LR/.22 WMR (plastic) . . . . NiB $135 Ex $115 Gd $75
Walnut grips add. $10

FAVORITE SINGLE-SHOT TARGET PISTOL $150
Replica of Stevens No. 35. Tip-up action. Caliber: .22 LR. Eight-inch bbl., 12 inches overall. Weight: 24 oz. Target sights. Chrome-plated frame. Blued bbl., Plastic or rosewood grips (add $5). Imported 1972-76.

Hawes
Deputy Denver Marshal

Hawes
Deputy Marshall

Hawes
Deputy Montana Marshal

Hawes
Deputy Silver City

Hawes
Deputy Texas Marshal

Hawes Sauer
Chief Marshal

Hawes Sauer
Federal Marshal

Hawes Sauer
Montana Marshal

Hawes Sauer
Montana Marshal .22

Hawes Sauer
Silver City Marshal

Hawes Sauer
Texas Marshal

SAUER CHIEF MARSHAL SA TARGET REVOLVER

Same as Western Marshal except has adj. rear sight and front sight, oversized rosewood grips. Not made in .22 caliber. Imported from 1973-81.

.357 Magnum or .45 Colt . . . . NiB $250 Ex $200 Gd $136
.44 Magnum . . . . NiB $281 Ex $225 Gd $153
Combination .357 Magnum
and 9mm Para.
.45 Colt and .45 Auto . . . . NiB $280 Ex $235 Gd $125
Combination
.44 Magnum and .44-40 . . . . NiB $275 Ex $225 Gd $150

SAUER FEDERAL MARSHAL

Same as Western Marshal except has color-casehardened frame, brass grip frame, one-piece walnut grip. Not made in .22 caliber. Imported from 1973-81.

.357 Magnum or .45 Colt . . . . NiB $235 Ex $185 Gd $125
.44 Magnum . . . . NiB $270 Ex $205 Gd $135
Combination
.357 Magnum and 9mm Para.,
.45 Colt and .45 Auto . . . . NiB $280 Ex $235 Gd $125
Combination .44 Magnum and .44-40 . . . . NiB $275 Ex $225 Gd $150

SAUER MONTANA MARSHAL

Same as Western Marshal except has brass grip frame. Imported from 1973-81.

.357 Magnum or .45 Colt . . . . NiB $250 Ex $200 Gd $136
.44 Magnum . . . . NiB $281 Ex $225 Gd $153
Combination .357 Magnum and 9mm Para.,
.45 Colt and .45 Auto . . . . NiB $300 Ex $240 Gd $163
Combination .44 Magnum and .44-40 . . . . NiB $313 Ex $250 Gd $170
.22 LR . . . . NiB $244 Ex $195 Gd $133
Combination .22 LR and .22 WMR . . . . NiB $263 Ex $210 Gd $143

SAUER SILVER CITY MARSHAL

Same as Western Marshal except has nickel plated frame, brass grip frame, blued cylinder and bbl., pearlite grips. Imported from 1973-81.

.44 Magnum . . . . NiB $300 Ex $240 Gd $163
Combination .357 Magnum and 9mm Para.
.45 Colt and .45 Auto . . . . NiB $275 Ex $205 Gd $125
Combination .44 Magnum and .44-40 . . . . NiB $300 Ex $215 Gd $150

SAUER TEXAS MARSHAL

Same as Western Marshal except nickel plated, has pearlite grips. Imported from 1973-81.

.357 Magnum or .45 Colt . . . . NiB $281 Ex $225 Gd $153
.44 Magnum . . . . NiB $300 Ex $240 Gd $163
Combination .357 Magnum and 9mm Para.,
.45 Colt and .45 Auto . . . . NiB $325 Ex $260 Gd $177
Combination .44 Magnum and .44-40 . . . . NiB $344 Ex $275 Gd $187
.22 LR . . . . NiB $244 Ex $195 Gd $133
Combination .22 LR and .22 WMR . . . . NiB $270 Ex $205 Gd $135

SAUER WESTERN MARSHAL SA REVOLVER

Calibers: .22 LR (disc.), .357 Magnum, .44 Magnum, .45 Auto. Also in two-cylinder combinations: .22 WMR (disc.), 9mm Para., .44-40, .45 Auto. Six-shot cylinder, bbl. lengths: 5.5-inch (disc.), 6-inch, 11.75 inches overall (with 6-inch bbl.). Weight: 46 oz. Fixed sights. Blued finish. Originally furnished w/simulated stag plastic grips. Recent production has smooth rosewood grips. Made from 1968 by J. P. Sauer & Sohn, Eckernforde, Germany. Imported from 1973-81.

.357 Magnum or .45 Colt	NiB $250	Ex $200	Gd $136
.44 Magnum	NiB $288	Ex $230	Gd $156
Combination .357 Magnum and 9mm Para., .45 Colt and .45 Auto	NiB $270	Ex $215	Gd $140
Combination .44 Magnum and .44-40	NiB $300	Ex $240	Gd $163
.22 LR	NiB $200	Ex $150	Gd $110
Combination .22 LR and .22 WMR	NiB $220	Ex $185	Gd $130

Hawes Sauer
Western Marshal

HECKLER & KOCH — Oberndorf/Neckar, West Germany, and Chantilly, Virginia

MODEL HK4 DA AUTO PISTOL

Calibers: .380 Automatic (9mm Short), .22 LR, .25 Automatic (6.35mm), .32 Automatic (7.65mm) w/conversion kits. Seven-shot magazine (.380 Auto), 8-shot in other calibers, 3.4-inch bbl., 6.19 inches overall. Weight: 18 oz. Fixed sights. Blued finish. Plastic grip. Disc. 1984.

.22 LR or .380 Automatic	NiB $385	Ex $295	Gd $190
.25 ACP or .32 ACP Automatic	NiB $385	Ex $295	Gd $190
.380 Automatic w/.22 conversion unit	NiB $494	Ex $395	Gd $269
.380 Automatic w/.22, .25, .32 conversion units	NiB $681	Ex $545	Gd $371

Heckler & Koch
Model HK4

MODEL MARK 23

DA AUTO PISTOL . . . . **NiB $2106 Ex $1595 Gd $1080**

Short-recoil semiautomatic pistol w/polymer frame and steel slide. Caliber: .45 ACP. 10-shot magazine, 5.87-inch bbl., 9.65 inches overall. Weight: 43 oz. Seven interchangeable rear sight adjustment units w/3-dot system. Developed primarily in response to specifications by the Special Operations Command (SOCOM) for a Special Operations Forces Offensive Handgun Weapon System. Imported 1996 to date.

MODEL P7K3 DA
AUTO PISTOL

Caliber: .380 ACP. Eight-round magazine, 3.8 inch-bbl., 6.3 inches overall. Weight: About 26 oz. Adj. rear sight. Imported 1988-94.

P7K3 in .380 Cal.	NiB $825	Ex $660	Gd $450
.22 LR conversion kit.	NiB $600	Ex $510	Gd $340
.32 ACP conversion kit	NiB $300	Ex $250	Gd $160

Heckler &Koch
Model P7K3

MODEL P7M8 . . . . **NiB $856 Ex $685 Gd $466**
Squeeze-cock SA semiautomatic pistol. Caliber: 9mm Para. Eight-shot magazine, 4.13-inch bbl., 6.73 inches overall. Weight: 29.9 oz. Matte black or nickel finish. Adj. rear sight. Imported 1985 to date. See illustration next page.

MODEL P7M10

Caliber: .40 S&W. Nine-shot magazine, 4.2-inch bbl., 6.9 inches overall. Weight: 43 oz. Fixed front sight blade, adj. rear w/3-dot system. Imported 1992-94.

Blued finish	NiB $1005	Ex $760	Gd $525
Nickel finish	NiB $1015	Ex $770	Gd $535

Heckler & Koch
Mark 23

Heckler & Koch
Model P7M8

Heckler & Koch USP45

Heckler & Koch
Model P7M13

Heckler & Koch
Model P7 (PSP)

Heckler & Koch
Model P9S DA

MODEL P7M13 . . . . NiB $900 Ex $705 Gd $490
Caliber: 9mm. 13-shot magazine, 4.13-inch bbl., 6.65 inches overall. Weight: 34.42 oz. Matte black finish. Adj. rear sight. Imported
1985-94.

MODEL P7(PSP)
AUTO PISTOL . . . . NiB $744 Ex $595 Gd $405
Caliber: 9mm Para. Eight-shot magazine, 4.13-inch bbl., 6.54 inches overall. DA. Weight: About 33.5 oz. Blued finish. Imported 1983-
85 and again in 1990 with limited availability.

MODEL P9S
DA AUTOMATIC PISTOL
Calibers: 9mm Para., .45 Automatic. Nine-shot (9mm) or 7-shot (.45
Auto) magazine. Four-inch bbl., 7.63 inches overall. Weight: 32
ounces. Fixed sights. Blued finish. Contoured plastic grips. Disc.
1986.
9mm . . . . NiB $725 Ex $545 Gd $380
.45 Automatic . . . . NiB $740 Ex $600 Gd $395

MODEL P9S TARGET
COMPETITION KIT
Same as Model P9S Target except comes w/extra 5.5-inch bbl. and
bbl. weights. Also available w/walnut competition grip.
W/standard grip . . . . NiB $1119 Ex $895 Gd $609
W/competition grip . . . . NiB $1188 Ex $950 Gd $646

MODEL SP89 . . . . NiB $3700 Ex $2950 Gd $2000
Semiautomatic, recoil-operated, delayed roller-locked bolt system.
Caliber: 9mm Para. 15-shot magazine, 4.5-inch bbl., 13 inches
overall. Weight: 68 oz. Hooded front sight, adj. rotary-aperture rear.
Imported 1989-93.

MODEL USP
AUTO PISTOL
Polymer integral grip/frame design w/recoil reduction system.
Calibers: 9mm Para., .40 S&W or .45 ACP. 15-shot (9mm) or 13-
shot (.40 S&W and .45ACP) magazine, 4.13- or 4.25-inch bbl.,
6.88 to 7.87 inches overall. Weight: 26.5-30.4 oz. Blade front
sight, adj. rear w/3-dot system. Matte black or stainless finish.
Stippled black polymer grip. Available in SA/DA or DAO.
Imported 1993 to date.
Matte
Black finish . . . . NiB $650 Ex $490 Gd $340
Stainless . . . . NiB $594 Ex $475 Gd $323
W/Tritium Sights, add $95
W/Ambidextrous Decocking Lever, add $20

**Heckler & Koch Model USP45
Compact 50th Anniversary**

**Heckler & Koch
Model USP9 Compact (Stainless)**

**Heckler & Koch
Model USP357 Compact**

**Heckler & Koch
Model USP Expert**

**Heckler & Koch
Model USP Tactical**

MODEL USP9 COMPACT
Caliber: 9mm. 10- shot magazine, 4.25- inch bbl., 7.64 inches overall. Weight: 25.5 oz. Short recoil w/modified Browning action. 3-dot sighting system. Polymer frame w/integral grips. Imported 1997 to date.
Blued finish . . . . NiB $600 Ex $490 Gd $330
Stainless finish . . . . NiB $635 Ex $515 Gd $350
W/Ambidextrous
decocking lever, add $15

MODEL USP40 COMPACT
Caliber: .40 S&W. 10-shot magazine, 3.58- inch bbl., 6.81 inches overall. Weight: 27 oz. Short recoil w/modified Browning action. 3-dot sighting system. Polymer frame w/integral grips. Imported 1997 to date.
Blued finish . . . . NiB $650 Ex $525 Gd $335
Stainless finish . . . . NiB $695 Ex $550 Gd $350
W/ambidextrous
decocking lever, add $15

MODEL USP45 COMPACT
Caliber: .45 ACP. Eight-shot magazine, 3.8- inch bbl., 7.09 inches overall. Weight: 28 oz. Short recoil w/modified Browning action. 3-dot sighting system. Polymer frame w/integral grips. Imported 1998 to date.
Blued finish . . . . NiB $650 Ex $525 Gd $335
Stainless finish . . . . NiB $695 Ex $550 Gd $350
W/ambidextrous
decocking lever, add $15
50th Anniversary
(1 of 1,000) . . . . NiB $1244 Ex $995 Gd $677

MODEL
USP EXPERT. . . . . NiB $1325 Ex $995 Gd $725
Caliber: .45 ACP. 10-shot magazine, 6.2- inch bbl., 9.65 inches overall. Weight: 30 oz. Adjustable 3-dot target sights. Short recoil modified Browning action w/recoil reduction system. Reinforced polymer frame w/integral grips and match-grade slide. Imported 1999 to date.

MODEL USP
TACTICAL . . . . NiB $1035 Ex $800 Gd $525
SOCOM Enhanced version of the USP Standard Model, w/4.92-inch threaded bbl. Chambered for .45 ACP only. Imported 1998 to date.

Heckler & Koch Model VP'7OZ

Heritage Rough Rider

Heritage Sentry

MODEL VP 70Z AUTO PISTOL . . . . NiB $550 Ex $425 Gd $300
Caliber: 9mm Para. 18-shot magazine, 4.5-inch bbl., 8 inches overall. Weight: 32.5 oz. DA Fixed sights. Blued slide, plastic receiver and grip. Disc. 1986.

HELWAN PISTOLS

See listings under Interarms.

HERITAGE MANUFACTURING — Opa Locka, Florida

MODEL HA25 AUTO PISTOL
Caliber: .25 ACP. Six-shot magazine, 2.5-inch bbl., 4.63 inches overall. Weight: 12 oz. Fixed sights. Blued or chrome finish. Made 1993 to date.
Blued . . . . NiB $120 Ex $95 Gd $65
Chrome . . . . NiB $125 Ex $100 Gd $70

ROUGH RIDER SA REVOLVER
Calibers: .22 LR, .22 Mag. Six-shot cylinder. bbl. lengths: 2.75, 3.75, 4.75, 6.5 or 9 inches. Weight: 31-38 oz. Blade front sight, fixed rear. High-polished blued finish w/gold accents. Smooth walnut grips. Made 1993 to date.
.22 LR . . . . NiB $110 Ex $85 Gd $65
.22 LR/.22 WRF combo . . . . NiB $140 Ex $110 Gd $80

SENTRY DA REVOLVER
Calibers: .22 LR, .22 Mag., .32 Mag., 9mm or .38 Special. Six- or 8-shot (rimfire) cylinder, 2- or 4-inch bbl., 6.25 inches overall (2-inch bbl.). Ramp front sight, fixed rear. Blued or nickel finish. Checkered polymer grips. Made from 1993-97.
Blued . . . . NiB $112 Ex $90 Gd $62
Nickel . . . . NiB $124 Ex $100 Gd $70

STEALTH DA AUTO PISTOL . . . . . . NiB $255 Ex $205 Gd $141
Calibers: 9mm, .40 S&W. 10-shot magazine, 3.9-inch bbl., weight: 20.2 oz. Gas-delayed blowback, double action only. Ambidextrous trigger safety. Blade front sight, drift-adj. rear. Black chrome or stainless slide. Black polymer grip frame. Made from 1996 to date.

HI-POINT FIREARMS — Mansfield, Ohio

MODEL JS-9MM
AUTO PISTOL . . . . NiB $120 Ex $95 Gd $60
Caliber: 9mm Para. Eight-shot magazine, 4.5-inch bbl., 7.75 inches overall. Weight: 39 oz. Fixed low-profile sights w/3-dot system. Matte blue, matte black or chrome finish. Checkered synthetic grips. Made from 1990-98.

MODEL JS-9MM COMPETITION PISTOL
(STALLARD) . . . . NiB $110 Ex $90 Gd $60
Similar to standard JS-9 except w/4-inch compensated bbl. w/ shortened slide and adj. sights. 10-shot magazine, 7.25 inches overall. Weight: 30 oz. Made from 1998 to date.

MODEL JS-9MM/C-9MM COMPACT PISTOL
(BEEMILLER) . . . . NiB $111 Ex $90 Gd $59
Similar to standard JS-9 except w/3.5-inch bbl. and shortened slide w/alloy or polymer frame. 6.72 inches overall. Weight: 29 oz. or 32 oz. Three-dot-style sights. Made from 1993 to date.

MODEL CF-.380
POLYMER . . . . NiB $75 Ex $55 Gd $35
Caliber: .380 ACP. Eight-shot magazine, 3.5-inch bbl., 6.72 inches overall. Weight: 32 oz. Three-dot sights. Made from 1994 to date.

MODEL JS-.40/J
C-.40 AUTO PISTOL
(IBERIA) . . . . NiB $138 Ex $110 Gd $75
Similar to Model JS-9mm except in caliber .40 S&W.

MODEL JS-.45/JH-.45
AUTO PISTOL
(HASKELL) . . . . NiB $155 Ex $120 Gd $80
Similar to Model JS-9mm except in caliber .45 ACP w/7-shot magazine and two-tone Polymer finish.

J. C. HIGGINS

See Sears, Roebuck & Company

HIGH STANDARD SPORTING FIREARMS — East Hartford, Connecticut Formerly High Standard Mfg. Co., Hamden, Connecticut

A long-standing producer of sporting arms, High Standard disc. its operations in 1984. See new High Standard models under separate entry, HIGH STANDARD MFG. CO., INC.

NOTE: *For ease in finding a particular firearm, High Standard handguns are grouped into three sections: Automatic pistols (below), derringers and revolvers. For a complete listing, please refer to the Index.*

AUTOMATIC PISTOLS

MODEL A
HAMMERLESS . . . . **NiB $750 Ex $595 Gd $405**
Caliber: .22 LR. 10-shot magazine, bbl. lengths: 4.5-, 6.75-inch. 11.5 inches overall (6.75-inch bbl.). Weight: 36 oz. (in 6.75-inch bbl.). Adj. target sights. Blued finish. Checkered walnut grips. Made 1938-42.

High Standard
Model A

MODEL B
AUTOMATIC PISTOL . . . . **NiB $440 Ex $355 Gd $280**
Original Standard pistol. Hammerless. Caliber: .22 LR. 10-shot magazine, bbl. lengths: 4.5-, 6.75-inch, 10.75 inches overall (with 6.75-inch bbl.). Weight: 33 oz. (6.75-inch bbl.). Fixed sights. Blued finish. Hard rubber grips. Made 1932-42.

High Standard
Model B

MODEL C
AUTOMATIC PISTOL . . . . **NiB $900 Ex $705 Gd $455**
Same as Model B except in .22 Short. Made 1935-42.

MODEL D
AUTOMATIC PISTOL . . . . **NiB $813 Ex $650 Gd $442**
Same general specifications as Model A but heavier bbl., weight: 40 oz. (6.75-inch bbl.). Made 1937-42.

High Standard
Model D

DURA-MATIC
AUTOMATIC PISTOL . . . . **NiB $306 Ex $245 Gd $167**
Takedown. Caliber: .22 LR. 10-shot magazine, 4.5 or 6.5 inch interchangeable bbl., 10.88 inches overall (6.5-inch bbl.). Weight: 35 oz. (in 6.5-inch bbl.). Fixed sights. Blued finish. Checkered grips. Made 1952-70.

High Standard
Dura-Matic

MODEL E
AUTOMATIC PISTOL . . . . **NiB $1679 Ex $1290 Gd $995**
Same general specifications as Model A but w/extra heavy bbl. and thumbrest grips. Weight: 42 oz. (6.75-inch bbl.). Made 1937-42.

FIELD-KING
AUTOMATIC PISTOL
FIRST MODEL
Same general specifications as Sport-King but w/heavier bbl. and target sights. Late model 6.75-inch bbls. have recoil stabilizer and lever take-down feature. Weight: 43 oz. (6.75-inch bbl.). Made 1951-58.
W/one bbl. . . . . **NiB $640 Ex $540 Gd $330**
W/both bbls. . . . . **NiB $707 Ex $612 Gd $438**

High Standard
Model E

FIELD-KING AUTOMATIC PISTOL
SECOND MODEL
Same general specifications as First Model Field-King but w/button take-down and marked FK 100 or FK 101.
W/one bbl. . . . . **NiB $625 Ex $500 Gd $225**
W/both bbls. . . . . **NiB $756 Ex $625 Gd $405**

**High Standard
G-.380**

**High Standard
Model G-B**

**High Standard
Model G-E**

**High Standard
Model H-A**

**High Standard
Model H-B**

FLITE-KING AUTOMATIC PISTOL — FIRST MODEL
Same general specifications as Sport-King except in .22. Short w/aluminum alloy frame and slide and marked FK 100 or FK 101. Weight: 26 oz. (6.5-inch bbl.). Made 1953-58.
W/one bbl. .NiB $494 Ex $395 Gd $269
W/both bbls. . . . . .NiB $594 Ex $475 Gd $323

FLITE-KING AUTOMATIC PISTOL — SECOND MODEL
Same as Flite-King—First Model except w/steel frame and marked in the 102 or 103 series. Made 1958-66.
Model 102. . . . . .NiB $577 Ex $415 Gd $295
Model 103. . . . . .NiB $533 Ex $395 Gd $275

MODEL G-.380
AUTOMATIC PISTOL . . . . .NiB $569 Ex $490 Gd $330
Lever takedown. Visible hammer. Thumb safety. Caliber: .380 Automatic. Six-shot magazine, 5-inch bbl., weight: 40 oz. Fixed sights. Blued finish. Checkered plastic grips. Made 1943-50.

MODEL G-B AUTOMATIC PISTOL
Lever takedown. Hammerless. Interchangeable bbls. Caliber: .22 LR. 10-shot magazine, bbl. lengths: 4.5, 6.75 inches, 10.75 inches overall (with 6.75-inch bbl.). Weight: 36 oz. (with 6.75-inch bbl.). Fixed sights. Blued finish. Checkered plastic grips. Made 1948-51.
W/one bbl. .NiB $550 Ex $415 Gd $295
W/both bbls. . . . . .NiB $569 Ex $490 Gd $330

MODEL G-D AUTOMATIC PISTOL
Lever takedown. Hammerless. Interchangeable bbls. Caliber: .22 LR. 10-shot magazine, bbl. lengths: 4.5, 6.75 inches. 11.5 inches overall (with 6.75-inch bbl.). Weight: 41 oz. (6.75-inch bbl.). Target sights. Blued finish. Checkered walnut grips. Made 1948-51.
W/one bbl. .NiB $905 Ex $690 Gd $495
W/both bbls. . . . . .NiB $1038 Ex $815 Gd $575

MODEL G-E AUTOMATIC PISTOL
Same general specifications as Model G-D but w/extra heavy bbl. and thumbrest grips. Weight: 44 oz. (with 6.75-inch bbl.). Made 1949-51.
W/one bbl. .NiB $1329 Ex $1125 Gd $860
W/both bbls. . . . . .NiB $1595 Ex $1265 Gd $995

MODEL H-A
AUTOMATIC PISTOL . . . . .NiB $1242 Ex $1100 Gd $745
Same as Model A but w/visible hammer, no thumb safety. Made 1939-42.

MODEL H-B
AUTOMATIC PISTOL . . . . .NiB $647 Ex $505 Gd $353
Same as Model B but w/visible hammer, no thumb safety. Made 1940-42.

MODEL H-D
AUTOMATIC PISTOL . . . . .NiB $1164 Ex $980 Gd $670
Same as Model D but w/visible hammer, no thumb safety. Made 1939-42.

MODEL H-DM
AUTOMATIC PISTOL . . . . .NiB $663 Ex $550 Gd $406
Also called H-D Military. Same as Model H-D but w/thumb safety. Made 1941-51.

MODEL H-E
AUTOMATIC PISTOL . . . . .NiB $2429 Ex $1895 Gd $1000
Same as Model E but w/visible hammer, no thumb safety. Made 1939-42.

**High Standard
Olympic Military**

**High Standard
Model H-E**

**High Standard Olympic
Automatic – First Model**

**High Standard Olympic
Automatic – Second Model**

**High Standard
Olympic I.S.U.**

**High Standard Olympic
I.S.U. Military**

OLYMPIC AUTOMATIC PISTOL FIRST MODEL (G-O)
Same general specifications as Model G-E but in .22 Short w/light alloy slide. Made 1950-51.
W/one bbl. . . . . NiB $1121 Ex $990 Gd $500
W/both bbls. . . . . NiB $1688 Ex $1350 Gd $918

OLYMPIC AUTOMATIC
SECOND MODEL
Same general specifications as Supermatic but in .22 Short w/light alloy slide. Weight: 39 oz. (6.75-inch bbl.). Made 1951-58.
W/one bbl. . . . . NiB $1044 Ex $920 Gd $605
W/both bbls. . . . . NiB $1329 Ex $1075 Gd $775

OLYMPIC AUTOMATIC PISTOL
THIRD MODEL . . . . NiB $1042 Ex $835 Gd $595
Same as Supermatic Trophy w/bull bbl. except in .22 Short. Made 1963-66.

OLYMPIC COMMEMORATIVE
Limited edition of Supermatic Trophy Military issued to commemorate the only American-made rimfire target pistol ever to win an Olympic gold medal. Highly engraved w/Olympic rings inlaid in gold. Deluxe presentation case. Two versions issued: In 1972 (.22 LR) and 1980 (.22 Short).
1972 issue . . . . NiB $5995 Ex $4995 Gd $3250
1980 issue . . . . NiB $1988 Ex $1650 Gd $1120

OLYMPIC I.S.U . . . . NiB $869 Ex $695 Gd $473
Same as Supermatic Citation except caliber .22 Short, 6.75- or 8-inch tapered bbl. w/stabilizer, detachable weights. Made from 1958-77. Eight-inch bbl. disc. in 1966.

OLYMPIC I.S.U. MILITARY . . . . . . NiB $2015 Ex $995 Gd $559
Same as Olympic I.S.U. except has military grip and bracket rear sight. Intro. in 1965. disc.

OLYMPIC MILITARY . . . . NiB $1015 Ex $825 Gd $625
Same as Olympic — Third Model except has military grip and bracket rear sight. Made in 1965.

PLINKER . . . . NiB $313 Ex $250 Gd $170
Similar to Dura-Matic w/same general specifications. Made 1971-73. See illustration next page.

SHARPSHOOTER
AUTOMATIC PISTOL . . . . NiB $703 Ex $575 Gd $395
Takedown. Hammerless. Caliber: .22 LR. 10-shot magazine, 5.5-inch bull bbl., 9 inches overall. Weight: 42 oz. Micrometer rear sight, blade front sight. Blued finish. Plastic grips. Made 1971-83. See illustration next page.

High Standard Plinker

High Standard — Sharpshooter

High Standard Sport-King
Automatic — First Model

High Standard Sport-King
Automatic — Second Model

High Standard Sport-King
Automatic — Third Model

High Standard Supermatic

SPORT-KING AUTOMATIC
FIRST MODEL
Takedown. Hammerless. Interchangeable bbls. Caliber: .22 LR. 10-shot magazine, bbl. lengths: 4.5-, 6.75-inches. 11.5 inches overall (with 6.75-inch bbl.). Weight: 39 oz. (with 6.75-inch bbl.). Fixed sights. Blued finish. Checkered plastic thumbrest grips. Made 1951-58. Note: 1951-54 production has lever takedown as in "G" series. Later version (illustrated) has push-button takedown.
W/one bbl. . . . . NiB $344 Ex $276 Gd $188
W/both bbls. . . . . NiB $424 Ex $340 Gd $231

SPORT-KING AUTOMATIC PISTOL
SECOND MODEL . . . . NiB $369 Ex $295 Gd $201
Caliber: .22 LR. 10-shot magazine, 4.5- or 6.75 inch interchangeable bbl. 11.25 inches overall (with 6.75-inch bbl.). Weight: 42 oz. (with 6.75-inch bbl.). Fixed sights. Blued finish. Checkered grips. Made 1958-70.

SPORT-KING AUTOMATIC PISTOL
THIRD MODEL . . . . NiB $331 Ex $265 Gd $180
Similar to Sport-King — Second Model w/same general specifications. Blued or nickel finish. Intro. in 1974. disc.

SPORT-KING LIGHTWEIGHT
Same as standard Sport-King except has forged aluminum alloy frame. Weight: 30 oz. w/6.75-inch bbl. Made 1954-65.
W/one bbl. . . . . NiB $351 Ex $249 Gd $160
W/both bbls. . . . . NiB $425 Ex $350 Gd $187

SUPERMATIC
AUTOMATIC PISTOL
Takedown. Hammerless. Interchangeable bbls. Caliber: .22 LR. 10-shot magazine, bbl. lengths: 4.5-, 6.75-inches. Late model 6.75-inch bbls. have recoil stabilizer feature. Weight: 43 oz. (with 6.75-inch bbl.) 11.5 inches overall (with 6.75-inch bbl.). Target sights. Elevated serrated rib between sights. Adj. bbl. weights add 2 or 3 oz. Blued finish. Checkered plastic thumbrest grips. Made 1951-58.
W/one bbl. . . . . NiB $688 Ex $550 Gd $374
W/both bbls. . . . . NiB $844 Ex $675 Gd $459

SUPERMATIC CITATION
Same as Supermatic Tournament except 6.75-, 8- or 10-inch tapered bbl. w/stabilizer and two removable weights. Also furnished w/Tournament's 5.5-inch bull bbl., adj. trigger pull, recoil-proof click-adj. rear sight (bbl.-mounted on 8- and 10-inch bbls.), checkered walnut thumbrest grips on bull bbl. model. Currently mfd. w/only bull bbl. Made 1958-66.
W/5.5-inch bull bbl. . . . . NiB $650 Ex $500 Gd $250
W/6.75-inch
tapered bbl. . . . . NiB $650 Ex $500 Gd $250
W/8-inch tapered bbl. . . . . NiB $880 Ex $695 Gd $490
W/10-inch tapered bbl. . . . . NiB $1069 Ex $895 Gd $670

**High Standard Victor
Solid Rib Barrel**

**High Standard
Supermatic Citation Bull Barrel**

**High Standard
Supermatic Citation Military Fluted Barrel**

**High Standard
Supermatic Tournament Bull Barrel**

**High Standard
Supermatic Tournament Military Tapered Barrel**

**High Standard
Supermatic Trophy Bull Barrel**

SUPERMATIC CITATION MILITARY

Same as Supermatic Citation except has military grip and bracket rear sight as in Supermatic Trophy. Made from 1965-73.
W/bull bbl. . . . . NiB $591 Ex $473 Gd $325
W/fluted bbl. . . . . NiB $819 Ex $675 Gd $490

SUPERMATIC
TOURNAMENT . . . . NiB $600 Ex $525 Gd $245

Takedown. Caliber: .22 LR. 10-shot magazine, interchangeable 5.5-inch bull or 6.75-inch heavy tapered bbl., notched and drilled for stabilizer and weights. 10 inches overall (with 5.5-inch bbl.). Weight: 44 oz. (5.5-inch bbl.). Click adj. rear sight, undercut ramp front. Blued finish. Checkered grips. Made 1958-66.

SUPERMATIC
TOURNAMENT
MILITARY . . . . NiB $590 Ex $470 Gd $315

Same as Supermatic Tournament except has military grip. Made 1965-71.

SUPERMATIC TROPHY

Same as Supermatic Citation except with 5.5-inch bull bbl., or 7.25-inch fluted bbl., w/detachable stabilizer and weights, extra magazine, High-luster blued finish, checkered walnut thumbrest grips. Made 1963-66.
W/bull bbl. . . . . NiB $1095 Ex $895 Gd $450
W/fluted bbl. . . . . NiB $1125 Ex $910 Gd $475

SUPERMATIC
TROPHY MILITARY

Same as Supermatic Trophy except has military grip and bracket rear sight. Made 1965-84.
W/bull bbl. . . . . NiB $925 Ex $825 Gd $430
W/fluted bbl. . . . . NiB $435 Ex $830 Gd $455

VICTOR
AUTOMATIC . . . . NiB $795 Ex $625 Gd $400

Takedown. Caliber: .22 LR. 10-shot magazine, 4.5-inch solid or vent rib and 5.5-inch vent rib, interchangeable bbl., 9.75 inches overall (with 5.5-inch bbl.). Weight: 52 oz. (with 5.5-inch bbl.). Rib mounted target sights. Blued finish. Checkered walnut thumbrest grips. Standard or military grip configuration. Made from 1972-84 (standard-grip model, 1974-75).

High Standard Derringer

High Standard Double-Nine — Steel Frame

High Standard Durango

High Standard Sierra

NOTE: *High Standard automatic pistols can be found in the preceding section, while revolvers immediately follow this derringer listing.*

DERRINGERS

DERRINGER
Hammerless, double action, two-shot, double bbl. (over/under). Calibers: .22 Short, Long, LR or .22 Magnum Rimfire, 3.5-inch bbls., 5 inches overall. Weight: 11 oz. Standard model has blued or nickel finish w/plastic grips. Presentation model is goldplated in walnut case. Standard model made from 1963 (.22 S-L-LR) and 1964 (.22 MRF) to 1984. Gold model, 1965-83.

(cont'd) **DERRINGER**
Gold Presentation One
Derringer . . . . NiB $688 Ex $550 Gd $374
Silver Presentation One
Derringer . . . . NiB $656 Ex $525 Gd $357
Presentation Set, matched
pair, consecutive numbers
(1965 only) . . . . NiB $1244 Ex $995 Gd $677
Standard model (blue) . . . . NiB $244 Ex $195 Gd $133
Standard model (nickel) . . . . NiB $269 Ex $215 Gd $146
Standard model
(Electroless nickel) . . . . NiB $281 Ex $225 Gd $153
Standard model (blue) . . . . NiB $244 Ex $195 Gd $133

REVOLVERS

NOTE: *Only High Standard revolvers can be found in this section. See the preceding sections for automatic pistols and derringers. For a complete listing of High Standard handguns, please refer to the Index.*

CAMP GUN . . . . NiB $250 Ex $200 Gd $136
Same as Sentinel Mark I/Mark IV except has 6-inch bbl., adj. rear sight, target-style checkered walnut grips. Caliber: .22 LR or .22 WMR. Made 1976-83.

DOUBLE-NINE DA REVOLVER —ALUMINUM FRAME
Western-style version of Sentinel. Blued or nickel finish w/simulated ivory, ebony or stag grips, 5.5-inch bbl., 11 inches overall. Weight: 27.25 oz. Made 1959-71.
Blue model . . . . NiB $210 Ex $165 Gd $95
Nickel model . . . . NiB $220 Ex $175 Gd $103

DOUBLE-NINE—STEEL FRAME
Similar to Double-Nine—Aluminum Frame, w/same general specifications except w/steel frame and has extra cylinder for .22 WMR, walnut grips. Intro. in 1971. disc.
Blue model . . . . NiB $267 Ex $213 Gd $145
Nickel model . . . . NiB $280 Ex $221 Gd $150

DOUBLE-NINE DELUXE . . . . NiB $276 Ex $221 Gd $150
Same as Double-Nine — Steel Frame except has adj. target rear sight. Intro. in 1971. disc.

DURANGO
Similar to Double-Nine—Steel Frame except .22 LR only, available w/4.5- or 5.5-inch bbl. Made 1971-73.
Blue model . . . . NiB $172 Ex $136 Gd $90
Nickel model . . . . NiB $184 Ex $145 Gd $95

HIGH SIERRA DA REVOLVER
Similar to Double-Nine—Steel Frame except has 7-inch octagon bbl., w/gold-plated grip frame, fixed or adj. sights. Made 1973-1983.
W/fixed sights . . . . NiB $335 Ex $268 Gd $182
W/adj. sights . . . . NiB $354 Ex $285 Gd $197

HOMBRE
Similar to Double-Nine—Steel Frame except .22 LR only, lacks single-action type ejector rod and tube, has 4.5-inch bbl. Made 1971-73.
Blue model . . . . NiB $166 Ex $133 Gd $88
Nickel model . . . . NiB $184 Ex $145 Gd $98

KIT GUN DA REVOLVER . . . . NiB $197 Ex $156 Gd $99
Solid frame, swing-out cylinder. Caliber: .22 LR. Nine-shot cylinder, 4-inch bbl., 9 inches overall. Weight: 19 oz. Adj. rear sight, ramp front. Blued finish. Checkered walnut grips. Made 1970-73.

High Standard Longhorn Steel Frame

High Standard Kit Gun

High Standard Sentinel

High Standard Longhorn Aluminum Frame

High Standard Natchez

High Standard Posse

LONGHORN
ALUMINUM FRAME
Similar to Double-Nine—Aluminum Frame except has Longhorn hammer spur, 4.5-, 5.5- or 9.5-inch bbl., Walnut, simulated pearl or simulated stag grips. Blued finish. Made 1960-1971.

W/4.5- or 5.5-inch bbl. . . . . NiB $230 Ex $184 Gd $125
W/9.5-inch bbl . . . . NiB $253 Ex $200 Gd $133

LONGHORN
STEEL FRAME
Similar to Double-Nine — Steel Frame except has 9.5-inch bbl. w/fixed or adj. sights. Made 1971-1983

W/fixed sights . . . . NiB $249 Ex $200 Gd $138
W/adj. sights . . . . NiB $381 Ex $315 Gd $220

NATCHEZ . . . . NiB $240 Ex $195 Gd $138
Similar to Double-Nine — Aluminum Frame except 4.5-inch bbl., 10 inches overall, weight: 25.25 oz., blued finish, simulated ivory bird's-head grips. Made 1961-66.

POSSE . . . . NiB $169 Ex $135 Gd $92
Similar to Double-Nine — Aluminum Frame except 3.5-inch bbl., 9 inches overall, weight: 23.25 oz. Blued finish, brass-grip frame and trigger guard, walnut grips. Made 1961-66.

SENTINEL DA REVOLVER
Solid frame, swing-out cylinder. Caliber: .22 LR. Nine-shot cylinder, 3- 4- or 6-inch bbl. Nine inches overall (with 4-inch-bbl.). Weight: 19 oz. (with 4-inch bbl.). Fixed sights. Aluminum frame. Blued or nickel finish. Checkered grips. Made 1955-56.

Blue model . . . . NiB $141 Ex $113 Gd $77
Blue/green model . . . . NiB $135 Ex $125 Gd $98
Gold model . . . . NiB $310 Ex $280 Gd $160
Nickel model . . . . NiB $150 Ex $135 Gd $85
Pink model . . . . NiB $325 Ex $290 Gd $160

SENTINEL DELUXE
Same as Sentinel except w/4- or 6-inch bbl., wide trigger, drift-adj. rear sight, two-piece square-butt grips. Made 1957-74. Note: Designated Sentinel after 1971.

Blue model . . . . NiB $140 Ex $125 Gd $90
Nickel model . . . . NiB $165 Ex $150 Gd $100

**High Standard
Sentinel I**

**High Standard
Sentinel Mark II**

**High Standard
Sentinel Mark III**

**High Standard
Sentinel Snub**

SENTINEL IMPERIAL
Same as Sentinel except has onyx-black or nickel finish, two-piece checkered walnut grips, ramp front sight. Made 1962-65.
Blue model . . . . NiB $140   Ex $125   Gd $80
Nickel model . . . . NiB $150   Ex $140   Gd $90

SENTINEL 1 DA REVOLVER
Steel frame. Caliber: .22 LR. Nine-shot cylinder, bbl. lengths: 2-, 3-, 4-inch, 6.88 inches overall (with 2-inch bbl.). Weight: 21.5 oz. (2-inch bbl.). Ramp front sight, fixed or adj. rear. Blued or nickel finish. Smooth walnut grips. Made 1974-83.
Blue model . . . . NiB $231   Ex $185   Gd $126
Nickel model . . . . NiB $294   Ex $235   Gd $160
W/adj. sights . . . . NiB $319   Ex $255   Gd $173

SENTINEL MARK II
DA REVOLVER. . . . . NiB $275   Ex $250   Gd $140
Caliber: .357 Magnum. Six-shot cylinder, bbl. lengths: 2.5-, 4-, 6-inch, 9 inches overall w/4-inch bbl., weight: 38 oz. (with 4-inch bbl.). Fixed sights. Blued finish. Walnut service or combat-style grips. Made 1974-76.

SENTINEL MARK III . . . . NiB $306   Ex $245   Gd $167
Same as Sentinel Mark II except has ramp front and adj. rear sights. Weight: 40 oz. (with 4-inch bbl.). Blued finish. Made 1974-76.

SENTINEL MARK IV
Same as Sentinel Mark I except in .22 WMR. Made 1974-83.
Blue model . . . . NiB $281   Ex $225   Gd $153
Nickel model . . . . NiB $306   Ex $245   Gd $167
W/adj. sights . . . . NiB $338   Ex $270   Gd $184

SENTINEL SNUB
Same as Sentinel Deluxe except w/2.75-inch bbl., (7.25 inches overall, weight: 15 oz.), checkered bird's head-type grips. Made 1957-74.
Blued finish . . . . NiB $145   Ex $140   Gd $90
Nickel finish . . . . NiB $155   Ex $150   Gd $100

HIGH STANDARD MFG. CO., INC. —
Houston, Texas
Distributed from Hartford, Connecticut

10X AUTOMATIC PISTOL . . . . NiB $925   Ex $725   Gd $425
Caliber: .22 LR. 10-shot magazine, 5.5-inch bbl., 9.5 inches overall. Weight: 45 oz. Checkered walnut grips. Blued finish. Made from 1994 to date.

OLYMPIC I.S.U. AUTOMATIC PISTOL
Same specifications as the 1958 I.S.U. issue. See listing under previous High Standard Section.
Olympic I.S.U. model . . . . NiB $550   Ex $450   Gd $200
Olympic I.S.U. military model. . . . . NiB $495   Ex $400   Gd $200
Military model . . . . NiB $419   Ex $335   Gd $228

SPORT KING AUTO PISTOL . . . . NiB $325   Ex $260   Gd $177
Caliber: .22 LR. 10-shot magazine, 4.5- or 6.75-inch bbl., 8.5 or 10.75 inches overall. Weight: 44 oz. (with 4.5-inch bbl.), 46 oz. (with 6.75-inch bbl.). Fixed sights, slide mounted. Checkered walnut grips. Parkerized finish. Advertised in 1996 to date. No resale value established.

SUPERMATIC CITATION AUTO PISTOL
Caliber: .22 LR. 10-shot magazine, 5.5- or 7.75-inch bbl., 9.5 or 11.75 inches overall. Weight: 44 oz. (with 5.5-inch bbl.), 46 oz. (with 7.75-inch bbl.). Frame-mounted, micro-adj. rear sight, undercut ramp

(cont'd) SUPERMATIC CITATION AUTO PISTOL
front sight. Blued or Parkerized finish. Made 1994 to date.
Supermatic Citation model . . . . . . NiB $415 Ex $325 Gd $185
.22 Short conversion . . . . NiB $320 Ex $260 Gd $175

CITATION MS AUTO PISTOL . . . . . NiB $628 Ex $550 Gd $300
Similar to the Supermatic Citation except has 10-inch bbl., 14 inches overall. Weight: 49 oz. Made 1994 to date.

SUPERMATIC TOURNAMENT . . . . . NiB $369 Ex $295 Gd $201
Caliber: .22 LR. 10-shot magazine, bbl. lengths: 4.5, 5.5, or 6.75 inches, overall length: 8.5, 9.5 or 10.75 inches. Weight: 43, 44 or 45 oz. depending on bbl. length. Micro-adj. rear sight, undercut ramp front sight. Checkered walnut grips. Parkerized finish. Made 1994 to date.

SUPERMATIC TROPHY
Caliber: .22 LR. 10-shot magazine, 5.5 or 7.25-inch bbl., 9.5 or 11.25 inches overall. Weight: 44 oz. (with 5.5-inch bbl.). Micro-adj. rear sight, undercut ramp front sight. Checkered walnut grips w/thumbrest. Blued or Parkerized finish. Made 1994 to date.
Supermatic Trophy. . . . . NiB $431 Ex $345 Gd $235
.22 Short Conversion. . . . . NiB $320 Ex $260 Gd $175

VICTOR AUTOMATIC
Caliber: .22 LR.10-shot magazine, 4.5- or 5.5-inch ribbed bbl., 8.5 or 9.5 inches overall. Weight: 45 oz. (with 4.5-inch bbl.), 46 oz. (with 5.5-inch bbl.). Micro-adj. rear sight, post front. Checkered walnut grips. Blued or Parkerized finish. Made 1994 to date.
Victor Model . . . . NiB $495 Ex $400 Gd $200
.22 Short conversion . . . . NiB $320 Ex $260 Gd $175

HOPKINS & ALLEN ARMS CO. — Norwich, Connecticut

HOPKINS & ALLEN REVOLVERS
See listings of comparable Harrington & Richardson and Iver Johnson models for values.

INGRAM — Mfd. by Military Armament Corp.

See listings under M.A.C. (Military Armament Corp.)

Note: *Military Armament Corp. ceased production of the select-fire automatic, M10 (9mm & .45 ACP) and M11 (.380 ACP) in 1977. Commercial production resumed on semiautomatic versions under the M.A.C. banner until 1982.*

INTERARMS — Alexandria, Virginia
See also Bersa Pistol.

HELWAN BRIGADIER
AUTO PISTOL . . . . NiB $195 Ex $150 Gd $90
Caliber: 9mm Para. Eight-shot magazine, 4.25-inch bbl., 8 inches overall. Weight: 32 oz. Blade front sight, dovetailed rear. Blued finish. Grooved plastic grips. Imported 1987-95.

VIRGINIAN DRAGOON SA REVOLVER
Calibers: .357 Magnum, .44 Magnum, .45 Colt. Six-shot cylinder. Bbls.: 5- (not available in .44 Magnum), 6-, 7.5-, 8.38-inch (latter only in .44 Magnum w/adj. sights), 11.88 inches overall with (6-inch bbl.). Weight: 48 oz. (with 6-inch bbl.). Fixed sights or micrometer rear and ramp front sights. Blued finish w/color-casetreated frame. Smooth walnut grips. SWISSAFE base pin safety system.

Interarms/Helwan
Brigadier

Interarms Virginian
SA Revolver

(cont'd) VIRGINIAN DRAGOON SA REVOLVER
Manufactured by Interarms Industries Inc., Midland, VA. 1977-84.
Standard Dragoon . . . . NiB $255 Ex $225 Gd $160
Engraved Dragoon . . . . NiB $545 Ex $470 Gd $320
Deputy model . . . . NiB $250 Ex $215 Gd $155
Stainless. . . . . NiB $255 Ex $225 Gd $200

VIRGINIAN REVOLVER
SILHOUETTE MODEL . . . . NiB $365 Ex $220 Gd $215
Same general specifications as regular model except designed in stainless steel w/untapered bull bbl., lengths of 7.5, 8.38 and 10.5 inches. Made 1985-86.

VIRGINIAN SA REVOLVER . . . . NiB $494 Ex $395 Gd $269
Similar to Colt Single-Action Army except has base pin safety system. Imported 1973-76. (See also listing under Hämmerli.)

INTRATEC U.S.A., INC. — Miami, Florida

CATEGORY 9 DAO
SEMIAUTOMATIC . . . . NiB $215 Ex $180 Gd $100
Blowback action w/polymer frame. Caliber: 9mm Para. Eight-shot magazine, 3-inch bbl., 7.7 inches overall. Weight: 18 oz. Textured black polymer grips. Matte black finish. Made 1993 to date.

CATEGORY 40
DAO SEMIAUTOMATIC . . . . NiB $213 Ex $170 Gd $116
Locking-breech action w/polymer frame. Caliber: .40 S&W. Seven-shot magazine, 3.25-inch bbl., 8 inches overall. Weight: 21 oz. Textured black polymer grips. Matte black finish. Made 1994 to date.

CATEGORY 45
DAO SEMIAUTOMATIC . . . . NiB $230 Ex $190 Gd $129
Locking-breech action w/polymer frame. Caliber: .45 ACP. Six-shot magazine, 3.25-inch bbl., 8 inches overall. Weight: 21 oz. Textured black polymer grips. Matte black finish. Made 1994 to date.

Japanese
Model 14 (1925)

Japanese
Model 26 DAO Revolver

MODEL PROTEC .22 DA SEMIAUTOMATIC
Caliber: .25 ACP. 10-shot magazine, 2.5-inch bbl., 5 inches overall. Weight: 14 oz. Wraparound composition grips. Black Teflon, satin grey or Tec-Kote finish. Advertised in 1992.
ProTec .22 standard . . . . NiB $110 Ex $80 Gd $30
ProTec .22 w/satin or Tec-Kote . . . . NiB $115 Ex $85 Gd $35

MODEL PROTEC .25 DA SEMIAUTOMATIC
Caliber: .25 ACP. Eight-shot magazine, 2.5-inch bbl., 5 inches overall. Weight: 14 oz. Fixed sights. Wraparound composition grips. Black Teflon, satin grey or Tec-Kote finish. Made 1991 to date. Note: Formerly Model Tec-.25.
ProTec .25 standard. . . . . NiB $88 Ex $70 Gd $48
ProTec .25 w/satin or Tec-Kote . . . . NiB $94 Ex $75 Gd $51

MODEL TEC-9 SEMIAUTOMATIC
Caliber: 9mm Para. 20- or 36-round magazine, 5-inch bbl., weight: 50-51 oz. Open fixed front sight, adj. rear. Military nonglare blued or stainless finish.
Tec-9 w/blued finish . . . . NiB $245 Ex $195 Gd $132
Tec-9 w/nickel finish. . . . . NiB $244 Ex $195 Gd $133
Tec 9S w/stainless finish . . . . NiB $325 Ex $260 Gd $175

MODEL TEC-9M SEMIAUTOMATIC
Same specifications as Model Tec-9 except has 3-inch bbl. without shroud and 20-round magazine, blued or stainless finish.
Tec-9M w/blued finish. . . . . NiB $219 Ex $175 Gd $119
Tec-9MS w/stainless finish. . . . . NiB $294 Ex $235 Gd $160

MODEL TEC-22T SEMIAUTOMATIC
Caliber: .22 LR. 10/.22-type 30-shot magazine, 4-inch bbl., 11.19 inches overall. Weight: 30 oz. Protected post front sight, adj. rear sight. Matte black or Tec-Kote finish. Made 1989 to date.

(cont'd) MODEL TEC-22T SEMIAUTOMATIC
Tec-22T standard. . . . . NiB $160 Ex $130 Gd $90
Tec-22TK Tec-Kote. . . . . NiB $194 Ex $155 Gd $105

MODEL TEC
DOUBLE DERRINGER. . . . . NiB $113 Ex $90 Gd $61
Calibers: .22 WRF, .32 H&R Mag., .38 Special. Two-shot capacity, 3-inch bbl., 4.63 inches overall. Weight: 13 oz. Fixed sights. Matte black finish. Made 1986-88.

ISRAEL ARMS — Kfar Sabs, Israel
Imported by Israel Arms International, Houston TX

MODEL BUL-M5 LOCKED
BREECH (2000) AUTO PISTOL . . . . NiB $395 Ex $265 Gd $230
Similar to the M1911 U.S. Government model. Caliber: .45 ACP. Seven-shot magazine, 5-inch bbl., 8.5 inches overall. Weight: 38 oz. Blade front and fixed, low-profile rear sights.

KAREEN MK II (1500) AUTO PISTOL
Single-action only. Caliber: 9mm Para. 10-shot magazine, 4.75-inch bbl., 8 inches overall. Weight: 33.6 oz. Blade front sight, rear adjustable for windage. Textured black composition or rubberized grips. Blued, two-tone, matte black finish. Imported 1996 to date.
Blued or matte black finish . . . . NiB $395 Ex $305 Gd $215
Two-tone finish . . . . NiB $595 Ex $460 Gd $331
Meprolite sights, add. $40

KAREEN MK II COMPACT
(1501) AUTO PISTOL . . . . NiB $385 Ex $320 Gd $225
Similar to standard Kareen MKII except w/3.85-inch bbl., 7.1 inches overall. Weight: 32 oz. Imported 1997 to date.

GOLAN MODEL (2500) AUTO PISTOL
Single or double action. Caliber: 9mm Para., .40 S&W. 10-shot magazine, 3.85-inch bbl., 7.1 inches overall. Weight: 34 oz. Steel slide and alloy frame w/ambidextrous safety and decocking lever. Matte black finish. Imported 1997 to date.
9mm Para. NiB $813 Ex $650 Gd $442
.40 S&W . . . . NiB $656 Ex $525 Gd $357

GAL MODEL
(5000) AUTO PISTOL . . . . NiB $344 Ex $275 Gd $187
Caliber: .45 ACP. Eight-shot magazine, 4.25-inch bbl., 7.25 inches overall. Weight: 42 oz. Low profile 3-dot sights. Combat-style black rubber grips. Imported 1997 to date.

JAPANESE MILITARY PISTOLS — Tokyo, Japan
Manufactured by Government Plant

MODEL 14 (1925)
AUTOMATIC PISTOL . . . . NiB $619 Ex $495 Gd $337
Modification of the Nambu Model 1914, changes chiefly intended to simplify mass production. Standard round trigger guard or oversized guard for use w/gloves. Caliber: 8mm Nambu. Eight-shot magazine, 4.75-inch bbl., 9 inches overall. Weight: About 29 oz. Fixed sights. Blued finish. Grooved wood grips. Intro. 1925 and mfd. through WW II.

MODEL 26 DAO REVOLVER. . . . . . NiB $550 Ex $370 Gd $241
Top-break frame. Caliber: 9mm. Six-shot cylinder w/automatic extractor/ejector, 4.7-inch bbl., adopted by the Japanese Army from 1893 to 1914, replaced by the Model 14 Automatic Pistol but remained in service through World War II.

MODEL 94 (1934)
AUTOMATIC PISTOL . . . . **NiB $270 Ex $200 Gd $125**
Poorly designed and constructed, this pistol is unsafe and can be fired merely by applying pressure on the sear, which is exposed on the left side. Caliber: 8mm Nambu. Six-shot magazine, 3.13-inch bbl., 7.13 inches overall. Weight: About 27 oz. Fixed sights. Blued finish. Hard rubber or wood grips. Intro. in 1934, principally for export to Latin American countries, production continued thru WW II.

NAMBU MODEL
1914 AUTOMATIC PISTOL . . . . . **NiB $1600 Ex $1400 Gd $680**
Original Japanese service pistol, resembles Luger in appearance and Glisenti in operation. Caliber: 8mm Nambu. Seven-shot magazine, 4.5-inch bbl., 9 inches overall. Weight: About 30 oz. Fixed front sight, adj. rear sight. Blued finish. Checkered wood grips. Made 1914-1925.

Japanese Model 94 (1934)

Jennings Model J Auto Pistol

Iver Johnson Enforcer

JENNINGS FIREARMS INC. — Currently Mfd. by Bryco Arms, Irvine, California
Previously by Calwestco, Inc. & B.L. Jennings
See additional listings under Bryco Arms.

MODEL J AUTO PISTOL
Calibers: .22 LR, .25 ACP. Six-shot magazine, 2.5-inch bbl., about 5 inches overall. Weight: 13 oz. Fixed sights. Chrome, satin nickel or black Teflon finish. Walnut, grooved black Cycolac or resin-impregnated wood grips. Made from 1981-85 under Jennings and Calwestco logos; from 1985 to date by Bryco Arms.
Model J-22. . . . . **NiB $70 Ex $55 Gd $35**
Model J-25. . . . . **NiB $65 Ex $50 Gd $30**

IVER JOHNSON ARMS, INC. — Jacksonville, Arkansas
Operation of this company dates back to 1871, when Iver Johnson and Martin Bye partnered to manufacture metallic cartridge revolvers. Johnson became the sole owner and changed the name to Iver Johnson's Arms & Cycle Works, which it was known as for almost 100 years. Modern management shortened the name, and after several owner changes the firm was moved from Massachusetts, its original base, to Jacksonville, Arkansas. In 1987, the American Military Arms Corporation (AMAC) acquired the operation, which subsequently ceased in 1993.

NOTE: *For ease in finding a particular firearm, Iver Johnson handguns are divided into two sections: Automatic Pistols (below) and Revolvers, which follow. For the complete handgun listing, please refer to the Index.*

AUTOMATIC PISTOLS

9MM DA AUTOMATIC . . . . **NiB $369 Ex $295 Gd $201**
Caliber: 9mm. Six-round magazine, 3-inch bbl., 6.5 inches overall. Weight: 26 oz. Blade front sight, adj. rear. Smooth hardwood grip. Blued or matte blued finish. Intro. 1986.

COMPACT .25 ACP . . . . **NiB $165 Ex $135 Gd $85**
Bernardelli V/P design. Caliber: .25 ACP. Five-shot magazine, 2.13-inch bbl., 4.13 inches overall. Weight: 9.3 oz. Fixed sights. Checkered composition grips. Blued slide, matte blued frame and color-casehardened trigger. Made 1991 to 93.

ENFORCER . . . . **NiB $450 Ex $345 Gd $239**
Semiautomatic. Caliber: .30 U.S. Carbine. Five-, 15-, or 30-round magazine, 9.5- inch bbl., weight: 5.5 lbs. Adj. sights. Walnut stock. Made mid-1980s to 1993.

PP30 SUPER
ENFORCER AUTOMATIC . . . . **NiB $420 Ex $330 Gd $200**
Caliber: .30 U.S. Carbine. Fifteen- or 30-shot magazine, 9.5-inch bbl., 17 inches overall. Weight: 4 pounds. Adj. peep rear sight, blade front. American walnut stock. Made 1984-86.

PONY AUTOMATIC PISTOL
Caliber: .380 Auto. Six-shot magazine, 3.1-inch bbl., 6.1 inches overall. Blue, matte blue, nickel finish or stainless. Weight: 20 oz. Wooden grips. Smallest of the locked breech automatics. Made 1982-88. Reintroduced 1990-93.
Blue or matte
blue model . . . . **NiB $300 Ex $250 Gd $169**
Nickel model . . . . **NiB $350 Ex $260 Gd $170**
Deluxe model . . . . **NiB $375 Ex $300 Gd $210**

Iver Johnson
Model TP

Iver Johnson
Model 55 Target

Iver Johnson
Model 55-S

Iver Johnson
Model 56 Blank Revolver

Iver Johnson
Model 57A Target

MODEL TP-22 DA
AUTOMATIC . . . . NiB $140 Ex $100 Gd $60
Calibers: .22 LR, Seven-shot magazine, 2.85-inch bbl., 5.39 inches
overall. Blued finish. Weight: 14.46 oz. Made 1982-93.

MODEL TP25 DA
POCKET PISTOL . . . . NiB $175 Ex $140 Gd $95
Double-action automatic. Caliber: .25 ACP. Seven-shot magazine,
3-inch bbl., 5.5 inches overall. Weight: 12 oz. Black plastic grips
and blued finish. Made 1982-93.

TRAILSMAN
AUTOMATIC PISTOL
Caliber: .22 LR. 10-shot magazine, 4.5 or 6-inch bbl., 8.75 inches
overall (with 4.5-inch bbl.). Weight: 46 oz. Fixed target-type sights.
Checkered composition grips. Made 1984-90.
Standard model . . . . NiB $206 Ex $165 Gd $112
Deluxe model . . . . NiB $244 Ex $195 Gd $133

REVOLVERS

MODEL 55 TARGET DA REVOLVER . . . . NiB $130 Ex $100 Gd $60
Solid frame. Caliber: .22 LR. Eight-shot cylinder, bbl. lengths: 4.5-,
6-inches. 10.75 inches overall (with 6-inch bbl.). Weight: 30.5 oz.
(with 6-inch bbl.). Fixed sights. Blued finish. Walnut grips. Note:
Original model designation was 55; changed to 55A when loading
gate was added in 1961. Made 1955-77.

MODEL 55-S REVOLVER . . . . NiB $140 Ex $100 Gd $60
Same general specifications as the Model 55 except for 2.5-inch
bbl. and small, molded pocket-size grip.

MODEL 56
BLANK REVOLVER . . . . NiB $81 Ex $65 Gd $44
Solid frame. Caliber: .22 blanks only. Eight-shot cylinder, 2.5-inch
solid bbl., 6.75 inches overall. Weight: 10 oz.

MODEL 57A
TARGET DA REVOLVER . . . . NiB $110 Ex $95 Gd $60
Solid frame. Caliber: .22 LR. Eight-shot cylinder, bbl. lengths: 4.5-,
and 6-inches. 10.75 inches overall. Weight: 30.5 oz. with 6-inch
bbl. Adj. sights. Blued finish. Walnut grips. Note: Original model
designation was 57, changed to 57A when loading gate was added
in 1961. Made 1956-75.

MODEL 66 TRAILSMAN
DA REVOLVER . . . . NiB $100 Ex $70 Gd $50
Hinged frame. Rebounding hammer. Caliber: .22 LR. Eight-shot
cylinder, 6-inch bbl., 11 inches overall. Weight: 34 oz. Adj. sights.
Blued finish. Walnut grips. Made 1958-75.

**Iver Johnson
Model 66 Trailsman**

**Iver Johnson
Model 67 Viking**

**Iver Johnson
Model 67S Viking Snub**

**Iver Johnson
Model 1900 Target**

**Iver Johnson
Cadet**

MODEL 67 VIKING DA REVOLVER . . . . NiB $138 Ex $110 Gd $75
Hinged frame. Caliber: .22 LR. Eight-shot cylinder, bbl. lengths: 4.5-
and 6-inches, 11 inches overall (with 6-inch bbl.). Weight: 34 oz.
(with 6-inch bbl.). Adj. sights. Walnut grips w/thumbrest. Made
1964-75.

**MODEL 67S VIKING
SNUB REVOLVER . . . . NiB $140 Ex $100 Gd $60**
DA. Hinged frame. Calibers: .22 LR, .32 S&W Short and Long, .38
S&W. Eight-shot cylinder in .22, 5-shot in .32 and .38 calibers; 2.75-
inch bbl. Weight: 25 oz. Adj. sights. Tenite grips. Made 1964-75.

MODEL 1900 DA REVOLVER . . . . . . NiB $120 Ex $100 Gd $55
Solid frame. Calibers: .22 LR, .32 S&W, .32 S&W Long, .38 S&W.
Seven-shot cylinder (.22 cal.), 6-shot (.32 S&W), 5-shot (.32 S&W
Long, .38 S&W); bbl. lengths: 2.5-, 4.5- and 6-inches. Weight: 12
oz. (in .32 S&W w/2.5-inch bbl.). Fixed sights. Blued or nickel fin-
ish. Hard rubber grips. Made 1900-47.

**MODEL 1900
TARGET DA REVOLVER. . . . . NiB $170 Ex $135 Gd $90**
Solid frame. Caliber: .22 LR. Seven-shot cylinder, bbl. lengths: 6-
and 9.5-inches. Fixed sights. Blued finish. Checkered walnut grips.
(This earlier model does not have counterbored chambers as in the
Target Sealed 8. Made 1925-42.)

AMERICAN BULLDOG DA REVOLVER
Solid frame. Calibers: .22 LR, .22 WMR, .38 Special. Six-shot cylinder in .22, 5-shot in .38. Bbl. lengths: 2.5-, 4-inch. 9 inches overall
(with 4-inch bbl.). Weight: 30 oz. (with 4-inch bbl.). Adj. sights.
Blued or nickel finish. Plastic grips. Made 1974-76.
.38 Special. NiB $160 Ex $130 Gd $80
Other calibers . . . . NiB $140 Ex $100 Gd $60

ARMSWORTH MODEL 855 SA. . . . NiB $225 Ex $160 Gd $115
Hinged frame. Caliber: .22 LR. Eight-shot cylinder, 6-inch bbl.,
10.75 inches overall. Weight: 30 oz. Adj. sights. Blued finish.
Checkered walnut one-piece grip. Adj. finger rest. Made 1955-57.

CADET DA REVOLVER . . . . NiB $138 Ex $115 Gd $65
Solid frame. Calibers: .22 LR, .22 WMR, .32 S&W Long, .38 S&W, .38
Special. Six- or 8-shot cylinder in .22, 5-shot in other calibers, 2.5-inch
bbl., 7 inches overall. Weight: 22 oz. Fixed sights. Blued finish or nickel finish. Plastic grips. Note: Loading gate added in 1961, .22 cylinder
capacity changed from 8 to 6 rounds in 1975. Made 1955-77.

CATTLEMAN SA REVOLVER
Patterned after the Colt Army SA revolver. Calibers: .357 Magnum, .44
Magnum, .45 Colt. Six-shot cylinder. Bbl. lengths: 4.75-, 5.5- (not avail-
able in .44), 6- (.44 only), 7.25-inch. Weight: About 41 oz. Fixed sights.
Blued bbl., and cylinder color-casehardened frame, brass grip frame.
One-piece walnut grip. Made by Aldo Uberti, Brescia, Italy, 1973-78.
.44 Magnum . . . . NiB $250 Ex $200 Gd $125
Other calibers . . . . NiB $220 Ex $179 Gd $110

Iver Johnson
Cattleman

Iver Johnson
Champion .22 Target

Iver Johnson
Sealed 8

Iver Johnson
Rookie

Iver Johnson
Safety Hammer

CATTLEMAN BUCKHORN
SA REVOLVER
Same as standard Cattleman except has adj. rear and ramp front sights. Bbl. lengths: 4.75- (.44 only), 5.75- (not available in .44), 6- (.44 only), 7.5- or 12-inches bbl., weight: About 44 oz. Made 1973-78.

.357 Magnum or .45
Colt w/12-inch bbl.............. NiB $300 Ex $220 Gd $150
.357 Magnum or .45
Colt w/5.75- or 7.5-inch bbl. ..... NiB $250 Ex $195 Gd $130
.44 Magnum, w/12-inch bbl....... NiB $375 Ex $300 Gd $204
.44 Magnum, other bbls......... NiB $300 Ex $250 Gd $160

CATTLEMAN BUNTLINE SA REVOLVER
Same as Cattleman Buckhorn except has 18-inch bbl., walnut shoulder stock w/brass fittings. Weight: About 56 oz. Made 1973-78.
.44 Magnum .... NiB $481 Ex $385 Gd $262
Other calibers .... NiB $431 Ex $345 Gd $235

CATTLEMAN TRAIL BLAZER ...... NiB $190 Ex $150 Gd $100
Similar to Cattleman Buckhorn except .22 caliber has interchangeable .22 LR and .22 WMR cylinders, 5.5- or 6.5-inch bbl., weight: About 40 oz. Made 1973-78.

CHAMPION
.22 TARGET SA .... NiB $231 Ex $185 Gd $126
Hinged frame. Caliber: .22 LR. Eight-shot cylinder. Single action. Counterbored chambers as in Sealed 8 model, 6-inch bbl., 10.75 inches overall. Weight: 28 oz. Adj. target sights. Blued finish. Checkered walnut grips, adj. finger rest. Made 1938-48.

DELUXE TARGET .... NiB $230 Ex $185 Gd $135
Same as Sportsman except has adj. sights. Made 1975-76.

PROTECTOR SEALED
8 DA REVOLVER .... NiB $175 Ex $125 Gd $89
Hinged frame. Caliber: .22 LR. Eight-shot cylinder, 2.5-inch bbl., 7.25 inches overall. Weight: 20 oz. Fixed sights. Blued finish. Checkered walnut grips. Made 1933-49.

ROOKIE
DA REVOLVER................... NiB $100 Ex $80 Gd $60
Solid frame. Caliber: .38 Special. Five-shot cylinder, 4-inch bbl., 9-inches overall. Weight: 30 oz. Fixed sights. Blued or nickel finish. Plastic grips. Made 1975-77.

SAFETY HAMMER
DA REVOLVER.................. NiB $140 Ex $110 Gd $70
Hinged frame. Calibers: .22 LR, .32 S&W, .32 S&W Long, .38 S&W. Seven-shot cylinder (.22 cal.), 6-shot (.32 S&W Long), 5-shot (.32 S&W, .38 S&W). bbl. lengths: 2, 3, 3.25, 4, 5 or 6 inches. Weight w/4-inch bbl.: 15 oz. (.22, .32 S&W), 19.5 oz. (.32 S&W Long) or 19 oz. (.38 S&W). Fixed sights. Blued or nickel finish. Hard rubber, round butt grips or square butt, rubber or walnut grips available. Note: .32 S&W Long and .38 S&W models built on heavy frame. Made 1892-1950.

SAFETY HAMMERLESS
DA REVOLVER.................. NiB $150 Ex $120 Gd $75
Similar to the Safety Hammer Model except w/shrouded hammerless frame. Made 1895-1950.

SIDEWINDER
DA REVOLVER.................. NiB $140 Ex $125 Gd $70
Solid frame. Caliber: .22 LR. Six- or 8-shot cylinder, bbl. lengths: 4.75, 6 inches; 11.25 inches overall (with 6-inch bbl.). Weight: 31 oz. (with 6-inch bbl.). Fixed sights. Blued or nickel finish w/plastic staghorn grips or color-casehardened frame w/walnut grips. Note: Cylinder capacity changed from 8 to 6 rounds in 1975. Intro. 1961. disc.

SIDEWINDER "S" .... NiB $150 Ex $125 Gd $85
Same as Sidewinder except has interchangeable cylinders in .22 LR and .22 WMR, adj. sights. Intro. 1974. disc.

SPORTSMAN
DA REVOLVER.................. NiB $129 Ex $100 Gd $70
Solid frame. Caliber: .22 LR. Six-shot cylinder. Bbl. lengths: 4.75-, 6-inches, 10.75 inches overall (with 6-inch bbl.). Weight: 30.5 oz. (with 6-inch bbl.). Fixed sights. Blued finish. Plastic grips. Made 1974-76.

SUPERSHOT 9-SHOT
DA REVOLVER.................. NiB $145 Ex $120 Gd $65
Same as Supershot Sealed 8 except has nine non-counterbored chambers. Made 1929-49.

SUPERSHOT .22 DA REVOLVER ...... NiB $99 Ex $80 Gd $50
Hinged frame. Caliber: .22 LR. Seven-shot cylinder, 6-inch bbl. Fixed sights. Blued finish. Checkered walnut grips. This earlier model does not have counterbored chambers as in the Supershot Sealed 8. Made 1929-49.

SUPERSHOT MODEL 844 DA...... NiB $175 Ex $135 Gd $89
Hinged frame. Caliber: .22 LR. Eight-shot cylinder, bbl. lengths: 4.5- or 6-inch, 9.25 inches overall (with 4.5-inch bbl.). Weight: 27 oz. (4.5-inch bbl.). Adj. sights. Blued finish. Checkered walnut one-piece grip. Made 1955-56.

SUPERSHOT SEALED
8 DA REVOLVER .... NiB $175 Ex $135 Gd $90
Hinged frame. Caliber: .22 LR. Eight-shot cylinder, 6-inch bbl., 10.75 inches overall. Weight: 24 oz. Adj. target sights. Blued finish. Checkered walnut grips. Postwar model does not have adj. finger rest as earlier version. Made 1931-57.

SWING-OUT DA REVOLVER
Calibers: .22 LR, .22 WMR, .32 S&W Long, .38 Special. Six-shot cylinder in .22, 5-shot in .32 and .38, 2-, 3-, 4-inch plain bbl., or 4-6-inch vent rib bbl., 8.75 inches overall (with 4-inch bbl.). Fixed or adj. sights. Blued or nickel finish. Walnut grips. Made in 1977.
W/plain barrel, fixed sights........ NiB $150 Ex $120 Gd $80
W/vent rib, adj. sights........... NiB $140 Ex $170 Gd $100

TARGET 9-SHOT DA REVOLVER .... NiB $181 Ex $145 Gd $99
Same as Target Sealed 8 except has nine non-counterbored chambers. Made 1929-46.

TARGET SEALED 8 DA REVOLVER .... NiB $170 Ex $130 Gd $95
Solid frame. Caliber: .22 LR. Eight-shot cylinder, bbl. lengths: 6- and 10-inches. 10.75 inches overall (with 6-inch bbl.). Weight: 24 oz. (with 6-inch bbl.). Fixed sights. Blued finish. Checkered walnut grips. Made 1931-57.

TRIGGER-COCKING SA TARGET .... NiB $235 Ex $185 Gd $130
Hinged frame. First pull on trigger cocks hammer, second pull releases hammer. Caliber: .22 LR. Eight-shot cylinder, counterbored chambers, 6-inch bbl., 10.75 inches overall. Weight: 24 oz. Adj. target sights. Blued finish. Checkered walnut grips. Made 1940-47.

Iver Johnson
Sidewinder

Iver Johnson
Supershot Sealed 8

Iver Johnson Target Sealed 8

Kahr Model K9

KAHR ARMS — Blauvelt, New York
MODEL K9
DAO AUTO PISTOL
Caliber: 9mm Para. Seven-shot magazine, 3.5-inch bbl., 6 inches overall. Weight: 24 oz. Fixed sights. Matte black, electroless nickel, Birdsong Black-T or matte stainless finish. Wraparound textured polymer or hardwood grips. Made 1994 to date.
Duo-Tone finish................ NiB $669 Ex $535 Gd $364
Matte black finish .... NiB $550 Ex $425 Gd $290
Electroless nickel finish .... NiB $575 Ex $460 Gd $313
Black-T finish................. NiB $785 Ex $575 Gd $420
Matte stainless finish............ NiB $531 Ex $425 Gd $289
Lady K9 model................. NiB $513 Ex $410 Gd $279
Elite model .... NiB $544 Ex $435 Gd $296
Tritium Night Sights, add............................ $90

Kel-Tec Model P-11

Kimber Model Classic .45

MODEL K40 DAO AUTO PISTOL
Similar to Model K9 except chambered .40 S&W w/5- or 6-shot magazine, Weight: 26 oz. Made 1997 to date.
Matte black finish . . . . NiB $506 Ex $405 Gd $275
Electroless nickel finish . . . . NiB $604 Ex $485 Gd $333
Black-T finish. . . . . NiB $639 Ex $505 Gd $334
Matte stainless finish . . . . NiB $531 Ex $420 Gd $278
Covert model
(shorter grip-frame) . . . . NiB $501 Ex $395 Gd $259
Elite model . . . . NiB $574 Ex $465 Gd $326
Tritium Night Sights, add. $90

MODEL MK9 DAO AUTO PISTOL
Similar to Model K9 except w/Micro-Compact frame. Six- or 7- shot magazine, 3- inch bbl., 5.5 inches overall. Weight: 22 oz. Stainless or Duo-Tone finish. Made 1998 to date.
Duo-Tone finish. . . . . NiB $689 Ex $555 Gd $384
Matte stainless
finish . . . . NiB $574 Ex $465 Gd $316
Elite model . . . . NiB $576 Ex $465 Gd $316
Tritium Night
Sights, add. $90

KBI, INC — Harrisburg, Pennsylvania

MODEL PSP-.25 AUTO PISTOL. . . . NiB $230 Ex $175 Gd $110
Caliber: .25 ACP. Six-shot magazine, 2.13-inch bbl., 4.13 inches overall. Weight: 9.5 oz. All-steel construction w/dual safety system. Made 1994 to date.

KEL-TEC CNC INDUSTRIES, INC. — Cocoa, Florida
MODEL P-11 DAO PISTOL
Caliber: 9mm Parabellum or .40 S&W. 10-shot magazine, 3.1- inch bbl., 5.6 inches overall. Weight: 14 oz. Blade front sight, drift adjustable rear. Aluminum frame w/steel slide. Checkered black, gray, or green polymer grips. Matte blue, nickel, stainless steel or Parkerized finish. Made 1995 to date.
9mm . . . . NiB $264 Ex $215 Gd $153
.40 S&W . . . . NiB $266 Ex $210 Gd $138
Parkerized finish, add $40
Nickel finish, add (disc. 1995). $30
Stainless finish, add
(1996 to date) $55
Tritium Night Sights, add. $80
.40 cal. conversion kit, add $175

KIMBER MANUFACTURING, INC. — Yonkers, New York (Formerly Kimber of America, Inc.)
MODEL CLASSIC .45
Similar to Government 1911 built on steel, polymer or alloy full-size or compact frame. Caliber: .45 ACP. Seven-, 8-, 10- or 14-shot magazine, 4- or 5-inch bbl., 7.7 or 8.75 inches overall. Weight: 28 oz. (Compact LW), 34 oz. (Compact or Polymer) or .38 oz. (Custom FS). McCormick low-profile combat or Kimber adj. target sights. Blued, matte black oxide or stainless finish. Checkered custom wood or black synthetic grips. Made from 1994 to date.
Custom (matte black) . . . . NiB $600 Ex $500 Gd $315
Custom Royal (polished blue) . . . . . NiB $656 Ex $525 Gd $357
Custom stainless (satin stainless). . . NiB $619 Ex $495 Gd $337
Custom Target (matte black) . . . . . . NiB $631 Ex $505 Gd $343
Target Gold Match
(polished blue). . . . . NiB $869 Ex $695 Gd $473
Target stainless Match
(polished stainless) . . . . NiB $699 Ex $795 Gd $540
Polymer (matte black) . . . . NiB $706 Ex $565 Gd $384
Polymer Stainless
(satin stainless slide) . . . . NiB $850 Ex $675 Gd $462
Polymer Target
(matte black slide). . . . . NiB $794 Ex $635 Gd $432
Compact (matte black) . . . . NiB $556 Ex $445 Gd $303
Compact stainless (satin stainless) . . . . NiB $619 Ex $495 Gd $337
Compact LW (matte
black w/alloy frame) . . . . NiB $639 Ex $480 Gd $330

KORTH PISTOLS — Ratzeburg, Germany
Currently imported by Keng's Firearms Specialty, Inc. Previously by Beeman Precision Arms; Osborne's and Mandall Shooting Supply
REVOLVERS COMBAT, SPORT, TARGET
Calibers: .357 Mag. and .22 LR w/interchangeable combination cylinders of .357 Mag./9mm Para. or .22 LR/.22 WMR also .22 Jet, .32 S&W and .32 H&R Mag. Bbls: 2.5-, 3-, 4-inch (combat) and 5.25- or 6-inch (target). Weight: 33 to 42 oz. Blued, stainless, matte silver or polished silver finish. Checkered walnut grips. Imported 1967 to date.
Standard rimfire model . . . . NiB $3150 Ex $2490 Gd $1650
Standard centerfire model. . . . . NiB $3195 Ex $2495 Gd $1690
ISU Match Target model . . . . . . NiB $3900 Ex $3160 Gd $2090
Custom stainless finish, add. $450
Matte silver finish, add $650
Polished silver finish, add $950

SEMIAUTOMATIC PISTOL

Calibers: 30 Luger, 9mm Para., .357 SIG, .40 S&W, 9x21mm. 10- or 14-shot magazine, 4- or 5-inch bbl., all-steel construction, recoil-operated. Ramp front sight, adj. rear. Blued, stainless, matte silver or polished silver finish. Checkered walnut grips. Imported 1988 to date.

Standard model	NiB $4744	Ex $3795	Gd $2581
Matte silver finish, add			$650
Polished silver finish, add			$950

Lahti Automatic Pistol

LAHTI PISTOLS — Mfd. by Husqvarna Vapenfabriks A. B. Huskvarna, Sweden, and Valtion Kivaar Tedhas ("VKT") Jyväskyla, Finland

AUTOMATIC PISTOL

Caliber: 9mm Para. Eight-shot magazine, 4.75-inch bbl., weight: About 46 oz. Fixed sights. Blued finish. Plastic grips. Specifications given are those of the Swedish Model 40 but also apply in general to the Finnish Model L-35, which differs only slightly. A considerable number of Swedish Lahti pistols were imported and sold in the U.S. The Finnish model, somewhat better made, is rare. Finnish Model L-35 adopted 1935. Swedish Model 40 adopted 1940 and mfd. through 1944.

Finnish L-35 model	NiB $2300	Ex $1790	Gd $1185
Swedish 40 model	NiB $460	Ex $340	Gd $200

L.A.R. MANUFACTURING, INC. — West Jordan, Utah

MARK I GRIZZLY WIN. MAG. AUTOMATIC PISTOL

Calibers: .357 Mag., .45 ACP, .45 Win. Mag. Seven-shot magazine, 6.5-inch bbl., 10.5 inches overall. Weight: 48 oz. Fully adj. sights. Checkered rubber combat-style grips. Blued finish. Made from 1983 to date. 8- or 10-inch bbl., Made 1987-99.

.357 Mag. (6.5 inch barrel)	NiB $1073	Ex $840	Gd $610
.45 Win. Mag.(6.5 inch barrel)	NiB $925	Ex $750	Gd $500
8-inch barrel	NiB $1200	Ex $1000	Gd $725
10-inch barrel	NiB $1275	Ex $1025	Gd $705

L.A.R. Mark I Grizzly

MARK IV GRIZZLY

AUTOMATIC PISTOL	NiB $1005	Ex $825	Gd $550

Same general specifications as the L.A.R. Mark I except chambered for .44 Magnum, has 5.5- or 6.5-inch bbl., beavertail grip safety, matte blued finish. Made 1991-99.

MARK V AUTO PISTOL	NiB $900	Ex $700	Gd $500

Similar to the Mark I except chambered in 50 Action Express. Six-shot magazine, 5.4- or 6.5-inch bbl., 10.6 inches overall (with 5.4-inch bbl.). Weight: 56 oz. Checkered walnut grips. Made 1993-99.

Laseraim Series I

LASERAIM TECHNOLOGIES INC. Little Rock, Arkansas

SERIES I SA AUTO PISTOL

Calibers: .40 S&W, .45 ACP, 10mm. Seven or 8- shot magazine, 3.875- or 5.5-inch dual-port compensated bbl., 8.75 or 10.5 inches overall. Weight: 46 or 52 oz. Fixed sights w/Laseraim or adjustable Millet sights. Textured black composition grips. Extended slide release, ambidextrous safety and beveled magazine well. Stainless or matte black Teflon finish. Made 1993 to date.

Series I w/adjustable sights	NiB $400	Ex $300	Gd $200
Series I w/fixed sights	NiB $350	Ex $270	Gd $190
Series I w/fixed sights (HotDot)	NiB $500	Ex $400	Gd $270
Series I Dream Team (RedDot)	NiB $740	Ex $590	Gd $390
Series I Illusion (Laseraim)	NiB $800	Ex $610	Gd $400

Laseraim Velocity 400 Series w/Laser Sight

**Laseraim Series III
w/LA93 Illusion III Scope**

**Llama Model IIIA
Deluxe Chrome Engraved First Issue**

**Llama Model IIIA
Deluxe Blue Engraved Second Issue**

SERIES II SA AUTO PISTOL
Similar to Series I except w/stainless finish and no bbl., compensator. Made 1993-96.

Series II w/adjustable sights ...... NiB $344 Ex $275 Gd $187
Series II w/fixed sights. .... NiB $313 Ex $250 Gd $170
Series II Dream Team. .... NiB $619 Ex $495 Gd $337
Series II Illusion. .... NiB $656 Ex $525 Gd $357

SERIES III SA AUTO PISTOL
Similar to Series II except w/serrated slide and 5-inch compensated bbl., only. Made 1994 to date.
**Series III w/
adjustable sights** .... NiB $544 Ex $435 Gd $296
Series III w/fixed sights .... NiB $494 Ex $395 Gd $269

VELOCITY SERIES SA AUTO PISTOL
Similar to Series I except chambered for .357 Sig. or .400 Cor-Bon, 3.875-inch unported bbl., (compact) or 5.5-inch dual-port compensated bbl. Made 1997 to date. See illustration previous page.
Compact model (unported) ...... NiB $344 Ex $275 Gd $187
Government model (ported) ...... NiB $406 Ex $325 Gd $221
**W/wireless laser
(HotDot), add** $150

LIGNOSE PISTOLS — Suhl, Germany
Aktien-Gesellschaft "Lignose" Abteilung

The following Lignose pistols were manufactured from 1920 to the mid-1930s. They were also marketed under the Bergmann name.

EINHAND MODEL 2A
POCKET AUTO PISTOL .... NiB $300 Ex $270 Gd $100
As the name implies, this pistol is designed for one-hand operation, pressure on a "trigger" at the front of the guard retracts the slide. Caliber: .25 Auto. (6.35 mm). Six-shot magazine, 2-inch bbl., 4.75 inches overall. Weight: About 14 oz. Blued finish. Hard rubber grips.

MODEL 2 POCKET
AUTO PISTOL .... NiB $330 Ex $250 Gd $180
Conventional Browning type. Same general specifications as Einhand Model 2A but lacks the one-hand operation.

EINHAND MODEL
3A POCKET AUTO PISTOL .... NiB $390 Ex $300 Gd $205
Same as the Model 2A except has longer grip, 9-shot magazine, weight: About 16 oz.

LLAMA HANDGUNS — Mfd. by Gabilondo y Cia, Vitoria, Spain (Imported by S.G.S., Wanamassa, New Jersey)

NOTE: *For ease in finding a particular Llama handgun, the listings are divided into two groupings: Automatic Pistols (below) and Revolvers, which follow. For a complete listing of Llama handguns, please refer to the Index.*

AUTOMATIC PISTOLS

MODEL IIIA
AUTOMATIC PISTOL .... NiB $210 Ex $185 Gd $130
Caliber: .380 Auto. Seven-shot magazine, 3.69-inch bbl., 6.5 inches overall. Weight: 23 oz. Adj. target sights. Blued finish. Plastic grips. Intro. 1951. disc.

MODELS IIIA, XA, XV DELUXE
Same as standard Model IIIA, XA and XV except engraved w/blued or chrome finish and simulated pearl grips. Disc. 1984.
Chrome-engraved finish. . . . . NiB $313 Ex $250 Gd $170
Blue-engraved finish . . . . NiB $281 Ex $225 Gd $153

MODEL VIII
AUTOMATIC PISTOL . . . . NiB $355 Ex $240 Gd $179
Caliber: .38 Super. Nine-shot magazine, 5-inch bbl., 8.5 inches overall. Weight: 40 oz. Fixed sights. Blued finish. Wood grips. Intro. in 1952. Disc.

MODELS VIII, IXA, XI DELUXE
Same as standard Models VIII, IXA and XI except finish (chrome engraved or blued engraved) and simulated pearl grips. Disc. 1984.
Chrome-engraved finish. . . . . NiB $406 Ex $325 Gd $221
Blue-engraved finish . . . . NiB $438 Ex $350 Gd $238

MODEL IXA AUTOMATIC PISTOL . . . . NiB $300 Ex $225 Gd $140
Same as model VIII except .45 Auto, 7-shot magazine,

MODEL XA AUTOMATIC PISTOL. . . . . NiB $210 Ex $180 Gd $100
Same as model IIIA except .32 Auto, 8-shot magazine,

MODEL XI AUTOMATIC PISTOL . . . . . NiB $306 Ex $245 Gd $167
Same as model VIII except 9mm Para.

MODEL XV AUTOMATIC PISTOL. . . . . NiB $250 Ex $200 Gd $125
Same as model XA except .22 LR.

MODELS BE-IIIA, BE-XA, BE-XV . . . . . . NiB $340 Ex $270 Gd $180
Same as models IIIA, XA and XV except w/blued-engraved finish. Made 1977-84.

MODELS BE-VIII,
BE-IXA, BE-XI DELUXE . . . . NiB $400 Ex $320 Gd $218
Same as models VIII, IXA and XI except w/blued-engraved finish. Made 1977-84.

MODELS C-IIIA, C-XA, C-XV . . . . . NiB $385 Ex $300 Gd $195
Same as models IIIA, XA and XV except in satin chrome.

MODELS C-VIII, C-IXA, C-XI . . . . . NiB $385 Ex $300 Gd $195
Same as models VIII, IXA and XI except in satin chrome.

MODELS CE-IIIA,
CE-XA, CE-XV . . . . NiB $425 Ex $360 Gd $240
Same as models IIIA, XA and XV except w/chrome engraved finish. Made 1977-84.

MODELS CE-VIII,
CE-IXA, CE-XI . . . . NiB $395 Ex $300 Gd $235
Same as models VIII, IXA and XI, w/except chrome engraved finish. Made 1977-84.

COMPACT FRAME
AUTO PISTOL . . . . NiB $400 Ex $305 Gd $200
Calibers: 9mm Para., .38 Super, .45 Auto. Seven-, 8- or 9-shot magazine, 5-inch bbl., 7.88 inches overall. Weight: 34 oz. Blued, satin-chrome or Duo-Tone finishes. Made 1990 to date. Duo-Tone disc. 1993.

DUO-TONE LARGE
FRAME AUTO PISTOL . . . . NiB $375 Ex $310 Gd $205
Caliber: .45 ACP. Seven-shot magazine, 5-inch bbl., 8.5 inches overall. Weight: 36 oz. Adj. rear sight. Blued finished w/satin chrome. Polymer black grips. Made 1990-93.

Llama Model XA First Issue

Llama Model C-XI

Llama Model CE-IIIA

Llama Model Compact

Llama Duo-Tone Large Frame

Llama M-82 DA Auto

Llama MINI-MAX II

Llama MAX-I

DUO-TONE SMALL
FRAME AUTO PISTOL . . . . NiB $340 Ex $250 Gd $160
Calibers: .22 LR, .32 and .380 Auto. Seven- or 8-shot magazine, 3.69 inch bbl., 6.5 inches overall. Weight: 23 oz. Square-notch rear sight, Partridge-type front. Blued finish w/chrome. Made 1990-93.

MODEL G-IIIA DELUXE . . . . NiB $1063 Ex $850 Gd $578
Same as Model IIIA except gold damascened w/simulated pearl grips. Disc. 1982.

LARGE-FRAME AUTOMATIC PISTOL (IXA)
Caliber: .45 Auto. Seven-shot magazine, 5-inch bbl., weight: 2 lbs., 8 oz. Adj. rear sight, Partridge-type front. Walnut grips or teakwood on satin chrome model. Later models w/polymer grips. Made from 1984 to date.
Blued finish . . . . NiB $335 Ex $230 Gd $150
Satin chrome finish . . . . NiB $380 Ex $300 Gd $200

M-82 DA AUTOMATIC PISTOL. . . . . NiB $700 Ex $550 Gd $345
Caliber: 9mm Para. 15-shot magazine, 4.25-inch bbl., 8 inches overall. Weight: 39 oz. Drift-adj. rear sight. Matte blued finish. Matte black polymer grips. Made from 1988-93.

M-87 COMPETITION PISTOL . . . . NiB $1040 Ex $831 Gd $565
Caliber: 9mm Para. 15-shot magazine, 5.5-inch bbl., 9.5 inches overall. Weight: 40 oz. Low-profile combat sights. Satin nickel finish. Matte black grip panels. Built-in ported compensator to minimize recoil and muzzle rise. Made 1989-93.

MICRO-MAX SA AUTOMATIC PISTOL
Caliber: .380 ACP. Seven-shot magazine, 3.125-inch bbl., weight: 23 oz. Blade front sight, drift adjustable rear w/3-dot system. Matte blue or satin chrome finish. Checkered polymer grips. Imported 1997 to date.
Matte blue finish . . . . NiB $260 Ex $210 Gd $146
Satin chrome finish . . . . NiB $295 Ex $235 Gd $166

MINI-MAX SA AUTOMATIC PISTOL
Calibers: 9mm, .40 S&W or .45 ACP. Six- or 8-shot magazine, 3.5-inch bbl., 8.3 inches overall. Weight: 35 oz. Blade front sight, drift adjustable rear w/3-dot system. Matte blue, Duo-Tone or satin chrome finish. Checkered polymer grips. Imported 1996 to date.
Duo-Tone finish . . . . NiB $300 Ex $250 Gd $160
Matte blue finish . . . . NiB $264 Ex $225 Gd $140
Satin chrome finish . . . . NiB $325 Ex $250 Gd $170
Stainless (disc.) . . . . NiB $344 Ex $275 Gd $190

MINI-MAX II SA AUTOMATIC PISTOL
Cal: .45 ACP only. 10-shot mag., 3.625 inch bbl., 7.375 inch overall. Wt: 37 oz. Blade front sight, drift adj. rear w/3-dot system. Shortened barrel and grip. Matte and Satin Chrome finish. Imp. 1998.
Matte blue finish . . . . NiB $412 Ex $330 Gd $225
Satin chrome finish . . . . NiB $446 Ex $355 Gd $245

MAX-I SA AUTOMATIC PISTOL
Calibers: 9mm or .45 ACP. 7- or 9-shot magazine, 4.25- to 5.125 inch bbl., weight: 34 or 36 oz. Blade front sight, drift adj. rear w/3-dot system. Matte blue, Duo-Tone or satin chrome finish. Checkered black rubber grips. Imported 1995 to date.
Duo-Tone finish . . . . NiB $260 Ex $210 Gd $135
Matte blue finish . . . . NiB $260 Ex $210 Gd $130
Satin chrome finish . . . . NiB $295 Ex $230 Gd $140

MAX-II SA AUTOMATIC PISTOL
Same as the MAX-I with 4.25 bbl. except w/10-shot mag. Weight: 39 oz. Matte blue or satin chrome finish. Imp. 1996 to date.
Matte Blue finish . . . . NiB $250 Ex $200 Gd $137
Satin Chrome finish . . . . NiB $285 Ex $230 Gd $145

OMNI 45
DOUBLE-ACTION
AUTOMATIC PISTOL . . . . **NiB $400 Ex $320 Gd $210**
Caliber: .45 Auto. Seven-shot magazine, 4.25-inch bbl., 7.75 inches overall. Weight: 40 oz. Adj. rear sight, ramp front. Highly polished deep blued finish. Made 1984-86.

OMNI 9MM
DOUBLE-ACTION
AUTOMATIC . . . . **NiB $438 Ex $350 Gd $238**
Same general specifications as .45 Omni except chambered for 9mm w/13-shot magazine. Made 1983-86.

SINGLE-ACTION
AUTOMATIC PISTOL . . . . **NiB $410 Ex $320 Gd $208**
Calibers: .38 Super, 9mm, .45 Auto. Nine-shot magazine (7-shot for .45 Auto), 5-inch bbl., 8.5 inches overall. Weight: 2 lbs., 8 oz. Intro. in 1981.

SMALL-FRAME
AUTOMATIC PISTOL
Calibers: .380 Auto (7-shot magazine), .22 RF (8 shot magazine), 3.69-inch bbl., weight: 23 oz. Partridge-blade front sight, adj. rear. Blued or satin-chrome finish.
Blued finish . . . . **NiB $325 Ex $250 Gd $160**
Satin-chrome finish . . . . **NiB $385 Ex $300 Gd $200**

REVOLVERS

MARTIAL DOUBLE-
ACTION REVOLVER . . . . **NiB $245 Ex $200 Gd $130**
Calibers: .22 LR, .38 Special. Six-shot cylinder, bbl. lengths: 4-inch (.38 Special only) or 6-inch; 11.25 inches overall (w/6-inch bbl.). Weight: About 36 oz. w/6-inch bbl. Target sights. Blued finish. Checkered walnut grips. Made 1969-76.

MARTIAL
DOUBLE-ACTION DELUXE
Same as standard Martial except w/satin chrome, chrome-engraved, blued engraved or gold damascened finish. Simulated pearl grips. Made 1969-78.
Satin-chrome finish . . . . **NiB $305 Ex $250 Gd $150**
Chrome-engraved finish. . . . . **NiB $360 Ex $290 Gd $190**
Blue-engraved finish . . . . **NiB $350 Ex $280 Gd $190**
Gold-damascened finish . . . . **NiB $1495 Ex $1200 Gd $900**

COMANCHE I
DOUBLE-ACTION
REVOLVER. . . . . **NiB $260 Ex $210 Gd $150**
Same general specifications as Martial .22. Made 1977-83.

COMANCHE II
. . . . **NiB $245 Ex $200 Gd $130**
Same general specifications as Martial .38. Made 1977-83.

COMANCHE III
DOUBLE-ACTION
REVOLVER. . . . . **NiB $260 Ex $210 Gd $135**
Caliber: .357 Magnum. Six-shot cylinder, 4-inch bbl., 9.25 inches overall. Weight: 36 oz. Adj. rear sight, ramp front. Blued finish. Checkered walnut grips. Made from 1975-95. Note: Prior to 1977, this model was designated "Comanche."

COMANCHE III
CHROME. **NiB $345 Ex $260 Gd $180**
Same gen. specifications as Comanche III except has satin chrome finish, 4- or 6-inch bbl. Made 1979-92.

Llama
Comanche I

Llama
Comanche III Chrome

Llama
Martial Double-Action Revolver

Llama
Martial Deluxe Gold-Damascened

Llama
Super Comanche IV

**Luger 1900
American Eagle**

SUPER COMANCHE IV DA REVOLVER ... NiB $340 Ex $275 Gd $185
Caliber: .44 Magnum. Six-shot cylinder, 6-inch bbl., 11.75 inches overall. Weight: 50 oz. Adj. rear sight, ramp front. Polished deep blued finish. Checkered walnut grips. Made from 1980-93.

SUPER COMANCHE V DA REVOLVER .... NiB $325 Ex $255 Gd $177
Caliber: .357 Mag. Six-shot cylinder, 4-, 6- or 8.5-inch bbl., weight: 48 ozs. Ramped front blade sight, click-adj. Rear. Made from 1980-89.

LORCIN Engineering Co., Inc. — Mira Loma, California

MODEL L-22 SEMIAUTOMATIC PISTOL ..... NiB $75 Ex $60 Gd $41
Caliber: 22 LR. Nine-shot magazine, 2.5-inch bbl., 5.25 inches overall. Weight: 16 oz. Blade front sight, fixed notch rear w/3-dot system. Black Teflon or chrome finish. Black, pink or pearl composition grips. Made 1990 to date.

MODEL L-25, LT-.25 SEMIAUTOMATIC PISTOL
Caliber: 25 ACP. Seven-shot magazine, 2.4-inch bbl., 4.8 inches overall. Weight: 12 oz. (LT-25) or 14.5 oz. (L-25). Blade front sight, fixed rear. Black Teflon or chrome finish. Black, pink or pearl composition grips. Made 1989 to date.
Model L-25 .... NiB $63 Ex $50 Gd $34
Model LT-25 .... NiB $75 Ex $60 Gd $41
Model Lady Lorcin .... NiB $81 Ex $65 Gd $44

MODEL L-32 SEMIAUTOMATIC PISTOL ..... NiB $81 Ex $65 Gd $44
Caliber: 32 ACP. Seven-shot magazine, 3.5-inch bbl., 6.6 inches overall. Weight: 27 oz. Blade front sight, fixed notch rear. Black Teflon or chrome finish. Black composition grips. Made 1992 to date.

MODEL L-380 SEMIAUTOMATIC PISTOL
Caliber: .380 ACP. Seven- or 10-shot magazine, 3.5-inch bbl., 6.6 inches overall. Weight: 23 oz. Blade front sight, fixed notch rear. Matte Black finish. Grooved black composition grips. Made 1994 to date.
Model L9MM (7-shot) .... NiB $88 Ex $70 Gd $48
Model L9MM (10-shot) .... NiB $119 Ex $95 Gd $65

MODEL L9MM SEMIAUTOMATIC PISTOL
Caliber: 9mm Parabellum. 10- or 13-shot magazine, 4.5-inch bbl., 7.5 inches overall. Weight: 31 oz. Blade front sight, fixed notch rear w/3-dot system. Black Teflon or chrome finish. Black composition grips. Made 1992 to date.
Model L-380 (10-shot) .... NiB $130 Ex $105 Gd $70
Model L-380 (13-shot) .... NiB $160 Ex $130 Gd $80

O/U DERRINGER .... NiB $94 Ex $75 Gd $51
Caliber: .38 Special/.357 Mag., .45LC. Two-shot derringer. 3.5-inch bbls.

(cont'd) **O/U DERRINGER**
6.5 inches overall. Weight: 12 oz. Blade front sight, fixed notch rear. Stainless finish. Black composition grips. Made 1996 to date.

LUGER PISTOLS

Mfd. by Deutsche Waffen und Munitionsfabriken (DWM), Berlin, Germany. Previously by Koniglich Gewehrfabrik Erfurt, Heinrich Krieghoff Waffenfabrik, Mauser-Werke, Simson & Co., Vickers Ltd., Waffenfabrik, Bern.

1900 AMERICAN EAGLE .... NiB $2950 Ex $1650 Gd $850
Caliber: 7.65 mm. Eight-shot magazine; thin, 4.75-inch; tapered bbl.; 9.5 inches overall. Weight: 32 oz. Fixed rear sight, dovetailed front sight. Grip safety. Checkered walnut grips. Early-style toggle, narrow trigger, wide guard, no stock lug. American Eagle over chamber. Estimated 8000 production.

1900 COMMERCIAL .... NiB $3000 Ex $2500 Gd $1325
Same specifications as Luger 1900 American Eagle except DWM on early-style toggle, no chamber markings. Estimated 8000 production.

1900 SWISS .... NiB $3750 Ex $3000 Gd $1350
Same specifications as Luger 1900 American Eagle except Swiss cross in sunburst over chamber. Estimated 9000 production.

1902 AMERICAN EAGLE ...... NiB $8500 Ex $6500 Gd $3500
Caliber: 9mm Para. Eight-shot magazine, 4-inch heavy tapered bbl., 8.75 inches overall. Weight: 30 oz. Fixed rear sight, dovetailed front sight. Grip safety. Checkered walnut grips. American Eagle over chamber, DWM on early-style toggle, narrow trigger, wide guard, no stock lug. Estimated 700 production.

1902 CARBINE .... NiB $11,875 Ex $9500 Gd $6460
Caliber: 7.65mm. Eight-shot magazine, 11.75-inch tapered bbl., 16.5 inches overall. Weight: 46 oz. Adj. 4-position rear sight, long ramp front sight. Grip safety. Checkered walnut grips and forearm. DWM on early-style toggle, narrow trigger, wide guard, no chamber markings, stock lug. Estimated 3200 production.
Model 1902 carbine (gun only) .... NiB $7562 Ex $6050 Gd $4114
Model 1902 carbine
(gun only, American Eagle) .... NiB $10,618 Ex $8495 Gd $5776
W/issued stock and matching numbers, add $4550
W/original stock and non-matching numbers, add $2550

1902 CARTRIDGE COUNTER .... NiB $26,000 Ex $16,500 Gd $8650
Caliber: 9mm Para. Eight-shot magazine, Heavy, tapered 4-inch bbl., 8.75 inches overall. Weight: 30 oz. Fixed rear sight, dovetailed front sight. Grip safety. Checkered walnut grips. DWM on dished toggle w/lock, American Eagle over chamber when marked. No stock lug. Estimated production unknown.

1902 COMMERCIAL .... NiB $8000 Ex $6500 Gd $3350
Same basic specifications as Luger 1902 Cartridge Counter except DWM on early-style toggle, narrow trigger, wide guard, no chamber markings, no stock lug. Estimated 400 production.

1902 AMERICAN EAGLE ...... NiB $8500 Ex $6500 Gd $3500
Same basic specifications as Luger 1902 Commercial except American Eagle over chamber, DWM on early-style toggle, narrow trigger, wide guard, no stock lug. Estimated 700 production.

**1902 AMERICAN EAGLE
CARTRIDGE COUNTER** .... NiB $25,900 Ex $16,500 Gd $8700
Same basic specifications as Luger 1902 Cartridge Counter except American Eagle over chamber, DWM on early-style toggle, narrow trigger, wide guard, no stock lug. Estimated 700 production.

1904 GL "BABY" . . . . **Nib $187,500 Ex $150,000 Gd $102,000**
Caliber: 9mm Para. Seven-shot magazine, 3.25-inch bbl., 7.75 inches overall. Weight: Approx. 20 oz. Serial number 10077B. "GL" marked on rear of toggle. Georg Luger's personal sidearm. Only one made in 1904.

1904 NAVAL (REWORKED) . . . . **Nib $12,188 Ex $9750 Gd $6630**
Caliber: 9mm Para. Eight-shot magazine, bbl., length altered to 4 inches., 8.75 inches overall. Weight: 30 oz. Adj. two-position rear sight, dovetailed front sight. Thumb lever safety. Checkered walnut grips. Heavy tapered bbl., DWM on new-style toggle w/lock, 1902 over chamber. W/or without grip safety and stock lug. Estimated 800 production.

1906 (11.35) . . . . **Nib $112,500 Ex $90,000 Gd $61,200**
Caliber: .45 ACP. Six-shot magazine, 5-inch bbl., 9.75 inches overall. Weight: 36 oz. Fixed rear sight, dovetailed front sight. Grip safety. Checkered walnut grips. GL monogram on rear toggle link, larger frame w/altered trigger guard and trigger, no proofs, no markings over chamber. No stock lug. Estimated production is 2. Note: This version of the Luger pistol is the most valuable next to the "GL" Baby Luger.

1906 AMERICAN EAGLE
(7.65) . . . . **Nib $2800 Ex $2000 Gd $950**
Caliber: 7.65mm. Eight-shot magazine, thin 4.75-inch tapered bbl., 9.5 inches overall. Weight: 32 oz. Fixed rear sight, dovetailed front sight. Grip safety. Checkered walnut grips. DWM on new-style toggle, American Eagle over chamber. No stock lug. Estimated 8000 production.

1906 AMERICAN EAGLE (9MM) . . . . . . **Nib $2680 Ex $2150 Gd $1200**
Same basic specifications as the 7.65mm 1906 except in 9mm Para. w/4-inch barrel, 8.75 inches overall, weight: 30 ounces. Estimated 3500 production.

1906 BERN (7.65MM) . . . . **Nib $2400 Ex $2100 Gd $1310**
Same basic specifications as the 7.65mm 1906 American Eagle except checkered walnut grips w/.38-inch borders, Swiss Cross on new-style toggle, Swiss proofs, no markings over chamber, no stock lug. Estimated 17,874 production.

1906 BRAZILIAN (7.65MM) . . . . **Nib $2500 Ex $1800 Gd $700**
Same general specifications as the 7.65mm 1906 American Eagle except w/Brazilian proofs, no markings over chamber, no stock lug. Estimated 4500 produced.

1906 BRAZILIAN (9MM) . . . . . . **Nib $2438 Ex $1950 Gd $1326**
Same basic specifications as the 9mm 1906 American Eagle except w/Brazilian proofs, no markings over chamber, no stock lug. Production unknown, but less than 4000 is estimated by collectors.

1906 COMMERCIAL
Calibers: 7.65mm, 9mm. Same specifications as the 1906 American Eagle versions (above) except no chamber markings and no stock lug. Estimated production: 6000 (7.65mm) and 3500 (9mm).
7.65mm . . . . **Nib $2800 Ex $1850 Gd $1200**
9mm . . . . **Nib $2800 Ex $1850 Gd $1200**

1906 DUTCH . . . . **Nib $1813 Ex $1450 Gd $986**
Caliber: 9mm Para. Same specifications as the 9mm 1906 American Eagle except tapered bbl., w/proofs, no markings over chamber, no stock lug. Estimated 3000 production.

1906 LOEWE AND COMPANY . . . . **Nib $4438 Ex $3550 Gd $2414**
Caliber: 7.65mm. Eight-shot magazine, 6-inch tapered bbl., 10.75 inches overall. Weight: 35 oz. Adj. two-position rear sight, dovetailed front sight. Grip safety. Checkered walnut grips. Loewe & Company over chamber, Naval proofs, DWM on new-style toggle, no stock lug. Estimated production unknown.

1906 NAVAL
Caliber: 9mm Para. Eight-shot magazine, 6-inch tapered bbl., 10.75 inches overall. Weight: 35 oz. Adj. two-position rear sight, dovetailed front sight. Grip safety and thumb safety w/lower marking (1st issue), higher marking (2nd issue). Checkered walnut grips. No chamber markings, DWM on new-style toggle w/o lock, but w/stock lug. Est. production: 9000 (1st issue); 2,000 (2nd issue).
First issue . . . . **Nib $3800 Ex $3000 Gd $1200**
Second issue . . . . **Nib $4000 Ex $3400 Gd $1200**

1906 NAVAL COMMERCIAL . . . . **Nib $3800 Ex $3000 Gd $1200**
Same as the 1906 Naval except lower marking on thumb safety, no chamber markings. DWM on new-style toggle, w/stock lug and commercial proofs. Estimated 3000 production.

1906 PORTUGUESE
ARMY . . . . **Nib $1800 Ex $1400 Gd $500**
Same specifications as the 7.65mm 1906 American Eagle except w/Portuguese proofs, crown and crest over chamber. No stock lug. Estimated 3500 production.

1906 PORTUGUESE NAVAL . . . . **Nib $9500 Ex $6000 Gd $2000**
Same as the 9mm 1906 American Eagle except w/Portuguese proofs, crown and anchor over chamber, no stock lug.

1906 RUSSIAN . . . . **Nib $15,000 Ex $9950 Gd $5500**
Same general specifications as the 9mm 1906 American Eagle except thumb safety has markings concealed in up position, DWM on new-style toggle, DWM bbl., proofs, crossed rifles over chamber. Estimated production unknown.

1906 SWISS . . . . **Nib $2400 Ex $1750 Gd $1200**
Same general specifications as the 7.65mm 1906 American Eagle Luger except Swiss Cross in sunburst over chamber, no stock lug. Estimated 10,300 production.

1906 SWISS (REWORK) . . . . **Nib $2400 Ex $1750 Gd $1200**
Same basic specifications as the 7.65mm 1906 Swiss except in bbl. lengths of 3.63, 4 and 4.75 inches, overall length 8.38 inches (with 4-inch bbl.). Weight 32 oz. (with 4-inch bbl.). DWM on new-style toggle, bbl., w/serial number and proof marks, Swiss Cross in sunburst or shield over chamber, no stock lug. Estimated production unknown.

1906 SWISS POLICE . . . . **Nib $2400 Ex $1750 Gd $1200**
Same general specifications as the 7.65mm 1906 Swiss except DWM on new-style toggle, Swiss Cross in matted field over chamber, no stock lug. Estimated 10,300 production.

1908 BULGARIAN . . . . **Nib $2500 Ex $1800 Gd $750**
Caliber: 9mm Para. Eight-shot magazine, 4-inch tapered bbl., 8.75 inches overall. Weight: 30 oz. Fixed rear sight dovetailed front sight. Thumb safety w/lower marking concealed. Checkered walnut grips. DWM chamber marking, no proofs, crown over shield on new-style toggle lanyard loop, no stock lug. Estimated production unknown.

1908 COMMERCIAL . . . . **Nib $1200 Ex $800 Gd $500**
Same basic specifications as the 1908 Bulgarian except higher marking on thumb safety. No chamber markings, commercial proofs, DWM on new-style toggle, no stock lug. Estimated 4000 production.

1908 ERFURT MILITARY . . . . **Nib $1219 Ex $995 Gd $709**
Caliber: 9mm Para. Eight-shot magazine, 4-inch tapered bbl., 8.75 inches overall. Weight: 30 oz. Fixed rear sight dovetailed front sight. Thumb safety w/higher marking concealed. Checkered walnut grips. Serial number and proof marks on barrel, crown and Erfurt on new-style toggle, dated chamber, but no stock lug. Estimated production unknown.

Luger 1923 Stoeger

1908 MILITARY

Same general specifications as the 9mm 1908 Erfurt Military Luger except first and second issue have thumb safety w/higher marking concealed, serial number on bbl., no chamber markings, proofs on frame, DWM on new-style toggle but no stock lug. Estimated production: 10,000 (first issue) and 5000 (second issue). Third issue has serial number and proof marks on barrel, dates over chamber, DWM on new-style toggle but no stock lug. Estimated 3000 production.

First issue.................... Nib $1200 Ex $800 Gd $500
Second issue .... Nib $1200 Ex $750 Gd $400
Third issue .... Nib $1500 Ex $950 Gd $600

1908 NAVAL .... Nib $3938 Ex $3150 Gd $2142

Same basic specifications as the 9mm 1908 military Lugers except w/6-inch bbl, adj. two-position rear sight, no chamber markings, DWM on new-style toggle, w/stock lug. Estimated 26,000 production.

1908 NAVAL
(COMMERCIAL) .... Nib $4500 Ex $3000 Gd $1500

Same specifications as the 1908 Naval Luger except no chamber markings or date. Commercial proofs, DWM on new-style toggle, w/stock lug. Estimated 1900 produced.

1914 ERFURT ARTILLERY ...... Nib $2500 Ex $1750 Gd $825

Caliber: 9mm Para. Eight-shot magazine, 8-inch tapered bbl., 12.75 inches overall. Weight: 40 oz. Artillery rear sight, Dovetailed front sight. Thumb safety w/higher marking concealed. Checkered walnut grips. Serial number and proof marks on barrel, crown and Erfurt on new-style toggle, dated chamber, w/stock lug. Estimated production unknown.

1914 ERFURT MILITARY .... Nib $1200 Ex $800 Gd $500

Same specifications as the 1914 Erfurt Artillery except w/4-inch bbl., and corresponding length, weight, etc.; fixed rear sight. Estimated 3000 production.

1914 NAVAL .... Nib $3250 Ex $2250 Gd $1000

Same specifications as 9mm 1914 Lugers except has 6-inch bbl. w/corresponding length and weight, adj. two-position rear sight. Dated chamber, DWM on new-style toggle, w/stock lug. Estimated 40,000 produced.

1914-1918 DWM ARTILLERY ...... Nib $2200 Ex $1800 Gd $875

Caliber: 9mm Para. Eight-shot magazine, 8-inch tapered bbl., 12.75 inches overall. Weight: 40 oz. Artillery rear sight, dovetailed front sight. Thumb safety w/higher marking concealed. Checkered walnut grips. Serial number and proof marks on barrel, DWM on new-style toggle, dated chamber, w/stock lug. Estimated 3000 production.

1914-1918 DWM MILITARY ..... Nib $1100 Ex $800 Gd $500

Same specifications as the 9mm 1914-1918 DWM Artillery except w/4-inch tapered bbl., and corresponding length, weight, etc., and fixed rear sight. Production unknown.

1920 CARBINE

Caliber: 7.65mm. Eight-shot magazine, 11.75-inch tapered bbl., 15.75 inches overall. Weight: 44 oz. Four-position rear sight, long ramp front sight. Grip (or thumb) safety. Checkered walnut grips and forearm. Serial numbers and proof marks on barrel, no chamber markings, various proofs, DWM on new-style toggle, w/stock lug. Estimated production unknown.

**Model 1920 Carbine
(gun only)** .... Nib $5400 Ex $4700 Gd $2500
**Model 1920 Carbine
(W/shoulder stock), add** $2500

1920 NAVY CARBINE .... Nib $3563 Ex $2850 Gd $1938

Caliber: 7.65mm. Eight-shot magazine, 11.75-inch tapered bbl., 15.75 inches overall. Two-position sliding rear sight. Naval military proofs and no forearm. Production unknown.

1920 COMMERCIAL .... Nib $825 Ex $625 Gd $350

Calibers: 7.65mm, 9mm Para. Eight-shot magazine, 3.63-, 3.75-, 4-, 4.75-, 6-, 8-, 10-, 12-, 16-, 18- or 20-inch tapered bbl., overall length: 8.375 to 24.75 inches. Weight: 30 oz. (with 3.63-inch bbl.). Varying rear sight configurations, dovetailed front sight. Thumb safety. Checkered walnut grips. Serial numbers and proof marks on barrel, no chamber markings, various proofs, DWM or crown over Erfurt on new-style toggle, w/stock lug. Production not documented.

1920 DWM OR ERFURT MILITARY ...... Nib $900 Ex $700 Gd $475

Caliber: 9mm Para. Eight-shot magazine, 4-inch tapered barrel, 8.75 inches overall. Weight: 30 oz. Fixed rear sight dovetailed front sight. Thumb safety. Checkered walnut grips. Serial numbers and proof marks on barrel, dated chamber, various proofs, DWM or crown over Erfurt on new-style toggle, w/stock lug. Esimated 3000 production.

1920 POLICE................. Nib $1180 Ex $915 Gd $620

Same specifications as 9mm 1920 DWM w/some dated chambers, various proofs, DWM or crown over Erfurt on new-style toggle, identifying marks on grip frame, w/stock lug. Estimated 3000 production.

1923 COMMERICAL .... Nib $825 Ex $525 Gd $285

Calibers: 7.65mm and 9mm Para. Eight-shot magazine, 3.63-, 3.75-, 4-, 6-, 8-, 12- or 16-inch tapered bbl., overall length: 8.38 inches (with 3.63-inch bbl.). Weight: 30 oz. (with 3.63-inch bbl.). Various rear sight configurations, dovetailed front sight. Thumb lever safety. Checkered walnut grips. DWM on new-style toggle, serial number and proofs on barrel, no chamber markings, w/stock lug. Estimated 15,000 production.

1923 DUTCH COMMERICAL .... Nib $1600 Ex $1400 Gd $600

Same basic specifications as 1923 Commercial Luger w/same caliber offerings, but only 3.63- or 4-inch bbl. Fixed rear sight, thumb lever safety w/arrow markings. Production unknown.

1923 KRIEGHOFF COMMERCIAL ..... Nib $1650 Ex $1300 Gd $770

Same specifications as 1923 Commercial Luger, w/same caliber offerings but bbl., lengths of 3.63, 4, 6, and 8 inches. "K" marked on new-style toggle. Serial number, proofs and Germany on barrel. No chamber markings, but w/ stock lug. Production unknown.

1923 SAFE AND LOADED ...... Nib $1450 Ex $1000 Gd $500

Same caliber offerings, bbl., lengths and specifications as the 1923 Commercial except thumb lever safety, safe markings, w/stock lug. Estimated 10,000 production.

1923 STOEGER

Same general specifications as the 1923 Commercial Luger with the same caliber offerings and bbl., lengths of 3.75, 4, 6, 8 and up to 24 inches. Thumb lever safety. DWM on new-style toggle, serial number and/or proof marks on barrel. American Eagle over chamber but no stock lug. Estimated production less than 1000 (also see Stoeger listings). Note: Qualified appraisals should be obtained on all Stoeger Lugers with bbl., lengths over 8 inches to ensure accurate values.

3.75-, 4-, or 6-inch bbl. . . . . **Nib $2744 Ex $2195 Gd $1493**
8-inch bbl. . . . . **Nib $3688 Ex $2950 Gd $2006**

1926 "BABY" PROTOTYPE . **Nib $106,250 Ex $85,000 Gd $57,800**

Calibers: 7.65mm Browning and 9mm Browning (short). Five-shot magazine, 2.31-inch bbl., about 6.25 inches overall. Small-sized-frame and toggle assembly. Prototype for a Luger "pocket pistol," but never manufactured commercially. Checkered walnut grips, slotted for safety. Only four known to exist, but as many as a dozen could have been made.

1929 SWISS . . . . **Nib $1750 Ex $1100 Gd $625**

Caliber: 7.65mm. Eight-shot magazine, 4.75-inch tapered bbl., 9.5 inches overall. Weight: 32 oz. Fixed rear sight, dovetailed front sight. Long grip safety and thumb lever w/S markings. Stepped receiver and straight grip frame. Checkered plastic grips. Swiss Cross in shield on new-style toggle. Serial numbers and proofs on barrel, no markings over chamber and no stock lug. Estimated 1900 produuction.

1934 KRIEGHOFF

COMMERCIAL (SIDE FRAME) . . . . **Nib $2750 Ex $2100 Gd $800**

Caliber: 7.65mm or 9mm Para. Eight-shot magazine, bbl. lengths: 4, 6, and 8 inches, overall length: 8.75 (with 4-inch bbl.). Weight: 30 oz. (with 4-inch bbl.). Various rear sight configurations w/dovetailed front sight. Thumb lever safety. Checkered brown plastic grips. Anchor w/H K Krieghoff Suhl on new-style toggle, but no chamber markings. Tapered bbl., w/serial number and proofs; w/stock lug. Estimated 1700 production.

1934 KRIEGHOFF S

Caliber: 9mm Para. Eight-shot magazine, 4-inch tapered bbl., 8.75 inches overall. Weight: 30 oz. Fixed rear sight, dovetailed front sight. Thumb lever safety. Anchor w/H K Krieghoff Suhl on new-style toggle, S dated chamber, bbl., proofs and stock lug. Early model: Checkered walnut or plastic grips. Estimated 2500 production. Late model: Checkered brown plastic grips. Est. 1200 production.

Early model . . . . **Nib $3369 Ex $2695 Gd $1833**
Late model . . . . **Nib $2438 Ex $1950 Gd $1326**

1934 BYF . . . . **Nib $1200 Ex $900 Gd $500**

Caliber: 9mm Para. Eight-shot magazine, 4-inch tapered bbl., 8.75 inches overall. Weight: 30 oz. Fixed rear sight, dovetailed front sight. Thumb lever safety. Checkered walnut or plastic grips. byf on new-style toggle, serial number and proofs on bbl., 41-42 dated chamber and w/stock lug. Estimated 3000 productlon.

1934 MAUSER S/42 K . . . . **Nib $4500 Ex $3800 Gd $1500**

Caliber: 9mm Para. Eight-shot magazine, 4-inch tapered bbl., 8.75 inches overall. Weight: 30 oz. Fixed rear sight dovetailed front sight. Thumb lever safety. Checkered walnut or plastic grips. 42 on new-style toggle, serial number and proofs on barrel, 1939-.40 dated chamber markings and w/stock lug. Estimated 10,000 production.

1934 MAUSER S/42 (DATED) . . . . **Nib $1000 Ex $775 Gd $400**

Same specifications as Luger 1934 Mauser 42 except 41 dated chamber markings and w/stock lug. Production unknown.

Luger S42

1934 MAUSER BANNER (MILITARY) . . . . . . **Nib $2600 Ex $1800 Gd $950**

Same specifications as Luger 1934 Mauser 42 except Mauser in banner on new-style toggle, tapered bbl., w/serial number and proofs usually, dated chamber markings and w/stock lug. Production unknown.

1934 MAUSER COMMERCIAL . . . . **Nib $1500 Ex $1050 Gd $600**

Same specifications as Luger 1934 Mauser 42 except checkered walnut grips. Mauser in banner on new-style toggle, tapered bbl., usually w/serial number and proofs, no chamber markings, but w/stock lug. Production unknown.

1934 MAUSER DUTCH . . . . **Nib $2800 Ex $1700 Gd $500**

Same specifications as Luger 1934 Mauser 42 except checkered walnut grips. Mauser in banner on new-style toggle, tapered bbl., w/caliber, 1940 dated chamber markings and w/stock lug. Production unknown.

1934 MAUSER LATVIAN . . . . . . **Nib $2851 Ex $1940 Gd $1700**

Caliber: 7.65mm. Eight-shot magazine, 4-inch tapered bbl., 8.75 inches overall. Weight: 30 oz. Fixed square-notched rear sight, dovetailed Partridge front sight. Thumb lever safety. Checkered walnut stocks. Mauser in banner on new-style toggle,1937 dated chamber markings and w/stock lug. Production unknown.

1934 MAUSER (OBERNDORF) . . . . **Nib $2813 Ex $2250 Gd $1530**

Same as 1934 Mauser 42 except checkered walnut grips. Oberndorf 1934 on new-style toggle, tapered bbl., w/proofs and caliber, Mauser banner over chamber and w/stock lug (also see Mauser).

1934 SIMSON-S TOGGLE . . . . . . **Nib $1850 Ex $1300 Gd $550**

Same as 1934 Mauser 42 except checkered walnut grips, S on new-style toggle, tapered bbl., w/serial number and proofs, no chamber markings; w/stock lug. Estimated 10,000 production.

42 MAUSER BANNER (BYF) . . . . . **Nib $1200 Ex $900 Gd $500**

Same specifications as Luger 1934 Mauser 42 except weight: 32 oz. Mauser in banner on new-style toggle, tapered bbl., w/serial number and proofs usually, dated chamber markings and w/stock lug. Estimated 3,500 production.

ABERCROMBIE AND FITCH . . . . **Nib $5750 Ex $4350 Gd $950**

Calibers: 7.65mm and 9mm Para. Eight-shot magazine, 4.75-inch tapered bbl., 9.5 inches overall. Weight: 32 oz. Fixed rear sight, dovetailed front sight. Grip safety. Checkered walnut grips. DWM on new-style toggle Abercrombie & Fitch markings on barrel, Swiss Cross in sunburst over chamber, no stock lug. Est. 100 production.

GRADING: **NiB** = New in Box **Ex** = Excellent or NRA 95% **Gd** = Good or NRA 68%

**Luna Model 200
Free Pistol**

DUTCH ROYAL AIR FORCE .... **Nib $2800 Ex $1700 Gd $500**
Caliber: 9mm Para. Eight-shot magazine, 4-inch tapered bbl., 8.75 inches overall. Weight: 30 oz. Fixed rear sight dovetailed front sight. Grip safety and thumb safety w/markings and arrow. Checkered walnut grips. DWM on new-style toggle, bbl., dated w/serial number and proofs, no markings over chamber, no stock lug. Estimated 4000 production.

DWM (G DATE)............... **Nib $1325 Ex $900 Gd $450**
Caliber: 9mm Para. Eight-shot magazine, 4-inch tapered bbl., 8.75 inches overall. Weight: 30 oz. Fixed rear sight, dovetailed front sight. Thumb lever safety. Checkered walnut grips. DWM on new-style toggle, serial number and proofs on barrel, G (1935 date) over chamber and w/stock lug. Production unknown.

DWM AND ERFURT .... **Nib $1119 Ex $895 Gd $609**
Caliber: 9mm Para. Eight-shot magazine, 4- or 6-inch tapered bbl., overall length: 8.75 or 10.75 inches. Weight: 30 or 38 oz. Fixed rear sight, dovetailed front sight. Thumb safety. Checkered walnut grips. Serial numbers and proof marks on barrel, double dated chamber, various proofs, DWM or crown over Erfurt on new-style toggle and w/stock lug. Production unknown.

KRIEGHOFF 36 .... **Nib $2994 Ex $2395 Gd $1629**
Caliber: 9mm Para. Eight-shot magazine, 4-inch tapered bbl., 8.75 inches overall. Weight: 30 oz. Fixed rear sight, dovetailed front sight. Thumb safety. Checkered brown plastic grips. Anchor w/H K Krieghoff Suhl on new-style toggle, 36 dated chamber, serial number and proofs on barrel and w/stock lug. Estimated 700 production.

**KRIEGHOFF-DATED
1936-1945** .... **Nib $3060 Ex $2500 Gd $1000**
Same specifications as Luger Krieghoff 36 except 1936-45 dated chamber, bbl. proofs. Est. 8600 production.

KRIEGHOFF (GRIP SAFETY) ... **Nib $4556 Ex $3645 Gd $2479**
Same specifications as Luger Krieghoff 36 except grip safety and thumb lever safety. No chamber markings, tapered bbl., w/serial number, proofs and caliber, no stock lug. Production unknown.

**MAUSER BANNER
(GRIP SAFETY)**............... **Nib $2600 Ex $1800 Gd $950**
Caliber: 7.65mm. Eight-shot magazine, 4.75-inch tapered bbl., 9.5 inches overall. Weight: 30 oz. Fixed rear sight, dovetailed front sight. Grip safety and thumb lever safety. Checkered walnut grips. Mauser in banner on new-style toggle, serial number and proofs on barrel, 1939 dated chamber markings, but no stock lug. Production unknown.

MAUSER BANNER 42 (DATED).... **Nib $1500 Ex $1050 Gd $600**
Caliber: 9mm Para. Eight-shot magazine, 4-inch tapered bbl., 8.75 inches overall. Weight: 30 oz. Fixed rear sight, dovetailed front sight. Thumb lever safety. Checkered walnut or plastic grips. Mauser in banner on new-style toggle serial number and proofs on bbl., (usually) 1942 dated chamber markings and stock lug. Production unknown.

**MAUSER BANNER
(SWISS PROOF)**............. **Nib $3150 Ex $2450 Gd $1250**
Same specifications as Luger Mauser Banner 42 above except checkered walnut grips and 1939 dated chamber.

MAUSER FREISE............. **Nib $4438 Ex $3550 Gd $2414**
Same specifications as Mauser Banner 42 except checkered walnut grips, tapered bbl. w/proofs on sight block and Freise above chamber. Production unknown.

S/42
Caliber: 9mm Para. Eight-shot magazine, 4-inch tapered barrel. 8.75 inches overall. Weight: 30 oz. Fixed rear sight, dovetailed front sight. Thumb lever safety. Checkered walnut grips. S/42 on new-style toggle, serial number and proofs on barrel and w/stock lug. Dated Model: Has dated chamber; estimated 3000 production. G Date: Has G (1935 date) over chamber; estimated 3000 production. K Date: Has K (1934 date) over chamber; prod. figures unknown.

Dated model	**Nib $1000**	**Ex $775**	**Gd $400**
G date model................	**Nib $1094**	**Ex $875**	**Gd $595**
K date model	**Nib $2369**	**Ex $1895**	**Gd $1289**

**RUSSIAN
COMMERCIAL**.............. **Nib $2688 Ex $2150 Gd $1462**
Caliber: 7.65mm. Eight-shot magazine, 3.63-inch tapered bbl., 8.38 inches overall. Weight: 30 oz. Fixed rear sight, dovetailed front sight. Thumb lever safety. Checkered walnut grips. DWM on new-style toggle, Russian proofs on barrel, no chamber markings but w/stock lug. Production unknown.

SIMSON AND COMPANY
Calibers: 7.65mm and 9mm Para. Eight-shot magazine, Weight: 32 oz. Fixed rear sight, dovetailed front sight. Thumb lever safety. Checkered walnut grips. Simson & Company Suhl on new-style toggle, serial number and proofs on barrel, date over chamber and w/stock lug. Estimated 10,000 production.

**Simson and
Company
(9mm w/1925 date)**..........	**Nib $2500**	**Ex $2000**	**Gd $675**
**Simson and
Company
(undated)**	**Nib $1450**	**Ex $800**	**Gd $450**
**Simson and
Company
(S code)**	**Nib $1850**	**Ex $1300**	**Gd $550**

VICKERS-DUTCH .... **Nib $2800 Ex $2000 Gd $800**
Caliber: 9mm Para. Eight-shot magazine, 4-inch tapered bbl., 8.75 inches overall. Weight: 30 oz. Fixed rear sight, dovetailed front sight. Grip safety and thumb lever w/arrow markings. Checkered walnut grips (coarse). Vickers LTD on new-style toggle, no chamber markings, dated barrel but no stock lug. Estimated 10,000 production.

LUNA FREE PISTOL — Zella-Mehlis, Germany Originally mfd. by Ernst Friedr. Buchel and later by Udo Anschutz

MODEL 200 FREE PISTOL .... **Nib $1100 Ex $990 Gd $600**
Single-shot. System Aydt action. Set trigger. Caliber: .22 LR. Eleven-inch bbl., weight: 40 oz. Target sights. Blued finish. Checkered and carved walnut grip and forearm; improved design w/adj. hand base on later models of Udo Anschutz manufacture. Made prior to WWII.

M.A.C. (Military Armament Corp.) — Stephensville, Texas, Dist. by Defense Systems International, Marietta, Georgia. Previously by Cobray, SWD and RPB Industries

INGRAM MODEL 10 AUTO PISTOL
Select fire (NFA-Title II-Class III) SMG based on Ingram M10 blowback system using an open bolt design with or without telescoping stock. Calibers: 9mm or .45 ACP. Cyclic rate: 750 RPM (9mm) or 900 RPM (.45 ACP). 32- or 30-round magazine, 5.75-inch threaded bbl. (to accept muzzle brake) bbl. extension or suppressor, 10.5 inches overall w/o stock or 10.6 (w/telescoped stock) and 21.5 (w/extended stock). Weight: 6.25 pounds. Front protected post sight, fixed aperture rear sight. Garand-style safety in trigger guard.

9mm model	Nib $850	Ex $775	Gd $550
.45 ACP model	Nib $850	Ex $775	Gd $550
W/bbl., extension, add			$195
W/suppressor, add			$495

INGRAM MODEL 10A1S SEMIAUTOMATIC
Similar to the Model 10 except (Class I) semiautomatic w/closed bolt design to implement an interchangable component system to easily convert to fire 9mm and .45 ACP.

9mm model	Nib $295	Ex $275	Gd $200
.45 ACP model	Nib $305	Ex $280	Gd $200
W/bbl., extension, add			$150
W/fake suppressor, add			$195

INGRAM MODEL 11 SEMIAUTOMATIC
Similar to the Model 10A1 except (Class I) semiautomatic chambered .380 ACP.

.380 ACP model	Nib $650	Ex $595	Gd $480
W/bbl., extension, add			$150
W/fake suppressor, add			$195

MAGNUM RESEARCH INC. — Minneapolis, Minnesota

BABY EAGLE SEMIAUTOMATIC . . . . Nib $415 Ex $350 Gd $210
DA. Calibers: 9mm, .40 S&W, .41 AE. 15-shot magazine (9mm), 9-shot magazine (.40 S&W), 10-shot magazine (.41 AE), 4.75-inch bbl., 8.15 inches overall. Weight: 35.4 oz. Combat sights. Matte blued finish. Imported 1991-96 and 1999 to date.

DESERT EAGLE MK VII SEMIAUTOMATIC
Gas-operated. Calibers: .357 Mag., .41 Mag., .44 Mag., .50 Action Express (AE). Eight- or 9-shot magazine, 6-inch w/standard bbl., or 10- and 14-inch w/polygonal bbl., 10.6 inches overall (with 6-inch bbl.). Weight: 52 oz. (w/alum. alloy frame) to 67 oz. (w/steel frame). Fixed or adj. combat sights. Combat-type trigger guard. finish: Military black oxide, nickel, chrome, stainless or blued. Wraparound rubber grips. Made by Israel Military Industries 1984-95.

.357 standard (steel) or alloy (6-inch bbl.)	Nib $850	Ex $650	Gd $395
.357 stainless steel (6-inch bbl.)	Nib $906	Ex $725	Gd $493
.41 Mag. standard (steel) or alloy 6-inch bbl.	Nib $844	Ex $675	Gd $459
.41 Mag. stainless steel (6-inch bbl.)	Nib $813	Ex $650	Gd $442
.44 Mag. standard (steel) or alloy (6-inch bbl.)	Nib $794	Ex $635	Gd $432
.44 Mag. stainless steel (6-inch bbl.)	Nib $869	Ex $695	Gd $473
.50 AE Magnum standard	Nib $938	Ex $750	Gd $510
Add for 10-inch bbl.	Nib $125	Ex $100	Gd $68
Add for 14-inch bbl.	Nib $156	Ex $125	Gd $85

Magnum Research Model Desert Eagle Mark XIX (Shown w/Optional Leupold Scope

Magnum Research Model One Pro .45

MODEL DESERT EAGLE MARK XIX SEMI-AUTOMATIC PISTOL
Interchangeable component system based on .50-caliber frame. Calibers: .357 Mag., .44 Mag., .50 AE. Nine-, 8-, 7-shot magazine, 6- or 10-inch bbl. w/dovetail design and cross slots to accept scope rings. Weight: 70.5 oz. (6-inch bbl.) or 79 oz. 10.75 or 14.75 inches overall. Sights: Post front and adjustable rear. Blue, chrome or nickel finish; available brushed, matte or polished. Hogue soft rubber grips. Made 1995 to date.

.357 Mag. (W/6-inch bbl.)	Nib $1025	Ex $875	Gd $400
.44 Mag. (W/6-inch bbl.)	Nib $956	Ex $765	Gd $520
.50 AE (W/6-inch bbl.)	Nib $994	Ex $795	Gd $541
W/10-inch bbl., add			$50
Two caliber conversion (bbl., bolt & mag.), add			$395
XIX Platform System			
3 caliber-conversion w/6 bbls.)	Nib $2744	Ex $2195	Gd $1493
XIX6 System (two caliber-conversion w/2 6-inch bbls.)	Nib $1813	Ex $1450	Gd $986
XIX10 System (two cal.-conv. w/ two 10 inch bbls.)	Nib $1969	Ex $1575	Gd $1071
Custom shop finish, add			$15%
24K gold finish, add			$35%

(ASAI) MODEL ONE PRO .45 PISTOL
Calibers: .45 ACP or .400 COR-BON, 3.75- inch bbl., 7.04 or 7.83 (IPSC Model) inches overall. Weight: 23.5 (alloy frame) or 31.1 oz. 10-shot magazine. Short recoil action. SA or DA mode w/de-cocking lever. Steel or alloy grip-frame. Textured black polymer grips. Imported 1998 to date.

Model 1P45	Nib $556	Ex $445	Gd $303
Model 1C45/400 (compensator kit), add			$175
Model 1C400NC (400 conversion kit), add			$125

**Magnum Research SSP-91 Lone Eagle Pistol
(w/Optional Leupold Scope)**

**Mauser
Model 80-SA**

**Mauser
Model 90-DA**

MOUNTAIN EAGLE SEMIAUTOMATIC
Caliber: .22 LR. 15-shot polycarbonate resin magazine, 6.5-inch injection-molded polymer and steel bbl., 10.6 inches overall. Weight: 21 oz. Ramp blade front sight, adj. rear. Injection-molded, checkered and textured grip. Matte black finish. Made 1992-96.
Mountain Eagle (standard, 6.5-inch bbl.) ... NiB $181 Ex $145 Gd $99
Mountain Eagle (compact 4.5-inch bbl.).... NiB $169 Ex $135 Gd $92

SSP-91 LONE EAGLE PISTOL
Single-shot action w/interchangeable rotating breech bbl., assembly. Calibers: .22 LR, .22 Mag., .22 Hornet, .22-250, .223 Rem., .243 Win., 6mm BR, 7mm-08, 7mm BR, .30-06, .30-30, .308 Win., .35 Rem., .357 Mag., .44 Mag., .444 Marlin. 14-inch interchangeable bbl. assembly, 15 inches overall. Weight: 4.5 lbs. Black or chrome finish. Made 1991 to date.
SSP-91 S/S pistol (complete gun w/black finish) ...... NiB $380 Ex $315 Gd $185
SSP-91 S/S pistol (complete gun w/chrome finish) ... NiB $559 Ex $475 Gd $368
Extra 14-inch bbl., action w/black finish...... NiB $625 Ex $564 Gd $486
Extra 14-inch bbl., action w/chrome finish.... NiB $715 Ex $644 Gd $553
Ambidextrous stock assembly .... NiB $94 Ex $75 Gd $51
W/muzzle brake, add $65
W/open sights, add $30

MAUSER PISTOLS — Oberndorf, Germany
Waffenfabrik Mauser of Mauser-Werke A.G.

MODEL 80-SA AUTOMATIC ...... NiB $450 Ex $325 Gd $190
Caliber: 9mm Para. 13-shot magazine, 4.66-inch bbl., 8 inches overall. Weight: 31.5 oz. Blued finish. Hardwood grips. Made 1991-94.

MODEL 90 DA AUTOMATIC ..... NiB $445 Ex $325 Gd $190
Caliber: 9mm Para. 14-shot magazine, 4.66-inch bbl., 8 inches overall. Weight: 35 oz. Blued finish. Hardwood grips. Made 1991-94.

MODEL 90 DAC COMPACT ...... NiB $450 Ex $325 Gd $190
Caliber: 9mm Para. 14-shot magazine, 4.13-inch bbl., 7.4 inches overall. Weight: 33.25 oz. Blued finish. Hardwood grips. Made 1991-94.

MODEL 1898 (1896) MILITARY AUTO PISTOL
Caliber: 7.63mm Mauser, but also chambered for 9mm Mauser and 9mm Para. w/the latter being identified by a large red "9" in the grips. 10-shot box magazine, 5.25-inch bbl., 12 inches overall. Weight: 45 oz. Adj. rear sight. Blued finish. Walnut grips. Made 1897-1939. Note: Specialist collectors recognize a number of variations at significantly higher values. Price here is for more common commercial and military types with original finish.
Commercial model (pre-war) .... NiB $3250 Ex $2500 Gd $925
Commercial model (wartime) .... NiB $1800 Ex $1350 Gd $500
Red 9 Commercial model (fixed sight) ...... NiB $1100 Ex $850 Gd $400
Red 9 WWI Contract (tangent sight)....... NiB $1950 Ex $1400 Gd $650
W/stock sssembly (matching SN), add $550

MODEL HSC DA AUTO PISTOL
Calibers: .32 Auto (7.65mm), .380 Auto (9mm Short). Eight-shot (.32) or 7-shot (.380) magazine, 3.4-inch bbl., 6.4 inches overall. Weight: 23.6 oz. Fixed sights. Blued or nickel finish. Checkered walnut grips. Made 1938-.45 and from 1968-96.
Commercial model (low grip screw)...... NiB $4000 Ex $3000 Gd $1850
Commercial model (wartime) .... NiB $400 Ex $325 Gd $180
Nazi military model (pre-war)............. NiB $750 Ex $550 Gd $200
Nazi military model (wartime) .... NiB $450 Ex $350 Gd $180
French production (postwar) .... NiB $375 Ex $300 Gd $175
Mauser production (postwar) .... NiB $350 Ex $295 Gd $150
Recent importation (Armes De Chasse) ...... NiB $475 Ex $425 Gd $240
Recent importation (Interarms)............. NiB $325 Ex $275 Gd $150
Recent importation (European Amer. Arms) ... NiB $265 Ex $225 Gd $125
Recent importation (Gamga, USA) .... NiB $395 Ex $330 Gd $220
American Eagle model (1 of 5000) .... NiB $438 Ex $350 Gd $238

LUGER LANGE PISTOL 08
Caliber: 9mm Para. Eight-inch bbl., Checkered grips. Blued finish. Accessorized w/walnut shoulder stock, front sight tool, spare magazine, leather case. Currently in production. Commemorative version made in limited quantities w/ivory grips and 14-carat gold monogram plate.

**Mauser Model 1898
(1896) Military**

Mauser Parabellum Luger

(cont'd) **LUGER LANGE PISTOL 08**
Commemorative model (100 produced) . . . NiB $2494 Ex $1995 Gd $1357
Commemorative matched pair . . . . NiB $4994 Ex $3995 Gd $2717
Cartridge counter model. . . . . NiB $3244 Ex $2595 Gd $1765
Carbine model (w/matching buttstock) . NiB $6063 Ex $4850 Gd $3298

PARABELLUM LUGER AUTO PISTOL
Current commercial model. Swiss pattern with grip safety. Calibers: 7.65mm Luger, 9mm Para. Eight-shot magazine, bbl. lengths: 4-, 6-inch, 8.75 inches overall (with 4-inch bbl.). Weight: 30 oz. (with 4-inch bbl.). Fixed sights. Blued finish. Checkered walnut grips. Made from 1970 to date. Note: Pistols of this model sold in the U.S. have the American Eagle stamped on the receiver.
Standard model (blue) . . . . NiB $1025 Ex $780 Gd $525

POCKET MODEL 1910 AUTO PISTOL
Caliber: .25 Auto (6.35mm). Nine-shot magazine, 3.1-inch bbl., 5.4 inches overall. Weight: 15 oz. Fixed sights. Blued finish. Checkered walnut or hard rubber grips. Made 1910-34.
Model 1910 (standard) . . . . NiB $425 Ex $300 Gd $140
Model 1910 (w/side latch) . . . . NiB $444 Ex $355 Gd $241

POCKET MODEL 1914 AUTOMATIC. . . . . . . NiB $425 Ex $300 Gd $145
Similar to Pocket Model 1910. Caliber: .32 Auto (7.65mm). Eight-shot magazine, 3.4-inch bbl., 6 inches overall. Weight: 21 oz. Fixed sights. Blued finish. Checkered walnut or hard rubber grips. Made 1914-34

POCKET MODEL 1934 . . . . NiB $450 Ex $325 Gd $150
Similar to Pocket Models 1910 and 1914 in the respective calibers. Chief difference is in the more streamlined, one-piece grips. Made 1934-39.

WTP MODEL I AUTO PISTOL. . . . . NiB $495 Ex $325 Gd $140
"Westentaschen-Pistole" (Vest Pocket Pistol). Caliber: .25 Automatic (6.35mm). Six-shot magazine, 2.5-inch bbl., 4 inches overall. Weight: 11.5 oz. Blued finish. Hard rubber grips. Made 1922-37.

WTP MODEL II AUTO PISTOL . . . . NiB $650 Ex $525 Gd $200
Similar to Model I but smaller and lighter. Caliber: .25 Automatic (6.35mm). Six-shot magazine, 2-inch bbl., 4 inches overall. Weight: 9.5 oz. Blued finish. Hard rubber grips. Made 1938-40.

MERWIN HULBERT & CO., — New York, NY

FIRST MODEL FRONTIER ARMY
Single action, .44 caliber, 7.5-inch bbl. Square butt, open top, scoop flutes on cylinder, two screws above trigger guard
. . . . NiB $3500 Ex $1800 Gd $750

SECOND MODEL FRONTIER ARMY
Similar to First Model except has only one screw above trigger guard. . . . . .NiB $5000 Ex $1700 Gd $900

SECOND MODEL POCKET ARMY
Similar to Second Model except has bird's-head butt instead of square butt, 3.5- or 7-inch (scarce) bbl. May be marked "Pocket Army." .NiB $5000 Ex $1250 Gd $800

THIRD MODEL FRONTIER ARMY
Caliber: .44, 7-inch round bbl. with no rib, single action. Square butt, top strap, usually has conventional fluting on cylinder but some have scoop flutes. . . . . .NiB $5000 Ex $1250 Gd $800

THIRD MODEL FRONTIER ARMY
Similar to Third Model Frontier Army except is double action.
. . . . .NiB $4750 Ex $1100 Gd $750

THIRD MODEL POCKET ARMY
Caliber: .44, 3.5- or 7.5-inch bbl. with no rib. Single action, bird's-head butt, top strap.
. . . . .NiB $4750 Ex $1100 Gd $750

THIRD MODEL POCKET ARMY
Similar to Third Model Pocket Army SA except is double action.
. . . . .NiB $4500 Ex $1000 Gd $700

FOURTH MODEL FRONTIER ARMY
Caliber: .44, 3.5- 5- or 7-inch unique ribbed bbl. Single action, square butt, top strap, conventional flutes on cylinder.
. . . . .NiB $6500 Ex $3500 Gd $1750

FOURTH MODEL FRONTIER ARMY
Similar to Fourth Model Frontier Army SA except is double action.
. . . . .NiB $6000 Ex $3000 Gd $1650

(The following handguns are foreign copies of Merwin Hulbert Co. guns and may be marked as such, or as "Sistema Merwin Hulbert," but rarely with the original Hopkins & Allen markings. These guns will usually bring half or less of a comparable genuine Merwin Hulbert product.)

FIRST POCKET MODEL
Caliber: .38 Special, 5-shot cylinder (w/cylinder pin exposed at front of frame), single action. Spur trigger; round loading hole in recoil shield, no loading gate.
. . . . .NiB $1500 Ex $450 Gd $225

SECOND POCKET MODEL
Similar to First Pocket Model except has sliding loading gate.
. . . . .NiB $1350 Ex. $375 Gd $200

THIRD POCKET MODEL
Similar to First Pocket Model except has enclosed cylinder pin.
. . . . .NiB $1250 Ex $350 Gd $185

THIRD POCKET MODEL W/TRIGGER GUARD
Similar to First Pocket Model except w/conventional trigger guard.
. . . . .NiB $1250 Ex $375 Gd $210

Mauser WTP Model I

Mitchell Arms Citation II

Mitchell Arms Sharpshooter II

MEDIUM FRAME POCKET MODEL
Caliber: .38 Spec., 5-shot cylinder, DA, may have hammer spur.
................................NiB $950 Ex $310 Gd $175

MEDIUM FRAME POCKET MODEL 32
Similar to Medium Frame Pocket Model except .32 caliber, 7-shot cylinder, double action. ....Nib $1100 Ex $350 Gd $200

TIP-UP MODEL 22
Similar to S&W Model One except .22 caliber, 7-shot cylinder, spur trigger. Scarce. ....NiB $1100 Ex $500 Gd $250.

MITCHELL ARMS, INC. — Santa Ana, California
MODEL 1911 GOLD SIGNATURE
Caliber: .45 ACP. Eight-shot magazine, 5-inch bbl., 8.75 inches overall. Weight: 39 oz. Interchangeable blade front sight, drift-adj. combat or fully adj. rear. Smooth or checkered walnut grips. Blued or stainless finish. Made 1994-96.

Blued model w/fixed sights	NiB $595	Ex $525	Gd $335
Blued model w/adj. sights	NiB $615	Ex $535	Gd $345
Stainless model w/fixed sights.....	NiB $765	Ex $650	Gd $550
Stainless model w/adj. sights......	NiB $795	Ex $675	Gd $575

ALPHA MODEL AUTO PISTOL
Dual action w/interchangeable trigger modules. Caliber: .45 ACP. Eight-shot magazine, 5-inch bbl., 8.75 inches overall. Weight: 39 oz. Interchangeable blade front sight, drift-adj. rear. Smooth or checkered walnut grips. Blued or stainless finish. Made from 1994 to date.Advertised 1995, but not manufactured.

Blued model w/fixed sights	NiB $873	Ex $698	Gd $475
Blued model w/adj. sights	NiB $906	Ex $725	Gd $493
Stainless model w/fixed sights..............	NiB $906	Ex $725	Gd $493
Stainless model w/adj. sights..............	NiB $936	Ex $749	Gd $509

AMERICAN EAGLE PISTOL .... NiB $581 Ex $465 Gd $316
Stainless-steel re-creation of the American Eagle Parabellum auto pistol. Caliber: 9mm Para. Seven-shot magazine, 4-inch bbl., 9.6 inches overall. Weight: 26.6 oz. Blade front sight, fixed rear. Stainless finish. Checkered walnut grips. Made 1993-94.

CITATION II AUTO PISTOL ...... NiB $395 Ex $295 Gd $170
Re-creation of the High Standard Supermatic Citation Military. Caliber: .22 LR. 10-shot magazine, 5.5-inch bull bbl. or 7.25 fluted bbl., 9.75 inches overall (5.5-inch bbl.). Weight: 44.5 oz. Ramp front sight, slide-mounted micro-adj. rear. Satin blued or stainless finish. Checkered walnut grips w/thumbrest. Made 1992-96.

OLYMPIC L.S.U. AUTO PISTOL.... NiB $825 Ex $550 Gd $275
Similar to the Citation II model except chambered in .22 Short, 6.75-inch round tapered bbl. w/stabilizer and removable counterweights. Made 1992-96.

SHARPSHOOTER II AUTO PISTOL....... NiB $320 Ex $280 Gd $170
Re-creation of the High Standard Sharpshooter. Caliber: .22 LR. 10-shot magazine, 5-inch bull bbl., 10.25 inches overall. Weight: 42 oz. Ramp front sight, slide-mounted micro-adj. rear. Satin blued or stainless finish. Checkered walnut grips w/thumbrest. Made 1992-96.

MODEL SA SPORT KING II....... NiB $269 Ex $215 Gd $146
Caliber: .22 LR. 10-shot magazine, 4.5- or 6.75-inch bbl., 9 or 11.25 inches overall. Weight: 39 or 42 oz. Checkered walnut or black plastic grips. Blade front sight and drift adjustable rear. Made 1993-94.

SA ARMY REVOLVER
Calibers: .357 Mag., .44 Mag., .45 Colt/.45 ACP. Six-shot cylinder. bbl., lengths: 4.75, 5.5, 7.5 inches, weight: 40-43 oz. Blade front sight, grooved top strap or adj. rear. Blued or nickel finish w/color-casehardened frame. Brass or steel backstrap/trigger guard. Smooth one-piece walnut grips. Imported 1987-94 and 1997 to date.

Standard model w/blued finish	NiB $369	Ex $295	Gd $201
Standard model w/nickel finish..........	NiB $406	Ex $325	Gd $221
Standard model w/stainless backstrap.....	NiB $438	Ex $350	Gd $238
.45 Combo w/blued finish	NiB $494	Ex $395	Gd $269
.45 Combo w/nickel finish	NiB $531	Ex $425	Gd $289

TROPHY II AUTO PISTOL........ NiB $425 Ex $350 Gd $170
Similar to the Citation II model except w/gold-plated trigger and gold-filled markings. Made 1992-96.

VICTOR II AUTO PISTOL . . . . **NiB $494 Ex $395 Gd $269**
Re-creation of the High Standard Victor w/full-length vent rib. Caliber: .22 LR. 10-shot magazine, 4.5- or 5.5-inch bbl., 9.75 inches overall (with 5.5-inch bbl.). Weight: 52 oz. (with 5.5-inch bbl.). Rib-mounted target sights. Satin blued or stainless finish. Checkered walnut grips w/thumbrest. Made 1992-96.

GUARDIAN ANGEL
DERRINGER . . . . **NiB $125 Ex $100 Gd $68**
Hammerless, double-action O/U derringer w/interchangeable drop-in breech block. Calibers: .22 LR, .22 WRM. Two-shot capacity. Two-inch bbl., 5 inches overall. Weight: 12 oz. Blue, nickel or gold finish. Blade front and fixed rear sights. Checkered black grips. Made 1996-97.

GUARDIAN II . . . . **NiB $238 Ex $190 Gd $129**
Caliber: .38 Special, Six-shot cylinder, 2-, 4- or 6-inch bbl., 8.5 inches overall (with 4-inch bbl.). Weight: 32 oz (with 4-inch bbl.). Blade ramp front and fixed rear sights. Checkered combat or target grips. Blued finish. Made 1995.

GUARDIAN III . . . . **NiB $275 Ex $225 Gd $140**
Same specifications as Guardian II model except w/adjustable rear sights. Made 1995.

TITAN II DA . . . . **NiB $305 Ex $240 Gd $165**
Caliber: .357 Mag. Six-shot cylinder. 2-, 4- or 6-inch bbl., 7.75 inches overall (with 4-inch bbl.). Weight: 38 oz (with 4-inch bbl.). Blade front and fixed rear sights. Crane mounted cylinder release. Blued or stainless finish. Made 1995.

TITAN III DA . . . . **NiB $345 Ex $270 Gd $180**
Same specification as the Titan II except w/adjustable rear sight. Made 1995.

MKE PISTOL — Ankara, Turkey
Mfd. by Makina ve Kimya Endüstrisi Kurumu

KIRIKKALE DA
AUTOMATIC PISTOL . . . . **NiB $365 Ex $295 Gd $170**
Similar to Walther PP. Calibers: .32 Auto (7.65mm), .380 Auto (9mm Short). Seven-shot magazine, 3.9-inch bbl., 6.7 inches overall. Weight: 24 oz. Fixed sights. Blued finish. Checkered plastic grips. Made 1948-88. Note: This is a Turkish Army standard service pistol.

MOA CORPORATION — Dayton, Ohio

MAXIMUM SINGLE-SHOT PISTOL
Calibers: .22 Hornet to .454 Casull Mag. Armoloy, Chromoloy or stainless falling block action fitted w/blued or stainless 8.75-, 10- or 14-inch Douglas bbl., weight: 60-68 oz. Smooth walnut grips. Made 1986 to date.
Chromoloy receiver
(blued bbl.) . . . . **NiB $799 Ex $695 Gd $350**
Armoloy receiver (blued bbl.) . . . . . **NiB $810 Ex $715 Gd $370**
Stainless receiver (blued bbl.) . . . . . **NiB $905 Ex $810 Gd $570**
W/stainless bbl., add **$95**
W/extra bbl., add **$250**

MAXIMUM CARBINE PISTOL
Similar to Maximum Pistol except w/18-inch bbl. Made 1986-88 and 1994 to date.
MOA Maximum (blued bbl.) . . . . . . **NiB $825 Ex $650 Gd $430**
MOA Maximum (stainless bbl.) . . . . **NiB $895 Ex $725 Gd $485**

**Mitchell Arms SA
Army Revolver**

**Mitchell Arms
Victor II**

MKE Kirikkale

**MOA Maximum
Carbine Pistol**

Mossberg Brownie "Pepperbox" Pistol

Navy Arms Model 1875 Schofield

Navy Arms Model 1875 SA Revolver

Navy Arms Frontier Standard

Navy Arms Frontier Target Model

O.F. MOSSBERG & SONS, INC. — North Haven, Connecticut

BROWNIE "PEPPERBOX" PISTOL....... NiB $350 Ex $300 Gd $170
Hammerless, top-break, double-action, four bbls. w/revolving firing pin. Caliber: .22 LR, 2.5-inch bbls., weight: 14 oz. Blued finish. Serated grips. Approximately 37,000 made 1919-.32.

NAMBU PISTOLS
See Listings under Japanese Military Pistols.

NAVY ARMS COMPANY — Martinsburg, West Virginia

MODEL 1873 SA REVOLVER
Calibers: .44-40, .45 Colt. Six-shot cylinder, bbl. lengths: 3, 4.75, 5.5, 7.5 inches, 10.75 inches overall (with 5.5-inch bbl.). Weight: 36 oz. Blade front sight, grooved topstrap rear. Blued w/color-case-hardened frame or nickel finish. Smooth walnut grips. Made 1991 to date.

Blued finish w/brass backstrap.... NiB $345 Ex $280 Gd $150
U.S. Artillery model w/5-inch bbl.... NiB $375 Ex $300 Gd $204
U.S. Cavalry model w/7-inch bbl... NiB $406 Ex $325 Gd $221
Bisley model................... NiB $345 Ex $295 Gd $150
Sheriff's model (disc. 1998)....... NiB $340 Ex $270 Gd $150

MODEL 1875 SCHOFIELD REVOLVER
Replica of S&W Model 3, top-break single-action w/auto ejector. Calibers: .44-40 or .45 LC. Six-shot cylinder, 5- or 7-inch bbl., 10.75 or 12.75 inches overall. Weight: 39 oz. Blade front sight, square-notched rear. Polished blued finish. Smooth walnut grips. Made 1994 to date.

Cavalry model (7-inch bbl.)....... NiB $600 Ex $525 Gd $250
Deluxe Cavalry model
(engraved)................... NiB $1438 Ex $1150 Gd $782
Wells Fargo model (5-inch bbl.) ...NiB $619 Ex $495 Gd $337
Deluxe Wells Fargo
model (engraved)............ NiB $1406 Ex $1125 Gd $765
Hideout model (3.5-inch bbl.)..... NiB $594 Ex $475 Gd $323

MODEL 1875 SA REVOLVER......
NiB $369 Ex $295 Gd $201
Replica of Remington Model 1875. Calibers: .357 Magnum, .44-40, .45 Colt. Six-shot cylinder, 7.5-inch bbl., 13.5 inches overall. Weight: About 48 oz. Fixed sights. Blued or nickel finish. Smooth walnut grips. Made in Italy c.1955-1980. Note: Originally marketed in the U.S. as Replica Arms Model 1875 (that firm was acquired by Navy Arms Co).

FRONTIER SA REVOLVER........
NiB $288 Ex $230 Gd $156
Calibers: .22 LR, .22 WMR, .357 Mag., .45 Colt. Six-shot cylinder, bbl. lengths: 4.5-, 5.5-, 7.5-inches, 10.25 inches overall (with 4.5-inch bbl.). Weight: About 36 oz. (with 4.5-inch bbl.). Fixed sights. Blued bbl., and cylinder, color-casehardened frame, brass grip frame. One-piece smooth walnut grip. Imported 1975-79.

FRONTIER TARGET MODEL......
NiB $313 Ex $250 Gd $170
Same as standard Frontier except has adj. rear sight and ramp front sight. Imported 1975-79.

BUNTLINE FRONTIER..........
NiB $469 Ex $375 Gd $255
Same as Target Frontier except has detachable shoulder stock and 16.5-inch bbl. Calibers: .357 Magnum and .45 Colt only. Made 1975-79.

HANDGUNS

LUGER (STANDARD) AUTOMATIC . . . . **NiB $156 Ex $125 Gd $85**
Caliber: .22 LR, standard or high velocity. 10-shot magazine, bbl. length: 4.5 inches, 8.9 inches overall. Weight: 1 lb., 13.5 oz. Square blade front sight w/square notch, stationary rear sight. Walnut checkered grips. Non-reflecting black finish. Made 1986-88.

**ROLLING BLOCK
SINGLE-SHOT PISTOL** . . . . **NiB $340 Ex $285 Gd $170**
Calibers: .22 LR, .22 Hornet, .357 Magnum. Eight-inch bbl., 12 inches overall. Weight: About 40 oz. Adjustable sights. Blued bbl., color-casehardened frame, brass trigger guard. Smooth walnut grip and forearm. Imported 1965-80.

TT-OLYMPIA PISTOL . . . . **NiB $250 Ex $225 Gd $150**
Reproduction of the Walther Olympia Target Pistol. Caliber: .22 LR. Eight inches overall 4.6-inch bbl., weight: 28 oz. Blade front sight, adj. rear. Blued finish. Checkered hardwood grips. Imported 1992-94.

Navy Arms
Rolling Block Single-Shot

Navy Arms
TT-Olympia Pistol

NEW ENGLAND FIREARMS — Gardner, Massachusetts

In 1987, New England Firearms was established as an independent company producing select H&R models under the NEF logo. In 1991, H&R 1871, Inc. was formed from the residual of the parent company and took over the New England Firearms facility. H&R 1871 produced firearms under both their logo and the NEF brand name until 1999, when the Marlin Firearms Company acquired the assets of H&R 1871.

MODEL R73 REVOLVER . . . . **NiB $125 Ex $95 Gd $60**
Caliber: .32 H&R Mag. Five-shot cylinder, 2.5- or 4-inch bbl., 8.5 inches overall (with 4-inch bbl.). Weight: 26 oz. (with 4 inch bbl.). Fixed or adjustable sights. Blued or nickel finish. Walnut-finish hardwood grips. Made from 1988-99.

MODEL R92 REVOLVER . . . . **NiB $125 Ex $95 Gd $60**
Same general specifications as Model R73 except chambered for .22 LR. Nine-shot cylinder. Weight: 28 oz. w/4 inch bbl., Made 1988-99.

MODEL 832 STARTER PISTOL . . . . **NiB $89 Ex $71 Gd $48**
Calibers: .22 Blank, .32 Blank. Nine- and 5-shot cylinders, respectively. Push-pin swing-out cylinder. Solid wood grips w/NEF medallion insert.

ULTRA REVOLVER . . . . **NiB $156 Ex $125 Gd $85**
Calibers: .22 LR, .22 Mag. Nine-shot cylinder in .22 LR, 6-shot cylinder in .22 Mag., 4- or 6-inch ribbed bull bbl., 10.75 inches overall (with 6-inch bbl.). Weight: 36 oz. (with 6-inch bbl.). Blade front sight, adj. square-notched rear. Blued or nickel finish. Walnut-finish hardwood grips. Made from 1989-99.

LADY ULTRA REVOLVER . . . . **NiB $150 Ex $115 Gd $70**
Same basic specifications as the Ultra except in .32 H&R Mag. w/5-shot cylinder and 3-inch ribbed bull bbl., 7.5 inches overall. Weight: 31 oz. Made 1992 -99.

New England Firearms
Model R73 Revolver

New England Firearms
Model 832 Starter Pistol

NORTH AMERICAN ARMS — Provo, Utah

MODEL 22LR . . . . **NiB $156 Ex $125 Gd $85**
Same as Model 22S except chambered for .22 LR., is 3.88-inches overall, weight: 4.5 oz. Made 1976 to date.

MODEL 22S MINI REVOLVER . . . . . . **NiB $169 Ex $135 Gd $92**
Single-Action. Caliber: .22 Short. Five-shot cylinder, 1.13-inch bbl., 3.5-inches overall. Weight: 4 oz. Fixed sights. Stainless steel. Plastic grips. Made from 1975 to date.

MODEL 450 MAGNUM EXPRESS
Single-Action. Calibers: .450 Magnum Express, .45 Win. Mag. Five-shot cylinder, 7.5- or 10.5-inch bbl., matte or polished stainless steel finish. Walnut grips. Presentation case. Disc. 1986.
Matte stainless model . . . . **NiB $1200 Ex $950 Gd $700**
Polished stainless model . . . . **NiB $1400 Ex $1100 Gd $850**
W/10-inch bbl., add $250
W/combo cylinder, add $225

Ortgies
Pocket Automatic Pistol

BLACK WIDOW REVOLVER
SA. Calibers: .22 LR., .22 WMR. Five-shot cylinder, 2-inch heavy vent bbl., 5.88-inches overall. Weight: 8.8 oz. Fixed or adj. sights. Full-size black rubber grips. Stainless steel brush finish. Made from 1990 to date.
Adj. sight model . . . . NiB $256 Ex $215 Gd $125
Adj. sight combo model . . . . NiB $295 Ex $240 Gd $170
Fixed sight model . . . . NiB $206 Ex $165 Gd $112
Fixed sight combo model. . . . . NiB $284 Ex $235 Gd $173

GUARDIAN DAO PISTOL . . . . NiB $355 Ex $285 Gd $290
Caliber: .32 ACP. Six-shot magazine, 2-inch bbl., 4.4 inches overall. Weight: 13.5 oz. Fixed sights. Black synthetic grips. Stainless steel. Made 1997 to date.

MINI-MASTER TARGET REVOLVER
SA. Calibers: .22 LR., .22 WMR. Five-shot cylinder, 4-inch heavy vent rib bbl., 7.75-inches overall. Weight: 10.75 oz. Fixed or adj. sights. Black rubber grips. Stainless steel brush finish. Made from 1990 to date.
Adj. sight model . . . . NiB $245 Ex $200 Gd $170
Adj. sight combo model . . . . NiB $351 Ex $288 Gd $208
Fixed sight model . . . . NiB $244 Ex $195 Gd $133
Fixed sight combo model. . . . . NiB $319 Ex $263 Gd $191

NORWEGIAN MILITARY PISTOLS
Mfd. by Kongsberg Vaapenfabrikk, Government Arsenal at Kongsberg, Norway

MODEL 1914
AUTOMATIC PISTOL . . . . NiB $406 Ex $325 Gd $221
Similar to Colt Model 1911 .45 Automatic w/same general specifications except has lengthened slide stop. Made 1919-46.

NORWEGIAN
MODEL 1912 . . . . NiB $2625 Ex $2100 Gd $1428
Same as the model 1914 except has conventional slide stop. Only 500 were made.

OLYMPIC ARMS, INC.
Olympia Washington

OA-93 AR SEMIAUTOMATIC PISTOL
AR-15 style receiver with no buffer tube or charging handle. Caliber: .223 Rem. or 7.62x39mm. Five-, 20- or 30-shot detachable

(cont'd) OA-93 AR SEMIAUTOMATIC PISTOL
magazine, 6-, 9- or 14-inch stainless steel bbl., 15.75 inches overall w/6-inch bbl., weight: 4 lbs., 3 oz. Flattop upper with no open sights. Vortex flash suppressor. A2 stowaway pistol grip and forward pistol grip. Made 1993-94. Note: All post-ban versions of OA-93 style weapons are classified by BATF as "Any Other Weapon" and must be transferred by a Class III dealer. Values listed here are for limited-production, pre-ban guns.
Model OA-93
(.223 Rem.) . . . . NiB $3500 Ex $2800 Gd $2550
Model OA-93
(7.62x39mm). . . . . NiB $4300 Ex $4100 Gd $3800

OA-96 AR SEMI-
AUTOMATIC PISTOL . . . . NiB $865 Ex $775 Gd $690
Similar to Model OA-93 AR except w/6.5-inch bbl. only chambered for .223 Rem. Additional compliance modifications include a fixed (nonremovable) well-style magazine and no forward pistol grip. Made 1996 to date.

ORTGIES PISTOLS — Erfurt, Germany
Manufactured by Deutsche Werke A.G.

POCKET AUTO-
MATIC PISTOL . . . . NiB $300 Ex $250 Gd $180
Calibers: .32 Auto (7.65mm), .380 Auto (9mm). Seven-shot magazine (.380 cal.), 8-shot (.32 cal.), 3.25-inch bbl., 6.5-inches overall. Weight: 22 oz. Fixed sights. Blued finish. Plain walnut grips. Made in 1920's.

VEST POCKET
AUTOMATIC PISTOL . . . . NiB $275 Ex $220 Gd $150
Caliber: .25 Auto (6.35mm). Six-shot magazine, 2.75-inch bbl., 5.19 inches overall. Weight: 13.5 oz. Fixed sights. Blued finish. Plain walnut grips. Made in 1920's.

PHOENIX ARMS — Ontario, California

MODEL HP22/HP25
SA AUTO PISTOLS. . . . . NiB $119 Ex $68 Gd $40
Caliber: .22 LR, .25 ACP. 10-shot magazine, 3-inch bbl., 5.5 inches overall. Weight: 20 oz. Checkered synthetic grips. Blade front sight, adjustable rear. Blue, chrome or nickel finish. Made 1994 to date.

MODEL HP
RANGE-MASTER TARGET SA
AUTO PISTOL . . . . NiB $128 Ex $100 Gd $70
Similar to Model HP .22 except w/5.5-inch target bbl. and extended magazine, Ramp front sight, adjustable notch rear on vent rib. Checkered synthetic grips. Blue or satin nickel finish. Made 1998 to date.

MODEL HP
RANGE-MASTER DELUXE TARGET
SA AUTO PISTOL . . . . NiB $225 Ex $130 Gd $90
Similar to Model HP Rangemaster Target model except w/dual-2000 laser sight and custom wood grips. Made 1998 to date.

"RAVEN" SA
AUTO PISTOL . . . . NiB $69 Ex $50 Gd $35
Caliber: .25 ACP. Six-shot magazine, 2.5 inch bbl., 4.75 inches overall. Weight: 15 oz. Ivory, pink pearl, or black slotted stocks. Fixed sights. Blue, chrome or nickel finish. Made 1993 to date.

PARA-ORDNANCE MFG. INC. — Scarborough, Ontario, Canada

LIMITED EDITION SERIES

Custom-tuned and fully accessorized "Limited Edition" versions of standard "P" Models. Enhanced-grip frame and serrated slide fitted w/match-grade bbl., and full-length recoil spring guide system. Beavertail grip safety and skeletonized hammer. Ambidextrous safety and trigger-stop adjustment. Fully adjustable or contoured low-mount sights. For pricing see individual models.

MODEL P-10 SA AUTO PISTOL

Super compact. Calibers: .40 S&W, .45 ACP. 10-shot magazine, 3-inch bbl., weight: 24 oz. (alloy frame) or 31 oz. (steel frame). Ramp front sight and drift adjustable rear w/3-dot system. Steel or alloy frame. Matte black, Duo-Tone or stainless finish. Made 1997 to date.

Alloy model	NiB $625	Ex $500	Gd $325
Duo-Tone model	NiB $619	Ex $495	Gd $337
Stainless steel model	NiB $706	Ex $575	Gd $407
Steel model	NiB $604	Ex $485	Gd $333
Limited model (tuned & accessorized), add			$125

P-12 COMPACT AUTO PISTOL

Calibers: .45 ACP. 11-shot magazine, 3.5-inch bbl., 7-inches overall. Weight: 24 oz. (alloy frame). Blade front sight, adj. rear w/3-dot system. Textured composition grips. Matte black alloy or steel finish. Made 1990 to date.

Model P1245 (alloy)	NiB $639	Ex $511	Gd $347
Model P1245C (steel)	NiB $763	Ex $610	Gd $414
Limited model (tuned & accessorized), add			$125

P-13 AUTO PISTOL

Same general specifications as Model P-12 except w/12-shot magazine, 4.5-inch bbl., 8-inches overall. Weight: 25 oz. (alloy frame). Blade front sight, adj. rear w/3-dot system. Textured composition grips. Matte black alloy or steel finish. Made 1990 to date.

Model P1345 (alloy)	NiB $765	Ex $550	Gd $350
Model P1345C (steel)	NiB $776	Ex $621	Gd $422
Limited model (tuned & accessorized), add			$125

P-14 AUTO PISTOL

Caliber: .45 ACP. 13-shot magazine, 5-inch bbl., 8.5 inches overall. Weight: 28 oz. Alloy frame. Blade front sight, adj. rear w/3-dot system. Textured composition grips. Matte black alloy or steel finish. Made from 1990 to date.

Model P1445 (alloy)	NiB $625	Ex $500	Gd $325
Model P1445C (steel)	NiB $691	Ex $555	Gd $381
Limited model (tuned & accessorized), add			$125

MODEL P-15 AUTO PISTOL

Caliber: .40 S&W. 10-shot magazine, 4.25-inch bbl., 7.75 inches overall. Weight: 28 to 36 oz. Steel, alloy or stainless receiver. Matte black, Duotone or stainless finish. Made 1996-99.

Model P1540 (alloy)	NiB $625	Ex $500	Gd $435
Model P1540C (steel)	NiB $591	Ex $475	Gd $326
Duotone stainless model	NiB $664	Ex $540	Gd $382
Stainless model	NiB $704	Ex $575	Gd $410

MODEL P-16 SA AUTO PISTOL

Caliber: .40 S&W. 10- or 16-shot magazine, 5-inch bbl., 8.5 inches overall. Weight: 40 oz. Ramp front sight and drift adjustable rear w/3-dot system. Carbon steel or stainless frame. Matte black, Duotone or stainless finish. Made 1997 to date.

Blue steel model	NiB $640	Ex $515	Gd $350
Duotone model	NiB $660	Ex $535	Gd $375

Para-Ordnance P-12 Compact

Para-Ordnance P-14 Auto Pistol

Plainfield Model 71

(cont'd) MODEL P-16 SA AUTO PISTOL

Stainless model	NiB $775	Ex $660	Gd $355
Limited model (tuned & accessorized), add			$125

MODEL P-18 SA AUTO PISTOL

Caliber: 9mm Parabellum. 10- or 18-shot magazine, 5-inch bbl., 8.5 inches overall. Weight: 40 oz. Dovetailed front sight and fully adjustable rear. Bright stainless finish. Made 1998 to date.

Stainless model	NiB $725	Ex $575	Gd $450
Limited model (tuned & accessorized), add			$125

Plainfield Model 72

Radom P-35

**Record-Match
Model 200 Free Pistol**

PLAINFIELD MACHINE COMPANY — Dunellen, New Jersey

This firm disc. operation about 1982.

MODEL 71 AUTOMATIC PISTOL
Calibers: .22 LR, .25 Automatic w/conversion kit available. 10-shot magazine (.22 LR) or 8-shot (.25 Auto), 2.5-inch bbl., 5.13 inches overall. Weight: 25 oz. Fixed sights. Stainless steel frame/slide. Checkered walnut grips. Made 1970-82. See illustration previous page.
.22 LR or .25 Auto only . . . . NiB $150 Ex $130 Gd $85
W/conversion kit . . . . NiB $180 Ex $150 Gd $90

MODEL 72 AUTOMATIC PISTOL
Same as Model 71 except has aluminum slide, 3.5-inch bbl., 6 inches overall. Made 1970-82
.22 LR or .25 Auto only . . . . NiB $160 Ex $135 Gd $70
W/conversion kit . . . . NiB $175 Ex $140 Gd $95

PROFESSIONAL ORDNANCE, INC. — Lake Havasu City, Arizona

MODEL CARBON-15 TYPE 20
SEMIAUTOMATIC PISTOL . . . . NiB $800 Ex $725 Gd $475
Similar to Carbon-15 Type 97 except w/unfluted barrel. Weight: 40 oz. Matte black finish. Made 1999 to date.

MODEL CARBON-15 TYPE 97
SEMIAUTOMATIC PISTOL . . . . NiB $875 Ex $825 Gd $500
AR-15 operating system w/recoil reduction system. Caliber: .223 Rem. 10-shot magazine, 7.25-inch fluted bbl., 20 inches overall. Weight: 46 oz. Ghost ring sights. Carbon-fiber upper and lower receivers w/Chromoly bolt carrier. Matte black finish. Checkered composition grip. Made 1996 to date.

RADOM PISTOL — Radom, Poland
Manufactured by the Polish Arsenal

P-35 AUTOMATIC PISTOL
Variation of the Colt Government Model .45 Auto. Caliber: 9mm Para. Eight-shot magazine, 4.75-inch bbl., 7.75 inches overall. Weight: 29 oz. Fixed sights. Blued finish. Plastic grips. Made 1935 thru WWII.
**Commercial model
(Polish Eagle)** . . . . NiB $2350 Ex $1600 Gd $450
**Nazi military model
(W/slotted backstrap)** . . . . NiB $900 Ex $700 Gd $190
**Nazi military model
(W/takedown lever)** . . . . NiB $550 Ex $375 Gd $185
**Nazi military model
(No takedown lever or slot)** . . . . . . NiB $375 Ex $300 Gd $180
Nazi military model (Parkerized) . . . . NiB $1000 Ex $800 Gd $200

RECORD-MATCH PISTOLS — Zella-Mehlis, Germany, Manufactured by Udo Anschütz

MODEL 200 FREE PISTOL . . . . NiB $990 Ex $935 Gd $700
Basically the same as Model 210 except w/different stock design and conventional set trigger, spur trigger guard. Made prior to WW II.

MODEL 210 FREE PISTOL . . . . . . NiB $1320 Ex $1260 Gd $701
System Martini action, set trigger w/button release. Caliber: .22 LR. Single-shot, 11-inch bbl., weight: 46 oz. Target sights micrometer rear. Blued finish. Carved and checkered walnut forearm and stock w/adj. hand base. Also made w/dual action (Model 210A); weight 35 oz. Made prior to WWII.

REISING ARMS CO. — Hartford, Connecticut

TARGET AUTOMATIC PISTOL . . . . . NiB $475 Ex $350 Gd $175
Hinged frame. Outside hammer. Caliber: .22 LR. 12-shot magazine, 6.5-inch bbl., fixed sights. Blued finish. Hard rubber grips. Made 1921-24.

REMINGTON ARMS COMPANY — Ilion, New York

MODEL 51 AUTOMATIC PISTOL
Calibers: .32 Auto, .380 Auto. Seven-shot magazine, 3.5-inch bbl., 6.63 inches overall. Weight: 21 oz. Fixed sights. Blued finish. Hard rubber grips. Made 1918-34.
.32 ACP . . . . NiB $750 Ex $625 Gd $325
.380 ACP . . . . NiB $650 Ex $525 Gd $275

Remington Model 51

MODEL 95 DOUBLE DERRINGER

SA. Caliber: 41 Short Rimfire. Three-inch double bbls. (superposed), 4.88 inches overall. Early models have long hammer spur and two-armed extractor, but later guns have short hammer spur and sliding extractor (a few have no extractor). Fixed blade front sight and grooved rear. finish: Blued, blued w/nickel-plated frame or fully nickel-plated; also w/factory engraving. Grips: Walnut, checkered hard rubber, pearl, ivory. Weight: 11 oz. Made 1866-1935. Approximately 150,000 were manufactured. Note: During the 70 years of its production, serial numbering of this model was repeated two or three times. Therefore, aside from hammer and extractor differences between the earlier and later models, the best clue to the age of a Double Derringer is the stamping of the company's name on the top of the bbl., or side rib. Prior to 1888, derringers were stamped "E. Remington & Sons, Ilion, N.Y." on one side rib and "Elliot's Patent Dec. 12, 1865" on the other (Type I-early & mid-production) and on the top rib (Type I-late production). In 1888-1911, "Remington Arms Co., Ilion, N.Y." and patent date were stamped on the top rib (Type II) and from 1912-35 "Remington Arms - U.M.C. Co., Ilion, N.Y." and patent date were stamped on the top rib.

Model 95 (Early Type I,
w/o extractor) . . . . NiB $2000 Ex $1950 Gd $700
Model 95 (Mid Type I,
w/extractor) . . . . NiB $2150 Ex $2000 Gd $795
Model 95 (Late Type I,
w/extractor) . . . . NiB $2200 Ex $2000 Gd $800
Model 95 (Type II,
produced 1988-11) . . . . NiB $1800 Ex $1400 Gd $600
Model 95 (Type III,
produced 1912-35) . . . . NiB $869 Ex $695 Gd $473
Factory-engraved model w/ivory
or pearl grips, add $35%

NEW MODEL SINGLE-SHOT TARGET PISTOL

Also called Model 1901 Target. Rolling-block action. Calibers: .22 Short & Long, .25 Stevens, .32 S&W, .44 S&W Russian. 10-inch half-octagon bbl., 14 inches overall. Weight: 45 oz. (.22 cal.). Target sights. Blued finish. Checkered walnut grips and forearm. Made 1901-09.

Model 1901 (.22 caliber). . . . . . . NiB $2500 Ex $2280 Gd $980
Model 1901
(.25 Stevens, .32 S&W) . . . . NiB $2188 Ex $1750 Gd $1190
Model 1901 (.44 Russian) . . . . . NiB $2700 Ex $2450 Gd $1050

MODEL XP-100 CUSTOM PISTOL . . . . NiB $495 Ex $395 Gd $210
Bolt-action, single-shot, long-range pistol. Calibers: .223 Rem., 7mm-08 or .35 Rem. 14.5-inch bbl., standard contour or heavy. Weight: About 4.25 lbs. Currently in production.

MODEL XP-100 SILHOUETTE. . . . . NiB $544 Ex $435 Gd $296
Same general specifications as Model XP-100 except chambered for 7mm BR Rem. and 35 Rem. 14.75-inch bbl., weight: 4.13 lbs. Made 1987-92.

**Remington
95 Double Derringer**

**Remington
XP-100 Custom**

**Remington
XP-100 Custom Heavy Barrel**

**Remington
XP-100 Silhouette**

**Remington
XP-100 Single-Shot**

**Remington
XP-100 Varmint Special**

Rossi Model 88
DA Revolver

Rossi Model 851
DA revolver

Rossi DA Revolver

MODEL XP-100 SINGLE-SHOT PISTOL ... NiB $419 Ex $335 Gd $228
Bolt action. Caliber: 221 Rem. Fireball. 10.5-inch vent rib bbl., 16.75 inches overall. Weight: 3.75 lbs. Adj. rear sight, blade front, receiver drilled and tapped for scope mounts. Blued finish. One-piece brown nylon stock. Made 1963-88.

MODEL XP-100 VARMINT SPECIAL ...... NiB $495 Ex $395 Gd $210
Bolt-action, single-shot, long-range pistol. Calibers: .223 Rem., 7mm BR. 14.5-inch bbl., 21.25 inches overall. Weight: About 4.25 lbs. One-piece Du Pont nylon stock w/universal grips. Made 1986-92.

MODEL XP-100R CUSTOM REPEATER
Same general specifications as Model XP-100 Custom except 4- or 5- shot repeater chambered for .22-250, .223 Rem., .250 Savage, 7mm-08 Rem., .308 Win., .35 Rem. and .350 Rem. Mag. Kevlar-reinforced synthetic or fiberglass stock w/blind magazine and sling swivel studs. Made 1992-94 and 1998 to date.
Model XP-100R (fiberglass stock) .... NiB $656 Ex $525 Gd $357
Model XP-100R KS (kevlar stock) .... NiB $595 Ex $550 Gd $350

XP-22R
RIMFIRE REPEATER .... NiB $544 Ex $435 Gd $296
Bolt-action clip repeater built on Model 541-style action. Calibers: .22 Short, Long, LR. Five-shot magazine, 14.5-inch bbl., weight: 4.25 lbs. Rem. synthetic stock. Announced 1991 but not produced.

RG REVOLVERS — Mfg. By Rohm Gmbh, Germany *(Imported by R.G. Industries, Miami, Florida)*

MODEL 23
SA/DA. 6-shot magazine, swing-out cylinder. Caliber: .22 LR. 1.75- or 3.38-inch bbl., Overall length: 5.13 and 7.5 inches. Weight: 16-17 oz. Fixed sights. Blued or nickel finish. Disc. 1986.
Blued finish .... NiB $95 Ex $80 Gd $50
Nickel finish .... NiB $95 Ex $80 Gd $50

MODEL 38S
SA/DA. Caliber: .38 Special. Six-shot magazine, swing-out cylinder. Three- or 4-inch bbl., overall length: 8.25 and 9.25 inches. Weight: 32-34 oz. Windage-adj. rear sight. Blued finish. Disc. 1986.
W/plastic grips .... NiB $131 Ex $105 Gd $71
W/wood grips .... NiB $150 Ex $120 Gd $82

ROSSI REVOLVERS — Sáo Leopoldo, Brazil Manufactured by Amadeo Rossi S.A. *(Imported by Interarms, Alexanderia, Virginia)*

MODEL 31 DA REVOLVER .... NiB $120 Ex $105 Gd $70
Caliber: .38 Special. Five-shot cylinder, 4-inch bbl., weight: 20 oz. Blued or nickel finish. Disc. 1985.

MODEL 51 DA REVOLVER .... NiB $125 Ex $110 Gd $80
Caliber: .22 LR. Six-shot cylinder, 6-inch bbl., weight: 28 oz. Blued finish. Disc. 1985.

MODEL 68 .... NiB $165 Ex $135 Gd $70
Caliber: .38 Special. Five-round magazine, 2- or 3-inch bbl., overall length: 6.5 and 7.5 inches. Weight: 21-23 oz. Blued finish. Nickel finish available w/3-inch bbl. Disc. 1998.

MODEL 84 DA REVOLVER .... NiB $190 Ex $155 Gd $125
Caliber: .38 Special. Six-shot cylinder, 3-inch bbl., 8 inches overall. Weight: 27.5 oz. Stainless steel finish. Imported 1984-86.

MODEL 85 DA REVOLVER .... NiB $206 Ex $165 Gd $112
Same as Model 84 except has vent rib. Imported 1985-86.

MODEL 88 DA REVOLVER
Caliber: .38 Special. Five-shot cylinder, 2- or 3-inch bbl., weight: 21 oz. Stainless steel finish. Imported 1988-98.
Model 88 (disc.) .... NiB $195 Ex $145 Gd $110
Model 88 Lady Rossi
(round butt) .... NiB $219 Ex $175 Gd $119

MODEL 88/2 DA REVOLVER....... NiB $181 Ex $145 Gd $99
Caliber: .38 Special. Five-shot cylinder, 2- or 3-inch bbl., 6.5 inches overall. Weight: 21 oz. Stainless steel finish. Imported 1985-87.

MODEL 89 DA REVOLVER .... NiB $175 Ex $135 Gd $115
Caliber: .32 S&W. Six-shot cylinder, 3-inch bbl., 7.5 inches overall. Weight: 17 oz. Stainless steel finish. Imported 1989-90.

MODEL 94 DA REVOLVER . . . . **NiB $160 Ex $140 Gd $95**
Caliber: .38 Special. Six-shot cylinder, 3-inch bbl., 8 inches overall. Weight: 29 oz. Imported 1985-88.

MODEL 95 (951) REVOLVER . . . . . **NiB $188 Ex $150 Gd $102**
Caliber: .38 Special. Six-round magazine, 3-inch bbl., 8 inches overall. Weight: 27.5 oz. Vent rib. Blued finish. Imported 1985-90.

MODEL 351/352 REVOLVERS
Caliber: .38 Special. Five-shot cylinder, 2-inch bbl., 6.87 inches overall. Weight: 22 oz. Ramp front and rear adjustable sights. Stainless or matte blued finish. Imported 1999 to date.
Model 351 (matte blue finish) . . . . . **NiB $250 Ex $200 Gd $130**
Model 352 (stainless finish) . . . . **NiB $200 Ex $160 Gd $109**

MODEL 461/462 REVOLVERS
Caliber: .357 Magnum. Six-shot cylinder, 2-inch heavy bbl., 6.87 inches overall. Weight: 26 oz. Rubber grips w/ serrated ramp front sight. Stainless or matte blued finish. Imported 1999 to date.
Model 461
(Matte blue finish) . . . . **NiB $250 Ex $200 Gd $130**
Model 462
(stainless finish) . . . . **NiB $275 Ex $230 Gd $165**

MODEL 511 DA REVOLVER . . . . . . **NiB $190 Ex $160 Gd $125**
Similar to the Model 51 except in stainless steel. Imported 1986-1990.

MODEL 515 DA REVOLVER . . . . . . **NiB $206 Ex $165 Gd $112**
Calibers: .22 LR, .22 Mag. Six-shot cylinder, 4-inch bbl., 9 inches overall. Weight: 30 oz. Red ramp front sight, adj. square-notched rear. Stainless finish. Checkered hardwood grips. Imported from 1992 to date.

MODEL 518 DA REVOLVER . . . . . . **NiB $194 Ex $155 Gd $105**
Similar to the Model 515 except in caliber .22 LR. Imported 1993 to date.

MODEL 677 DA REVOLVER . . . . . . **NiB $216 Ex $175 Gd $122**
Caliber: .357 Mag. Six-shot cylinder, 2-inch bbl., 6.87 inches overall. Weight: 26 oz. Serrated front ramp sight, channel rear. Matte blue finish. Contoured rubber grips. Imported 1997 to date.

MODEL 720 DA REVOLVER . . . . . . **NiB $219 Ex $175 Gd $119**
Caliber: .44 Special. Five-shot cylinder, 3-inch bbl., 8 inches overall. Weight: 27.5 oz. Red ramp front sight, adj. square-notched rear. Stainless finish. Checkered Neoprene combat-style grips. Imported from 1992 to date.

MODEL 841 DA REVOLVER . . . . . . **NiB $206 Ex $165 Gd $112**
Same general specifications as Model 84 except has 4-inch bbl., (9 inches overall), weight: 30 oz. Imported 1985-86.

MODEL 851 DA REVOLVER . . . . . . **NiB $204 Ex $175 Gd $115**
Same general specifications as Model 85 except w/3-or 4-inch bbl., 8 inches overall (with 3-inch bbl.). Weight: 27.5 oz. (with 3-inch bbl.). Red ramp front sight, adj. square-notched rear. Stainless finish. Checkered hardwood grips. Imported 1991 to date.

MODEL 877 DA REVOLVER . . . . . . **NiB $226 Ex $185 Gd $132**
Same general specifications as Model 677 except stainless steel. Made 1996 to date.

MODEL 941 DA REVOLVER . . . . . . **NiB $188 Ex $150 Gd $102**
Caliber: .38 Special. Six-shot cylinder, 4-inch bbl., 9 inches overall. Weight: 30 oz. Blued finish. Imported 1985-86.

Rossi Model 971
DA Revolver

MODEL 951 DA REVOLVER . . . . . **NiB $210 Ex $170 Gd $119**
Previous designation M95 w/same general specifications.

MODEL 971 DA REVOLVER
Caliber: .357 Magnum. Six-shot cylinder, 2.5-, 4- or 6-inch bbl., 9 inches overall (with 4-inch bbl.). Weight: 36 oz. (with 4-inch bbl.). Blade front sight, adj. square-notched rear. Blued or stainless finish. Checkered hardwood grips. Imported 1990 to date.
Blued finish . . . . **NiB $194 Ex $155 Gd $105**
Stainless finish . . . . **NiB $206 Ex $165 Gd $112**
W/compensated
bbl., add **$15**

MODEL 971 VRC
DA REVOLVER . . . . **NiB $267 Ex $215 Gd $130**
Same general specifications as Model 971 stainless except w/ventilated rib and compensated bbl. Made 1996 to date.

CYCLOPS DA REVOLVER . . . . **NiB $385 Ex $300 Gd $230**
Caliber: .357 Mag. Six-shot cylinder, 6- or 8-inch compensated slab-sided bbl., 11.75 or 13.75 inches overall. Weight: 44 oz. or 51 oz. Undercut blade front sight, fully adjustable rear. B-Square scope mount and rings. Stainless steel finish. Checkered rubber grips. Made 1997 to date.

DA REVOLVER . . . . **NiB $156 Ex $125 Gd $85**
Calibers: .22 LR, .32 S&W Long, .38 Special. Five-shot (.38) or 6-shot cylinder (other calibers), bbl. lengths: 3-, 6-inches. Weight: 22 oz. (3-inch bbl.). Adj. Rear sight, ramp front. Blued or nickel finish. Wood or plastic grips. Imported 1965-91.

SPORTSMAN'S .22 . . . . **NiB $219 Ex $175 Gd $119**
Caliber: .22 LR. Six-round magazine, 4-inch bbl., 9 inches overall. Weight: 30 oz. Stainless steel finish. Disc. 1991.

RUBY PISTOL
Manufactured by Gabilondo y Urresti, Eibar, Spain, and others

7.65MM
AUTOMATIC PISTOL . . . . **NiB $265 Ex $200 Gd $70**
Secondary standard service pistol of the French Army in world wars I and II. Essentially the same as the Alkartasuna (see separate listing). Other manufacturers: Armenia Elgoibarresa y Cia., Eceolaza y Vicinai y Cia., Hijos de Angel Echeverria y Cia., Bruno Salaverria y Cia., Zulaika y Cia., all of Eibar, Spain-Gabilondo y Cia., Elgoibar Spain; Ruby Arms Company, Guernica, Spain. Made 1914-.22.

Ruger Mark I Target W/5.5-inch Untapered Bull Barrel

Ruger Mark II

Ruger Mark II .22/.45 KP4

Ruger Mark II Stainless W/10-inch Bull Barrel

RUGER HANDGUNS — Southport, Connecticut
Manufactured by Sturm, Ruger & Co.

Rugers made in 1976 are designated "Liberty" in honor of the U.S. Bicentennial and bring a premium of approximately 25 percent in value over regular models.

NOTE: *For ease in finding a particular Ruger handgun, the listings are divided into two groups: Automatic/Single-Shot Pistols (below) and Revolvers, which follow. For a complete listing, please refer to the index.*

AUTOMATIC/SINGLE-SHOT PISTOLS

HAWKEYE SINGLE-SHOT PISTOL . . . . . NiB $1300 Ex $1100 Gd $600
Built on a SA revolver frame w/cylinder replaced by a swing-out breechblock and fitted w/a bbl., w/integral chamber. Caliber: .256 Magnum. 8.5-inch bbl., 14.5 inches overall. Weight: 45 oz. Blued finish. Ramp front sight, click adj. rear. Smooth walnut grips. Made 1963-65 (3300 produced).

MARK I TARGET MODEL AUTOMATIC PISTOL
Caliber: .22 LR. 10-shot magazine, 5.25- and 6.88-inch heavy tapered or 5.5-inch untapered bull bbl., 10.88 inches overall (with 6.88-inch bbl.). Weight: 42 oz. (in 5.5- or 6.88-inch bbl.). Undercut target front sight, adj. rear. Blued finish. Hard rubber grips or checkered walnut thumbrest grips. Made 1951-81.
Standard . . . . NiB $250 Ex $200 Gd $130
W/red medallion . . . . NiB $500 Ex $425 Gd $275
Walnut grips, add $15

MARK II AUTOMATIC PISTOL
Caliber: .22 LR, standard or high velocity 10-shot magazine, 4.75- or 6-inch tapered bbl., 8.31 inches overall (with 4.75-inch bbl.). Weight: 36 oz. Fixed front sight, square notch rear. Blued or stainless finish. Made 1982 to date.
Blued. . . . . NiB $275 Ex $240 Gd $120
Stainless . . . . NiB $340 Ex $270 Gd $105
Bright stainless (ltd.
prod. 5,000 in 1982). . . . . NiB $494 Ex $395 Gd $269

MARK II .22/.45 AUTOMATIC PISTOL
Same general specifications as Ruger Mark II .22 LR except w/blued or stainless receiver and bbl., in four lengths: 4-inch tapered w/adj. sights (P4), 4.75-inch tapered w/fixed sights (KP4), 5.25-inch tapered w/adj. sights (KP 514) and 5.5-inch bull (KP 512). Fitted w/Zytel grip frame of the same design as the Model 1911 45 ACP. Made 1993 to date.
Model KP4 (4.75-inch bbl.). . . . . NiB $215 Ex $188 Gd $115
Model KP512, KP514
(w/5.5- or 5.25-inch bbl.). . . . . NiB $266 Ex $236 Gd $180
Model P4, P512
(Blued w/4- or 5.5-inch bbl.) . . . . NiB $206 Ex $165 Gd $112

MARK II BULL BARREL MODEL
Same as standard Mark II except for bull bbl. (5.5- or 10-inch). Weight: About 2.75 lbs.
Blued finish . . . . NiB $231 Ex $185 Gd $126
Stainless finish (intro. 1985) . . . . . . NiB $313 Ex $250 Gd $170

MARK II GOVERNMENT MODEL AUTO PISTOL
Civilian version of the Mark II used by U.S. Armed Forces. Caliber: .22 LR. 10-shot magazine, 6.88-inch bull bbl., 11.13 inches overall. Weight: 44 oz. Blued or stainless finish. Made from 1986 to date.
Blued model (MK687G commercial) . . . . . NiB $335 Ex $270 Gd $140
Stainless steel model
(KMK678G commercial). . . . . NiB $325 Ex $260 Gd $177
W/U.S. markings (military model) . . . . NiB $550 Ex $500 Gd $330

MARK II TARGET MODEL
Caliber: .22 LR. 10-shot magazine, 4-, 5.5- and 10-inch bull bbl. or 5.25- and 6.88-inch heavy tappered bbl., weight: 38 oz. to 52 oz. 11.13 inches overall (with 6.88-inch bbl.). Made from 1982 to date.
Blued. . . . . NiB $275 Ex $240 Gd $125
Stainless steel . . . . NiB $340 Ex $270 Gd $105

**Ruger Mark II
Target Model**

**Ruger P-89
DAC/DAO**

Ruger P-90

**Ruger P-93
Compact**

MODEL P-85 AUTOMATIC PISTOL
Caliber: 9mm. DA, recoil-operated. 15-shot capacity, 4.5 inch bbl., 7.84 inches overall. Weight: 32 oz. Fixed rear sight, square-post front. Available w/decocking levers, ambidextrous safety or in DA only. Blued or stainless finish. Made 1987-92.
Blued finish . . . . NiB $335 Ex $295 Gd $200
Stainless steel finish. . . . . NiB $350 Ex $315 Gd $280

MODEL P-89 AUTOMATIC PISTOL
Caliber: 9mm. DA w/slide-mounted safety levers. 15-shot magazine, 4.5-inch bbl., 7.84 inches overall. Weight: 32 oz. Square-post front sight, adj. rear w/3-dot system. Blued or stainless steel finish. Grooved black Xenoy grips. Made from 1992 to date.
P-89 blued. NiB $380 Ex $330 Gd $200
P-89 stainless . . . . NiB $425 Ex $360 Gd $300

MODEL P-89 DAC/DAO AUTO PISTOLS
Similar to the standard Model P-89 except the P-89 DAC has ambidextrous decocking levers. The P-89 DAO operates in double-action-only mode. Made 1991 to date.
P-89 DAC blued. . . . . NiB $380 Ex $325 Gd $200
P-89 DAC stainless . . . . NiB $425 Ex $350 Gd $250
P-89 DAO stainless . . . . NiB $425 Ex $350 Gd $250

MODEL P-90, KP90 DA AUTOMATIC PISTOL
Caliber: .45 ACP. Seven-shot magazine, 4.5-inch bbl., 7.88 inches overall. Weight: 33.5 oz. Square-post front sight adj. square-notched rear w/3-dot system. Grooved black Xenoy composition grips. Blued or stainless finish. DAC model has ambidextrous decocking levers. Made 1991 to date.
Model P-90 blued . . . . NiB $425 Ex $350 Gd $200
Model P-90 DAC (decockers) . . . . . NiB $435 Ex $360 Gd $210
Model KP-90 DAC stainless. . . . . . . NiB $435 Ex $365 Gd $310
Model KP-90 DAC (decockers) . . . . NiB $440 Ex $370 Gd $315

MODEL P-91 DA AUTOMATIC PISTOL
Same general specifications as the Model P-90 except chambered for .40 S&W w/12-shot double-column magazine, Made 1992-94.
Model P-91 Standard. . . . . NiB $385 Ex $335 Gd $280
Model P-91 DAC (decockers) . . . . . NiB $400 Ex $320 Gd $260
Model P-91 DAO (DA only) . . . . . . NiB $406 Ex $325 Gd $260

MODEL P-93 COMPACT AUTO PISTOL
Similar to the standard Model P-89 except w/3.9-inch bbl., (7.3 inches overall) and weight: 31 oz. Stainless steel finish. Made 1993 to date.
Model P-93 DAC (decocker) (disc. 1994) . . . . . NiB $450 Ex $370 Gd $245
Model P-93 DAO (DA only) . . . . NiB $430 Ex $340 Gd $235

MODEL P-94 AUTOMATIC PISTOL
Similar to the Model P-91 except w/4.25-inch bbl., Calibers: 9mm or .40 S&W. Blued or stainless finish. Made 1994 to date.
Model KP-94 DAC (S/S decocker). . . . . NiB $450 Ex $365 Gd $320
Model KP-94 DAO (S/S dble. action only) . . . . NiB $425 Ex $360 Gd $315
Model P-94 DAC (Blued decocker). . . . . NiB $400 Ex $315 Gd $280
Model P-94 DAO (blued dble. action only) . . . NiB $390 Ex $299 Gd $260

Ruger Bearcat SA
(Old Model)

Ruger Bisley
Colt .45 Long (New Model)

Ruger Bisley
Single-Six Small Frame

Ruger Blackhawk

Ruger Blackhawk
SA .44

Ruger P-97

MODEL P-95 AUTOMATIC PISTOL
Caliber: 9mm Parabellum. 10-shot magazine, 3.9-inch bbl., 7.3 inches overall. Weight: 27 oz. Square-post front sight, drift adjustable rear w/3-dot system. Molded polymer grip-frame fitted w/stainless or chrome-moly slide. Ambidextrous decocking levers (P-95D) or double action only (DAO). Matte black or stainless finish. Made 1997 to date.

P-95 blued.................... **NiB $345 Ex $280 Gd $160**
P-95 stainless................. **NiB $380 Ex $305 Gd $165**

MODEL P-97 AUTOMATIC PISTOL
Caliber: .45 ACP. Eight-shot magazine, 4.5- inch bbl., 7.25 inches overall. Weight: 30.5 oz. Square-post front sight adj. square-notched rear w/3-dot system. Grooved black Xenoy composition grips. Blued or stainless finish. DAC model has ambidextrous decocking levers. Made 1999 to date.

Model KP-97
DAO stainless .... **NiB $395 Ex $315 Gd $200**
Model KP-97
DAC (decockers) .... **NiB $395 Ex $315 Gd $200**

STANDARD MODEL AUTOMATIC PISTOL
Caliber: .22 LR. Nine-shot magazine, 4.75- or 6-inch bbl., 8.75 inches overall (with 4.75-inch bbl.). Weight: 36 oz. (with 4.75 inch bbl.). Fixed sights. Blued finish. Hard rubber or checkered walnut grips. Made from 1949 to date. Note: After the death of Alexander Sturm in 1951, the color of the eagle on the grip medallion was changed from red to black as a memorial. Known as the "Red Eagle Automatic," this early type is now a collector's item. Made 1951-81.

W/red eagle medallion .... **NiB $525 Ex $425 Gd $230**
W/black eagle medallion......... **NiB $195 Ex $175 Gd $100**
Walnut grips, add **$15**

NOTE: *This section contains only Ruger Revolvers. Automatic and Single-Shot Pistols may be found on the preceding pages. For a complete listing of Ruger handguns, please refer to the index.*

REVOLVERS

BEARCAT SA (OLD MODEL)
Aluminum frame. Caliber: .22 LR. Six-shot cylinder, 4-inch bbl., 8.88 inches overall. Weight: 17 oz. Fixed sights. Blued finish. Smooth walnut grips. Made 1958-73.

W/brass trigger guard .... **NiB $350 Ex $300 Gd $200**
W/aniodized
aluminum trigger .... **NiB $600 Ex $580 Gd $300**

BEARCAT, SUPER (OLD MODEL) . . . . **NiB $350 Ex $290 Gd $190**
Same general specifications as Bearcat except has steel frame.
Weight: 25 oz. Made 1971-73.

NEW MODEL BEARCAT REVOLVER
Same general specifications as Super Bearcat except all steel frame
and trigger guard. Interlocked mechanism and transfer bar. Calibers:
.22 LR and .22WMR. Interchangeable 6-shot cylinders (disc. 1996).
Smooth walnut stocks w/Ruger medallion. Made 1994 to date.
Convertible model (disc.
1996 after factory recall) . . . . **NiB $350 Ex $275 Gd $200**
Standard model (.22 LR only) . . . . **NiB $310 Ex $250 Gd $150**

BISLEY SA REVOLVER, LARGE FRAME
Calibers: .357 Mag., .41 Mag. .44 Mag., .45 Long Colt. 7.5-inch bbl., 13
inches overall. Weight: 48 oz. Non-fluted or fluted cylinder, no engraving.
Ramp front sight, adj. rear. Satin blued or stainless. Made 1986 to date.
Blued finish . . . . **NiB $420 Ex $335 Gd $180**
Vaquero/Bisley (blued w/case colored fr.) . . . . **NiB $420 Ex $335 Gd $180**
Vaquero/Bisley (stainless steel) . . . **NiB $425 Ex $320 Gd $190**
W/ivory grips, add **$35**

BISLEY SINGLE-SIX REVOLVER, SMALL FRAME
Calibers: .22 LR and .32 Mag. Six-shot cylinder, 6.5-inch bbl., 11.5
inches overall. Weight: 41 oz. Fixed rear sight, blade front. Blue finish. Goncalo Alves grips. Made 1986 to date.
.22 caliber . . . . **NiB $335 Ex $250 Gd $150**
.32 H&R Mag. . . . . **NiB $385 Ex $300 Gd $260**

BLACKHAWK SA CONVERTIBLE (OLD MODEL)
Same as Blackhawk except has extra cylinder. Caliber combinations: .357
Magnum and 9mm Para., .45 Colt and .45 Automatic. Made 1967-72.
.357/9mm combo (early w/o prefix SN) . . . **NiB $400 Ex $350 Gd $195**
.357/9mm combo (late w/prefix SN) . . . . . **NiB $394 Ex $315 Gd $214**
.45 LC/.45 ACP combo
(1967-85 & 1999 to date) . . . . **NiB $500 Ex $450 Gd $290**

BLACKHAWK SA REVOLVER (OLD MODEL)
Calibers: .30 Carbine, .357 Magnum, .41 Magnum, .45 Colt. Six-
shot cylinder, bbl. lengths: 4.63-inch (.357, .41, .45 caliber), 6.5-
inch (.357, .41 caliber), 7.5-inch (.30, .45 caliber). 10.13 inches
overall (.357 Mag. w/4.63-inch bbl.). Weight: 38 oz. (.357 w/4.63-
inch bbl.). Ramp front sight, adj. rear. Blued finish. Checkered hard
rubber or smooth walnut grips. Made 1956-73.
.30 Carbine, .357 Mag. . . . . **NiB $400 Ex $350 Gd $195**
.41 Mag. . . . . **NiB $400 Ex $300 Gd $195**
.45 Colt . . . . **NiB $420 Ex $360 Gd $200**

BLACKHAWK SA "FLAT-TOP" REVOLVER (OLD MODEL)
Similar to standard Blackhawk except w/"Flat Top" cylinder strap.
Calibers: .357 or .44 Magnum. Six-shot fluted cylinder, 4.625-, 6.5-,
7.5- or 10-inch bbl., adj. rear sight, ramp front. Blued finish. Black
rubber or smooth walnut grips. Made 1956-63.
.357 Mag. (w/4.625-inch bbl.) . . . . **NiB $500 Ex $450 Gd $225**
.357 Mag. (w/6.5-inch bbl.) . . . . **NiB $700 Ex $550 Gd $300**
.357 Mag. (w/10-inch bbl.) . . . . **NiB $1200 Ex $1050 Gd $600**
.44 Mag. (w/fluted cylinder/ 4.625-inch bbl.) . . **NiB $700 Ex $550 Gd $300**
.44 Mag. (w/fluted cylinder/ 6.5-inch bbl.) . . **NiB $750 Ex $600 Gd $350**
.44 Mag. (w/fluted cylinder/ 10-inch bbl.) . . **NiB $1200 Ex $1050 Gd $600**

GP-100 DA REVOLVER
Caliber: .357 Magnum. Three- to 4-inch heavy bbl., or 6-inch stan-
dard or heavy bbl., Overall length: 9.38 or 11.38 inches. Cushioned
grip panels. Made from 1986 to date.
Blued finish . . . . **NiB $400 Ex $315 Gd $185**
Stainless steel finish . . . . **NiB $425 Ex $325 Gd $225**

**Ruger GP-100
DA Revolver**

Ruger New Model Blackhawk Convertible

**Ruger Blackhawk High-Gloss Stainless
(New Model) .357 Magnum**

NEW MODEL BLACKHAWK CONVERTIBLE
Same as New Model Blackhawk except has extra cylinder. Blued finish only.
Caliber combinations: .357 Magnum/9mm Para., .44 Magnum/.44-40, .45
Colt/.45 ACP. (Limited Edition Buckeye Special .32-20/.32 H&R Mag. or .38-
40/10mm). Made 1973 to date.
.32-20/.32 H&R Mag. (1989-90) . . . . **NiB $370 Ex $295 Gd $160**
.38-40/10mm (1990-91) . . . . **NiB $344 Ex $275 Gd $187**
.357/9mm combo . . . . **NiB $370 Ex $295 Gd $160**
.44/.44-40 combo (disc.1982) . . . . **NiB $406 Ex $325 Gd $221**
.45 LC/.45 ACP combo (disc. 1985) . . . . . . **NiB $375 Ex $300 Gd $204**

NEW MODEL BLACKHAWK SA REVOLVER
Interlocked mechanism. Calibers: .30 Carbine, .357 Magnum, .357
Maximum, .41 Magnum, .44 Magnum, .44 Special, .45 Colt. Six-shot cylin-
der, bbl. lengths: 4.63-inch (.357, .41, .45 Colt); 5.5 inch (.44 Mag., .44
Spec.); 6.5-inch (.357, .41, .45 Long Colt); 7.5-inch (.30, .45, .44 Special, .44
Mag.); 10.5-inch in .44 Mag; 10.38 inches overall (.357 Mag. w/4.63-inch
bbl.). Weight: 40 oz. (.357 w/4.63-inch bbl.). Adj. rear sight, ramp front.
Blued finish or stainless steel; latter only in .357 or .45 LC. Smooth walnut
grips. Made 1973 to date.
Blued finish . . . . **NiB $350 Ex $245 Gd $135**
High-gloss stainless (.357 Mag., .45 LC) . . . **NiB $344 Ex $275 Gd $187**
Satin stainless (.357 Mag., .45 LC) . . . . **NiB $331 Ex $265 Gd $180**
.357 Maximum SRM (1984-85) . . . . **NiB $370 Ex $295 Gd $175**

Ruger Blackhawk
Blued finish (New Model

Ruger Single-Six SSM
(New Model)

Ruger Super Blackhawk
(New Model)

Ruger Super Single-Six
Convertible (New Model)

Ruger Police Service-Six
Stainless Steel

Ruger Redhawk

Ruger Super Redhawk
Stainless DA Scope-Ring

NEW MODEL SINGLE-SIX SSM REVOLVER............ NiB $300 Ex $275 Gd $150
Same general specifications as standard Single-Six except chambered for .32 H&R Magnum cartridge. Bbl. lengths: 4.63, 5.5, 6.5 or 9.5 inches.

NEW MODEL SUPER BLACKHAWK SA REVOLVER
Interlocked mechanism. Caliber: .44 Magnum. Six-shot cylinder, 5.5-inch, 7.5-inch and 10.5-inch bull bbl. 13.38 inches overall. Weight: 48 oz. Adj. rear sight, ramp front. Blued and stainless steel finish. Smooth walnut grips. Made 1973 to date, 5.5-inch bbl. made 1987 to date.
Blued finish .... NiB $375 Ex $300 Gd $190
High-gloss stainless
(1994-96)..................... NiB $369 Ex $295 Gd $201
Satin stainless steel .... NiB $356 Ex $285 Gd $194

NEW MODEL SUPER SINGLE-SIX CONVERTIBLE REVOLVER
SA w/interlocked mechanism. Calibers: .22 LR and .22 WMR. Interchangeable 6-shot cylinders. Bbl. lengths: 4.63, 5.5, 6.5, 9.5 inches. 10.81 inches overall (with 4.63 inch bbl.). Weight: 33 oz. (with 4.63-inch bbl.). Adj. rear sight, ramp front. Blued finish or stainless steel; latter only w/5.5- or 6.5-inch bbl., smooth walnut grips. Made 1972 to date.
Blued finish .... NiB $290 Ex $220 Gd $110
High-gloss stainless (1994-96)..... NiB $231 Ex $185 Gd $126
Stainless steel .... NiB $325 Ex $255 Gd $200

POLICE SERVICE-SIX
Same general specifications as Speed-Six except has square butt. Stainless steel models and 9mm Para. caliber available w/only 4-inch bbl., Made 1971-88.
.38 Special, blued finish .... NiB $250 Ex $220 Gd $170
.38 Special, stainless steel .... NiB $270 Ex $235 Gd $210
.357 Magnum or 9mm Para.,
blued finish .... NiB $250 Ex $220 Gd $170
.357 Magnum, stainless steel...... NiB $275 Ex $240 Gd $210

REDHAWK DA REVOLVER

Calibers: .357 Mag., .41 Mag., .45 LC, .44 Mag. Six-shot cylinder, 5.5- and 7.5-inch bbl., 11 and 13 inches overall, respectively. Weight: About 52 oz. Adj. rear sight, interchangeable front sights. Stainless finish. Made 1979 to date; .357 Mag. disc. 1986. Alloy steel model w/blued finish intro. in 1986 in .41 Mag. and .44 Mag. calibers.

Blued finish . . . . **NiB $480 Ex $320 Gd $180**
Stainless steel . . . . **NiB $515 Ex $405 Gd $325**

Ruger
Super Redhawk Stainless

SUPER REDHAWK STAINLESS DA SCOPE-RING REVOLVER

Calibers: .44 Mag., .454 Casull and .45 LC. Six-shot cylinder, 7.5- to 9.5- inch bbl., 13 to 15 inches overall. Weight: 53 to 58 oz. Integral scope mounting system w/stainless rings. Adjustable rear sight. Cushioned grip panels. Made 1987 to date.

Model .44 Mag. 7.5- inch
bbl., stainless . . . . **NiB $550 Ex $450 Gd $325**
Model .44 Mag. 9.5- inch
bbl., stainless . . . . **NiB $550 Ex $450 Gd $325**
Model .454 Casull & 45 LC
Stainless/target gray stainless . . . . . **NiB $640 Ex $520 Gd $395**

SECURITY-SIX DA REVOLVER

Caliber: .357 Magnum, handles .38 Special. Six-shot cylinder, bbl. lengths: 2.25-, 4-, 6-inch, 9.25 inches overall (with 4-inch bbl.). Weight: 33.5 oz. (with 4-inch bbl.). Adj. rear sight, ramp front. Blued finish or stainless steel. Square butt. Checkered walnut grips. Made 1971-85.

Blued finish . . . . **NiB $250 Ex $200 Gd $136**
Stainless steel . . . . **NiB $294 Ex $235 Gd $160**

Ruger
Single-Six

SINGLE-SIX SA REVOLVER (OLD MODEL)

Calibers: .22 LR, .22 WMR. Six-shot cylinder. bbl., lengths: 4.63, 5.5, 6.5, 9.5 inches, 10.88 inches overall (with 5.5-inch bbl.). Weight: About 35 oz. Fixed sights. Blued finish. Checkered hard rubber or smooth walnut grips. Made 1953-73. Note: Pre-1956 model w/flat loading gate is worth about twice as much as later version.

Standard . . . . **NiB $300 Ex $225 Gd $115**
Convertible (w/two cylinders,
.22 LR/.22 WMR) . . . . **NiB $450 Ex $400 Gd $200**

SINGLE-SIX — LIGHTWEIGHT . . . . **NiB $500 Ex $400 Gd $175**
Same general specifications as Single-Six except has 4.75-inch bbl., lightweight alloy cylinder and frame, 10 inches overall length, weight: 23 oz. Made in 1956.

Ruger
Single-Six Lightweight

SP101 DA REVOLVER

Calibers: .22 LR, .32 Mag., 9mm, .38 Special+P, .357 Mag. Five- or 6-shot cylinder, 2.25-, 3.06- or 4-inch bbl., weight: 25-34 oz. Stainless steel finish. Cushioned grips. Made 1988 to date. See illustration next page.

Standard model . . . . **NiB $385 Ex $245 Gd $240**
DAO model (DA only,
spurless hammer) . . . . **NiB $365 Ex $280 Gd $240**

Ruger
Super Single-Six Convertible

SPEED-SIX DA REVOLVER

Calibers: .38 Special, .357 Magnum, 9mm Para. Six-shot cylinder, 2.75-, 4-inch bbl., (9mm available only w/2.75-inch bbl.). 7.75 inches overall (2.75-inch bbl.). Weight: 31 oz. (with 2.75-inch bbl.). Fixed sights. Blued or stainless steel finish; latter available in .38 Special (with 2.75 inch bbl.), .357 Magnum and 9mm w/either bbl., Round butt. Checkered walnut grips. Made 1973-87.

.38 Special, blued finish . . . . **NiB $230 Ex $205 Gd $156**
.38 Special, stainless steel . . . . **NiB $280 Ex $245 Gd $120**
.357 Magnum or 9mm Para.,
blued finish . . . . **NiB $300 Ex $250 Gd $180**
.357 Magnum or 9mm Para.,
stainless steel. . . . . **NiB $300 Ex $250 Gd $180**

Ruger Single-Six Fixed Sight

Ruger Vaquero Stainless Steel

Ruger Vaquero Blued

Ruger SP101

SUPER BLACKHAWK
SA .44 MAGNUM REVOLVER (OLD MODEL)
SA w/heavy frame and unfluted cylinder. Caliber: .44 Magnum. Six-shot cylinder. 6.5- or 7.5-inch bbl., Adj. rear sight, ramp front. Steel or brass grip frame w/square-back trigger guard. Smooth walnut grips. Blued finish. Made 1956-73.

W/6.5-inch bbl., ... NiB $385 Ex $295 Gd $170
W/7.5-inch bbl., ... NiB $385 Ex $295 Gd $170
W/brass gripframe . . . . NiB $869 Ex $695 Gd $473

VAQUERO SA REVOLVER
Calibers: .357 Mag., .44-40, .44 Magnum, .45 Colt. Six-shot cylinder. Bbl. lengths: 4.625, 5.5, 7.5 inches, 13.63 inches overall (with 7.5-inch bbl.). Weight: 41 oz. (with 7.5-inch bbl.). Blade front sight, grooved topstrap rear. Blued w/color casehardened frame or polished stainless finish. Smooth rosewood grips w/Ruger medallion. Made 1993 to date.

Blued w/color-case
hardened frame . . . . NiB $420 Ex $320 Gd $270
Stainless finish . . . . NiB $420 Ex $320 Gd $270
W/ivory grips, add. $41

RUSSIAN SERVICE PISTOLS Mfd. by Government plants at Tula and elsewhere

Tokarev-type pistols have also been made in Hungary, Poland, Yugoslavia, People's Republic of China, N. Korea.

MODEL 30 TOKAREV SERVICE AUTOMATIC
Modified Colt-Browning type. Caliber: 7.62mm Russian Auto (also uses 7.63mm Mauser Auto cartridge). Eight-shot magazine, 4.5-inch bbl., 7.75 inches overall. Weight: About 29 oz. Fixed sights. Made 1930 mid-1950s. Note: A slightly modified version w/improved locking system and different disconnector was adopted in 1933.
Standard Service Model TT30 . . . . . NiB $325 Ex $290 Gd $165
Standard Service Model TT33 . . . . . NiB $325 Ex $290 Gd $165
Recent imports (distinguished
by importer marks) . . . . NiB $140 Ex $110 Gd $60

MODEL PM
MAKAROV AUTO PISTOL. . . . . NiB $450 Ex $400 Gd $190
Double-action, blowback design. Caliber: 9mm Makarov. Eight-shot magazine, 3.8-inch bbl., 6.4 inches overall. Weight: 26 oz. Blade front sight, square-notched rear. Checkered composition grips.
Standard Service Model PM
(Pistole Makarov) . . . . NiB $469 Ex $375 Gd $255
Recent imports (distinguished
by importer marks) . . . . NiB $188 Ex $150 Gd $102

SAKO HANDGUNS — Riihimaki, Finland Manufactured by Oy Sako Ab

.22-.32 OLYMPIC PISTOL (TRIACE)
Calibers: .22 LR, .22 Short, .32 S&W Long. Five-round magazine, 6- or 8.85- (.22 Short) inch bbl., weight: About 46 oz. (.22 LR); 44 oz. (.22 Short); 48 oz. (.32). Steel frame. ABS plastic, anatomically designed grip. Non-reflecting matte black upper surface and chromium-plated slide. Equipped w/carrying case and tool set. Limited importation 1983-89.
Sako .22 or .32
Single pistol. . . . . NiB $1300 Ex $1150 Gd $650
Sako Triace, triple-barrel set
w/wooden grip . . . . NiB $2500 Ex $2200 Gd $1200

SAUER HANDGUNS
Mfd. through WW II by J. P. Sauer & Sohn, Suhl, Germany. Now mfd. by J. P. Sauer & Sohn, GmbH, Eckernförde, West Germany

See also listings under Sig Sauer.

MODEL 1913 POCKET
AUTOMATIC PISTOL . . . . **NiB $295 Ex $225 Gd $145**
Caliber: .32 Automatic (7.65mm). Seven-shot magazine, 3-inch bbl., 5.88 inches overall. Weight: 22 oz. Fixed sights. Blued finish. Black hard rubber grips. Made 1913-30.

MODEL 1930 POCKET AUTOMATIC PISTOL
Authority Model (Behorden Model). Successor to Model 1913, has improved grip and safety. Caliber: .32 Auto (7.65mm). Seven-shot magazine, 3-inch bbl., 5.75 inches overall. Weight: 22 oz. Fixed sights. Blued finish. Black hard rubber grips. Made 1930-38. Note: Some pistols made w/indicator pin showing when cocked. Also mfd. w/dual slide and receiver; this type weight: about 7 oz. less than the standard model.
Steel model . . . . **NiB $325 Ex $230 Gd $145**
Dural (alloy) model . . . . **NiB $1563 Ex $1250 Gd $850**

MODEL 38H DA AUTOMATIC PISTOL
Calibers: .25 Auto (6.35mm), .32 Auto (7.65mm), .380 Auto (9mm). Specifications shown are for .32 Auto model. Seven-shot magazine, 3.25-inch bbl., 6.25 inches overall. Weight: 20 oz. Fixed sights. Blued finish. Black plastic grips. Also made in dual model weighing about 6 oz. less. Made 1938-1945. Note: This pistol, designated Model .38, was mfd. during WW II for military use. Wartime models are inferior in design to earlier production, as some lack safety lever.
.22 caliber . . . . **NiB $4000 Ex $3000 Gd $1250**
.32 ACP . . . . **NiB $395 Ex $325 Gd $185**
.32 ACP (w/Nazi proofs) . . . . **NiB $494 Ex $395 Gd $269**
.380 ACP . . . . **NiB $3500 Ex $2700 Gd $1250**

POCKET .25 (1913)
AUTOMATIC PISTOL . . . . **NiB $300 Ex $240 Gd $145**
Smaller version of Model 1913, issued about same time as .32 caliber model. Caliber: .25 Auto (6.35mm). Seven-shot magazine, 2.5-inch bbl., 4.25 inches overall. Weight: 14.5 oz. Fixed sights. Blued finish. Black hard rubber grips. Made 1913-30.

SINGLE-ACTION REVOLVERS
See listings under Hawes.

SAVAGE ARMS CO. — Utica, New York

MODEL 101 SA
SINGLE-SHOT PISTOL . . . . **NiB $150 Ex $120 Gd $60**
Barrel integral w/swing-out cylinder. Calibers: .22 Short, Long, LR. 5.5-inch bbl. Weight: 20 oz. Blade front sight, slotted rear, adj. for windage. Blued finish. Grips of compressed, impregnated wood. Made 1960-68.

MODEL 501/502F "STRIKER" SERIES PISTOLS
Calibers: .22 LR., and .22 WMR. 5- or 10- shot magazine, 10-inch bbl., 19 inches overall. Weight: 4 lbs. Drilled and tapped sights for scope mount (installed). Ambidextrous rear grip. Made 2000 to date.
Model 501F, .22 LR . . . . **NiB $185 Ex $165 Gd $125**
Model 502F, .22 WMR. . . . . **NiB $205 Ex $180 Gd $130**

MODEL 510/516 "STRIKER" SERIES PISTOLS
Calibers: 223 Rem., .22-250 Rem., .243 Win., 7mm-08 Rem., .260 Rem., and .308 Win. Three-shot magazine, 14-inch bbl., .22.5 inches overall. Drilled and tapped for scope mounts. Left hand bolt with right hand ejection. Stainless steel finish. Made 1998 to date.

Sako Model .22-.32 Olympic

Sauer 1930 Pocket

Savage Model 101

(cont'd.) MODEL 510/516 "STRIKER" SERIES PISTOLS
Model 510F . . . . **NiB $385 Ex $335 Gd $180**
Model 516FSAK . . . . **NiB $475 Ex $390 Gd $335**
Model 516FSS . . . . **NiB $380 Ex $335 Gd $320**
Model 516BSAK . . . . **NiB $475 Ex $390 Gd $335**
Model 516BSS . . . . **NiB $535 Ex $430 Gd $350**

MODEL 1907 AUTOMATIC PISTOL
Caliber: .32 ACP, 10-shot magazine, 3.25-inch bbl., 6.5 inches overall. Weight: 19 oz. Checkered hard rubber or steel grips marked "Savage Quality," circling an Indian-head logo. Optional pearl grips. Blue, nickel, silver or gold finish. Made 1908-20.
Blued model (.32 ACP) . . . . **NiB $425 Ex $300 Gd $115**
Blued model (.380 ACP) . . . . **NiB $550 Ex $450 Gd $200**
W/ optional nickel,
silver or gold finish, add . . . . **$750-$1200**
W/optional pearl grips, add . . . . **$225-$950**

Sears/J.C. Higgins Model 88 DA Revolver

Security Model PM 357

Security Model PPM 357

Security Model PSS38

MODEL 1910 AUTOMATIC PISTOL
Calibers: .32 Auto, .380 Auto. 10-shot magazine (.32 cal.), 9-shot (.380 cal.). 3.75-inch bbl., (.32 cal.), 4.25-inch (.380 cal.). 6.5 inches overall (.32 cal.), 7 inches (.380 cal.). Weight: About 23 oz. Fixed sights. Blued finish. Hard rubber grips. Made in hammerless type w/grip safety or w/exposed hammer spur. Made 1910-17.
.32 ACP . . . . NiB $300   Ex $250   Gd $160
.380 ACP . . . . NiB $470   Ex $380   Gd $250

MODEL 1915 AUTOMATIC PISTOL
Same general specifications as the Savage Model 1907 except the Model 1915 is hammerless and has a grip safety. It is also chambered for both the .32 and .380 ACP. Made 1915-17.
.32 ACP . . . . NiB $525   Ex $450   Gd $225
.380 ACP . . . . NiB $656   Ex $525   Gd $357

U.S. ARMY TEST MODEL 1910 . NiB $7500   Ex $5500   Gd $2500
Caliber: .45 ACP, Seven-shot magazine w/exposed hammer. An enlarged version of the Model 1910 manufactured for military trials between 1907 and 1911. Note: Most "Trial Pistols" were refurbished and resold as commercial models. Values are for original Government Test Issues Models.

MODEL 1917 AUTOMATIC PISTOL
Same specifications as 1910 Model except has spur-type hammer and redesigned, heavier grip. Made 1917-28.
.32 ACP . . . . NiB $300   Ex $250   Gd $110
.380 ACP . . . . NiB $650   Ex $575   Gd $250

SEARS, ROEBUCK & COMPANY — Chicago, Illinois

J.C. HIGGINS MODEL 80
AUTO PISTOL . . . . NiB $175   Ex $125   Gd $95
Caliber: .22 LR. 10-shot magazine, 4.5- or 6.5-inch interchangeable bbl., 10.88 inches overall (with 6.5-inch bbl.). Weight: 41 oz. (with 6.5-inch bbl.). Fixed Partridge sights. Blued finish. Checkered grips w/thumbrest.

J.C. HIGGINS MODEL 88
DA REVOLVER. . . . . NiB $115   Ex $90   Gd $60
Caliber: .22 LR. Nine-shot cylinder, 4- or 6-inch bbl., 9.5 inches (with 4-inch bbl.). Weight: 23 oz. (with 4-inch bbl.). Fixed sights. Blued or nickel finish. Checkered plastic grips.

J.C. HIGGINS RANGER
DA REVOLVER. . . . . NiB $140   Ex $110   Gd $70
Caliber: .22 LR. Nine-shot cylinder, 5.5-inch bbl., 10.75 inches overall. Weight: 28 oz. Fixed sights. Blued or chrome finish. Checkered plastic grips.

SECURITY INDUSTRIES OF AMERICA — Little Ferry, New Jersey

MODEL PM 357 DA REVOLVER . . . . . . NiB $225   Ex $175   Gd $125
Caliber: .357 Magnum. Five-shot cylinder, 2.5-inch bbl., 7.5 inches overall. Weight: 21 oz. Fixed sights. Stainless steel. Walnut grips. Made 1975-78.

MODEL PPM357 DA REVOLVER . . . . . NiB $225   Ex $175   Gd $125
Caliber: .357 Magnum. Five-shot cylinder, 2-inch bbl., 6.13 inches overall. Weight: 18 oz. Fixed sights. Stainless steel. Walnut grips. Made from 1976-78. Note: Spurless hammer (illustrated) was disc. in 1977; this model has the same conventional hammer as other Security revolvers.

MODEL PSS 38
DA REVOLVER . . . . **NiB $175 Ex $150 Gd $110**
Caliber: .38 Special. Five-shot cylinder, 2-inch bbl., 6.5 inches over-all. Weight: 18 oz. Fixed sights. Stainless steel. Walnut grips. Intro. 1973. disc.

R. F. SEDGLEY. INC. — Philadelphia, Pennsylvania

BABY HAMMERLESS
EJECTOR REVOLVER . . . . **NiB $550 Ex $450 Gd $200**
DA. Solid frame. Folding trigger. Caliber: .22 Long. Six-shot cylinder, 4 inches overall. Weight: 6 oz. Fixed sights. Blued or nickel finish. Rubber grips. Made c. 1930-39.

L. W. SEECAMP, INC. — Milford, Connecticut

MODEL LWS .25
DAO PISTOL . . . . **NiB $400 Ex $325 Gd $220**
Caliber: .25 ACP. Seven-shot magazine, 2-inch bbl., 4.125 inches overall. Weight: 12 oz. Checkered black polycarbonate grips. Matte stainless finish. No sights. Made 1981-85.

MODEL LWS .32 DAO PISTOL
Caliber: .32 ACP. Six-shot magazine, 2-inch bbl., 4.25 inches over-all. Weight: 12.9 oz. Ribbed sighting plane with no sights. Checkered black Lexon grips. Stainless steel. Made 1985 to date. Limited production results in inflated resale values.
Matte stainless finish . . . . **NiB $575 Ex $525 Gd $395**
Polished stainless finish . . . . **NiB $600 Ex $535 Gd $400**

SHERIDAN PRODUCTS, INC. — Racine, Wisconsin

KNOCKABOUT
SINGLE-SHOT PISTOL . . . . **NiB $100 Ex $90 Gd $40**
Tip-up type. Caliber: .22 LR, Long, Short; 5-inch bbl., 6.75 inches overall. Weight: 24 oz. Fixed sights. Checkered plastic grips. Blued finish. Made 1953-60.

SIG PISTOLS — Neuhausen am Rheinfall, Switzerland, Mfd. by SIG Schweizerische Industrie-Gesellschaft

See also listings under SIG-Sauer.

MODEL P210-1
AUTOMATIC PISTOL . . . . **NiB $2000 Ex $1675 Gd $980**
Calibers: .22 LR, 7.65mm Luger, 9mm Para. Eight-shot magazine, 4.75-inch bbl., 8.5 inches overall. Weight: 33 oz. (.22 cal.) or 35 oz. (7.65mm, 9mm). Fixed sights. Polished blued finish. Checkered wood grips. Made 1949-86.

MODEL P210-2 . . . . **NiB $1500 Ex $1275 Gd $750**
Same as Model P210-1 except has sandblasted finish, plastic grips. Not avail. in .22 LR. Disc. 1987.

MODEL P210-5
TARGET PISTOL . . . . **NiB $1995 Ex $1750 Gd $975**
Same as Model P210-2 except has 6-inch bbl., micrometer adj. rear sight, target front sight, adj. trigger stop, 9.7 inches overall. Weight: About 38.3 oz. Disc. 1997.

SIG
Model P210-1

SIG
Model P210-6 Target Pistol

MODEL P210-6 TARGET PISTOL . . . . . . **NiB $1875 Gd $1500 Gd $875**
Same as Model P210-2 except has micrometer adj. rear sight, target front sight, adj. trigger stop. Weight: About 37 oz. Disc. 1987.

P210 .22 CONVERSION UNIT . . . . **NiB $744 Ex $595 Gd $405**
Converts P210 pistol to .22 LR. Consists of bbl., w/recoil spring, slide and magazine,

SIG SAUER HANDGUNS
Mfd. by J. P. Sauer & Sohn of West Germany, SIG of Switzerland, and other manufacturers

MODEL P220 DA/DAO AUTOMATIC PISTOL
Calibers: 22LR, 7.65mm, 9mm Para., .38 Super, .45 Automatic. Seven-shot in .45, 9-shot in other calibers, 4.4-inch bbl., 8 inches overall. Weight: 26.5 oz.(9mm). Fixed sights. Blue, electroless nickel, K-Kote, Duo/nickel or Ilaflon finish. Alloy frame. Checkered plastic grips. Imported 1976 to date. Note: Also sold in U.S. as Browning BDA. See illustration next page.
Blue finish . . . . **NiB $670 Ex $580 Gd $350**
Duo/nickel finish . . . . **NiB $710 Ex $575 Gd $394**
Nickel finish . . . . **NiB $740 Ex $650 Gd $420**
K-Kote finish . . . . **NiB $710 Ex $575 Gd $344**
Ilaflon finish . . . . **NiB $710 Ex $575 Gd $394**
.22 conversion kit, add **$680**
W/Siglite sights, add **$92**

MODEL P220 SPORT AUTOMATIC . . . . . **NiB $1175 Ex $950 Gd $750**
Similar to Model P220 except .45 ACP only w/4.5-inch compensated bbl., 10-shot magazine, adj. target sights. Weight: 46.1 oz. Stainless finish. Made 1999 to date.

SIG Sauer
P220

SIG Sauer
P225

SIG Sauer
P230

MODEL P225 DA AUTOMATIC
Caliber: 9mm Para. Eight-shot magazine, 3.85-inch bbl., 7 inches overall. Weight: 26.1 oz. Blue, nickel, K-Kote, Duo/nickel or Ilaflon finish.

Blued finish	NiB $525	Ex $450	Gd $350
Duo/nickel finish	NiB $570	Ex $495	Gd $395
Nickel finish	NiB $595	Ex $520	Gd $420
K-Kote finish	NiB $595	Ex $520	Gd $420
W/Siglite sights, add			$105

MODEL P226 DA/DAO AUTOMATIC
Caliber: .357 SIG, 9mm Para., .40 S&W, 10- or 15-shot magazine, 4.4-inch bbl., 7.75 inches overall. Weight: 29.5 oz. Alloy frame. Blue, electroless nickel, K-Kote, Duo/nickel or Nitron finish. Imported 1983 to date.

Blued finish	NiB $740	Ex $610	Gd $350
Duo/nickel finish	NiB $780	Ex $690	Gd $375
Nickel finish	NiB $688	Ex $550	Gd $374
K-Kote finish	NiB $656	Ex $525	Gd $357
Nitron finish (Blacken stainless)	NiB $663	Ex $530	Gd $360
W/Siglite sights, add			$85

MODEL P228 DA AUTOMATIC
Same general specifications as Model P226 except w/3.86-inch bbl., 7.13 inches overall. 10- or 13-shot magazine, Imported 1990-97.

Blued finish	NiB $675	Ex $575	Gd $350
Duo/nickel finish	NiB $716	Ex $616	Gd $391
Electroless nickel finish	NiB $745	Ex $645	Gd $420
K-Kote finish	NiB $720	Ex $620	Gd $395
For Siglite nite sights, add			$102

MODEL P229 DA/DAO AUTOMATIC
Same general specifications as Model P228 except w/3.86-inch bbl., 10- or 12-shot magazine, weight: 32.5 oz. Nitron or Satin Nickel finish. Imported 1991 to date.

Nitron finish (Blackened stainless)	NiB $725	Ex $625	Gd $350
Satin nickel finish	NiB $765	Ex $665	Gd $390
For Siglite nite sights, add			$100

MODEL P229
SPORT AUTOMATIC . . . . NiB $1175 Ex $925 Gd $750
Similar to Model P229 except .357 SIG only w/4.5-inch compensated bbl., adj. target sights. Weight: 43.6 oz. Stainless finish. Made 1998 to date.

MODEL P230 DA AUTOMATIC PISTOL
Calibers: .22 LR, .32 Auto (7.65mm), .380 Auto (9mm Short), 9mm Ultra. 10-shot magazine in .22, 8-shot in .32, 7-shot in 9mm; 3.6-inch bbl., 6.6 inches overall. Weight: 18.2 oz. or 22.4 oz. (steel frame). Fixed sights. Blued or stainless finish. Plastic grips. Imported 1976-96.

Blued finish	NiB $425	Ex $325	Gd $215
Stainless finish (P230SL)	NiB $480	Ex $400	Gd $380

MODEL P232 DA/DAO AUTOMATIC PISTOL
Caliber: .380 ACP. Seven-shot magazine, 3.6-inch bbl., 6.6 inches overall. Weight: 16.2 oz. or 22.4 oz. (steel frame). Double/single action or double action only. Blade front and notch rear drift adjustable sights. Alloy or steel frame. Automatic firing pin lock and heelmounted magazine release. Blue, Duo or stainless finish. Stippled black composite stocks. Imported 1997 to date.

Blued finish	NiB $450	Ex $390	Gd $217
Duo finish	NiB $470	Ex $410	Gd $237
Stainless finish	NiB $485	Ex $430	Gd $360
For Siglite nite sights, add			$40

MODEL P239 DA/DAO AUTOMATIC PISTOL
Caliber: .357 SIG, 9mm Parabellum or .40 S&W. Seven- or 8-shot magazine, 3.6-inch bbl., 6.6 inches overall. Weight: 28.2 oz. Double/single action or double action only. Blade front and notch rear adjustable sights. Alloy frame w/stainless slide. Ambidextrous frame- mounted magazine release. Matte black or Duo finish. Stippled black composite stocks. Made 1996 to date.

Matte black finish	NiB $500	Ex $440	Gd $220
DAO finish	NiB $538	Ex $430	Gd $292
For Siglite nite sights, add			$100

SMITH & WESSON, INC. — Springfield, Massachusetts

NOTE: *For ease in locating a particular S&W handgun, the listings are divided into two groupings: Automatic/Single-Shot Pistols (below) and Revolvers (page 153). For a complete handgun listing, please refer to the index.*

AUTOMATIC/SINGLE-SHOT PISTOLS

.32 AUTOMATIC PISTOL . . . . . NiB $2800 Ex $2100 Gd $1500
Caliber: .32 Automatic. Same general specifications as .35 caliber model, but barrel is fastened to the receiver instead of hinged. Made 1924-37.

MODEL .22 SPORT SERIES
Caliber: .22 LR. 10-shot magazine, 4-, 5.5- or 7-inch standard (A-series) or bull bbl., (S-series). Single action. Eight, 9.5 or 11 inches overall. Weight: 28 oz. to 33 oz. Partridge front sight, fully adjustable rear. Alloy frame w/stainless slide. Blued finish. Black polymer or Dymondwood grips. Made 1997 to date.

Model 22A (w/4-inch bbl.) . . . . NiB $210	Ex $185	Gd $110
Model 22A (w/5.5-inch bbl.). . . . . . NiB $239	Ex $214	Gd $138
Model 22A (w/7-inch bbl.) . . . . NiB $277	Ex $252	Gd $177
Model 22S (w/5.5-inch bbl.) . . . . . . NiB $310	Ex $285	Gd $210
Model 22S (w/7-inch bbl.) . . . . NiB $244	Ex $195	Gd $133

W/bull bbl., add $40
W/Dymondwood grips, add $75

35 (1913) AUTOMATIC PISTOL . . . NiB $775 Ex $650 Gd $375
Caliber: 35 S&W Auto. Seven-shot magazine, 3.5-inch bbl., (hinged to frame). 6.5 inches overall. Weight: 25 oz. Fixed sights. Blued or nickel finish. Plain walnut grips. Made 1913-21.

MODEL 39 9MM DA AUTO PISTOL
Calibers: 9mm Para. Eight-shot magazine, 4-inch barrel. Overall length: 7.44-inches. Steel or alloy frames. Weight: 26.5 oz. (w/alloy frame). Click adjustable rear sight, ramp front. Blued or nickel finish. Checkered walnut grips. Made 1954-82. Note: Between 1954 and 1966, 927 pistols were produced w/steel instead of alloy. In 1970, Model 39-1 w/alloy frame and steel slide. In 1971, Model 39-2 was introduced as an improved version of the original Model 39 w/modified extractor.

Model 39 (early production) 1954-70
First series (SN range 1000-2600) . . . . . NiB $1450 Ex $1250 Gd $625
9mm blue(w/steel frame & slide,
produced 1966) . . . . NiB $1200 Ex $975 Gd $580
9mm blue (w/alloy frame) . . . . NiB $406 Ex $325 Gd $221
Nickel finish, add $35
Models 39-1, 39-2 (late production)
1970-82 9mm blue (w/alloy frame) . . . . . . NiB $360 Ex $250 Gd $200
Nickel finish, add $35

MODEL 41 .22 AUTOMATIC PISTOL
Caliber: .22 LR, .22 Short (not interchangeably). 10-shot magazine, bbl. lengths: 5-, 5.5-, 7.75-inches; latter has detachable muzzle brake, 12 inches overall (with 7.75-inch bbl.). Weight: 43.5 oz. (with 7.75-inch bbl.). Click adj. rear sight, undercut Partridge front. Blued finish. Checkered walnut grips w/thumbrest. 1957 to date.
.22 LR model . . . . NiB $675 Ex $535 Gd $250
.22 Short model
(w/counter-
weights & muzzle brake) . . . . NiB $1094 Ex $875 Gd $595
W/extended sight, add $95
W/muzzle brake, add $45

Smith & Wesson
Model 22A Sport Series

Smith & Wesson
Model 22S Sport Series w/Dymondwood Grips

Smith & Wesson
Model 41 .22

MODEL 46 .22 AUTO PISTOL . . . . . NiB $450 Ex $335 Gd $200
Caliber: .22 LR. 10-shot magazine, bbl. lengths: 5-, 5.5-, 7-inches. 10.56 inches overall (with 7-inch bbl.). Weight: 42 oz. (with 7-inch bbl.). Click adj. rear sight, undercut Partridge front. Blued finish. Molded nylon grips w/thumbrest. Only 4,000 produced. Made 1959-68. See illustration next page.

MODEL 52 .38 MASTER AUTO
Caliber: .38 Special (midrange wadcutter only). Five-shot magazine, 5-inch bbl., overall length: 8.63 inches. Weight: 41 oz. Micrometer click rear sight, Partridge front on ramp base. Blued finish. Checkered walnut grips. Made 1961-94. See illustration next page.
Model 52 (1961-63) . . . . NiB $875 Ex $775 Gd $395
Model 52-1 (1963-71) . . . . NiB $675 Ex $550 Gd $295
Model 52-2 (1971-93) . . . . NiB $675 Ex $550 Gd $295
Model 52-A USA Marksman
(fewer than 100 mfg.) . . . . NiB $3000 Ex $2550 Gd $1700

Smith & Wesson
Model 46

Smith & Wesson
Model 52

Smith & Wesson
Model 59

Smith & Wesson
Model 422

Smith & Wesson
Model 439

MODEL 59
9MM DA AUTO
Similar specifications as Model 39 except has 14-shot staggered column magazine, checkered nylon grips. Made 1971-82.
Model 59, blue . . . . NiB $385 Ex $340 Gd $215
Model 59, nickel . . . . NiB $421 Ex $370 Gd $225
Model 59
(early production
w/smooth grip frame) . . . . NiB $563 Ex $450 Gd $306

MODEL 61
ESCORT POCKET AUTOMATIC PISTOL
Caliber: .22 LR. Five-shot magazine, 2.13-inch bbl., 4.69 inches overall. Weight: 14 oz. Fixed sights. Blued or nickel finish. Checkered plastic grips. Made 1970-73.
Model 61, blue . . . . NiB $250 Ex $210 Gd $110
Model 61, nickel . . . . NiB $275 Ex $230 Gd $110

MODEL 410
AUTO PISTOL . . . . NiB $460 Ex $330 Gd $175
Caliber: .40 S&W. Double action. 10-shot magazine, 4-inch bbl., 7.5 inches overall. Weight: 28.5 oz. Alloy frame w/steel slide. Post front sight, fixed rear w/3-dot system. Matte blue finish. Checkered synthetic grips w/straight backstrap. Made 1996 to date.

MODEL 411
AUTO PISTOL . . . . NiB $440 Ex $375 Gd $275
Similar to S&W Model 915 except in caliber .40 S&W. 11-shot magazine, made 1994-96.

MODEL 422 SA
AUTO PISTOL
Caliber: .22 LR. 10-shot magazine, 4.5- or 6-inch bbl., 7.5 inches overall (with 4.5-inch bbl.). Weight: 22-23.5 oz. Fixed or adjustable sights. Checkered plastic or walnut grips. Blued finish. Made from 1987-96.
Standard model . . . . NiB $185 Ex $150 Gd $100
Target model . . . . NiB $225 Ex $175 Gd $105

MODEL 439
9MM AUTOMATIC
DA. Caliber: 9mm Para. Two 8-round magazines, 4-inch bbl., 7.44 inches overall. Alloy frame. Weight: 30 oz. Serrated ramp square front sight, square notch rear. Checkered walnut grips. Blued or nickel finish. Made 1979-88.
Model 439, blue . . . . NiB $385 Ex $315 Gd $210
Model 439, nickel . . . . NiB $419 Ex $349 Gd $290
W/adjustable sights, add $24

Smith & Wesson
Model 645

Smith & Wesson
Model 459

MODEL 457
COMPACT AUTO PISTOL . . . . **NiB $466 Ex $335 Gd $180**
Caliber: .45 ACP. Double action. Seven-shot magazine, 3.75-inch
bbl., 7.25 inches overall. Weight: 29 oz. Alloy frame w/steel slide.
Post front sight, fixed rear w/3-dot system. Bobbed hammer. Matte
blue finish. Wraparround synthetic grip w/straight backstrap. Made
1996 to date.

MODEL 459 DA AUTOMATIC
Caliber: 9mm Para. Two 14-round magazines, 4-inch bbl., 7.44
inches overall. Alloy frame. Weight: 28 oz. Blued or nickel finish.
Made 1979-87.
Model 459, blue . . . . **NiB $410 Ex $345 Gd $240**
Model 459, nickel . . . . **NiB $454 Ex $390 Gd $270**
FBI Model (brushed finish) . . . . **NiB $650 Ex $600 Gd $330**

MODEL 469
(MINI) AUTOMATIC . . . . **NiB $370 Ex $320 Gd $220**
DA. Caliber: 9mm Para. Two 12-round magazines, 3.5-inch bbl.,
6.88 inches overall. Weight: 26 oz. Yellow ramp front sight, dovetail
mounted square-notch rear. Sandblasted blued finish. Optional
ambidextrous safety. Made 1982-88.

MODEL 539 DA AUTOMATIC
Similar to Model 439 except w/steel frame. Caliber: 9mm Para. Two
8-round magazines, 4-inch bbl., 7.44 inches overall. Weight: 36 oz.
Blued or nickel finish. Made 1980-83.
Model 539, blue . . . . **NiB $450 Ex $395 Gd $300**
Model 539, nickel . . . . **NiB $485 Ex $430 Gd $325**
W/adjustable sights, add **$30**

Smith & Wesson
Model 469

MODEL 559 DA AUTOMATIC
Similar to Model 459 except w/steel frame. Caliber: 9mm Para. Two
14-round magazines, 4-inch bbl., 7.44 inches overall. Weight: 39.5
oz. Blued or nickel finish. (3750 produced) Made 1980-83.
Model 559, blue . . . . **NiB $485 Ex $435 Gd $250**
Model 559, nickel . . . . **NiB $515 Ex $470 Gd $280**
W/adjustable sights, add **$30**

MODEL 622 SA AUTO PISTOL
Same general specifications as Model 422 except w/stainless finish.
Made from 1989-96.
Standard model . . . . **NiB $220 Ex $175 Gd $160**
Target model . . . . **NiB $275 Ex $225 Gd $175**

MODEL 639 AUTOMATIC . . . . **NiB $420 Ex $300 Gd $275**
Caliber: 9mm Para. Two 12-round magazines, 3.5-inch bbl., 6.9
inches overall. Weight: 36 oz. Stainless. Made 1982-88.

Smith & Wesson
Model 639

**Smith & Wesson
Model 659**

**Smith & Wesson
Model 745**

**Smith & Wesson
Model 1026**

MODEL 645 DA AUTOMATIC
Caliber: .45 ACP. Eight-shot. 5-inch bbl., overall length: 8.5 inches. Weight: Approx. 38 oz. Red ramp front, fixed rear sights. Stainless. Made 1986-88. See illustration previous page.
Model 645 (w/fixed sights) . . . . NiB $475 Ex $365 Gd $300
Model 645 (w/adjustable sights) . . . NiB $500 Ex $390 Gd $325

MODEL 659 9MM AUTOMATIC
DA. Similar to S&W Model 459 except weight: 39.5 oz. and finish is satin stainless steel finish. Made 1983-88.
Model 659 (w/fixed sights) . . . . NiB $445 Ex $335 Gd $300
Model 659 (w/adjustable sights) . . . . NiB $470 Ex $360 Gd $325

MODEL 669 AUTOMATIC. . . . . . . NiB $425 Ex $305 Gd $207
Caliber: 9mm. 12-shot magazine, 3.5 inch bbl., 6.9 inches overall. Weight: 26 oz. Serrated ramp front sight w/red bar, fixed rear. Nonglare stainless steel finish. Made 1986-88.

MODEL 745 AUTOMATIC PISTOL
Caliber: .45 ACP. Eight-shot magazine, 5-inch bbl., 8.63 inches overall. Weight: 38.75 oz. Fixed sights. Blued slide, stainless frame. Checkered walnut grips. Similar to the model 645, but w/o DA capability. Made 1987-90.
W/standard competition features . . . . NiB $575 Ex $440 Gd $335
IPSC Commemorative (first 5,000) . . . . NiB $681 Ex $545 Gd $371

MODEL 908/909/910 AUTO PISTOLS
Caliber: 9mm Parabellum. Double action. Eight-shot (Model 908), 9-shot (Model 909) or 10-shot (Model 910) magazine; 3.5- or 4-inch bbl.; 6.83 or 7.38 inches overall. Weight: 26 oz. to 28.5 oz. Post front sight, fixed rear w/3-dot system. Matte blue steel slide w/alloy frame. Delrin synthetic wrap-around grip w/straight backstrap. Made 1994 to date.
Model 908. . . . . NiB $420 Ex $310 Gd $175
Model 909 (disc 1996) . . . . NiB $360 Ex $275 Gd $175
Model 910 . . . . NiB $420 Ex $310 Gd $175

MODEL 915 AUTO PISTOL . . . . . . NiB $350 Ex $255 Gd $175
DA. Caliber: 9mm Para. 15-shot magazine, 4-inch bbl., 7.5 inches overall. Weight: 28.5 oz. Post front sight, fixed square-notched rear w/3-dot system. Xenoy wraparound grip. Blued steel slide and alloy frame. Made 1992-94.

MODEL 1000 SERIES DA AUTO
Caliber: 10mm. Nine-shot magazine, 4.25- or 5-inch bbl., 7.88 or 8.63 inches overall. Weight: About 38 oz. Post front sight, adj. or fixed square-notched rear w/3-dot system. One-piece Xenoy wrap-around grips. Stainless slide and frame. Made 1990-94.
Model 1006 (fixed sights, 5 inch bbl.) . . . . NiB $635 Ex $525 Gd $400
Model 1006 (Adj. sights, 5 inch bbl.) . . . . . NiB $662 Ex $552 Gd $427
Model 1026 (fixed sights, 5 inch bbl.,
decocking lever) . . . . NiB $630 Ex $525 Gd $400
Model 1066 (fixed
sights, 4.25 inch bbl.) . . . . NiB $610 Ex $515 Gd $395
Model 1076 (fixed sights, 4.25 inch bbl.,
frame-mounted decocking lever,
straight backstrap). . . . . NiB $645 Ex $530 Gd $400
Model 1076 (same as above
w/Tritium night sight) . . . . NiB $685 Ex $570 Gd $440
Model 1086 (same as model
1076 in DA only) . . . . NiB $710 Ex $515 Gd $395

MODEL 2206 SA AUTOMATIC PISTOL
Similar to Model 422 except w/stainless-steel slide and frame, weight: 35-39 oz. Partridge front sight on adj. sight model; post w/white dot on fixed sight model. Plastic grips. Made 1990-96.
Standard model . . . . NiB $290 Ex $225 Gd $175
Target model . . . . NiB $360 Ex $275 Gd $230

MODEL 2213
SPORTSMAN AUTO . . . . NiB $255 Ex $200 Gd $160
Caliber: .22 LR. Eight-shot magazine, 3-inch bbl., 6.13 inches overall. Weight: 18 oz. Partridge front sight, fixed square-notched rear w/3-dot system. Black synthetic molded grips. Stainless steel slide w/alloy frame. Made 1992-99.

MODEL 2214
SPORTSMAN AUTO . . . . NiB $230 Ex $185 Gd $130
Same general specifications as Model 2214 except w/blued slide and matte black alloy frame. Made from 1990-99.

MODEL 3904/3906 DA AUTO PISTOL

Caliber: 9mm. Eight-shot magazine, 4-inch bbl., 7.5 inches overall. Weight: 25.5 oz. (Model 3904) or 34 oz. (Model 3906). Fixed or adj. sights. Delrin one-piece wraparound, checkered grips. Alloy frame w/blued carbon steel slide (Model 3904) or satin stainless (Model 3906). Made 1989-91.

Model 3904 w/adjustable sights	NiB $470	Ex $405	Gd $325
Model 3904 w/fixed sights	NiB $450	Ex $385	Gd $280
Model 3904 w/Novak LC sight	NiB $475	Ex $370	Gd $250
Model 3906 w/adjustable sights	NiB $538	Ex $463	Gd $393
Model 3906 w/Novak LC sight	NiB $510	Ex $435	Gd $365

MODEL 3913/3914 DA AUTOMATIC

Caliber: 9mm Parabellum (Luger). Eight-shot magazine, 3.5-inch bbl., 6.88 inches overall. Weight: 25 oz. Post front sight, fixed or adj. square-notched rear. One-piece Xenoy wraparound grips w/straight backstrap. Alloy frame w/stainless or blued slide. Made 1990 to date.

Model 3913 stainless	NiB $615	Ex $475	Gd $380
Model 3913LS Lady Smith stainless w/contoured trigger guard	NiB $630	Ex $480	Gd $380
Model 3913TSW (intro. 1998)	NiB $615	Ex $475	Gd $380
Model 3914 blued compact (disc 1995)	NiB $465	Ex $385	Gd $280

MODEL 3953/3954 DA AUTO PISTOL

Same general specifications as Model 3913/3914 except double action only. Made from 1991 to date.

Model 3953 stainless, double action only	NiB $615	Ex $475	Gd $380
Model 3954 blued, double action only (disc. 1992)	NiB $445	Ex $380	Gd $280

MODEL 4000 SERIES DA AUTO

Caliber: .40 S&W. 11-shot magazine, 4-inch bbl., 7.88 inches overall. Weight: 28-30 oz. w/alloy frame or 36 oz. w/stainless frame. Post front sight, adj. or fixed square-notched rear w/2 white dots. Straight backstrap. One-piece Xenoy wraparound grips. Blued or stainless finish. Made between 1990-93.

Model 4003 stainless w/alloy frame	NiB $585	Ex $495	Gd $395
Model 4003 TSW w/ S&W Tactical options	NiB $740	Ex $645	Gd $360
Model 4004 blued w/alloy frame	NiB $531	Ex $425	Gd $289
Model 4006 stainless frame, fixed sights	NiB $540	Ex $460	Gd $280
Model 4006 stainless frame, Adj. sights	NiB $655	Ex $545	Gd $400
Model 4006 TSW w/ S&W Tactical options	NiB $745	Ex $645	Gd $360
Model 4013 stainless frame, fixed sights	NiB $595	Ex $485	Gd $285
Model 4013 TSW w/ S&W Tactical options	NiB $730	Ex $580	Gd $420
Model 4014 blued, fixed sights (disc. 1993)	NiB $510	Ex $425	Gd $275
Model 4026 w/decocking Lever (disc. 1994)	NiB $620	Ex $520	Gd $400
Model 4043 DA only, stainless w/alloy frame	NiB $740	Ex $640	Gd $360
Model 4044 DA only, blued w/alloy frame	NiB $540	Ex $460	Gd $295
Model 4046 DA only, stainless frame, fixed sights	NiB $655	Ex $540	Gd $400
Model 4046 TSW w/ S&W Tactical options	NiB $755	Ex $650	Gd $350
Model 4046 DA only, stainless frame, Tritium night sight	NiB $888	Ex $783	Gd $517

Smith & Wesson
Model 3906

Smith & Wesson
Model 3953

Smith & Wesson
Model 4013

Smith & Wesson
Model 4046

Smith & Wesson
Model 4053

Smith & Wesson
Model 4586

Smith & Wesson Model 5904
w/Adjustable Sights

MODEL 4013/4014 DA AUTOMATIC

Caliber: .40 S&W. Eight-shot capacity, 3.5-inch bbl., 7 inches overall. Weight: 26 oz. Post front sight, fixed Novak LC rear w/3-dot system. One-piece Xenoy wraparound grips. Stainless or blued slide w/alloy frame. Made 1991 to date.

Model 4013 w/stainless slide (disc. 1996) .... NiB $595 Ex $480 Gd $280
Model 4013 Tactical w/stainless slide .... NiB $730 Ex $580 Gd $420
Model 4014 w/blued slide (disc. 1993) ...... NiB $510 Ex $425 Gd $235

MODEL 4053/4054 DA AUTO PISTOL

Same general specifications as Model 4013/4014 except double action only. Alloy frame fitted w/blued steel slide. Made 1991-97.

(cont'd) MODEL 4053/4054 DA AUTO PISTOL

Model 4053 DA only w/stainless slide .... NiB $510 Ex $425 Gd $375
Model 4053 TSW w/ S&W Tactical options ... NiB $730 Ex $580 Gd $415
Model 4054 DA only w/blued slide
(disc. 1992)............................ NiB $510 Ex $425 Gd $375

MODEL 4500 SERIES DA AUTOMATIC

Caliber: .45 ACP. Six-, 7- or 8-shot magazine, bbl. lengths: 3.75, 4.25 or 5 inches; 7.13 to 8.63 inches overall. Weight: 34.5 to 38.5 oz. Post front sight, fixed Novak LC rear w/3-dot system or adj. One-piece Xenoy wraparound grips. Satin stainless finish. Made 1990 to date.

Model 4505 w/fixed sights, 5-inch bbl........ NiB $575 Ex $500 Gd $300
Model 4505 w/Novak LC sight, 5-inch bbl. ... NiB $602 Ex $527 Gd $327
Model 4506 w/fixed sights, 5-inch bbl........ NiB $680 Ex $550 Gd $410
Model 4506 w/Novak LC sight, 5-inch bbl. ... NiB $713 Ex $583 Gd $440
Model 4513T (TSW) w/3.75-inch bbl.
Tactical Combat .... NiB $655 Ex $535 Gd $400
Model 4516 w/3.75-inch bbl............... NiB $655 Ex $530 Gd $350
Model 4526 w/5-inch bbl., alloy frame,
decocking lever, fixed sights .... NiB $635 Ex $530 Gd $400
Model 4536, decocking lever .... NiB $640 Ex $540 Gd $410
Model 4546, w/3.75-inch bbl., DA only ..... NiB $640 Ex $540 Gd $410
Model 4553T (TSW) w/3.75-inch bbl.
Tactical Combat .... NiB $602 Ex $527 Gd $322
Model 4556, w/3.75-inch bbl., DA only ..... NiB $575 Ex $500 Gd $300
Model 4563 TSW w/4.25-inch bbl.
Tactical Combat .... NiB $655 Ex $535 Gd $400
Model 4566 w/4.25-inch bbl.,
ambidextrous safety, fixed sights .... NiB $625 Ex $525 Gd $350
Model 4566 TSW w/4.25-inch bbl.
Tactical Combat .... NiB $655 Ex $535 Gd $400
Model 4576 w/4.25-inch bbl.,
decocking lever .... NiB $635 Ex $530 Gd $350
Model 4583T TSW w/4.25-inch bbl.
Tactical Combat .... NiB $602 Ex $527 Gd $410
Model 4586 w/4.25-inch bbl., DA only ...... NiB $680 Ex $550 Gd $400
Model 4586 TSW w/4.25-inch bbl.
Tactical Combat .... NiB $655 Ex $535 Gd $340

MODEL 5900 SERIES DA AUTOMATIC

Caliber: 9mm. 15-shot magazine, 4-inch bbl., 7.5 inches overall. Weight: 26-38 oz. Fixed or adj. sights. One-piece Xenoy wraparound grips. Alloy frame w/stainless-steel slide (Model 5903) or blued slide (Model 5904) stainless-steel frame and slide (Model 5906). Made 1989/90 to date.

Model 5903 w/adjustable sights .... NiB $695 Ex $560 Gd $275
Model 5903 w/Novak LC rear sight .... NiB $$695 Ex $560 Gd $275
Model 5903 TSW w/4-inch bbl.,
Tactical Combat .... NiB $695 Ex $560 Gd $275
Model 5904 w/adjustable sights .... NiB $538 Ex $430 Gd $292
Model 5904 w/Novak LC rear sight .... NiB $530 Ex $415 Gd $280
Model 5905 w/Adjustable Sights .... NiB $550 Ex $435 Gd $325
Model 5905 w/Novak LC rear sight .... NiB $635 Ex $530 Gd $350
Model 5906 w/adjustable sights .... NiB $630 Ex $525 Gd $325
Model 5906 w/Novak LC rear sight .... NiB $610 Ex $425 Gd $300
Model 5906 w/Tritium night sight.......... NiB $730 Ex $615 Gd $475
Model 5906 TSW w/4-inch bbl.,
Tactical Combat .... NiB $725 Ex $630 Gd $455
Model 5924 anodized frame, blued slide ..... NiB $570 Ex $425 Gd $235
Model 5926 Stain. frame, decocking lever .... NiB $655 Ex $530 Gd $400
Model 5943 alloy frame/
stainless slide, DA only .... NiB $630 Ex $525 Gd $325
Model 5943 TSW w/4-inch bbl., DA only .... NiB $600 Ex $480 Gd $326
Model 5944 alloy frame/
blued slide, DA only .... NiB $540 Ex $440 Gd $310
Model 5946 stainless frame/slide, DA only ... NiB $595 Ex $400 Gd $280
Model 5946 TSW w/4-inch bbl., DA only..... NiB $602 Ex $527 Gd $140

MODEL 6900 COMPACT SERIES

Double action. Caliber: 9mm. 12-shot magazine, 3.5-inch bbl., 6.88 inches overall. Weight: 26.5 oz. Ambidextrous safety. Post front sight, fixed Novak LC rear w/3-dot system. Alloy frame w/blued carbon steel slide (Model 6904) or stainless steel slide (Model 6906). Made 1989 to date.

Model 6904	NiB $570	Ex $410	Gd $280
Model 6906 w/fixed sights	NiB $585	Ex $470	Gd $380
Model 6906 w/Tritium night sight	NiB $705	Ex $511	Gd $440
Model 6926 same as model			
6906 w/decocking lever	NiB $595	Ex $480	Gd $280
Model 6944 same as model			
6904 in DA only	NiB $510	Ex $425	Gd $235
Model 6946 same as model			
6906 in DA only ,fixed sights	NiB $595	Ex $480	Gd $280
Model 6946 w/Tritium night sight	NiB $655	Ex $535	Gd $340

SIGMA SW380 AUTOMATIC PISTOL . . . . . NiB $285 Ex $245 Gd $170

Caliber: .380 ACP. Double-action only. Six-shot magazine, 3-inch bbl., weight: 14 oz. Black integral polymer gripframe w/checkered back and front straps. Fixed channel sights. Polymer frame w/hammerless steel slide. Made 1996 to date.

SIGMA SW9 SERIES AUTOMATIC PISTOL

Caliber: 9mm Parabellum. Double action only. 10-shot magazine, 3.25-, 4- or 4.5-inch bbl., weight: 17.9 oz. to 24.7 oz. Polymer frame w/hammerless steel slide. Post front sight and drift adjustable rear w/3-dot system. Gray or black integral polymer gripframe w/checkered back and front straps. Made 1994 to date.

Model SW9C (compact w/3.25-inch bbl.)	NiB $450	Ex $355	Gd $265
Model SW9F (blue slide w/4.5-inch bbl.)	NiB $485	Ex $390	Gd $280
Model SW9M (compact w/3.25-inch bbl.)	NiB $300	Ex $270	Gd $175
Model SW9V (stainless slide w/4-inch bbl.)	NiB $360	Ex $300	Gd $250
Tritium night sight, add			$210

SW40 SERIES AUTOMATIC PISTOL

Same general specifications as SW9 series except chambered for .40 S&W w/4- or 4.5-inch bbl., weight: 24.4 to 26 oz. Made 1994 to date.

Model SW40C (compact w/4inch bbl.)	NiB $450	Ex $355	Gd $265
Model SW40F (blue slide w/4.5inch bbl.)	NiB $450	Ex $355	Gd $265
Model SW40V (stainless slide w/4inch bbl.)	NiB $360	Ex $300	Gd $250
Tritium night sight, add			$210

MODEL 1891 SINGLE-SHOT TARGET PISTOL, FIRST MODEL

Hinged frame. Calibers: .22 LR, .32 S&W, .38 S&W. Bbl. lengths: 6-, 8- and 10-inches, approx. 13.5 inches overall (with 10-inch bbl.). Weight: About 25 oz. Target sights, barrel catch rear adj. for windage and elevation. Blued finish. Square butt, hard rubber grips. Made 1893-1905. Note: This model was available also as a combination arm w/accessory .38 revolver bbl. and cylinder enabling conversion to a pocket revolver. It has the frame of the .38 SA revolver Model 1891 w/side flanges, hand and cylinder stop slots.

Single-shot pistol, .22 LR.	NiB $800	Ex $650	Gd $325
Single-shot pistol, .32 S&W or .38 S&W.	NiB $1119	Ex $895	Gd $609
Combination set, revolver and single-shot barrel	NiB $1244	Ex $995	Gd $677

MODEL 1891 SINGLE-SHOT TARGET PISTOL, SECOND MODEL . . . . NiB $1100 Ex $750 Gd $375

Similar to the First Model except side flanges, hand and stop slots eliminated, cannot be converted to revolver, redesigned rear sight. Caliber: .22 LR only, 10-inch bbl. only. Made 1905-09.

PERFECTED SINGLE-SHOT TARGET PISTOL

Similar to Second Model except has double-action lockwork. Caliber: .22 LR only, 10-inch bbl. Checkered walnut grips, extended

Smith & Wesson
Model 1

(cont'd) PERFECTED SINGLE-SHOT TARGET PISTOL

square-butt target type. Made 1909-23. Note: In 1920 and thereafter, this model was made w/barrels having bore diameter of .223 instead of .226 and tight, short chambering. The first group of these pistols was produced for the U.S. Olympic Team of 1920, thus the designation Olympic Model.

Pre-1920 type	NiB $1700	Ex $750	Gd $300
Olympic model	NiB $1400	Ex $995	Gd $595

STRAIGHT LINE SINGLE-SHOT
TARGET PISTOL . . . . NiB $1750 Ex $1200 Gd $550

Frame shaped like that of an automatic pistol, barrel swings to the left on pivot for extracting and loading, straight-line trigger and hammer movement. Caliber: .22 LR. 10-inch bbl., 11.25 inches overall. Weight: 34 oz. Target sights. Blued finish. Smooth walnut grips. Supplied in metal case w/screwdriver and cleaning rod. Made 1925-36.

NOTE: *The following section contains only S&W Revolvers. For a complete listing of S&W handguns, please refer to the index.*

REVOLVERS

MODEL 1 HAND EJECTOR
DA REVOLVER. . . . . NiB $700 Ex $600 Gd $385

First Model. Forerunner of the .32 Hand Ejector and Regulation Police models, this was the first S&W revolver of the solid-frame, swing-out cylinder type. Top strap of this model is longer than those of later models, and it lacks the usual S&W cylinder latch. Caliber: .32 S&W Long. Bbl., lengths: 3.25-, 4.25-, and 6-inches. Fixed sights. Blued or nickel finish. Round butt, hard rubber stocks. Made 1896-1903.

NO. 3 SA FRONTIER. . . . . NiB $9060 Ex $6000 Gd $1900

Caliber: .44-40 WCF. Bbl., lengths: 4-, 5- and 6.5-inch. Fixed or target sights. Blued or nickel finish. Round, hard rubber or checkered walnut grips. Made 1885-1908.

NO. 3 SA (NEW MODEL) . . . . . NiB $3744 Ex $2995 Gd $2037

Hinged frame. Six-shot cylinder. Caliber: .44 S&W Russian. Bbl., lengths: 4-, 5-, 6-, 6.5-, 7.5- and 8-inches. Fixed or target sights. Blued or nickel finish. Round, hard rubber or checkered walnut grips. Made 1878-1908. Note: Value shown is for standard model. Specialist collectors recognize numerous variations w/a range of higher values.

NO. 3 SA TARGET . . . . NiB $6500 Ex $3250 Gd $1190

Hinged frame. Six-shot cylinder. Calibers: .32/.44 S&W, .38/.44 S&W Gallery & Target. 6.5-inch bbl. only. Fixed or target sights. Blued or nickel finish. Round, hard rubber or checkered walnut grips. Made 1887-1910.

**Smith & Wesson
Model 10 (Two-inch Barrel)**

**Smith & Wesson
Model 12 (Two-inch Barrel**

**Smith & Wesson Model 13
(Heavy Barrel)**

**Smith & Wesson
Model 14**

MODEL 10 .38 MILITARY & POLICE DA

Also called Hand Ejector Model of 1902, Hand Ejector Model of 1905, Model K. Manufactured substantially in its present form since 1902, this model has undergone numerous changes, most of them minor. Round- or square-butt models, the latter intro. in 1904. Caliber: .38 Special. Six-shot cylinder, bbl. lengths: 2-(intro. 1933), 4-, 5-, 6- and 6.5-inch (latter disc. 1915) also 4-inch heavy bbl., (intro. 1957); 11.13 inches overall (square-butt model w/6-inch bbl.). Round-butt model is 1/4-inch shorter, weight: About 1/2 oz. less. Fixed sights. Blued or nickel finish. Checkered walnut grips, hard rubber available in round-butt style. Current Model 10 has short action. Made 1902 to date. Note: S&W Victory Model, wartime version of the M & P .38, was produced for the U.S. Government from 1940 to the end of the war. A similar revolver, designated .38/200 British Service Revolver, was produced for the British Government during the same period. These arms have either brush-polish or sandblast blued finish, and most of them have plain, smooth walnut grips, lanyard swivels.

Model of 1902 (1902-05) . . . . NiB $600 Ex $470 Gd $200
Model of 1905 (1905-40) . . . . NiB $500 Ex $385 Gd $200
.38/200 British Service (1940-45) . . . NiB $350 Ex $255 Gd $110
Victory Model (1942-45) . . . . NiB $356 Ex $285 Gd $194
Model of 1944 (1945-48) . . . . NiB $219 Ex $175 Gd $119
Model 10 (1948 - date) . . . . NiB $350 Ex $255 Gd $110

MODEL 10 .38 MILITARY
& POLICE HEAVY BARREL . . . . NiB $350 Ex $255 Gd $110
Same as standard Model 10 except has heavy 4-inch bbl., weight: 34 oz. Made 1957 to date.

MODEL 12 .38 M
& PAIRWEIGHT . . . . NiB $365 Ex $260 Gd $140
Same as standard Military & Police except has light alloy frame, furnished w/2- or 4-inch bbl. only, weight: 18 oz. (w/2-inch bbl.). Made 1952-86.

MODEL 12/13 (AIR FORCE MODEL)
DA REVOLVER . . . . NiB $800 Ex $725 Gd $475
Special "Air Force" Model designed with alloy cylinder and frame to be used as a "Survival Weapon" for air crews. Athough this weapon was actually a first-series Model 12, the Air Force stamped "M13" on the top strap. Issued 1953 but recalled for function problems in 1954.

MODEL 13 .357
MILITARY/POLICE . . . . NiB $310 Ex $230 Gd $125
Same as Model 10 .38 Military & Police Heavy Barrel except chambered for .357 Magnum and .38 Special w/3- or 4-inch bbl. Round or square butt configuration. Made 1974-98.

MODELS 14 (K38) AND 16 (K32) MASTERPIECE REVOLVERS
Calibers: .22 LR, .22 Magnum Rimfire, .32 S&W Long, .38 Special. Six-shot cylinder. DA/SA. Bbl. lengths: 4- (.22 WMR only), 6-, 8.38-inch (latter not available in K32), 11.13 inches overall (with 6-inch bbl.). Weight: 38.5 oz. (with 6-inch bbl.). Click adj. rear sight, Partridge front. Blued finish. Checkered walnut grips. Made 1947 to date. (Model 16 disc. 1974, w/only 3,630 produced; reissued 1990-93.)
Model 14 (K-38 double-
action) . . . . NiB $300 Ex $250 Gd $150
Model 14 (K-38 single action,
6-inch bbl.) . . . . NiB $325 Ex $260 Gd $160
Model 14 (K-38 single action,
8.38-inch bbl.) . . . . NiB $356 Ex $285 Gd $194
Model 16 (K-32 double-
action) 1st Issue . . . . NiB $1350 Ex $1150 Gd $750
Model 16 (K-32 double-
action) . . . . NiB $425 Ex $275 Gd $190

MODELS 15 (.38) AND 18 (.22) COMBAT MASTERPIECE DA REVOLVERS
Same as K-.22 and K-.38 Masterpiece but w/2- (.38) or 4-inch bbl., and Baughman quick-draw front sight. 9.13 inches overall w/4-inch bbl., Weight: 34 oz. (.38 cal.). Made 1950 to date.
Model 15 . . . . NiB $340 Ex $200 Gd $180
Model 18 (disc. 1985) . . . . NiB $350 Ex $275 Gd $190
W/target options TH & TT, add $35

MODEL 17 K-.22 MASTERPIECE DA REVOLVER
Caliber: 22LR. Six-shot cylinder, Bbl lengths: 4, 6 or 8.38 inches. 11.13 inches overall (with 6-inch bbl.). Weight: 38 oz. (with 6-inch bbl.). Partridge-type front sight, S&W micrometer click rear. Checkered walnut Service grips with S&W momogram. S&W blued finish. Made 1947-93 and 1996-98.
Model 17 (4-inch bbl.) . . . . .NiB $575 Ex $500 Gd $300
Model 17 (6-inch bbl.) . . . . NiB $575 Ex $500 Gd $300
Model 17 (8.38-inch bbl.) . . . . NiB $600 Ex $550 Gd $380
W/target options TH & TT, add $35

MODEL 19 .357 COMBAT MAGNUM DA REVOLVER
Caliber: .357 Magnum. Six-shot cylinder, bbl. lengths: 2.5 (round butt), 4, or 6 inches, 9.5 inches overall (with 4-inch bbl.). Weight: 35 oz. (with 4-inch bbl.). Click adj. rear sight, ramp front. Blued or nickel finish. Target grips of checkered Goncalo Alves. Made 1956 to date (2.5- and 6-inch bbls. were disc. in 1991).
Model 19 (2.5-inch bbl.) . . . . NiB $345 Ex $265 Gd $170
Model 19 (4-inch bbl.) . . . . NiB $354 Ex $275 Gd $179
Model 19 (6-inch bbl.) . . . . NiB $360 Ex $280 Gd $184
Model 19 (8.38-inch bbl.) . . . . NiB $344 Ex $275 Gd $187
W/target options TH & TT, add $60

MODEL 20 .38/.44 HEAVY DUTY DA
Caliber: .38 Special. Six-shot cylinder, bbl. lengths: 4, 5 and 6.5 inches;10.38 inches overall (with 5-inch bbl.). Weight: 40 oz. (with 5-inch bbl.). Fixed sights. Blued or nickel finish. Checkered walnut grips. Short action after 1948. Made 1930-56 and 1957-67.
Pre-World War II . . . . NiB $595 Ex $490 Gd $340
Postwar . . . . NiB $350 Ex $285 Gd $150

MODEL 21 1950 .44 MILITARY DA REVOLVER
Postwar version of the 1926 Model 44 Military. Caliber: .44 Special, 6-shot cylinder. Bbl. lengths: 4-, 5- and 6.5-inches. 11.75 inches overall (w/6.5-inch bbl.) Weight: 39.5 oz. (w/6.5-inch bbl.). Fixed front sight w/square-notch rear sight; target model has micrometer click rear sight adj. for windage and elevation. Checkered walnut grips w/S&W monogram. Blued or nickel finish. Made 1950-67.
Model 21 (4- or 5-inch bbl.) . . . . NiB $1750 Ex $1575 Gd $650
Model 21 (6.5-inch bbl.) . . . . NiB $2625 Ex $2362 Gd $975

MODEL .22 1950 ARMY DA . . . . . . NiB $1750 Ex $1575 Gd $650
Postwar version of the 1917 Army w/same general specifications except redesigned hammer. Made 1950-67.

.22/.32 TARGET DA REVOLVER
Also known as the "Bekeart Model." Design based upon ".32 Hand Ejector." Caliber: .22 LR (recessed head cylinder for high-speed cartridges intro. 1935). Six-shot cylinder, 6-inch bbl., 10.5 inches overall. Weight: 23 oz. Adj. target sights. Blued finish. Checkered walnut grips. Made 1911-53. Note: In 1911, San Francisco gun dealer Phil Bekeart, who suggested this model, received 292 pieces. These are the true "Bekeart Model" revolvers and are marked with separate identification numbers on the base of the wooden grip.
.22/.32 Target model . . . . NiB $300 Ex $250 Gd $130
.22/.32 Target model (early prod. 1-3000) . . . . NiB $425 Ex $300 Gd $180
.22/.32 Target model (Bekeart model). . . . . . . NiB $1075 Ex $875 Gd $200

.22/.32 KIT GUN. . . . . NiB $300 Ex $235 Gd $175
Same as .22/.32 Target except has 2- or 4-inch bbl., round grips, 6 or 8 inches overall, weight: 19-21oz. Made 1935-53.

Smith & Wesson
Model 15

Smith & Wesson
Model 17 K-22

Smith & Wesson
Model 18 (See Model 15 for description)

Smith & Wesson
Model 19 (Round Butt)

Smith & Wesson
Model 19 (Square Butt)

Smith & Wesson
Model 20

Smith & Wesson
Model 21

Smith & Wesson
Model 22

Smith & Wesson
Model 22/32 Kit Gun

Smith & Wesson
Model 22/32 Target Revolver

Smith & Wesson
Model 23

MODEL 23 .38/.44 OUTDOORSMAN DA REVOLVER

Target version of the .38/44 Heavy Duty. 6.5- or 8.75-inch bbl., weight: 41.75 oz. Target sights, micrometer-click rear on postwar models. Blued or nickel finish. 1950 transition model has ribbed barrel, redesigned hammer. Made 1930-67.

Prewar model (plain bbl.) . . . . NiB $650 Ex $550 Gd $280
Postwar (ribbed bbl.). . . . . NiB $780 Ex $660 Gd $336

MODEL 24 1950 .44 TARGET DA REVOLVER

Postwar version of the 1921 Model .44 with 4-, 5- or 6.5-inch ribbed bbl., redesigned hammer, micrometer click rear sight. Matte or polished blue finish. Made 1950-67. Model 24 reintroduced 1983 only.

Model 24 (1950)
w/4-inch bbl. . . . . NiB $960 Ex $790 Gd $510
Model 24 (1950)
w/5-inch bbl. . . . . NiB $973 Ex $805 Gd $525
Model 24 (1950)
w/6.5-inch bbl. . . . . NiB $695 Ex $575 Gd $375
Model 24 (1950) w/polished
blue finish, add 20%
Model 24 (1950)
w/nickel finish, add. 50%
Model 24
.44 Target reintroduced
(7,500 produced in 1983-84)
Model 24 (w/4-inch bbl.) . . . . NiB $450 Ex $425 Gd $325
Model 24 (w/6.5-inch bbl.). . . . . NiB $400 Ex $375 Gd $275
Model 24-3 .44
Lew Horton Special (produced in 1983)
Model 24-3 (w/3-inch bbl.). . . . . NiB $380 Ex $325 Gd $250

MODEL .25 1955 .45 TARGET DA REVOLVER
Same as 1950 Model .44 Target, but chambered for .45 ACP, .45 Auto Rim or .45 LC w/4-, 6- or 6.5-inch bbl. Made 1955 to 1991 in several variations. Note: In 1961, the .45 ACP was designated Model .25-2, and in 1978 the .45 LC was designated Model .25-5.
Model 25 1955 .45 Target
Model 25 (.45 ACP w/4- or 6-inch bbl.) . . . . . . NiB $450 Ex $400 Gd $200
Model 25 (.45 ACP w/6.5-inch pinned bbl.) . . . NiB $650 Ex $550 Gd $350
Model 25 (.45 LC early production) . . . . NiB $1350 Ex $1200 Gd $600
Model 25-2 .45 ACP
Model 25 (w/3-inch bbl., Lew Horton Special) NiB $500 Ex $450 Gd $375
Model 25 (w/4-inch bbl.) . . . . NiB $456 Ex $365 Gd $248
Model 24-3 (w/6.5-inch bbl.) . . . . NiB $469 Ex $375 Gd $255
Model 25-5 .45 LC
Model 25 (w/4-inch bbl.) . . . . NiB $456 Ex $365 Gd $248
Model 24-3 (w/6.5-inch bbl.) . . . . NiB $494 Ex $395 Gd $269

MODEL 26 1950 .45 LIGHT TARGET DA REVOLVER
Similar to 1950 Model Target except w/lighter bbl. Note: Lighter profile was not well received. (Only 2768 produced)
Model 26 (.45 ACP or .45 Auto Rim
**w/6.5-inch bbl.) . . . . NiB $770 Ex $660 Gd $275
Model 26 (.45 LC, < 200 produced) . . . . NiB $2310 Ex $1980 Gd $825
W/4- or 5-inch bbl., add. 25%

MODEL 27 .357 MAGNUM DA
Caliber: .357 Magnum. Six-shot cylinder, bbl. lengths: 3.5-, 4-, 5-, 6-, 6.5-and 8.38-inches, 11.38 inches overall (with 6-inch bbl.). Weight: 44 oz. (with 6-inch bbl.). Adj. target sights, Baughman quick-draw ramp front sight on 3.5-inch bbl., Blued or nickel finish. Checkered walnut grips. Made 1935-94. Note: Until 1938, the .357 Magnum was custom made in any barrel length from 3.5-inch to 8.75-inch. Each of these revolvers was accompanied by a registration certificate and has its registration number stamped on the inside of the yoke. Postwar magnums have a redesigned hammer w/shortened fall and the new S&W micrometer click rear sight.
Prewar registered model
(Reg Number on yoke). . . . . NiB $1244 Ex $995 Gd $677
Prewar model without registration number . . . NiB $380 Ex $300 Gd $205
Early model w/pinned bbl., recessed cyl. . . . . . NiB $418 Ex $330 Gd $225
Late model w/8.38-inch bbl. . . . . NiB $388 Ex $308 Gd $213
Late model, w/3.5-5-inch bbl. . . . . NiB $425 Ex $365 Gd $240
Late model, other bbl. lengths. . . . . NiB $425 Ex $365 Gd $240

MODEL 28 HIGHWAY PATROLMAN
Caliber: .357 Magnum. Six-shot cylinder, bbl. lengths: 4- or 6-inches, 11.25 inches overall (with 6-inch bbl.). Weight: 44 oz. (with 6-inch bbl.). Adj.rear sight, ramp front. Blued finish. Checkered walnut grips, Magna or target type. Made 1954-86.
Prewar registered model
(reg number on yoke) . . . . NiB $1244 Ex $995 Gd $677
Prewar model without registration number . . . NiB $869 Ex $695 Gd $473
Early model w/pinned bbl.,
recessed cylinder, 5-screws . . . . NiB $351 Ex $305 Gd $247
Late model, all bbl. lengths . . . . NiB $270 Ex $235 Gd $190

MODEL 29 .44 MAGNUM DA REVOLVER
Caliber: .44 Magnum. Six-shot cylinder. bbl., lengths: 4-, 5-, 6.5-, 8.38-inches. 11.88 inches overall (with 6.5-inch bbl.). Weight: 47 oz. (with 6.5-inch bbl.). Click adj. rear sight, ramp front. Blued or nickel finish. Checkered Goncalo Alves target grips. Made 1956-98.
Early Production Standard Series (disc. 1983)
3-Screw model (1962-83) . . . . NiB $650 Ex $550 Gd $300
4-Screw model (1957-61) . . . . NiB $695 Ex $650 Gd $425
5-Screw model (1956-57) . . . . NiB $906 Ex $725 Gd $493
W/5-inch bbl., 3- or 4-screw models, add 95%

Smith & Wesson Model 24 Target

Smith & Wesson Model 25 Target

Smith & Wesson Model 27

Smith & Wesson Model 28

(cont'd) **MODEL 29 .44 MAGNUM DA REVOLVER**
Late Production standard series (disc. 1998)
Model 29 (w/4- or 6.5-inch bbl.) . . . . NiB $431 Ex $345 Gd $235
Model 29 (w/3-inch bbl., Lew Horton Special) . . NiB $425 Ex $350 Gd $295
Model 29 (w/8.38-inch bbl.) . . . . NiB $483 Ex $383 Gd $298
Model 29 Classic (w/5- or 6.5-inch bbl.) . . . . . NiB $475 Ex $375 Gd $270
Model 29 Classic (w/8.38-inch bbl.) . . . . NiB $483 Ex $388 Gd $298
Model 29 Classic DX (w/6.5-inch bbl.). . . . . . . NiB $625 Ex $525 Gd $300
Model 29 Classic DX (w/8.38-inch bbl.) . . . . . NiB $633 Ex $533 Gd $308
Model 29 Magna Classic (w/7.5-inch ported bbl.)
. . . . NiB $850 Ex $725 Gd $395
Model 29 Silhouette (w/10.63-inch bbl.) . . . . . NiB $550 Ex $475 Gd $298

Smith & Wesson
Model 29

Smith & Wesson
Model 31

Smith & Wesson
Model 32

Smith & Wesson
Model 34

MODEL 30 .32 HAND
EJECTOR DA REVOLVER . . . . **NiB $300 Ex $260 Gd $175**
Caliber: .32 S&W Long. Six-shot cylinder, bbl. lengths: 2-(intro. 1949), 3-, 4- and 6-inches, 8 inches overall (with 4-inch bbl.). Weight: 18 oz. (with 4-inch bbl.). Fixed sights. Blued or nickel finish. Round, checkered walnut or hard rubber grips. Made 1903-76.

MODELS 31 & 33 REGULATION POLICE DA REVOLVER
Same basic type as .32 Hand Ejector except has square buttgrips. Calibers: .32 S&W Long (Model 31) .38 S&W (Model 33). Six-shot cylinder in .32 cal., 5-shot in .38 caliber. Bbl., lengths: 2- (intro. 1949), 3-, 4- and 6-inches in .32 cal., 4-inch only in .38 cal., 8.5 inches overall (with 4-inch bbl.). Weight: 18 oz. (.38 cal. w/4-inch bbl.), 18.75 oz. (.32 cal. w/4-inch bbl.). Fixed sights. Blued or nickel finish. Checkered walnut grips. Made from 1917. Model 33 disc. in 1974; Model 31 disc. in 1992.
Model 31 . . . . **NiB $290 Ex $235 Gd $175**
Model 33 . . . . **NiB $325 Ex $275 Gd $175**

.32 DOUBLE-ACTION
REVOLVER . . . . **NiB $425 Ex $380 Gd $145**
Hinged frame. Caliber: .32 S&W. Five-shot cylinder, bbl. lengths: 3-, 3.5- and 6-inches. Fixed sights. Blued or nickel finish. Hard rubber grips. Made from 1880-1919. Note: Value shown applies generally to the several varieties. Exception is the rare first issue of 1880 (identified by squared sideplate and serial no. 1 to 30) valued up to $2,500.

MODEL .32 TERRIER DA . . . . NiB $330 Ex $220 Gd $125
Caliber: .38 S&W. Five-shot cylinder, 2-inch bbl., 6.25 inches overall. Weight: 17 oz. Fixed sights. Blued or nickel finish. Checkered walnut or hard rubber grips. Built on .32 Hand Ejector frame. Made 1936-74.

.32-20 MILITARY & POLICE DA . . . NiB $390 Ex $265 Gd $200
Same as M & P 38 except chambered for .32-20 Winchester cartridge. First intro. in the 1899 model, M & P revolvers were produced in this caliber until about 1940. Values same as M & P .38 models.

MODEL 34 1953
.22/.32 KIT GUN . . . . **NiB $300 Ex $235 Gd $175**
Same general specifications as previous .22/.32 Kit Gun except w/2-inch or 4-inch bbl. and round or square grips, blued or nickel finish. Made 1936-91.

MODEL 35 1953
.22/.32 TARGET . . . . **NiB $425 Ex $300 Gd $200**
Same general specifications as previous model .22/.32 Target except has micrometer-click rear sight. Magna type target grips. Weight: 25 oz. Made 1953-74.

MODEL 36 CHIEFS SPECIAL DA
Based on .32 Hand Ejector w/frame lengthened to permit longer cylinder for .38 Special cartridge. Caliber: .38 Special. Five-shot cylinder, bbl. lengths: 2- or 3-inches, 6.5 inches overall (with 2-inch bbl.). Weight: 19 oz. Fixed sights. Blued or nickel finish. Checkered walnut grips, round or square butt. Made 1952 to date.
Blued model . . . . **NiB $295 Ex $230 Gd $155**
Nickel model . . . . **NiB $307 Ex $242 Gd $167**
Early model (5-screw, small trigger guard, SN 1-2500) . . . . **NiB $369 Ex $295 Gd $20**

MODEL 37 AIRWEIGHT
CHIEFS SPECIAL . . . . NiB $410 Ex $285 Gd $185
Same general specifications as standard Chiefs Special except has light alloy frame, weight: 12.5 oz. w/2-inch bbl., blued finish only. Made 1954 to date.

MODEL 38 BODYGUARD AIRWEIGHT DA REVOLVER
Shrouded hammer. Light alloy frame. Caliber: .38 Special. Five-shot cylinder, 2- or 3-inch bbl., 6.38 inches overall (w/2-inch bbl). Weight: 14.5 oz. Fixed sights. Blued or nickel finish. Checkered walnut grips. Made 1955-98.
Blued model . . . . NiB $350 Ex $260 Gd $170
Nickel model . . . . NiB $365 Ex $275 Gd $185
**Early model (pinned &
recessed, pre-1981)** . . . . NiB $313 Ex $250 Gd $170

.38 DA REVOLVER. . . . . NiB $500 Ex $350 Gd $195
Hinged frame. Caliber: .38 S&W. Five-shot cylinder, bbl. lengths: 4-, 4.25-, 5-, 6-, 8- and 10-inch. Fixed sights. Blued or nickel finish. Hard rubber grips. Made 1880-1911. Note: Value shown applies generally to the several varieties. Exceptions are the first issue of 1880 (identified by squared sideplate and serial no. 1 to 4,000) and the 8- and 10-inch bbl. models of the third issue (1884-95).

MODEL .38 HAND EJECTOR DA
Military & Police — First Model. Resembles Colt New Navy in general appearance, lacks bbl., lug and locking bolt common to all later S&W hand ejector models. Caliber: .38 Long Colt. Six-shot cylinder, bbl. lengths: 4-, 5-, 6- and 6.5-inch, 11.5 inches overall (with 6.5-inch bbl.). Fixed sights. Blued or nickel finish. Round, checkered walnut or hard rubber grips. Made 1899-1902.
**Standard model
(civilian issue)** . . . . NiB $650 Ex $550 Gd $205
**Army Model (marked U.S.
Army Model, 1000 issued)** . . . . . NiB $1900 Ex $1600 Gd $625
**Navy Model (marked USN,
1000 issued)** . . . . NiB $1400 Ex $1600 Gd $625

.38 MILITARY &
POLICE TARGET DA . . . . NiB $600 Ex $450 Gd $210
Target version of the Military & Police w/standard features of that model. Caliber: .38 Special, six-inch bbl. Weight: 32.25 oz. Adj. target sights. Blued finish. Checkered walnut grips. Made 1899-1940. For values, add $175 for corresponding M&P 38 models.

MODEL .38 PERFECTED DA . . . . . . NiB $800 Ex $500 Gd $200
Hinged frame. Similar to earlier .38 DA Model but heavier frame, side latch as in solid-frame models, improved lockwork. Caliber: .38 S&W. Five-shot cylinder, bbl. lengths: 3.25, 4, 5 and 6 inches. Fixed sights. Blued or nickel finish. Hard rubber grips. Made 1909-20.

MODEL .40 CENTENNIAL
DA HAMMERLESS REVOLVER . . . . . NiB $475 Ex $425 Gd $260
Similar to Chiefs Special but has Safety Hammerless-type mechanism w/grip safety. Two-inch bbl. Weight: 19 oz. Made 1953-74.

MODEL 42 CENTENNIAL AIRWEIGHT
Same as standard Centennial model except has light alloy frame, weight: 13 oz. Made 1954-74.
Blued model . . . . NiB $475 Ex $425 Gd $260
Nickel model . . . . NiB $1000 Ex $950 Gd $550

MODEL 43 1955 .22/.32
KIT GUN AIRWEIGHT . . . . NiB $425 Ex $350 Gd $185
Same as Model 34 Kit Gun except has light alloy frame, square grip. Furnished w/3.5-inch bbl., weight: 14.25 oz. Made 1954-74.

Smith & Wesson
Model 36

Smith & Wesson
Model 37

Smith & Wesson
Model 38 Bodyguard Airweight

MODEL 44 1926 MILITARY DA REVOLVER
Basically the same as the early New Century model with extractor rod casing but lacking the "Triple Lock" feature. Caliber: .44 S&W Special. Six-shot cylinder, bbl. lengths: 4, 5 and 6.5 inches, 11.75 inches overall (with 6.5-inch bbl.). Weight: 39.5 oz. (with 6.5-inch bbl.). Fixed sights. Blued or nickel finish. Checkered walnut grips. Made 1926-41.
Standard model . . . . NiB $869 Ex $695 Gd $473
**Target model w/6.5-inch bbl.,
target sights, blued** . . . . NiB $3688 Ex $2950 Gd $2006

.44 AND .38 DA REVOLVERS
Also called Wesson Favorite (lightweight model), Frontier (caliber .44-40). Hinged frame. Six-shot cylinder. Calibers: .44 S&W Russian, .38-40, .44-40. Bbl. lengths: 4-, 5-, 6- and 6.5-inch. Weight: 37.5 oz. (with 6.5-inch bbl.). Fixed sights. Blued or nickel finish. Hard rubber grips. Made 1881-1913, Frontier disc. 1910.
Standard model, .44 Russian . . . NiB $4500 Ex $1900 Gd $680
Standard model, .38-40 . . . . NiB $4500 Ex $1900 Gd $680
Frontier model . . . . NiB $4500 Ex $1900 Gd $680
Favorite model . . . . NiB $10,000 Ex $8000 Gd $2800

Smith & Wesson
Model 48

Smith & Wesson
Model 63

Smith & Wesson
Model 49 Bodyguard

Smith & Wesson
Model 64

Smith & Wesson
Model 57

Smith & Wesson
Model 60

.44 HAND EJECTOR MODEL DA REVOLVER
First Model, New Century, also called "Triple Lock" because of its third cylinder lock at the crane. Six-shot cylinder. Calibers: .44 S&W Special, .450 Eley, .455 Mark II. Bbl. lengths: 4-, 5-, 6.5- and 7.5-inch. Weight: 39 oz. (with 6.5-inch bbl.). Fixed sights. Blued or nickel finish. Checkered walnut grips. Made 1907-66.
Second Model is basically the same as New Century except crane lock ("Triple Lock" feature) and extractor rod casing eliminated. Calibers: .44 S&W Special .44-40 Win. .45 Colt. Bbl. lengths: 4-, 5-, 6.5- and 7.5-inch; 11.75 inches overall (with 6.5-inch bbl.). Weight: 38 oz. (with 6.5-inch bbl.). Fixed sights. Blued or nickel finish. Checkered walnut grips. Made 1915-37.
First Model series w/triple lock (1907-15)
Standard model,
.44 S&W Special . . . . NiB $2275 Ex $1875 Gd $840
Standard model w/
special calibers . . . . NiB $2275 Ex $1875 Gd $850
British 455
Target model . . . . NiB $3200 Ex $2950 Gd $640
Second Model series w/o triple lock (1915-37)
Standard model,
.44 S&W Special . . . . NiB $1700 Ex $1525 Gd $715
Standard model
w/special calibers . . . . NiB $2275 Ex $1875 Gd $840
Third Model series (see S&W Model .44/1926)
Fourth Model series (see S&W Model .44/1950)

.44 HAND EJECTOR,
SECOND MODEL
DA REVOLVER . . . . NiB $675 Ex $595 Gd $290
Basically the same as New Century except crane lock ("Triple Lock" feature) and extractor rod casing eliminated. Calibers: .44 S&W Special .44-40 Win. .45 Colt. Bbl. lengths: 4-, 5-, 6.5- and 7.5-inches, 11.75 inches overall (with 6.5-inch bbl.). Weight: .38 oz. (with 6.5-inch bbl.). Fixed sights. Blued or nickel finish. Checkered walnut grips. Made 1915-37.

MODEL 48 (K-.22) MASTERPIECE M.R.F. DA REVOLVER
Caliber: .22 Mag. and .22 RF. Six-shot cylinder, bbl. lengths: 4, 6 and 8.38 inches, 11.13 inches overall (w/ 6-inch bbl.). Weight: 39 oz. Adj. rear sight, ramp front. Made 1959-86.
Model 48 (4- or 6-inch bbl.) . . . . . . NiB $275 Ex $245 Gd $175
Model 48 (8.38-inch bbl.) . . . . NiB $310 Ex $290 Gd $190
W/target options TH & TT, add $50

MODEL 49 BODYGUARD
Same as Model 38 Bodyguard Airweight except has steel frame, weight: 20.5 oz. Made 1959-96.
Blued model . . . . NiB $300 Ex $260 Gd $160
Nickel model . . . . NiB $325 Ex $285 Gd $185

MODEL 51 1960 .22/.32 KIT GUN . . . . . . NiB $400 Ex $350 Gd $225
Same as Model 34 Kit Gun except chambered for .22 WMR 3.5-inch bbl., weight: 24 oz. Made 1960-74.

MODEL 53 .22 MAGNUM DA
Caliber: .22 Rem. Jet C.F. Magnum. Six-shot cylinder (inserts permit use of .22 Short, Long, or LR cartridges). Bbl. lengths: 4, 6, 8.38 inches, 11.25 inches overall (with 6-inch bbl.). Weight: 40 oz. (with 6-inch bbl.). Micrometer-click rear sight ramp front. Checkered walnut grips. Made 1960-74.
Model 53 (4- or 6-inch bbl.) . . . . . . NiB $735 Ex $650 Gd $385
Model 53 (8.38-inch bbl.) . . . . NiB $755 Ex $680 Gd $405
W/target options TH & TT, add $35

MODEL 57 41 MAGNUM DA REVOLVER
Caliber: 41 Magnum. Six-shot cylinder, bbl. lengths: 4-, 6-, 8.38-inch. Weight: 40 oz. (with 6-inch bbl.). Micrometer click rear sight, ramp front. Target grips of checkered Goncalo Alves. Made 1964-93.
Model 57 (w/4- or 6-inch bbl.) . . . . NiB $350 Ex $255 Gd $175
Model 57 (w/8.63-inch bbl.) . . . . NiB $370 Ex $275 Gd $195
Model 57 (w/pinned bbl., recessed cylinder), add 10%

MODEL 58 41 MILITARY
& POLICE DA REVOLVER . . . . NiB $495 Ex $450 Gd $295
Caliber: 41 Magnum. Six-shot cylinder, 4-inch bbl. 9.25 inches overall. Weight: 41 oz. Fixed sights. Checkered walnut grips. Made 1964-82.

MODEL 60 STAINLESS DA
Caliber: .38 Special or .357 Magnum. Five-shot cylinder, bbl. lengths: 2, 2.1 or 3 inches, 6.5 or 7.5 inches overall. Weight: 19 to 23 oz. Square-notch rear sight, ramp front. Satin finish stainless steel. Made 1965-96 (.38 Special) and 1996 to date .357/.38).
.38 Special (disc. 1996) . . . . NiB $350 Ex $250 Gd $190
.357 Mag. . . . . NiB $400 Ex $295 Gd $210
Lady Smith (W/smaller grip) . . . . . . NiB $430 Ex $285 Gd $215

MODEL 63 (1977) KIT GUN DA . . . . NiB $365 Ex $245 Gd $195
Caliber: .22 LR. Six-shot cylinder, 2- or 4-inch bbl., 6.5 or 8.5 inches overall. Weight: 19 to 24.5 oz. Adj. rear sight, ramp front. Stainless steel. Checkered walnut or synthetic grips.

MODEL 64 .38 M&P STAINLESS. . . . . NiB $390 Ex $265 Gd $200
Same as standard Model 10 except satin-finished stainless steel, square butt w/4-inch heavy bbl., or round butt w/2-inch bbl. Made 1970 to date.

MODEL 65 .357 MILITARY/POLICE STAINLESS
Same as Model 13 except satin-finished stainless steel. Made 1974 to date.
Model 65 M&P . . . . NiB $395 Ex $270 Gd $205
Model 65 Lady Smith (W/smaller grip) . . . . NiB $430 Ex $300 Gd $225

**Smith & Wesson
Model 66 Combat Magnum**

**Smith & Wesson
Model 67 Combat Masterpiece**

MODEL 66 .357 COMBAT MAGNUM STAINLESS
Same as Model 19 except satin-finished stainless steel. Made 1971 to date.
Model 66 (2.5-inch bbl.) . . . . NiB $461 Ex $321 Gd $236
Model 66 (3-inch bbl.) . . . . NiB $450 Ex $310 Gd $225
Model 66 (4-inch bbl.) . . . . NiB $450 Ex $310 Gd $225
Model 66 (6-inch bbl.) . . . . NiB $470 Ex $399 Gd $254
W/target options TH & TT, add $48

MODEL 67 .38 COMBAT
MASTERPIECE STAINLESS . . . . NiB $455 Ex $310 Gd $225
Same as Model 15 except satin-finished stainless steel available only w/4-inch bbl. Made 1972-88 and 1991 to date.

MODEL 68 .38 COMBAT
MASTERPIECE STAINLESS . . . . NiB $750 Ex $625 Gd $495
Same as Model 66 except w/4- or 6-inch bbl., chambered for .38 Special. Made to accommodate CA Highway Patrol because they were not authorized to carry .357 magnums. Made 1976-83. (7500 produced)

125th Anniversary Commemorative
Issued to celebrate the 125th anniversary of the 1852 partnership of Horace Smith and Daniel Baird Wesson. Standard Edition is Model 25 revolver in .45 Colt w/6.5-inch bbl., bright blued finish, gold-filled bbl., roll mark "Smith & Wesson 125th Anniversary," sideplate marked w/gold-filled Anniversary seal, smooth Goncalo Alves grips, in presentation case w/nickel silver Anniversary medallion and book, "125 Years w/Smith & Wesson," by Roy Jinks. Deluxe Edition is same except revolver is Class A engraved w/gold-filled seal on sideplate, ivory grips, Anniversary medallion is sterling silver and book is leather bound. Limited to 50 units. Total issue is 10,000 units, of which 50 are Deluxe Edition and two are a Custom Deluxe Edition and not for sale. Made in 1977.
Standard edition . . . . NiB $744 Ex $595 Gd $405
Deluxe edition . . . . NiB $2119 Ex $1695 Gd $1153

Smith & Wesson
125th Commemorative Deluxe Edition

Smith & Wesson
Model 629 Classic

Smith & Wesson
Model 586 Distinguished Combat Magnum

Smith & Wesson
Model 625

Smith & Wesson
Model 629

317 AIRLITE DA REVOLVER
Caliber: .22 LR. Eight-shot cylinder, 1.88- or 3-inch bbl., 6.3 or 7.2 inches overall. Weight: 9.9 oz. or 11 oz. Ramp front sight, notched frame rear. Aluminum, carbon fiber, stainless and titanium construction. Brushed aluminum finish. Synthetic or Dymondwood grips. Made 1997 to date.
Model 317
(w/1.88-inch bbl.) .... NiB $425 Ex $300 Gd $220
Model 317
(w/3-inch bbl.) .... NiB $425 Ex $300 Gd $220
Model 317
(w/Dymondwood grips), add. $68

MODEL 520
DA REVOLVER. .... NiB $325 Ex $275 Gd $125
Caliber: .357 Mag. Six-shot cylinder. N-Frame w/4-inch bbl. Weight: 40 oz. Fixed sights. In 1980, 3000 were made for the N.Y. State Police, but that agency did not purchase those firearms. (Sold commercially).

MODEL 547
DA REVOLVER. .... NiB $295 Ex $265 Gd $185
Caliber: 9mm. Six-shot cylinder, bbl. length: 3 or 4 inches, 7.31 inches overall. Weight: 32 oz. Square-notch rear sight, ramp front. Disc. 1986.

MODEL 581 REVOLVER
Caliber: .357 Magnum. Bbl. lengths: 4 inches, weight: 34 oz. Serrated ramp front sight, square notch rear. Checkered walnut grips. Made 1985-92.
Blued finish .... NiB $275 Ex $225 Gd $160
Nickel finish .... NiB $295 Ex $245 Gd $180

MODEL 586 DISTINGUISHED COMBAT MAGNUM
Caliber: .357 Magnum. Six-shot cylinder, bbl. lengths: 4, 6 and 8.38 inches, overall length: 9.75 inches (with 4-inch bbl.). Weight: 42, 46, 53 oz., respectively. Red ramp front sight, micrometer-click adj. rear. Checkered grip. Blued or nickel finish. Made 1980-99.
Model 586
(w/4- or 6-inch bbl.) .... NiB $370 Ex $285 Gd $185
Model 586
(w/8.63-inch bbl.) .... NiB $392 Ex $307 Gd $207
Model 586 (w/adjustable
front sight), add. $35
Model 586
(w/nickel finish), add. $45

MODEL 610 DA REVOLVER ...... NiB $640 Ex $500 Gd $395
Similar to Model 625 except in caliber 10mm. Magna classic grips. Made 1990-91 and 1998 to date.

MODEL 617 DA REVOLVER
Similar to Model 17 except in stainless. Made 1990 to date.
Semi-target model w/4- or 6-inch bbl. . . . . . . NiB $470 Ex $320 Gd $225
Target model w/6-inch bbl. . . . . NiB $470 Ex $320 Gd $225
Target model w/8.38-inch bbl. . . . . NiB $470 Ex $320 Gd $225
W/10-shot cylinder, add $94

MODEL 624 DOUBLE-ACTION REVOLVER
Same general specifications as Model 24 except satin finished stainless steel. Limited production of 10,000. Made 1985-86.
Model 624 w/4-inch bbl. . . . . NiB $340 Ex $250 Gd $225
Model 624 w/6.5-inch bbl. . . . . NiB $364 Ex $264 Gd $239
**Model 624 w/3-inch bbl., round
butt (Lew Horton spec.)** . . . . NiB $395 Ex $350 Gd $395

MODEL 625 DA REVOLVER . . . . . . NiB $480 Ex $340 Gd $235
Same general specifications as Model 25 except 3-, 4- or 5-inch bbl., round-butt Pachmayr grips and satin stainless steel finish. Made 1989 to date.

MODEL 627 DA REVOLVER . . . . . . NiB $480 Ex $340 Gd $235
Same general specifications as Model 27 except satin stainless steel finish. Made 1989-91.

MODEL 629 DA REVOLVER
Same as Model 29 in .44 Magnum except in stainless steel. Classic made 1990 to date.
Model 629 (3-inch bbl., Backpacker) . . . . NiB $575 Ex $445 Gd $325
Model 629 (4- and 6-inch bbl.) . . . . NiB $597 Ex $467 Gd $345
Model 629 (8.38-inch bbl.) . . . . NiB $613 Ex $463 Gd $363
Model 629 Classic (5- and 6.5-inch bbl.) . . . . . NiB $600 Ex $455 Gd $345
Model 629 Classic (8.38-inch bbl.) . . . . NiB $625 Ex $480 Gd $370
Model 629 Classic DX (6.5-inch bbl.) . . . . . . NiB $795 Ex $635 Gd $510
Model 629 Classic DX (8.38-inch bbl.) . . . . . NiB $827 Ex $667 Gd $542
**Model 629 Magna Classic (w/7.5-inch
ported bbl.)** . . . . NiB $969 Ex $775 Gd $527

MODEL 631 DA REVOLVER
Similar to Model 31 except chambered for .32 H&R Mag. Goncalo Alves combat grips. Made 1991-92.
Fixed sights, 2-inch bbl. . . . . NiB $340 Ex $275 Gd $200
Adjustable sights, 4-inch bbl. . . . . NiB $344 Ex $275 Gd $187
Lady Smith, 2-inch bbl. . . . . NiB $365 Ex $295 Gd $225
Lady Smith, 2-inch bbl. (black stainless). . . . . . NiB $369 Ex $295 Gd $201

MODEL 632 CENTENNIAL DA
Same general specifications as Model 640 except chambered for .32 H&R Mag. 2- or 3-inch bbl., weight: 15.5 oz. Stainless slide w/alloy frame. Fixed sights. Santoprene combat grips. Made in 1991-92.
Model 632 w/2-inch bbl. . . . . NiB $315 Ex $240 Gd $195
Model 632 w/3-inch bbl. . . . . NiB $315 Ex $240 Gd $195

MODEL 637 CHIEFS
SPECIAL AIRWEIGHT DA . . . . NiB $405 Ex $275 Gd $210
Same general specifications as Model 37 except w/clear anodized fuse alloy frame and stainless cylinder. 560 made in 1991 and reintroduced in 1996.

MODEL 638 BODYGUARD
AIRWEIGHT DA . . . . NiB $420 Ex $300 Gd $230
Same general specifications as Model .38 except w/clear anodized fuse alloy frame and stainless cylinder. 1200 made in 1989 and reintroduced in 1998.

MODEL 640 CENTENNIAL DA . . . . NiB $420 Ex $300 Gd $230
Caliber: .38 Special. Five-shot cylinder, 2, 2.1 or 3-inch bbl., 6.31 inches overall. Weight: 20-22 oz. Fixed sights. Stainless finish. Smooth hardwood service grips. Made 1990 to date.

Smith & Wesson
Model 640

Smith & Wesson
Model 642 Centennial Airweight

MODEL 642 CENTENNIAL AIRWEIGHT DA REVOLVER
Same general specifications as Model 640 except w/stainless steel/aluminum alloy frame and finish. Weight 15.8 oz. Santoprene combat grips. Made 1990-93 and reintroduced 1996.
**Model 642
Centennial** . . . . NiB $420 Ex $300 Gd $220
**Model 642 Lady Smith
(W/smaller grip)** . . . . NiB $420 Ex $300 Gd $220

MODEL 648
DA REVOLVER . . . . NiB $350 Ex $250 Gd $195
Same general specifications as Models 17/617 except in stainless and chambered for .22 Mag. Made 1990-93.

MODEL 649
BODYGUARD DA . . . . NiB $445 Ex $300 Gd $220
Caliber: .38 Special. Five-shot cylinder, bbl. length: 2 inches, 6.25 inches overall. Weight: 20 oz. Square-notch rear sight ramp front. Stainless frame and finish. Made 1986 to date.

MODEL 650
REVOLVER . . . . NiB $250 Ex $200 Gd $190
Caliber: .22 Mag. Six-shot cylinder, 3-inch bbl., 7 inches overall. Weight: 23.5 oz. Serrated ramp front sight, fixed square-notch rear. Round butt, checkered walnut monogrammed grips. Stainless steel finish. Made 1983-86.

**Smith & Wesson
Model 696**

**Smith & Wesson
Model K-22 Outdoorsman**

**Smith & Wesson
Lady Smith First Model**

**Smith & Wesson
Lady Smith Second Model**

MODEL 651 STAINLESS DA

Caliber: .22 Mag. Rimfire. Six-shot cylinder, bbl. length: 3 and 4 inches, 7 and 8.63 inches, respectively, overall. Weight: 24.5 oz. Adj. rear sight, ramp front. Made 1983-87 and 1990-98. Note: Optional .22 LR cylinder available during early production.

Model 651 w/3- or 4-inch bbl.,.... NiB $355 Ex $250 Gd $190
Model 651 w/extra cylinder ...... NiB $555 Ex $475 Gd $375

MODEL 657 REVOLVER

Caliber: 41 Mag. Six-shot cylinder. Bbl. lengths: 4, 6 or 8.4 inches; 9.6, 11.4, and 13.9 inches overall. Weight: 44.2, 48 and 52.5 oz. Serrated black ramp front sight on ramp base click rear, adj. for windage and elevation. Satin finished stainless steel. Made 1986 to date.

W/4- or 6-inch bbl., ... NiB $535 Ex $375 Gd $290
W/8.4-inch bbl., ... NiB $552 Ex $392 Gd $307

MODEL 681 .... NiB $320 Ex $231 Gd $195

Same as S&W Model 581 except in stainless finish only. Made 1991-93.

MODEL 686

Same as S&W Model 586 Distinguished Combat Magnum except in stainless finish w/additional 2.5-inch bbl. Made 1991 to date.

Model 686 (w/2.5-inch bbl.)............ NiB $475 Ex $350 Gd $320
Model 686 (w/4- or 6-inch bbl.)........ NiB $500 Ex $375 Gd $345
Model 686 (w/8.63-inch bbl.).......... NiB $530 Ex $405 Gd $395
Model 686 (w/adjustable
front sight), add.......................................$35

MODEL 686 PLUS

Same as standard Model 686 Magnum except w/7-shot cylinder and 2.5-, 4- or 6-inch bbl. Made 1996 to date.

Model 686 Plus (w/2.5-inch bbl.) .... NiB $490 Ex $330 Gd $250
Model 686 Plus (w/4-inch bbl.) .... NiB $512 Ex $352 Gd $270
Model 686 Plus (w/6-inch bbl.) .... NiB $406 Ex $325 Gd $221

MODEL 696 .... NiB $485 Ex $315 Gd $250

Caliber: .44 S&W Special. L-Frame w/five-shot cylinder, 3-inch shrouded bbl., 8.38 inches overall. Weight: 48 oz. Red ramp front sight, micrometer-click adj. rear. Checkered synthetic grip. Satin stainless steel. Made 1997 to date.

MODEL 940 CENTENNIAL DA .... NiB $390 Ex $265 Gd $220

Same general specifications as Model 640 except chambered for 9mm. Two- or 3-inch bbl., Weight: 23-25 oz. Santoprene combat grips. Made 1991 to date.

MODEL 1891 SA REVOLVER

Hinged frame. Caliber: .38 S&W. Five-shot cylinder, bbl. lengths: 3.25, 4, 5 and 6-inches. Fixed sights. Blued or nickel finish. Hard rubber grips. Made 1891-1911. Note: Until 1906, an accessory single-shot target bbl. (see Model 1891 Single-Shot Target Pistol) was available for this revolver.

Revolver only................. NiB $2300 Ex $1650 Gd $780
Set w/.22 single-shot bbl. ..... NiB $3000 Ex $2000 Gd $1500

1917 ARMY DA REVOLVER

Caliber: .45 Automatic, using 3-cartridge half-moon clip or .45 Auto Rim, without clip. Six-shot cylinder, 5.5-inch bbl., 10.75 inches overall. Weight: 36.25 oz. Fixed sights. Blued finish (blue-black finish on commercial model, brush polish on military). Checkered walnut grips (commercial model, smooth on military). Made under U.S. Government contract 1917-19 and produced commercially 1919-1941. Note: About 175,000 of these revolvers were produced during WW I. The DCM sold these to NRA members during the 1930s at $16.15 each.

Commercial model .... NiB $650 Ex $500 Gd $285
Military model................. NiB $800 Ex $600 Gd $220

K-22 MASTERPIECE DA . . . . NiB $1200 Ex $1050 Gd $600
Improved version of K-22 Outdoorsman w/same specifications but w/micrometer-click rear sight, short action and antibacklash trigger. Fewer than 1100 manufactured in 1940.

K-22 OUTDOORSMAN DA . . . . . . NiB $575 Ex $500 Gd $285
Design based on the .38 Military & Police Target. Caliber: .22 LR. Six-shot cylinder, 11.13 inches overall. Weight: 35 oz. Adj. target sights. Blued finish. Checkered walnut grip. Made 1931-40.

K32 AND K38 HEAVY MASTERPIECES
Same as K32 and K38 Masterpiece but w/heavy bbl. Weight: 38.5 oz. Made 1950-53. Note: All K32 and K38 revolvers made after September 1953 have heavy bbls. and the "Heavy Masterpiece" designation was disc. Values for Heavy Masterpiece models are the same as shown for Models 14 and 16. (See separate listing).

K-32 TARGET DA REVOLVER . . . . NiB $1350 Ex $1090 Gd $750
Same as .38 Military & Police Target except chambered for .32 S&W Long cartridge, slightly heavier bbl., weight: 34 oz. Only 98 produced. Made 1938-.40.

LADY SMITH (MODEL M HAND EJECTOR) DA REVOLVER
Caliber: .22 LR. Seven-shot cylinder, bbl. length: 2.25-, 3-, 3.5- and 6-inch (Third Model only), approximately 7 inches overall w/3.5-inch bbl., weight: About 9.5 oz. Fixed sights, adj. target sights available on Third Model. Blued or nickel finish. Round butt, hard rubber grips on First and Second models; checkered walnut or hard rubber square buttgrips on Third Model. First Model —1902-06: Cylinder locking bolt operated by button on left side of frame, no bbl., lug and front locking bolt. Second Model —1906-11: Rear cylinder latch eliminated, has bbl. lug, forward cylinder lock w/draw-bolt fastening. Third Model —1911-21: Same as Second Model except has square grips, target sights and 6-inch bbl. available. Note: Legend has it that a straight-laced D.B. Wesson ordered discontinuance of the Lady Smith when he learned of the little revolver's reputed popularity w/ladies of the evening. The story, which undoubtedly has enhanced the appeal of this model to collectors, is not true: The Lady Smith was disc. because of difficulty of manufacture and high frequency of repairs.

First model . . . . NiB $2800 Ex $1800 Gd $435
Second model . . . . NiB $2000 Ex $1500 Gd $425
Third model, w/fixed sights,
2.25- or 3.5-inch bbl. . . . . NiB $2000 Ex $1500 Gd $435
Third model, w/fixed sights,
6-inch bbl.. . . . . NiB $2000 Ex $1475 Gd $425
Third model, w/adj. sights,
6-inch bbl.. . . . . NiB $3900 Ex $1590 Gd $695

REGULATION POLICE
DA (I FRAME) . . . . NiB $594 Ex $475 Gd $323
Calibers: .32 S&W (6-shot) or .38 S&W (5-shot) built on .32 Hand Ejector frames. Two-, 3-, 3.25-, 4-, 4.25- or 6-inch bbl., weight: 20-24 oz. Fixed sights. Blue or nickel finish. Checkered walnut grips. Made 1917-57. Note: After 1957 "J" Frames replaced the older "I" Frames and designations changed to Model 31 and 33 respectively.
Regulation Police, .32 S&W. . . . . . . NiB $325 Ex $275 Gd $125
Regulation Police, .38 S&W. . . . . . . NiB $325 Ex $275 Gd $125

REGULATION POLICE TARGET DA
Target version of the Regulation Police w/standard features of that model. Calibers: .32 S&W Long or .38 S&W. 6-inch bbl., 10.25 inches overall. Weight: 20 oz. Adjustable target sights. Blue or nickel finish. Checkered walnut grips. Made about 1917-57.
Regulation Police Target, .32 S&W . . . . NiB $650 Ex $550 Gd $250
Regulation Police Target, .38 S&W . . . . NiB $650 Ex $550 Gd $250

Smith & Wesson Regulation Police Target

Smith & Wesson Safety Hammerless

SAFETY HAMMERLESS
REVOLVER . . . . NiB $1200 Ex $800 Gd $325
Also called New Departure Double Action. Hinged frame. Calibers: .32 S&W, .38 S&W. Five-shot cylinder, bbl. lengths: 2, 3- and 3.5-inch (.32 cal.) or 2-, 3.25-, 4-, 5- and 6-inch (.38 cal.); 6.75 inches overall (.32 cal. w/3-inch bbl.) or 7.5 inches (.38 cal. w/3.25-inch bbl.). Weight: 14.25 oz. (.32 cal. w/3-inch bbl.) or 18.25 oz. (.38 cal. 2.5-inch bbl.). Fixed sights. Blued or nickel finish. Hard rubber grips. Made 1888-1937 (.32 cal.); 1887-1941 (.38 cal. w/various minor changes.)

TEXAS RANGER
COMMEMORATIVE. . . . . NiB $1200 Ex $915 Gd $650
Issued to honor the 150th anniversary of the Texas Rangers. Model 19 .357 Combat Magnum w/4-inch bbl., sideplate stamped w/Texas Ranger Commemorative Seal, smooth Goncalo Alves grips. Special Bowie knife in presentation case. 8,000 sets made in 1973. Top value is for set in new condition.

SPHINX ENGINEERING SA. — Porrentruy, Switzerland

MODEL AT-380 DA PISTOL
Caliber: .380 ACP. 10-shot magazine, 3.27- inch bbl., 6.03 inches overall. Weight: 25 oz. Stainless steel frame w/blued slide or Palladium finish. Slide latch w/ambidextrous magazine release. Imported 1993-96.
Model AT-380 two-tone
(w/blued slide) . . . . NiB $435 Ex $375 Gd $275
Model AT-380 N/pall
(w/Palladium finish) . . . . NiB $506 Ex $446 Gd $346

NOTE: *The AT-88 pistol series was previously manufactured by ITM in Switzerland and imported by Action Arms before Sphinx-Muller resumed production of these firearms, now designated as the AT-2000 series.*

Springfield Armory
1911-A1 Post '90 Series Trophy Model

Springfield Armory
1911-A1 PDP Series Defender

Springfield Armory
1911-A1 Champion

Springfield Armory
1911-A1 Compact

Sphinx
Model AT2000S Scope Optional

MODEL AT2000S DA AUTOMATIC PISTOL

Calibers: 9mm Parabellum, .40 S&W. 15- or 11-shot magazine respectively, 4.53-inch bbl., (S-standard), 3.66-inch bbl., (P-compact), 3.34-inch bbl., (H-subcompact), 8.25 inches overall. Weight: 36.5 oz. Fixed sights w/3-dot system. Stainless frame w/blued slide or Palladium finish. Ambidextrous safety. Checkered walnut or neoprene grips. Imported 1993-96.

Model AT2000S (standard) . . . . NiB $965 Ex $750 Gd $450
Model AT2000P (compact) . . . . NiB $850 Ex $625 Gd $410
Model AT2000H (subcompact) . . . . NiB $850 Ex $625 Gd $410
.40 S&W, add $90
For Palladium finish (disc. 1994). . . . . . NiB $200 Ex $177 Gd $148

MODEL AT2000C/2000CS COMPETITOR

Similar to the Model AT2000S except also chambered for 9x21mm. 10-shot magazine, 5.31-inch compensated bbl., 9.84 inches overall. Weight: 40.56 oz. Fully adjustable BoMar or ProPoint sights. Made 1993-96.

Model 2000C (w/BoMar sight) . . . . NiB $1725 Ex $1275 Gd $850
Model 2000CS (w/ProPoint sight) . . . . . . NiB $1725 Ex $1275 Gd $850

MODEL AT2000GM/GMS GRAND MASTER

Similar to the AT2000C except single action only w/square trigger guard and extended beavertail grip. Imported 1993-96.

Model 2000GM (w/BoMar sight) . . . . NiB $2244 Ex $1795 Gd $1221
Model 2000GMS (w/ProPoint sight) . . . . . . NiB $2369 Ex $1895 Gd $1289

SPRINGFIELD, INC. — Geneseo, Illinois (Formerly Springfield Armory)

MODEL M1911 SERIES AUTO PISTOL

Springfield builds the "PDP" (Personal Defense Pistol) Series based on the self-loading M 1911-A1 pistol (military specifications model) as adopted for a standard service weapon by the U.S. Army. With enhancements and modifications they produce a full line of firearms including Ultra-Compacts, Lightweights, Match Grade and Competition Models. For values see specific models.

MODEL 1911-A1 GOVERNMENT

Calibers: 9mm Para., .38 Super, .40 S&W, 10mm or .45 ACP., 7-, 8-, 9- or 10-shot magazine, 4- or 5-inch bbl., 8.5 inches overall. Weight: 36 oz. Fixed combat sights. Blued, Parkerized or Duo-Tone finish. Checkered walnut grips. Note: This is an exact duplicate of the Colt M1911-A1 that was used by the U.S. Armed Forces as a service weapon.

Blued finish . . . . NiB $400 Ex $360 Gd $280
Parkerized finish . . . . NiB $400 Ex $360 Gd $280

MODEL 1911-A1 (PRE '90 SERIES)
Calibers: 9mm Parabellum, .38 Super, 10mm, .45 ACP. Seven-, 8-, 9- or 10-shot magazine, bbl. length: 3.63, 4, 4.25 or 5 inches, 8.5 inches overall. Weight: 36 oz. Fixed combat sights. Blued, Duo-Tone or Parkerized finish. Checkered walnut stocks. Made 1985-90.

Government model (blued)	NiB $400	Ex $360	Gd $280
Government model (Parkerized)	NiB $400	Ex $360	Gd $280
Bullseye model (wadcutter)	NiB $1415	Ex $1200	Gd $750
Combat Commander model (blued)	NiB $435	Ex $385	Gd $275
Combat Commander model (Parkerized)	NiB $435	Ex $385	Gd $275
Commander model (blued)	NiB $450	Ex $415	Gd $285
Commander model (Duo-Tone)	NiB $450	Ex $445	Gd $315
Commander model (Parkerized)	NiB $450	Ex $415	Gd $285
Compact model (blued)	NiB $480	Ex $445	Gd $280
Compact model (Duo-Tone)	NiB $530	Ex $495	Gd $330
Compact model (Parkerized)	NiB $450	Ex $415	Gd $250
Defender model (blued)	NiB $515	Ex $470	Gd $315
Defender model (Parkerized)	NiB $485	Ex $435	Gd $280
Defender model (Custom Carry)	NiB $800	Ex $725	Gd $460
National Match model (Hardball)	NiB $780	Ex $650	Gd $460
Trophy Master (Competition)	NiB $1300	Ex $1100	Gd $750
Trophy Master (Distinguished)	NiB $2000	Ex $1675	Gd $1025
Trophy Master (Competition)	NiB $1664	Ex $1450	Gd $890

MODEL 1911-A1 (POST '90 SERIES)
SA linkless operating system w/steel or alloy frame. Calibers: 9mm Parabellum, .38 Super, .40 S&W, 10mm, .45 ACP. Seven-, 8-, 9- or 10-shot magazine, bbl. length: 3.63, 4, 4.25 or 5 inches; 8.5 inches overall. Weight: 28 oz. to 36 oz. Fixed combat sights. Blued, Duo-Tone, Parkerized or stainless finish. Checkered composition or walnut stocks. Made 1990 to date.

Mil-Spec model (blued)	NiB $465	Ex $375	Gd $280
Mil-Spec model (Parkerized)	NiB $465	Ex $375	Gd $280
Standard model (blued)	NiB $456	Ex $365	Gd $248
Standard model (Parkerized)	NiB $650	Ex $500	Gd $350
Standard model (stainless)	NiB $675	Ex $525	Gd $400
Trophy model (blued)	NiB $970	Ex $775	Gd $425
Trophy model (Duo-Tone)	NiB $950	Ex $785	Gd $435
Trophy model (stainless)	NiB $1011	Ex $846	Gd $496

MODEL 1911-A1 PDP SERIES
PDP Series (Personal Defense Pistol). Calibers: .38 Super, .40 S&W, .45 ACP. Seven-, 8-, 9-, 10-, 13- or 17-shot magazine, bbl. length: 4, 5, 5.5 or 5.63 inches, 9 to 11 inches overall w/compensated bbl. Weight: 34.5 oz. to 42.8 oz. Post front sight, adjustable rear w/3-dot system. Blued, Duo-Tone, Parkerized or stainless finish. Checkered composition or walnut stocks. Made 1991 to date.

Defender model (blued)	NiB $850	Ex $735	Gd $450
Defender model (Duo-Tone)	NiB $850	Ex $735	Gd $450
Defender model (Parkerized)	NiB $850	Ex $735	Gd $450
.45 ACP Champion Comp model (blued)	NiB $695	Ex $500	Gd $325
.45 ACP Compact Comp HC model (blued)	NiB $780	Ex $690	Gd $480
.38 Sup Factory Comp model (blued)	NiB $780	Ex $690	Gd $450
.45 ACP Factory Comp model (blued)	NiB $780	Ex $690	Gd $450
.38 Sup Factory Comp HC model (blued)	NiB $780	Ex $690	Gd $450
.45 ACP Factory Comp HC model (blued)	NiB $780	Ex $690	Gd $450

MODEL M1911-A1 CHAMPION
Calibers: .38 ACP, .45 ACP. Six- or 7-shot magazine, 4-inch bbl.

Springfield Armory
M1911-A1 Ultra Compact Parkerized

(cont'd) MODEL M1911-A1 CHAMPION
Weight: 26.5 to 33.4 oz. Low profile post front sight and drift adjustable rear w/3-dot sighting system. Commander-style hammer and slide. Checkered walnut grips. Blue, Bi-Tone, Parkerized or stainless finish. Made 1992 to date.

.380 ACP standard (disc. 1995)	NiB $375	Ex $300	Gd $200
.45 ACP Parkerized	NiB $450	Ex $350	Gd $200
.45 ACP blued	NiB $450	Ex $360	Gd $225
.45 ACP Bi-Tone (B/H Model)	NiB $695	Ex $500	Gd $295
.45 ACP stainless	NiB $700	Ex $495	Gd $395
.45 super tuned	NiB $875	Ex $550	Gd $450

MODEL M1911-A1 COMPACT
Similar to the standard M1911 w/champion length slide on a steel or alloy frame w/a shortened grip. Caliber: .45 ACP. Six- or 7-shot magazine (10+ law enforcement only), 4-inch bbl. weight: 26.5 to 32 oz. Low profile sights w/3-dot system. Checkered walnut grips. Matte blue, Duo-Tone or Parkerized finish. Made 1991-96.

Compact Parkerized	NiB $415	Ex $355	Gd $225
Compact blued	NiB $481	Ex $421	Gd $291
Compact Duo-Tone	NiB $415	Ex $355	Gd $225
Compact stainless	NiB $725	Ex $550	Gd $475
Compact comp (ported)	NiB $830	Ex $725	Gd $450
High capacity blue	NiB $540	Ex $405	Gd $330
High capacity stainless	NiB $579	Ex $504	Gd $369

MODEL M1911-A1 ULTRA COMPACT
Similar to M1911 Compact except chambered for .380 ACP or .45 ACP. 6- or 7-shot magazine, 3.5-inch bbl., weight: 22 oz. to 30 oz. Matte Blue, Bi-Tone, Parkerized (military specifiactions) or stainless finish. Made 1995 to date. See illustration next page.

.380 ACP Ultra (disc. 1996)	NiB $665	Ex $475	Gd $265
.45 ACP Ultra Parkerized	NiB $665	Ex $475	Gd $265
.45 ACP Ultra blued	NiB $665	Ex $475	Gd $265
.45 ACP Ultra Bi-Tone	NiB $775	Ex $585	Gd $375
.45 ACP Ultra stainless	NiB $745	Ex $525	Gd $425
.45 ACP ultra high capacity Parkerized	NiB $735	Ex $525	Gd $300
.45 ACP ultra high capacity blue	NiB $735	Ex $525	Gd $300
.45 ACP ultra high capacity stainless	NiB $745	Ex $525	Gd $425
.45 ACP V10 ultra comp Parkerized	NiB $690	Ex $485	Gd $275
.45 ACP V10 ultra comp blue	NiB $690	Ex $485	Gd $275
.45 ACP V10 ultra comp stainless	NiB $745	Ex $525	Gd $425
.45 ACP V10 ultra super tuned	NiB $925	Ex $775	Gd $425

Springfield Armory
M1911-A1 Ultra Compact Bi-Tone

Springfield Armory
P9 Combat

Springfield Armory
M1911-A1 Ultra Compact Stainless

Springfield Armory Panther

Springfield Armory
M1911-A1 Ultra Compact Super Tuned

FIRECAT
AUTOMATIC PISTOL
Calibers: 9mm, .40 S&W. Eight-shot magazine (9mm) or 7-shot magazine (.40 S&W), 3.5-inch bbl., 6.5 inches overall. Weight: 25.75 oz. Fixed sights w/3-dot system. Checkered walnut grip. Matte blued finish. Made 1991-93.

9mm . . . . NiB $495 Ex $425 Gd $275
.40 S&W . . . . NiB $495 Ex $425 Gd $275

PANTHER
AUTO PISTOL . . . . NiB $535 Ex $450 Gd $275
Calibers: 9mm, .40 S&W. 15-shot magazine (9mm) or 11-shot magazine (.40 S&W), 3.8-inch bbl., 7.5 inches overall. Weight: 28.95 oz. Blade front sight, rear adj. for windage w/3-dot system. Checkered walnut grip. Matte blued finish. Made 1991-93.

MODEL P9 DA COMBAT SERIES
Calibers: 9mm, .40 S&W, .45 ACP. Magazine capacity: 15-shot (9mm), 11-shot (.40 S&W) or 10-shot (.45 ACP), 3.66-inch bbl., (Compact and Sub-Compact), or 4.75-inch bbl., (Standard), 7.25 or 8.1 inches overall. Weight: 32 to 35 oz. Fixed sights w/3-dot system. Checkered walnut grip. Matte blued, Parkerized, stainless or Duo-Tone finish. Made 1990-94.

Compact model (9mm,
Parkerized) . . . . NiB $430 Ex $375 Gd $240
Sub-Compact model (9mm,
Parkerized) . . . . NiB $470 Ex $415 Gd $280
Standard model (9mm,
Parkerized) . . . . NiB $450 Ex $375 Gd $240
W/blued finish, add $25
W/Duo-Tone finish, add $235
W/stainless finish, add. $20
.40 S&W, add. $35
.45 ACP add. $95

MODEL P9 COMPETITION SERIES

Same general specifications as Model P9 except in target configuration w/5-inch bbl., (LSP Ultra) or 5.25-inch bbl. Factory Comp model w/dual port compensator system, extended safety and magazine release.

Factory Comp model
(9mm Bi-Tone) . . . . NiB $594 Ex $475 Gd $323
Factory Comp model
(9mm stainless) . . . . NiB $706 Ex $565 Gd $384
LSP Ultra model
(9mm Bi-Tone) . . . . NiB $544 Ex $435 Gd $296
LSP Ultra model
(9mm stainless) . . . . NiB $581 Ex $465 Gd $316
.40 S&W, .45 ACP: add $90

STALLARD ARMS — Mansfield, Ohio
See listings under Hi-Point.

STAR PISTOLS — Eibar, Spain
Star, Bonifacio Echeverria, S.A.

MODEL 30M DA AUTO PISTOL . . . NiB $350 Ex $295 Gd $215
Caliber: 9mm Para. 15-shot magazine, 4.38-inch bbl., 8 inches overall. Weight: 40 oz. Steel frame w/combat features. Adj. sights. Checkered composition grips. Blued finish. Made 1984-91.

MODEL 30PK DA AUTO PISTOL . . . . NiB $350 Ex $295 Gd $215
Same gen. specifications as Star Model 30M except 3.8-inch bbl., weight: 30 oz. Alloy frame. Made 1984-89.

MODEL 31P DA AUTO PISTOL
Same general specifications as Model 30M except removable backstrap houses complete firing mechanism. Weight: 39.4 oz. Made 1990-94.
Blued finish . . . . NiB $350 Ex $295 Gd $210
Starvel finish . . . . NiB $380 Ex $325 Gd $240

MODEL 31 PK DA AUTO PISTOL . . . . NiB $350 Ex $295 Gd $210
Same general specifications as Model 31P except w/alloy frame. Weight: 30 oz. Made 1990-97.

MODEL A AUTOMATIC PISTOL . . . NiB $325 Ex $275 Gd $150
Modification of the Colt Government Model .45 Auto, which it closely resembles, but lacks grip safety. Caliber: .38 Super. Eight-shot magazine, 5-inch bbl., 8 inches overall. Weight: 35 oz. Fixed sights. Blued finish. Checkered grips. Made 1934-97. (No longer imported.)

MODELS AS, BS, PS. . . . . NiB $330 Ex $300 Gd $210
Same as Models A, B and P except have magazine safety. Made in 1975.

MODEL B . . . . NiB $325 Ex $250 Gd $140
Same as Model A except in 9mm Para. Made 1934-75.

MODEL BKM. . . . . NiB $310 Ex $270 Gd $170
Similar to Model BM except has aluminum frame weight: 25.6 oz. Made 1976-92.

MODEL BKS STARLIGHT
AUTOMATIC PISTOL . . . . NiB $265 Ex $130 Gd $145
Light alloy frame. Caliber: 9mm Para. Eight-shot magazine, 4.25-inch bbl., 7 inches overall. Weight: 25 oz. Fixed sights. Blued or chrome finish. Plastic grips. Made 1970-81.

Star Model 30M

Star Model 30PK

Star Model AS

Star Model BKS

MODEL BM AUTOMATIC PISTOL

Caliber: 9mm. Eight-shot magazine, 3.9-inch bbl., 6.95 inches overall. Weight: 34.5 oz. Fixed sights. Checkered walnut grips. Blued or Starvel finish. Made 1976-92.

Blued
finish . . . . NiB $285 Ex $245 Gd $155
Starvel
finish . . . . NiB $315 Ex $275 Gd $185

MODEL CO POCKET

AUTOMATIC PISTOL . . . . NiB $250 Ex $190 Gd $110
Caliber: .25 Automatic (6.35mm), 2.75-inch bbl., 4.5 inches overall. Weight: 13 oz. Fixed sights. Blued finish. Plastic grips. Made 1941-57.

MODEL CU STARLET

POCKET PISTOL . . . . NiB $235 Ex $200 Gd $110
Light alloy frame. Caliber: .25 Auto (6.35mm). Eight-shot magazine, 2.38-inch bbl., 4.75 inches overall. Weight: 10.5 oz. Fixed sights. Blued or chrome-plated slide w/frame anodized in black, blue, green, gray or gold. Plastic grips. Made 1957-97. (U.S. importation disc. 1968.)

MODEL F

AUTOMATIC PISTOL . . . . NiB $325 Ex $225 Gd $100
Caliber: .22 LR. 10-shot magazine, 4.5-inch bbl., 7.5 inches overall. Weight: 25 oz. Fixed sights. Blued finish. Plastic grips. Made 1942-67.

MODEL F

OLYMPIC RAPID-FIRE. . . . . NiB $450 Ex $325 Gd $120
Caliber: .22 Short. Nine-shot magazine, 7-inch bbl., 11.06 inches overall. Weight: 52 oz. w/weights. Adj. target sight. Adj. 3-piece bbl. weight. Aluminum alloy slide. Muzzle brake. Plastic grips. Made 1942-67.

MODEL FM . . . . NiB $300 Ex $225 Gd $90
Similar to Model FR except has heavier frame w/web in front of trigger guard, 4.25-inch heavy bbl., Weight: 32 oz. Made 1972-91.

MODEL FR . . . . NiB $325 Ex $225 Gd $90
Similar to Model F w/same general specifications but restyled, has slide stop and adj. rear sight. Made 1967-72.

MODEL FRS. . . . . NiB $350 Ex $250 Gd $90
Same as Model FR except has 6-inch bbl., weight: 28 oz. Also avail. in chrome finish. Made 1967-91.

MODEL FS. NiB $325 Ex $225 Gd $90
Same as regular Model F but w/6-inch bbl. and adj. sights. Weight: 27 oz. Made 1942-67.

MODEL H . . . . NiB $350 Ex $250 Gd $90
Same as Model HN except .32 Auto (7.65mm), 7-shot magazine, weight: 20 oz. Made 1934-41.

MODEL HK LANCER

AUTOMATIC PISTOL . . . . NiB $245 Ex $215 Gd $120
Similar to Starfire w/same general specifications except .22 LR. Made 1955-68.

MODEL HN

AUTOMATIC PISTOL . . . . NiB $375 Ex $265 Gd $100
Caliber: .380 Auto (9mm Short). Six-shot magazine, 2.75-inch bbl., 5.56 inches overall. Weight: 20 oz. Fixed sights. Blued finish. Plastic grips. Made 1934-41.

Star Model F

Star Model F
Olympic Rapid-Fire

Star Model FS

MODEL I

AUTOMATIC PISTOL . . . . NiB $350 Ex $250 Gd $95
Caliber: .32 Auto (7.65mm). Nine-shot magazine, 4.81-inch bbl., 7.5 inches overall. Weight: 24 oz. Fixed sights. Blued finish. Plastic grips. Made 1934-36.

MODEL IN . . . . NiB $395 Ex $265 Gd $95
Same as Model I except caliber .380 Auto (9mm Short), 8-shot magazine, weight: 24.5 oz. Made 1934-36.

MODEL M MILITARY

AUTOMATIC PISTOL . . . . NiB $325 Ex $275 Gd $160
Modification of the Colt Government Model .45 Auto, which it closely resembles, but without grip safety. Calibers: 9mm Bergmann (Largo), .45 ACP, 9mm Para. Eight-shot magazine except 7-shot in .45 caliber, 5-inch bbl., 8.5 inches overall. Weight: 36 oz. Fixed sights. Blued finish. Checkered grips. Made 1934-39.

MODELS M40, M43, M45 FIRESTAR AUTO PISTOLS
Calibers: 9mm, .40 S&W, .45 ACP. Seven-shot magazine (9mm) or 6-shot (other calibers). 3.4-inch bbl., 6.5 inches overall. Weight: 30.35 oz. Blade front sight, adj. rear w/3-dot system. Checkered rubber grips. Blued or Starvel finish. Made 1990-97.

M40 blued (.40 S&W)	NiB $295	Ex $250	Gd $150
M40 Starvel (.40 S&W)	NiB $315	Ex $270	Gd $170
M43 blued (9mm)	NiB $295	Ex $255	Gd $170
M43 Starvel (9mm)	NiB $315	Ex $270	Gd $170
M45 blued (.45 ACP)	NiB $325	Ex $295	Gd $170
M45 Starvel (.45 ACP)	NiB $345	Ex $315	Gd $190

MEGASTAR AUTOMATIC PISTOL
Calibers: 10mm, .45 ACP. 12-shot magazine, 4.6-inch bbl., 8.44 inches overall. Weight: 47.6 oz. Blade front sight, adj. rear. Checkered composition grip. finishes: Blued or Starvel. Made from 1992-97.

Blued finish, 10mm or .45 ACP	NiB $450	Ex $375	Gd $275
Starvel finish, 10mm or .45 ACP	NiB $479	Ex $404	Gd $304

MODEL P . . . . NiB $350 Ex $285 Gd $160
Same as Model A except caliber .45 Auto, has 7-shot magazine. Made 1934-75.

MODEL PD AUTOMATIC PISTOL
Caliber: .45 Auto. Six-shot magazine, 3.75-inch bbl., 7 inches overall. Weight: 25 oz. Adj. rear sight, ramp front. Blued or Starvel finish. Checkered walnut grips. Made 1975-92.

Blued finish	NiB $345	Ex $290	Gd $170
Starvel finish	NiB $365	Ex $310	Gd $190

MODEL S . . . . NiB $235 Ex $200 Gd $100
Same as Model SI except caliber .380 Auto (9mm), 7-shot magazine, weight: 19 oz. Made 1941-65.

MODEL SL AUTOMATIC PISTOL . . . . NiB $275 Ex $235 Gd $150
Reduced-size modification of the Colt Government Model .45 Auto, lacks grip safety. Caliber: .32 Auto (7.65mm). Eight-shot magazine, 4-inch bbl., 6.5 inches overall. Weight: 20 oz. Fixed sights. Blued finish. Plastic grips. Made 1941-65.

STARFIRE DK AUTOMATIC PISTOL . . . . . . NiB $460 Ex $350 Gd $180
Light alloy frame. Caliber: .380 Automatic (9mm Short). Seven-shot magazine, 3.13-inch bbl.. 5.5 inches overall. Weight: 14.5 oz. Fixed sights. Blued or chrome-plated slide w/frame anodized in black, blue, green, gray or gold. Plastic grips. Made 1957-97. U.S. importation disc. 1968.

MODEL SUPER A AUTOMATIC PISTOL . . . NiB $395 Ex $325 Gd $150
Caliber: .38 Super. Improved version of Model A but has disarming bolt permitting easier takedown, cartridge indicator, magazine safety, take-down magazine, improved sights w/luminous spots for aiming in darkness. This is the standard service pistol of the Spanish Armed Forces, adopted 1946.

MODEL SUPER B AUTOMATIC PISTOL
Caliber: 9mm Para. Similar to Model B except w/improvements described under Model Super A. Made c. 1946-89/90.

Super blued finish	NiB $325	Ex $250	Gd $140
Starvel finish	NiB $355	Ex $280	Gd $170

MODELS SUPER M, SUPER P . . . . . NiB $790 Ex $650 Gd $290
Calibers: .45 ACP, 9mm Parabellum or 9mm Largo, (Super M) and 9mm Parabellum (Super P). Improved versions of the Models M & P w/same general specifications, but has disarming bolt permitting easier takedown, cartridge indicator, magazine safety, take-down magazine, improved sights w/luminous spots for aiming in darkness.

MODELS SUPER SL, SUPER S . . . . . NiB $275 Ex $235 Gd $150
Same general specifications as the regular Model SI and S except w/improvements described under Super Star. Made c. 1946-72.

Star
Model M Military

Star
Model PD

MODEL SUPER SM . . . . NiB $275 Ex $235 Gd $175
Similar to Model Super S except has adj. rear sight, wood grips. Made 1973-81.

SUPER TARGET MODEL . . . . NiB $1250 Ex $950 Gd $500
Same as Super Star model except w/adj. target rear sight. (Disc.)

ULTRASTAR DA AUTOMATIC PISTOL . . . . NiB $295 Ex $250 Gd $165
Calibers: 9mm Parabellum or .40 S&W. Nine-shot magazine, 3.57-inch bbl., 7 inches overall. Weight: 26 oz. Blade front, adjustable rear w/3-dot system. Polymer frame. Blue metal finish. Checkered black polymer grips. Imported 1994-97.

STENDA-WERKE PISTOL — Suhl, Germany

POCKET AUTOMATIC PISTOL . . . . NiB $225 Ex $170 Gd $100
Essentially the same as the Beholla (see listing of that pistol for specifications). Made c. 1920-.25. Note: This pistol may be marked "Beholla" along w/the Stenda name and address.

STERLING ARMS CORPORATION — Gasport, New York

MODEL 283 TARGET 300
AUTO PISTOL . . . . NiB $155 Ex $100 Gd $85
Caliber: .22 LR. 10-shot magazine, bbl. lengths: 4.5-, 6- 8-inch. 9 inches overall w/4.5-inch bbl., Weight: 36 oz. w/4.52-inch bbl. Adj. sights. Blued finish. Plastic grips. Made 1970-71.

Sterling
Model 283Target 300

Sterling
Model 284 Target 300L

Sterling
Model 285 Husky

Sterling
Model 286 Trapper

Sterling
Model 300

Sterling
Model 400

MODEL 284 TARGET 300L . . . . NiB $175 Ex $125 Gd $90
Same as Model 283 except has 4.5- or 6-inch Luger-type bbl. Made
1970-71.

MODEL 285 HUSKY . . . . NiB $175 Ex $125 Gd $90
Same as Model 283 except has fixed sights, 4.5-inch bbl only. Made
1970-71.

MODEL 286 TRAPPER . . . . NiB $175 Ex $125 Gd $90
Same as Model 284 except w/fixed sights. Made 1970-71.

MODEL 287 PPL-.380
AUTOMATIC PISTOL . . . . NiB $125 Ex $100 Gd $68
Caliber: .380 Auto. Six-shot magazine, 1-inch bbl., 5.38 inches
overall. Weight: 22.5 oz. Fixed sights. Blued finish. Plastic grips.
Made 1971-72.

MODEL 300
AUTOMATIC PISTOL . . . . NiB $125 Ex $95 Gd $50
Caliber: .25 Auto. Six-shot magazine, 2.33-inch bbl., 4.5 inches
overall. Weight: 13 oz. Fixed sights. Blued or nickel finish. Plastic
grips. Made 1972-83.

MODEL 300S. . . . . NiB $135 Ex $100 Gd $60
Same as Model 300 except in stainless steel. Made 1976-83.

MODEL 302 . . . . NiB $125 Ex $95 Gd $50
Same as Model 300 except in .22 LR. Made 1973-83.

MODEL 302S. . . . . NiB $125 Ex $95 Gd $50
Same as Model 302 except in stainless steel. Made 1976-83.

MODEL 400 DA
AUTOMATIC PISTOL . . . . NiB $170 Ex $140 Gd $110
Caliber: .380 Auto. Seven-shot magazine, 3.5-inch bbl., 6.5 inches
overall. Weight: 24 oz. Adj. rear sight. Blued or nickel finish.
Checkered walnut grips. Made 1975-83.

MODEL 400S. . . . . NiB $195 Ex $150 Gd $110
Same as Model 400 except stainless steel. Made 1977-83.

**MODEL 450 DA
AUTO PISTOL** . . . . NiB $225 Ex $195 Gd $150
Caliber: .45 Auto. Eight-shot magazine, 4-inch bbl., 7.5 inches over-all. Weight: 36 oz. Adj. rear sight. Blued finish. Smooth walnut grips. Made 1977-83.

**MODEL PPL-22
AUTOMATIC PISTOL** . . . . NiB $175 Ex $125 Gd $90
Caliber: .22 LR. 10-shot magazine, 1-inch bbl., 5.5 inches overall. Weight: About 24 oz. Fixed sights. Blued finish. Wood grips. Only 382 made 1970-71.

J. STEVENS ARMS & TOOL CO. — Chicopee Falls, Mass.

This firm was established in Civil War era by Joshua Stevens, for whom the company was named. In 1936 it became a subsidiary of Savage Arms.

**NO. 10
SINGLE-SHOT
TARGET PISTOL** . . . . NiB $220 Ex $200 Gd $120
Caliber: .22 LR. 8-inch bbl., 11.5 inches overall. Weight: 37 oz. Target sights. Blued finish. Hard rubber grips. In external appearance this arm resembles an automatic pistol but it has a tip-up action. Made 1919-39.

**NO. 35
OFFHAND MODEL SINGLE-SHOT
TARGET PISTOL** . . . . NiB $350 Ex $300 Gd $185
Tip-up action. Caliber: .22 LR. Bbl. lengths: 6, 8, 10, 12.25 inches. Weight: 24 oz. w/6-inch bbl. Target sights. Blued finish. Walnut grips. Note: This pistol is similar to the earlier "Gould" model. Made 1907-39.

**OFFHAND NO. 35 SINGLE-SHOT
PISTOL/SHOTGUN** . . . . NiB $350 Ex $300 Gd $150
Same general specifications as the standard No. 35 pistol except chambered for the .410 shotshell. Six-, 8-, 10-, or 12-inch half-ocatagonal bbl., iron frame either blued, nickel plated, or case-hardened. BATF Class 3 license required to purchase. Made 1923-42.

**NO. 36
SINGLE-SHOT PISTOL** . . . . NiB $720 Ex $550 Gd $350
Tip-up action. Calibers: .22 Short and LR, .22 WRF, .25 Stevens, .32 Short Colt, .38 Long Colt, .44 Russian. 10- or 12-inch half-octagonal bbl., iron or brass frame w/nickel plated finish. Blued bbl. Checkered walnut grips. Made 1880-1911.

**NO. 37
SINGLE-SHOT PISTOL** . . . . NiB $900 Ex $725 Gd $450
Similar specifications to the No. 38 except the finger spur on the trigger guard has been omitted. Made 1889-1903.

**NO. 38
SINGLE-SHOT PISTOL** . . . . NiB $425 Ex $390 Gd $275
Tip-up action. Calibers: .22 Short and LR, .22 WRF, .25 Stevens, .32 Stevens, .32 Short Colt. Iron or brass frame. Checkered grips. Made 1884-1903.

Stevens No. 10

Stevens No. 35

Stevens No. 38

**NO. 41
TIP-UP SINGLE-SHOT PISTOL** . . . . NiB $275 Ex $225 Gd $145
Tip-up action. Caliber: .22 Short, 3.5-inch half-octagonal bbl. Blued metal parts w/optional nickel frame. Made 1896-1915.

STEYR PISTOLS — Steyr, Austria

GB SEMIAUTOMATIC PISTOL
Caliber: 9mm Para. 18-round magazine, 5.4-inch bbl., 8.9 inches overall. Weight: 2.9 lbs. Post front sight, fixed, notched rear. Double, gas-delayed, blow-back action. Made 1981-88.
Commercial model . . . . NiB $600 Ex $525 Gd $335
**Military model
(Less than 1000 imported)** . . . . NiB $550 Ex $450 Gd $380

M12 AUTOMATIC PISTOL
Caliber: 9mm Steyr. Eight-shot fixed magazine, charger loaded; 5.1-inch bbl., 8.5 inches overall. Weight: 35 oz. Fixed sights. Blued finish. Checkered wood grips. Made 1911-19. Adopted by the Austro-Hungarian Army in 1912. Note: Confiscated by the Germans in 1938, an estimated 250,000 of these pistols were converted to 9mm Para. and stamped w/an identifying "08" on the left side of the slide. Mfd. by Osterreichische Waffenfabrik-Gesellschaft.
Commercial model (9mm Steyr) . . . NiB $450 Ex $375 Gd $295
**Military model (9mm Steyr-
Austro-Hungarian Army)** . . . . NiB $455 Ex $380 Gd $145
**Military model (9mm Parabellum
Conversion marked "08")** . . . . NiB $900 Ex $750 Gd $390

**Stoeger
American Eagle Luger P08 Stainless**

**Stoeger
American Eagle Luger Navy Model**

**Stoeger
Standard Luger**

**Targa
Model GT380XE**

STOEGER LUGERS
Formerly mfd. by Stoeger Industries, So. Hackensack, N.J.; later by Classic Arms, Union City, N.J.

AMERICAN EAGLE LUGER
Caliber: 9mm Para. Seven-shot magazine, 4- or 6-inch bbl., 8.25 inches overall (with 4-inch bbl.). or 10.25 inches (with 6-inch bbl.). Weight: 30 or 32 oz. Checkered walnut grips. Stainless steel w/brushed or matte black finish. Made from 1994 to date.
Model P-08
stainless
(4-inch bbl.)................... NiB $640 Ex $350 Gd $280
Navy model
(6-inch bbl.)................... NiB $640 Ex $350 Gd $280
W/matte black
finish, add $50

STANDARD LUGER .22
AUTOMATIC PISTOL .... NiB $145 Ex $120 Gd $70
Caliber: .22 LR. 10-shot magazine, 4.5- or 5.5-inch bbl., 8.88 inches overall (with 4.5-inch bbl.). Weight: 29.5 oz. (with 4.5-inch bbl.). Fixed sights. Black finish. Smooth wood grips. Made 1969-86.

STEEL FRAME LUGER
.22 AUTO PISTOL .... NiB $150 Ex $125 Gd $85
Caliber: .22 LR. 10-shot magazine, 4.5-inch bbl., 8.88 inches overall. Blued finish. Checkered wood grips. Features one piece forged and machined steel frame. Made 1980-86.

TARGET LUGER
.22 AUTO PISTOL .... NiB $180 Ex $175 Gd $133
Same as Standard Luger .22 except has target sights 9.38 inches overall w/4.5-inch bbl., Checkered wood grips. Made 1975-86.

TARGA PISTOLS — Italy
Manufactured by Armi Tanfoglio Guiseppe

MODEL GT26S
AUTO PISTOL .... NiB $94 Ex $75 Gd $51
Caliber: .25 ACP. Six-shot magazine, 2.5-inch bbl., 4.63 inches overall. Weight: 15 oz. fixed sights. Checkered composition grips. Blued or chrome finish. Disc. 1990.

MODEL GT32
AUTO PISTOL
Caliber: .32 ACP. Six-shot magazine, 4.88-inch bbl., 7.38 inches overall. Weight: 26 oz. fixed sights. Checkered composition or walnut grips. Blued or chrome finish.
Blued finished .... NiB $125 Ex $100 Gd $70
Chrome finish .... NiB $140 Ex $105 Gd $80

MODEL GT380
AUTOMATIC PISTOL
Same as the Targa GT32 except chambered for .380 ACP.
Blued finish .... NiB $144 Ex $115 Gd $78
Chrome finish .... NiB $156 Ex $125 Gd $85

MODEL GT380XE
AUTOMATIC PISTOL .... NiB $175 Ex $135 Gd $95
Caliber: .380 ACP. 11-shot magazine, 3.75-inch bbl., 7.38 inches overall. Weight: 28 oz. Fixed sights. Blued or satin nickel finish. Smooth wooden grips. Made 1980-90.

Taurus Model .44

Taurus Model 66

Taurus
Model 74 Target Grade

Taurus Model 80

FORJAS TAURUS S.A. — Porto Alegre, Brazil

MODEL 44 DA REVOLVER
Caliber: .44 Mag. Six-shot cylinder, 4-, 6.5-, or 8.38-inch bbl. Weight: 44.75 oz., 52.5 or 57.25 oz. Brazilian hardwood grips. Blued or stainless steel finish. Made 1994 to date.
Blued finish . . . . NiB $400 Ex $325 Gd $160
Stainless. . . . . NiB $455 Ex $365 Gd $295

MODEL 65 DA REVOLVER
Caliber: .357 Magnum. 6-shot cylinder, 3- or 4-inch bbl., weight: 32 oz. Front ramp sight, square notch rear. Checkered walnut target grip. Royal blued or satin nickel finish. Imported 1992-97 and 1999 to date.
Blue . . . . NiB $345 Ex $260 Gd $100
Stainless. . . . . NiB $350 Ex $265 Gd $110

MODEL 66 DA REVOLVER
Calibers: .357 Magnum, .38 Special. Six-shot cylinder, 3-, 4- and 6-inch bbl., weight: 35 oz. Serrated ramp front sight, rear click adj. Checkered walnut grips. Royal blued or nickel finish. Imported 1992-97 and 1999 to date.
Blue . . . . NiB $305 Ex $235 Gd $140
Stainless. . . . . NiB $365 Ex $245 Gd $195

MODEL 73 DA REVOLVER . . . . NiB $175 Ex $150 Gd $100
Caliber: .32 Long. Six-shot cylinder, 3-inch heavy bbl., weight: 20 oz. Checkered grips. Blued or satin nickel finish. Disc. 1993.

MODEL 74 TARGET
GRADE DA REVOLVER . . . . NiB $185 Ex $175 Gd $110
Caliber: .32 S&W Long. Six-shot cylinder, 3-inch bbl., 8.25 inches overall. Weight: 20 oz. Adj. rear sight, ramp front. Blued or nickel finish. Checkered walnut grips. Made 1971-90.

MODEL 80 DA REVOLVER
Caliber: .38 Special. Six-shot cylinder, bbl. lengths: 3, 4 inches, 9.25 inches overall (with 4-inch bbl.). Weight: 30 oz. (with 4-inch bbl.) Fixed sights. Blued or nickel finish. Checkered walnut grips. Made 1996-97.
Blued . . . . NiB $190 Ex $145 Gd $85
Stainless. . . . . NiB $245 Ex $180 Gd $130

MODEL 82 HEAVY BARREL
Same as Model 80 except has heavy bbl., weight: 33 oz. w/4-inch bbl., Made 1971 to date.
Blued . . . . NiB $195 Ex $150 Gd $90
Stainless. . . . . NiB $200 Ex $160 Gd $100

MODEL 83 HEAVY BARREL TARGET GRADE
Same as Model 84 except has heavy bbl., weight: 34.5 oz. Made 1977 to date. See illustration next page.
Blued . . . . NiB $215 Ex $155 Gd $95
Stainless. . . . . NiB $250 Ex $185 Gd $135

Taurus Model 82

Taurus Model 83

**Taurus
Model 85 w/Spur Hammer**

Taurus Model 84

**Taurus
Model 85 Concealed Hammer**

Taurus Model 86

MODEL 84 TARGET
GRADE REVOLVER . . . . NiB $250 Ex $195 Gd $130
Caliber: .38 Special. Six-shot cylinder, 4-inch bbl., 9.25 inches over-all. Weight: 31 oz. Adj. rear sight, ramp front. Blued or nickel finish. Checkered walnut grips. Made 1971-89.

MODEL 85 DA REVOLVER
Caliber: .38 Special. Five-shot cylinder, 2- or 3-inch. bbl., weight: 21 oz. Fixed sights. Checkered walnut grips. Blued, satin nickel or stainless-steel finish. Currently in production. Model 85CH is the same as the standard version except for concealed hammer.
Blued or satin nickel . . . . NiB $265 Ex $200 Gd $95
Stainless steel . . . . NiB $325 Ex $235 Gd $175

MODEL 86 TARGET
MASTER DA REVOLVER . . . . NiB $270 Ex $200 Gd $130
Caliber: .38 Special. Six-shot cylinder, 6-inch bbl., 11.25 inches overall. Weight: 34 oz. Adj. rear sight, Partridge-type front. Blued finish. Checkered walnut grips. Made 1971-94.

MODEL 94 TARGET GRADE
Same as Model 74 except .22 LR. w/9-shot cylinder, 3- or 4-inch bbl., weight: 25 oz. Blued or stainless finish. Made 1971 to date.
Blued finish . . . . NiB $245 Ex $180 Gd $95
Stainless finish . . . . NiB $290 Ex $210 Gd $150

MODEL 96 TARGET MASTER . . . . . NiB $275 Ex $200 Gd $130
Same as Model 86 except in .22 LR. Made 1971 to date.

MODEL 431 DA REVOLVER
Caliber: .44 Spec. Five-shot cylinder, 3- or 4-inch solid-rib bbl. w/ejector shroud. Weight: 35 oz. w/4-inch bbl., Serrated ramp front sight, notched topstrap rear. Blued or stainless finish. Made 1992-97.
Blued finish . . . . NiB $220 Ex $170 Gd $100
Stainless finish . . . . NiB $285 Ex $215 Gd $170

MODEL 441 DA REVOLVER
Similar to the Model 431 except w/6-inch bbl. and fully adj. target sights. Weight: 40 oz. Made 1991-97.
Blued finish . . . . NiB $240 Ex $180 Gd $100
Stainless finish . . . . NiB $355 Ex $250 Gd $190

MODEL 445 DA REVOLVER
Caliber: .44 Special. Five-shot cylinder, 2-inch bbl., 6.75 inches overall. Weight: 28.25 oz. Serrated ramp front sight, notched frame rear. Standard or concealed hammer. Santoprene I grips. Blue or stainless finish. Imported 1997 to date.
Blue model . . . . NiB $270 Ex $205 Gd $100
Stainless model . . . . NiB $360 Ex $225 Gd $155

MODEL .454 DA RAGING BULL REVOLVER

Caliber: .454 Casull. Five-shot cylinder, ported 6.5- or 8.4-inch vent rib bbl., 12 inches overall (w/6.5-inch bbl.). Weight: 53 or 63 oz. Partridge front sight, micrometer adj. rear. Santoprene I or walnut grips. Blue or stainless finish. Imported 1997 to date.

Blue model . . . . NiB $795 Ex $645 Gd $475
Stainless model . . . . NiB $780 Ex $710 Gd $635

MODEL 669/669VR DA REVOLVER

Caliber: .357 Mag. Six-shot cylinder, 4- or 6-inch solid-rib bbl. w/ejector shroud Model 669VR has vent rib bbl., weight: 37 oz. w/4-inch bbl., Serrated ramp front sight, micro-adj. rear. Royal blued or stainless finish. Checkered Brazilian hardwood grips. Made 1989 to date.

Model 669 blued . . . . NiB $260 Ex $190 Gd $115
Model 669 stainless . . . . NiB $325 Ex $245 Gd $190
Model 669VR blued . . . . NiB $270 Ex $200 Gd $125
Model 669VR stainless . . . . NiB $335 Ex $255 Gd $200

MODEL 741/761 DA REVOLVER

Caliber: .32 H&R Mag. Six-shot cylinder, 3- or 4-inch solid-rib bbl. w/ejector shroud. Weight: 20 oz. w/3-inch bbl., Serrated ramp front sight, micro-adj. rear. Blued or stainless finish. Checkered Brazilian hardwood grips. Made 1991-97.

Model 741
blued. . . . . NiB $205 Ex $155 Gd $95
Model 741
stainless . . . . NiB $275 Ex $215 Gd $150
Model 761
(6-inch bbl.,
blued, 34 oz.) . . . . NiB $250 Ex $185 Gd $100

MODEL 941 TARGET REVOLVER

Caliber: .22 Magnum. Eight-shot cylinder. Solid-rib bbl. w/ejector shroud. Micro-adj. rear sight. Brazilian hardwood grips. Blued or stainless finish.

Blued finish . . . . NiB $260 Ex $190 Gd $95
Stainless finish . . . . NiB $295 Ex $230 Gd $150

MODEL PT .22 DA

AUTOMATIC PISTOL . . . . NiB $175 Ex $135 Gd $70
Caliber: .22 LR. Nine-shot magazine, 2.75-inch bbl., weight: 12.3 oz. Fixed open sights. Brazilian hardwood grips. Blued finish. Made 1991 to date.

MODEL PT .25 DA

AUTOMATIC PISTOL . . . . NiB $175 Ex $135 Gd $70
Same general specifications as Model PT 22 except in .25 ACP w/eight-shot magazine, Made from 1992 to date.

MODEL PT-58 SEMI-

AUTOMATIC PISTOL . . . . NiB $325 Ex $275 Gd $190
Caliber: .380 ACP. Twelve-shot magazine, 4-inch bbl., 7.2 inches overall. Weight: 30 oz. Blade front sight, rear adj. for windage w/3-dot sighting system. Blued, satin nickel or stainless finish. Made 1988-96.

MODEL PT 92AF SEMIAUTOMATIC PISTOL

Double action. Caliber: 9mm Para. Fifteen-round magazine, 5-inch bbl., 8.5 inches overall. Weight: 24 oz. Blade front sight, notched bar rear. Smooth Brazilian walnut grips. Blued, satin nickel or stainless finish. Made 1991 to date.

Blued finish . . . . NiB $430 Ex $340 Gd $195
Satin nickel finish . . . . NiB $470 Ex $380 Gd $235
Stainless finish . . . . NiB $440 Ex $350 Gd $280

Taurus
Model 669

Taurus
Model PT-.22

Taurus
Model PT-58

Taurus
Model PT92

Taurus
Model PT-99AF

Taurus
Model PT-908

Texas Arms
Defender Derringer

MODEL PT-92AFC COMPACT PISTOL
Same general specifications as Model PT-92AF except w/13-shot magazine, 4.25-inch bbl., 7.5 inches overall. Weight: 31 oz. Made 1991-96
Blued finish . . . . NiB $335 Ex $285 Gd $190
Satin nickel finish . . . . NiB $372 Ex $323 Gd $228
Stainless finish . . . . NiB $400 Ex $310 Gd $250

MODEL PT 99AF SEMI-
AUTOMATIC PISTOL . . . . NiB $465 Ex $355 Gd $200
Same general specifications as Model PT-92AF except rear sight is adj. for elevation and windage, and finish is blued or satin nickel.

MODEL PT 100 DA AUTOMATIC PISTOL
Caliber: .40 S&W. Eleven-shot magazine, 5-inch bbl., weight: 34 oz. Fixed front sight, adj. rear w/3-dot system. Smooth hardwood grip. Blued, satin nickel or stainless finish. Made 1991-97.
Blued finish . . . . NiB $450 Ex $345 Gd $200
Satin finish. . . . . NiB $440 Ex $385 Gd $240
Stainless finish . . . . NiB $405 Ex $355 Gd $225

MODEL PT 101 DA AUTOMATIC PISTOL
Same general specifications as Model 100 except w/micrometer click adj. sights. Made 1992-96.
Blued finish . . . . NiB $465 Ex $355 Gd $200
Satin nickel finish . . . . NiB $510 Ex $400 Gd $245
Stainless finish . . . . NiB $470 Ex $395 Gd $275

MODEL PT 111 MILLENNIUM DAO PISTOL
Caliber: 9mm Parabellum. 10-shot magazine, 3.12-inch bbl., 6 inches overall. Weight: 19.1 oz. Fixed low-profile sights w/3-dot system. Black polymer grip/frame. Blue or stainless slide. Imported 1998 to date.
Blue model . . . . NiB $355 Ex $190 Gd $135
Stainless model . . . . NiB $355 Ex $290 Gd $135

MODEL PT 908 SEMIAUTOMATIC PISTOL
Caliber: 9mm Para. Eight-shot magazine, 3.8-inch bbl., 7 inches overall. Weight: 30 oz. Post front sight, drift-adj. combat rear w/3-dot system. Blued, satin nickel or stainless finish. Made 1993-97.
Blued finish . . . . NiB $330 Ex $285 Gd $190
Satin nickel finish . . . . NiB $330 Ex $295 Gd $190
Stainless finish . . . . NiB $535 Ex $420 Gd $275

MODEL PT 911 COMPACT SEMIAUTOMATIC PISTOL
Caliber: 9mm Parabellum. 10-shot magazine, 3.75-inch bbl., 7.05 inches overall. Weight: 28.2 oz. Fixed low-profile sights w/3-dot system. Santoprene II grips. Blue or stainless finish. Imported 1997 to date.
Blue model . . . . NiB $415 Ex $335 Gd $185
Stainless model . . . . NiB $535 Ex $420 Gd $275

MODEL PT 938 COMPACT SEMIAUTOMATIC PISTOL
Caliber: 380 ACP. 10-shot magazine, 3.72-inch bbl., 6.75 inches overall. Weight: 27 oz. Fixed low-profile sights w/3-dot system. Santoprene II grips. Blue or stainless finish. Imported 1997 to date.
Blue model . . . . NiB $400 Ex $335 Gd $180
Stainless model . . . . NiB $356 Ex $285 Gd $194

MODEL PT 940 COMPACT SEMIAUTOMATIC PISTOL
Caliber: .40 S&W. 10-shot magazine, 3.75-inch bbl., 7.05 inches overall. Weight: 28.2 oz. Fixed low-profile sights w/3-dot system. Santoprene II grips. Blue or stainless finish. Imported 1997 to date.
Blue model . . . . NiB $425 Ex $355 Gd $190
Stainless model . . . . NiB $435 Ex $360 Gd $290

MODEL PT 945 COMPACT SEMIAUTOMATIC PISTOL
Caliber: .45 ACP. Eight-shot magazine, 4.25-inch bbl., 7.48 inches overall. Weight: 29.5 oz. Fixed low-profile sights w/3-dot system. Santoprene II grips. Blue or stainless finish. Imported 1995 to date.
Blue model . . . . NiB $450 Ex $365 Gd $210
Stainless model . . . . NiB $475 Ex $385 Gd $310

TEXAS ARMS — Waco, Texas

DEFENDER DERRINGER . . . . NiB $275 Ex $235 Gd $140
Calibers: 9mm, .357 Mag., .44 Mag., .45 ACP, .45 Colt/.410. Three-inch bbl., 5 inches overall. Weight: 21 oz. Blade front sight, fixed rear. Matte gun-metal gray finish. Smooth grips. Made 1993 to date.

TEXAS LONGHORN ARMS — Richmond, Texas

"THE JEZEBEL" PISTOL . . . . NiB $263 Ex $210 Gd $143
Top-break, single-shot. Caliber: .22 Short, Long or LR. Six-inch half-round bbl., 8 inches overall. Weight: 15 oz. Bead front sight, adj. rear. One-piece walnut grip. Stainless finish. Intro. in 1987.

SA REVOLVER CASED SET
Set contains one each of the Texas Longhorn Single Actions. Each chambered in the same caliber and w/the same serial number. Intro. in 1984.
Standard set. . . . . NiB $5500 Ex $4400 Gd $2992
Engraved set . . . . NiB $7188 Ex $5750 Gd $3910

SOUTH TEXAS ARMY LIMITED
EDITION SA REVOLVER . . . . NiB $1695 Ex $1250 Gd $975
Calibers: All popular centerfire pistol calibers. Six-shot cylinder, 4.75-inch bbl.,10.25 inches overall. Weight: 40 oz. Fixed sights. Color casehardened frame. One-piece deluxe walnut grips. Blued bbl., Intro. in 1984.

SESQUICENTENNIAL SA REVOLVER . . . . . NiB $2369 Ex $1895 Gd $1289
Same as South Texas Army Limited Edition except engraved and nickel-plated w/one-piece ivory grip. Intro. in 1986.

TEXAS BORDER SPECIAL
SA REVOLVER . . . . NiB $1494 Ex $1195 Gd $813
Same as South Texas Army Limited Edition except w/3.5-inch bbl. and bird's-head grips. Intro. in 1984.

WEST TEXAS FLAT TOP
TARGET SA REVOLVER . . . . NiB $1495 Ex $1250 Gd $973
Same as South Texas Army Limited Edition except w/choice of bbl. lengths from 7 .5 to 15 inches. Same special features w/flat-top style frame and adj. rear sight. Intro. in 1984.

THOMPSON PISTOL — West Hurley, New York Mfd. by Auto-Ordnance Corporation

MODEL 27A-5 SEMIAUTOMATIC PISTOL
Similar to Thompson Model 1928A submachine gun except has no provision for automatic firing, does not have detachable buttstock. Caliber: .45 Auto, 20-shot detachable box magazine (5-, 15- and 30-shot box magazines, 39-shot drum also available), 13-inch finned bbl., overall length: 26 inches. Weight: About 6.75 lbs. Adj. rear sight, blade front. Blued finish. Walnut grips. Intro. 1977. See Auto-Ordnance in Handgun Section.

THOMPSON/CENTER ARMS — Rochester, New Hampshire

CONTENDER SINGLE-SHOT PISTOL
Break frame, underlever action. Calibers: (rimfire) .22 LR. .22 WMR, 5mm RRM; (standard centerfire), .218 Bee, .22 Hornet, .22 Rem. Jet, .221 Fireball, .222 Rem., .25-35, .256 Win. Mag., .30 M1 Carbine, .30-30, .38 Auto, .38 Special .357 Mag./Hot Shot, 9mm Para., .45 Auto, .45 Colt, .44 Magnum/Hot Shot; (wildcat centerfire) .17 Ackley Bee, .17 Bumblebee, .17 Hornet, .17 K Hornet, .17 Mach IV, .17-.222, .17-.223, .22 K Hornet, .30 Herrett, .357 Herrett, .357-4 B&D. Interchangeable bbls.: 8.75- or 10-inch standard octagon (.357 Mag., .44 Mag. and .45 Colt available w/detachable choke for use w/Hot Shot cartridges); 10-inch w/vent rib and detachable internal choke tube for Hot Shots, .357 and .44 Magnum only; 10-inch

Thompson
Contender Single-Shot Pistol

Thompson
Center Contender Bull Barrel

(cont'd) **CONTENDER SINGLE-SHOT PISTOL**
bull bbl., .30 or .357 Herrett only. 13.5 inches overall w/10-inch bbl., Weight: 43 oz. (w/standard 10-inch bbl.). Adj. rear sight, ramp front; vent rib model has folding rear sight, adj. front; bull bbl., available w/or w/o sights. Lobo 1.5/ scope and mount (add $40 to value). Blued finish. Receiver photoengraved. Checkered walnut thumbrest grip and forearm (pre-1972 model has different grip w/silver grip cap). Made 1967 to date, w/the following revisions and variations.
Standard model. . . . . NiB $300 Ex $250 Gd $140
Vent rib model . . . . NiB $400 Ex $300 Gd $165
Bull bbl. model, w/sights . . . . NiB $380 Ex $295 Gd $160
Bull bbl. model, without sights . . . . NiB $370 Ex $280 Gd $145
Extra standard bbl. . . . . NiB $225 Ex $175 Gd $75
Extra vent rib or bull bbl. . . . . NiB $270 Ex $185 Gd $90

CONTENDER BULL BARREL . . . . . . NiB $380 Ex $295 Gd $160
Caliber offerings of the bull bbl. version expanded in 1973 and 1978, making it the Contender model w/the widest range of caliber options: .22 LR, .22 Win. Mag., .22 Hornet, .223 Rem., 7mm T.C.U., 7x30 Waters, .30 M1 Carbine, .30-30 Win., .32 H&R Mag., .32-20 Win., .357 Rem. Max., .357 Mag., 10mm Auto, .44 Magnum, .445 Super Magnum. 10-inch heavy bbl., Partridge-style iron sights. Contoured Competitor grip. Blued finish.

CONTENDER INTERNAL CHOKE MODEL
Originally made in 1968-69 w/octagonal bbl., this Internal Choke version in .45 Colt/.410 caliber only was reintroduced in 1986 w/10-inch bull bbl. Vent rib also available. Fixed iron rear sight, bead front. Detachable choke screws into muzzle. Blued finish. Contoured American black walnut Competitor grip, also since 1986, has nonslip rubber insert permanently bonded to back of grip.
W/bull bbl. . . . . NiB $400 Ex $315 Gd $180
W/vent rib . . . . NiB $425 Ex $340 Gd $231

CONTENDER OCTAGON BARREL . . . . NiB $355 Ex $260 Gd $170
The original Contender design, this octagonal bbl., version began to see the discontinuance of caliber offerings in 1980. Now it is available in .22 LR only, 10-inch octagonal bbl., Partridge-style iron sights. Contoured Competitor grip. Blued finish.

**Thompson Center
Contender Octagon Barrel**

**Thompson Center
Contender Super 14**

**Thompson Center
Contender TC Alloy II w/Vent Rib**

CONTENDER STAINLESS
Similar to the standard Contender models except stainless steel w/blued sights. Black Rynite forearm and ambidextrous finger-groove grip. Made from 1993 to date.
Standard SS model (10-inch bbl.) . . . . NiB $435 Ex $315 Gd $220
SS Super 14. . . . . NiB $445 Ex $325 Gd $230
SS Super 16. . . . . NiB $450 Ex $330 Gd $235

CONTENDER SUPER 14/16
Calibers: .22 LR, .222 Rem., .223 Rem., 6mm T.C.U., 6.5mm T.C.U., 7mm T.C.U., 7x30 Waters, .30 Herrett, .30-30 Win., .357 Herrett, .357 Rem. Max., .35 Rem., 10mm Auto, .44 Mag., .445 Super Mag. 14- or 16.25-inch bull bbl., 18 or 20.25 inches overall. Weight: 43-65 oz. Partridge-style ramp front sight, adj. target rear. Blued finish. Made 1978 to date.
Super 14 . . . . NiB $360 Ex $255 Gd $170
Super 16 . . . . NiB $365 Ex $260 Gd $175

CONTENDER TC ALLOY II
Calibers: .22 LR, .223 Rem., .357 Magnum, .357 Rem. Max., .44 Magnum, 7mm T.C.U., .30-30 Win., .45 Colt/.410 (w/internal choke), .35 Rem. and 7-30 Waters (14-inch bbl.). 10- or 14-inch bull bbl. or 10-inch vent rib bbl. (w/internal choke). All metal parts permanently electroplated w/T/C Alloy II, which is harder than stainless steel, ensuring smoother action, 30 percent longer bbl. life. Other design specifications the same as late model Contenders. Made 1986-89.
T/C Alloy II 10-inch bull bbl. . . . . NiB $355 Ex $295 Gd $240
T/C Alloy II vent rib bbl. w/choke . . . . NiB $406 Ex $325 Gd $221
T/C Alloy II Super 14 . . . . NiB $438 Ex $350 Gd $238

ENCORE SINGLE-SHOT PISTOL
Similar to the standard Contender models except w/10-, 12- or 15-inch bbl., Calibers: .22-250 Rem., .223 Rem., .243 Win., .260 Rem., .270 Win., 7mm BR Rem., 7mm-08 Rem., 7.62x39mm, .308 Win., .30-06 Spfd., .44 Rem. Mag., .444 Marlin, .45-70 Govt., .45 LC/410. Blue or stainless finish. Walnut or composition, ambidextrous finger-groove grip. Hunter Model w/2.5-7x pistol scope. Note: Encore bbls. are not interchangeable with Contenter models. Made from 1998 to date.
Encore model w/10-inch
bbl. (blue, disc.) . . . . NiB $430 Ex $365 Gd $195
Encore model w/12-inch bbl. (blue) . . . . . . NiB $430 Ex $365 Gd $195
Encore model w/15-inch bbl. (blue) . . . . . . NiB $438 Ex $473 Gd $203
Hunter model w/2.5-7x scope . . . . NiB $700 Ex $600 Gd $360
Encore model (stainless), add $55

UBERTI HANDGUNS — Mfd. by Aldo Uberti, Ponte Zanano, Italy
(Imported by Uberti USA, Inc.)

MODEL 1871 ROLLING BLOCK
TARGET PISTOL . . . . NiB $335 Ex $275 Gd $165
Single shot. Calibers: .22 LR, .22 Magnum, .22 Hornet and .357 Magnum; 9.5-inch bbl., 14 inches overall. Weight: 44 oz. Ramp front sight, fully adjustable rear. Smooth walnut grip and forearm. Color casehardened frame w/brass trigger guard. Blued half-octagon or full round barrel.

MODEL 1873 CATTLEMAN SA REVOLVER
Calibers: .357 Magnum, .38-40, .44-40, .44 Special, .45 Long Colt, .45 ACP. Six-shot cylinder, Bbl length: 3.5, 4.5, 4.75, 5.5, 7.5 or 18 inches; 10.75 inches overall (5.5-inch bbl.). Weight: 38 oz. (5.5-inch bbl.). Color casehardened steel frame w/steel or brass back strap and trigger guard. Nickel-plated or blued barrel and cylinder. Imported 1997 to date.
First issue . . . . NiB $365 Ex $310 Gd $170
Bisley . . . . NiB $365 Ex $310 Gd $175
Bisley (flattop) . . . . NiB $365 Ex $310 Gd $175
Buntline (reintroduced 1992) . . . . NiB $365 Ex $310 Gd $175
Quick Draw . . . . NiB $365 Ex $310 Gd $175
Sabre (bird head) . . . . NiB $365 Ex $310 Gd $175
Sheriff's model . . . . NiB $365 Ex $310 Gd $175
Convertible cylinder, add $51
Stainless steel, add $125
Steel backstrap and trigger guard, add $55
Target sights, add $60

MODEL 1875 REMINGTON OUTLAW
Replica of Model 1875 Remington. Calibers: .357 Mag., .44-40, .45 ACP, .45 Long Colt. Six-shot cylinder, 5.5- to 7.5-inch bbl., 11.75 to 13.75 inches overall. Weight: 44 oz. (with 7.5 inch bbl). Color casehardened steel frame w/steel or brass back strap and trigger guard. Blue or nickel finish.
Blue model . . . . NiB $395 Ex $295 Gd $150
Nickel model (disc. 1995). . . . . NiB $500 Ex $415 Gd $260
Convertible cylinder
(.45 LC/.45 ACP), add. $92

MODEL 1890 REMINGTON POLICE
Similar to Model 1875 Remington except without the web under the ejector housing.
Blue Model . . . . NiB $395 Ex $295 Gd $150
Nickel Model (disc. 1995) . . . . NiB $500 Ex $415 Gd $260
Convertible Cylinder (.45 LC/.45 ACP), add. $92

ULTRA LIGHT ARMS, INC — Granville, WV.

MODEL 20 SERIES PISTOLS
Calibers: .22-250 thru .308 Win. Five-shot magazine, 14-inch bbl., weight: 4 lbs. Composite Kevlar, graphite reinforced stock. Benchrest grade action available in right- or left-hand models. Timney adjustable trigger w/three function safety. Bright or matte finish. Made 1987-99.

Model 20 Hunter's Pistol (disc. 1989). . . NiB $1295 Ex $1150 Gd $650
Model 20 Reb Pistol (disc. 1999) . . . . . . NiB $1475 Ex $1200 Gd $675

UNIQUE PISTOLS — Hendaye, France
Mfd. by Manufacture d'Armes des Pyrénées
Currently imported by Nygord Precision Products(Previously by Beeman Precision Arms)

MODEL B/CF AUTOMATIC PISTOL . . . . . . NiB $205 Ex $195 Gd $130
Calibers: .32 ACP, .380 ACP. Nine-shot (.32) or 8-shot (.38) magazine, 4-inch bbl., 6.6 inches overall. Weight: 24.3 oz. Blued finish. Plain or thumbrest plastic grips. Intro. 1954. Disc.

MODEL D2 . . . . NiB $300 Ex $250 Gd $195
Same as Model D6 except has 4.5-inch bbl., 7.5 inches overall, weight: 24.5 oz. Made 1954 to date.

MODEL D6 AUTOMATIC PISTOL. . . . . NiB $300 Ex $250 Gd $140
Caliber: .22 LR. 10-shot magazine, 6-inch bbl., 9.25 inches overall. Weight: About 26 oz. Adj. sights. Blued finish. Plain or thumbrest plastic grips. Intro. in 1954. Disc.

MODEL DES/32U RAPID FIRE PISTOL
Caliber: .32 S&W Long (wadcutter). Five- or 6-shot magazine, 5.9-inch bbl., weight: .40.2 oz. Blade front sight, micro-adj. rear. Trigger adj. for weight and position. Blued finish. Stippled handrest grips. Imported 1990 to date.

Right-hand model . . . . NiB $1350 Ex $1225 Gd $625
Left-hand model . . . . NiB $1412 Ex $1287 Gd $687

MODEL DES/69-U TARGET PISTOL
Caliber: .22 LR. Five-shot magazine, 5.9-inch bbl., w/250 gm counterweight. 10.6 inches overall. Trigger adjusts for position and pull. Weight: 35.3 oz. Blade front sight, micro-adj. rear. Checkered walnut thumbrest grips w/adj. handrest. Blued finish. Imported 1969 to date.

Right-hand model . . . . NiB $1150 Ex $995 Gd $500
Left-hand model . . . . NiB $1180 Ex $1025 Gd $530

MODEL DES/VO RAPID FIRE
MATCH AUTOMATIC PISTOL . . . . NiB $1000 Ex $770 Gd $525
Caliber: .22 Short. Five-shot magazine, 5.9-inch bbl., 10.4 inches overall. Weight: 43 oz. Click adj. rear sight blade front. Checkered walnut thumbrest grips w/adj. handrest. Trigger adj. for length of pull. Made 1974 to date.

KRIEGS MODELL L AUTOMATIC PISTOL . . . . NiB $325 Ex $250 Gd $160
Caliber: .32 Auto (7.65mm). Nine-shot magazine, 3.2-inch bbl., 5.8 inches overall. Weight: 26.5 oz. Fixed sights. Blued finish. Plastic grips. Mfd. during German occupation of France 1940-45. Note: Bears the German military acceptance marks and may have grips marked "7.65m/m 9 SCHUSS."

MODEL L AUTOMATIC PISTOL . . . . NiB $250 Ex $200 Gd $100
Calibers: .22 LR, .32 Auto (7.65mm), .380 Auto (9mm Short). 10-shot magazine in .22, 7 in .32, 6 in .380; 3.3-inch bbl.; 5.8 inches overall. Weight: 16.5 oz. (.380 Auto w/light alloy frame), 23 oz. (w/steel frame). Fixed sights. Blued finish. Plastic grips. Intro. 1955. Disc.

Unique D6

Unique
DES/69 Standard Match

Unique
Model DES/VO Rapid Fire Match

MODEL MIKROS POCKET
AUTOMATIC PISTOL . . . . NiB $200 Ex $155 Gd $100
Calibers: .22 Short, .25 Auto (6.35mm). Six-shot magazine, 2.25-inch bbl., 4.44 inches overall. Weight: 9.5 oz. (light alloy frame), 12.5 oz. (steel frame.). Fixed sights. Blued finish. Plastic grips. Intro. 1957. Disc. See illustration next page.

MODEL RR
AUTOMATIC PISTOL . . . . NiB $180 Ex $170 Gd $110
Postwar commercial version of WWII Kriegsmodell w/same general specifications. Intro. 1951. Disc.

MODEL 2000-U MATCH PISTOL
Caliber: .22 Short. Designed for U.I.T. rapid fire competition. Five-shot top-inserted magazine, 5.5-inch bbl., w/five vents for recoil reduction. 11.4 inches overall. Weight: 43.4 oz. Special light alloy frame, solid steel slide and shock absorber. Stippled French walnut w/adj. handrest. Imported 1990-96.

Right-hand model . . . . NiB $1300 Ex $1050 Gd $500
Left-hand model . . . . NiB $1330 Ex $1080 Gd $530

Unique
Mikros Pocket

U.S. Arms Abilene

Universal Enforcer (3000)

Uzi
Semi-automatic Pistol

UNITED STATES ARMS CORPORATION — Riverhead, New York

ABILENE SA REVOLVER
Safety Bar action. Calibers: .357 Mag., .41 Mag., .44 Mag., .45 Colt and .357/9mm convertible model w/two cylinders. Six-shot cylinder, bbl. lengths: 4.63-, 5.5-, 6.5-inch, 7.5- and 8.5-inches in .44

(cont'd) ABILENE SA REVOLVER
Mag. only. Weight: About 48 oz. Adj. rear sight, ramp front. Blued finish or stainless steel. Smooth walnut grips. Made 1976-83.
.44 Magnum, blued finish . . . . NiB $300 Ex $250 Gd $165
.44 Magnum, stainless steel. . . . . . . NiB $350 Ex $290 Gd $200
Other calibers, blued finish. . . . . . . NiB $281 Ex $225 Gd $153
.357 Magnum, stainless steel. . . . . . NiB $344 Ex $275 Gd $187
Convertible, .357 Mag./9mm
Para., blued finish . . . . NiB $300 Ex $250 Gd $165

UNIVERSAL FIREARMS CORPORATION — Hialeah, Florida
This company was purchased by Iver Johnson Arms in the mid-1980s, when the Enforcer listed below was disc.. An improved version was issued under the Iver Johnson name (see separate listing).

ENFORCER (3000)
SEMIAUTOMATIC PISTOL . . . . NiB $275 Ex $275 Gd $160
M-1 Carbine-type action. Caliber: 30 Carbine. Five-, 15- or 30-shot clip magazine, 10.25-inch bbl., 17.75 inches overall. Weight: 4.5 lbs. (with 30-shot magazine). Adj. rear sight, blade front. Blued finish. Walnut stock w/pistol grip and handguard. Made 1964-83.

UZI PISTOLS — Mfd. by Israel Military Industries, Israel
(Currently imported by UZI America)

SEMIAUTOMATIC PISTOL . . . . NiB $975 Ex $850 Gd $650
Caliber: 9mm Para. 20-round magazine, 4.5-inch bbl., about 9.5 inches overall. Weight: 3.8 lbs. Front post-type sight, rear open-type, both adj. Disc. 1993.

"EAGLE" SERIES
SEMIAUTOMATIC DA PISTOL
Caliber: 9mm Parabellum, .40 S&W, .45 ACP (Short Slide). 10-shot magazine, 3.5-, 3.7- and 4.4-inch bbl., weight: 32 oz. to 35 oz. Blade front sight, drift adjustable tritium rear. Matte blue finish. Black synthetic grips. Imported 1997 to date.
Compact model
(DA or DAO) . . . . NiB $485 Ex $440 Gd $330
Polymer compact model . . . . NiB $485 Ex $440 Gd $330
Full-size model . . . . NiB $485 Ex $440 Gd $330
Short slide model. . . . . NiB $485 Ex $440 Gd $330

WALTHER PISTOLS — Manufactured by German, French and Swiss firms
The following Walther pistols were made before and during World War II by Waffenfabrik Walther, Zella-Mehlis (Thür.), Germany.

MODEL 1
AUTOMATIC PISTOL . . . . NiB $650 Ex $525 Gd $225
Caliber: .25 Auto (6.35mm). Six-shot. 2.1-inch bbl., 4.4 inches overall. Weight: 12.8 oz. Fixed sights. Blued finish. Checkered hard rubber grips. Intro. 1908.

MODEL 2
AUTOMATIC PISTOL
Caliber: .25 Auto (6.35mm). Six-shot magazine, 2.1-inch bbl., 4.2 inches overall. Weight: 9.8 oz. Fixed sights. Blued finish. Checkered hard rubber grips. Intro. 1909.
Standard model . . . . NiB $450 Ex $425 Gd $135
Pop-up sight model . . . . NiB $1395 Ex $995 Gd $550

MODEL 3 AUTOMATIC PISTOL . . . . NiB $1500 Ex $1250 Gd $550
Caliber: .32 Auto (7.65mm). Six-shot magazine, 2.6-inch bbl., 5 inches overall. Weight: 16.6 oz. Fixed sights. Blued finish. Checkered hard rubber grips. Intro. 1910.

MODEL 4 AUTOMATIC PISTOL . . . . NiB $400 Ex $325 Gd $150
Caliber: .32 Auto (7.65mm). Eight-shot magazine, 3.5-inch bbl., 5.9 inches overall. Weight: 18.6 oz. Fixed sights. Blued finish. Checkered hard rubber grips. Made 1910-18.

MODEL 5 AUTOMATIC PISTOL . . . . NiB $485 Ex $425 Gd $135
Improved version of Model 2 w/same general specifications, distinguished chiefly by better workmanship and appearance. Intro. in 1913.

MODEL 6 AUTOMATIC PISTOL . . . . . . NiB $6000 Ex $4500 Gd $1050
Caliber: 9mm Para. Eight-shot magazine, 4.75-inch bbl., 8.25 inches overall. Weight: 34 oz. Fixed sights. Blued finish. Checkered hard rubber grips. Made 1915-17. Note: The powerful 9mm Para. cartridge is too much for the simple blow-back system of this pistol, so firing is not recommended.

MODEL 7 AUTOMATIC PISTOL . . . . NiB $650 Ex $500 Gd $200
Caliber: .25 Auto. (6.35mm). Eight-shot magazine, 3-inch bbl., 5.3 inches overall. Weight: 11.8 oz. Fixed sights. Blued finish. Checkered hard rubber grips. Made 1917-18.

MODEL 8 AUTOMATIC PISTOL . . . . NiB $495 Ex $450 Gd $150
Caliber: .25 Auto. (6.35mm). Eight-shot magazine, 2.88-inch bbl., 5.13 inches overall. Weight: 12.38 oz. Fixed sights. Blued finish. Checkered plastic grips. Made 1920-45.

MODEL 8 LIGHTWEIGHT
AUTOMATIC PISTOL . . . . NiB $494 Ex $395 Gd $269
Same as standard Model Eight except about 25 percent lighter due to use of aluminum alloys.

MODEL 9 VEST POCKET
AUTOMATIC PISTOL . . . . NiB $600 Ex $525 Gd $160
Caliber: .25 Auto. (6.35mm). Six-shot magazine, 2-inch bbl., 3.94 inches overall. Weight: 9 oz. Fixed sights. Blued finish. Checkered plastic grips. Made 1921-45.

MODEL HP DOUBLE-ACTION AUTOMATIC
Prewar commercial version of the P38 marked with an "N" proof over an "Eagle" or "Crown." The "HP" is an abbreviation of "Heeres Pistole" (Army Pistol). Caliber: 9mm Para. 8-shot magazine, 5-inch bbl., 8.38 inches overall. Weight: About 34.5 oz. Fixed sights. Blued finish. Checkered wood or plastic grips. The Model HP is distinguished by its notably fine material and workmanship. Made 1937-44. (SN range 1000-25900)
First production (Swedish Trials
model H1000-H2000) . . . . NiB $2938 Ex $2350 Gd $1598
Standard commercial production
(2000-24,000) . . . . NiB $1500 Ex $1300 Gd $795
War production - marked "P38"
(24,000-26,000) . . . . NiB $1200 Ex $995 Gd $650
W/Nazi proof "Eagle/359," add $240

OLYMPIA FUNFKAMPF
MODEL AUTOMATIC . . . . NiB $1725 Ex $1400 Gd $550
Caliber: .22 LR. 10-shot magazine, 9.6-inch bbl., 13 inches overall. Weight: 33 oz., less weight. Set of 4 detachable weights. Adj. target sights. Blued finish. Checkered grips. Intro. 1936.

OLYMPIA HUNTING
MODEL AUTOMATIC . . . . NiB $1600 Ex $1200 Gd $440
Same general specifications as Olympia Sport Model but w/4-inch bbl., Weight: 28.5 oz.

Walther Model 5

Walther Model 8

Walther Model 9

OLYMPIA RAPID FIRE
MODEL AUTOMATIC . . . . NiB $1600 Ex $1200 Gd $540
Caliber: .22 Short. Six-shot magazine, 7.4-inch bbl., 10.7 inches overall. Weight: (without 12.38 oz. detachable muzzle weight,) 27.5 oz. Adj. target sights. Blued finish. Checkered grips. Made about 1936-40.

OLYMPIA SPORT
MODEL AUTOMATIC . . . . NiB $975 Ex $825 Gd $420
Caliber: .22 LR. 10-shot magazine, 7.4-inch bbl., 10.7 inches overall. Weight: 30.5 oz., less weight. Adj. target sights. Blued finish. Checkered grips. Set of four detachable weights was supplied at extra cost. Made about 1936-40.

**Walther PP
(Prewar)**

P38 MILITARY DA AUTOMATIC
Modification of the Model HP adopted as an official German Service arm in 1938 and produced throughout WW II by Walther (code "ac"), Mauser (code "byf") and a few other manufacturers. General specifications and appearance same as Model HP, but w/a vast difference in quality, the P38 being a mass-produced military pistol. Some of the late wartime models were very roughly finished and tolerances were quite loose.

War Production w/Walther banner (1940)
Zero Ser. 1st Iss. (SN 01-01,000) . . . . NiB $7500 Ex $5700 Gd $2000
Zero Ser. 2nd Iss. (SN 01,000-03,500) . . . . . . NiB $6000 Ex $4650 Gd $1900
Zero Ser. 3rd Iss. (SN 03,500-013,000) . . . . . . NiB $2750 Ex $2000 Gd $800

WALTHER CONTRACT PISTOLS (LATE 1940-44)
"480" code Series (SN 1-7,600) . . . . NiB $5250 Ex $3500 Gd $1200
"ac" code Ser. w/no date (SN 7,350-9,700). . . NiB $5500 Ex $4200 Gd $1800
"ac" code Ser. w/.40 below
code (SN 9,700-9,900A) . . . . NiB $4000 Ex $3500 Gd $1500
"ac40" code inline Ser. (SN 1-9,900B) . . . . NiB $2000 Ex $1600 Gd $600
"ac" code Ser. w/41 below code (SN 1-4,5001) . . . . . NiB $1500 Ex $1350 Gd $700
"ac" code Ser. w/42 below code
(SN 4,500I-9,300K) . . . . NiB $1250 Ex $1100 Gd $500
"ac" code Ser. w/43 date (inline or below) . . . . . . NiB $600 Ex $450 Gd $300
"ac" code Ser. w/45 (inline or below) . . . . NiB $550 Ex $450 Gd $275

MAUSER CONTRACT PISTOLS (LATE 1942-44)
"byf" code Ser. w/42 date (19,000 prod.) . . . . . NiB $1100 Ex $1000 Gd $600
"bcf" code Ser. w/43, 44 or 45 date
(inline or below) . . . . NiB $700 Ex $600 Gd $450
"svw" code Ser. (French prod. w/Nazi proofs). . . NiB $1100 Ex $925 Gd $450
"svw" code Ser. (French prod. w/star proof) . . . . . NiB $450 Ex $365 Gd $250

SPREEWERKE CONTRACT PISTOLS (LATE 1942-45)
"cyq" code 1st Ser. w/Eagle over
359 (500 prod.) . . . . NiB $1619 Ex $1295 Gd $881
"cyq" code Standard Ser. (300,000 prod.) . . . . . . NiB $775 Ex $400 Gd $300
"cyq" code "0" Ser. (5,000 prod.). . . . . NiB $1000 Ex $995 Gd $425

MODEL PP DA AUTOMATIC PISTOL
Polizeipistole (Police Pistol). Calibers: .22 LR (5.6mm), .25 Auto (6.35mm), .32 Auto (7.65mm), .380 Auto (9mm). Eight-shot magazine, (7-shot in .380), 3.88-inch bbl., 6.94 inches overall. Weight: 23 oz. Fixed sights. Blued finish. Checkered plastic grips. 1929-45. Post-War production and importation 1952 to present.

NOTE: Wartime models are inferior in quality to prewar commercial pistols.

COMMERCIAL MODEL W/CROWN "N" PROOF
.22 cal. (w/comm. Crown "N" proof) . . . . NiB $995 Ex $850 Gd $541
.25 cal. (w/comm. Crown "N" proof) . . . . . . NiB $3453 Ex $3100 Gd $1500
.32 cal. (w/comm. Crown "N" proof) . . . . NiB $495 Ex $425 Gd $250
.32 cal. (w/Dural (alloy) frame) . . . . NiB $569 Ex $489 Gd $287

(cont'd) **Commercial Model w/Crown "N" Proof**
.32 cal. (w/Verchromt Fin., pre-war) . . . . NiB $1000 Ex $1400 Gd $485
.32 cal. (A.F.Stoeger Contract, pre-war) . . . . . . NiB $1650 Ex $1200 Gd $425
.32 cal. (Allemagne French contract,
pre-war) . . . . NiB $1200 Ex $1000 Gd $425
.380 cal. (w/Comm. Crown "N" proof). . . . . NiB $1250 Ex $995 Gd $541
.380 cal. (w/Verchromt Fin., pre-war) . . . . NiB $2400 Ex $2100 Gd $727

WARTIME MODEL WITH EAGLE "N" PROOF
.32 cal. (w/Waffenampt proofs). . . . . NiB $550 Ex $465 Gd $522
.32 cal. (w/Eagle "C" Nazi Police markings) . . . . . NiB $825 Ex $695 Gd $380
.32 cal. (w/Eagle "F" Nazi Police markings) . . . . . NiB $825 Ex $695 Gd $380
.32 cal. (w/NSKK markings). . . . . NiB $2875 Ex $2050 Gd $700
.32 cal. (w/NSDAP Gruppe markings) . . . . NiB $2275 Ex $1925 Gd $650
.380 cal. (w/Waffenampt proofs) . . . . NiB $1250 Ex $995 Gd $646

COMMERCIAL MODEL (POST-WAR)
.22 cal. (German manufacture) . . . . NiB $925 Ex $800 Gd $400
.32 cal. (German manufacture) . . . . NiB $825 Ex $475 Gd $350
.380 cal. (German manufacture) . . . . NiB $950 Ex $800 Gd $275
.22 cal. (French manufacture) . . . . NiB $450 Ex $395 Gd $165
.32 cal. (French manufacture) . . . . NiB $450 Ex $395 Gd $165
.380 cal. (French manufacture) . . . . NiB $495 Ex $434 Gd $181
.22, .32 or .380 Cal. (other foreign manuf.) . . . . . NiB $300 Ex $235 Gd $150

MODEL PP SPORT DA AUTOMATIC PISTOL
Target version of the Model PP. Caliber: .22 LR. Eight-shot magazine, 5.75- to 7.75 inch bbl. w/adjustable sights. Blue or nickel finish. Checkered plastic grips w/thumbrest. Made 1953-70.
PP Sport (Walther manufacture) . . . . NiB $875 Ex $775 Gd $525
PP Sport (Manurhin manufacture) . . . . NiB $700 Ex $650 Gd $430
PP Sport C model (comp./single act.) . . . . NiB $895 Ex $815 Gd $525
W/nickel finish, add $170
W/matched bbl., weights, add $75

MODEL PP DELUXE ENGRAVED
These elaborately engraved models are available in blued finish, silver- or gold-plated.
Blued finish . . . . NiB $1380 Ex $1200 Gd $1000
Silver-plated. . . . . NiB $1700 Ex $1290 Gd $1100
Gold-plated . . . . NiB $1900 Ex $1590 Gd $1200
W/ivory grips, add. $250
W/presentation case, add $700
.22 caliber, add $50
.380 caliber, add 95%

MODEL PP LIGHTWEIGHT
Same as standard Model PP except about 25 percent lighter due to use of aluminum alloys (Dural). Values 40 percent higher. (See individual listings).

WALTHER MODEL PP
SUPER DA PISTOL. . . . . NiB $813 Ex $650 Gd $442
Caliber: 9x18mm. Seven-shot magazine, 3.6-inch bbl., 6.9 inches overall. Weight: 30 oz. Fixed sights. Blued finish. Checkered plastic grips. Made 1974-81.

MODEL PP 7.65MM
PRESENTATION. . . . . NiB $1813 Ex $1450 Gd $986
Made of soft aluminum alloy in green-gold color, these pistols were not intended to be fired.

MODEL PPK DOUBLE-ACTION AUTOMATIC PISTOL
Polizeipistole Kriminal (Detective Pistol). Calibers: .22 LR (5.6mm), .25 Auto (6.35mm), .32 Auto (7.65mm), .380 Auto (9mm). Seven-shot magazine, (6-shot in .380), 3.25-inch bbl., 5.88 inches overall. Weight: 19 oz. Fixed sights. Blued finish. Checkered plastic grips.
Note: Wartime models are inferior in workmanship to prewar commercial pistols. Made 1931-45.

NOTE: *After both World Wars, the Walther manufacturing facility was required to cease the production of "restricted" firearms as part of the armistice agreements. Following WW II, Walther moved its manufacturing facility from the original location in Zella/Mehilis, Germany to Ulm/Donau. In 1950, the firm Manufacture de Machines du Haut Rhine at Mulhouse, France was licensed by Walther and started production of PP and PPK models at the Manurhin facility in 1952. The MK II Walthers as produced at Manurhin were imported into the U.S. until 1968 when CGA importation requirements restricted the PPK firearm configuration from further importation. As a result, Walther developed the PPK/S to conform to the new regulations and licensed Interarms to produce the firearm in the U.S. from 1986-99. From 1984-86, Manurhin imported PP and PPK/S type firearms under the Manurhin logo. Additional manufacturing facilities (both licensed & unlicensed) that produced PP and PPK type firearms were established after WW II in various locations and other countries including: China, France, Hungary, Korea, Romania and Turkey. In 1996, Walther was sold to Umarex Sportwaffen GmbH and manufacturing facilities were relocated in Arnsberg, Germany. In 1999, Walther formed a partnership with Smith and Wesson and selected Walther firearms are licensed for production in the U.S.*

**Walther PPK
(WW II)**

**Walther PPK
Silver-Plated**

COMMERCIAL MODEL W/EAGLE "N" PROOF (PREWAR)

.22 cal. (w/Comm. Eagle "N" proof)....... NiB $1250 Ex $1100 Gd $470
.25 cal. (w/Comm. Eagle "N" proof)...... NiB $5000 Ex $3000 Gd $2600
.32 cal. (w/Comm. Eagle "N" proof)...... NiB $650 Ex $450 Gd $350
.380 cal. (w/Comm. Eagle "N" proof)..... NiB $2500 Ex $2000 Gd $800

WARTIME MODEL W/EAGLE "N" PROOF

.22 cal. (w/Comm. Eagle "N" proof)....... NiB $1244 Ex $995 Gd $677
.22 cal. (w/Dural frame) .... NiB $1500 Ex $1200 Gd $1100
.32 cal. (w/Comm. Eagle "N" proof)........ NiB $550 Ex $450 Gd $250
.32 cal. (w/Dural frame) .... NiB $781 Ex $625 Gd $425
.32 cal. (w/Verchromt Fin., Pre-War) ...... NiB $2100 Ex $1600 Gd $650
.380 cal. (w/Comm. Eagle "N" proof)...... NiB $2600 Ex $2000 Gd $700
.380 cal. (w/Dural frame) .... NiB $2800 Ex $2100 Gd $750
.380 cal. (w/Verchromt Fin., Pre-War) .... NiB $3150 Ex $2400 Gd $1725
.22 cal. (w/Comm. Eagle "N" proof)...... NiB $700 Ex $690 Gd $475
.32 cal. (w/Waffenampt proofs)............ NiB $925 Ex $650 Gd $300
.32 cal. (w/Eagle "C" Nazi Police markings)... NiB $925 Ex $650 Gd $260
.32 cal. (w/Eagle "F" Nazi Police markings)...... NiB $1250 Ex $900 Gd $375
.32 cal. (w/NSKK markings)............. NiB $1994 Ex $1595 Gd $1085
.32 cal. (w/NSDAP Gruppe markings) ..... NiB $1900 Ex $1400 Gd $975
.380 cal. (w/Waffenampt proofs) .... NiB $1200 Ex $900 Gd $650

COMMERCIAL MODEL (POST-WAR)

.22 cal. (German manufacture)............. NiB $925 Ex $800 Gd $300
.32 cal. (German manufacture)............. NiB $825 Ex $475 Gd $275
.380 cal. (German manufacture)............ NiB $950 Ex $475 Gd $375
.22 cal. (French manufacture) .... NiB $2000 Ex $750 Gd $375
.32 cal. (French manufacture) .... NiB $750 Ex $550 Gd $325
.380 cal. (French manufacture)............ NiB $1050 Ex $725 Gd $350
.22, .32 or .380 cal. (other foreign manuf.) ... NiB $281 Ex $225 Gd $153

COMMERCIAL MODEL (U.S. PRODUCTION)

.380 cal. (w/blue finish)................... NiB $475 Ex $365 Gd $320
.380 cal. (w/nickel finish)................. NiB $475 Ex $365 Gd $320
.32 or .380 Cal. (stainless steel)............. NiB $475 Ex $365 Gd $320

MODEL PPK DELUXE ENGRAVED

These elaborately engraved models are available in blued finish, chrome-, silver- or gold-plated.
Blued finish .... NiB $1650 Ex $1300 Gd $975
Chrome-plated .... NiB $2700 Ex $1350 Gd $995
Silver-plated .... NiB $1925 Ex $1400 Gd $2309

(cont'd) MODEL PPK DELUXE ENGRAVED

Gold-plated .... NiB $2250 Ex $1675 Gd $1200
W/ivory grips, add $250
W/Presentation case, add $700
.22 cal, add $50
.25 cal, add $100
.380 cal, add $95

MODEL PPK LIGHTWEIGHT

Same as standard Model PPK except about 25 percent lighter due to aluminum alloys. Values 50 percent higher.

MODEL PPK 7.65MM

PRESENTATION.............. NiB $1575 Ex $1130 Gd $650
Made of soft aluminum alloy in green-gold color, these pistols were not intended to be fired.

MODEL PPK/S DA AUTOMATIC PISTOL

Designed to meet the requirements of the U.S. Gun Control Act of 1968, this model has the frame of the PP and the shorter slide and bbl., of the PPK. Overall length: 6.1 inches. Weight: 23 oz. Other specifications are the same as those of standard PPK except steel frame only. German, French and U.S. production 1971 to date. U.S. version made by Interarms 1978-99.

.22 cal. (German manufacture) ... NiB $1050 Ex $750 Gd $375
.32 cal. (German manufacture) .... NiB $750 Ex $550 Gd $295
.380 cal. (German manufacture) .. NiB $1050 Ex $725 Gd $300
.22 cal. (French manufacture) ..... NiB $725 Ex $500 Gd $350
.32 cal. (French manufacture) ..... NiB $730 Ex $425 Gd $289
.380 cal. (French manufacture) .... NiB $775 Ex $475 Gd $335
.22, .32 or .380 cal., blue
(U.S. manufacture) .... NiB $475 Ex $365 Gd $250
.22, .32 or .380 cal., stainless
(U.S. manuf.) .... NiB $475 Ex $365 Gd $325

NOTE: *Interarms (Interarmco) acquired a license from Walther in 1978 to manufacturer PP and PPK models at the Ranger Manufacturing Co., Inc. in Gadsden, Alabama. In 1988 the Ranger facility was licensed as EMCO and continued to produce Walther firearms for Interarms until 1996. From 1996-99, Black Creek in Gadsden, Alabama produced Walther pistols for Interarms. In 1999, Smith & Wesson acquired manufacturing rights for Walther firearms at the Black Creek facility.*

Walther
Free Pistol

MODELS PPK/S DELUXE ENGRAVED
These elaborately engraved models are available in blued finish, chrome-, silver- or gold-plated.

Blued finish . . . . NiB $1400 Ex $1000 Gd $950
Chrome-plated. . . . . NiB $1290 Ex $1000 Gd $700
Silver-plated. . . . . NiB $1450 Ex $1050 Gd $960
Gold-plated . . . . NiB $1619 Ex $1295 Gd $881

NOTE: *The following Walther pistols are now manufactured by Carl Walther, Waffenfabrik, Ulm/Donau, Germany.*

SELF-LOADING
SPORT PISTOL . . . . NiB $700 Ex $650 Gd $425
Caliber: .22 LR. 10-shot magazine, bbl. lengths: 6- and 9-inch, 9.88 inches overall w/6-inch bbl. Target sights. Blued finish. One-piece, wood or plastic grips, checkered. Intro. in 1932.

MODEL FREE PISTOL
MODEL FREE PISTOL . . . . NiB $1750 Ex $1325 Gd $690
Single-Shot. Caliber: .22 LR. 11.7-inch heavy bbl., Weight: 48 oz. Adj. grips and target sights w/electronic trigger. Importation disc. 1991.

Walther GSP

MODEL GSP TARGET AUTOMATIC PISTOL
Calibers: .22 LR, .32 S&W Long Wadcutter. Five-shot magazine, 4.5-inch bbl., 11.8 inches overall. Weights: 44.8 oz. (.22 cal.) or 49.4 oz. (.32 cal.). Adj. target sights. Black finish. Walnut thumbrest grips w/adj. handrest. Made 1969-94.
.22 LR . . . . NiB $1395 Ex $1200 Gd $475
.32 S&W Long
Wadcutter . . . . NiB $1595 Ex $1100 Gd $495
Conversion unit.
.22 Short
or .22 LR add. . . . . NiB $895 Ex $780 Gd $800

MODEL OSP RAPID
FIRE TARGET PISTOL. . . . . NiB $1475 Ex $1025 Gd $475
Caliber: .22 Short. Five-shot magazine, 4.5-inch bbl., 11.8 inches overall. Weight: 42.3 oz. Adj. target sights. Black finish. Walnut thumbrest grips w/adj. handrest. .22 LR conversion unit available (add $275). Made 1968-94.

MODEL P4 (P38-LV)
DA PISTOL . . . . NiB $695 Ex $595 Gd $290
Similar to P38 except has an uncocking device instead of a manual safety. Caliber: 9mm Para. 4.3-inch bbl., 7.9 inches overall. Other general specifications same as for current model P38. Made 1974-82.

MODEL P5 DA PISTOL
MODEL P5 DA PISTOL . . . . NiB $775 Ex $650 Gd $425
Alloy frame w/frame-mounted decocking levers. Caliber: 9mm Para. Eight-shot magazine, 3.5-inch bbl., 7 inches overall. Weight: 28 oz. blued finish. Checkered walnut or synthetic grips. Made 1988 to date.

MODEL P5
COMPACT PISTOL . . . . NiB $950 Ex $825 Gd $400
Similar to model P5 except w/3.1-inch bbl. and weight: 26 oz. Made 1988-96.

Walther P5

MODEL P38 (P1) DA AUTOMATIC
Postwar commercial version of the P38, has light alloy frame. Calibers: .22 LR, 7.65mm Luger, 9mm Para. Eight-shot magazine, bbl., lengths: 5.1-inch in .22 caliber, 4.9- inch in 7.65mm and 9mm, 8.5 inches overall. Weight: 28.2 oz. Fixed sights. Nonreflective black finish. Checkered plastic grips. Made 1957-89. Note: The "P1" is W. German Armed Forces official pistol.
.22 LR . . . . NiB $700 Ex $590 Gd $350
Other calibers . . . . NiB $650 Ex $550 Gd $295

MODEL P38 DELUXE ENGRAVED PISTOL
Elaborately engraved, available in blued or chrome-, silver- or gold-plated finish.
Blued finish . . . . NiB $1800 Ex $1325 Gd $750
Chrome-plated. . . . . NiB $1475 Ex $1150 Gd $725
Silver-plated. . . . . NiB $1450 Ex $1150 Gd $750
Gold-plated . . . . NiB $1800 Ex $1500 Gd $1000

MODEL P38K . . . . **NiB $695 Ex $600 Gd $275**
Short-barreled version of current P38, the "K" standing for "kurz" (meaning short). Same general specifications as standard model except 2.8-inch bbl., 6.3 inches overall, weight: 27.2 oz. Front sight is slide mounted. Caliber: 9mm Para. Made 1974-80.

MODEL P 88
DA AUTOMATIC
PISTOL . . . . **NiB $1325 Ex $1175 Gd $460**
Caliber: 9mm Para. 15-shot magazine, 4-inch bbl., 7.38 inches overall. Weight: 31.5 oz. Blade front sight, adj. rear. Checkered black synthetic grips. External hammer w/ambidextrous decocking levers. Alloy frame w/matte blued steel slide. Made 1987-93.

MODEL P 88 DA COMPACT
Similar to the standard P 88 Model except w/10- or 13-shot magazine, 3.8-inch bbl., 7.1 inches overall. Weight: 29 oz. Imported 1993 to date.
Model P88
(early importation) . . . . **NiB $850 Ex $725 Gd $475**
Model P88
(post 94 importation) . . . . **NiB $750 Ex $625 Gd $400**

MODEL P99 DA
AUTOMATIC PISTOL . . . . **NiB $550 Ex $475 Gd $325**
Calibers: 9mm Para., .40 S&W or 9x21mm. 10-shot magazine, 4-inch bbl., 7.2 inches overall. Weight: 22-25 oz. Ambidextrous magazine release, decocking lever and 3-function safety. Interchangeable front post sight, micro-adj. rear. Polymer gripframe w/blued slide. Imported 1997 to date.

MODEL TPH DA POCKET PISTOL
Light alloy frame. Calibers: .22 LR, .25 ACP (6.35mm). Six-shot magazine, 2.25-inch bbl., 5.38 inches overall. Weight: 14 oz. Fixed sights. Blued finish. Checkered plastic grips. Made 1968 to date. Note: Few Walther-made models reached the U.S. because of import restrictions. A U.S.-made version was mfd. by Interarms from 1986-99.
German model . . . . **NiB $775 Ex $625 Gd $270**
U.S. model . . . . **NiB $365 Ex $330 Gd $200**

NOTE: The Walther Olympia Model pistols were manufactured 1952-1963 by Hämmerli AG Jagd-und Sportwaffenfabrik, Lenzburg, Switzerland, and marketed as "Hämmerli-Walther." See Hämmerli listings for specific data.

OLYMPIA MODEL
200 AUTO PISTOL,
1952 TYPE . . . . **NiB $660 Ex $600 Gd $385**
Similar to 1936 Walther Olympia Funfkampf Model.

For the following Hammerelli-Walther Models
(200, 201, 202, 203, 204, and 205)
See listings under Hammerli Section.

WARNER PISTOL — Norwich, Connecticut
Warner Arms Corp. (or Davis-Warner Arms Co.)

INFALLIBLE POCKET
AUTOMATIC PISTOL . . . . **NiB $450 Ex $350 Gd $100**
Caliber: .32 Auto. Seven-shot magazine, 3-inch bbl., 6.5 inches overall. Weight: About 24 oz. Fixed sights. Blued finish. Hard rubber grips. Made 1917-19.

Walther P38

Walther P38K

Walther P88

Walther TPH
(Current)

Hamerelli-Walther
Model 200, 1952 Type

Webley Mark III
38 Military & Police Revolver

WEBLEY & SCOTT LTD. — London and Birmingham, England

MODEL 9MM MILITARY
& POLICE AUTOMATIC . . . . NiB $950 Ex $850 Gd $475
Caliber: 9mm Browning Long. Eight-shot magazine, 8 inches overall. Weight: 32 oz. Fixed sights. Blued finish. Checkered Vulcanite grips. Made 1909-30.

MODEL 25
HAMMER AUTOMATIC . . . . NiB $325 Ex $250 Gd $125
Caliber: .25 Automatic. Six-shot magazine, overall length: 4.75 inches. Weight: 11.75 oz. No sights. Blued finish. Checkered Vulcanite grips. Made 1906-40.

MODEL 25 HAMMERLESS
AUTOMATIC . . . . NiB $375 Ex $225 Gd $125
Caliber: .25 Automatic. Six-shot magazine, overall length: 4.25 inches, weight: 9.75 oz. Fixed sights. Blued finish. Checkered Vulcanite grips. Made 1909-.40.

MARK I 455
AUTOMATIC PISTOL . . . . NiB $1750 Ex $1300 Gd $550
Caliber: .455 Webley Auto. Seven-shot magazine, 5-inch bbl., 8.5 inches overall. Weight: About 39 oz. Fixed sights. Blued finish. Checkered Vulcanite grips. Made 1913-31. Reissued during WWII. Total production about 9,300. Note: Mark I No. 2 is same pistol w/adj. rear sight and modified manual safety.

MARK III 38 MILITARY
& POLICE REVOLVER . . . . NiB $350 Ex $295 Gd $140
Hinged frame. DA. Caliber: .38 S&W. Six-shot cylinder, bbl. lengths: 3- and 4-inches. 9.5 inches overall (with 4-inch bbl.). Weight: 21 oz. (with 4-inch bbl.). Fixed sights. Blued finish. Checkered walnut or Vulcanite grips. Made 1897-45.

MARK IV 22 CALIBER
TARGET REVOLVER . . . . NiB $675 Ex $550 Gd $200
Same frame and general appearance as Mark IV .38. Caliber: .22 LR. Six-shot cylinder, 6-inch bbl., 10.13 inches overall. Weight: 34 oz. Target sights. Blued finish. Checkered grips. Disc. 1945.

MARK IV 38 MILITARY
& POLICE REVOLVER . . . . NiB $450 Ex $375 Gd $187
Identical in appearance to the double-action Mark IV .22 w/hinged frame except chambered for .38 S&W. Six-shot cylinder, bbl. length: 3-, 4- and 5-inches; 9.13 inches overall (with 5-inch bbl.). Weight: 27 oz. (with 5-inch bbl.). Fixed sights. Blued finish. Checkered grips. Made 1929-c. 1957.

MARK VI NO. 1 BRITISH
SERVICE REVOLVER . . . . NiB $300 Ex $250 Gd $160
DA. Hinged frame. Caliber: 455 Webley. Six-shot cylinder, bbl. lengths: 4-, 6- and 7.5-inches; 11.25 inches overall (with 6-inch bbl.). Weight: 38 oz. (with 6-inch bbl.). Fixed sights. Blued finish. Checkered walnut or Vulcanite grips. Made 1915-1947.

MARK VI 22
TARGET REVOLVER . . . . NiB $450 Ex $375 Gd $180
Same frame and general appearance as the Mark VI 455. Caliber: .22 LR. Six-shot cylinder, 6-inch bbl., 11.25 inches overall. Weight: 40 oz. Target sights. Blued finish. Checkered walnut or Vulcanite grips. Disc. 1945.

METROPOLITAN POLICE
AUTOMATIC PISTOL . . . . NiB $450 Ex $300 Gd $165
Calibers: .32 Auto, .380 Auto. Eight-shot (.32) or 7-shot (.380) magazine, 3.5-inch bbl., 6.25 inches overall. weight: 20 oz. Fixed sights. Blued finish. Checkered Vulcanite grips. Made 1906-40 (.32) and 1908-20 (.380).

RIC MODEL DA REVOLVER . . . . . . NiB $295 Ex $250 Gd $110
Royal Irish Constabulary or Bulldog Model. Solid frame. Caliber: .455 Webley. Five-shot cylinder, 2.25-inch bbl., weight: 21 oz. Fixed sights. Blued finish. Checkered walnut or vulcanite grips. Disc.

SEMIAUTOMATIC
SINGLE-SHOT PISTOL . . . . NiB $950 Ex $750 Gd $475
Similar in appearance to the Webley Metropolitan Police Automatic, this pistol is "semiautomatic" in the sense that the fired case is extracted and ejected and the hammer cocked as in a blow-back automatic pistol; it is loaded singly and the slide manually operated in loading. Caliber: .22 Long, 4.5- or 9-inch bbl., 10.75 inches overall (with 9-inch bbl.). Weight: 24 oz. (with 9-inch bbl.). Adj. sights. Blued finish. Checkered Vulcanite grips. Made 1911-27.

SINGLE-SHOT TARGET PISTOL . . . . . . NiB $375 Ex $250 Gd $100
Hinge frame. Caliber: .22 LR. 10-inch bbl., 15 inches overall. Weight: 37 oz. Fixed sights on earlier models, current production has adj. rear sight. Blued finish. Checkered walnut or Vulcanite grips. Made 1909 to date.

FOSBERY AUTOMATIC REVOLVER
Hinged frame. Recoil action revolves cylinder and cocks hammer. Caliber: 455 Webley. Six-shot cylinder, 6-inch bbl., 12 inches overall. Weight: 42 oz. Fixed or adjustable sights. Blued finish. Checkered walnut grips. Made 1901-1939. Note: A few were produced in caliber .38 Colt Auto w/an 8-shot cylinder (very rare).
1901 model . . . . NiB $6000 Ex $5500 Gd $3000
1902 model . . . . NiB $5500 Ex $4000 Gd $1500
1904 model . . . . NiB $5500 Ex $4000 Gd $1500
.38 Colt (8-shot), add 100%
Target model w/adjustable

WESSON FIREARMS CO., INC. — Palmer, Massachusetts
Formerly Dan Wesson Arms, Inc.

MODEL 8 SERVICE
Same general specifications as Model 14 except caliber .38 Special. Made 1971-75. Values same as for Model 14.

MODEL 8-2 SERVICE
Same general specifications as Model 14-2 except caliber .38 Special. Made 1975 to date. Values same as for Model 14-2.

MODEL 9 TARGET
Same as Model 15 except caliber .38 Special. Made 1971-75. Values same as for Model 15.

MODEL 9-2 TARGET
Same as Model 15-2 except caliber .38 Special. Made 1975 to date. Values same as for Model 15-2.

MODEL 9-2H HEAVY BARREL
Same general specifications as Model 15-2H except caliber .38 Special. Made 1975 to date. Values same as for Model 15-2H. Disc. 1983.

MODEL 9-2HV VENT RIB HEAVY BARREL
Same as Model 15-2HV except caliber .38 Special. Made 1975 to date. Values same as for Model 15-2HV.

MODEL 9-2V VENT RIB
Same as Model 15-2V except caliber .38 Special. Made 1975 to date. Values same as for Model 15-2H.

MODEL 11 SERVICE DA REVOLVER
Caliber: .357 Magnum. Six-shot cylinder. bbl. lengths: 2.5-, 4-, 6-inches interchangeable bbl. assemblies, 9 inches overall (with 4-inch bbl.). Weight: 38 oz. (with 4-inch bbl.). Fixed sights. Blued finish. Interchangeable grips. Made 1970-71. Note: The Model 11 has an external bbl., nut.
W/one bbl. assembly and grip..... NiB $200 Ex $175 Gd $130
Extra bbl. assembly $60
Extra grip..$45

MODEL 12 TARGET
Same general specifications as Model 11 except has adj. sights. Made 1970-71.
W/one-bbl. assembly and grip.... NiB $245 Ex $200 Gd $140
Extra bbl. assembly $60
Extra grip..$25

MODEL 14 SERVICE DA REVOLVER
Caliber: .357 Magnum. Six-shot cylinder, bbl. length: 2.25-, 3.75, 5.75-inches; interchangeable bbl. assemblies, 9 inches overall (with 3.75-inch bbl.). Weight: 36 oz. (with 3.75-inch bbl.). Fixed sights. Blued or nickel finish. Interchangeable grips. Made 1971-75. Note: Model 14 has recessed bbl., nut.
W/one-bbl. assembly and grip..... NiB $225 Ex $185 Gd $140
Extra bbl. assembly $60
Extra grip..$25

MODEL 14-2 SERVICE DA REVOLVER
Caliber: .357 Magnum. Six-shot cylinder, bbl. lengths: 2.5-, 4-, 6-, 8-inch; interchangeable bbl. assemblies, 9.25 inches overall (with 4-inch bbl.) Weight: 34 oz. (with 4-inch bbl.). Fixed sights. Blued finish. Interchangeable grips. Made 1975 to date. Note: Model 14-2 has recessed bbl. nut.

**Dan Wesson
Model 14-2 Service**

(cont'd) MODEL 14-2 SERVICE DA REVOLVER
W/one bbl. assembly
(8 inch) and grip ....NiB $215 Ex $170 Gd $120
W/one bbl. assembly
(other lengths) and grip..........NiB $215 Ex $170 Gd $120
Extra bbl. assembly, 8 inch $65
Extra bbl. assembly,
other lengths $50
Extra grip..$25

MODEL 15 TARGET
Same general specifications as Model 14 except has adj. sights. Made 1971-75.
W/one bbl. assembly
and grip...................NiB $270 Ex $220 Gd $125
Extra bbl. assembly $60
Extra grip..$25

MODEL 15-2 TARGET
Same general specifications as Model 14-2 except has adj. rear sight and interchangeable blade front; also avail. w/10-, 12- or 15-inch bbl., Made 1975 to date.
W/one bbl. assembly (8 inch) and grip. NiB $280 Ex $230 Gd $125
W/one bbl. assembly (10 inch) and grip.. NiB $280 Ex $230 Gd $125
W/one bbl. assembly
(12 inch)/grip. Disc...............NiB $280 Ex $230 Gd $125
W/one bbl. assembly
(15 inch)/grip. Disc...............NiB $280 Ex $230 Gd $125
W/one-bbl. assembly
(other lengths)/grip................NiB $175 Ex $140 Gd $95
Extra bbl. assembly (8 inch) $65
Extra bbl. assembly (10 inch) $65
Extra bbl. assembly (12 inch). Disc...................$65
Extra bbl. assembly (15 inch). Disc...................$65
Extra bbl. assembly (other lengths) $65
Extra grip..$25

MODEL 15-2H HEAVY BARREL
Same as Model 15-2 except has heavy bbl., assembly weight: with 4-inch bbl., 38 oz. Made 1975-83.
W/one bbl. assembly (8 inch) and grip ......NiB $200 Ex $165 Gd $110
W/one bbl. assembly (10 inch) and grip .....NiB $200 Ex $165 Gd $110
W/one bbl. assembly (12 inch) and grip .....NiB $200 Ex $165 Gd $110
W/one bbl. assembly (15 inch) and grip .....NiB $200 Ex $165 Gd $110
W/one bbl. assembly
(other lengths)/grip ....NiB $200 Ex $165 Gd $110
Extra bbl. assembly (8 inch) $65
Extra bbl. assembly (10 inch).........................$65
Extra bbl. assembly (12 inch) $65
Extra bbl. assembly (15 inch) $65
Extra bbl. assembly
(other lengths) $65
Extra grip..$25

**Dan Wesson
Model 15-2H Interchangeable Heavy**

MODEL 15-2HV VENT RIB HEAVY BARREL
Same as Model 15-2 except has vent rib heavy bbl. assembly; weight: (w/4-inch bbl.) 37 oz. Made 1975 to date.

W/one bbl. assembly (8 inch) and grip . . . . . . NiB $235 Ex $200 Gd $125
W/one bbl. assembly (10 inch) and grip . . . . . NiB $235 Ex $200 Gd $125
W/one bbl. assembly (12 inch) and grip . . . . . NiB $235 Ex $200 Gd $125
W/one bbl. assembly
(15 inch) and grip . . . . NiB $250 Ex $235 Gd $160
W/one bbl. assembly (other
lengths) and grip . . . . NiB $213 Ex $170 Gd $116
Extra bbl. assembly (8 inch) $65
Extra bbl. assembly (10 inch) $65
Extra bbl. assembly (12 inch) $65
Extra bbl. assembly (15 inch) $65
Extra bbl. assembly
(other lengths) $65
Extra grip $25

MODEL 15-2V VENT RIB
Same as Model 15-2 except has vent rib bbl. assembly, weight: 35 oz. (with 4-inch bbl.). Made 1975 to date. Values same as for 15-2H.

HUNTER PACS
Dan Wesson Hunter Pacs are offered in all Magnum calibers and include heavy vent rib 8-inch shrouded bbl., Burris scope mounts, bbl. changing tool in a case.

HP22M-V. . . . . NiB $750 Ex $575 Gd $360
HP22M-2 . . . . NiB $606 Ex $485 Gd $330
HP722M-V. NiB $706 Ex $565 Gd $384
HP722M-2 . . . . NiB $681 Ex $545 Gd $371
HP32-V . . . . NiB $656 Ex $525 Gd $357
HP32-2 . . . . NiB $569 Ex $455 Gd $309
HP732-V . . . . NiB $688 Ex $550 Gd $374
HP732-2 . . . . NiB $644 Ex $515 Gd $350
HP15-V . . . . NiB $644 Ex $515 Gd $350
HP15-2 . . . . NiB $594 Ex $475 Gd $323
HP715-V . . . . NiB $694 Ex $555 Gd $377
HP715-2 . . . . NiB $644 Ex $515 Gd $350
HP41-V . . . . NiB $563 Ex $450 Gd $306
HP741-V . . . . NiB $744 Ex $595 Gd $405
HP741-2 . . . . NiB $644 Ex $515 Gd $350
HP44-V . . . . NiB $731 Ex $585 Gd $398
HP44-2 . . . . NiB $644 Ex $515 Gd $350
HP744-V . . . . NiB $806 Ex $645 Gd $439
HP744-2 . . . . NiB $781 Ex $625 Gd $425
HP40-V . . . . NiB $494 Ex $395 Gd $269
HP40-2 . . . . NiB $706 Ex $565 Gd $384
HP740-V . . . . NiB $844 Ex $675 Gd $459
HP740-2 . . . . NiB $781 Ex $625 Gd $425
HP375-V . . . . NiB $481 Ex $385 Gd $262
HP375-2 . . . . NiB $820 Ex $656 Gd $446
HP45-V . . . . NiB $619 Ex $495 Gd $337

WHITNEY FIREARMS COMPANY — Hartford, Connecticut

WOLVERINE AUTOMATIC PISTOL
Dural frame/shell contains all operating components. Caliber: .22 LR. 10-shot magazine, 4.63-inch bbl., 9 inches overall. Weight: 23 oz. Partridge-type sights. Blued or nickel finish. Plastic grips. Made 1955-62.
Wolverine model, blue . . . . NiB $425 Ex $350 Gd $200
Wolverine model, nickel . . . . NiB $600 Ex $475 Gd $230

WICHITA ARMS — Wichita, Kansas

CLASSIC PISTOL
Caliber: Chambered to order. Bolt-action, single-shot. 11.25-inch octagonal bbl., 18 inches overall. Weight: 78 oz. Open micro sights. Custom-grade checkered walnut stock. Blued finish. Made 1980-97.
Standard . . . . NiB $3280 Ex $2250 Gd $2000
Presentation grade
(engraved) . . . . NiB $5250 Ex $3550 Gd $2750

HUNTER PISTOL. . . . . NiB $1250 Ex $875 Gd $700
Bolt-action, single-shot. Calibers: .22 LR, .22 WRF, 7mm Super Mag., 7-30 Waters, .30-30 Win., .32 H&R Mag., .357 Mag., .357 Super Mag. 10.5-inch bbl., 16.5 inches overall, weight: 60 oz. No sights (scope mount only). Stainless steel finish. Walnut stock. Made 1983-94.

INTERNATIONAL PISTOL . . . . NiB $680 Ex $465 Gd $350
Top-break, single-shot. SA. Calibers: 7-30 Waters, 7mm Super Mag., 7R (.30-30 Win. necked to 7mm), .30-30 Win. .357 Mag., .357 Super Mag., .32 H&R Mag., .22 Mag., .22 LR. 10- and 14-inch bbl. (10.5 inch for centerfire calibers). Weight: 50-71 oz. Partridge front sight, adj. rear. Walnut forend and grips.

MK-40
SILHOUETTE PISTOL . . . . NiB $1520 Ex $1050 Gd $850
Calibers: .22-250, 7mm IHMSA, .308 Win. Bolt-action, single-shot. 13-inch bbl., 19.5 inches overall. Weight: 72 oz. Wichita Multi-Range sight system. Aluminum receiver w/blued bbl., gray Fiberthane glass stock. Made 1981 to date.

SILHOUETTE
PISTOL (WSP) . . . . NiB $1875 Ex $1505 Gd $1200
Calibers: .22-250, 7mm IHMSA 308 Win. Bolt-action, single-shot. 14.94-inch bbl., 21.38 inches overall. Weight: 72 oz. Wichita Multi-Range sight system. Blued finish. Walnut or gray Fiberthane glass stock. Walnut center or rear grip. Made 1979 to date.

WILKINSON ARMS — Parma, Idaho

"LINDA" SEMI-
AUTOMATIC PISTOL . . . . NiB $675 Ex $625 Gd $350
Caliber: 9mm Para. Luger. 31-shot magazine, 8.25-inch bbl., 12.25 inches overall. Weight: 77 oz. Rear peep sight w/blade front. Blued finish. Checkered composition grips.

"SHERRY" SEMI-
AUTOMATIC PISTOL . . . . NiB $248 Ex $200 Gd $110
Caliber: .22 LR. Eight-shot magazine, 2.13-inch bbl., 4.38 inches overall. Weight: 9.25 oz. Crossbolt safety. Fixed sights. Blued or blue-gold finish. Checkered composition grips.

Learn the thrill of speed

The hunter who pursues grouse or woodcock needs a gun that can be carried all day and then move like lightning to a fast-disappearing target.

The Franchi Veloce Squire is for those who never stop chasing the most elusive game.

It's a no-compromise speedster whose very name means "fast." An aluminum receiver, reinforced on the breech face with steel, is fitted with 20-ga. and 28-ga. barrel sets that keep weight a just $5^{1}/_{2}$ pounds. It's no slowpoke in the looks department, with select walnut stock, gold-embellished game scenes, a rugged monobloc, even a filigreed top lever.

Veloce: learn the thrill of speed!

VELOCE SQUIRE & VELOCE   THINK SAFETY!

NEW! Veloce Squire™ 28-ga. and 20-ga. set

Veloce™ English Stock

Veloce Squire™ two gauge set

Franchi.

Uberti . . .
Home on the Range

Reach back across the
centuries and fill your hand
with a real piece of
Americana. Follow the trail
of inventors and adventurers
through the 19th century as
they set the standard for
design and craftsmanship
across the globe.
Uberti historical arms

faithfully replicate
the guns that helped forge
a new nation.
These replicas are the
ultimate in fit, finish,
attention to authentic
detail and accuracy.
More than just classic looks,
these firearms are the choice
of today's collectors
and competitive shooters.

A. Uberti
HISTORY REPEATS ITSELF

Stoeger Industries • 17603 Indian Head Highway, Suite 200 Accokeek, MD 20607-2501 • tel: (301) 283-6300 • fax: (301) 283-6986 • www.StoegerIndustries.com
Imported by Stoeger Industries®   Part of the Benelli USA® family

Twenty-Sixth Edition
GUN TRADER'S GUIDE

Rifles

Action Arms Timber Wolfe

Alpha Arms Custom

Alpha Arms Alaskan

Alpha Arms Jaguar

AA ARMS — Monroe, North Carolina

AR-9 SEMIAUTOMATIC CARBINE .... NiB $750 Ex $625 Gd $350
Semiautomatic recoil-operated rifle w/side-folding metal stock design. Fires from a closed bolt. Caliber: 9mm Parabellum. 20-shot magazine. 16.25-inch bbl., 33 inches overall. Weight: 6.5 lbs. Fixed blade, protected postfront sight adjustable for elevation, winged square notched rear. Matte phosphate/blue or nickel finish. Checkered polymer grip/frame. Made 1991-94.

ACTION ARMS — Philadelphia, Pennsylvania

MODEL B SPORTER
SEMI-AUTOMATIC CARBINE ..... NiB $545 Ex $475 Gd $300
Similar to Uzi Carbine (see separate listing) except w/thumbhole stock. Caliber: 9mm Parabellum, 10-shot magazine. 16-inch bbl. Weight: 8.75 lbs. Post front sight; adj. rear. Imported 1993-94.

TIMBER WOLFE REPEATING RIFLE
Calibers: .357 Mag./.38 Special and .44 Mag. slide-action. Tubular magazine holds 10 and 8 rounds, respectively. 18.5-inch bbl. 36.5 inches overall. Weight: 5.5 lbs. Fixed blade front sight; adj. rear. Receiver w/integral scope mounts. Checkered walnut stock. Imported 1989-94.

(cont'd.) TIMBER WOLFE REPEATING RIFLE
Blued model .... NiB $280 Ex $225 Gd $150
Chrome model, add................................$50
.44 Mag., add $100

ALPHA ARMS, INC. — Dallas, Texas

CUSTOM BOLT-ACTION RIFLE .... NiB $1525 Ex $1200 Gd $750
Calibers: .17 Rem. thru .338 Win. Mag. Right or left-hand action in three action lengths w/three-lug locking system and 60-degree bolt rotation. 20- to 24-inch round or octagonal bbl. Weight: 6 to 7 lbs. No sights. Presentation-grade California Claro walnut stock w/hand-rubbed oil finish, custom inletted sling swivels and ebony forend tip. Made 1984-89.

ALASKAN BOLT-ACTION RIFLE .... NiB $1525 Ex $1200 Gd $750
Similar to Custom model except w/stainless-steel bbl. and receiver w/all other parts coated w/Nitex. Weight: 6.75 to 7.25 lbs. Open sights w/bbl-band sling swivel. Classic-style Alpha wood stock w/Niedner-style steel grip cap and solid recoil pad. Made 1984-89.

GRAND SLAM
BOLT-ACTION RIFLE........... NiB $1200 Ex $950 Gd $650
Same as Custom model except w/Alphawood (fiberglass and wood) classic-style stock featuring Niedner-style grip cap. Weight: 6.5 lbs. Left-hand models. Made 1984-89.

AMT Magnum Hunter

JAGUAR BOLT-ACTION RIFLE

Same as Custom Rifle except designed on Mauser-style action w/claw extractor drilled and tapped for scope. Originally designated Alpha Model 1. Calibers: .243, 7mm-08, .308 original chambering (1984-85) up to .338 Win. Mag. in standard model; .338 thru .458 Win. Mag. in Big Five model (1984-85). Teflon-coated trigger guard/floorplate assembly. Made 1984-88.

Jaguar Grade I . . . . NiB $950 Ex $750 Gd $540
Jaguar Grade II . . . . NiB $1150 Ex $550 Gd $500
Jaguar Grade III . . . . NiB $1200 Ex $950 Gd $650
Jaguar Grade IV . . . . NiB $1300 Ex $950 Gd $650
Big Five model . . . . NiB $1550 Ex $1100 Gd $850

AMERICAN ARMS — N. Kansas City, Missouri

1860 HENRY . . . . NiB $835 Ex $625 Gd $350
Replica of 1860 Henry rifle. Calibers: .44-40 or .45 LC. 24.25-inch half-octagonal bbl. 43.75 inches overall. Weight: 9.25 lbs. Brass frame and appointments. Straight-grip walnut buttstock.

1866 WINCHESTER
Replica of 1866 Winchester. Calibers: .44-40 or .45 LC. 19-inch round tapered bbl. (carbine) or 24.25-inch tapered octagonal bbl. (rifle). 38 to 43.25 inches overall. Weight: 7.75 or 8.15 lbs. Brass frame, elevator and buttplate. Walnut buttstock and forend.
Carbine . . . . NiB $650 Ex $550 Gd $335
Rifle . . . . NiB $650 Ex $550 Gd $335

1873 WINCHESTER
Replica of 1873 Winchester rifle. Calibers: .44-40 or .45 LC. 24.25-inch tapered octagonal bbl. w/tubular magazine. Color casehardened steel frame w/brass elevator and ejection port cover. Walnut buttstock w/steel buttplate.
Standard model . . . . NiB $775 Ex $625 Gd $350
Deluxe model . . . . NiB $1012 Ex $810 Gd $550

AMT (ARCADIA MACHINE & TOOL) — Irwindale, California

BOLT-ACTION REPEATING RIFLE

Winchester-type push-feed or Mauser-type controlled-feed short-, medium- or long-action. Calibers: .223 Rem., .22-250 Rem., .243 A, .243 Win., 6mm PPC, .25-06 Rem., 6.5x08, .270 Win., 7x57 Mauser, 7mm-08 Rem., 7mm Rem Mag., 7.62x39mm, .308 Win., .30-06, .300 Win. Mag., .338 Win. Mag., .375 H&H, .416 Rem., .416 Rigby, .458 Win. Mag. 22- to 28-inch number 3 contour bbl. Weight: 7.75 to 8.5 lbs. Sights: None furnished; drilled and tapped for scope mounts. Classic composite or Kevlar stock. Made 1996-97.
Standard model . . . . NiB $800 Ex $625 Gd $450
Deluxe model . . . . NiB $1000 Ex $800 Gd $500

BOLT-ACTION SINGLE-SHOT RIFLE

Winchester-type cone breech push-feed or Mauser-type controlled-feed action. Calibers: .22 Hornet, .22 PPC, .222 Rem., .223 Rem., .22-250 Rem., .243 A, .243 Win., 6mm PPC, 6.5x08, .270 Win., 7mm-08 Rem., .308 Win. 22- to 28-inch #3 contour bbl. Weight: 7.75 to 8.5 lbs. Sights: None furnished; drilled and tapped for scope mounts. Classic composite or Kevlar stock. Made 1996-97.
Standard model . . . . NiB $825 Ex $650 Gd $500
Deluxe model . . . . NiB $995 Ex $800 Gd $600

CHALLENGER AUTOLOADING TARGET RIFLE SERIES I, II & III

Similar to Small Game Hunter except w/McMillan target fiberglass stock. Caliber: .22 LR. 10-shot magazine. 16.5-, 18-, 20- or 22-inch bull bbl. Drilled and tapped for scope mount; no sights. Stainless steel finish. Made 1994-98.
Challenger I Standard . . . . NiB $700 Ex $500 Gd $325
Challenger II w/muzzle brake . . . . . NiB $831 Ex $675 Gd $475
Challenger III w/bbl extension . . . . NiB $738 Ex $600 Gd $424
W/jewelled trigger, add $200

LIGHTNING 25/22

AUTOLOADING RIFLE . . . . NiB $220 Ex $175 Gd $110
Caliber: .22 LR. 25-shot magazine. 18-inch tapered or bull bbl. Weight: 6 lbs. 37 inches overall. Sights: Adj. rear; ramp front. Folding stainless-steel stock w/matte finish. Made 1984-94.

LIGHTNING SMALL GAME HUNTER SERIES

Similar to AMT 25/22 except w/conventional matte black fiberglass/nylon stock. 10-shot rotary magazine. 22-inch bbl. 40.5 inches overall. Weight: 6 lbs. Grooved for scope; no sights. Made 1987-94 (Series I), 1992-93 (Series II).
Hunter I . . . . NiB $208 Ex $170 Gd $110
Hunter II (w/22-inch
heavy target bbl.) . . . . NiB $225 Ex $180 Gd $120

MAGNUM HUNTER AUTO RIFLE . . . . NiB $369 Ex $295 Gd $201
Similar to Lightning Small Game Hunter II model except chambered in .22 WRF w/22-inch match-grade bbl. Made 1993 to date.

ANSCHUTZ RIFLES — Ulm, Germany Mfd. by J.G. Anschutz GmbH Jagd und Sportwaffenfabrik

Currently imported by AcuSport Corp.; Accuracy International; Champion's Choice; Champion Shooter's Supply, Go Sportsmen's Supply, Inc.; Gunsmithing Inc. (Previously by Precision Sales Int'l., Inc.)

Anschutz models 1407 ISU, 1408-ED, 1411, 1413, 1418, 1432, 1433, 1518 and 1533 were marketed in the U.S by Savage Arms. Further, Anschutz models 1403, 1416, 1422D, 1441, 1516 and 1522D were sold as Savage/Anschutz with Savage model designations (see also listings under Savage Arms.)

GRADING: NiB = New in Box   Ex = Excellent or NRA 95%   Gd = Good or NRA 68%

Anschutz Model 54.18MS-REP

Anschutz Model 1411

Anschutz Model 1413

MODEL 54 18MS . . . . **NiB $1200 Ex $950 Gd $650**
Bolt-action, single-shot, Caliber: .22 LR. 22-inch bbl. European hardwood stock w/cheekpiece. Stipple-checkered forend and Wundhammer swell pistol-grip. Receiver grooved, drilled and tapped for scope blocks. Weight: 8.4 lbs. Imported 1982-97.

MODEL 54.18MS-REP REPEATING RIFLE
Same as model 54.18MS except w/repeating action and 5-shot magazine. 22- to 30-inch bbl. 41-49 inches overall. Avg. weight: 7 lbs., 12 oz. Hardwood or synthetic gray thumbhole stock. Imported 1989-97.
Standard MS-
REP model . . . . **NiB $1350 Ex $1100 Gd $700**
MS-REP Deluxe
w/Fibergrain stock . . . . **NiB $1225 Ex $1000 Gd $650**

MODEL 64S BOLT-ACTION SINGLE-SHOT RIFLE
Bolt-action, single-shot. Caliber: .22 LR. 26-inch bbl. Checkered European hardwood stock w/Wundhammer swell pistol-grip and adj. buttplate. Single-stage trigger. Aperture sights. Weight: 8.25 lbs. Imported 1963-82.
Standard . . . . **NiB $500 Ex $350 Gd $250**
Left-hand model . . . . **NiB $500 Ex $350 Gd $275**

MODEL 64MS BOLT-ACTION SINGLE-SHOT RIFLE
Bolt-action, single-shot. Caliber: .22 LR. 21.25-inch bbl. European hardwood silhouette-style stock w/cheekpiece. Forend base and Wundhammer swell pistol-grip, stipple-checkered. Adj. two-stage trigger. Receiver grooved, drilled and tapped for scope blocks. Weight: 8 lbs. Imported 1982-96.
Standard or Featherweight
(disc. 1988) . . . . **NiB $775 Ex $675 Gd $325**
Left-hand model . . . . **NiB $800 Ex $680 Gd $440**

MODEL 64MSR BOLT-ACTION REPEATER
Similar to Anschutz Model 64MS except repeater w/5-shot magazine. Imported 1996 to date.
Standard model . . . . **NiB $775 Ex $675 Gd $400**
Left-hand model . . . . **NiB $800 Ex $675 Gd $400**

MODEL 520/61 SEMIAUTOMATIC. . . . . . . **NiB $395 Ex $250 Gd $100**
Caliber: .22 LR. 10-shot magazine. 24-inch bbl. Sights: Folding leaf rear, hooded ramp front. Receiver grooved for scope mounting. Rotary-style safety. Monte Carlo stock and beavertail forend, checkered. Weight: 6.5 lbs. Imported 1982-83.

MODEL 525 AUTOLOADER
Caliber: .22 LR. 10-shot magazine. 20- or 24-inch bbl. 39 to 43 inches overall. Weight: 6.1 to 6.5 lbs. Adj. folding rear sight; hooded ramp front. Checkered European hardwood Monte Carlo style buttstock and beavertail forend. Sling swivel studs. Imported since 1982.
Carbine model
(disc. 1986) . . . . **NiB $3800 Ex $250 Gd $150**
Rifle model (24-inch bbl.) . . . . **NiB $469 Ex $375 Gd $255**

MODEL 1403B . . . . **NiB $850 Ex $650 Gd $350**
A lighter-weight model designed for Biathlon competition. Caliber: .22 LR. 21.5-inch bbl. Adj. two-stage trigger. Adj. grooved wood buttplate, stipple-checkered deep thumb-rest flute and straight pistol-grip. Weight: 9 lbs. w/sights. Imported 1982-1992.

MODEL 1403D MATCH SINGLE-SHOT TARGET RIFLE
Caliber: .22 LR. 25-inch bbl. 43 inches overall. Weight: 8.6 lbs. No sights, receiver grooved for Anschutz target sights. Walnut-finished hardwood target stock w/adj. buttplate. Importation disc. 1992.
Standard model . . . . **NiB $619 Ex $495 Gd $337**
W/match sights . . . . **NiB $869 Ex $695 Gd $473**

Anschutz Model 1416D

Anschutz Model 1418

Anschutz Model 1422D

MODEL 1407 ISU MATCH 54 RIFLE
Bolt-action, single-shot, caliber: .22 LR. 26.88-inch bbl. Scope bases. Receiver grooved for Anschutz sights. Single-stage adj. trigger. Select walnut target stock w/deep forearm for position shooting, adj. buttplate, hand stop and swivel. Weight: 10 lbs. Imported 1970-81.
Standard model . . . . NiB $550 Ex $475 Gd $225
Left-hand model . . . . NiB $550 Ex $475 Gd $225
W/international sights, add $65

MODEL 1408-ED
SUPER RUNNING BOAR . . . . NiB $400 Ex $350 Gd $300
Bolt-action, single-shot, caliber: .22 LR. 23.5-inch bbl. w/sliding weights. No metallic sights. Receiver drilled and tapped for scope-sight bases. Single-stage adj. trigger. Oversize bolt knob. Select walnut stock w/thumbhole, adj. comb and buttplate. Weight: 9.5 lbs. Intro. 1976. Disc.

MODEL 1411 MATCH 54 RIFLE
Bolt-action, single-shot. Caliber: .22 LR. 27.5-inch extra heavy bbl. w/mounted scope bases. Receiver grooved for Anschutz sights. Single-stage adj. trigger. Select walnut target stock w/cheekpiece (adj. in 1973 and later production), full pistol-grip, beavertail forearm, adj. buttplate, hand stop and swivel. Model 1411-L has left-hand stock. Weight: 11 lbs. Disc.
W/Non-adj. cheekpiece . . . . NiB $400 Ex $350 Gd $200
W/adj. cheekpiece . . . . NiB $563 Ex $450 Gd $306
with Anschutz
International Sight set . . . . NiB $306 Ex $125 Gd $85

MODEL 1413 SUPER MATCH 54 RIFLE
Freestyle international target rifle w/specifications similar to those of Model 1411, except w/special stock w/thumbhole, adj. pistol grip, adj. cheekpiece in 1973 and later production, adj. hook buttplate, adj. palmrest. Model 1413-L has left-hand stock. Weight: 15.5 lbs. Disc.
W/Non-adj. cheekpiece . . . . NiB $725 Ex $650 Gd $330
W/Adj. cheekpiece . . . . NiB $606 Ex $485 Gd $300
With Anschutz
International Sight set $275

MODEL 1416D . . . . NiB $518 Ex $500 Gd $300
Bolt-action sporter. Caliber: .22 LR. 22.5-inch bbl. Sights: Folding leaf rear; hooded ramp front. Receiver grooved for scope mounting. Select European stock w/cheekpiece, skip-checkered pistol grip and forearm. Weight: 6 lbs. Imported 1982 to date.

MODEL 1416D CLASSIC/CUSTOM SPORTERS
Same as Model 1416D except w/American classic-style stock (Classic) or modified European-style stock w/Monte Carlo roll-over cheekpiece and Schnabel forend (Custom). Weight: 5.5 lbs. (Classic); 6 lbs. (Custom). Imported 1986 to date.
Model 1416D Classic . . . . NiB $575 Ex $460 Gd $313
Model 1416D Classic,
"True" left-hand . . . . NiB $619 Ex $495 Gd $337
Model 1416D Custom . . . . NiB $556 Ex $445 Gd $303
Model 1416D fiberglass (1991-92) . . . . NiB $681 Ex $545 Gd $371

MODEL 1418 BOLT-ACTION
SPORTER . . . . NiB $350 Ex $275 Gd $150
Caliber: .22 LR. 5- or 10-shot magazine. 19.75-inch bbl. Sights: Folding leaf rear; hooded ramp front. Receiver grooved for scope mounting. Select walnut stock, Mannlicher type w/cheekpiece, pistol-grip and forearm skip checkered. Weight: 5.5 lbs. Intro. 1976. Disc.

MODEL 1418D BOLT-ACTION
SPORTER . . . . NiB $895 Ex $785 Gd $450
Caliber: .22 LR. 5- or 10-shot magazine. 19.75-inch bbl. European walnut Monte Carlo stock, Mannlicher type w/cheekpiece, pistol-grip and forend skip-line checkered, buffalo horn Schnabel tip. Weight: 5.5 lbs. Imported from 1982-95 and 1998 to date.

MODEL 1422D CLASSIC/CUSTOM RIFLE
Bolt-action sporter. Caliber: .22 LR. 5-shot removable straight-feed clip magazine. 24-inch bbl. Sights: Folding leaf rear; hooded ramp front. Select European walnut stock, classic type (Classic); Monte Carlo w/hand-carved rollover cheekpiece (Custom). Weight: 7.25 lbs. (Classic) 6.5 lbs. (Custom). Imported 1982-89.
Model 1422D Classic . . . . NiB $725 Ex $575 Gd $350
Model 1422D Custom . . . . NiB $800 Ex $725 Gd $400

Anschutz Model 1427B

Anschutz Model 1432

Anschutz Model 1432D

MODEL 1427B BIATHLON RIFLE

Bolt-action clip repeater. Caliber: .22 LR. 21.5-inch bbl. Two-stage trigger w/wing-type safety. Hardwood stock w/deep fluting, pistol grip and deep forestock with adj. hand stop rail. Target sights w/adjustable weights. Advertised in 1981 but imported from 1982 to date as Model 1827B. (See that model designation for current values)

MODEL 1430D MATCH . . . . NiB $675 Ex $550 Gd $330

Improved version of Model 64S. Bolt-action, single-shot. Caliber: .22 LR. 26-inch medium-heavy bbl. Walnut Monte Carlo stock w/cheekpiece, adj. buttplate, deep midstock tapered to forend. Pistol-grip and contoured thumb groove w/stipple checkering. Single-stage adj. trigger. Target sights. Weight: 8.38 lbs. Imported 1982-83.

MODEL 1432 BOLT-ACTION SPORTER

Caliber: .22 Hornet. 5-shot box magazine. 24-inch bbl. Sights: Folding leaf rear, hooded ramp front. Receiver grooved for scope mounting. Select walnut stock w/Monte Carlo comb and cheekpiece, pistol-grip and forearm skip-checkered. Weight: 6.75 lbs. Imported 1974-87. (Reintroduced as 1700/1730 series)

Early model
(1974-85). . . . . NiB $1190 Ex $850 Gd $600
Late model
(1985-87). . . . . NiB $1025 Ex $800 Gd $525

MODEL 1432D CLASSIC/CUSTOM RIFLE

Bolt-action sporter similar to Model 1422D except chambered for Caliber: .22 Hornet. 4-shot magazine. 23.5-inch bbl. Weight: 7.75 lbs. (Classic); 6.5 lbs. (Custom). Classic stock on Classic model; fancy-grade Monte Carlo w/hand-carved rollover cheekpiece (Custom). Imported 1982-87. (Reintroduced as 1700/1730 series)

Model 1432D Classic . . . . NiB $1190 Ex $850 Gd $600
Model 1432D Custom. . . . . NiB $1025 Ex $800 Gd $525

MODEL 1433 BOLT-ACTION SPORTER . . . . . NiB $1005 Ex $800 Gd $550

Caliber: .22 Hornet. 5-shot box magazine. 19.75-inch bbl. Sights: Folding leaf rear, hooded ramp front. Receiver grooved for scope mounting. Single-stage or double-set trigger. Select walnut Mannlicher stock; cheekpiece, pistol-grip and forearm skip-checkered. Weight: 6.5 lbs. Imported 1976-86.

MODEL 1448D CLAY BIRD. . . . . . . NiB $295 Ex $265 Gd $180

Similar to Model 1449 except chambered for Caliber: .22 LR. w/22.5-inch smooth bore bbl. and no sights. Walnut-finished hardwood stock. Imported 1999 to date.

MODEL 1449 YOUTH SPORTER . . . . NiB $230 Ex $185 Gd $125

Bolt-action sporter version of Model 2000. Caliber: .22 LR. 5-shot box magazine. 16.25-inch bbl. Weight: 3.5 lbs. Hooded ramp front sight, addition. Walnut-finished hardwood stock. Imported 1989-92.

MODEL 1450B TARGET RIFLE . . . . NiB $625 Ex $450 Gd $300

Biathlon rifle developed on 2000 Series action. 19.5-inch bbl. Weight: 5.5 lbs. Adj. buttplate. Target sights. Imported 1993-94.

MODEL 1451 E/R SPORTER/TARGET

Bolt-action, single-shot (1451E) or repeater (1451R). Caliber: .22 LR. 22- or 22.75-inch bbl. w/o sights. Select hardwood stock w/stippled pistolgrip and vented forearm. beavertail forend, adj. cheekpiece, and deep thumb flute. Weight: 6.5 lbs. Imported 1996 to date.
Model 1451E (disc. 1997) . . . . NiB $400 Ex $300 Gd $200
Model 1451R . . . . NiB $435 Ex $395 Gd $260

MODEL 1451D CLASSIC/CUSTOM RIFLE

Same as Model 1451R except w/walnut-finished hardwood stock (Classic) or modified European-style walnut stock w/Monte Carlo rollover cheekpiece and Schnabel forend (Custom). Weight: 5 lbs. Imported 1996 to date.
Model 1451D Classic (Super) . . . . . NiB $300 Ex $225 Gd $150
Model 1451D Custom. . . . . NiB $435 Ex $395 Gd $260

Anschutz Model 1700

Anschutz Model 1803D

Anschutz Model 1907

MODEL 1451 ST- R RIFLE . . . . NiB $435 Ex $395 Gd $280
Same as Model 1451R except w/two-stage trigger and walnut-finished hardwood uncheckered stock. Imported 1999 to date.

MODEL 1516D CLASSIC/CUSTOM RIFLE
Same as Model 1416D except chambered for Caliber: .22 Magnum RF, with American classic-style stock (Classic) or modified European-style stock w/Monte Carlo rollover cheekpiece and Schnabel forend (Custom). Weight: 5.5 lbs. (Classic), 6 lbs. (Custom). Imported 1986 to date.
Model 1516D Classic . . . . NiB $650 Ex $500 Gd $325
Model 1516D Custom . . . . NiB $675 Ex $550 Gd $350

MODELS 1516D/1518D LUXUS RIFLES
The alpha designation for these models was changed from Custom to Luxus in 1996-98. (See current Custom listings for Luxus values.)

MODELS 1518/1518D SPORTING RIFLES
Same as Model 1418 except chambered for .22 Magnum RF, 4-shot box magazine. Model 1518 intro. 1976. Disc. Model 1518D has full Mannlicher-type stock. Imported 1982 to date.
Model 1518. . . . . NiB $700 Ex $580 Gd $350
Model 1518D . . . . NiB $895 Ex $700 Gd $475
W/set trigger, add $125

MODEL 1522D CLASSIC/CUSTOM RIFLE
Same as Model 1422D except chambered for .22 Magnum RF, 4-shot magazine. Weight: 6.5 lbs. (Custom). Fancy-grade Classic or Monte Carlo stock w/hand-carved rollover cheekpiece. Imported 1982-89. (Reintroduced as 1700D/1730D series)
Model 1522D Classic . . . . NiB $1000 Ex $800 Gd $550
Model 1522D Custom . . . . NiB $1000 Ex $800 Gd $550

MODEL 1532D CLASSIC/CUSTOM RIFLE
Same as Model 1432D except chambered for .222 Rem. Three-shot mag. Weight: 6.5 lbs. (Custom). Classic stock on Classic Model; fancy-grade Monte Carlo stock w/handcarved rollover cheekpiece (Custom). Imported 1982-89. (Reintroduced as 1700D/174 D0 series)
Model 1532D Classic . . . . NiB $895 Ex $700 Gd $350
Model 1532D Custom . . . . NiB $1190 Ex $900 Gd $600

MODEL 1533 . . . . NiB $1000 Ex $750 Gd $500
Same as Model 1433 except chambered for .222 Rem. Three-shot box magazine. Imported 1976-94.

MODEL 1700 SERIES BOLT-ACTION REPEATER
Match 54 Sporter. Calibers: .22 LR., .22 Magnum, .22 Hornet, .222 Rem. Five-shot removable magazine 24-inch bbl. 43 inches overall. Weight: 7.5 lbs. Folding leaf rear sight, hooded ramp front. Select European walnut stock w/cheekpiece and Schnabel forend tip. Imported 1989 to date.
Standard Model 1700
Bavarian — rimfire cal. . . . . NiB $915 Ex $835 Gd $475
Standard Model 1700
Bavarian — centerfire cal. . . . . NiB $1225 Ex $950 Gd $600
**Model 1700D Classic (Classic
stock, 6.75 lbs.) rimfire cal. . . . . . . NiB $1075 Ex $895 Gd $600**
Model 1700D Classic — centerfire cal. . . . . . NiB $1188 Ex $950 Gd $646
Model 1700D Custom — rimfire cal. . . . . NiB $994 Ex $795 Gd $541
Model 1700D Custom — centerfire cal. . . . . . NiB $1219 Ex $975 Gd $663
**Model 1700D Graphite Cust. (McMillian graphite
reinforced stock, 22 inch bbl., intro. 1991) . . NiB $1050 Ex $875 Gd $550**
Select walnut and gold trigger . . . . add $181
**Model 1700 FWT Feather-
weight (6.5 lbs.) rimfire calibers . . . . NiB $1031 Ex $825 Gd $561**
Model 1700 FWT — centerfire cal. . . . . NiB $1200 Ex $1050 Gd $650

Anschutz Model 2013

MODEL 1733D MANNLICHER........ NiB $1255 Ex $1050 Gd $750
Same as Model 1700D except w/19-inch bbl. and Mannlicher-style stock. 39 inches overall. Weight: 6.25 lbs. Imported 1993-96 (Reintroduced in 1998).

MODEL 1740 MONTE CARLO SPORTER
Caliber: .22 Hornet or .222 Rem. Three and 5-shot magazines respectively. 24-inch bbl. 43.25 inches overall. Weight: 6.5 lbs. Hooded ramp front, folding leaf rear. Drilled and tapped for scope mounts. Select European walnut stock w/roll-over cheekpiece, checkered grip and forend. Imported 1997 to date.
Model 1740 Custom .... NiB $1208 Ex $950 Gd $600
Model 1740 Classic
(Meistergrade) .... NiB $1369 Ex $1095 Gd $745

MODEL 1743 MONTE CARLO
SPORTER .... NiB $1225 Ex $1000 Gd $650
Similar to Model 1740 except w/Mannlicher full stock. Imported 1997 to date.

MODEL 1803D MATCH SINGLE-SHOT TARGET RIFLE
Caliber: .22 LR. 25.5-inch bbl. 43.75 inches overall. Weight: 8.5 lbs. No sights; receiver grooved, drilled and tapped for scope mounts. Blonde or walnut-finished hardwood stock w/adj. cheekpiece, stippled grip and forend. Left-hand version. Imported 1987-92.
Right-hand model
(Reintroduced as 1903D) .... NiB $900 Ex $750 Gd $450
Left-hand model .... NiB $969 Ex $775 Gd $527

MODEL 1807 ISU
STANDARD MATCH .... NiB $1225 Ex $950 Gd $600
Bolt-action single-shot. Caliber: 22 LR. 26-inch bbl. Improved Super Match 54 action. Two-stage match trigger. Removable cheekpiece, adj. buttplate, thumbpiece and forestock w/stipple-checkered. Weight: 10 lbs. Imported 1982-88. (Reintroduced as 1907 ISU)

MODEL 1808ED SUPER RUNNING TARGET
Bolt-action single-shot. Caliber: .22 LR. 23.5-inch bbl. w/sliding weights. Improved Super Match 54 action. Heavy beavertail forend w/adj.cheekpiece and buttplate. Adj. single-stage trigger. Weight: 9.5 lbs. Imported from 1982-96.
Right-hand model .... NiB $1490 Ex $1200 Gd $750
Left-hand model .... NiB $1531 Ex $1225 Gd $833

MODEL 1808MS-R
METALLIC SILHOUETTE .... NiB $1850 Ex $1400 Gd $800
Bolt-action repeater. Caliber: .22 LR. 19.2-inch bbl. w/o sights. Thumbhole Monte Carlo stock w/grooved forearm enhanced w/ "Anschutz" logo. Weight: 8.2 lbs. Imported from 1998 to date.

MODEL 1810 SUPER MATCH II....... NiB $1825 Ex $1300 Gd $800
A less detailed version of the Super Match 1813 model. Tapered forend w/deep receiver area. Select European hardwood stock.

Weight: 13.5 lbs. Imported 1982-88 (reintroduced as 1910 series).
MODEL 1811 PRONE MATCH....... NiB $1680 Ex $1475 Gd $740
Bolt-action single-shot. Caliber: .22 LR. 27.5-inch bbl. Improved Super Match 54 action. Select European hardwood stock w/beavertail forend, adj. cheekpiece, and deep thumb flute. Thumb groove and pistol grip w/stipple checkering. Adj. buttplate. Weight: 11.5 lbs. Imported 1982-88. (Reintroduced as 1911Prone Match)

MODEL 1813 SUPER MATCH........ NiB $2120 Ex $1800 Gd $750
Bolt-action single-shot. Caliber: .22 LR. 27.5-inch bbl. Improved Super Match 54 action w/light firing pin, one-point adj. trigger. European walnut thumbhole stock, adj. palm rest, forend and pistol grip stipple checkered. Adj. cheekpiece and hook buttplate. Weight: 15.5 lbs. Imported 1982-88. (Reintroduced as 1913 Super Match)

MODEL 1827 BIATHLON RIFLE
Bolt-action clip repeater. Caliber: .22 LR. 21.5-inch bbl. 42.5 inches overall. Weight: 8.5 to 9 lbs. Slide safety. Adj. target sight set w/snow caps. European walnut stock w/cheekpiece, stippled pistol grip and forearm w/adj. weights. Fortner straight pull bolt option offered in 1986. Imported 1982 to date.
Mdl. 1827B w/Sup. Mat. 54 action .... NiB $2200 Ex $2000 Gd $900
Model 1827B, left-hand .... NiB $1954 Ex $1580 Gd $1102
Model 1827BT w/Fortner
Option, right-hand .... NiB $2300 Ex $2100 Gd $900
Model 1827BT, left-hand .... NiB $2454 Ex $1980 Gd $1374
Model 1827BT w/laminated stock, add $175
W/stainless steel bbl., add $205

MODEL 1907 ISU INTERNATIONAL MATCH RIFLE
Updated version of Model 1807 w/same general specifications as Model 1913 except w/26-inch bbl. 44.5 inches overall. Weight: 11 lbs. Designed for ISU 3-position competition. Fitted w/vented beechwood or walnut, blonde or color-laminated stock. Imported 1989 to date.
Right-hand model .... NiB $1435 Ex $1250 Gd $750
Left-hand model .... NiB $1616 Ex $1310 Gd $918
W/laminated stock, add $135
W/walnut stock, add $100
W/stainless steel bbl., add $130

MODEL 1910 INTERNATIONAL SUPER MATCH RIFLE
Updated version of Model 1810 w/same general specifications Model 1913 except w/less-detailed hardwood stock w/tapered forend. Weight: 13.5 lbs. Imported 1989 to date.
Right-hand model .... NiB $2400 Ex $1925 Gd $980
Left-hand model .... NiB $2394 Ex $1945 Gd $1371

MODEL 1911 PRONE MATCH RIFLE
Updated version of Model 1811 w/same general specifications Model 1913 except w/specialized prone match hardwood stock w/beavertail forend. Weight: 11.5 lbs. Imported 1989 to date.
Right-hand model .... NiB $2200 Ex $2000 Gd $900

Anschutz Achiever

Armalite AR-10

RIFLES

MODEL 1912
LADIES' SPORT RIFLE . . . . NiB $1690 Ex $1480 Gd $750
Similar to the Model 1907 designed for ISU 3-position competition w/same general U.I.T. specifications except w/shorter dimensions to accomode smaller competitors. Weight: 11.4 lbs. Imported 1999 to date.

MODEL 1913 STANDARD RIFLE . . . . . . NiB $1458 Ex $1100 Gd $750
Similar to 1913 Super Match w/economized appointments. Imported 1997 to date.

MODEL 1913 SUPER MATCH RIFLE
Bolt-action single-shot Super Match (updated version of Model 1813). Caliber: .22 LR. 27.5-inch bbl. Weight: 14.2 lbs. Adj. two-stage trigger. Vented International thumbhole stock w/adj. cheekpiece, hand and palm rest, fitted w/10-way butthook. Imported 1989 to date.

Right-hand model	NiB $2120	Ex $1800	Gd $750
Left-hand model	NiB $2188	Ex $1750	Gd $1190
W/laminated stock, add			$130
W/stainless			
steel bbl., add			$140

MODEL 2007 ISU STANDARD RIFLE
Bolt-action single-shot. Caliber: .22 LR. 19.75-inch bbl. 43.5 to 44.5 inches overall. Weight: 10.8 lbs. Two-stage trigger. Standard ISU stock w/adj. cheekpiece. Imported 1992 to date.

Right-hand model	NiB $1825	Ex $1375	Gd $780
Left-hand model	NiB $1929	Ex $1560	Gd $1088
W/stainless steel bbl., add			$140

MODEL 2013
LADIES' SPORT RIFLE . . . . NiB $2025 Ex $1850 Gd $790
Similar to the Model 2007 designed for ISU 3-position competition w/same general U.I.T. specifications except w/shorter dimensions to acco-modate smaller competitors. Weight: 11.4 lbs. Imported 1999 to date.

MODEL 2013
BENCHREST RIFLE (BR-50) . . . . . NiB $1635 Ex $1475 Gd $750
Bolt-action single-shot. Caliber: .22 LR. 19.6-inch bbl. 43 inches overall. Weight: 10.3 lbs. Adjustable trigger for single or two-stage function. Benchrest-configuration stock. Imported 1999 to date.

MODEL 2013 SILHOUETTE RIFLE . . . . NiB $2010 Ex $1500 Gd $800
Bolt-action single-shot. Caliber: .22 LR. 20-inch bbl. 45.5 inches overall. Weight: 11.5 lbs. Two-stage trigger. Thumbhole black synthetic or laminat-ed stock w/adj. cheekpiece, hand and palm rest. Imported 1994 to date.

MODEL 2013 SUPER MATCH RIFLE
Bolt-action single-shot. Caliber: .22 LR. 19.75- or 27.1-inch bbl. 43 to 50.1 inches overall. Weight: 15.5 lbs. Two-stage trigger. International thumbhole, black synthetic or laminated stock w/adj. cheekpiece, hand and palm rest; fitted w/10-way butthook. Imported 1992 to date.

Right-hand model	NiB $2350	Ex $2120	Gd $1000
Left-hand model	NiB $2329	Ex $1880	Gd $1306
W/laminated stock, add			$180

ACHIEVER BOLT-ACTION RIFLE . . . . NiB $350 Ex $275 Gd $150
Caliber: .22 LR. 5-shot magazine. Mark 2000-type repeating action. 19.5-inch bbl. 36.5 inches overall. Weight: 5 lbs. Adj. open rear sight; hooded ramp front. Plain European hardwood target-style stock w/vented forend and adj. buttplate. Imported since 1987.

ACHIEVER ST-SUPER TARGET . . . . . NiB $475 Ex $350 Gd $200
Same as Achiever except single-shot w/22-inch bbl. and adj. stock. 38.75 inches overall. Weight: 6.5 lbs. Target sights. Imported since 1994.

BR-50 BENCH REST RIFLE . . . . . NiB $1950 Ex $1525 Gd $900
Single-shot. Caliber: .22 LR. 19.75-inch bbl. (23 inches w/muzzle weight). 37.75-42.5 inches overall. Weight: 11 lbs. Grooved receiver, no sights. Walnut-finished hardwood or synthetic benchrest stock w/adj. cheekpiece. Imported 1994-97. (Reintroduced as Model 2013 BR-50)

KADETT BOLT-ACTION
REPEATING RIFLE . . . . NiB $300 Ex $200 Gd $125
Caliber: .22 LR. 5-shot detachable box magazine. 22-inch bbl. 40 inches overall. Weight: 5.5 lbs. Adj. folding leaf rear sight; hooded ramp front. Checkered European hardwood stock w/walnut-finish. Imported 1987-88.

MARK 2000 MATCH . . . . NiB $395 Ex $290 Gd $175
Takedown, bolt-action single-shot. Caliber: .22 LR. 26-inch heavy bbl. Walnut stock w/deep-fluted thumb-groove, Wundhammer swell pistol grip, beavertail forend. Adj. buttplate, single-stage adj. trigger. Weight: 8 lbs. Imported 1982-89.

Armalite AR-10 (T) Target Carbine

Armalite M-15A2 National Match

Armalite M-15A2 HBAR

ARMALITE, INC. — Geneseo, Illinois (Formerly Costa Mesa, California)

Armalite was in Costa Mesa, California from 1959-73. Following the acquisition by Eagle Arms in 1995, production resumed under the Armalite, Inc. Logo in Geneseo, Illinois.

Production by ARMALITE

AR-7 EXPLORER SURVIVAL RIFLE. . . NiB $135 Ex $110 Gd $60
Takedown. Semiautomatic. Caliber: .22 LR. Eight-shot box magazine. 16-inch cast aluminum bbl. w/steel liner. Sights: Peep rear; blade front. Brown plastic stock, recessed to stow barrel, action, and magazine. Weight: 2.75 lbs. Will float stowed or assembled. Made 1959-1973 by Armalite; 1974-90 by Charter Arms; 1990-97 by Survival Arms, Cocoa, FL.; 1997 to date by Henry Repeating Arms Co., Brooklyn, NY.

AR-7 EXPLORER CUSTOM RIFLE . . . NiB $185 Ex $150 Gd $75
Same as AR-7 Survival Rifle except w/deluxe walnut stock w/cheekpiece and pistol grip. Weight: 3.5 lbs. Made 1964-70.

AR-180 SEMIAUTOMATIC RIFLE
Commercial version of full automatic AR-18 Combat Rifle. Gas-operated semiautomatic. Caliber: .223 Rem. (5.56mm). Five, 20-, 30-round magazines. 18.25-inch bbl. w/flash hider/muzzle brake. Sights: Flip-up "L" type rear, adj. for windage; post front, adj. for

(cont'd.) AR-180 SEMIAUTOMATIC RIFLE
elevation. Accessory: 3x scope and mount (add $60 to value). Folding buttstock of black nylon, rubber buttplate and pistol grip, heat dissipating fiberglass forend (hand guard), swivels, sling. 38 inches overall, 28.75 inches folded. Weight: 6.5 lbs. Note: Made by Armalite Inc. 1969-72, manufactured for Armalite by Howa Machinery Ltd., Nagoya, Japan, 1972-73; by Sterling Armament Co. Ltd., Dagenham, Essex, England, 1976 to 94. Importation disc.
Armalite AR-180 (Mfg. by
Armalite-Costa Mesa) . . . . NiB $1200 Ex $1000 Gd $700
Armalite AR-180 (Mfg. by Howa) . . . . . . NiB $1369 Ex $1095 Gd $745
Armalite AR-180 (Mfg. by Sterling). . . . . . . NiB $994 Ex $795 Gd $541
W/3x scope and mount, add. $225

Production by ARMALITE, Inc.

AR-10 (A) SEMIAUTOMATIC SERIES
Gas-operated semiautomatic action. Calibers: .243 Win. or .308 Win. (7.62 x 51mm). 10-shot magazine. 16- or 20-inch bbl. 35.5 or 39.5 inches overall. Weight: 9 to 9.75 lbs. Post front sight, adj. aperature rear. Black or green composition stock. Made 1995 to date.
AR-10 A2 (Std. carbine). . . . . NiB $1825 Ex $1525 Gd $600
AR-10 A2 (Std. rifle) . . . . NiB $1175 Ex $995 Gd $575
AR-10 A4 (S.P. carbine) . . . . NiB $1225 Ex $995 Gd $575
AR-10 A4 (S.P. rifle). . . . . NiB $1225 Ex $995 Gd $575
W/stainless steel bbl., add. $120

Armi Jager AP-74 Wood Stock

AR-10 (T) TARGET
Similar to Armalite Model AR-10A except in National Match configuration w/three-slot short Picatinny rail system and case deflector. 16- or 24-inch bbl. Weight: 8.25 to 10.4 lbs. Composite stock and handguard. No sights. Optional National Match carry handle and detachable front sight. Made 1995 to date.
AR-10 T (Rifle)............. NiB $1825 Ex $1525 Gd $900
AR-10 T (Carbine) .... NiB $1825 Ex $1525 Gd $900

MODEL AR-50 SS BOLT-ACTION
RIFLE..................... NiB $2300 Ex $1950 Gd $1200
Caliber: .50 BMG. 31-inch bbl. w/muzzle brake. 59 inches overall. Weight: 41 lbs. Modified octagonal-form receiver, drilled and slotted for scope rail. Single-stage trigger. Triple front-locking bolt lug w/spring-loaded plunger for automatic ejection. Magnesium phosphate steel, hard-anodized aluminum finish. Made 1999 to date.

M15 SERIES
Gas-operated semiautomatic w/A2-style forward-assist mechanism and push-type pivot pin for easy takedown. Caliber: .223. 7-shot magazine. 16-, 20- or 24-inch bbl. Weight: 7-9.2 lbs. Composite or retractable stock. Fully adj. sights. Black anodized finish. Made 1995 to date.
M-15A2 (Carbine) ....NiB $825 Ex $700 Gd $550
M-15A2 (Service Rifle) ....NiB $875 Ex $750 Gd $560
M-15A2 (National Match)............NiB $1225 Ex $995 Gd $650
M-15A2
(Golden Eagle heavy bbl.)..........NiB $1200 Ex $975 Gd $625
M-15A2 M4C
(retractable stock, disc. 1997)..........NiB $1150 Ex $890 Gd $575
M-15A4 (Action Master, disc. 1997).....NiB $1031 Ex $825 Gd $561
M-15A4 (Predator) ....NiB $875 Ex $750 Gd $560
M-15A4 (S.P. Rifle) ....NiB $850 Ex $700 Gd $450
M-15A4 (S.P. Carbine)................NiB $800 Ex $650 Gd $400
M-15A4T (Eagle Eye Carbine)..........NiB $1200 Ex $950 Gd $650
M-15A4T (Eagle Eye Rifle)............NiB $1250 Ex $925 Gd $650

ARMI JAGER — Turin, Italy

AP-74 COMMANDO............ NiB $250 Ex $190 Gd $120
Similar to standard AP-74 but styled to resemble original version of Uzi 9mm submachine gun w/wood buttstock. Lacks carrying handle and flash suppressor. Has different type front sight mount and guards, wood stock, pistol grip and forearm. Intro. 1976. Disc.

AP-74 SEMIAUTOMATIC RIFLE
Styled after U.S. M16 military rifle. Caliber: .22 LR, .32 Auto (pistol cartridge). Detachable clip magazine; capacity: 14 rounds caliber .22 LR, 9 rounds .32 ACP. 20-inch bbl. w/flash suppressor. Weight: 6.5 lbs. M16 type sights. Stock, pistol-grip and forearm of black plastic, swivels and sling. Intro. 1974. Disc.
.22 LR....................... NiB $300 Ex $250 Gd $150
.32 Auto..................... NiB $325 Ex $275 Gd $160

AP-74 WOOD STOCK MODEL
Same as standard AP-74 except w/wood stock, pistol-grip and forearm weight: 7 lbs. Disc.
.22 LR .... NiB $375 Ex $300 Gd $190
.32 Auto..................... NiB $400 Ex $300 Gd $190

ARMSCOR (Arms Corp.) — Manila, Philippines (Imported until 1991 by Armscor Precision, San Mateo, CA; 1991-95 by Ruko Products, Inc., Buffalo NY: Currently imported by K.B.I., Harrisburg, PA)

MODEL 20 AUTO RIFLE
Caliber: .22 LR. 15-shot magazine. 21-inch bbl. 39.75 inches overall. Weight: 6.5 lbs. Sights: Hooded front; adj. rear. Checkered or plain walnut finished mahogany stock. Blued finish. Imported 1990-91. (Reinstated by Ruko in the M series.)
Model 20 (checkered stock) .... NiB $119 Ex $95 Gd $65
Model 20C (carbine-style stock) ..... NiB $106 Ex $85 Gd $58
Model 20P (plain stock) .... NiB $94 Ex $75 Gd $51

MODEL 1600 AUTO RIFLE
Caliber: .22 LR. 15-shot magazine. 19.5-inch bbl. 38 inches overall. Weight: 6 lbs. Sights: Post front; aperture rear. Plain mahogany stock. Matte black finish. Imported 1987-91. (Reinstated by Ruko in the M series.)
Standard model .... NiB $140 Ex $100 Gd $70
Retractable stock model .... NiB $150 Ex $115 Gd $75

MODEL AK22 AUTO RIFLE
Caliber: .22 LR. 15- or 30-shot magazine. 18.5-inch bbl. 36 inches overall. Weight: 7 lbs. Sights: Post front; adj. rear. Plain mahogany stock. Matte black finish. Imported 1987-91.
Standard model .... NiB $185 Ex $165 Gd $100
Folding stock model .... NiB $200 Ex $170 Gd $125

MODEL M14 SERIES BOLT-ACTION RIFLE
Caliber: .22 LR. 10-shot magazine. 23-inch bbl. Weight: 6.25 lbs. Open sights. Walnut or walnut finished mahogany stock. Imported 1991-97.
M14P Standard model.............. NiB $95 Ex $70 Gd $45
M14D Deluxe model
(checkered stock, disc. 1995) .... NiB $81 Ex $65 Gd $44

MODEL M20 SERIES SEMIAUTOMATIC RIFLE
Caliber: .22 LR. 10- or 15-shot magazine. 18.25- or 20.75-inch bbl. Weight:5.5 to 6.5 lbs. 38 to 40.5 inches overall. Hooded front sight w/windage adj. rear. Walnut finished mahogany stock. Imported 1990-97.
M20C carbine model .... NiB $100 Ex $80 Gd $50
M20P standard model.................. NiB $90 Ex $70 Gd $50
M20S Sporter Deluxe (checkered
mahogany stock)...................... NiB $125 Ex $110 Gd $60
M20SC Super Classic (checkered
walnut stock) .... NiB $250 Ex $195 Gd $80

A-Square — Hannibal

MODEL M1400 BOLT-ACTION RIFLE
Similar to Model 14P except w/checkered stock w/Schnabel forend. Weight: 6 lbs. Imported 1990-97.
M1400LW (Lightweight, disc. 1992) . . . . . . NiB $190 Ex $160 Gd $100
M1400S (Sporter) . . . . NiB $125 Ex $100 Gd $70
M1400SC (Super Classic) . . . . NiB $244 Ex $195 Gd $133

MODEL M1500 BOLT-ACTION RIFLE
Caliber: .22 Mag. 5-shot magazine. 21.5-inch bbl. Weight: 6.5 lbs. Open sights. Checkered mahogany stock. Imported 1991-97.
M1500 (standard) . . . . NiB $125 Ex $100 Gd $70
M1500LW (Euro-style walnut
stock, disc. 1992) . . . . NiB $175 Ex $150 Gd $100
M1500SC (Monte Carlo stock) . . . . NiB $180 Ex $150 Gd $110

MODEL M1600 AUTO RIFLE
Rimfire replica of Armalite Model AR 180 (M16) except chambered for Caliber .22 LR. 15-shot magazine. 18-inch bbl. Weight: 5.25 lbs. Composite or retractable buttstock w/composite handguard and pistol grip. Carrying handle w/adj. aperture rear sight and protected post front. Black anodized finish. Imported 1991-97.
M-1600 (standard w/fixed stock) . . . . . . NiB $144 Ex $115 Gd $78
M-1600R (retractable stock) . . . . NiB $156 Ex $125 Gd $85

MODEL M1800 BOLT-ACTION RIFLE
Caliber: .22 Hornet. 5-shot magazine. 22-inch bbl. Weight: 6.6 lbs. Checkered hardwood or walnut stock. Sights: Post front; adj. rear. Imported 1995 to date.
M-1800 (standard) . . . . NiB $250 Ex $180 Gd $125
M-1800SC (checkered walnut stock) . . . . . NiB $350 Ex $280 Gd $200

MODEL M2000 AUTO RIFLE
Similar to Model 20P except w/checkered mahogany stock and adj. sights. Imported 1991 to date.
M2000S (standard) . . . . NiB $125 Ex $100 Gd $68
M2000SC (checkered walnut stock) . . . . . . NiB $231 Ex $185 Gd $126

ARNOLD ARMS — Arlington, Washington

AFRICAN SAFARI
Calibers: .243 to .458 Win. Magnum. 22- to 26-inch bbl. Weight: 7-9 lbs. Scope mount standard or w/optional M70 Express sights. Chrome-moly in four finishes. "A" and "AA" Fancy Grade English walnut stock with number 5 standard wraparound checkering pattern. Ebony forend tip. Made 1996 to date.
With "A" Grade English
walnut: matte blue . . . . NiB $4369 Ex $3495 Gd $2377
Std. polish . . . . NiB $4619 Ex $3695 Gd $2513
Hi-Luster . . . . NiB $4813 Ex $3850 Gd $2618
Stainless steel matte . . . . NiB $4369 Ex $3495 Gd $2377
With "AA" Grade English
Walnut: C-M matte blue . . . . NiB $4344 Ex $3475 Gd $2363
Std. polish . . . . NiB $4619 Ex $3695 Gd $2513
Hi-Luster . . . . NiB $4813 Ex $3850 Gd $2618
Stainless steel matte . . . . NiB $4369 Ex $3495 Gd $2377

ALASKAN TROPHY
Calibers: .300 Magnum to .458 Win. Magnum. 24- to 26-inch bbl. Weight: 7-9 lbs. Scope mount w/Express sights standard. Stainless steel or chrome-moly Apollo action w/fibergrain or black synthetic stock. Barrel band on 357 H&H and larger magnums. Made 1996 to date.
Matte finish . . . . NiB $2994 Ex $2395 Gd $1629
Std. polish . . . . NiB $3244 Ex $2595 Gd $1765
Stainless steel . . . . NiB $3063 Ex $2450 Gd $1666

A-SQUARE COMPANY INC. — Louisville, Kentucky (Formerly Bedford, KY)

CAESAR BOLT-ACTION RIFLE
Custom rifle built on Remington's 700 receiver. Calibers: Same as Hannibal, Groups I, II and III. 20- to 26-inch bbl. Weight: 8.5 to 11 lbs. Express 3-leaf rear sight, ramp front. Synthetic or classic Claro oil-finished walnut stock w/flush detachable swivels and Coil-Chek recoil system. Three-way adj. target trigger; 3-position safety. Right- or left-hand. Made 1984 to date.
Synthetic stock model . . . . NiB $3100 Ex $2500 Gd $1700
Walnut stock model . . . . NiB $2750 Ex $2100 Gd $1500

GENGHIS KHAN BOLT-ACTION RIFLE
Custom varmint rifle developed on Winchester's M70 receiver; fitted w/heavy tapered bbl. and Coil-Chek stock. Calibers: .22-250 Rem., .243 Win., .25-06 Rem., 6mm Rem. Weight: 8-8.5 lbs. Made 1994 to date.
Synthetic stock model . . . . NiB $3800 Ex $2990 Gd $2050
Walnut stock model . . . . NiB $3150 Ex $2550 Gd $1750

HAMILCAR BOLT-ACTION RIFLE
Similar to Hannibal Model except lighter. Calibers: .25-06, .257 Wby., 6.5x55 Swedish, .270 Wby., 7x57, 7mm Rem., 7mm STW, 7mm Wby., .280 Rem., .30-06, .300 Win., .300 Wby., .338-06, 9.3x62. Weight: 8-8.5 lbs. Made 1994 to date.
Synthetic stock model . . . . NiB $3619 Ex $2895 Gd $1969
Walnut stock model . . . . NiB $3188 Ex $2550 Gd $1734

HANNIBAL BOLT-ACTION RIFLE
Custom rifle built on reinforced P-17 Enfield receiver. Calibers: Group I: 30-06; Group II: 7mm Rem. Mag., .300 Win. Mag., .416 Taylor, .425 Express, .458 Win. Mag.; Group III: .300 H&H, .300 Wby. Mag., 8mm Rem. Mag., .340 Wby. Mag., .375 H&H, .375 Wby. Mag., .404 Jeffery, .416 Hoffman, .416 Rem Mag., .450 Ackley, .458 Lott; Group IV: .338 A-Square Mag., .375 A-Square Mag., .378 Wby. Mag., .416 Rigby, .416 Wby. Mag., .460 Short Square Mag., .500 A-Square Mag. 20- to 26-inch bbl. Weight: 9 to 11.75 lbs. Express 3-leaf rear sight, ramp front. Classic Claro oil-finished walnut stock or synthetic stock w/flush detachable swivels and Coil-Chek recoil system. Adj. trigger w/2-position safety. Made 1983 to date.
Synthetic stock model . . . . NiB $3563 Ex $2850 Gd $1938
Walnut stock model . . . . NiB $3369 Ex $2695 Gd $1833

Auto-Ordnance
Thompson Model 27A-1
Deluxe

Auto-Ordnance
Thompson Model 27A-1
Standard Carbine

Auto-Ordnance
Thompson M1 Carbine

AUSTRIAN MILITARY RIFLES — Steyr, Austria
Manufactured at Steyr Armory

MODEL 90
STEYR-MANNLICHER RIFLE . . . . . . **NiB $275 Ex $150 Gd $100**
Straight-pull bolt action. Caliber: 8mm. 5-shot magazine. Open
sights. 10-inch bayonet. Cartridge clip forms part of the magazine
mechanism. Some of these rifles were provided with a laced canvas
hand guard, others were of wood.

MODEL 90
STEYR-MANNLICHER CARBINE . . . **NiB $275 Ex $180 Gd $100**
Same general specifications as Model 90 rifle except w/19.5-inch
bbl., weight 7 lbs. No bayonet stud or supplemental forend grip.

MODEL 95
STEYR-MANNLICHER CARBINE . . . **NiB $275 Ex $180 Gd $100**
Same general specifications as Model 95 rifle except w/19.5-inch
bbl., weight 7 lbs. Post front sight; adj. rear carbine sight.

MODEL 95
STEYR-MANNLICHER
SERVICE RIFLE. . . . . **NiB $250 Ex $130 Gd $95**
Straight-pull bolt action. Caliber: 8x50R Mannlicher (many of these
rifles were altered during World War II to use the 7.9mm German
service ammunition). 5-shot Mannlicher-type box magazine. 30-
inch bbl. Weight: 8.5 lbs. Sights: Blade front; rear adj. for elevation.
Military-type full stock.

AUTO-ORDNANCE CORPORATION — West
Hurley, New York (Manufacturing rights
acquired by Kahr Arms 1999)

THOMPSON MODEL 22-27A-3 . . . **NiB $695 Ex $575 Gd $400**
Same-bore version of Deluxe Model 27A-1. Same general specifications except 22 LR w/lightweight alloy receiver, weight 6.5 lbs.
Magazines include 5-, 20-, 30- and 50-shot box types, 80-shot
drum. Made 1977-94.

THOMPSON MODEL 27A-1 DELUXE
Same as Standard Model 27A-1 except w/finned bbl. w/compen-
sator, adj. rear sight, pistol-grip forestock. Caliber: .22 LR, l0mm
(1991-93) or 45 ACP. Weight: 11.5 lbs. Made 1976-99.
.22 LR (Limited production) . . . . **NiB $1244 Ex $995 Gd $677**
10mm or 45 ACP . . . . **NiB $695 Ex $575 Gd $450**
50-round drum magazine, add **$250**
100-round drum magazine, add **$450**
Violin carrying case, add. **$100**

THOMPSON MODEL 27A-1
STANDARD SEMIAUTO CARBINE. . . . . . . **NiB $600 Ex $550 Gd $350**
Similar to Thompson submachine gun ("Tommy Gun") except has
no provision for automatic firing. Caliber: .45 Auto. 20-shot detachable box magazine (5-,15- and 30-shot box magazines, 39-shot
drum also available). 16-inch plain bbl. Weight: 14 lbs. Sights:
Aperture rear; blade front. Walnut buttstock, pistol grip and grooved
forearm, sling swivels. Made 1976-86.

THOMPSON 27A-1C
LIGHTWEIGHT CARBINE . . . . NiB $719 Ex $575 Gd $391
Similar to Model 27A-1 except w/lightweight alloy receiver. Weight: 9.25 lbs. Made 1984 to date.

THOMPSON M1
SEMI-AUTOMATIC CARBINE . . . . . NiB $695 Ex $575 Gd $400
Similar to Model 27A-1 except in M-1 configuration w/side cocking lever and horizontal forearm. Weight: 11.5 lbs. Made 1986 to date.

BARRETT FIREARMS MFG., INC. — Murfreesboro, Tennessee

MODEL 82 A-1
SEMI-AUTOMATIC RIFLE . . . . . NiB $6750 Ex $5200 Gd $3200
Caliber: .50 BMG. 10-shot detachable box magazine. 29-inch recoiling bbl. w/muzzle brake. 57 inches overall. Weight: 28.5 lbs. Open iron sights and 10x scope. Composit stock w/Sorbothance recoil pad and self-leveling bipod. Blued finish. Made 1985 to date.

MODEL 90
BOLT-ACTION RIFLE . . . . NiB $3450 Ex $2950 Gd $1800
Caliber: .50 BMG. Five shot magazine. 29-inch match bbl. 45 inches overall. Weight: 22 lbs. Composite stock w/retractable bipod. Made 1990-95.

MODEL 95 BOLT-ACTION . . . . NiB $4475 Ex $3450 Gd $2550
Similar to Model 90 bullpup design chambered for .50 BMG except w/improved muzzle brake and extendable bipod. Made 1995 to date.

BEEMAN PRECISION ARMS INC. — Santa Rosa, California

Since 1993 all European firearms imported by Beeman have been distributed by Beeman Outdoor Sports, Div., Roberts Precision Arms, Inc., Santa Rosa, CA.

WEIHRAUCH HW MODELS 60J AND 60J-ST
BOLT-ACTION RIFLES
Calibers: .22 LR (60J-ST), .222 Rem. (60J). 22.8-inch bbl. 41.7 inches overall. Weight: 6.5 lbs. Sights: Hooded blade front; open adj. rear. Blued finish. Checkered walnut stock w/cheekpiece. Made 1988-94.
Model 60J . . . . NiB $450 Ex $680 Gd $550
Model 60J-ST . . . . NiB $563 Ex $450 Gd $306

WEIHRAUCH HW MODEL 60M
SMALL BORE RIFLE . . . . NiB $600 Ex $500 Gd $320
Caliber: .22 LR. Single-shot. 26.8-inch bbl. 45.7 inches overall. Weight: 10.8 lbs. Adj. trigger w/push-button safety. Sights: Hooded blade front on ramp, precision aperture rear. Target-style stock w/stippled forearm and pistol grip. Blued finish. Made 1988-94.

WEIHRAUCH HW
MODEL 660 MATCH RIFLE . . . . . . NiB $850 Ex $725 Gd $350
Caliber: .22 LR. 26-inch bbl. 45.3 inches overall. Weight: 10.7 lbs. Adj. match trigger. Sights: globe front, precision aperture rear. Match-style walnut stock w/adj. cheekpiece and buttplate. Made 1988-94.

FEINWERKBAU MODEL 2600 SERIES TARGET RIFLE
Caliber: .22 LR. Single-shot. 26.3-inch bbl. 43.7 inches overall.

(cont'd) FEINWERKBAU MODEL 2600 SERIES TARGET RIFLE
Weight: 10.6 lbs. Match trigger w/fingertip weight adjustment dial. Sights: Globe front; micrometer match aperture rear. Laminated hardwood stock w/adj. cheekpiece. Made 1988-94.
Standard Model 2600
(left-hand) . . . . NiB $1570 Ex $1200 Gd $800
Standard Model 2600
(right-hand) . . . . NiB $1400 Ex $1100 Gd $700
Free Rifle Model 2602
(left-hand) . . . . NiB $2000 Ex $1600 Gd $900
Free Rifle Model 2602
(right-hand) . . . . NiB $2000 Ex $1600 Gd $900

BELGIAN MILITARY RIFLES
Mfd. by Fabrique Nationale D'Armes de Guerre, Herstal, Belgium; Fabrique D'Armes de L'Etat, Lunich, Belgium

Hopkins & Allen Arms Co. of Norwich, Conn., as well as contractors in Birmingham, England, also produced these guns during World War I.

MODEL 1889 MAUSER
MILITARY RIFLE . . . . NiB $200 Ex $130 Gd $80
Caliber: 7.65mm Belgian Service (7.65mm Mauser). 5-shot projecting box magazine. 30.75-inch bbl. w/jacket. Weight: 8.5 lbs. Adj. rear sight, blade front. Straight-grip military stock. This, and the carbine version, was the principal weapon of the Belgian Army at the start of WWII. Made 1889 to c.1935.

MODEL 1916
MAUSER CARBINE . . . . NiB $225 Ex $175 Gd $90
Same as Model 1889 Rifle except w/20.75-inch bbl. Weighs 8 lbs. and has minor differences in the rear sight graduations, lower band closer to the muzzle and swivel plate on side of buttstock.

MODEL 1935 MAUSER
MILITARY RIFLE . . . . NiB $300 Ex $225 Gd $125
Same general specifications as F.N. Model 1924; minor differences. Caliber: 7.65mm Belgian Service. Mfd. by Fabrique Nationale D'Armes de Guerre.

MODEL 1936 MAUSER
MILITARY RIFLE . . . . NiB $225 Ex $180 Gd $122
An adaptation of Model 1889 w/German M/98-type bolt, Belgian M/89 protruding box magazine. Caliber: 7.65mm Belgian Service. Mfd. by Fabrique Nationale D'Armes de Guerre.

BENTON & BROWN FIREARMS, INC. — Fort Worth, Texas

MODEL 93 BOLT-ACTION RIFLE
Similar to Blaser Model R84 (the B&B rifle is built on the Blaser action, see separate listing) with an interchangeable bbl. system. Calibers: .243 Win., 6mm Rem., .25-06, .257 Wby., .264 Win., .270 Win., .280 Rem., 7mm Rem Mag., .30-06, .308, .300 Wby., .300 Win. Mag., .338 Win., .375 H&H. 22- or 24-inch bbl. 41 or 43 inches overall. Bbl.-mounted scope rings and one-piece base; no sights. Two-piece walnut or fiberglass stock. Made 1993 to date.
Walnut stock model . . . . NiB $1750 Ex $1600 Gd $890
Fiberglass stock model . . . . NiB $1550 Ex $1200 Gd $850
Extra bbl. assembly, add $475
Extra bolt assembly, add $425

Beretta 501
Bolt-Action Sporter

Beretta AR-70

BERETTA U.S.A. CORP. — Accokeek, Maryland, Manufactured by Fabbrica D'Armi Pietro Beretta, S.p.A., Gardone Val Trompia (Brescia), Italy

455 SxS EXPRESS DOUBLE RIFLE
Sidelock action w/removable sideplates. Calibers: .375 H&H, .458 Win. Mag., .470 NE, .500 NE (3 inches), .416 Rigby. Bbls.: 23.5 or 25.5-inch. Weight: 11 lbs. Double triggers. Sights: Blade front; V-notch folding leaf rear. Checkered European walnut forearm and buttstock w/recoil pad. Color casehardened receiver w/blued bbls. Made 1990 to date.
Model 455 . . . . NiB $40,938 Ex $32,750 Gd $22,270
Model 455EELL . . . . NiB $51,875 Ex $41,500 Gd $28,220

500 BOLT-ACTION SPORTER
Centerfire bolt-action rifle w/Sako A I short action. Calibers: .222 Rem., .223 Rem. Five shot magazine. 23.63-inch bbl. Weight: 6.5 lbs. Available w/ or w/o iron sights. Tapered dovetailed receiver. European walnut stock. Disc. 1986.
Standard . . . . NiB $595 Ex $500 Gd $350
DL Model . . . . NiB $1438 Ex $1150 Gd $782
500 EELL
Engraved . . . . NiB $1500 Ex $1300 Gd $850
W/iron sights, add 10%

501 BOLT-ACTION SPORTER
Same as Model 500 except w/Sako A II medium action. Calibers: .243 Win., .308 Win. Weight: 7.5 lbs. Disc. 1986.
Standard . . . . NiB $619 Ex $495 Gd $337
Standard
w/iron sights . . . . NiB $595 Ex $550 Gd $350
DL model. . . . . NiB $1420 Ex $1150 Gd $800
501 EELL (engraved) . . . . NiB $1550 Ex $1300 Gd $850
W/iron sights, add 10%

502 BOLT-ACTION SPORTER
Same as Model 500 except w/Sako A III long action. Calibers: .270 Win., 7mm Rem. Mag., .30/06, 375 H&H. Weight: 8.5 lbs. Disc. 1986.
Standard model . . . . NiB $681 Ex $545 Gd $371
DL model. . . . . NiB $1600 Ex $1250 Gd $850
502 EELL (engraved) . . . . NiB $1744 Ex $1395 Gd $949
W/iron sights, add 10%

AR-70 SEMIAUTOMATIC RIFLE . . . . NiB $1850 Ex $1625 Gd $950
Caliber: .223 Rem. (5.56mm). 30-shot magazine. 17.75-inch bbl. Weight: 8.25 lbs. Sights: Rear peep adj. for windage and elevation; blade front. High-impact synthetic buttstock. Imported 1984-89.

EXPRESS S686/S689 SABLE O/U RIFLE
Calibers: .30-06 Spfld., 9.3x74R, and .444 Marlin. 24-inch bbl. Weight: 7.7 lbs. Drilled and tapped for scope mount. European-style cheek rest and ventilated rubber recoil pad. Imported 1995 to date.
Model S686/S689 Silver Sable II. . . . . . NiB $4500 Ex $3500 Gd $2000
Model S689 Gold Sable . . . . NiB $6000 Ex $5000 Gd $2900
Model S686/S689 EELL
Diamond Sable. . . . . NiB $12,500 Ex $9000 Gd $6000
W/extra bbl. set, add $325
W/detachable claw mounts, add $595

EXPRESS SSO O/U EXPRESS DOUBLE RIFLE
Sidelock. Calibers: .375 H&H Mag., .458 Win. Mag., 9.3 x 74R. 23-24- or 25.5-inch blued bbls. Weight: 11 lbs. Double triggers. Express sights w/blade front and V-notch folding leaf rear. Optional Zeiss scope w/claw mounts. Color casehardened receiver w/scroll engraving, game scenes and gold inlays on higher grades. Checkered European walnut forearm and buttstock w/cheekpiece and recoil pad. Imported 1985 to date.
Model SS0 (disc. 1989) . . . . NiB $9000 Ex $7900 Gd $5000
Model SS05 (disc. 1990) . . . . NiB $10,000 Ex $8500 Gd $6000
Model SS06 Custom. . . . . NiB $25,500 Ex $19,500 Gd $12,000
Model SS06 EELL Gold Custom . . . . NiB $28,900 Ex $25,500 Gd $14,500
Extra bbl. assembly, add $6250
Claw mounts, add. $550

Beretta Mato
Deluxe Grade

Beretta Mato
Synthetic Grade

Blaser Model R84

MATO
Calibers: .270 Win., .280 Rem., 7mm Rem. Mag, .300 Win. Mag., .338 Win. Mag., .375 H&H. 23.6-inch bbl. Weight: 8 lbs. Adjustable trigger. Drop-out box magazine. Drilled and tapped for scope w/ or w/o adj. sights. Walnut or synthetic stock. Manufactured based on Mauser 98 action. Made in 1997 to date.
Standard model . . . . NiB $1200 Ex $900 Gd $600
Deluxe model . . . . NiB $1850 Ex $1500 Gd $800
.375 H&H w/iron sights, add. $300

SMALL BORE SPORTING CARBINE/TARGET RIFLE
Semiautomatic w/bolt handle in raised or conventional single-shot bolt-action w/handle in lowered position. Caliber: .22 LR. Four, 5-, 8-, 10- or 20-shot magazines. 20.5-inch standard or heavy bbl. Sights: 3-leaf folding rear, partridge front. Target or sporting stock w/checkered pistol grip and forend and sling swivels. Weight: 5.5 to 6 lbs.
Sporter model (Super Sport X) . . . . NiB $375 Ex $300 Gd $195
Target model (Olympia X) . . . . NiB $252 Ex $425 Gd $275

BLASER USA, INC. — Fort Worth, Texas Mfd. by Blaser Jagdwaffen GmbH, Germany (Imported by Sigarms, Exeter, NH; Autumn Sales, Inc., Fort Worth, TX)

MODEL R84 BOLT-ACTION RIFLE
Calibers: .22-250, .243, 6mm Rem., .25-06, .270, .280 Rem., .30-06- .257 Wby. Mag., .264 Win. Mag., 7mm Rem Mag., .300 Win. Mag., .300 Wby. Mag., .338 Win. Mag., .375 H&H. Interchangeable bbls. w/standard or Magnum bolt assemblies. Bbl. length: 23 inches (standard); 24 inches (Magnum). 41 to 42 inches overall. Weight: 7 to 7.25 lbs. No sights. Bbl.-mounted scope system. Two-piece Turkish walnut stock w/solid black recoil pad. Imported 1989-94.

(cont'd.) MODEL R84 BOLT-ACTION RIFLE
Model R84 Standard . . . . NiB $2100 Ex $1600 Gd $995
Model R84 Deluxe
(game scene) . . . . NiB $2900 Ex $1900 Gd $1190
Model R84 Super Deluxe
(Gold and silver inlays) . . . . NiB $3500 Ex $1900 Gd $1300
Left-hand model, add $125
Extra bbl. assembly, add $650

MODEL R93 SAFARI SERIES BOLT-ACTION REPEATER
Similar to Model R84 except restyled action w/straight-pull bolt, unique safety and searless trigger mechanism. Additional chamberings: 6.5x55, 7x57, .308, .416 Rem. Optional open sights. Imported 1994-98.
Model R93 Safari . . . . NiB $3575 Ex $3000 Gd $1900
Model R93 Safari Deluxe . . . . NiB $4000 Ex $3800 Gd $3000
Model R84 Safari
Super Deluxe . . . . NiB $4500 Ex $4000 Gd $3150
Extra bbl. assembly, add $525

MODEL R93 CLASSIC SERIES BOLT-ACTION REPEATER
Similar to Model R93 Safari except w/expanded model variations. Imported 1998 to date.
Model R93 Attache
(Premium wood, fluted bbl.) . . . . NiB $4200 Ex $3550 Gd $2800
Model R93 Classic
(.22-250 to .375 H&H) . . . . NiB $3244 Ex $2595 Gd $1765
Model R93 Classic Safari (.416 Rem.) . . . . NiB $3619 Ex $2895 Gd $1969
Model R93 LX (.22-250 to .416 Rem.) . . . . . NiB $1619 Ex $1295 Gd $881
Model R93 Synthetic (.22-250
to .375 H&H) . . . . NiB $1244 Ex $995 Gd $677
Extra bbl. assembly, add $550

Brno Model II

Brno Model 21H
Bolt-Action Sporting Rifle

Brno Model 22F

Brno Hornet
Bolt-Action Sporting Rifle

BRITISH MILITARY RIFLES
Mfd. at Royal Small Arms Factory, Enfield Lock, Middlesex, England, as well as private contractors

RIFLE NO. 1 MARK III. . . . . NiB $250 Ex $150 Gd $100
Short magazine Lee-Enfield (S.M.L.E.). Bolt action. Caliber: .303 British. 10-shot box magazine. 25.25-inch bbl. Weight: 8.75 lbs. Sights: Adj. rear; blade front w/guards. Two-piece, full-length military stock. Note: The earlier Mark III (approved 1907) is virtually the same as Mark III (adopted 1918) except for sights and different magazine cut-off that was eliminated on the latter.

RIFLE NO. 3 MARK I (PATTERN 14) . . . . . . NiB $275 Ex $200 Gd $100
Modified Mauser-type bolt action. Except for caliber .303 British and long-range sight, this rifle is the same as U.S. Model 1917 Enfield. See listing of the latter for general specifications.

RIFLE NO. 4 MARK I . . . . NiB $225 Ex $175 Gd $100
Post-World War I modification of the S.M.L.E. intended to simplify mass production. General specifications same as Rifle No. 1 Mark III except w/aperture rear sight and minor differences in construction and weighs 9.25 lbs.

LIGHT RIFLE NO. 4 MARK I . . . . . . NiB $175 Ex $125 Gd $90
Modification of the S.M.L.E. Caliber: .303 British. 10-shot box magazine. 23-inch bbl. Weight: 6.75 lbs. Sights: Micrometer click rear peep; blade front. One-piece military-type stock w/recoil pad. Made during WWII.

RIFLE NO. 5 MARK I . . . . NiB $300 Ex $200 Gd $125
Jungle Carbine. Modification of the S.M.L.E. similar to Light Rifle No. 4 Mark I except w/20.5-inch bbl. w/flash hider, carbine-type stock. Made during WWII, originally designed for use in the Pacific Theater.

BRNO SPORTING RIFLES — Brno, Czech Republic, Manufactured by Ceska Zbrojovka
Imported by Euro-Imports, El Cajon, CA (Previously by Bohemia Arms & Magnum Research)

See also CZ rifles.

MODEL I BOLT-ACTION
SPORTING RIFLE. . . . . NiB $600 Ex $525 Gd $350
Caliber: .22 LR. Five shot detachable magazine. 22.75-inch bbl. Weight: 6 lbs. Sights: three-leaf open rear; hooded ramp front. Sporting stock w/checkered pistol grip, swivels. Made 1946-73.

MODEL II BOLT-ACTION
SPORTING RIFLE. . . . . NiB $650 Ex $550 Gd $350
Same as Model I except w/deluxe grade stock. Made 1949-57.

MODEL III BOLT-ACTION
TARGET RIFLE . . . . NiB $700 Ex $650 Gd $400
Same as Model I except w/heavy bbl. and target stock. Made 1948-56.

MODEL IV BOLT-ACTION
TARGET RIFLE . . . . NiB $750 Ex $590 Gd $400
Same as Model III except w/improved target trigger mechanism. Made 1956-62.

MODEL V BOLT-ACTION
SPORTING RIFLE. . . . . NiB $700 Ex $530 Gd $350
Same as Model I except w/improved trigger mechanism. Made 1956-73.

Brno Model-ZKM 611

Brown Precision High Country Youth Rifle

MODEL 21H BOLT-ACTION
SPORTING RIFLE.............. **NiB $750 Ex $600 Gd $400**
Mauser-type action. Calibers: 6.5x57mm, 7x57mm 8x57mm. Five shot box magazine. 20.5-inch bbl. Double set trigger. Weight: 6.75 lbs. Sights: Two-leaf open rear-hooded ramp front. Half-length sporting stock w/cheekpiece, checkered pistol-grip and forearm, swivels. Made 1946-55.

MODEL 22F.................. **NiB $994 Ex $795 Gd $541**
Same as Model 21H except w/full-length Mannlicher-type stock, weight: 6 lbs., 14 oz. Disc.

MODEL 98 STANDARD
Calibers: .243 Win., .270 Win., .30-06, .308 Win., .300 Win. Mag., 7x57mm, 7x64mm, or 9.3x62mm. 23.8-inch bbl. Overall 34.5 inches. Weight: 7.25 lbs. Checkered walnut stock w/Bavarian cheekpiece. Imported 1998 to date.
Standard calibers .... **NiB $431 Ex $345 Gd $235**
Calibers .300 Win., Mag., 9.3x62mm ..... **NiB $481 Ex $385 Gd $262**
W/single set trigger, add................................. **$100**

MODEL 98 MANNLICHER
Similar to Model 98 Standard except full length stock and set triggers. Imported 1998 to date.
Standard calibers .... **NiB $594 Ex $475 Gd $323**
Calibers .300 Win. Mag., 9.3x62mm...... **NiB $656 Ex $525 Gd $357**

ZBK-110 SINGLE-SHOT
Calibers: .22 Hornet, .222 Rem., 5.6x52R, 5.6x50 Mag., 6.5x57R, 7x57R, and 8x57JRS. 23.8-inch bbl. Weight: 6.1 lbs. Walnut checkered buttstock and forearm w/Bavarian cheekpiece. Imported 1998 to date.
Standard model...................... **NiB $225 Ex $170 Gd $120**
Lux model.......................... **NiB $375 Ex $250 Gd $175**
Calibers 7x57R and 8x57 JRS, add **$25**
W/interchangeable 12 ga.
shotgun bbl., add **$132**

HORNET BOLT-ACTION
SPORTING RIFLE.............. **NiB $950 Ex $825 Gd $450**
Miniature Mauser action. Caliber: .22 Hornet. Five-shot detachable box magazine. 23-inch bbl. Double set trigger. Weight: 6.25 lbs.

(cont'd.) **HORNET BOLT-ACTION SPORTING RIFLE**
Sights: Three-leaf open rear hooded ramp front. Sporting stock w/checkered pistol grip and forearm, swivels. Made 1949-74. Note: This rifle was also marketed in U.S. as "Z-B Mauser Varmint Rifle." (Reintroduced as Model ZKB 680)

MODEL ZKB 680
BOLT-ACTION RIFLE........... **NiB $469 Ex $375 Gd $255**
Calibers: .22 Hornet, .222 Rem. 5-shot detachable box magazine. 23.5-inch bbl. Weight: 5.75 lbs. Double-set triggers. Adj. open rear sight, hooded ramp front. Walnut stock. Imported 1985-92.

MODEL ZKM 611 SEMIAUTOMATIC RIFLE
Caliber: .22 WMR. Six-round magazine. 20-inch bbl. 37 inches overall. Weight: 6.2 lbs. Hooded front sight; mid-mounted rear sight. Checkered walnut or beechwood stock. Single thumbscrew takedown. Grooved receiver for scope mounting. Imported 1992 to date.
Standard beechwood model ...... **NiB $406 Ex $325 Gd $221**
Deluxe walnut model .... **NiB $505 Ex $400 Gd $250**

BROWN PRECISION COMPANY — Los Molinos, California

MODEL 7 SUPER LIGHT SPORTER ...... **NiB $995 Ex $900 Gd $650**
Lightweight sporter built on a Remington Model 7 barreled action w/18-inch factory bbl. Weight: 5.25 lbs. Kevlar stock. Made 1984-92.

HIGH COUNTRY BOLT-ACTION SPORTER
Custom sporting rifles built on Blaser, Remington 700, Ruger 77 and Winchester 70 actions. Calibers: .243 Win., .25-06, .270 Win., 7mm Rem. Mag., .308 Win., .30-06. Five-shot magazine (4-shot in 7mm Mag.). 22- or 24-inch bbl. Weight: 6.5 lbs. Fiberglass stock w/recoil pad, sling swivels. No sights. Made 1975 to date.
Standard High Country .... **NiB $1100 Ex $950 Gd $700**
Custom High Country .... **NiB $2000 Ex $1590 Gd $900**
Left-hand action, add............................... **$200**
Stainless bbl., add **$200**
70, 77 or Blaser actions, add.......................... **$125**
70 SG action, add **$350**

Brown Precision Pro-Hunter

Brown Precision Tactical Elite

HIGH COUNTRY YOUTH RIFLE . . . . **NiB $1200 Ex $900 Gd $600**
Similar to standard Model 7 Super Light except w/Kevlar or graphite stock, scaled-down to youth dimensions. Calibers: .223, .243, 6mm, 7mm-08, .308. Made 1992 to date.

PRO-HUNTER BOLT-ACTION RIFLE
Custom sporting rifle built on Remington 700 or Winchester 70 SG action fitted w/match-grade Shilen bbl. chambered in customer's choice of caliber. Matte blued, nickel or Teflon finish. Express-style rear sight hooded ramp front. Synthetic stock. Made 1989 to date
Standard Pro-Hunter . . . . **NiB $2350 Ex $1950 Gd $1100**
Pro-Hunter Elite (1993 to date) . . . . . . **NiB $3350 Ex $2600 Gd $1750**

PRO-VARMINTER BOLT-ACTION RIFLE
Custom varminter built on a Remington 700 or 40X action fitted w/Shilen stainless steel benchrest bbl. Varmint or benchrest-style stock. Made 1993 to date.
Standard Pro-Varminter . . . . **NiB $1790 Ex $1350 Gd $900**
Pro-Hunter w/Rem 40X action . . . . . . **NiB $2350 Ex $1790 Gd $1190**

SELECTIVE TARGET MODEL . . . . . **NiB $1190 Ex $900 Gd $575**
Tactical law-enforcement rifle built on a Remington 700V action. Caliber: .308 Win. 20-, 22- or 24-inch bbl. Synthetic stock. Made 1989-92.

TACTICAL ELITE RIFLE . . . . **NiB $2500 Ex $2200 Gd $1200**
Similar to Selective Target Model except fitted w/select match-grade Shilen benchrest heavy stainless bbl. Calibers: .223, .308, .300 Win. Mag. Black or camo Kevlar/graphite composite fiberglass stock w/adj. buttplate. Non-reflective black Teflon metal finish. Made 1993 to date.

**BROWNING RIFLES — Morgan, Utah
Mfd. for Browning by Fabrique Nationale d'Armes de Guerre (now Fabrique Nationale Herstal), Herstal, Belgium; Miroku Firearms Mfg. Co., Tokyo, Japan; A.T.I., Salt Lake City, Ut; Oy Sako Ab, Riihimaki, Finland.**

.22 AUTOMATIC RIFLE, GRADE I
Similar to discontinued Remington Model 241A. Autoloading. Take-down. Calibers: .22 LR. .22 Short (not interchangeably). Tubular magazine in butt-stock holds 11 LR. 16 Short. Bbl. lengths: 19.25 inches (.22 LR), 22.25 inches (.22 Short). Weight: 4.75 lbs. (.22 LR); 5 lbs. (.22 Short). Receiver scroll engraved. Open rear sight, bead front. Checkered pistol-grip butt-stock, semibeavertail forearm. Made 1965-72 by FN; 1972 to date by Miroku. Note: Illustrations are of rifles manufactured by FN.
FN manufacture. . . . . **NiB $575 Ex $400 Gd $200**
Miroku manufacture . . . . **NiB $300 Ex $200 Gd $150**

.22 AUTOMATIC RIFLE, GRADE II
Same as Grade I except satin chrome-plated receiver engraved w/small game animal scenes, gold-plated trigger select walnut stock and forearm. .22 LR only. Made 1972-84.
FN manufacture. . . . . **NiB $975 Ex $645 Gd $450**
Miroku manufacture . . . . **NiB $400 Ex $325 Gd $200**

.22 AUTOMATIC RIFLE, GRADE III
Same as Grade I except satin chrome-plated receiver elaborately hand-carved and engraved w/dog and game-bird scenes, scrolls and leaf clusters: gold-plated trigger, extra-fancy walnut stock and forearm, skip-checkered. .22 LR only. Made 1972-84.
FN manufacture. . . . . **NiB $2000 Ex $1600 Gd $995**
Miroku manufacture . . . . **NiB $800 Ex $490 Gd $395**

.22 AUTOMATIC, GRADE VI. . . . . . **NiB $700 Ex $500 Gd $325**
Same general specifications as standard .22 Automatic except for engraving, high-grade stock w/checkering and glossy finish. Made by Miroku 1986 to date.

MODEL 52 BOLT-ACTION RIFLE . . . . **NiB $700 Ex $550 Gd $350**
Limited edition of Winchester Model 52C Sporter. Caliber: .22 LR. 5-shot magazine. 24-inch bbl. Weight: 7 lbs. Micro-Motion trigger. No sights. Checkered select walnut stock w/rosewood forend and metal grip cap. Blued finish. Only 5000 made in 1991-92.

MODEL 53 LEVER-ACTION RIFLE . . . . **NiB $725 Ex $600 Gd $390**
Limited edition of Winchester Model 53. Caliber: .32-20. 7-shot tubular half-magazine. 22-inch bbl. Weight: 6.5 lbs. Adj. rear sight, bead front. Select walnut checkered pistol-grip stock w/high-gloss finish. Classic-style forearm. Blued finish. Only 5000 made in 1990. See illustration next page.

Browning Model 53
Lever-Action Limited Edition

Browning Model 71
Grade I Lever-Action

Browning Model 71
High-Grade Carbine

Browning Model 71
High-Grade

Browning Model 78
Single-Shot .45-70

MODEL 65 GRADE I
LEVER-ACTION RIFLE . . . . NiB $700 Ex $450 Gd $350
Caliber: .218 Bee. 7-shot tubular half-magazine. 24-inch bbl. Weight: 6.75 lbs. Sights: Adj. buckhorn-style rear, hooded bead front. Select walnut pistol-grip stock w/high-gloss finish. Semibeavertail forearm. Limited edition of 3500 made in 1989.

MODEL 65 HIGH GRADE RIFLE . . . . NiB $1750 Ex $900 Gd $600
Same general specifications as Model 65 Grade I except w/engraving and gold-plated animals on grayed receiver. Cut checkering on pistol grip and forearm. Limited edition of 1500 made in 1989.

MODEL 71 GRADE I CARBINE . . . . NiB $700 Ex $525 Gd $350
Same general specifications as Model 71 Grade I Rifle except carbine w/20-inch round bbl. and weighs 8 lbs. Limited edition of 4000 made in 1986-87.

MODEL 71 GRADE I
LEVER-ACTION RIFLE . . . . NiB $790 Ex $600 Gd $400
Caliber: .348 Win. 4-shot magazine. 24-inch round bbl. Weight: 8 lbs., 2 oz. Open buckhorn sights. Select walnut straight grip stock w/satin finish. Classic-style forearm, flat metal buttplate. Limited edition of 3000 made in 1986-87.

MODEL 71 HIGH-GRADE CARBINE . . . . . . NiB $1150 Ex $975 Gd $550
Same general specifications as Model 71 High Grade Rifle, except carbine w/20-inch round bbl. Limited edition of 3000 made in 1986-88.

MODEL 71 HIGH-GRADE RIFLE . . . . NiB $1225 Ex $950 Gd $675
Caliber: .348 Win. Four shot magazine. 24-inch round bbl. Weight: 8 lbs., 2 oz. Engraved receiver. Open buckhorn sights. Select walnut checkered pistol-grip stock w/high-gloss finish. Classic-style forearm, flat metal buttplate. Limited edition of 3000 made in 1987.

78 BICENTENNIAL SET . . . . NiB $3500 Ex $2875 Gd $1900
Special Model 78 .45-70 w/same specifications as standard type, except sides of receiver engraved w/bison and eagle, scroll engraving on top of receiver, lever, both ends of bbl. and buttplate; high-grade walnut stock and forearm. Accompanied by an engraved hunting knife and stainless steel commemorative medallion, all in an alder wood presentation case. Each item in set has matching serial number beginning with "1776" and ending with numbers 1 to 1,000. Edition limited to 1,000 sets. Made in 1976.

78 SINGLE-SHOT RIFLE
Falling-block lever-action similar to Winchester 1885 High Wall single-shot rifle. Calibers: .22-250, 6mm Rem., .243 Win., .25-06, 7mm Rem. Mag., .30-06, .45-70 Govt. 26-inch octagon or heavy round bbl.; 24-inch octagon bull bbl. on .45-70 model. Weight: 7.75 lbs. w/octagon bbl.; w/round bbl., 8.5 lbs.; .45-70, 8.75 lbs. Furnished w/o sights except .45-70 model w/open rear sight, blade front. Checkered fancy walnut stock and forearm. .45-70 model w/straight-grip stock and curved buttplate; others have Monte Carlo comb and cheekpiece, pistol-grip w/cap, recoil pad. Made 1973-83 by Miroku. Reintroduced in 1985 as Model 1885.
All calibers except .45-70 . . . . NiB $750 Ex $625 Gd $390
.45-70 . . . . NiB $825 Ex $650 Gd $400

Browning Model 1885
High-Wall Single-Shot

Browning Model 1885
High-Wall Traditional Hunter

Browning Model 1885
Low-Wall Single-Shot

Browning Model 1885
BPCR Single-Shot

MODEL 1885 SINGLE-SHOT RIFLE

Calibers: .22 Hornet, .223, .243, (Low Wall); .357 Mag., .44 Mag., .45 LC (L/W Traditional Hunter); .22-250, .223 Rem., .270 Win., 7mm Rem. Mag., .30-06, .454 Casull Mag., .45.70 (High Wall); .30.30 Win., .38-55 WCF, .45 Govt. (H/W Traditional Hunter); .40-65, .45 Govt. and .45.90 (BPCR). 24-, 28-, 30 or 34-inch round, octagonal or octagonal and round bbl. 39.5, 43.5, 44.25 or 46.125 inches overall. Weight: 6.25, 8.75, 9, 11, or 11.75 lbs. respectively. Blued or color casehardened receiver. Gold-colored adj. trigger. Drilled and tapped for scope mounts w/no sights or vernier tang rear sight w/globe front and open sights on .45-70 Govt. Walnut straight-grip stock and Schnabel forearm w/cut checkering and high-gloss or oil finish. Made 1985 to date.

Low Wall model w/o sights (Intro. 1995) . . NiB $750 Ex $650 Gd $425
Traditional Hunter model (Intro. 1998) . . . NiB $900 Ex $850 Gd $475
High Wall model w/o sights (Intro. 1985) . . . . NiB $700 Ex $550 Gd $400
Traditional Hunter model (Intro. 1997) . . . NiB $975 Ex $775 Gd $450
**BPCR model w/no
ejector (Intro. 1996)** . . . . NiB $1550 Ex $1250 Gd $895
**BPCR Creedmoor Model .45-90
(Intro. 1998)** . . . . NiB $1550 Ex $1200 Gd $850

MODEL 1886 MONTANA
CENTENNIAL RIFLE . . . . NiB $1850 Ex $1490 Gd $925
Same general specifications as Model 1886 High Grade lever-action except w/specially engraved receiver designating Montana Centennial; also different stock design. Made in 1986 in limited issue by Miroku.

MODEL 1886 GRADE I
LEVER-ACTION RIFLE . . . . NiB $1190 Ex $875 Gd $650
Caliber: .45-70 Govt., 8-round magazine. 26-inch octagonal bbl. 45 inches overall. Weight: 9 lbs., 5 oz. Deep blued finish on receiver. Open buckhorn sights. Straight-grip walnut stock. Classic-style forearm. Metal buttplate. Satin finish. Made in 1986 in limited issue 7,000 by Miroku.

MODEL 1886 HIGH-
GRADE LA RIFLE . . . . NiB $1450 Ex $1100 Gd $795
Same general specifications as the Model 1886 Grade I except receiver is grayed, steel embellished w/scroll; elk and American bison engraving. High-gloss stock. Made in 1986 in limited issue of 3,000 by Miroku.

MODEL 1895 GRADE I LA RIFLE . . . . NiB $750 Ex $700 Gd $650
Caliber: .30-06, .30-40 Krag. Four shot magazine. 24-inch round bbl. 42 inches overall. Weight: 8 lbs. French walnut stock and Schnabel forend. Sights: Rear buckhorn; gold bead on elevated ramp front. Made in 1984 in limited issue of 8,000 (2,000 chambered for .30-40 Krag and 6,000 chambered for .30-06). Mfd. by Miroku.

MODEL 1895 HIGH-
GRADE LA RIFLE . . . . NiB $1350 Ex $1200 Gd $850
Same general specifications as Model 1895 Grade I except engraved receiver and Grade III French walnut stock and forend w/fine checkering. Made in 1985 in limited issue of 1000 in each caliber by

**Browning Model 1886
Grade I**

**Browning Model 1886
High-Grade**

**Browning Model 1895
Grade I**

**Browning
A-Bolt Eclipse**

MODEL A-BOLT .22 RIFLE

Calibers: .22 LR. .22 Magnum. 5- and 15-shot magazines. 22-inch round bbl. 40.25 inches overall. Weight: 5 lbs., 9 oz. Gold-colored adj. trigger. Laminated walnut stock w/checkering. Rosewood forend grip cap; pistol grip. With or w/o sights. Ramp front and adj. folding leaf rear on open sight model. 22 LR made 1985-96; 22 Magnum, 1990-96.

Grade I .22 LR . . . . NiB $350 Ex $275 Gd $185
Grade I .22 Magnum . . . . NiB $425 Ex $345 Gd $200
Deluxe Grade
Gold Medallion . . . . NiB $525 Ex $400 Gd $290

MODEL A-BOLT ECLIPSE BOLT RIFLE

Same general specifications as Hunter Grade except fitted w/gray and black laminated thumbhole stock. Available in both short and long action w/two bbl. configurations w/BOSS. Mfd. by Miroku 1996 to date.

Eclipse w/standard bbl. . . . . NiB $850 Ex $725 Gd $590
Eclipse Varmint w/heavy bbl. . . . . NiB $995 Ex $850 Gd $725
Eclipse M-1000
(Target .300 Win. Mag.) . . . . NiB $1150 Ex $890 Gd $650

MODEL A-BOLT EURO-BOLT RIFLE

Same general specifications as Hunter Grade except w/checkered satin-finished walnut stock. W/continental-style cheekpiece, palm-swell grip and Schnabel forend. Mannlicher-style spoon bolt handle and contoured bolt shroud. 22- or 26-inch bbl. w/satin blued finish. Weight: 6.8 to 7.4 lbs. Calibers: .22-250 Rem., .243 Win., .270 Win., .30.06, .308 Win., 7mm Rem. Mag. Mfd. by Miroku 1993-94; 1994-96 (Euro-Bolt II).

Euro-Bolt . . . . NiB $590 Ex $450 Gd $295
Euro-Bolt II . . . . NiB $625 Ex $550 Gd $395
BOSS option, add $90

MODEL A-BOLT HUNTER GRADE RIFLE

Calibers: .22 Hornet, .223 Rem., .22-250 Rem., .243 Win., .257 Roberts, 7mm-08 Rem., .308 Win., (short action) .25-06 Rem., .270 Win., .280 Rem., .284 Win., .30-06, 7mm Rem. Mag., .300 Win. Mag., .338 Win. Mag. Four-shot magazine (standard), 3-shot (magnum). 22-inch bbl. (standard), 24-inch (magnum). Weight: 7.5 lbs. (standard), 8.5 lbs. (magnum). With or w/o sights. Classic-style walnut stock. Produced in two action lengths w/nine locking lugs, fluted bolt w/60 degree rotation. Mfd. by Miroku 1985-93; 1994 to date (Hunter II).

Hunter . . . . NiB $600 Ex $550 Gd $390
Hunter II . . . . NiB $695 Ex $500 Gd $425
Hunter Micro. . . . . NiB $700 Ex $550 Gd $450
BOSS option, add $90
Open sights, add $50

MODEL A-BOLT MEDALLION GRADE RIFLE

Same as Hunter Grade except w/high-gloss deluxe stock rosewood grip cap and forend; high-luster blued finish. Also in .375 H&H w/open sights. Left-hand models available in long action only. Mfd. by Miroku 1988-93; 1994 to date (Medallion II). Bighorn Sheep Ltd. Ed.

(600 made 1986, .270 Win.) . . . . NiB $1250 Ex $950 Gd $650
Gold Medallion Deluxe Grade . . . . NiB $656 Ex $525 Gd $357
Gold Medallion II Deluxe Grade . . . . NiB $681 Ex $545 Gd $371
Medallion, Standard Grade . . . . NiB $525 Ex $450 Gd $275
Medallion II, Standard Grade . . . . NiB $531 Ex $425 Gd $289
Medallion, .375 H&H . . . . NiB $890 Ex $675 Gd $400
Medallion II, .375 H&H . . . . NiB $900 Ex $650 Gd $450
Micro Medallion . . . . NiB $575 Ex $450 Gd $300
Micro Medallion II . . . . NiB $600 Ex $475 Gd $325
Pronghorn Antelope Ltd. Ed.
(500 made 1987, .243 Win.) . . . . NiB $1190 Ex $950 Gd $775
BOSS option, add $90

Browning A-Bolt .22

Browning A-Bolt
Euro-Bolt

Browning A-Bolt
Hunter

Browning A-Bolt
Hunter with BOSS

Browning A-Bolt
Medallion Custom Trophy

Browning A-Bolt
Medallion White Gold

Browning A-Bolt
Medallion

Browning A-Bolt
Medallion (Left-Handed)

RIFLES

Browning A-Bolt
Composite Stalker

Browning A-Bolt
Stainless Stalker

Browning BAR, Grade IV

Browning BAR, Grade V

MODEL A-BOLT STALKER RIFLE
Same general specifications as Model A-Bolt Hunter Rifle except w/checkered graphite-fiberglass composite stock and matte blued or stainless metal. Non-glare matte finish of all exposed metal surfaces. 3 models: Camo Stalker orig. w/multi-colored laminated wood stock, matte blued metal; Composite Stalker w/graphite-fiberglass stock, matte blued metal; w/composite stock, stainless metal. Mfd. by Miroku 1987-93; 1994 to date. (Stalker II).

Camo Stalker (orig. laminated stock)	NiB $550	Ex $395	Gd $225
Composite Stalker	NiB $590	Ex $450	Gd $325
Composite Stalker II	NiB $590	Ex $450	Gd $325
Stainless Stalker	NiB $625	Ex $525	Gd $425
Stainless Stalker II	NiB $650	Ex $550	Gd $450
Stainless Stalker, .375 H&H	NiB $795	Ex $675	Gd $550
BOSS option, add			$90
Left-hand model, add			$90

MODEL A-BOLT
VARMINT II RIFLE . . . . NiB $700 Ex $650 Gd $495
Same general specifications as Stalker model except w/22-inch heavy bbl. w/BOSS system and varmint-style black laminated wood stock. Calibers: .22-250, .223 or .308. No sights. Bright blue or satin finish. Mfd. by Miroku 1994 to date.

MODEL B-92 LEVER-ACTION RIFLE . . . . . NiB $450 Ex $390 Gd $200
Calibers: .357 Mag. and .44 Rem. Mag. 11-shot magazine. 20-inch round bbl. 37.5 inches overall. Weight: 5.5 to 6.4 lbs. Seasoned French walnut stock w/high gloss finish. Cloverleaf rear sight; steel post front. Made 1979-89 by Miroku.

BAR AUTOMATIC RIFLE,
GRADE I, STANDARD CALIBERS . . . . . NiB $690 Ex $525 Gd $375
Gas-operated semiautomatic. Calibers: .243 Win., .270 Win., .280 Rem., .308 Win., .30-06. Four-round box magazine. 22-inch bbl. Weight: 7.5 lbs. Folding leaf rear sight, hooded ramp front. French walnut stock and forearm checkered, QD swivels. Made 1967-92 by FN.

BAR, GRADE I, MAGNUM CALIBERS . . . . NiB $700 Ex $650 Gd $490
Same as BAR in standard calibers, except w/24-inch bbl. chambered 7mm Rem. Mag. or .300 Win. Mag. .338 Win. Mag. w/3-round box magazine and recoil pad. Weight: 8.5 lbs. Made 1969-92 by FN.

BAR, GRADE II
Same as Grade I except receiver engraved w/big-game heads (deer and antelope on standard-caliber rifles, ram and grizzly on Magnum-caliber) and scrollwork, higher grade wood. Made 1967-74 by FN.

Standard calibers	NiB $890	Ex $750	Gd $550
Magnum calibers	NiB $995	Ex $725	Gd $495

BAR, GRADE III
Same as Grade I except receiver of grayed steel engraved w/big-game heads (deer and antelope on standard-caliber rifles, moose and elk on Magnum-caliber) framed in fine-line scrollwork, gold-plated trigger, stock and forearm of highly figured French walnut, hand-checkered and carved. Made 1971-74 by FN.

Standard calibers	NiB $950	Ex $890	Gd $500
Magnum calibers	NiB $1200	Ex $1125	Gd $625

BAR, GRADE IV
Same as Grade I except receiver of grayed steel engraved w/full detailed rendition of running deer and antelope on standard-caliber rifles, moose and elk on Magnum-caliber gold-plated trigger, stock and forearm of highly figured French walnut, hand checkered and carved. Made 1971-86 by FN.

Standard calibers	NiB $1563	Ex $1250	Gd $850
Magnum calibers	NiB $1813	Ex $1450	Gd $986

BAR, GRADE V
Same as Grade I except receiver w/complete big-game scenes executed by a master engraver and inlaid w/18K gold (deer and antelope on standard-caliber rifles, moose and elk on Magnum caliber), gold-plated trigger, stock and forearm of finest French walnut, intricately hand-checkered and carved. Made 1971-74 by FN.

Standard calibers	NiB $3063	Ex $2450	Gd $1666
Magnum calibers	NiB $3500	Ex $2850	Gd $1950

Browning BAR
Mark II Safari

Browning BAR
Mark II Safari

Browning BAR .22

Browning BAR .22
('82 Model)

MODEL BAR MARK II SAFARI AUTOMATIC RIFLE
Same general specifications as standard BAR semiautomatic rifle, except w/redesigned gas and buffer systems, new bolt release lever, and engraved receiver. Made 1993 to date.

Standard calibers	NiB $650	Ex $590	Gd $400
Magnum calibers	NiB $725	Ex $625	Gd $425
Lightweight (Alloy receiver w/20-inch bbl.)	NiB $575	Ex $490	Gd $300
BAR Mk II Grade III (intro. 1996)	NiB $2100	Ex $1925	Gd $1100
BAR Mk II Grade IV (intro. 1996)	NiB $2295	Ex $1675	Gd $1250
W/BOSS option, add			$60
W/open sights, add			$15

BAR .22 AUTOMATIC RIFLE
Semiautomatic. Caliber: .22 LR. Tubular magazine holds 15 rounds. 20.25-inch bbl. Weight: 6.25 lbs. Sights: Folding-leaf rear, gold bead front on ramp. Receiver grooved for scope mounting. French walnut pistol-grip stock and forearm checkered. Made 1977-85.

Grade I	NiB $350	Ex $290	Gd $160
Grade II	NiB $425	Ex $390	Gd $200

BBR LIGHTNING BOLT-ACTION RIFLE . . . NiB $525 Ex $425 Gd $315
Bolt-action rifle w/short bolt throw of 60 degrees. Calibers: .25-06 Rem., .270 Win., .30-06, 7mm Rem. Mag., .300 Win. Mag. 24-inch bbl. Weight: 8 lbs. Made 1979-84.

BL-.22 LEVER-ACTION REPEATING RIFLE
Short-throw lever-action. Caliber: .22 LR, Long, Short. Tubular magazine holds 15 LR, 17 Long 22 Short. 20-inch bbl. Weight: 5 lbs. Sights: Folding leaf rear; bead front. Receiver grooved for scope

(cont'd.) **BL .22 LEVER-ACTION REPEATING RIFLE**
mounting. Walnut straight-grip stock and forearm, bbl. band. Made 1970 to date by Miroku.

Grade I	NiB $325	Ex $195	Gd $130
Grade II w/scroll engraving	NiB $350	Ex $225	Gd $160

BLR LEVER-ACTION REPEATING RIFLE
Calibers: (short action only) .243 Win., .308 Win., .358 Win. Four round detachable box magazine. 20-inch bbl. Weight: 7 lbs. Sights: Windage and elevation adj. open rear; hooded ramp front. Walnut straight-grip stock and forearm, checkered, bbl. band, recoil pad. Made 1966 by BAC/USA; 1969-73 by FN; 1974-80 by Miroku. Note: USA manufacture of this model was limited to prototypes and pre-production guns only and may be identified the "MADE IN USA" roll stamp on the bbl.

FN model	NiB $695	Ex $475	Gd $325
Miroku model	NiB $425	Ex $300	Gd $200
USA model	NiB $1100	Ex $950	Gd $550

BLR LIGHTNING MODEL
Lightweight version of the Browning BLR '81 w/forged alloy receiver and redesigned trigger group. Calibers: Short Action— .22-250 Rem., .223 Rem., .243 Win., 7mm-08 Rem., .308 Win.; Long Action— .270 Win., 7mm Rem. Mag., .30-06, .300 Win. Mag. Three or 4-round detachable box magazine. 20-, 22- or 24-inch bbl. Weight: 6.5 to 7.75 lbs. Pistol-grip style walnut stock and forearm, cut checkering and recoil pad. Made by Miroku 1995 to date.

BLR Lightning model short action	NiB $450	Ex $390	Gd $200
BLR Lightning model long action	NiB $475	Ex $425	Gd $275

Browning BBR Lightning

Browning BL-.22, Grade I

Browning BPR Pump Rifle

BLR MODEL '81
Redesigned version of the Browning BLR. Calibers: .222-50 Rem., .243 Win., .308 Win., .358 Win; Long Action— .270 Win., 7mm Rem. Mag., .30-06. Fourround detachable box magazine. 20-inch bbl. Weight: 7 lbs. Walnut straight-grip stock and forearm, cut checkering, recoil pad. Made by Miroku 1981-95; Long Action intro. 1991.
BLR Model '81 short action . . . . . . NiB $550 Ex $395 Gd $250
BLR Model '81 long action . . . . . . NiB $590 Ex $400 Gd $290

BPR-22 PUMP RIFLE
Hammerless slide-action repeater. Specifications same as for BAR-.22, except also available chambered for .22 Magnum RF; magazine capacity, 11 rounds. Made 1977-82 by Miroku.
Model I . . . . NiB $250 Ex $200 Gd $140
Model II. . . . . NiB $450 Ex $395 Gd $225

BPR PUMP RIFLE
Slide-action repeater based on proven BAR designs w/forged alloy receiver and slide that cams down to clear bbl. and receiver. Calibers: .243 Win., .308 Win., .270 Win., .30-06, 7mm Rem. Mag. .300 Win. Mag. Three or 4-round detachable box magazine. 22- or 24-inch bbl. w/ramped front sight and open adj. rear. Weight: 7.2 to 7.4 lbs. Made 1997 to date by Miroku.
BPR Model standard calibers. . . . . . NiB $795 Ex $625 Gd $395
BPR Model magnum calibers. . . . . . NiB $875 Ex $650 Gd $425

HIGH-POWER BOLT-ACTION
RIFLE, MEDALLION GRADE . . . . NiB $1650 Ex $1495 Gd $895
Same as Safari Grade except receiver and bbl. scroll engraved, ram's head engraved on floorplate; select walnut stock w/rosewood forearm tip, grip cap. Made 1961-74.

HIGH-POWER BOLT-ACTION
RIFLE, OLYMPIAN GRADE . . . . NiB $3600 Ex $3225 Gd $1750
Same as Safari Grade except bbl. engraved; receiver, trigger guard and floorplate satin chrome-plated and engraved w/game scenes appropriate to caliber; finest figured walnut stock w/rosewood forearm tip and grip cap, latter w/18K-gold medallion. Made 1961-74.

HIGH-POWER BOLT-ACTION RIFLE,
SAFARI GRADE, MEDIUM ACTION . . . . . . NiB $995 Ex $750 Gd $525
Same as Standard except medium action. Calibers: .22-250, .243 Win., .264 Win. Mag., .284 Win. Mag., .308 Win. Bbl.: 22-inch lightweight bbl.; .22-250 and .243 also available w/24-inch heavy bbl. Weight: 6 lbs., 12 oz. w/lightweight bbl.; 7 lbs. 13 oz. w/heavy bbl. Made 1963-74 by Sako.

HIGH-POWER BOLT-ACTION RIFLE,
SAFARI GRADE, SHORT ACTION. . . . . . . NiB $995 Ex $750 Gd $525
Same as Standard except short action. Calibers: .222 Rem., .222 Rem. Mag. 22-inch lightweight or 24-inch heavy bbl. No sights. Weight: 6 lbs., 2 oz. w/lightweight bbl.; 7.5 lbs. w/heavy bbl. Made 1963-74 by Sako.

HIGH-POWER BOLT-ACTION RIFLE,
SAFARI GRADE, STANDARD ACTION . . . NiB $1275 Ex $995 Gd $795
Mauser-type action. Calibers: .270 Win., .30-06, 7mm Rem. Mag., .300 H&H Mag., .300 Win. Mag., .308 Norma Mag. .338 Win. Mag., .375 H&H Mag., .458 Win. Mag. Cartridge capacity: 6 rounds in .270, .30-06; 4 in Magnum calibers. Bbl. length: 22 in., in .270, .30-06; 24 in., in Magnum calibers. Weight: 7 lbs., 2 oz., in .270, .30-06; 8.25 lbs. in Mag. calibers. Folding leaf rear sight, hooded ramp front. Checkered stock w/pistol grip, Monte Carlo cheekpiece, QD swivels; recoil pad on Magnum models. Made 1959-74 by FN.

"T-BOLT" T-1 .22 REPEATING RIFLE
Straight-pull bolt action. Caliber: .22 LR. Five shot clip magazine. 24-inch bbl. Peep rear sight w/ramped blade front. Plain walnut stock w/pistol grip and laquered finish. Weight: 6 lbs. Also left-hand model. Made 1965-74 by FN.
Right-hand model . . . . NiB $450 Ex $390 Gd $225
Left-hand model . . . . NiB $475 Ex $395 Gd $225

"T-BOLT" T-2
Same as T-1 Model except w/checkered fancy figured walnut stock. Made 1966-74 by FN. (Reintroduced briefly during the late 1980's with oil-finished stock)
Original model . . . . NiB $475 Ex $395 Gd $225
Reintroduced model . . . . NiB $425 Ex $350 Gd $200

Browning
BL-22 II

Browning
BLR Model '81

Browning High-Power
Bolt-Action Rifle, Medallion Grade

Browning High-Power
Safari Grade Medium Action, Heavy Barrel

Browning High-Power
Safari Grade Short Action, Heavy Barrel

Browning High-Power
Safari Grade Standard Action

F.N. BROWNING FAL SEMIAUTOMATIC RIFLE
Same as F.N. FAL Semiautomatic Rifle. See F.N. listing for specifications. Sold by Browning for a brief period c. 1960.
F.N. FAL standard
model (G-series). . . . . NiB $3750 Ex $2650 Gd $1875
F.N. FAL lightweight
model (G-series). . . . . NiB $4525 Ex $3995 Gd $2500
F.N. FAL heavy bbl..
model (G-series). . . . . NiB $7025 Ex $5775 Gd $4550
BAC FAL model. . . . . NiB $2875 Ex $2550 Gd $1590

BSA GUNS LTD. — Birmingham, England (Previously Imported by Samco Global Arms, BSA Guns Ltd and Precision Sports)

NO. 12 MARTINI SINGLE-SHOT
TARGET RIFLE. . . . . NiB $575 Ex $450 Gd $325
Caliber .22 LR. 29-inch bbl. Weight: 8.75 lbs. Parker-Hale Model 7 rear sight and Model 2 front sight. Straight-grip stock, checkered forearm. Note: This model was also available w/open sights or w/BSA No. 20 and 30 sights. Made before WWII.

Browning "T-Bolt" T-1

Browning "T-Bolt" T-2

MODEL 12/15 MARTINI HEAVY .... **NiB $595 Ex $450 Gd $290**
Same as Standard Model 12/15 except w/extra heavy bbl., weighs 11 lbs.

MODEL 12/15 MARTINI
SINGLE-SHOT TARGET RIFLE ..... **NiB $525 Ex $395 Gd $275**
Caliber: .22 LR. 29-inch bbl. Weight: 9 lbs. Parker-Hale No. PH-7A rear sight and No. FS-22 front sight. Target stock w/high comb and cheekpiece, beavertail forearm. Note: This is a post-WWII model; however, a similar rifle, the BSA-Parker Model 12/15, was produced c. 1938.

NO. 13 MARTINI SINGLE-SHOT
TARGET RIFLE .... **NiB $500 Ex $395 Gd $250**
Caliber: .22 LR. Lighter version of the No.12 w/same general specifications except w/25-inch bbl., weighs 6.5lbs. Made before WWII.

NO. 13 SPORTING RIFLE
Same as No. 13 Target except fitted w/Parker-Hale "Sportarget" rear sight and bead front sight. Also available in .22 Hornet. Made before WWII.
.22 Long Rifle .... **NiB $550 Ex $395 Gd $260**
.22 Hornet .... **NiB $750 Ex $595 Gd $395**

MODEL 15 MARTINI
SINGLE-SHOT TARGET RIFLE .... **NiB $525 Ex $395 Gd $250**
Caliber: .22 LR. 29-inch bbl. Weight: 9.5 lbs. BSA No. 30 rear sight and No. 20 front sight. Target stock w/cheekpiece and pistol-grip, long, semi-beavertail forearm. Made before WWII.

CENTURION MODEL
MATCH RIFLE .... **NiB $495 Ex $350 Gd $250**
Same general specifications as Model 15 except w/"Centurion" match bbl. Made before WWII.

CF-2 BOLT-ACTION
HUNTING RIFLE .... **NiB $400 Ex $325 Gd $195**
Mauser-type action. Calibers: 7mm Rem. Mag., .300 Win. Mag. 3-shot magazine. 23.6-inch bbl. Weight: 8 lbs. Sights: Adj. rear; hooded ramp front. Checkered walnut stock w/Monte Carlo comb, rollover cheekpiece, rosewood forend tip, recoil pad, sling swivels. Made 1975-87. See Ithaca-BSA CF-2.

CF-2 STUTZEN RIFLE .... **NiB $495 Ex $350 Gd $250**
Calibers: .222 Rem., .22-250, .243 Win., .270 Win., .308 Win. .30-06. Four round capacity (5 in 222 Rem.). 20.6-inch bbl. 41.5 inches (approx.) overall length. Weight: 7.5 to 8 lbs. Williams front and rear sights. Hand-finished European walnut stock. Monte Carlo cheekpiece and Wundhammer palm swell. Double-set triggers. Importation disc. 1987.

CFT TARGET RIFLE .... **NiB $795 Ex $595 Gd $425**
Single-shot bolt action. Caliber: 7.62mm. 26.5-inch bbl. About 47.5 inches overall. Weight: 11 lbs., incl. accessories. Bbl. and action weight: 6 lbs., 12 oz. Importation disc. 1987.

MAJESTIC DELUXE FEATHERWEIGHT BOLT-ACTION HUNTING RIFLE
Mauser-type action. Calibers: .243 Win., .270 Win., .308 Win., .30-06, .458 Win. Mag. Four shot magazine. 22-inch bbl. w/BESA recoil reducer. Weight: 6.25 lbs.; 8.75 lbs. in 458. Folding leaf rear sight, hooded ramp front. Checkered European-style walnut stock w/cheekpiece, pistol-grip, Schnabel forend, swivels, recoil pad. Made 1959-65.
.458 Win. Mag. caliber .... **NiB $550 Ex $425 Gd $275**
Other calibers .... **NiB $450 Ex $395 Gd $225**

BSA MAJESTIC DELUXE
STANDARD WEIGHT .... **NiB $425 Ex $250 Gd $170**
Same as Featherweight model except heavier bbl. w/o recoil reducer. Calibers: .22 Hornet, .222 Rem., .243 Win., 7x57mm, .308 Win., .30-06. Weight: 7.25 to 7.75 lbs. Disc.

MARTINI-INTERNATIONAL
ISU MATCH RIFLE .... **NiB $925 Ex $700 Gd $465**
Similar to MK III, but modified to meet International Shooting Union "Standard Rifle" specifications. 28-inch standard weight bbl. Weight: 10.75 lbs. Redesigned stock and forearm, latter attached to bbl. w/"V" section alloy strut. Intro. 1968. Disc.

MARTINI-INTERNATIONAL
MARK V MATCH RIFLE .... **NiB $950 Ex $725 Gd $495**
Same as ISU model except w/heavier bbl. Weight: 12.25 lbs. Intro. 1976. Disc.

MARTINI-INTERNATIONAL
MATCH RIFLE SINGLE-SHOT
HEAVY PATTERN .... **NiB $675 Ex $525 Gd $425**
Caliber: .22 LR. 29-inch heavy bbl. Weight: 14 lbs. Parker-Hale "International" front and rear sights. Target stock w/full cheekpiece and pistol-grip, broad beavertail forearm, handstop, swivels. Right- or left-hand models. Mfd. 1950-53.

MARTINI-INTERNATIONAL
MATCH RIFLE — LIGHT PATTERN .... **NiB $650 Ex $525 Gd $400**
Same general specifications as Heavy Pattern except w/26-inch lighter weight bbl. Weight: 11 lbs. Disc.

MARTINI-INTERNATIONAL
MK II MATCH RIFLE .... **NiB $850 Ex $550 Gd $425**
Same general specifications as original model. Heavy and Light Pattern. Improved trigger mechanism and ejection system. Redesigned stock and forearm. Made 1953-59.

MARTINI-INTERNATIONAL
MK III MATCH RIFLE .... **NiB $950 Ex $725 Gd $495**
Same general specifications as MK II Heavy Pattern. Longer action frame w/I-section alloy strut to which forearm is attached; bbl. is fully floating. Redesigned stock and forearm. Made 1959-67.

BSA
Model 12/15 Martini

BSA
Model 15 Martini

BSA CFT Target

BSA
Martini-International ISU Match

BSA
Martini-International Mark V Match

BSA
Martini-International MK III Match

MONARCH DELUXE BOLT-ACTION
HUNTING RIFLE . . . . **NiB $325 Ex $290 Gd $195**
Same as Majestic Deluxe Standard Weight model except w/redesigned
stock of U.S. style w/contrasting hardwood forend tip and grip cap.
Calibers: .222 Rem., .243 Win., .270 Win., 7mm Rem. Mag., .308
Win., .30-06. 22-inch bbl. Weight: 7 to 7.25 lbs. Made 1965-74.

MONARCH DELUXE
VARMINT RIFLE . . . . **NiB $425 Ex $350 Gd $225**
Same as Monarch Deluxe except w/24-inch heavy bbl. and weighs
9 lbs. Calibers: .222 Rem., .243 Win. See illustration next page.

BUSHMASTER FIREARMS —
(Quality Parts Company), Windham, Maine

M17S BULLPUP . . . . **NiB $825 Ex $695 Gd $475**
Caliber: .223. 21.5-inch bbl. Weight: 8.2 lbs. Polymer stocks.
Handle w/fixed open sights w/Weaver-type rail for any optics.
Semi-auto, self-compensating short stroke gas piston. Forward trig-
ger/grip w/rear chamber. Bullpup style. Alloy receiver. Synthetic
lower receiver is hinged to upper w/hinged takedown system.
Accepts M-16 type magazines. Made 1992 to date.

BSA Monarch Deluxe Varmint

MODEL XM15 E2S SERIES
Caliber: .223. 16-, 20-, 24- or 26-inch bbl. Weight: 7 to 8.6 lbs. Polymer stocks. Adjustable sights w/dual flip-up aperture; optional flattop rail accepts scope. Direct gas-operated w/rotating bolt. Forged alloy receiver. All steel-coated w/manganese phosphate. Accepts M-16 type magazines. Made 1989 to date.

XM15 E2S Carbine. . . . . NiB $1050 Ex $875 Gd $625
XM15 E2S Target Rifle . . . . NiB $1100 Ex $825 Gd $575

CALICO LIGHT WEAPONS SYSTEMS — Bakersville, California

LIBERTY 50/100 SEMIAUTOMATIC RIFLE
Retarded blowback action. Caliber: 9mm. 50- or 100-shot helical-feed magazine. 16.1-inch bbl. 34.5 inches overall. Weight: 7 lbs. Adjustable post front sight and aperture rear. Ambidextrous rotating safety. Glass-filled polymer or thumbhole-style wood stock. Made 1995 to date.

Model Liberty 50. . . . . NiB $725 Ex $575 Gd $325
Model Liberty 100. . . . . NiB $800 Ex $775 Gd $400

MODEL M-100 SEMIAUTOMATIC SERIES
Similar to the Liberty 100 Model except chambered for .22 LR. Weight: 5 lbs. 34.5 inches overall. Folding or glass-filled polymer stock and forearm. Made 1986 to date.

Model M-100 w/folding
stock (disc. 1994) . . . . NiB $425 Ex $290 Gd $150
Model M-100 FS w/fixed
stock (1996) . . . . NiB $595 Ex $400 Gd $275

MODEL M-105
SEMI-AUTOMATIC SPORTER . . . . . NiB $295 Ex $225 Gd $150
Similar to the Liberty 100 Model except fitted w/walnut buttstock and forearm. Made 1986 to date.

MODEL M-900 SEMIAUTOMATIC CARBINE
Caliber: 9mm Parabellum. 50- or 100-shot magazine. 16.1-inch bbl. 28.5 inches overall. Weight: 3.7 lbs. Post front sight adj. for windage and elevation, fixed notch rear. Collapsible steel buttstock and glass-filled polymer grip. Matte black finish. Made 1989-94.

Model M-100 w/folding
stock (disc. 1994) . . . . NiB $525 Ex $400 Gd $250
Model M-100 FS w/fixed
stock (Intro. 1996) . . . . NiB $495 Ex $350 Gd $225

MODEL M-951 TACTICAL CARBINE
Similar to Model 900 except w/long compensator and adj. forward grip. Made 1990-94.

Model 951. NiB $495 Ex $350 Gd $255
Model 951-S . . . . NiB $525 Ex $295 Gd $275

CANADIAN MILITARY RIFLES — Quebec, Canada, Manufactured by Ross Rifle Co.

MODEL 1907 MARK II
ROSS MILITARY RIFLE . . . . NiB $325 Ex $225 Gd $195
Straight-pull bolt action. Caliber: .303 British. 5-shot box magazine. 28-inch bbl. Weight: 8.5 lbs. Sights: adj. rear; blade front. Military-type full stock. Note: The Ross was originally issued as a Canadian service rifle in 1907. There were several variations; it was the official weapon at the start of WWI, but has been obsolete for many years. For Ross sporting rifle, see listing under Ross Rifle company.

CENTURY INTERNATIONAL ARMS, INC. — Boca Raton, Florida; (Formerly St. Albans, Vermont)

CENTURION M38/M96 BOLT-ACTION SPORTER
Sporterized Swedish M38/96 Mauser action. Caliber: 6.5x55mm. 5-shot magazine. 24-inch bbl. 44 inches overall. Adj. rear sight. Blade front. Black synthetic or checkered European hardwood Monte Carlo stock. Holden Ironsighter see-through scope mount. Imported 1987 to date.

W/hardwood stock . . . . NiB $175 Ex $125 Gd $80
W/synthetic stock . . . . NiB $190 Ex $150 Gd $100

CENTURION M98 BOLT-ACTION SPORTER
Sporterized VZ24 or 98 Mauser action. Calibers: .270 Win., 7.62x39mm, .308 Win., .30-06. Five shot magazine. 22-inch bbl. 44 inches overall. Weight: 7.5 lbs. W/Millet or Weaver scope base(s), rings and no iron sights. Classic or Monte Carlo laminated hardwood, black synthetic or checkered European hardwood stock. Imported 1992 to date.

M98 Action W/black
synthetic stock (w/o rings). . . . . NiB $225 Ex $175 Gd $119
M98 Action W/hardwood
Stock (w/o rings) . . . . NiB $195 Ex $150 Gd $90
VZ24 Action W/laminated
Hardwood Stock (Elite) . . . . NiB $295 Ex $225 Gd $150
VZ24 Action W/black
synthetic stock . . . . NiB $281 Ex $225 Gd $153
W/Millet base and rings, add $25

CENTURION P-14 SPORTER
Sporterized P-14 action. Caliber: 7mm Rem. Mag., .300 Win. Mag. 5-shot magazine. 24-inch bbl. 43.4 inches overall. Weight: 8.25 lbs. Weaver-type scope base. Walnut stained hardwood or fiberglass stock. Imported 1987 to date.

W/hardwood stock . . . . NiB $215 Ex $175 Gd $115
W/fiberglass stock. . . . . NiB $250 Ex $175 Gd $125

ENFIELD SPORTER 4 BOLT-ACTION RIFLE
Sporterized Lee-Enfield action. Caliber: .303 British. 10-shot magazine. 25.25-inch bbl. 44.5 inches overall. Blade front sight, adj. aperture rear. Sporterized beechwood military stock or checkered walnut Monte Carlo stock. Blued finish. Imported 1987 to date.

W/sporterized military stock . . . . NiB $125 Ex $95 Gd $55

Chipmunk Bolt-Action
Single-Shot

Charter Arms AR-7 Explorer Survival Rifle
(Disassembled and Stowed in Stock)

L1A1 FAL SPORTER . . . . NiB $825 Ex $650 Gd $495
Sporterized L1A1 FAL semiautomatic. Caliber: .308 Win. 20.75-inch
bbl. 41 inches overall. Weight: 9.75 lbs. Protected front post sight,
adj. aperture rear. Matte blued finish. Black or camo Bell & Carlson
thumbhole sporter stock w/rubber buttpad. Imported 1988-98.

M-14 SPORTER . . . . NiB $395 Ex $275 Gd $175
Sporterized M-14 gas operated semiautomatic action. Caliber: .308
Win. 10-shot magazine. 22-inch bbl. 41 inches overall. Weight:
8.25 lbs. Blade front sight, adj. aperture rear sight. Parkerized finish.
Walnut stock w/rubber recoil pad. Forged receiver. Imported 1991
to date.

TIGER DRAGUNOV . . . . NiB $35000 Ex 2575 Gd $1225
Russian SVD semiautomatic sniper rifle. Caliber: 7.62x54R. 5-shot
magazine. 21-inch bbl. 43 inches overall. Weight: 8.5 lbs. Blade
front sight, open rear adj. for elevation. Blued finish. European laminated hardwood thumbhole stock. 4x range-finding scope w/light-
ed reticle and sunshade. Quick detachable scope mount. Imported
1994-95.

CHARTER ARMS CORPORATION — Stratford, Connecticut

**AR-7 EXPLORER
SURVIVAL RIFLE** . . . . NiB $125 Ex $90 Gd $60
Same as Armalite AR-7, except w/black, instead of brown, "wood
grain" plastic stock. See listing of that rifle for specifications. Made
1973-90.

CHIPMUNK RIFLES — Prospect, Oregon MFD. by Rogue Rifle Company (Formerly Oregon Arms Company and Chipmunk Manufacturing, Inc.)

BOLT-ACTION SINGLE-SHOT RIFLE
Calibers: .22 LR. or .22 WMR. 16.13-inch standard or 18.13-inch
bull bbl. Weight: 2.5 lbs. (standard) or 4 lbs. (Bull bbl.) Peep sight
rear; ramp front. Plain or checkered American walnut, laminated or
black hardwood stock. Made 1982 to date.
Standard model
w/plain walnut stock . . . . NiB $160 Ex $105 Gd $60
Standard model
w/black hardwood stock . . . . NiB $140 Ex $95 Gd $60
Standard model
w/camouflage stock . . . . NiB $170 Ex $125 Gd $75
Standard model w/laminated stock . . . . NiB $156 Ex $125 Gd $85
Deluxe grade
w/checkered walnut stock . . . . NiB $225 Ex $170 Gd $105
.22 WMR, add $20

CHURCHILL RIFLES — Mfd. in England.
*Imported by Ellett Brothers, Inc., Chapin, SC
(Previously by Kassnar Imports, Inc.)*

HIGHLANDER BOLT-ACTION RIFLE . . . . NiB $438 Ex $350 Gd $238
Calibers: .243 Win., .25-06 Rem., .270 Win., .308 Win., .30-06, 7mm Rem. Mag.,
.300 Win. Mag. Four shot magazine (standard); 3-shot (magnum). Bbl. length: 22-
inch (standard); 24-inch (magnum). 42.5 to 44.5 inches overall. Weight: 7.5 lbs.
Adj. rear sight, blade front. Checkered European walnut pistol-grip stock. Imported
1986-91.

"ONE OF ONE THOUSAND" RIFLE . . . . . . NiB $2500 Ex $1995 Gd $890
Made for Interarms to commemorate that firm's 20th anniversary.
Mauser-type action. Calibers: .270, 7mm Rem. Mag., .308, .30-06,
.300 Win. Mag., .375 H&H Mag., .458 Win. Mag. Five shot magazine (3-shot in Magnum calibers). 24-inch bbl. Weight: 8 lbs.
Classic-style French walnut stock w/cheekpiece, black forend tip,
checkered pistol grip and forearm, swivel-mounted recoil pad w/car-
tridge trap, pistol-grip cap w/trap for extra front sight, barrel-mounted sling swivel. Limited issue of 1,000 rifles made in 1973. See illustration next page.

REGENT BOLT-ACTION RIFLE . . . . NiB $550 Ex $495 Gd $375
Calibers: .243 Win., .25-06 Rem., .270 Win., .308 Win., .30-06, 7mm
Rem. Mag., .300 Win. Mag. Four shot magazine. 22-inch round bbl.
42.5 inches overall. Weight: 7.5 lbs. Ramp front sight w/gold bead;
adj. rear. Hand-checkered Monte Carlo-style stock of select European
walnut; recoil pad. Made 1986-90. See illustration next page.

CIMARRON ARMS — Fredericksburg, Texas

1860 HENRY LEVER-ACTION
Replica of 1860 Henry w/original Henry loading system. Calibers: .44-
40, .44 Special, .45 Colt. 13-shot magazine. 22-inch bbl. (carbine) or
24.25-inch bbl. (rifle). 43 inches overall (rifle). Weight: 9.5 lbs. (rifle).
Bead front sight, open adj. rear. Brass receiver and buttplate. Smooth
European walnut buttstock. Imported 1991 to date.
Carbine model . . . . NiB $850 Ex $695 Gd $425
Rifle model . . . . NiB $875 Ex $625 Gd $450
Civil War model
(U.S. issue martially marked) . . . . . . NiB $875 Ex $715 Gd $475
W/A-engraving, add $395

Churchill "One of One Thousand"

Churchill Regent

1866 YELLOWBOY LEVER-ACTION
Replica of 1866 Winchester. Calibers: .22 LR, 22WMR, .38 Special, .44-40, .45 Colt. 16-inch round bbl. (Trapper), 19-inch round bbl. (Carbine) or 24.25-inch octagonal bbl. (rifle). 43 inches overall (rifle). Weight: 9 lbs. (rifle). Bead front sight, open adj. rear. Brass receiver, buttplate and forend cap. Smooth European walnut stock. Imported 1991 to date.

Carbine . . . . NiB $675 Ex $525 Gd $325
Rifle . . . . NiB $795 Ex $550 Gd $350
Indian model (disc.) . . . . NiB $650 Ex $525 Gd $325
Trapper Model (.44-40 WCF only, disc.) . . . . . . NiB $525 Ex $400 Gd $250
W/A-engraving, add $425
W/B-engraving, add. $595
W/C-engraving, add $995

1873 LEVER-ACTION
Replica of 1873 Winchester. Calibers: .22 LR. .22WMR, .357 Magnum, .44-40 or .45 Colt. 16-inch round bbl. (Trapper), 19-inch round bbl. (SRC), 20-inch octagonal bbl. (short rifle), 24.25-inch octagonal bbl. (sporting rifle) and 30-inch octagonal bbl. (express rifle). 43 inches overall (sporting rifle). Weight: 8 lbs. Fixed blade front sight, adj. semi-buckhorn rear or tang peep sight. Walnut stock and forend. Color case-hardened receiver. Imported 1989 to date.

Express Rifle . . . . NiB $850 Ex $625 Gd $450
Short Rifle (disc.) . . . . NiB $825 Ex $575 Gd $390
Sporting Rifle . . . . NiB $700 Ex $550 Gd $370
SRC Carbine . . . . NiB $725 Ex $550 Gd $375
Trapper (disc.) . . . . NiB $595 Ex $475 Gd $290
One of 1000 engraved model . . . . NiB $2150 Ex $1750 Gd $1100

1874 FALLING BLOCK SPORTING RIFLE
Replica of 1874 Sharps Sporting Rifle. Calibers: .45-65, .45-70, .45-90 or .45-120. 32- or 34-inch round or octagonal bbl. Weight: 9.5 to 10 lbs. Blade or globe front sight w/adj. open rear or sporting tang peep sight. Single or double set triggers. Checkered walnut stock and forend w/nose cap. Color case-hardened receiver. Imported 1997 to date.
1874 Sporting Rifle - Billy Dixon Model . . . NiB $1050 Ex $950 Gd $720
1874 Sporting Rifle - Quigley Model . . . NiB $1450 Ex $1275 Gd $750
Sharps Sporting No. 1 Rifle . . . . NiB $995 Ex $775 Gd $525

CLERKE RECREATION PRODUCTS — Santa Monica, California

DELUXE HI-WALL . . . . NiB $360 Ex $290 Gd $195
Same as standard model, except w/adj. trigger, half-octagon bbl., select wood, stock w/cheekpiece and recoil pad. Made 1972-74.

HI-WALL
SINGLE-SHOT RIFLE . . . . NiB $350 Ex $295 Gd $175
Falling-block lever-action similar to Winchester 1885 High Wall S.S. Color casehardened investment-cast receiver. Calibers: .222 Rem., .22-250, .243 Rem., 6mm Rem., .25-06, .270 Win., 7mm Rem. Mag., .30-06, .45-70 Govt. 26-inch medium-weight bbl. Weight: 8 lbs. Furnished w/o sights. Checkered walnut pistol-grip stock and Schnabel forearm. Made 1972-74.

CLIFTON ARMS — Medina, Texas

SCOUT BOLT-ACTION RIFLE
Custom rifle built on the Dakota .76, Ruger .77 or Winchester .70 action. Shilen match-grade barrel cut and chambered to customer's specification. Clifton composite stock fitted and finished to customer's preference. Made 1992-97.
African
Scout . . . . NiB $3500 Ex $2850 Gd $2195
Pseudo
Scout . . . . NiB $3375 Ex $1995 Gd $1225
Standard
Scout . . . . NiB $3350 Ex $1950 Gd $1200
Super
Scout . . . . NiB $3475 Ex $2775 Gd $1275

COLT INDUSTRIES, FIREARMS DIVISION — Hartford, Connecticut

NOTE: *On Colt AR-15 Sporter models currently produced (i.e., Competition H-BAR, Sporter Match Target Lightweight, and Sporter Target Rifle), add $200 to pre-ban models made prior to 10-13-94.*

AR-15 A2 DELTA
MATCH H-BAR RIFLE . . . . NiB $1600 Ex $1525 Gd $1300
Similar to AR-15A2 Government Model except w/standard stock and heavy refined bbl. Furnished w/3-9x rubber armored scope and removeable cheekpiece. Made 1986-91.

AR-15 A2 GOVERNMENT
MODEL CARBINE . . . . NiB $2125 Ex $1800 Gd $995
Caliber: .223 Rem., 5-shot magazine. 16-inch bbl. w/flash suppressor. 35 inches overall. Weight: 5.8 lbs. Telescoping aluminum buttstock; sling swivels. Made 1985-91.

Colt AR-15 A2

Colt AR-15 A2 Delta Match H-BAR

Colt AR-15 A2 Government Model

Colt AR-15 Sporter Competition H-BAR

AR-15 A2 SPORTER II . . . . **NiB $1250 Ex $1100 Gd $995**
Same general specifications as standard AR-15 Sporter except heavier bbl., improved pistol-grip. Weight 7.5 lbs.; optional 3x or 4x scope. Made 1985-89.

AR-15 COMPACT 9MM CARBINE . . . . **NiB $1650 Ex $1400 Gd $1000**
Semiautomatic. Caliber: 9mm NATO. 20-round detachable magazine. Bbl.: 16-inch round. Weight: 6.3 lbs. Adj. rear and front sights. Adj. buttstock. Ribbed round handguard. Made 1985-86.

Colt Stagecoach

Colteer 1-.22

Colteer .22 Autoloader

Coltsman Deluxe

Coltsman 1957 Standard

AR-15 SEMIAUTOMATIC SPORTER
Commercial version of U.S. M16 rifle. Gas-operated. Takedown. Caliber: .223 Rem. (5.56mm). 20-round magazine w/spacer to reduce capacity to 5 rounds. 20-inch bbl. w/flash suppressor. Sights: Rear peep w/windage adjustment in carrying handle; front adj. for windage. 3x scope and mount optional. Black molded buttstock of high-impact synthetic material, rubber buttplate. Barrel surrounded by handguard of black fiberglass w/heat-reflecting inner shield. Swivels, black web sling strap. Weight: w/o accessories, 6.3 lbs. Made 1964-94.
Standard Sporter . . . . NiB $1244 Ex $995 Gd $677
W/adj. stock, redesigned
forearm (disc. 1988), add $200
W/3x scope and mount, add. $100

AR-15 SPORTER
COMPETITION
H-BAR RIFLE . . . . NiB $1250 Ex $995 Gd $625
Similar to AR-15 Sporter Target model except w/integral Weaver-type mounting system on a flat-top receiver. 20-inch bbl. w/counter-bored muzzle and 1:9 rifling twist. Made 1991 to date.

AR-15 SPORTER
COMPETITION H-BAR (RS) . . . . NiB $1625 Ex $1300 Gd $795
Similar to AR-15 Sporter Competition H-BAR Model except "Range Selected" for accuracy w/3x9 rubber-clad scope w/mount. Carrying handle w/iron sights. Made 1992-94.

AR-15 SPORTER MATCH TARGET LIGHTWEIGHT
Calibers: .223 Rem., 7.62x39mm, 9mm. 5-shot magazine. 16-inch bbl. (non-threaded after 1994). 34.5-35.5 inches overall. Weight: 7.1 lbs. Redesigned stock and shorter handguard. Made 1991 to date.
Standard LW Sporter (except 9mm) . . . . . . NiB $975 Ex $750 Gd $510
Standard LW Sporter, 9mm . . . . NiB $925 Ex $650 Gd $450
.22 LR conversion (disc. 1994), add $175

AR-15 SPORTER TARGET RIFLE
Caliber: .223 Rem. 5-shot magazine. 20-inch bbl. w/flash suppressor (non-threaded after 1994). 39 inches overall. Weight: 7.5 lbs. Black composition stock, grip and handguard. Sights: post front; adj. aperture rear. Matte black finish. Made 1993 to date.
Sporter Target Rifle . . . . NiB $1100 Ex $925 Gd $600
.22 LR conversion (disc. 1994), add $200

LIGHTNING MAGAZINE RIFLE - LARGE FRAME
Similar to Medium Frame model except w/large frame to accommodate larger calibers: .38-56, .44-60, .45-60, .45-65, .45-85, or .50-95 Express. Standard 22-inch (carbine & baby carbine) or 28-inch round or octagonal bbl. (rifle). Note: Additional bbl. lengths optional. Weight: 8 to 10.5 lbs. Sights: Open rear; bead or blade front. Walnut stock and checkered forearm. Made 1887-94. (6,496 produced)
Rifle . . . . NiB $4000 Ex $2975 Gd $2100
Carbine . . . . NiB $7900 Ex $6000 Gd $4000
Baby Carbine. . . . . NiB $9994 Ex $7995 Gd $5437
.50-95 Express, add 35%

Coltsman 1961 Custom

Coltsman 1961 Standard

Colt-Sauer Grand African

LIGHTNING MAGAZINE RIFLE - MEDIUM FRAME
Slide-action w/12-shot tubular magazine Carbine & Baby Carbine) or 15-shot tubular magazine (rifle). Calibers: .32-20, .38-40, .44-40. Standard 20-inch (Carbine & Baby Carbine) or 26-inch round or octagonal bbl.(rifle). Note: Additional bbl. lengths optional. Weight: 5.5 lbs. (Baby Carbine), 6.25 lbs. (carbine) or 7 to 9 lbs. (rifle). Sights: Open rear; bead or blade front. Walnut stock and checkered forearm. Blue finish w/color casehardened hammer. Made 1884-1902. (89,777 produced)

Rifle . . . . NiB $2200 Ex $1650 Gd $1100
Carbine . . . . NiB $3500 Ex $2675 Gd $1825
Baby Carbine . . . . NiB $5000 Ex $3900 Gd $2700
Military model
w/bayonet
lug & sling swivels . . . . NiB $4313 Ex $3450 Gd $2346

LIGHTNING MAGAZINE RIFLE - SMALL FRAME
Similar to Medium Frame model except w/smaller frame and chambered for .22 caliber only. Standard 24-inch round or octagonal bbl. w/half magazine. Note: Additional bbl. lengths optional. Weight: 6 lbs. Sights: Open rear; bead or blade front. Walnut stock and checkered forearm. Made 1884-1902. (89,912 produced)

Standard Rifle model . . . . NiB $1315 Ex $995 Gd $675
W/Deluxe or optional features, add 20%

STAGECOACH .22 AUTOLOADER . . . . . . NiB $350 Ex $275 Gd $150
Same as Colteer .22 Autoloader except w/engraved receiver, saddle ring, 16.5-inch bbl. Weight: 4 lbs., 10 oz. Made 1965-75.

1-.22 SINGLE-SHOT
BOLT-ACTION RIFLE . . . . NiB $300 Ex $225 Gd $150
Caliber: .22 LR. Long, Short. 20- or 22-inch bbl. Sights: Open rear; ramp front. Pistol-grip stock w/Monte Carlo comb. Weight: 5 lbs. Made 1957-67.

.22 AUTOLOADER . . . . NiB $300 Ex $225 Gd $150
Caliber: .22 LR. 15-round tubular magazine. 19.38-inch bbl. Sights: Open rear; hooded ramp front. Straight-grip stock, Western carbine-style forearm w/bbl. band. Weight: 4.75 lbs. Made 1964-75.

CUSTOM BOLT-ACTION
SPORTING RIFLE . . . . NiB $500 Ex $395 Gd $250
FN Mauser action, side safety, engraved floorplate. Calibers: .30-06, .300 H&H Mag. Five shot box magazine. 24-inch bbl., rampfront sight. Fancy walnut stock. Monte Carlo comb, cheekpiece, pistol-grip, checkered, QD swivels. Weight: 7.25 lbs. Made 1957-61.

DELUXE RIFLE . . . . NiB $850 Ex $650 Gd $450
FN Mauser action. Same as Custom model, except plain floorplate, plainer wood and checkering. Made 1957-61. Value shown is for rifle as furnished by manufacturer w/o rear sight.

MODELS OF 1957 RIFLES
Sako medium action. Calibers: .243, .308. Weight: 6.75 lbs. Other specifications similar to those of models w/FN actions. Made 1957-61.

Custom . . . . NiB $800 Ex $600 Gd $400
Deluxe . . . . NiB $800 Ex $625 Gd $400
Standard . . . . NiB $650 Ex $400 Gd $325

MODEL OF 1961,
CUSTOM RIFLE . . . . NiB $625 Ex $475 Gd $300
Sako action. Calibers: .222, .222 Mag., .223, .243, .264, .270, .308, .30-06, .300 H&H. 23-, 24-inch bbl. Sights: Folding leaf rear; hooded ramp front. Fancy French walnut stock w/Monte Carlo comb, rosewood forend tip and grip cap skip checkering, recoil pad, sling swivels. Weight: 6.5 - 7.5 lbs. Made 1963-65.

MODEL OF 1961, STANDARD RIFLE . . . . . NiB $625 Ex $500 Gd $325
Same as Custom model except plainer, American walnut stock. Made 1963-65.

STANDARD RIFLE . . . . NiB $600 Ex $450 Gd $300
FN Mauser action. Same as Deluxe model except in .243, .30-06, .308, .300 Mag. and stock w/o cheekpiece, bbl. length 22 inches. Made 1957-61. Value shown is for rifle as furnished by manufacturer w/o rear sight.

COLT-SAUER DRILLINGS See Colt shotgun listings.

Colt-Sauer Grand Alaskan

Colt-Sauer Short Action

Cooper Arms — Model 22 Pro Varmint

GRAND AFRICAN . . . . NiB $1800 Ex $1400 Gd $925
Same specifications as standard model except .458 Win. Mag., weight: 9.5 lbs. Sights: Adj. leaf rear; hooded ramp front. Magnum-style stock of Bubinga. Made 1973-85. See illustration previous page.

GRAND ALASKAN . . . . NiB $1795 Ex $1225 Gd $800
Same specifications as standard model except .375 H&H, weight: 8.5 lbs. Sights: Adj. leaf rear; hooded ramp front. Magnum-style stock of walnut.

MAGNUM . . . . NiB $1350 Ex $950 Gd $650
Same specifications as standard model except calibers 7mm Rem. Mag., .300 Win. Mag., .300 Weatherby. Weight: 8.5 lbs. Made 1973-85.

SHORT ACTION . . . . NiB $1200 Ex $925 Gd $625
Same specifications as standard model except shorter action chambered for the following calibers: .22-250, .243 Win., .308 Win. and similar length cartridges. Weight: 7.5 lbs.; 8.25 lbs. (.22-250). Drilled and tapped for scope mount. No front or rear open sights. Made 1973-88.

**SPORTING RIFLE,
STANDARD MODEL** . . . . NiB $1225 Ex $950 Gd $650
Sauer 80 non-rotating bolt action. Calibers: .25-06, .270 Win., .30-06. Three-round detachable box magazine. 24-inch bbl. Weight: 7.75 lbs., 8.5 lbs. (.25-06). Furnished w/o sights. American walnut stock w/Monte Carlo cheekpiece, checkered pistol grip and forearm, rosewood forend tip and pistol-grip cap, recoil pad. Made 1973-88.

COMMANDO CARBINES — Knoxville,
Tennessee,
(Formerly Volunteer Enterprises, Inc.)
MARK III SEMIAUTOMATIC CARBINE
Blow-back action, fires from closed bolt. Caliber: .45 ACP. 15- or 30-shot magazine. 16.5-inch bbl. w/cooling sleeve and muzzle brake. Weight: 8 lbs. Sights: peep rear; blade front. "Tommy Gun" style stock and forearm or grip. Made 1969-76.
W/horizontal forearm . . . . NiB $425 Ex $325 Gd $225

MARK 9
Same specifications as Mark III and Mark 45 except caliber 9mm Luger. Made 1976-81.
W/horizontal forearm . . . . NiB $450 Ex $360 Gd $245
W/vertical foregrip . . . . NiB $469 Ex $375 Gd $255

MARK 45
Same specifications as Mark III. Has redesigned trigger housing and magazines. Made 1976-88.
W/horizontal forearm . . . . NiB $450 Ex $390 Gd $250
W/vertical f oregrip . . . . NiB $544 Ex $435 Gd $296

CONTINENTAL RIFLES — Manufactured in Belgium for Continental Arms, Corp., New York, N.Y.

DOUBLE RIFLE
Calibers: .270, .303 Sav., .30-40, .348 Win., .30-06, .375 H&H, .400 Jeffrey, .465, .470, .475 No. 2, .500, .600. Side-by-side. Anson-Deeley reinforced boxlock action w/triple bolting lever work. Two triggers. Nonautomatic safety. 24- or 26-inch bbls. Sights: Express rear; bead front. Checkered cheekpiece stock and forend. Weight: From 7 lbs., depending on caliber. Imported 1956-75.

CZ Model ZKK 600

COOPER FIREARMS of MONTANA, INC. — (Previously COOPER ARMS), Stevensville, Montana

MODEL 21

Similar to Model 36C except in calibers .17 Rem., .17 Mach IV, .221 Fireball, .222, .223, 6x45, 6x47. 24-inch stainless or chrome-moly bbl. 43.5 inches overall. Weight: 8.75 lbs. Made 1994 to date.

21 Benchrest	NiB $1850	Ex $1550	Gd $995
21 Classic	NiB $950	Ex $795	Gd $450
21 Custom Classic	NiB $1700	Ex $1100	Gd $500
21 Western Classic	NiB $1700	Ex $1100	Gd $500
21 Varminter	NiB $925	Ex $725	Gd $450
21 Varmint Extreme	NiB $1700	Ex $995	Gd $725

MODEL 22

Bolt-action, single-shot. Calibers: .22 BR. .22-250 Rem., .220 Swift, .243 Win., 6mm PPC, 6.5x55mm, 25-06 Rem., 7.62x39mm 26-inch bbl, 45.63 inches overall. Weight: 8 lbs., 12 oz. Single-stage trigger. AAA Claro walnut stock. Made 1996 to date.

22 Benchrest	NiB $1750	Ex $1425	Gd $950
22 Classic	NiB $1700	Ex $1160	Gd $600
22 Custom Classic	NiB $1200	Ex $1100	Gd $750
22 Western Classic	NiB $1795	Ex $1195	Gd $800
22 Varminter	NiB $1000	Ex $795	Gd $500
22 Pro-Varmint Extreme	NiB $1690	Ex $995	Gd $700
22 Black Jack	NiB $1690	Ex $995	Gd $700

MODEL 36 RF/BR 50

	NiB $1725	Ex $1100	Gd $725

Caliber: .22 LR. Bolt-action. Single-shot. 22-inch bbl. 40.5 inches overall. Weight: 6.8 lbs. No sights. Fully-adj. match-grade trigger. Stainless barrel. McMillan benchrest stock. Three mid-bolt locking lugs. Made 1994 to date.

MODEL 36 CF BOLT-ACTION RIFLE

Calibers: .17 CCM, .22 CCM, .22 Hornet. 4-shot mag. 23.75 inch bbl. 42.5 inch overall. Weight: 7 lbs. Walnut or synthetic stock. Made 1992-94.

Marksman	NiB $925	Ex $700	Gd $495
Sportsman	NiB $825	Ex $625	Gd $425
Classic Grade	NiB $1690	Ex $995	Gd $725
Custom Grade	NiB $1000	Ex $800	Gd $550
Custom Classic Grade	NiB $1700	Ex $1100	Gd $750

MODEL 36 RF BOLT-ACTION RIFLE

Similar to Model 36CF except in caliber .22 LR. Five shot magazine. Weight: 6.5-7 lbs. Made 1992 to date.

BR-50 (22-inch stainless bbl.)	NiB $1300	Ex $998	Gd $650
Custom Grade	NiB $1000	Ex $780	Gd $525
Custom Classic Grade	NiB $1100	Ex $800	Gd $550
Featherweight	NiB $1063	Ex $850	Gd $578

MODEL 36 TRP-1 SERIES

Similar to Model 36RF except in target configuration w/ ISU or silhouette-style stock. Made 1991-93.

TRP-1 (ISU single-shot)	NiB $900	Ex $725	Gd $425
TRP-1S (Silhouette)	NiB $900	Ex $725	Gd $425

MODEL 38 SINGLE SHOT

Similar to Model 36CF except in calibers .17 or .22 CCM w/3-shot magazine. Weight: 8 lbs. Walnut or synthetic stock. Made 1992-93.

Sporter Standard	NiB $900	Ex $700	Gd $550
Classic Grade	NiB $995	Ex $795	Gd $550
Custom Grade	NiB $1125	Ex $950	Gd $550
Custom Classic Grade	NiB $1390	Ex $1100	Gd $725

MODEL 40 CLASSIC BOLT-ACTION RIFLE

Calibers: .17 CCM, .17 Ackley Hornet, .22 Hornet, .22K Hornet, .22 CCM, 4- or 5-shot magazine. 23.75-inch bbl. Checkered oil-finished AAA Claro walnut stock. Made 1995-97.

Classic	NiB $1390	Ex $1100	Gd $725
Custom Classic	NiB $1490	Ex $1195	Gd $800
Classic Varminter	NiB $1500	Ex $1195	Gd $800

CUMBERLAND MOUNTAIN ARMS — Winchester, Tennessee

PLATEAU RIFLE

Falling block action w/underlever. Calibers: .40-65, and .45-70. 32-inch round bbl. 48 inches overall. Weight: 10.5 lbs. American walnut stock. Bead front sight, adj. buckhorn rear. Blued finish. Lacquer finish walnut stock w/crescent buttplate. Made 1995 to date.

Standard model	NiB $900	Ex $725	Gd $500
Deluxe model	NiB $1300	Ex $1025	Gd $690

CZ RIFLES — Strankonice, Czechoslovakia (Currently Uhersky Brod and Brno, Czecho.) Mfd. by Ceska Zbrojovka-Nardoni Podnik (Formerly Bohmische Waffenfabrik A.G.)

See also listings under Brno Sporting Rifles and Springfield, Inc.

ZKK 600 BOLT-ACTION RIFLE

Calibers: .270 Win., 7x57, 7x64, .30-06. Five shot magazine. 23.5-inch bbl. Weight: 7.5 lbs. Adj. folding-leaf rear sight, hooded ramp front. Pistol-grip walnut stock. Imported 1990 to date.

Standard model	NiB $531	Ex $425	Gd $289
Deluxe model	NiB $619	Ex $495	Gd $337

ZKK 601 BOLT-ACTION RIFLE

Similar to Model ZKK 600 except w/short action in calibers .223 Rem., .243 Win., .308 Win. 43 inches overall. Weight: 6 lbs., 13 oz. Checkered walnut pistol-grip stock w/Monte Carlo cheekpiece. Imported 1990 to date.

Standard model	NiB $500	Ex $425	Gd $350
Deluxe model	NiB $550	Ex $490	Gd $350

ZKK 602 BOLT-ACTION RIFLE

Similar to Model ZKK 600 except w/Magnum action in calibers .300 Win. Mag., 8x68S, .375 H&H, .458 Win. Mag. 25-inch bbl. 45.5 inches overall. Weight: 9.25 lbs. Imported 1990 to date.

Standard model	NiB $675	Ex $575	Gd $390
Deluxe model	NiB $800	Ex $650	Gd $425

RIFLES

CA Model ZKM 452 LUX Model

CZ 511

CZ Model ZKM 527

CZ 550 LUX Model

ZKM 452 BOLT-ACTION REPEATING RIFLE

Calibers: .22 LR. or .22 WMR. Five, 6- or 10-shot magazine. 25-inch bbl. 43.5 inches overall. Weight: 6 lbs. Adj. rear sight, hooded bead front. Oil-finished beechwood or checkered walnut stock w/Schnabel forend. Imported 1995 to date.

Standard model (22 LR)	NiB $350	Ex $280	Gd $133
Deluxe model (22 LR)	NiB $390	Ex $250	Gd $175
Varmint model (22 LR)	NiB $325	Ex $250	Gd $175
.22 WMR, add			$35

ZKM 527 BOLT-ACTION RIFLE

Calibers: .22 Hornet, .222 Rem., .223 Rem., 7.62x39mm. Five shot magazine. 23.5-inch bbl. 42.5 inches overall. Weight: 6.75 lbs. Adj. rear sight, hooded ramp front. Grooved receiver. Adj. double-set triggers. Oil-finished beechwood or checkered walnut stock . Imported 1995 to date.

Standard model	NiB $495	Ex $390	Gd $275
Classic model	NiB $500	Ex $390	Gd $275
Carbine model (shorter configuration)	NiB $525	Ex $395	Gd $275
Deluxe model	NiB $580	Ex $490	Gd $300

ZKM 537 SPORTER BOLT-ACTION RIFLE

Calibers: .243 Win., .270 Win., 7x57mm, .308 Win., .30-06. Four or 5-shot magazine. 19- or 23.5-inch bbl. 40.25 or 44.75 inches overall. Weight: 7 to 7.5 lbs. Adj. folding leaf rear sight, hooded ramp front. Shrouded bolt. Standard or Mannlicher-style checkered walnut stock. Imported 1992-94.

Standard model	NiB $525	Ex $395	Gd $275
Mannlicher model	NiB $750	Ex $500	Gd $350
Mountain Carbine model	NiB $525	Ex $390	Gd $250

511 SEMI-AUTO RIFLE

511 SEMI-AUTO RIFLE . . . . NiB $195 Ex $175 Gd $100
Caliber: .22 LR. 8- shot magazine. 22- inch bbl., 38.6 inches

(cont'd.) 511 SEMI-AUTO RIFLE

overall. Weight: 5.39 lbs. Receiver top fitted for telescopic sight mounts. Walnut wood-lacquered checkering stock. Imported 1998 to date.

550 BOLT-ACTION SERIES

Calibers: .243 Win., 6.5x55mm, .270 Win., 7mm Mag., 7x57, 7x64, .30-06, .300 Win Mag., .375 H&H, .416 Rem., .416 Rigby, .458 Win. Mag., 9.3x62. Four or 5-shot detachable magazine. 20.5- or 23.6-inch bbl. Weight: 7.25 to 8 lbs. No sights or Express sights on magnum models. Receiver drilled and tapped for scope mount. Standard or Mannlicher-style checkered walnut stock w/buttpad. Imported 1995 to date.

Standard	NiB $450	Ex $375	Gd $250
Magnum	NiB $575	Ex $455	Gd $300
Delux	NiB $495	Ex $390	Gd $275
Mannlicher	NiB $560	Ex $425	Gd $300
Calibers .416 Rem., .416 Rigby, .458 Win. Mag., add			$70

CZECHOSLOVAKIAN MILITARY RIFLES — Brno, Czechoslovakia, Manufactured by Ceska Zbrojovka

MODEL 1924 (VZ24)

MAUSER MILITARY RIFLE . . . . NiB $250 Ex $190 Gd $125
Basically same as German Kar., 98k and F.N. (Belgian Model 1924.) Caliber: 7.9mm Mauser. Five shot box magazine. 23.25-inch bbl. Weight: 8.5 lbs. Sights: Adj. rear; blade front w/guards. of Belgian-type military stock, full handguard. Mfd. 1924 thru WWII. Many of these rifles were made for export. As produced during the German occupation, this model was known as Gewehr 24t.

Daisy V/L Collector's Kit

Daisy V/L Standard

MODEL 1933 (VZ33) MAUSER
MILITARY CARBINE . . . . **NiB $325 Ex $250 Gd $175**
Modification of German M/98 action w/smaller receiver ring. Caliber: 7.9mm Mauser. 19.25-inch bbl. Weight: 7.5 lbs. Sights: Adj. rear; blade front w/guards. Military-type full stock. Mfd. 1933 thru WWII. A similar model, produced during the German occupation, was designated Gew. 33/40.

DAEWOO PRECISION INDUSTRIES — Manufactured in Korea (Previously Imported by Kimber of America; Daewoo Precision Industries; Nationwide Sports and KBI, Inc.)

DR200 SA SEMIAUTOMATIC SPORTER
Caliber: .223 Rem. (5.56mm). Six or 10-shot magazine. 18.4-inch bbl. 39.25 inches overall. Weight: 9 lbs. Protected post front sight, fully-adj. aperture rear. Forged aluminum receiver w/rotating locking bolt assembly. Synthetic sporterized thumbhole stock. Imported 1994-96.
Sporter model . . . . **NiB $650 Ex $500 Gd $375**
Varmint model. . . . . **NiB $550 Ex $500 Gd $275**

DR300 SA SEMIAUTO-
MATIC SPORTER. . . . . **NiB $575 Ex $490 Gd $325**
Similar to Model Daewoo DR200 except chambered for 7.62x39mm. Imported 1994-96.

DAISY RIFLES — Rogers, Arkansas

Daisy V/L rifles carry the first and only commercial caseless cartridge system. These rifles are expected to appreciate considerably in future years. The cartridge, no longer made, is also a collector's item. Production was discontinued following BATF ruling the V/L model to be a firearm.

COLLECTOR'S KIT. . . . . **NiB $406 Ex $325 Gd $221**
Presentation-grade rifle w/gold plate inscribed w/owner's name and gun serial number mounted on the stock. Also includes a special gun case, pair of brass gun cradles for wall-hanging, 300 rounds of 22 V/L ammunition and a certificate signed by Daisy president Cass S. Hough. Approx. 1,000 manufactured 1968-69.

PRESENTATION
GRADE . . . . **NiB $290 Ex $225 Gd $190**
Same specifications as standard model except w/walnut stock. Approx. 4,000 manufactured 1968-69.

STANDARD RIFLE . . . . **NiB $225 Ex $175 Gd $120**
Single-shot under-lever action. Caliber: .22 V/L (caseless cartridge, propellant ignited by jet of hot air). 18-inch bbl. Weight: 5 lbs. Sights: Adj. open rear, ramp w/blade front. Wood-grained Lustran stock (foam-filled). Approx. 19,000 manufactured 1968-69.

Dakota Model 10 Single-Shot Rifle

Dakota Arms Model 76
African Grade

Dakota Arms Model 76
Classic Grade

Dakota Arms Model 97
Hunter

DAKOTA ARMS, INC. — Sturgis, South Dakota

MODEL 10 SINGLE-SHOT RIFLE
Chambered for most commercially-loaded calibers. 23-inch bbl. 39.5 inches overall. Weight: 5.5 lbs. Top tang safety. No sights. Checkered pistol-grip buttstock and semi-beavertail forearm, QD swivels, rubber recoil pad. Made 1992 to date.
Standard calibers . . . . NiB $3180 Ex $2775 Gd $1725
Magnum calibers . . . . NiB $3650 Ex $2925 Gd $1975

MODEL 22 BOLT-ACTION
SPORTER RIFLE . . . . NiB $1300 Ex $1050 Gd $690
Calibers: .22 LR. .22 Hornet. Five shot magazine. 22-inch bbl. Weight: 6.5 lbs. Adj. trigger. Checkered classic-style Claro or English walnut stock w/black recoil pad. Made 1992 to date.

MODEL 76 AFRICAN
BOLT-ACTION RIFLE . . . . NiB $4130 Ex $3700 Gd $2300
Same general specifications as Model 76 Safari. Calibers: .404 Jeffery, .416 Rigby, .416 Dakota, .450 Dakota. 24-inch bbl. Weight: 8 lbs. Checkered select walnut stock w/two crossbolts. Made 1989 to date.

MODEL 76 ALPINE
BOLT-ACTION RIFLE . . . . NiB $2195 Ex $1550 Gd $1035
Same general specifications as Model 76 Classic except short action w/blind magazine. Calibers: .22-250, .243, 6mm Rem., .250-3000, 7mm-08, .308. 21-inch bbl. Weight: 7.5 lbs. Made 1989-93.

MODEL 76 CLASSIC
BOLT-ACTION RIFLE . . . . NiB $2825 Ex $2195 Gd $1500
Calibers: .257 Roberts, .270 Win., .280 Rem., .30-06, 7mm Rem. Mag., .300 Win. Mag., .338 Win. Mag., .375 H&H Mag., .458 Win. Mag. 21- or 23-inch bbl. Weight: 7.5 lbs. Receiver drilled and

(cont'd.) **MODEL 76 CLASSIC BOLT-ACTION RIFLE**
tapped for sights. Adj. trigger. Classic-style checkered walnut stock w/steel grip cap and solid recoil pad. Right- and left-hand models. Made 1988 to date.

MODEL 76 LONGBOW TACTICAL
BOLT-ACTION RIFLE . . . . NiB $4050 Ex $3095 Gd $2095
Calibers: .300 Dakota Mag., .330 Dakota Mag., .338 Lapua Mag. Blind magazine. Ported 28-inch bbl. 50 to 51 inches overall. Weight: 13.7 lbs. Black or oliver green fiberglass stock w/adj. cheekpiece and buttplate. Receiver drilled and tapped w/one-piece rail mount and no sights. Made 1997 to date.

MODEL 76 SAFARI
BOLT-ACTION RIFLE . . . . NiB $4075 Ex $3075 Gd $2025
Calibers: .300 Win. Mag., .338 Win. Mag., .375 H&H Mag. .458 Win. Mag. 23-inch bbl. w/bbl. band swivel. Weight: 8.5 lbs. Ramp front sight, standing leaf rear. Checkered fancy walnut stock w/ebony forend tip and solid recoil pad. Made 1988 to date.

MODEL 76 TRAVELER SERIES RIFLES
Threadless take-down action w/interchangeable bbl. capability based on the Dakota 76 design. Calibers: .257 through .458 Win (Standard-Classic & Safari) and .416 Dakota, .404 Jeffery, .416 Rigby, .338 Lapua and .450 Dakota Mag. (E/F Family-African Grade). 23- to 24- inch bbl. Weight: 7.5 to 9.5 lbs. Right or left-hand action. X grade (Classic) or XXX grade (Safari or African) oil finish English Bastogne or Claro walnut stock. Made 1999 to date.
Classic Grade. . . . . NiB $4150 Ex $3125 Gd $2095
Safari Grade . . . . NiB $4125 Ex $3150 Gd $2550
African Grade . . . . NiB $5244 Ex $4195 Gd $2853
Interchangeable bbl. assemblies
Classic Grade, add. $1150
Safari Grade, add. $1450
African Grade, add $1595

RIFLES

MODEL 76 VARMINT

BOLT-ACTION RIFLE.......... **NiB $2275 Ex $1775 Gd $995**
Similar to Model 76 Classic except single-shot action w/ heavy bbl. chambered for .17 Rem. to 6mm PPC. Weight: 13.7 lbs. Checkered walnut or synthetic stock. Receiver drilled and tapped for scope mounts and no sights. Made 1994-98.

MODEL 97 HUNTER BOLT-ACTION SERIES

Calibers: .22-250 Rem. to .330 Dakota Mag.(Lightweight), .25-06 to .375 Dakota Mag. (Long Range). 22-, 24- or 26-inch bbl. 43 to 46 inches overall. Weight: 6.16 lbs. to 7.7 lbs. Black composite fiberglass stock w/recoil pad. Fully adj. match trigger. Made 1997 to date.
Lightweight .... **NiB $1795 Ex $1450 Gd $790**
Long Range .... **NiB $1563 Ex $1250 Gd $850**

MODEL 97 VARMINT HUNTER

BOLT-ACTION RIFLE.......... **NiB $1600 Ex $1375 Gd $750**
Similar to Model 97 Hunter except single-shot action w/ heavy bbl. chambered .22-250 Rem. to .308 Win. Checkered walnut stock. Receiver drilled and tapped for scope mounts and no sights. Made 1998 to date.

CHARLES DALY RIFLE — Harrisburg, Pennsylvania, *Imported by K.B.I., Inc., Harrisburg, PA, (Previously by Outdoor Sports Headquarters, Inc.)*

EMPIRE GRADE BOLT-ACTION RIFLE (RF)

Similar to Superior Grade except w/checkered California walnut stock w/rosewood grip cap and forearm cap. High polished blued finish and damascened bolt. Made 1998 to date.
Empire Grade (.22 LR) .... **NiB $306 Ex $245 Gd $167**
Empire Grade (.22WMR)........ **NiB $331 Ex $265 Gd $180**
Empire Grade (.22 Hornet) .... **NiB $469 Ex $375 Gd $255**

FIELD GRADE BOLT-ACTION RIFLE (RF)

Caliber: .22 LR. 16.25-, 17.5- or 22.63-inch bbl. 32 to 41 inches overall. Single-shot (True Youth) and 6- or 10-shot magazine. Plain walnut-finished hardwood or checkered polymer stock. Blue or stainless finish. Imported 1998 to date.
Field Grade (Standard w/22.63-inch bbl.).... **NiB $106 Ex $85 Gd $58**
Field Grade (Youth w/17.5-inch bbl.) .... **NiB $113 Ex $90 Gd $61**
Field Grade (True Youth w/16.25-inch bbl.) .... **NiB $149 Ex $119 Gd $81**
Field Grade (Polymer w/stainless action) .... **NiB $119 Ex $95 Gd $65**

FIELD GRADE HUNTER BOLT-ACTION RIFLE

Calibers: .22 Hornet, .223 Rem., .243 Win., .270 Win., 7mm Rem. Mag. .308 Win., .30-06, .300 Win. Mag., .300 Rem. Ultra Mag., .338 Win. Mag. Three, 4-, or 5-shot magazine. 22- or 24-inch bbl. w/o sights. Weight: 7.2 to 7.4 lbs. Checkered walnut or black polymer stock. Receiver drilled and tapped. Blue or stainless finish. Imported 1998 to date.
Field Grade Hunter (walnut stock) .... **NiB $475 Ex $380 Gd $258**
Field Grade Hunter (polymer stock) ...... **NiB $494 Ex $395 Gd $269**
w/Left-hand model, add **$35**

HAMMERLESS DRILLING

See listing under Charles Daly shotguns.

HORNET RIFLE .... **NiB $1188 Ex $950 Gd $646**
Same as Herold Rifle. See listing of that rifle for specifications. imported during the 1930s

MAUSER 98

Calibers: .243 Win., .270 Win., 7mm Rem. Mag. .308 Win., .30-06, .300 Win. Mag., .375 H&H, or .458 Win. Mag. Three, 4-, or 5-shot magazine. 23-inch bbl. 44.5 inches overall. Weight: 7.5 lbs. Checkered European walnut (Superior) or fiberglass/graphic (Field) stock w/recoil pad. Ramped front sight, adj. rear. Receiver drilled and tapped w/side saftey. Imported 1998 to date.
Field Grade (standard calibers)......... **NiB $395 Ex $345 Gd $100**
Field Grade (375 H&H and 458 Win. Mag.) .... **NiB $595 Ex $495 Gd $295**
Superior Grade (standard calibers)....... **NiB $595 Ex $450 Gd $295**
Superior Grade (magnum calibers)....... **NiB $819 Ex $695 Gd $537**

MINI-MAUSER 98

Similar to Mauser 98 except w/19.25-inch bbl. chambered for .22 Hornet, .22-250 Rem., .223 Rem., or 7.62x39mm. Five shot magazine. Imported 1998 to date.
Field Grade....................... **NiB $350 Ex $300 Gd $185**
Superior Grade.................... **NiB $460 Ex $375 Gd $200**

SUPERIOR GRADE BOLT-ACTION RIFLE

Calibers: .22 LR. .22 WMR, .22 Hornet. 20.25- to 22.63-inch bbl. 40.5 to 41.25 inches overall. Five, 6-, or 10-shot magazine. Ramped front sight, adj. rear w/grooved receiver. Checkered walnut stock. Made 1998 to date.
Superior Grade (.22 LR) .... **NiB $150 Ex $120 Gd $70**
Superior Grade (.22WMR) .... **NiB $175 Ex $135 Gd $90**
Superior Grade (.22 Hornet) ...... **NiB $335 Ex $285 Gd $175**

SEMIAUTOMATIC RIFLE

Caliber: .22 LR. 20.75-inch bbl. 40.5 inches overall. 10-shot magazine. Ramped front sight, adj. rear w/grooved receiver. Plain walnut-finished hardwood stock (Field), checkered walnut (Superior), checkered polymer stock or checkered California walnut stock w/rosewood grip cap and forearm cap (Empire). Blue or stainless finish. Imported 1998 to date.
Field Grade .... **NiB $110 Ex $90 Gd $55**
Field Grade (Polymer w/stainless action)............... **NiB $120 Ex $100 Gd $60**
Superior Grade .... **NiB $175 Ex $150 Gd $90**
Empire Grade .... **NiB $290 Ex $225 Gd $150**

EAGLE ARMS INC. — Geneseo, Illinois (Previously Coal Valley, Illinois)

In 1995, Eagle Arms Inc., became a division of ArmaLite and reintroduced that logo. For current ArmaLite production see models under that listing.

MODEL EA-15 CARBINE

Caliber: .223 Rem. (5.56mm). 30-shot magazine. 16-inch bbl. and collapsible buttstock. Weight: 5.75 lbs. (E1); 6.25 lbs. (E2 w/heavy bbl. & National Match sights). Made 1989 to 94.
E1 Carbine.................... **NiB $781 Ex $625 Gd $425**
E2 Carbine.................... **NiB $844 Ex $675 Gd $459**

MODEL EA-15 GOLDEN

EAGLE MATCH RIFLE .... **NiB $1095 Ex $850 Gd $550**
Same general specifications as EA-15 Standard, except w/E2-style National Match sights. 20-inch Douglas Heavy Match bbl. NM trigger and bolt-carrier group. Weight: 12.75 lbs. Made 1991 to 94.

EMF AP-74 Semiautomatic

EMF AP74-W Sporter

EMF AP-74 Paratrooper

EMF COMPANY, INC. — Santa Ana, California

MODEL AP-74
SEMI-AUTOMATIC CARBINE . . . . . **NiB $295 Ex $250 Gd $155**
Calibers: .22 LR or .32 ACP, 15-shot magazine. 20-inch bbl. w/flash reducer. 38 inches overall. Weight: 6.75 lbs. Protected pin front sight; protected rear peep sight. Lightweight plastic buttstock; ventilated snap-out forend. Importation. disc. 1989.

MODEL AP74-W
SPORTER CARBINE . . . . **NiB $325 Ex $260 Gd $150**
Sporterized version of AP-74 w/wood buttstock and forend. Importation disc. 1988.

MODEL AP74 PARATROOPER . . . . **NiB $280 Ex $195 Gd $175**
Same general specifications as Model AP74-W except w/folding tubular buttstock. Made in .22 LR. only. Importation disc. 1987.

MODEL 1860 HENRY RIFLE
Calibers: .44-40 and .45 LC. 24.25-inch bbl.; upper-half octagonal w/magazine tube in one-piece steel. 43.75-inches overall. Weight: 9.25 lbs. Varnished American walnut wood stock. Polished brass frame and brass buttplate. Original rifle was patented by B. Tyler Henry and produced by the New Haven Arms Company, when Oliver Winchester was president. Imported 1987 to date.
Deluxe model . . . . **NiB $775 Ex $600 Gd $270**
Engraved model . . . . **NiB $995 Ex $725 Gd $475**

MODEL 1866
YELLOW BOY RIFLE . . . . **NiB $575 Ex $495 Gd $290**
Calibers: .44-40, .45 LC and .38 Special. Lever-action. Bbl: 24 inches, 43 inches overall. Bead front sight. Exact reproduction. Offered w/blued finish, walnut stock and brass frame.

MODEL 1866 YELLOW BOY CARBINE
Same features as 1866 Yellow Boy Rifle except carbine.
Standard carbine . . . . **NiB $595 Ex $390 Gd $250**
Engraved carbine . . . . **NiB $600 Ex $475 Gd $275**

MODEL 1873 SPORTING RIFLE
Calibers: .22 LR. .22 WMR, .357 Mag., .44-40 and .45 LC. 24.25-inch octagonal bbl. 43.25 inches overall. Weight: 8.16 lbs. Color casehardened frame w/blued steel magazine tube. Walnut stock and forend.
Standard Rifle . . . . **NiB $750 Ex $600 Gd $375**
Engraved Rifle . . . . **NiB $875 Ex $575 Gd $390**
Boy's Rifle
(Youth Model, .22 LR) . . . . **NiB $590 Ex $475 Gd $300**

MODEL 1873 SPORTING RIFLE CARBINE
Same features as 1873 sporting rifle except w/19-inch bbl. Overall length: 38.25 inches. Weight: 7.38 lbs. Color casehardened or blued frame.
Standard carbine . . . . **NiB $750 Ex $600 Gd $375**
Boy's carbine (Youth Model, .22 LR) . . . . . . **NiB $590 Ex $475 Gd $300**

Erma — EG712

Erma — EGM1

Erma — EM1 22

ERMA-WERKE — Dachau, Germany (Previously imported by Precision Sales International; Nygord Precision Products; Mandall's Shooting Supplies)

MODEL EG72
PUMP-ACTION REPEATER . . . . **NiB $125 Ex $95 Gd $70**
Visible hammer. Caliber: .22 LR. 15-shot magazine. 18.5-inch bbl. Weight: 5.25 lbs. Sights: open rear; hooded ramp front. Receiver grooved for scope mounting. Straight-grip stock, grooved slide handle. Imported 1970-76.

MODEL EG73 . . . . NiB $265 Ex $230 Gd $125
Same as Model EG712 except chambered for .22 WMR w/12-shot tubular magazine, 19.3-inch bbl. Imported 1973-97.

MODEL EG712 LEVER-ACTION
REPEATING CARBINE. . . . . **NiB $260 Ex $230 Gd $125**
Styled after Winchester Model 94. Caliber: .22 LR. Long, Short. Tubular magazine holds 15 LR, 17 Long, 21 Short. 18.5-inch bbl. Weight: 5.5 lbs. Sights: Open rear; hooded ramp front. Receiver grooved for scope mounting. Western carbine-style stock and forearm w/bbl. band. Imported 1976-97. Note: A similar carbine of Erma manufacture is marketed in U.S. as Ithaca Model 72 Saddle Gun.

MODEL EGM1. . . . . NiB $265 Ex $225 Gd $125
Same as Model EM1 except w/unslotted buttstock, ramp front sight, 5-shot magazine standard. Imported 1970-95.

MODEL EM1 .22
SEMIAUTOMATIC CARBINE . . . . . . **NiB $350 Ex $275 Gd $175**
Styled after U.S. Carbine cal. 30 M1. Caliber: .22 LR. 10- or 15-round magazine. 18-inch bbl. Weight: 5.5 lbs. Carbine-type sights. Receiver grooved for scope mounting. Military stock/handguard. Imported 1966-97.

EUROPEAN AMERICAN ARMORY — Sharpes, Florida

MODEL HW 660 BOLT-ACTION
SINGLE-SHOT RIFLE. . . . . **NiB $795 Ex $650 Gd $400**
Caliber: .22 LR. 26.8-inch bbl., 45.7 inches overall. Weight: 10.8 lbs. Match-type aperture rear sight; Hooded ramp front. Stippled walnut stock. Imported 1992-96.

MODEL HW BOLT-ACTION
SINGLE-SHOT TARGET RIFLE . . . . . **NiB $790 Ex $650 Gd $450**
Same general specification as Model HW 660 except equipped w/ target stock. Imported 1995-96.

MODEL SABITTI SP1822
Caliber: .22 LR. 10-round detachable magazine. 18.5 inch bbl. 37.5 inches overall. Weight: 5.25 to 7.15 lbs. No sights. Hammer-forged heavy non-tapered bbl. Scope-mounted rail. Flush-mounted magazine release. Alloy receiver w/non-glare finish. Manual bolt lock. Wide claw extractor. Blowback action. Cross-trigger safety. Imported 1994-96.
Traditional Sporter model. . . . . NiB $194 Ex $155 Gd $105
**Thumbhole Sporter
model (synthetic stock)**. . . . . NiB $313 Ex $250 Gd $170

FABRIQUE NATIONALE HERSTAL — Herstal & Liege, Belgium, (Formerly Fabrique Nationale d'Armes de Guerre)

MODELS 1924, 1934/30 AND
1930 MAUSER MILITARY RIFLES . . . . **NiB $375 Ex $275 Gd $175**
Similar to German Kar. 98k w/straight bolt handle. Calibers: 7mm, 7.65mm and 7.9mm Mauser. Five shot box magazine. 23.5-inch bbl. Weight: 8.5 lbs. Sights: Adj. rear; blade front. Military stock of M/98 pattern w/slight modification. Model differences are minor. Also produced in a short carbine model w/17.25-inch bbl. Note: These rifles were manufactured under contract for Abyssinia, Argentina, Belgium, Bolivia, Brazil, Chile, China, Colombia, Ecuador, Iran, Luxembourg, Mexico, Peru, Turkey, Uruguay and Yugoslavia. Such arms usually bear the coat of arms of the country for which they were made together with the contractor's name and date of manufacture. Also sold commercially and exported to all parts of the world.

F.N. Model 1949

F.N. Model 1950 Mauser

F.N. Deluxe Mauser

F.N. Supreme Mauser

F.N. FAL Semiautomatic

MODEL 1949 SEMIAUTOMATIC
MILITARY RIFLE . . . . NiB $700 Ex $575 Gd $250
Gas-operated. Calibers: 7mm, 7.65mm, 7.92mm, .30-06. 10-round box magazine, clip fed or loaded singly. 23.2-inch bbl. Weight: 9.5 lbs. Sights: Tangent rear-shielded post front. Pistol-grip stock, handguard. Note: Adopted by Belgium in 1949; also by Belgian Congo, Brazil, Colombia, Luxembourg, Netherlands, East Indies, and Venezuela. Approx. 160,000 were made.

MODEL 1950 MAUSER
MILITARY RIFLE . . . . NiB $450 Ex $300 Gd $225
Same as previous F.N. models of Kar. 98k type except chambered for .30-06.

DELUXE MAUSER BOLT-ACTION
SPORTING RIFLE. . . . . NiB $695 Ex $600 Gd $350
American calibers: .220 Swift, .243 Win., .244 Rem., .250/3000, .257 Roberts, .270 Win., 7mm, .300 Sav., .308 Win. .30-06. European calibers: 7x57, 8x57JS, 8x60S, 9.3x62, 9.5x57, 10.75x68mm. Fiveshot box magazine. 24-inch bbl. Weight: 7.5-8.25 lbs. American model is standard w/hooded ramp front sight and Tri-Range rear; Continental model w/two-leaf rear. Checkered stock w/cheekpiece, pistol-grip, swivels. Made 1947-63.

DELUXE MAUSER —
PRESENTATION GRADE . . . . NiB $1200 Ex $950 Gd $650
Same as regular model except w/select grade stock; engraving on receiver, trigger guard, floorplate and bbl. breech. Disc. 1963.

FAL/FNC/LAR SEMIAUTOMATIC
Same as standard FAL military rifle except w/o provision for automatic firing. Gas-operated. Calibers: 7.62mm NATO (.308 Win.) or 5.56mm (.223 Rem.). 10- or 20-round box magazine. 25.5-inch bbl. (including flash hider). Weight: 9 lbs. Sights: Post front; aperture rear. Fixed wood or folding buttstock, pistol-grip, forearm/handguard w/carrying handle and sling swivels. Disc. 1988.
**F.N. FAL/LAR model (Light
Automatic Rifle)** . . . . NiB $2375 Ex $2050 Gd $1250
F.N. FAL/HB model (heavy bbl.) . . . . . . NiB $2688 Ex $2150 Gd $1462
F.N. FAL/PARA (Paratrooper) . . . . NiB $3300 Ex $2650 Gd $1650
**F.N. FNC Carbine
model (.223 cal.)** . . . . NiB $2500 Ex $1790 Gd $1150
**F.N. FNC Carbine model w/flash
suppresser (.223 cal.)** . . . . NiB $2600 Ex $1850 Gd $1200

SUPREME MAUSER BOLT-ACTION
SPORTING RIFLE. . . . . NiB $700 Ex $850 Gd $350
Calibers: .243, .270, 7mm, .308, .30-06. Four shot magazine in .243 and .308; 5-shot in other calibers. 22-inch bbl. in .308; 24-inch in other calibers. Sights: Hooded ramp front, Tri-Range peep rear. Checkered stock w/ Monte Carlo cheekpiece, pistol-grip, swivels. Weight: 7.75 lbs. Made 1957-75.

SUPREME MAGNUM MAUSER
. . . . NiB $750 Ex $600 Gd $375
Calibers: .264 Mag., 7mm Mag., .300 Win. Mag. Specifications same as for standard caliber model except 3-shot magazine capacity.

Finnish Lion Champion

Finnish Lion Match

FEATHER INDUSTRIES, INC. — Boulder, Colorado

See MITCHELL ARMS. For current production.

MODEL AT-9 SEMIAUTOMATIC RIFLE
Caliber: 9mm Parabellum. 10-, 25-, 32-, or 100-shot magazine. 17-inch bbl. 35 inches overall (extended). Hooded post front sight, adj. aperture rear. Weight: 5 lbs. Telescoping wire stock w/composition pistol-grip and barrel-shroud handguard. Matte black finish. Made 1988-95.

Model AT-9	NiB $700	Ex $625	Gd $400
W/32-shot magazine, add			$75
W/100-shot drum magazine, add			$250

MODEL AT-22 . . . . NiB $225 Ex $175 Gd $120
Caliber: .22 LR. 20-shot magazine. 17-inch bbl. 35 inches overall (extended). Hooded post front sight; adj. aperture rear. Weight: 3.25 lbs. Telescoping wire stock w/composition pistol-grip and barrel shroud handguard. Matte black finish.

MODEL F2 SA CARBINE . . . . NiB $250 Ex $190 Gd $110
Similar to AT-22, except w/fixed Polymer stock and pistol-grip. Made 1992-95.

MODEL F9 SA CARBINE . . . . NiB $575 Ex $525 Gd $325
Similar to AT-9, except w/fixed Polymer stock and pistol-grip. Made 1992-95.

FINNISH LION RIFLES — Jyväkylylä, Finland Manufactured by Valmet Oy, Tourula Works

CHAMPION FREE RIFLE . . . . NiB $594 Ex $475 Gd $323
Bolt-action single-shot target rifle. Double-set trigger. Caliber: .22 LR. 28.75-inch heavy bbl. Weight: 16 lbs. Sights: Extension rear peep; aperture front. Walnut free-rifle stock w/full pistol-grip, thumbhole, beavertail forend, hook buttplate, palm rest, hand stop, swivel. Made 1965-72.

STANDARD ISU
TARGET RIFLE . . . . NiB $350 Ex $275 Gd $150
Bolt-action, single-shot. Caliber: .22 LR. 27.5-inch bbl. Weight: 10.5 lbs. Sights: extension rear peep; aperture front. Walnut target stock w/full pistol-grip, checkered beavertail forearm, adj. buttplate, sling swivel. Made 1966-77.

MATCH RIFLE . . . . NiB $494 Ex $395 Gd $269
Bolt-action, single-shot. Caliber: .22 LR. 28.75-inch heavy bbl. Weight: 14.5 lbs. Sights: Extension rear peep; aperture front. Walnut free-rifle stock w/full pistol-grip, thumbhole, beavertail forearm, hook buttplate, palm rest, hand stop, swivel. Made 1937-72.

STANDARD TARGET RIFLE
Bolt-action, single-shot. Caliber: .22 LR. 27.5-inch bbl. 44.5 inches overall. Weight: 10.5 lbs. No sights; micrometer rear and globe front International-style sights available. Select walnut stock in target configuration. Currently in production.

Standard model	NiB $725	Ex $595	Gd $375
Thumbhole stock model	NiB $781	Ex $625	Gd $425
Standard model	NiB $350	Ex $250	Gd $150
Deluxe model	NiB $375	Ex $300	Gd $200

LUIGI FRANCHI, S.P.A. — Brescia, Italy

CENTENNIAL AUTOMATIC RIFLE
Commemorates Franchi's 100th anniversary (1868-1968). Centennial seal engraved on receiver. Semiautomatic. Take-down. Caliber: .22 LR. 11-shot magazine in buttstock. 21-inch bbl. Weight: 5.13 lbs. Sights: Open rear; gold bead front on ramp. Checkered walnut stock and forend. Deluxe model w/fully engraved receiver, premium grade wood. Made 1968.

Standard model	NiB $350	Ex $260	Gd $175
Engraved model	NiB $415	Ex $325	Gd $220

Franchi Deluxe Centennial

Francotte Sidelock Double Rifle

Francotte Boxlock Mountain Rifle
w/claw mounts and scope

Galil .223 AR Semiautomatic Rifle

FRANCOTTE RIFLES — Leige, Belgium
Imported by Armes de Chasse, Hertford, NC
(Previously by Abercrombie & Fitch)

BOLT-ACTION RIFLE
Custom rifle built on Mauser style bolt action. Available in three action lengths. Calibers: .17 Bee to .505 Gibbs. Barrel length: 21- to 24.5-inches. Weight: 8 to 12 lbs. Stock dimensions, wood type and style to customer's specifications. Engraving, appointments and finish to customer's preference. Note: Deduct 25% for models w/o engraving.
Short action . . . . NiB $9400 Ex $7350 Gd $4500
Standard action . . . . NiB $7825 Ex $6000 Gd $3600
Magnum Francotte action . . . . . NiB $13,750 Ex $10,800 Gd $7000

BOXLOCK MOUNTAIN RIFLE
Custom single-shot rifle built on Anson & Deeley style boxlock or Holland & Holland style sidelock action. 23- to 26-inch barrels chambered to customer's specification. Stock dimensions, wood type and style to customer's specifications. Engraving, appointments and finish to customer's preference. Note: Deduct 30% for models w/o engraving.
Boxlock . . . . NiB $13,900 Ex $11,700 Gd $7500
Sidelock . . . . NiB $22,438 Ex $17,950 Gd $12,206

DOUBLE RIFLE
Custom side-by-side rifle. Built on Francotte system boxlock or back-action sidelock. 23.5- to 26-inch barrels chambered to customer's specification. Stock dimensions, wood type and style to customer's specifications. Engraving, appointments and finish to customer's preference. Note: Deduct 30% for models w/o engraving.
Boxlock . . . . NiB $18,500 Ex $15,500 Gd $9500
Sidelock . . . . NiB $29,450 Ex $25,000 Gd $15,700

FRENCH MILITARY RIFLE — Saint Etienne, France

MODEL 1936
MAS MILITARY RIFLE . . . . NiB $150 Ex $110 Gd $60
Bolt-action. Caliber: 7.5mm MAS. 5-shot box magazine. 22.5-inch bbl. Weight: 8.25 lbs. Sights: Adj. rear; blade front. Two-piece military-type stock. Bayonet carried in forend tube. Made 1936-1940 by Manufacture Francaise d'Armes et de Cycles de St. Etienne (MAS).

GALIL RIFLES — Manufactured by Israel Military Industries, Israel, Imported by UZI America Inc., North Haven, CT
(Previously by Action Arms, Springfield Armory and Magnum Research, Inc.)

AR SEMIAUTOMATIC RIFLE
Calibers: .308 Win. (7.62 NATO), .223 Rem. (5.56mm). 25-shot (.308) or 35-shot (.223) magazine. 16-inch (.223) or 18.5-inch (.308) bbl. w/flash suppressor. Weight: 9.5 lbs. Folding aperture rear sight, post front. Folding metal stock w/carrying handle. Imported 1982-94. Currently select fire models available to law enforcement only.
Model .223 AR . . . . NiB $2200 Ex $1750 Gd $1000
Model .308 AR . . . . NiB $2200 Ex $1750 Gd $1000
Model .223 ARM . . . . NiB $2625 Ex $2000 Gd $1425
Model .308 ARM . . . . NiB $2625 Ex $2000 Gd $1425

SPORTER SEMIAUTOMATIC RIFLE...... NiB $998 Ex $900 Gd $575
Same general specifications as AR Model except w/hardwood thumb-hole stock and 5-shot magazine. Weight: 8.5 lbs. Imported 1991-94.

GARCIA CORPORATION — Teaneck, New Jersey

BRONCO 22 SINGLE-SHOT RIFLE......... NiB $95 Ex $75 Gd $50
Swing-out action. Takedown. Caliber: .22 LR. Long, Short. 16.5-inch bbl. Weight: 3 lbs. Sights: Open rear-blade front. One-piece stock and receiver, crackle finish. Intro. 1967. Discontinued.

GERMAN MILITARY RIFLES — Mfd. by Ludwig Loewe & Co., Berlin, other contractors and by German arsenals and various plants under German government control

MODEL 24T (GEW. 24T) MAUSER RIFLE .... NiB $500 Ex $350 Gd $225
Same general specifications as Czech Model 24 (VZ24) Mauser Rifle w/minor modification and laminated wood stock. Weight: 9.25 lbs. Made in Czechoslovakia during German occupation; adopted 1940.

MODEL 29/40 (GEW. 29/40)
MAUSER RIFLE .... NiB $350 Ex $250 Gd $150
Same general specifications as Kar. 98K w/minor differences. Made in Poland during German occupation; adopted 1940.

MODEL 33/40 (GEW. 33/40)
MAUSER RIFLE .... NiB $950 Ex $725 Gd $450
Same general specifications as Czech Model 33 (VZ33) Mauser Carbine w/minor modifications and laminated wood stock as found in war-time Model 98K carbines. Made in Czechoslovakia during German occupation; adopted 1940.

MODELS 41 AND 41-W (GEW. 41, GEW. 41-W)
SEMIAUTOMATIC MILITARY RIFLES
Gas-operated, muzzle cone system. Caliber: 7.9mm Mauser. 10-shot box magazine. 22.5-inch bbl. Weight: 10.25 lbs. Sights: Adj. leaf rear; blade front. Military-type stock w/semi-pistol grip, plastic handguard. Note: Model 41 lacks bolt release found on Model 41-W; otherwise, the models are the same. These early models were mfd. in Walther's Zella-Mehlis plant. Made c.1941-43.
Model 41................... NiB $4063 Ex $3250 Gd $2210
Model 41-W .... NiB $3119 Ex $2495 Gd $1697

MODEL 43 (GEW. 43, KAR. 43)
SEMIAUTO MILITARY RIFLES.......... NiB $1188 Ex $950 Gd $646
Gas-operated, bbl. vented as in Russian Tokarev. Caliber: 7.9mm Mauser. 10-shot detachable box magazine. 22- or 24-inch bbl. Weight: 9 lbs. Sights: Adj. rear; hooded front. Military-type stock w/semi-pistol-grip, wooden handguard. Note: These rifles are alike except for minor details, have characteristic late WWII mfg. short cuts: cast receiver and bolt cover, stamped steel parts, etc. Gew. 43 may have either 22- or 24-inch bbl. The former length was standardized in late 1944, when weapon designation was changed to "Kar. 43." Made 1943-45.

MODEL 1888 (GEW. 88) MAUSER-
MANNLICHER SERVICE RIFLE.......... NiB $350 Ex $200 Gd $150
Bolt-action w/straight bolt handle. Caliber: 7.9mm Mauser (8x57mm). Five shot Mannlicher box magazine. 29-inch bbl. w/jacket. Weight: 8.5 lbs. Fixed front sight, adj. rear. Military-type full stock. Mfd. by Ludwig Loewe & Co., Haenel, Schilling and other contractors.

MODEL 1888 (KAR. 88) MAUSER-
MANNLICHER CARBINE........ NiB $250 Ex $200 Gd $150
Same general specifications as Gew. 88 except w/18-inch bbl., w/o jacket, flat turned-down bolt handle, weight: 6.75 lbs. Mfd. by Ludwig Loewe & Co., Haenel, Schilling and other contractors.

MODEL 1898 (GEW. 98)
MAUSER MILITARY RIFLE........ NiB $475 Ex $350 Gd $200
Bolt action with straight bolt handle. Caliber: 7.9mm Mauser (8x57mm). Five shot box magazine. 29-inch stepped bbl. Weight: 9 lbs. Sights: Blade front; adj. rear. Military-type full stock w/rounded bottom pistol grip. Adopted 1898.

MODEL 1898A (KAR. 98A)
MAUSER CARBINE .... NiB $395 Ex $350 Gd $150
Same general specifications as Model 1898 (Gew.98) Rifle except has turned-down bolt handle, smaller receiver ring, light 23.5-inch-straight taper bbl., front sight guards, sling is attached to left side of stock, weight: 8 lbs. Note: Some of these carbines are marked "Kar. 98;" the true Kar. 98 is the earlier original M/98 carbine w/17-inch bbl. and is rarely encountered.

MODEL 1898B (KAR. 98B)
MAUSER CARBINE .... NiB $425 Ex $350 Gd $250
Same general specifications as Model 1898 (Gew.98) Rifle except has turned-down bolt handle and sling attached to left side of stock. This is post-WWI model.

MODEL 1898K (KAR. 98K)
MAUSER CARBINE .... NiB $425 Ex $350 Gd $250
Same general specifications as Model 1898 (Gew.98) Rifle except has turned-down bolt handle, 23.5-inch bbl., may have hooded front sight, sling attached to left side of stock, weighs about 8.5 lbs. Adopted in 1935, this was the standard German service rifle of WWII. Note: Late-war models had stamped sheet steel trigger guards and many of the Model 98K carbines made during WWII had laminated wood stocks These weigh .5 to .75 pound more than the previous Model 98K. Value shown is for earlier type.

MODEL VK 98
PEOPLE'S RIFLE ("VOLKSAEWEHR").. NiB $219 Ex $175 Gd $119
Kar. 98K-type action. Caliber: 7.9mm. Single-shot or repeater (latter w/rough hole-in-the-stock 5-shot "magazine" or fitted w/10-shot clip of German Model 43 semiauto rifle). 20.9-inch bbl. Weight: 7 lbs. Fixed V-notch rear sight dovetailed into front receiver ring; front blade welded to bbl. Crude, unfinished, half-length stock w/o buttplate. Last ditch weapon made in 1945 for issue to German civilians. Note: Of value only as a military arms collector's item, this hastily-made rifle should be regarded as unsafe to shoot.

GÉVARM RIFLE — Saint Etienne, France Manufactured by Gevelot

E-1 AUTOLOADING RIFLE .... NiB $175 Ex $150 Gd $100
Caliber: .22 LR. 8-shot clip magazine. 19.5-inch bbl. Sights: Open rear; post front. Pistol-grip stock and forearm of French walnut.

GOLDEN EAGLE RIFLES — Houston, Texas Mfd. by Nikko Firearms Ltd., Tochigi, Japan

MODEL 7000 GRADE I AFRICAN .... NiB $650 Ex $500 Gd $395
Same as Grade I Big Game except: Caliber: .375 H&H Mag. and .458 Win. Mag. two-shot magazine in .458, weight: 8.75 lbs. in .375 and 10.5 lbs. in .458, furnished w/sights. Imported 1976-81.

RIFLES

Golden Eagle Model 7000

Carl Gustaf Model 2000

Carl Gustaf Deluxe

Carl Gustaf Grand Prix

Carl Gustaf Sporter

MODEL 7000 BIG GAME SERIES

Bolt action. Calibers: .22-250, .243 Win., .25-06, .270 Win., Weatherby Mag., 7mm Rem. Mag., .30-06, .300 Weatherby Mag., .300 Win. Mag., .338 Win. Mag. Magazine capacity: 4 rounds in .22-250, 3 rounds in other calibers. 24- or 26-inch bbl. (26-inch only in 338). Weight: 7 lbs., .22-250; 8.75, lbs., other calibers. Furnished w/o sights. Fancy American walnut stock, skip checkered, contrasting wood forend tip and grip cap w/gold eagle head, recoil pad. Imported 1976-81.

Model 7000 Grade I . . . . NiB $681 Ex $545 Gd $371
Model 7000 Grade II . . . . NiB $744 Ex $595 Gd $405

GREIFELT & CO. — Suhl, Germany

SPORT MODEL 22 HORNET
BOLT-ACTION RIFLE . . . . NiB $2119 Ex $1695 Gd $1153
Caliber: .22 Hornet. Five shot box magazine. 22-inch Krupp steel bbl. Weight: 6 lbs. Sights: Two-leaf rear; ramp front. Walnut stock, checkered pistol-grip and forearm. Made before WWII.

CARL GUSTAF RIFLES — Eskilstuna, Sweden
Mfd. by Carl Gustaf Stads Gevärsfaktori

MODEL 2000 BOLT-ACTION RIFLE
Calibers: .243, 6.5x55, 7x64, .270, .308 Win., .30-06, 7mm Rem. Mag., .300 Win. Mag. Three shot magazine. 24-inch bbl. 44 inches overall. Weight: 7.5 lbs. Receiver drilled and tapped. Hooded ramp front sight, open rear. Adj. trigger. Checkered European walnut stock w/Monte Carlo cheekpiece and Wundhammer palmswell grip. Imported 1991-95

Model 2000
w/o sights . . . . NiB $1369 Ex $1095 Gd $745
Model 2000 w/sights . . . . NiB $1563 Ex $1250 Gd $850
Model 2000 LUXE . . . . NiB $1695 Ex $1500 Gd $900

DELUXE . . . . NiB $719 Ex $575 Gd $391
Same specifications as Monte Carlo Standard. Calibers: 6.5x55, 308 Win., .30-06, 9.3x62. Four shot magazine in 9.3x62. Jeweled bolt. Engraved floorplate and trigger guard. Deluxe French walnut stock w/rosewood forend tip. Imported 1970-77.

Hammerli Model 45

Hammerli-Tanner 300M

GRAND PRIX SINGLE-SHOT
TARGET RIFLE . . . . **NiB $595 Ex $495 Gd $330**
Special bolt action with "world's shortest lock time." Single-stage trigger adjusts down to 18 oz. Caliber: .22 LR. 26.75-inch heavy bbl. w/adj. trim weight. Weight: 9.75 lbs. Furnished w/o sights. Target-type Monte Carlo stock of French walnut, adj. cork buttplate. Imported 1970-77.

MONTE CARLO STANDARD
BOLT-ACTION SPORTING RIFLE . . . . **NiB $450 Ex $395 Gd $350**
Carl Gustaf 1900 action. Calibers: 6.5x55, 7x64, .270 Win., 7mm Rem. Mag., .308 Win., .30-06, 9.3x62. Five shot magazine, except 4-shot in 9.3x62 and 3-shot in 7mm Rem. Mag. 23.5-inch bbl. Weight: 7 lbs. Sights: Folding leaf rear; hooded ramp front. French walnut Monte Carlo stock w/cheekpiece, checkered forearm and pistol grip, sling swivels. Also available in left-hand model. Imported 1970-77.

SPECIAL . . . . **NiB $500 Ex $425 Gd $295**
Also designated "Grade II" in U.S. and "Model 9000" in Canada. Same specifications as Monte Carlo Standard. Calibers: .22-250, .243 Win., .25-06, .270 Win., 7mm Rem. Mag., .308 Win., .30-06, .300 Win. Mag. Three shot magazine in magnum calibers. Select wood stock w/rosewood forend tip. Left-hand model avail. Imported 1970-77.

SPORTER . . . . **NiB $594 Ex $475 Gd $323**
Also designated "Varmint-Target" in U.S. Fast bolt action w/large Bakelite bolt knob. Trigger pull adjusts down to 18 oz. Calibers: .222 Rem., .22-250, .243 Win., 6.5x55. Five shot magazine except 6-shot in .222 Rem. 26.75-inch heavy bbl. Weight: 9.5 lbs. Furnished w/o sights. Target-type Monte Carlo stock of French walnut. Imported 1970 to date.

STANDARD . . . . **NiB $550 Ex $450 Gd $300**
Same specifications as Monte Carlo Standard. Calibers: 6.5x55, 7x64, .270 Win., .308 Win., .30-06, 9.3x62. Classic-style stock w/o Monte Carlo. Imported 1970-77.

TROFÉ . . . . **NiB $795 Ex $600 Gd $410**
Also designated "Grade III" in U.S. and "Model 8000" in Canada. Same specifications as Monte Carlo Standard. Calibers: .22-250, .25-06, 6.5x55, .270 Win., 7mm Rem. Mag., .308 Win., .30-06, .300 Win. Mag. Three shot magazine in magnum calibers. Furnished w/o sights. Fancy wood stock w/rosewood forend tip, high-gloss lacquer finish. Imported 1970-77.

C.G. HAENEL — Suhl, Germany

'88 MAUSER SPORTER . . . . **NiB $525 Ex $405 Gd $300**
Same general specifications as Haenel Mauser-Mannlicher except w/Mauser 5-shot box magazine.

MAUSER-MANNLICHER
BOLT-ACTION SPORTING RIFLE . . **NiB $475 Ex $375 Gd $225**
Mauser M/88-type action. Calibers: 7x57, 8x57, 9x57mm. Mannlicher clip-loading box magazine, 5-shot. 22- or 24-inch half or full octagon bbl. w/raised matted rib. Double-set trigger. Weight: 7.5 lbs. Sights: Leaf-type open rear; ramp front. Sporting stock w/cheekpiece, checkered pistol-grip, raised side-panels, Schnabel tip, swivels.

HÄMMERLI AG JAGD-UND — SPORTWAF-FENFABRIK

Lenzburg, Switzerland, Imported by Sigarms, Exetre, NH, (Previously by Hammerli USA; Mandall Shooting Supplies, Inc. & Beeman Precision Arms)

MODEL 45 SMALLBORE BOLT-ACTION
SINGLE-SHOT MATCH RIFLE . . . . **NiB $660 Ex $550 Gd $350**
Calibers: .22 LR. 22 Extra Long. 27.5-inch heavy bbl. Weight: 15.5 lbs. Sights: Micrometer peep rear; globe front. Free-rifle stock w/cheekpiece, full pistol-grip, thumbhole, beavertail forearm, palm-rest, Swiss-type buttplate, swivels. Made 1945-57.

MODEL 54 SMALLBORE
MATCH RIFLE . . . . **NiB $670 Ex $550 Gd $325**
Bolt-action, single-shot. Caliber: .22 LR. 27.5-inch heavy bbl. Weight: 15 lbs. Sights: Micrometer peep rear; globe front. Free-rifle stock w/cheekpiece, thumbhole, adj. hook buttplate, palm rest, swivel. Made 1954-57.

MODEL 503 FREE RIFLE . . . . **NiB $650 Ex $550 Gd $325**
Bolt-action, single-shot. Caliber: .22 LR. 27.5-inch heavy bbl. Weight: 15 lbs. Sights: Micrometer peep rear; globe front. Free-rifle stock w/cheekpiece, thumbhole, adj. hook buttplate, palm rest, swivel. Made 1957-62.

Harrington & Richardson
Model 60 Reising

Harrington & Richardson
Model 65 Military

Harrington & Richardson
Model 150 Leatherneck

MODEL 506 SMALLBORE MATCH RIFLE . . . . NiB $675 Ex $550 Gd $350
Bolt-action, single-shot. Caliber: .22 LR. 26.75-inch heavy bbl. Weight: 16.5 lbs. Sights: Micrometer peep rear; globe front. Free-rifle stock w/cheekpiece, thumbhole adj. hook buttplate, palmrest, swivel. Made 1963-66.

MODEL OLYMPIA 300 METER BOLT-ACTION SINGLE-SHOT FREE RIFLE . . . . NiB $875 Ex $750 Gd $450
Calibers: .30-06, .300 H&H Magnum for U.S.A.; ordinarily produced in 7.5mm, other calibers available on special order. 29.5-inch heavy bbl. Double-pull or double-set trigger. Sights: Micrometer peep rear, globe front. Free-rifle stock w/cheekpiece, full pistol grip, thumbhole, beavertail forend, palmrest, Swiss-type buttplate, swivels. Made 1945-59.

TANNER 300 METER FREE RIFLE . . . . NiB $900 Ex $825 Gd $450
Bolt-action, single-shot. Caliber: 7.5mm standard, available in most popular centerfire calibers. 29.5-inch heavy bbl. Weight: 16.75 lbs. Sights: Micrometer peep rear; globe front. Free-rifle stock w/cheekpiece, thumbhole, adj. hook buttplate, palmrest, swivel. Intro. 1962. Disc. See Illustration previous page.

HARRINGTON & RICHARDSON, INC. — Gardner, Massachusetts (Now H&R 1871, INC., Gardner, Mass.)

Formerly Harrington & Richardson Arms Co. of Worcester, Mass. One of the oldest and most distinguished manufacturers of handguns, rifles and shotguns, H&R suspended operations on January 24, 1986. In 1987, New England Firearms was established as an independent company producing selected H&R models under the NEF logo. In 1991, H&R 1871, Inc. was formed from the residual of the parent company and that took over the New England Firearms facility. H&R 1871 produced firearms under both its logo and the NEF brand name until 1999 when the Marlin Firearms Company acquired the assets of H&R 1871.

MODEL 60 REISING SEMI-AUTOMATIC RIFLE . . . . NiB $500 Ex $475 Gd $225
Caliber: .45 Automatic. 12- and 20-shot detachable box magazines. 18.25-inch bbl. Weight: 7.5 lbs. Sights: Open rear; blade front. Plain pistol-grip stock. Made 1944-46.

MODEL 65 MILITARY AUTOLOADING RIFLE . . . . NiB $300 Ex $240 Gd $125
Also called "General." Caliber: .22 LR. 10-shot detachable box magazine. 23-inch heavy bbl. Weight: 9 lbs. Sights: Redfield 70 rear peep, blade front w/protecting "ears." Plain pistol-grip stock, "Garand" dimensions. Made 1944-46. Note: This model was used as a training rifle by the U.S. Marine Corps.

MODEL 150 LEATHERNECK AUTOLOADER . . . . NiB $100 Ex $80 Gd $60
Caliber: .22 LR. only. Five shot detachable box magazine. 22-inch bbl. Weight: 7.25 lbs. Sights: Open rear; blade front, on ramp. Plain pistol-grip stock. Made 1949-53.

MODEL 151 . . . . NiB $150 Ex $85 Gd $70
Same as Model 150 except w/Redfield 70 rear peep sight.

MODEL 155 SINGLE-SHOT RIFLE . . . . NiB $180 Ex $130 Gd $80
Model 158 action. Calibers: .44 Rem. Mag., .45-70 Govt. 24- or 28-inch bbl. (latter in .44 only). Weight: 7 or 7.5 lbs. Sights: Folding leaf rear; blade front. Straight-grip stock, forearm w/bbl. band, brass cleaning rod. Made 1972-82.

MODEL 157 SINGLE-SHOT RIFLE . . . . NiB $180 Ex $100 Gd $70
Model 158 action. Calibers: .22 WMR, .22 Hornet, .30-30. 22-inch bbl. Weight: 6.25 lbs. Sights: Folding leaf rear; blade front. Pistol-grip stock, full-length forearm, swivels. Made 1976-86.

Harrington & Richardson
Model 155

Harrington & Richardson
Model 157

Harrington & Richardson
Model 158 Topper Jet

Harrington & Richardson
Model 158C w/extra shotgun barrel

MODEL 158 TOPPER JET SINGLE-SHOT COMBINATION RIFLE

Shotgun-type action w/visible hammer, side lever, auto ejector. Caliber: .22 Rem. Jet. 22-inch bbl. (interchanges with .30-30, .410 ga., 20 ga. bbls.). Weight: 5 lbs. Sights: Lyman folding adj. open rear; ramp front. Plain pistol-grip stock and forearm, recoil pad. Made 1963-67.

Rifle only . . . . NiB $150 Ex $125 Gd $80
Interchangeable bbl.
.30-30, shotgun . . . . NiB $50 Ex $40 Gd $25

MODEL 158C . . . . NiB $150 Ex $135 Gd $80

Same as Model 158 Topper Jet except calibers .22 Hornet, .30-30, .357 Mag., .357 Mag., .44 Mag. Straight-grip stock. Made 1963-86.

MODEL 163 MUSTANG

SINGLE-SHOT RIFLE . . . . NiB $150 Ex $130 Gd $75
Same as Model 158 Topper except w/gold-plated hammer and trigger, straight-grip stock and contoured forearm. Made 1964-67.

MODEL 165 LEATHERNECK AUTOLOADER . . . NiB $125 Ex $110 Gd $75

Caliber: .22 LR. 10-shot detachable box magazine. 23-inch bbl. Weight: 7.5 lbs. Sights: Redfield 70 rear peep; blade front, on ramp. Plain pistol-grip stock, swivels, web sling. Made 1945-61.

MODEL 171 . . . . NiB $350 Ex $300 Gd $190

Model 1873 Springfield Cavalry Carbine replica. Caliber: .45-70. 22-inch bbl. Weight: 7 lbs. Sights: Leaf rear; blade front. Plain walnut stock. Made 1972-81.

MODEL 171 DELUXE . . . . NiB $400 Ex $350 Gd $250

Same as Model 171 except engraved action and different sights. Made 1972-86. See illustration next page.

MODEL 172 . . . . NiB $1244 Ex $995 Gd $677

Same as Model 171 Deluxe except silver-plated, w/fancy walnut stock, checkered, w/grip adapter; tang-mounted aperture sight. Made 1972-86.

MODEL 173 . . . . NiB $406 Ex $325 Gd $221

Model 1873 Springfield Officer's Model replica, same as 100th Anniversary Commemorative except w/o plaque on stock. Made 1972-86.

MODEL 174 . . . . NiB $400 Ex $350 Gd $250

Little Big Horn Commemorative Carbine. Same as Model 171 Deluxe except w/tang-mounted aperture sight, grip adapter. Made 1972-84.

MODEL 178 . . . . NiB $400 Ex $350 Gd $250

Model 1873 Springfield Infantry Rifle replica. Caliber: .45-70. 32-inch bbl. Weight: 8 lbs. 10 oz. Sights: Leaf rear; blade front. Full-length stock w/bbl. bands, swivels, ramrod. Made 1973-86.

MODEL 250 SPORTSTER BOLT-ACTION

REPEATING RIFLE . . . . NiB $95 Ex $75 Gd $50
Caliber: .22 LR. 5-shot detachable box magazine. 23-inch bbl. Weight: 6.5 lbs. Sights: Open rear; blade front, on ramp. Plain pistol-grip stock. Made 1948-61.

Harrington & Richardson
Model 171

Harrington & Richardson
Model 171 Deluxe

Harrington & Richardson
Model 172

Harrington & Richardson
Model 173

Harrington & Richardson
Model 174 Little Big Horn Commemorative

Harrington & Richardson
Model 178

MODEL 251 . . . . NiB $106 Ex $85 Gd $58
Same as Model 250 except w/Lyman No. 55H rear sight.

**MODEL 265 "REG'LAR" BOLT-
ACTION REPEATING RIFLE.** . . . . NiB $100 Ex $80 Gd $54
Caliber: .22 LR. 10-shot detachable box magazine. 22-inch bbl.
Weight: 6.5 lbs. Sights: Lyman No. 55 rear peep; blade front, on
ramp. Plain pistol-grip stock. Made 1946-49.

**MODEL 300 ULTRA
BOLT-ACTION RIFLE.** . . . . NiB $500 Ex $425 Gd $225
Mauser-type action. Calibers: .22-250, .243 Win., .270 Win., .30-06,
.308 Win., 7mm Rem. Mag., .300 Win. Mag. Three round magazine
in 7mm and .300 Mag. calibers, 5-round in others. 22- or 24-inch bbl.
Sights: Open rear; ramp front. Checkered stock w/rollover cheekpiece
and full pistol grip, contrasting wood forearm tip and pistol grip, rubber buttplate, sling swivels. Weight: 7.25 lbs. Made 1965-82.

Harrington & Richardson
Model 300

Harrington & Richardson
Model 301 Carbine

Harrington & Richardson
Model 317P

Harrington & Richardson
Model 330

Harrington & Richardson
Model 360 Ultra

Harrington & Richardson
Model 370 Ultra Medalist

MODEL 301 CARBINE . . . . **NiB $425 Ex $350 Gd $225**
Same as Model 300 except w/18-inch bbl., Mannlicher-style stock, weighs 7.25 lbs.; not available in caliber .22-250. Made 1967-82.

MODEL 308 AUTOMATIC RIFLE. . . **NiB $406 Ex $325 Gd $221**
Original designation of the Model 360 Ultra. Made 1965-67.

**MODEL 317 ULTRA WILDCAT
BOLT-ACTION RIFLE**. . . . . **NiB $595 Ex $550 Gd $325**
Sako short action. Calibers: .17 Rem. 17/.223 (handload), .222 Rem.,

(cont'd.) MODEL 317 ULTRA WILDCAT BOLT-ACTION RIFLE
.223 Rem. Six round magazine. 20-inch bbl. No sights, receiver dovetailed for scope mounts. Checkered stock w/cheekpiece and full pistol grip, contrasting wood forearm tip and pistol-grip cap, rubber buttplate. Weight: 5.25 lbs. Made 1968-76.

**MODEL 317P
PRESENTATION GRADE** . . . . **NiB $700 Ex $575 Gd $400**
Same as Model 317 except w/select grade fancy walnut stock w/basket weave carving on forearm and pistol-grip. Made 1968-76.

Harrington & Richardson
Model 700 Deluxe

Harrington & Richardson
Model 750 Pioneer

Harrington & Richardson
"New" Model 750

Harrington & Richardson
Model 755

MODEL 330 HUNTER'S RIFLE .... NiB $300 Ex $250 Gd $175
Similar to Model 300, but w/plainer stock. Calibers: .243 Win., .270 Win., .30-06, .308 Win., 7mm Rem. Mag., .300 Win. Mag. Weight: 7.13 lbs. Made 1967-72.

MODEL 333 .... NiB $250 Ex $225 Gd $125
Plainer version of Model 300 w/uncheckered walnut-finished hardwood stock. Calibers: 7mm Rem. Mag. and .30-06. 22-inch bbl. Weight: 7.25 lbs. No sights. Made in 1974.

MODEL 340 .... NiB $375 Ex $300 Gd $195
Mauser-type action. Calibers: .243 Win., .308 Win., .270 Win., .30-06, 7x57. 22-inch bbl. Weight: 7.25 lbs. Hand-checkered American walnut stock. Made 1982-84.

MODEL 360
ULTRA AUTOMATIC RIFLE .... NiB $405 Ex $325 Gd $225
Gas-operated semiautomatic. Calibers: .243 Win., .308 Win. Three round detachable box magazine. 22-inch bbl. Sights: Open rear; ramp front. Checkered stock w/rollover cheekpiece, full pistol grip, contrasting wood forearm tip and pistol-grip cap, rubber buttplate, sling swivels. Weight: 7.25 lbs. Made 1967-78.

MODEL 361 .... NiB $450 Ex $375 Gd $250
Same as Model 360 except w/full rollover cheekpiece for right- or left-hand shooters. Made 1970-73.

MODEL 365 ACE BOLT-ACTION
SINGLE-SHOT RIFLE .... NiB $100 Ex $95 Gd $50
Caliber: .22 LR. 22-inch bbl. Weight: 6.5 lbs. Sights: Lyman No. 55 rear peep, blade front, on ramp. Plain pistol-grip stock. Made 1946-47.

MODEL 370 ULTRA MEDALIST ... NiB $475 Ex $450 Gd $258
Varmint and target rifle based on Model 300. Calibers: .22-250, .243 Win., 6mm Rem. Three round magazine. 24-inch varmint weight bbl. No sights. Target-style stock w/semibeavertail forearm. Weight: 9.5 lbs. Made 1968-73.

MODEL 422 SLIDE-ACTION
REPEATER .... NiB $125 Ex $95 Gd $75
Caliber: .22 LR. Long, Short. Tubular magazine holds 21 Short, 17 Long, 15 LR. 24-inch bbl. Weight: 6 lbs. Sights: Open rear; ramp front. Plain pistol-grip stock grooved slide handle. Made 1956-58.

MODEL 450 .... NiB $110 Ex $95 Gd $50
Same as Model 451 except w/o front and rear sights.

MODEL 451 MEDALIST
BOLT-ACTION TARGET RIFLE ...... NiB $175 Ex $150 Gd $80
Caliber: .22 LR. Five shot detachable box magazine. 26-inch bbl. Weight: 10.5 lbs. Sights: Lyman No. 524F extension rear; Lyman No. 77 front, scope bases. Target stock w/full pistol-grip and forearm, swivels and sling. Made 1948-61.

RIFLES

Harrington & Richardson
Model 760

Harrington & Richardson
Model 866

Harrington & Richardson
Model 1873 — 100th Anniversary

Harrington & Richardson
Model 5200 Sporter

Harrington & Richardson
Ultra Varmint

MODEL 465 TARGETEER SPECIAL
BOLT-ACTION REPEATER . . . . **NiB $160 Ex $125 Gd $80**
Caliber: .22 LR. 10-shot detachable box magazine. 25-inch
bbl. Weight: 9 lbs. Sights: Lyman No. 57 rear peep; blade front,
on ramp. Plain pistol-grip stock, swivels, web sling strap. Made
1946-47.

MODEL 700 AUTOLOADER . . . . . . **NiB $275 Ex $250 Gd $125**
Caliber: .22 WMR. 5-shot magazine. 22-inch bbl. Weight: 6.5 lbs.
Sights: Folding leaf rear; blade front, on ramp. Monte Carlo-style
stock of American walnut. Made 1977-86.

MODEL 700 DELUXE . . . . **NiB $400 Ex $325 Gd $250**
Same as Model 700 Standard except w/select custom polished and
blued finish, select walnut stock, hand checkering, and no iron
sights. Fitted w/H&R Model 432 4x scope. Made 1980-86.

MODEL 750 PIONEER BOLT-ACTION
SINGLE-SHOT RIFLE . . . . **NiB $90 Ex $70 Gd $50**
Caliber: .22 LR. Long, Short. 22- or 24-inch bbl. Weight: 5 lbs. Sights: Open rear;
bead front. Plain pistol-grip stock. Made 1954-81; redesigned 1982; discont. 1985.

MODEL 751 SINGLE-SHOT RIFLE . . . . **NiB $75 Ex $55 Gd $35**
Same as Model 750 except w/Mannlicher-style stock. Made 1971.

MODEL 755 SAHARA
SINGLE-SHOT RIFLE . . . . **NiB $75 Ex $55 Gd $35**
Blow-back action, automatic ejection. Caliber: .22 LR. Long, Short.
18-inch bbl. Weight: 4 lbs. Sights: Open rear; military-type front.
Mannlicher-style stock. Made 1963-71.

MODEL 760 SINGLE-SHOT . . . . **NiB $90 Ex $70 Gd $50**
Same as Model 755 except w/conventional sporter stock. Made 1965-70.

MODEL 765 PIONEER BOLT-ACTION
SINGLE-SHOT RIFLE . . . . NiB $70 Ex $55 Gd $35
Caliber: .22 LR. Long, Short. 24-inch bbl. Weight: 5 lbs. Sights: Open rear; hooded bead front. Plain pistol-grip stock. Made 1948-54.

MODEL 800 LYNX
AUTOLOADING RIFLE. . . . . NiB $125 Ex $100 Gd $65
Caliber: .22 LR. Five or 10-shot clip magazine. 22-inch bbl. Open sights. Weight: 6 lbs. Plain pistol-grip stock. Made 1958-60.

MODEL 852 FIELDSMAN
BOLT-ACTION REPEATER . . . . NiB $110 Ex $55 Gd $60
Caliber: .22 LR. Long, Short. Tubular magazine holds 21 Short, 17 Long, 15 LR. 24-inch bbl. Weight: 5.5 lbs. Sights: Open rear; bead front. Plain pistol-grip stock. Made 1952-53.

MODEL 865 PLAINSMAN
BOLT-ACTION REPEATER . . . . NiB $100 Ex $80 Gd $50
Caliber .22 LR. Long, Short. Five shot detachable box magazine. 22- or 24-inch bbl. Weight: 5.25 lbs. Sights: Open rear, bead front. Plain pistol-grip stock. Made 1949-86.

MODEL 866
BOLT-ACTION REPEATER . . . . NiB $100 Ex $80 Gd $50
Same as Model 865, except w/Mannlicher-style stock. Made 1971.

MODEL 1873 100TH ANNIVERSARY
(1871-1971) COMMEMORATIVE
OFFICER'S SPRINGFIELD REPLICA. . . . . . . NiB $750 Ex $550 Gd $375
Model 1873 "trap door" single-shot action. Engraved breech block, receiver, hammer, lock, band and buttplate. Caliber: .45-70. 26-inch bbl. Sights: Peep rear; blade front. Checkered walnut stock w/anniversary plaque. Ramrod. Weight: 8 lbs. 10,000 made 1971.

MODEL 5200 SPORTER . . . . NiB $595 Ex $500 Gd $308
Turn-bolt repeater. Caliber: .22 LR. 24-inch bbl. Classic-style American walnut stock. Adj. trigger. Sights: Peep receiver; hooded ramp front. Weight: 6.5 lbs. Disc. 1983.

MODEL 5200 MATCH RIFLE. . . . . . NiB $400 Ex $395 Gd $300
Same action as 5200 Sporter. Caliber: .22 LR. 28-inch target weight bbl. Target stock of American walnut. Weight: 11 lbs. Made 1982-86.

CUSTER MEMORIAL ISSUE
Limited Edition Model 1873 Springfield Carbine replica, richly engraved and inlaid w/gold, fancy walnut stock, in mahogany display case. Made 1973.
Officers' Model
Limited to 25 pieces. . . . . NIB $5625 EX $4500 GD $3060
Enlisted Men's model,
limited to 243 pieces. . . . . NiB $3125 Ex $2500 Gd $1700

TARGETEER JR. BOLT-ACTION RIFLE . . . . . NiB $125 Ex $100 Gd $65
Caliber: .22 LR. 5-shot detachable box magazine. 20-inch bbl. Weight: 7 lbs. Sights: Redfield 70 rear peep; Lyman No. 17A front. Target stock, junior-size w/pistol grip, swivels and sling. Made 1948-51.

ULTRA SINGLE-SHOT RIFLE
Side-lever single-shot. Calibers: .22-250 Rem., .223 Rem., .25-06 Rem., .308 Win. 22- to 26-inch bbl. Weight: 7-8 lbs. Curly maple or laminated stock. Barrel-mounted scope mount, no sights. Made 1993 to date.
Ultra Hunter (.25-06, .308). . . . . . . NiB $190 Ex $125 Gd $100
Ultra Varmint. . . . . NiB $225 Ex $175 Gd $125

HARRIS GUNWORKS — Phoenix, Arizona (Formerly McMillan Gun Works)

SIGNATURE ALASKAN
BOLT-ACTION RIFLE. . . . . NiB $3400 Ex $2700 Gd $1800
Same general specifications as Classic Sporter except w/match-grade bbl. Rings and mounts. Sights: Single-leaf rear, bbl. band front. Checkered Monte Carlo stock w/palmswell and solid recoil pad. Nickel finish. Calibers: LA (long): .270 Win., .280 Rem., .30-06, MA (Magnum): 7mm Rem. Mag., .300 Win. Mag., .300 Wby. Mag., .340 Wby. Mag., .358 Win., .375 H&H Mag. Made 1990 to date.

SIGNATURE CLASSIC SPORTER
The prototype for Harris' Signature Series, this bolt-action rifle is available in three lengths: SA (standard/ short) — from .22-250 to .350 Rem Mag.; LA (long) — .25-06 to .30-06; MA (Magnum) — 7mm STW to .416 Rem. Mag. Four-shot or 3-shot (Magnum) magazine. Bbl. lengths: 22, 24 or 26 inches. Weight: 7 lbs. (short action). No sights; rings and bases provided. Harris fiberglass stock, Fibergrain or wood stock optional. Stainless, matte black or black chrome sulfide finish. Available in right- and left-hand models. Made 1987 to date. Has pre-64 Model 70-style action for dangerous game.
Classic Sporter Standard . . . . . . NiB $2400 Ex $2100 Gd $1200
Classic Sporter Stainless . . . . . . NiB $2590 Ex $2125 Gd $1225
Talon Sporter. . . . . NiB $2600 Ex $1900 Gd $1300

SIGNATURE MOUNTAIN RIFLE. . . . . NiB $2950 Ex $2600 Gd $1325
Same general specifications as Harris (McMillan) Classic Sporter except w/titanium action and graphite-reinforced fiberglass stock. Weight: 5.5 lbs. Calibers: .270 Win., .280 Rem., .30-06, 7mm Mag., .300 Win. Mag. Other calibers on special order. Made 1995 to date.

SIGNATURE SUPER VARMINTER . . . . . NiB $2400 Ex $2000 Gd $1200
Same general specifications as Harris (McMillan) Classic Sporter except w/heavy, contoured bbl., adj. trigger, fiberglass stock and field bipod. Calibers: .223, .22-250, .220 Swift, .244 Win., 6mm Rem., .25-06, 7mm-08, .308 Win., .350 Win. Mag. Made 1995 to date.

TALON SAFARI RIFLE
Same general specifications as Harris (McMillan) Classic Sporter except w/Harris Safari-grade action, match-grade bbl. and "Safari" fiberglass stock. Calibers: Magnum — .300 H&H Mag., .300 Win Mag., .300 Wby. Mag., .338 Win. Mag., .340 Wby. Mag., .375 H&H Mag., .404 Jeffrey, .416 Rem. Mag., .458 Win., Super Mag. — .300 Phoenix, .338 Lapua, .378 Wby. Mag., .416 Rigby, .416 Wby. Mag., .460 Wby. Mag. Matte black finish. Other calibers available on special order, and at a premium, but the "used gun" value remains the same. Imported 1989 to date.
Safari Magnum . . . . NiB $3650 Ex $2850 Gd $1850
Safari Super Magnum . . . . NiB $4044 Ex $3295 Gd $2337

HECKLER & KOCH, GMBH — Oberndorf/Neckar, Germany
Imported by Heckler & Koch, Inc., Sterling, VA

MODEL 911 SEMIAUTO RIFLE. . . . . NiB $1750 Ex $1550 Gd $850
Caliber: .308 (7.62mm). 5-shot magazine. 19.7-inch bull bbl. 42.4 inches overall. Sights: Hooded post front; adj. aperture rear. Weight: 11 lbs. Kevlar-reinforced fiberglass thumbhole-stock. Imported 1989-93.

MODEL HK91 A-2 SEMIAUTO . . . . NiB $2200 Ex $1900 Gd $1190
Delayed roller-locked blow-back action. Caliber: 7.62mm X 51 NATO (308 Win.) 5- or 20-round box magazine. 19-inch bbl. Weight: W/o magazine, 9.37 lbs. Sights L "V" and aperture rear, post front. Plastic buttstock and forearm. Disc. 1991.

Heckler & Koch
Model HK91 A-2

Heckler & Koch
Model HK91 A-3

Heckler & Koch
Model HK93 A-2

Heckler & Koch
Model HK940 Carbine

MODEL HK91 A-3 . . . . **NiB $2500 Ex $2250 Gd $1400**
Same as Model HK91 A-2 except w/retractable metal buttstock, weighs 10.56 lbs. Disc. 1991.

MODEL HK93 SEMIAUTOMATIC
Delayed roller-locked blow-back action. Caliber: 5.56mm x 45 (.223 Rem.). 5- or 20-round magazine. 16.13-inch bbl. Weight: W/o magazine, 7.6 lbs. Sights: "V" and aperture rear; post front. Plastic buttstock and forearm. Disc. 1991.
HK93 A-2 . . . . **NiB $2308 Ex $2150 Gd $995**
HK93 A-3 w/retractable stock. . . . . **NiB $2350 Ex $2100 Gd $1850**

MODEL HK94 SEMIAUTOMATIC CARBINE
Caliber: 9mm Para. 15-shot magazine. 16-inch bbl. Weight: 6.75 lbs. Aperture rear sight, front post. Plastic buttstock and forend or retractable metal stock. Imported 1983-91.

(cont'd.) **MODEL HK94 SEMIAUTOMATIC CARBINE**
HK94-A2 w/standard stock . . . . **NiB $3000 Ex $2950 Gd $2500**
HK94-A3 w/retractable stock . . . . **NiB $4530 Ex $3625 Gd $2465**

MODEL HK300
SEMIAUTOMATIC . . . . **NiB $690 Ex $625 Gd $400**
Caliber: .22 WMR. 5- or 15-round box magazine. 19.7-inch bbl. w/polygonal rifling. Weight: 5.75 lbs. Sights: V-notch rear; ramp front. High-luster polishing and bluing. European walnut stock w/cheekpiece, checkered forearm and pistol-grip. Disc. 1989.

MODEL HK630 SEMIAUTOMATIC . . . . . . **NiB $1175 Ex $950 Gd $575**
Caliber: .223 Rem. Four or 10-round magazine. 24-inch bbl. Overall length: 42 inches. Weight: 7 lbs. Sights: Open rear; ramp front. European walnut stock w/Monte Carlo cheekpiece. Imported 1983-90.

GRADING: NiB = New in Box   **Ex** = Excellent or NRA 95%   **Gd** = Good or NRA 68%   **249**

Heckler & Koch
Model HK PSG-1

Heckler & Koch
Model SL-8

Heckler & Koch
Model USC Carbine

MODEL HK770 SEMIAUTOMATIC . . . . NiB $1825 Ex $1500 Gd $800
Caliber: .308 Win. Three or 10-round magazine. Overall length: 44.5 inches. Weight: 8 lbs. Sights: Open rear; ramp front. European walnut stock w/Monte Carlo cheekpiece. Imported 1983-90.

MODEL HK940 SEMIAUTOMATIC . . . . NiB $1950 Ex $1750 Gd $925
Caliber: .30-06 Springfield. Three or 10-round magazine. Overall length: 47 inches. Weight: 8.8 lbs. Sights: Open rear; ramp front. European walnut stock w/Monte Carlo cheekpiece. Imported 1983-90.

MODEL HK PSG-1
MARKSMAN'S RIFLE . . . . NiB $10,313 Ex $8250 Gd $5610
Caliber: .308 (7.62mm). Five and 20-shot magazine. 25.6-inch bbl. 47.5 inches overall. Hensoldt 6x42 telescopic sight. Weight: 17.8 lbs. Matte black composite stock w/pistol-grip. Imported 1988 to date.

MODEL SL8-1 RIFLE . . . . NiB $1600 Ex $1250 Gd $850
Caliber: .223 Win. 10-shot magazine. 20.80- inch bbl. 38.58 inches overall. Weight: 8.6 lbs. Gas-operated, short-stroke piston w/rotary locking bolt. Rear adjustable sight w/ambidextrous safety selector lever. Polymer receiver w/adjustable buttstock. Introduced 1999.

MODEL SR-9
SEMIAUTO RIFLE . . . . NiB $1750 Ex $1600 Gd $900
Caliber: .308 (7.62mm). Five shot magazine. 19.7-inch bull bbl. 42.4 inches overall. Hooded post front sight; adj. aperture rear. Weight: 11 lbs. Kevlar-reinforced fiberglass thumbhole-stock w/wood grain finish. Imported 1989-93.

MODEL SR-9
TARGET RIFLE. . . . . NiB $2500 Ex $1950 Gd $1300
Same general specifications as standard SR-9 except w/ PSG-1 trigger group and adj. buttstock. Imported 1992-94.

MODEL USC
CARBINE RIFLE. . . . . NiB $1100 Ex $975 Gd $650
Caliber: 45 ACP. 10-shot magazine. 16- inch bbl., 35.43 inches overall. Weight: 6 lbs. Blow-back operating system. Polymer receiver w/integral grips. Rear adjustable sight w/ambidextrous safety selector lever. Introduced 1999.

HERCULES RIFLES

See listings under "W" for Montgomery Ward.

Heym
Model SR-20 Standard

Heym
Model SR-20L Mannlicher

HEROLD RIFLE — Suhl, Germany
Made by Franz Jaeger & Company

BOLT-ACTION REPEATING
SPORTING RIFLE. . . . . NiB $1250 Ex $995 Gd $625
"Herold-Repetierbüchse." Miniature Mauser-type action w/unique 5-shot box magazine on hinged floorplate. Double-set triggers. Caliber: .22 Hornet. 24-inch bbl. Sights: Leaf rear; ramp front. Weight: 7.75 lbs. Fancy checkered stock. Made before WWII. Note: These rifles were imported by Charles Daly and A.F. Stoeger Inc. of New York City and sold under their names.

HEYM RIFLES AMERICA, INC. — Mfd. By Heym, GmbH & Co JAGWAFFEN KD., Gleichamberg, Germany, *(Previously imported by Heym America, Inc.; Heckler & Koch; JagerSport, Ltd.)*

MODEL 55B O/U DOUBLE RIFLE
Kersten boxlock action w/double cross bolt and cocking indicators. Calibers: .308 Win., .30-06, .375 H&H, .458 Win. Mag., .470 N.E. 25-inch bbl. 42 inches overall. Weight: 8.25 lbs. Sights: fixed V-type rear; front ramp w/silver bead. Engraved receiver w/optional sidelocks, interchangeable bbls. and claw mounts. Checkered European walnut stock. Imported from Germany.
Model 55 (boxlock) . . . . NiB $7500 Ex $6100 Gd $5500
Model 55 (sidelock) . . . . NiB $11,938 Ex $9550 Gd $6494
W\Extra rifle bbls., add $5500
W/Extra shotgun bbls., add $2800

MODEL 88B DOUBLE RIFLE
Modified Anson & Deeley boxlock action w/standing gears, double under-locking lugs and Greener extension w/crossbolt. Calibers: 8x57 JRS, 9.3x74R, .30-06, .375 H&H, .458 Win. Mag., .470 Nitro Express, .500 Nitro Express. Other calibers available on special order. Weight: 8 to 10 lbs. Top tang safety and cocking indicators. Double triggers w/front set. Fixed or 3-leaf express rear sight, front ramp w/silver bead. Engraved receiver w/optional sidelocks. Checkered French walnut stock. Imported from Germany.
Model 88B Boxlock . . . . NiB $10,969 Ex $8775 Gd $5967
Model 88B/SS Sidelock . . . . NiB $13,438 Ex $10,750 Gd $7310
Model 88B Safari (Magnum) . . . . . . NiB $14,938 Ex $11,950 Gd $8126

EXPRESS BOLT-ACTION RIFLE
Same general specifications as Model SR-20 Safari except w/modified magnum Mauser action. Checkered AAA-grade European walnut stock w/cheekpiece, solid rubber recoil pad, rosewood forend tip and grip

(cont'd.) **EXPRESS BOLT-ACTION RIFLE**
cap. Calibers: .338 Lapua Magnum, .375 H&H, .378 Wby. Mag., .416 Rigby .450 Ackley, .460 Wby. Mag., .500 A-Square, .500 Nitro Express, .600 Nitro Express. Other calibers available on special order, but no change in used gun value. Imported from Germany 1989-95.
Standard Express Magnum . . . . NiB $5188 Ex $4150 Gd $2822
600 Nitro Express . . . . NiB $5500 Ex $4800 Gd $2800
Left-hand models, add $600

SR-20 BOLT-ACTION RIFLE
Calibers: .243 Win., .270 Win., .308 Win., .30-06, 7mm Rem. Mag., .300 Win. Mag., .375 H&H. Five shot (standard) or 3-shot (Magnum) magazine. Bbl. length: 20.5-inch (SR-20L); 24-inch (SR-20N); 26-inch (SR-20G). Weight: 7.75 lbs. Adj. rear sight, blade front. Checkered French walnut stock in Monte Carlo style (N&G Series) or full Mannlicher (L Series). Imported from Germany. Disc. 1992.
SR-20L . . . . NiB $1825 Ex $1425 Gd $800
SR-20N . . . . NiB $1990 Ex $1595 Gd $950
SR-20G . . . . NiB $2500 Ex $1950 Gd $1275

SR-20 CLASSIC BOLT-ACTION RIFLES
Same as SR-20 except w/.22-250 and .338 Win. Mag. plus metric calibers on request. 24-inch (standard) or 25-inch (Magnum) bbl. Checkered French walnut stock. Left-hand models. Imported from Germany since 1985; Sporter version 1989-93.
Classic (Standard) . . . . NiB $2092 Ex $1674 Gd $1138
Classic (Magnum) . . . . NiB $2325 Ex $1860 Gd $1264
Left-hand models, add $300
Classic Sporter (Std.
w/.22-inch bbl.) . . . . NiB $2242 Ex $1794 Gd $1220
Classic Sporter (Mag.
w/.24-inch bbl.) . . . . NiB $2475 Ex $1980 Gd $1346

SR-20 ALPINE, SAFARI AND TROPHY SERIES
Same general specifications as Model SR-20 Classic Sporter except Alpine Series w/20-inch bbl., Mannlicher stock, chambered in standard calibers only; Safari Series w/24-inch bbl., 3-leaf express sights and magnum action in calibers .375 H & H, .404 Jeffrey, .425 Express, .458 Win. Mag.; Trophy Series w/Krupp-Special tapered octagon bbl. w/quarter rib and open sights, standard and Magnum calibers. Imported from Germany 1989-93.
Alpine Series . . . . NiB $2242 Ex $1794 Gd $1220
Safari Series . . . . NiB $2287 Ex $1830 Gd $1244
Trophy Series (Stand. calibers) . . . . NiB $2925 Ex $2340 Gd $1591
Trophy Series
(Magnum calibers) . . . . NiB $3187 Ex $2550 Gd $1734

J.C. HIGGINS RIFLES

See Sears, Roebuck & Company.

High Standard
Flite-King Pump

High Standard
Hi-Power Deluxe

High Standard
Sport-King Autoloading Carbine

High Standard
Sport-King Deluxe Auto

High Standard
Sport-King Field Auto

High Standard
Sport-King Special Auto

HI-POINT FIREARMS — Dayton, Ohio

MODEL 995 CARBINE

Semiautomatic recoil-operated carbine. Calibers: 9mm Parabellum or 40 S&W. 10-shot magazine. 16.5-inch bbl. 31.5 inches overall. Protected post front sight, aperture rear w/integral scope mount. Matte blue, chrome or Parkerized finish. Checkered polymer grip/frame. Made 1996 to date.

Model 995, 9mm (blue or Parkerized) . . . . . NiB $156 Ex $125 Gd $85
Model 995, .40 S&W (blue or Parkerized) . . . NiB $188 Ex $150 Gd $102
W/laser sights, add $35
W/chrome finish, add $15

HIGH STANDARD SPORTING FIREARMS — East Hartford, Connecticut, (Formerly High Standard Mfg. Co., Hamden, CT)

A long-standing producer of sporting arms, High Standard discontinued its operations in 1984.

FLITE-KING

PUMP RIFLE . . . . NiB $150 Ex $100 Gd $60
Hammerless slide-action. Caliber: .22 LR. .22 Long, .22 Short. Tubular mag. holds 17 LR, 19 Long, or 24 Short. 24-inch bbl. Weight: 5.5 lbs. Sights: Partridge rear; bead front. Monte Carlo stock w/pistol grip, serrated semibeavertail forearm. Made 1962-75.

HI-POWER

DELUXE RIFLE . . . . NiB $525 Ex $350 Gd $200
Mauser-type bolt action, sliding safety. Calibers: .270, .30-06. Four shot magazine. 22-inch bbl. Weight: 7 lbs. Sights: Folding open rear; ramp front. Walnut stock w/checkered pistol-grip and forearm, Monte Carlo comb, QD swivels. Made 1962-66.

Holland & Holland
Best Quality Magazine

Holland & Holland
Royal Deluxe Double

Howa
Model 1500 Hunter

Howa
Model 1500 Lightning

HI-POWER FIELD BOLT-ACTION RIFLE.....NiB $450 Ex $300 Gd $175
Same as Hi-Power Deluxe except w/plain field style stock. Made 1962-66.

**SPORT-KING AUTO-
LOADING CARBINE ....NiB $150 Ex $90 Gd $70**
Same as Sport-King Field Autoloader except w/18.25-inch bbl., Western-style straight-grip stock w/bbl. band, sling and swivels. Made 1964-73.

SPORT-KING DELUXE AUTOLOADER ....NiB $225 Ex $175 Gd $75
Same as Sport-King Special Autoloader except w/checkered stock. Made 1966-75.

SPORT-KING FIELD AUTOLOADER ....NiB $110 Ex $90 Gd $55
Calibers: .22 LR. .22 Long, .22 Short (high speed). Tubular magazine holds 15 LR, 17 Long, or 21 Short. 22.25-inch bbl. Weight: 5.5 lbs. Sights: Open rear; beaded post front. Plain pistol-grip stock. Made 1960-66.

SPORT-KING SPECIAL AUTOLOADER ....NiB $175 Ex $130 Gd $75
Same as Sport-King Field except stock w/Monte Carlo comb and semibeavertail forearm. Made 1960-66.

HOLLAND & HOLLAND, LTD. — London, England, *Imported by Holland & Holland, NY, NY*

**NO. 2 MODEL HAMMERLESS
EJECTOR DOUBLE RIFLE ....NiB $14,938 Ex $11,950 Gd $8126**
Same general specifications as Royal Model except plainer finish. Disc. 1960.

BEST QUALITY MAGAZINE RIFLE ....NiB $14,375 Ex $11,500 Gd $7820
Mauser or Enfield action. Calibers: .240 Apex, .300 H&H Mag., .375 H&H Magnum. Four shot box magazine. 24-inch bbl. Weight: 7.25 lbs., 240 Apex; 8.25 lbs., .300 Mag. and .375 Mag. Sights: Folding leaf rear; hooded ramp front. Detachable French walnut stock w/cheekpiece, checkered pistol-grip and forearm, swivels. Currently mfd. Specifications given apply to most models.

DELUXE MAGAZINE RIFLE.......NiB $15,938 Ex $12,750 Gd $8670
Same specifications as Best Quality except w/exhibition-grade stock and special engraving. Currently mfd.

ROYAL DELUXE DOUBLE RIFLE....NiB $56,875 Ex $45,500 Gd $30,940
Formerly designated "Modele Deluxe." Same specifications as Royal Model except w/exhibition-grade stock and special engraving. Currently mfd.

**ROYAL HAMMERLESS
EJECTOR RIFLE.........NiB $40,625 Ex $32,500 Gd $22,100**
Sidelock. Calibers: .240 Apex, 7mm H&H Mag., .300 H&H Mag., .300 Win. Mag., .30-06, .375 H&H Mag., .458 Win. Mag., .465 H&H Mag. 24- to 28-inch bbls. Weight: From 7.5 lbs. Sights: Folding leaf rear, ramp front. Cheekpiece stock of select French walnut, checkered pistol-grip and forearm. Currently mfd. Same general specifications apply to prewar model.

Husqvarna
Series 1100 Deluxe

Husqvarna
1951 Hi-Power

HOWA RIFLES — Mfg. By Howa Machinery Ltd., Shinkawa-Chonear, Nagoya 452, Japan, *Imported by Interarms, Alexandria, VA*

See also Mossberg (1500) Smith & Wesson (1500 & 1700) and Weatherby (Vanguard).

MODEL 1500 HUNTER
Similar to Trophy Model except w/standard walnut stock. No Monte Carlo cheekpiece or grip cap. Imported 1988-89.

Standard calibers . . . . NiB $450 Ex $400 Gd $275
Magnum calibers . . . . NiB $431 Ex $350 Gd $246
Stainless steel, add. $85

MODEL 1500 LIGHTNING BOLT-ACTION RIFLE
Similar to Hunter Model except fitted w/black Bell & Carlson Carbelite stock w/checkered grip and forend. Weight: 7.5 lbs. Imported 1988-89.

Standard calibers . . . . NiB $415 Ex $330 Gd $195
Magnum calibers . . . . NiB $431 Ex $350 Gd $246

MODEL 1500 PCS BOLT-ACTION RIFLE
Similar to Hunter Model except in Police Counter Sniper configuration and chambered for .308 Win. only. Walnut or synthetic stock w/checkered grip and forend. Receiver drilled and tapped but w/o sights. Weight: 8.5 to 9.3 lbs. Imported 1999 to date.

PCS Model w/walnut stock . . . . . . NiB $415 Ex $330 Gd $195
PCS Model w/synthetic stock . . . . . NiB $394 Ex $325 Gd $237
Stainless steel, add $85

MODEL 1500 REALTREE
CAMO RIFLE . . . . NiB $475 Ex $400 Gd $275
Similar to Trophy Model except fitted w/Camo Bell & Carlson Carbelite stock w/checkered grip and forend. Weight: 8 lbs. Stock, action and barrel finished in Realtree camo. Available in standard calibers only. Imported 1993 to date.

MODEL 1500 TROPHY/VARMINT BOLT-ACTION RIFLE
Calibers: .22-250, .223, .243 Win., .270 Win., .308 Win., .30-06, 7mm Mag.,. .300 Win. Mag.,. .338 Win. Mag. 22-inch bbl. (standard); 24-inch bbl. (Magnum). 42.5 inches overall (standard). Weight: 7.5 lbs. Adj. rear sight hooded ramp front. Checkered walnut stock w/Monte Carlo cheekpiece. Varmint Model w/24-inch heavy bbl., weight of 9.5 lbs. in calibers .22-250, .223 and .308 only. Imported 1979-93.

Trophy Standard . . . . NiB $528 Ex $410 Gd $240
Trophy Magnum . . . . NiB $489 Ex $395 Gd $275
Varmint (Parkerized finish) . . . . NiB $400 Ex $320 Gd $218
Stainless steel, add $85

MODEL 1500 WOODGRAIN LIGHTNING RIFLE
Calibers: .243, .270, 7mm Rem. Mag., .30-06. Mag. Five shot magazine 22-inch. 42 inches overall. Weight: 7.5 lbs. Receiver drilled and tapped for scope mount, no sights. Checkered woodgrain synthetic polymer stock. Imported 1993-94.

Standard calibers . . . . NiB $450 Ex $390 Gd $225
Magnum calibers . . . . NiB $514 Ex $415 Gd $289

H-S PRECISION — Rapid City, South Dakota

PRO-SERIES
Custom rifle built on Remington 700 bolt action. Calibers: .22 to .416, 24- or 26-inch bbl. w/fluted option. Aluminum bedding block system w/take-down option. Kevlar/carbon fiber stock to customer's specifications. Appointments and options to customer's preference. Made 1990 to date.

Sporter model . . . . NiB $1975 Ex $1650 Gd $950
Pro-Hunter model (PHR). . . . . NiB $1656 Ex $1325 Gd $901
Long-Range Model . . . . NiB $1875 Ex $1575 Gd $875
Long-Range
takedown model . . . . NiB $2188 Ex $1750 Gd $1190
Marksman model . . . . NiB $1975 Ex $1650 Gd $950
Marksman takedown model . . . . NiB $2290 Ex $1825 Gd $1200
Varmint takedown
model (VTD). . . . . NiB $1950 Ex $1625 Gd $925
Left-hand models, add. $200

HUNGARIAN MILITARY RIFLES — Budapest, Hungary, Manufactured at Government Arsenal

MODEL 1935M MANN-
LICHER MILITARY RIFLE . . . . NiB $275 Ex $225 Gd $125
Caliber: 8x52mm Hungarian. Bolt action, straight handle. Five shot projecting box magazine. 24-inch bbl. Weight: 9 lbs. Adj. leaf rear sight, hooded front blade. Two-piece military-type stock. Made 1935-40.

MODEL 1943M (GERMAN
GEW 98/40) MANNLICHER
MILITARY RIFLE . . . . NiB $325 Ex $250 Gd $150
Modification, during German occupation, of Model 1935M. Caliber: 7.9mm Mauser. Turned-down bolt handle and Mauser M/98-type box magazine; other differences are minor. Made 1940 to end of war in Europe.

Husqvarna 3000
Crown Grade

Husqvarna 4100
Lightweight

Husqvarna 6000
Imperial Custom

RIFLES

HUSQVARNA VAPENFABRIK A.B. — Husqvarna, Sweden

MODEL 456 LIGHTWEIGHT
FULL-STOCK SPORTER . . . . NiB $500 Ex $400 Gd $275
Same as Series 4000/4100 except w/sporting style full stock w/slope-away cheekrest. Weight: 6.5 lbs. Made 1959-70.

SERIES 1000 SUPER GRADE . . . . . . NiB $494 Ex $395 Gd $269
Same as 1951 Hi-Power except w/European walnut sporter stock w/Monte Carlo comb and cheekpiece. Made 1952-56.

SERIES 1100 DELUXE MODEL HI-POWER
BOLT-ACTION SPORTING RIFLE . . . . NiB $500 Ex $400 Gd $272
Same as 1951 Hi-Power, except w/jeweled bolt, European walnut stock. Made 1952-56.

1950 HI-POWER SPORTING RIFLE . . . . . . NiB $438 Ex $350 Gd $238
Mauser-type bolt action. Calibers: .220 Swift, .270 Win. .30-06 (see note below), 5-shot box magazine. 23.75-inch bbl. Weight: 7.75 lbs. Sights: Open rear; hooded ramp front. Sporting stock of Arctic beech, checkered pistol grip and forearm, swivels. Note: Husqvarna sporters were first intro. in U.S. about 1948; earlier models were also available in calibers 6.5x55, 8x57 and 9.3x57. Made 1946-1951.

1951 HI-POWER RIFLE . . . . NiB $469 Ex $375 Gd $255
Same as 1950 Hi-Power except w/high-comb stock, low safety.

SERIES 3000 CROWN GRADE . . . . NiB $475 Ex $350 Gd $225
Same as Series 3100, except w/Monte Carlo comb stock.

SERIES 3100 CROWN GRADE . . . . NiB $475 Ex $350 Gd $225
HVA improved Mauser action. Calibers: .243, .270, 7mm, .30-06, .308 Win. Five shot box magazine. 23.75-inch bbl. Weight: 7.75 lbs. Sights: Open rear; hooded ramp front. European walnut stock, checkered, cheekpiece, pistol-grip cap, black forend tip, swivels. Made 1954-72.

SERIES 4000 LIGHTWEIGHT RIFLE . . . . . . NiB $475 Ex $350 Gd $225
Same as Series 4100 except w/Monte Carlo comb stock and no rear sight.

SERIES 4100 LIGHTWEIGHT RIFLE . . . . . . NiB $470 Ex $350 Gd $200
HVA improved Mauser action. Calibers: .243, .270, 7mm, .30-06, .308 Win. Five shot box magazine. 20.5-inch bbl. Weight: 6.25 lbs. Sights: Open rear; hooded ramp front. Lightweight walnut stock w/cheekpiece, pistol grip, Schnabel forend tip, checkered, swivels. Made 1954-72. See illustration previous page.

SERIES 6000 IMPERIAL CUSTOM GRADE . NiB $625 Ex $500 Gd $325
Same as Series 3100 except fancy-grade stock, 3-leaf folding rear sight, adj. trigger. Calibers: .243, .270, 7mm Rem. Mag. .308, .30-06. Made 1968-70. See illustration previous page.

SERIES 7000 IMPERIAL
MONTE CARLO LIGHTWEIGHT. . . NiB $650 Ex $500 Gd $325
Same as Series 4000 Lightweight except fancy-grade stock, 3-leaf folding rear sight, adj. trigger. Calibers: .243, .270, .308, .30-06. Made 1968-70.

MODEL 8000 IMPERIAL GRADE RIFLE . . . NiB $650 Ex $500 Gd $325
Same as Model 9000 except w/jeweled bolt, engraved floorplate, deluxe French walnut checkered stock, no sights. Made 1971-72.

MODEL 9000 CROWN GRADE RIFLE . . . . NiB $500 Ex $400 Gd $300
New design Husqvarna bolt action. Adj. trigger. Calibers: .270, 7mm Rem. Mag., .30-06, .300 Win. Mag. Five shot box magazine, hinged floorplate. 23.75-inch bbl. Sights: Folding leaf rear; hooded ramp front. Checkered walnut stock w/Monte Carlo cheekpiece, rosewood forend tip and pistol-grip cap. Weight: 7 lbs. 3 oz. Made 1971-72.

SERIES P-3000 PRESENTATION RIFLE . . . . NiB $800 Ex $650 Gd $425
Same as Crown Grade Series 3000 except w/selected stock, engraved action, adj. trigger. Calibers: .243, .270, 7mm Rem. Mag., .30-06. Made 1968-70.

Interarms Mark X
Lightweight Sporter

Interarms Mini-Mark X

Italian Model 38 Military Rifle

INTERARMS RIFLES — Alexandria, Virginia

The following Mark X rifles are manufactured by Zavodi Crvena Zastava, Belgrade, Yugoslavia.

MARK X ALASKAN . . . . **NiB $475 Ex $350 Gd $250**
Same specifications as Mark X Sporter, except chambered for .375 H&H Mag. and .458 Win. Mag. w/3-round magazine. Stock w/recoil-absorbing cross bolt and heavy duty recoil pad. Weighs 8.25 lbs. Made 1976-84.

MARK X BOLT-ACTION SPORTER SERIES
Mauser-type action. Calibers: .22-250, .243, .25-06, .270, 7x57, 7mm Rem. Mag., .308, .30-06, .300 Win. Mag. Five shot magazine (3-shot in magnum calibers). 24-inch bbl. Weight: 7.5 lbs. Sights: Adj. leaf rear; ramp front, w/hood. Classic-style stock of European walnut w/Monte Carlo comb and cheekpiece, checkered pistol grip and forearm, black forend tip, QD swivels. Made 1972-97.
Mark X Standard . . . . **NiB $369 Ex $295 Gd $201**
Mark X Camo (Realtree) . . . . **NiB $469 Ex $375 Gd $255**
American Field, std.
(rubber recoil pad) . . . . **NiB $581 Ex $465 Gd $316**
American Field, Magnum
(rubber recoil pad) . . . . **NiB $619 Ex $495 Gd $337**

MARK X CAVALIER . . . . **NiB $375 Ex $300 Gd $200**
Same specifications as Mark X Sporter except w/contemporary-style stock w/rollover cheekpiece, rosewood forend tip/grip cap, recoil pad. Intro. 1974; Disc.

MARK X CONTINENTAL
MANNLICHER STYLE CARBINE . . . . **NiB $400 Ex $350 Gd $225**
Same specifications as Mark X Sporter except straight European-style comb stock w/sculptured cheekpiece. Precise double-set triggers and classic "butterknife" bolt handle. French checkering. Weight: 7.25 lbs. Disc.

MARK X LIGHTWEIGHT SPORTER . . . . . . **NiB $350 Ex $290 Gd $200**
Calibers: .22-250 Rem., .270 Win., 7mm Rem. Mag., .30-06 or 7mm Mag. Four or 5-round magazine. 20-inch bbl. Synthenic Carbolite stock Weight: 7 lbs. Imported 1988-90. (Reintroduced

1994-97.)
MARK X MARQUIS
MANNLICHER STYLE CARBINE . . . . **NiB $431 Ex $345 Gd $235**
Same specifications as Mark X Sporter except w/20-inch bbl., full-length Mannlicher-type stock w/metal forend/muzzle cap. Calibers: .270, 7x57, .308, .30-06. Imported 1976-84.

MINI-MARK X BOLT-ACTION
RIFLE . . . . **NiB $375 Ex $295 Gd $200**
Miniature M98 Mauser action. Caliber: .223 Rem. Five shot magazine. 20-inch bbl. 39.75 inches overall. Weight: 6.25 lbs. Adj. rear sight, hooded ramp front. Checkered hardwood stock. Imported 1987-94.

MARK X VISCOUNT . . . . **NiB $375 Ex $300 Gd $200**
Same specifications as Mark X Sporter except w/plainer field grade stock. Imported 1974-87.

AFRICAN SERIES . . . . **NiB $625 Ex $540 Gd $350**
Mauser-type bolt-action. Calibers: .375 H&H Mag., .458 Win. Mag. Three shot magazine. 24-inch bbl. Weight: 8 lbs. Sights: 3-leaf express open rear, ramp front w/hood. English-style stock of European walnut, w/cheekpiece, black forend tip, checkered pistol grip and forearm, recoil pad, QD swivels. Imported 1974-96 by Whitworth Rifle Co., England.

ITALIAN MILITARY RIFLES
Manufactured by government plants at Brescia, Gardone, Terni and Turin, Italy

MODEL 38 MILITARY RIFLE . . . . **NiB $100 Ex $90 Gd $50**
Modification of Italian Model 1891 Mannlicher-Carcano Military Rifle w/turned-down bolt handle, detachable folding bayonet. Caliber: 7.35mm Italian Service (many arms of this model were later converted to the old 6.5mm caliber). Six shot box magazine. 21.25-inch bbl. Weight: 7.5 lbs. Sights: Adj. rear-blade front. Military straight-grip stock. Adopted 1938.

Ithaca Model 49

Ithaca Model 49
Presentation

Ithaca Model 49R
Sporter

Ithaca Model 72
Saddlegun

Ithaca Model 72
Saddlegun Deluxe

ITHACA GUN COMPANY, INC. — King Ferry, New York, (Formerly Ithaca, NY)

MODEL 49
SADDLEGUN LEVER ACTION

SINGLE-SHOT RIFLE . . . . **NiB $145 Ex $130 Gd $60**
Martini-type action. Hand-operated rebounding hammer. Caliber: .22 LR. Long, Short. 18-inch bbl. Open sights. Western carbine-style stock. Weight: 5.5 lbs. Made 1961-78.

MODEL 49 SADDLEGUN — DELUXE . . . . . **NiB $175 Ex $125 Gd $75**
Same as standard Model 49 except w/gold-plated hammer and trigger, figured walnut stock, sling swivels. Made 1962-75.

MODEL 49 SADDLEGUN — MAGNUM . . . **NiB $170 Ex $150 Gd $90**
Same as standard Model 49 except chambered for .22 WMR cartridge. Made 1962-78.

MODEL 49 SADDLEGUN
—PRESENTATION. . . . . **NiB $290 Ex $275 Gd $120**
Same as standard Model 49 Saddlegun except w/gold-plated hammer and trigger, engraved receiver, full fancy-figured walnut stock w/gold nameplate. Available in .22 LR or .22 WMR. Made 1962-74.

MODEL 49 SADDLEGUN
— ST. LOUIS BICENTENNIAL . . . . . **NiB $290 Ex $275 Gd $120**
Same as Model 49 Deluxe except w/commemorative inscription. 200 made in 1964. Top value is for rifle in new, unfired condition.

MODEL 49R SADDLEGUN
REPEATING RIFLE . . . . **NiB $265 Ex $245 Gd $100**
Similar in appearance to Model 49 Single-Shot. Caliber: .22 LR. Long, Short. Tubular magazine holds 15 LR, 17 Long, 21 Short. 20-inch bbl. Weight: 5.5 lbs. Sights: Open rear-bead front. Western-style stock, checkered grip. Made 1968-71.

Ithaca
Model LSA-65 Standard

Ithaca
Model X5-T

Ithaca
Model X-15

Ithaca
BSA CF-2

MODEL 49 YOUTH SADDLEGUN . . . . **NiB $135 Ex $100 Gd $70**
Same as standard Model 49 except shorter stock for young shooters.
Made 1961-78.

REPEATING CARBINE . . . . **NiB $325 Ex $250 Gd $150**
Caliber: .22 LR. Long, Short. Tubular magazine holds 15 LR, 17
Long, 21 Short. 18.5-inch bbl. Weight: 5.5 lbs. Sights: Open rear;
hooded ramp front. Receiver grooved for scope mounting. Western
carbine stock and forearm of American walnut. Made 1973-78.

MODEL 72 SADDLEGUN — DELUXE . . . . **NiB $375 Ex $300 Gd $190**
Same as standard Model 72 except w/silver-finished and engraved
receiver, octagon bbl., higher grade walnut stock and forearm.
Made 1974-76.

**MODEL LSA-65 BOLT
ACTION STANDARD GRADE** . . . . . **NiB $425 Ex $375 Gd $250**
Same as Model LSA-55 Standard Grade except calibers .25-06,
.270, .30-06; 4-shot magazine, 23-inch bbl., weight: 7 lbs. Made
1969-77.

MODEL LSA-65 DELUXE . . . . **NiB $500 Ex $450 Gd $275**
Same as Model LSA-65 Standard Grade except w/special features of
Model LSA-55 Deluxe. Made 1969-77.

**MODEL X5-C LIGHTNING
AUTOLOADER** . . . . **NiB $175 Ex $125 Gd $75**
Takedown. Caliber: .22 LR. Seven shot clip magazine. 22-inch bbl.
Weight: 6 lbs. Sights: Open rear; Ray-bar front. Pistol-grip stock,
grooved forearm. Made 1958-64.

**MODEL X5-T LIGHTNING
AUTOLOADER TUBULAR
REPEATING RIFLE** . . . . **NiB $175 Ex $125 Gd $75**
Same as Model X5-C except w/16-shot tubular magazine, stock
w/plain forearm.

**MODEL X-15 LIGHTNING
AUTOLOADER** . . . . **NiB $180 Ex $140 Gd $75**
Same general specifications as Model X5-C except forend is not
grooved. Made 1964-67.

**BSA CF-2 BOLT-ACTION
REPEATING RIFLE** . . . . **NiB $300 Ex $275 Gd $170**
Mauser-type action. Calibers: 7mm Rem. Mag., .300 Win. Mag.
Three shot magazine. 23.6-inch bbl. Weight: 8 lbs. Sights: Adj. rear;
hooded ramp front. Checkered walnut stock w/Monte Carlo comb,
rollover cheekpiece, rosewood forend tip, recoil pad, sling swivels.
Imported 1976-77. Mfd. by BSA Guns Ltd., Birmingham, England.

Johnson Model 1941

Johnson Sporting Rifle

Iver Johnson Model M-1

JAPANESE MILITARY RIFLES — Tokyo, Japan Manufactured by Government Plant

MODEL 38 ARISAKA SERVICE RIFLE . . . . . NiB $475 Ex $325 Gd $175
Mauser-type bolt action. Caliber: 6.5mm Japanese. Five shot box magazine. Bbl. lengths: 25.38 and 31.25 inches. Weight: 9.25 lbs. w/long bbl. Sights: fixed front, adj. rear. Military-type full stock. Adopted in 1905, the 38th year of the Meiji reign hence, the designation "Model 38."

MODEL 38 ARISAKA CARBINE. . . . NiB $475 Ex $325 Gd $175
Same general specifications as Model 38 Rifle except w/19-inch bbl., heavy folding bayonet, weight 7.25 lbs.

MODEL 44 CAVALRY CARBINE . . . NiB $650 Ex $575 Gd $300
Same general specifications as Model 38 Rifle except w/19-inch bbl., heavy folding bayonet, weight 8.5 lbs. Adopted in 1911, the 44th year of the Meiji reign, hence the designation, "Model 44."

MODEL 99 SERVICE RIFLE . . . . . . NiB $380 Ex $200 Gd $150
Modified Model 38. Caliber: 7.7mm Japanese. Five shot box magazine. 25.75-inch bbl. Weight: 8.75 lbs. Sights: Fixed front; adj. aperture rear; anti-aircraft sighting bars on some early models; fixed rear sight on some late WWII rifles. Military-type full stock, may have bipod. Takedown paratroop model was also made during WWII. Adopted in 1939, (Japanese year 2599) from which the designation "Model 99" is taken. Note: The last Model 99 rifles made were of poor quality; some with cast steel receivers. Value shown is for earlier type.

JARRETT CUSTOM RIFLES — Jackson, South Carolina

MODEL NO. 2 WALKABOUT
BOLT-ACTION RIFLE. . . . . NiB $2890 Ex $2550 Gd $1550
Custom lightweight rifle built on Remington M700 action. Jarrett match-grade barrel cut and chambered to customer's specification in short action calibers only. McMillan fiberglass stock pillar-bedded to action and finished to customer's preference.

MODEL NO. 3 CUSTOM
BOLT-ACTION RIFLE. . . . . NiB $2875 Ex $2400 Gd $1475
Custom rifle built on Remington M700 action. Jarrett match grade barrel cut

(cont'd.) **MODEL NO. 3 CUSTOM BOLT-ACTION RIFLE**
and chambered to customer's specification. McMillan classic fiberglass stock pillar-bedded to action and finished to customer's preference. made 1989 to date.

MODEL NO. 4 PROFESSIONAL
HUNTER BOLT-ACTION RIFLE . . . . . . NiB $6450 Ex $5400 Gd $4100
Custom magnum rifle built on Winchester M70 "controlled feed" action. Jarrett match grade barrel cut and chambered to customer's specification in magnum calibers only. Quarter rib w/iron sights and two Leupold scopes w/Q-D rings and mounts. McMillan classic fiberglass stock fitted and finished to customer's preference.

JOHNSON AUTOMATICS, INC. — Providence, Rhode Island

MODEL 1941 SEMIAUTO
MILITARY RIFLE . . . . NiB $2500 Ex $1575 Gd $1200
Short-recoil operated. Removable, air-cooled, 22-inch bbl. Caliber: .30-06, 7mm Mauser. 10-shot rotary magazine. Two-piece wood stock, pistol grip, perforated metal radiator sleeve over rear half of bbl. Sights: Receiver peep; protected post front. Weight: 9.5 lbs. Note: The Johnson M/1941 was adopted by the Netherlands government in 1940-41 and the major portion of the production of this rifle, 1941-43, was on Dutch orders. A quantity was also bought by the U.S. government for use by Marine Corps parachute troops (1943) and for Lend Lease. All these rifles were caliber .30-06; the 7mm Johnson rifles were made for the South American government.

SPORTING RIFLE PROTOTYPE. . . . NiB $13,750 Ex $11,000 Gd $7480
Same general specifications as military rifle except fitted w/sporting stock, checkered grip and forend. Blade front sight; receiver peep sight. Less than a dozen made prior to World War II.

IVER JOHNSON ARMS, INC. — Jacksonville, Arkansas, (Formerly of Fitchburg, Massachusetts, and Middlesex, New Jersey)

LI'L CHAMP BOLT-ACTION RIFLE . . . . NiB $90 Ex $65 Gd $50
Caliber: .22 S. L. LR. Single-shot. 16.25-inch bbl. 32.5 inches overall. Weight: 3.25 lbs. Adj. rear sight, blade front. Synthetic composition stock. Made 1986-88.

Iver Johnson Model SC30FS

Iver Johnson Survival
Semiautomatic Carbine

Iver Johnson Trailblazer

Iver Johnson Model XX (2X) Bolt-Action Rifle

MODEL M-1 SEMIAUTOMATIC CARBINE

Similar to U.S. M-1 Carbine. Calibers: 9mm Parabellum 30 U.S. Carbine. 15- or 30-shot magazine. 18-inch bbl. 35.5 inches overall. Weight: 6.5 lbs. Sights: blade front, w/guards; adj. peep rear. Walnut, hardwood or collapsible wire stock. Parkerized finish.

Model M-1 (30 cal. w/hardwood)	NiB $325	Ex $250	Gd $150
Model M-1 (30 cal. w/walnut)	NiB $350	Ex $260	Gd $160
Model M-1 (30 cal. w/wire)	NiB $400	Ex $325	Gd $165
Model M-1 (9mm w/hardwood)	NiB $235	Ex $220	Gd $185
Model M-1 (9mm w/walnut)	NiB $295	Ex $250	Gd $190
Model M-1 (9mm w/wire)	NiB $350	Ex $290	Gd $180

MODEL PM.30

SEMIAUTOMATIC CARBINE . . . . . . NiB $330 Ex $250 Gd $150
Similar to U.S. Carbine, Cal. 30 M1. 18-inch bbl. Weight: 5.5 lbs. 15- or 30-round detachable magazine. Both hardwood and walnut stock.

MODEL SC30FS

SEMIAUTOMATIC CARBINE . . . . . . NiB $400 Ex $325 Gd $165
Similar to Survival Carbine except w/folding stock. Made 1983 to date.

SURVIVAL SEMIAUTOMATIC CARBINE . . NiB $375 Ex $350 Gd $175
Similar to Model PM.30 except in stainless steel. Made 1983 to date. W/folding high-impact plastic stock add $35.

TRAILBLAZER SEMIAUTO RIFLE . . . . NiB $125 Ex $110 Gd $90
Caliber: .22 LR. 18-inch bbl. Weight: 5.5 lbs. Sights: Open rear, blade front. Hardwood stock. Made 1983-85

MODEL X BOLT-ACTION RIFLE . . . . . NiB $115 Ex $95 Gd $65
Takedown, Single-shot. Caliber: .22 Short, Long and LR. 22-inch bbl. Weight: 4 lbs. Sights: Open rear; blade front. Pistol-grip stock w/knob forend tip. Made 1928-32.

MODEL XX (2X) BOLT-ACTION RIFLE . . . . . NiB $125 Ex $90 Gd $70
Improved version of Model X w/heavier 24-inch bbl. larger stock (w/o knob tip), weight: 4.5 lbs, Made 1932-55.

MODEL 5100A1

BOLT-ACTION RIFLE . . . . NiB $4994 Ex $3995 Gd $2717
Single-shot long-range rifle w/removable bolt for breech loading. Caliber: 50BMG. Fluted 29-inch bbl. w/muzzle brake. 51.5 inches overall. Adj. composition stock w/folding bipod. Scope rings; no sights.

K.B.I., INC. — Harrisburg, Pennsylvania

See listing under Armscor; Charles Daly; FEG; Liberty and I.M.I.

SUPER CLASSIC

Calibers: .22 LR, .22 Mag., RF, .22 Hornet. Five or 10-round capacity. Bolt and semiauto action. 22.6- or 20.75-inch bbl. 41.25 or 40.5 inches overall. Weight: 6.4 to 6.7 lbs. Blue finish. Oil-finished American walnut stock w/hardwood grip cap and forend tip. Checkered Monte Carlo comb and cheekpiece. High polish blued barreled action w/damascened bolt. Dovetailed receiver and iron sights. Recoil pad. QD swivel posts.

.22 Long Rifle (M-1500 SC)	NiB $206	Ex $165	Gd $112
.22 Magnum Rimfire (M-1500 SC)	NiB $231	Ex $185	Gd $126
.22 Hornet (M-1800-S)	NiB $369	Ex $295	Gd $201
.22 Long Rifle Semiauto (M-2000 SC)	NiB $231	Ex $185	Gd $126

K.D.F. INC. — Sequin, Texas

MODEL K15 BOLT-ACTION RIFLE

Calibers: (Standard) .22-250, .243 Win., 6mm Rem., .25-06, .270 Win., .280 Rem., 7mm Mag., .30-60; (Magnum) .300 Wby., .300 Win., .338 Win., .340 Wby., .375 H&H, .411 KDF, .416 Rem., .458 Win. Four shot magazine (standard), 3-shot (magnum). 22-inch (standard) or 24-inch (magnum) bbl. 44.5 to 46.5 inches overall. Weight: 8 lbs. Sights optional. Kevlar composite or checkered walnut stock in Classic, European or thumbhole-style. Note: U.S. Manufacture limited to 25 prototypes and pre-production variations.

Standard model . . . . NiB $1725 Ex $1550 Gd $850

KDF Model K15
Bolt-Action Rifle

Kel-Tec
Sub-Series Semiautomatic Rifles

KEL-TEC CNC INDUSTRIES, INC. — Cocoa, Florida

SUB-SERIES SEMIAUTOMATIC RIFLES

Semiautomatic blow-back action w/pivoting bbl., takedown. 9mm Parabellum or 40 S&W. Interchangeable grip assembly accepts most double column, high capacity handgun magazines. 16.1-inch bbl. 31.5 inches overall. Weight: 4.6 lbs. Hooded post front sight, flip-up rear. Matte black finish. Tubular buttstock w/grooved polymer buttplate and vented handguard. Made 1997 to date.

Sub-9 Model (9mm) . . . . NiB $390 Ex $275 Gd $200
Sub-40 Model (40 S&W) . . . . NiB $475 Ex $390 Gd $250

KIMBER RIFLES — Mfd. By Kimber Manufacturing, Inc., Yonkers, NY (Formerly Kimber of America, Inc.; Kimber of Oregon, Inc.)

Note: From 1980-91, Kimber of Oregon produced Kimber firearms. A redesigned action designated by serialization with a "B" suffix was introduced 1986. Pre-1986 production is recognized as the "A" series but is not so marked. These early models in rare configurations and limited-run calibers command premium prices from collectors. Kimber of America, in Clackamas, Oregon, acquired the Kimber trademark and resumed manufactured of Kimber rifles. During this transition, Nationwide Sports Distributors, Inc. in Pennsylvania and Nevada became exclusive distributors of Kimber products. In 1997, Kimber Manufacturing acquired the trademark with manufacturing rights and expanded production to include a 1911-A1-style semiautomatic pistol, the Kimber Classic 45.

Rifle production resumed in late 1998 with the announcement of an all-new Kimber .22 rifle and a refined Model 84 in both single shot and repeater configurations.

MODEL 82 BOLT-ACTION RIFLE

Small action based on Kimber's "A" Model 82 rimfire receiver w/twin rear locking lugs. Calibers: .22 LR. .22 WRF, .22 Hornet, .218 Bee, .25-20. 5- or 10-shot magazine (.22 LR); 5-shot magazine (22WRF); 3-shot magazine (.22 Hornet). .218 Bee and .25-20 are single-shot. 18- to 25-inch bbl. 37.63 to 42.5 inches overall. Weight: 6 lbs. (Light Sporter), 6.5 lbs. (Sporter), 7.5 lbs. (Varmint); 10.75 lbs. (Target). Right- and left-hand actions are available in distinctive stock styles.

Cascade (disc. 1987) . . . . NiB $850 Ex $775 Gd $500
Classic (disc. 1988) . . . . NiB $850 Ex $775 Gd $500
Continental . . . . NiB $1313 Ex $1050 Gd $714
Custom Classic
(disc. 1988) . . . . NiB $906 Ex $725 Gd $493
Mini Classic . . . . NiB $569 Ex $455 Gd $309
Super America . . . . NiB $1550 Ex $975 Gd $725
Super Continental . . . . NiB $1490 Ex $1250 Gd $750
1990 Classifications
All-American
Match . . . . NiB $875 Ex $750 Gd $525
Deluxe Grade
(disc. 1990) . . . . NiB $1250 Ex $975 Gd $775
Hunter
(Laminated stock) . . . . NiB $800 Ex $650 Gd $425
Super America . . . . NiB $1250 Ex $995 Gd $650
Target
(Government Match) . . . . NiB $850 Ex $795 Gd $625

MODEL 82C CLASSIC BOLT-ACTION RIFLE

Caliber: .22 LR. Four shot or 10-shot magazine. 21-inch air-gauged bbl. 40.5 inches overall. Weight: 6.5 lbs. Receiver drilled and tapped for Warne scope mounts; no sights. Single-set trigger. Checkered Claro walnut stock w/red buttpad and polished steel grip cap. Reintroduced 1993.

Classic model . . . . NiB $825 Ex $690 Gd $400
Left-hand model, add. $75

Kimber Model 82 Rimfire Classic

Kimber Model 82C Rimfire Classic

Kimber Model 84 Classic

Kimber Model 89 Big Game 375 Caliber

Kimber Model 89 Big Game 375 H&H Caliber

Model 84 Bolt-Action Rifle

Classic (disc. 1988) Compact-medium action based on a scaled-down Mauser-type receiver, designed to accept small base centerfire cartridges. Calibers: .17 Rem., .221 Fireball, .222 Rem., .223 Rem. Five shot magazine. Same general barrel and stock specifications as Model 82.

Classic (discontinued 1988)	NiB $894	Ex $695	Gd $469
Continental	NiB $1188	Ex $950	Gd $646
Custom Classic (disc. 1988)	NiB $1069	Ex $855	Gd $581
Super America (disc. 1988)	NiB $1219	Ex $975	Gd $663
Super Continental (disc. 1988)	NiB $1281	Ex $1025	Gd $697
1990 Classifications			
Deluxe Grade (disc. 1990)	NiB $1119	Ex $895	Gd $609
Hunter/Sporter (laminated stock)	NiB $994	Ex $795	Gd $541
Super America (disc. 1991)	NiB $1244	Ex $995	Gd $677
Super Varmint (disc. 1991)	NiB $1281	Ex $1025	Gd $697
Ultra Varmint (disc. 1991)	NiB $1194	Ex $955	Gd $649

MODEL 89 BIG-GAME RIFLE

Large action combining the best features of the pre-64 Model 70 Winchester and the Mauser 98. Three action lengths are offered in three stock styles. Calibers: .257 Roberts, .25-06, 7x57, .270 Win., .280 Win., .30-06, 7mm Rem. Mag., .300 Win. Mag., .300 H&H, .338 Win., 35

(cont'd.) MODEL 89 BIG-GAME RIFLE

Whelen, .375 H&H, .404 Jeffrey, .416 Rigby, .460 Wby., .505 Gibbs (.308 cartridge family to follow). Five shot magazine (standard calibers); 3-shot magazine (Magnum calibers). 22- to 24-inch bbl. 42 to 44 inches overall. Weight: 7.5 to 10.5 lbs. Model 89 African features express sights on contoured quarter rib, banded front sight. Barrel-mounted recoil lug w/integral receiver lug and twin recoil crosspins in stock.

BGR Long Action

Classic (disc. 1988)	NiB $869	Ex $695	Gd $473
Custom Classic (disc. 1988)	NiB $1119	Ex $895	Gd $609
Super America	NiB $1369	Ex $1095	Gd $745
1990 Classifications			
Deluxe Grade: Featherweight	NiB $1619	Ex $1295	Gd $881
Medium	NiB $1656	Ex $1325	Gd $901
.375 H&H	NiB $1744	Ex $1395	Gd $949
Hunter Grade (laminated stock)			
.270 and .30-06	NiB $1188	Ex $950	Gd $646
.375 H&H	NiB $1494	Ex $1195	Gd $813
Super America: Featherweight	NiB $1869	Ex $1495	Gd $1017
Medium	NiB $1963	Ex $1570	Gd $1068
.375 H&H	NiB $2500	Ex $2000	Gd $1360
African — All calibers	NiB $4494	Ex $3595	Gd $2445

Krico Model 400

KNIGHT'S MANUFACTURING COMPANY — Vero Beach, Florida

SR-15 SEMIAUTOMATIC
MATCH RIFLE . . . . **NiB $1600 Ex $1350 Gd $900**
AR-15 configuration. Caliber: .223 Rem. (5.56mm). Five or 10-shot magazine. 20-inch w/free-floating, match-grade bbl., 38 inches overall. Weight: 7.9 lbs. Integral Weaver-style rail. Two-stage target trigger. Matte black oxide finish. Black synthetic AR-15A2-style stock and forearm. Made 1997 to date.

SR-15 M-4 SEMIAUTOMATIC CARBINE
Similar to SR-15 rifle except w/16-inch bbl. Sights and mounts optional. Fixed synthetic or collapsible buttstock. Made 1997 to date.
Model SR-15 Carbine (w/collapsible stock) . . . . . NiB $1330 Ex $1200 Gd $850
Model SR-15 Carbine (w/fixed stock) . . . . . . NiB $1330 Ex $1200 Gd $850

SR-15 M-5 SEMIAUTOMATIC RIFLE . . . . **NiB $1450 Ex $1275 Gd $950**
Caliber: .223 Rem. (5.56mm). Five or 10-shot magazine. 20-inch bbl. 38 inches overall. Weight: 7.6 lbs. Integral Weaver-style rail. Two-stage target trigger. Matte black oxide finish. Black synthetic AR-15A2-style stock and forearm. Made 1997 to date.

SR-25 MATCH RIFLE
Similar to SR-25 Sporter except w/free floating 20- or 24-inch match bbl. 39.5-43.5 inches overall. Weight: 9.25 and 10.75 lbs., respectively. Integral Weaver-style rail. Sights and mounts optional. 1 MOA guaranteed. Made 1993 to date.
Model SR-25 LW Match (w/20-inch bbl.) . . . . NiB $2650 Ex $2250 Gd $1425
Model SR-25 Match (w/24-inch bbl.) . . . NiB $2650 Ex $2250 Gd $1425
W/RAS (Rail Adapter System), add $300

SR-25 SEMIAUTOMATIC CARBINE
Similar to SR-25 Sporter except w/free floating 16-inch bbl. 35.75 inches overall. Weight: 7.75 lbs. Integral Weaver-style rail. Sights and mounts optional. Made 1995 to date.
Model SR-25 Carbine (w/o sights) . . . . NiB $2600 Ex $2350 Gd $1400
W/RAS (Rail Adapter System), add $300

SR-25 SEMIAUTOMATIC
SPORTER RIFLE . . . . **NiB $2700 Ex $2200 Gd $1500**
AR-15 configuration. Caliber: .308 Win. (7.62 NATO). Five, 10- or 20-shot magazine. 20-inch bbl. 39.5 inches overall. Weight: 8.75 lbs. Integral Weaver-style rail. Protected post front sight adjustable for elevation, detachable rear adjustable for windage. Two-stage target trigger. Matte black oxide finish. Black synthetic AR-15A2-style stock and forearm. Made 1993-97.

SR-50 SEMIAUTOMATIC LONG
RANGE PRECISION RIFLE . . . . . **NiB $6300 Ex $5500 Gd $3200**
Gas-operated semiautomatic action. Caliber: .50 BMG. 10-shot magazine. 35.5-inch bbl. 58.5 inches overall. Weight: 31.75 lbs. Integral Weaver-style rail. Two-stage target trigger. Matte black oxide finish. Tubular-style stock. Made 1996 to date.

KONGSBERG RIFLES — Kongsberg, Norway
(Imported by Kongsberg America L.L.C., Fairfield, CT)

MODEL 393 CLASSIC SPORTER
Calibers: .22-250 Rem., .243 Win., 6.5x55, .270 Win., 7mm Rem. Mag., .30-06, .308 Win. .300 Win. Mag., .338 Win. Mag. Three or 4-shot rotary magazine. 23-inch bbl. (Standard) or 26-inch bbl. (magnum). Weight: 7.5 to 8 lbs. 44 to 47 inches overall. No sights w/ dovetailed receiver or optional hooded blade front sight, adjustable rear. Blue finish. Checkered European walnut stock w/rubber buttplate. Imported 1994-98.
Standard calibers . . . . NiB $875 Ex $750 Gd $450
Magnum calibers . . . . NiB $1146 Ex $940 Gd $676
Left-hand model, add $135
W/optional sights, add $50

MODEL 393 DELUXE SPORTER
Similar to Classic Model except w/deluxe European walnut stock. Imported 1994-98.
Standard calibers . . . . NiB $950 Ex $795 Gd $475
Magnum calibers . . . . NiB $1178 Ex $965 Gd $693
Left-hand model, add $135
W/optional sights, add $50

MODEL 393 THUMBHOLE SPORTER
Calibers: 22-250 Rem. or 308 Win. Four shot rotary magazine. 23-inch heavy bbl. Weight: 8.5 lbs. 44 inches overall. No sights, dovetailed receiver. Blue finish. Stippled American walnut thumbhole stock w/adjustable cheekpiece. Imported 1993-98.
Right-hand model . . . . NiB $1350 Ex $1175 Gd $500
Left-hand model . . . . NiB $1629 Ex $1330 Gd $948

KRICO RIFLES — Stuttgart-Hedelfingen, Germany, Mfd. by Sportwaffenfabrik, Kriegeskorte GmbH, *Imported by Mandall Shooting Supplies, Scottsdale, AZ, (Previously by Beeman Precision Arms, Inc.)*

MODEL 260 SEMIAUTOMATIC RIFLE . . . . **NiB $610 Ex $550 Gd $350**
Caliber: .22 LR. 10-shot magazine. 20-inch bbl. 38.9 inches overall. Weight: 6.6 lbs. Hooded blade front sight; adj. rear. Grooved receiver. Beech stock. Blued finish. Imported 1991 to date.

MODEL 300 BOLT-ACTION RIFLE
Calibers: .22 LR. .22 WMR. .22 Hornet. 19.6-inch bbl. (22 LR), 23.6-inch (22 Hornet). 38.5 inches overall. Weight: 6.3 lbs. Double-set triggers. Sights: Ramped blade front, adj. open rear. Checkered walnut-finished hardwood stock. Blued finish. Imported 1993 to date.
Model 300 Standard . . . . NiB $625 Ex $475 Gd $325
Model 300 Deluxe . . . . NiB $650 Ex $500 Gd $350
Model 300 SA (Monte Carlo walnut stock) . . . . NiB $756 Ex $615 Gd $434
Model 300 Stutzen (full-length walnut stock) . . . . NiB $875 Ex $750 Gd $500

Krico Model 420

Krico 640 Varmint

MODEL 311 SMALL-BORE RIFLE
Bolt action. Caliber: .22 LR. Five or 10-shot clip magazine. 22-inch bbl. Weight: 6 lbs. Single- or double-set trigger. Sights: Open rear; hooded ramp front; available w/factory-fitted Kaps 2.5x scope. Checkered stock w/cheekpiece, pistol-grip and swivels. Disc.
W/scope sight . . . . **NiB $425 Ex $375 Gd $225**
W/iron sights only . . . . **NiB $350 Ex $250 Gd $200**

MODEL 320 BOLT-ACTION SPORTER . . . . **NiB $675 Ex $525 Gd $350**
Caliber: .22 LR. Five shot detachable box magazine. 19.5-inch bbl. 38.5 inches overall. Weight: 6 lbs. Adj. rear sight, blade ramp front. Checkered European walnut Mannlicher-style stock w/low comb and cheekpiece. Single or double-set triggers. Imported 1986-91.

**MODEL 340 METALLIC
SILHOUETTE
BOLT-ACTION RIFLE** . . . . **NiB $690 Ex $575 Gd $390**
Caliber: .22 LR. Five shot magazine. 21-inch heavy, bull bbl. 39.5 inches overall. Weight: 7.5 lbs. No sights. Grooved receiver for scope mounts. European walnut stock in off-hand, match-style configuration. Match or double-set triggers. Imported 1983-86.

MODEL 360S BIATHLON RIFLE . . . . . . **NiB $1300 Ex $1050 Gd $575**
Caliber: .22 LR. Five 5-shot magazines. 21.25-inch bbl. w/snow cap. 40.5 inches overall. Weight: 9.25 lbs. Straight-pull action. Match trigger w/17-oz. pull. Sights: Globe front, adj. match peep rear. Biathlon-style walnut stock w/high comb and adj. butt-plate. Imported 1991 to date.

MODEL 360 S2 BIATHLON RIFLE . . . . . **NiB $1275 Ex $1000 Gd $550**
Similar to Model 360S except w/pistol-grip activated action. Biathlon-style walnut stock w/black epoxy finish. Imported 1991 to date.

MODEL 400 BOLT-ACTION RIFLE . . . . **NiB $844 Ex $675 Gd $459**
Caliber: .22 Hornet. Five shot detachable box magazine. 23.5-inch bbl. Weight: 6.75 lbs. Adj. open rear sight, ramp front. European walnut stock. Disc. 1990.

MODEL 420 BOLT-ACTION RIFLE . . . . **NiB $875 Ex $700 Gd $475**
Same as Model 400 except w/full-length Mannlicher-style stock and double-set triggers. Scope optional, extra. Disc. 1989.

MODEL 440 S BOLT-ACTION RIFLE . . . . . **NiB $819 Ex $655 Gd $445**
Caliber: .22 Hornet. Detachable box magazine. 20-inch bbl. 36.5 inches overall. Weight: 7.5 lbs. No sights. French walnut stock w/ventilated forend. Disc. 1988.

MODEL 500 MATCH RIFLE . . . . **NiB $3313 Ex $2650 Gd $1802**
Caliber: .22 LR. Single-shot. 23.6-inch bbl. 42 inches overall. Weight: 9.4 lbs. Kricotronic electronic ignition system. Sights: Globe front; match micrometer aperture rear. Match-style European walnut stock w/adj. butt.

MODEL 600 BOLT-ACTION RIFLE . . . . . . **NiB $1119 Ex $895 Gd $609**
Same general specifications as Model 700 except w/short action. Calibers: .17 Rem., .222, .223, .22-250, .243, 5.6x50 Mag. and 308.

MODEL 620 BOLT-ACTION RIFLE . . . . . . **NiB $1170 Ex $970 Gd $600**
Same as Model 600 except w/short-action-chambered for .308 Win. only and full-length Mannlicher-style stock w/Schnabel forend tip. 20.75-inch bbl. Weight: 6.5 lbs. No longer imported.

**MODEL 640 SUPER SNIPER
BOLT-ACTION REPEATING RIFLE NiB $1369 Ex $1095 Gd $745**
Calibers: .223 Rem., .308 Win. Three shot magazine. 26-inch bbl. 44.25 inches overall. Weight: 9.5 lbs. No sights drilled and tapped for scope mounts. Single or double-set triggers. Select walnut stock w/adj. cheekpiece and recoil pad. Disc. 1989.

MODEL 640 VARMINT RIFLE . . . . **NiB $875 Ex $750 Gd $450**
Caliber: .222 Rem. Four shot magazine. 23.75-inch bbl. Weight: 9.5 lbs. No sights. European walnut stock. No longer imported.

MODEL 700 BOLT-ACTION RIFLE
Calibers: .17 Rem., .222, .222 Rem. Mag., .223, .22-250, 5.6x50 Mag., .243, 5.6x57 RSW, 6x62, 6.5x55, 6.5x57, 6.5x68 .270 Win., 7x64, 7.5 Swiss, 7mm Mag., .30-06, .300 Win., 8x68S, 9.3x64. 24-inch (standard) or 26-inch (magnum) bbl. 44 inches overall (standard). Weight: 7.5 lbs. Adj. rear sight; hooded ramp front. Checkered European-style walnut stock w/Bavarian cheekpiece and rosewood Schnabel forend tip. Imported 1983 to date.
Model 700 . . . . **NiB $1063 Ex $850 Gd $578**
Model 700 Deluxe . . . . **NiB $1119 Ex $895 Gd $609**
Model 700 Deluxe S . . . . **NiB $1369 Ex $1095 Gd $745**
Model 700 Stutzen . . . . **NiB $1188 Ex $950 Gd $646**

Krieghoff Teck Boxlock Over/Under

Krieghoff Teck Sidelock Over/Under

Lakefield Model 64B

Lakefield Model 92S Target

Lakefield Mark I

MODEL 720 BOLT-ACTION RIFLE
Same general specifications as Model 700 except in calibers .270 Win. and .30-06 w/full-length Mannlicher-style stock and Schnabel forend tip. 20.75-inch bbl. Weight: 6.75 lbs. Disc. importing 1990.
Sporter Model . . . . **NiB $1119 Ex $895 Gd $609**
Ltd. Edition . . . . **NiB $2300 Ex $1990 Gd $1000**

BOLT-ACTION SPORTING RIFLE . . . . **NiB $600 Ex $550 Gd $375**
Miniature Mauser action. Single- or double-set trigger. Calibers: .22 Hornet, .222 Rem. Four shot clip magazine. 22-24- or 26-inch bbl. Weight: 6.25 lbs. Sights: Open rear; hooded ramp front. Checkered stock w/cheekpiece, pistol-grip, black forend tip, sling swivels. Imported 1956-62.

CARBINE . . . . **NiB $650 Ex $525 Gd $350**
Same as Krico Sporting Rifle except w/20- or 22-inch bbl., full-length Mannlicher-type stock.

SPECIAL VARMINT RIFLE . . . . **NiB $650 Ex $525 Gd $350**
Same as Krico Rifle except w/heavy bbl., no sights, weight: 7.25 lbs. Caliber: .222 Rem. only.

KRIEGHOFF RIFLES — Ulm (Donau), Germany, Mfd. by H. Krieghoff Jagd und Sportwaffenfabrik

See also Combination Guns under Krieghoff shotgun listings.

TECK OVER/UNDER RIFLE
Kersten action, double crossbolt, double underlugs. Boxlock. Calibers: 7x57r5, 7x64, 7x65r5, .30-30, .308 Win. .30-06, .300 Win. Mag., 9.3x74r5, .375 H&H Mag. .458 Win. Mag. 25-inch bbls. Weight: 8 to 9.5 lbs. Sights: Express rear; ramp front. Checkered walnut stock and forearm. Made 1967 to date.
Standard calibers . . . .**NiB $8700 Ex $6400 Gd $5000**
.375 H&H Mag.
(Disc. 1988)
.458 Win. Mag . . . .**NiB $9000 Ex $6700 Gd $6000**

ULM OVER/
UNDER RIFLE . . . . **NiB $14,300 Ex $10,300 Gd $6000**
Same general specifications as Teck model except w/sidelocks w/leaf Arabesque engraving. Made 1963 to date.

**Magnum Research Mountain Eagle
Bolt-Action Rifle**

ULM-PRIMUS OVER/UNDER RIFLE... NiB $14,063 Ex $11,250 Gd $7650
Delux version of Ulm model, w/detachable sidelocks, higher grade engraving and stock wood. Made 1963 to date.

LAKEFIELD ARMS LTD. — Ontario, Canada

See also listing under Savage for production since 1994.

MODEL 64B SEMIAUTOMATIC RIFLE ...... NiB $140 Ex $80 Gd $60
Caliber: .22 LR. 10-shot magazine. 20-inch bbl. Weight: 5.5 lbs. 40 inches overall. Bead front sight, adj. rear. Grooved receiver for scope mounts. Stamped checkering on walnut-finished hardwood stock w/Monte Carlo cheekpiece. Imported 1990-94.

**MODEL 90B
BOLT-ACTION TARGET RIFLE ..... NiB $425 Ex $300 Gd $175**
Caliber: .22 LR. Five shot magazine. 21-inch bbl. w/snow cap. 39.63 inches overall. Weight: 8.25 lbs. Adj. receiver peep sight; globe front w/colored inserts. Receiver drilled and tapped for scope mounts. Biathlon-style natural finished hardwood stock w/shooting rails, hand stop and butthook. Made 1991-94.

MODEL 91T/91TR BOLT-ACTION TARGET RIFLE
Calibers: .22 Short, Long, LR. 25-inch bbl. 43.63 inches overall. Weight: 8 lbs. Adj. rear peep sight; globe front w/inserts. Receiver drilled and tapped for scope mounts. Walnut-finished hardwood stock w/shooting rails and hand stop. Model 91TR is a 5-shot clip-fed repeater. Made 1991-94.
Model 91T single-shot. .... NiB $340 Ex $255 Gd $100
Model 91TR repeater (.22 LR only). ...... NiB $350 Ex $200 Gd $110

MODEL 92S TARGET RIFLE ...... NiB $281 Ex $225 Gd $153
Same general specifications as Model 90B except w/conventional target-style stock. 8 lbs. No sights, but drilled and tapped for scope mounts. Made 1993-95.

MODEL 93M BOLT ACTION ...... NiB $138 Ex $110 Gd $75
Caliber: .22 WMR. Five shot magazine. 20.75-inch bbl. 39.5 inches overall. Weight: 5.75 lbs. Bead front sight, adj. open rear. Receiver grooved for scope mount. Thumb-operated rotary safety. Checkered walnut-finished hardwood stock. Blued finish. Made 1995.

MARK I BOLT-ACTION RIFLE .... NiB $88 Ex $70 Gd $48
Calibers: .22 Short, Long, LR. Single-shot. 20.5-inch bbl. (19-inch Youth Model); available in smoothbore. Weight: 5.5 lbs. 39.5 inches overall. Bead front sight; adj. rear. Grooved receiver for scope mounts. Checkered walnut-finished hardwood stock w/Monte Carlo and pistol-grip. Blued finish. Made 1990-94.

MARK II BOLT-ACTION RIFLE
Same general specifications as Mark I except has repeating action w/10-shot detachable box magazine. .22 LR. only. Made 1992-94.
(contd.) **MARK II BOLT-ACTION RIFLE**
Mark II Standard .... NiB $94 Ex $75 Gd $51
Mark II Youth (19-inch barrel)....... NiB $106 Ex $85 Gd $58
Mark II left-hand .... NiB $131 Ex $105 Gd $71

LAURONA RIFLES — Mfg. in Eibar, Spain Imported by Galaxy Imports, Victoria, TX

MODEL 2000X O/U EXPRESS RIFLE
Calibers: .30-06, 8x57 JRS, 8x75 JR, .375 H&H, 9.3x74R Five shot magazine. 24-inch separated bbls. Weight: 8.5 lbs. Quarter rib drilled and tapped for scope mount. Open sights. Matte black chrome finish. Monte Carlo-style checkered walnut buttstock; tulip forearm. Imported 1993 to date.
Standard calibers............ NiB $2813 Ex $2250 Gd $1530
Magnum calibers............ NiB $3495 Ex $2796 Gd $1901

L.A.R. MANUFACTURING, INC. — West Jordan, Utah

**BIG BOAR COMPETITOR
BOLT-ACTION RIFLE........ NiB $2313 Ex $1850 Gd $1258**
Single-shot, bull-pup action. Caliber: .50 BMG. 36-inch bbl. 45.5 inches overall. Weight: 28.4 lbs. Made 1994 to date.

LUNA RIFLE — Mehlis, Germany Mfg. by Ernst Friedr. Büchel

SINGLE-SHOT TARGET RIFLE ..... NiB $990 Ex $850 Gd $550
Falling block action. Calibers: .22 LR. .22 Hornet. 29-inch bbl. Weight: 8.25 lbs. Sights: Micrometer peep rear tang; open rear; ramp front. Cheekpiece stock w/full pistol-grip, semibeavertail forearm, checkered, swivels. Made before WWII.

MAGNUM RESEARCH, INC. — Minneapolis, Minnesota

MOUNTAIN EAGLE BOLT-ACTION RIFLE SERIES
Calibers: .222 Rem., .223 Rem., .270 Win., .280 Rem., 7mm Rem. Mag., 7mm STW, .30-06, .300 Win. Mag., .338 Win. Mag., .340 Wby. Mag., .375 H&H, .416 Rem. Mag. Five shot (std.) or 4-shot (Mag.). 24- or 26-inch bbl. 44 to 46 inches overall. Weight: 7.75 to 9.75 lbs. Receiver drilled and tapped for scope mount; no sights. Blued finish. Fiberglass composite stock. Made 1994 to date.
Standard model................... NiB $1328 Ex $1075 Gd $600
Magnum model.................... NiB $1328 Ex $1075 Gd $600
Varmint model (Intro. 1996)......... NiB $1328 Ex $1075 Gd $600

Mannlicher Model L Rifle

Mannlicher
Model M Carbine

Mannlicher Model M Professional

Mannlicher
Model M Rifle

RIFLES

MAGTECH — Las Vegas, Nevada
Mfg. by CBC, Brazil

MODEL MT 122.2/S BOLT-ACTION RIFLE . . . NiB $110 Ex $90 Gd $50
Calibers: .22 Short, Long, Long Rifle. Six or 10-shot clip. Bolt action. 25-inch free-floating bbl. 43 inches overall. Weight: 6.5 lbs. Double locking bolt. Red cocking indicator. Safety lever. Brazilian hardwood finish. Double extractors. Beavertail forearm. Sling swivels. Imported 1994 to date.

MODEL MT 122.2/R BOLT-ACTION RIFLE . . . NiB $106 Ex $85 Gd $58
Same as Model MT 122.2/S except adj. rear sight and post front sight.

MODEL MT 122.2T BOLT-ACTION RIFLE . . . NiB $113 Ex $90 Gd $61
Same as Model MT 122.2/S except w/adj. micrometer-type rear sight and ramp front sight.

MANNLICHER SPORTING RIFLES — Steyr, Austria, Mfg. by Steyr-Daimler-Puch, A.-G.

NOTE: *Certain Mannlicher-Schoenauer models were produced before WWII. Manufacture of sporting rifles and carbines was resumed at the Steyr-Daimler-Puch plant in Austria in 1950 during which time the Model 1950 rifles and carbines were introduced.*

In 1967, Steyr-Daimler-Puch introduced a series of sporting rifles with a bolt action that is a departure from the Mannlicher-Schoenauer system of earlier models. In the latter, the action is locked by lugs symmetrically arranged behind the bolt head as well as by placing the bolt handle ahead of the right flank of the receiver, the rear section of which is open on top for backward movement of the bolt handle. The current action, made in four lengths to accommodate different ranges of cartridges, has a closed-top receiver; the bolt locking lugs are located toward the rear of the bolt (behind the magazine). The Mannlicher-Schoenauer rotary magazine has been redesigned as a detachable box type made of Makrolon. Imported by Gun South, Inc. Trussville, AL

MODEL L CARBINE. . . . . NiB $1313 Ex $1050 Gd $714
Same general specifications as Model SL Carbine except w/type "L" action, weight: 6.2 lbs. Calibers same as for Model L Rifle. Imported 1968-96.

**Mannlicher Model SL
Rifle w/Single-Set Trigger**

MODEL L RIFLE . . . . NiB $1875 Ex $1350 Gd $800
Same general specifications as Model SL Rifle except w/type "L" action, weighs 6.3 lbs. Calibers: .22-250, 5.6x57 (disc. 1991), ..243 Win., 6mm Rem. .308 Win. Imported 1968-96.

MODEL L VARMINT RIFLE . . . . . NiB $1900 Ex $1390 Gd $790
Same general specifications as Model SL Varmint Rifle except w/type "L" action. Calibers: .22-250, .243 Win., .308 Win. Imported 1969-96.

MODEL LUXUS BOLT-ACTION RIFLE
Same general specifications as Models L and M except w/3-shot detachable box magazine and single-set trigger. Full or half-stock w/low-luster oil or high-gloss lacquer finish. Disc. 1996.
Full stock . . . . NiB $1944 Ex $1595 Gd $1149
Half stock . . . . NiB $2495 Ex $1750 Gd $780

MODEL M CARBINE
Same general specifications as Model SL Carbine except w/type "M" action, stock w/recoil pad, weighs 6.8 lbs. Left-hand version w/additional 6.5x55 and 9.3x62 calibers intro. 1977. Imported 1969-96.
Right-hand carbine . . . . NiB $1995 Ex $1400 Gd $750
Left-hand carbine . . . . NiB $2144 Ex $1795 Gd $1349

MODEL M PROFESSIONAL RIFLE . . . . . NiB $1900 Ex $1350 Gd $700
Same as standard Model M Rifle except w/synthetic (Cycolac) stock, weighs 7.5 lbs. Calibers: 6.5x55, 6.5x57, .270 Win., 7x57, 7x64, 7.5 Swiss, .30-06, 8x57JS, 9.3x62. Imported 1977-93.

MODEL M RIFLE
Same general specifications as Model SL Rifle except w/type "M" action, stock w/forend tip and recoil pad; weighs 6.9 lbs. Calibers: 6.5x57, .270 Win., 7x57, 7x64, .30-06, 8x57JS, 9.3x62. Made 1969 to date. Left-hand version also in calibers 6.5x55 and 7.5 Swiss. Imported 1977-96.
Right-hand rifle . . . . NiB $1500 Ex $1050 Gd $700
Left-hand rifle . . . . NiB $2144 Ex $1795 Gd $1349

MODEL S RIFLE . . . . NiB $1500 Ex $1050 Gd $700
Same general specifications as Model SL Rifle except w/type "S" action, 4-round magazine, 25.63-inch bbl., stock w/forend tip and recoil pad, weighs 8.4 lbs. Calibers: 6.5x68, .257 Weatherby Mag., .264 Win. Mag., 7mm Rem. Mag., .300 Win. Mag., .300 H&H Mag., .308 Norma Mag., 8x68S, .338 Win. Mag., 9.3x64, .375 H&H Mag. Imported 1970-96.

MODEL SL CARBINE . . . . NiB $1500 Ex $1050 Gd $700
Same general specifications as Model SL Rifle except w/20-inch bbl. and full-length stock, weight: 6 lbs. Imported 1968-96.

MODEL SL RIFLE . . . . NiB $1500 Ex $1050 Gd $700
Steyr-Mannlicher SL bolt action. Calibers: .222 Rem., .222 Rem., .222 Rem. Mag., .223 Rem. Five shot rotary magazine, detachable. 23.63-inch bbl. Weight: 6 lbs. Single- or double-set trigger (mechanisms interchangeable). Sights: Open rear; hooded ramp front. Half stock of European walnut w/Monte Carlo comb and cheekpiece, skip-checkered forearm and pistol grip, rubber buttpad, QD swivels. Imported 1967-96.

MODEL SL
VARMINT RIFLE . . . . NiB $1100 Ex $1075 Gd $725
Same general specifications as Model SL Rifle except caliber .222 Rem. only, w/25.63-inch heavy bbl., no sights, weighs 7.92 lbs. Imported 1969-96.

MODEL SSG MATCH TARGET RIFLE
Type "L" action. Caliber: .308 Win. (7.62x51 NATO). Five or 10-round magazine, single-shot plug. 25.5-inch heavy bbl. Weight: 10.25 lbs. Single trigger. Sights: Micrometer peep rear; globe front. Target stock, European walnut or synthetic, w/full pistol-grip, wide forearm w/swivel rail, adj. rubber buttplate. Imported 1969 to date.
W/walnut stock . . . . NiB $2200 Ex $1750 Gd $1102
W/synthetic stock . . . . NiB $1319 Ex $995 Gd $581

MODEL S/T RIFLE . . . . NiB $1995 Ex $1400 Gd $600
Same as Model S Rifle except w/heavy 25.63-inch bbl., weight: 9 lbs. Calibers: 9.3x64, .375 H&H Mag., .458 Win. Mag. Option of 23.63-inch bbl. in latter caliber. Imported 1975-96.

MODEL 1903
BOLT-ACTION
SPORTING CARBINE . . . . NiB $3900 Ex $3800 Gd $500
Caliber: 6.5x53mm (referred to in some European gun catalogs as 6.7x53mm, following the Austrian practice of designating calibers by bullet diameter). Five shot rotary magazine. 450mm (17.7-inch) bbl. Weight: 6.5 lbs. Double-set trigger. Sights: Two-leaf rear; ramp front. Full-length sporting stock w/cheekpiece, pistol-grip, trap buttplate, swivels. Pre-WWII.

MODEL 1905 CARBINE . . . . NiB $1200 Ex $775 Gd $500
Same as Model 1903 except w/19.7-inch bbl. chambered 9x56mm and weight: 6.75 lbs. Pre-WWII.

MODEL 1908 CARBINE . . . . NiB $1300 Ex $1100 Gd $800
Same as Model 1905 except calibers 7x57mm and 8x56mm Pre-WWII.

MODEL 1910 CARBINE . . . . NiB $1500 Ex $1200 Gd $550
Same as Model 1905 except in 9.5x57mm. Pre-WWII.

MODEL 1924 CARBINE . . . . NiB $1600 Ex $1400 Gd $900
Same as Model 1905 except caliber .30-06 (7.62x63mm). Pre-WWII.

MODEL 1950
BOLT-ACTION
SPORTING RIFLE . . . . NiB $1450 Ex $1300 Gd $450
Calibers: .257 Roberts, .270 Win., .30-06. Five shot rotary magazine. 24-inch bbl. Weight: 7.25 lbs. Single trigger or double-set trigger. Redesigned low bolt handle, shotgun-type safety. Sights: Folding leaf open rear; hooded ramp front. Improved half-length stock w/cheekpiece, pistol grip, checkered, ebony forend tip, swivels. Made 1950-52.

Mannlicher-Schoenauer
Model 1905 Carbine

Mannlicher-Schoenauer
Model 1905 Carbine

Mannlicher-Schoenauer
Model 1905 Carbine

Mannlicher-Schoenauer
Model 1905 Carbine

Mannlicher-Schoenauer
Model 1905 Carbine

MODEL 1950 CARBINE . . . . **NiB $1700 Ex $1400 Gd $850**
Same general specifications as Model 1950 Rifle except w/20-inch bbl., full-length stock, weighs 7 lbs. Made 1950-52.

**MODEL 1950
6.5 CARBINE** . . . . **NiB $1800 Ex $1600 Gd $890**
Same as other Model 1950 Carbines except caliber 6.5x53mm, w/18.25-inch bbl., weighs 6.75 lbs. Made 1950-52.

**MODEL 1952
IMPROVED CARBINE** . . . . **NiB $1900 Ex $1295 Gd $780**
Same as Model 1950 Carbine except w/swept-back bolt handle, redesigned stock. Calibers: .257, .270, 7mm, .30-06. Made 1952-56.

**MODEL 1952 IMPROVED
6.5 CARBINE** . . . . **NiB $1050 Ex $950 Gd $500**
Same as Model 1952 Carbine except caliber 6.5x53mm, w/18.25-inch bbl. Made 1952-56.

**MODEL 1952 IMPROVED
SPORTING RIFLE.** . . . . **NiB $1400 Ex $1200 Gd $750**
Same as Model 1950 except w/swept-back bolt handle, redesigned stock. Calibers: .257, .270, .30-06, 9.3x62mm. Made 1952-56 and imported exclusively by Stoeger Arms Corp.

MODEL 1956 CUSTOM CARBINE . . . . **NiB $875 Ex $700 Gd $475**
Same general specifications as Models 1950 and 1952 Carbines except w/redesigned stock w/high comb. Drilled and tapped for scope mounts. Calibers: .243, 6.5mm, .257, .270, 7mm, .30-06, .308. Made 1956-60.

CARBINE, MODEL 1961-MCA . . **NiB $2000 Ex $1850 Gd $500**
Same as Model 1956 Carbine except w/universal Monte Carlo design stock. Calibers: .243 Win., 6.5mm, .270, .308, .30-06. Made 1961-71.

RIFLE, MODEL 1961-MCA . . . . . **NiB $1650 Ex $1200 Gd $550**
Same as Model 1956 Rifle except w/universal Monte Carlo design stock. Calibers: .243, .270, .30-06. Made 1961-71.

**HIGH VELOCITY
BOLT-ACTION SPORTING RIFLE** . . . **NiB $2100 Ex $1900 Gd $875**
Calibers: 7x64 Brenneke, .30-06 (7.62x63), 8x60 Magnum, 9.3x62, 10.75x68mm. 23.6-inch bbl. Weight: 7.5 lbs. Sights: British-style 3-leaf open rear; ramp front. Half-length sporting stock w/cheekpiece, pistol grip, checkered, trap buttplate, swivels. Also produced in a takedown model. Pre-WWII. See illustration next page.

M72 MODEL L/M CARBINE . . . . . . **NiB $900 Ex $650 Gd $400**
Same general specifications as M72 Model L/M Rifle except w/20-inch bbl. and full-length stock, weight: 7.2 lbs. Imported 1972 to date.

Mannlicher Schoenauer
High Velocity Bolt-Action Sporting Rifle

Marlin Model 9 9mm Carbine

Marlin Model 9N Nickel-Teflon

M72 MODEL L/M RIFLE . . . . NiB $800 Ex $725 Gd $500
M72 bolt-action, type L/M receiver front-locking bolt internal rotary magazine (5-round). Calibers: .22-250, 5.6x57, 6mm Rem., .243 Win., 6.5x57, .270 Win., 7x57, 7x64, .308 Win., .30-06. 23.63-inch bbl. Weight: 7.3 lbs. Single- or double-set trigger (mechanisms interchangeable). Sights: Open rear; hooded ramp front. Half stock of European walnut, checkered forearm and pistol-grip, Monte Carlo cheekpiece, rosewood forend tip, recoil pad QD swivels. Imported 1972-81.

M72 MODEL S RIFLE . . . . NiB $775 Ex $675 Gd $450
Same general specifications as M72 Model L/M Rifle except w/magnum action, 4-round magazine, 25.63-inch bbl., weighs 8.6 lbs. Calibers: 6.5x68, 7mm Rem. Mag., 8x68S, 9.3x64, .375 H&H Mag. Imported 1972-81.

M72 MODEL S/T RIFLE . . . . NiB $1325 Ex $1025 Gd $680
Same as M72 Model S Rifle except w/heavy 25.63-inch bbl., weighs 9.3 lbs. Calibers: .300 Win. Mag. 9.3x64, .375 H&H Mag., .458 Win. Mag. Option of 23.63-inch bbl. in latter caliber. Imported 1975-81.

MODEL SBS FORESTER RIFLE
Calibers: .243 Win., .25-06 Rem., .270 Win., .6.5x55mm, 6.5x57mm, 7x64mm, 7mm-08 Rem., .30-06, .308 Win. 9.3x64mm. Four shot detachable magazine. 23.6-inch bbl. 44.5 inches overall. Weight: 7.5 lbs. No sights w/drilled and tapped for Browning A-Bolt configuration. Checkered American walnut stock w/Monte Carlo cheekpiece and Pachmayr swivels. Polished or matte blue finish. Imported 1997 to date.
SBS Forester Rifle (standard calibers) . . . . . NiB $790 Ex $625 Gd $395
SBS Forester Mountain Rifle (20-inch bbl.) . . . . NiB $756 Ex $600 Gd $390
For magnum calibers, add. $25
For metric calibers, add $100

MODEL SBS PRO-HUNTER RIFLE
Similar to the Forester Model, except w/ASB black synthetic stock. Matte blue finish. Imported 1997 to date.

(cont'd.) MODEL SBS PRO-HUNTER RIFLE
SBS Pro-Hunter Rifle (standard calibers) . . . . . NiB $740 Ex $600 Gd $390
SBS Pro-Hunter Rifle
Mountain Rifle (20-inch bbl.) . . . . NiB $790 Ex $590 Gd $385
SBS Pro-Hunter Rifle (.376 Steyr) . . . . NiB $781 Ex $625 Gd $425
SBS Pro-Hunter Youth/Ladies Rifle . . . . NiB $790 Ex $625 Gd $395
For magnum calibers, add. $25
For metric calibers, add. $100
W/walnut stock . . . . NiB $2144 Ex $1745 Gd $1235
W/synthetic stock . . . . NiB $1719 Ex $1395 Gd $981

MARLIN FIREARMS CO. — North Haven, Connecticut

MODEL 9 SEMIAUTOMATIC CARBINE
Calibers: 9mm Parabellum. 12-shot magazine. 16.5-inch bbl. 35.5 inches overall. Weight: 6.75 lbs. Manual bolt hold-open. Sights: Hooded post front; adj. open rear. Walnut-finished hardwood stock w/rubber buttpad. Blued or nickel-Teflon finish. Made 1985 to date.
Model 9 . . . . NiB $340 Ex $225 Gd $105
Model 9N, Nickel-Teflon (disc. 1994) . . . . NiB $375 Ex $250 Gd $110

MODEL 15Y/15YN
Bolt-action, single-shot "Little Buckaroo" rifle. Caliber: .22 Short, Long or LR. 16.25-inch bbl. Weight: 4.25 lbs. Thumb safety. Ramp front sight; adj. open rear. One-piece walnut Monte Carlo stock w/full pistol-grip. Made 1984-88. Reintroduced in 1989 as Model 15YN.
Model 15Y . . . . NiB $120 Ex $90 Gd $55
Model 15YN . . . . NiB $125 Ex $95 Gd $60

MODEL 18 BABY SLIDE-ACTION
REPEATER . . . . NiB $290 Ex $275 Gd $150
Exposed hammer. Solid frame. Caliber: .22 LR, Long Short. Tubular magazine holds 14 Short cartridges. 20-inch bbl., round or octagon. Weight: 3.75 lbs. Sights: Open rear; bead front. Plain straight-grip stock and slide handle. Made 1906-09.

Marlin Model 15Y "Little Buckaroo"

Marlin Model 15YN

Marlin Model 20

Marlin Model 25M Bolt-Action Rifle

Marlin Model 25MB
Midget Magnum

MODEL 20 SLIDE-ACTION
REPEATING RIFLE . . . . **NiB $295 Ex $280 Gd $150**
Exposed hammer. Takedown. Caliber: .22 LR. Long, Short. Tubular magazine: Half-length holds 15 Short, 12 Long, 10 LR; full-length holds 25 Short, 20 Long, 18 LR. 24-inch octagon bbl. Weight: 5 lbs. Sights: Open rear; bead front. Plain straight-grip stock, grooved slide handle. Made 1907-22. Note: After 1920 was designated "Model 20-S."

MODEL 25 BOLT-ACTION RIFLE . . . . **NiB $150 Ex $125 Gd $75**
Caliber: .22 Short, Long or LR 7-shot clip. 22-inch bbl. Weight: 5.5 lbs. Ramp front sight, adj. open rear. One-piece walnut Monte Carlo stock w/full pistol-grip Mar-Shield finish. Made 1984-88.

MODEL 25
SLIDE-ACTION REPEATER . . . . **NiB $415 Ex $275 Gd $150**
Exposed hammer. Takedown. Caliber: .22 Short (also handles 22 CB caps). Tubular magazine holds 15 Short. 23-inch bbl. Weight: 4 lbs. Sights: Open rear; beaded front. Plain straight-grip stock and slide handle. Made 1909-10.

MODEL 25M BOLT ACTION W/SCOPE . . . . **NiB $144 Ex $115 Gd $78**
Caliber: .22 WMR. 7-shot clip. 22-inch bbl. Weight: 6 lbs. Ramp front sight w/brass bead, adj. open rear. Walnut-finished stock w/Monte Carlo styling and full pistol-grip. Sling swivels. Made 1986-88.

MODEL 25MB MIDGET MAGNUM . . . . **NiB $150 Ex $115 Gd $75**
Bolt action. Caliber: .22 WMR. Seven shot capacity. 16.25-inch bbl. Weight: 4.75 lbs. Walnut-finished Monte Carlo-style stock w/full pistol grip and abbreviated forend. Sights: Ramp front w/brass bead, adj. open rear. Thumb safety. Made 1986-88.

MODEL 25MG/25MN/25N/25NC BOLT-ACTION RIFLE
Caliber: .22 WMR (Model 25MN) or .22 LR. (Model 25N). Seven shot clip magazine. 22-inch bbl. 41 inches overall. Weight: 5.5 to 6 lbs. Adj. open rear sight, ramp front; receiver grooved for scope mounts. One piece walnut-finished hardwood Monte Carlo stock w/pistol grip. Made 1989 to date.
Marlin Model 25MG (Garden Gun) . . . . **NiB $163 Ex $130 Gd $88**
Marlin Model 25MN . . . . **NiB $144 Ex $115 Gd $78**
Marlin Model 25N . . . . **NiB $131 Ex $105 Gd $71**
Marlin Model 25NC (camouflage stock) . . . . **NiB $163 Ex $130 Gd $88**

Marlin Model 39
Carbine

Marlin Model 39
Century Ltd.

Marlin Model 39 Carbine
90th Anniversary

Marlin Model 39 Rifle
Original First Issue

Marlin Model 39A
90th Anniversary Rifle

MODEL 27 SLIDE-ACTION
REPEATING RIFLE . . . . **NiB $390 Ex $225 Gd $150**
Exposed hammer. Takedown. Calibers: .25-20, .32-20. Magazine (tubular) holds 7 shots. 24-inch octagon bbl. Weight: 5.75 lbs. Sights: Open rear; bead front. Plain, straight-grip stock, grooved slide handle. Made 1910-16.

MODEL 27S . . . . **NiB $300 Ex $208 Gd $125**
Same as Model 27 except w/round bbl., also chambered for .25 Stevens rimfire Made 1920-32.

MODEL 29 SLIDE-ACTION REPEATER . . . . **NiB $300 Ex $225 Gd $125**
Similar to Model 20 w/23-inch round bbl., half magazine only, weight 5.75 lbs. Made 1913-16.

MODEL 30/30A AND 30AS LEVER-ACTION
Caliber: .30/30 Win. 6-shot tubular magazine. 20-inch bbl. w/Micro-Groove rifling. 38.25 inches overall. Weight: 7 lbs. Brass bead front sight, adj. rear. Solid top receiver, offset hammer spur for scope use. Walnut-finished hardwood stock w/pistol-grip. Mar-Shield finish. Made 1964-2000.
Model 30/30A . . . . **NiB $220 Ex $150 Gd $100**
Model 30AS . . . . **NiB $220 Ex $150 Gd $100**
Model 30AS w/4x scope, add $10

MODEL 32 SLIDE-ACTION REPEATER . . . . **NiB $550 Ex $400 Gd $225**
Hammerless. Takedown. Caliber: .22 LR. Long, Short. Tubular magazine holds 15 Short, 12 Long, 10 LR; full magazine, 25 Short, 20 Long, 18 LR. 24-inch octagon bbl. Weight: 5.5 lbs. Sights: Open rear; bead front. Plain pistol-grip stock, grooved slide handle. Made 1914-15.

MODEL 36 LEVER-ACTION REPEATING CARBINE
Calibers: .30-30, .32 Special. 7-shot tubular magazine. 20-inch bbl. Weight: 6.5 lbs. Sights: Open rear; bead front. Pistol-grip stock, semibeavertail forearm w/carbine bbl. band. Early production w/receiver, lever and hammer color casehardened and the remaining metal blued. Late production w/blued receiver. Made 1936-48. Note: In 1936, this was designated "Model 1936" and was so marked on the upper tang. In 1937, the model designation was shortened to "36". An "RC" serial number suffix identifies a "Regular/Carbine".
Model 1936 (CC receiver,
w/long tang, w/o SN prefix) . . . . **NiB $750 Ex $625 Gd $400**
Model 1936 (CC receiver,
w/short tang, w/o SN prefix) . . . . **NiB $531 Ex $425 Gd $289**
Model 1936 (CC receiver, w/SN prefix) . . . **NiB $438 Ex $350 Gd $238**
Model 36 (CC receiver, w/SN prefix) . . . . . **NiB $406 Ex $325 Gd $221**
Model 36 (blued receiver, w/SN prefix) . . . **NiB $369 Ex $295 Gd $201**

Marlin Model 39 — ADL

Marlin Model 39AS

MODEL 36 SPORTING CARBINE
Same as M36 carbine except w/6-shot, (2/3 magazine) and weighs 6.25 lbs.
Model 1936 (CC receiver,
w/long tang, w/o SN prefix) . . . . NiB $750 Ex $600 Gd $400
Model 1936 (CC receiver,
w/short tang, w/o SN prefix) . . . . NiB $550 Ex $475 Gd $300
Model 1936 (CC receiver, w/SN prefix) . . . NiB $494 Ex $395 Gd $269
Model 36 (CC receiver, w/SN prefix) . . . . . NiB $450 Ex $360 Gd $245
Model 36 (blued receiver, w/SN prefix) . . . NiB $406 Ex $325 Gd $221

MODEL 36A/36A-DL LEVER-ACTION REPEATING RIFLE
Same as Model 36 Carbine except has 24-inch bbl. w/hooded front
sight and 2/3 magazine holding 6 cartridges. Weight: 6.75 lbs. Note:
An "A" serial number suffix identifies a Rifle while an "A-DL" suffix
designates a Deluxe Model w/checkered stock, semibeavertail fore-
arm, swivels and sling. Made 1936-48.
Model 1936 (CC receiver,
w/long tang, w/o SN prefix) . . . . NiB $1150 Ex $1000 Gd $300
Model 1936 (CC receiver,
w/short tang, w/o SN prefix) . . . . NiB $550 Ex $475 Gd $300
Model 1936 (CC receiver, w/SN prefix) . . . NiB $531 Ex $425 Gd $289
Model 36 (CC receiver, w/SN prefix) . . . . . NiB $469 Ex $375 Gd $255
Model 36 (blued receiver, w/SN prefix) . . . NiB $438 Ex $350 Gd $238
For ADL model, add 25%

MODEL 37 SLIDE-ACTION
REPEATING RIFLE . . . . NiB $400 Ex $350 Gd $150
Similar to Model 29 except w/24-inch bbl. and full magazine.
Weight: 5.25 lbs. Made 1913-16.

MODEL 38 SLIDE-ACTION
REPEATING RIFLE . . . . NiB $350 Ex $250 Gd $150
Hammerless. Takedown. Caliber: .22 LR, Long, Short. 2/3 magazine (tubular) holds 15 Short, 12 Long, 10 LR. 24-inch octagon or round bbls. Weight:
5.5 lbs. Sights: Open rear; bead front. Plain shotgun-type pistol-grip buttstock w/hard rubber buttplate, grooved slide handle. Ivory bead front sight;
adj. rear. About 20,000 Model 38 rifles were made between 1920-30.

MODEL 39 CARBINE . . . . NiB $250 Ex $175 Gd $125
Same as 39M except w/lightweight bbl., 3/4 magazine (capacity: 18 Short,
14 Long, 12 LR), slimmer forearm. Weight: 5.25 lbs. Made 1963-67.

MODEL 39 90TH
ANNIVERSARY CARBINE . . . . NiB $1000 Ex $925 Gd $690
Carbine version of 90th Anniversary Model 39A. 500 made in 1960.
Top value is for carbine in new, unfired condition.

MODEL 39 CENTURY LTD. . . . . NiB $450 Ex $300 Gd $190
Commemorative version of Model 39A. Receiver inlaid w/brass
medallion, "Marlin Centennial 1870-1970." Square lever. 20-inch
octagon bbl. Fancy walnut straight-grip stock and forearm; brass
forend cap, buttplate, nameplate in buttstock. 35,388 made in
1970.

MODEL 39 LEVER-ACTION
REPEATER . . . . NiB $2000 Ex $1850 Gd $990
Takedown. Casehardened receiver. Caliber: .22 LR, Long, Short.
Tubular magazine holds 25 Short, 20 Long, 18 LR. 24-inch octagon
bbl. Weight: 5.75 lbs. Sights: Open rear; bead front. Plain pistol-grip
stock and forearm. Made 1922-38.

MODEL 39A
General specifications same as Model 39 except w/blued receiver,
round bbl., heavier stock w/semibeavertail forearm, weight 6.5 lbs.
Made 1938-60.
Early model (no prefix) . . . . NiB $1156 Ex $925 Gd $629
Late model ("B" prefix) . . . . NiB $938 Ex $750 Gd $510

MODEL 39A 90TH
ANNIVERSARY RIFLE . . . . NiB $1000 Ex $950 Gd $690
Commemorates Marlin's 90th anniversary. Same general specifications as Golden 39A except w/chrome-plated bbl. and action, stock
and forearm of select walnut-finely checkered, carved figure of a
squirrel on right side of buttstock. 500 made in 1960. Top value is
for rifle in new, unfired condition.

MODEL 39A
ARTICLE II RIFLE . . . . NiB $475 Ex $350 Gd $250
Commemorates National Rifle Association Centennial 1871-1971.
"The Right to Bear Arms" medallion inlaid in receiver. Similar to
Model 39A. Magazine capacity: 26 Short, 21 Long, 19 LR. 24-inch
octagon bbl. Fancy walnut pistol-grip stock and forearm; brass
forend cap, buttplate. 6,244. Made in 1971.

GRADING: **NiB** = New in Box **Ex** = Excellent or NRA 95% **Gd** = Good or NRA 68% **273**

Marlin Model 56

Marlin Model 57

Marlin Model 60C

Marlin Model 60SS

Marlin Model 62

GOLDEN 39A/39AS RIFLE
Same as Model 39A except w/gold-plated trigger, hooded ramp front sight, sling swivels. Made 1960-87 (39A); Model 39AS 1988 to date.
Golden 39A . . . . NiB $350 Ex $250 Gd $125
Golden 39AS (W/hammer block safety) . . . NiB $230 Ex $150 Gd $110

MODEL 39A "MOUNTIE" LEVER-
ACTION REPEATING RIFLE . . . . NiB $350 Ex $300 Gd $175
Same as Model 39A except w/lighter, straight-grip stock, slimmer forearm. Weight: 6.25 lbs. Made 1953-60.

MODEL 39A OCTAGON . . . . NiB $650 Ex $500 Gd $300
Same as Golden 39A except w/oct. bbl., plain bead front sight, slimmer stock and forearm, no pistol-grip cap or swivels. Made 1973. (2551 produced)

MODEL 39D . . . . NiB $225 Ex $180 Gd $125
Same as Model 39M except w/pistol-grip stock, forearm w/bbl. band. Made 1970-74.

39M ARTICLE II CARBINE . . . . NiB $450 Ex $395 Gd $225
Same as 39A Article II Rifle except w/straight-grip buttstock, square lever, 20-inch octagon bbl., reduced magazine capacity. 3,824m, made in 1971.

GOLDEN 39M
Calibers: .22 Short, Long and LR. Tubular magazine holds 21 Short, 16 Long or 15 LR cartridges. 20-inch bbl. 36 inches overall. Weight: 6 lbs. Gold-plated trigger. Hooded ramp front sight, adj. folding semi-buckhorn rear. Two-piece, straight-grip American black walnut stock. Sling swivels. Mar-Shield finish. Made 1960-87.
Model Golden 39M . . . . NiB $357 Ex $250 Gd $200
Model 39M Octagon
(octagonal bbl.,
made 1973 only) . . . . NiB $425 Ex $395 Gd $300

MODEL 39M "MOUNTIE" CARBINE
Same as Model 39A "Mountie" Rifle except w/20-inch bbl. Weight: 6 lbs. 500 made in 1960. (For values See Marlin 39 90th Anniversary Carbine)

MODEL 39TDS
CARBINE . . . . NiB $300 Ex $200 Gd $125
Same general specifications as Model 39M except takedown style w/16.5-inch bbl. and reduced magazine capacity. 32.63 inches overall. Weight: 5.25 lbs. Made 1988-95.

Marlin Model 70HC w/7-Shot Clip

Marlin Model 70P

MODEL 45 . . . . **NiB $280 Ex $225 Gd $125**
Semiautomatic action. Caliber: .45 Auto. Seven shot clip.16.5-inch bbl. 35.5 inches overall. Weight: 6.75 lbs. Manual bolt hold-open. Sights: Ramp front sight w/brass bead, adj. folding rear. Receiver drilled and tapped for scope mount. Walnut-finished hardwood stock. Made 1986 to date.

MODEL 49/49DL AUTOLOADING RIFLE
Same as Model 99C except w/two-piece stock, checkered after 1970. Made 1968-71. Model 49DL w/scrollwork on sides of receiver, checkered stock and forearm; made 1971-78.
Model 49 . . . . **NiB $150 Ex $120 Gd $82**
Model 49DL . . . . **NiB $156 Ex $125 Gd $85**

MODEL 50/50E AUTOLOADING RIFLE
Takedown. Cal: .22 LR. Six shot detachable box mag. 22 inch bbl. Wt: 6 lbs. Sights: Open rear; bead front; Mdl. 50E w/peep rear sight, hooded front. Plain pistol-grip stock, forearm w/finger grooves. Made 1931-34.
Model 50 . . . . **NiB $165 Ex $125 Gd $75**
Model 50E . . . . **NiB $175 Ex $125 Gd $80**

MODEL 56 LEVERMATIC RIFLE . . . **NiB $250 Ex $190 Gd $100**
Same as Model 57 except clip-loading. Magazine holds eight rounds. Weight: 5.75 lbs. Made 1955-64.

MODEL 57 LEVERMATIC RIFLE . . . **NiB $250 Ex $190 Gd $100**
Lever-action. Cal: .22 LR. 22 Long, 22 Short. Tubular mag. holds 19 LR, 21 Long, 27 Short. 22 inch bbl. Wt: 6.25 lbs. Sights: Open rear, adj. for windage and elevation; hooded ramp front. Monte Carlo-style stock w/pistol-grip. Made 1959-65.

MODEL 57M LEVERMATIC . . . . **NiB $250 Ex $190 Gd $110**
Same as Model 57 except chambered for 22 WMR cartridge, w/24-inch bbl., 15-shot magazine. Made 1960-69.

MODEL 60 SEMIAUTOMATIC RIFLE . . . . **NiB $100 Ex $75 Gd $50**
Caliber: .22 LR. 14-shot tubular magazine. 22-inch bbl. 40.5 inches overall. Weight: 5.5 lbs. Grooved receiver. Ramp front sight w/removable hood; adj. open rear. Anodized receiver w/blued bbl. Monte Carlo-style walnut-finished hardwood stock w/Mar-Shield finish. Made 1981 to date. Note: Marketed 1960-1980 under Glenfield promotion logo and w/slightly different stock configuration.

MODEL 60C SELF-LOADING RIFLE . . . . **NiB $105 Ex $95 Gd $70**
Cal: .22 LR. 14- shot tubular mag. 22 inch Micro-Groove bbl., 40.5 inch overall. Wt: 5.5 lbs. Screw-adjustable open rear and ramp front sights. Aluminum receiver, grooved for scope mount. Hardwood Monte Carlo stock w/Mossy Oak "Break-Up" camouflage pattern. Made 1998 to date.

MODEL 60SS SEMIAUTOMATIC RIFLE
Same general specifications as Model 60 except w/stainless bbl. and magazine tube. Synthetic, uncheckered birch or laminated black/gray birch stock w/nickel-plated swivel studs. Made 1993 to date.
Model 60SB w/uncheckered
birch stock . . . . **NiB $200 Ex $150 Gd $90**
Model 60SS w/laminated
birch stock . . . . **NiB $210 Ex $150 Gd $90**
Model 60SSK w/fiberglass stock . . . . **NiB $200 Ex $150 Gd $90**

MODEL 62
LEVERMATIC RIFLE . . . . **NiB $475 Ex $350 Gd $225**
Lever-action. Calibers: .256 Magnum, .30 Carbine. Four shot clip magazine. 23-inch bbl. Weight: 7 lbs. Sights: Open rear; hooded ramp front. Monte Carlo-style stock w/pistol-grip, swivels and sling. Made in .256 Magnum 1963-66; in .30 Carbine 1966-69.

MODEL 65 BOLT-ACTION
SINGLE-SHOT RIFLE . . . . **NiB $90 Ex $60 Gd $40**
Takedown. Caliber: .22 LR. Long, Short. 24-inch bbl. Weight: 5 lbs. Sights: Open rear; bead front. Plain pistol-grip stock w/grooved forearm. Made 1932-38. Model 65E is same as Model 65 except w/rear peep sight and hooded front sight.

MODEL 70HC SEMIAUTOMATIC
Caliber: .22 LR. Seven and 15-shot magazine. 18-inch bbl. Weight: 5.5 lbs. 36.75 inches overall. Ramp front sight; adj. open rear. Grooved receiver for scope mounts. Walnut-finished hardwood stock w/Monte Carlo and pistol-grip. Made 1988-96.
Marlin model . . . . **NiB $145 Ex $120 Gd $75**
Glenfield model . . . . **NiB $100 Ex $80 Gd $50**

MODEL 70P
SEMIAUTOMATIC . . . . **NiB $150 Ex $125 Gd $70**
"Papoose" takedown. Caliber: .22 LR. Seven shot clip. 16.25-inch bbl. 35.25 inches overall. Weight: 3.75 lbs. Sights: Ramp front, adj. open rear. Side ejection, manual bolt hold-open. Cross-bolt safety. Walnut-finished hard-wood stock w/abbreviated forend, pistol-grip. Made 1984-94.

MODEL 70PSS
SELF-LOADING CARBINE . . . . **NiB $160 Ex $125 Gd $75**
"Papoose" takedown carbine. Caliber: .22 LR. Seven shot clip. 16.25- inch bbl., 35.25 inches overall. Weight: 3.25 lbs. Ramp front and adjustable open rear sights. Automatic last-shot hold open (1996). Black fiberglass synthetic stock. Made 1995 to date.

Marlin Model 75C

Marlin Model 80C

Marlin Model 80DL

Marlin Model 81DL

MODEL 75C
SEMIAUTOMATIC . . . . **NiB $150 Ex $100 Gd $75**
Caliber: .22 LR. 13-shot tubular magazine.18-inch bbl. 36.5 inches overall. Weight: 5 lbs. Side ejection. Cross-bolt safety. Sights: Ramp-mounted blade front; adj. open rear. Monte Carlo-style walnut-finished hardwood stock w/pistol-grip. Made 1975-92.

MODEL 80 BOLT-ACTION REPEATING RIFLE
Takedown. Caliber: .22 LR. Long, Short. Eight shot detachable box magazine. 24-inch bbl. Weight: 6 lbs. Sights: Open rear; bead front. Plain pistol-grip stock. Made 1934-39. Model 80E, w/peep rear sight; hooded front, made 1934-40.
Model 80 Standard . . . . **NiB $120 Ex $90 Gd $60**
Model 80E . . . . **NiB $110 Ex $75 Gd $55**

MODEL 80C/80DL BOLT-ACTION REPEATER
Improved version of Model 80. Model 80C w/bead from sight, semi-beavertail forearm; made 1940-70. Model 80DL w/peep rear sight; hooded blade front sight on ramp, swivels; made 1940-65.
Model 80C . . . . **NiB $120 Ex $90 Gd $60**
Model 80DL . . . . **NiB $110 Ex $75 Gd $60**

MODEL 81/81E BOLT-ACTION REPEATER
Takedown. .22 LR. Long, Short. Tubular magazine holds 24 Short, 20 Long, 18 LR. 24-inch bbl. Weight: 6.25 lbs. Sights: Open rear, bead front. Plain pistol-grip stock. Made 1937-40. Model 81E w/peep rear sight; hooded front w/ramp.
Model 81 . . . . **NiB $130 Ex $125 Gd $60**
Model 81E . . . . **NiB $150 Ex $100 Gd $90**

MODEL 81C/81DL BOLT-ACTION REPEATER
Improved version of Model 81 w/same general specifications. Model 81C w/bead front sight, semibeavertail forearm; made 1940-70. Model 81 DL w/peep rear sight, hooded front, swivels; disc. 1965.
Model 81C . . . . **NiB $150 Ex $125 Gd $60**
Model 81DL . . . . **NiB $165 Ex $130 Gd $75**

MODEL 88-C/88-DL AUTOLOADING
Takedown. Caliber: .22 LR. Tubular magazine in buttstock holds 14 cartridges. 24-inch bbl. Weight: 6.75 lbs. Sights: Open rear; hooded front. Plain pistol-grip stock. Made 1947-56. Model 88-DL w/received peep sight, checkered stock and sling swivels, made 1953-56.
Model 88-C . . . . **NiB $175 Ex $150 Gd $90**
Model 88-DL . . . . **NiB $180 Ex $160 Gd $95**

Marlin Model 93 Musket

Marlin Model 93 Lever Action

Marlin Model 94 Sporting Carbine

MODEL 89-C/89-DL AUTOLOADING RIFLE
Clip magazine version of Model 88-C. Seven shot clip (12-shot in later models); other specifications same. Made 1950-61. Model 89-DL w/receiver peep sight, sling swivels.

Model 89-C	**NiB $165 Ex $130 Gd $90**
Model 89-DL	**NiB $170 Ex $150 Gd $95**

MODEL 92 LEVER-ACTION REPEATING RIFLE
Calibers: .22 Short, Long, LR. .32 Short, Long (rimfire or centerfire by changing firing pin). Tubular magazines holding 25 Short, 20 Long, 18 LR (.22); or 17 Short, 14 Long (.32); 16-inch bbl. model w/shorter magazine holding 15 Short, 12 Long, 10 LR. Bbl. lengths: 16 (.22 cal. only) 24, 26, 28 inches. Weight: 5.5 lbs. w/24-inch bbl. Sights: open rear; blade front. Plain straight-grip stock and forearm. Made 1892-1916. Note: Originally designated "Model 1892."

Model 92 (.22 caliber)	**NiB $1800 Ex $1250 Gd $650**
Model 92 (.32 caliber)	**NiB $1390 Ex $1100 Gd $780**

MODEL 93/93SC CARBINE
Same as Standard Model 93 Rifle except in calibers .30-30 and .32 Special only. Model 93 w/7-shot magazine. 20-inch round bbl., carbine sights, weight: 6.75 lbs. Model 93SC magazine capacity 5 shots, weight 6.5 lbs.

Model 93 Carbine (w/saddle ring)	**NiB $1500 Ex $1250 Gd $975**
Model 93 Carbine ("Bullseye" w/o saddle ring)	**NiB $1000 Ex $890 Gd $550**
Model 93SC Sporting Carbine	**NiB $1600 Ex $1300 Gd $900**

MODEL 93 LEVER-ACTION
REPEATING RIFLE . . . . **NiB $2200 Ex $1800 Gd $1195**
Solid frame or takedown. Calibers: .25-36 Marlin, .30-30, .32 Special, .32-40, .38-55. Tubular magazine holds 10 cartridges. 26-inch round or octagon bbl. standard; also made w/28-, 30- and 32-inch bbls. Weight: 7.25 lbs. Sights: Open rear; bead front. Plain straight-grip stock and forearm. Made 1893-1936. Note: Before 1915 designated "Model 1893."

MODEL 93 MUSKET . . . . **NiB $3900 Ex $2890 Gd $1590**
Same as Standard Model 93 except w/30-inch bbl., angular bayonet, ramrod under bbl., musket stock, full-length military-style forearm. Weight: 8 lbs. Made 1893-1915.

MODEL 94 LEVER-ACTION
REPEATING RIFLE . . . . **NiB $2500 Ex $2000 Gd $1875**
Solid frame or takedown. Calibers: .25-20, .32-20, .38-40, .44-40. 10-shot tubular magazine. 24-inch round or octagon bbl. Weight: 7 lbs. Sights open rear; bead front. Plain straight-grip stock and forearm (also available w/pistol-grip stock). Made 1894-1934. Note: Before 1906 designated "Model 1894."

MODEL 94 LEVER-ACTION COWBOY SERIES
Calibers: .357 Mag., .44-40, .44 Mag., .45 LC. 10-shot magazine. 24-inch tapered octagon bbl. Weight: 7.5 lbs. 41.5 inches overall. Marble carbine front sight, adjustable semi-buckhorn rear. Blue finish. Checkered, straight-grip American black walnut stock w/hard rubber buttplate. Made 1996 to date. Cowboy II introduced in 1997.

Cowboy model (.45 LC)	**NiB $500 Ex $375 Gd $250**
Cowboy II model (.357 Mag., .44-40, .44 Mag)	**NiB $500 Ex $375 Gd $250**

MODEL 97 LEVER-ACTION
REPEATING RIFLE . . . . **NiB $2450 Ex $1980 Gd $1900**
Takedown. Caliber: .22 LR. Long, Short. Tubular magazine; full length holds 25 Short, 20 Long, 18 LR; half length holds 16 Short, 12 Long and 10 LR. Bbl. lengths: 16, 24, 26, 28 inches. Weight: 6 lbs. Sights: Open rear; bead front. Plain, straight-grip stock and forearm (also avail. w/pistol-grip stock). Made 1897-1922. Note: Before 1905 designated "Model 1897."

MODEL 98 AUTOLOADING RIFLE . . . . **NiB $150 Ex $95 Gd $75**
Solid frame. Caliber: .22 LR. Tubular magazine holds 15 cartridges. 22-inch bbl. Weight: 6.75 lbs. Sights: Open rear; hooded ramp front. Monte Carlo stock w/cheekpiece. Made 1950-61.

MODEL 99 AUTOLOADING RIFLE . . . . **NiB $150 Ex $95 Gd $75**
Caliber: .22 LR. Tubular magazine holds 18 cartridges. 22-inch bbl. Weight: 5.5 lbs. Sights: Open rear; hooded ramp front. Plain pistol-grip stock. Made 1959-61.

MODEL 99C . . . . **NiB $160 Ex $125 Gd $80**
Same as Model 99 except w/gold-plated trigger, receiver grooved for tip-off scope mounts, Monte Carlo stock (checkered in later production). Made 1962-78.

MODEL 99DL . . . . **NiB $200 Ex $175 Gd $95**
Same as Model 99 except w/gold-plated trigger, jeweled breech bolt, Monte Carlo stock w/pistol-grip, swivels and sling. Made 1960-65.

Marlin Model 336 Cowboy

Marlin Model 336M

Marlin Model 336 Marauder

Marlin Model 336 Sporting Carbine

Marlin Model 336 Zane Grey Century

Marlin Model 336A

Marlin Model 336A-DL

MODEL 99M1 CARBINE . . . . **NiB $210 Ex $150 Gd $100**
Same as Model 99C except styled after U.S. .30 M1 Carbine; 9-shot tubular magazine, 18-inch bbl. Sights: Open rear; military-style ramp front; carbine stock w/handguard and bbl. band, sling swivels. Weight: 4.5 lbs. Made 1966-79.

**MODEL 100 BOLT-ACTION
SINGLE-SHOT RIFLE** . . . . **NiB $125 Ex $90 Gd $50**
Takedown. Caliber: .22 LR, Long, Short. 24-inch bbl. Weight: 4.5 lbs. Sights: Open rear; bead front. Plain pistol-grip stock. Made 1936-60.

MODEL 100SB . . . . **NiB $120 Ex $95 Gd $60**
Same as Model 100 except smoothbore for use w/22 shot cartridges, shotgun sight. Made 1936-41.

Marlin Model 336DT Deluxe Texan

Marlin Model 336T Texan

MODEL 100 TOM MIX SPECIAL . . . . NiB $380 Ex $295 Gd $200
Same as Model 100 except w/peep rear sight; hooded front; sling.
Made 1936-46.

MODEL 101 . . . . NiB $95 Ex $75 Gd $40
Improved version of Model 100 w/same general specifications,
except w/stock w/beavertail forearm, weighs 5 lbs. Intro. 1951. Disc.

MODEL 101 DL . . . . NiB $100 Ex $70 Gd $40
Same as Model 101 except has peep rear sight; hooded front,
swivels. Disc.

MODEL 122 SINGLE-SHOT
JUNIOR TARGET RIFLE . . . . NiB $75 Ex $50 Gd $35
Bolt action. Caliber: .22 LR, .22 Long, .22 Short. 22-inch bbl.
Weight: 5 lbs. Sights: Open rear; hooded ramp front. Monte Carlo
stock w/pistol-grip, swivels, sling. Made 1961-65.

MODEL 322 BOLT-ACTION
VARMINT RIFLE . . . . NiB $550 Ex $500 Gd $295
Sako short Mauser action. Caliber: .222 Rem. Three shot clip magazine. 24-inch medium weight bbl. Checkered stock. Sights: Two-
position peep rear; hooded ramp front. Weight: 7.5 lbs. Made 1954-
57.

MODEL 336A
LEVER-ACTION RIFLE . . . . NiB $300 Ex $175 Gd $158
Improved version of Model 36A Rifle w/same general specifications
except w/improved action w/round breech bolt. Calibers: .30-30,
.32 Special (disc. 1963), .35 Rem. (intro. 1952). Made 1948-63;
reintroduced 1973, disc. 1980.

MODEL 336A-DL . . . . NiB $525 Ex $450 Gd $275
Same as Model 336A Rifle except w/deluxe checkered stock and
forearm, swivels and sling. Made 1948-63.

MODEL 336AS
LEVER-ACTION RIFLE . . . . NiB $225 Ex $160 Gd $110
Similar to Model 30AS. Caliber: .30-30 Win., Six shot tubular maga-
zine. 20- inch Micro-Groove bbl. 38.25 inches overall. Weight: 7 lbs.
Maine birch pistol grip stock w/swivel studs and hard rubber butt plate.
Tapped for scope mount and receiver sight. Screw-adjustable open
rear and ramp front sight. Checkered walnut finish. Made 1999 to date.

MODEL 336C
LEVER-ACTION CARBINE . . . . NiB $275 Ex $220 Gd $150
Improved version of Model 36 Carbine w/same general specifications except w/improved action w/round breech bolt. Original calibers: .30-30 and .32 Win. Spec. Made 1948-83. Note: Caliber .35

Rem. intro. 1953. Caliber .32 Winchester Special disc. 1963.
MODEL 336 COWBOY
LEVER-ACTION RIFLE . . . . NiB $550 Ex $400 Gd $275
Calibers: .30-30 Win., or .38-55 Win., 6- shot tubular magazine. 24- inch
tapered octagon bbl. 42.5 inches overall. Weight: 7.5 lbs. American black
walnut checkering stock. Marble carbine front sight w/solid top receiver
drilled and tapped for scope mount. Mar-Shield finish. Made 1998 to date.

MODEL 336CS
W/SCOPE . . . . NiB $350 Ex $245 Gd $150
Lever-action w/hammer block safety. Caliber: .30/30 Win. or .35 Rem. Six
shot tubular magazine. 20-inch round bbl. w/Micro-Groove rifling. 38.5
inches overall. Weight: 7 lbs. Ramp front sight w/hood, adj. semi-buckhorn folding rear. Solid top receiver drilled and tapped for scope mount or
receiver sight; offset hammer spur for scope use. American black walnut
stock w/pistol-grip, fluted comb. Mar-Shield finish. Made 1984 to date.

MODEL 336DT
DELUXE TEXAN . . . . NiB $400 Ex $395 Gd $300
Same as Model 336T except w/select walnut stock and forearm, hand-
carved longhorn steer and map of Texas on buttstock. Made 1962-64.

MODEL 336M
LEVER-ACTION RIFLE . . . . NiB $500 Ex $400 Gd $275
Calibers: .30-30 Win., 6- shot tubular magazine. 20- inch stainless
steel Micro Groove bbl., 38.5 inches overall. Weight: 7 lbs.
American black walnut w/checkered pistol-grip stock. Adjustable
folding semi-buckhorn rear and ramp front sight w/brass bead and
removable Wide-Scan hood. Tapped for receiver sight and scope
mount. Mar-Shield finish. Made 1999 to date.

MODEL 336 MARAUDER . . . . NiB $450 Ex $400 Gd $220
Same as Model 336 Texan Carbine except w/16.25-inch bbl.,
weight: 6.25 lbs. Made 1963-64.

MODEL 336-MICRO GROOVE ZIPPER . . . NiB $525 Ex $450 Gd $295
General specifications same as Model 336 Sporting Carbine except
caliber .219 Zipper. Made 1955-61.

MODEL 336 OCTAGON . . . . NiB $500 Ex $435 Gd $180
Same as Model 336T except chambered for .30-30 only w/22-inch
octagon bbl. Made 1973.

MODEL 336 SPORTING CARBINE . . . . . . NiB $400 Ex $300 Gd $150
Same as Model 336A rifle except w/20-inch bbl., weight: 6.25 lbs.
Made 1948-63.

MODEL 336T TEXAN CARBINE . . . . NiB $250 Ex $200 Gd $175
Same as Model 336 Carbine except w/straight-grip stock and is not available

Marlin Model 336TS Carbine

Marlin Model 444SS

Marlin Model 455 Sporter

MODEL 336TS. . . . . NiB $325 Ex $275 Gd $125
Lever-action w/hammer-block safety. Caliber: .30-30 Win. Six shot
tubular magazine. 18.5-inch Micro-Groove bbl. 37 inches overall.
Weight: 6.5 lbs. Ramp front sight, adj. semi-buckhorn folding rear.
Straight-grip American black walnut stock. Made 1983-87.

**MODEL 336 ZANE
GREY CENTURY . . . . NiB $450 Ex $350 Gd $225**
Similar to Model 336A except w/22-inch octagonal bbl., caliber
.30-30, Zane Grey Centennial 1872-1972 medallion inlaid in
receiver; select walnut stock w/classic pistol-grip and forearm; brass
buttplate, forend cap. Weight: 7 lbs. 10,000 produced (numbered
ZG1 through ZG10,000). Made 1972.

**MODEL 444 LEVER-ACTION
REPEATING RIFLE . . . . NiB $375 Ex $325 Gd $150**
Action similar to Model 336. Caliber: .444 Marlin. Four shot tubu-
lar magazine. 24-inch bbl. Weigh: 7.5 lbs. Sights: Open rear; hood-
ed ramp front. Monte Carlo stock w/straight grip, recoil pad.
Carbine-style forearm w/bbl. band. Swivels, sling. Made 1965-71.

MARLIN MODEL 444 SPORTER . . . . NiB $380 Ex $350 Gd $160
Same as Model 444 Rifle except w/22-inch bbl., pistol-grip stock
and forearm as on Model 336A, recoil pad, QD swivels and sling.
Made 1972-83.

**MODEL 444P (OUTFITTER)
LEVER-ACTION RIFLE . . . . NiB $475 Ex $350 Gd $175**
Caliber: .444 Marlin. Five shot tubular magazine. 18.5-inch ported
bbl., 37 inches overall. Weight: 6.75 lbs. Ramp front and adjustable
folding rear sights. Black walnut straight grip stock w/cut checkering
and Mar-Shield finish. Made 1998 to date.

MODEL 444SS. . . . . NiB $475 Ex $350 Gd $175
Same general specifications as Model 444 except w/hammer safety.
Made 1984 to date.

MODEL 455 BOLT-ACTION SPORTER
FN Mauser action w/Sako trigger. Calibers: .30-06 or .308. Five shot
box magazine. 24-inch medium weight stainless-steel bbl. Monte

Carlo *(cont'd.)* **MODEL 455 BOLT-ACTION SPORTER**
stock w/cheekpiece, checkered pistol grip and forearm. Lyman No. 48
receiver sight; hooded ramp front. Weight: 8.5 lbs. Made 1957-59.
**Model 455 (chambered for .30-06,
1079 produced) . . . . NiB $550 Ex $425 Gd $225**
Model 455 (chambered for .308, 59 produced). . . . NiB $550 Ex $425 Gd $225

MODEL 780 BOLT-ACTION REPEATER SERIES
Caliber: .22 LR. Long, Short. Seven shot clip magazine. 22-inch bbl.
Weight: 5.5 to 6 lbs. Sights: Open rear; hooded ramp front. Receiver
grooved for scope mounting. Monte Carlo stock w/checkered pistol-
grip and forearm. Made 1971-88.
Model 780 Standard . . . . NiB $110 Ex $80 Gd $55
Model 781 (w/17-shot tubular magazine) . . . NiB $110 Ex $80 Gd $55
Model 782 (.22 WMR, w/swivels, sling) . . . . . NiB $110 Ex $80 Gd $55
Model 783 (w/12-shot tubular magazine) . . . NiB $110 Ex $80 Gd $55

MODEL 795 SELF-LOADING RIFLE . . . . NiB $125 Ex $100 Gd $80
Caliber: .22 LR. 10- shot clip. 18- inch Micro-Groove bbl., 37 inches overall. Weight: 5 lbs. Screw-adjustable open rear and ramp front
sight. Monte Carlo synthetic stock with checkering swivel studs.
Made 1999 to date.

MODEL 880 BOLT-ACTION REPEATER SERIES
Caliber: .22 rimfire. 7-shot magazine. 22-inch bbl. 41 inches over-
all. Weight: 5.5 to 6 lbs. Hooded ramp front sight; adj. folding rear.
Grooved receiver for scope mounts. Checkered Monte Carlo-style
walnut stock w/QD studs and rubber recoil pad. Made 1989-97.
Model 880 (.22 LR) . . . . NiB $180 Ex $130 Gd $75
Model 880SS (Stainless .22 LR) . . . . NiB $200 Ex $160 Gd $109
Model 880SQ (Squirrel .22 LR) . . . . NiB $213 Ex $170 Gd $116
Model 881 (w/7-shot tubular magazine . . . . NiB $185 Ex $135 Gd $75
Model 882 (.22 WMR) . . . . NiB $175 Ex $140 Gd $95
Model 882L (w/laminated hardwood stock) . . . . . . NiB $185 Ex $135 Gd $75
Model 882SS (Stainless w/fire sights) . . . . . NiB $219 Ex $175 Gd $119
Model 882SSV (Stainless .22 LR) . . . . NiB $219 Ex $175 Gd $119
**Model 883 (.22 WMR w/12-
shot tubular magazine) . . . . NiB $180 Ex $130 Gd $75**
Model 883N (w/nickel-Teflon finish) . . . . . NiB $216 Ex $175 Gd $122
Model 883SS (stainless w/laminated stock) . . . . NiB $234 Ex $190 Gd $134

Marlin Model 780

Marlin Model 781

Marlin Model 783

Marlin Model 882L

Marlin Model 883N

MODEL 922 MAGNUM
SELF-LOADING RIFLE . . . . NiB $350 Ex $275 Gd $100
Similar to Model 9 except chambered for .22 WMR. Seven shot magazine. 20.5-inch bbl. 39.5 inches overall. Weight: 6.5 lbs. American black walnut stock w/Monte Carlo. Blued finish. Made 1993 to date.

MODEL 980 .22 MAGNUM . . . . NiB $160 Ex $110 Gd $75
Bolt action. Caliber: .22 WMR. Eight shot clip magazine. 24-inch bbl. Weight: 6 lbs. Sights: Open rear; hooded ramp front. Monte Carlo stock, swivels, sling. Made 1962-70.

MODEL 989 AUTOLOADING RIFLE . . . . NiB $140 Ex $95 Gd $70
Caliber: .22 LR. Seven shot clip magazine. 22-inch bbl. Weight: 5.5 lbs. Sights: Open rear; hooded ramp front. Monte Carlo walnut stock w/pistol grip. Made 1962-66.

MODEL 989M2
CARBINE . . . . NiB $140 Ex $90 Gd $67
Same as Model 99M1 except clip-loading, 7-shot magazine. Made 1966-79.

MODEL 990 SEMIAUTOMATIC
Caliber: .22 LR. 17-shot tubular magazine. 22-inch bbl. 40.75 inches overall. Weight: 5.5 lbs. Side ejection. Cross-bolt safety. Ramp front sight w/brass bead; adj. semi-buckhorn folding rear. Receiver grooved for scope mount. Monte Carlo-style American black walnut stock w/checkered pistol grip and forend. Made 1979-87.
Model 990 Semiautomatic . . . . NiB $140 Ex $110 Gd $70
Model 990L (w/14 rounds,
laminated hardwood stock, QD studs,
black recoil pad; 1992 to date) . . . . NiB $125 Ex $95 Gd $70

Marlin Model 980

Marlin Model 989

Marlin Model 989M2

Marlin Model 990

Marlin Model 990L

Marlin Model 995

MODEL 995 SEMIAUTOMATIC .... NiB $160 Ex $120 Gd $75
Caliber: .22 LR. Seven shot clip magazine.18-inch bbl. 36.75 inches overall. Weight: 5 lbs. Cross-bolt safety. Sights: Ramp front w/brass bead; adj. folding semi-buckhorn rear. Monte Carlo-style American black walnut stock w/checkered pistol grip and forend. Made 1979-94.

MODEL 1870-1970
CENTENNIAL MATCHED
PAIR, MODELS 336 AND 39 .... NiB $1875 Ex $1550 Gd $1000
Presentation-grade rifles in luggage-style case. Matching serial numbers. Fancy walnut straight-grip buttstock and forearm brass buttplate and forend cap. Engraved receiver w/inlaid medallion; square lever. 20-inch octagon bbl. Model 336: .30-30, 7-shot, 7 lbs.

Model 39: .22 Short, Long, LR, tubular magazine holds 21 Short, 16
(cont'd.) **MODEL 1870-1970 CENTENNIAL MATCHED PAIR, MODELS 336 AND 39**
Long, 15 LR. 1,000 sets produced. Made 1970. Top value is for rifles in new, unfired condition. See illustration on page 277.

MODEL 1892 LEVER-ACTION RIFLE
See Marlin Model 92.

MODEL 1893 LEVER-ACTION RIFLE
See Marlin Model 93.

MODEL 1894 LEVER-ACTION RIFLE
See Marlin Model 94 Lever-Action Rifle listed previously under

Marlin 1870-1970 Matched Pair

Marlin Model 1894 Carbine

Marlin Model 1894CL

MODEL 1894 CARBINE
Replica of original Model 94. Caliber: .44 Rem. 10-shot magazine. 20-inch round bbl. Weight: 6 lbs. Sight: Open rear; ramp front. Straight-grip stock. Made 1969-84.
Standard Model 1894 Carbine . . . . **NiB $375 Ex $250 Gd $175**
Model 1894 Octagon
(made 1973) . . . . **NiB $400 Ex $325 Gd $180**
Model 1894 Sporter (w/22-inch bbl.,
made 1973) . . . . **NiB $375 Ex $250 Gd $225**

MODEL 1894CL CLASSIC . . . . **NiB $450 Ex $325 Gd $175**
Calibers: .218 Bee, .25-20 Win., .32-20 Win. Six shot tubular magazine. 22-inch bbl. 38.75 inches overall. Weight: 6.25 lbs. Adj. semibuckhorn folding rear sight, brass bead front. Receiver tapped for scope mounts. Straight-grip American black walnut stock w/Mar-Shield finish. Made 1988-94.

MODEL 1894 COWBOY/COWBOY II
See Marlin Model 94 Cowboy/Cowboy II.

MODEL 1894CS LEVER-ACTION . . . . **NiB $400 Ex $350 Gd $150**
Caliber: .357 Magnum, .38 Special. Nine shot tubular magazine. 18.5-inch bbl. 36 inches overall. Weight: 6 lbs. Side ejection. Hammer block safety. Square finger lever. Bead front sight, adj. semi-buckhorn folding rear. Offset hammer spur for scope use. Two-piece straight grip American black walnut stock w/white buttplate spacer. Mar-Shield finish. Made 1984 to date.

MODEL 1894M LEVER-ACTION . . . . **NiB $300 Ex $250 Gd $150**
Caliber: .22 WMR.11-shot tubular magazine. 20-inch bbl. Weight: 6.25 lbs. Sights: Ramp front w/brass bead and Wide-Scan hood; adj. semi-buckhorn folding rear. Offset hammer spur for scope use. Straight-grip American black walnut stock w/white buttplate spacer. Squared finger lever. Made 1986-88.

MODEL 1894S LEVER-ACTION . . . . **NiB $350 Ex $275 Gd $175**
Calibers: .41 Mag., .44 Rem. Mag., .44 S&W Special, .45 Colt.10-shot tubular magazine. 20-inch bbl.37.5 inches overall. Weight: 6 lbs. Sights and stock same as Model 1894M. Made 1984 to date.

Marlin Model 1894CS

Marlin Model 1894M

Marlin Model 1894S

Marlin Model 1895
.45-70 (New Model)

MODEL 1895 .45-70 REPEATER . . . NiB $600 Ex $300 Gd $150
Model 336-type action. Caliber: .45-70 Government. Four shot magazine. 22-inch bbl. Weight: 7 lbs. Sights: Open rear; bead front. Straight-grip stock, forearm w/metal end cap, QD swivels, leather sling. Made 1972-79.

MODEL 1895
LEVER-ACTION REPEATER . . . . NiB $3000 Ex $2700 Gd $2000
Solid frame or takedown. Calibers: .33 WCF, .38-56, .40-65, .40-70, .40-82, .45-70. Nine shot tubular magazine. 24-inch round or octagongon bbl. standard (other lengths available). Weight: 8 lbs. Sights: Open rear; bead front. Plain stock and forearm (also available w/pistol-grip stock). Made 1895-1915.

MODEL 1895G (GUIDE GUN)
LEVER-ACTION RIFLE . . . . NiB $369 Ex $295 Gd $201
Caliber: .45-70 Govt., 4- shot magazine. 18.5-inch ported bbl., 37 inches overall. Weight: 6.75 lbs. Ramp front and adjustable folding rear sights. Black walnut straight grip stock w/cut checkering and Mar-Shield finish. Made 1998 to date.

MODEL 1895M
LEVER-ACTION RIFLE . . . . NiB $500 Ex $450 Gd $275
Caliber: .450 Marlin. Four shot tubular magazine., 18.5- inch ported bbl. w/Ballard-type rifling. 37 inches overall. Weight: 6.75 lbs. Genuine American black walnut straight-grip stock w/checkering. Ventilated recoil pad. Adjustable folding semi-buckhorn rear and ramp front sights. Mar-Shield finish. Made 1999 to date.

MODEL 1895SS
LEVER-ACTION . . . . NiB $325 Ex $250 Gd $175
Caliber: .45-70 Govt. Four shot tubular magazine. 22-inch bbl. w/Micro-Groove rifling. 40.5 inches overall. Weight: 7.5 lbs. Ramp front sight w/brass bead and Wide-Scan hood; adj. semi-buckhorn folding rear. Solid top receiver tapped for scope mount or receiver sight. Off-set hammer spur for scope use. Two-piece American black walnut stock w/fluted comb, pistol-grip, sling swivels. Made 1984 to date.

MODEL 1897 LEVER-ACTION RIFLE
See Marlin Model 97.

Marlin Model 1895G

Marlin Model 1895M

Marlin Model 1895SS

Marlin Model 1895 Rifle
(Old Model — 1895-1915)

Marlin Model 1897
Cowboy

MODEL 1897 COWBOY
LEVER-ACTION RIFLE . . . . **NiB $600 Ex $500 Gd $275**
Caliber: .22 LR., capacity: 19LR,- 21L,- or 26S,- tubular magazine. 24-inch tapered octagon bbl., 40 inches overall. Weight: 6.5 lbs. Marble front and adjustable rear sight, tapped for scope mount. Black walnut straight grip stock w/cut checkering and Mar-Shield finish. Made 1999 to date.

MODEL 1936 LEVER-ACTION CARBINE
See Marlin Model 36.

MODEL 2000 TARGET RIFLE
Bolt-action single-shot. Caliber: .22 LR. Optional 5-shot adapter kit available. 22-inch bbl. 41 inches overall. Weight: 8 lbs. Globe front sight, adj. peep or aperture rear. two-stage target trigger. Textured composite Kevlar or black/gray laminated stock. Made 1991 to date.
Model 2000 (disc. 1995). . . . . **NiB $475 Ex $405 Gd $250**
Model 2000A w/Adj. comb
(Made 1994 only) . . . . **NiB $525 Ex $425 Gd $250**
Model 2000L w/laminated
stock (intro. 1996) . . . . **NiB $554 Ex $450 Gd $317**

MODEL 7000 . . . . **NiB $206 Ex $165 Gd $112**
Caliber: .22 LR. 10-shot magazine. 18-inch bbl. Weight: 5.5 lbs. Synthetic stocks. No sights; receiver grooved for scope. Semi-auto. Side ejection. Manual bolt hold-open. Cross-bolt safety. Matte finish. Made 1997 to date.
Model 7000 . . . . **NiB $225 Ex $175 Gd $125**
Model 7000T . . . . **NiB $375 Ex $300 Gd $250**

MODEL A-1
AUTOLOADING RIFLE . . . . **NiB $175 Ex $100 Gd $75**
Takedown. Caliber: .22 LR. Six shot detachable box magazine. 24-inch bbl. Weight: 6 lbs. Open rear sight. Plain pistol-grip stock. Made 1935-46.

MODEL A-1C
AUTOLOADING RIFLE . . . . **NiB $150 Ex $90 Gd $60**
Improved version of Model A-1 w/same general specifications, stock w/semibeavertail forend. Made 1940-46.

MODEL A-1DL . . . . **NiB $150 Ex $90 Gd $60**
Same as Model A-1C except w/peep rear sight; hooded front, swivels.

Marlin Model 2000

Marlin Model 2000L

Marlin Model 7000

Marlin Model 7000T

MODEL A-1E . . . . NiB $150 Ex $90 Gd $60
Same as Model A-1 except w/peep rear sight; hooded front.

MODEL MR-7 BOLT-ACTION RIFLE
Calibers: .25-06 Rem., .270 Win., .280 Rem., .308 Win. or .30-06.
Four shot magazine. 22-inch bbl. w/ or w/o sights. 43.31 inches
overall. Weight: 7.5 lbs. Checkered American walnut or birch stock
w/recoil pad and sling-swivel studs. Jeweled bolt w/cocking indica-
tor and 3-position safety. Made from 1996-99.
Model MR-7 . . . . NiB $450 Ex $325 Gd $225
Model MR7B w/birch
stock (Intro. 1998) . . . . NiB $130 Ex $125 Gd $95
Open sights, add $35

MODEL 10 . . . . NiB $100 Ex $80 Gd $54
Same as Marlin Model 101 except w/walnut-finished hardwood
stock. Made 1966-79. Note: Later production w/hot-iron-
stamped wood pistol grip to simulate checkering/carving; plain
forend.

MODEL 20 . . . . NiB $100 Ex $80 Gd $54
Same as Marlin Model 80/780 except w/bead front sight, walnut-
finished hardwood stock. Made 1966-82. Note: Recent production
has stamped pistol-grip to simulate checkering; plain forend.

MODEL 30 . . . . NiB $150 Ex $90 Gd $60
Same as Marlin Model 336C except chambered for .30-30 only,
w/4-shot magazine, plainer stock and forearm of walnut-finished
hardwood. Made 1966-68.

MODEL 30A . . . . NiB $225 Ex $150 Gd $100
Same as Marlin Model 336C except chambered for .30-30 only,
w/checkered stock of walnut-finished hardwood. Made 1969-83.

MODEL 36G . . . . NiB $250 Ex $150 Gd $95
Same as Marlin Model 336C except chambered for .30-30 only,
w/5-shot magazine, plainer stock. Made 1960-65.

MODEL 60 . . . . NiB $75 Ex $50 Gd $35
Same as Marlin Model 99C except w/walnut-finished hardwood
stock. Made 1960-80.

MODEL 70 . . . . NiB $80 Ex $60 Gd $40
Same as Marlin Model 989M2 except w/walnut-finished hardwood
stock; no handguard. Made 1966-69.

MODEL 80G . . . . NiB $80 Ex $60 Gd $40
Same as Marlin Model 80C except w/plain stock, bead front sight.
Made 1960-65.

Marlin Model A-1 Autoloader

Marlin-Glenfield Model 10

Marlin-Glenfield Model 30A

Marlin-Glenfield Model 60

Marlin-Glenfield Model 70

Marlin-Glenfield Model 80G

MODEL 81G . . . . **NiB $75 Ex $50 Gd $40**
Same as Marlin Model 81C except w/plain stock, bead front sight.
Made 1960-65.

MODEL 99G . . . . **NiB $80 Ex $65 Gd $50**
Same as Marlin Model 99C except w/plain stock, bead front sight.
Made 1960-65.

MODEL 101G . . . . **NiB $75 Ex $50 Gd $40**
Same as Marlin Model 101 except w/plain stock. Made 1960-65.

MODEL 989G
AUTOLOADING RIFLE . . . . **NiB $75 Ex $50 Gd $40**
Same as Marlin Model 989 except w/plain stock, bead front sight.
Made 1962-64.

MAUSER SPORTING RIFLES — Oberndorf am Neckar, Germany, Mfg. by Mauser-Werke GmbH, *Imported by Brolin Arms, Pomona, CA, (Previously by Gun South, Inc.; Gibbs Rifle Co.; Precision Imports, Inc. and KDF, Inc.)*

Before the end of WWI the name of the Mauser firm was "Waffenfabrik Mauser A.-G." Shortly after WWI it was changed to "Mauser-Werke A.-G." This information may be used to determine the age of genuine original Mauser sporting rifles made before WWII because all bear either of these firm names as well as the Mauser banner trademark.

The first four rifles listed were manufactured before WWI. Those that follow were produced between World Wars I and II. The early Mauser models can generally be identified by the pistol grip, which is rounded instead of capped, and the M/98 military-type magazine floorplate and catch. The later models have hinged magazine floorplates with lever or button release.

Mauser Model ES340

Mauser Model ES350

NOTE: *The "B" series of Mauser 22 rifles (Model ES340B, MS350B, etc.) were improved versions of their corresponding models and were introduced about 1935.*

PRE-WORLD WAR I MODELS

BOLT-ACTION SPORTING CARBINE
Calibers: 6.5x54, 6.5x58, 7x57, 8x57, 957mm. 19.75-inch bbl. Weight: 7 lbs. Full-stocked to muzzle. Other specifications same as for standard rifle.
Sporting Carbine w/20-inch
bbl. (Type M) . . . . NiB $2244 Ex $1795 Gd $1221
Sporting Carbine w/20-
or 24-inch bbl. (Type S) . . . . NiB $2313 Ex $1850 Gd $1258

BOLT-ACTION SPORTING RIFLE
Calibers: 6.5x55, 6.5x58, 7x57, 8x57, 9x57, 9.3x62 10.75x68.5-shot box magazine, 23.5-inch bbl. Weight: 7 to 7.5 lbs. Pear-shaped bolt handle. Double-set or single trigger. Sights: Tangent curve rear; ramp front. Pistol-grip stock, forearm w/Schnabel tip and swivels.
Sporting Rifle (Type A, English export) . NiB $2494 Ex $1995 Gd $1357
Sporting Rifle (Type B) . . . . NiB $1619 Ex $1295 Gd $881

BOLT-ACTION SPORTING RIFLE,
MILITARY MODEL TYPE C . . . . NiB $688 Ex $550 Gd $374
So called because of stepped M/98-type bbl., military front sight and double-pull trigger. Calibers: 7x57, 8x57, 9x57mm. Other specifications same as for standard rifle.

BOLT-ACTION SPORTING RIFLE
SHORT MODEL TYPE K . . . . NiB $3563 Ex $2850 Gd $1938
Calibers: 6.5x54, 8x51mm. 19.75-inch bbl. Weight: 6.25 lbs. Other specifications same as for standard rifle.

PRE-WORLD WAR II MODELS

MODEL DSM34 BOLT-ACTION
SINGLE-SHOT SPORTING RIFLE . . . . NiB $469 Ex $375 Gd $255
Also called "Sport-model." Caliber: .22 LR. 26-inch bbl. Weight: 7.75 lbs. Sights: Tangent curve open rear; Barleycorn front. M/98 military-type stock, swivels. Intro. c. 1935.

MODEL EL320 BOLT-ACTION
SINGLE-SHOT SPORTING RIFLE . . . . NiB $450 Ex $360 Gd $245
Caliber: .22 LR. 23.5-inch bbl. Weight: 4.25 lbs. Sights: Adj. open rear; bead front. Sporting stock w/checkered pistol grip, swivels.

MODEL EN310 BOLT-ACTION
SINGLE-SHOT SPORTING RIFLE . . . . NiB $406 Ex $325 Gd $221
Caliber: .22 LR. ("22 Lang fur Buchsen.") 19.75-inch bbl. Weight: 4 lbs. Sights: Fixed open rear, blade front. Plain pistol-grip stock.

MODEL ES340 BOLT-ACTION
SINGLE-SHOT TARGET RIFLE . . . . NiB $469 Ex $375 Gd $255
Caliber: .22 LR. 25.5-inch bbl. Weight: 6.5 lbs. Sights: Tangent curve rear; ramp front. Sporting stock w/checkered pistol-grip and grooved forearm, swivels.

MODEL ES340B
BOLT-ACTION SINGLE-SHOT
TARGET RIFLE . . . . NiB $469 Ex $375 Gd $255
Caliber: .22 LR. 26.75-inch bbl. Weight: 8 lbs. Sights: Tangent curve open rear; ramp front. Plain pistol-grip stock, swivels.

MODEL ES350
BOLT-ACTION SINGLE-SHOT
TARGET RIFLE . . . . NiB $656 Ex $525 Gd $357
"Meistershaftsbuchse" (Championship Rifle). Caliber: .22 LR. 27.5-inch bbl. Weight: 7.75 lbs. Sights: Open micrometer rear; ramp front. Target stock w/checkered pistol-grip and forearm, grip cap, swivels.

MODEL ES350B
BOLT-ACTION SINGLE-SHOT
TARGET RIFLE . . . . NiB $594 Ex $475 Gd $323
Same general specifications as Model MS350B except single-shot, weight: 8.25 lbs.

MODEL KKW BOLT-ACTION
SINGLE-SHOT TARGET RIFLE . . . . NiB $469 Ex $375 Gd $255
Caliber: .22 LR. 26-inch bbl. Weight: 8.75 lbs. Sights: Tangent curve open rear; Barleycorn front. M/98 military-type stock, swivels. Note: This rifle has an improved design Mauser 22 action w/separate nonrotating bolt head. In addition to being produced for commercial sale, this model was used as a training rifle by the German armed forces; it was also made by Walther and Gustoff. Intro. just before WWII.

MODEL M410 BOLT-ACTION
REPEATING SPORTING RIFLE . . . . NiB $844 Ex $675 Gd $459
Caliber: .22 LR. Five shot detachable box magazine. 23.5-inch bbl. Weight: 5 lbs. Sights: Tangent curve open rear; ramp front. Sporting stock w/checkered pistol-grip, swivels.

Mauser Type "A" Pattern No. 1

Mauser Type "B" Pattern No. 60

Mauser Type "M" Pattern No. 270

MODEL MM410B BOLT-ACTION
REPEATING SPORTING RIFLE . . . . **NiB $869 Ex $695 Gd $473**
Caliber: .22 LR. Five shot detachable box magazine. 23.5-inch bbl. Weight: 6.25 lbs. Sights: Tangent curve open rear; ramp front. Lightweight sporting stock w/checkered pistol-grip, swivels.

MODEL MS350B BOLT-ACTION
REPEATING TARGET RIFLE . . . . **NiB $869 Ex $695 Gd $473**
Caliber: .22 LR. Five shot detachable box magazine. Receiver and bbl. grooved for detachable rear sight or scope. 26.75-inch bbl. Weight: 8.5 lbs. Sights: Micrometer open rear; ramp front. Target stock w/checkered pistol grip and forearm, grip cap, sling swivels.

MODEL MS420 BOLT-ACTION
REPEATING SPORTING RIFLE . . . . **NiB $938 Ex $750 Gd $510**
Caliber: .22 LR. Five shot detachable box magazine. 25.5-inch bbl. Weight: 6.5 lbs. Sights: Tangent curve open rear; ramp front. Sporting stock w/checkered pistol grip, grooved forearm swivels.

MODEL MS420B BOLT-ACTION
REPEATING TARGET RIFLE . . . . **NiB $781 Ex $625 Gd $425**
Caliber: .22 LR. Five shot detachable box magazine. 26.75-inch bbl. Weight: 8 lbs. Sights: Tangent curve open rear; ramp front. Target stock w/checkered pistol grip, grooved forearm, swivels.

STANDARD MODEL RIFLE . . . . **NiB $656 Ex $525 Gd $357**
Refined version of German Service Kar. 98k. Straight bolt handle. Calibers: 7mm Mauser (7x57mm), 7.9mm Mauser (8x57mm). Five shot box magazine. 23.5-inch bbl. Weight: 8.5 lbs. Sights: Blade front; adj. rear. Walnut stock of M/98 military-type. Note: These rifles were made for commercial sale and are of the high quality found in the Oberndorf Mauser sporters. They bear the Mauser trademark on the receiver ring.

TYPE "A" BOLT-ACTION
SPORTING RIFLE. . . . . **NiB $2494 Ex $1995 Gd $1357**
Special British Model. 7x57, 30-06 (7.62x63), 8x60, 9x57, 9.3x62mm. Five shot box mag. 23.5-inch round bbl. Weight: 7.25 lbs. Mil.-type single trigger. Sights: Express rear; hooded ramp front. Circassian walnut sporting stock w/checkered pistol-grip and forearm, w/ or w/o cheekpiece, buffalo horn forend tip and grip cap, detachable swivels. Variations: Octagon bbl., double-set trigger, shotgun-type safety, folding peep rear sight, tangent curve rear sight, three-leaf rear sight.

TYPE "A" BOLT-ACTION
SPORTING RIFLE,
MAGNUM MODEL . . . . **NiB $2744 Ex $2195 Gd $1493**
Same general specifications as standard Type "A" except w/Magnum action, weighs 7.5 to 8.5 lbs. Calibers: .280 Ross, .318 Westley Richards Express, 10.75x68mm, .404 Nitro Express.

TYPE "A" BOLT-ACTION
SPORTING RIFLE,
SHORT MODEL . . . . **NiB $2244 Ex $1795 Gd $1221**
Same as standard Type "A" except w/short action, 21.5-inch round bbl., weight 6 lbs. Calibers: .250-3000, 6.5x54, 8x51mm.

TYPE "B" BOLT-ACTION
SPORTING
RIFLE . . . . **NiB $1688 Ex $1350 Gd $918**
Normal Model. Calibers: 7x57, .30-06 (7.62x63), 8x57, 8x60, 9x57, 9.3x62, 10.7568mm. Five shot box magazine. 23.5-inch round bbl. Weight: 7.25 lbs. Double-set trigger. Sights: Three-leaf rear, ramp front. Fine walnut stock w/checkered pistol-grip, Schnabel forend tip, cheekpiece, grip cap, swivels. Variations: Octagon or half-octagon bbl., military-type single trigger, shotgun-type safety, folding peep rear sight, tangent curve rear sight, telescopic sight.

TYPE "K"
BOLT-ACTION
SPORTING RIFLE. . . . . **NiB $3563 Ex $2850 Gd $1938**
Light Short Model. Same specifications as Normal Type "B" model except w/short action, 21.5-inch round bbl., weight: 6 lbs. Calibers: .250-3000, 6.5x54, 8x51mm.

TYPE "M"
BOLT-ACTION
SPORTING CARBINE . . . . **NiB $2244 Ex $1795 Gd $1221**
Calibers: 6.5x54, 7x57, .30-06 (7.62x63), 8x51, 8x60, 9x57mm. Five shot box magazine. 19.75-inch round bbl. Weight: 6 to 6.75 lbs. Double-set trigger, flat bolt handle. Sights: Three-leaf rear; ramp front. Stocked to muzzle, cheekpiece, checkered pistol-grip and forearm, grip cap, steel forend cap, swivels. Variations: Military-type single trigger, shotgun-type trigger, shotgun-type safety, tangent curve rear sight, telescopic sight.

Mauser Model 66S Standard

Mauser Model 66S Deluxe

Mauser Model 66SP
Super Match Target Rifle

Mauser Model 66ST Carbine

TYPE "S" BOLT-ACTION
SPORTING CARBINE . . . . **NiB $2325 Ex $1950 Gd $1225**
Calibers: 6.5x54 7x57, 8x51, 8x60, 9x57mm. Five shot box magazine. 19.75-inch round bbl. Weight: 6 to 6.75 lbs. Double-set trigger. Sights: Three-leaf rear; ramp front. Stocked to muzzle, Schnabel
forend tip, cheekpiece, checkered pistol-grip w/cap, swivels.
Variations: Same as listed for Normal Model Type "B."

POST-WORLD WAR II MODELS

NOTE: *Production of original Mauser sporting rifles (66 series)
resumed at the Oberndorf plant in 1965 by Mauser-Jagdwaffen
GmbH, now Mauser-Werke Oberndorf GmbH. The Series 2000-
3000-4000 rifles, however, were made for Mauser by Friedrich
Wilhelm Heym Gewehrfabrik, Muennerstadt, West Germany.*

MODEL 66S BOLT-ACTION STANDARD SPORTING RIFLE
Telescopic short action. Bbls. interchangeable within cal. group.
Single- or double-set trigger (interchangeable). Cal: .243 Win.,
6.5x57, .270 Win., 7x64, .308 Win., .30-06. Three round mag. 23.6
inch bbl. (25.6inch in 7x64). Wt: 7.3 lbs. (7.5 lbs. in 7x64). Sights:
Adj. open rear, hooded ramp front. Select Eur. walnut stock, Monte
Carlo w/cheekpiece, rosewood forend tip and pistol-grip cap, skip
checkering, recoil pad, sling swivels. Made 1965 to date, export to

(cont'd.) **MODEL 66S BOLT-ACTION STANDARD SPORTING RIFLE**
U.S. disc. 1974. Note: U.S.designation, 1971-73, was "Model 660."
Model 66S . . . . **NiB $2300 Ex $2000 Gd $1000**
W/extra bbl. assembly, add $550

MODEL 66S DELUXE SPORTER
Limited production special order. Model 66S rifles and carbines are available with /elaborate engraving, gold and silver
inlays and carved select walnut stocks. Added value is upward
of $4500.

MODEL 66S ULTRA
Same general specifications as Model 66S Standard except with
20.9-inch bbl., weight: 6.8 lbs.
Model 66S Ultra . . . . **NiB $1575 Ex $1490 Gd $950**
W/extra bbl. assembly, add $550

MODEL 66SG BIG GAME
Same general specifications as Model 66S Standard except
w/25.6-inch bbl., weight 9.3 lbs. Calibers: .375 H&H Mag., .458
Win. Mag. Note: U.S. designation, 1971-73, was "Model 660
Safari."
Model 66SG . . . . **NiB $2900 Ex $1875 Gd $1150**
W/ extra bbl. assembly, add $550

Mauser Model 99

Mauser Model 201

Mauser Model 3000

Mauser Model 4000

MODEL 66SH HIGH PERFORMANCE . . NiB $1575 Ex $1400 Gd $975
Same general specifications as Model 66S Standard except w/25.6-inch bbl., weighs 7.5 lbs. (9.3 lbs. in 9.3x64). Calibers: 6.5x68, 7mm Rem. Mag., 7mm S.E.v. Hoffe, .300 Win. Mag., 8x68S, 9.3x64.

MODEL 66SP SUPER MATCH
BOLT-ACTION TARGET RIFLE. . . . . . . NiB $4000 Ex $3400 Gd $1750
Telescopic short action. Adj. single-stage trigger. Caliber: .308 Win. (chambering for other cartridges available on special order). Three shot magazine. 27.6-inch heavy bbl. w/muzzle brake, dovetail rib for special scope mount. Weight: 12 lbs. Target stock w/wide and deep forearm, full pistol-grip, thumbhole adj. cheekpiece, adj. rubber buttplate.

MODEL 66ST CARBINE
Same general specifications as Model 66S Standard except w/20.9-inch bbl., full-length stock, weight: 7 lbs.
Model 66ST . . . . NiB $1575 Ex $1400 Gd $975
W/extra bbl. assembly, add $550

MODEL 83 BOLT-ACTION RIFLE . . . . . NiB $2325 Ex $1950 Gd $1200
Centerfire single-shot, bolt-action rifle for 300-meter competition. Caliber: .308 Win. 25.5-inch fluted bbl. Weight: 10.5 lbs. Adj. micrometer rear sight globe front. Fully adj. competition stock. Disc. 1988.

MODEL 96 . . . . NiB $656 Ex $525 Gd $357
Calibers: .25-06, .270 Win., 7x64, .308 Win., .30-06, 7mm Rem. Mag., .300 Win. Mag. 22-inch bbl.; magnums 24-inch. Weight: 6.25 lbs. No sights; drilled and tapped for scope. Walnut stock. 5-shot top-loading magazine. 3-position safety.

MODEL 99 CLASSIC BOLT-ACTION RIFLE
Calibers: .243 Win., .25-06, .270 Win., .30-06, .308 Win., .257 Wby., .270 Wby., 7mm Rem. Mag., .300 Win., .300 Wby. .375 H&H. Four shot magazine (standard), 3-shot (Magnum). Bbl.: 24-inch (standard) or 26-inch (Magnum). 44 inches overall (standard). Weight: 8 lbs. No sights. Checkered European walnut stock w/rosewood grip cap available in Classic and Monte Carlo styles w/High-Luster or oil finish. Disc. importing 1994.
Standard Classic or
Monte Carlo (oil finish) . . . . NiB $1120 Ex $925 Gd $600
Magnum Classic or
Monte Carlo (oil finish) . . . . NiB $1208 Ex $970 Gd $666
Standard Classic or
Monte Carlo (H-L finish) . . . . NiB $1150 Ex $950 Gd $625
Magnum Classic or
Monte Carlo (H-L finish) . . . . NiB $1264 Ex $1015 Gd $697

MODEL 107 BOLT-ACTION RIFLE . . . . NiB $350 Ex $250 Gd $150
Caliber: .22 LR. Mag. Five shot magazine. 21.5-inch bbl. 40 inches overall. Weight: 5 lbs. Receiver drilled and tapped for rail scope mounts. Hooded front sight, adj. rear. Disc. importing 1994.

MODEL 201/201 LUXUS BOLT-ACTION RIFLE
Calibers: .22 LR. .22 Win. Mag. 5-shot magazine. 21-inch bbl. 40 inches overall. Weight: 6.5 lbs. Receiver drilled and tapped for scope mounts. Sights optional. Checkered walnut-stained beech stock w/Monte Carlo. Model 201 Luxus w/checkered European walnut stock QD swivels, rosewood forend and rubber recoil pad. Made 1989 to date. Disc. importing 1994.
Model 201 Standard . . . . NiB $700 Ex $650 Gd $370
Model 201 Magnum . . . . NiB $644 Ex $520 Gd $362
Model 201 Luxus Standard . . . . NiB $725 Ex $650 Gd $375
Model 201 Luxus Magnum . . . . NiB $831 Ex $675 Gd $475

Midland Model 2700 Bolt-Action Rifle

Merkel Model 220

**MODEL 2000 BOLT-ACTION
SPORTING RIFLE**. . . . . **NiB $570 Ex $475 Gd $300**
Modified Mauser-type action. Calibers: .270 Win., .308 Win., .30-06. Five shot magazine. 24-inch bbl. Weight: 7.5 lbs. Sights: Folding leaf rear; hooded ramp front. Checkered walnut stock w/Monte Carlo comb and cheekpiece, forend tip, sling swivels. Made 1969-71. Note: Model 2000 is similar in appearance to Model 3000.

MODEL 2000 CLASSIC BOLT-ACTION SPORTING RIFLE
Calibers: .22-250 Rem., .234 Win., .270 Win., 7mm Mag., .308 Win., .30-06, .300 Win. Mag. Three or 5-shot magazine. 24-inch bbl. Weight: 7.5 lbs. Sights: Folding leaf rear; hooded ramp front. Checkered walnut stock w/Monte Carlo comb and cheekpiece, forend tip, sling swivels. Imported 1998. Note: The Model 2000 Classic is designed to interchange bbl. assemblies within a given caliber group.
Model 2000 Classic. . . . . **NiB $1531 Ex $1225 Gd $833**
**Model 2000 Professional
w/Recoil Compensator** . . . . **NiB $3119 Ex $2495 Gd $1697**
Model 2000 Sniper. . . . . **NiB $1744 Ex $1395 Gd $949**
Model 2000 Varmint. . . . . **NiB $1688 Ex $1350 Gd $918**
Extra bbl. assembly, add **$895**

**MODEL 3000 BOLT-ACTION
SPORTING RIFLE**. . . . . **NiB $575 Ex $450 Gd $320**
Modified Mauser-type action. Calibers: .243 Win., .270 Win., .308 Win., .30-06. Five shot magazine. 22-inch bbl. Weight: 7 lbs. No sights. Select European walnut stock, Monte Carlo style w/cheekpiece, rosewood forend tip and pistol-grip cap, skip checkering, recoil pad, sling swivels. Made 1971-74.

MODEL 3000 MAGNUM . . . . **NiB $575 Ex $500 Gd $400**
Same general specifications as standard Model 3000, except w/3-shot magazine, 26-inch bbl., weight: 8 lbs. Calibers: 7mm Rem. Mag., .300 Win. Mag., .375 H&H Mag.

MODEL 4000 VARMINT RIFLE . . . . **NiB $500 Ex $400 Gd $290**
Same general specifications as standard Model 3000, except w/smaller action, folding leaf rear sight; hooded ramp front, rubber buttplate instead of recoil pad, weight 6.75 lbs. Calibers: .222 Rem., .223 Rem. 22-inch bbl. Select European walnut stock w/rosewood forend tip and pistol-grip cap. French checkering and sling swivels.

McMILLAN GUN WORKS — Phoenix, Arizona
Harris Gunworks

See Harris Gunworks.

GEBRÜDER MERKEL — Suhl, Germany

For Merkel combination guns and drillings, see listings under Merkel shotguns.

OVER/UNDER RIFLES ("BOCK-DOPPELBÜCHSEN")
Calibers: 5.6x35 Vierling, 6.5x58r5, 7x57r5, 8x57JR, 8x60R Magnum, 9.3x53r5, 9.3x72r5, 9.3x74r5, 10.3x60R as well as most of the British calibers for African and Indian big game. Various bbl. lengths, weights. In general, specifications correspond to those of Merkel over/under shotguns. Values of these over/under rifles (in calibers for which ammunition is obtainable) are about the same as those of comparable shotgun models currently manufactured. For more specific data, see Merkel shotgun models indicated below.
Model 220. . . . . **NiB $9000 Ex $8000 Gd $4000**
Model 220E. . . . . **NiB $9575 Ex $8400 Gd $7400**
Model 221. . . . . **NiB $7438 Ex $5950 Gd $4046**
Model 221E. . . . . **NiB $9813 Ex $7850 Gd $5338**
Model 320. . . . . **NiB $8125 Ex $6500 Gd $4420**
Model 320E. . . . . **NiB $15,000 Ex $12,000 Gd $8160**
Model 321. . . . . **NiB $16,563 Ex $13,250 Gd $9010**
Model 321E. . . . . **NiB $17,500 Ex $14,000 Gd $9520**
Model 322. . . . . **NiB $18,125 Ex $14,500 Gd $9860**
Model 323E . . . . **NiB $23,125 Ex $18,500 Gd $12,580**
Model 324 . . . . **NiB $26,875 Ex $21,500 Gd $14,620**

MEXICAN MILITARY RIFLE
Mfd. by Government Arsenal, Mexico, D.F.

MODEL 1936 MAUSER MILITARY RIFLE . . . **NiB $200 Ex $150 Gd $95**
Same as German Kar.98k w/minor variations and U.S. M/1903 Springfield-type knurled cocking piece.

Mossberg Model 25

MIDLAND RIFLES — Mfg. by Gibbs Rifle Company, Inc., Martinsburg, WV

MODEL 2100 BOLT-ACTION
RIFLE . . . . **NiB $331 Ex $265 Gd $180**
Calibers: .22-250, .243 Win., 6mm Rem., .270 Win., 6.5x55, 7x57, 7x64, .308 Win., and .30-06. Springfield 1903 action. Four shot magazine. 22-inch bbl. 43 inches overall. Weight: 7 lbs. Flip-up rear sight; hooded ramp front. Finely finished and checkered walnut stock w/pistol-grip cap and sling swivels. Steel recoil bar. Action drilled and tapped for scope mounts. Production disc.1997.

MODEL 2600 BOLT-ACTION RIFLE . . . . . . **NiB $350 Ex $280 Gd $160**
Same general specifications as Model 2100 except no pistol-grip cap, and stock is walnut-finished hardwood. Made 1992-97.

MODEL 2700 BOLT-ACTION RIFLE . . . . . **NiB $350 Ex $275 Gd $175**
Same general specifications as Model 2100 except the weight of this rifle as been reduced by utilizing a tapered bbl., anodized aluminum trigger housing and lightened stock. Weight: 6.5 lbs. Disc.

MODEL 2800 LIGHTWEIGHT RIFLE . . . . . **NiB $356 Ex $285 Gd $194**
Same general specifications as Model 2100 except w/laminated birch stock. Made 1992-94 and 1996-97.

MITCHELL ARMS. INC. — Fountain Valley, California, (Formerly Santa Ana, CA)

MODEL 15/22 SEMIAUTOMATIC
High Standard-style action. Caliber: .22 LR. 15-shot magazine (10-shot after 10/13/94). 20.5-inch bbl. 37.5 inches overall. Weight: 6.25 lbs. Ramp front sight; adj. open rear. Blued finish. Mahogany stock; Monte Carlo-style American walnut stock on Deluxe model. Made 1994-96.
Model 15/22 SP (Special)
w/plastic buttplate . . . . **NiB $94 Ex $75 Gd $51**
Model 15/22 Carbine . . . . **NiB $131 Ex $105 Gd $71**
Model 15/22D Deluxe . . . . **NiB $156 Ex $125 Gd $85**

MODEL 9300 SERIES BOLT-ACTION RIFLE
Calibers: .22 LR. .22 Mag. Five or 10-shot magazine. 22.5-inch bbl. 40.75 inches overall. Weight: 6.5 lbs. Beaded ramp front sight; adj. open rear. Blued finish. American walnut stock. Made 1994-95.
Model 9302 (.22 LR,
checkered, rosewood caps) . . . . **NiB $231 Ex $185 Gd $126**
Model 9302 (.22 Mag.,
checkered, rosewood caps) . . . . **NiB $244 Ex $195 Gd $133**
Model 9303 (.22 LR, plain stock) . . . . **NiB $181 Ex $145 Gd $99**
Model 9304 (.22 Mag.,
checkered, No rosewood caps) . . . . **NiB $194 Ex $155 Gd $105**
Model 9305 (.22 LR, special stock) . . . . **NiB $156 Ex $125 Gd $85**

AK-22 SEMIAUTOMATIC RIFLE . . . . **NiB $231 Ex $185 Gd $126**
Replica of AK-47 rifle. .22 LR. .22 WMR. 20-shot magazine (.22 LR), 10-shot (.22 WMR). 18-inch bbl. 36 inches overall. Weight: 6.5 lbs. Sights: Post front; open adj. rear. European walnut stock and forend. Matte black finish. Made 1985-94.

CAR-15 22 SEMIAUTOMATIC RIFLE. . . . . . **NiB $231 Ex $185 Gd $126**
Replica of AR-15 CAR rifle. Caliber: .22 LR. 15-shot magazine.16.25-inch bbl. 32 inches overall. Sights: Adj. post front; adj. aperture rear. Telescoping buttstock and ventilated forend. Matte black finish. Made 1990-94.

GALIL 22 SEMIAUTOMATIC RIFLE. . . . . . **NiB $275 Ex $225 Gd $140**
Replica of Israeli Galil rifle. Calibers: .22 LR. .22 WMR. 20-shot magazine (.22 LR), 10-shot (.22 WMR). 18-inch bbl. 36 inches overall. Weight: 6.5 lbs. Sights: Adj. post front; rear adj. for windage. Folding metal stock w/European walnut grip and forend. Matte black finish. Made 1987-93.

M-16A 22 SEMIAUTOMATIC RIFLE . . . . . **NiB $231 Ex $185 Gd $126**
Replica of AR-15 rifle. Caliber: .22 LR. 15-shot magazine. 20.5-inch bbl. 38.5 inches overall. Weight: 7 lbs. Sights: Adj. post front, adj. aperture rear. Black composite stock and forend. Matte black finish. Made 1990-94.

MAS 22 SEMIAUTOMATIC RIFLE. . . . . . . **NiB $275 Ex $220 Gd $150**
Replica of French MAS bullpup rifle. Caliber: .22 LR. 20-shot magazine. 18-inch bbl. 28 inches overall. Weight: 7.5 lbs. Sights: Adj. post front, folding aperture rear. European walnut buttstock and forend. Matte black finish. Made 1987-93.

PPS SEMIAUTOMATIC RIFLE
Caliber: .22 LR. 20-shot magazine, 50-shot drum. 16.5-inch bbl. 33.5 inches overall. Weight: 5.5 lbs. Sights: Blade front; adj. rear. European walnut stock w/ventilated bbl. shroud. Matte black finish. Made 1989-94.
Model PPS (20-shot) . . . . **NiB $250 Ex $200 Gd $136**
Model PPS/50 (50-shot drum) . . . . . **NiB $506 Ex $425 Gd $321**

O.F. MOSSBERG & SONS, INC. — North Haven, Connecticut, (Formerly New Haven, CT)

MODEL 10 BOLT-ACTION
SINGLE-SHOT RIFLE . . . . **NiB $150 Ex $100 Gd $75**
Takedown. Caliber: .22 LR, Long, Short. 22-inch bbl. Weight: 4 lbs. Sights: Open rear; bead front. Plain pistol-grip stock w/swivels, sling. Made 1933-35.

MODEL 14 BOLT-ACTION
SINGLE-SHOT RIFLE . . . . **NiB $160 Ex $100 Gd $75**
Takedown. Caliber: .22 LR. Long, Short. 24-inch bbl. Weight: 5.25 lbs. Sights: Peep rear; hooded ramp front. Plain pistol-grip stock w/semi-beavertail forearm, 1.25-inch swivels. Made 1934-35.

MODEL 20 BOLT-ACTION
SINGLE-SHOT RIFLE . . . . **NiB $160 Ex $100 Gd $70**
Takedown. Caliber: .22 LR. Long, Short. 24-inch bbl. Weight: 4.5 lbs. Sights: Open rear; bead front. Plain pistol-grip stock and forearm w/finger grooves, sling and swivels. Made 1933-35.

MODEL 25/25A BOLT-ACTION SINGLE-SHOT RIFLE
Takedown. Caliber: .22 LR. Long, Short. 24-inch bbl. Weight: 5 lbs. Sights: Peep rear; hooded ramp front. Plain pistol-grip stock w/semi-beavertail forearm. 1.25-inch swivels. Made 1935-36.
Model 25. . . . . **NiB $160 Ex $100 Gd $70**
Model 25A (Improved Model 25, 1936-38) . . . . . **NiB $170 Ex $100 Gd $75**

Mossberg Model 35A

Mossberg Model L42A

Mossberg Model 42B

MODEL 26B/26C BOLT-ACTION SINGLE-SHOT
Takedown. Caliber: .22 LR. Long, Short. 26-inch bbl. Weight: 5.5 lbs. Sights; Rear, micrometer click peep or open; hooded ramp front. Plain pistol-grip stock swivels. Made 1938-41.
Model 26B . . . . NiB $170 Ex $130 Gd $75
Model 26C
(No rear sight/swivels) . . . . NiB $150 Ex $100 Gd $60

MODEL 30 BOLT-ACTION
SINGLE-SHOT RIFLE . . . . NiB $130 Ex $100 Gd $70
Takedown. Caliber: .22 LR. Long, Short. 24-inch bbl. Weight: 4.5 lbs. Sights: Peep rear; bead front, on hooded ramp. Plain pistol-grip stock, forearm w/finger grooves. Made 1933-35.

MODEL 34 BOLT-ACTION
SINGLE-SHOT RIFLE . . . . NiB $150 Ex $100 Gd $70
Takedown. Caliber: .22 LR. Long, Short. 24-inch bbl. Weight: 5.5 lbs. Sights: Peep rear; hooded ramp front. Plain pistol-grip stock w/semibeavertail forearm, 1.25-inch swivels. Made 1934-35.

MODEL 35 TARGET GRADE
BOLT-ACTION SINGLE-SHOT RIFLE . . . . NiB $325 Ex $220 Gd $80
Caliber: .22 LR. 26-inch heavy bbl. Weight: 8.25 lbs. Sights: Micrometer click rear peep; hooded ramp front. Large target stock w/full pistol grip, cheekpiece, full beavertail forearm, 1.25-inch swivels. Made 1935-37.

MODEL 35A BOLT-ACTION
SINGLE-SHOT RIFLE . . . . NiB $325 Ex $220 Gd $80
Caliber: .22 LR. 26-inch heavy bbl. Weight: 8.25 lbs. Sights: Micrometer click peep rear; hooded front. Target stock w/cheekpiece full pistol grip and forearm, 1.25-inch sling swivels. Made 1937-38.

MODEL 35A-LS . . . . NiB $380 Ex $250 Gd $165
Caliber .22 LR. Same as Model 35A but w/Lyman No. 57 rear sight, 17A front. Target stock w/checkpiece, full pistol-grip and forearm.

MODEL 35B . . . . NiB $370 Ex $240 Gd $160
Same specifications as Model 44B except single-shot. Made 1938-40.

MODEL 40 BOLT-ACTION REPEATER. . . . . . NiB $150 Ex $100 Gd $70
Takedown. Caliber: .22 LR. Long, Short, 16-round tubular magazine. 24-inch bbl. Weight: 5 lbs. Sights: Peep rear; bead front, on hooded ramp. Plain pistol-grip stock, forearm w/finger grooves. Made 1933-35.

MODEL 42 BOLT-ACTION REPEATER. . . . . . NiB $150 Ex $100 Gd $70
Takedown. Caliber: .22 LR. Long, Short. Seven shot detachable box magazine. 24-inch bbl. Weight: 5 lbs. Sights: Receiver peep, open rear; hooded ramp front. Pistol-grip stock. 1.25-inch swivels. Made 1935-37.

MODEL 42A/L42A BOLT-ACTION REPEATERS
Takedown. Caliber: .22 LR. Long, Short. Seven shot detachable box magazine. 24-inch bbl. Weight: 5 lbs. Sights: Receiver peep, open rear; ramp front. Plain pistol-grip stock. Made 1937-38. Model L42A (left-hand action) made 1937-1941.
Model 42A. NiB $150 Ex $120 Gd $82
Model L42A. . . . . NiB $231 Ex $185 Gd $126

MODEL 42B/42C BOLT-ACTION REPEATERS
Takedown. Caliber: .22 LR. Long, Short. Five shot detachable box magazine. 24-inch bbl. Weight: 6 lbs. Sights: Micrometer click receiver peep, open rear hooded ramp front. Plain pistol-grip stock, swivels. Made 1938-41.
Model 42B. NiB $150 Ex $125 Gd $60
Model 42C (No rear peep sight) . . . . . NiB $119 Ex $95 Gd $65

Mossberg Model 42C

Mossberg Model L-43

Mossberg Model 43B

Mossberg Model 44US

Mossberg Model L45A
Left-Hand Model

Mossberg Model 45B

Mossberg Model L46A-LS

Mossberg Model 46B

MODEL 42M BOLT-ACTION REPEATER . . . . NiB $175 Ex $150 Gd $80
Caliber: .22 LR. Long, Short. Seven shot detachable box magazine.
23-inch bbl. Weight: 6.75 lbs. Sights: Microclick receiver peep,
open rear; hooded ramp front. Two-piece Mannlicher-type stock
w/cheekpiece and pistol-grip, swivels. Made 1940-50.

**MODEL 43/L43 BOLT-ACTION
REPEATERS . . . . NiB $406 Ex $325 Gd $221**
Speedlock, adj. trigger pull. Caliber: .22 LR. Seven shot detachable box

(cont'd.) MODEL 43/L43 BOLT-ACTION REPEATERS
magazine. 26-inch heavy bbl. Weight: 8.25 lbs. Sights: Lyman No.
57 rear; selective aperture front. Target stock w/cheekpiece, full pistol-grip, beavertail forearm, adj. front swivel. Made 1937-38. Model
L43 is same as Model 43 except w/left-hand action.

MODEL 43B . . . . NiB $350 Ex $250 Gd $95
Same as Model 44B except w/Lyman No. 57 receiver sight and No.
17A front sight. Made 1938-39.

Mossberg Model 46M

Mossberg Model 50

Mossberg Model 51

Mossberg Model 51M

MODEL 44 BOLT-ACTION REPEATER.....NiB $250 Ex $200 Gd $90
Takedown. Caliber: .22 LR. Long, Short. Tubular magazine holds 16 LR. 24-inch bbl. Weight: 6 lbs. Sights: Peep rear; hooded ramp front. Plain pistol-grip stock w/semi-beavertail forearm, 1.25-inch swivels. Made 1934-35. Note: Do not confuse this rifle w/later Models 44B and 44US, which are clip repeaters.

**MODEL 44B BOLT-ACTION
TARGET RIFLE................NiB $270 Ex $200 Gd $100**
Caliber: .22 LR. Seven shot detachable box magazine. Made 1938-41.

MODEL 44US BOLT-ACTION REPEATER
Caliber: .22 LR. Seven shot detachable box magazine. 26-inch heavy bbl. Weight: 8.5 lbs. Sights: Micrometer click receiver peep, hooded front. Target stock, swivels. Made 1943-48. Note: This model was used as a training rifle by the U.S. Armed Forces during WWII.
Model 44US ....NiB $250 Ex $225 Gd $90
Model 44US (marked U.S. Property) .....NiB $325 Ex $275 Gd $200

MODEL 45 BOLT-ACTION REPEATER......NiB $175 Ex $150 Gd $90
Takedown. Caliber: .22 LR. Long, Short. Tubular magazine holds 15 LR. 18 Long, 22 Short. 24-inch bbl. Weight: 6.75 lbs. Sights: Rear peep; hooded ramp front. Plain pistol-grip stock, 1.25-inch swivels. Made 1935-37.

MODEL 45A, L45A, 45AC BOLT-ACTION REPEATERS
Takedown. Caliber: .22 LR. Long, Short. Tubular magazine holds 15 LR, 18 Long, 22 Short. 24-inch bbl. Weight: 6.75 lbs. Sights: Receiver peep, open rear; hooded blade front sight mounted on ramp. Plain pistol-grip stock, 1.25-inch sling swivels. Made 1937-38. See illustration on previous page.

(cont'd.) MODEL 45A, L45A, 45AC BOLT-ACTION REPEATERS
Model 45A ....NiB $175 Ex $140 Gd $95
Model L45A (Left-hand action).........NiB $225 Ex $180 Gd $122
Model 45AC (No receiver peep sight)......NiB $160 Ex $120 Gd $80

MODEL 45B/45C BOLT-ACTION REPEATERS
Takedown. Caliber: .22 LR. Long, Short. Tubular magazine holds 15 LR, 18 Long, 22 Short. 24-inch bbl. Weight: 6.25 lbs. Open rear sight; hooded blade front sight mounted on ramp. Plain pistol-grip stock w/sling swivels. Made 1938-40.
Model 45B ....NiB $156 Ex $125 Gd $85
Model 45C (No sights, made 1935-37).....NiB $138 Ex $110 Gd $75

MODEL 46 BOLT-ACTION REPEATER......NiB $175 Ex $180 Gd $90
Takedown. Caliber: .22 LR. Long, Short. Tubular magazine holds 15 LR, 18 Long, 22 Short. 26-inch bbl. Weight: 7.5 lbs. Sights: Micrometer click rear peep; hooded ramp front. Pistol-grip stock w/cheekpiece, full beavertail forearm, 1.25-inch swivels. Made 1935-37.

MODEL 46A, 46A-LS, L46A-LS BOLT-ACTION REPEATERS
Takedown. Caliber: .22 LR. Long, Short. Tubular magazine holds 15 LR, 18 Long, 22 Short. 26-inch bbl. Weight: 7.25 lbs. Sights: Micrometer click receiver peep, open rear; hooded ramp front. Pistol-grip stock w/cheekpiece and beavertail forearm, quick-detachable swivels. Made 1937-38.
Model 46A ....NiB $181 Ex $145 Gd $99
Mdl. 46A-LS (w/Lyman No. 57 receiver sight)....NiB $244 Ex $195 Gd $133
Model L46A-LS (Left-hand action).......NiB $356 Ex $285 Gd $194

Mossberg Model 140B

Mossberg Model 140K

Mossberg Model 144LS

Mossberg Model 146B

MODEL 46B BOLT-ACTION REPEATER . . . . **NiB $144 Ex $115 Gd $78**
Takedown. Caliber: .22 LR. Long, Short. Tubular magazine holds 15 LR, 18 Long, 22 Short. 26-inch bbl. Weight: 7 lbs. Sights: Micrometer click receiver peep, open rear, hooded front. Plain pistol-grip stock w/cheekpiece, swivels. Note: Postwar version of this model has full magazine holding 20 LR, 23 Long, 30 Short. Made 1938-50.

MODEL 46BT . . . . **NiB $206 Ex $165 Gd $112**
Same as Model 46B except w/heavier bbl. and stock. Weight: 7.75 lbs. Made 1938-39.

MODEL 46C . . . . **NiB $200 Ex $150 Gd $90**
Same as Model 46 except w/a heavier bbl. and stock than that model. Weight: 8.5 lbs. Made 1936-37.

MODEL 46M BOLT-ACTION REPEATER . . . . **NiB $200 Ex $150 Gd $90**
Caliber: .22 LR. Long, Short. Tubular magazine holds 22 Short, 18 Long, 15 LR. 23-inch bbl. Weight: 7 lbs. Sights: Microclick receiver peep, open rear; hooded ramp front. Two-piece Mannlicher-type stock w/cheekpiece and pistol-grip, swivels. Made 1940-52.

MODEL 50 AUTOLOADING RIFLE . . . . **NiB $175 Ex $140 Gd $95**
Same as Model 51 except w/plain stock w/o beavertail cheekpiece, swivels or receiver peep sight. Made 1939-42.

MODEL 51 AUTOLOADING RIFLE . . . . **NiB $170 Ex $125 Gd $95**
Takedown. Caliber: .22 LR. 15-shot tubular magazine in buttstock. 24-inch bbl. Weight: 7.25 lbs. Sights: Micrometer click receiver peep, open rear; hooded ramp front. Cheekpiece stock w/full pistol grip and beavertail forearm, swivels. Made 1939 only.

MODEL 51M AUTOLOADING RIFLE . . . . . . **NiB $170 Ex $125 Gd $95**
Caliber: .22 LR. 15-shot tubular magazine. 20-inch bbl. Weight: 7 lbs. Sights: Microclick receiver peep, open rear; hooded ramp front. Two-piece Mannlicher-type stock w/pistol-grip and cheekpiece, hard-rubber buttplate and sling swivels. Made 1939-46.

MODEL 140B SPORTER-TARGET RIFLE . . . . **NiB $170 Ex $125 Gd $95**
Same as Model 140K except w/peep rear sight, hooded ramp front sight. Made 1957-58.

MODEL 140K BOLT-ACTION REPEATER . . . **NiB $150 Ex $120 Gd $82**
Caliber: .22 LR. .22 Long, .22 Short. Seven shot clip magazine. 24.5-inch bbl. Weight: 5.75 lbs. Sights: Open rear; bead front. Monte Carlo stock w/cheekpiece and pistol-grip, sling swivels. Made 1955-58.

MODEL 142-A BOLT-ACTION REPEATING CARBINE . . . . **NiB $188 Ex $150 Gd $102**
Caliber: .22 Short Long, LR. Seven shot detachable box magazine. 18-inch bbl. Weight: 6 lbs. Sights: Peep rear, military-type front. Monte Carlo stock w/pistol-grip, hinged forearm pulls down to form hand grip; sling swivels mounted on left side of stock. Made 1949-57.

Mossberg Model 151K

Mossberg Model 151M

Mossberg Model 152

MODEL 142K . . . . NiB $131 Ex $105 Gd $71
Same as Model 142 except w/open rear sight. Made 1953-57.

**MODEL 144 BOLT-ACTION
TARGET RIFLE** . . . . NiB $400 Ex $325 Gd $175
Caliber: .22 LR. Seven shot detachable box magazine. 26-inch
heavy bbl. Weight: 8 lbs. Sights: Microclick receiver peep; hooded
front. Pistol-grip target stock w/beavertail forearm, adj. hand stop,
swivels. Made 1949-54. Note: This model designation was resumed
c.1973 to replace Model 144LS, and then disc. again in 1985.

MODEL 144LS. . . . . NiB $450 Ex $390 Gd $165
Same as Model 144 except w/Lyman No. 57MS or Mossberg S331
receiver sight and Lyman 17A front sight. Made 1954 to date. Note:
Since 1973, this model has been marketed as Model 144.

MODEL 146B BOLT-ACTION REPEATER . . NiB $200 Ex $150 Gd $100
Takedown. Caliber: .22 LR. Long, Short. Tubular magazine holds 30
Short, 23 Long, 20 LR. 26-inch bbl. Weight: 7 lbs. Sights: Micrometer
click rear peep, open rear; hooded front. Plain stock w/pistol-grip, Monte
Carlo comb and cheekpiece, knob forend tip, swivels. Made 1949-54.

MODEL 151K . . . . NiB $180 Ex $140 Gd $90
Same as Model 151M except w/24-inch bbl., weight: 6 lbs., w/o
peep sight, plain stock w/Monte Carlo comb and cheekpiece, pistol-
grip knob, forend tip, w/o swivels. Made 1950-51.

MODEL 151M AUTOLOADING RIFLE . . . . . NiB $180 Ex $140 Gd $90
Improved version of Model 51M w/same general specifications, complete action is instantly removable w/o use of tools. Made 1946-58.

MODEL 152 AUTOLOADING CARBINE . . . NiB $180 Ex $140 Gd $90
Caliber: .22 LR. Seven shot detachable box magazine. 18-inch bbl.
Weight: 5 lbs. Sights: Peep rear; military-type front. Monte Carlo
stock w/pistol-grip, hinged forearm pulls down to form hand grip,
sling mounted on swivels on left side of stock. Made 1948-57.

MODEL 152K . . . . NiB $160 Ex $125 Gd $80
Same as Model 152 except w/open instead of peep rear sight. Made
1950-57.

MODEL 320B BOY SCOUT TARGET RIFLE . . . . . NiB $163 Ex $130 Gd $88
Same as Model 340K except single-shot w/auto. safety. Made 1960-71.

**MODEL 320K HAMMERLESS
BOLT-ACTION SINGLE-SHOT** . . . . . . NiB $125 Ex $100 Gd $68
Same as Model 346K except single-shot, w/drop-in loading plat-
form, automatic safety. Weight: 5.75 lbs. Made 1958-60.

MODEL 321B . . . . NiB $144 Ex $115 Gd $78
Same as Model 321K except w/receiver peep sight. Made 1972-75.

**MODEL 321K BOLT-ACTION
SINGLE-SHOT** . . . . NiB $150 Ex $120 Gd $82
Same as Model 341 except single-shot. Made 1972-80.

MODEL 333 AUTOLOADING CARBINE . . NiB $150 Ex $125 Gd $100
Caliber: .22 LR. 15-shot tubular magazine. 20-inch bbl. Weight:
6.25 lbs. Sights: Open rear; ramp front. Monte Carlo stock w/check-
ered pistol grip and forearm, bbl. band, swivels. Made 1972-73.

MODEL 340B TARGET SPORTER . . . . NiB $180 Ex $150 Gd $100
Same as Model 340K except w/peep rear sight, hooded ramp front
sight. Made 1958-81.

**MODEL 340K HAMMERLESS
BOLT-ACTION REPEATER** . . . . NiB $150 Ex $125 Gd $100
Same as Model 346K except clip type, 7-shot magazine. Made
1958-71.

MODEL 340M . . . . NiB $288 Ex $230 Gd $156
Same as Model 340K except w/18.5-inch bbl., Mannlicher-style
stock w/swivels and sling. Weight: 5.25 lbs. Made 1970-71.

Mossberg Model 320B

Mossberg Model 320K

Mossberg Model 333

Mossberg Model 340B

Mossberg Model 340K

Mossberg Model 341

Mossberg Model 342K

Mossberg Model 346B

Mossberg Model 346K

RIFLES

Mossberg Model 350K
Autoloading — Clip Type

Mossberg Model 351K
Automatic Sporter

Mossberg Model 352K
Carbine

Mossberg Model 353
Carbine

Mossberg Model 377
Plinkster

MODEL 341 BOLT-ACTION REPEATER...... NiB $125 Ex $95 Gd $70
Caliber: .22 Short. Long, LR. Seven shot clip magazine. 24-inch bbl. Weight: 6.5 lbs. Sights: Open rear, ramp front. Monte Carlo stock w/checkered pistol-grip and forearm, sling swivels. Made 1972-85.

**MODEL 342K HAMMERLESS
BOLT-ACTION CARBINE.........** NiB $150 Ex $125 Gd $90
Same as Model 340K except w/18-inch bbl., stock w/no cheekpiece, extension forend is hinged, pulls down to form hand grip; sling swivels and web strap on left side of stock. Weight: 5 lbs. Made 1958-74.

MODEL 346B .... NiB $150 Ex $125 Gd $90
Same as Model 346K except w/peep rear sight, hooded ramp front sight. Made 1958-67.

**MODEL 346K HAMMERLESS
BOLT-ACTION REPEATER ....** NiB $144 Ex $115 Gd $78
Caliber: .22 Short. Long, LR. Tubular magazine holds 25 Short, 20 Long, 18 LR. 24-inch bbl. Weight: 6.5 lbs. Sights: Open rear; bead front. Walnut stock w/Monte Carlo comb, cheekpiece, pistol-grip, sling swivels. Made 1958-71.

**MODEL 350K AUTOLOADING
RIFLE — CLIP TYPE ....** NiB $140 Ex $95 Gd $70
Caliber: .22 Short (High Speed), Long, LR. Seven shot clip magazine.

(cont'd.) MODEL 350K AUTOLOADING RIFLE — CLIP TYPE
23.5-inch bbl. Weight: 6 lbs. Sights: Open rear; bead front. Monte Carlo stock w/pistol-grip. Made 1958-71.

MODEL 351C AUTOLOADING CARBINE .. NiB $160 Ex $130 Gd $90
Same as Model 351K except w/18.5-inch bbl., Western carbine-style stock w/barrel band and sling swivels. Weight: 5.5 lbs. Made 1965-71.

**MODEL 351K AUTOLOADING
SPORTER............................** NiB $160 Ex $130 Gd $90
Caliber: .22 LR. 15-shot tubular magazine in buttstock. 24-inch bbl. Weight: 6 lbs. Sights: Open rear; bead front. Monte Carlo stock w/pistol-grip. Made 1960-71.

MODEL 352K AUTOLOADING CARBINE...... NiB $160 Ex $130 Gd $90
Caliber: .22 Short, Long, LR. Seven shot clip magazine. 18-inch bbl. Weight: 5 lbs. Sights: Open rear; bead front. Monte Carlo stock w/pistol grip; extension forend of Tenite is hinged, pulls down to form hand grip; sling swivels, web strap. Made 1958-71.

MODEL 353 AUTOLOADING CARBINE ... NiB $160 Ex $130 Gd $90
Caliber: .22 LR. 7-shot clip magazine. 18-inch bbl. Weight: 5 lbs. Sights: Open rear; ramp front. Monte Carlo stock w/checkered pistol-grip and forearm; black Tenite extension forend pulls down to form hand grip. Made 1972-85.

Mossberg Model 400

Mossberg Model 402

Mossberg Model 472
Brush Gun

Mossberg Model 472
Carbine (Pistol Grip)

Mossberg Model 472
Carbine (Straight Grip)

Mossberg Model 472
"One in Five Thousand"

MODEL 377 PLINKSTER AUTOLOADER . . . NiB $180 Ex $140 Gd $95
Caliber: .22 LR. 15-shot tubular magazine. 20-inch bbl. Weight: 6.25 lbs. 4x scope sight. Thumbhole stock w/rollover cheekpiece, Monte Carlo comb, checkered forearm; molded of modified polystyrene foam in walnut-finish; sling swivel studs. Made 1977-79.

MODEL 380 SEMIAUTOMATIC RIFLE . . . . . NiB $150 Ex $120 Gd $82
Caliber: .22 LR. 15-shot buttstock magazine. 20-inch bbl. Weight: 5.5 lbs. Sights: Open rear; bead front. Made 1980-85.

MODEL 400 PALOMINO LEVER-ACTION . . . . NiB $250 Ex $190 Gd $100
Hammerless. Caliber: .22 Short, Long, LR. Tubular magazine holds 20 Short, 17 Long, 15 LR. 24-inch bbl. Weight: 5.5 lbs. Sights: Open rear; bead front. Monte Carlo stock w/checkered pistol-grip; beavertail forearm. Made 1959-64.

MODEL 402 PALOMINO CARBINE . . . . . . NiB $250 Ex $200 Gd $175
Same as Model 400 except w/18.5-inch (1961-64) or 20-inch bbl. (1964-71), forearm w/bbl. band, swivels; magazine holds two fewer rounds. Weight: 4.75 lbs. Made 1961-71.

MODEL 430 AUTOLOADING RIFLE. . . . . . NiB $144 Ex $115 Gd $78
Caliber: .22 LR. 18-shot tubular magazine. 24-inch bbl. Weight: 6.25 lbs. Sights: Open rear; bead front. Monte Carlo stock w/checkered pistol grip; checkered forearm. Made 1970-71.

MODEL 432 WESTERN-STYLE AUTO . . . . . . NiB $138 Ex $110 Gd $75
Same as Model 430 except w/plain straight-grip carbine-type stock and forearm, bbl. band, sling swivels. Magazine capacity: 15 cartridges. Weight: 6 lbs. Made 1970-71.

GRADING: **NiB** = New in Box   **Ex** = Excellent or NRA 95%   **Gd** = Good or NRA 68%

Mossberg Model 640K
Chuckster

Mossberg Model 640KS

Mossberg Model 640M

Mossberg Model 642K

MODEL 472 BRUSH GUN . . . . **NiB $200 Ex $175 Gd $100**
Same as Model 472 Carbine w/straight-grip stock except w/18-inch
bbl., weight: 6.5 lbs. Caliber: .30-30. Magazine capacity: 5 rounds.
Made 1974-76.

MODEL 472 LEVER-ACTION CARBINE . . . **NiB $180 Ex $150 Gd $100**
Calibers: .30-30, .35 Rem. Six shot tubular magazine. 20-inch bbl.
Weight: 6.75 to 7 lbs. Sights: Open rear; ramp front. Pistol-grip or
straight-grip stock, forearm w/bbl. band; sling swivels on pistol-grip
model saddle ring on straight-grip model. Made 1972-79.

MODEL 472 ONE IN FIVE THOUSAND . . . **NiB $425 Ex $300 Gd $140**
Same as Model 472 Brush Gun except w/Indian scenes etched on
receiver; brass buttplate, saddle ring and bbl. bands, gold-plated
trigger, bright blued finish, select walnut stock and forearm. Limited
edition of 5,000; serial numbered 1 to 5,000. Made in 1974.

MODEL 472 RIFLE. . . . . **NiB $200 Ex $175 Gd $100**
Same as Model 472 Carbine w/pistol-grip stock except w/24-inch
bbl., 5-shot magazine, weight: 7 lbs. Made 1974-76.

MODEL 479
Calibers: .30-30. 6-shot tubular magazine. 20-inch bbl. Weight:
6.75 to 7 lbs. Sights: Open rear; ramp front. Made 1983-85.
Model 479 Rifle . . . . **NiB $190 Ex $175 Gd $120**
Model 479PCA
(Carbine w/20-inch bbl.). . . . . **NiB $190 Ex $175 Gd $120**
Model 479RR
(Roy Rogers, 5000 Ltd. Edition) . . . . **NiB $325 Ex $275 Gd $120**

MODEL 620K HAMMERLESS SINGLE-SHOT
BOLT-ACTION RIFLE. . . . . **NiB $160 Ex $140 Gd $95**
Single shot. Caliber: .22 WMR. 24-inch bbl. Weight: 6 lbs. Sights:
Open rear; bead front. Monte Carlo stock w/cheekpiece, pistol-grip,
sling swivels. Made 1959-60.

MODEL 620K-A. . . . . **NiB $156 Ex $125 Gd $85**
Same as Model 640K except w/sight modification. Made 1960-68.

MODEL 640K CHUCKSTER HAMMERLESS
BOLT-ACTION RIFLE. . . . . **NiB $160 Ex $140 Gd $95**
Caliber: .22 WMR. Five shot detachable clip magazine. 24-inch bbl.
Weight: 6 lbs. Sights: Open rear; bead front. Monte Carlo stock
w/cheekpiece, pistol grip, sling swivels. Made 1959-84.

MODEL 640KS . . . . **NiB $200 Ex $150 Gd $100**
Deluxe version of Model 640K w/select walnut stock hand checkering;
gold-plated front sight, rear sight elevator, and trigger. Made 1960-64.

MODEL 640M. . . . . **NiB $300 Ex $275 Gd $175**
Similar to Model 640K except w/heavy receiver and jeweled bolt. 20-inch
bbl., full length Mannlicher-style stock w/Monte Carlo comb and cheekpiece,
swivels and leather sling. 40.75 inches overall. Weight: 6 lbs. Made 1971-73.

MODEL 642K CARBINE . . . . **NiB $225 Ex $175 Gd $125**
Caliber: .22 WMR. Five shot detachable clip magazine. 18-inch bbl.
Weight: 5 lbs. 38.25 inches overall. Sights: Open rear; bead front.
Monte Carlo walnut stock w/black Tenite forearm extension that
pulls down to form hand grip. Made 1961-68.

Mossberg Model 800

Mossberg Model 800D

Mossberg Model 800M

Mossberg Model 810

Mossberg Model L

Mossberg Model R

MODEL 800 BOLT-ACTION
CENTERFIRE RIFLE . . . . **NiB $219 Ex $175 Gd $119**
.222 Rem., .22-250, .243 Win., .308 Win. Four shot mag., 3-shot in .222. 22-inch bbl. Weight: 7.5 lbs. Sights: Folding leaf rear; ramp front. Monte Carlo stock w/cheekpiece, checkered pistol-grip and forearm, sling swivels. Made 1967-79.

MODEL 800D SUPER GRADE. . . . . **NiB $356 Ex $285 Gd $194**
Deluxe version of Model 800 except w/stock w/rollover comb and cheekpiece, rosewood forend tip and pistol-grip cap. Weight: 6.75 lbs. Chambered for all calibers listed for the Model 800 except for .222 Rem. Sling swivels. Made 1970-73.

MODEL 800M. . . . . **NiB $275 Ex $250 Gd $150**
Same as Model 800 except w/flat bolt handle, 20-inch bbl., Mannlicher-style stock. Weight: 6.5 lbs. Calibers: .22-250, .243 Win., .308 Win. Made 1969-72.

MODEL 800VT VARMINT/TARGET . . . . . . **NiB $225 Ex $175 Gd $125**
Similar to Model 800 except w/24-inch heavy bbl., no sights. Weight: 9.5 lbs. Calibers: .222 Rem., .22-250, .243 Win. Made 1968-79.

MODEL 810 BOLT-ACTION CENTERFIRE RIFLE
Calibers: .270 Win., .30-06, 7mm Rem. Mag., .338 Win. Mag. Detachable box magazine (1970-75) or internal magazine w/hinged floorplate (1972 to date). Capacity: Four shot in .270 and .30-06, 3-shot in Magnums. 22-inch bbl. in .270 and .30-06, 24-inch in Magnums. Weight: 7.5 to 8 lbs. Sights: Leaf rear; ramp front. Stock w/Monte Carlo comb and cheekpiece, checkered pistol-grip and forearm, grip cap, sling swivels. Made 1970-79.
Standard calibers. . . . . **NiB $325 Ex $260 Gd $177**
Magnum calibers. . . . . **NiB $350 Ex $275 Gd $190**

MODEL 1500
MOUNTAINEER
GRADE I CENTERFIRE RIFLE. . . . . . **NiB $375 Ex $300 Gd $225**
Calibers: .223, .243, .270, .30-06, 7mm Mag. 22-inch or 24-inch (7mm Mag.) bbl. Weight: 7 lbs. 10 oz. Hardwood walnut-finished checkered stock. Sights: Hooded ramp front w/gold bead; fully adj. rear. Drilled and tapped for scope mounts. Sling swivel studs. Imported 1986-87.

Musgrave Premier NR5

Musgrave RSA NR1

Musgrave Valiant NR6

Musketeer Mauser Sporter

MODEL 1500 VARMINT BOLT-ACTION RIFLE
Same as Model 1500 Grade I except w/22-inch heavy bbl. Chambered in .222, .22-250, .223 only. High-luster blued finish or Parkerized satin finished stock. Imported from Japan 1986-87.
High-luster blue. . . . . NiB $375 Ex $300 Gd $225
Parkerized satin finish . . . . NiB $394 Ex $315 Gd $214

MODEL 1700LS CLASSIC
HUNTER BOLT-ACTION RIFLE . . . . NiB $425 Ex $350 Gd $225
Same as Model 1500 Grade I except w/checkered classic-style stock and Schnabel forend. Chambered in 243, 270, 30-06 only. Imported from Japan 1986-87.

MODEL B BOLT-ACTION RIFLE . . . . NiB $175 Ex $150 Gd $70
Takedown. Caliber: .22 LR. Long, Short. Single-shot. 22-inch bbl. Sights: Open rear; bead front. Plain pistol-grip stock. Made 1930-32.

MODEL K SLIDE-ACTION REPEATER . . . . . . NiB $180 Ex $125 Gd $80
Hammerless. Takedown. Caliber: .22 LR. Long, Short. Tubular magazine holds 20 Short, 16 Long, 14 LR. 22-inch bbl. Weight: 5 lbs. Sights: Open rear; bead front. Plain, straight-grip stock. Grooved slide handle. Made 1922-31.

MODELS L42A, L43, L45A, L46A-LS
See Models 42A, 43, 45A and 46A-LS respectively; "L" refers to a left-hand version of those rifles.

MODEL L SINGLE-SHOT RIFLE . . . . NiB $431 Ex $345 Gd $235
Martini-type falling-block lever-action. Takedown. Caliber: .22 LR, Long, Short. 24-inch bbl. Weight: 5 lbs. Sights: Open rear; bead front. Plain pistol-grip stock and forearm. Made 1929-32.

MODEL M SLIDE-ACTION REPEATER . . . . NiB $281 Ex $225 Gd $153
Specifications same as for Model K except w/24-inch octagon bbl., pistol-grip stock, weighs 5.5 lbs. Made 1928-31.

MODEL R BOLT-ACTION REPEATER . . . . . NiB $269 Ex $215 Gd $146
Takedown. Caliber: .22 LR, Long, Short. Tubular magazine. 24-inch bbl. Sights: Open rear; bead front. Plain pistol-grip stock. Made 1930-32.

MUSGRAVE RIFLES, MUSGRAVE MFRS. & DIST. (PTY) LTD. — Bloemfontein, South Africa

PREMIER NR5 BOLT-
ACTION HUNTING RIFLE . . . . NiB $430 Ex $350 Gd $225
Calibers: .243 Win., .270 Win., .30-06, .308 Win., 7mm Rem. Mag. Five shot magazine. 25.5-inch bbl. Weight: 8.25 lbs. Furnished w/o sights, but drilled and tapped for scope mount. Select walnut Monte Carlo stock w/cheekpiece, checkered pistol-grip and forearm, contrasting pistol-grip cap and forend tip, recoil pad, swivel studs. Made 1971-76.

Navy Arms .45-70 Mauser

Navy Arms 1873 Carbine

Navy Arms Henry
Lever-Action

Navy Arms Model 1873 Carbine

Navy Arms 1874 Sharps Cavalry Carbine

Navy Arms 1874
Sharps Sniper Rifle

RSA NR1 BOLT-ACTION
SINGLE-SHOT TARGET RIFLE . . . . . NiB $431 Ex $345 Gd $235
Caliber: .308 Win. (7.62mm NATO). 26.4-inch heavy bbl. Weight:
10 lbs. Sights: Aperture receiver; tunnel front. Walnut target stock
w/beavertail forearm, handguard, bbl. band, rubber buttplate, sling
swivels. Made 1971-76.

VALIANT NR6 HUNTING RIFLE . . . NiB $395 Ex $300 Gd $195
Similar to Premier except w/24-inch bbl.; stock w/straight comb,
skip French-style checkering, no grip cap or forend tip. Sights:
Leaf rear; hooded ramp front bead sight. Weight: 7.7lbs. Made
1971-76.

MUSKETEER RIFLES — Washington, D.C.
Mfd. by Firearms International Corp.

MAUSER SPORTER
FN Mauser bolt action. .243, .25-06, .270, .264 Mag., .308, .30-06,
7mm Mag., .300 Win. Mag. Magazine holds 5 standard, 3 Magnum
cartridges. 24-inch bbl. Weight: 7.25 lbs. No sights. Monte Carlo
stock w/checkered pistol-grip and forearm, swivels. Made 1963-72.
Standard Sporter . . . . NiB $375 Ex $325 Gd $195
Deluxe Sporter . . . . NiB $425 Ex $350 Gd $200
Standard Carbine. . . . . NiB $360 Ex $300 Gd $195

Navy Arms
Revolving Carbine

Navy Arms
Rolling Block Baby Carbine

Navy Arms
Rolling Block Buffalo Rifle

NAVY ARMS — Ridgefield, New Jersey

.45-70 MAUSER CARBINE. . . . . NiB $225 Ex $175 Gd $120
Same as .45-70 Mauser Rifle except w/18-inch bbl., straight-grip stock w/low comb, weight: 7.5 lbs. Disc.

.45-70 MAUSER RIFLE. . . . . NiB $200 Ex $160 Gd $109
Siamese Mauser bolt action. Caliber: .45-70 Govt. Three round magazine. 24-0r 26-inch bbl. Weight: 8.5 lbs. w/26-inch bbl. Sights: Open rear; ramp front: Checkered stock w/Monte Carlo comb. Intoduced 1973. Disc.

MODEL 1873 WINCHESTER
BORDER RIFLE . . . . NiB $775 Ex $650 Gd $295
Replica of Winchester Model 1873 Short Rifle. Calibers: .357 Mag., .44-40, and .45 Colt. 20- inch bbl., 39.25 inches overall. Weight: 7.6 lbs. Blued full octagonal barrel, color casehardened receiver w/walnut stocks. Made 1999 to date.

MODEL 1873 CARBINE . . . . NiB $750 Ex $650 Gd $325
Similar to Model 1873 Rifle except w/blued receiver, 10-shot magazine, 19-inch round bbl. carbine-style forearm w/bbl. band, weighs 6.75 lbs. Disc. Reissued in 1991 in 44-40 or 45 Colt.

MODEL 1873 LEVER-ACTION RIFLE . . . . . NiB $750 Ex $675 Gd $350
Replica of Winchester Model 1873. Casehardened receiver. Calibers: .22 LR. .357 Magnum, .44-40. 15-shot magazine. 24-inch octagon bbl. Weight: 8 lbs. Sights: Open rear; blade front. Straight-grip stock, forearm w/end cap. Disc. Reissued in 1991 in .44-40 or .45 Colt w/12-shot magazine. Disc. 1994.

MODEL 1873 TRAPPER'S . . . . NiB $580 Ex $475 Gd $340
Same as Model 1873 Carbine, except w/16.5-inch bbl., 8-shot magazine, weighs 6.25 lbs. Disc.

MODEL 1873 SPORTING CARBINE/RIFLE
Replica of Winchester Model 1873 Sporting Rifle. Calibers: .357 Mag. (24.25-inch bbl. only), .44-40 and .45 Colt. 24.25-inch bbl. (Carbine) or 30-inch bbl. (Rifle). 48.75 to 53 inches overall. Weight: 8.14 to 9.3 lbs. Octagonal barrel, casehardened receiver and checkered walnut pistol-grip. Made 1992 to date.
Carbine model. . . . . NiB $850 Ex $725 Gd $375
Rifle model . . . . NiB $900 Ex $825 Gd $425

MODEL 1874 SHARPS
CAVALRY CARBINE. . . . . NiB $725 Ex $550 Gd $400
Replica of Sharps 1874 Cavalry Carbine. Similar to Sniper Model, except w/22-inch bbl. and carbine stock. Caliber: .45-70. Imported 1994 to date.

MODEL 1874 SHARPS SNIPER RIFLE
Replica of Sharps 1874 Sharpshooter's Rifle. Caliber: .45-70. Falling breech, single-shot. 30-inch bbl. 46.75 inches overall. Weight: 8.5 lbs. Double-set triggers. Color casehardened receiver. Blade front sight; rear sight w/elevation leaf. Polished blued bbl. Military three-band stock w/patch box. Imported 1994 to date.
Infantry model (single trigger) . . . . NiB $1100 Ex $975 Gd $575
Sniper model (double set trigger) . . . . . . NiB $1600 Ex $1400 Gd $675

ENGRAVED MODELS
Yellowboy and Model 1873 rifles are available in deluxe models w/select walnut stocks and forearms and engraving in three grades. Grade "A" has delicate scrollwork in limited areas. Grade "B" is more elaborate with 40 percent coverage. Grade "C" has highest grade engraving. Add to value:
Grade "A" . . . . NiB $219 Ex $175 Gd $119
Grade "B" . . . . NiB $244 Ex $195 Gd $133
Grade "C" . . . . NiB $619 Ex $495 Gd $337

HENRY LEVER-ACTION RIFLE
Replica of the Winchester Model 1860 Henry Rifle. Caliber: .44-40. 12-shot magazine. 16.5-, 22- or 24.25-inch octagon bbl. Weight: 7.5 to 9 lbs. 35.4 to 43.25 inches overall. Sights: Blade front, adjustable ladder rear. European walnut straight grip buttstock w/bbl. and side stock swivels. Imported 1985 to date. Brass or steel receiver. Blued or color casehardened metal.
Carbine model w/22-inch bbl.,
introduced 1992) . . . . NiB $775 Ex $600 Gd $375
Military rifle model (w/brass frame) . . . . . . NiB $775 Ex $600 Gd $375
Trapper model (w/brass frame) . . . . NiB $775 Ex $600 Gd $375
Trapper model (w/iron frame). . . . . NiB $825 Ex $725 Gd $395
W/"A" engraving, add $300
W/"B" engraving, add $500
W/"C" engraving, add $900

Navy Arms
Yellowboy Carbine

MARTINI TARGET RIFLE . . . . **NiB $475 Ex $400 Gd $260**
Martini single-shot action. Calibers: .444 Marlin, .45-70. 26- or 30-inch half-octagon or full-octagon bbl. Weight: 9 lbs. w/26-inch bbl. Sights: Creedmoor tang peep, open middle, blade front. Stock w/cheekpiece and pistol-grip, forearm w/Schnabel tip, both checkered. Intro. 1972. Disc.

REVOLVING CARBINE . . . . **NiB $575 Ex $475 Gd $325**
Action resembles that of Remington Model 1875 Revolver. Casehardened frame. Calibers: .357 Magnum, .44-40, .45 Colt. Six shot cylinder. 20-inch bbl. Weight: 5 lbs. Sights: Open rear; blade front. Straight-grip stock brass trigger guard and buttplate. Intro. 1968. Disc.

ROLLING BLOCK BABY CARBINE . . . . **NiB $219 Ex $175 Gd $119**
Replica of small Remington Rolling Block single-shot action. Casehardened frame, brass trigger guard. Calibers: .22 LR. .22 Hornet, .357 Magnum, .44-40. 20-inch octagon or 22-inch round bbl. Weight: 5 lbs. Sights: Open rear; blade front. Straight-grip stock, plain forearm, brass buttplate. Imported 1968-81.

ROLLING BLOCK BUFFALO CARBINE . . . . **NiB $385 Ex $350 Gd $300**
Same as Buffalo Rifle except w/18-inch bbl., weigh: 10 lbs.

ROLLING BLOCK BUFFALO RIFLE . . . . **NiB $600 Ex $500 Gd $250**
Replica Remington Rolling Block single-shot action. Casehardened frame, brass trigger guard. Calibers: .444 Marlin, .45-70, .50-70. 26- or 30-inch heavy half-octagon or full-octagon bbl. Weight: 11 to 12 lbs. Sights: Open rear; blade front. Straight-grip stock w/brass buttplate, forearm w/brass bbl. band. Made 1971 to date.

ROLLING BLOCK CREEDMOOR RIFLE
Same as Buffalo Rifle except calibers .45-70 and .50-70 only, 28- or 30-inch heavy half-octagon or full-octagon bbl., Creedmoor tang peep sight.
Target model . . . . **NiB $785 Ex $565 Gd $300**
Deluxe target model (disc. 1998) . . . . . . **NiB $1475 Ex $1200 Gd $975**

YELLOWBOY CARBINE . . . . **NiB $531 Ex $425 Gd $289**
Similar to Yellowboy Rifle except w/19-inch bbl., 10-shot magazine (14-shot in 22 Long Rifle), carbine-style forearm. Weight: 6.75 lbs. Disc. Reissued 1991 in .44-40 only.

YELLOWBOY LEVER-ACTION REPEATER . . . . **NiB $625 Ex $500 Gd $300**
Replica of Winchester Model 1866. Calibers: .38 Special, .44-40. 15-shot magazine. 24-inch octagon bbl. Weight: 8 lbs. Sights: Folding leaf rear; blade front. Straight-grip stock, forearm w/end cap. Intro. 1966. Disc. Reissued 1991 in .44-40 only w/12-shot magazine and adj. ladder-style rear sight.

YELLOWBOY TRAPPER'S MODEL . . . . **NiB $556 Ex $445 Gd $303**
Same as Yellowboy Carbine except w/16.5-inch bbl., 8-round magazine, weighs 6.25 lbs. Disc.

NEW ENGLAND FIREARMS — Gardner, Massachusetts

In 1987, New England Firearms was established as an independent company producing selected H&R models under the NEF logo. In 1991, H&R 1871, Inc. was formed from the residual of the parent company and that took over the New England Firearms facility. H&R 1871 produced firearms under both its logo and the NEF brand name until 1999, when the Marlin Firearms Company acquired the assets of H&R 1871.

HANDI-RIFLE
Single-shot, break-open action w/side-lever release. Calibers: .22 Hornet, .22-250, .223, .243, .270, .30-30, .30-06, .45-70. 22-inch bbl. Weight: 7 lbs. Sights: Ramp front; folding rear. Drilled and tapped for scope mounts. Walnut-finished hardwood or synthetic stock. Blued finish. Made 1989 to date.
Calibers: .22-250, .243,
.270 and .30-06 . . . . **NiB $200 Ex $140 Gd $95**
Calibers: .22 Hornet, .223,
.30-30 and .45-70 . . . . **NiB $200 Ex $140 Gd $95**

NEWTON SPORTING RIFLES — Buffalo, New York
Mfd. by Newton Arms Co., Charles Newton Rifles Corp. and Buffalo Newton Rifle Co.

BUFFALO SPORTING RIFLE . . . . **NiB $1250 Ex $1050 Gd $750**
Same general specifications as Standard Model — Second Type. Made c. 1922-32 by Buffalo Newton Rifle Co.

MAUSER SPORTING RIFLE . . . . . **NiB $1200 Ex $1090 Gd $700**
Mauser (Oberndorf) action. Caliber: .256 Newton. Five shot box magazine, hinged floorplate. Double-set triggers. 24-inch bbl. Open rear sight, ramp front sight. Sporting stock w/checkered pistol-grip. Weight: 7 lbs. Made c. 1914 by Newton Arms Co.

STANDARD MODEL
SPORTING RIFLE — FIRST TYPE . . . . **NiB $1150 Ex $975 Gd $590**
Newton bolt action, interrupted screw-type breech-locking mechanism, double-set triggers. Calibers: .22, .256, .280, .30, .33, .35 Newton; .30-06. 24-inch bbl. Sights: Open rear or cocking-piece peep; ramp front. Checkered pistol-grip stock. Weight: 7 to 8 lbs., depending on caliber. Made c. 1916-18 by Newton Arms Co.

STANDARD MODEL
SPORTING RIFLE
SECOND TYPE. . . . . **NiB $919 Ex $735 Gd $500**
Newton bolt action, improved design; distinguished by reversed-set trigger and 1917-Enfield-type bolt handle. Calibers: .256, .30, .35 Newton and .30-06. Five shot box magazine. 24-inch bbl. Sights: Open rear; ramp front. Checkered pistol-grip stock. Weight: 7.75 to 8.25 lbs. Made c. 1921 by Charles Newton Rifle Corp.

RIFLES

Noble Model 10

Noble Model 33

Noble Model 222

Noble Model 236

Noble Model 275

NIKKO FIREARMS, LTD. — Tochiga, Japan

See listings under Golden Eagle Rifles.

NOBLE MFG. CO. — Haydenville, Massachusetts

MODEL 10 BOLT-ACTION
SINGLE-SHOT RIFLE . . . . **NiB $81 Ex $65 Gd $44**
Caliber: .22 LR. Long, Short. 24-inch bbl. Plain pistol-grip stock. Sights: Open rear, bead front. Weight: 4 lbs. Made 1955-58.

MODEL 20 BOLT-ACTION
SINGLE-SHOT RIFLE . . . . **NiB $75 Ex $60 Gd $41**
Manually cocked. Caliber: .22 LR. Long, Short. 22-inch bbl. Weight: 5 lbs. Sights: Open rear; bead front. Walnut stock w/pistol grip. Made 1958-63.

MODEL 33 SLIDE-ACTION REPEATER . . . . **NiB $94 Ex $75 Gd $51**
Hammerless. Caliber: .22 LR. Long, Short. Tubular magazine holds 21 Short, 17 Long, 15 LR. 24-inch bbl. Weight: 6 lbs. Sights: Open rear; bead front. Tenite stock and slide handle. Made 1949-53.

MODEL 33A . . . . **NiB $81 Ex $65 Gd $44**
Same general specifications as Model 33 except w/wood stock and slide handle. Made 1953-55.

MODEL 222 BOLT-ACTION
SINGLE-SHOT RIFLE . . . . **NiB $94 Ex $75 Gd $51**
Manually cocked. Caliber: .22 LR. Long, Short. Barrel integral w/receiver. Overall length: 38 inches. Weight: 5 lbs. Sights: Interchangeable V-notch and peep rear; ramp front. Scope mounting base. Pistol-grip stock. Made 1958-71.

MODEL 236 SLIDE-ACTION
REPEATING RIFLE . . . . **NiB $106 Ex $85 Gd $58**
Hammerless. Caliber: .22 Short, Long, LR. Tubular magazine holds 21 Short, 17 Long, 15 LR. 24-inch bbl. Weight: 5.5 lbs. Sights: Open rear; ramp front. Pistol-grip stock, grooved slide handle. Made 1951 to date.

MODEL 275 LEVER-ACTION RIFLE . . . . **NiB $150 Ex $95 Gd $70**
Hammerless. Caliber: .22 Short, Long, LR. Tubular magazine holds 21 Short, 17 Long, 15 LR. 24-inch bbl. Weight: 5.5 lbs. Sights: Open rear; ramp front. Stock w/semipistol-grip. Made 1958-71.

Parker-Hale
Model 81 Classic

Parker-Hale
Model 87

NORINCO — Mfd. by Northern China Industries Corp., Beijing, China, *Imported by Century International Arms; Interarms; KBI and China Sports, Inc.*

MODEL 81S/AK SEMIAUTOMATIC RIFLE

Semiautomatic Kalashnikov style AK-47 action. Caliber: 7.62x39mm. Five, 30- or 40-shot magazine. 17.5-inch bbl. 36.75 inches overall. Weight: 8.5 lbs. Hooded post front sight, 500 meters leaf rear sight. Oil-finished hardwood (military style) buttstock, pistol grip, forearm and handguard or folding metal stock. Black oxide finish. Imported 1988-89.

Model 81S (w/wood stock)	NiB $975	Ex $725	Gd $500
Model 81S-1 (w/under-folding metal stock)	NiB $1119	Ex $895	Gd $609
Model 81S-5/56S-2 (w/side-folding metal stock)	NiB $994	Ex $795	Gd $541

MODEL 84S/AK SEMIAUTOMATIC RIFLE

Semiautomatic Kalashnikov style AK-47 action. Caliber: .223 (5.56mm). 30-shot magazine. 16.25-inch bbl. 35.5 inches overall. Weight: 8.75 lbs. Hooded post front sight, 800 meters leaf rear sight. Oil-finished hardwood (military style) buttstock, pistol grip, forearm and handguard; sporterized composite fiberglass stock or folding metal stock. Black oxide finish. Imported 1988-89.

Model 84S (w/wood stock)	NiB $556	Ex $445	Gd $303
Model 84S-1 (w/under-folding metal stock)	NiB $688	Ex $550	Gd $374
Model 84S-3 (w/fiberglass stock)	NiB $656	Ex $525	Gd $357
Model 84S-5 (w/side-folding metal stock)	NiB $1119	Ex $895	Gd $609

MODEL AK-47 THUMBHOLE SPORTER

Semiautomatic AK-47 sporterized variant. Calibers: .223 (5.56mm) or 7.62x39mm. Five shot magazine. 16.25-inch bbl. or 23.25-inch bbl. 35.5 or 42.5 inches overall. Weight: 8.5 to 10.3 lbs. Adj. post front sight, open adj. rear. Forged receiver w/black oxide finish. Walnut-finished thumbhole stock w/recoil pad. Imported 1991-93.

Model AK-47 Sporter (5.56mm)	NiB $494	Ex $395	Gd $269
Model AK-47 Sporter (7.62x39mm)	NiB $469	Ex $375	Gd $255

MODEL MAK 90/91 SPORT

Similar to Model AK-47 Thumbhole Sporter except w/minor modifications implemented to meet importation requirements. Imported 1994-95.

Model Mak 90 (w/16.25-inch bbl.)	NiB $475	Ex $400	Gd $275
Model Mak 91 (w/23.25-inch bbl.)	NiB $475	Ex $400	Gd $275

OLYMPIC ARMS — Olympia, Washington

PCR SERIES

Gas-operated semi-auto action. Calibers: .17 Rem., .223, 7.62x39, 6x45, 6PPC or 9mm, .40 S&W, 4.5ACP (in carbine version only). 10-shot magazine. 16-, 20- or 24-inch bbl. Weight: 7 to 10.2 lbs. Black composite stocks. Post front, rear adj. sights; scope ready flat-top. Barrel fluting. William set trigger. Made 1994 to date.

PCR-1/Ultra Match	NiB $960	Ex $850	Gd $500
PCR-2/MultiMatch ML-1	NiB $994	Ex $795	Gd $541
PCR-3/MultiMatch ML-2	NiB $1050	Ex $850	Gd $550
PCR-4/AR-15 Match	NiB $1199	Ex $959	Gd $652
PCR-5/CAR-15 (.223 Rem.)	NiB $960	Ex $700	Gd $425
PCR-5/CAR-15 (9mm, 40S&W, 45ACP)	NiB $800	Ex $695	Gd $450
PCR-5/CAR-15 (.223 Rem.)	NiB $744	Ex $595	Gd $405
PCR-6/A-2 (7.62x39mm)	NiB $781	Ex $625	Gd $425

PARKER-HALE LIMITED — Birmingham, England

MODEL 81 AFRICAN . . . . NiB $875 Ex $700 Gd $450

Same general specifications as Model 81 Classic except in caliber .375 H&H only. Sights: African Express rear; hooded blade front. Barrel-band swivel. All-steel trigger guard. Checkered European walnut stock w/pistol grip and recoil pad. Engraved receiver. Imported 1986-91.

MODEL 81 CLASSIC
BOLT-ACTION RIFLE . . . . NiB $720 Ex $550 Gd $350

Calibers: .22-250, .243 Win., .270 Win., 6mm Rem., 6.5x55, 7x57, 7x64, .308 Win., .30-06, .300 Win. Mag., 7mm Rem. Mag. Four shot magazine. 24-inch bbl. Weight: 7.75 lbs. Sights: Adj. open rear, hooded ramp front. Checkered pistol-grip stock of European walnut. Imported 1984-91.

MODEL 85 SNIPER RIFLE . . . . . . NiB $1750 Ex $1425 Gd $850

Caliber: .308 Win. 10- or 20-shot M-14-type magazine. 24.25-inch bbl. 45 inches overall. Weight: 12.5 lbs. Blade front sight, folding aperture rear. McMillan fiberglass stock w/detachable bipod.

Parker-Hale Model 1100
Lightweight

Parker-Hale Model 1200
Super Clip

MODEL 87 BOLT-ACTION
REPEATING TARGET RIFLE . . . . . NiB $1375 Ex $1100 Gd $650
Calibers: .243 Win., 6.5x55, .308 Win., .30-06 Springfield, .300 Win. Mag. Five shot detachable box magazine. 26-inch bbl. 45 inches overall. Weight: 10 lbs. No sights; grooved for target-style scope mounts. Stippled walnut stock w/adj. buttplate. Sling swivel studs. Parkerized finish. Folding bipod. Imported 1988-91.

MODEL 1000 STANDARD RIFLE . . . . NiB $400 Ex $325 Gd $195
Calibers: .22-250, .243 Win., .270 Win., 6mm Rem., .308 Win., .30-06. Four shot magazine. Bolt action. 22-inch or 24-inch (22-250) bbl. 43 inches overall. 7.25 lbs. Checkered walnut Monte Carlo-style stock w/satin finish. Imported 1984-88.

MODEL 1100 LIGHTWEIGHT
BOLT-ACTION RIFLE . . . . NiB $475 Ex $400 Gd $270
Same general specifications as Model 1000 Standard except w/22-inch lightweight profile bbl., hollow bolt handle, alloy trigger guard and floorplate, 6.5 lbs., Schnabel forend. Imported 1984-91.

MODEL 1100M AFRICAN
MAGNUM RIFLE . . . . NiB $800 Ex $650 Gd $425
Same as Model 1000 Standard except w/24-inch bbl. in calibers .404 Jeffery, .458 Win. Mag. Weight: 9.5 lbs. Sights: Adj. rear; hooded post front. Imported 1984-91.

MODEL 1200 SUPER CLIP
BOLT-ACTION RIFLE . . . . NiB $540 Ex $450 Gd $275
Same as Model 1200 Super except w/detachable box magazine in calibers .243 Win., 6mm Rem., .270 Win. .30-06 and .308 Win., .300 Win. Mag., 7mm Rem. Mag. Imported 1984-91.

MODEL 1200 SUPER BOLT-ACTION
SPORTING RIFLE . . . . NiB $540 Ex $450 Gd $275
Mauser-type bolt action. Calibers: .22-250, .243 Win., 6mm Rem., .25-06, .270 Win., .30-06, .308 Win. Four shot magazine. 24-inch bbl. Weight: 7.25 lbs. Sights: Folding open rear, hooded ramp front. European walnut stock w/rollover Monte Carlo cheekpiece, rosewood forend tip and pistol-grip cap, skip checkering, recoil pad, sling swivels. Imported 1968-91.

MODEL 1200 SUPER MAGNUM . . . . NiB $590 Ex $475 Gd $300
Same general specifications as 1200 Super except calibers 7mm Rem. Mag. and .300 Win. Mag., 3-shot magazine. Imported 1988-91.

MODEL 1200P PRESENTATION . . . . NiB $494 Ex $395 Gd $269
Same general specifications as 1200 Super except w/scroll-engraved action, trigger guard and floorplate, no sights. QD swivels. Calibers: .243 Win. and .30-06. Imported 1969-75.

MODEL 1200V VARMINT . . . . NiB $525 Ex $425 Gd $370
Same general specifications as 1200 Super, except w/24-inch heavy bbl., no sights, weight: 9.5 lbs. Calibers: .22-250, 6mm Rem., .25-06, .243 Win. Imported 1969-89.

MODEL 1300C SCOUT . . . . NiB $700 Ex $600 Gd $475
Calibers: .243, .308 Win. 10-round magazine. 20-inch bbl. w/muzzle brake. 41 inches overall. Weight: 8.5 lbs. No sights, drilled and tapped for scope. Checkered laminated birch stock w/QD swivels. Imported 1991.

MODEL 2100 MIDLAND
BOLT-ACTION RIFLE . . . . NiB $325 Ex $270 Gd $175
Calibers: .22-250, .243 Win., 6mm Rem., .270 Win., 6.5x55, 7x57, 7x64, .308 Win, .30-06. Four shot box magazine. 22-inch or 24-inch (22-250) bbl. 43-inches overall. Weight: 7 lbs. Sights: Adj. folding rear; hooded ramp front. Checkered European walnut Monte Carlo stock w/pistol-grip. Imported 1984-91.

MODEL 2700 LIGHTWEIGHT . . . . NiB $350 Ex $275 Gd $175
Same general specifications as Model 2100 Midland except w/tapered lightweight bbl. and aluminum trigger guard. Weight: 6.5 lbs. Imported 1991.

MODEL 2800 MIDLAND . . . . NiB $300 Ex $250 Gd $150
Same general specifications as model 2100 except w/laminated birch stock. Imported 1991.

PEDERSEN CUSTOM GUNS — North Haven, Connecticut, Division of O.F. Mossberg & Sons, Inc.

MODEL 3000 GRADE I
BOLT-ACTION RIFLE . . . . NiB $994 Ex $795 Gd $541
Richly engraved w/silver inlays, full-fancy American black walnut stock. Mossberg Model 810 action. Calibers: .270 Win., .30-06, 7mm Rem. Mag., .338 Win. Mag. Three shot magazine, hinged floorplate. 22-inch bbl. in .270 and .30-06, 24-inch in Magnums. Weight: 7 to 8 lbs. Sights: Open rear; hooded ramp front. Monte Carlo stock w/roll-over cheekpiece, wraparound hand checkering on pistol grip and forearm, rosewood pistol-grip cap and forend tip, recoil pad or steel buttplate w/trap, detachable swivels. Imported 1973-75.

MODEL 3000 GRADE II . . . . NiB $744 Ex $595 Gd $405
Same as Model 3000 Grade I except less elaborate engraving, no inlays, fancy grade walnut stock w/recoil pad. Imported 1973-75.

MODEL 3000 GRADE III . . . . NiB $619 Ex $495 Gd $337
Same as Model 3000 Grade I except no engraving or inlays, select

Pedersen Model 3000
Grade I Bolt-Action Rifle

Pedersen Model 3000
Grade III

Plainfield M-1 Carbine

MODEL 4700 CUSTOM
DELUXE LEVER-ACTION RIFLE.........NiB $244 Ex $195 Gd $133
Mossberg Model .472 action. Calibers: .30-30, 35 Rem. Five shot tubular magazine. 24-inch bbl. Weight: 7.5 lbs. Sights: Open rear, hooded ramp front. Hand-finished black walnut stock and beavertail forearm, barrel band swivels. Imported 1975.

J.C. PENNEY CO., INC. — Dallas, Texas

Firearms sold under the J.C. Penney label were mfd. by Marlin, High Standard, Stevens, Savage and Springfield.

MODEL 2025 BOLT-ACTION REPEATER.....NiB $70 Ex $40 Gd $35
Takedown. Caliber: .22 RF. 8-shot detachable box magazine. 24-inch bbl. Weight: 6 lbs. Sights: Open rear; bead front. Plain pistol-grip stock. Mfd. by Marlin.

MODEL 2035 BOLT-ACTION REPEATER.....NiB $70 Ex $40 Gd $35
Takedown. Caliber: .22 RF. Eight shot detachable box magazine. 24-inch bbl. Weight: 6 lbs. Sights: Open rear; bead front. Plain pistol-grip stock. Mfd. by Marlin.

MODEL 2935 LEVER-ACTION RIFLE......NiB $175 Ex $140 Gd $90
Same general specifications as Marlin Model 336.

MODEL 6400 BOLT-ACTION
CENTERFIRE RIFLE ....NiB $160 Ex $125 Gd $80
Same general specifications as Savage Model 340.

MODEL 6660
AUTOLOADING RIFLE..................NiB $75 Ex $60 Gd $50
Caliber: .22 RF. Tubular magazine. 22-inch bbl. Weight: 5.5 lbs. Sights: Open rear; hooded ramp front. Plain pistol-grip stock. Mfd. by Marlin.

PLAINFIELD MACHINE COMPANY — Dunellen, New Jersey

M-1 CARBINE ....NiB $175 Ex $130 Gd $95
Same as U.S. Carbine, Cal. .30, M-1 except also available in caliber 5.7mm (.22 caliber w/necked-down .30 Carbine cartridge case). Current production w/ventilated metal handguard and barrel band w/o bayonet lug; earlier models have standard military-type fittings. Made 1960-77.

M-1 CARBINE,
COMMANDO MODEL................NiB $180 Ex $150 Gd $105
Same as M-1 Carbine except w/paratrooper-type stock w/telescoping wire shoulderpiece. Made 1960-77.

M-1 CARBINE, MILITARY SPORTER......NiB $175 Ex $145 Gd $110
Same as M-1 Carbine except w/unslotted buttstock and wood handguard. Made 1960-77.

M-1 DELUXE SPORTER ....NiB $180 Ex $150 Gd $105
Same as M-1 Carbine except w/Monte Carlo sporting stock Made 1960-73.

Polish Model 1929 Mauser

Purdey Double Rifle

Purdey Bolt-Action Rifle

POLISH MILITARY RIFLES — Manufactured by Government Arsenals at Radom and Warsaw, Poland

MODEL 1898 (KARABIN 98, K98)
MAUSER MILITARY CARBINE . . . . Nib $270 Ex $175 Gd $125
Same as German Kar. 98A except for minor details. First manufactured during early 1920s.

MODEL 1898 (KARABIN 98, WZ98A)
MAUSER MILITARY RIFLE . . . . NiB $250 Ex $145 Gd $110
Same as German Kar. 98 used in WWI except for minor details. Manufacture began c. 1921.

MODEL 1929 (KARABIN 29, WZ29)
MAUSER MILITARY RIFLE . . . . NiB $270 Ex $175 Gd $125
Same as Czech Model 24, mfd. 1929 thru WWII except for minor details. A similar model produced during German occupation was designated Gew. 29/40.

WILLIAM POWELL & SON LTD. — Birmingham, England

DOUBLE-BARREL RIFLE . . . . NiB $31,250 Ex $25,000 Gd $17,000
Boxlock. Made to order in any caliber during the time that rifle was manufactured. Bbls.: Made to order in any legal length, but 26 inches recommended. Highest grade French walnut buttstock and forearm w/fine checkering. Metal is elaborately engraved. Imported by Stoeger 1938-51.

BOLT-ACTION RIFLE . . . . NiB $2625 Ex $2100 Gd $1428
Mauser-type bolt action. Calibers: 6x54 through .375 H&H Magnum. Three and 4-shot shot magazine, depending upon chambering. 24-inch bbl. Weight: 7.5 to 8.75 lbs. Sights: Folding leaf rear; hooded ramp front. Cheekpiece stock, checkered forearm and pistol grip, swivels. Imported by Stoeger 1938-51.

JAMES PURDEY & SONS LTD. — London, England

DOUBLE RIFLE
Sidelock action, hammerless, ejectors. Almost any caliber is available but the following are the most popular: .375 Flanged Magnum Nitro Express, .500/465 Nitro Express .470 Nitro Express, .577 Nitro Express. 25.5-inch bbls. (25-inch in .375). Weight: 9.5 to 12.75 lbs. Sights: Folding leaf rear; ramp front. Cheekpiece stock, checkered forearm and pistol-grip, recoil pad, swivels. Currently manufactured to individual measurements and specifications; same general specifications apply to pre-WWII model.
H&H calibers . . . . NiB $69,375 Ex $55,500 Gd $37,740
NE calibers . . . . NiB $85,000 Ex $55,500 Gd $37,774

BOLT-ACTION RIFLE . . . . NiB $22,000 Ex $19,000 Gd $12,000
Mauser-type bolt action. Calibers: 7x57, .300 H&H Magnum, .375 H&H Magnum, 10.75x73. Three shot magazine. 24-inch bbl. Weight: 7.5 to 8.75 lbs. Sights: Folding leaf rear; hooded ramp front. Cheekpiece stock, checkered forearm and pistol-grip, swivels. Currently manufactured; same general specifications apply to pre-WWII model.

RAPTOR ARMS COMPANY, INC. — Newport, New Hampshire

BOLT-ACTION RIFLE
Calibers: .243 Win., .270 Win., .30-06 or .308 Win. Four shot magazine. 22-inch sporter or heavy bbl. Weight: 7.3 to 8 lbs. 42.5 inches overall. No sights w/drilled and tapped receiver or optional blade front, adjustable rear. Blue, stainless or "Taloncote" rust-resistant finish. Checkered black synthetic stock w/Monte Carlo cheepiece and vented recoil pad. Imported 1997 to date.
Raptor Sporter model . . . . NiB $244 Ex $195 Gd $133
Raptor Deluxe Peregrine model (Disc. 1998) . . . . NiB $294 Ex $235 Gd $160
Raptor heavy barrel model . . . . NiB $281 Ex $225 Gd $153
Raptor stainless barrel model . . . . NiB $306 Ex $245 Gd $167

Remington No. 7
Target and Sporting Rifle

REMINGTON ARMS COMPANY — Ilion, New York

To facilitate locating Remington firearms, models are grouped into four categories: Single-shot rifles, bolt-action repeating rifles, slide-action (pump) rifles, and semiautomatic rifles. For a complete listing, please refer to the index.

SINGLE-SHOT RIFLES

NO. 1 SPORTING RIFLE . . . . . . NiB $1850 Ex $1600 Gd $995
Single-Shot, rolling-block action. Calibers: .40-50, .40-70, .44-77, .50-45, .50-70 Gov't. centerfire and .44 Long, .44 Extra Long, .45-70, .46 Long, .46 Extra Long, .50-70 rimfire. Bbl. lengths: 28- or 30-inch part octagon. Weight: 5 to 7.5 lbs. Sights: Folding leaf rear sight; sporting front, dovetail bases. Plain walnut straight stock; flanged-top, semicarbine buttplate. Plain walnut forend with thin, rounded front end. Made 1868 to 1902.

NO. 1 1/2 SPORTING RIFLE . . . . NiB $3500 Ex $3000 Gd $650
Single-Shot, rolling-block action. Calibers: .22 Short, Long, or Extra Long. 25 Stevens, .32, and .38 rimfire cartridges. .32-20, .38-40 and .44-40 centerfire. Bbl. lengths: 24-, 26-, 28- or 30-inch part octagon. Remaining features similar to Remington No. 1. Made from 1869 to 1902.

NO. 2 SPORTING RIFLE
Single-shot, rolling-block action. Calibers: .22, .25, .32, .38, .44 rimfire or centerfire. Bbl. lengths: 24, 26, 28 or 30 inches. Weight: 5 to 6 lbs. Sights: Open rear; bead front. Straight-grip sporting stock and knobtip forearm of walnut. Made 1873-1910.
Calibers: .22, .25, .32 . . . . NiB $800 Ex $600 Gd $275
Calibers: .38, .44 . . . . NiB $850 Ex $625 Gd $300

NO. 3 CREEDMOOR
AND SCHUETZEN RIFLES
. . . . NiB $6875 to $31,250 Ex $55,000 to $25,000 Gd $3740 to $17,000
Produced in a variety of styles and calibers, these are collector's items and bring far higher prices than the sporting types. The Schuetzen Special, which has an under-lever action, is especially rare — perhaps fewer than 100 have been made.

NO. 3 HIGH POWER RIFLE
Single-shot, Hepburn falling-block action w/side lever. Calibers: .30-30, .30-40, .32 Special, .32-40, .38-55, .38-72 (high-power cartridges). Bbl. lengths: 26-, 28-, 30-inch. Weight: About 8 lbs. Open sporting sights. Checkered pistol-grip stock and forearm. Made 1893-1907.
Calibers: .30-30, .30-40,
.32 Special, .32-40 . . . . NiB $2000 Ex $1500 Gd $950
Calibers: .38-55, .38-72 . . . . NiB $2188 Ex $1750 Gd $1190

NO. 3 SPORTING RIFLE . . . . NiB $2500 Ex $2000 Gd $995
Single-shot, Hepburn falling-block action w/side lever. Calibers: .22 WCF, .22 Extra Long, .25-20 Stevens, .25-21 Stevens, .25-25 Stevens, .32 WCF, .32-40 Ballard & Marlin, .32-40 Rem., .38 WCF, .38-40 Rem., 38-

(cont'd.) NO. 3 SPORTING RIFLE
.38-50 Rem., .38-55 Ballard & Marlin, .40-60 Ballard & Marlin, .40-60 WCF, .40-65 Rem. Straight, .40-82 WCF, .45-70 Gov., .45-90 WCF, also was supplied on special order in bottle-necked .40-50, .40-70, .40-90, .44-77, .44-90, .44-105, .50-70 Gov., .50-90 Sharps Straight. Bbl. lengths: 26-inch (22, 25, 32 cal. only), 28-inch, 30-inch; half-octagon or full-octagon. Weight: 8 to 10 lbs. Sights: Open rear; blade front. Checkered pistol-grip stock and forearm. Made 1880 to c. 1911.

NO. 4 SINGLE-SHOT RIFLE . . . . NiB $875 Ex $650 Gd $400
Rolling-block action. Solid frame or takedown. Calibers: .22 Short and Long, .22 LR. .25 Stevens R.F., .32 Short and Long R.F. 22.5-inch octagon bbl., 24-inch available in 32 caliber only. Weight: About 4.5 lbs. Sights: Open rear; blade front. Plain walnut stock and forearm. Made 1890-1933.

NO. 4S MILITARY MODEL 22
SINGLE-SHOT RIFLE . . . . NiB $850 Ex $725 Gd $500
Rolling-block action. Calibers: .22 Short only, .22 LR. only. 28-inch bbl. Weight: About 5 lbs. Sights: Military-type rear; blade front. Military-type stock w/handguard, stacking swivel, sling. Has a bayonet stud on the barrel; bayonet and scabbard were regularly supplied. Note: At one time the Military Model was the official rifle of the Boy Scouts of America and was called the Boy Scout Rifle. Made 1913-33.

NO. 5 SPECIAL SINGLE-SHOT RIFLE
Single-shot, rolling-block action. Calibers: 7mm Mauser, .30-30, .30-40 Krag, .303 British, .32-40, .32 Special, .38-55 (high-power cartridges). Bbl. lengths: 24, 26 and 28 inches. Weight: About 7 lbs. Open sporting sights. Plain straight-grip stock and forearm. Made 1902-18. Note: Models 1897 and 1902 Military Rifles, intended for the export market, are almost identical with the No. 5, except for 30-inch bbl. full military stock and weight (about 8.5 lbs.); a carbine was also supplied. The military rifles were produced in caliber 8mm Lebel for France, 7.62mm Russian for Russia and 7mm Mauser for the Central and South American government trade. At one time, Remington also offered these military models to retail buyers.
Sporting model . . . . NiB $813 Ex $650 Gd $442
Military model . . . . NiB $594 Ex $475 Gd $323

NO. 6 TAKEDOWN RIFLE . . . . NiB $525 Ex $375 Gd $200
Single-shot, rolling-block action. Calibers: .22 Short, .22 Long, .22 LR, .32 Short/Long RF. 20-inch bbl. Weight: Avg. 4 lbs. Sights: Open front and rear; tang peep. Plain straight-grip stock, forearm. Made 1901-33.

NO. 7 TARGET AND SPORTING RIFLE . . . . NiB $2438 Ex $1950 Gd $1326
Single-shot. Rolling-block Army Pistol frame. Calibers: .22 Short, .22 LR. 25-10 Stevens R.F. (other calibers as available in No. 2 Rifle were supplied on special order). Half-octagon bbls.: 24-, 26-, 28-inch. Weight: About 6 lbs. Sights: Lyman combination rear; Beach combination front. Fancy walnut stock and forearm, Swiss buttplate available as an extra. Made 1903-11.

Remington
Model 40X Standard Rimfire

Remington
Model 40-XB Centerfire

Remington
Model 40-XB Rimfire

MODEL 33 BOLT-ACTION
SINGLE-SHOT RIFLE . . . . **NiB $200 Ex $140 Gd $95**
Takedown. Caliber: .22 Short, Long, LR. 24-inch bbl. Weight: About
4.5 lbs. Sights: Open rear, bead front. Plain, pistol-grip stock, forearm with grasping grooves. Made 1931-36.

MODEL 33 NRA
JUNIOR TARGET RIFLE . . . . **NiB $300 Ex $250 Gd $100**
Same as Model 33 Standard except has Lyman peep rear sight,
Partridge-type front sight, 0.88-inch sling and swivels, weighs about
5 lbs.

MODEL 40X
CENTERFIRE RIFLE . . . . **NiB $1200 Ex $750 Gd $325**
Specifications same as for Model 40X Rimfire (heavy weight).
Calibers: .222 Rem., .222 Rem. Mag., 7.62mm NATO, .30-06 (oth-
ers were available on special order). Made 1961-64. Value shown is
for rifle w/o sights.

MODEL 40X HEAVYWEIGHT BOLT-ACTION TARGET RIFLE (RIMFIRE)
Caliber: .22 LR. Single shot. Action similar to Model 722. Click adj.
trigger. 28-inch heavy bbl. Redfield Olympic sights. Scope bases.
High-comb target stock bedding device, adj. swivel, rubber
buttplate. Weight: 12.75 lbs. Made 1955-1964.
With sights. . . . . **NiB $1190 Ex $995 Gd $475**
Without sights . . . . **NiB $1090 Ex $895 Gd $375**

MODEL 40-X SPORTER . . . . **NiB $1563 Ex $1250 Gd $850**
Same general specifications as Model 700 C Custom (see that listing
in this section) except in caliber .22 LR. Made 1972-77.

MODEL 40X STANDARD BARREL
Same as Model 40X Heavyweight except has lighter bbl. Weight:
10.75 lbs.
With sights. . . . . **NiB $700 Ex $540 Gd $200**
Without sights . . . . **NiB $790 Ex $650 Gd $290**

MODEL 40-XB CENTERFIRE MATCH RIFLE .. **NiB $1200 Ex $750 Gd $370**
Bolt-action, single-shot. Calibers: .222 Rem., .222 Rem. Mag.,
.223 Rem., .22-250, 6x47mm, 6mm Rem., .243 Win., .25-06,
7mm Rem. Mag., .30-06, .308 Win. (7.62mm NATO), .30-338,

(cont'd.) **MODEL 40-XB CENTERFIRE MATCH RIFLE**
(7.62mm NATO), .30-338, .300 Win. Mag. 27 25-inch standard or
heavy bbl. Target stock w/adj. front swivel block on guide rail, rubber buttplate. Weight w/o sights: Standard bbl., 9.25 lbs.; heavy
bbl., 11.25 lbs. Value shown is for rifle without sights. Made 1964
to date.

MODEL 40-XB RANGEMASTER CENTERFIRE
Single-shot target rifle with same basic specifications as Model 40-
XB Centerfire Match. Additional calibers in .220 Swift, 6mm BR
Rem. and 7mm BR Rem., and stainless bbl. only. American walnut
or Kevlar (weighs 1 lb. less) target stock with forend stop.
Discontinued 1994.
Model 40-XB right-hand model. . . . . **NiB $994 Ex $795 Gd $541**
Model 40-XB left-hand model. . . . . **NiB $1063 Ex $850 Gd $578**
For 2-oz. trigger, add **$100**
Model 40-XB KS (Kevlar stock, R.H.) . . . . **NiB $1119 Ex $895 Gd $609**
Model 40-XB KS (Kevlar stock, L.H.). . . . . . **NiB $1063 Ex $850 Gd $578**
For 2-oz. trigger, add **$100**
For Repeater model, add. **$100**

MODEL 40-XB RANGEMASTER
RIMFIRE MATCH RIFLE . . . . **NiB $800 Ex $690 Gd $325**
Bolt-action, single-shot. Caliber: .22 LR. 28-inch standard or heavy
bbl. Target stock with adj. front swivel block on guide rail, rubber
buttplate. Weight w/o sights: Standard bbl., 10 lbs.; heavy bbl.,
11.25 lbs. Value shown is for rifle without sights. Made 1964-74.

MODEL 40-XB
VARMINT SPECIAL RIFLE . . . . **NiB $1200 Ex $750 Gd $370**
Same general specifications as Model 40-XB Repeater except has
synthetic stock (Kevlar). Made 1987-94.

MODEL 40-XBBR BENCH REST RIFLE
Bolt action, single shot. Calibers: .222 Rem., .222 Rem. Mag., .223
Rem., 6x47mm, .308 Win. (7.62mm NATO). 20- or 26-inch
unblued stainless-steel bbl. Supplied w/o sights. Weight: With 20-
inch bbl., 9.25 lbs., with 26-inch bbl.,12 lbs. (Heavy Varmint class;
7.25 lbs. w/Kevlar stock (Light Varmint class). Made 1969 to date.
Model 40-XBBR (discontinued) . . . . **NiB $869 Ex $695 Gd $473**
Model 40-XBBR KS (Kevlar stock) . . . . . . **NiB $1119 Ex $895 Gd $609**

Remington
Model 40-XB Varmint Special

Remington
Model 40-XBR

Remington
Model 40-XC

Remington
Model 40-XR Custom Sporter Grade II

Remington
Model 40-XR Rimfire Position Rifle

RIFLES

MODEL 40-XC NATIONAL MATCH COURSE RIFLE

Bolt-action repeater. Caliber: .308 Win. (7.62mm NATO). Five shot magazine, clip slot in receiver. 24-inch bbl. Supplied w/o sights. Weight: 11 lbs. Thumb groove stock w/adj. hand stop and sling swivel, adj. buttplate. Made 1974 to date.

Mdl. 40-XC (wood stock) (disc.) . . . . NiB $870 Ex $650 Gd $425
Mdl. 40-XC KS (Kevlar stk. disc. 1994) . . . NiB $1100 Ex $900 Gd $575

MODEL 40-XR CUSTOM SPORTER RIFLE

Caliber: .22 RF. 24-inch contoured bbl. Supplied w/o sights. Made in four grades of checkering, engraving and other custom features. Made 1987 to date.

Grade I . . . . NiB $1100 Ex $925 Gd $700
Grade II . . . . NiB $1995 Ex $1650 Gd $1000
Grade III . . . . NiB $2900 Ex $2150 Gd $1100
Grade IV . . . . NiB $4875 Ex $4700 Gd $2600

MODEL 40-XR RIMFIRE POSITION RIFLE

Bolt action, single shot. Caliber: .22 LR. 24-inch heavy bbl. Supplied w/o sights. Weight: 10 lbs. Position-style stock w/thumb groove, adj. hand stop and sling swivel on guide rail, adj. buttplate. Made 1974 to date.

Model 40-XR . . . . NiB $1100 Ex $925 Gd $525
Model 40-XR KS (Kevlar stock) . . . . NiB $1200 Ex $995 Gd $600

MODEL 41A TARGETMASTER BOLT-ACTION

SINGLE-SHOT RIFLE . . . . NiB $200 Ex $150 Gd $95
Takedown. Caliber: .22 Short, Long, LR. 27-inch bbl. Weight: About 5.5 lbs. Sights: Open rear; bead front. Plain pistol-grip stock. Made 1936-40.

MODEL 41AS . . . . NiB $200 Ex $150 Gd $95
Same as Model 41A except chambered for .22 Remington Special (.22 W.R.F.).

MODEL 41P . . . . NiB $200 Ex $150 Gd $95
Same as Model 41A except has peep rear sight, hooded front sight.

MODEL 41SB . . . . NiB $180 Ex $125 Gd $100
Same as Model 41A except smoothbore for use with shot cartridges.

MODEL 510A TARGETMASTER

BOLT-ACTION SINGLE-SHOT RIFLE . . . . NiB $156 Ex $125 Gd $85
Takedown. Caliber: 22 Short, Long, LR. 25-inch bbl. Weight: About 5.5 lbs. Sights: Open rear; bead front. Plain pistol-grip stock. Made 1939-62.

MODEL 510P . . . . NiB $168 Ex $135 Gd $93
Same as Model 510A except has peep rear sight, Partridge front on ramp.

Remington
Model 540X

Remington
Model 580

Remington
International Match

Remington
Nylon 10

MODEL 510SB . . . . **NiB $300 Ex $200 Gd $150**
Same as Model 510A except smoothbore for use with shot cartridges, shotgun bead front sight, no rear sight.

MODEL 510X BOLT-ACTION
SINGLE-SHOT RIFLE . . . . **NiB $200 Ex $150 Gd $90**
Same as Model 510A except improved sights. Mfd.1964-66.

MODEL 514 BOLT-ACTION
SINGLE-SHOT . . . . **NiB $150 Ex $125 Gd $90**
Takedown. Caliber: .22 Short, Long, LR. 24-inch bbl. Weight: 4.75
lbs. Sights: Open rear; bead front. Plain pistol-grip stock. Made
1948-71.

MODEL 514BC BOY'S CARBINE . . . . **NiB $160 Ex $130 Gd $95**
Same as Model 514 except has 21-inch bbl., 1-inch shorter stock.
Made 1961-71.

MODEL 514P . . . . **NiB $160 Ex $130 Gd $95**
Same as Model 514 except has receiver peep sight.

MODEL 540-X RIMFIRE TARGET RIFLE . . . **NiB $325 Ex $250 Gd $100**
Bolt-action, single-shot. Caliber: .22 R. 26-inch heavy bbl. Supplied
w/o sights. Weight: About 8 lbs. Target stock w/Monte Carlo cheekpiece and thumb groove, guide rail for hand stop and swivel, adj.
buttplate. Made 1969-74.

MODEL 540-XR POSITION RIFLE . . . . **NiB $350 Ex $275 Gd $150**
Bolt-action, single-shot. Caliber: .22 LR. 26-inch medium-weight bbl.
Supplied w/o sights. Weight: 8 lbs., 13 oz. Position-style stock w/thumb
groove, guide rail for hand stop and swivel, adj. buttplate. Made 1974-84.

MODEL 540-XRJR . . . . **NiB $350 Ex $275 Gd $150**
Same as Model 540-XR except 1.75-inch shorter stock. Made
1974-84.

MODEL 580 BOLT-ACTION
SINGLE-SHOT . . . . **NiB $150 Ex $120 Gd $82**
Caliber: .22 Short, Long, LR. 24-inch bbl. Weight: 4.75 lbs. Sights:
Bead front; U-notch rear. Monte Carlo stock. Made 1967-78.

MODEL 580BR BOY'S RIFLE . . . . **NiB $163 Ex $130 Gd $88**
Same as Model 580 except w/1-inch shorter stock. Made 1971-78.

MODEL 580SB SMOOTH BORE . . . **NiB $219 Ex $175 Gd $119**
Same as Model 580 except smooth bore for .22 Long Rifle shot cartridges. Made 1967-78.

INTERNATIONAL FREE RIFLE . . . . . **NiB $950 Ex $700 Gd $400**
Same as Model 40-XB rimfire and centerfire except has free rifle-
type stock with adj. buttplate and hook, adj. palm rest, movable
front sling swivel, 2-oz. trigger. Weight: About 15 lbs. Made
1964-74. Value shown is for rifle with professionally finished
stock, no sights.

INTERNATIONAL MATCH FREE RIFLE . . . **NiB $1000 Ex $875 Gd $475**
Calibers: .22 LR, .222 Rem., .222 Rem. Mag., 7.62mm NATO, .30-
06 (others were available on special order). Model 40X-type bolt-
action, single-shot. 2-oz. adj. trigger. 28-inch heavy bbl. Weight:
About 15.5 lbs. Free rifle-style stock with thumbhole (furnished
semifinished by mfr.); interchangeable and adj. rubber buttplate and
hook buttplate, adj. palm rest, sling swivel. Made 1961-64. Value
shown is for rifle with professionally-finished stock, no sights.

Remington Model 7

Remington Model Seven FS

Remington Model Seven
KS Custom Rifle

NYLON 10 BOLT-ACTION
SINGLE-SHOT RIFLE . . . . **NiB $150 Ex $125 Gd $95**
Caliber: .22 Short, Long, LR. 19.13-inch bbl. Weight: 4.25 lbs. Open rear sight; ramped blade front. Receiver grooved for scope mount. Brown nylon stock. Made 1962-1966.

BOLT-ACTION REPEATING RIFLES

MODEL SEVEN (7) CF BOLT-ACTION RIFLE
Calibers: .17 Rem., .222 Rem., .223 Rem., .243 Win., 6mm Rem., 7mm-08 Rem., .308 Win. Magazine capacity: 5-shot in .17 Rem., .222 Rem., .223 Rem., 4-shot in other calibers. 18.5-inch bbl. Weight: 6.5 lbs. Walnut stock checkering, and recoil pad. Made 1983 to date. .223 Rem. added in 1984.
Standard calibers except
.17 Rem. & .222 Rem. . . . . **NiB $450 Ex $375 Gd $250**
Caliber .17 Rem & .222 Rem. . . . . **NiB $475 Ex $395 Gd $260**

MODEL SEVEN (7)
FS RIFLE. . . . . **NiB $531 Ex $425 Gd $289**
Calibers: .243, 7mm-08 Rem., .308 Win. 18.5-inch bbl. 37.5 inches overall. Weight: 5.25 lbs. Hand layup fiberglass stock, reinforced with DuPont Kevlar at points of bedding and stress. Made 1987-90.

MODEL SEVEN (7) KS RIFLE . . . . . . **NiB $775 Ex $625 Gd $400**
Calibers: .223 Rem., 7mm-08, .308, .35 Rem. and .350 Rem. Mag. 20-inch bbl. Custom-made in Remington's Custom Shop with Kevlar stock. Made 1987 to date.

MODEL SEVEN (7) LS RIFLE . . . . . . **NiB $500 Ex $425 Gd $250**
Calibers: .223 Rem., .243 Win., .260 Rem., 7mm-08 and 308 Win. 20-inch matte bbl. Laminated hardwood stock w/matte brown finish. Weight: 6.5 lbs. Made 2000 to date.

MODEL SEVEN (7) LSS RIFLE . . . . . **NiB $550 Ex $425 Gd $275**
Similar to Model 7 LS except stainless bbl. w/o sights. Calibers: .22-250 Rem., .243 Win. or 7mm-08. Made 2000 to date.

MODEL SEVEN (7) MS CUSTOM RIFLE . . . **NiB $950 Ex $825 Gd $475**
Similar to the standard Model 7 except fitted with a laminated full Mannlicher-style stock. Weight: 6.75 lbs. Calibers: .222 Rem., .22-250, .243, 6mm Rem.,7mm-08, .308, .350 Rem. Additional calibers available on special order. Made 1993 to date.

MODEL SEVEN (7) SS RIFLE . . . . . . **NiB $525 Ex $400 Gd $275**
Same as Model 7 except 20-inch stainless bbl., receiver and bolt; black synthetic stock. Calibers: .243, 7mm-08 or .308. Made 1994 to date.

MODEL SEVEN (7) YOUTH RIFLE. . . . . . . **NiB $350 Ex $300 Gd $225**
Similar to the standard Model 7 except fitted with hardwood stock with a 12.19-inch pull. Calibers: .243, 6mm, 7mm-08 only. Made 1993 to date.

MODEL 30A BOLT-ACTION
EXPRESS RIFLE. . . . . **NiB $556 Ex $445 Gd $303**
Standard Grade. Modified M/1917 Enfield Action. Calibers: .25, .30, .32 and .35 Rem., 7mm Mauser, .30-06. Five shot box magazine. 22-inch bbl. Weight: About 7.25 lbs. Sights: Open rear; bead front. Walnut stock w/checkered pistol grip and forearm. Made 1921-40. Note: Early Model 30s had a slender forend with Schnabel tip, military-type double-pull trigger.

MODEL 30R CARBINE . . . . **NiB $569 Ex $475 Gd $355**
Same as Model 30A except has 20-inch bbl., plain stock weighs about 7 lbs.

MODEL 30S SPORTING RIFLE . . . . **NiB $681 Ex $545 Gd $371**
Special Grade. Same action as Model 30A. Calibers: .257 Roberts, 7mm Mauser, .30-06. Five shot box magazine. 24-inch bbl. Weight: About 8 lbs. Lyman No. 48 Receiver sight, bead front sight. Special high comb stock with long, full forearm, checkered. Made 1930-40.

MODEL 34 BOLT-ACTION REPEATER. . . . . . **NiB $150 Ex $125 Gd $90**
Takedown. Caliber: .22 Short, Long, LR. Tubular magazine holds 22 Short, 17 Long or 15 LR. 24-inch bbl. Weight: 5.25 lbs. Sights: Open rear; bead front. Plain, pistol-grip stock, forearm w/grasping grooves. Made 1932-36.

Remington Model 30A

Remington Model 30R

Remington Model 30S

Remington Model 34

Remington Model 37 (1937)

Remington Model 37 (1940)

MODEL 34 NRA TARGET RIFLE . . . . NiB $400 Ex $325 Gd $200
Same as Model 34 Standard except has Lyman peep rear sight, Partridge-type front sight, .88-inch sling and swivels, weight: About 5.75 lbs.

MODEL 37 RANGEMASTER BOLT-ACTION TARGET RIFLE (I)
Model of 1937. Caliber: .22 LR. Five shot box magazine, single shot adapter also supplied as standard equipment. 28-inch heavy bbl. Weight: About 12 lbs. Remington front and rear sights, scope bases. Target stock, swivels, sling. Note: Original 1937 model had a stock with outside bbl. band similar in appearance to that of the old-style Winchester Model 52, forearm design was modified and bbl. band eliminated in 1938. Made 1937-40.
With factory sights . . . . NiB $550 Ex $425 Gd $300
Without sights . . . . NiB $475 Ex $400 Gd $225

MODEL 37 RANGEMASTER BOLT-ACTION TARGET RIFLE (II)
Model of 1940. Same as Model of 1937 except has "Miracle" trigger mechanism and Randle-design stock with high comb, full pistol-grip and wide beavertail forend. Made 1940-54.
With factory sights . . . . NiB $688 Ex $550 Gd $374
Without sights . . . . NiB $494 Ex $395 Gd $269

MODEL 40-XB
CENTERFIRE REPEATER. . . . . NiB $1044 Ex $835 Gd $568
Same as Model 40-XB Centerfire except 5-shot repeater. Calibers: .222 Rem., .222 Rem. Mag., .223 Rem., .22-250, 6x47mm, 6mm Rem., .243 Win., .308 Win. (7.62mm NATO). Heavy bbl. only. Discontinued.

MODEL 78 SPORTSMAN
BOLT-ACTION RIFLE . . . . NiB $281 Ex $225 Gd $153
Similar to Model 700 ADL except with straight-comb walnut-finished hardwood stock in calibers .223 Rem., .243 Win., .270 Win., .30-06 Springfield and .308 Win. 22-inch bbl. Weight: 7 lbs. Adj. sights. Made 1984-91.

MODEL 341A SPORTSMASTER
BOLT-ACTION REPEATER . . . . NiB $169 Ex $135 Gd $92
Takedown. Caliber: .22 Short, Long, LR. Tubular magazine holds 22 Short, 17 Long, 15 LR. 27-inch bbl. Weight: About 6 lbs. Sights: Open rear; bead front. Plain pistol-grip stock. Made 1936-40.

Remington Model 511X

Remington Model 512A

Remington Model 513S

Remington Model 513TR

MODEL 341P . . . . NiB $194 Ex $155 Gd $105
Same as Model 341A except has peep rear sight, hooded front sight.

MODEL 341SB . . . . NiB $200 Ex $225 Gd $150
Same as Model 341A except smoothbore for use with shot cartridges.

MODEL 511A SCOREMASTER BOLT-ACTION
BOX MAGAZINE REPEATER . . . . NiB $181 Ex $145 Gd $99
Takedown. Caliber: 22 Short, Long, LR. Six shot detachable box magazine. 25-inch bbl. Weight: About 5.5 lbs. Sights: Open rear; bead front. Plain pistol-grip stock. Made 1939-62.

MODEL 511P . . . . NiB $188 Ex $150 Gd $102
Same as Model 511A except has peep rear sight, Partridge-type blade front on ramp.

MODEL 511X BOLT-ACTION REPEATER . . NiB $194 Ex $155 Gd $105
Clip type. Same as Model 511A except improved sights. Made 1964-66.

MODEL 512A SPORTSMASTER
BOLT-ACTION REPEATER . . . . NiB $169 Ex $135 Gd $92
Takedown. Caliber: .22 Short, Long, LR. Tubular magazine holds 22 Short, 17 Long, 15 LR. 25-inch bbl. Weight: About 5.75 lbs. Sights: Open rear; bead front. Plain pistol-grip stock w/semibeavertail forend. Made 1940-62.

MODEL 512P . . . . NiB $219 Ex $175 Gd $119
Same as Model 512A except has peep rear sight, blade front, on ramp.

MODEL 512X BOLT-ACTION REPEATER . . NiB $231 Ex $185 Gd $126
Tubular magazine type. Same as Model 512A except has improved sights. Made 1964-66.

MODEL 513S BOLT-ACTION RIFLE . . . . . NiB $500 Ex $450 Gd $275
Caliber: .22 LR. Six shot detachable box magazine. 27-inch bbl. Weight: About 6.75 lbs. Marble open rear sight, Partridge-type front. Checkered sporter stock. Made 1941-56.

MODEL 513TR MATCHMASTER
BOLT-ACTION TARGET RIFLE . . . . NiB $331 Ex $265 Gd $180
Caliber: .22 LR. Six shot detachable box magazine. 27-inch bbl. Weight: About 9 lbs. Sights: Redfield No. 75 rear; globe front. Target stock. Sling and swivels. Made 1941-69.

MODEL 521TL JUNIOR TARGET
BOLT-ACTION REPEATER . . . . NiB $294 Ex $235 Gd $160
Takedown. Caliber: .22 LR. Six shot detachable box magazine. 25-inch bbl. Weight: About 7 lbs. Sights: Lyman No. 57RS rear; dovetailed blade front. Target stock. Sling and swivels. Made 1947-69.

MODEL 522 VIPER . . . . NiB $150 Ex $100 Gd $75
Calibers: .22 LR. 10-shot magazine. 20-inch bbl. 40 inches overall. Weight: 4.63 lbs. Checkered black PET resin stock with beavertail forend. Dupont high-tech synthetic lightweight receiver. Matte black finish on all exposed metal. Made 1993 to date.

MODEL 541-S CUSTOM SPORTER . . . . . . NiB $688 Ex $550 Gd $374
Bolt-action repeater. Scroll engraving on receiver and trigger guard. Caliber: .22 Short, Long, LR. 5-shot clip magazine. 24-inch bbl. Weight: 5.5 lbs. Supplied w/o sights. Checkered walnut stock w/rosewood-finished forend tip, pistol-grip cap and buttplate. Made 1972-84.

MODEL 541-T BOLT-ACTION RIFLE
Caliber: .22 RF. Clip-fed, Five shot. 24-inch bbl. Weight: 5.88 lbs. Checkered walnut stock. Made 1986 to date; heavy bbl. model intro. 1993.
Model 541-T Standard . . . . NiB $400 Ex $275 Gd $160
Model 541-T-HB heavy bbl. . . . . NiB $425 Ex $300 Gd $215

Remington Model 521TL

Remington Model 541-S

Remington Model 581-S

MODEL 581 CLIP REPEATER
Same general specifications as Model 580 except has 5-shot clip magazine. Made 1967-84.
Model 581...........................NiB $156 Ex $125 Gd $85
Model 581 left hand
(made 1969-1984) ....NiB $188 Ex $150 Gd $102

MODEL 581-S BOLT-ACTION RIFLE.....NiB $175 Ex $150 Gd $100
Caliber: .22 RF. Clip-fed, 5-shot. 24-inch bbl. Weight: 4.75 lbs. Plain walnut-colored stock. Made 1987-92.

MODEL 582 TUBULAR REPEATER ....NiB $163 Ex $130 Gd $88
Same general specifications as Model 580 except has tubular magazine holding 20 Short,15 Long,14 LR. Weight: About 5 lbs. Made 1967-84.

MODEL 591 BOLT-ACTION
CLIP REPEATER.....................NiB $244 Ex $195 Gd $133
Caliber: 5mm Rimfire Magnum. Four shot clip magazine. 24-inch bbl. Weight: 5 lbs. Sights: Bead front; U-notch rear. Monte Carlo stock. Made 1970-73.

MODEL 592 TUBULAR REPEATER ....NiB $181 Ex $145 Gd $99
Same as Model 591 except has tubular magazine holding 10 rounds, weight: 5.5 lbs. Made 1970-73.

MODEL 600 BOLT-ACTION CARBINE
Calibers: .222 Rem., .223 Rem., .243 Win., 6mm Rem., .308 Win., 35 Rem., 5-shot magazine (6-shot in .222 Rem.) 18.5-inch bbl. with ventilated rib. Weight: 6 lbs. Sights: Open rear; blade ramp front. Monte Carlo stock w/pistol-grip. Made 1964-67.
.222 Rem. ....NiB $800 Ex $725 Gd $425
.223 Rem....................NiB $1313 Ex $1050 Gd $714
.35 Rem....................NiB $781 Ex $625 Gd $425
Standard calibers..............NiB $619 Ex $495 Gd $337

MODEL 600 MAGNUM ....NiB $994 Ex $795 Gd $541
Same as Model 600 except calibers 6.5mm Mag. and .350 Rem. Mag., 4-shot magazine, special Magnum-type bbl. with bracket for scope back-up, laminated walnut and beech stock w/recoil pad. QD swivels and sling; weight: About 6.5 lbs. Made 1965-67.

MODEL 600 MONTANA
TERRITORIAL CENTENNIAL $750
Same as Model 600 except has commemorative medallion embedded in buttstock. Made 1964. Value is for rifle in new, unfired condition.

MODEL 660 STP
Calibers: .222 Rem., 6mm Rem., .243 Win., .308 Win., 5-shot magazine. (6-shot in .222 Rem.) 20-inch bbl. Weight: 6.5 lbs. Sights: Open rear; bead front on ramp. Monte Carlo stock, checkered, black pistol-grip cap and forend tip. Made 1968-71.
.222 Rem.....................NiB $606 Ex $485 Gd $330
Other calibers ....NiB $563 Ex $450 Gd $306

MODEL 660 MAGNUM ....NiB $850 Ex $675 Gd $550
Same as Model 660 except calibers 6.5mm Rem. Mag. and .350 Rem. Mag., 4-shot magazine, laminated walnut-and-beech stock with recoil pad. QD swivels and sling. Made 1968-71.

MODEL 700 ADL CENTERFIRE RIFLE.....NiB $375 Ex $295 Gd $195
Calibers: .22-250, .222 Rem., .25-06, 6mm Rem., .243 Win., .270 Win., .30-06, .308 Win., 7mm Rem. Mag. Magazine capacity: 6-shot in .222 Rem.; 4-shot in 7mm Rem. Mag. Five shot in other calibers. Bbl. lengths: 24-inch in .22-250, .222 Rem., .25-06, 7mm Rem. Mag.; 22-inch in other calibers. Weight: 7 lbs. standard; 7.5 lbs. in 7mm Rem. Mag. Sights: Ramp front; sliding ramp open rear. Monte Carlo stock w/cheekpiece, skip checkering, recoil pad on Magnum. Laminated stock also avail. Made 1962-93.

MODEL 700 APR BOLT-ACTION RIFLE .. NiB $1188 Ex $950 Gd $646
Acronym for African Plains Rifle. Calibers: 7mm Rem. Mag., 7mm STW, 300 Win. Mag., 300 Wby. Mag., 300 Rem. Ultra Mag., 338 Win. Mag., 375 H&H. Three shot magazine. 26-inch bbl. on a magnum action. 46.5 inches overall. Weight: 7.75 lbs. Matte blue finish. Checkered classic-style laminated wood stock w/black magnum recoil pad. Made 1994 to date.

MODEL 700 AS BOLT-ACTION RIFLE
Similar to the Model 700 BDL except with nonreflective matte black metal finish, including the bolt body. Weight: 6.5 lbs. Straight comb synthetic stock made of Arylon, a fiberglass-reinforced thermoplastic resin with nonreflective matte finish. Made 1988-92.
Standard caliber ....NiB $456 Ex $365 Gd $248
Magnum caliber ....NiB $494 Ex $395 Gd $269

Remington Model 581

Remington Model 581-S

Remington Model 582

Remington Model 591

Remington Model 592

Remington Model 600

Remington Model 600
Montana Territorial Centennial

Remington Model 660

Remington Model 700 ADL

RIFLES

**Remington Model 700
ADL w/Laminated Stock**

**Remington
Model 700 ADL Left Hand**

MODEL 700 AWR
BOLT-ACTION RIFLE . . . . NiB $1300 Ex $1100 Gd $950
Acronym for Alaskan Wilderness Rifle, similar to Model 700 APR except w/24-inch stainless bbl. and black chromed action. Matte gray or black Kevlar stock w/straight comb and raised cheekpiece fitted w/black magnum recoil pad. Made 1994 to date.

MODEL 700 BDL CENTERFIRE RIFLE
Same as Model 700 ADL except has hinged floorplate hooded ramp front sight, stock w/black forend tip and pistol-grip cap, cut checkering, QD swivels and sling. Additional calibers: .17 Rem., .223 Rem., .264 Win. Mag., 7mm-08, .280, .300 Sav., .300 Win. Mag., 8mm Rem. Mag., .338 Win. Mag., .35 Whelen. All have 24-inch bbls. Magnums have 4-shot magazine, recoil pad, weighs 7.5 lbs; .17 Rem. has 6-shot magazine, weighs 7 lbs. Made 1962 to date. Made 1973 to date.
Standard calibers except .17 Rem. . . . . . . NiB $481 Ex $385 Gd $262
Magnum calibers and .17 Rem. . . . . NiB $544 Ex $435 Gd $296
Left-hand, .270 Win. and .30-06 . . . . NiB $494 Ex $395 Gd $269
Left-hand, 7mm
Rem. Mag and .222 Rem. . . . . NiB $550 Ex $475 Gd $400

MODEL 700 BDL EUROPEAN RIFLE
Same general specifications as Model 700 BDL, except has oil-finished walnut stock. Calibers: .243, .270, 7mm-08, 7mm Mag., .280 Rem., .30-06. Made 1993-95.
Standard calibers . . . . NiB $500 Ex $400 Gd $275
Magnum calibers . . . . NiB $500 Ex $450 Gd $350

MODEL 700 BDL SS BOLT-ACTION RIFLE
Same as Model 700 BDL except w/24-inch stainless bbl., receiver and bolt plus black synthetic stock. Calibers: .223 Rem., .243 Win., 6mm Rem., .25-06 Rem., .270 Win. .280 Rem., 7mm-08, 7mm Rem. Mag., 7mm Wby. Mag., .30-06, .300 Win., .308 Win., .338 Win. Mag. .375 H&H. Made 1992 to date.
Standard calibers . . . . NiB $550 Ex $475 Gd $280
Magnum calibers, add $80
DM (detachable magazine), add $40
DM-B (muzzle brake), add $90

MODEL 700 BDL
VARMINT SPECIAL . . . . NiB $500 Ex $400 Gd $270
Same as Model 700 BDL except has 24-inch heavy bbl., no sights, weighs 9 lbs. (8.75 lbs. in 308 Win.). Calibers: .22-250, .222 Rem., .223 Rem., .25-06, 6mm Rem., .243 Win., .308 Win. Made 1967-94.

REMINGTON MODEL 700 CS BOLT-ACTION RIFLE
Similar to Model 700 BDL except with nonreflective matte black metal finish, including the bolt body. Straight comb synthetic stock camouflaged in Mossy Oak Bottomland pattern. Made 1992-94.
Standard calibers . . . . NiB $494 Ex $395 Gd $269
Magnum calibers . . . . NiB $531 Ex $425 Gd $289

MODEL 700 CLASSIC
Same general specifications as Model 700 BDL except has "Classic" stock of high-quality walnut with full-pattern cut-checkering, special satin wood finish; Schnabel forend. Brown rubber buttpad. Hinged floorplate. No sights. Weight: 7 lbs. Also chambered for "Classic" cartridges such as .257 Roberts and .250-3000. Intro. 1981.
Standard calibers . . . . NiB $500 Ex $350 Gd $250
Magnum calibers . . . . NiB $550 Ex $400 Gd $270

MODEL 700 CUSTOM BOLT-ACTION RIFLE
Same general specifications as Model 700 BDL except custom-built; available in choice of grades, each with higher quality wood, different checkering patterns, engraving, high-gloss blued finish. Introduced in 1965.
Model 700 C Grade I . . . . NiB $1188 Ex $950 Gd $646
Model 700 C Grade II . . . . NiB $2063 Ex $1650 Gd $1122
Model 700 C Grade III . . . . NiB $2688 Ex $2150 Gd $1462
Model 700 C Grade IV . . . . NiB $4938 Ex $3950 Gd $2686
Model 700 D Peerless . . . . NiB $1744 Ex $1395 Gd $949
Model 700 F Premier . . . . NiB $3319 Ex $2655 Gd $1805

MODEL 700 FS BOLT-ACTION RIFLE
Similar to Model 700 ADL except with straight comb fiberglass stock reinforced with DuPont Kevlar, finished in gray or gray camo with Old English-style recoil pad. Made 1987-89.
Standard calibers . . . . NiB $560 Ex $500 Gd $300
Magnum calibers . . . . NiB $600 Ex $500 Gd $350

MODEL 700 KS CUSTOM MOUNTAIN RIFLE
Similar to standard Model 700 MTN Rifle, except with custom Kevlar reinforced resin synthetic stock with standard or wood-grain finish. Calibers: .270 Win., .280 Rem., 7mm Rem Mag., .30-06, .300 Win., .300 Wby. Mag., 8mm Rem. Mag., .338 Win. Mag., .35 Whelen, .375 H&H. Four shot magazine. 24-inch bbl. Weight: 6.75 lbs. Made 1986 to date.
Standard KS stock (disc. 1993) . . . . NiB $1025 Ex $850 Gd $450
Wood-grain KS stock . . . . NiB $950 Ex $725 Gd $493
SS Model Stainless Synthetic (1995-97) . . NiB $1156 Ex $965 Gd $720
Left-hand model, add $75

Remington Model 700 APR

Remington Model 700 BDL

Remington Model 700 BDL Magnum

Remington Model 700 Classic

Remington Model 700 Custom Grade I

Remington Model 700 Custom Grade II

Remington Model 700 Custom Grade III

Remington Model 700 Custom Grade IV

Remington Model 700 FS

RIFLES

Remington Model 700 KS
Custom Mountain Rifle

Remington Model 700
Mountain Rifle Deluxe

Remington Model 700 RS

Remington Model 700 Sendero

Remington Model 700 Safari

MODEL 700 LS BOLT-ACTION RIFLE
Similar to Model 700 ADL except with checkered Monte Carlo-style laminated wood stock with alternating grain and wood color, impregnated with phenolic resin and finished with a low satin luster. Made 1988-93
Standard calibers . . . . NiB $550 Ex $450 Gd $300
Magnum calibers . . . . NiB $575 Ex $460 Gd $325

MODEL 700 LSS BOLT-ACTION RIFLE
Similar to Model 700 BDL except with stainless steel barrel and action. Checkered Monte Carlo-style laminated wood stock with alternating grain and gray tinted color impregnated with phenolic resin and finished with a low satin luster. Made 1996 to date.
Standard calibers . . . . NiB $550 Ex $475 Gd $325
Magnum calibers . . . . NiB $600 Ex $525 Gd $350

MODEL 700 MTN RIFLE
Lightweight version of Model 700. Calibers: .243 Win., .25-06, .257 Roberts, .270 Win., 7x57, 7mm-08 Rem., .280 Rem., .30-06 and .308 Win. Four shot magazine. 22-inch bbl. Weight: 6.75 lbs. Satin blue or stainless finish. Checkered walnut stock and redesigned pistol grip, straight comb, contoured cheekpiece, Old English-style recoil pad and satin oil finish or black synthetic stock with pressed checkering and blind magazine. Made 1986 to date.

(cont'd.) MODEL 700 MOUNTAIN RIFLE
Standard w/blind magazine . . . . NiB $450 Ex $350 Gd $225
Standard w/hinged floorplate (disc. 1994) . NiB $508 Ex $420 Gd $308
DM Model (New 1995) . . . . NiB $560 Ex $450 Gd $300
SS Model stainless synthetic (disc. 1993) . . NiB $460 Ex $350 Gd $250

MODEL 700 RS BOLT-ACTION RIFLE
Similar to the Model 700 BDL except with straight comb DuPont Rynite stock finished in gray or gray camo with Old English style recoil pad. made 1987-90.
Standard calibers . . . . NiB $550 Ex $450 Gd $300
Magnum calibers . . . . NiB $575 Ex $450 Gd $325
.280 Rem. calibers (Limited production) . . . NiB $688 Ex $550 Gd $374

MODEL 700 SAFARI GRADE
Big game heavy magnum version of the Model 700 BDL. 8mm Rem. Mag., .375 H&H Mag., .416 Rem. Mag. and .458 Win. Mag. 24-inch heavy bbl. Weight: 9 lbs. Blued or stainless finish. Checkered walnut stock in synthetic/Kevlar stock with standard matte or wood-grain finish with old English style recoil pad. made 1962 to date.
Safari Classic/Monte Carlo . . . . NiB $1025 Ex $900 Gd $475
Safari KS (Kevlar stock) intro. 1989 . . . . . NiB $1194 Ex $995 Gd $741
Safari KS (Wood-grain) intro. 1992 . . . . . . NiB $1113 Ex $900 Gd $628
Safari KS SS (Stainless) intro. 1993 . . . . . NiB $1388 Ex $1150 Gd $846
Safari left-hand, add $95

Remington Model 721A Deluxe

Remington Model 722A

MODEL 700 SENDERO BOLT-ACTION RIFLE
Same as Model 700 VS except chambered in long action and magnum .25-06 Rem., .270 Win., .280 Rem., 7mm Rem. Mag., .300 Win. Made 1994 to date.

Standard calibers	NiB $650	Ex $550	Gd $325
Magnum calibers, add			$30
SF Model (stainless fluted), add			$115

MODEL 700 VLS (VARMIT LAMINATED STOCK)
BOLT-ACTION RIFLE. . . . . NiB $575 Ex $450 Gd $300
Same as Model 700 BDL Varmint Special except with 26-inch polished blue barrel. Laminated wood stock with alternating grain and wood color impregnated with phenolic resin and finished with a satin luster. Calibers: .222 Rem., .223 Rem., .22-250 Rem., .243 Win., 7mm-08 Rem., .308 Win. Weight: 9.4 lbs. Made 1995 to date.

MODEL 700 VS BOLT-ACTION RIFLE
Same as Model 700 BDL Varmint Special except w/26-inch matte blue or fluted stainless barrel. Textured black or gray synthetic stock reinforced with Kevlar, fiberglass and graphite with full length aluminum bedding block. Calibers: .22-250 Rem., .220 Swift, .223 Rem., .308 Win. Made 1992 to date.

Model 700 VS	NiB $650	Ex $475	Gd $350
Model 700 VS SF (fluted barrel)	NiB $694	Ex $570	Gd $412
Model 700 VS SF/SF-P (Fluted & ported barrel)	NiB $856	Ex $725	Gd $557

MODEL 720A BOLT-ACTION
HIGH POWER . . . . NiB $1275 Ex $1100 Gd $950
Modified M/1917 Enfield action. .257 Roberts, .270 Win., .30-06. Five shot box magazine. 22-inch bbl. Weight: About 8 lbs. Sights: Open rear; bead front, on ramp. Pistol-grip stock, checkered. Model 720R has 20-inch bbl.; Model 720S has 24-inch bbl. Made 1941.

MODEL 721A STANDARD GRADE
BOLT-ACTION HIGH-POWER RIFLE . . . . . NiB $400 Ex $350 Gd $290
Calibers: .270 Win., .30-06. Fourshot box magazine. 24-inch bbl. Weight: About 7.25 lbs. Sights: Open rear; bead front, on ramp. Plain sporting stock. Made 1948-62.

MODEL 721A MAGNUM
STANDARD GRADE . . . . NiB $550 Ex $425 Gd $350
Caliber: .264 Win. Mag. or .300 H&H Mag. Same as standard model except has 26-inch bbl. Three shot magazine and recoil pad. Weight: 8.25 lbs.

MODEL 721ADL/BDL DELUXE
Same as Model 721A Standard or Magnum except has deluxe checkered stock and/or select wood.

Model 721ADL Deluxe Grade	NiB $625	Ex $550	Gd $425
Model 721ADL .300 Magnum Deluxe	NiB $744	Ex $625	Gd $473
Model 721BDL Deluxe Special Grade	NiB $631	Ex $525	Gd $389
Model 721BDL .300 Magnum Deluxe	NiB $703	Ex $590	Gd $446

MODEL 722A STANDARD GRADE SPORTER
Same as Model 721A bolt-action except shorter action. .222 Rem. mag., .243 Win., .257 Roberts, .308 Win., .300 Savage. Four or 5-shot magazine. Weight: 7-8 lbs. .222 Rem. introduced 1950; .244 Rem. introduced 1955. Made 1948-62.

.222 Rem.	NiB $406	Ex $325	Gd $221
.244 Rem.	NiB $369	Ex $295	Gd $201
.222 Rem. Mag. & .243 Win.	NiB $469	Ex $375	Gd $255
Other Calibers	NiB $400	Ex $325	Gd $200

MODEL 722ADL DELUXE GRADE
Same as Model 722A except has deluxe checkered stock.

Standard calibers	NiB $550	Ex $450	Gd $300
.222 Rem. Deluxe Grade	NiB $600	Ex $500	Gd $375
.244 Rem. Deluxe Grade	NiB $700	Ex $625	Gd $375

MODEL 722BDL DELUXE SPECIAL GRADE
Same as Model 722ADL except select wood.

Standard calibers	NiB $550	Ex $500	Gd $400
.222 Rem. Deluxe Special Grade	NiB $550	Ex $500	Gd $400
.224 Rem. Deluxe Special Grade	NiB $600	Ex $495	Gd $375

MODEL 725 KODIAK
MAGNUM RIFLE . . . . NiB $4000 Ex $3300 Gd $2000
Similar to Model 725ADL. Calibers: .375 H&H Mag., .458 Win. Mag. Three shot magazine. 26-inch bbl. with recoil reducer built into muzzle. Weight: About 9 lbs. Deluxe, reinforced Monte Carlo stock with recoil pad, black forend tip swivels, sling. Fewer than 100 made in 1961.

MODEL 725ADL BOLT-ACTION REPEATING RIFLE
Calibers: .222, .243, .244, .270, .280, .30-06. Four shot box mag. (5-shot in 222). 22-inch bbl. (24-inch in .222). Weight: About 7 lbs. Sights: Open rear, hooded ramp front. Monte Carlo comb stock w/pistol-grip, checkered, swivels. Made 1958-61.

.222 Rem., .243 Win., .244 Rem	NiB $719	Ex $575	Gd $391
.270 Win.	NiB $700	Ex $550	Gd $350
.280 Win.	NiB $800	Ex $675	Gd $400
.30-06	NiB $575	Ex $450	Gd $350

MODEL 788 CENTERFIRE BOLT-ACTION
Calibers: .222 Rem., .22-250, .223 Rem., 6mm Rem., .243 Win., 7mm-08 Rem., .308 Win., .30-30, .44 Rem. Mag. Three shot clip magazine (4-shot in .222 and .223 Rem.). 24-inch bbl. in .22s, 22-inch in other calibers. Weight: 7.5 lbs. with 24-inch bbl.; 7.25 lbs. with 22-inch bbl. Sights: Blade front on ramp; U-notch rear. Plain Monte Carlo stock. Made 1967-84.

.22-250, .223 Rem., 6mm Rem., .243 Win., .308 Win.	NiB $375	Ex $275	Gd $190
.30-30 Win.	NiB $436	Ex $355	Gd $251
7mm-08 Rem.	NiB $438	Ex $350	Gd $238
.44 Mag.	NiB $481	Ex $385	Gd $262

RIFLES

Remington Nylon 11

Remington Nylon 12

NYLON 11 BOLT-ACTION
REPEATER . . . . NiB $250 Ex $150 Gd $90
Clip type. Caliber: .22 Short, Long, LR. six or 10-shot clip mag.
19.63-inch bbl. Weight: 4.5 lbs. Sights: Open rear; blade front.
Nylon stock. Made 1962-66.

NYLON 12 BOLT-ACTION
REPEATER . . . . NiB $250 Ex $150 Gd $90
Same as Nylon 11 except has tubular magazine holding 22 Short,
17 Long, 15 LR. Made 1962-66.

SLIDE- AND LEVER-ACTION RIFLES

MODEL SIX (6) SLIDE-ACTION
REPEATER . . . . NiB $406 Ex $325 Gd $221
Hammerless. Calibers: 6mm Rem., .243 Win., .270 Win. 7mm
Express Rem., .30-06, .308 Win. 22-inch bbl. Weight: 7.5 lbs.
Checkered Monte Carlo stock and forearm. Made 1981-88.

MODEL SIX (6) SLIDE-ACTION
REPEATER, PEERLESS GRADE . . . . NiB $1750 Ex $1500 Gd $900
Same as Model Six Standard except has engraved receiver. Made
1981-88.

MODEL SIX (6) SLIDE-ACTION REPEATER, PREMIUM GRADES
Same as Model Six Standard except has engraved receiver with gold
inlay. Made 1981-88.
Peerless D Grade . . . . NiB $1750 Ex $1550 Gd $925
Premier F Grade . . . . NiB $4063 Ex $3250 Gd $2210
Premier Gold F Grade . . . . NiB $5744 Ex $4595 Gd $3125

MODEL 12A, 12B, 12C, 12CS SLIDE-ACTION REPEATERS
Standard Grade. Hammerless. Takedown. Caliber: .22 Short, Long
or LR. Tubular magazine holds 15 Short, 12 Long or 10 LR cartridges. 22- or 24-inch round or octagonal bbl. Open rear sight,
bead front. Plain, half-pistol-grip stock and grooved slide handle of
walnut. Made 1909-36.
Model 12A . . . . NiB $500 Ex $300 Gd $200
Model 12B
(22 Short only w/octagon bbl.) . . . . NiB $625 Ex $475 Gd $300
Model 12C
(w/24-inch octagon bbl.) . . . . NiB $525 Ex $450 Gd $275
Model 12CS
(22 WRF w/24-inch octagon bbl.) . . . . NiB $500 Ex $375 Gd $250

MODEL 14A HIGH POWER
SLIDE-ACTION REPEATING RIFLE . . . . NiB $535 Ex $400 Gd $350
Standard grade. Hammerless. Takedown. Calibers: .25, .30, .32 and
.35 Rem. Five shot tubular magazine. 22-inch bbl. Weight: About
6.75 lbs. Sights: Open rear; bead front. Plain half-pistol-grip stock
and grooved slide handle of walnut. Made 1912-35.

MODEL 14R CARBINE . . . . NiB $850 Ex $675 Gd $400
Same as Model 14R except has 18.5-inch bbl., straight-grip stock,
weight: About 6 lbs.

MODEL 14.5 CARBINE . . . . NiB $850 Ex $650 Gd $375
Same as Model 14A Rifle except has 9-shot magazine, 18.5-inch
bbl.

MODEL 14.5 RIFLE . . . . NiB $950 Ex $675 Gd $450
Similar to Model 14A except calibers: .38-40 and .44-40, 11-shot
full magazine, 22.5-inch bbl. Made 1912 to early 1920's.

MODEL 25A SLIDE-ACTION
REPEATER . . . . NiB $850 Ex $500 Gd $375
Standard Grade. Hammerless. Takedown. Calibers: .25-20, .32-20.
10-shot tubular magazine. 24-inch bbl. Weight: About 5.5 lbs.
Sights: Open rear; bead front. Plain, pistol-grip stock, grooved slide
handle. Made 1923-36.

MODEL 25R CARBINE . . . . NiB $900 Ex $525 Gd $400
Same as Model 25A except has 18-inch bbl. Six shot magazine,
straight-grip stock, weight: About 4.5 lbs.

MODEL 121A
FIELDMASTER
SLIDE-ACTION REPEATER. . . . . NiB $550 Ex $400 Gd $250
Standard Grade. Hammerless. Takedown. Caliber: .22 Short, Long,
LR. Tubular magazine holds 20 Short, 15 Long or 14 LR cartridges.
24-inch round bbl. Weight: 6 lbs. Plain, pistol-grip stock and
grooved semi-beavertail slide handle. Made 1936-54.

MODEL 121S. . . . . NiB $531 Ex $425 Gd $289
Same as Model 121A except chambered for .22 Remington Special
(.22 W.R.F.). Magazine holds 12 rounds. Disc.

MODEL 121SB . . . . NiB $619 Ex $495 Gd $337
Same as Model 121A except smoothbore. Disc.

Remington Model 121A

Remington Model 141A
Gamemaster

Remington Model 572A

Remington Model 572BDL

RIFLES

MODEL 141A GAMEMASTER
SLIDE-ACTION REPEATER....... **NiB $400 Ex $275 Gd $190**
Standard Grade. Hammerless. Takedown. Calibers: .30, .32 and .35
Rem. Five shot tubular magazine. 24-inch bbl. Weight: About 7.75
lbs. Sights: Open rear; bead front, on ramp. Plain, pistol-grip stock,
semibeavertail forend (slide-handle). Made 1936-50.

MODEL 572A FIELDMASTER
SLIDE-ACTION REPEATER........ **NiB $250 Ex $125 Gd $90**
Hammerless. Caliber: .22 Short, Long, LR. Tubular magazine holds 20
Short, 17 Long, 15 LR. 23-inch bbl. Weight: About 5.5 lbs. Sights: Open
rear; ramp front. Pistol-grip stock, grooved forearm. Made 1955-88.

MODEL 572BDL DELUXE........ **NiB $300 Ex $200 Gd $100**
Same as Model 572A except has blade ramp front sight, sliding
ramp rear; checkered stock and forearm. Made 1966 to date.

MODEL 572SB SMOOTH BORE... **NiB $313 Ex $250 Gd $170**
Same as Model 572A except smoothbore for .22 LR shot cartridges.
Made 1961 to date.

MODEL 760 BICENTENNIAL
COMMEMORATIVE............ **NiB $700 Ex $500 Gd $375**
Same as Model 760 except has commemorative inscription on
receiver. Made 1976.

MODEL 760 CARBINE .... **NiB $550 Ex $425 Gd $200**
Same as Model 760 Rifle except made in calibers .270 Win., .280 Rem., .30-
06 and .308 Win. only, has 18.5-inch bbl., weight: 7.25 lbs. Made 1961-80.

MODEL 760 GAMEMASTER
STANDARD GRADE SLIDE-ACTION REPEATING RIFLE
Hammerless. Calibers: .223 Rem., 6mm Rem., .243 Win., .257
Roberts, .270 Win. .280 Rem., .30-06, .300 Sav., .308 Win., .35
Rem. 22-inch bbl. Weight: About 7.5 lbs. Sights: Open rear; bead
front, on ramp. Plain pistol-grip stock, grooved slide handle on early
models; current production has checkered stock and slide handle.
Made 1952-80.
.222 Rem. ....**NiB $1175 Ex $900 Gd $550**
.223 Rem. ....**NiB $1350 Ex $990 Gd $600**
.257 Roberts ....**NiB $890 Ex $675 Gd $400**
Other calibers ....**NiB $850 Ex $700 Gd $225**

MODEL 760ADL
DELUXE GRADE .... **NiB $475 Ex $375 Gd $250**
Same as Model 760 except has deluxe checkered stock, standard or
high comb, grip cap, sling swivels. Made 1953-63.

MODEL 760BDL
CUSTOM DELUXE .... **NiB $456 Ex $365 Gd $248**
Same as Model 760 Rifle except made in calibers .270, .30-06 and
.308 only, has Monte Carlo cheekpiece stock forearm with black tip,
basket-weave checkering. Available also in left-hand model. Made
1953-80.

MODEL 760D
PEERLESS GRADE .... **NiB $1250 Ex $1000 Gd $750**
Same as Model 760 except scroll engraved, fancy wood. Made
1953-80.

GRADING: NiB = New in Box   **Ex** = Excellent or NRA 95%   **Gd** = Good or NRA 68%

Remington Model 760
Bicentennial Commemorative

Remington Model 760
Gamemaster

Remington Model 7600 Carbine

Remington Model 7600 Rifle

Remington Nylon 76 Lever-Action

Remington Sportsman 76

MODEL 760F PREMIER GRADE
Same as Model 760 except extensively engraved with game scenes and scroll, finest grade wood. Also available with receiver inlaid with gold; adds 50 percent to value. Made 1953-80.
Premier F Grade . . . . NiB $2438 Ex $1950 Gd $1326
Premier Gold F Grade . . . . NiB $5744 Ex $4595 Gd $3125

MODEL 7600 SLIDE-ACTION
CARBINE . . . . NiB $500 Ex $325 Gd $225
Same general specifications as Model 7600 Rifle except has 18.5-inch bbl. and weighs 7.25 lbs. Made 1987 to date.

MODEL 7600 SLIDE-ACTION RIFLE. . . . . . NiB $475 Ex $380 Gd $225
Similar to Model Six except has lower grade finishes. Made 1981 to date.

MODEL 7600 SPECIAL PURPOSE. . . . . . . NiB $450 Ex $350 Gd $200
Same general specification as the Model 7600, except chambered only in .270 or .30-06. Special Purpose matte black finish on all exposed metal. American walnut stock with SP nonglare finish.

NYLON 76 LEVER-ACTION REPEATER. . . . NiB $300 Ex $250 Gd $150
Short-throw lever action. Caliber: .22 LR. 14-shot buttstock tubular magazine. Weight: 4 lbs. Black or brown nylon stock and forend. Made 1962-64. Remington's only lever-action rifle.

SPORTSMAN 76 SLIDE-ACTION RIFLE . . . NiB $290 Ex $225 Gd $150
Caliber: .30-06, 4-shot magazine. 22-inch bbl. Weight: 7.5 lbs. Open rear sight; front blade mounted on ramp. Uncheckered hardwood stock and forend. Made 1985-87.

SEMIAUTOMATIC RIFLES

MODEL FOUR (4) AUTOLOADING RIFLE
Hammerless. Calibers: 6mm Rem., .243 Win., .270 Win. 7mm Express Rem., .30-06, .308 Win. 22-inch bbl. Weight: 7.5 lbs. Sights: Open rear; bead front, on ramp. Monte Carlo checkered stock and forearm. Made 1981-88.
Standard . . . . NiB $700 Ex $575 Gd $250
Peerless Grade (Engr. receiver) . . . . NiB $2000 Ex $1800 Gd $750
Premier Grade (Engr. receiver) . . . . NiB $3688 Ex $2950 Gd $2006
Prem. Gr. (Engr. rec., gold inlay) . . . . . . NiB $6063 Ex $4850 Gd $3298

MODEL FOUR DIAMOND
ANNIVERSARY LTD. EDITION $1000
Same as Model Four Standard except has engraved receiver w/inscription, checkered high-grade walnut stock and forend. Only 1,500 produced. Made 1981 only. (Value for new condition)

MODEL 8A AUTOLOADING RIFLE . . . . . . NiB $750 Ex $600 Gd $375
Standard Grade. Takedown. Calibers: .25, .30, .32 and .35 Rem. Five-shot, clip-loaded magazine. 22-inch bbl. Weight: 7.75 lbs. Sights: Adj. and dovetailed open rear; dovetailed bead front. Half-moon metal buttplate on plain straight-grip walnut stock; plain walnut forearm with thin curved end. Made 1906-1936.

MODEL 16 AUTOLOADING RIFLE. . . . . . NiB $400 Ex $300 Gd $175
Takedown. Closely resembles the Winchester Model 03 semiautomatic rifle. Calibers: .22 Short, .22 LR, 22 Rem. Auto. 15-shot tubular magazine in buttstock. 22-inch bbl. Weight: 5.75 lbs. Sights: Open rear; dovetailed bead front. Plain straight-grip stock and forearm. Made 1914-1928. Note: In 1918 this model was discontinued in all calibers except .22 Rem. Auto; specifications are for that model.

MODEL 24A AUTOLOADING RIFLE . . . . . NiB $400 Ex $275 Gd $175
Standard Grade. Takedown. Calibers: .22 Short only, .22 LR. only. Tubular magazine in buttstock, holds 15 Short or 10 LR. 21-inch bbl. Weight: About 5 lbs. Sights: Dovetailed adj. open rear; dovetailed bead front. Plain walnut straight-grip buttstock; plain walnut forearm. Made 1922-35.

MODEL 81A WOODSMASTER
AUTOLOADER . . . . NiB $525 Ex $400 Gd $225
Standard Grade. Takedown. Calibers: .30, .32 and .35 Rem., .300 Sav. Five shot box magazine (not detachable). 22-inch bbl. Weight: 8.25 lbs. Sights: Open rear; bead front. Plain walnut pistol-grip stock, forearm. Made 1936-50.

MODEL 241A SPEEDMASTER
AUTOLOADER . . . . NiB $300 Ex $250 Gd $150
Standard Grade. Takedown. Calibers: .22 Short only, .22 LR. only. Tubular magazine in buttstock, holds 15 Short or 10 LR. 24-inch bbl. Weight: About 6 lbs. Sights: Open rear, bead front. Plain walnut stock and forearm. Made 1935-51.

MODEL 550A AUTOLOADER . . . . . . NiB $225 Ex $150 Gd $75
Has "Power Piston" or floating chamber, which permits interchangeable use of 22 Short, Long or LR cartridges. Tubular magazine holds 22 Short, 17 Long, 15 LR. 24-inch bbl. Weight: About 6.25 lbs. Sights: Open rear; bead front. Plain, one-piece pistol-grip stock. Made 1941-71.

MODEL 550P . . . . NiB $225 Ex $150 Gd $75
Same as Model 550A except has peep rear sight, blade front, on ramp.

MODEL 550-2G . . . . NiB $300 Ex $225 Gd $125
"Gallery Special." Same as Model 550A except has 22-inch bbl., screweye for counter chain and fired shell deflector.

**Remington Sportsman 742
Canadian Centennial**

MODEL 552A SPEEDMASTER
AUTOLOADER . . . . NiB $225 Ex $150 Gd $75
Caliber: .22 Short, Long, LR. Tubular magazine holds 20 Short, 17 Long, 15 LR. 25-inch bbl. Weight: About 5.5 lbs. Sights: Open rear; bead front. Pistol-grip stock, semi-beavertail forearm. Made 1957-88.

MODEL 552BDL DELUXE . . . . NiB $290 Ex $190 Gd $125
Same as Model 552A except has checkered walnut stock and forearm. Made 1966 to date.

MODEL 552C CARBINE . . . . NiB $250 Ex $150 Gd $100
Same as Model 552A except has 21-inch bbl. Made 1961-77.

MODEL 552GS GALLERY SPECIAL. . . . . . NiB $290 Ex $190 Gd $125
Same as Model 552A except chambered for .22 Short only. Made 1957-77.

MODEL 740A WOODSMASTER AUTOLOADER
Standard Grade. Gas-operated. Calibers: .30-06 or .308. Four shot detachable box magazine. 22-inch bbl. Weight: About 7.5 lbs. Plain pistol-grip stock, semibeavertail forend with finger grooves. Sights: Open rear; ramp front. Made 1955-60.
Rifle model . . . . NiB $375 Ex $300 Gd $190
Carbine model. . . . . NiB $425 Ex $350 Gd $225

MODEL 740ADL/BDL DELUXE
Same as Model 740A except has deluxe checkered stock, standard or high comb, grip cap, sling swivels. Model 740 BDL also has select wood. Made 1955-60.
Model 740 ADL Deluxe Grade . . . . NiB $575 Ex $450 Gd $225
Model 740 BDL Deluxe Special Grade . . . NiB $650 Ex $500 Gd $350

MODEL 742 BICENTENNIAL
COMMEMORATIVE. $700
Same as Model 742 Woodsmaster rifle except has commemorative inscription on receiver. Made 1976. (Value for new condition)

MODEL 742
CANADIAN CENTENNIAL $700
Same as Model 742 rifle except has commemorative inscription on receiver. Made 1967. Value is for rifle in new, unfired condition.

MODEL 742 CARBINE . . . . NiB $650 Ex $450 Gd $190
Same as Model 742 Woodsmaster Rifle except made in calibers .30-06 and .308 only, has 18.5-inch bbl., weight 6.75 lbs. Made 1961-80.

MODEL 742 WOODSMASTER
AUTOMATIC BIG GAME RIFLE . . . . NiB $590 Ex $400 Gd $195
Gas-operated semiautomatic. Calibers: 6mm Rem., .243 Win., .280 Rem., .30-06, .308 Win. Four shot clip magazine. 22-inch bbl. Weight: 7.5 lbs. Sights: Open rear; bead front, on ramp. Checkered pistol-grip stock and forearm. Made 1960-80.

Remington Model 7400

Remington Model 7400 Carbine

Remington Nylon 66
Bicentennial Commemorative

Remington Nylon 66 Mohawk

Remington Sportsman 74

MODEL 742BDL CUSTOM DELUXE...... NiB $550 Ex $450 Gd $225
Same as Model 742 Rifle except made in calibers .30-06 and .308 only, has Monte Carlo cheekpiece stock, forearm with black tip, basket-weave checkering. Available in left-hand model. Made 1966-80.

MODEL 742D PEERLESS GRADE .... NiB $1725 Ex $1425 Gd $900
Same as Model 742 except scroll engraved, fancy wood. Made 1961-80.

MODEL 742F PREMIER GRADE
Same as Model 742 except extensively engraved with game scenes and scroll, finest grade wood. Also available with receiver inlaid with gold; adds 50 percent to value. Made 1961-1980.
Premier F Grade .... NiB $3688 Ex $2950 Gd $2006
Premier Gold F Grade........ NiB $5744 Ex $4595 Gd $3125

MODEL 7400 AUTOLOADER
Similar to Model Four w/lower grade finishes. Made 1981 to date.
Model 7400 Standard .... NiB $425 Ex $350 Gd $195
Model 7400 HG
(High gloss finish) .... NiB $431 Ex $345 Gd $235

MODEL 7400 CARBINE .... NiB $425 Ex $300 Gd $225
Caliber: .30-06 only. Similar to the Model 7400 rifle except has 18.5-inch bbl. and weight: 7.25 lbs. Made 1988 to date.

MODEL 7400 SPECIAL PURPOSE......... NiB $425 Ex $325 Gd $200
Same general specification as the Model 7400 except chambered only in .270 or .30-06. Special Purpose matte black finish on metal. American walnut stock with SP nonglare finish. Made 1993-95.

NYLON 66 APACHE BLACK .... NiB $200 Ex $125 Gd $90
Same as Nylon 66 Mohawk Brown except bbl. and receiver cover chrome-plated, black stock. Made 1962-84.

**NYLON 66 BICENTENNIAL
COMMEMORATIVE ....** NiB $225 Ex $150 Gd $100
Same as Nylon 66 except has commemorative inscription on receiver. Made 1976.

NYLON 66MB AUTOLOADING RIFLE..... NiB $200 Ex $125 Gd $90
Similar to the early production Nylon 66 Black Apache except with blued bbl. and receiver cover. Made 1978-87.

**NYLON 66 MOHAWK
BROWN AUTOLOADER ....** NiB $150 Ex $100 Gd $85
Caliber: .22 LR. Tubular magazine in buttstock holds14 rounds. 19.5-inch bbl. Weight: About 4 lbs. Sights: Open rear; blade front. Brown nylon stock and forearm. Made 1959-87.

NYLON 77 CLIP REPEATER....... NiB $175 Ex $125 Gd $90
Same as Nylon 66 except has 5-shot clip magazine. Made 1970-71.

Rossi Model 62 Stainless Rifle

Rossi Model 62 Stainless Carbine

Rossi Model 62 WMR Rifle

Rossi Model 62 SAC Carbine

Rossi Model 62 Gallery Rifle

SPORTSMAN 74 AUTOLOADING RIFLE . . . . . **NiB $325 Ex $230 Gd $150**
Caliber: .30-06, 4-shot magazine. 22-inch bbl. Uncheckered buttstock and forend. Open rear sight; ramped blade front sight. Made 1985-88.

JOHN RIGBY & CO. — London, England

MODEL 275 MAGAZINE SPORTING RIFLE **NiB $6250 Ex $5000+ Gd $3400**
Mauser action. Caliber: .275 High Velocity or 7x57mm 5-shot box magazine. 25-inch bbl. Weight: about 7.5 lbs. Sights: Folding leaf rear; bead front. Sporting stock w/half-pistol-grip, checkered. Specifications given are those of current model; however, in general, they apply also to prewar model.

MODEL 275 LIGHTWEIGHT
MAGAZINE RIFLE . . . . **NiB $5000 Ex $4000+ Gd $2720**
Same as standard .275 rifle except has 21-inch bbl. Weight: 6.75 lbs.

MODEL 350 MAGNUM
MAGAZINE SPORTING RIFLE . . . . . . **NiB $4375 Ex $3500+ Gd $2380**
Mauser action. Caliber: .350 Magnum. Five shot box magazine. 24-inch bbl. Weight: About 7.75 lbs. Sights: Folding leaf rear; bead front. Sporting stock with full pistol-grip, checkered. Currently mfd.

MODEL 416 BIG GAME
MAGAZINE SPORTING RIFLE . . . . . . **NiB $7500 Ex $6000+ Gd $4080**
Mauser action. Caliber: .416 Big Game. Four shot box magazine. 24-inch bbl. Weight: 9 to 9.25 lbs. Sights: Folding leaf rear; bead front. Sporting stock with full pistol-grip, checkered. Currently mfd.

BEST QUALITY HAMMERLESS
EJECTOR DOUBLE RIFLE . . . . . . **NiB $48,750 Ex $39,000+ Gd $26,520**
Sidelocks. Calibers: .275 Magnum, .350 Magnum, .470 Nitro Express. 24- to 28-inch bbls. Weight: 7.5 to 10.5 lbs. Sights: Folding leaf rear; bead front. Checkered pistol-grip stock and forearm.

SECOND QUALITY HAMMERLESS
EJECTOR DOUBLE RIFLE . . . . . . **NiB $21,875 Ex $17,500 Gd $11,900**
Same general specifications as Best Quality double rifle except boxlock.

THIRD QUALITY HAMMERLESS
EJECTOR DOUBLE RIFLE . . . . **NiB $12,375 Ex $9900 Gd $6732**
Same as Second Quality double rifle except plainer finish and not of as high quality.

ROSS RIFLE CO. — Quebec, Canada

MODEL 1910 BOLT-ACTION
SPORTING RIFLE . . . . **NiB $600 Ex $195 Gd $175**
Straight-pull bolt-action with interrupted screw-type lugs. Calibers: .280 Ross, .303 British. Four shot or 5-shot magazine. Bbl. lengths: 22, 24, 26 inches. Sights: Two-leaf open rear; bead front. Checkered sporting stock. Weight: About 7 lbs. Made c. 1910 to end of World War I. Note: Most firearm authorities agree that this and other Ross models with interrupted screw-type lugs are unsafe to fire.

ROSSI RIFLES — Sao Leopoldo, Brazil
Manufactured by Amadeo Rossi, S.A.

62 GALLERY MODEL SAC CARBINE
Same as standard Gallery Model except in .22 LR only with 16.25-inch bbl.; weight 5.5 lbs. Imported 1975-98.
Blued finish . . . . **NiB $185 Ex $150 Gd $90**
Nickel finish . . . . **NiB $200 Ex $160 Gd $115**
Stainless . . . . **NiB $250 Ex $180 Gd $120**

62 GALLERY MODEL MAGNUM . . . . **NiB $190 Ex $160 Gd $100**
Same as standard Gallery Model except chambered for .22 WMR, 10-shot magazine. Imported 1975-98.

Ruger Number One (1)
Light Sporter

Ruger Number One (1)
Medium Sporter

Ruger Number One
"North Americans"

62 GALLERY MODEL SLIDE-ACTION REPEATER
Similar to Winchester Model 62. Calibers: .22 LR. Long, Short or .22 WMR. Tubular magazine holds 13 LR, 16 Long, 20 Short. 23-inch bbl. 39.25 inches overall. Weight: 5.75 lbs. Sights: Open rear; bead front. Straight-grip stock, grooved slide handle. Blued, nickel or stainless finish. Imported 1970-98. Values same as SAC Model.

LEVER-ACTION 65/92 CARBINE
Similar to Winchester Model 92. Caliber: .38 Special/.357 Mag., .44 Mag., .44-40, .45 LC. 8- or 10-shot magazine. 16-, 20- or 24-inch round or half-octagonal bbl. Weight: 5.5 to 6 lbs. 33.5- to 41.5-inches overall. Satin blue, chrome or stainless finish. Brazilian hardwood buttstock and forearm. Made 1978-98.

Model M92 SRC .45LC	NiB $350	Ex $275 Gd $190
Model M92 SRC .38/357, .44 Mag	NiB $350	Ex $275 Gd $190
Model M92 w/octagon bbl	NiB $375	Ex $200 Gd $195
Model M92 LL Lever	NiB $350	Ex $225 Gd $175
Engraved, add		$75
Chrome, add		$25
Stainless, add		$75

RUGER RIFLES — Southport, Connecticut
Manufactured by Sturm, Ruger & Co.

NUMBER ONE (1) LIGHT SPORTER . . . . . . NiB $650 Ex $525 Gd $250
Same as No.1 Standard except has 22-inch bbl., folding leaf rear sight on quarter-rib and ramp front sight, Henry pattern forearm. Made 1966 to date.

NUMBER ONE (1) MEDIUM SPORTER . . . NiB $600 Ex $475 Gd $275
Same as No. 1 Light Sporter except has 26-inch bbl. 22-inch in 45-70); weight: 8 lbs (7.25 lbs. in .45-70). Calibers: 7mm Rem. Mag., .300 Win. Mag., .45-70. Made 1966 to date.

NUMBER ONE (1) "NORTH AMERICANS"
PRESENTATION RIFLE $52,000
Same general specifications as the Ruger No. 1 Standard except highly

(cont'd.) **NUMBER ONE (1) "NORTH AMERICANS" PRESENTATION RIFLE** customized with elaborate engravings, carvings, fine-line checkering and gold inlays. A series of 21 is planned, each rifle depicting a North American big-game animal, chambered in the caliber appropriate to the game. Stock is of Northern California English walnut. Comes in trunk-style Huey case with Leupold scope and other accessories.

NUMBER ONE (1) RSI INTERNATIONAL
SINGLE-SHOT RIFLE . . . . NiB $600 Ex $450 Gd $290
Similar to the No. 1 Light Sporter except with lightweight 20-inch bbl. and full Mannlicher-style forend, in calibers .243 Win., .270 Win., 7x57mm, .30-06. Weight: 7.25 lbs.

NUMBER ONE (1)
SPECIAL VARMINTER . . . . NiB $600 Ex $450 Gd $290
Same as No. 1 Standard except has heavy 24-inch bbl. with target scope bases, no quarter-rib. Weight: 9 lbs. Calibers: .22-250, .25-06, 7mm Rem. Mag., .300 Win. Mag. Made 1966 to date.

NUMBER ONE (1)
STANDARD RIFLE . . . . NiB $590 Ex $425 Gd $275
Falling-block single-shot action with Farquharson-type lever. Calibers: .22-250, .243 Win., 6mm Rem., .25-06, .270 Win., .30-06, 7mm Rem. Mag., .300 Win. Mag. 26-inch bbl. Weight: 8 lbs. No sights, has quarter-rib for scope mounting. Checkered pistol-grip buttstock and semi-beavertail forearm, QD swivels, rubber buttplate. Made 1966 to date.

NUMBER ONE (1) TROPICAL RIFLE . . . . . . NiB $650 Ex $520 Gd $300
Same as No. 1 Light Sporter except has heavy 24-inch bbl.; calibers are .375 H&H .404 Jeffery, .416 Rigby, and .458 Win. Mag. Weight: 8.25 to 9 lbs. Made 1966 to date.

NUMBER THREE (3) SINGLE-SHOT
CARBINE . . . . NiB $450 Ex $400 Gd $225
Falling-block action with American-style lever. Calibers: .22 Hornet .223 Rem., .30-40 Krag, .357 Win., .44 Mag., .45-70. 22-inch bbl. Weight: 6 lbs. Sights: Folding leaf rear; gold bead front. Carbine-style stock w/curved buttplate, forearm with bbl. band. Made 1972-87.

RIFLES

Ruger Number One "North Americans" Presentation Set

Ruger No. 1
International

Ruger No. 1
Special Varminter

Ruger No. 1
Standard Rifle

Ruger No. 1 Tropical Rifle

Ruger No. 3 Single-Shot Carbine

Ruger Model 10/22
Standard Rifle

Ruger Model 10/22
Deluxe Rifle

Ruger Model 44
Autoloading Carbine

MODEL 10/22 AUTOLOADING CARBINE
Caliber: .22 LR. Detachable 10-shot rotary magazine. 18.5-inch bbl. Weight: 5 lbs. Sights: Folding leaf rear; bead front. Carbine-style stock with bbl. band and curved buttplate (walnut stock discontinued 1980). Made 1964 to date. International and Sporter versions discontinued 1971.

10/22 Standard Carbine (Walnut stock)	NiB $250	Ex $190	Gd $100

10/22 Int'l. (w/Mannlicher
style stock, swivels) Disc.1971............ NiB $550 Ex $400 Gd $300
10/22 RB (Birch stock, blued) .... NiB $175 Ex $125 Gd $90
K10/22 RB (Birch stock, stainless) .... NiB $180 Ex $150 Gd $100
10/22 Sporter (MC stock,
flat buttplate, swivels) Disc.1971.......... NiB $180 Ex $150 Gd $100
10/22 SP Deluxe Sporter (made since 1966).... NiB $231 Ex $185 Gd $126
10/22 RBI Int'l. (blued); made since 1994... NiB $219 Ex $175 Gd $119
10/22 RBI Int'l. (stainless); made since 1995 .... NiB $244 Ex $195 Gd $133

MODEL 44 AUTOLOADING CARBINE
Gas-operated. Caliber: .44 Magnum. Four shot tubular magazine (with magazine release button since 1967). 18.5-inch bbl. Weight: 5.75 lbs. Sights: Folding leaf rear; gold bead front. Carbine-style stock w/bbl. band and curved buttplate. Made 1961-86. International and Sporter versions discontinued 1971.

Model 44 Standard autoloading carbine... NiB $450 Ex $350 Gd $240
Model 44 Int'l (w/Mannlicher-
style stock, swivels)................... NiB $690 Ex $500 Gd $400
Mdl. 44 Sporter (MC stk. w/fingergroove)... NiB $600 Ex $650 Gd $450
Model 44RS Carbine
(w/rear peep sight, disc. 1978).......... NiB $550 Ex $400 Gd $295

MODEL 77 BOLT-ACTION RIFLE
Receiver with integral scope mount base or with round top. Short stroke or magnum length action (depending on caliber) in the former type receiver, magnum only in the latter. .22-250, .220 Swift, 6mm Rem., .243 Win., .250-3000, .25-06, .257 Roberts, 6.5 Rem. Mag., .270 Win., 7x57mm,

7mm-08 7mm Rem. Mag., .280 Rem., .284 Win., .308 Win., .30-06, .300
(cont'd.) MODEL 77 BOLT-ACTION RIFLE
Win. Mag. .338 Win. Mag., .350 Rem. Mag., .458 Win. Mag. Five shot magazine standard, 4-shot in .220 Swift, 3-shot in magnum calibers. 22 24- or 26-inch bbl. (depending on caliber). Weight: About 7 lbs.; .458 Mag. model, 8.75 lbs. Round-top model furnished w/folding leaf rear sight and ramp front; integral base model furnished w/scope rings, with or w/o open sights. Stock w/checkered pistol grip and forearm, pistol-grip cap, rubber recoil pad, QD swivel studs. Made 1968-92.

Model 77, integral base, no sights .... NiB $450 Ex $380 Gd $200
6.5 Rem. Mag., add................................... $75
.284 Win., add $30
.338 Win. Mag., add $50
.350 Rem. Mag., 6.5 Rem. Mag., add $75
Model 77RL Ultra Light, no sights, ... NiB $450 Ex $350 Gd $225
Model 77RL Ultra Light, open sights, ... NiB $460 Ex $370 Gd $250
Model 77RS, integral base, open sights ... NiB $456 Ex $365 Gd $248
.338 Win. Mag., .458 Win. Mag.,
with standard stock, add................................. $75
Model 77RSC, .458 Win. Mag. with
fancy Circassian walnut stock, add $525
Model 77RSI International, Mannlicher
stock, short action, 18.5-inch bbl., 7 lbs. ... NiB $450 Ex $350 Gd $225
Model 77ST, round top, open sights ...... NiB $460 Ex $360 Gd $280
.338 Win. Mag., add $50
Model 77V, Varmint,
integral base, no sights .... NiB $450 Ex $380 Gd $200
Model 77NV, Varmint, integral base, no sights, stainless
steel barrel, laminated wood stock....... NiB $475 Ex $390 Gd $250

MODEL 77 MARK II ALL-WEATHER RIFLE ... NiB $450 Ex $350 Gd $225
Revised Model 77 action. Same general specifications as Model M-77 Mark II except with stainless bbl. and action. Zytel injection-molded stock. Calibers: .223, .243, .270, .308, .30-06, 7mm Mag.,

Ruger Model 77 Round Top Receiver

Ruger Model 77 Ultra-Light Carbine

Ruger Model 77 International Carbine

Ruger Model 77 Varmint Rifle

Ruger Model 77 Mark II All-Weather Rifle

MODEL 77 MARK II BOLT-ACTION RIFLE

Revised Model 77 action. Same general specifications as Model M-77 except with new 3-position safety and fixed blade ejector system. Calibers .22 PPC, .223 Rem., 6mm PPC, 6.5x55 Swedish, .375 H&H, .404 Jeffery and .416 Rigby also available. Weight: 6 to 10.25 lbs. Made 1989 to date.

Model 77 MKIIR, integral base, no sights . . NiB $450 Ex $350 Gd $225
Left-hand Model 77LR MKII, add $25
Model 77RL MKII, Ultra Light, no sights. . . NiB $450 Ex $380 Gd $200
Model 77RLS MKII, Ultra
Light, open sights . . . . NiB $450 Ex $390 Gd $250
Model 77RS MKII, integral base, open sights . . . NiB $456 Ex $365 Gd $248
Model 77RS MKII, Express, with fancy French
walnut stock, integral base, open sights . . NiB $1200 Ex $975 Gd $650
Model 77RSI MKII,
International, Mannlicher . . . . NiB $494 Ex $395 Gd $269
Model 77RSM MKII magnum, with fancy Circassian
walnut stock, integral base, open sights. . . . . . NiB $1290 Ex $990 Gd $690
Model 77VT (VBZ or VTM)
MKII Varmint/Target stainless steel action,
laminated wood stock. . . . . NiB $475 Ex $390 Gd $250

MODEL 77/.22 HORNET BOLT-ACTION RIFLE

Mini-Sporter built on the 77/.22 action in caliber .22 Hornet. Six shot rotary magazine. 20- inch bbl. 40 inches overall. Weight: 6 lbs. Receiver machined for Ruger rings (included). Beaded front sight and open adj. rear, or no sights. Blued or stainless finish. Checkered American walnut stock. Made 1994 to date.

(cont'd.) MODEL 77/.22 HORNET BOLT-ACTION RIFLE

Model 77/.22RH (rings, no sights) . . . . NiB $325 Ex $300 Gd $200
Model 77/.22RSH (rings & sights). . . . . NiB $350 Ex $300 Gd $200
Model 77/.22VHZ (S/S w/
laminated wood stock) . . . . NiB $375 Ex $350 Gd $225

MODEL 77/.22 RIMFIRE BOLT-ACTION RIFLE

Calibers: .22 LR. or .22 WMR. 10-shot (.22 LR) or 9-shot (.22 WMR) rotary magazine. 20-inch bbl. 39.75 inches overall. Weight: 5.75 lbs. Integral scope bases; with or w/o sights. Checkered American walnut or Zytel injection-molded stock. Stainless or blued finish. Made 1983 to date. (Blued); stainless. Introduced 1989.

77/.22 R, rings, no sights, walnut stock . . . . . . NiB $344 Ex $275 Gd $187
77/.22 RS, rings, sights, walnut. . . . . NiB $350 Ex $275 Gd $200
77/.22 RP, rings, no sights, synthetic stock . . . . NiB $281 Ex $225 Gd $153
77/.22 RSP, rings, sights, synthetic stock . . . . . NiB $306 Ex $245 Gd $167
K77/.22 RP, S/S rings, no sights, synthetic . . . . NiB $356 Ex $285 Gd $194
K77/.22 RSP, S/S, rings, sights, synthetic . . . . . NiB $369 Ex $295 Gd $201
77/.22 RM, .22 WMR,
rings, no sights, walnut . . . . NiB $350 Ex $275 Gd $190
77/.22 RSM, .22 WMR, rings, sights, walnut . . . NiB $375 Ex $290 Gd $200
K77/.22 RSMP, .22 WMR, S/S, rings,
sights, synthetic. . . . . NiB $369 Ex $295 Gd $201
K77/.22 RMP, .22 WMR,
S/S, no sights, synthetic . . . . NiB $344 Ex $275 Gd $187
K77/.22 VBZ, .22 WMR,
no sights, laminated. (1993) . . . . NiB $369 Ex $295 Gd $201

Ruger Model 77 Mark II

Ruger Model 77/.22 Rimfire

Ruger Model 77/.22
All Weather

Ruger Model 77/.44
All Weather

MODEL 77/.44 BOLT-ACTION
Short-action, carbine-style M77 similar to the 77/.22RH. Chambered .44 Rem. Mag. Four shot rotary magazine. 18.5-inch bbl. 38.25 inches overall. Weight: 6 lbs. Gold bead front sight, folding adjustable rear w/integral scope base and Ruger rings. Blue or stainless finish. Synthetic or checkered American walnut stock w/rubber buttpad and swivels. Made 1997 to date.
Model 77/.44 blued............. NiB $475 Ex $350 Gd $225
Model 77/.44 stainless.......... NiB $490 Ex $360 Gd $230

MODEL 96 LEVER ACTION CARBINE
Caliber: .22 LR. .22 Mag., .44 Mag. Detachable 10-, 9- or 4-shot magazine. 18.5-inch bbl. Weight: 5.25 lbs. Front gold bead sights. Drilled and tapped for scope. American hardwood stock. Made 1996 to date.
.22 Long Rifle .... NiB $250 Ex $200 Gd $130
.22 Magnum .... NiB $260 Ex $225 Gd $140
.44 Magnum .... NiB $431 Ex $345 Gd $235

MINI-14 SEMIAUTOMATIC RIFLE
Gas-operated. Caliber: .223 Rem. (5.56mm). 5-, 10- or 20-shot box magazine. 18.5-inch bbl. Weight: About 6.5 lbs. Sights: Peep rear; blade front mounted on removable barrel band. Pistol-grip stock w/curved buttplate, handguard. Made 1976 to date.
Mini-14/5 blued .... NiB $525 Ex $490 Gd $300
K-Mini-14/5 stainless steel .... NiB $550 Ex $500 Gd $350

(cont'd.) MINI-14 SEMIAUTOMATIC RIFLE
Mini-14/5F blued, folding stock .... NiB $700 Ex $590 Gd $400
K-Mini-14/5F stainless, folding stock ..... NiB $725 Ex $600 Gd $425
Mini-14 Ranch Rifle,
scope model, 6.25 lbs. .... NiB $550 Ex $500 Gd $300
K-Mini-1H Ranch Rifle,
scope model, stainless................. NiB $575 Ex $525 Gd $325

MINI-THIRTY (30) AUTOLOADER
Caliber: 7.62 x 39mm. 5-shot detachable magazine. 18.5-inch bbl. 37.25 inches overall. Weight: 7 lbs. 3 oz. Designed for use with telescopic sights. Walnut stained stock. Sights: Peep rear; blade front mounted on bbl. band. Blued or stainless finish. Made 1986 to date.
Blued....................... NiB $550 Ex $500 Gd $290
Stainless..................... NiB $575 Ex $550 Gd $300

PC SERIES SEMIAUTOMATIC CARBINES
Calibers: 9mm Parabellum or .40 S&W. 10-shot magazine. 15.25-inch bbl. Weight: 6.25 lbs. Integral Ruger scope mounts with or without sights. Optional blade front sight, adjustable open rear. Matte black oxide finish. Matte black Zytel stock w/checkered pistol-grip and forearm. Made 1997 to date.
Model PC9 (w/o sights).......... NiB $425 Ex $375 Gd $225
Model PC40 (w/o sights)......... NiB $450 Ex $400 Gd $250
W/adjustable sights, add $40

Ruger Model 96 Lever-Action

Ruger Model 96/44M Lever-Action

Ruger Mini-14 Semiautomatic

Ruger Mini-14 with Folding Stock

Ruger Mini-Thirty Autoloader

Ruger Model PC9 Carbine

Ruger Model PC9 w/Ghost Ring Sights

RIFLES

RUSSIAN MILITARY RIFLES — Principal U.S.S.R. Arms Plant, Tula

MODEL 1891
MOSIN MILITARY RIFLE . . . . NiB $400 Ex $100 Gd $55
Nagant system bolt action. Caliber: 7.62mm Russian. Five shot box magazine. 31.5-inch bbl. Weight: About 9 lbs. Sights: Open rear; blade front. Full stock w/straight grip. Specifications given are for WWII version; earlier types differ slightly. Note: In 1916, Remington Arms Co. and New England Westinghouse Co. produced 250,000 of these rifles on a contract from the Imperial Russian Government. Few were delivered to Russia and the balance bought by the U.S. Government for training in 1918. Eventually, many of these rifles were sold to N.R.A. members for about $3 each by the director of Civilian Marksmanship.

TOKAREV MODEL 40 SEMIAUTOMATIC
MILITARY RIFLE . . . . NiB $750 Ex $350 Gd $200
Gas-operated. Caliber: 7.62mm Russian. 10-shot detachable box magazine. 24.5-inch bbl. Muzzle brake. Weight: About 9 lbs. Sights: Leaf rear, hooded post front. Full stock w/pistol grip. Differences among Models 1938,1940 and 1941 are minor.

SAKO RIFLES — Riihimaki, Finland Manufactured by Sako L.T.D.

Formerly imported by Stoeger Industries, Wayne NJ (formerly by Garcia Corp.) until 2000. Imported by Beretta USA 2001 to date.

MODEL 72 . . . . NiB $950 Ex $750 Gd $550
Single model designation replacing Vixen Sporter, Vixen Carbine, Vixen Heavy Barrel, Forester Sporter, Forester Carbine, Forester Heavy Barrel, Finnbear Sporter, and Finnbear Carbine, with same specifications, except all but heavy barrel models fitted with open rear sight. Values same as for corresponding earlier models. Imported 1972-74.

MODEL 73 LEVER-ACTION RIFLE . . . . . . NiB $1000 Ex $850 Gd $550
Same as Finnwolf except has 3-shot clip magazine, flush floorplate; stock has no cheekpiece. Imported 1973-75.

MODEL 74 CARBINE . . . . NiB $950 Ex $625 Gd $490
Long Mauser-type bolt action. Caliber: .30-06. Five shot magazine. 20-inch bbl. Weight: 7.5 lbs. No sights. Checkered Mannlicher-type full stock of European walnut, Monte Carlo cheekpiece. Imported 1974-78.

MODEL 74 HEAVY BARREL RIFLE,
LONG ACTION. . . . . NiB $950 Ex $625 Gd $400
Same specifications as short action except w/24-inch heavy bbl., weighs 8.75 lbs.; magnum w/4-shot magazine. Calibers: .25-06, 7mm Rem. Mag. Imported 1974-78.

MODEL 74 HEAVY BARREL RIFLE,
MEDIUM ACTION . . . . NiB $950 Ex $625 Gd $400
Same specifications as short action except w/23-inch heavy bbl., weighs 8.5 lbs. Calibers: .220 Swift, .22-250, .243 Win., .308 Win. Imported 1974-78.

MODEL 74 HEAVY BARREL RIFLE,
SHORT ACTION . . . . NiB $1000 Ex $800 Gd $450
Mauser-type bolt action. Calibers: .222 Rem., .223 Rem. Five shot magazine. 23.5-inch heavy bbl. Weight: 8.25 lbs. No sights. Target-style checkered European walnut stock w/beavertail forearm. Imported 1974-78.

MODEL 74 SUPER SPORTER,
LONG ACTION. NiB $950 Ex $658 Gd $400
Same specifications as short action except w/24-inch bbl., weight: 8 lbs.; magnums have 4-shot magazine, recoil pad. Calibers: .25-06, .270 Win. 7mm Rem. Mag., .30-06, .300 Win. Mag., .338 Win. Mag., .375 H&H Mag. Imported 1974-78.

MODEL 74 SUPER SPORTER,
MEDIUM ACTION. . . . . NiB $975 Ex $675 Gd $425
Same specifications as short action except weight: 7.25 lbs. Calibers: .220 Swift, .22-250, .243 Win. Imported 1974-78.

MODEL 74 SUPER SPORTER,
SHORT ACTION . . . . NiB $975 Ex $650 Gd $400
Mauser-type bolt action. Calibers: .222 Rem., .223 Rem. Five shot magazine. 23.5-inch bbl. Weight: 6.5 lbs. No sights. Checkered European walnut stock w/Monte Carlo cheekpiece, QD swivel studs. Imported 1974, now disc.

MODEL 75 DELUXE . . . . NiB $1244 Ex $995 Gd $677
Same specifications as Sako 75 Hunter Model except w/hinged floor plate, deluxe high gloss checkered walnut stock w/rosewood forend cap and grip cap w/silver inlay. Imported 1998 to date.

MODEL 75 HUNTER. . . . . NiB $975 Ex $725 Gd $500
New bolt action design available in four action lengths fitted with a new bolt featuring three front locking lugs with an external extractor positioned under the bolt. Calibers: .17 Rem., .222 Rem., .223 Rem., (I); .22-250 Rem., .243 Win., 7mm-08 Rem., .308 Win., (III); .25-06 Rem., .270 Win., .280 Rem., .30-06, (IV); 7mm Rem Mag., .300 Win. Mag., .300 Wby. Mag., .338 Win. Mag. 7mm STW, .300 Wby. Mag., .340 Wby. Mag., .375 H&H Mag. and .416 Rem. Mag.,(V). 4-, 5- or 6-shot magazine w/detachable magazine. 22-, 24-, and 26-inch bbls. 41.75 to 45.6 inches over all. Weight: 6.3 to 9 lbs. Sako dovetail scope base integral with receiver with no sights. Checkered high-grade walnut stock w/recoil pad and sling swivels. Made 1997 to date.

MODEL 75 STAINLESS SYNTHETIC . . . . . NiB $1031 Ex $825 Gd $561
Similar to Model 75 Hunter except chambered for .22-250 Rem., .243 Win., .25-06 Rem., .270 Win., 7mm-08 Rem., 7mm STW, .30-06, .308 Win., 7mm Rem Mag., .300 Win. Mag., .338 Win. Mag. or .375 H&H Mag. 22-, 24-, and 26-inch bbls. Black composite stock w/soft rubber grips inserts. Matte stainless steel finish. Made 1997 to date.

MODEL 75 VARMINT RIFLE . . . . . . NiB $750 Ex $550 Gd $375
Similar to Model 75 Hunter except chambered .17 Rem., .222 Rem., .223 Rem. and .22-250 Rem. 24-inch bbl. Matte lacquered walnut stock w/beavertail forearm. Made 1998 to date.

MODEL 78 SUPER HORNET SPORTER. . . . NiB $550 Ex $425 Gd $275
Same specifications as Model 78 Rimfire except chambered for .22 Hornet, 4-shot magazine. Imported 1977-87.

MODEL 78 SUPER RIMFIRE SPORTER . . . . NiB $500 Ex $400 Gd $225
Bolt action. Caliber: .22 LR. Five shot magazine. 22.5-inch bbl. Weight, 6.75 lbs. No sights. Checkered European walnut stock, Monte Carlo cheekpiece. Imported 1977-86.

CLASSIC BOLT-ACTION RIFLE
Medium Action (.243. Win.) or Long Action (.270 Win. .30-06, 7mm Rem. Mag.). American walnut stock. Made 1980-86. Reintroduced in 1993 w/matte lacquer finish stock, 22- or 24-inch bbl., overall length of 42 to 44 inches, weight 6.88 to 7.25lbs. Imported 1992-97.
Standard calibers. . . . . NiB $844 Ex $675 Gd $459
Magnum caliber . . . . NiB $906 Ex $725 Gd $493
Left-hand models. . . . . NiB $919 Ex $735 Gd $500

Sako Model 73

Sako Model 74 Carbine

Sako Model 74 Super Sporter

Sako Model 74 Super Rimfire

Sako Model 75 Hunter

Sako 75 Stainless Synthetic

Sako Model 75 Varmint Rifle

Sako Classic

Sako Deluxe Lightweight

Sako Fiberglass

Sako Finnfire

Sako Finnfire Heavy Barrel

Sako Finnwolf

DELUXE GRADE AI . . . . NiB $950 Ex $650 Gd $425
Same specifications as Standard Grade except w/22 lines to the inch
French checkering, rosewood grip cap and forend tip, semibeaver-
tail forend. Disc.

DELUXE GRADE AII . . . . NiB $975 Ex $675 Gd $450
Same specifications as Standard Grade except w/22 lines per inch
French checkering, rosewood grip cap and forend tip, semi beaver-
tail forend. Disc.

DELUXE GRADE AIII . . . . NiB $1275 Ex $980 Gd $600
Same specifications as w/standard except w/French checkering,
rosewood grip cap and forend tip, semibeavertail forend. Disc.

**DELUXE LIGHTWEIGHT
BOLT-ACTION RIFLE** . . . . NiB $1056 Ex $845 Gd $575
Same general specifications as Hunter Lightweight except w/beauti-
fully grained French walnut stock; superb high-gloss finish, fine
hand-cut checkering, rosewood forend tip and grip cap. Imported
1985-97.

**FIBERCLASS BOLT-ACTION
RIFLE** . . . . NiB $1000 Ex $900 Gd $525
All-weather fiberglass stock version of Sako barreled long action.
Calibers: .25-06, .270, .30-06, 7mm Rem. Mag., .300 Win. Mag.,
.338 Win. Mag., .375 H&H Mag. Bbl. length: 22.5 inches. Overall
length: 44.25 inches. Weight: 7.25 lbs. Imported 1984-96.

FINNBEAR CARBINE . . . . NiB $1100 Ex $800 Gd $475
Same as Finnbear Sporter except w/20-inch bbl., Mannlicher-type
full stock. Imported 1971. Disc.

FINNBEAR SPORTER . . . . NiB $1050 Ex $800 Gd $475
Long Mauser-type bolt action. Calibers: .25-06, .264 Mag. .270,
.30-06, .300 Win. Mag., .338 Mag., 7mm Mag., .375 H&H Mag.
Magazine holds 5 standard or 4 magnum cartridges. 24-inch bbl.
Weight: 7 lbs. Hooded ramp front sight. Sporter stock w/Monte
Carlo cheekpiece, checkered pistol-grip and forearm, recoil pad,
swivels. Imported 1961-71.

FINNFIRE BOLT-ACTION RIFLE
Mini-Sporter built for rimfires on a scaled-down Sako design.
Caliber: .22 LR. 5- or 10-shot magazine. 22-inch bbl. 39.5 inches
overall. Weight: 5.25 lbs. Receiver machined for 11mm dovetail
scope rings. Beaded blade front sight, open adj. rear. Blued finish.
Checkered European walnut stock. Imported 1994 to date.
Hunter model . . . . NiB $700 Ex $590 Gd $425
Varmint model . . . . NiB $795 Ex $600 Gd $450
Sporter model . . . . NiB $906 Ex $725 Gd $493

FINNWOLF LEVER-ACTION RIFLE . . . . NiB $969 Ex $775 Gd $527
Hammerless. Calibers: .243 Win., .308 Win. Four shot clip magazine. 23-inch bbl. Weight: 6.75 lbs. Hooded ramp front sight. Sporter
stock w/Monte Carlo cheekpiece, checkered pistol-grip and forearm,
swivels (available w/right- or left-hand stock). Imported 1963-72.

Sako Forester Sporter

Sako Golden Anniversary

Sako Hunter Lightweight

FINSPORT 2700 . . . . **NiB $850 Ex $700 Gd $450**
Bolt-action centerfire rifle. Calibers: .270, .30-06, 7mm Rem. Mag., .300 Win. Mag. Bbl. length: 24 inches. Weight: 8 lbs. Imported 1984-86.

FORESTER CARBINE . . . . **NiB $1050 Ex $925 Gd $475**
Same as Forester Sporter except w/20-inch bbl., Mannlicher-type full stock. Imported 1958-71.

FORESTER HEAVY BARREL . . . . . . **NiB $1000 Ex $900 Gd $425**
Same as Forester Sporter except w/24-inch heavy bbl. Weight 7.5 lbs. Imported 1958-71.

FORESTER SPORTER . . . . **NiB $1100 Ex $925 Gd $450**
Medium-length Mauser-type bolt action. Calibers: .22-250, .243 Win., .308 Win. Five shot magazine. 23-inch bbl. Weight: 6.5 lbs. Hooded ramp front sight. Sporter stock w/Monte Carlo cheekpiece, checkered pistol grip and forearm, swivels. Imported 1957-71.

GOLDEN ANNIVERSARY MODEL . . . . **NiB $2590 Ex $1975 Gd $1300**
Special presentation-grade rifle issued in 1973 to commemorate Sako's 50th anniversary. 1,000 (numbered 1 to 1,000) made. Same specifications as Deluxe Sporter: Long action, 7mm Rem. Mag. receiver, trigger guard and floorplate decorated w/gold oak leaf and acorn motif. Stock of select European walnut, checkering bordered w/hand-carved oak leaf pattern.

HIGH-POWER MAUSER SPORTING RIFLE . . . . . . **NiB $1000 Ex $900 Gd $700**
FN Mauser action. Calibers: .270, .30-06. Five shot magazine. 24-inch bbl. Sights: Open rear leaf; Partridge front; hooded ramp. Checkered stock w/Monte Carlo comb and cheekpiece. Weight: 7.5 lbs. Imported 1950-57.

HUNTER LIGHTWEIGHT BOLT-ACTION RIFLE
5- or 6-shot magazine. Bbl. length: 21.5 inches, AI; 22 inches, AII; 22.5 inches, AIII. Overall length: 42.25-44.5 inches. Weight: 5.75 lbs., AI; 6.75 lbs. AII; 7.25 lbs., AIII. Monte Carlo-style European walnut stock, oil finished. Hand-checkered pistol-grip and forend. Imported 1985-97. Left-hand version intro. 1987.
AI (Short Action) .17 Rem. . . . . **NiB $975 Ex $700 Gd $500**
.222 Rem., .223 Rem. . . . . **NiB $950 Ex $725 Gd $500**
AII (medium action)
.22-250 Rem., .243 Win., .308 Win. . . . . . . **NiB $850 Ex $700 Gd $450**

(cont'd.) **HUNTER LIGHTWEIGHT BOLT-ACTION RIFLE**
AII1 (long action) .25-06 Rem.,
.270 Win., .30-06 . . . . **NiB $906 Ex $725 Gd $493**
.338 Win. Mag. . . . . **NiB $1039 Ex $845 Gd $597**
.375 H&H Mag. . . . . **NiB $1133 Ex $920 Gd $648**
Left-hand model (standard cal.) . . . . **NiB $1162 Ex $930 Gd $632**
Magnum calibers. . . . . **NiB $1413 Ex $1145 Gd $803**

LAMINATED STOCK BOLT-ACTION RIFLES
Similar in style and specifications to Hunter Grade except w/stock of resin-bonded hardwood veneers. Available 18 calibers in AI (Short), AII (Medium) or AV action, left-hand version in 10 calibers, AV only. Imported 1987-95.
Short or medium action . . . . **NiB $950 Ex $775 Gd $500**
Long action/Magnum . . . . **NiB $975 Ex $800 Gd $525**

MAGNUM MAUSER . . . . **NiB $1400 Ex $1100 Gd $775**
Similar specifications as Standard Model except w/recoil pad and redesigned longer AIII action to handle longer magnum cartridges. Calibers: .300 H&H Magnum, .375 H&H Magnum, standard at time of introduction. Disc.

MANNLICHER-STYLE CARBINE
Similar to Hunter Model except w/full Mannlicher-style stock and 18.5-inch bbl. Weighs 7.5 lbs. Chambered in .243, .25-06, .270, .308, .30-06, 7mm Rem. Mag., .300 Win. Mag., .338 Win. Mag., .375 H&H. Intro. in 1977. Disc.
Standard calibers . . . . **NiB $1150 Ex $875 Gd $550**
Magnum calibers (except .375) . . . . **NiB $1175 Ex $900 Gd $600**
.375 H&H . . . . **NiB $1190 Ex $925 Gd $625**

SAFARI GRADE . . . . **NiB $2325 Ex $1780 Gd $975**
Classic bolt-action. Calibers: .300 Win. Mag., .338 Win. Mag., .375 H&H. Oil-finished European walnut stock w/hand-checkering. Barrel band swivel, express-type sight rib; satin or matte blue finish. Imported 1980-96.

SPORTER DELUXE . . . . **NiB $1150 Ex $875 Gd $550**
Same as Vixen, Forester, Finnbear and Model 74 except w/fancy French walnut stock w/skip checkering, rosewood forend tip and pistol-grip cap, recoil pad, inlaid trigger guard and floorplate. Disc.

Sako Mannlicher-Style Carbine

Sako Sporter Deluxe

Sako TRG-21
Target Rifle

STANDARD GRADE AI . . . . **NiB $950 Ex $675 Gd $350**
Short bolt-action. Calibers: .17 Rem., .222 Rem., .223 Rem. Five shot magazine. 23.5-inch bbl. Weight: 6.5 lbs. No sights. Checkered European walnut
stock w/Monte Carlo cheekpiece, QD swivel studs. Imported 1978-85.

STANDARD GRADE AII. . . . . **NiB $960 Ex $690 Gd $375**
Medium bolt-action. Calibers: .22-250 Rem., .243 Win., .308 Win.
23.5-inch bbl. in .22-250; 23-inch bbl. in other calibers. Five shot
magazine. Weight: 7.25 lbs. Checkered European walnut stock
w/Monte Carlo cheekpiece, QD swivel studs. Imported 1978-85.

STANDARD GRADE AIII . . . . **NiB $995 Ex $725 Gd $425**
Long bolt action. Calibers: .25-06 Rem., .270 Win., .30-06, 7mm
Rem. Mag., .300 Win. Mag., .338 Win. Mag., .375 H&H. 24-inch
bbl. 4-shot magazine. Weight: 8 lbs. Imported 1978-84.

SUPER DELUXE RIFLE . . . . **NiB $2250 Ex $1975 Gd $1150**
Available in AI, AII, AIII action calibers. Select European walnut
stock, hand-checkered, deep oak leaf hand-engraved design.
Disc.

TRG-BOLT-ACTION TARGET RIFLE
Caliber: .308 Win., .330 Win. or .338 Lapua Mag. Detachable 10-shot
magazine. 25.75- or 27.2-inch bbl. Weight: 10.5 to 11 lbs. Blued action
w/stainless barrel. Adjustable two-stage trigger. modular reinforced
polyurethane target stock w/adj. cheekpiece and buttplate. Options:
Muzzle break; detachable bipod; QD sling swivels and scope mounts
w/1-inch or 30mm rings. Imported 1993 to date.

(cont'd.) TRG-BOLT-ACTION TARGET RIFLE
TRG-21 .308 Win . . . . NiB $2500 Ex $1990 Gd $1350
TRG-22 .308 Win. . . . . NiB $2563 Ex $2050 Gd $1394
TRG-41 .338 Lapua. . . . . NiB $2994 Ex $2395 Gd $1629
TRG-42 .300 Win. or .338 Lapua . . . . . NiB $3063 Ex $2450 Gd $1666

TRG-S BOLT-ACTION RIFLE
Calibers: .243, 7mm-08, .270, .30-06, 7mm Rem. Mag., .300 Win.
Mag., .338 Win. Mag. Five shot magazine (standard calibers), 4-shot
(magnum), 22- or 24-inch bbl. 45.5 inches overall. Weight: 7.75 lbs. No
sights. Reinforced polyurethane stock w/Monte Carlo. Intro. in 1993.
Standard calibers. . . . . NiB $700 Ex $625 Gd $375
Magnum calibers. . . . . NiB $744 Ex $595 Gd $405

VIXEN CARBINE . . . . **NiB $1050 Ex $925 Gd $800**
Same as Vixen Sporter except w/20-inch bbl., Mannlicher-type full
stock. Imported 1947-71.

VIXEN HEAVY BARREL . . . . **NiB $1000 Ex $800 Gd $425**
Same as Vixen Sporter except calibers .222 Rem., .222 Rem. Mag.,
.223 Rem., heavy bbl., target-style stock w/beavertail forearm.
Weight: 7.5 lbs. Imported 1947-71.

VIXEN SPORTER . . . . **NiB $1050 Ex $950 Gd $450**
Short Mauser-type bolt-action. Cals.: .218 Bee, .22 Hornet, .222 Rem.,
.222 Rem. Mag., .223 Rem. Five shot magazine. 23.5-inch bbl. Weight:
6.5 lbs. Hooded ramp front sight. Sporter stock w/Monte Carlo cheekpiece, checkered pistol-grip and forearm, swivels. Imported 1946-71.

Sako TRG-S Bolt-Action Rifle

Sako Vixen Heavy Barrel

Sako Vixen Sporter

J. P. SAUER & SOHN — Eckernforde, Germany, (Formerly Suhl, Germany), Imported by Sigarms Exeter, NH, (Previously by Paul Company Inc. and G.U. Inc.)

MAUSER BOLT-ACTION
SPORTING RIFLE . . . . **NiB $1250 Ex $990 Gd $675**
Calibers: 7x57 and 8x57mm most common, but these rifles were produced in a variety of calibers including most of the popular Continental calibers as well as our .30-06. Five shot box magazine. 22- or 24-inch Krupp steel bbl., half-octagon w/raised matted rib. Double-set trigger. Weight: 7.5 lbs. Sights: Three-leaf open rear; ramp front. Sporting stock w/cheekpiece, checkered pistol grip, raised side-panels, Schnabel tip, swivels. Also made w/20-inch bbl. and full-length stock. Mfd. before WWII.

MODEL S-90 BOLT-ACTION RIFLES
Calibers: .243 Win., .308 Win. (Short action); .25-06, .270 Win., .30-06 (Medium action); 7mm Rem. Mag., .300 Win. Mag., .300 Wby., .338 Win., .375 H&H (Magnum action). Four shot (standard) or 3-shot magazine (magnum). Bbl. length: 20-inch (Stutzen), 24-inch. Weight: 7.6 to 10.75 lbs. Adjustable (Supreme) checkered Monte Carlo style stock. contrasting forend and pistol grip cap w/high-gloss finish or European (Lux) checkered Classic-style European walnut stock w/satin oil finish. Imported 1983-89.
S-90 Standard	**NiB $1000 Ex $875 Gd $475**
S-90 Lux	**NiB $1200 Ex $950 Gd $500**
S-90 Safari.	**NiB $1175 Ex $925 Gd $500**
S-90 Stutzen	**NiB $1000 Ex $875 Gd $475**
S-90 Supreme	**NiB $1300 Ex $1050 Gd $700**
Grade I engraving, add	**$600**
Grade II engraving, add	**$800**
Grade III engraving add	**$1000**
Grade IV engraving, add	**$1500**

MODEL 200 BOLT-ACTION RIFLES
Calibers: .243 Win., .25-06, .270 Win., 7mm Rem Mag., .30-06, .308 Win., .300 Win. Mag., Detachable box magazine. 24-inch (American) or 26-inch (European) interchangeable bbl. Standard (steel) or lightweight (alloy) action. Weight: 6.6 to 7.75 lbs. 44 inches overall. Stock options: American Model w/checkered Monte Carlo style 2-piece stock contrasting forend and pistol grip cap w/high gloss finish and no sights. European walnut stock w/Schnabel forend, satin oil finish and iron sights. Contemporary Model w/synthetic carbon fiber stock. Imported 1986-93.
Standard model.	**NiB $1225 Ex $925 Gd $575**

(cont'd.) MODEL 200 BOLT-ACTION RIFLES
Lightweight model	**NiB $1000 Ex $875 Gd $475**
Contemporary model	**NiB $1100 Ex $925 Gd $525**
American model	**NiB $1200 Ex $950 Gd $525**
European model	**NiB $1225 Ex $975 Gd $550**
Left-hand model, add	**$125**
Magnum calibers, add.	**$115**
Interchangeable barrel assembly, add	**$295**

MODEL 202 BOLT-ACTION RIFLES
Calibers: .243 Win., 6.5x55, 6.5x57, 6.6x68, .25-06, .270 Win., .280 7x64, .308, .30-06, Springfield, 7mm Rem. Mag., .300 Win. Mag., .300 Wby. Mag., 8x68S, .338 Win. Mag., .375 H&H Mag. Removable 3-shot box magazine. 23.6- and 26-inch interchangable bbl. 44.3 and 46 inches overall. Modular receiver drilled and tapped for scope bases. Adjustable two-stage trigger w/dual release safety. Weight: 7.7 to 8.4 lbs. Stock options: Checkered Monte Carlo-style select American walnut two-piece stock; Euro-classic French walnut two-piece stock w/semi Schnabel forend and satin oil finish; Super Grade Claro walnut two-piece stock fitted w/rosewood forend and grip cap w/high-gloss epoxy finish. Imported 1994 to date.
Standard model.	**NiB $1150 Ex $725 Gd $475**
Euro-Classic model	**NiB $1190 Ex $750 Gd $475**
Super Grade model.	**NiB $1200 Ex $775 Gd $500**
Left-hand model, add	**$150**
Magnum calibers, add.	**$125**
Interchangeable barrel assembly, add	**$295**

SAVAGE INDUSTRIES — Westfield, Massachusetts, (Formerly Chicopee Falls, MA and Utica, NY)

MODEL 3 BOLT-ACTION
SINGLE-SHOT RIFLE . . . . **NiB $150 Ex $125 Gd $75**
Takedown. Caliber: .22 Short, Long, LR. 26-inch bbl. on prewar rifles, postwar production w/24-inch bbl. Weight: 5 lbs. Sights: Open rear; bead front. Plain pistol-grip stock. Made 1933-52.

MODEL 3S. . . . . **NiB $185 Ex $150 Gd $90**
Same as Model 3 except w/peep rear sight, hooded front. Made 1933-42.

MODEL 3ST. . . . . **NiB $190 Ex $175 Gd $95**
Same as Model 3S except fitted w/swivels and sling. Made 1933-42.

Savage Model 3

Savage Model 4

Savage Model 5

Savage Model 6

Savage Model 19 NRA (1933)

Savage Model 20

MODEL 4 BOLT-ACTION REPEATER. . . . . . . NiB $175 Ex $135 Gd $95
Takedown. Caliber: .22 Short, Long, LR. Five shot detachable box magazine. 24-inch bbl. Weight: 5.5 lbs. Sights: Open rear; bead front. Checkered pistol-grip stock on prewar models, early production had grooved forearm; postwar rifles have plain stocks. Made 1933-65.

MODEL 4M. . . . . NiB $150 Ex $85 Gd $70
Same as Model 4 except chambered for .22 Rimfire Magnum. Made 1961-65.

MODEL 4S. . . . . NiB $190 Ex $95 Gd $75
Same as Model 4 except w/peep rear sight, hooded front. Made 1933-42.

**MODEL 5 BOLT-ACTION
REPEATER** . . . . NiB $175 Ex $95 Gd $75
Same as Model 4 except w/tubular magazine (holds 21 Short, 17 Long, 15 LR), weight: 6 lbs. Made 1936-61.

MODEL 5S. . . . . NiB $175 Ex $140 Gd $95
Same as Model 5 except w/peep rear sight, hooded front. Made 1936-42.

MODEL 6 AUTOLOADING RIFLE. . . . . NiB $175 Ex $150 Gd $100
Takedown. Caliber: .22 Short, Long, LR. Tubular magazine holds 21 Short, 17 Long, 15 LR. 24-inch bbl. Weight: 6 lbs. Sights: Open rear; bead front. Checkered pistol-grip stock on prewar models, postwar rifles have plain stocks. Made 1938-68.

MODEL 6S. . . . . NiB $190 Ex $160 Gd $105
Same as Model 6 except w/peep rear sight, bead front. Made 1938-42.

MODEL 7 AUTOLOADING RIFLE. . . . . NiB $200 Ex $175 Gd $110
Same general specifications as Model 6 except w/5-shot detachable box magazine. Made 1939-51.

MODEL 7S. . . . . NiB $180 Ex $120 Gd $100
Same as Model 7 except w/peep rear sight, hooded front. Made 1938-42.

MODEL 19 BOLT-ACTION TARGET RIFLE. . . . . . NiB $350 Ex $250 Gd $150
Model of 1933. Speed lock. Caliber: .22-LR. Five shot detachable box magazine. 25-inch bbl. Weight: 8 lbs. Adj. rear peep sight, blade front on early models, later production equipped w/extension rear sight, hooded front. Target stock w/full pistol-grip and beavertail forearm. Made 1933-46.

Savage Model 23AA

Savage Model 29

Savage Model 40

Savage Model 45

RIFLES

MODEL 19 NRA BOLT-ACTION
MATCH RIFLE . . . . **NiB $500 Ex $450 Gd $225**
Model of 1919. Caliber: .22 LR. Five shot detachable box magazine. 25-inch bbl. Weight: 7lbs. Sights: Adj. rear peep; blade front. Full military stock w/pistol-grip. Made 1919-33.

MODEL 19H . . . . **NiB $575 Ex $475 Gd $300**
Same as standard Model 19 (1933) except chambered for .22 Hornet, w/Model 23D-type bolt mechanism, loading port and magazine. Made 1933-42.

MODEL 19L. . . . . **NiB $350 Ex $250 Gd $150**
Same as standard Model 19 (1933) except equipped w/Lyman No. 48Y receiver sight, 17A front sight. Made 1933-42.

MODEL 19M. . . . . **NiB $450 Ex $400 Gd $175**
Same as standard Model 19 (1933) except w/heavy 28-inch bbl. w/scope bases, weight: 9.25 lbs. Made 1933-42.

MODEL 20-1926
HI-POWER . . . . **NiB $450 Ex $350 Gd $250**
Same as Model 1920 except w/24-inch medium weight bbl., improved stock, Lyman 54 rear peep sight, weight: 7 lbs. Made 1926-29.

MODEL 23A BOLT-ACTION
SPORTING RIFLE. . . . . **NiB $240 Ex $165 Gd $130**
Caliber: 22 LR. Five shot detachable box magazine. 23-inch bbl. Weight: 6 lbs. Sights: Open rear, blade or bead front. Plain pistol-grip stock w/slender forearm and Schnabel tip. Made 1923-33.

MODEL 23AA . . . . **NiB $295 Ex $250 Gd $160**
Model of 1933. Improved version of Model 23A w/same general specifications except w/speed lock, improved stock, weighs 6.5 lbs. Made 1933-42.

MODEL 23B . . . . **NiB $275 Ex $175 Gd $125**
Same as Model 23A except caliber .25-20, 25-inch bbl. Model of 1933 w/improved stock w/full forearm instead of slender forearm w/Schnabel found on earlier production. Weight: 6.5 lbs. Made 1923-42.

MODEL 23C . . . . **NiB $300 Ex $220 Gd $130**
Same as Model 23B except caliber .32-20. Made 1923-42.

MODEL 23D . . . . **NiB $375 Ex $250 Gd $175**
Same as Model 23B except caliber .22 Hornet. Made 1933-47.

MODEL 25 SLIDE-ACTION REPEATER . . . . **NiB $500 Ex $350 Gd $200**
Takedown. Hammerless. Caliber: .22 Short, Long, LR. Tubular magazine holds 20 Short, 17 Long, 15 LR. 24-inch octagon bbl. Weight: 5.75 lbs. Sights: Open rear; blade front. Plain pistol-grip stock, grooved slide handle. Made 1925-29.

MODEL 29 SLIDE-ACTION
REPEATER . . . . **NiB $425 Ex $300 Gd $200**
Takedown. Hammerless. Caliber: .22 Short, Long, LR. Tubular magazine holds 20 Short, 17 Long, 15 LR. 24-inch bbl., octagon on prewar, round on postwar production. Weight: 5.5 lbs. Sights: Open rear; bead front. Stock w/checkered pistol grip and slide handle on prewar, plain stock and grooved forearm on postwar production. Made 1929-67.

MODEL 40 BOLT-ACTION
SPORTING RIFLE. . . . . **NiB $375 Ex $225 Gd $180**
Standard Grade. Calibers: .250-3000, .300 Sav., .30-30, .30-06. Four shot detachable box magazine. 22-inch bbl. in calibers .250-3000 and .30-30; 24-inch in .300 Sav. and .30-06. Weight: 7.5 lbs. Sights: Open rear; bead front, on ramp. Plain pistol-grip stock w/tapered forearm and Schnabel tip. Made 1928-40.

MODEL 45 SUPER SPORTER . . . . . . **NiB $525 Ex $395 Gd $250**
Special Grade. Same as Model 40 except w/checkered pistol-grip

Savage Model 60

Savage Model 63K

Savage Model 71 "Stevens Favorite"

MODEL 60 AUTOLOADING RIFLE....... NiB $150 Ex $100 Gd $78
Caliber: .22 LR. 15-shot tubular magazine. 20-inch bbl. Weight: 6
lbs. Sights: Open rear, ramp front. Monte Carlo stock of walnut
w/checkered pistol-grip and forearm. Made 1969-72.

MODEL 63K KEY LOCK BOLT-ACTION
SINGLE-SHOT RIFLE.............. NiB $100 Ex $70 Gd $50
Trigger locked w/key. Caliber: .22 Short, Long, LR. 18-inch bbl.
Weight: 4 lbs. Sights: Open rear; hooded ramp front. Full-length
stock w/pistol grip, swivels. Made 1970-72.

MODEL 63KM.................. NiB $115 Ex $75 Gd $60
Same as Model 63K except chambered for .22 WMR. Made 1970-72.

MODEL 64F AUTOLOADING RIFLE........ NiB $100 Ex $75 Gd $60
Same general specifications as Model 64G except w/black
graphite/polymer stock. Weight: 5 lbs. Made 1997 to date.

MODEL 64G AUTOLOADING RIFLE....... NiB $110 Ex $90 Gd $70
Caliber: 22 LR. 10-shot magazine. 20-inch bbl. Weight: 5.5 lbs. 40
inches overall. Sights: Adj. open rear; bead front. Grooved receiver
for scope mounts. Stamped checkering on walnut-finished hardwood stock w/Monte Carlo cheekpiece. Made 1996 to date.

MODEL 71 "STEVENS FAVORITE"
SINGLE-SHOT LEVER-ACTION RIFLE..... NiB $250 Ex $175 Gd $125
Replica of original Stevens Favorite issued as a tribute to Joshua
Stevens, "Father of .22 Hunting." Caliber: .22 LR. 22-inch full-octagon bbl. Brass-plated hammer and lever. Sights: Open rear; brass
blade front. Weight: 4.5 lbs. Plain straight-grip buttstock and
Schnabel forend; brass commemorative medallion inlaid in buttstock, brass crescent-shaped buttplate. 10,000 produced. Made in
1971 only. Top value is for new, unfired gun.

MODEL 90 AUTO-LOADING
CARBINE......................... NiB $150 Ex $120 Gd $82
Similar to Model 60 except w/16.5-inch bbl. w/folding leaf rear
sight, bead front. 10-shot tubular magazine. Unchecked, carbine-

(cont'd.) **MODEL 90 AUTOLOADING CARBINE**
style walnut stock w/bbl. Band and sling swivels. Weight: 5.75 lbs.
Made 1969-72.

MODEL 93G BOLT-ACTION RIFLE....... NiB $150 Ex $125 Gd $90
Caliber: .22 Win Mag. 5-shot magazine. 20.75-inch bbl. 39.5 inches
overall. Weight: 5.75 lbs. Sights: Adj. open rear; bead front. Grooved
receiver for scope mounts. Stamped checkering on walnut-finished
hardwood stock w/Monte Carlo cheekpiece. Made 1996 to date.

MODEL 93F BOLT-ACTION RIFLE........ NiB $125 Ex $80 Gd $75
Same general specifications as Model 93G except w/black
graphite/polymer stock. Weight: 5.2 lbs. Made 1997 to date.

NOTE: MODEL 99 LEVER-ACTION REPEATER
*Introduced in 1899, this model has been produced in a variety of
styles and calibers. Original designation "Model 1899" was changed
to "Model 99" c.1920. Earlier rifles and carbines — similar to Models
99A, 99B and 99H — were supplied in calibers .25-35, .30-30, .303
Sav., .32-40 and .38-55. Post-WWII Models 99A, 99C, 99CD, 99DE,
99DL, 99F and 99PE have top tang safety other 99s have slide safety
on right side of trigger guard. Models 99C and 99CD have detachable
box magazine instead of traditional Model 99 rotary magazine.*

MODEL 99A (I) .... NiB $850 Ex $650 Gd $275
Hammerless. Solid frame. Calibers: .30-30, .300 Sav., .303 Sav.
Five-shot rotary magazine. 24-inch bbl. Weight: 7.25 lbs. Sights:
Open rear; bead front, on ramp. Plain straight-grip stock, tapered
forearm. Made 1920-36.

MODEL 99A (II) .... NiB $800 Ex $750 Gd $450
Current model. Similar to original Model 99A except w/top tang
safety, 22-inch bbl., folding leaf rear sight, no crescent buttplate.
Calibers: .243 Win., .250 Sav., .300 Sav., .308 Win. Made 1971-82.

MODEL 99B .... NiB $995 Ex $795 Gd $475
Takedown. Otherwise same as Model 99A except weight: 7.5 lbs.
Made 1920-36.

Savage Model 90

Savage Model 99A 1971 Issue

Savage Model 99C

Savage Model 99CD

Savage Model 99DE

MODEL 99C . . . . **NiB $995 Ex $900 Gd $300**
Current model. Same as Model 99F except w/clip magazine instead of rotary. Calibers: .243 Win., .284 Win., .308 Win. Four shot detachable magazine holds one round less in .284. Weight: 6.75 lbs. Made 1965 to date.

MODEL 99CD . . . . **NiB $600 Ex $525 Gd $300**
Deluxe version of Model 99C. Calibers: .243 Win., .250 Sav., .308 Win. Hooded ramp front sight. Weight: 8.25 lbs. Stock w/Monte Carlo comb and cheekpiece, checkered pistol-grip, grooved forearm, swivels and sling. Made 1975 to 81.

MODEL 99DE CITATION GRADE . . . . **NiB $850 Ex $575 Gd $400**
Same as Model 99PE except w/less elaborate engraving. Made 1968-70.

MODEL 99DL DELUXE . . . . **NiB $400 Ex $300 Gd $200**
Postwar model. Calibers: .243 Win., .308 Win. Same as Model 99F, except w/high comb Monte Carlo stock, sling swivels. Weight: 6.75 lbs. Made 1960-73.

MODEL 99E CARBINE (I) . . . . **NiB $750 Ex $600 Gd $325**
Pre-WWII type. Solid frame. Calibers: .22 Hi-Power, .250/3000, .30/30, .300 Sav., .303 Sav. w/22-inch bbl.; .300 Sav. 24-inch. Weight: 7 lbs. Other specifications same as Model 99A. Made 1920-36.

MODEL 99E CARBINE (II) . . . . **NiB $390 Ex $260 Gd $150**
Current model. Solid frame. Calibers: .250 Sav., .243 Win., .300 Sav., .308 Win. 20- or 22-inch bbl. Checkered pistol-grip stock and forearm. Made 1960-89.

Savage Model 99E 1969 Issue

Savage Model 99EG (Post WWII)

Savage Model 99F

Savage Model 99G

Savage Model 99PE Early Issue

Savage Model 99PE Late Issue

MODEL 99EG (I) . . . . **NiB $780 Ex $650 Gd $375**
Pre-WWII type. Solid frame. Plain pistol-grip stock and forearm. Otherwise same as Model G. Made 1936-41.

MODEL 99EG (II) . . . . **NiB $600 Ex $400 Gd $300**
Post-WWII type. Same as prewar model except w/checkered stock and forearm. Calibers: .250 Sav., .300 Sav., .308 Win. (intro. 1955), .243 Win., and .358 Win. Made 1946-60.

MODEL 99F
FEATHERWEIGHT (I) . . . . **NiB $850 Ex $600 Gd $415**
Pre-WWII type. Takedown. Specifications same as Model 99E, except weight: 6.5 lbs. Made 1920-42.

MODEL 99F
FEATHERWEIGHT (II) . . . . **NiB $550 Ex $350 Gd $200**
Postwar model. Solid frame. Calibers: .243 Win., .300 Sav., .308 Win. 22-inch bbl. Checkered pistol-grip stock and forearm. Weight: 6.5 lbs. Made 1955-73.

MODEL 99G . . . . **NiB $850 Ex $600 Gd $415**
Takedown. Checkered pistol-grip stock and forearm. Weight: 7.25 lbs. Other specifications same as Model 99E. Made 1920-42.

MODEL 99H CARBINE . . . . **NiB $800 Ex $500 Gd $350**
Solid frame. Calibers: .250/3000, .30/30, .303 Sav. 20-inch special weight bbl. Walnut carbine stock w/metal buttplate; walnut forearm w/bbl. band. Weight: 6.5 lbs. Open rear sights; ramped blade front sight. Other specifications same as Model 99A. Made 1931-42.

MODEL 99K . . . . **NiB $2200 Ex $1875 Gd $990**
Deluxe version of Model G w/similar specifications except w/fancy stock and engraving on receiver and bbl. Lyman peep rear sight and folding middle. Made 1931-42.

MODEL 99PE PRESENTATION GRADE. . . **NiB $1800 Ex $1550 Gd $700**
Same as Model 99DL except w/engraved receiver (game scenes on sides), tang and lever, fancy walnut Monte Carlo stock and forearm w/hand checkering, QD swivels. Calibers: .243, .284, .308. Made 1968-70.

Savage Model 99R (Pre-WWII)

Savage Model 99R (Post-WWII)

Savage Model 99RS (Pre-WWII)

Savage Model 99T

MODEL 99R (I) . . . . NiB $850 Ex $600 Gd $425
Pre-WWII type. Solid frame. Calibers: .250-3000 (22-inch bbl.), .300 Sav. (24-inch bbl.). Weight: 7.5 lbs. Special large pistol-grip stock and forearm, checkered. General specifications same as other Model 99 rifles. Made 1936-42.

MODEL 99R (II) . . . . NiB $780 Ex $400 Gd $275
Post-WWII type. Same as prewar mod except w/24-inch bbl. only, w/screw eyes for sling swivels. Calibers: .250 Sav., .300 Sav., .308 Win., .243 Win. and .358 Win. Made 1946-60.

MODEL 99RS (I) . . . . NiB $775 Ex $525 Gd $400
Pre-WWII type. Same as prewar Model 99R except equipped w/Lyman rear peep sight and folding middle sight, quick detachable swivels and sling. Made 1936-42.

MODEL 99RS (II) . . . . NiB $775 Ex $500 Gd $375
Post-WWII type. Same as postwar Model 99RS except equipped w/Redfield 70LH receiver sight, blank in middle sight slot. Made 1946-58.

MODEL 99T . . . . NiB $780 Ex $425 Gd $315
Featherweight. Solid frame. Calibers: .22 Hi-Power, .30/30, .303 Sav. w/20-inch bbl.; .300 Sav. w/22-inch bbl. Checkered pistol-grip stock and beavertail forearm. Weight: 7 lbs. General specifications same as other Model 99 rifles. Made 1936-42.

MODEL 99-358 . . . . NiB $550 Ex $400 Gd $300
Similar to current Model 99A except caliber .358 Win. has grooved forearm, recoil pad, swivel studs. Made 1977-80.

**MODEL 110 SPORTER
BOLT-ACTION RIFLE** . . . . NiB $210 Ex $150 Gd $100
Calibers: .243, .270, .308, .30-06. Four shot box magazine. 22-inch bbl. Weight: About 6.75 lbs. Sights: Open rear; ramp front. Standard sporter stock with checkered pistol-grip. Made 1958-63.

MODEL 110B BOLT-ACTION RIFLE
Same as Model 110E except with checkered select walnut Monte Carlo-style stock (early models) or brown laminated stock (late models). Calibers: .243 Win., .270 Win. .30-06, 7mm Rem. Mag., .338 Win. Mag. Made 1976 to date.
Early model . . . . NiB $313 Ex $250 Gd $170
**Laminated
stock model** . . . . NiB $331 Ex $265 Gd $180

MODEL 110BL . . . . NiB $369 Ex $295 Gd $201
Same as Model 110B except has left-hand action.

MODEL 110C
Calibers: .22-250, .243, .25-06, .270, .308, .30-06, 7mm Rem. Mag., .300 Win. Mag. Four shot detachable clip magazine (3-shot in Magnum calibers). 22-inch bbl. (24-inch in .22-250 Magnum calibers). Weight: 6.75 lbs., Magnum, 7.75 to 8 lbs. Sights: Open rear; ramp front. Checkered Monte Carlo-style walnut stock (Magnum has recoil pad). Made 1966-88.
**Standard
calibers** . . . . NiB $580 Ex $350 Gd $175
**Magnum
calibers** . . . . NiB $625 Ex $375 Gd $200

Savage Model 110

Savage Model 110B

Savage Model 110BL

Savage Model 110C

Savage Model 110E

Savage Model 110 MCL

MODEL 110CL
Same as Model 110C except has left-hand action. (Available only in .243 Win., .30-06, .270 Win. and 7mm Mag.) Made 1963-66.
Standard calibers . . . . NiB $350 Ex $275 Gd $190
Magnum calibers . . . . NiB $375 Ex $280 Gd $200

MODEL 110CY
YOUTH/LADIES RIFLE . . . . NiB $350 Ex $300 Gd $175
Same as Model 110G except with walnut-finished hardwood stock with 12.5-inch pull. Calibers: .243 Win. and .300 Savage. Made 1991 to date.

MODEL 110D
Similar to Model 110C except has internal magazine with hinged floorplate. Calibers: .243 Win., .270 Win., .30-06, 7mm Rem. Mag., .300 Win. Mag. Made 1972-88.
Standard calibers . . . . NiB $344 Ex $275 Gd $187
Magnum calibers . . . . NiB $369 Ex $295 Gd $201

MODEL 110DL
Same as Model 110D except has left-hand action. Discontinued.
Standard calibers . . . . NiB $406 Ex $325 Gd $221
Magnum calibers . . . . NiB $438 Ex $350 Gd $238

Savage Model 110P

Savage Model 110PE

MODEL 110E.................. **NiB $290 Ex $200 Gd $150**
Calibers: .22-250, .223 Rem., .243 Win., .270 Win., .308, 7mm Rem. Mag., .30-06. Four shot box magazine (3-shot in Magnum). 20- or 22-inch bbl. (24-inch stainless steel in Magnum). Weight: 6.75 lbs.; Magnum, 7.75 lbs. Sights: Open rear; ramp front. Plain Monte Carlo stock on early production; current models have checkered stocks of walnut-finished hardwood (Magnum has recoil pad). Made 1963-89.

MODEL 110EL................. **NiB $306 Ex $245 Gd $167**
Same as Model 110E except has left-hand action made in .30-06 and 7mm Rem. Mag. only. Made 1969-73.

MODEL 110F/110K BOLT-ACTION RIFLE
Same as Model 110E except Model 110F has black Rynite synthetic stock, swivel studs; made 1988-93. Model 110K has laminated camouflage stock; made 1986-88.
Model 110F, adj. sights .... **NiB $344 Ex $275 Gd $187**
Model 110FNS, no sights .... **NiB $356 Ex $285 Gd $194**
Model 110K, standard calibers .... **NiB $369 Ex $295 Gd $201**
Model 110K, magnum calibers .... **NiB $419 Ex $335 Gd $228**

MODEL 110FM SIERRA ULTRA LIGHT.... **NiB $350 Ex $275 Gd $180**
Calibers: .243 Win., .270 Win., .30-06, .308 Win. Five shot magazine. 20-inch bbl. 41.5 inches overall. Weight: 6.25 lbs. No sights w/drilled and tapped receiver. Black graphite/fiberglass composition stock. Non-glare matte blue finish. Made 1996 to date.

MODEL 110FP POLICE RIFLE..... **NiB $385 Ex $290 Gd $190**
Calibers: .223, .308 Win. Four shot magazine. 24-inch bbl. 45.5 inches overall. Weight: 9 lbs. Black Rynite composite stock. Matte blue finish. Made 1990 to date.

MODEL 110G BOLT-ACTION RIFLE
Calibers: .223, .22-250, .243 Win., .270, 7mm Rem. Mag., .308 Win., .30-06, .300 Win. Mag. Five shot (standard) or 4-shot magazine (magnum). 22- or 24-inch bbl. 42.38 overall (standard). Weight: 6.75 to 7.5 lbs. Ramp front sight, adj. rear. Checkered walnut-finished hardwood stock with rubber recoil pad. Made 1989-93.
Model 110G, standard calibers.......... **NiB $350 Ex $250 Gd $150**
Model 110G, magnum calibers.......... **NiB $375 Ex $275 Gd $190**
Model 110GLNS, left-hand, no sights..... **NiB $381 Ex $305 Gd $207**

MODEL 110GV VARMINT RIFLE .... **NiB $350 Ex $275 Gd $175**
Similar to the Model 110G except fitted with medium-weight varmint bbl. with no sights. Receiver drilled and tapped for scope mounts. Calibers .22-250 and .223 only. Made 1989-93.

MODEL 110M MAGNUM
Same as Model 110MC except calibers: 7mm Rem. Mag. .264, .300 and .338 Win. 24-inch bbl. Stock with recoil pad. Weight: 7.75 to 8 lbs. Made 1963-69.
Model 110M Magnum .... **NiB $390 Ex $375 Gd $200**
Model 110ML Magnum................ **NiB $415 Ex $400 Gd $375**

MODEL 110MC
Same as Model 110 except has Monte Carlo-style stock. Calibers: .22-250, .243 Win., .270, .308, .30-06. 24-inch bbl. in .22-250. Made 1959-69.
Model 110MC....................... **NiB $225 Ex $175 Gd $110**
Model 110MCL...................... **NiB $231 Ex $185 Gd $126**

MODEL 110P PREMIER GRADE
Calibers: .243 Win., 7mm Rem. Mag., .30-06. Four shot magazine (3-shot in Magnum). 22-inch bbl. (24-inch stainless steel in Magnum). Weight: 7 lbs.; Magnum, 7.75 lbs. Sights: Open rear folding leaf; ramp front. French walnut stock w/Monte Carlo comb and cheekpiece, rosewood forend tip and pistol-grip cap, skip checkering, sling swivels (Magnum has recoil pad). Made 1964-70.
Calibers .243 Win. and .30-06..... **NiB $450 Ex $325 Gd $225**
Caliber 7mm Rem. Mag. .... **NiB $465 Ex $350 Gd $250**

MODEL 110PE PRESENTATION GRADE
Same as Model 110P except has engraved receiver, floorplate and trigger guard, stock of choice grade French walnut. Made 1968-70.
Calibers .243 Win. and .30-06..... **NiB $688 Ex $550 Gd $374**
Caliber 7mm Rem. Mag. .... **NiB $744 Ex $595 Gd $405**

MODEL 110PEL PRESENTATION GRADE
Same as Model 110PE except has left-hand action.
Calibers .243 Win. and .30-06..... **NiB $744 Ex $595 Gd $405**
Caliber 7mm Rem. Mag. .... **NiB $813 Ex $650 Gd $442**

MODEL 110PL PREMIER GRADE
Same as Model 110P except has left-hand action.
Calibers .243 Win. and .30-06..... **NiB $475 Ex $350 Gd $225**
Caliber 7mm Rem. Mag. .... **NiB $495 Ex $350 Gd $250**

MODEL 110S/110V
Same as Model 110E except Model 110S in .308 Win. only; discontinued 1985. Model 110V in .22-250 and .223 Rem. w/heavy 2-inch barrel, 47 inches overall, weight: 9 lbs. Discontinued. 1989.
Model 110S.................. **NiB $344 Ex $275 Gd $187**
Model 110V.................. **NiB $369 Ex $295 Gd $201**

Savage Model 111 Chieftain

Savage Model 111F

Savage Model 112V

Savage Model 116FCSAK

MODEL 111 CHIEFTAIN BOLT-ACTION RIFLE
Calibers: .243 Win., .270 Win., 7x57mm, 7mm Rem. Mag. .30-06. 4-shot clip magazine (3-shot in Magnum). 22-inch bbl. (24-inch in Magnum). Weight: 7.5 lbs., 8.25 lbs. Magnum. Sights: Leaf rear; hooded ramp front. Select walnut stock w/Monte Carlo comb and cheekpiece, checkered, pistol-grip cap, QD swivels and sling. Made 1974-79.

Standard calibers	NiB $400	Ex $325	Gd $200
Magnum calibers	NiB $451	Ex $365	Gd $255

MODELS 111F, 111FC, 111FNS CLASSIC HUNTERS
Similar to the Model 111G except with graphite/fiberglass composite stock. Weight: 6.25 lbs. Made 1994 to date.

Model 111F (Box mag., right/left hand)	NiB $350	Ex $225	Gd $175
Model 111FC (Detachable magazine)	NiB $425	Ex $300	Gd $200
Model 111FNS (Box mag., no sights, R/L hand)	NiB $325	Ex $260	Gd $177

MODELS 111G, 111GC, 111GNS CLASSIC HUNTERS
Calibers: .22-250 Rem., .223 Rem., .243 Win., .25-06 Rem. .250 Sav., .270 Win., 7mm-08 Rem., 7mm Rem. Mag., .30-06, .300 Sav., .300 Win. Mag., .308 Win., .338 Win. 22- or 24-inch bbl. Weight: 7 lbs. Ramp front sight, adj. open rear. Walnut-finished hardwood stock. Blued finish. Made 1994 to date.

Model 111G (Box mag., right/left hand)	NiB $350	Ex $275	Gd $150
Model 111GC (Detachable mag., R/L hand)	NiB $370	Ex $280	Gd $160
Model 111GNS (Box mag., no sights)	NiB $330	Ex $250	Gd $125

MODEL 112BV,112BVSS HEAVY VARMINT RIFLES
Similar to the Model 110G except fitted with 26-inch heavy bbl. Laminated wood stock with high comb. .22-250 and .223 only.

(cont'd.) MODEL 112BV,112BVSS HEAVY VARMINT RIFLES
Model 112BV (Made 1993-94)	NiB $550	Ex $400	Gd $290
Model 112BVSS (Fluted stainless bbl.; made since 1994)	NiB $575	Ex $425	Gd $325

MODEL 112FV,112FVS,112FVSS VARMINT RIFLES
Similar to the Model 110G except fitted with 26-inch heavy bbl. and Dupont Rynite stock. Calibers: .22-250, .223 and .220 Swift (112FVS only). Blued or stainless finish. Made 1991 to date.

Model 112FV (blued)	NiB $344	Ex $275	Gd $187
Model 112FV-S (blued, single shot), disc. 1993	NiB $375	Ex $350	Gd $210
Model 112FVSS (stainless)	NiB $500	Ex $425	Gd $250
Model 112 FVSS-S (stainless, single shot)	NiB $525	Ex $450	Gd $275

MODEL 112V VARMINT RIFLE
	NiB $394	Ex $315	Gd $214

Bolt action, single shot. Caliber: .220 Swift, .222 Rem., .223 Rem. .22-250, .243 Win., .25-06. 26-inch heavy bbl. with scope bases. Supplied w/o sights. Weight: 9.25 lbs. Select walnut stock in varmint style w/checkered pistol-grip, high comb, QD sling swivels. Made 1975-79.

MODEL 114C, 114CE, 114CU RIFLES
Calibers: .270 Win., 7mm Rem. Mag., .30-06, .300 Win. Mag. 22- or 24-inch bbl. Weight: 7 lbs. Detachable 3- or 4-shot magazine. Ramp front sight; adjustable, open rear; (114CU has no sights). Checkered select walnut stock w/oil finish, red butt pad. Schnabel forend and skip-line checkering (114CE). High-luster blued finish. Made 1991 to date.

Model 114C (Classic)	NiB $475	Ex $400	Gd $230
Model 114CE (Classic European)	NiB $480	Ex $400	Gd $235
Model 114CU (Classic Ultra)	NiB $495	Ex $375	Gd $250

Savage Model 170C Carbine

Savage Model 219

Savage Model 219L

MODELS 116FSAK, 116FCSAK BOLT-ACTION RIFLES
Similar to the Model 116FSK except in calibers .270 Win., .30-06, 7mm Mag., .300 Win. Mag., .338 Win. Mag. Fluted 22-inch stainless bbl. w/adj. muzzle brake. Weight: 6.5 lbs. Made 1994 to date.
Model 116FSAK . . . . NiB $500 Ex $450 Gd $275
Model 116FCSAK (detachable mag.). . . . . . NiB $550 Ex $455 Gd $300

MODELS 116FSC, 116FSS BOLT-ACTION RIFLES
Improved Model 110 with satin stainless action and bbl. Calibers: .223, .243, .270, .30-06, 7mm Rem. Mag., .300 Win. Mag., .338 Win. Mag. 22- or 24-inch bbl. Four or 5-shot capacity. Weight: About 7.5 lbs. Black Rynite stock w/recoil pad and swivel studs. Receiver drilled and tapped for scope mounts, no sights. Made 1991 to date.
Model 116FSS . . . . NiB $525 Ex $450 Gd $275
Model 116FSC, detachable magazine . . . . . NiB $550 Ex $475 Gd $300

MODEL 116FSK KODIAK RIFLE . . . . NiB $575 Ex $400 Gd $300
Similar to the Model 116FSS except with 22-inch bbl. chambered for 338 Win. Mag. only. "Shock Suppressor" recoil reducer. Made 1993 to date.

MODEL 116SE, 116US RIFLES
Calibers: .270 Win., 7mm Rem Mag., .30-06, .300 Win. Mag. (116US); .300 Win. Mag., .338 Win. mag., .425 Express, .458 Win. Mag. (116SE). 24-inch stainless barrel (with muzzle brake 116SE only). 45.5 inches overall. Weight: 7.2 to 8.5 lbs. Three shot magazine. 3-leaf Express sights 116SE only. Checkered Classic style select walnut stock with ebony forend tip. Stainless finish. Made 1994 to date.
Model 116SE (Safari Express) . . . . . NiB $875 Ex $675 Gd $450
Model 116US (Ultra Stainless) . . . . NiB $650 Ex $500 Gd $325

MODEL 170 PUMP-ACTION
CENTERFIRE RIFLE . . . . NiB $240 Ex $190 Gd $125
Calibers: .30-30, .35 Rem. Three shot tubular magazine. 22-inch bbl. Weight: 6.75 lbs. Sights: Folding leaf rear; ramp front. Select walnut stock w/checkered pistol-grip Monte Carlo comb, grooved slide handle. Made 1970-81.

MODEL 170C CARBINE . . . . NiB $275 Ex $195 Gd $125
Same as Model 170 Rifle except has 18.5-inch bbl., straight comb stock, weight: 6 lbs.; caliber .30-30 only. Made 1974-81.

MODEL 219 SINGLE-SHOT RIFLE
Hammerless. Takedown. Shotgun-type action with top lever. Calibers: .22 Hornet, .25-20, .32-20, .30-30. 26-inch bbl. Weight: about 6 lbs. Sights: Open rear; bead front. Plain pistol-grip stock and forearm. Made 1938-65.
Model 219 . . . . NiB $250 Ex $175 Gd $120
Model 219L (w/side lever, made 1965-67) . . NiB $175 Ex $125 Gd $90

MODEL 221-229 UTILITY GUNS
Same as Model 219 except in various calibers, supplied in combination with an interchangeable shotgun bbl. All versions discontinued.
Model 221 (.30-30,12-ga. 30-inch bbl.) . . . . NiB $175 Ex $140 Gd $95
Model 222 (.30-30,16-ga. 28-inch bbl.) . . . . NiB $156 Ex $125 Gd $85
Model 223 (.30-30, 20-ga. 28-inch bbl.) . . . . NiB $138 Ex $110 Gd $75
Model 227 (.22 Hornet, 12-ga. 30-inch bbl.) . . . NiB $188 Ex $150 Gd $102
Model 228 (.22 Hornet, 16-ga. 28-inch bbl.) . . NiB $181 Ex $145 Gd $99
Model 229 (.22 Hornet, 20-ga. 28-inch bbl.) . . NiB $175 Ex $140 Gd $95

MODEL 340 BOLT-ACTION REPEATER
Calibers: .22 Hornet, .222 Rem., .223 Rem., .225 Win., .30-30. Clip magazine; 4-shot capacity (3-shot in 30-30). Bbl. lengths: Originally 20-inch in .30-30, 22-inch in .22 Hornet; later 22-inch in .30-30, 24-inch in other calibers. Weight: 6.5 to 7.5 lbs. depending on caliber and vintage. Sights: Open rear (folding leaf on recent production); ramp front. Early models had plain pistol-grip stock, checkered since 1965. Made 1950-85. (Note: Those rifles produced between 1947-1950 were .22 Hornet Stevens Model .322 and .30-30 Model .325. The Savage model, however, was designated Model .340 for all calibers.)
Pre-1965 with plain stock . . . . NiB $300 Ex $190 Gd $125
Current model . . . . NiB $200 Ex $160 Gd $109
Savage Model 340C Carbine . . . . . . NiB $300 Ex $190 Gd $125

Savage Model 340

Savage Model 340C Carbine

Savage Model 1895 Replica

MODEL 340S DELUXE . . . . NiB $350 Ex $250 Gd $140
Same as Model 340 except has checkered stock, screw eyes for sling, peep rear sight, hooded front. Made 1955-60.

MODEL 342 . . . . NiB $340 Ex $250 Gd $150
Designation, 1950 to 1955, of Model 340 .22 Hornet.

MODEL 342S DELUXE . . . . NiB $375 Ex $275 Gd $150
Designation, 1950 to 1955, of Model 340S .22 Hornet.

ANNIVERSARY MODEL
1895 LEVER-ACTION . . . . NiB $1500 Ex $1300 Gd $1000
Replica of Savage Model 1895 Hammerless Lever-Action Rifle issued to commemorate the 75th anniversary (1895-1970) of Savage Arms. Caliber: .308 Win. Five shot rotary magazine. 24-inch full-octagon bbl. Engraved receiver. Brass-plated lever. Sights: Open rear; brass blade front. Plain straight-grip buttstock, Schnabel-type forend; brass medallion inlaid in buttstock, brass crescent-shaped buttplate. 9,999 produced. Made in 1970 only. Top value is for new, unfired specimen.

MODEL 1903 SLIDE-ACTION
REPEATER . . . . NiB $375 Ex $250 Gd $190
Hammerless. Takedown. Caliber: .22 Short, Long, LR. Detachable box magazine. 24-inch octagon bbl. Weight: About 5 lbs. Sights: Open rear; bead front. Pistol-grip stock, grooved slide handle. Made 1903-21.

MODEL 1904 BOLT-ACTION
SINGLE-SHOT RIFLE . . . . NiB $150 Ex $100 Gd $50
Takedown. .22 Short, Long, LR. 18-inch bbl. Weight: About 3 lbs. Sights: Open rear; bead front. Plain, straight-grip, one-piece stock. Made 1904-17.

MODEL 1905 BOLT-ACTION
SINGLE-SHOT RIFLE . . . . NiB $150 Ex $100 Gd $50
Takedown. .22 Short, Long, LR. 22-inch bbl. Weight: About 5 lbs. Sights: Open rear; bead front. Plain, straight-grip one-piece stock. Made 1905-19.

MODEL 1909 SLIDE-ACTION
REPEATER . . . . NiB $370 Ex $250 Gd $175
Hammerless. Takedown. Similar to Model 1903 except has 20-inch round bbl., plain stock and forearm, weight: about 4.75 lbs. Made 1909-15.

MODEL 1912
AUTOLOADING RIFLE . . . . NiB $475 Ex $290 Gd $150
Takedown. Caliber: 22 LR. only. Seven shot detachable box magazine. 20-inch bbl., plain stock and forearm. Made 1912-16.

MODEL 1914 SLIDE-ACTION
REPEATER . . . . NiB $370 Ex $250 Gd $175
Hammerless. Takedown. Caliber: .22 Short, Long, LR, Tubular magazine holds 20 Short, 17 Long, 15 LR. 24-inch octagon bbl. Weight: About 5.75 lbs. Sights: Open rear; bead front. Plain pistol-grip stock, grooved slide handle. Made 1914-24.

MODEL 1920 HI-POWER BOLT-ACTION RIFLE
Short Mauser-type action. Calibers: .250/3000, .300 Sav. Five shot box magazine. 22-inch bbl. in .250 cal.; 24-inch in .300 cal. Weight: About 6 lbs. Sights: Open rear; bead front. Checkered pistol-grip stock w/slender forearm and Schnabel tip. Made 1920-26.
Model 1920
Hi-Power
(.250-3000 Sav.) . . . . NiB $550 Ex $375 Gd $225
Model 1920
Hi-Power
(.300 Sav.) . . . . NiB $500 Ex $325 Gd $200

NOTE: *In 1965, Savage began the importation of rifles manufactured by J. G. Anschutz GmbH, Ulm, West Germany. Models designated "Savage/Anschutz" are listed in this section, those marketed in the U.S. under the "Anschutz" name are included in that firm's listings. Anschutz rifles are now distributed in the U.S. by Precision Sales Int'l., Westfield, Mass. See "Anschutz" for detailed specifications.*

Savage/Anschutz Mark 10D

Savage-Stevens Model 34

Savage-Stevens Model 35

MARK 10 BOLT-ACTION
TARGET RIFLE...................... **NiB $450 Ex $295 Gd $200**
Single shot. Caliber: .22 LR. 26-inch bbl. Weight: 8.5 lbs. Sights: Anschutz micrometer rear; globe front. Target stock w/full pistol-grip and cheekpiece, adj. hand stop and swivel. Made 1967-72.

MARK 10D .... **NiB $475 Ex $300 Gd $200**
Same as Mark 10 except has redesigned stock with Monte Carlo comb, different rear sight. Weight: 7.75 lbs. Made 1972.

MODEL 54
CUSTOM SPORTER................... **NiB $675 Ex $550 Gd $300**
Same as Anschutz Model 1422D.

MODEL 54M.................. **NiB $825 Ex $575 Gd $350**
Same as Anschutz Model 1522D.

MODEL 64 BOLT-ACTION
TARGET RIFLE................. **NiB $550 Ex $400 Gd $250**
Same as Anschutz Model 1403.

MODEL 153 BOLT-ACTION
SPORTER .... **NiB $600 Ex $400 Gd $275**
Caliber: .222 Rem. Three shot clip magazine. 24-inch bbl. Sights: Folding leaf open rear; hooded ramp front. Weight: 6.75 lbs. French walnut stock w/cheekpiece, skip checkering, rosewood forend tip and grip cap, swivels. Made 1964-67.

MODEL 153S.................. **NiB $675 Ex $475 Gd $300**
Same as Model 153 except has double-set trigger. Made 1965-67.

MODEL 164 CUSTOM SPORTER....... **NiB $500 Ex $350 Gd $200**
Same as Anschutz Model 1416.

MODEL 164M.................. **NiB $575 Ex $375 Gd $225**
Same as Anschutz Model 1516.

MODEL 184 SPORTER .... **NiB $550 Ex $400 Gd $200**
Same as Anschutz Model 1441.

NOTE: *Since J. Stevens Arms (see also separate listing) is a division of Savage Industries, certain Savage models carry the "Stevens" name.*

MODEL 34 BOLT-ACTION
REPEATER .... **NiB $140 Ex $85 Gd $50**
Caliber: .22 Short, Long, LR. 20-inch bbl. Weight: 4.75 lbs. Sights: Open rear; bead front. Plain pistol-grip stock. Made 1965-80.

MODEL 34M.................... **NiB $125 Ex $90 Gd $60**
Same as Model 34 except chambered for 22 WMR. Made 1969-73.

MODEL 35 .... **NiB $125 Ex $90 Gd $60**
Bolt-action repeater. Caliber: 22 LR. Six shot clip magazine. 22-inch bbl. Weight: About 5 lbs. Sights: Open rear; ramp front. Monte Carlo stock w/checkered pistol grip and forearm. Made 1982 to date.

MODEL 35M.................... **NiB $150 Ex $100 Gd $65**
Same as Model 35 except chambered for 22 WMR. Made 1982 to date.

MODEL 46 BOLT-ACTION
RIFLE........................... **NiB $135 Ex $90 Gd $60**
Caliber: .22 Short, Long, LR. Tubular magazine holds 22 Short, 17 Long, 15 LR. 20-inch bbl. Weight: 5 lbs. Plain pistol-grip stock on early production; later models have Monte Carlo stock w/checkering. Made 1969-73.

MODEL 65
BOLT-ACTION RIFLE.............. **NiB $150 Ex $100 Gd $60**
Caliber: .22 Short, Long, LR. Five shot clip magazine. 20-inch bbl. Weight: 5 lbs. Sights: Open rear; ramp front. Monte Carlo stock w/checkered pistol grip and forearm. Made 1969-73.

Savage-Stevens Model 46

Savage-Stevens Model 65

Savage-Stevens Model 72 — Crackshot

Savage-Stevens Model 73

Savage-Stevens Model 80

MODEL 65M . . . . NiB $150 Ex $110 Gd $70
Same as Model 65 except chambered for .22 WMR, has 22-inch bbl., weighs 5.25 lbs. Made 1969-81.

NOTE: *The Model 72 is a "Favorite"-type single-shot unlike the smaller, original "Crackshot" made by Stevens from 1913-39.*

**MODEL 72 CRACKSHOT SINGLE-SHOT
LEVER-ACTION RIFLE** . . . . NiB $250 Ex $200 Gd $125
Falling-block action. Casehardened frame. Caliber: .22 Short, Long, LR. 22-inch octagon bbl. Weight: 4.5lbs. Sights: Open rear; bead front. Plain straight-grip stock and forend of walnut. Made 1972 to date.

MODEL 73 BOLT-ACTION SINGLE-SHOT . . . NiB $100 Ex $80 Gd $60
Caliber: .22 Short, Long, LR. 20-inch bbl. Weight: 4.75 lbs. Sights: Open rear; bead front. Plain pistol-grip stock. Made 1965-80.

MODEL 73Y YOUTH MODEL . . . . . . NiB $105 Ex $85 Gd $60
Same as Model 73 except has 18-inch bbl., 1.5-inch shorter butt-stock, weight: 4.5 lbs. Made 1965-80.

**MODEL 74
LITTLE FAVORITE** . . . . NiB $170 Ex $158 Gd $90
Same as Model 72 Crackshot except has black-finished frame, 22-inch round bbl., walnut-finished hardwood stock. Weight: 4.75 lbs. Made 1972-74.

**MODEL 80
AUTOLOADING RIFLE** . . . . NiB $150 Ex $120 Gd $82
Caliber: 22 LR. 15-shot tubular magazine. 20-inch bbl. Weight: 6 lbs. Sights: Open rear, bead front. Monte Carlo stock of walnut w/checkered pistol-grip and forearm. Made 1976 to date. (Note: This rifle is essentially the same as the Model 60 of 1969-72 except for a different style of checkering, side instead of top safety and plain bead instead of ramp front sight.)

**MODEL 88
AUTOLOADING RIFLE** . . . . NiB $160 Ex $150 Gd $90
Similar to Model 60 except has walnut-finished hardwood stock, plain bead front sight. Weight: 5.75 lbs. Made 1969-72.

Savage-Stevens Model 89

Savage-Stevens Model 987-T

MODEL 89 SINGLE-SHOT
LEVER-ACTION CARBINE . . . . NiB $90 Ex $75 Gd $50
Martini-type action. Caliber: .22 Short, Long, LR. 18.5-inch bbl. Weight: 5 lbs. Sights: Open rear; bead front. Western-style carbine stock w/straight grip, forearm with bbl. band. Made 1976-89.

MODEL 987-T
AUTOLOADING RIFLE . . . . NiB $150 Ex $120 Gd $82
Caliber: .22 LR. 15-shot tubular magazine. 20-inch bbl. Weight: 6 lbs. Sights: Open rear; ramp front. Monte Carlo stock w/checkered pistol grip and forearm. Made 1981-89.

"STEVENS FAVORITE"
See Savage Model 71.

V.C. SCHILLING — Suhl, Germany

MAUSER-MANNLICHER
BOLT ACTION SPORTING RIFLE . . NiB $813 Ex $650 Gd $442
Same general specifications as given for the Haenel Mauser-Mannlicher Sporter. See separate listing.

'88 MAUSER SPORTER . . . . NiB $781 Ex $625 Gd $425
Same general specifications as Haenel '88 Mauser Sporter. See separate listing.

SCHULTZ & LARSEN GEVAERFABRIK — Otterup, Denmark

MATCH RIFLE NO. 47 . . . . NiB $700 Ex $650 Gd $475
Caliber: .22 LR. Bolt-action, single-shot, set trigger. 28.5-inch heavy bbl. Weight: 14 lbs. Sights: Micrometer receiver, globe front. Free-rifle stock w/cheekpiece, thumbhole, adj. Schuetzen-type buttplate, swivels, palmrest.

FREE RIFLE MODEL 54 . . . . NiB $950 Ex $775 Gd $500
Calibers: 6.5x55mm or any standard American centerfire caliber. Schultz & Larsen M54 bolt-action, single-shot, set trigger. 27.5-inch heavy bbl. Weight: 15.5 lbs. Sights: Micrometer receiver; globe front. Free-rifle stock w/cheekpiece, thumbhole, adj. Schuetzen-type buttplate, swivels, palm rest.

MODEL 54J
SPORTING RIFLE. . . . . NiB $675 Ex $550 Gd $350
Calibers: .270 Win., .30-06, 7x61 Sharpe & Hart. Schultz & Larsen bolt action. Three shot magazine. 24-inch bbl. in .270 and .30-06, 26-inch in 7x61 S&H. Checkered stock w/Monte Carlo comb and cheekpiece. Value shown is for rifle less sights.

SEARS, ROEBUCK & COMPANY — Chicago, Illinois

The most encountered brands or model designations used by Sears are J. C. Higgins and Ted Williams. Firearms sold under these designations have been mfd. by various firms including Winchester, Marlin, Savage, Mossberg, etc.

MODEL 2C
BOLT-ACTION RIFLE . . . . NiB $100 Ex $80 Gd $60
Caliber: .22RF. Seven shot clip mag. 21-inch bbl. Weight: 5 lbs. Sights: Open rear; ramp front. Plain Monte Carlo stock. Mfd. by Win.

MODEL 42
BOLT-ACTION REPEATER . . . . NiB $100 Ex $80 Gd $54
Takedown. Caliber: .22RF. Eight shot detachable box magazine. 24-inch bbl. Weight: 6 lbs. Sights: Open rear; bead front. Plain pistol-grip stock. Mfd. by Marlin.

MODEL 42DL
BOLT-ACTION REPEATER . . . . NiB $100 Ex $80 Gd $60
Same general specifications as Model 42 except fancier grade w/peep sight, hooded front sight and swivels.

MODEL 44DL
LEVER-ACTION RIFLE . . . . NiB $175 Ex $135 Gd $90
Caliber: .22RF. Tubular magazine holds 19 LR cartridges. 22-inch bbl. Weight: 6.25 lbs. Sights: Open rear; hooded ramp front. Monte Carlo-style stock w/pistol grip. Mfd. by Marlin.

MODEL 53
BOLT-ACTION RIFLE . . . . NiB $225 Ex $150 Gd $110
Calibers: .243, .270, .308, .30-06. Four shot magazine. 22-inch bbl. Weight: 6.75 lbs. Sights: Open rear; ramp front. Standard sporter stock w/pistol-grip, checkered. Mfd. by Savage.

Sedgley Springfield Sporter

Sedgley Springfield — Left Hand

Sedgley Springfield Mannlicher

MODEL 54 LEVER-ACTION
RIFLE . . . . NiB $175 Ex $150 Gd $100
Similar general specifications as Winchester Model 94 carbine. Made in .30-30 caliber only. Mfd. by Winchester.

MODEL 103 SERIES
BOLT-ACTION REPEATER . . . . NiB $180 Ex $75 Gd $55
Same general specifications as Model 103.2 w/minor changes. Mfd. by Marlin.

MODEL 103.2 BOLT-ACTION
REPEATER . . . . NiB $100 Ex $75 Gd $55
Takedown. Caliber: .22RF. 8-shot detachable box magazine. 24-inch bbl. Weight: 6 lbs. Sights: Open rear; bead front. Plain pistol-grip stock. Mfd. by Marlin.

R. F. SEDGLEY, INC. — Philadelphia, Pennsylvania

SPRINGFIELD SPORTER . . . . NiB $1275 Ex $1000 Gd $500
Springfield '03 bolt action. Calibers: .220 Swift, .218 Bee, .22-3000, R, .22-4000, .22 Hornet, .25-35, .250-3000, .257 Roberts, .270 Win., 7mm, .30-06. 24-inch bbl. Weight: 7.5 lbs. Sights: Lyman No. 48 receiver; bead front on matted ramp. Checkered walnut stock, grip cap, sling swivels. Disc. 1941.

SPRINGFIELD LEFT-HAND SPORTER . . . NiB $1450 Ex $1190 Gd $775
Bolt-action reversed for left-handed shooter; otherwise the same as standard Sedgley Springfield Sporter. Disc. 1941.

SEDGLEY SPRINGFIELD
MANNLICHER-TYPE SPORTER . . . . NiB $1550 Ex $1275 Gd $900
Same as standard Sedgley Springfield Sporter except w/20-inch bbl., Mannlicher-type full stock w/cheekpiece, weight: 7.75 lbs. Disc. 1941.

SHILEN RIFLES, INC. — Ennis, Texas

DGA BENCHREST RIFLE . . . . NiB $1450 Ex $1075 Gd $800
DGA single-shot bolt-action. Calibers as listed for Sporter. 26-inch medium-heavy or heavy bbl. Weight: From 10.5 lbs. No sights. Fiberglass or walnut stock, classic or thumbhole pattern. Currently manufactured.

DGA SPORTER . . . . NiB $1500 Ex $995 Gd $690
DGA bolt action. Calibers: .17 Rem., .222 Rem., .223 Rem. .22-250, .220 Swift, 6mm Rem., .243 Win., .250 Sav., .257 Roberts, .284 Win., .308 Win., .358 Win. Three shot blind magazine. 24-inch bbl. Average weight: 7.5 lbs. No sights. Select Claro walnut stock w/cheekpiece, pistol grip, sling swivel studs. Currently manufactured.

DGA VARMINTER . . . . NiB $1395 Ex $1050 Gd $715
Same as Sporter except w/25-inch medium-heavy bbl. Weight: 9 lbs.

SHILOH RIFLE MFG. Co. — Big Timber, Montana (Formerly Shiloh Products)

SHARPS MODEL 1874 BUSINESS RIFLE . . . . . NiB $1050 Ex $975 Gd $600
Replica of 1874 Sharps similar to No. 3 Sporting Rifle. .32-40, .38-55, .40-50 BN, .40-70 BN, .40-90 BN, .45-70 ST, .45-90 ST, .50-70 ST, .50-100 ST. 28-inch round heavy bbl. Blade front sight, buckhorn rear. Double-set triggers. Straight-grip walnut stock w/steel crescent buttplate. Made 1986 to date.

SHARPS MODEL 1874 LONG
RANGE EXPRESS RIFLE . . . . NiB $1600 Ex $1550 Gd $995
Replica of 1874 Sharps w/single-shot falling breech action. .32-40, .38-55, .40-50 BN, .40-70 BN, .40-90 BN, .45-70 ST, .45-90 ST, .45-110 ST, .50-70 ST, .50-90 ST, .50-110 ST. 34-inch tapered octagon bbl. 51 inches overall. Weight: 10.75 lbs. Globe front sight, sporting tang peep rear. Walnut buttstock w/pistol-grip and Schnabel-style forend. Color casehardened action w/double-set triggers Made 1986 to date.

Shilen DGA
Benchrest Rifle

Shilen DGA Sporter

Shilen DGA Varminter

SHARPS MODEL 1874 SADDLE RIFLE . . . NiB $1100 Ex $995 Gd $600
Similar to 1874 Express Rifle except w/30-inch bbl., blade front sight and buckhorn rear. Made 1986 to date.

**SHARPS MODEL 1874
SPORTING RIFLE NO. 1 . . . . NiB $1190 Ex $995 Gd $625**
Similar to 1874 Express Rifle except w/30-inch bbl., blade front sight and buckhorn rear. Made 1986 to date.

**SHARPS MODEL 1874
SPORTING RIFLE NO. 3 . . . . NiB $1000 Ex $875 Gd $575**
Similar to 1874 Sporting Rifle No. 1 except w/straight-grip stock w/steel crescent buttplate. Made 1986 to date.

SHARPS MODEL 1874 MONTANA ROUGHRIDER
Similar to 1874 Sporting Rifle No. 1 except w/24- to 34-inch half-octagon or full-octagon bbl. Standard or deluxe walnut stock w/pistol-grip or military-style buttstock. Made 1989 to date.
Standard model . . . . NiB $995 Ex $600 Gd $525
Deluxe model . . . . NiB $1125 Ex $850 Gd $500

SIG SWISS INDUSTRIAL COMPANY — Neuhausen-Rhine Falls, Switzerland

AMT SEMIAUTOMATIC RIFLE . . . . . . NiB $4025 Ex $3975 Gd $2700
.308 Win.(7.62 NATO). 5, 10, or 20-shot magazine. 18.5-inch bbl. w/flash suppressor. Weight: 9.5 lbs. Sights: Adj. aperture rear, post front. Walnut buttstock and forend w/synthetic pistol grip. Imported 1980-88.

AMT SPORTING RIFLE . . . . NiB $3750 Ex $2750 Gd $1995
Semiautomatic version of SG510-4 automatic assault rifle based on Swiss Army SIGW57. Roller-delayed blowback action. Caliber: 7.62x51mm NATO (.308 Win.). Five, 10- and 20-round magazines. 19-inch bbl. Weight: 10 lbs. Sights, aperture rear, post front. Wood buttstock and forearm, folding bipod. Imported 1960-88.

PE57 SEMIAUTOMATIC RIFLE . . . . . . NiB $4994 Ex $3995 Gd $2717
Caliber: 7.5 Swiss. 24-shot magazine. 23.75-inch bbl. Weight: 12.5 lbs. Sights: Adj. aperture rear; post front. High-impact synthetic stock. Imported from Switzerland during the 1980s.

Smith & Wesson
Model 1500DL

Smith & Wesson
Model 1700 LS Classic Hunter

Springfield Armory
BM-59

SMITH & WESSON — Springfield, Massachusetts, Mfd. by Husqvarna, Vapenfabrik A.B., Huskvarna, Sweden & Howa Machonery LTD., Shinkawa-Chonear, Nagota 452, Japan

MODEL 1500 . . . . NiB $350 Ex $275 Gd $175
Bolt-action. .243 Win., .270 Win., .30-06, 7mm Rem. Mag. 22-inch bbl. (24-inch in 7mm Rem. Mag.). Weight: 7.5 lbs. American walnut stock w/Monte Carlo comb and cheekpiece, cut checkering. Sights: Open rear, hooded ramp, gold beadfront. This model was also imported by Mossberg (see separate listings); Imported 1979-84.

MODEL 1500DL DELUXE . . . . NiB $350 Ex $275 Gd $180
Same as standard model, except w/o sights; w/engine-turned bolt, decorative scroll on floorplate, French checkering. Imported 1983-84.

MODEL 1700 LS "CLASSIC HUNTER" . . . . NiB $400 Ex $350 Gd $200
Bolt action. Calibers: .243 Win., .270 Win., .30-06, 5-shot magazine. 22-inch bbl. Weight: 7.5 lbs. Solid recoil pad, no sights, Schnabel forend, checkered walnut stock. Imported 1983-84.

MODEL A BOLT-ACTION RIFLE . . . . NiB $475 Ex $350 Gd $240
Similar to Husqvarna Model 9000 Crown Grade. Mauser-type bolt action. Calibers: .22-250, .243 Win., .270 Win., .308 Win., .30-06, 7mm Rem. Mag., .300 Win. Mag. Five shot magazine except 3-round capacity in latter two calibers. 23.75-inch bbl. Weight: 7 lbs. Sights: Folding leaf rear; hooded ramp front. Checkered walnut stock w/Monte Carlo cheekpiece, rosewood forend tip and pistol-grip cap, swivels. Made 1969-72.

MODEL B . . . . NiB $425 Ex $305 Gd $175
Same as Model A except w/20.25-inch extra-light bbl., Monte Carlo cheekpiece w/Schnabel-style forearm, weight: 6 lbs., 10 oz. Calibers: .243 Win., .30-06.

MODEL C . . . . NiB $425 Ex $310 Gd $175
Same as Model B except w/cheekpiece stock w/straight comb.

MODEL D . . . . NiB $550 Ex $400 Gd $275
Same as Model C except w/full-length Mannlicher-style forearm.

MODEL E. . . . . NiB $550 Ex $400 Gd $275
Same as Model B except w/full-length Mannlicher-style forearm.

SPRINGFIELD, INC. — Colona, Illinois (Formerly Springfield Armory of Geneseo, Ill.)

This is a private firm not to be confused with the former U.S. Government facility in Springfield, Mass.

BM-59 SEMIAUTOMATIC RIFLE
Gas-operated. Caliber: .308 Win. (7.62mm NATO). 20-shot detachable box magazine. 19.3-inch bbl. w/flash suppressor. About 43 inches overall. Weight: 9.25 lbs. Adj. military aperture rear sight, square post front; direct and indirect grenade launcher sights. European walnut stock w/handguard or folding buttstock (Alpine Paratrooper). Made 1981-90.
**Standard
model** . . . . NiB $1994 Ex $1595 Gd $1085
**Paratrooper
model** . . . . NiB $2000 Ex $1625 Gd $1275

**Springfield Armory
SAR-8 Sporter Rifle**

M-1 GARAND SEMIAUTOMATIC RIFLE
Gas-operated. Calibers: .308 Win. (7.62 NATO), .30-06. Eight shot stripper clip. 24-inch bbl. 43.5 inches overall. Weight: 9.5 lbs. Adj. aperture rear sight, military square blade front. Standard "Issue-grade" walnut stock or folding buttstock. Made 1979-90.

Standard model	NiB $895	Ex $675	Gd $450
National match	NiB $900	Ex $700	Gd $500
Ultra match	NiB $950	Ex $850	Gd $550
Sniper model	NiB $950	Ex $850	Gd $550
Tanker model	NiB $750	Ex $650	Gd $375
Paratrooper w/folding stock	NiB $975	Ex $750	Gd $525

MATCH M1A
Same as Standard M1A except w/National Match-grade bbl. w/modified flash suppressor, National Match sights, turned trigger pull, gas system assembly in one unit, modified mainspring guide glass-bedded walnut stock. Super Match M1A w/premium-grade heavy bbl. (weighs 10 lbs).

Match M1A	NiB $1500	Ex $1290	Gd $800
Super Match M1A	NiB $1700	Ex $1300	Gd $925

STANDARD M1A SEMIAUTOMATIC
Gas-operated. Similar to U.S. M14 service rifle except w/o provision for automatic firing. Caliber: 7.65mm NATO (.308 Win.). Five, 10- or 20-round detachable box magazine. 25.13-inch bbl w/flash suppressor. Weight: 9 lbs. Sights: Adj. aperture rear; blade front. Fiberglass, birch or walnut stock, fiberglass handguard, sling swivels. Made 1974 to date.

W/fiberglass or birch stock	NiB $1020	Ex $775	Gd $500
W/walnut stock	NiB $1161	Ex $955	Gd $691

M-6 SCOUT RIFLE/SHOTGUN COMBO
Similar to (14-inch) short-barrel Survival Gun provided as backup weapon to U.S. combat pilots. Calibers: .22 LR/.410 and .22 Hornet/.410. 18.5-inch bbl. 32 inches overall. Weight: 4 lbs. Parkerized or stainless steel finish. Folding detachable stock w/storage for fifteen .22 LR cartridges and four .410 shells. Drilled and tapped for scope mounts. Intro. 1982 and imported from Czech Republic 1995 to date.

First Issue (no trigger guard)	NiB $190	Ex $150	Gd $100
Second Issue (w/trigger guard)	NiB $160	Ex $125	Gd $90

SAR-8 SPORTER RIFLE
Similar to H&K 911 semiautomatic rifle. Calibers: .308 Win., (7.62x51) NATO. Detachable 5- 10- or 20-shot magazine. 18- or 20-inch bbl. 38.25 or 45.3 inches overall. Weight: 8.7 to 9.5 lbs. Protected front post and rotary adj. rear sight. Delayed roller-locked blow-back action w/fluted chamber. Kevlar-reinforced fiberglass thumb-hole style wood stock. Imported 1990 to date.

SAR-8 w/wood stock (disc. 1994)	NiB $1288	Ex $1050	Gd $746
SAR-8 w/thumb-hole stock	NiB $1025	Ex $850	Gd $575

SAR-48, SAR-4800
Similar to Browning FN FAL/LAR semiautomatic rifle. Calibers: .233 Rem. (5.56x45) and 3.08 Win. (7.62x51) NATO. Detachable 5- 10- or 20-shot magazine. 18- or 21-inch chrome-lined bbl. 38.25 or 45.3 inches overall. Weight: 9.5 to 13.25 lbs. Protected post front and adj. rear sight. Forged receiver and bolt w/adj. gas system. Pistol-grip or thumb-hole style; synthetic or wood stock. Imported 1985; reintroduced 1995.

SAR-48 w/pistol-grip stock (disc. 1989)	NiB $1150	Ex $975	Gd $575
SAR-48 w/wood stock (disc. 1989)	NiB $2288	Ex $1850	Gd $1290
SAR-48 w/folding stock (disc. 1989)	NiB $2574	Ex $2075	Gd $1437
SAR-48 w/thumb-hole stock	NiB $1176	Ex $945	Gd $649

SQUIRES BINGHAM CO., INC. —
Makati, Rizal, Philippines

MODEL 14D DELUXE BOLT-ACTION
REPEATING RIFLE . . . . NiB $100 Ex $75 Gd $50
Caliber: .22 LR. Five shot box magazine. 24-inch bbl. Sights: V-notch rear; hooded ramp front. Receiver grooved for scope mounting. Pulong Dalaga stock w/contrasting forend tip and grip cap, checkered forearm and pistol-grip. Weight: 6 lbs. Disc.

MODEL 15 . . . . NiB $125 Ex $80 Gd $75
Same as Model 14D except chambered for .22 WMR. Importation. Disc.

MODEL M16 SEMIAUTOMATIC RIFLE . . . . . NiB $120 Ex $125 Gd $90
Styled after U.S. M16 military rifle. Caliber: .22 LR. 15-shot box magazine. 19.5-inch bbl. w/muzzle brake/flash hider. Rear sight in carrying handle, post front on high ramp. Black-painted mahogany buttstock and forearm. Weight: 6.5 lbs. Importation. Disc.

MODEL M20D DELUXE . . . . NiB $200 Ex $175 Gd $95
Caliber: .22 LR. 15-shot box magazine. 19.5-inch bbl. w/muzzle brake/flash hider. Sights: V-notch rear; blade front. Receiver grooved for scope mounting. Pulong Dalaga stock w/contrasting forend tip and grip cap, checkered forearm/pistol-grip. Weight: 6 lbs. Importation. Disc.

STANDARD ARMS COMPANY —
Wilmington, Delaware

MODEL G AUTOMATIC RIFLE . . . . NiB $600 Ex $300 Gd $195
Gas-operated. Autoloading. Hammerless. Takedown. .25-35, .30-30, .25 Rem., .30 Rem., .35 Rem. Magazine capacity: 4 rounds in .35 Rem., 5 rounds in other calibers. 22.38-inch bbl. Weight: 7.75 lbs. Sights: Open sporting rear; ivory bead front. Shotgun-type stock. Made c. 1910. Note: This was the first gas-operated rifle manufactured in the U.S. While essentially an autoloader, the gas port can be closed and the rifle may be operated as a slide-action repeater.

**Star
Rolling Block Carbine**

MODEL M HAND-OPERATED RIFLE ..... NiB $300 Ex $275 Gd $150
Slide-action repeater w/same general specifications as Model G except lacks autoloading feature. Weight: 7 lbs.

STAR — Eibar, Spain
Mfd. by Bonifacio Echeverria, S.A.

ROLLING BLOCK CARBINE ...... NiB $200 Ex $160 Gd $109
Single-shot action similar to Remington Rolling Block. .30-30, .357 Mag., .44 Mag. 20-inch bbl. Weight: 6 lbs. Sights: Folding leaf rear; ramp front. Walnut straight-grip stock w/crescent buttplate, forearm w/bbl. band. Imported 1973-75.

STERLING — Imported by Lanchester U.S.A., Inc., Dallas, Texas

MARK 6 SEMIAUTOMATIC CARBINE ..... NiB $750 Ex $575 Gd $395
Caliber: 9mm Para.34-shot magazine. Bbl.: 16.1 inches. Weight: 7.5 lbs. Flip-type rear peep sight, ramp front. Folding metal skeleton stock. Made 1983-94.

J. STEVENS ARMS CO. — Chicopee Falls, Massachusetts, Div. of Savage Industries, Westfield, Mass.

J. Stevens Arms eventually became a division of Savage Industries. Consequently, the "Stevens" brand name is used for some rifles by Savage; see separate Savage-Stevens listings under Savage.

NO. 12 MARKSMAN SINGLE-SHOT RIFLE. . NiB $200 Ex $150 Gd $75
Lever-action, tip-up. Takedown. Calibers: .22 LR, .25 R.F., .32 R.F. 22-inch bbl. Plain straight-grip stock, small tapered forearm.

**NO. 14 LITTLE SCOUT
SINGLE-SHOT RIFLE** .... NiB $200 Ex $95 Gd $50
Caliber: .22 RF. 18-inch bbl. One-piece slab stock readily distinguishes it from the No. 14X that follows. Made 1906-1910.

**NO. 14.5 LITTLE SCOUT
SINGLE-SHOT RIFLE** .... NiB $200 Ex $100 Gd $75
Rolling block. Takedown. Caliber: .22 LR. 18- or 20-inch bbl. Weight: 2.75 lbs. Sights: open rear; blade front. Plain straight-grip stock, small tapered forearm.

MODEL 15 .... NiB $175 Ex $100 Gd $90
Same as Stevens-Springfield Model 15 except w/24-inch bbl., weight: 5 lbs., w/redesigned stock. Made 1948-65.

MODEL 15Y YOUTH'S RIFLE .... NiB $150 Ex $95 Gd $80
Same as Model 15 except w/21-inch bbl., short buttstock, weight: 4.75 lbs. Made 1958-65.

**NO. 44 IDEAL
SINGLE-SHOT RIFLE** .... NiB $744 Ex $595 Gd $405
Rolling block. Lever-action. Takedown. Calibers: .22 LR. .25 R.F., .32 R.F., .25-20 S.S., .32-20, .32-40, .38-40, .38-55, .44-40. Bbl. lengths: 24-inch, 26-inch (round, half-octagon, full-octagon). Weight: 7 lbs w/26-inch round bbl. Sights: Open rear; Rocky Mountain front. Plain straight-grip stock and forearm. Made 1894-32.

NO. 44.5 IDEAL SINGLE-SHOT RIFLE .... NiB $938 Ex $750 Gd $510
Falling-block. Lever-action rifle. Aside from the new design action intro. 1903, specifications of this model are the same as those of Model 44. Model 44X disc. 1916.

NOS. 45 TO 54 IDEAL SINGLE-SHOT RIFLES
These are higher-grade models, differing from the standard No. 44 and 44.5 chiefly in finish, engraving, set triggers, levers, bbls., stock, etc. The Schuetzen types (including the Stevens-Pope models) are in this series. Model Nos. 45 to 54 were intro. 1896 and originally had the No. 44-type rolling-block action, which was superseded in 1903 by the No. 44.5-type falling-block action. These models were all disc. about 1916. Generally speaking, the 45-54 series rifles, particularly the Stevens Pope and higher grade Schuetzen models are collector's items, bringing much higher prices than the ordinary No. 44 and 44.5.

**MODEL 66 BOLT-ACTION
REPEATING RIFLE** .... NiB $175 Ex $100 Gd $85
Takedown. Caliber: .22 Short, Long, LR. Tubular magazine holds 13 LR, 15 Long, 19 Short. 24-inch bbl. Weight: 5 lbs. Sights: Open rear, bead front. Plain pistol-grip stock w/grooved forearm. Made 1931-35.

**NO. 70 VISIBLE LOADING
SLIDE-ACTION** .... NiB $300 Ex $250 Gd $100
Exposed hammer. Caliber: .22 LR., Long, Short. Tubular magazine holds 11 LR., 13 Long, 15 Short. 22-inch bbl. Weight: 4.5 lbs. Sights: Open rear; bead front. Plain straight-grip stock, grooved slide handle. Made 1907-34. Note: Nos. 702, 71, 712, 72, 722 essentially the same as No. 70, differing chiefly in bbl. length or sight tooling.

MODEL 87 AUTOLOADING RIFLE........ NiB $175 Ex $125 Gd $90
Takedown. Caliber: .22 LR. 15-shot tubular magazine. 24-inch bbl. (20-inch on current model). Weight: 6 lbs. Sights: Open rear, bead front. Pistol-grip stock. Made 1938 to date. Note: This model originally bore the "Springfield" brand name, disc. in 1948.

**MODEL 322 HI-POWER
BOLT-ACTION CARBINE**........ NiB $300 Ex $250 Gd $125
Caliber: .22 Hornet. 4-shot detachable magazine. 21-inch bbl. Weight: 6.75 lbs. Sights: Open rear; ramp front. Pistol-grip stock. Made 1947-50 (See Savage models 340, 342.)

Stevens No. 14 Little Scout

Stevens No. 14.5 Little Scout

Stevens No. 44 Ideal

Stevens Ideal Schuetzen Rifle

Stevens Model 87

MODEL 322-S . . . . **NiB $350 Ex $275 Gd $150**
Same as Model 325 except w/peep rear sight. (See Savage models 340S, 342S.)

MODEL 325 HI-POWER
BOLT-ACTION CARBINE . . . . **NiB $300 Ex $250 Gd $125**
Caliber: .30-30. Three shot detachable box magazine. 21-inch bbl. Weight: 6.75 lbs. Sights: Open rear; bead front. Plain pistol-grip stock. Made 1947-50. (See Savage Model 340.)

MODEL 325-S . . . . **NiB $350 Ex $275 Gd $150**
Same as Model 325 except w/peep rear sight. (See Savage Model 340S.)

NO. 414 ARMORY MODEL
SINGLE-SHOT RIFLE . . . . **NiB $500 Ex $425 Gd $275**
No. 44-type lever-action. Calibers: .22 LR only, .22 Short only. 26-inch bbl. Weight: 8 lbs. Sights: Lyman receiver peep; blade front. Plain straight-grip stock, military-type forearm, swivels. Made 1912-32.

MODEL 416 BOLT-ACTION
TARGET RIFLE . . . . **NiB $325 Ex $225 Gd $180**
Caliber: .22 LR. Five shot detachable box magazine. 26-inch heavy bbl. Weight: 9.5 lbs. Sights: Receiver peep; hooded front. Target stock, swivels, sling. Made 1937-49.

NO. 419 JUNIOR TARGET MODEL
BOLT-ACTION SINGLE-SHOT RIFLE . . . . . **NiB $350 Ex $250 Gd $175**
Takedown. Caliber: .22 LR. 26-inch bbl. Weight: 5.5 lbs. Sights: Lyman No. 55 rear peep; blade front. Plain junior target stock w/pistol grip and grooved forearm, swivels, sling. Made 1932-36.

BUCKHORN MODEL 053 BOLT-ACTION
SINGLE-SHOT RIFLE . . . . **NiB $138 Ex $110 Gd $75**
Takedown. Calibers: .22 Short, Long, LR., .22 WRF. .25 Stevens R.F. 24-inch bbl. Weight: 5.5 lbs. Sights: Receiver peep; open middle; hooded front. Sporting stock w/pistol-grip and black forend tip. Made 1935-48.

BUCKHORN MODEL 53 . . . . **NiB $180 Ex $150 Gd $90**
Same as Buckhorn Model 053 except w/open rear sight and plain bead front sight.

Stevens No. 414 Armory

Stevens Model 416

Stevens Buckhorn Model 53

Stevens Buckhorn Model 055

Stevens Buckhorn Model 56

BUCKHORN 055 . . . . **NiB $180 Ex $150 Gd $90**
Takedown. Same as Model 056 except in single-shot configuration. Weight: 5.5 lbs. Caliber: .22 LR., Long, Short. 24-inch bbl. Weight: 6 lbs. Sights: Receiver peep, open middle, hooded front. Made 1935-48.

BUCKHORN MODEL 056
BOLT-ACTION . . . . **NiB $185 Ex $150 Gd $95**
Takedown. Caliber: .22 LR., Long, Short. Five shot detachable box magazine. 24-inch bbl. Weight: 6 lbs. Sights: Receiver peep, open middle, hooded front. Sporting stock w/pistol grip and black forend tip. Made 1935-48.

BUCKHORN
MODEL 56 . . . . **NiB $175 Ex $125 Gd $90**
Same as Buckhorn Model 056 except w/open rear sight and plain bead front sight.

BUCKHORN NO. 057 . . . . **NiB $160 Ex $100 Gd $75**
Same as Buckhorn Model 076 except w/5-shot detachable box magazine. Made 1939-48.

BUCKHORN NO. 57 . . . . **NiB $160 Ex $100 Gd $75**
Same as Buckhorn Model 76 except w/5-shot detachable box magazine. Made 1939-48.

BUCKHORN MODEL 066
BOLT-ACTION REPEATING RIFLE . . . . **NiB $225 Ex $175 Gd $100**
Takedown. Caliber: .22 LR, Long, Short. Tubular magazine holds 21 Short, 17 Long, 15 LR. 24-inch bbl. Weight: 6 lbs. Sights: Receiver peep; open middle; hooded front. Sporting stock w/pistol grip and black forend tip. Made 1935-48.

BUCKHORN MODEL 66 . . . . **NiB $160 Ex $100 Gd $75**
Same as Buckhorn Model 066 except w/open rear sight, plain bead front sight.

BUCKHORN NO. 076
AUTOLOADING RIFLE . . . . **NiB $175 Ex $150 Gd $95**
Takedown. Caliber: .22 LR. 15-shot tubular magazine. 24-inch bbl. Weight: 6 lbs. Sights: Receiver peep; open middle; hooded front. Sporting stock w/pistol grip, black forend tip. Made 1938-48.

BUCKHORN NO. 76 . . . . **NiB $175 Ex $150 Gd $90**
Same as Buckhorn No. 076 except w/open rear sight, plain bead front sight.

CRACKSHOT NO. 26
SINGLE-SHOT RIFLE . . . . **NiB $250 Ex $195 Gd $125**
Lever-action. Takedown. Calibers: .22 LR, .32 R.F. 18-inch or 22-inch bbl. Weight: 3.25 lbs. Sights: Open rear; blade front. Plain straight-grip stock, small tapered forearm. Made 1913-39.

Stevens Buckhorn Model 066

Stevens Buckhorn Model 66

Stevens Buckhorn Model 76

Stevens Crackshot No. 26

RIFLES

CRACKSHOT NO. 26.5 . . . . **NiB $290 Ex $175 Gd $150**
Same as Crackshot No. 26 except w/smoothbore bbl. for shot cartridges.

FAVORITE NO. 17
SINGLE-SHOT RIFLE . . . . **NiB $275 Ex $175 Gd $125**
Lever-action. Takedown. Calibers: .22 LR, .25 R.F., .32 R.F. 24-inch round bbl; other lengths were available. Weight: 4.5 lbs. Sights: Open rear; Rocky Mountain front. Plain straight-grip stock, small tapered forearm. Made 1894-1935.

FAVORITE NO. 18 . . . . **NiB $350 Ex $250 Gd $125**
Same as Favorite No. 17 except w/Vernier peep rear sight, leaf middle sight, Beach combination front sight.

FAVORITE NO. 19 . . . . **NiB $375 Ex $275 Gd $150**
Same as Favorite No. 17 except w/Lyman combination rear sight, leaf middle sight, Lyman front sight.

FAVORITE NO. 20 . . . . **NiB $350 Ex $275 Gd $175**
Same as Favorite No. 17 except w/smoothbore barrel.

FAVORITE NO. 27 . . . . **NiB $375 Ex $275 Gd $190**
Same as Favorite No. 17 except w/octagon bbl.

FAVORITE NO. 28 . . . . **NiB $350 Ex $250 Gd $175**
Same as Favorite No. 18 except w/octagon bbl.

FAVORITE NO. 29 . . . . **NiB $375 Ex $250 Gd $175**
Same as Favorite No. 19 except w/octagon bbl.

WALNUT HILL NO. 417-0
SINGLE-SHOT TARGET RIFLE . . . . **NiB $875 Ex $675 Gd $425**
Lever-action. Calibers: .22 LR only, .22 Short only, .22 Hornet. 28-inch heavy bbl. (extra heavy 29-inch bbl. also available). Weight: 10.5 lbs. Sights: Lyman No. 52L extension rear; 17A front, scope bases mounted on bbl. Target stock w/full pistol-grip, beavertail forearm, bbl. band, swivels, sling. Made 1932-47.

WALNUT HILL NO. 417-1 . . . . **NiB $900 Ex $875 Gd $500**
Same as No. 417-0 except w/Lyman No. 48L receiver sight.

WALNUT HILL NO. 417-2 . . . . **NiB $950 Ex $875 Gd $525**
Same as No. 417-0 except w/Lyman No. 144 tang sight.

WALNUT HILL NO. 417-3 . . . . **NiB $890 Ex $750 Gd $400**
Same as No. 417-0 except w/o sights.

WALNUT HILL NO. 417.5
SINGLE-SHOT RIFLE . . . . **NiB $900 Ex $825 Gd $450**
Lever-action. Calibers: .22 LR, .22 WMR, .25 R.F., .22 Hornet. 28-inch bbl. Weight: 8.5 lbs. Sights: Lyman No. 144 tang peep, folding middle; bead front. Sporting stock w/pistol-grip, semi-beavertail forearm, swivels, sling. Made 1932-40.

WALNUT HILL NO. 418
SINGLE-SHOT RIFLE . . . . **NiB $550 Ex $400 Gd $325**
Lever-action. Takedown. Calibers: .22 LR only, .22 Short only. 26-inch bbl. Weight: 6.5 lbs. Sights: Lyman No. 144 tang peep; blade front. Pistol-grip stock, semi-beavertail forearm, swivels, sling. Made 1932-40.

Stevens Walnut Hill
No. 417-1

Stevens Walnut Hill
No. 417.5

Stevens Walnut Hill
No. 418

WALNUT HILL NO. 418.5 . . . . **NiB $625 Ex $550 Gd $390**
Same as No. 418 except also available in calibers .22 WRF and .25
Stevens R.F., w/Lyman No. 2A tang peep sight, bead front sight.

MODEL 15 SINGLE-SHOT
BOLT-ACTION RIFLE . . . . **NiB $150 Ex $100 Gd $75**
Takedown. Caliber: .22 LR, Long, Short. 22-inch bbl. Weight: 4 lbs.
Sights: Open rear, bead front. Plain pistol-grip stock. Made 1937-48.

MODEL 82 BOLT-ACTION
SINGLE-SHOT RIFLE . . . . **NiB $125 Ex $105 Gd $75**
Takedown. Caliber: .22 LR, Long, Short. 22-inch bbl. Weight: 4 lbs.
Sights: Open rear; gold bead front. Plain pistol-grip stock w/grooved
forearm. Made 1935-39.

MODEL 83 BOLT-ACTION
SINGLE-SHOT RIFLE . . . . **NiB $150 Ex $90 Gd $70**
Takedown. Calibers: .22 LR, Long, Short; .22 WRF, .25 Stevens R.F.
24-inch bbl. Weight: 4.5 lbs. Sights: Peep rear; open middle; hooded front. Plain pistol-grip stock w/grooved forearm. Made 1935-39.

MODEL 84 . . . . **NiB $175 Ex $150 Gd $95**
Same as Model 86 except w/5-shot detachable box magazine. Pre-
1948 rifles of this model were designated Springfield Model 84,
later known as Stevens Model 84. Made 1940-65.

MODEL 84-S (084) . . . . **NiB $175 Ex $150 Gd $95**
Same as Model 84 except w/peep rear sight and hooded front sight.
Pre-1948 rifles of this model were designated Springfield Model
084, later known as Stevens Model 84-S. Disc.

MODEL 85 . . . . **NiB $190 Ex $110 Gd $80**
Same as Stevens Model 87 except w/5-shot detachable box magazine. Made
1939 to date. Pre-1948 rifles of this model were designated Springfield Model 85,
currently known as Stevens Model 85. Earlier models command slight premiums.

MODEL 85-S (085) . . . . **NiB $175 Ex $125 Gd $90**
Same as Model 85 except w/peep rear sight and hooded front sight.
Pre-1948 models were designated Springfield Model 085; also
known as Stevens Model 85-S.

MODEL 86
BOLT-ACTION . . . . **NiB $175 Ex $125 Gd $90**
Takedown. Caliber: .22 LR, Long, Short. Tubular magazine holds 15
LR, 17 Long, 21 Short. 24-inch bbl. Weight: 6 lbs. Sights: Open
rear, gold bead front. Pistol-grip stock, black forend tip on later
production. Made 1935-65. Note: The Springfield brand name was
disc. in 1948.

MODEL 86-S (086) . . . . **NiB $180 Ex $150 Gd $100**
Same as Model 86 except w/peep rear sight and hooded front sight.
Pre-1948 rifles of this model were designated as Springfield Model
086, later known as Stevens Model 86-S. Disc.

MODEL 87-S (087) . . . . **NiB $190 Ex $175 Gd $105**
Same as Stevens Model 87 except w/peep rear sight and
hooded front sight. Pre-1948 rifles of this model were designated as Springfield Model 087, later known as Stevens Model
87-S. Disc.

STEYR-DAIMLER-PUCH A.-G. — Steyr, Austria
See also listings under Mannlicher.

AUG-SA
SEMIAUTOMATIC RIFLE . . . . **NiB $3744 Ex $2995 Gd $2037**
Gas-operated. Caliber: .223 Rem. (5.56mm). 30- or 40-shot magazine. 20-inch bbl. standard; optional 16-inch or 24-inch heavy bbl.
w/folding bipod. 31 inches overall. Weight: 8.5 lbs. Sights: Integral
1.5x scope and mount. Green high-impact synthetic stock w/folding
vertical grip.

Stevens-Springfield
Model 15

Stevens-Springfield
Model 82

Stevens-Springfield
Model 83

Stevens-Springfield
Model 84

Stevens-Springfield
Model 85

Stevens-Springfield
Model 86-S

RIFLES

SMALL BORE CARBINE. . . . . **NiB $531 Ex $425 Gd $289**
Bolt-action repeater. Caliber: .22 LR. Five shot detachable box magazine. 19.5-inch bbl. Sights: Leaf rear; hooded bead front. Mannlicher-type stock, checkered, swivels. Made 1953-67.

STOEGER RIFLE — Mfd. by Franz Jaeger & Co., Suhl, Germany; dist. in the U.S. by A. F. Stoeger, Inc., New York, N.Y.

HORNET RIFLE . . . . **NiB $1250 Ex $875 Gd $550**
Same specifications as Herold Rifle, designed and built on a Miniature Mauser-type action. See listing under Herold Bolt-Action Repeating Sporting Rifle for additional specifications. Imported during the 1930s.

SURVIVAL ARMS — Orange, CT

AR-7 EXPLORER . . . . **NiB $140 Ex $100 Gd $60**
Caliber: .22 LR. Eight shot magazine. Weight: 3 lbs. Polymer stocks. Drift adj. sights. Disassembles into five separate elements, allowing

(cont'd.) **AR-7 EXPLORER**
barrel, action and magazine to fit into buttstock; assembles quickly w/o tools. Choice of camo, silvertone or black matte finishes. Made 1992-95.

THOMPSON/CENTER ARMS — Rochester, New Hampshire

CONTENDER CARBINE
Calibers: .22 LR, .22 Hornet, .222 Rem., .223 Rem., 7mm T.C.U., 7x30 Waters, .30-30 Win., .35 Rem., .44 Mag., .357 Rem. Max. and .410 bore. 21-inch interchangeable bbls. 35 inches overall. Adj. iron sights. Checkered American walnut or Rynite stock and forend. Made 1985 to date.

Standard model (rifle calibers)	NiB $400	Ex $300	Gd $225
Standard model (.410 bore)	NiB $458	Ex $370	Gd $258
Rynite stock model (rifle calibers)	NiB $519	Ex $450	Gd $362
Rynite stock model (.410 bore).	NiB $544	Ex $470	Gd $376
Extra bbls. (rifle calibers)	NiB $249	Ex $205	Gd $149
Extra bbls. (.410 bore).	NiB $264	Ex $215	Gd $153
Youth model (all calibers and .410 bore)	NiB $350	Ex $275	Gd $175

Thompson/Center
Contender Carbine

Thompson/Center
TCR '83 Aristocrat

Thompson/Center
TCR '87 Hunter

CONTENDER CARBINE

SURVIVAL SYSTEM . . . . NiB $575 Ex $400 Gd $300
Similar to standard Contender Carbine w/Rynite stock and forend.
Comes w/two 16.25-inch bbls. chambered in .223 and .45/.410
bore. Camo Cordura case.

STAINLESS CONTENDER CARBINE

Same as standard Contender Carbine Model, except stainless steel
w/blued sights. Calibers: .22 LR, .22 Hornet, .223 Rem., 7-30
Waters, .30-30 Win., .410. Walnut or Rynite stock and forend.
Made 1993 to date.
Walnut stock model . . . . NiB $450 Ex $375 Gd $250
Rynite stock model . . . . NiB $425 Ex $350 Gd $240
Youth stock model . . . . NiB $400 Ex $325 Gd $225
Extra bbls. (rifle calibers) . . . . NiB $219 Ex $175 Gd $119

TCR '83 ARISTOCRAT MODEL

Break frame, overlever action. Calibers: .223 Rem., .22/250 Rem.,
.243 Win., 7mm Rem. Mag., .30-06 Springfield. Interchangeable
bbls.: 23 inches in length. Weight: 6 lbs., 14 oz. American walnut
stock and forearm, checkered, black rubber recoil pad, cheekpiece.
Made 1983-87.
TCR '83 Standard model . . . . NiB $425 Ex $375 Gd $200
TCR '83 Aristocrat . . . . NiB $495 Ex $350 Gd $225
Extra bbls. (rifle calibers) . . . . NiB $219 Ex $175 Gd $119

TCR '87 HUNTER RIFLE

Similar to TCR '83 except in calibers .22 Hornet, ..222 Rem., 223
Rem., .22-250 Rem., .243 Win., .270 Win., 7mm-08, .308 Win.,
.30-06, .32-40 Win. Also 12-ga. slug and 10- and 12-ga. field bbls.
23-inch standard or 25.88-inch heavy bbl. interchangeable. 39.5 to
43.38 inches overall. Weight: 6 lbs., 14 oz. to 7.5 lbs. Iron sights
optional. Checkered American black walnut buttstock w/fluted end.
Disc. 1993.

(cont'd.) TCR '87 HUNTER RIFLE
Standard model . . . . NiB $500 Ex $400 Gd $225
**Extra bbl. (rifle calibers and
10- or 12-ga. Field)** . . . . NiB $238 Ex $190 Gd $129
Extra bbl. (12-ga. slug) . . . . NiB $281 Ex $225 Gd $153

TIKKA RIFLES — Mfg. by Sako, Ltd. of Riihimaki, Finland & Armi Marocchi in Italy

Imported by Beretta USA

Note: *Tikka New Generation, Battue and Continental series bolt
action rifles are being manufactured by Sako, Ltd., in Finland. Tikka
O/U rifles (previously Valmet) are being manufactured in Italy by
Armi Marocchi. For earlier importation see additional listings under
Ithaca LSA and Valmet 412S models.*

MODEL 412S DOUBLE RIFLE

Calibers: .308 Win., .30-06, 9.3x74R. 24-inch bbl. w/quarter rib
machined for scope mounts; automatic ejectors (9.3x74R only). 40
inches overall. Weight: 8.5 lbs. Ramp front and folding adj. rear
sight. Barrel selector on trigger and cocking indicators in tang.
European walnut buttstock and forearm. Model 412S was replaced
by the 512S version in 1994. Imported 1989-93.
Model 412S
(disc. 1993) . . . . NiB $1390 Ex $1000 Gd $750
**Extra barrel assembly
(O/U shotgun), add** $650
**Extra barrel assembly
(O/U Combo), add** $775
**Extra barrel assembly
(O/U rifle), add** $995

Tikka Model 412S
Double Rifle

Tikka Model LSA55
Deluxe

Tikka Model LSA65
Deluxe

Tikka Model M55
Deluxe

Tikka Model M55
Standard

RIFLES

MODEL 512S DOUBLE RIFLE
Formerly Valmet 412S. In 1994, following the joint venture of 1989, the model designation was changed to 512S. Imported 1994 to date.
Model 512S. . . . . NiB $1400 Ex $1275 Gd $925
Extra barrel assembly
(O/U rifle), add. $755

LSA55 DELUXE . . . . NiB $500 Ex $450 Gd $375
Same as LSA55 Standard except w/rollover cheekpiece, rosewood grip cap and forend tip, skip checkering, high-luster blue. Imported 1965-88.

LSA55 SPORTER . . . . NiB $494 Ex $395 Gd $269
Same as LSA55 except has 22.8-inch heavy bbl. w/o sights, special stock w/beavertail forearm, not available in 6mm Rem. Weighs 9 lbs. Imported 1965-88.

LSA55 STANDARD
BOLT-ACTION REPEATER . . . . NiB $450 Ex $325 Gd $200
Mauser-type action. Calibers: .222 Rem., .22-250, 6mm Rem. Mag., .243 Win., .308 Win. Thrree shot clip magazine. 22.8-inch bbl. Weight: 6.8 lbs. Sights: Folding leaf rear; hooded ramp front. Checkered walnut stock w/Monte Carlo cheekpiece, swivels. Made 1965-88.

LSA65 DELUXE . . . . NiB $525 Ex $450 Gd $300
Same as LSA65 Standard except w/special features of LSA55 Deluxe. Imported 1970-88.

LSA65 STANDARD . . . . NiB $425 Ex $325 Gd $200
Same as LSA55 Standard except calibers: .25-06, 6.5x55 .270 Win., .30-06. Five shot magazine, 22-inch bbl., weight: 7.5 lbs. Imported 1970-88.

MODEL M 55
Bolt action. Calibers: .222 Rem., .22-250 Rem., .223 Rem. .243 Win., .308 Win. (6mm Rem. and 17 Rem. available in Standard and Deluxe models only). 23.2-inch bbl. (24.8-inch in Sporter and Heavy Barrel models). 42.8 inches overall (44 inches in Sporter and Heavy Barrel models). Weight: 7.25 to 9 lbs. Monte Carlo-style stock w/pistol-grip. Sling swivels. Imported 1965-88.
Continental . . . . NiB $650 Ex $475 Gd $330
Deluxe model . . . . NiB $690 Ex $480 Gd $350
Sporter. . . . . NiB $625 Ex $500 Gd $325
Sporter w/sights . . . . NiB $650 Ex $475 Gd $330
Standard . . . . NiB $575 Ex $450 Gd $300
Super Sporter . . . . NiB $725 Ex $590 Gd $350
Super Sporter w/sights . . . . NiB $790 Ex $375 Gd $400
Trapper . . . . NiB $660 Ex $450 Gd $325

Tikka
Model M65 Sporter

Tikka
Model M65 Wild Boar

MODEL M65

Bolt action. Calibers: .25-06, .270 Win., .308 Win., .30-06, 7mm Rem. Mag., .300 Win. Mag. (Sporter and Heavy Bbl. models in .270 Win., .308 Win. and .30-06 only). 22.4-inch bbl. (24.8-inch in Sporter and Heavy Bbl. models). 43.2 inches overall (44 inches in Sporter, 44.8 inches in Heavy Bbl.). Weight: 7.5 to 9.9 lbs. Monte Carlo-style stock w/pistol-grip. Disc. 1989.

Continental	NiB $650	Ex $475	Gd $330
Deluxe Magnum	NiB $725	Ex $590	Gd $395
Deluxe model	NiB $675	Ex $475	Gd $325
Magnum	NiB $625	Ex $425	Gd $350
Sporter	NiB $500	Ex $450	Gd $300
Sporter w/sights	NiB $680	Ex $550	Gd $350
Standard	NiB $575	Ex $450	Gd $300
Super Sporter	NiB $795	Ex $600	Gd $400
Super Sporter w/sights	NiB $800	Ex $625	Gd $450
Super Sporter Master	NiB $1000	Ex $825	Gd $500

MODEL M65 WILDBOAR . . . . NiB $675 Ex $550 Gd $390
Same general specifications as Model M 65 except 20.8-inch bbl., overall length of 41.6 inches, weight: of 7.5 lbs. Disc. 1989.

NEW GENERATION RIFLES
Short-throw bolt available in three action lengths. Calibers: .22-250 Rem., .223 Rem., .243 Win., .308 Win., (medium action) .25-06 Rem., .270 Win., .30.06, (Long Action) 7mm Rem. Mag., .300 Win. Mag., .338 Win. Mag., (Magnum Action). 22- to 26-inch bbl. 42.25 to 46 inches overall. Weight: 7.2 to 8.5 lbs. Available w/o sights or w/hooded front and open rear sight on quarter rib. Quick-release 3- or 5-shot detachable magazine w/recessed side release. Barrel selector on trigger and cocking indicators in tang. European walnut buttstock and forearm matte lacquer finish. Imported 1989-94.

Standard calibers	NiB $750	Ex $590	Gd $375
Magnum calibers	NiB $775	Ex $600	Gd $400

PREMIUM GRADE RIFLE
Similar to New Generation rifles except w/hand-checkered deluxe wood stock w/roll-over check-piece and rosewood grip cap and forend tip. High polished blued finish. Imported 1989-94.

Standard calibers	NiB $795	Ex $650	Gd $400
Magnum calibers	NiB $875	Ex $650	Gd $475

WHITETAIL BOLT-ACTION RIFLE SERIES
New Generation design in multiple model configurations and three action lengths chambered .22-250 to .338 Win. Mag.

BATTUE MODEL
Similar to Hunter Model except designed for snapshooting w/hooded front and open rear sights on quarter rib. Blued finish. Checkered select walnut stock w/matt lacquered finish. Imported 1991-97.

Battue model (standard w/sights)	NiB $570	Ex $450	Gd $300
Magnum calibers, add			$40

CONTINENTAL MODEL
Similar to Hunter Model except w/prone-style stock w/wider forearm and 26-inch heavy bbl. chambered for 17 Rem., .22-250 Rem., .223 Rem., .308 Win. (Varmint); .25-06 Rem., .270 Win., 7mm Rem. Mag., .300 Win. Mag. (Long Range). Weight: 8.6 lbs. Imported 1991 to date.

Continental Long-Range model	NiB $675	Ex $475	Gd $330
Continental Varmint model	NiB $625	Ex $475	Gd $325
Magnum calibers, add			$40

SPORTER MODEL . . . . NiB $850 Ex $675 Gd $525
Similar to Hunter Model except 23.5-inch bbl. Five shot detachable mazigine. Chambered .22-250 Rem., .223 Rem., .308 Win. Weight: 8.6 lbs. Adjustable buttplate and cheekpiece w/stippled pistol grip and forend. Imported 1998 to date.

WHITETAIL HUNTER MODEL
Calibers: .22-250 Rem., .223 Rem., .243 Win., .25-06 Rem., .270 Win., 7mm Rem. Mag., .308 Win .30.06, .300 Win. Mag., .338 Win. Mag. Three or 5-shot detachable box magazine. 20.5- to 24.5-inch bbl. with no sights. 42 to 44.5 inches overall. Weight: 7 to 7.5 lbs. Adj. single-stage or single-set trigger. Blued or stainless finish. All-Weather synthetic or checkered select walnut stock w/matt lacquered finish. Imported 1991 to date.

Standard model	NiB $575	Ex $450	Gd $300
Deluxe model	NiB $700	Ex $550	Gd $375
Synthetic model	NiB $675	Ex $450	Gd $325
Stainless model	NiB $680	Ex $495	Gd $325
Magnum calibers, add			$40
Left-hand model, add			$70

Tikka
Continental/Varmint

Tikka
New Generation

Tikka
Premium Grade

Tikka
Whitetail/Battue

Tikka
Whitetail Hunter Deluxe

Tikka
Whitetail Hunter Synthetic

Tikka
Whitetail Hunter Stainless Synthetic

RIFLES

UBERTI RIFLES — Lakeville, Connecticut
Mfd. By Aldo Uberti, Ponte Zanano, Italy
Imported by Stoeger Industries, Accokeek, MD

MODEL 1866 SPORTING RIFLE
Replica of Winchester Model 1866 lever-action repeater. Calibers: .22 LR, .22 WMR, .38 Spec., .44-40, .45 LC. 24.25-inch octagonal bbl. 43.25 inches overall. Weight: 8.25 lbs. Blade front sight,rear elevation leaf. Brass frame and buttplate. Bbl., magazine tube, other metal parts blued. Walnut buttstock and forearm.

	NiB	Ex	Gd
Model 1866 Rifle	$750	$575	$300
Model 1866 Carbine (19-inch round bbl.)	$645	$525	$325
Model 1866 Trapper (16-inch bbl.) Disc. 1989	$575	$450	$320
Model 1866 Rimfire (Indian Rifle)	$525	$425	$300
Model 1866 Rimfire (Indian Carbine)	$500	$405	$295

GRADING: **NiB** = New in Box   **Ex** = Excellent or NRA 95%   **Gd** = Good or NRA 68%

Uberti Model 1873 Carbine

Ultra Model 2200

Ultra Light Model 28

MODEL 1873 SPORTING RIFLE
Replica of Winchester Model 1873 lever-action repeater. Calibers: .22 LR, .22 WMR, .38 Spec., .357 Mag., .44-40, .45 LC. 24.25- or 30-inch octagonal bbl. 43.25 inches overall. Weight: 8 lbs. Blade front sight; adj. open rear. Color case-hardened frame. Bbl., magazine tube, hammer, lever and buttplate blued. Walnut buttstock and forearm.
Model 1873 Rifle . . . . NiB $825 Ex $590 Gd $350
Model 1873 Carbine
(19-inch round bbl.) . . . . NiB $725 Ex $560 Gd $340
Model 1873 Trapper
(16-inch bbl.)
Disc. 1990 . . . . NiB $675 Ex $500 Gd $325

HENRY RIFLE
Replica of Henry lever-action repeating rifle. Calibers: .44-40, .45 LC. 24.5-inch half-octagon bbl. 43.75 inches overall. Weight: 9.25 lbs. Blade front sight; rear sight adj. for elevation. Brass frame, buttplate and magazine follower. Bbl., magazine tube and remaining parts blued. Walnut buttstock.
Henry Rifle . . . . NiB $775 Ex $550 Gd $375
Henry Carbine (22.5-inch bbl.) . . . . NiB $750 Ex $525 Gd $350
Henry Trapper
(16- or 18-inch bbl.) . . . . NiB $700 Ex $560 Gd $381
Steel frame, add $85

ULTRA-HI PRODUCTS COMPANY — Hawthorne, New Jersey

MODEL 2200 SINGLE-SHOT
BOLT-ACTION RIFLE . . . . NiB $150 Ex $110 Gd $75
Caliber: .22 LR, Long, Short. .23-inch bbl. Weight: 5 lbs. Sights: Open rear; blade front. Monte Carlo stock w/pistol grip. Made in Japan. Intro. 1977; Disc.

ULTRA LIGHT ARMS COMPANY — Granville, West Virginia

MODEL 20 BOLT-ACTION RIFLE
Calibers: .22-250 Rem., .243 Win., 6mm Rem., .250-3000 Savage, .257 Roberts, .257 Ack., 7mm Mauser, 7mm Ack., 7mm-08 Rem., .284 Win., .300 Savage, .308 Win., .358 Win. Box magazine. 22-inch ultra light bbl. Weight: 4.75 lbs. No sights. Synthetic stock of Kevlar or graphite finished, seven different colors. Nonglare matte or bright metal finish. Medium-length action available L.H. models. Made 1985 to date.
Standard model . . . . NiB $2225 Ex $1850 Gd $995
Left-hand model . . . . NiB $2006 Ex $1625 Gd $1137

MODEL 20S BOLT-ACTION RIFLE
Same general specifications as Model 20 except w/short action in calibers 17 Rem., .222 Rem., .223 Rem., .22 Hornet only.
Standard model . . . . NiB $2250 Ex $1875 Gd $1000
Left-hand model . . . . NiB $2094 Ex $1695 Gd $1185

MODEL 24 BOLT-ACTION RIFLE
Same general specifications as Model 20 except w/long action in calibers .25-06, .270 Win., .30-06 and 7mm Express only.
Standard model . . . . NiB $2325 Ex $1890 Gd $995
Left-hand model . . . . NiB $2038 Ex $1650 Gd $1154

MODEL 28 BOLT-ACTION RIFLE . . . . . NiB $2500 Ex $1790 Gd $1100
Same general specifications as Model 20 except w/long magnum action in calibers .264 Win. Mag., 7mm Rem. Mag., .300 Win. Mag., .338 Win. Mag. only. Offered w/recoil arrester. Left-hand model available.

MODEL 40 BOLT-ACTION RIFLE
Similar to Model 28 except in calibers .300 Wby. and .416 Rigby. Weight: 5.5 lbs. Made 1994 to date.
Standard model . . . . NiB $2500 Ex $1790 Gd $1100
Left-hand, model . . . . NiB $2469 Ex $1995 Gd $1389

U.S. Model 1903-A1
Springfield

U.S. Model 1903-A3
Springfield

U.S. Model 1917
Enfield

UNIQUE RIFLE — Hendaye, France
Mfd. by Manufacture d'Armes des Pyrénées Francaises

T66 MATCH RIFLE . . . . NiB $475 Ex $400 Gd $275
Single-shot bolt-action rifle. Caliber: .22 LR. 25.5-inch bbl. Weight: 10.5 lbs. Sights: Micrometer aperture rear; globe front. French walnut target stock w/Monte Carlo comb, bull pistol-grip, wide and deep forearm, stippled grip surfaces, adj. swivel on accessory track, adj. rubber buttplate. Made 1966. Disc.

U.S. MILITARY RIFLES — Mfd. by Springfield Armory, Remington Arms Co., Winchester Repeating Arms Co., Inland Mfg. Div. of G.M.C., and other contractors. See notes.

Unless otherwise indicated, the following U.S. military rifles were mfg. at Springfield Armory, Springfield, Mass.

MODEL 1898
KRAG-JORGENSEN CARBINE . . . NiB $1875 Ex $1675 Gd $950
Same general specifications as Model 1898 Rifle except w/22-inch bbl., weight: 8 lbs., carbine-type stock. Note: The foregoing specifications apply, in general, to Carbine models 1896 and 1899, which differed from Model 1898 only in minor details.

MODEL 1898
KRAG-JORGENSEN MILITARY RIFLE . . . NiB $1875 Ex $1675 Gd $950
Bolt action. Caliber: .30-40 Krag. 5-shot hinged box magazine. 30-inch bbl. Weight: 9 lbs. Sights: Adj. rear; blade front. Military-type stock, straight grip. Note: The foregoing specifications apply, in general, to Rifle models 1892 and 1896, which differed from Model 1898.

MODEL 1903 MARK I SPRINGFIELD . . . NiB $1850 Ex $1650 Gd $775
Same as Standard Model 1903 except altered to permit use of the Pedersen Device. This device, officially designated "U.S. Automatic Pistol Model 1918," converted the M/1903 to a semiautomatic weapon firing a .30 caliber cartridge similar to .32 automatic pistol ammunition. Mark I rifles have a slot milled in the left side of the receiver to serve as an ejection port when the Pedersen Device was in

(cont'd.) **MODEL 1903 MARK I SPRINGFIELD**
use; these rifles were also fitted w/a special sear and cut-off. Some 65,000 of these devices were manufactured and, presumably, a like number of M/1903 rifles were converted to handle them. During the early 1930s, all Pedersen Devices were ordered destroyed and the Mark I rifles were reconverted by replacement of the special sear and cut-off w/standard components. Some 20-odd specimens are known to have escaped destruction and are in government museums and private collections. Probably more are extant. Rarely is a Pedersen Device offered for sale, so a current value cannot be assigned. However, many of the altered rifles were bought by members of the National Rifle Association through the Director of Civilian Marksmanship. Value shown is for the Mark I rifle w/o the Pedersen Device.

MODEL 1903 NATIONAL
MATCH SPRINGFIELD . . . . NiB $1550 Ex $1375 Gd $795
Same general specifications as Standard Model 1903 except specially selected w/star-gauged bbl., Type C pistol-grip U.S. Model 1903 National Match Springfield (Con't) stock, polished bolt assembly; early types have headless firing pin assembly and reversed safety lock. Produced especially for target shooting.

MODEL 1903 SPRINGFIELD MILITARY RIFLE
Modified Mauser-type bolt action. Caliber: .30-06. 5-shot box magazine. 23.79-inch bbl. Weight: 8.75 lbs. Sights: Adj. rear; blade front. Military-type stock straight grip. Note: M/1903 rifles of Springfield manufacture w/serial numbers under 800,000 (1903-1918) have case-hardened receivers; those between 800,000 and 1,275,767 (1918-1927) were double heat-treated; rifles numbered over 1,275,767 have nickle steel bolts and receivers. Rock Island production from No. 1 to 285,507 have case-hardened receivers. Improved heat treatment was adopted in May 1918 with No. 285,207; about three months later, with No. 319,921, the use of nickel steel was begun, but the production of some double-heat-treated carbon-steel receivers and bolts continued. Made 1903-30 at Springfield Armory during WWI, M/1903 rifles were also made at Rock Island Arsenal, Rock Island, Ill.
W/case-hardened receiver . . . . . NiB $5000 Ex $4250 Gd $1850
W/double heat-treated receiver . . . NiB $3950 Ex $3250 Gd $1300
W/nickel steel receiver . . . . NiB $1450 Ex $1250 Gd $750

MODEL 1903 SPRINGFIELD SPORTER . . . NiB $1244 Ex $995 Gd $677
Same general specifications as National Match except w/sporting design stock, Lyman No. 48 receiver sight.

GRADING: **NiB** = New in Box   **Ex** = Excellent or NRA 95%   **Gd** = Good or NRA 68%

U.S. Carbine Caliber .30, M1 (Grand)

U.S. Carbine Caliber .30, M1

MODEL 1903 STYLE T
SPRINGFIELD MATCH RIFLE . . . . NiB $1438 Ex $1150 Gd $782
Same specifications as Springfield Sporter except w/heavy bbl. (26-, 28- or 30-inch), scope bases, globe front sight, weight: 12.5 lbs. w/26-inch bbl.

MODEL 1903 TYPE A
SPRINGFIELD FREE RIFLE . . . . . NiB $1719 Ex $1375 Gd $935
Same as Style T except made w/28-inch bbl. only, w/Swiss buttplate, weight: 13.25 lbs.

MODEL 1903 TYPE B
SPRINGFIELD FREE RIFLE . . . . . NiB $2281 Ex $1825 Gd $1241
Same as Type A, except w/cheekpiece stock, palm rest, Woodie double-set triggers, Garand fast firing pin, weight: 14.75 lbs.

MODEL 1903-A1 SPRINGFIELD
Same general specifications as Model 1903 except may have Type C pistol-grip stock adopted in 1930. The last Springfields produced at the Springfield Armory were of this type; final serial number was 1,532,878, made in 1939. Note: Late in 1941, Remington Arms Co., Ilion, N.Y., began production, under government contract, of Springfield rifles of this type w/a few minor modifications. These rifles are numbered 3,000,001-3,348,085 and were manufactured before the adoption of Model 1903-A3.
Springfield manufacture . . . . NiB $1250 Ex $1100 Gd $600
Remington manufacture . . . . NiB $813 Ex $650 Gd $442

MODEL 1903-A3 SPRINGFIELD . . . . . . NiB $1500 Ex $1300 Gd $325
Same general specifications as Model 1903-A1, except modified to permit increased production and lower cost; may have either straight-grip or pistol-grip stock, bolt is not interchangeable w/earlier types, w/receiver peep sight, many parts are stamped sheet steel, including the trigger guard and magazine assembly. Quality of these rifles, lower than that of other 1903 Springfields, reflects the emergency conditions under which they were produced. Mfd. during WWII by Remington Arms Co. and L. C. Smith Corona Typewriters, Inc.

MODEL 1922-M1 22
SPRINGFIELD TARGET RIFLE . . . . NiB $1094 Ex $875 Gd $595
Modified Model 1903. Caliber: .22 LR. Five shot detachable box magazine. 24.5-inch bbl. Weight: 9 lbs. Sights: Lyman No. 48C receiver, blade front. Sporting-type stock similar to that of Model 1903 Springfield Sporter. Issued 1927. Note: The earlier Model 1922, which is seldom encountered, differs from the foregoing chiefly in the bolt mechanism and magazine.

M2 22 SPRINGFIELD TARGET RIFLE . . . . NiB $1195 Ex $925 Gd $500
Same general specifications as Model 1922-M1 except w/speedlock, improved bolt assembly adj. for headspace. Note: These improvements were later incorporated in many rifles of the preceding models (M1922, M1922MI) and arms so converted were marked "M1922M2" or "M1922MII."

NOTE: *The WWII-vintage 30-caliber U.S. Carbine was mfd. by Inland Mfg. Div. of G.M.C., Dayton, OH; Winchester Repeating Arms Co., New Haven, CT, and other contractors: International Business Machines Corp., Poughkeepsie, NY; National Postal Meter Co., Rochester, NY; Quality Hardware & Machine Co., and Rock-Ola Co., Chicago, IL; Saginaw Steering Gear Div. of G.M.C., Saginaw, MI; Standard Products Co., Port Clinton, OH; Underwood-Elliott-Fisher Co., Hartford, CT.*

CALIBER .30, M1
(GARAND) MIL. RIFLE . . . . NiB $1250 Ex $1050 Gd $975
Clip-fed, gas-operated, air-cooled semiautomatic. Uses a clip containing 8 rounds. 24-inch bbl. Weight: W/o bayonet, 9.5 lbs. Sights: Adj. peep rear; blade front w/guards. Pistol-grip stock, handguards. Made 1937-57. Note: Garand rifles have also been produced by Winchester Repeating Arms Co., Harrington & Richardson Arms Co., and International Harvester Co. Deduct 25% for arsenal-assembled mismatches.

CALIBER .30, M1,
NATIONAL MATCH . . . . NiB $2100 Ex $1550 Gd $600
Accurized target version of the Garand. Glass-bedded stock; match grade bbl., sights, gas cylinder. "NM" stamped on bbl. forward of handguard.

NOTE: *The U.S. Model 1917 Enfield was mfd. 1917-18 by Remington Arms Co. of Delaware (later Midvale Steel & Ordnance Co., Eddystone, PA); Remington Arms Co., Ilion, NY; Winchester Repeating Arms Co., New Haven, CT.*

MODEL 1917 ENFIELD MILITARY RIFLE . . NiB $795 Ex $675 Gd $250
Modified Mauser-type bolt action. Caliber: .30-06. Five shot box magazine. 26-inch bbl. Weight: 9.25 lbs. Sights: Adj. rear; blade front w/guards. Military-type stock w/semi-pistol-grip. This design originated in Great Britain as the, "Pattern 14" and was mfd. in caliber .303 for the British Government in three U.S. plants. In 1917, the U.S. Government contracted w/these firms to produce the same rifle in caliber .30-06; over two million of these Model 1917 Enfields were mfd. While no more were produced after WWI, the U.S. supplied over a million of them to Great Britain during WWII.

Uzi Semiautomatic
Model B Carbine

Valmet M-62S

Valmet Hunter

**CARBINE,
CALIBER 30, M1** . . . . **NiB $719 Ex $575 Gd $391**
Gas-operated (short-stroke piston), semiautomatic. 15- or 30-round
detachable box magazine. 18-inch bbl. Weight: 5.5 lbs. Sights: adj.
rear; blade front sight w/guards. Pistol-grip stock w/handguard, side-
mounted web sling. Made 1942-45. In 1963, 150,000 surplus M1
Carbines were sold at $20 each to members of the National Rifle
Assn. by the Dept. of the Army. Note: For Winchester and Rock-Ola,
add 30%; for Irwin Pedersen, add 80%. Quality Hardware did not
complete its production run. Guns produced by other manufacturers were marked "Unquality" & command premium prices.

U.S. REPEATING ARMS CO.

See Winchester Rifle listings.

UNIVERSAL SPORTING GOODS, INC. — Miami, Florida

DELUXE CARBINE. . . . . **NiB $325 Ex $275 Gd $150**
Same as standard model except also available in caliber .256,
w/deluxe walnut Monte Carlo stock and handguard. Made 1965 to
date.

STANDARD M-1 CARBINE . . . . **NiB $225 Ex $175 Gd $125**
Same as U.S. Carbine, Cal. .30, M1 except may have either wood
or metal handguard, bbl. band w/ or w/o bayonet lug; 5-shot magazine standard. Made 1964 to date.

UZI CARBINE — Mfd. by Israel Military Industries, Israel

SEMIAUTOMATIC MODEL B CARBINE
Calibers: 9mm Parabellum, .41 Action Express, .45 ACP. 20- to 50-
round magazine. 16.1-inch bbl. Weight: 8.4 lbs. Metal folding
stock. Front post-type sight, open rear, both adj. Imported by Action
Arms 1983-89. NFA (Selective Fire) models imported by UZI
America, INC., 1994 to date.
Model B Carbine (9mm or .45 ACP). . . . **NiB $1275 Ex $1050 Gd $675**
Model B Carbine (.41 AE) . . . . **NiB $1494 Ex $1195 Gd $813**
Centerfire conversion unit, add $250
Rimfire conversion unit, add. $175

SEMIAUTOMATIC
MINI CARBINE . . . . **NiB $2450 Ex $2000 Gd $1400**
Similar to Uzi Model B except with 19.75-inch bbl.and chambered
9mm Parabellum only. 20-round magazine. Weight: 7.2 lbs.
Imported 1989.

**Vickers Jubilee
Single-Shot Target Rifle**

VALMET OY — Jyväskylä, Finland

M-62S SEMIAUTOMATIC RIFLE . . . . NiB $1781 Ex $1425 Gd $969
Semiautomatic version of Finnish M-62 automatic assault rifle based on Russian AK-47. Gas-operated rotating bolt action. Caliber: 7.62mmX39 Russian. 15- and 30-round magazines. 16.63-inch bbl. Weight: 8 lbs. w/metal stock. Sights: Tangent aperture rear; hooded blade front w/luminous flip-up post for low-light use. Tubular steel or wood stock. Intro. 1962. Disc.

M-71S . . . . NiB $1800 Ex $1575 Gd $875
Same specifications as M-62S except caliber 5.56mmx45 (.223 Rem.), w/open rear sight, reinforced resin or wood stock, weight: 7.75 lbs. w/former. Made 1971-89.

M-76 SEMIAUTOMATIC RIFLE
Semiautomatic assault rifle. Gas-operated, rotating bolt action. Caliber: 223 Rem. 15- and 30-shot magazines. Made 1984-89.
Wood stock . . . . NiB $1494 Ex $1195 Gd $813
Folding stock . . . . NiB $1869 Ex $1495 Gd $1017

M-78 SEMIAUTOMATIC RIFLE . . . . NiB $1688 Ex $1350 Gd $918
Caliber: 7.62x51 (NATO). 24.13-inch bbl. Overall length: 43.25 inches. Weight: 10.5 lbs.

M-82 SEMIAUTOMATIC CARBINE . . . . . NiB $2500 Ex $1950 Gd $975
Caliber: .223 Rem. 15- or 30-shot magazine. 17-inch bbl. 27 inches overall. Weight: 7.75 lbs.

MODEL 412 S DOUBLE RIFLE . . . . NiB $1313 Ex $1050 Gd $714
Boxlock. Manual or automatic extraction. Calibers: .243, .308, .30-06, .375 Win., 9.3x74R. Bbls.: 24-inch over/under. Weight: 8.63 lbs. American walnut checkered stock and forend.

HUNTER SEMIAUTOMATIC RIFLE . . . . . . NiB $950 Ex $750 Gd $500
Similar to M-78 except in calibers .223 Rem. (5.56mm), .243 Win., .308 Win. (7.62 NATO) and .30-06. Five , 9- or 15-shot magazine. 20.5-inch plain bbl. 42 inches overall. Weight: 8 lbs. Sights: Adj. combination scope mount/rear; blade front, mounted on gas tube. Checkered European walnut buttstock and extended checkered forend and handguard. Imported 1986-89.

VICKERS LTD. — Crayford, Kent, England

**JUBILEE MODEL SINGLE-SHOT-
TARGET RIFLE** . . . . NiB $425 Ex $325 Gd $200
Round-receiver Martini-type action. Caliber: .22 LR. 28-inch heavy bbl. Weight: 9.5 lbs. Sights: Parker-Hale No. 2 front; Perfection rear peep. One-piece target stock w/full forearm and pistol-grip. Made before WWII.

EMPIRE MODEL . . . . NiB $475 Ex $350 Gd $225
Similar to Jubilee Model except w/27- or 30-inch bbl., straight-grip stock, weight: 9.25 lbs. w/30-inch bbl. Made before WWII.

VOERE — Manufactured in Kufstein, Austria Imported by JagerSport, Cranston, Rhode Island

**VEC-91 LIGHTNING
BOLT-ACTION RIFLE** . . . . NiB $2438 Ex $1950 Gd $1326
Features unique electronic ignition system to activate or fire caseless ammunition. Calibers: .5.56 UCC (.222 Cal.), 6mm UCC caseless. Five shot magazine. 20-inch bbl. 39 inches overall. Weight: 6 lbs. Open adj. rear sight. Drilled and tapped for scope mounts. European walnut stock w/cheekpiece. Twin forward locking lugs. Imported 1992 to date.

VOERE, VOELTER & COMPANY — Vaehrenbach, Germany

Mauser-Werke acquired Voere in 1987 and all models are now marketed under new designations.

MODEL 1007 BIATHLON REPEATER . . . . . NiB $350 Ex $275 Gd $175
Caliber: 22 LR. Five shot magazine. 19.5-inch bbl. 39 inches overall. Weight: 5.5 lb. Sights: Adj. rear, blade front. Plain beechwood stock. Imported 1984-86.

MODEL 1013 BOLT-ACTION REPEATER . . . . . NiB $650 Ex $450 Gd $300
Same as Model 1007 except w/military-style stock in 22 WMR caliber. Double-set triggers optional. Imported 1984-86 by KDF, Inc.

MODEL 2107 BOLT-ACTION REPEATER
Caliber: 22 LR. Five or 8-shot magazine. 19.5-inch bbl. 41 inches overall. Weight: 6 lbs. Sights: Adj. rear sight, hooded front. European hardwood Monte Carlo-style stock. Imported 1986 by KDF, Inc.
Standard model . . . . NiB $350 Ex $225 Gd $150
Deluxe model . . . . NiB $400 Ex $275 Gd $200

WALTHER RIFLES — Mfd. by the German firms of Waffenfabrik Walther and Carl Walther Sportwaffenfabrik

The following Walther rifles were mfd. before WWII by Waffenfabrik Walther, Zella-Mehlis (Thür.), Germany.

**MODEL 1 AUTOLOADING
RIFLE (LIGHT)** . . . . NiB $695 Ex $600 Gd $350
Similar to Standard Model 2 but w/20-inch bbl., lighter stock, weight: 4.5 lbs.

MODEL 2 AUTOLOADING RIFLE . . . . NiB $675 Ex $550 Gd $325
Bolt-action, may be used as autoloader, manually operated repeater or single-shot. Caliber: .22 LR. Five or 9-shot detachable box magazine. 24.5-inch bbl. Weight: 7 lbs. Sights: Tangent-curve rear; ramp front. Sporting stock w/checkered pistol grip, grooved forearm, swivels. Disc.

Walther Model 1

Walther Model 2

Walther Model GX-1

Walther Model KKM-S

Walther Model U.I.T.
Super Match

OLYMPIC BOLT-ACTION
MATCH RIFLE . . . . **NiB $1156 Ex $925 Gd $629**
Single-shot. Caliber: .22 LR. 26-inch heavy bbl. Weight: 13 lbs. Sights: Micrometer extension rear; interchangeable front. Target stock w/checkered pistol-grip, thumbhole, full beavertail forearm covered w/corrugated rubber, palm rest, adj. Swiss-type buttplate, swivels. Disc.

MODEL V BOLT-ACTION
SINGLE-SHOT RIFLE . . . . **NiB $550 Ex $390 Gd $275**
Caliber: .22 LR. 26-inch bbl. Weight: 7 lbs. Sights: Open rear; ramp front. Plain pistol-grip stock w/grooved forearm. Disc.

MODEL V MEISTERBÜCHSE
(CHAMPION) . . . . **NiB $625 Ex $450 Gd $295**
Same as standard Model V except w/micrometer open rear sight and checkered pistol-grip. Disc.

POST WWII MODELS
The Walther rifles listed below have been manufactured since WWII by Carl Walther Sportwaffenfabrik, Ulm (Donau), Germany.

MODEL GX-1 FREE RIFLE . . . . . . **NiB $1875 Ex $1375 Gd $775**
Bolt-action, single-shot. Caliber: .22 LR. 25.5-inch heavy bbl. Weight: 15.9 lbs. Sights: Micrometer aperture rear; globe front. Thumbhole stock w/adj. cheekpiece and buttplate w/removable hook, accessory rail. Left-hand stock available. Accessories furnished include hand stop and sling swivel, palm rest, counterweight assembly.

MODEL KKJ SPORTER . . . . **NiB $1200 Ex $975 Gd $495**
Bolt action. Caliber: .22 LR. Five shot box magazine. 22.5-inch bbl. Weight: 5.5 lbs. Sights: Open rear; hooded ramp front. Stock w/cheekpiece, checkered pistol-grip and forearm, sling swivels. Disc.

MODEL KKJ-HO . . . . NiB $1450 Ex $1250 Gd $925
Same as Model KKJ except chambered for .22 Hornet. Disc.

MODEL KKJ-MA . . . . NiB $1250 Ex $1100 Gd $490
Same as Model KKJ except chambered for .22 WMR. Disc.

MODEL KKM INTERNATIONAL
MATCH RIFLE . . . . NiB $925 Ex $750 Gd $500
Bolt-action, single-shot. Caliber: .22 LR. 28-inch heavy bbl. Weight: 15.5 lbs. Sights: Micrometer aperture rear; globe front. Thumbhole stock w/high comb, adj. hook buttplate, accessory rail. Left-hand stock available. Disc.

MODEL KKM-S . . . . NiB $975 Ex $800 Gd $525
Same specifications as Model KKM, except w/adj. cheekpiece. Disc.

MOVING TARGET MATCH RIFLE . . . . NiB $925 Ex $675 Gd $430
Bolt-action, single-shot. Caliber: .22 LR. 23.6-inch bbl. w/weight. Weight: 8.6 lbs. Supplied w/o sights. Thumbhole stock w/adj. cheekpiece and buttplate. Left-hand stock available.

PRONE 400 TARGET RIFLE . . . . NiB $775 Ex $625 Gd $400
Bolt-action, single-shot. Caliber: .22 LR. 25.5-inch heavy bbl. Weight: 10.25 lbs. Supplied w/o sights. Prone stock w/adj. cheekpiece and buttplate, accessory rail. Left-hand stock available. Disc.

MODEL SSV VARMINT RIFLE . . . . . NiB $720 Ex $600 Gd $400
Bolt-action, single-shot. Calibers: .22 LR, .22 Hornet. 25.5-inch bbl. Weight: 6.75 lbs. Supplied w/o sights. Monte Carlo stock w/high cheekpiece, full pistol grip and forearm. Disc.

MODEL U.L.T. SPECIAL MATCH RIFLE . . . . . NiB $1250 Ex $925 Gd $650
Bolt-action, single-shot. Caliber: .22 LR. 25.5-inch bbl. Weight: 10.2 lbs. Sights: Micrometer aperture rear; globe front. Target stock w/high comb, adj. buttplate, accessory rail. Left-hand stock avail. Disc. 1993.

MODEL U.L.T. SUPER MATCH RIFLE . . . . . . NiB $1275 Ex $950 Gd $675
Bolt-action, single-shot. Caliber: .22 LR. 25.5-inch heavy bbl. Weight: 10.2 lbs. Micrometer aperture rear; globe front. Target stock w/support for off-hand shooting, high comb, adj. buttplate and swivel. Left-hand stock available. Disc. 1993.

MONTGOMERY WARD — Chicago, Illinois
Western Field and Hercules Models

Firearms under the "private label" names of Western Field and Hercules are manufactured by such firms as Mossberg, Stevens, Marlin, and Savage for distribution and sale by Montgomery Ward.

MODEL 14M-497B WESTERN FIELD
BOLT-ACTION RIFLE . . . . NiB $100 Ex $80 Gd $54
Caliber: .22 RF. Seven shot detachable box magazine. 24-inch bbl. Weight: 5 lbs. Sights: Receiver peep; open rear; hooded ramp front. Pistol-grip stock. Mfg. by Mossberg.

MODEL M771 WESTERN FIELD
LEVER-ACTION RIFLE . . . . NiB $150 Ex $125 Gd $95
Calibers: .30-30, .35 Rem. Six shot tubular magazine. 20-inch bbl. Weight: 6.75 lbs. Sights: Open rear; ramp front. Pistol-grip or straight stock, forearm w/barrel band. Mfg. by Mossberg.

MODEL M772 WESTERN FIELD
LEVER-ACTION RIFLE . . . . NiB $175 Ex $150 Gd $100
Calibers: .30-30, .35 Rem. Six shot tubular magazine. 20-inch bbl. Weight: 6.75 lbs. Sights: Open rear; ramp front. Pistol-grip or straight stock, forearm w/bbl. band. Mfg. by Mossberg.

MODEL M775
BOLT-ACTION RIFLE . . . . NiB $110 Ex $95 Gd $70
Calibers: .222 Rem., .22-250, .243 Win., .308 Win. Four shot magazine. Weight: 7.5 lbs. Sights: Folding leaf rear; ramp front. Monte Carlo stock w/cheekpiece, pistol-grip. Mfg by Mossberg.

MODEL M776
BOLT-ACTION RIFLE . . . . NiB $200 Ex $175 Gd $125
Calibers: .222 Rem., .22-250, .243 Win., .308 Win. Four shot magazine. Weight: 7.5 lbs. Sights: Folding leaf rear; ramp front. Monte Carlo stock w/cheekpiece, pistol-grip. Mfg. by Mossberg.

MODEL M778
LEVER-ACTION . . . . NiB $195 Ex $150 Gd $100
Calibers: .30-30, .35 Rem. 6-shot tubular magazine. 20-inch bbl. Weight: 6.75 lbs. Sights: Open rear; ramp front. Pistol-grip or straight stock, forearm w/bbl. band. Mfg. by Mossberg.

MODEL M780
BOLT-ACTION RIFLE . . . . NiB $200 Ex $175 Gd $125
Calibers: .222 Rem., .22-250, .243 Win., .308 Win. Four shot magazine. Weight: 7.5 lbs. Sights: Folding leaf rear; ramp front. Monte Carlo stock w/cheekpiece, pistol grip. Mfg. by Mossberg.

MODEL M782
BOLT-ACTION RIFLE . . . . NiB $200 Ex $175 Gd $125
Same general specifications as Model M780.

MODEL M808 . . . . NiB $105 Ex $85 Gd $59
Takedown. Caliber: .22RF. 15-shot tubular magazine. Bbls.: 20- and 24-inch. Weight: 6 lbs. Sights: Open rear; bead front. Pistol-grip stock. Mfg. by Stevens.

MODEL M832 BOLT-ACTION RIFLE . . . . NiB $110 Ex $90 Gd $60
Caliber: .22 RF. Seven shot clip magazine. 24-inch bbl. Weight: 6.5 lbs. Sights: Open rear; ramp front. Mfg. by Mossberg.

MODEL M836 . . . . NiB $115 Ex $90 Gd $70
Takedown. Caliber: .22RF. 15-shot tubular magazine. Bbls.: 20- and 24-inch. Weight: 6 lbs. Sights: Open rear; bead front. Pistol-grip stock. Mfg. by Stevens.

MODEL M865 LEVER-ACTION CARBINE . . . NiB $140 Ex $100 Gd $85
Hammerless. Caliber: .22RF. Tubular magazine. Made w/both 18.5-inch and 20-inch bbls., forearm w/bbl. band, swivels. Weight: 5 lbs. Mfg. by Mossberg.

MODEL M894
AUTO-LOADING CARBINE . . . . NiB $125 Ex $100 Gd $75
Caliber: .22 RF. 15-shot tubular magazine. 20-inch bbl. Weight: 6 lbs. Sights: Open rear; ramp front. Monte Carlo stock w/pistol-grip. Mfg. by Mossberg.

MODEL M-SD57 . . . . NiB $110 Ex $90 Gd $60
Takedown. Caliber: .22RF. 15-shot tubular magazine. Bbls.: 20- and 24-inch. Weight: 6 lbs. Sights: Open rear; bead front. Pistol-grip stock. Mfg. by Stevens.

WEATHERBY, INC. — Atascadero, CA
(Formerly South Gate, CA)

CROWN CUSTOM RIFLE . . . . . NiB $5700 Ex $3875 Gd $1975
Calibers: .240, .30-06, .257, .270, 7mm, .300, and .340. Bbl.: Made to order. Super fancy walnut stock. Also available w/engraved barreled action including gold animal overlay.

Weatherby Mark V Classicmark I

Weatherby Crown Custom

Weatherby Fiberguard

Weatherby Fibermark

RIFLES

DELUXE .378 MAGNUM RIFLE ...... **NiB $2600 Ex $1875 Gd $1250**
Same general specifications as Deluxe Magnum in other calibers
except caliber .378 W. M. Schultz & Larsen action; 26-inch bbl.
Disc. 1958.

DELUXE MAGNUM RIFLE ..... **NiB $1895 Ex $1400 Gd $1000**
Calibers: .220 Rocket, .257 Weatherby Mag., .270 W.M. 7mm
W.M., .300 W.M., .375 W.M. Specially processed FN Mauser
action. 24-inch bbl. (26-inch in .375 cal.). Monte Carlo-style stock
w/cheekpiece, black forend tip, grip cap, checkered pistol-grip and
forearm, quick-detachable sling swivels. Value shown is for rifle w/o
sights. Disc. 1958.

DELUXE RIFLE .... **NiB $1350 Ex $1025 Gd $725**
Same general specifications as Deluxe Magnum except chambered
for standard calibers such as .270, .30-06, etc. Disc. 1958.

FIBERGUARD RIFLE .... **NiB $675 Ex $550 Gd $375**
Same general specifications as Vanguard except for fiberglass stock
and matte metal finish. Disc, 1988.

FIBERMARK RIFLE .... **NiB $1195 Ex $875 Gd $575**
Same general specifications as Mark V except w/molded fiberglass
stock, finished in a nonglare black wrinkle finish. The metal is finished in a non-glare matte finish. Disc. 1993.

MARK V ACCUMARK BOLT-ACTION REPEATING
Weatherby Mark V magnum action. Calibers: .257 Wby., .270 Wby.,
7mm Rem. Mag., 7mm Wby., 7mm STW, .300 Win. Mag., .300 Wby.

(cont'd.) **MARK V ACCUMARK BOLT ACTION REPEATING**
Mag., .30-338 Wby., .30-378 Wby. and .340 Wby. 26- or 28-inch
stainless bbl. w/black oxide flutes. 46.5 or 48.5 inches overall.
Weight: 8 to 8.5 lbs. No sights, drilled and tapped for scope.
Stainless finish w/blued receiver. H-S Precision black synthetic stock
w/aluminum bedding plate, recoil pad and sling swivels. Imported
1996 to date.

Mark V Accumark (.30-338
& .30-378 Wby. Mag.) .... **NiB $1313 Ex $1050 Gd $714**
Mark V Accumark (All other calibers) .... **NiB $1119 Ex $895 Gd $609**
Mark V Left-Action, add **$75**

MARK V ACCUMARK
LIGHT WEIGHT RIFLE .... **NiB $1215 Ex $1025 Gd $600**
Similar to the Mark V Accumark except w/LightWeight Mark V
action designed for standard calibers w/sixlocking lugs rather than
nine. 24-inch stainless bbl. Weight: 5.75 lbs. Gray or black Monte
Carlo-style composite Kevlar/fiberglass stock w/Pachmayr
"Decelerator" pad. No sights. Imported 1997 to date.

MARK V CLASSICMARK I RIFLE
Same general specifications as Mark V except w/checkered select
American Claro walnut stock w/oil finish and presentation recoil
pad. Satin metal finish. Imported 1992-93.

Calibers .240 to .300 Wby. ...... **NiB $1075 Ex $750 Gd $450**
Caliber .340 Wby. .... **NiB $1095 Ex $775 Gd $450**
Caliber .378 Wby. .... **NiB $1275 Ex $775 Gd $450**
Caliber .416 Wby. .... **NiB $1150 Ex $825 Gd $450**
Caliber .460 Wby. .... **NiB $1250 Ex $900 Gd $475**

Weatherby Mark V Deluxe

Weatherby Mark V Euromark

Weatherby Mark V Lazermark

Weatherby Mark V Safari Grade

MARK V CLASSICMARK LL RIFLE

Same general specifications as Classicmark I except w/checkered select American walnut stock w/oil finish steel grip cap and Old English recoil pad. Satin metal finish. Right-hand only. Imported 1992-93.

Calibers .240 to .340 Wby.
(26-inch bbl.) . . . . NiB $1350 Ex $1050 Gd $700
Caliber .378 Wby. . . . . NiB $1400 Ex $1075 Gd $750
Caliber .416 Wby. . . . . NiB $1525 Ex $1295 Gd $895
Caliber .460 Wby. . . . . NiB $1575 Ex $1325 Gd $925

MARK V DELUXE RIFLE . . . . NiB $995 Ex $725 Gd $480
Similar to Mark V Sporter except w/Lightweight Mark V action designed for standard calibers w/sixlocking lugs rather than nine, 4- or 5-shot magazine. 24-inch bbl. 44 inches overall. Weight: 6.75 lbs. Checkered Monte Carlo American walnut stock w/rosewood forend and pistol grip and diamond inlay. Imported 1997 to date.

WEATHERBY MARK V DELUXE BOLT-ACTION SPORTING RIFLE

Mark V action, right or left hand. Calibers: .22-250, .30-06- .224 Weatherby Varmintmaster; .240, .257, .270, 7mm, .300, .340, .375, .378, .416, .460 Weatherby Magnums. Box magazine holds 2 to 5 cartridges depending on caliber. 24- or 26-inch bbl. Weight: 6.5 to 10.5 lbs. Monte Carlo-style stock w/cheekpiece, skip checkering, forend tip, pistol-grip cap, recoil pad, QD swivels. Values shown are for rifles w/o sights. Made in Germany 1958-69; in Japan 1970-94. Values shown for Japanese production.

Calibers .22-250, .224 . . . . NiB $1025 Ex $785 Gd $540
Caliber .375 H&H Magnum . . . . NiB $1100 Ex $925 Gd $625
Caliber .378 Weatherby Magnum . . . . . . NiB $1275 Ex $1000 Gd $775
Caliber .416 Weatherby Magnum . . . . . . NiB $1350 Ex $1050 Gd $700
Caliber .460 Weatherby Magnum . . . . . . NiB $1725 Ex $1325 Gd $950

MARK V EUROMARK BOLT-ACTION RIFLE

Same general specifications as other Mark V rifles except w/hand-rubbed, satin oil finish Claro walnut stock and nonglare special process blue matte barreled action. Left-hand models available. Imported 1986-93. Reintroduced 1995.

Caliber .378 Wby. Mag. . . . . NiB $1350 Ex $1050 Gd $700
Caliber .416 Wby. Mag. . . . . NiB $1450 Ex $1125 Gd $800
Caliber .460 Wby Mag. . . . . NiB $1725 Ex $1325 Gd $950
Other calibers . . . . NiB $925 Ex $695 Gd $450

MARK V LAZERMARK RIFLE

Same general specifications as Mark V except w/laser-carved stock.

Caliber .378 Wby. Mag. . . . . NiB $1825 Ex $1425 Gd $795
Caliber .416 Wby. Mag. . . . . NiB $1825 Ex $1425 Gd $795
Caliber .460 Wby. Mag. . . . . NiB $2150 Ex $1500 Gd $975
Other calibers . . . . NiB $1295 Ex $995 Gd $625

MARK V SAFARI GRADE RIFLE. . . . . . . NiB $2119 Ex $1695 Gd $1153
Same general specifications as Mark V except extra capacity magazine, bbl. sling swivel, and express rear sight typical "Safari" style.

MARK V SPORTER RIFLE

Sporter version of Mark V Magnum w/low-luster metal finish. Checkered Carlo walnut stock w/o grip cap or forend tip. No sights. Imported 1993 to date.

Calibers .257 to .300 Wby. . . . . NiB $935 Ex $775 Gd $400
.340 Weatherby . . . . NiB $995 Ex $625 Gd $425
.375 H&H . . . . NiB $1025 Ex $725 Gd $525

MARK V LIGHTWEIGHT SPORTER RIFLE. . NiB $900 Ex $725 Gd $400
Similar to Mark V Sporter except w/Lightweight Mark V action designed for standard calibers w/six locking lugs rather than nine. Imported 1997 to date.

Weatherby Mark XXII Deluxe
.22 Automatic Sporter

Weatherby Vanguard (I) VGL
Bolt-Action Sporting Rifle

Weatherby Varmintmaster

RIFLES

MARK V STAINLESS RIFLE
Similar to the Mark V Magnum except in 400-series stainless steel w/bead-blasted matte finish. Weight: 8 lbs. Monte Carlo synthetic stock w/aluminum bedding block. Imported 1995 to date.

Mark V Stainless (.30-.378 Wby.). . NiB $1125 Ex $915 Gd $475
Mark V Stainless (.375 H&H.) . . . . NiB $1125 Ex $915 Gd $475
All other calibers. . . . . NiB $975 Ex $695 Gd $475
W/fluted bbl., add. $100

MARK V (LW) STAINLESS RIFLE . . . . NiB $775 Ex $595 Gd $395
Similar to the Mark V (standard calibers) except in 400-series stainless steel w/bead-blasted matte finish. Five shot magazine. 24-inch bbl. 44 inches overall. Weight: 6.5 lbs. Monte Carlo synthetic stock w/aluminum bedding block. Imported 1995 to date.

MARK V SLS RIFLE
Acronym for Stainless Laminated Sporter. Similar to the Mark V Magnum Sporter, except w/stainless 400-series action and 24- or 26-inch stainless bbl. Laminated wood stock. Weight: 8.5 lbs. Black oxide bead-blasted matte blue finish. Imported 1997 to date.

Mark V SLS (.340 Wby.). . . . . NiB $1125 Ex $915 Gd $475
All other calibers. . . . . NiB $975 Ex $695 Gd $475

MARK V SYNTHETIC RIFLE
Similar to the Mark V Magnum except w/Monte Carlo synthetic stock w/aluminum bedding block. 24- or 26-inch standard tapper or fluted bbl. Weight: 7.75 to 8 lbs. Matte blue finish. Imported 1995 to date.

Mark V Synthetic (.340 Wby.) . . . . NiB $975 Ex $695 Gd $450
Mark V Synthetic (.30-378 Wby.) . . . . NiB $995 Ex $675 Gd $450
All other calibers . . . . NiB $725 Ex $550 Gd $375
W/fluted bbl., add. $100

MARK V ULTRA LIGHT WEIGHT RIFLE
Similar to the Mark V Magnum except w/skeletonized bolt handle. 24- or 26-inch fluted stainless bbl. chambered .257 Wby., .270 Wby., 7mm Rem. Mag., 7mm Wby., .300 Win. Mag., .300 Wby. Monte Carlo synthetic stock w/aluminum bedding block. Weight: 6.75 lbs. Imported 1998 to date.

(cont'd.) MARK V ULTRA LIGHT WEIGHT RIFLE
Mark V Ultra Lightweight
(standard calibers). . . . . NiB $1825 Ex $1400 Gd $725
Mark V Ultra Lightweight
(Weatherby calibers) . . . . NiB $1850 Ex $1450 Gd $750
Mark V Ultra Lightweight
(Left-hand action), add $100

MARK XXII DELUXE .22 AUTOMATIC
SPORTER, CLIP-FED MODEL . . . . NiB $495 Ex $450 Gd $325
Semiautomatic w/single-shot selector. Caliber: .22 LR. Five and 10-shot clip magazines. 24-inch bbl. Weight: 6 lbs. Sights: Folding leaf open rear; ramp front. Monte Carlo-type stock w/cheekpiece, pistol-grip, forend tip, grip cap, skip checkering, QD swivels. Intro. 1964. Made in Italy 1964-69; in Japan, 1970-1981; in the U.S., 1982-90.

MARK XXII, TUBULAR
MAGAZINE MODEL . . . . NiB $395 Ex $320 Gd $195
Same as Mark XXII, clip-fed model except w/15-shot tubular magazine. Made in Japan 1973-81; in the U.S.,1982-90.

VANGUARD (I) BOLT-ACTION SPORTING RIFLE
Mauser-type action. Calibers: .243 Win., .25-06, .270 Win., 7mm Rem. Mag., .30-06, .300 Win. Mag. Five shot magazine; (3-shot in Magnum calibers). 24-inch bbl. Weight: 7 lbs. 14 oz. No sights. Monte Carlo-type stock w/cheekpiece, rosewood forend tip and pistol-grip cap, checkering, rubber buttpad, QD swivels. Imported 1970-84.

Vanguard Standard . . . . NiB $450 Ex $375 Gd $225
Vanguard VGL (w/shorter
20-inch bbl., plain checkered
stock matte finish, 6.5 lbs . . . . NiB $425 Ex $350 Gd $230
Vanguard VGS (w/24-inch
bbl., plain checkered stock,
matte finish . . . . NiB $475 Ex $360 Gd $250
Vanguard VGX
(w/higher grade finish) . . . . NiB $525 Ex $425 Gd $275

Westley Richards
Best Quality Double

Westley Richards
Best Quality Magazine Rifle

VANGUARD CLASSIC I RIFLE.....NiB $480 Ex $370 Gd $255
Same general specifications as Vanguard VGX Deluxe except w/hand-checkered classic-style stock, black buttpad and satin finish. Calibers .223 Rem., .243 Win. .270 Win., 7mm-08, 7mm Rem. Mag., .30-06 and .308 Win. Imported 1989-94.

VANGUARD CLASSIC II RIFLE....NiB $695 Ex $575 Gd $375
Same general specifications as Vanguard VGX Deluxe except custom checkered classic-style American walnut stock w/black forend tip, grip cap and solid black recoil pad, satin finish. Imported 1989-94.

VANGUARD VGX DELUXE.......NiB $625 Ex $495 Gd $350
Calibers: .22-250 Rem., .243 Rem., .270 Wby. Mag., .270 Win., 7mm Rem. Mag., .30-06, .300 Win. Mag., .300 Wby. Mag., .338 Win. Mag. Three or 5-round capacity. 24-inch bbl. About 44 inches overall. Weight: 7 to 8.5 lbs. Custom checkered American walnut stock w/Monte Carlo and recoil pad. Rosewood forend tip and pistol-grip cap. High-luster finish. Disc. 1994.

VARMINTMASTER BOLT-ACTION RIFLE..NiB $1800 Ex $1395 Gd $750
Calibers: .224 Wby., .22-250, 4-shot magazine. 26-inch bbl. 45 inches overall. Weight: 7.75 lbs. Checkered walnut stock. No sights. Disc.

WEATHERMARK RIFLE
Same gen. specs. as Classicmark except w/checkered blk. Weathermark composite stock. Mark V bolt act. Cal: .240, .257, .270, .300, .340, .378, .416 and .460 Weatherby Mag.; plus .270 Win., 7mm Rem. Mag., .30-06 and .375 H&H Mag. Wt: 8 to 10 lbs. Right-hand only. Imp. 1992-94.
Calibers .257 to .300 Wby........NiB $695 Ex $525 Gd $350
Caliber .340 Weatherby..........NiB $725 Ex $550 Gd $360
Caliber .375 H&H...............NiB $950 Ex $650 Gd $450
Other non-Wby. calibers........NiB $695 Ex $495 Gd $350

WEATHERMARK ALASKAN RIFLE.......NiB $775 Ex $625 Gd $425
Same general specifications as Weathermark except w/nonglare electroless nickel finish. Right-hand only. Imported 1992-94.

WEIHRAUCH — Melrichstadt, West Germany
Imported by European American Armory, Sharpes, FL.

MODEL HW 60 TARGET RIFLE....NiB $625 Ex $550 Gd $350
Single-shot. Caliber: .22 LR. 26.75-inch bbl. Walnut stock. Adj. buttplate and trigger. Hooded ramp front sight. Push button safety. Imported 1995-97.

MODEL HW 66 BOLT-ACTION RIFLE....NiB $575 Ex $490 Gd $300
Caliber: .22 Hornet. 22.75-inch bbl. 41.75 inches overall. Weight: 6.5 lbs. Walnut stock w/cheekpiece. Hooded blade ramp front sight. Checkered pistol grip and forend. Imported 1989-90.

MODEL HW 660 MATCH
BOLT-ACTION RIFLE...........NiB $850 Ex $725 Gd $400
Caliber: .22 LR. 26-inch bbl. 45.33 inches overall. Weight: 10.75 lbs. Walnut or laminated stock w/adj. cheekpiece and buttplate. Checkered pistol grip and forend. Adj. trigger. Imported 1991 to date.

WESTERN FIELD RIFLES

See listings under "W" for Montgomery Ward.

WESTLEY RICHARDS & CO., LTD. — London, England

BEST QUALITY
DOUBLE RIFLE.........NiB $34,375 Ex $27,500 Gd $18,700
Boxlock, hammerless, ejector. Hand-detachable locks. Calibers: .30-06, .318 Accelerated Express, .375 Mag., .425 Mag. Express, .465 Nitro Express, .470 Nitro Express. 25-inch bbls. Weight: 8.5 to 11 lbs. Sights: leaf rear; hooded front. French walnut stock w/cheekpiece, checkered pistol grip and forend.

BEST QUALITY MAGAZINE RIFLE
Mauser or Magnum Mauser action. Calibers: 7mm High Velocity, .30-06, .318 Accelerated Express, .375 Mag., .404 Nitro Express, .425 Mag. Bbl. lengths: 24-inch; 7mm, 22-inch; .425 caliber, 25-inch. Weight 7.25 to 9.25 lbs. Sights: Leaf rear; hooded front.
Standard action.............NiB $8688 Ex $6950 Gd $4726
Magnum action.........NiB $12,813 Ex $10,250 Gd $6970

WICHITA ARMS — Wichita, Kansas

MODEL WCR CLASSIC BOLT-ACTION RIFLE
Single-shot. Calibers: .17 Rem through .308 Win. 21-inch octagon bbl. Hand-checkered walnut stock. Drilled and tapped for scope w/no sights. Right or left-hand action w/Canjar trigger. Non-glare blued finish. Made 1978 to date.
Right-hand model ....NiB $3250 Ex $2500 Gd $1600
Left-hand model ....NiB $3169 Ex $2570 Gd $1804

MODEL WSR SILHOUETTE BOLT-ACTION RIFLE
Single-shot, bolt action, chambered in most standard calibers. Right or left-hand action w/fluted bolt. Drilled and tapped for scope mount with no sights. 24-inch bbl. Canjar trigger. Metallic gray Fiberthane stock w/vented rubber recoil pad. Made 1983-95.
Right-hand model ....NiB $2450 Ex $1775 Gd $1200
Left-hand model ....NiB $2394 Ex $1950 Gd $1382

Wickliffe '76 Standard
Single-Shot Rifle

Winchester Model 1873
Lever-Action Rifle

MODEL WMR STAINLESS
MAGNUM BOLT-ACTION RIFLE . . . . **NiB $2000 Ex $1695 Gd $995**
Single-shot or w/blind magazine action chambered .270 Win. through .458 Win. Mag. Drilled and tapped for scope with no sights. Fully adj. trigger. 22- or 24-inch bbl. Hand-checkered select walnut stock. Made 1980-84.

MODEL WVR VARMINT RIFLE
Calibers: .17 Rem through .308 Win. Three shot magazine. Right or left-hand action w/jeweled bolt. 21-inch bbl. w/o sights. Drilled and tapped for scope. Hand-checkered American walnut pistol-grip stock. Made 1978 to date.
Right-hand model . . . . **NiB $2500 Ex $1790 Gd $1100**
Left-hand model . . . . **NiB $2456 Ex $2000 Gd $1416**

WICKLIFFE RIFLES — Wickliffe, Ohio
Mfd. by Triple S Development Co., Inc.

'76 COMMEMORATIVE
MODEL . . . . **NiB $1200 Ex $950 Gd $775**
Limited edition of 100. Same as Deluxe Model except w/filled etching on receiver sidewalls, U.S. silver dollar inlaid in stock, 26-inch bbl. only, comes in presentation case. Made in 1976 only.

'76 DELUXE MODEL . . . . **NiB $494 Ex $395 Gd $269**
Same as Standard Model except w/22-inch bbl. in .30-06 only; high-luster blued finish, fancy-grade figured American walnut stock w/nickel silver grip cap.

'76 STANDARD MODEL
SINGLE-SHOT RIFLE . . . . **NiB $419 Ex $335 Gd $228**
Falling-block action. Calibers: .22 Hornet, .223 Rem., .22-250, .243 Win., .25-06, .308 Win., .30-06, .45-70. 22-inch lightweight bbl. (.243 and .308 only) or 26-inch heavy sporter bbl. Weight: 6.75 or 8.5 lbs., depending on bbl. No sights. Select American walnut Monte Carlo stock w/right or left cheekpiece and pistol-grip, semi-beavertail forearm. Intro. 1976. Disc.

STINGER MODEL . . . . **NiB $438 Ex $350 Gd $238**
Falling block, single-shot. Calibers: .22 Hornet and .223 Rem. .22-inch bbl. w/no sights. American walnut Monte Carlo stock w/continental-type forend. Made 1979-80.

TRADITIONALIST MODEL . . . . **NiB $440 Ex $340 Gd $235**
Falling block single-shot. Calibers: .30-06, .45-70. 24-inch bbl. w/open sights. Hand-checkered. American walnut classic-style buttstock and forearm. Made 1979-80.

WILKINSON ARMS CO. — Covina, California

TERRY CARBINE . . . . **NiB $475 Ex $365 Gd $250**
Caliber: 9mm Para. Semiautomatic. 30-shot magazine. 16-inch bbl. 30 inches overall. Weight: 6 lbs. Dovetailed receiver for scope mounting. Bolt-type safety. Ejection port w/automatic trap door. Blowback action. Fires from closed bolt. Made 1975 to date.

TED WILLIAMS RIFLES

See Sears, Roebuck and Company.

WINCHESTER RIFLES — Winchester Repeating Arms Company, New Haven, Connecticut

EARLY MODELS 1873 – 1918

NOTE: *Most Winchester rifles manufactured prior to 1918 used the date of approximate manufacture as the model number. For example, the Model 1894 repeating rifle was manufactured from 1894 to 1937. When Winchester started using two-digit model numbers after 1918, the "18" was dropped and the rifle was then called the Model 94. The Model 1892 was called the Model 92, etc.*

Winchester Model 1886
w/Case-colored Receiver

Winchester Model 1886
w/Blued Receiver

Winchester Model 1886 Saddle-Ring Carbine

At Right: Close-up barrel engraving on Winchester
Model 1873 One of One Thousand.

MODEL 1873 LEVER-ACTION
CARBINE . . . . **NiB $9313 Ex $7450 Gd $5066**
Same as Standard Model 1873 Rifle except w/20-inch bbl., 12-shot magazine, weight: 7.25 lbs.

MODEL 1873 LEVER-ACTION
RIFLE . . . . **NiB $8688 Ex $6950 Gd $4726**
Calibers: .32-20, .38-40, .44-40; a few were chambered for .22 rimfire. 15-shot magazine, also made w/6-shot half magazine. 24-inch bbl. (round, half-octagon, octagon). Weight: 8.5 lbs. Sights: Open rear; bead or blade front. Plain straight-grip stock and forearm. Made 1873-1924. 720,610 rifles of this model were mfd.

MODEL 1873 —
ONE OF ONE THOUSAND . . . . **NiB $190,000+ Ex $80,000+ Gd $50,000+**
During the late 1870s, Winchester offered Model 1873 rifles of superior accuracy and extra finish, designated "One of One Thousand" grade, at $100. These rifles are marked "1 of 1000" or "One of One Thousand." Only 136 of this model are known to have been manufactured. This is one of the rarest of shoulder arms and, because so few have been sold in recent years, it is extremely difficult to assign a value; however, an "excellent" specimen would probably bring a price upward of $200,000.

MODEL 1873 SPECIAL
SPORTING RIFLE . . . . **NiB $10,000 Ex $8500 Gd $5000**
Same as Standard Model 1873 Rifle except this type has receiver case-hardened in colors, pistol-grip stock of select walnut, octagon bbl. only.

MODEL 1885 SINGLE-SHOT RIFLE
Designed by John M. Browning, this falling-block, lever-action rifle was manufactured from 1885 to 1920 in a variety of models and chambered for most of the popular cartridges of the period — both rimfire and centerfire — from .22 to .50 caliber. There are two basic styles of frames,

(cont'd.) MODEL 1885 SINGLE-SHOT RIFLE
low-wall and high-wall. The low-wall was chambered only for the lower-powered cartridges, while the high-wall was supplied in all calibers and made in three basic types. The standard model for No. 3 and heavier barrels is the type commonly encountered; the thin-walled version was supplied with No. 1 and No. 2 light barrels and the thick-walled action in the heavier calibers. Made in both solid frame and takedown versions. Barrels were available in five weights ranging from the lightweight No. 1 to the extra-heavy No. 5 in round, half-octagon and full-octagon styles. Many other variations were also offered.

MODEL 1885 HIGH-WALL
SPORTING RIFLE . . . . **NiB $3500+ Ex $1900+ Gd $1500**
Solid frame or takedown. No. 3, 30-inch bbl., standard. Weight: 9.5 lbs. Standard trigger and lever. Open rear sights; blade front sight. Plain stock and forend.

MODEL 1885 LOW-WALL
SPORTING RIFLE . . . . **NiB $1619 Ex $1295 Gd $881**
Solid frame. No. 1, 28-inch round or octagon bbl. Weight: 7 lbs. Open rear sight; blade front sight. Plain stock and forend.

MODEL 1885
SCHUETZEN RIFLE . . . . **NiB $5494 Ex $4395 Gd $2989**
Solid frame or takedown. High-wall action. Schuetzen double-set trigger. Spur finger lever. No. 3, 30-inch octagon bbl. Weight: 12 lbs. Vernier rear peep sight; wind-gauge front sight. Fancy walnut Schuetzen stock with checkered pistol-grip and forend. Schuetzen buttplate; adj. palm rest.

MODEL 1885
SPECIAL SPORTING RIFLE . . . . . **NiB $2500+ Ex $2000+ Gd $1400**
Same general specifications as the standard high-wall model except with checkered fancy walnut stock and forend.

Winchester Model 1890

Winchester Model 1892

MODEL 1885 SINGLE-SHOT
MUSKET . . . . **NiB $1244 Ex $995 Gd $677**
Solid frame. Low-wall. .22 Short and Long Rifle. 28-inch round bbl. Weight: 8.6 lbs. Lyman rear peep sight; blade front sight. Military-type stock and forend. Note: The U.S. Government purchased a large quantity of these muskets during World War I for training purposes.

MODEL 1885 SINGLE-SHOT
"WINDER" MUSKET . . . . **NiB $950 Ex $790 Gd $500**
Solid frame or takedown. High-wall. Plain trigger. 28-inch round bbl. Weight: 8.5 lbs. Musket rear sight; blade front sight. Military-type stock and forend w/bbl. band and sling stud/rings.

MODEL 1886 LEVER-ACTION RIFLE
Solid frame or takedown. .33 Win., .38-56, .38-70, .40-65, .40-70, .40-82, .45-70, .45-90, .50-100, .50-110. The .33 Win. and .45-70 were the last calibers in which this model was supplied. Eight shot tubular magaine; also 4-shot half-magazine. 26-inch bbl. (round, half-octagon, octagon). Weight: 7.5 lbs. Sights: Open rear; bead or blade front. Plain straight-grip stock and forend or standard models. Made 1886-1935.
Standard model . . . . **NiB $4938 Ex $3950 Gd $2686**
Takedown model . . . . **NiB $6119 Ex $4895 Gd $3329**
**Deluxe model (pistol-grip and
high-quality walnut)** . . . . **NiB $10,000 Ex $9500 Gd $6000**

MODEL 1886 SADDLE-RING
CARBINE . . . . **NiB $12063 Ex $9650 Gd $6562**
Same as standard rifle except with 22-inch bbl., carbine buttstock and forend. Carbine rear sight. Saddle ring on left side of receiver.

MODEL 1890 SLIDE-ACTION RIFLE
Visible hammer. Calibers: .22 Short, Long, LR; .22 WRF (not interchangeable). Tubular magazine holds 15 Short, 12 Long, 11 LR; 12 WRF. 24-inch octagon bbl. Weight: 5.75 lbs. Sights: Open rear; bead front. Plain straight-grip stock, grooved slide handle. Originally solid frame; after No. 15,499, all rifles of this model were takedown-type. Fancy checkered pistol-grip stock, nickel-steel bbl. supplied at extra cost, which can also increase the value by 100% or more. Made 1890-1932.
Blue WRF . . . . **NiB $1850 Ex $1500 Gd $950**
Blue (.22 LR) . . . . **NiB $1900 Ex $1850 Gd $975**
Color casehardened receiver . . . . **NiB $6119 Ex $4895 Gd $3329**

MODEL 1892 LEVER-ACTION
RIFLE . . . . **NiB $2369 Ex $1895 Gd $1289**
Solid frame or takedown. Calibers: .25-20, .32-20, .38-40, .44-40. 13-shot tubular magazine; also 7-shot half-magazine. 24-inch bbl. (round, octagon, half-octagon). Weight: from 6.75 lbs. up. Sights: Open rear; bead front. Plain straight-grip stock and forend. Pistol-grip fancy walnut stocks were available at extra cost and also doubles the value of the current value for standard models.

MODEL 1892 SADDLE-RING
CARBINE . . . . **NiB $2500 Ex $2200 Gd $1600**
Same general specifications as the Model 1892 rifle except carbine buttstock, forend and sights. 20-inch bbl. Saddle ring on left side of receiver.

MODEL 1894 LEVER-ACTION
RIFLE . . . . **NiB $1869 Ex $1495 Gd $1017**
Solid frame or takedown. .25-35, .30-30, .32-40, .32 Special, .38-55. Seven shot tubular magazine or 4-shot half-magazine. 26-inch bbl. (round, octagon, half-octagon). Weight: about 7.35 lbs. Sights: Open rear; bead front. Plain straight-grip stock and forearm on standard model; crescent-shaped or shotgun-style buttplate. Made 1894-1937. See also Winchester Model 94 for later variations of this model.

MODEL 1894 LEVER-ACTION DELUXE. NiB $2313 Ex $1850 Gd $1258
Same general specifications as the standard rifle except checkered pistol-grip buttstock and forend using high-grade walnut. Engraved versions are considerably higher in value.

MODEL 1894 SADDLE-RING
CARBINE . . . . **NiB $1500 Ex $1395 Gd $950**
Same general specifications as the Model 1894 standard rifle except 20-inch bbl., carbine buttstock, forend, and sights. Saddle ring on left side of receiver. Weight: about 6.5 lbs.

MODEL 1894 STANDARD CARBINE . . . . **NiB $1244 Ex $995 Gd $677**
Same general specifications as Saddle-Ringle Carbine except shotgun type buttstock and plate, no saddle ring, standard open rear sight. Sometimes called "Eastern Carbine." See also Winchester Model 94 carbine.

1895 LEVER-ACTION
CARBINE . . . . **NiB $2688 Ex $2150 Gd $1462**
Same as Model 95 Standard Rifle except has 22-inch bbl., carbine-style buttstock and forend, weight: About 8 lbs., calibers .30-40 Krag, .30-03, .30-06 and .303, solid frame only.

1895 LEVER-ACTION RIFLE . . . . **NiB $3000 Ex $1850 Gd $1000**
Calibers: .30-40 Krag, .30-03, .30-60, .303 British, 7.62mm Russian, .35 Win., .38-72, .40-72, .405 Win. Four shot box magazine except .30-40 and .303, which have 5-shot magazines. Bbl. lengths: 24-, 26-, 28-inches (round, half-octagon, octagon). Weight: About 8.5 lbs. Sights: Open rear; bead or blade front. Plain straight-grip stock and forend (standard). Both solid frame and takedown models were made from1897-1931.

MODEL (1897) LEE BOLT-ACTION RIFLE
Straight-pull bolt-action. .236 U.S. Navy, 5-shot box magazine, clip loaded. 24- and 28-inch bbl. Weight: 7.5 to 8.5 lbs. Sights: Folding leaf rear sight on musket; open sporting sight on sporting rifle.
Musket model . . . . **NiB $1750 Ex $1600 Gd $975**
Sporting rifle . . . . **NiB $1850 Ex $1650 Gd $995**

Winchester Model 1894

Winchester Model 1894
Fancy-Grade Takedown

Winchester Model 1894
Saddle-Ring Carbine

Winchester Model 1895
Carbine

Winchester Model 1895
Rifle

Winchester Model 1897
Lee Sporting Rifle

MODEL 1900 BOLT-ACTION
SINGLE-SHOT RIFLE . . . . **NiB $531 Ex $425 Gd $289**
Takedown. Caliber: .22 Short and Long. 18-inch bbl. Weight: 2.75 lbs. Open rear sight; blade front sight. One-piece, straight-grip stock. Made from 1899 to 1902.

MODEL 1902
BOLT-ACTION
SINGLE-SHOT RIFLE . . . . **NiB $400 Ex $300 Gd $200**
Takedown. Basically the same as Model 1900 with minor improvements. Calibers: .22 Short and Long, .22 Extra Long, .22 LR. Weight: 3 lbs. Made 1902-1931.

MODEL 1903
SELF-LOADING RIFLE . . . . **NiB $975 Ex $750 Gd $475**
Takedown. Caliber: .22 WRA. 10-shot tubular magazine in butt-stock. 20-inch bbl. Weight: 5.75 lbs. Sights: Open rear; bead front. Plain straight-grip stock and forearm (fancy grade illustrated). Made 1903-36.

MODEL (1904) 99 THUMB-TRIGGER BOLT-ACTION
SINGLE-SHOT RIFLE . . . . **NiB $744 Ex $595 Gd $405**

(cond't) MODEL (1904) 99
Takedown. Same as Model 1902 except fired by pressing a button behind the cocking piece. Made 1904-23.

MODEL 1904 BOLT-ACTION
SINGLE-SHOT RIFLE . . . . **NiB $400 Ex $300 Gd $200**
Similar to Model 1902. Takedown. Caliber: 22 Short, Long Extra Long, LR. 21-inch bbl. Weight: 4 lbs. Made 1904-31.

MODEL 1905 SELF-LOADING RIFLE. . **NiB $725 Ex $500 Gd $425**
Takedown. Calibers: .32 Win. S. and L., .35 Win. S. and L. Five or 10-shot detachable box magazine. 22-inch bbl. Weight: 7.5 lbs. Sights: Open rear; bead front. Plain pistol-grip stock and forearm. Made 1905-20.

MODEL 1906
SLIDE-ACTION REPEATER . . . . . **NiB $800 Ex $750 Gd $500**
Takedown. Visible hammer. Caliber: .22 Short, Long, LR. Tubular magazine holds 20 Short, 16 Long or 14 LR. 20-inch bbl. Weight: 5 lbs. Sights: Open rear; bead front. Straight-grip stock and grooved forearm. Made 1906-32.

Winchester Model 1902

Winchester Model 1903

Winchester Model 1904

Winchester Model 1905

Winchester Model 1906

Winchester Model 1907

Winchester Model 1910

MODEL 1907 SELF-LOADING RIFLE . . . . . NiB $619 Ex $495 Gd $337
Takedown. Caliber: .351 Win. S. and L. Five or 10-shot detachable box magazine. 20-inch bbl. Weight: 7.75 lbs. Sights: Open rear; bead front. Plain pistol-grip stock and forearm. Made 1907-57.

MODEL 1910 SELF-LOADING RIFLE . . . . . NiB $744 Ex $595 Gd $405
Takedown. Caliber: .401 Win. S. and L. Four shot detachable box magazine. 20-inch bbl. Weight: 8.5 lbs. Sights: Open rear; bead front. Plain pistol-grip stock and forearm. Made 1910-36.

Winchester Model 43
Special Grade

MODEL 43 BOLT-ACTION
SPORTING RIFLE. . . . . **NiB $755 Ex $600 Gd $400**
Standard Grade. Calibers: .218 Bee, .22 Hornet, .25-20, .32-20 (latter two discontinued 1950). Three shot detachable box magazine. 24-inch bbl. Weight: 6 lbs. Sights: Open rear, bead front on hooded ramp. Plain pistol-grip stock with swivels. Made 1949-57.

MODEL 43 SPECIAL GRADE. . . . . . **NiB $980 Ex $750 Gd $495**
Same as Standard Model 43 except has checkered pistol-grip and forearm, grip cap.

MODEL 47 BOLT-ACTION
SINGLE-SHOT RIFLE . . . . **NiB $350 Ex $275 Gd $175**
Caliber: .22 Short, Long, LR. 25-inch bbl. Weight: 5.5 lbs. Sights: Peep or open rear; bead front. Plain pistol-grip stock. Made 1949-54.

MODEL 52 BOLT-ACTION TARGET RIFLE
Standard bbl. First type. .22 LR. Five shot box magazine. 28-inch bbl. Weight: 8.75 lbs. Sights: Folding leaf peep rear; blade front sight; standard sights various other combinations available. Scope bases. Semi-military-type target stock w/pistol grip; original model has grasping grooves in forearm; higher comb and semi-beavertail forearm on later models. Numerous changes were made in this model; the most important was the adoption of the speed lock in 1929. Model 52 rifles produced before this change are generally referred to as "slow lock" models. Last arms of this type bore serial numbers followed by the letter "A." Made 1919-37.
Slow Lock model . . . . **NiB $531 Ex $425 Gd $289**
Speed Lock model . . . . **NiB $719 Ex $575 Gd $391**

MODEL 52 HEAVY BARREL . . . . . . **NiB $781 Ex $625 Gd $425**
First type speed lock. Same general specifications as Standard Model 52 of this type except has heavier bbl., Lyman No. 17G front sight, weight: 10 lbs.

MODEL 52 INTERNATIONAL MATCH RIFLE
Similar to Model 52-D Heavy Barrel except has special lead-lapped bbl., laminated "free rifle"-style stock with high comb, thumbhole, hook buttplate, accessory rail, handstop/swivel assembly, palm rest. Weight: 13.5 lbs. Made 1969-78.
With standard trigger . . . . **NiB $1000 Ex $950 Gd $775**
With Kenyon or I.S.U. trigger . . . . . **NiB $688 Ex $550 Gd $374**

MODEL 52 INTERNATIONAL PRONE . . . **NiB $1025 Ex $995 Gd $780**
Similar to Model 52-D Heavy Barrel except has special lead-lapped bbl., prone stock with full pistol-grip, rollover cheekpiece removable for bore-cleaning. Weight 11.5 lbs. Made 1975-80.

MODEL 52 SPORTING RIFLE
First type. Same as Standard Model 52 of this type except has lightweight 24-inch bbl., Lyman No. 48 receiver sight and gold bead front sight on hooded ramp, deluxe checkered sporting stock with cheekpiece, black forend tip, etc. Weight: 7.75 lbs. Made 1934-58. Reintroduced 1993.

(cont'd.) **MODEL 52 SPORTING RIFLE**
Model 52 Sporter . . . . **NiB $2438 Ex $1950 Gd $1326**
Model 52A Sporter . . . . **NiB $3494 Ex $2795 Gd $1901**
Model 52B Sporter . . . . **NiB $2744 Ex $2195 Gd $1493**
Model 52C Sporter . . . . **NiB $3438 Ex $2750 Gd $1870**
Model 52 C Sporter
(1993 BAC re-issue) . . . . **NiB $650 Ex $495 Gd $330**

MODEL 52-B BOLT-ACTION RIFLE
Standard bbl. Extensively redesigned action. Supplied with choice of "Target" stock, an improved version of the previous Model 52 stock, or "Marksman" stock with high comb, full pistol grip and beavertail forearm. Weight: 9 lbs. Offered with a wide choice of target sight combinations (Lyman, Marble-Goss, Redfield, Vaver, Winchester), value shown is for rifle less sight equipment. Other specifications as shown for first type. Made 1935-47. Reintroduced 1997.
Target model . . . . **NiB $800 Ex $650 Gd $925**
BAC model
(1997 BAC re-issue) . . . . **NiB $619 Ex $495 Gd $337**
USRAC Sporting model . . . . **NiB $650 Ex $495 Gd $350**

MODEL 52-B BULL GUN
HEAVY BARREL . . . . **NiB $844 Ex $675 Gd $459**
Same specifications as Standard Model 52-B except Bull Gun has extra heavy bbl., Marksman stock only, weight: 12 lbs. Heavy Bbl. model weight: 11 lbs. Made 1940-47.

MODEL 52-C BOLT-ACTION RIFLE
Improved action with "Micro-Motion" trigger mechanism and new-type "Marksman" stock. General specifications same as shown for previous models. Made 1947-61, Bull Gun from 1952. Value shown is for rifle less sights.
Bull Gun (extra heavy barrel,
Wt. 12 lbs.) . . . . **NiB $1000 Ex $800 Gd $550**
Standard barrel
(Wt. 9.75 lbs.) . . . . **NiB $800 Ex $650 Gd $540**
Target model
(heavy barrel) . . . . **NiB $850 Ex $675 Gd $550**

NOTE: *Following WWI, Winchester had financial difficulties and, like many other firearm firms of the day, failed. However, Winchester continued to operate in the hands of receivers. Then, in 1931, The Western Cartridge Co. — under the leadership of John Olin — purchased all assets of the firm. After that, Winchester leaped ahead of all other firms of the day in firearm and ammunition development.*
The first sporting firearm to come out of the Winchester plant after WWI was the Model 20 shotgun, but this was quickly followed by the famous Model 52 bolt-action rifle. This was also a time when Winchester dropped the four-digit model numbers and began using two-digit numbers instead. This model-numbering procedure, with one exception (Model 677), continued for the next several years.

Winchester Model 47

Winchester Model 52
Standard Barrel

Winchester Model 52
International Match

Winchester Model 52
International Prone Target

MODEL 52-D BOLT-ACTION
TARGET RIFLE . . . . **NiB $800 Ex $750 Gd $395**
Redesigned Model 52 action, Single-Shot. Caliber: .22 LR. 28-inch standard or heavy bbl., free-floating, with blocks for standard target scopes. Weight: With standard bbl., 9.75 lbs., with heavy barrel, 11 lbs. Restyled Marksman stock with accessory channel and forend stop, rubber buttplate. Made 1961-78. Value shown is for rifle without sights.

MODEL 53 LEVER-ACTION
REPEATER . . . . **NiB $2119 Ex $1695 Gd $1153**
Modification of Model 92. Solid frame or takedown. Calibers: .25-20, .32-20, .44-40. Six shot tubular half-magazine in solid frame model. 7-shot in takedown. 22-inch nickel steel bbl. Weight: 5.5 to 6.5 lbs. Sights: Open rear; bead front. Redesigned straight-grip stock and forearm. Made 1924-32.

MODEL 54 BOLT-ACTION
HIGH POWER SPORTING RIFLE (I) . . . . . . **NiB $900 Ex $800 Gd $550**
First type. Calibers: .270 Win., 7x57mm, .30-30, .30-06, 7.65x53mm, 9x57mm. Five shot box magazine. 24-inch bbl. Weight: 7.75 lbs. Sights: Open rear; bead front. Checkered stock w/pistol grip, tapered forearm w/Schnabel tip. This type has two-piece firing pin. Made 1925-30.

MODEL 54 BOLT-ACTION
HIGH POWER SPORTING RIFLE (II) . . . . . **NiB $950 Ex $825 Gd $500**
Standard Grade. Improved type with speed lock and one-piece firing pin. Calibers: .22 Hornet, .220 Swift, .250/3000, .257 Roberts, .270 Win., 7x57mm, .30-06. Five shot box magazine. 24-inch bbl., 26-inch in cal. .220 Swift. Weight: About 8 lbs. Sights: Open rear, bead front on ramp. NRA-type stock w/checkered pistol-grip and forearm. Made 1930-36. Add $200 for .22 Hornet caliber.

MODEL 54 CARBINE (I) . . . . **NiB $1000 Ex $800 Gd $525**
First type. Same as Model 54 rifle except has 20-inch bbl., plain lightweight stock with grasping grooves in forearm. Weight: 7.25 lbs.

MODEL 54 CARBINE (II) . . . . **NiB $1000 Ex $850 Gd $550**
Improved type. Same as Model 54 Standard Grade Sporting Rifle of this type except has 20-inch bbl. Weight: About 7.5 lbs. This model may have either NRA-type stock or the lightweight stock found on the first-type Model 54 Carbine.

MODEL 54 NATIONAL
MATCH RIFLE . . . . **NiB $1031 Ex $825 Gd $561**
Same as Standard Model 54 except has Lyman sights, scope bases, Marksman-type target stock, weighs 9.5 lbs. Same calibers as Standard Model.

MODEL 54 SNIPER'S
MATCH RIFLE . . . . **NiB $1500 Ex $1250 Gd $500**
Similar to the earlier Model 54 Sniper's Rifle except has Marksman-type target stock, scope bases, weight: 12.5 lbs. Available in same calibers as Model 54 Standard Grade.

MODEL 54 SNIPER'S RIFLE . . . . . . **NiB $1125 Ex $900 Gd $600**
Same as Standard Model 54 except has heavy 26-inch bbl., Lyman No. 48 rear peep sight and blade front sight semi-military stock, weight: 11.75 pounds, cal. .30-06 only.

MODEL 54 SUPER GRADE . . . . . **NiB $1500 Ex $1250 Gd $800**
Same as Standard Model 54 Sporter except has deluxe stock with cheekpiece, black forend tip, pistol-grip cap, quick detachable swivels, 1-inch sling strap. See illustration previous page.

Winchester Model 52-B
Standard Barrel

Winchester Model 52-B
Sporter

Winchester Model 52-C
Heavy Barrel

Winchester Model 53

Winchester Model 54
Super Grade

MODEL 54 TARGET RIFLE . . . . NiB $1031 Ex $825 Gd $561
Same as Standard Model 54 except has 24-inch medium-weight bbl. (26-inch in cal. .220 Swift), Lyman sights, scope bases, Marksman-type target stock, weight: 10.5 lbs., same calibers as Standard Model.

MODEL 55 "AUTOMATIC"
SINGLE-SHOT . . . . NiB $300 Ex $225 Gd $150
Caliber: .22 Short, Long, LR. 22-inch bbl. Sights: Open rear, bead front. One-piece walnut stock. Weight: About 5.5 lbs. Made 1958-60.

MODEL 55 LEVER-ACTION REPEATER
Modification of Model 94. Solid frame or takedown. Calibers: .25-35, .30-30, .32 Win. Special. Three shot tubular half magazine. 24-inch nickel steel bbl. Weight: About 7 lbs. Sights: Open rear; bead front. Made 1924-32.
Standard model (straight grip) . . . . NiB $1188 Ex $950 Gd $646
Deluxe model (pistol grip) . . . . NiB $3119 Ex $2495 Gd $1697

MODEL 56 BOLT-ACTION
SPORTING RIFLE. . . . . NiB $1200 Ex $995 Gd $575
Solid frame. Caliber: .22 LR., .22 Short. Five or 10-shot detachable box magazine. 22-inch bbl. Weight: 4.75 lbs. Sights: Open rear; bead front. Plain pistol-grip with Schnabel forend. Made 1926-29.

MODEL 57 BOLT-ACTION RIFLE
Solid frame. Same as Model 56 except available (until 1929) in .22 Short as well as LR with 5- or 10-shot magazine. Has semi-military style target stock, bbl. band on forend, swivels and web sling, Lyman peep rear sight, weight: 5 lbs. Mfd. 1926-36.
Sporter model . . . . NiB $675 Ex $550 Gd $400
Target model . . . . NiB $625 Ex $575 Gd $425

MODEL 58 BOLT-ACTION
SINGLE-SHOT. . . . . NiB $406 Ex $325 Gd $221
Similar to Model 52. Takedown. Caliber. .22 Short, Long LR. 18-inch bbl. Weight: 3 lbs. Sights, Open rear; blade front. Plain, flat, straight-grip hardwood stock. Not serial numbered. Made 1928-31.

MODEL 59 BOLT-ACTION
SINGLE-SHOT. . . . . NiB $525 Ex $400 Gd $275
Improved version of Model 58, has 23-inch bbl., redesigned stock w/pistol grip, weight: 4.5 lbs. Made 1930.

MODEL 60, 60A BOLT-ACTION SINGLE-SHOT
Redesign of Model 59. Caliber: .22 Short, Long, LR. 23-inch bbl. (27-inch after 1933). Weight: 4.25 lbs. Sights: Open rear, blade front. Plain pistol-grip stock. Made 1930-34 (60), 1932-39 (60A).
Model 60 . . . . NiB $300 Ex $200 Gd $140
Model 60A . . . . NiB $375 Ex $210 Gd $150

Winchester Model 55
"Automatic" Single-Shot

Winchester Model 55
Lever-Action

Winchester Model 56

Winchester Model 57
Target

MODEL 60A TARGET RIFLE . . . . . . NiB $450 Ex $375 Gd $250
Essentially the same as Model 60 except has Lyman peep rear sight
and square top front sight, semi-military target stock and web sling,
weight: 5.5 lbs. Made 1932-39.

MODEL 61 HAMMERLESS SLIDE-ACTION REPEATER
Takedown. Caliber: .22 Short, Long, LR. Tubular magazine holds 20
Short, 16 Long, 14 LR. 24-inch round bbl. Weight: 5.5 lbs. Sights:
Open rear; bead front. Plain pistol-grip stock, grooved semi-beaver-
tail slide handle. Also available with 24-inch full-octagon bbl. and
only calibers .22 Short, .22 LR or .22 WRF. Note: Octagon barrel
model discontinued 1943-44; assembled 1948.
Model 61 (round barrel) . . . . NiB $744 Ex $595 Gd $405
Model 61 (grooved receiver) . . . . . NiB $938 Ex $750 Gd $510
Model 61 (octagon barrel) . . . . . NiB $1619 Ex $1295 Gd $881

MODEL 61 MAGNUM . . . . NiB $925 Ex $750 Gd $475
Same as Standard Model 61 except chambered for .22 WMR; magazine holds 12 rounds. Made 1960-63.

MODEL 62 VISIBLE HAMMER. . . . . NiB $625 Ex $500 Gd $350
Modernized version of Model 1890. Caliber: .22 Short, Long, LR.
23-inch bbl. Weight: 5.5 lbs. Plain straight-grip stock, grooved semi-
beavertail slide handle. Also available in Gallery Model chambered
for .22 Short only. Made 1932-1959. Note: Pre-WWII model (small
forearm) commands 25% higher price.

MODEL 63 SELF-LOADING RIFLE
Takedown. Caliber: .22 LR High Speed only. 10-shot tubular magazine
in buttstock. 23-inch bbl. Weight: 5.5 lbs. Sights: Open rear, bead
front. Plain pistol-grip stock and forearm. Originally available with 20-
inch bbl. as well as 23-inch. Made 1933-59. Reintroduced 1997.
Model 63 w/23-inch bbl. . . . . NiB $869 Ex $695 Gd $473
Model 63 w/20-inch bbl. . . . . NiB $1313 Ex $1050 Gd $714

(cont'd.) **MODEL 63 SELF-LOADING RIFLE**
Model 63 grooved receiver) . . . . NiB $1206 Ex $965 Gd $656
Model 63 Grade I (1997 BAC reissue) . . . . NiB $706 Ex $565 Gd $384
Model 63 High Grade (1997 BAC reissue). . . . NiB $1275 Ex $975 Gd $650

MODEL 64 DELUXE DEER RIFLE . . . . NiB $1244 Ex $995 Gd $677
Same as Standard Model 64 calibers .30-30 and .32 Win. Special,
except has checkered pistol-grip and semi-beavertail forearm,
swivels and sling, weighs 7.75 lbs. Made 1933-56.

MODEL 64 LEVER-ACTION REPEATER
Standard Grade. Improved version of Models 94 and 55. Solid
frame. Calibers: .25-35, .30-30, .32 Win. Special. Five shot tubular
two-thirds magazine. 20- or 24-inch bbl. Weight: About 7 lbs.
Sights: Open rear; bead front on ramp w/sight cover. Plain pistol-
grip stock and forearm. Made 1933-56. Production resumed in
1972 (caliber .30-30, 24-inch bbl.). Discontinued 1974.
Original model . . . . NiB $825 Ex $700 Gd $525
1972-74 model . . . . NiB $650 Ex $475 Gd $350

MODEL 64 .219 ZIPPER . . . . . . NiB $2369 Ex $1895 Gd $1289
Same as Standard Grade Model 64 except has 26-inch bbl., peep
rear sight. Made 1937-47.

**MODEL 65 LEVER-ACTION
REPEATER** . . . . NiB $2494 Ex $1995 Gd $1357
Improved version of Model 53. Solid frame. Calibers: .25-20 and
.32-20. Six-shot tubular half-magazine. 22-inch bbl. Weight: 6.5
lbs. Sights: Open rear, bead front on ramp base. Plain pistol-grip
stock and forearm. made 1933-47.

MODEL 65 .218 BEE . . . . NiB $2688 Ex $2150 Gd $1462
Same as Standard Model 65 except has 24-inch bbl., peep rear
sight. Made 1938-47.

Winchester Model 58

Winchester Model 59

Winchester Model 60A

Winchester Model 61

Winchester Model 62

Winchester Model 63

MODEL 67 BOLT-ACTION
SINGLE-SHOT RIFLE . . . . NiB $200 Ex $175 Gd $100
Takedown. Calibers: .22 Short, Long, LR, .22 LR shot (smoothbore), .22 WRF. 27-inch bbl. Weight: 5 lbs. Sights: Open rear, bead front. Plain pistol-grip stock (original model had grasping grooves in forearm). Made 1934-63.

MODEL 67 BOY'S RIFLE . . . . NiB $225 Ex $175 Gd $110
Same as Standard Model 6 except has shorter stock, 20-inch bbl., weighs 4.25 lbs.

MODEL 68 BOLT-ACTION
SINGLE-SHOT . . . . NiB $250 Ex $175 Gd $135
Same as Model 67 except has rear peep sight. Made 1934-1946.

MODEL 69 BOLT-ACTION RIFLE . . NiB $360 Ex $275 Gd $150
Takedown. Caliber: .22 S, L, LR. Five or 10-shot box magazine. 25-inch bbl. Weight: 5.5 lbs. Peep or open rear sight. Plain pistol-grip stock. Rifle cocks on closing motion of the bolt. Made 1935-37.

MODEL 69A BOLT-ACTION RIFLE
Same as the Model 69 except cocking mechanism was changed to cock the rifle by the opening motion of the bolt. Made 1937-63. Note: Models with grooved receivers command 20% higher prices.
Model 69A standard . . . . NiB $406 Ex $325 Gd $221

Cont'd) **MODEL 69A BOLT-ACTION RIFLE**
Match Mdl. w/Lyman No. 57E
W receiver sight . . . . NiB $494 Ex $395 Gd $269
(Target Model w/Winchester
peep rear sight, swivels, sling . . . . . NiB $594 Ex $475 Gd $323

MODEL 70
Introduced in 1937, the Model 70 Bolt-Action Repeating Rifle was offered in several styles and calibers. Only minor design changes were made over a period of 27 years and more than 500,000 of these rifles were sold. The original model was dubbed "The Rifleman's Rifle." In 1964, the original Model 70 was superseded by a revised version with redesigned action, improved bolt, swaged (free-floating) barrel, restyled stock. This model again underwent major changes in 1972. Most visible: New stock with contrasting forend tip and grip cap, cut checkering (instead of impressed as in predecessor) knurled bolt handle. The action was machined from a solid block of steel with barrels made from chrome molybdenum steel. Other changes in the design and style of the Model 70 continued. The XTR models were added in 1978 along with the Model 70A, the latter omitting the white liners, forend caps and floor plates. In 1981, an XTR Featherweight Model was added to the line, beginning with serial number G1,440,000. This version featured lighter barrels, fancy-checkered stocks with Schnabel forend. After U.S. Repeating Arms took over the Winchester plant, the Model 70 went through even more changes as described under that section of Winchester rifles.

Winchester Model 64
Deer Rifle

Winchester Model 64
Standard

Winchester Model 64
1972-74 Type

Winchester Model 65

Winchester Model 67

Winchester Model 68

Winchester Model 69

Winchester Model 69 Match

RIFLES

Winchester Model 70
Basic Post-WWII Model

Winchester Model 70
Standard Model

Winchester Model 70
Super Grade

Winchester Model 70
African (1964)

Winchester Model 70
Deluxe (1964)

PRE-1964 MODEL 70

MODEL 70
AFRICAN RIFLE . . . . NiB $5000 Ex $4450 Gd $2500
Same general specifications as Super Grade Model 70 except w/25-inch bbl., 3-shot magazine, Monte Carlo stock w/recoil pad. Weight: 9.5 lbs. Caliber: .458 Winchester Magnum. Made 1956–63.

MODEL 70 ALASKAN
Same as Standard Model 70 except calibers .338 Win. Mag., .375 H&H Mag.; 3-shot magazine in .338, 4-shot in .375 caliber; 25-inch bbl.; stock w/recoil pad. Weight: 8 lbs. in .338; 8.75 lbs. in .375 caliber. Made 1960–63.
.338 Win.
Mag. . . . . NiB $1744 Ex $1395 Gd $949
.375 H&H . . . . NiB $2244 Ex $1795 Gd $1221

MODEL 70 BULL GUN . . . . NiB $4000 Ex $3500 Gd $2000
Same as Standard Model 70 except w/heavy 28-inch bbl., scope bases, Marksman stock, weighs 13.25 lbs., caliber .300 H&H Magnum and .30-06 only. Disc. 1963.

MODEL 70 FEATHERWEIGHT SPORTER
Same as Standard Model 70 except w/redesigned stock and 22-inch bbl., aluminum trigger guard, floorplate and buttplate. Calibers: .243 Win., .264 Win. Mag., .270 Win., .308 Win., .30-06, .358 Win. Weight: 6.5 lbs. Made 1952–63.
.243 Win. NiB $994 Ex $795 Gd $541
.264 Win. . . . . NiB $1494 Ex $1195 Gd $813
.270 Win. . . . . NiB $1244 Ex $995 Gd $677
.30-06 Springfield . . . . NiB $938 Ex $750 Gd $510
.308 Win. NiB $869 Ex $695 Gd $473
.358 Win. . . . . NiB $2119 Ex $1695 Gd $1153

Winchester Model 70
Standard Weight Target Rifle

Winchester Model 70
Heavy Weight Target Rifle

Winchester Model 70
Bull Gun

Winchester Model 70
(Pre-1964) Standard Model

RIFLES

MODEL 70 NATIONAL
MATCH RIFLE . . . . **NiB $2000 Ex $1925 Gd $1400**
Same as Standard Model 70 except w/scope bases, Marksman-type target stock, weight: 9.5 lbs. caliber .30-06 only. Disc. 1960.

MODEL 70 STANDARD GRADE
Calibers: .22 Hornet, .220 Swift, .243 Win., .250-3000, .257 Roberts, .270 Win., 7x57mm, .30-06, .308 Win., .300 H&H Mag., .375 H&H Mag. Five shot box magazine (4-shot in Magnum calibers). 24-inch bbl. standard; 26-inch in .220 Swift and .300 Mag.; 25-inch in .375 Mag.; at one time a 20-inch bbl. was available. Sights: Open rear; hooded ramp front. Checkered walnut stock; Monte Carlo comb standard on later production. Weight: From 7.75 lbs. depending on caliber and bbl. length. Made 1937–63.

.22 Hornet (1937-58)	NiB $1938 Ex $1550 Gd $1054	
.220 Swift (1937-63).	NiB $1369 Ex $1095 Gd $745	
.243 Win. (1955-63)	NiB $1119 Ex $895 Gd $609	
.250-3000 Sav. (1937-49)	NiB $2494 Ex $1995 Gd $1357	
.257 Roberts (1937-59).	NiB $1744 Ex $1395 Gd $949	
.264 Win. Mag. (1959-63) limited.	NiB $1244 Ex $995 Gd $677	
.270 Win. (1937-63)	NiB $994 Ex $795 Gd $541	
7x57mm Mauser (1937-49)	NiB $2744 Ex $2195 Gd $1493	
7.65 Argentine (1937 only) limited	Very Rare	
.30-06 Springfield (1937-63).	NiB $813 Ex $650 Gd $442	
.308 Win. (1952-63) special order.	Very Rare	
.300 H&H (1937-63).	NiB $1438 Ex $1150 Gd $782	
.300 Sav. (1944-50) limited	Rare	
.300 Win. Mag. (1962-63).	NiB $1869 Ex $1495 Gd $1017	
.338 Win. Mag. (1959-63)		
special order only	NiB $1781 Ex $1425 Gd $969	
.35 Rem. (1941-47) limited	Very Rare	
.358 Win. (1955-58)	Very Rare	
.375 H&H (1937-63).	NiB $2244 Ex $1795 Gd $1221	
.458 Win. Mag. (1956-63)		
Super Grade only	NiB $4494 Ex $3595 Gd $2445	
9x57 Mauser (1937 only) limited.	Very Rare	

MODEL 70 SUPER GRADE
Same as Standard Grade Model 70 except w/deluxe stock w/cheek-piece, black forend tip, pistol-grip cap, quick detachable swivels, sling. Disc. 1960. Prices for Super Grade models also reflect rarity in both production and caliber. Values are generally twice that of standard models of similar configuration.

MODEL 70 SUPER GRADE FEATHERWEIGHT
Same as Standard Grade Featherweight except w/deluxe stock w/cheekpiece, black forend tip, pistol-grip cap, quick detachable swivels, sling. Disc. 1960. Note: SG-FWs are very rare, but unless properly documented will not command premium prices. Prices for authenticated Super Grades Featherweight models are generally 4 to 5 times that of a standard production Featherweight model w/similar chambering.

MODEL 70 TARGET RIFLE
Same as Standard Model 70 except w/24-inch medium-weight bbl., scope bases, Marksman stock, weight 10.5 lbs. Originally offered in all of the Model 70 calibers, this rifle was available later in calibers .243 Win. and .30-06. Disc. 1963. Values are generally twice that of standard models of similar configuration.

MODEL 70 TARGET
HEAVY WEIGHT . . . . **NiB $3600 Ex $1795 Gd $1175**
Same general specifications as Standard Model 70 except w/either 24- or 26-inch heavy weight bbl. weight: 10.5 lbs. No checkering. .243 and .30-06 calibers.

MODEL 70 TARGET
BULL BARREL . . . . **NiB $4000 Ex $2200 Gd $1595**
Same general specifications as Standard Model 70 except 28-inch heavy weight bbl. and chambered for either .30-06 or .300 H&H Mag. Drilled and tapped for front sight base. Receiver slotted for clip loading. Weight: 13.25 lbs.

Winchester Model 70
International Army Match (1964)

Winchester Model 70
Mannlicher (1964)

Winchester Model 70
Standard (1964)

Winchester Model 70
Target (1964)

MODEL 70
VARMINT RIFLE . . . . NiB $1200 Ex $1125 Gd $975
Same general specifications as Standard Model 70 except w/26-inch heavy bbl., scope bases, special varminter stock. Calibers: .220 Swift, .243 Win. Made 1956–63.

MODEL 70
WESTERNER . . . . NiB $1150 Ex $995 Gd $875
Same as Standard Model 70 except calibers .264 Win. Mag., .300 Win. Mag.; 3-shot magazine; 26-inch bbl. in former caliber, 24-inch in latter. Weight: 8.25 lbs. Made 1960–63.

1964-TYPE MODEL 70

MODEL 70 AFRICAN . . . . NiB $1100 Ex $675 Gd $495
Caliber: .458 Win. Mag. Three shot magazine. 22-inch bbl. Weight: 8.5 lbs. Special "African" sights. Monte Carlo stock w/ebony forend tip, hand-checkering, twin stock-reinforcing bolts, recoil pad, QD swivels. Made 1964–71.

MODEL 70 DELUXE . . . . NiB $995 Ex $725 Gd $425
Calibers: .243, .270 Win., .30-06, .300 Win. Mag. Five shot box magazine (3-shot in Magnum). 22-inch bbl. (24-inch in Magnum). Weight: 7.5 lbs. Sights: Open rear; hooded ramp front. Monte Carlo stock w/ebony forend tip, hand-checkering, QD swivels, recoil pad on Magnum. Made 1964–71.

MODEL 70 INTERNATIONAL
ARMY MATCH RIFLE . . . . NiB $950 Ex $790 Gd $575
Caliber: .308 Win. (7.62 NATO). Five shot box magazine. 24-inch heavy barrel. Externally adj. trigger. Weight: 11 lbs. ISU stock w/military oil finish, forearm rail for standard accessories, vertically adj. buttplate. Made in 1971. Value shown is for rifle w/o sights.

MODEL 70 MAGNUM
Calibers: 7mm Rem. Mag.; .264, .300, .338 Win. Mag.; .375 H&H Mag. Three shot magazine. 24-inch bbl. Weight: 7.75 to 8.5 lbs. Sights: Open rear; hooded ramp front. Monte Carlo stock w/cheekpiece, checkering, twin stock-reinforcing bolts, recoil pad, swivels. Made 1964–71.
Caliber .375 H&H Mag. . . . . NiB $688 Ex $550 Gd $374
Other calibers . . . . NiB $469 Ex $375 Gd $255

MODEL 70 MANNLICHER . . . . NiB $700 Ex $600 Gd $500
Calibers: .243, .270, .308 Win., .30-06. Five shot box magazine. 19-inch bbl. Sights: open rear; hooded ramp front. Weight: 7.5 lbs. Mannlicher-style stock w/Monte Carlo comb and cheekpiece, checkering, steel forend cap, QD sling swivels. Made 1969–71.

MODEL 70 STANDARD. . . . . NiB $425 Ex $350 Gd $230
Calibers: .22-250, .222 Rem., .225, .243, .270, .308 Win., .30-06. Five shot box magazine. 22-inch bbl. Weight: 7.5 lbs. Sights: Open rear; hooded ramp front. Monte Carlo stock w/cheekpiece, checkering, swivels. Made 1964–71.

**Winchester Model 70
African (1972)**

MODEL 70 TARGET . . . . NiB $656 Ex $525 Gd $357
Calibers: .308 Win. (7.62 NATO) and .30-06. Five shot box magazine. 24-inch heavy bbl. Blocks for target scope. No factory sights installed, but drilled and tapped for front and rear sights. Weight: 10.25 lbs. High-comb Marksman-style stock, aluminum hand stop, swivels. Straight-grain, one-piece stock w/sling swivels, but no checkering. Made 1964–71.

MODEL 70 VARMINT . . . . NiB $470 Ex $375 Gd $280
Same as Model 70 Standard except w/24-inch target weight bbl., blocks for target scope. No factory sights installed, but drilled and tapped for front and rear sights. Available in calibers .22-250, .222 Rem., and .243 Win. only. Weight: 9.75 lbs. Made 1964–71.

1972-TYPE MODEL 70

MODEL 70 AFRICAN . . . . NiB $744 Ex $595 Gd $405
Similar to Model 70 Magnum except w/22-inch bbl. caliber .458 Win. Mag. w/special African open rear sight, reinforced stock w/ebony forend tip, detachable swivels and sling; front sling swivel stud attached to bbl. Weight: 8.5 lbs. Made 1972-92.

MODEL 70 CLASSIC SM
Similar to Model 70 Classic Sporter except w/checkered black composite stock and matte metal finish. Made 1994-96.
Model 70 Classic SM . . . . NiB $470 Ex $395 Gd $250
Caliber .375 H&H . . . . NiB $575 Ex $450 Gd $300
W/BOSS, add $100
W/open sights, add $40

MODEL 70 CLASSIC SPORTER
Similar to Model 70 Sporter except w/pre-64-style action w/controlled round feeding, classic-style stock. Optional open sights. Made 1994 to date.
Standard model . . . . NiB $430 Ex $360 Gd $100
W/BOSS, add $100
W/open sights, add $40

MODEL 70 CLASSIC SPORTER STAINLESS
Similar to Model 70 Classic Sporter except w/matte stainless steel finish. Weight: 7.5 lbs. No sights. Made 1994 to date.
Standard model . . . . NiB $615 Ex $525 Gd $275
Magnum model . . . . NiB $675 Ex $550 Gd $325
W/BOSS, add $100

MODEL 70 CUSTOM SHARPSHOOTER
Calibers: .22-250, .223, .308 Win., .300 Win. Mag. 24- or 26-inch bbl. 44.5 inches overall (24-inch bbl.). Weight: 11 lbs. Custom-fitted, hand-honed action. McMillan A-2 target-style stock. Matte blue or stainless finish. Made 1992-96.
Model 70 Custom
Sharpshooter (blued) . . . . NiB $1775 Ex $1350 Gd $875
Model 70 Custom
Sharpshooter (stainless) . . . . NiB $1858 Ex $1400 Gd $925

MODEL 70 CUSTOM SPORTING SHARPSHOOTER
Similar to Custom Sharpshooter Model except w/sporter-style gray composite stock. Stainless 24- or 26-inch bbl. w/blued receiver. Calibers: .270, 7mm STW, .300 Win. Mag. Made 1993 to date.
Model 70 Custom Sharpshooter
blued (disc. 1995) . . . . NiB $1775 Ex $1350 Gd $875
Model 70 Custom Sharpshooter, stainless . NiB $1850 Ex $1400 Gd $925

**MODEL 70 GOLDEN 50TH ANNIVERSARY EDITION
BOLT-ACTION RIFLE** $1000
Caliber: .300 Win. Three shot magazine. 24-inch bbl. 44.5 inches overall. Weight: 7.75 lbs. Checkered American walnut stock. Hand-engraved American scroll pattern on bbl., receiver, magazine cover, trigger guard and pistol-grip cap. Sights: Adj. rear; hooded front ramp. Inscription on bbl. reads "The Rifleman's Rifle 1937–1987." Only 500 made 1986–87. (Value for guns in new condition)

MODEL 70 FEATHERWEIGHT CLASSIC . . . . . . NiB $531 Ex $425 Gd $289
Similar to Model 70 XTR Featherweight except w/controlled-round feeding system. Calibers: .270, .280 and .30-06. Made 1992 to date.

**MODEL 70 INTERNATIONAL
ARMY MATCH** . . . . NiB $900 Ex $775 Gd $500
Caliber: .308 Win. (7.62mm NATO). Five shot magazine, clip slot in receiver bridge. 24-inch heavy barrel. Weight: 11 lbs. No sights, but drilled and tapped for front and rear iron sights, and/or scope mounts. ISU target stock. Intro. 1973; disc.

MODEL 70 LIGHTWEIGHT . . . . NiB $575 Ex $350 Gd $140
Calibers: .22-250 and .223 Rem.; .243, .270 and .308 Win.; .30-06 Springfield. Five shot mag. capacity (6-shot .223 Rem.). 22-inch barrel. 42 to 42.5 inches overall. Weight: 6 to 6.25 lbs. Checkered classic straight stock. Sling swivel studs. Made 1986-95.

MODEL 70 MAGNUM
Same as Model 70 except w/3-shot magazine, 24-inch bbl., reinforced stock w/recoil pad. Weight: 7.75 lbs. (except 8.5 lbs. in .375 H&H Mag.). Calibers: .264 Win. Mag., 7mm Rem. Mag., .300 Win. Mag., .338 Win. Mag., .375 H&H Mag. Made 1972-80.
.375 H&H Magnum . . . . NiB $650 Ex $500 Gd $300
Other magnum calibers . . . . NiB $550 Ex $375 Gd $295

MODEL 70 STANDARD . . . . NiB $406 Ex $325 Gd $221
Same as Model 70A except w/5-shot magazine, Monte Carlo stock w/cheekpiece, black forend tip and pistol-grip cap w/white spacers, checkered pistol grip and forearm, detachable sling swivels. Same calibers plus .225 Win. Made 1972-80.

MODEL 70 STANDARD CARBINE . . . . NiB $413 Ex $330 Gd $224
Same general specifications as Standard Model 70 except 19-inch bbl. and weight: 7.25 lbs. Shallow recoil pad. Walnut stock and forend w/traditional Model 70 checkering. Swivel studs. No sights, but drilled and tapped for scope mount.

RIFLES

Winchester Model 70
Featherweight

Winchester Model 70
Golden 50th Anniversary

Winchester Model 70
Featherweight Classic

Winchester Model 70
Lightweight

Winchester Model 70
Magnum

Winchester Model 70
Carbine

MODEL 70 SPORTER DBM
Same general specifications as Model 70 Sporter SSM except w/detachable box magazine. Calibers: .22-250 (disc. 1994), .223 (disc. 1994), .243 (disc. 1994), .270, 7mm Rem. Mag., .308 (disc. 1994), .30-06, .300 Win. Mag. Made 1992-94.
Model 70 DBM . . . . NiB $475 Ex $395 Gd $250
Model 70 DBM-S (w/iron sights) . . . . NiB $494 Ex $395 Gd $269

MODEL 70 STAINLESS SPORTER SSM . . . . NiB $494 Ex $395 Gd $269
Same general specifications as Model 70 XTR Sporter except w/checkered black composite stock and matte finished receiver, bbl. and other metal parts. Calibers: .270, 7mm Rem. Mag., .30-06, .300 Win. Mag., .338 Win. Mag. Weight: 7.75 lbs. Made 1992-94.

MODEL 70 CLASSIC SUPER GRADE . . . . . NiB $800 Ex $725 Gd $395
Calibers: .270, 7mm Rem. Mag., .30-06, .300 Win. Mag., .338 Win. Mag. Five shot magazine (standard), 3-shot (magnum). 24-inch bbl.

(cont'd.) MODEL 70 CLASSIC SUPER GRADE
44.5 inches overall. Weight: 7.75 lbs. Checkered walnut stock w/sculptured cheekpiece and tapered forend. Scope bases and rings, no sights. Controlled-round feeding system. Made 1990 to date.

MODEL 70 TARGET . . . . NiB $825 Ex $750 Gd $400
Calibers: .30-06 and .308 Win. (7.62mm NATO). 5-shot magazine. 26-inch heavy bbl. Weight: 10.5 lbs. No sights, but drilled and tapped for scope mount and open sights. High-comb Marksman-style target stock, aluminum hand stop and swivels. Intro. 1972. Disc.

MODEL 70 ULTRA MATCH . . . . . . NiB $850 Ex $775 Gd $425
Similar to Model 70 Target but custom grade w/26-inch heavy bbl. w/deep counterbore, glass bedding, externally adj. trigger. Intro. 1972. Disc.

Winchester Model 70
XTR Sporter

Winchester Model 70A

MODEL 70 VARMINT (HEAVY BARREL)

Same as Model 70 Standard except w/medium-heavy, counter-bored 26-inch bbl., no sights, stock w/less drop. Weight: 9 lbs. Calibers: .22-250 Rem., .223 Rem., .243 Win., .308 Win. Made 1972-93. Model 70 SHB, in .308 Win. only w/black synthetic stock and matte blue receiver/bbl. Made 1992-93.

Model 70 Varmint . . . . NiB $650 Ex $525 Gd $280
Model 70 SHB (synthetic heavy barrel) . . . NiB $460 Ex $375 Gd $250

MODEL 70 WIN-CAM RIFLE . . . . . NiB $450 Ex $350 Gd $200

Caliber: .270 Win. and .30-06 Springfield. 24-inch barrel. Camouflage one-piece laminated stock. Recoil pad. Drilled and tapped for scope. Made 1986 to date.

MODEL 70 WINLITE BOLT-ACTION RIFLE . . . . . NiB $625 Ex $450 Gd $330

Calibers: .270 Win., .280 Rem., .30-06 Springfield, 7mm Rem., .300 Win. Mag., and .338 Win. Mag. Five shot magazine; 3-shot for Magnum calibers. 22-inch bbl.; 24-inch for Magnum calibers. 42.5 inches overall; 44.5, Magnum calibers. Weight: 6.25 to 7 lbs. Fiberglass stock w/rubber recoil pad, sling swivel studs. Made 1986-90.

MODEL 70 WIN-TUFF BOLT-ACTION RIFLE

Calibers: .22-250, .223, .243, .270, .308 and .30-06 Springfield. 22-inch bbl. Weight: 6.25–7 lbs. Laminated dye-shaded brown wood stock w/recoil pad. Barrel drilled and tapped for scope. Swivel studs. FWT Model made 1986–94. LW Model intro. 1992.

Featherweight model . . . . NiB $500 Ex $375 Gd $260
Lightweight model (Made 1992–93) . . . . . . NiB $450 Ex $340 Gd $230

MODEL 70 XTR FEATHERWEIGHT . . . . NiB $469 Ex $375 Gd $255

Similar to Standard Win. Model 70 except lightweight American walnut stock w/classic Schnabel forend, checkered. 22-inch bbl., hooded blade front sight, folding leaf rear sight. Stainless-steel magazine follower. Weight: 6.75 lbs. Made 1984-94.

MODEL 70 XTR SPORTER RIFLE . . . . NiB $500 Ex $375 Gd $250

Calibers: .264 Win. Mag., 7mm Rem. Mag., .300 Win. Mag., .200 Weatherby Mag., and .338 Win. Mag. Three shot magazine. 24-inch barrel. 44.5 inches overall. Weight: 7.75 lbs. Walnut Monte Carlo stock. Rubber buttpad. Receiver tapped and drilled for scope mounting. Made 1986-94.

MODEL 70 XTR SPORTER MAGNUM . . . . NiB $500 Ex $375 Gd $260

Calibers: .264 Win. Mag., 7mm Rem. Mag., .300 Win. Mag., .338 Win. Mag. Three shot magazine. 24-inch bbl. 44.5 inches overall. Weight: 7.75 lbs. No sights furnished, optional adj. folding leaf rear; hooded ramp. Receiver drilled and tapped for scope. Checkered

American walnut Monte Carlo-style stock w/satin finish. Made 1986-94.

MODEL 70 XTR

SPORTER VARMINT . . . . NiB $460 Ex $375 Gd $250
Same general specifications as Model 70 XTR Sporter, except in calibers .223, .22-250, .243 only. Checkered American walnut Monte Carlo-style stock w/cheekpiece. Made 1986-94.

MODEL 70A . . . . NiB $360 Ex $275 Gd $195

Calibers: .222 Rem., .22-250, .243 Win., .25-06, .270 Win., .30-06, .308 Win. Four shot magazine. 22-inch bbl. (except 24- or 26-inch in 25-06). Weight: 7.5 lbs. Sights: Open rear; hooded ramp front. Monte Carlo stock w/checkered pistol grip and forearm, sling swivels. Made 1972-78.

MODEL 70A MAGNUM . . . . NiB $375 Ex $275 Gd $200

Same as Model 70A except w/3-shot magazine, 24-inch bbl., recoil pad. Weight: 7.75 lbs. Calibers: .264 Win. Mag., 7mm Rem. Mag., .300 Win. Mag. Made 1972-78

MODEL 70 ULTIMATE CLASSIC BOLT-ACTION RIFLE

Calibers: .25-06 Rem., .264 Win., .270 Win., .270 Wby. Mag., .280 Rem., 7mm Rem. Mag., 7mm STW, .30-06, Mag., .300 Win. Mag., .300 Wby. Mag., .300 H&H Mag., .338 Win. Mag., .340 Wby. Mag., .35 Whelen, .375 H&H Mag., .416 Rem. Mag. and .458 Win. Mag. Three, 4- or 5-shot magazine. 22- 24- 26-inch stainless bbl. in various configurations including: full-fluted tapered round, half round and half octagonal or tapered full octagonal. Weight: 7.75 to 9.25 lbs. Checkered fancy walnut stock. Made 1995 to date.

Model 70
Ultimate Classic . . . . NiB $2300 Ex $1850 Gd $975
For Mag. calibers (.375 H&H,
.416 and .458), add $250

MODEL 70 LAMINATED STAINLESS

BOLT-ACTION RIFLE . . . . NiB $850 Ex $725 Gd $395
Calibers: .270 Win., .30-06 Spfld., 7mm Rem. Mag., .300 Win. Mag., and .338 Win. Mag. Five shot magazine. 24-inch bbl. 44.75 inches overall. Weight: 8 to 8.525 lbs. Gray/Black laminated stock. Made 1998 to date.

MODEL 70 CHARACTERISTICS

MODEL 70 FIRST MODEL (SERIAL NUMBERS 1 – 80,000)

First manufactured in 1936; first sold in 1937. Receiver drilled for Lyman No. 57W or No. 48WJS receiver peep sights. Also drilled and tapped for Lyman or Fecker scope sight block. Weight w/24-inch bbl. in all calibers except .375 H&H Mag.: 8.25 lbs. 9 lbs. in H&H

Cross-sectional view of the pre-1964 Winchester Model 70's speed lock action. This action cocks on the opening movement of the bolt with polished, smooth-functioning cams and guide lug, insuring fast and smooth operation.

MODEL 70 SECOND MODEL (SERIAL NUMBERS 80,000 – 350,000)

All civilian production of Winchester Model 70 rifles halted during World War II. Production resumed in 1947 w/improved safety and integral front-sight ramp. Serial numbers started at around 80,000. This model type was produced until 1954, ending around serial number 350,000.

MODEL 70 THIRD MODEL (SERIAL NUMBERS 350,000 – 400,000)

This variety was manufactured from 1954 to 1960 and retained many features of the Second Model except that a folding rear sight replaced the earlier type and front-sight ramps were brazed onto the bbl. rather than being an integral part of the bbl. The Model 70 Featherweight Rifle was intro. in 1954 in .308 WCF caliber. It was fitted w/light 22-inch bbl. and was also available w/either a Monte Carlo or Standard stock. The .243 Win. cartridge was added in 1955 in all grades of the Winchester Model 70 except the National Match and Bull Gun models. The .358 Win. cartridge was also intro. in 1955, along w/new Varmint Model chambered in .243 caliber only.

MODEL 70 FOURTH MODEL (SERIAL NUMBERS 400,000 – 500,000)

Different markings were inscribed on the barrels of these models and new magnum calibers were added; that is, .264 Win Mag., .338 Win. Mag, and .458 Win. Mag. All bbls. of this variation were about 0.13 inch shorter than previous ones. The .22 Hornet and .257 Roberts were disc. in 1962; the .358 Win. caliber in 1963.

MODEL 70 FIFTH MODEL (SERIAL NUMBERS 500,000 TO ABOUT 570,000)

These rifles may be recognized by slightly smaller checkering patterns and slightly smaller lightweight stocks. Featherweight bbls. were marked "Featherweight." Webbed recoil pads were furnished on magnum calibers.

POST-1964 MODEL 70 RIFLES

In 1964, the Winchester-Western Division of Olin Industries claimed that they were losing money on every Model 70 they produced. Both labor and material costs had increased to a level that could no longer be ignored. Other models followed suit. Consequently, sweeping changes were made to the entire Winchester line. Many of the older, less popular models were discontinued. Models that were to remain in production were modified for lower production costs.

1964 WINCHESTER MODEL 70 RIFLES SERIAL NUMBERS 570,000 TO ABOUT 700,000)

The first version of the "New Model 70s" utilized a free-floating barrel, swaged rifle bore, new stock and sights, new type of bolt and receiver, and a different finish throughout on both the wood and metal parts. The featherweight grade was dropped, but six other grades were available in this new line:

Standard
Deluxe (Replaced Previous Super Grade)
Magnum
Varmint
Target
African

1966 MODEL 70 RIFLES (SERIAL NUMBERS 700,000-G TO ABOUT 1,005,000)

In general, this group of Model 70s had fancier wood checkering, cross-bolt stock reinforcement, improved wood finish and improved action. One cross-bolt reinforcement was used on standard guns. Magnum calibers, however, used an additional forward cross-bolt and red recoil pad. The free-floating barrel clearance forward of the breech taper was reduced in thickness. Impressed checkering was used on the Deluxe models until 1968. Hand checkering was once again used on Deluxe and Carbine models in 1969; the big, red "W" was removed from all grip caps. A new, red safety-indicator and undercut cheekpiece was introduced in 1971.

1972 MODEL 70 RIFLES (SERIAL NUMBERS G1,005,000 TO ABOUT G1,360,000)

Both the barrels and receivers for this variety of Model 70s were made from chrome molybdenum (C-M) steel. The barrels were tapered w/spiral rifling, ranging in length from 22 to 24 inches. Calibers .222 Rem., .225 Win. .22-250, .243 Win., .25-06, .270, .308 Win., .30-06 and .458 WM used the 22-inch length, while the following calibers used the 24-inch length: .222 Rem., .22-250, .243 Win., .264 Win. Mag., 7mm Mag., .300 and .375 H&H Mag. The .225 Win caliber was dropped in 1973; Mannlicher stocks were also disc. in 1973. The receiver for this variety of Model 70s was machined from a block of C-M steel. A new improved anti-bind bolt was introduced along with a new type of ejector. Other improvements included hand-cut checkering, pistol-grip stocks with pistol-grip and dark forend caps. An improved satin wood finish was also utilized.

1978 MODEL 70 RIFLES (SERIAL NUMBERS BEGAN AROUND G1,360,000)

This variety of Model 70 was similar to the 1972 version except that a new XTR style was added which featured high-luster wood and metal finishes, fine-cut checkering, and similar embellishments. All Model 70 rifles made during this period used the XTR style; no standard models were available. In 1981, beginning with serial number G1,440,000 (approximately), a Featherweight version of the Model 70 XTR was introduced. The receiver was identical to the 1978 XTR, but lighter barrels were fitted. Stocks were changed to a lighter design with larger scroll checkering patterns and a Schnabel forend with no Monte Carlo comb. A satin sheen stock finish on the featherweight version replaced the high-luster finish used on the other XTR models. A new-style red buttplate with thick, black rubber liner was used on the Featherweight models. The grip cap was also redesigned for this model.

Winchester Model 70
Black Shadow

Winchester Model 70
Classic Camo

U.S. REPEATING ARMS MODEL 70 — 1982 TO DATE

In the early 1980s, negotiations began between Olin Industries and an employee-based corporation. The result of these negotiations ended with Olin selling all tools, machinery, supplies, etc. at the New Haven plant to the newly-formed corporation which was eventually named U.S. Repeating Arms Company. Furthermore, U.S. Repeating Arms Company purchased the right to use the Winchester name and logo. Winchester Model 70s went through very few changes the first two years after the transition. However, in 1984, the Featherweight Model 70 XTR rifles were offered in a new short action for .22-250 Rem., .223 Rem., .243 Win. and .308 Win. calibers, in addition to their standard action which was used for the longer cartridges. A new Model 70 lightweight carbine was also introduced this same year. Two additional models were introduced in 1985 — the Model 70 Lightweight Mini-Carbine Short Action and the Model 70 XTR Sporter Varmint. The Model 70 Winlite appeared in the 1986 "Winchester" catalog, along with two economy versions of the Model 70 — the Winchester Ranger and the Ranger Youth Carbine. Five or six different versions of the Winchester Model 70 had been sufficient for 28 years (1937 - 1964). Now, changes in design and the addition of new models each year seemed to be necessary to keep the rifle alive. New models were added, old models dropped, changed in design, etc., on a regular basis. The trend continues. Still, the Winchester Model 70 Bolt-Action Repeating Rifle — in any of its variations — is the most popular bolt-action rifle ever built.

MODEL 70 BLACK SHADOW . . . . . NiB $385 Ex $300 Gd $225
Calibers: .243 Win., .270 Win., .300 Win. Mag., .308 Win., .338 Win. Mag., .30-06 Spfld., 7mm STW, 7mm Rem. Mag. and 7mm-08 Rem. Three 4- or 5-shot magazine. 20- 24- 25- or 26-inch bbls. 39.5 to 46.75 inches overall.Weight: 6.5 to 8.25 lbs. Composite, Walnut or Gray/Black laminated stocks. Made 1998 to date.

MODEL 70 CLASSIC
CAMO BOLT-ACTION RIFLE . . . . . . NiB $825 Ex $750 Gd $400
Calibers: .270 Win., 30-06 Spfld., 7mm Rem. Mag., .300 Win. Mag. Three or 5-shot magazine. 24- or 26-inch bbl. 44.75 to 46.75 inches overall. Weight; 7.25 to 7.5 lbs. Mossy Oak finish and composite stock. Made 1998 to date.

MODEL 70 CLASSIC
COMPACT BOLT-ACTION RIFLE . . . NiB $494 Ex $395 Gd $269
Calibers: .243 Win., .308 Win., and 7mm-08 Rem. Three shot magazine. 20-inch bbl. 39.5 inches overall. Weight: 6.5 lbs. Walnut stock. Made 1998 to date.

MODEL 70 CLASSIC LAREDO RANGE HUNTER
BOLT-ACTION RIFLE
Calibers: 7mm STW, 7mm Rem. mag., .300 Win. Mag. Three shot magazine. 26-inch bbl. 46.75 inches overall. Weight: 9.5 lbs. Composite stock. Made 1996 to date.
Classic Laredo . . . . NiB $650 Ex $525 Gd $395
Classic Laredo Fluted
(Made 1998 to date) . . . . NiB $675 Ex $550 Gd $375
Bossâ Classic Laredo . . . . NiB $656 Ex $525 Gd $357

MODEL 70 COYOTE . . . . NiB $545 Ex $450 Gd $275
Calibers: .22-250 Rem., .223 Rem., and .243 Win. Five or 6-shot magazine. 24- inch bbl., 44 inches overall. Weight: 9 lbs. Medium-heavy stainless steel barrel w/laminated stock. Reverse taper forend. Made 1999 to date.

MODEL 70 RANGER
COMPACT RIFLE. NiB $375 Ex $285 Gd $175
Calibers: .22-250 Rem., .223 Rem., .243 Win., 7mm-08 Rem., Mag., and .308 Win. Five or 6-shot magazine. 20- or 22-inch bbl. 41 inches overall. Weight: 6.5 lbs. Adjustable TRUGLO front and rear fiber optic sights. Push-feed action. Made 1999 to date.

MODEL 70
STEALTH RIFLE . . . . NiB $675 Ex $585 Gd $323
Varminter style bolt-action rifle. Calibers: .22-250 Rem., .223 Rem., and .308 Win. Five or 6-shot magazine. 26- inch bbl. 46 inches overall. Weight: 10.75 lbs. Black synthetic stock w/Pillar Plus Accu Block and full-length aluminum bedding block. Matte blue finish. Made 1999 to date.

MODEL 71 LEVER-ACTION REPEATER
Solid frame. Caliber: .348 Win. Four shot tubular magazine. 20- or 24-inch bbl. Weight: 8 lbs. Sights: Open or peep rear; bead front on ramp w/hood. Walnut stock. Made 1935–57.
Special Grade (checkered pistol-grip
and forearm, grip cap, quick-detachable
swivels and sling . . . . NiB $1875 Ex $1500 Gd $975
Special Grade Carbine
(20-inch bbl.; disc. 1940) . . . . NiB $2369 Ex $1895 Gd $1289
Standard Grade
(lacks checkering,
grip cap, sling and swivels) . . . . NiB $1100 Ex $950 Gd $525
Standard Grade
Carbine (20-inch
bbl.; disc. 1940) . . . . NiB $2000 Ex $1600 Gd $995

Winchester Model 72

Winchester Model 74

Winchester Model 75
Sporting

Winchester Model 88
Pre-1965

MODEL 72 BOLT-ACTION REPEATER. . . . . NiB $450 Ex $325 Gd $200
Tubular magazine. Takedown. Caliber: .22 Short, Long, LR. Magazine holds 20 Short, 16 Long or 15 LR. 25-inch bbl. Weight: 5.75 lbs. Sights: Peep or open rear; bead front. Plain pistol-grip stock. Made 1938–59.

MODEL 73 LEVER-ACTION REPEATER
See Model 1873 rifles, carbines, "One of One Thousand" and other variations of this model at the beginning of Winchester Rifle Section. Note: The Winchester Model 1873 was the first lever-action repeating rifle bearing the Winchester name.

MODEL 74 SELF-LOADING RIFLE . . . . NiB $275 Ex $225 Gd $150
Takedown. Calibers: .22 Short only, .22 LR only. Tubular magazine in buttstock holds 20 Short, 14 LR. 24-inch bbl. Weight: 6.25 lbs. Sights: Open rear; bead front. Plain pistol-grip stock, one-piece. Made 1939–55.

MODEL 75 SPORTING RIFLE . . . . . NiB $795 Ex $700 Gd $400
Same as Model 75 Target except has 24-inch bbl., checkered sporter stock, open rear sight; bead front on hooded ramp, weight: 5.5 lbs.

MODEL 75 TARGET RIFLE. . . . . . . NiB $550 Ex $400 Gd $250
Caliber: .22 LR. 5- or 10-shot box magazine. 28-inch bbl. Weight: 8.75 lbs. Target sights (Lyman, Redfield or Winchester). Target stock w/pistol grip and semi-beavertail forearm, swivels and sling. Made 1938–59.

**MODEL 77 SEMIAUTOMATIC RIFLE,
CLIP TYPE . . . . NiB $275 Ex $225 Gd $140**
Solid frame. Caliber: .22 LR. Eight shot clip magazine. 22-inch bbl. Weight: About 5.5 lbs. Sights: Open rear; bead front. Plain, one-piece pistol-grip stock. Made 1955–63.

**MODEL 77,
TUBULAR MAGAZINE . . . . NiB $275 Ex $225 Gd $150**
Same as Model 77. Clip type except has tubular magazine holding 15 rounds. Made 1955–63.

MODEL 86 CARBINE AND RIFLE
See Model 1886 at beginning of Winchester Rifle section.

MODEL 88 CARBINE
Same as Model 88 Rifle except has 19-inch bbl., plain carbine-style stock and forearm with bbl. band. Weight: 7 lbs. Made 1968-73.
88 Carbine. . . . . NiB $625 Ex $495 Gd $325
.284 Win. NiB $1300 Ex $1200 Gd $900

MODEL 88 LEVER-ACTION RIFLE
Hammerless. Calibers: .243 Win., .284 Win., .308 Win., .358 Win. Four shot box magazine. 3-shot in pre-1963 models and in .284. 22-inch bbl. Weight: About 7.25 lbs. One-piece walnut stock with pistol-grip, swivels (1965 and later models have basket-weave ornamentation instead of checkering). Made 1955–1973. Note: .243 and .358 introduced 1956, later discontinued 1964; .284 introduced 1963.
Model 88 (checkered stock) . . . . NiB $650 Ex $500 Gd $335
Model 88 (basketweave stock) . . . . NiB $550 Ex $450 Gd $306
.284 Win. . . . . NiB $1063 Ex $850 Gd $578
.358 Win. . . . . NiB $1244 Ex $995 Gd $677

MODEL 92 LEVER-ACTION RIFLE
Similar to the original Model 1892. Calibers: .357 Mag., .44-40, .44 Mag., .45 LC. 10-shot magazine. 24-inch round bbl. Weight: 6.25 lbs. 41.25 inches overall. Bead front sight, adjustable buckhorn rear. Etched receiver and gold trigger. Blue finish. Smooth straight-grip walnut stock and forewarm w/ metal grip cap. Made 1997 to date.
Standard Rifle . . . . NiB $563 Ex $450 Gd $306
Short Rifle w/20-inch bbl. (.44 Mag. only) . . . . NiB $544 Ex $435 Gd $296

Winchester Model 70
Coyote

Winchester Model 70
Ranger Compact

RIFLES

Winchester Model 70
Stealth

Winchester Model 94
Traditional

MODEL 94
ANTIQUE CARBINE . . . . **NiB $275 Ex $250 Gd $175**
Same as standard Post-64 Model 94 Carbine except has decorative scrollwork and casehardened receiver, brass-plated loading gate, saddle ring; caliber .30-30 only. Made 1964–84.

MODEL 94 CARBINE
Same as Model 1894 Rifle except 20-inch round bbl., 6-shot full-length magazine. Weight: About 6.5 lbs. Originally made in calibers .25-35, .30-30, .32 Special and .38-55. Original version discontinued 1964. See 1894 Models at beginning of Winchester Rifle Section.
Pre-World War II
(under No. 1,300,000) . . . . **NiB $1244 Ex $995 Gd $677**
Postwar, pre-1964
(under No. 2,700,000) . . . . **NiB $688 Ex $550 Gd $374**

MODEL 94
CLASSIC CARBINE . . . . **NiB $380 Ex $275 Gd $225**
Same as Canadian Centennial '67 Commemorative Carbine except without commemorative details; has scroll-engraved receiver, gold-plated loading gate. Made 1968–70.

MODEL 94
CLASSIC RIFLE . . . . **NiB $360 Ex $250 Gd $225**
Same as Model 67 Rifle except without commemorative details; has scroll-engraved receiver, gold-plated loading gate. Made 1968–70.

MODEL 94
DELUXE CARBINE . . . . **NiB $356 Ex $285 Gd $194**
Caliber: .30-30 Win. Six shot magazine. 20-inch bbl. 37.75 inches overall. Weight: 6.5 lbs. Semi-fancy American walnut stock with rubber buttpad, long forearm and specially cut checkering. Engraved with "Deluxe" script. Made 1987 to date.

MODEL 94 LONG BARREL RIFLE . . . . **NiB $325 Ex $275 Gd $150**
Caliber: .30-30 Win. Seven round magazine. 24-inch bbl. 41.75 inches overall. Weight: 7 lbs. American walnut stock. Blade front sight. Made 1987 to date.

MODEL 94 TRAPPER . . . . **NiB $325 Ex $250 Gd $160**
Same as Winchester Model 94 Carbine except 16-inch bbl. and weight: 6 lbs., 2 oz. Made 1980 to date.

MODEL 94 WIN-TUFF RIFLE . . . . . **NiB $300 Ex $225 Gd $160**
Caliber: .30-30 Win. Six round magazine. 20-inch bbl. 37.75 inches overall. Weight: 6.5 lbs. Brown laminated wood stock. Made 1987 to date.

MODEL 94 WRANGLER CARBINE
Same as standard Model 94 Carbine except has 16-inch bbl., engraved receiver and chambered for .32 Special & .38-55 Win.
Wrangler, Top
Eject (disc.1984) . . . . **NiB $325 Ex $250 Gd $175**
Wrangler II,
Angle Eject (disc. 1985) . . . . **NiB $275 Ex $190 Gd $150**

Winchester Model 94
Long Barrel

Winchester Model 94
Win-Tuff

Winchester Model 94
Wrangler II Angle Eject

Winchester Model 94
XTR Big Bore

Winchester Model 94
XTR 7-30 Waters

MODEL 94 XTR BIG BORE . . . . **NiB $355 Ex $255 Gd $160**
Modified Model 94 action for added strength. Caliber: .375 Win.
20-inch bbl. Rubber buttpad. Checkered stock and forearm. Weight:
6.5 lbs. Made 1978 to date.

MODEL 94 XTR
LEVER-ACTION RIFLE . . . . **NiB $300 Ex $200 Gd $140**
Same general specifications as standard Angle Eject M94 except
chambered .30-30 and 7-30 Waters and has 20- or 24-inch bbl.
Weight: 7 lbs. Made 1985 to date by U.S. Repeating Arms.

MODEL 94 COMMEMORATIVES

MODEL 94 ANTLERED GAME . . . . . **NiB $656 Ex $525 Gd $357**
Standard Model 94 action. Gold-colored medallion inlaid in
stock. Antique gold-plated receiver, lever tang and bbl. bands.
Medallion and receiver engraved with elk, moose, deer and cari-
bou. 20.5-inch bbl. Curved steel buttplate. In .30-30 caliber.
19,999 made in 1978.

MODEL 94 BICENTENNIAL
'76 CARBINE . . . . **NiB $800 Ex $675 Gd $490**
Same as Standard Model 94 Carbine except caliber .30-30 Win.
only; antique silver-finished, engraved receiver; stock and forearm
of fancy walnut, checkered, Bicentennial medallion embedded in
buttstock, curved buttplate. 20,000 made in 1976.

MODEL 94 BUFFALO BILL COMMEMORATIVE
Same as Centennial '66 Rifle except receiver is black-chromed,
scroll-engraved and bears name "Buffalo Bill"; hammer, trigger,
loading gate, saddle ring, forearm cap, and buttplate are nickel-
plated; Buffalo Bill Memorial Assn. commemorative medallion
embedded in buttstock; "Buffalo Bill Commemorative" inscribed
on bbl., facsimile signature "W.F. Cody, Chief of Scouts" on tang.
Carbine has 20-inch bbl., 6-shot magazine, 7-lb. weight. 112,923
made in 1968.
Carbine . . . . **NiB $563 Ex $450 Gd $306**
Rifle . . . . **NiB $594 Ex $475 Gd $323**
Matched carbine rifle set . . . . **NiB $1369 Ex $1095 Gd $745**

Winchester Model 66
Commemorative

Winchester Model 94
Chief Crazy Horse Commemorative

CANADIAN CENTENNIAL '67 COMMEMORATIVE

Same as Centennial '66 Rifle except receiver engraved with maple leaves and forearm cap is black-chromed, buttplate is blued, commemorative inscription in gold on barrel and top tang: "Canadian Centennial 1867–1967." Carbine has 20-inch bbl., 6-shot magazine, weight: 7 lb., 90,398 made in 1967.

Carbine	NiB $563	Ex $450	Gd $306
Rifle	NiB $594	Ex $475	Gd $323
Matched carbine/rifle set	NiB $1313	Ex $1050	Gd $714

CENTENNIAL '66 COMMEMORATIVE

Commemorates Winchester's 100th anniversary. Standard Model 94 action. Caliber: .30-30. Full-length magazine holds 8 rounds. 26-inch octagon bbl. Weight: 8 lbs. Gold-plated receiver and forearm cap. Sights: Open rear; post front. Saddle ring. Walnut buttstock and forearm with high-gloss finish, solid brass buttplate. Commemorative inscription on bbl. and top tang of receiver. 100,478 made in 1966.

Carbine	NiB $563	Ex $450	Gd $306
Rifle	NiB $594	Ex $475	Gd $323
Matched carbine/rifle set	NiB $1369	Ex $1095	Gd $745

MODEL 94 CHEYENNE

COMMEMORATIVE . . . . **NiB $988 Ex $825 Gd $674**
Available in Canada only. Same as Standard Model 94 Carbine except chambered for .44-40. 11,225 made in 1977.

MODEL 94
CHIEF CRAZY HORSE

COMMEMORATIVE . . . . **NiB $688 Ex $550 Gd $374**
Cailber: .38-55, 7-shot tubular magazine. 24-inch bbl., 41.75 inches overall. Walnut stock with medallion of the United Sioux Tribes; buttstock and forend also decorated with brass tacks. Engraved receiver. Open rear sights; bead front sight. 19,999 made in 1983.

MODEL 94 COLT COMMEMORATIVE

CARBINE SET . . . . **NiB $3744 Ex $2995 Gd $2037**
Standard Model 94 action. Caliber: .44-40 Win. 20-inch bbl. Weight: 6.25 lbs. Features the horse-and-rider trademark and distinctive WC monogram in gold etching on left side of receiver. Sold in set with Colt Single Action Revolver chambered for same caliber. See illustration next page.

MODEL 94 COWBOY COMMEMORATIVE CARBINE

Same as Standard Model 94 Carbine except caliber .30-30 only; nickel-plated receiver, tangs, lever, bbl. bands; engraved receiver, "Cowboy Commemorative" on bbl., commemorative medallion embedded in buttstock; curved buttplate. 20,915 made in 1970. Nickel-silver medallion inlaid in stock. Antique silver-plated receiver engraved with scenes of the old frontier. Checkered walnut stock and forearm. 19,999 made in 1970.

Cowboy Carbine	NiB $563	Ex $450	Gd $306
Cowboy Carbine (1 of 300)	NiB $3619	Ex $2895	Gd $1969

MODEL 94 GOLDEN SPIKE COMMEMORATIVE

CARBINE . . . . **NiB $494 Ex $395 Gd $269**
Same as Standard Model 94 Carbine except caliber .30-30 only; gold-plated receiver, tangs and bbl. bands; engraved receiver, commemorative medallion embedded in stock. 64,758 made in 1969.

MODEL 94 ILLINOIS
SESQUICENTENNIAL

COMMEMORATIVE CARBINE . . . . . **NiB $494 Ex $395 Gd $269**
Same as Standard Model 94 Carbine except caliber .30-30 only; gold-plated buttplate, trigger, loading gate, and saddle ring; receiver engraved with profile of Lincoln, commemorative inscription on receiver, bbl.; souvenir medallion embedded in stock. 31,124 made in 1968.

MODEL 94 LEGENDARY
FRONTIERSMEN

COMMEMORATIVE . . . . **NiB $656 Ex $525 Gd $357**
Standard Model 94 action. Caliber: .39-55. 24-inch round bbl. Nickel-silver medallion inlaid in stock. Antique silver-plated receiver engraved with scenes of the old frontier. Checkered walnut stock and forearm. 19,999 made in 1979.

MODEL 94
LEGENDARY LAWMEN

COMMEMORATIVE . . . . **NiB $656 Ex $525 Gd $357**
Same as Standard Model 94 Carbine except .30-30 Win. only; antique silver-plated receiver engraved with action law-enforcement scenes. 16-inch Trapper bbl., antique silver-plated bbl. bands. 19,999 made in 1978.

**Winchester Colt
Commemorative Set**

**Winchester Model 94
NRA Centennial**

MODEL 94 LONE STAR COMMEMORATIVE
Same as Theodore Roosevelt Rifle except yellow-gold plating; "Lone Star" engraving on receiver and bbl., commemorative medallion embedded in buttstock. 30,669 made in 1970.
Rifle or carbine . . . . NiB $563 Ex $450 Gd $306
Matched carbine/rifle set . . . . . . NiB $1369 Ex $1095 Gd $745

MODEL 94 NRA
CENTENNIAL MUSKET . . . . NiB $531 Ex $425 Gd $289
Commemorates 100th anniversary of National Rifle Association of America. Standard Model 94 action. Caliber: .30-30. Seven shot magazine. 26-inch bbl. Sights: Military folding rear; blade front. Black chrome-finished receiver engraved "NRA 1871–1971" plus scrollwork. Barrel inscribed "NRA Centennial Musket." Musket-style buttstock and full-length forearm; commemorative medallion embedded in buttstock. Weight: 7.13 lbs. Made in 1971.

MODEL 94 NRA
CENTENNIAL RIFLE . . . . NiB $563 Ex $450 Gd $306
Same as Model 94 Rifle except has commemorative details as in NRA Centennial Musket (barrel inscribed "NRA Centennial Rifle"); caliber .30-30, 24-inch bbl., QD sling swivels. Made in 1971.

MODEL 94 NRA
CENTENNIAL MATCHED SET . . . . NiB $1188 Ex $950 Gd $646
Rifle and musket were offered in sets with consecutive serial numbers. Note: Production figures not available. These rifles offered in Winchester's 1972 catalog.

MODEL 94
NEBRASKA CENTENNIAL
COMMEMORATIVE CARBINE . . . . NiB $1688 Ex $1325 Gd $918
Same as Standard Model 94 Carbine except caliber .30-30 only; gold-plated hammer, loading gate, bbl. band, and buttplate; souvenir medallion embedded in stock, commemorative inscription on bbl. 2,500 made in 1966.

MODEL 94 THEODORE ROOSEVELT
COMMEMORATIVE RIFLE/CARBINE
Standard Model 94 action. Caliber: .30-30. Rifle has 6-shot half-magazine, 26-inch bbl., weight: 7.5-lb. Carbine has 6-shot full magazine, 20-inch bbl., weight: 7-lb. White gold-plated receiver, upper tang, and forend cap; receiver engraved with American Eagle, "26th President 1901–1909," and Roosevelt's signature. Commemorative medallion embedded in buttstock. Saddle ring. Half pistol-grip, contoured lever. 49,505 made in 1969.
Carbine . . . . NiB $531 Ex $425 Gd $289
Rifle . . . . NiB $563 Ex $450 Gd $306
Matched set . . . . NiB $1313 Ex $1050 Gd $714

MODEL 94
TEXAS RANGER
ASSOCIATION CARBINE . . . . . NiB $3244 Ex $2595 Gd $1765
Same as Texas Ranger Commemorative Model 94 except special edition of 150 carbines, numbered 1 through 150, with hand-checkered full-fancy walnut stock and forearm. Sold only through Texas Ranger Association. Made in 1973.

Winchester Model 100

MODEL 94 TEXAS RANGER
COMMEMORATIVE CARBINE..... **NiB $931 Ex $745 Gd $507**
Same as Standard Model 94 Carbine except caliber .30-30 Win. only, stock and forearm of semi-fancy walnut, replica of Texas Ranger star embedded in buttstock, curved buttplate. 5,000 made in 1973.

MODEL 94 TRAPPER
Same as Winchester Model 94 Carbine except w/16-inch bbl. and weighs 6 lbs. 2 oz. Angle Eject introduced in 1985 also chambered for .357 Mag., .44 Mag. and .45 LC. Made 1980 to date.
94 Trapper, Top Eject (disc. 1984)........ NiB $325 Ex $250 Gd $175
94 Trapper, Angle Eject (.30-30)......... NiB $300 Ex $195 Gd $125
.357 Mag., .44 Mag. or .45 LC., add......................... $25

MODEL 94 JOHN WAYNE
COMMEMORATIVE CARBINE.... **NiB $1188 Ex $950 Gd $646**
Standard Model 94 action. Caliber: .32-40. 18.5-inch bbl. Receiver is pewter-plated with engraving of Indian attack and cattle drive scenes. Oversized bow on lever. Nickel-silver medallion in buttstock bears a bas-relief portrait of Wayne. Selected American walnut stock with deep-cut checkering. Introduced by U.S. Repeating Arms in 1981.

MODEL 94 WELLS FARGO & CO.
COMMEMORATIVE CARBINE..... **NiB $656 Ex $525 Gd $357**
Same as Standard Model 94 Carbine except .30-30 Win. only; antique silver-finished, engraved receiver; stock and forearm of fancy walnut, checkered, curved buttplate. Nickel-silver stagecoach medallion (inscribed "Wells Fargo & Co. —1852–1977—125 Years") embedded in buttstock. 20,000 made in 1977.

MODEL 94 O. F. WINCHESTER
COMMEMORATIVE RIFLE.............. **NiB $906 Ex $725 Gd $493**
Standard Model 94 action. Caliber: .38-55. 24-inch octagonal bbl. Receiver is satin gold-plated with distinctive engravings. Stock and forearm semi-fancy American walnut with high grade checkering.

MODEL 94 WRANGLER CARBINE
Same as standard Model 94 Carbine except w/16-inch bbl., engraved receiver and chambered for .32 Special and .38-55 Win. Angle Eject introduced in 1985 as Wrangler II, also chambered for .30-30 Win., .44 Mag. and .45 LC. Made 1980-86. Re-introduced in 1992.
94 Wrangler, Top Eject (disc. 1984)...... NiB $280 Ex $225 Gd $150
94 Wrangler II, Angle Eject (.30-30)...... NiB $275 Ex $200 Gd $140
.44 Mag. or .45 LC., add.................................... $25

MODEL 94 WYOMING DIAMOND JUBILEE
COMMEMORATIVE CARBINE....... **NiB $1869 Ex $1495 Gd $1017**
Same as Standard Model 94 Carbine except caliber .30-30 Win. only, receiver engraved and casehardened in colors, brass saddle ring and loading gate, souvenir medallion embedded in buttstock, commemorative inscription on bbl. 1,500 made in 1964.

MODEL 94 ALASKAN PURCHASE CENTENNIAL
COMMEMORATIVE CARBINE....... **NiB $1994 Ex $1595 Gd $1085**
Same as Wyoming issue except different medallion and inscription. 1,501 made in 1967.

MODEL 94 XTR BIG BORE
Modified Model 94 action for added strength. Calibers: .307 Win., .356 Win., .375 Win. or .444 Marlin. 20-inch bbl. Six shot magazine. Rubber buttpad. Checkered stock and forearm. Weight: 6.5 lbs. Made 1978 to date.
94 XTR BB, Top Eject (disc. 1984)........ NiB $355 Ex $250 Gd $150
94 XTR BB, Angle Eject (intro. 1985)..... NiB $275 Ex $195 Gd $130
.356 Win. or .375 Win., add.............................. $150

MODEL 94 XTR LEVER-ACTION RIFLE
Same general specifications as standard M94 and Angle Eject M94 except chambered for .30-30 Win. and 7-30 Waters and has 20- or 24-inch bbl. Weight: 6.5 to 7 lbs. Made 1978-88 by U.S. Repeating Arms.
94 XTR Top Eject (disc. 1984)........... NiB $325 Ex $235 Gd $150
94 XTR Angle Eject (.30-30)............. NiB $295 Ex $225 Gd $135
94 XTR Deluxe Angle Eject (.30-30)...... NiB $375 Ex $295 Gd $190
7-30 Waters, add.. $80

MODEL 100 AUTOLOADING RIFLE......
NiB $550 Ex $425 Gd $275
Gas-operated semiautomatic. Calibers: .243, .284, .308 Win. Four shot clip magazine (3-shot in .284). 22-inch bbl. Weight: 7.25 lbs. Sights: Open rear; hooded ramp front. One-piece stock w/pistol grip, basket-weave checkering, grip cap, sling swivels. Made 1961–73.

MODEL 100 CARBINE ....
NiB $600 Ex $475 Gd $300
Same as Model 100 Rifle except has 19-inch bbl., plain carbine-style stock and forearm with bbl. band. Weight: 7 lbs. Made 1967–73.

MODEL 121 DELUXE ....
NiB $156 Ex $125 Gd $85
Same as Model 121 Standard except has ramp front sight, stock with fluted comb and sling swivels. Made 1967–73.

MODEL 121 STANDARD
BOLT-ACTION SINGLE SHOT...... **NiB $150 Ex $120 Gd $82**
Caliber: .22 Short, Long, LR. 20.75-inch bbl. Weight: 5 lbs. Sights: Open rear; bead front. Monte Carlo-style stock. Made 1967–73.

MODEL 121 YOUTH.............
NiB $150 Ex $120 Gd $90
Same as Model 121 Standard except has 1.25-inch shorter stock. Made 1967–73.

MODEL 131 BOLT-ACTION REPEATER.....
NiB $169 Ex $135 Gd $92
Caliber: .22 Short, Long or LR. Seven shot clip magazine. 20.75-inch bbl. Weight: 5 lbs. Sights: Open rear; ramp front. Plain Monte Carlo stock. Made 1967–73.

MODEL 135 ....
NiB $156 Ex $125 Gd $85
Same as Model 131 except chambered for .22 WMR cartridge. Magazine holds 5 rounds. Made in 1967.

MODEL 141
BOLT-ACTION
TUBULAR REPEATER............. **NiB $190 Ex $150 Gd $95**
Same as Model 131 except has tubular magazine in buttstock; holds 19 Short, 15 Long, 13 LR. Made 1967–73.

RIFLES

Winchester Model 250
Standard

Winchester Model 270
Standard

MODEL 145 . . . . NiB $180 Ex $150 Gd $95
Same as Model 141 except chambered for .22 WMR; magazine holds 9 rounds. Made in 1967.

MODEL 150 LEVER-ACTION CARBINE . . . . NiB $150 Ex $125 Gd $75
Same as Model 250 except has straight loop lever, plain carbine-style straight-grip stock and forearm with bbl. band. Made 1967-73.

MODEL 190 CARBINE . . . . NiB $150 Ex $125 Gd $75
Same as Model 190 rifle except has carbine-style forearm with bbl. band. Made 1967-73.

MODEL 190 SEMIAUTOMATIC RIFLE . . . . NiB $130 Ex $100 Gd $65
Same as current Model 290 except has plain stock and forearm. Made 1966-78.

MODEL 250 DELUXE RIFLE . . . . . . NiB $225 Ex $175 Gd $100
Same as Model 250 Standard Rifle except has fancy walnut Monte Carlo stock and forearm, sling swivels. Made 1965-71.

**MODEL 250 STANDARD
LEVER-ACTION RIFLE** . . . . NiB $150 Ex $120 Gd $82
Hammerless. Caliber: .22 Short, Long or LR. Tubular magazine holds 21 Short, 17 Long, 15 LR. 20.5-inch bbl. Sights: Open rear; ramp front. Weight: About 5 lbs. Plain stock and forearm on early production; later model has checkering. Made 1963-73.

MODEL 255 DELUXE RIFLE . . . . NiB $225 Ex $190 Gd $80
Same as Model 250 Deluxe Rifle except chambered for .22 WMR cartridge. Magazine holds 11 rounds. Made 1965-73.

MODEL 255 STANDARD RIFLE . . . . NiB $188 Ex $150 Gd $102
Same as Model 250 Standard Rifle except chambered for .22 WMR cartridge. Magazine holds 11 rounds. Made 1964-70.

MODEL 270 DELUXE RIFLE . . . . NiB $195 Ex $150 Gd $90
Same as Model 270 Standard Rifle except has fancy walnut Monte Carlo stock and forearm. Made 1965-73.

**MODEL 270 STANDARD
SLIDE-ACTION RIFLE** . . . . NiB $130 Ex $100 Gd $70
Hammerless. Caliber: .22 Short, Long or LR. Tubular magazine holds 21 Short, 17 Long, 15 LR. 20.5-inch bbl. Sights: Open rear; ramp front. Weight: About 5 lbs. Early production had plain walnut stock and forearm (slide handle); latter also furnished in plastic (Cycolac); last model has checkering. Made 1963-73.

MODEL 275 DELUXE RIFLE . . . . . . NiB $225 Ex $175 Gd $100
Same as Model 270 Deluxe Rifle except chambered for .22 WMR cartridge. Tubular magazine holds 11 rounds. Made 1965-70.

**MODEL 275
STANDARD RIFLE** . . . . NiB $160 Ex $125 Gd $90
Same as Model 270 Standard Rifle except chambered for .22 WMR cartridge. Magazine holds 11 rounds. Made 1964-70.

MODEL 290 DELUXE RIFLE . . . . NiB $225 Ex $190 Gd $80
Same as Model 290 Standard Rifle except has fancy walnut Monte Carlo stock and forearm. Made 1965-73.

MODEL 290 STANDARD SEMIAUTOMATIC RIFLE
Caliber: .22 Long or LR. Tubular magazine holds 17 Long, 15 LR. 20.5-inch bbl. Sights: Open rear; ramp front. Weight: About 5 lbs. Plain stock and forearm on early production; current model has checkering. Made 1963-77.
W/plain stock/forearm . . . . NiB $225 Ex $190 Gd $80
W/checkered
stock/forearm . . . . NiB $250 Ex $200 Gd $95

**MODEL 310 BOLT-ACTION
SINGLE SHOT** . . . . NiB $250 Ex $195 Gd $135
Caliber: .22 Short, Long, LR. 22-inch bbl. Weight: 5.63 lbs. Sights: Open rear; ramp front. Monte Carlo stock w/checkered pistol-grip and forearm, sling swivels. Made 1972-75.

**MODEL 320 BOLT-ACTION
REPEATER** . . . . NiB $290 Ex $250 Gd $150
Same as Model 310 except has 5-shot clip magazine. Made 1972-74.

**MODEL 490
SEMIAUTOMATIC RIFLE** . . . . NiB $290 Ex $225 Gd $150
Caliber: .22 LR. 5-shot clip magazine. 22-inch bbl. Weight: 6 lbs. Sights: Folding leaf rear; hooded ramp front. One-piece walnut stock w/checkered pistol grip and forearm. Made 1975-77.

**MODEL 670 BOLT-ACTION
SPORTING RIFLE** . . . . NiB $350 Ex $250 Gd $180
Calibers: .225 Win., .243 Win., .270 Win., .30-06, .308 Win. Four shot magazine. 22-inch bbl. Weight: 7 lbs. Sights: Open rear; ramp front. Monte Carlo stock w/checkered pistol-grip and forearm. Made 1967-73.

Winchester Model 310

Winchester Model 320

Winchester Model 490
Rifle

Winchester Model 670
Bolt-Action Rifle

Winchester Model 670
Magnum

Winchester Model 770

RIFLES

MODEL 670 CARBINE . . . . **NiB $350 Ex $280 Gd $185**
Same as Model 670 Rifle except has 19-inch bbl. Weight: 6.75 lbs.
Calibers: .243 Win., .270 Win., .30-06. Made 1967–70.

MODEL 670 MAGNUM . . . . **NiB $395 Ex $275 Gd $215**
Same as Model 670 Rifle except has 24-inch bbl., reinforced
stock with recoil pad with slightly different checkering pattern.
Weight: 7.25 lbs. Calibers: .264 Win. Mag., 7mm Rem. Mag.,
.300 Win. Mag. Open rear sight; ramp front sight with hood.
Made 1967–70.

**MODEL 770 BOLT-ACTION
SPORTING RIFLE.** . . . . **NiB $375 Ex $275 Gd $200**
Model 70-type action. Calibers: .22-250, .222 Rem., .243, .270
Win., .30-06. Four shot box magazine. 22-inch bbl. Sights: Open
rear; hooded ramp front. Weight: 7.13 lbs. Monte Carlo stock,
checkered pistol-grip and forend; sling swivels. Made 1969–71.

MODEL 770 MAGNUM . . . . **NiB $400 Ex $325 Gd $250**
Same as Standard Model 770 except 24-inch bbl., weight: 7.25 lbs., recoil
pad. Calibers: 7mm Rem. Mag., .264 and .300 Win. Mag. Made 1969–71.

Winchester Model 9422
Boy Scouts of America Commemorative

Winchester Model 9422
Eagle Scout Limited Edtion

Winchester Model 9422
WinCam

Winchester Model 9422
XTR Classic

MODEL 9422 LEVER-ACTION RIMFIRE RIFLES

Similar to the standard Model 94 except chambered for .22 Rimfire. Calibers: .22 Short, Long, LR. (9422) or .22 WMR (9422M). Tubular magazine holds 21 or 15 Short.17 or 12 Long, 15 or 11 LR (9422 or Trapper) or 11 or 8 WRM (9422M or Trapper M). 16.5- or 20.5 inch bbl. 33.125- to 37.125 inches overall. Weight: 5.75 to 6.25 lbs. Open rear sight; hooded ramp front. Carbine-style stock and barrel-band forearm. Stock options: Walnut (Standard), laminated brown (WinTuff), laminated green (WinCam). Made 1972 to date.

Walnut (Standard)	NiB $345	Ex $275	Gd $175
WinCam	NiB $350	Ex $280	Gd $180
WinTuff	NiB $294	Ex $235	Gd $160
Legacy	NiB $380	Ex $325	Gd $175
Trapper (16.5-inch bbl.)	NiB $335	Ex $260	Gd $175
XTR Classic	NiB $475	Ex $450	Gd $300
High Grade Series I	NiB $415	Ex $350	Gd $220
High Grade Series II	NiB $375	Ex $275	Gd $200
25th Anniversary Edition Grade I(1of 2500)	NiB $550	Ex $450	Gd $350
25th Anniversary Edition High Grade (1of 250)	NiB $1195	Ex $975	Gd $675
Boy Scout Commemorative (1of 15,000)	NiB $650	Ex $540	Gd $350
Eagle Scout Commemorative (1of 1000)	NiB $3369	Ex $2695	Gd $1833
22 WRM, add			10%

DOUBLE XPRESS RIFLE . . . . NiB $2744 Ex $2195 Gd $1493
Over/under double rifle. Caliber: .30-06. 23.5-inch bbl. Weight: 8.5 lbs. Made for Olin Corp. by Olin-Kodensha in Japan. Introduced 1982.

RANGER YOUTH
BOLT-ACTION CARBINE . . . . NiB $350 Ex $250 Gd $150
Calibers: .223 (discontinued 1989), .243 Win., and .308 Win. Four and 5-shot magazine. Bbl.: 20-inch. Weight: 5.75 lbs. American hardwood stock. Open rear sight. Made 1985 to date by U.S. Repeating Arms.

RANGER LEVER-ACTION CARBINE . . . . . . NiB $244 Ex $195 Gd $133
Caliber: .30-30. Five shot tubular magazine. Bbl.: 20-inch round. Weight: 6.5 lbs. American hardwood stock. Economy version of Model 94. Made 1985 to date by U.S. Repeating Arms.

RANGER BOLT-ACTION CARBINE . . . . NiB $325 Ex $260 Gd $177
Calibers: .223 Rem., .243 Win., .270, .30-06, 7mm Rem. (discontinued 1985), Mag. Three and 4-shot magazine. Bbl.: 24-inch in 7mm; 22-inch in .270 and .30-06. Open sights. American hardwood stock. Made 1985 to date by U.S. Repeating Arms.

MODEL 1892 GRADE I LEVER-ACTION RIFLE
Similar to the original Model 1892. Calibers: .357 Mag., .44-40, .44 Mag., .45 LC. 10-shot magazine. 24-inch round bbl. Weight: 6.25 lbs. 41.25 inches overall. Bead front sight, adjustable buckhorn rear. Etched receiver and gold trigger. Blue finish. Smooth straight-grip walnut stock and forearm w/ metal grip cap. Made 1997 to date.
Standard Rifle . . . . NiB $665 Ex $580 Gd $325
Short Rifle w/20-inch bbl.
(.44 Mag. only) . . . . NiB $544 Ex $435 Gd $296

MODEL 1892 GRADE
II LEVER-ACTION RIFLE . . . . NiB $1125 Ex $975 Gd $595
Similar to the Grade I Model 1892 except w/gold appointments and receiver game scene. Chambered .45 LC only. Limited production of 1,000 in 1997.

Winslow Commander Grade

Winslow Crown Grade

Winslow Regent Grade
Bushmaster Stock

WINSLOW ARMS COMPANY — Camden, South Carolina

BOLT-ACTION SPORTING RIFLE
Action: FN Supreme Mauser, Mark X Mauser, Remington 700 and 788, Sako, Winchester 70. Standard calibers: .17-222, .17-223, .222 Rem., .22-250, .243 Win., 6mm Rem., .25-06, .257 Roberts, .270 Win., 7x57, .280 Rem., .284 Win., .308 Win., .30-06, .358 Win. Magnum calibers: .17-222 Mag., .257 Wby., .264 Win., .270 Wby., 7mm Rem., 7mm Wby., .300 H&H, .300 Wby., .300 Win., .308 Norma, 8mm Rem., .338 Win., .358 Norma, .375 H&H, .375 Wby., .458 Win. Three-shot magazine in standard calibers, 2-shot in magnum. 24-inch barrel in standard calibers, 26-inch in magnum. Weight: With 24-inch bbl., 7 to 7.5 lbs.; with 26-inch bbl., 8 to 9 lbs. No sights. Stocks: "Bushmaster" with slender pistol-grip and beavertail forearm, "Plainsmaster" with full curl pistol-grip and flat forearm; both styles have Monte Carlo cheekpiece. Values shown are for basic rifle in each grade; extras such as special fancy wood, more elaborate carving, inlays and engraving can increase these figures considerably. Made 1962–89.

Commander
Grade . . . . .NiB $500 Ex $475 Gd $335
Regal Grade . . . . .NiB $615 Ex $590 Gd $400

(cont'd.) **BOLT-ACTION SPORTING RIFLE**
Regent Grade . . . . .NiB $750 Ex $650 Gd $470
Regimental Grade . . . . .NiB $995 Ex $895 Gd $600
Crown
Grade . . . . NiB $1400 Ex $1200 Gd $950
Royal
Grade . . . . NiB $1600 Ex $1400 Gd $1050
Imperial
Grade . . . . NiB $3500 Ex $3000 Gd $2200
Emperor
Grade . . . . .NiB $6500 Ex $5700 Gd $3995

ZEPHYR DOUBLE RIFLES
Manufactured by Victor Sarasqueta Company — Eibar, Spain

DOUBLE RIFLE . . . . .NiB $20,625 Ex $16,500 Gd $1122
Boxlock. Calibers: Available in practically every caliber from .22 Hornet to .505 Gibbs. Bbls.: 22 to 28 inches standard, but any lengths were available on special order. Weight: 7 lbs. for the smaller calibers up to 12 or more lbs. for the larger calibers. Imported by Stoeger from about 1938 to 1951.

Twenty-Sixth Edition
GUN TRADER'S GUIDE

Shotguns

American Arms
Bristol (Sterling) Over/Under

American Arms
Derby Hammerless Double

American Arms
Gentry/York Hammerless Double

American Arms
Silver Over/Under

American Arms
Camper Special

ALDENS SHOTGUN — Chicago, Illinois

MODEL 670 CHIEFTAIN SLIDE ACTION . . NiB $213 Ex $170 Gd $116
Hammerless. Gauges: 12, 20 and others. Three shot tubular magazine. Bbl.: 26- to 30-inch; various chokes. Weight: 6.25 to 7.5 lbs. depending on bbl. length and ga. Walnut-finished hardwood stock.

AMERICAN ARMS — N. Kansas City, Missouri

See also Franchi Shotguns.

BRISTOL (STERLING) O/U . . . . NiB $695 Ex $550 Gd $375
Boxlock w/Greener crossbolt and engraved sideplates. Single selective trigger. Selective automatic ejectors. Gauges: 12, 20; 3-inch chambers. 26-, 28-, 30-, or 32-inch vent-rib bbls. w/screw-in choke tubes (Improved Cylinder/Modified/Full). Weight: 7 lbs. Antique-silver receiver w/game scene or scroll engraving. Checkered full pistol-grip-style buttstock and forearm w/high-gloss finish. Imported 1986-88 with the model designation Bristol; redesignated Sterling 1989-90.

BRITTANY HAMMERLESS DOUBLE . . . . . . NiB $690 Ex $560 Gd $375
Boxlock w/engraved case-colored receiver. Single selective trigger. Selective automatic ejectors. Gauges: 12, 20. 3-inch chambers. Bbls.:

(cont'd.) BRITTANY HAMMERLESS DOUBLE
25- or 27-inch w/screw-in choke tubes (IC/M/F). Weight: 6.5 lbs. (20 ga.). Checkered English-style walnut stock w/semi-beavertail forearm or pistol-grip stock w/high-gloss finish. Imported 1989 to date.

CAMPER SPECIAL . . . . NiB $106 Ex $85 Gd $58
Similar to the Single Barrel except takedown model w/21-inch bbl., M choke and pistol-grip stock. Made in 1989 only.

COMBO . . . . NiB $194 Ex $155 Gd $105
Similar to the Single-Barrel model except available w/interchangeable rifle and shotgun bbls. .22 LR/20-ga. shotgun or .22 Hornet/12-ga. shotgun. Rifle bbl. has adj. rear sights; blade-type front sight. Made in 1989.

DERBY HAMMERLESS DOUBLE
Sidelock w/engraved sideplates. Single non-selective or double triggers. Selective automatic ejectors. Gauges: 12, 20, 28 and .410., 3-inch chambers. Bbls.: 26-inch (IC/M) or 28-inch (M/F). Weight: 6 lbs. (20 ga.). Checkered English-style walnut stock and splinter forearm w/hand-rubbed oil finish. Engraved frame/sideplates w/antique silver finish. Imported 1986-94.
12 or 20 ga. . . . . NiB $875 Ex $750 Gd $450
28 or .410 ga. (disc. 1991) . . . . NiB $938 Ex $750 Gd $510

**American Arms
WS/SS Hammerless Double**

F.S. SERIES O/U
Greener crossbolt in Trap and Skeet configuration. Single selective trigger. Selective automatic ejectors. 12 gauge only. 26-, 28-, 30-, or 32-inch separated bbls. Weight: 6.5 to 7.25 lbs. Black or chrome receiver. Checkered walnut buttstock and forearm. Imported 1986-87.

Model F.S. 200 Boxlock . . . . NiB $690 Ex $550 Gd $375
Model F.S. 300 Boxlock . . . . NiB $825 Ex $675 Gd $475
Model F.S. 400 Sidelock . . . . NiB $1150 Ex $945 Gd $650
Model F.S. 500 Sidelock . . . . NiB $1150 Ex $950 Gd $650

GENTRY/YORK HAMMERLESS DOUBLE
Chrome, coin-silver or color casehardened boxlock receiver w/scroll engraving. Double triggers. Extractors. Gauges: 12, 16, 20, 28, .410. 3-inch chambers (16 and 28 have 2.75-inch). Bbls.: 26-inch (IC/M) or 28-inch (M/F, 12, 16 and 20). Weight: 6.75 lbs. (12 ga.). Checkered walnut buttstock w/pistol-grip and beavertail forearm; both w/semi-gloss oil finish. Imported as York from 1986-88, redesignated Gentry 1989 to date.

Gentry 12, or 16 or 20 ga. . . . . NiB $625 Ex $450 Gd $300
Gentry 28 or .410 ga. . . . . NiB $675 Ex $550 Gd $390
York 12, 16 or 20 ga. (disc. 1988) . . . . . . NiB $494 Ex $395 Gd $269
York 28 or .410 ga. (disc. 1988) . . . . NiB $594 Ex $475 Gd $323

GRULLA NO. 2 HAMMERLESS DOUBLE
True sidelock w/engraved detachable sideplates. Double triggers. Extractors and cocking indicators. Gauges: 12, 20, .410 w/3-inch chambers; 28 w/2.75-inch. 26-inch bbl. Imported 1989 to date.

Standard model . . . . NiB $3119 Ex $2495 Gd $1697
Two-bbl. set (disc. 1995) . . . . . . NiB $4063 Ex $3250 Gd $2210

SILVER I O/U
Boxlock. Single selective trigger. Extractors. Gauges: 12, 20 and .410 w/3-inch chambers; 28 w/2.75 inch. Bbls.: 26-inch (IC/M), 28-inch (M/F, 12 and 20 ga. only). Weight: 6.75 lbs. (12 ga.). Checkered walnut stock and forearm. Antique-silver receiver w/scroll engraving. Imported 1987 to date.

12 or 20 ga. . . . . NIB $525 EX. $425 GD $275
28 or .410 ga. . . . . NIB $563 EX $450 GD $306

SILVER II O/U
Similar to Model Silver I except w/selective automatic ejectors and 26-inch bbls. w/screw-in tubes (12 and 20 ga.). Fixed chokes (28 and .410). Made 1987 to date.

12 or 20 ga . . . . NiB $656 Ex $525 Gd $357
28 or .410 ga. . . . . NiB $719 Ex $575 Gd $391
Upland Lite II . . . . NiB $794 Ex $635 Gd $432
Two-bbl. set . . . . NiB $1031 Ex $825 Gd $561

SILVER LITE O/U
Similar to Model Silver II except w/blued, engraved alloy receiver. Available in 12 and 20 ga. only. Imported from 1990-92.

Standard Model . . . . NiB $675 Ex $550 Gd $400
Two-bbl. Set . . . . NiB $1063 Ex $850 Gd $578

SILVER SKEET/TRAP . . . . NiB $813 Ex $650 Gd $442
Similar to the Silver II Model except has 28-inch (Skeet) or 30-inch (Trap) ported bbls. w/target-style rib and mid-bead sight. Imported 1992-94.

SILVER SPORTING O/U . . . . NiB $825 Ex $690 Gd $450
Boxlock. Single selective trigger. Selective automatic ejectors. Gauges: 12, 2.75-inch chambers. 28-inch bbls.w/Franchoke tubes (SK, IC, M and F). Weight: 7.5 lbs. Checkered walnut stock and forearm. Special broadway rib and vented side ribs. Engraved receiver w/chrome-nickel finish. Imported from 1990 to date.

SINGLE-SHOT SHOTGUN
Break-open action. Gauges: 10 (3.5), 12, 20, .410, 3-inch chamber. Weight: about 6.5 lbs. Bead front sight. Walnut-finished hardwood stock w/checkered grip and forend. Made from 1988 to 1990.

10 ga. (3.5-inch) . . . . NiB $125 Ex $100 Gd $68
12, 20 or .410 ga. . . . . NiB $106 Ex $85 Gd $58
Multi-choke bbl., add $30

SLUGGER SINGLE-SHOT SHOTGUN . . . . NiB $119 Ex $95 Gd $65
Similar to the Single-Shot model except in 12 and 20 ga. only w/24-inch slug bbl. Rifle-type sights and recoil pad. Made from 1989 to 1990.

TS/OU 12 SHOTGUN . . . . NiB $700 Ex $575 Gd $390
Turkey Special. Boxlock. Single selective trigger. Selective automatic ejectors. Gauge: 12, 3.5-inch chambers. Bbls.: 24-inch O/U w/screw-in choke tubes (IC, M, F). Weight: 6 lbs. 15 oz. Checkered European walnut stock and beavertail forearm. Matte blue metal finish. Imported 1987 to date.

TS/SS 10 HAMMERLESS DOUBLE . . . . NiB $656 Ex $525 Gd $357
Turkey Special. Same general specifications as Model WS/ SS 10, except w/26-inch side-by-side bbls., screw-in choke tubes (F/F) and chambered for 10-ga. 3.5-inch shells. Weight: 10 lbs., 13 oz. Imported 1987 to 1993.

TS/SS 12 HAMMERLESS DOUBLE . . . . NiB $600 Ex $500 Gd $325
Same general specifications as Model WS/SS 10 except in 12 ga. w/26-inch side-by-side bbls. and 3 screw-in choke tubes (IC/M/F). Weight: 7 lbs., 6 oz. Imported 1987 to date.

WS/OU 12 SHOTGUN . . . . NiB $635 Ex $500 Gd $335
Waterfowl Special. Boxlock. Single selective trigger. Selective automatic ejectors. Gauge: 12; 3.5-inch chambers. Bbls.: 28-inch O/U w/screw-in tubes (IC/M/F). Weight: 7 lbs. Checkered European walnut stock and beavertail forearm. Matte blue metal finish. Imported 1987 to date.

WS/SS 10 HAMMERLESS DOUBLE . . . . NiB $700 Ex $575 Gd $390
Waterfowl Special. Boxlock. Double triggers. Extractors. Gauge: 10; 3.5-inch chambers. Bbls.: 32-inch side/side choked F/F. Weight: About 11 lbs. Checkered walnut stock and beavertail forearm w/satin finish. Parkerized metal finish. Imported from 1987 to 1995.

SHOTGUNS

Armalite AR-17
Golden Gun

Armsport 1050

Armsport 1125

WT/OU 10 Shotgun . . . . **NiB $900 Ex $725 Gd $490**
Same general specifications as Model WS/OU 12 except chambered
for 10-ga. 3.5-inch shells. Extractors. Satin wood finish and matte
blue metal. Imported 1987 to date.

ARMALITE, INC. — Costa Mesa, California

AR-17 GOLDEN GUN. . . . . **NiB $625 Ex $500 Gd $390**
Recoil-operated semiautomatic. High-test aluminum bbl. and
receiver housing. 12 ga. only. Two-shot magazine. 24-inch bbl.
w/interchangeable choke tubes: IC/M/F. Weight: 5.6 lbs.
Polycarbonate stock and forearm recoil pad. Gold-anodized
finish standard, also made w/black finish. Made 1964-65.
Fewer than 2,000 produced.

ARMSCOR (Arms Corp.) — Manila, Philippines, *Imported until 1991 by Armscor Precision, San Mateo, CA; 1991-95 by Ruko Products, Inc., Buffalo NY: Currently imported by K.B.I., Harrisburg, PA*

MODEL M-30 FIELD PUMP SHOTGUN
Double slide-action bars w/damascened bolt. Gauge: 12 only w/3-
inch chamber. Bbl.: 28-inch w/fixed chokes or choke tubes. Weight:
7.6 lbs. Walnut or walnut finished hardwood stock.
Model M30-F (w/hard-
wood stock and fixed chokes) . . . . . . **NiB $225 Ex $175 Gd $90**
Model M-30F (w/hard-
wood stock and choke tubes) . . . . . . **NiB $250 Ex $180 Gd $95**
Model M-30F/IC (w/walnut
stock and choke tubes) . . . . **NiB $260 Ex $185 Gd $100**

MODEL M-30 RIOT PUMP
Double-action slide bar w/damascened bolt. Gauge: 12 only w/3-
inch chamber. Bbls: 18.5 and 20-inch w/IC bore. Five or 7-shot
magazine. Weight: 7 lbs, 2 ozs. Walnut finished hardwood stock.

(cont'd.) MODEL M-30 RIOT PUMP
Model M-30R6 (5-shot magazine). . . . . **NiB $175 Ex $150 Gd $98**
Model M-30R8 (7-shot magazine). . . . . **NiB $185 Ex $160 Gd $100**

MODEL M-30 SPECIAL COMBO
Simlar to Special Purpose Model except has detachable synthetic
stock that removes to convert to pistol-grip configuration.
Model M-30C (disc. 1995) . . . . **NiB $210 Ex $175 Gd $120**
Model M-30RP (disc. 1995) . . . . . **NiB $219 Ex $175 Gd $119**

MODEL M-30 SPECIAL PURPOSE
Double-action slide bar w/damascened bolt. Seven shot magazine.
Gauge: 12 only w/3-inch chamber. 20-inch bbl. w/cylinder choke.
Iron sights (DG Model) or venter handguard (SAS Model). Weight:
7.5 lbs. Walnut finished hardwood stock.
Model M-30DG (Deer Gun) . . . . **NiB $206 Ex $165 Gd $112**
Model M-30SAS (Special Air Services) . . . . **NiB $231 Ex $185 Gd $126**

ARMSPORT, INC. — Miami, Florida

1000 SERIES HAMMERLESS DOUBLES
Side-by-side w/engraved receiver, double triggers and extractors.
Gauges: 10 (3.5), 12, 20, .410- 3-inch chambers. Model 1033: 10 ga.,
32-inch bbl. Model 1050/51: 12 ga., 28-inch bbl., M/F choke. Model
1052/53: 20 ga., 26-inch bbl., I/M choke. Model 1054/57: .410 ga., 26-
inch bbl., I/M. Model 1055: 28 ga., Weight: 5.75 to 7.25 lbs. European
walnut buttstock and forend. Made in Italy. Importation disc. 1993.
Model 1033 (10 ga. disc. 1989) . . . . . . **NiB $721 Ex $577 Gd $392**
Model 1050 (12 ga. disc. 1993) . . . . . . **NiB $638 Ex $590 Gd $374**
Model 1051 (12 ga. disc. 1985) . . . . . **NiB $405 Ex $324 Gd $221**
Model 1052 (20 ga. disc. 1985) . . . . . **NiB $378 Ex $302 Gd $205**
Model 1053 (20 ga. disc. 1993) . . . . . **NiB $680 Ex $544 Gd $370**
Model 1054 (.410 disc. 1992). . . . . **NiB $756 Ex $605 Gd $411**
Model 1055 (28 ga. disc. 1992) . . . . . **NiB $446 Ex $357 Gd $243**
Model 1057 (.410 disc. 1985). . . . . **NiB $481 Ex $385 Gd $261**

MODEL 1125 SINGLE-SHOT SHOTGUN . . . . **NiB $90 Ex $75 Gd $50**
Bottom-opening lever. Gauges: 12, 20. Three inch chambers. Bead
front sight. Plain stock and forend. Imported 1987-89.

HUNT BUCKS
FEDERAL   PREMIUM
LOADED FOR BEAR.

Like a ghost out of nowhere, suddenly he's there and you're face to face with the biggest buck in the county. For a once in a lifetime shot like this, there's just no such thing as overkill. You need all the bullet you can get - one with the knockdown power to drop him right where he stands. That's the idea behind **Federal® Premium® Trophy Bonded Bear Claw**. With its fusion-bonded core, this bullet delivers 95% of its weight during penetration. The bullet jacket features a hard, solid, copper base tapering to a soft, copper nose section for controlled expansion. Trophy Bonded Bear Claw—the ultimate big game bullet.

FOR YOUR NEAREST FEDERAL DEALER AND TO CONTACT US VISIT WWW.FEDERALCARTRIDGE.COM.

NO EXCUSES

THE ULTIMATE
BIG GAME BULLET

Armsport 2700

Armsport 2741

Armsport 2900
Tri-Barrel

MODEL 2700 GOOSE GUN

Similar to the 2700 Standard Model except 10 ga. w/3.5-inch chambers. Double triggers w/28-inch bbl. choked IC/M or 32-inch bbl., F/F. 12mm wide vent rib. Weight: 9.5 lbs. Canada geese engraved on receiver. Antiqued silver-finished action. Checkered European walnut stock w/rubber recoil pad. Imported from Italy 1986 to 1993.

W/fixed chokes .... NiB $975 Ex $775 Gd $525
W/choke tubes .... NiB $1075 Ex $850 Gd $575

MODEL 2700 OVER/UNDER SERIES

Hammerless, takedown shotgun w/engraved receiver. Selective single or double triggers. Gauges: 10, 12, 20, 28 and .410. Bbl.: 26-or 28-inch w/fixed chokes or choke tubes. Weight: 8 lbs. Checkered European walnut buttstock and forend. Made in Italy. Importation disc. 1993.

Model 2701 12 ga. (disc. 1985) .... NiB $494 Ex $395 Gd $269
Model 2702 12 ga. .... NiB $531 Ex $425 Gd $289
Model 2703 20 ga. (disc. 1985) .... NiB $519 Ex $415 Gd $282
Model 2704 20 ga. .... NiB $563 Ex $450 Gd $306
Model 2705 (.410, DT, fixed chokes) ..... NiB $656 Ex $525 Gd $357
Model 2730/31 (Boss-style action,
SST Choke tubes) .... NiB $744 Ex $595 Gd $405
Model 2733/35 (Boss-style
action, extractors)..................... NiB $688 Ex $550 Gd $374
Model 2741 (Boss-style
action, ejectors) .... NiB $594 Ex $475 Gd $323
Model 2742 Sporting Clays
(12 ga./choke tubes)................. NiB $719 Ex $575 Gd $391
Model 2744 Sporting Clays
(20 ga./choke tubes)................. NiB $731 Ex $585 Gd $398
Model 2750 Sporting Clays
(12 ga./sideplates)................. NiB $781 Ex $625 Gd $425
Model 2751 Sporting Clays
(20 ga./sideplates)................. NiB $813 Ex $650 Gd $442

MODEL 2755 SLIDE-ACTION SHOTGUN

Gauge: 12 w/3-inch chamber. Tubular magazine. Bbls.: 28- or 30-inch w/fixed choke or choke tubes. Weight: 7 lbs. European walnut stock. Made in Italy 1986-87.

Standard model, fixed choke...... NiB $325 Ex $275 Gd $170
Standard model, choke tubes ..... NiB $500 Ex $390 Gd $270
Police model, 20-inch bbl......... NiB $295 Ex $250 Gd $160

MODEL 2900 TRI-BARREL (TRILLING) SHOTGUN

Boxlock. Double triggers w/top-tang bbl. selector. Extractors. Gauge: 12; 3-inch chambers. Bbls.: 28-inch (IC, M and F). Weight: 7.75 lbs. Checkered European walnut stock and forearm. Engraved silver receiver. Imported 1986-87 and 1990-93.

Model 2900 (fixed chokes) .... NiB $2031 Ex $1625 Gd $1105
Model 2900 (choke tubes)..... NiB $2744 Ex $2195 Gd $1493
Deluxe grades, add $500

ASTRA SHOTGUNS — Guernica, Spain Manufactured by Unceta y Compania

MODEL 650 O/U SHOTGUN

Hammerless, takedown w/double triggers. 12 ga. w/.75-inch chambers. Bbls.: 28-inch (M/F or SK/SK); 30-inch (M/F). Weight: 6.75 lbs. Checkered European walnut buttstock and forend.

W/extractors .... NiB $550 Ex $425 Gd $300
W/ejectors .... NiB $675 Ex $540 Gd $350

MODEL 750 O/U SHOTGUN

Similar to the Model 650 except w/selective single trigger and ejectors. Made in field, skeet and trap configurations since 1980.

Field model w/extractors........ NiB $625 Ex $500 Gd $340
Field model w/ejectors .... NiB $744 Ex $595 Gd $405
Trap or Skeet................. NiB $869 Ex $695 Gd $473

AYA (Aguirre Y Aranzabal) — Eibar, Spain (Previously Mfd. by Diarm, *Imported by Armes De Chasse, Hertford, NC*

MODEL 1 HAMMERLESS DOUBLE

A Holland & Holland sidelock similar to the Model 2 except in 12 and 20 ga. only, w/special engraving and exhibition-grade wood. Weight: 5-8 lbs., depending on ga. Imported by Diarm until 1987, since 1992 by Armes de Chasse.

Model 1 Standard .... NiB $6275 Ex $2995 Gd $1800
Model 1 Deluxe............. NiB $7700 Ex $3500 Gd $2000
Extra set of bbls., add $2550

SHOTGUNS

AyA Model 53E

AyA Model 76

AyA Model 117

MODEL 2 HAMMERLESS DOUBLE
Sidelock action w/selective single or double triggers automatic ejectors and safety. Gauges: 12, 20, 28, (2.75-inch chambers); .410 (3-inch chambers). Bbls.: 26- or 28-inch w/various fixed choke combinations. Weight: 7 lbs. (12 ga.). English-style straight walnut butt-stock and splinter forend. Imported by Diarm until 1987, since 1992 by Armes de Chasse.

12 or 20 ga. w/double triggers ..... NiB $2895 Ex $1450 Gd $1100
12 or 20 ga. w/single trigger .... NiB $2950 Ex $2250 Gd $1195
28 or .410 ga. w/double triggers.... NiB $2975 Ex $2255 Gd $1225
28 or .410 ga. w/single trigger ..... NiB $3000 Ex $2295 Gd $1225
Extra set of bbls., add $1325

MODEL 4
HAMMERLESS DOUBLE
Lightweight Anson & Deely boxlock, scalloped frame. Gauges: 12, 16, 20, 28, and .410. Bbls.: 25- to 28-inch w/concave rib. Importation disc. 1987 and resumed in 1992 by Armes de Chasse.
12 ga. .... NiB $1150 Ex $1100 Gd $500
16 ga. (early importation) .... NiB $594 Ex $475 Gd $323
20 ga. .... NiB $850 Ex $675 Gd $450
28 ga. .... NiB $975 Ex $750 Gd $425
.410 ga. .... NiB $980 Ex $750 Gd $450
Deluxe grades, add $500

MODEL 37 SUPER
O/U SHOTGUN .... NiB $3244 Ex $2595 Gd $1765
Sidelock. automatic ejectors. Selective single trigger. Made in all gauges, bbl. lengths and chokes. Vent rib bbls. Elaborately engraved. Checkered stock (w/straight or pistol grip) and forend. Disc. 1995.

MODEL 37 SUPER A
O/U SHOTGUN .... NiB $5744 Ex $4595 Gd $3125
Similar to the Standard Model 37 Super except has nickel steel frame and is fitted w/detachable sidelocks engraved w/game scenes. Importation disc. 1987 and resumed 1992 by Armes de Chasse.

MODEL 53E. .... NiB $2244 Ex $1795 Gd $1221
Same general specifications as Model 117 except more elaborate engraving and select figured wood. Importation disc. 1987 and resumed 1992 by Armes de Chasse.

MODEL 56 HAMMERLESS DOUBLE
Pigeon weight Holland & Holland sidelock w/Purdey-style third lug and sideclips. Gauges: 12, 16, 20. Receiver has fine-line scroll and rosette engraving; gold-plated locks. Importation disc. 1987 and resumed 1992 by Armes de Chasse.
12 ga. .... NiB $7100 Ex $3350 Gd $2800
16 ga. (early importation) ..... NiB $6500 Ex $2250 Gd $1530
20 ga. (early importation) ..... NiB $7250 Ex $3475 Gd $2100

MODEL 76 HAMMERLESS DOUBLE. . . NiB $688 Ex $550 Gd $374
Anson & Deeley boxlock. Auto ejectors. Selective single trigger. Gauges: 12, 20 (3-inch). Bbls.: 26-, 28-, 30-inch (latter in 12 ga. only), any standard choke combination. Checkered pistol-grip stock/beavertail forend. Disc.

MODEL 76—.410 GA.. .... NiB $813 Ex $650 Gd $442
Same general specifications as 12 and 20 ga. Model 76 except chambered for 3-inch shells in .410, has extractors, double triggers, 26-inch bbls. only, English-style stock w/straight grip and small forend. Disc.

MODEL 117 HAMMERLESS DOUBLE..... NiB $906 Ex $725 Gd $493
Holland & Holland-type sidelocks, hand-detachable. Engraved action. Automatic ejectors. Selective single trigger. Gauges: 12, 20 (3-inch). Bbls.: 26-, 27-, 28-, 30-inch; 27- and 30-inch in 12 ga. only; any standard choke combination. Checkered pistol-grip stock and beavertail forend of select walnut. Manufactured in 1985.

BOLERO .... NiB $475 Ex $390 Gd $275
Same general specifications as Matador except non-selective single trigger and extractors. Gauges: 12 16, 20, 20 Magnum (3-inch), .410 (3-inch). Note: This model, prior to 1956, was designated F. I. Model 400 by the importer. Made 1955-63.

CONTENTO OVER/UNDER SHOTGUN
Boxlock w/Woodward side lugs and double internal bolts. Gauge: 12 (2.75-inch chambers). Bbls.: 26-, 28-inch field; 30-, 32-inch trap; fixed chokes as required or screw-in choke tubes. Hand-checkered European walnut stock and forend. Single selective trigger and automatic ejectors.
M.K.2. .... NiB $906 Ex $725 Gd $493
M.K.3. .... NiB $1575 Ex $1260 Gd $857
W/Interchangeable single bbl., add.................... $400

AyA Matador II

AyA Model XXV Boxlock

MATADOR
HAMMERLESS DOUBLE . . . . **NiB $469 Ex $375 Gd $255**
Anson & Deeley boxlock. Selective automatic ejectors. Selective single trigger. Gauges: 12, 16, 20, 20 Magnum (3-inch). Bbls.: 26-, 28-, 30-inch; any standard choke combination. Weight: 6.5 to 7.5 lbs., depending on ga. and bbl. length. Checkered pistol-grip stock and beavertail forend. Note: This model, prior to 1956, was designated F. I. Model 400E by the U.S. importer, Firearms Int'l. Corp. of Washington, D.C. Made 1955-63.

MATADOR II . . . . **NiB $531 Ex $425 Gd $289**
Improved version of Matador w/same general specifications except has vent-rib bbls. Made 1964-69.

MATADOR III . . . . **NiB $781 Ex $625 Gd $425**
Same general specifications as AyA Matador II. Made 1970-85.

MODEL XXV BOXLOCK
Anson & Deeley boxlock w/double locking lugs. Gauges: 12 and 20. 25-inch chopper lump, satin blued bbls. w/Churchill rib. Weight: 5 to 7 lbs. Double triggers. Automatic safety and ejectors. Color-casehardened receiver w/Continental-style scroll and floral engraving. European walnut stock. Imported 1979-86 and 1991 to date.
12 or 20 ga. . . . . **NiB $2500 Ex $1395 Gd $800**
Extra set of bbls., add **$1050**

MODEL XXV SIDELOCK
Holland & Holland-type sidelock. Gauges: 12, 20, 28 and .410; 25-, 26-, 27- 28-, 29-, and 32-inch bbls. Chopper lump, satin blued bbls. w/Churchill rib. Weight: 5 to 7 lbs. Double triggers standard or selective or non-selective single trigger optional. Automatic safety and ejectors. Cocking indicators. Color-casehardened or coin-silver-finished receiver w/Continental-style scroll and floral engraving. Select European walnut stock w/hand-cut checkering and oil finish. Imported 1979-86 and 1991 to date.
12 or 20 ga. . . . . **NiB $3600 Ex $1750 Gd $995**
28 ga. (disc. 1997) . . . . **NiB $2193 Ex $1754 Gd $1193**
.410 ga. (disc. 1997) . . . . **NiB $2516 Ex $2012 Gd $1368**
Single trigger, add **$75**
Single selective trigger, add **$120**
Extra set of bbls., add **$1700**

BAIKAL SHOTGUNS — Izhevsk and Tula, Russia

MODEL IJ-18M SINGLE SHOT . . . . **NiB $63 Ex $50 Gd $34**
Hammerless w/cocking indicator. Automatic ejector. Manual safety.

(cont'd.) **MODEL IJ**
Gauges: 12 , 20, 16 w/2.75-inch chamber or .410 w/3-inch chamber. Bbls.: 26-, 28-inch w/fixed chokes (IC, M, F). Weight: 5.5 to 6 lbs. Made in Russia.

MODEL IJ-27 FIELD O/U . . . . **NiB $350 Ex $275 Gd $190**
Boxlock. Double triggers w/extractors. 12 ga.; 2.75-inch chambers. Bbls.: 26-inch, IC/M; 28-inch, M/F w/fixed chokes. Weight: 6.75 lbs. Made in Russia.

MODEL IJ-43 FIELD SIDE-BY-SIDE
Side-by-side; boxlock. Double triggers; extractors. 12 or 20 ga. w/2.75-inch chambers. Bbls: 20-inch cylinder bbl and 26-or 28-inch modified full bbl. Weight: 6.75 to 7 lbs. Checkered walnut stock, forend. Blued, engraved receiver. Imported 1994-96.
Model IJ-43 Field w/20-inch bbls . . . . . **NiB $231 Ex $185 Gd $126**
Model IJ-43 Field
w/26- or 28-inch bbls . . . . **NiB $206 Ex $165 Gd $112**

IZH-43 SERIES SIDE-BY-SIDE
Boxlock. Gauges: 12, 16, 20 or .410 w/2.75- or 3-inch chambers. Bbls.: 20-, 24-, 26- or 28-inch w/fixed chokes or choke tubes. Single selective or double triggers. Weight: 6.75 lbs. Checkered hardwood (standard on Hunter II Model) or walnut stock and forend (standard on Hunter Model). Blued, engraved receiver. Imported 1994 to date.
Model IZH-43Hunter
(12 ga. w/walnut stock) . . . . **NiB $330 Ex $285 Gd $130**
Model IZH-43 Hunter
(20, 16 or .410 ga.) . . . . **NiB $331 Ex $265 Gd $180**
Model IZH-43 Hunter II
(12 ga. w/external hammers) . . . . . **NiB $344 Ex $275 Gd $187**
Model IZH-43 Hunter II
(12 ga. hammerless) . . . . **NiB $219 Ex $175 Gd $119**
Model IZH-43 Hunter II
(20, 16 or .410 ga.) . . . . **NiB $231 Ex $185 Gd $126**
Hunter II w/walnut stock, add **$35**
Hunter II w/single selective trigger, add **$45**

MODEL IJ-27 O/U
Boxlock. Single selective trigger w/automatic ejectors or double triggers w/extractors. Gauges: 12 or 20 w/2.75-inch chambers. Bbls.: 26-inch or 28-inch w/fixed chokes. Weight: 7 lbs. Checkered European hardwood stock and forearm. Made in Russia.
Model IJ-27 (w/double
triggers and extractors.) . . . . **NiB $330 Ex $275 Gd $130**
Model IJ-27
(single selective
trigger and ejectors) . . . . **NiB $350 Ex $290 Gd $150**

SHOTGUNS

Baker Paragon
Expert and Deluxe Grades

Baker
Black Beauty Special

BAKER SHOTGUNS — Batavia, New York
Made 1903-1933 by Baker Gun Company

BATAVIA LEADER HAMMERLESS DOUBLE
Sidelock. Plain extractors or automatic ejectors. Double triggers.
Gauges: 12, 16, 20. Bbls.: 26- to 32-inch; any standard boring.
Weight: About 7.75 lbs. (12 ga. w/30-inch bbls.). Checkered pistol-
grip stock and forearm.
W/plain extractors . . . . NiB $795 Ex $350 Gd $250
W/automatic ejectors . . . . NiB $825 Ex $425 Gd $250

BATAVIA EJECTOR . . . . NiB $1050 Ex $795 Gd $540
Same general specifications as the Batavia Leader except higher
quality and finer finish throughout; has Damascus or homotensile
steel bbls., checkered pistol-grip stock and forearm of select walnut;
automatic ejectors standard; 12 and 16 ga. only. Deduct 60% for
Damascus bbls.

BATAVIA SPECIAL . . . . NiB $500 Ex $300 Gd $200
Same general specifications as the Batavia Leader except 12 and 16
ga. only; extractors, homotensile steel bbls.

BLACK BEAUTY
Same general specifications as the Batavia Leader except higher
quality and finer finish throughout; has line engraving, special steel
bbls., select walnut stock w/straight, full or half-pistol-grip.
Black Beauty w/plain extractors . . . NiB $550 Ex $325 Gd $250
Black Beauty Special
w/plain extractors . . . . NiB $995 Ex $625 Gd $400
Black Beauty Special
w/automatic ejectors. . . . . NiB $1050 Ex $750 Gd $500

GRADE R
High-grade gun w/same general specifications as the Batavia Leader
except has fine Damascus or Krupp fluid steel bbls., engraving in line,
scroll and game scene designs, checkered stock and forearm of fancy
European walnut; 12 and 16 ga. only. Deduct 60% for Damascus bbls.
Non-ejector . . . . NiB $1350 Ex $980 Gd $650
W/automatic ejectors . . . . NiB $1350 Ex $980 Gd $650

GRADE S
Same general specifications as the Batavia Leader except higher
quality and finer finish throughout; has Flui-tempered steel bbls.,
line and scroll engraving, checkered stock w/half-pistol-grip and

(cont'd.) GRADE S
forearm of semi-fancy imported walnut; 10, 12 and 16 ga.
Non-ejector . . . . NiB $1050 Ex $750 Gd $500
W/automatic ejectors . . . . NiB $1350 Ex $980 Gd $650

PARAGON, EXPERT AND DELUXE GRADES
Made to order only, these are the higher grades of Baker hammerless sidelock double-bbl. shotguns. After 1909, the Paragon Grade,
as well as the Expert and Deluxe intro. that year, had a crossbolt in
addition to the regular Baker system taper wedge fastening. There
are early Paragon guns w/Damascus bbls. and some are non-ejector,
but this grade was also produced w/automatic ejectors and w/the
finest fluid steel bbls., in lengths to 34 inches, standard on Expert
and Deluxe guns.
Differences among the three models are in overall quality, finish,
engraving and grade of fancy figured walnut in the stock and forearm; Expert and Deluxe wood may be carved as well as checkered.
Choice of straight, full or half-pistol grip was offered. A single trigger was available in the two higher grades. The Paragon was available in 10 ga (Damascus bbls. only), and the other two models were
regularly produced in 12, 16 and 20 ga.
Paragon grade, non-ejector . . . . . NiB $1744 Ex $1395 Gd $949
Paragon grade,
Automatic ejectors . . . . NiB $1994 Ex $1595 Gd $1085
Expert grade . . . . NiB $2869 Ex $2295 Gd $1561
Deluxe grade . . . . NiB $4063 Ex $3250 Gd $2210
For single trigger, add $250

BELKNAP SHOTGUNS — Louisville, Kentucky

MODEL B-68 SINGLE-SHOT SHOTGUN . . NiB $119 Ex $95 Gd $65
Takedown. Visible hammer. Automatic ejector. Gauges: 12, 16, 20
and .410. Bbls.: 26-inch to 36-inch; F choke. Weight: 6 lbs. Plain
pistol-grip stock and forearm.

MODEL B-63 SINGLE-SHOT SHOTGUN . . . . NiB $106 Ex $85 Gd $58
Takedown. Visible hammer. Automatic ejector. Gauges: 12, 20 and
.410. Bbls.: 26- to 36-inch, F choke. Weight: Average 6 lbs. Plain
pistol-grip stock and forearm.

MODEL B-63E SINGLE-SHOT SHOTGUN . . . . NiB $106 Ex $85 Gd $58
Same general specifications as Model B-68 except has side lever
opening instead of top lever.

Benelli Executive Grade I

Benelli Executive Grade II

Benelli Executive Grade III

MODEL B-64 SLIDE-ACTION
SHOTGUN.............................NiB $219 Ex $175 Gd $119
Hammerless. Gauges: 12, 16, 20 and .410. Three shot tubular magazine. Various bbl. lengths and chokes from 26-inch to 30-inch. Weight: 6.25 to 7.5 lbs. Walnut-finished hardwood stock.

MODEL B-65C AUTOLOADING
SHOTGUN ....NiB $356 Ex $285 Gd $194
Browning-type lightweight alloy receiver. 12 ga. only. Four shot tubular magazine. Bbl.: plain, 28-inch. Weight: About 8.25 lbs. Disc. 1949.

BENELLI SHOTGUNS — Urbino, Italy
Imported by Benelli USA, Accokeek, MD

MODEL 121 M1 MILITARY/POLICE
AUTOLOADING SHOTGUN ....NiB $450 Ex $385 Gd $250
Gauge: 12. Seven shot magazine. 19.75-inch bbl. 39.75 inches overall. Cylinder choke, 2.75-inch chamber. Weight: 7.4 lbs. Matte black finish and European hardwood stock. Post front sight, fixed buckhorn rear sight. Imported in 1985.

BLACK EAGLE AUTOLOADING SHOTGUN
Two-piece aluminum and steel receiver. Ga: 12; 3-inch chamber. Four shot magazine. Screw-in choke tubes (SK, IC, M, IM, F). Bbls.: Ventilated rib; 21, 24, 26 or 28 inches w/bead front sight; 24-inch rifled slug. 42.5 to 49.5 inches overall. Weight: 7.25 lbs. (28-inch bbl.). Matte black lower receiver w/blued upper receiver and bbl. Checkered walnut stock w/high-gloss finish and drop adjustment. Imported from 1989-90 and 1997-98.
Limited edition.......................NiB $1750 Ex $1500 Gd $1000
Competition model ....NiB $1025 Ex $790 Gd $450
Slug model (disc. 1992) ....NiB $725 Ex $500 Gd $350
Standard model (disc. 1992) ....NiB $825 Ex $650 Gd $390

BLACK EAGLE EXECUTIVE
Custom Black Eagle Series. Montefeltro-style rotating bolt w/three locking lugs. All-steel lower receiver engraved, gold inlay by Bottega Incisione di Cesare Giovanelli. 12 ga. only. 21-, 24-, 26-, or 28-inch vent-rib bbl. w/5 screw-in choke tubes (Type I) or fixed chokes. Custom deluxe walnut stock and forend. Built to customer specifications on special order.

(cont'd.) BLACK EAGLE EXECUTIVE
Executive Grade I ....NiB $3744 Ex $2995 Gd $2037
Executive Grade II...........NiB $4063 Ex $3250 Gd $2210
Executive Grade III ....NiB $4781 Ex $3825 Gd $2601

LEGACY AUTOLOADING SHOTGUN
Gauges: 12 and 20 ga. w/3-inch chambers. 24- 26- or 28-inch bbl. 47.63 to 49.62 inches overall. Weight: 5.8 to 7.5 lbs. Four shot magazine. Five screw-in choke tubes. Lower alloy receiver and upper steel reciever cover. Features Benelli's inertia recoil operating system. Imported 1998 to date. See illustration next page.
Legacy model ....NiB $1125 Ex $900 Gd $750
Legacy model Limited edition ...NiB $1700 Ex $1425 Gd $850

M1 SUPER 90
AUTO-LOADING SHOTGUN .....NiB $800 Ex $675 Gd $400
Gauge: 12. 7-shot magazine. Cylinder choke. 19.75-inch bbl. 39.75 inches overall. Weight: 7 lbs., 4 oz. to 7 lbs., 10 oz. Matte black finish. Stock and forend made of fiberglass-reinforced polymer. Sights: Post front, fixed buckhorn rear, drift adj. Introduced 1985; when the model line expanded in 1989, this configuration was discontinued.

M1 SUPER 90 DEFENSE AUTOLOADER......NiB $925 Ex $725 Gd $375
Same general specifications as Model Super 90 except w/pistol-grip stock. Available w/Ghost-Ring sight option. Imported 1986-98.

M1 SUPER 90
ENTRY AUTOLOADER. ....NiB $800 Ex $675 Gd $350
Same gen. specifications as Model Super 90 except w/5-shot magazine. 14-inch bbl. 35.5 inches overall. Weight: 6.5 lbs. Standard or pistol-grip stock. Imported 1992 to date. *Special permit required for under 18 inch bbl. firearms.*

M1 SUPER 90 FIELD
Inertia-recoil semiautomatic shotgun. Gauge: 12; 3-inch chamber. Three shot magazine. Bbl.: 21, 24, 26 or 28 inches. 42.5 to 49.5 inches overall. Choke: SK, IC, M, IM, F. Matte receiver. Standard polymer stock or satin walnut (26- or 28-inch bbl. only). Bead front sight. Imported from 1990 to date.
W/Realtree camo ....NiB $700 Ex $575 Gd $350
W/polymer stock ....NiB $590 Ex $425 Gd $300
W/walnut stock ....NiB $625 Ex $450 Gd $325

SHOTGUNS

Benelli Legacy
Limited Edition (Only 250 Made)

12 GA·LEGACY·Limited Edition 1 OF 250

Benelli M1 – Super 90

Benelli M1 – Super 90 w/Pistol Grip

M1 SUPER 90 SLUG AUTOLOADER
Same general specifications as M1 Super 90 Field except w/5-shot magazine. 18.5-inch bbl. Cylinder bore. 39.75 inches overall. Weight: 6.5 lbs. Polymer standard stock. Rifle or Ghost-Ring sights. Imported 1986-98.

W/rifle sights . . . . NiB $650 Ex $500 Gd $400
W/ghost-ring sights . . . . NiB $700 Ex $525 Gd $400
W/Realtree camo finish, add $100

M1 SUPER 90 SPORTING
SPECIAL AUTOLOADER . . . . NiB $750 Ex $650 Gd $375
Same general specifications as M1 Super 90 Field except w/18.5-inch bbl. 39.75 inches overall. Weight: 6.5 lbs. Ghost-ring sights. Polymer stock. Imported 1994-98.

M1 SUPER 90 TACTICAL AUTOLOADER
Same general specifications as M1 Super 90 Field except w/18.5-inch bbl. Five shot magazine. IC, M, or F choke. 39.75 inches overall. Weight: 6.5 lbs. Rifle or Ghost-Ring sights. Polymer pistol-grip or standard stock. Imported1994 to date.

W/rifle sights . . . . NiB $750 Ex $650 Gd $375
W/ghost-ring sights . . . . NiB $794 Ex $645 Gd $455
W/pistol-grip stock, add $25

M3 SUPER 90 PUMP/AUTOLOADER
Inertia-recoil semiautomatic and/or pump action. Gauge: 12. Seven shot magazine. Cylinder choke. 19.75-inch bbl. 41 inches overall (31 inches folded). Weight: 7 to 7.5 lbs. Matte black finish. Stock:

stan-
(cont'd.) M3 SUPER 90 PUMP/AUTOLOADER
dard synthetic, pistol-grip or folding tubular steel. Standard rifle or Ghost-Ring sights. Imported 1989 to date. Caution: Increasing the magazine capacity to more than 5 rounds in M3 shotguns w/pistol-grip stocks violates provisions of the 1994 Crime Bill. This model may be used legally only by the military and law-enforcement agencies.

Standard model . . . . NiB $820 Ex $680 Gd $395
Pistol-grip model . . . . NiB $938 Ex $750 Gd $510
W/folding stock . . . . NiB $994 Ex $795 Gd $541
W/laser sight . . . . NiB $1244 Ex $995 Gd $677
For ghost ring sights, add $50

MONTEFELTRO/SUPER 90 SEMIAUTOMATIC
Gauges: 12 or 20 gauge w/3-inch chamber. 21- 24- 26- or 28-inch bbl. 43.7 to 49.5 inches overall. Weight: 5.3 to 7.5 lbs. 4-shot magazine. Five screw-in choke tubes (C, IC, M, IM, F). High gloss or satin walnut or Realtree Camo stock. Blued metal finish. Imported 1987 to date.

Standard Hunter model . . . . NiB $820 Ex $680 Gd $395
Slug model (disc. 1992). . . . . NiB $650 Ex $500 Gd $300
Turkey model . . . . NiB $650 Ex $575 Gd $300
Uplander model . . . . NiB $650 Ex $500 Gd $300
Limited Edition (1995-96) . . . . NiB $1781 Ex $1425 Gd $96
20 ga. w/Realtree camo . . . . NiB $688 Ex $550 Gd $374
20 ga. Youth Model w/short stock, add. $40

Benelli Montefeltro
Super 90 Left-Handed Model

Benelli Montefeltro
Realtree Camo

Beretta Model 57E

Beretta
Model 409PB

SL 121V SEMIAUTO (SL-80 SERIES) . . . NiB $525 Ex $300 Gd $250
Recoil-operated semiautomaticw/split receiver design. Gauge: 12.
Five shot capacity. 26-, 28- or 30-inch ventilated rib bbl. (26-inch
choked M, IM, IC, 28-inch, F, M, IM; 30-inch, F choke - Mag.).
Straight walnut stock w/hand-checkered pistol grip and forend.
Importation disc. in 1985.

**SL 121V SLUG SHOTGUN
(SL-80 SERIES)** . . . . NiB $535 Ex $325 Gd $260
Same general specifications as Benelli SL 121V except designed for
rifled slugs and equipped w/rifle sights. Disc. in 1985.

SL 123V SEMIAUTO (SL-80 SERIES) . . . NiB $450 Ex $360 Gd $245
Gauge: 12. 26- and 28-inch bbls. 26-inch choked IM, M, IC; 28-
inch choked F, IM, M. Disc. in 1985.

**SL 201 SEMIAUTOMATIC
(SL-80 SERIES)** . . . . NiB $400 Ex $320 Gd $218
Gauge: 20. 26-inch bbl. Mod. choke. Weight: 5 lbs., 10 oz.
Ventilated rib. Disc. in 1985.

SPORT AUTOLOADING SHOTGUN . . NiB $938 Ex $750 Gd $510
Similar to the Black Eagle Competition model except has one-piece
matte- finished alloy receiver w/inscribed red Benelli logo. 26 or 28
inches bbl. w/2 inchangable carbon fiber vent ribs. Oil-finished
checkered walnut stock w/adjustable buttpad and buttstock.
Imported 1997 to date.

SUPER BLACK EAGLE AUTOLOADING SHOTGUN
Same general specifications as Black Eagle except w/3.5-inch cham-
ber that accepts 2.75-, 3- and 3.5-inch shells. Two shot magazine
(3.5-inch), 3-shot magazine (2.75- or 3-inch). High-gloss, satin fin-
ish or camo stock. Realtree camo, matte black or blued metal finish.
Imported 1991 to date.
Standard model . . . . NiB $994 Ex $795 Gd $541
Realtree camo . . . . NiB $1119 Ex $895 Gd $609
Custom slug model . . . . NiB $938 Ex $750 Gd $510
Limited edition . . . . NiB $1781 Ex $1425 Gd $969

(cont'd.) **SUPER BLACK EAGLE AUTOLOADING SHOTGUN**
W/wood stock, add $25
Left-hand model, add. $30

BERETTA USA CORP. — Accokeek, Maryland
Mfd. by Fabbrica D'Armi Pietro Beretta S.p.A.
in Gardone Val Trompia (Brescia), Italy
Imported by Beretta USA (Previously by Garcia Corp.)

MODEL 57E O/U
Same general specifications as Golden Snipe, but higher quality
throughout. Imported 1955-67.
W/non-selective single trigger . . . . NiB $995 Ex $875 Gd $475
W/selective single trigger . . . . NiB $1031 Ex $825 Gd $561

**MODEL 409PB
HAMMERLESS DOUBLE** . . . . NiB $950 Ex $650 Gd $395
Boxlock. Double triggers. Plain extractors. Gauges: 12, 16, 20, 28.
Bbls.: 27.5-, 28.5- and 30-inch, IC/M choke or M/F choke. Weight:
from 5.5 to 7.75 lbs., depending on ga. and bbl. length. Straight or
pistol-grip stock and beavertail forearm, checkered. Imported
1934-64.

MODEL 410E
Same general specifications as Model 409PB except has automatic
ejectors and is of higher quality throughout. Imported 1934-64.
Model 410E (12 ga.) . . . . NiB $1250 Ex $1100 Gd $700
Model 410E (20 ga.) . . . . NiB $1719 Ex $1375 Gd $935
Model 410E (28 ga.) . . . . NiB $4375 Ex $3500 Gd $2380

MODEL 410 10-GA. MAGNUM . . NiB $1188 Ex $950 Gd $646
Same as Model 410E except heavier construction. Plain extractors.
Double triggers. 10-ga. Magnum, 3.5-inch chambers. 32-inch bbls.,
both F choke. Weight: about 10 lbs. Checkered pistol-grip stock and
forearm, recoil pad. Imported 1934-84.

SHOTGUNS

Beretta Model 682 Over/Under Sporting

Beretta Model 682 Over/Under Trap

Beretta Model 610E

MODEL 411E
Same general specifications as Model 409PB except has sideplates, automatic ejectors and is of higher quality throughout. Imported 1934-64.

Model 411E (12 ga.) . . . . NiB $1869 Ex $1495 Gd $1017
Model 411E (20 ga.) . . . . NiB $2438 Ex $1950 Gd $1326
Model 411E (28 ga.) . . . . NiB $4494 Ex $3595 Gd $2445

MODEL 424 HAMMERLESS
DOUBLE . . . . NiB $1369 Ex $1095 Gd $745
Boxlock. Light border engraving. Plain extractors. Gauges: 12, 20; chambers 2.75-inch in former, 3-inch in latter. Bbls.: 28-inch M/F choke, 26-inch IC/M choke. Weight: 5 lbs. 14 oz. to 6 lbs. 10 oz., depending on ga. and bbl. length. English-style straight-grip stock and forearm, checkered. Imported 1977-84.

MODEL 426E. . . . . NiB $1850 Ex $1400 Gd $975
Same as Model 424 except action body is finely engraved, silver pigeon inlaid in top lever; has selective automatic ejectors and selective single trigger, stock and forearm of select European walnut. Imported 1977-84.

MODEL 450 SERIES HAMMERLESS DOUBLES
Custom English-style sidelock. Single, non-selective trigger or double triggers. Manual safety. Selective automatic ejectors. Gauge: 12; 2.75- or 3-inch chambers. Bbls.: 26, 28 or 30 inches choked to customers' specifications. Weight: 6.75 lbs. Checkered high-grade walnut stock. Receiver w/coin-silver finish. Imported 1948 to date.

Model 450 EL (disc. 1982). . . . . NiB $7369 Ex $5895 Gd $4009
Model 450 EELL (disc. 1982). . . NiB $7813 Ex $6250 Gd $4250
Model 451 (disc. 1987). . . . . . . NiB $6369 Ex $5095 Gd $3465
Model 451 E (disc. 1989) . . . . . NiB $6994 Ex $5595 Gd $3805
Model 451 EL (disc. 1985) . . . . . . NiB $12,438 Ex $9950 Gd $6766
Model 451 EELL (disc. 1990) . . . NiB $13,656 Ex $10,925 Gd $7429
Model 452 (Intro. 1990) . . . . . NiB $21,875 Ex $17,500 Gd $11,900
Model 452 EELL (intro. 1992) . . NiB $29,063 Ex $23,250 Gd $15,810
Extra set of bbls., add 30%

MODEL 470 SERIES HAMMERLESS DOUBLE
Gauge: 12 and 20 ga. w/3-inch chambers. 26- or 28-inch bbl. Weight: 5.9 to 6.5 lbs. Low profile, improved box lock action w/single selective trigger. Selected walnut, checkered stock and forend. Metal front bead sight. Scroll-engraved receiver w/gold inlay and silver chrome finish. Imported 1999 to date.

(cont'd.) MODEL 470 SERIES HAMMERLESS DOUBLE
Model 470 Silver Hawk 12 ga.. . . . . . NiB $2313 Ex $1850 Gd $1258
Model 470 Silver Hawk 20 ga.. . . . . . NiB $2494 Ex $1995 Gd $1357
Model 470 EL Silver Hawk 12 ga. . . . NiB $3869 Ex $3095 Gd $2105
Model 470 EL Silver Hawk 20 ga. . . . NiB $4031 Ex $3225 Gd $2193
Model 470 EELL (Jubilee II) 12 ga. . . . NiB $7619 Ex $6095 Gd $4145
Model 470 EELL (Jubilee II) 20 ga. . . . NiB $8063 Ex $6450 Gd $4386
Extra set of bbls., add. 30%

MODEL 625 S/S HAMMERLESS DOUBLE
Boxlock. Gauges: 12 or 20. Bbls.: 26-, 28- or 30-inch w/fixed choke combinations. Single selective or double triggers w/extractors. Checkered English-style buttstock and forend. Imported 1984-87.

W/double triggers . . . . NiB $906 Ex $725 Gd $493
W/single selective trigger . . . . NiB $1063 Ex $850 Gd $578
20 ga., add. $150

MODEL 626 S/S HAMMERLESS DOUBLE
Field Grade side-by-side. Boxlock action w/single selective trigger, extractors and automatic safety. Gauges: 12 (2.75-inch chambers); 20 (3-inch chambers). Bbls.: 26- or 28-inch w/Mobilchoke or various fixed-choke combinations. Weight: 6.75 lbs. (12 ga.). Bright chrome finish. Checkered European walnut buttstock and forend in straight English style. Imported 1985-94.

Model 626 Field (disc. 1988). . . . . NiB $1150 Ex $950 Gd $475
Model 626 Onyx . . . . NiB $1275 Ex $1025 Gd $725
Model 626 Onyx (3.5-inch
Magnum, disc. 1993). . . . . NiB $1369 Ex $1095 Gd $745
20 ga., add. $200

MODEL 627 S/S HAMMERLESS DOUBLE
Same as Model 626 S/S except w/engraved sideplates and pistol-grip or straight English-style stock. Imported 1985-94.

Model 627 EL Field . . . . NiB $2369 Ex $1895 Gd $1289
Model 627 EL Sport. . . . . NiB $2438 Ex $1950 Gd $1326
Model 627 EELL. . . . . NiB $4313 Ex $3450 Gd $2346

MODEL 682 O/U SHOTGUN
Hammerless takedown w/single selective trigger. Gauges: 12, 20, 28, .410. Bbls.: 26- to 34-inch w/fixed chokes or Mobilchoke tubes. Checkered European walnut buttstock/forend in various grades and configurations. Imported 1984 to date.

Model 682 Comp Skeet . . . . . . NiB $1869 Ex $1495 Gd $1017
Model 682 Comp Skeet Deluxe. . . . . NiB $2744 Ex $2195 Gd $1493

Beretta Model 687EL

Beretta Model 687EEL

(cont'd.) MODEL 682 O/U SHOTGUN

Mdl. 682 Comp Super Skeet . . . . NiB $2244 Ex $1795 Gd $1221
Mdl. 682 Comp Skeet 2-bbl.
set (disc. 1989) . . . . NiB $4619 Ex $3695 Gd $2513
Mdl. 682 Comp Skeet
4 bbl. Set (disc. 1996) . . . . NiB $5313 Ex $4250 Gd $2890
Mdl. 682 Sporting Continental . . . . NiB $1869 Ex $1495 Gd $1017
Mdl. 682 Sporting Combo . . . . NiB $2938 Ex $2350 Gd $1598
Mdl. 682 Sporting Gold . . . . NiB $1744 Ex $1395 Gd $949
Mdl. 682 Sporting Super Sport . . . . NiB $1906 Ex $1525 Gd $1037
Mdl. 682 Comp Trap Gold X . . . . NiB $1869 Ex $1495 Gd $1017
Mdl. 682 Comp Trap Top Sgle. (1986-95) . . . NiB $1813 Ex $1450 Gd $986
Mdl. 682 Comp Trap Live Pig. (1990-98) . . . NiB $2406 Ex $1925 Gd $1309
Mdl. 682 Comp Mono/ComboTrp. Gld. X . . NiB $2688 Ex $2150 Gd $1462
Mdl. 682 Comp Mono Trap (1985-88) . . . . . . NiB $1619 Ex $1295 Gd $881
Mdl. 682 Super Trap Gold X (1991-95) . . . . . NiB $1938 Ex $1550 Gd $1054
Mdl. 682 Sup. Trap
Combo Gld. X (1991-97) . . . . NiB $2744 Ex $2195 Gd $1493
Mdl. 682 Super Trap
Top Sgle. Gld. X (1991-95) . . . . NiB $1994 Ex $1595 Gd $1085
Mdl. 682 Sup. Trap Unsingle (1992-94) . . . . NiB $1869 Ex $1495 Gd $1017

MODEL 686 O/U SHOTGUN

Low-profile improved boxlock action. Single selective trigger. Selective automatic ejectors. Gauges: 12, 20, 28 w/3.5- 3- or 2.75-inch chambers, depending upon ga. Bbls.: 26-, 28-, 30-inch w/fixed chokes or Mobilchoke tubes. Weight: 5.75 to 7.5 lbs. Checkered American walnut stock and forearm of various qualities, depending upon model. Receiver finishes also vary, but all have blued bbls. Sideplates to simulate sidelock action on EL models. Imported 1988 to date.

Model 686 Field Onyx . . . . NiB $1285 Ex $955 Gd $550
Mdl. 686 (3.5-inch Mag., disc.
1993 & reintro.1996) . . . . NiB $1350 Ex $975 Gd $650
Model 686 EL Gold Perdiz (1992-97) . . . . NiB $1619 Ex $1295 Gd $881
Model 686 Essential (1994-96) . . . . NiB $894 Ex $715 Gd $486
Model 686 Silver Essential (1997-98) . . . . NiB $996 Ex $797 Gd $542
Model 686 Sil. Pig. Onyx (intro. 1996) . . . . NiB $1307 Ex $1045 Gd $710
Mdl. 686 Sil. Perdiz Onyx (disc. 1996) . . . . . . NiB $1271 Ex $1017 Gd $691
Model 686 Sil. Pig./Perdiz Onyx Combo . . . . . NiB $1821 Ex $1457 Gd $791
Model 686 L Silver Perdiz (disc. 1994) . . . . NiB $1031 Ex $825 Gd $561
Model 686 Skeet Silver Pigeon (1996-98) . . . . . NiB $1093 Ex $874 Gd $595
Model 686 Skeet Silver Perdiz (1994-96) . . . . NiB $1306 Ex $1045 Gd $710
Model 686 Skeet Sil. Pig./Perdiz Combo . . . . . NiB $1306 Ex $1045 Gd $710
Model 686 Sporting Special (1987-93) . . . . NiB $1505 Ex $1204 Gd $819
Model 686 Sporting English (1991-92) . . . . NiB $1581 Ex $1265 Gd $860
Model 686 Sporting Onyx
w/fixed chokes (1991-92) . . . . NiB $1505 Ex $1204 Gd $819
Model 686 Sporting Onyx
w/tubes (intro. 1992) . . . . NiB $1134 Ex $907 Gd $619
Mdl. 686 Sporting Onyx Gld. (disc. 1993) . . . NiB $1643 Ex $1314 Gd $894
Mdl. 686 Sporting Sil. Pig. (intro. 1996) . . . . . NiB $1340 Ex $1072 Gd $729
Model 686 Sporting Sil. Perdiz (1993-96) . . . . NiB $1306 Ex $1045 Gd $710

(cont'd.) MODEL 686 O/U SHOTGUN

Mdl. 686 Sporting Coll. Sport (1996-97) . . . . . NiB $996 Ex $797 Gd $542
Model 686 Sporting Combo . . . . NiB $2330 Ex $1864 Gd $1268
Model 686 Trap International (1994-95) . . . . . NiB $955 Ex $764 Gd $520
Model 686 Trap Silver Pigeon (intro. 1997) . . . NiB $1031 Ex $825 Gd $561
Model 686 Trap Top Mono (intro. 1998) . . . . NiB $1065 Ex $852 Gd $579
Model 686 Ultralight Onyx (intro. 1992) . . . NiB $1368 Ex $1094 Gd $744
Mdl. 686 Ultralight Del. Onyx (intro. 1998) . . . . NiB $1719 Ex $1375 Gd $935

MODEL 687 O/U SHOTGUN

Same as Model 686 except w/decorative sideplates and varying grades of engraving and game-scene motifs.

Model 687 L Onyx (disc. 1991) . . . . NiB $1271 Ex $1017 Gd $691
Model 687 L Onyx Gold Field (1988-89) . . NiB $1444 Ex $1155 Gd $785
Model 687 L Onyx Silver Pigeon . . . . NiB $1856 Ex $1485 Gd $1009
Model 687 EL Onyx (disc. 1990) . . . . NiB $2509 Ex $2007 Gd $1365
Model 687 EL Gold Pigeon . . . . NiB $2880 Ex $2304 Gd $1567
Model 687 EL Gold Pigeon Sm. Fr. . . . . . . NiB $2681 Ex $2145 Gd $1458
Mdl. 687 EL Gld. Pig. Sporting (Int. 1993) . . . . NiB $3980 Ex $3184 Gd $2165
Model 687 EELL Diamond Pigeon . . . . . . NiB $3980 Ex $3184 Gd $2165
Mdl. 687 EELL Diamond Pig. Skeet . . . . . . NiB $3843 Ex $3074 Gd $2091
Mdl. 687 EELL Diam. Pig. Sporting . . . . . . NiB $4056 Ex $3245 Gd $2206
Mdl. 687 EELL Diam. Pig. X Trap . . . . NiB $3540 Ex $2832 Gd $1926
Mdl. 687 EELL Diam. Pig. Mono Trap . . . . NiB $3644 Ex $2915 Gd $1982
Mdl. 687 EELL Diam. Pig. Trap Combo . . . NiB $4943 Ex $3954 Gd $2689
Model 687 EELL Field Combo . . . . NiB $4118 Ex $3294 Gd $2240
Model 687 EELL Skeet 4-bbl. set . . . . NiB $6806 Ex $5445 Gd $3702
Model 687 EELL Gallery Special . . . . NiB $6318 Ex $5054 Gd $3437
Model 687 EELL
Gallery Special Combo . . . . NiB $7631 Ex $6105 Gd $4151
Model 687 EELL Gallery Special pairs . NiB $15,125 Ex $12,100 Gd $8228
Model 687 Sporting English (1991-92) . . . NiB $1994 Ex $1595 Gd $1084
Mdl. 687 Sporting Sil. Pig. (intro. 1996) . . . NiB $1780 Ex $1424 Gd $969
Mdl. 687 Sporting Sil. Perdiz (1993-96) . . NiB $1856 Ex $1485 Gd $1009

MODEL 1200 SERIES SEMIAUTOLOADING SHOTGUN

Short recoil action. Gauge: 12; 2.75- or 3-inch chamber. Six shot magazine. 24-, 26- or 28-inch vent-rib bbl. w/fixed chokes or Mobilchoke tubes. Weight: 7.25 lbs. Matte black finish. Adj. technopolymer stock and forend. Imported 1988 to date.

Model 1200 w/fixed choke (disc. 1989) . . . . . . NiB $525 Ex $420 Gd $285
Model 1200 Riot (disc. 1989) . . . . NiB $538 Ex $431 Gd $293
Model 1201 w/Mobilchoke (disc. 1994) . . . . . . NiB $553 Ex $442 Gd $301
Model 1201 Riot . . . . NiB $594 Ex $476 Gd $323
W/Pistol-grip stock, add $72
W/Tritium sights, add $56

MODEL A-301 AUTOLOADING

SHOTGUN . . . . NiB $431 Ex $345 Gd $235
Field Gun. Gas-operated. Scroll-decorated receiver. Gauge: 12 or 20; 2.75-inch chamber in former, 3-inch in latter. Three shot magazine. Bbl.: Ventilated rib; 28-inch F or M choke, 26-inch IC. Weight: 6 lbs., 5 oz. – 6 lbs., 14 oz., depending on gauge and bbl. length. Checkered pistol-grip stock/forearm. Imported 1977-

SHOTGUNS

Beretta Model A-303

Beretta Model A-390 Field

Beretta Model AL-2

MODEL A-301 MAGNUM . . . . NiB $444 Ex $355 Gd $241
Same as Model A-301 Field Gun except chambered for 12 ga. Three inch Magnum shells, 30-inch F choke bbl. only, stock w/recoil pad. Weight: 7.25 lbs.

MODEL A-301 SKEET GUN . . . . . . NiB $469 Ex $375 Gd $255
Same as Model A-301 Field Gun except 26-inch bbl. SK choke only, skeet-style stock, gold-plated trigger.

MODEL A-301 SLUG GUN . . . . NiB $438 Ex $350 Gd $238
Same as Model A-301 Field Gun except has plain 22-inch bbl., slug choke, w/rifle sights. Weight: 6 lbs., 14 oz.

MODEL A-301 TRAP GUN . . . . NiB $469 Ex $375 Gd $255
Same as Model A-301 Field Gun except has 30-inch bbl. in F choke only, checkered Monte Carlo stock w/recoil pad, gold-plated trigger. Blued bbl. and receiver. Weight: 7 lbs., 10 oz. Imported 1978-82.

MODEL A-302 SEMIAUTOLOADING SHOTGUN
Similar to gas-operated Model 301. Hammerless, takedown shotgun w/tubular magazine and Mag-Action that handles both 2.75- and 3-inch Magnum shells. Gauge: 12 or 20; 2.75- or 3-inch Mag. chambers. Bbl.: Vent or plain; 22-inch/Slug (12 ga.); 26-inch/IC (12 or 20) 28-inch/M (20 ga.), 28-inch/Multi-choke (12 or 20 ga.) 30-inch/F (12 ga.). Weight: 6.5 lbs., 20 ga.; 7.25.lbs., 12 ga. Blued/ black finish. Checkered European walnut, pistol-grip stock and forend. Imported 1983 to c. 1987.
Standard model w/fixed choke . . . . NiB $444 Ex $355 Gd $241
Standard model w/multi-choke . . . . NiB $494 Ex $395 Gd $269

MODEL A-302 SUPER LUSSO . . NiB $2200 Ex $1975 Gd $1300
A custom A-302 in presentation grade w/hand-engraved receiver and custom select walnut stock.

MODEL A-303 SEMIAUTOLOADER
Similar to Model 302, except w/target specifications in Trap, Skeet and Youth configurations, and weighs 6.5 to 8 lbs. Imported 1983-96.
Field and Upland models . . . . NiB $523 Ex $493 Gd $456
Skeet and Trap (disc. 1994) . . . . . . NiB $648 Ex $518 Gd $352
Slug model (disc. 1992) . . . . NiB $711 Ex $568 Gd $386

(cont'd.) MODEL A-303 SEMIAUTOLOADER
Sporting Clays . . . . NiB $72 Ex $593 Gd $403
Super Skeet . . . . NiB $1086 Ex $868 Gd $591
Super Trap . . . . NiB $1031 Ex $825 Gd $561
Waterfowl/Turkey (disc. 1992) . . . . NiB $680 Ex $543 Gd $370
Mobil choke, add $50

MODEL A-303 YOUTH GUN . . . . . NiB $650 Ex $450 Gd $250
Locked-breech, gas-operated action. Ga: 12 and 20; 2-shot magazine. Bbls.: 24, 26, 28, 30 or 32-inches, vent rib. Weight: 7 lbs. (12 ga.), 6 lbs. (20 ga.). Crossbolt safety. Length of pull shortened to 12.5 inches. Imported 1988-96.

MODEL A-390 SEMIAUTOMATIC SHOTGUN
Gas-operated, self-regulating action designed to handle any size load. Gauges: 12 or 20 w/ 3-inch chamber. 3-shot magazine. Bbl.: 24, 26, 28 or 30 inches w/vent rib and Mobilchoke tubes. Weight: 7.5 lbs. Select walnut stock w/adj. comb. Blued or matte black finish. Imported 1992-96. Superseded by AL-390 series.
Standard model/Slug model . . . . . . NiB $544 Ex $435 Gd $296
Field model/Silver Mallard . . . . NiB $556 Ex $445 Gd $303
Deluxe model/Gold Mallard . . . . . . NiB $606 Ex $485 Gd $330
Turkey/Waterfowl model (matte finish) . . . NiB $569 Ex $455 Gd $309
For 20 ga., add $35

MODEL A-390 TARGET
Similar to the Model 390 Field except w/2.75-inch chamber. Skeet: 28-inch ported bbl. w/wide vent rib and fixed choke (SK). Trap: 30- or 32-inch w/Mobilchoke tubes. Weight: 7.5 lbs. Fully adj. buttstock. Imported from 1993-96.
Sport Trap model . . . . NiB $556 Ex $445 Gd $303
Sport Skeet model . . . . NiB $544 Ex $435 Gd $296
Sporting Clays model (unported) . . . NiB $563 Ex $450 Gd $306
Super Trap model (ported) . . . . NiB $744 Ex $595 Gd $405
Super Skeet model (ported) . . . . NiB $731 Ex $585 Gd $398
W/ported bbl., add $85
20 ga., add $35

MODEL AL-1 FIELD GUN . . . . NiB $431 Ex $345 Gd $235
Same as Model AL-2 gas-operated Field Gun except has bbl. w/o rib, no engraving on receiver. Imported 1971-73.

Beretta Model AL-391
Urika Gold Sporting

Beretta Model AL-391
Urika Gold Trap

MODEL AL-2 AUTOLOADING SHOTGUN

Field Gun. Gas-operated. Engraved receiver (1968 version, 12 ga. only, had no engraving). Gauge: 12 or 20. 2.75-inch chamber. Three shot magazine. Bbls.: Vent rib; 30-inch F choke, 28-inch F or M choke, 26-inch IC. Weight: 6.5 to 7.25 lbs, depending on ga. and bbl. length. Checkered pistol-grip stock and forearm. Imported 1968-75.

W/Plain receiver . . . . NiB $356 Ex $285 Gd $194
W/Engraved receiver . . . . NiB $494 Ex $395 Gd $269

MODEL AL-2 MAGNUM . . . . NiB $444 Ex $355 Gd $241

Same as Model AL-2 Field Gun except chambered for 12 ga. 3-inch Magnum shells; 30-inch F or 28-inch M choke bbl. only. Weight: About 8 lbs. Imported 1973-75.

MODEL AL-2 SKEET GUN . . . . NiB $419 Ex $335 Gd $228

Same as Model AL-2 Field Gun except has wide rib, 26-inch bbl. in SK choke only, checkered pistol-grip stock and beavertail forearm. Imported 1973-75.

MODEL AL-2 TRAP GUN . . . . NiB $406 Ex $325 Gd $221

Same as Model AL-2 Field Gun except has wide rib, 30 inch bbl. in F choke only, beavertail forearm. Monte Carlo stock w/recoil pad. Weight: About 7.75 lbs. Imported 1973-75.

MODEL AL-3

Similar to corresponding AL-2 models in design and general specifications. Imported 1975-76.
Field model . . . . NiB $419 Ex $335 Gd $228
Magnum model . . . . NiB $431 Ex $345 Gd $235
Skeet model . . . . NiB $438 Ex $350 Gd $238
Trap model . . . . NiB $394 Ex $315 Gd $214

MODEL AL-3 DELUXE TRAP GUN . . . . NiB $856 Ex $685 Gd $466

Same as standard Model AL-3 Trap Gun except has fully-engraved receiver, gold-plated trigger and safety, stock and forearm of premium-grade European walnut, gold monogram escutcheon inlaid in buttstock. Imported 1975-76.

AL390 FIELD SHOTGUN

Lightweight version of A-390 series. Gauges: 12 or 20 ga. 22- 24-, 26-, 28-, or 30-inch bbl., 41.7 to 47.6 inches overall. Weight: 6.4 to 7.5 lbs. Imported 1997 to date.
Mdl. AL390 Field/Sil. Mallard (12 or 20 ga.) . . . NiB $652 Ex $522 Gd $355
Mdl. AL390 Field/Sil. Mallard Yth. (20 ga.) . . . . NiB $660 Ex $528 Gd $358
Model AL390 Field/Slug (12 ga. only) . . . . NiB $637 Ex $510 Gd $346
Model AL390 Silver Mallard camouflage . . NiB $712 Ex $570 Gd $386
Model AL390 Silver Mallard synthetic . . . . NiB $667 Ex $534 Gd $363
Model AL390 Gold Mallard (12 or 20 ga.) . NiB $742 Ex $594 Gd $404
Model AL390 NWTF Spec. camouflage . . . NiB $892 Ex $714 Gd $486
Model AL390 NWTF Spec. synthetic . . . . . NiB $712 Ex $570 Gd $387

Mdl. AL390 NWTF Spec. Yth. . . . . NiB $760 Ex $425 Gd $270
AL390 SPORT SPORTING SHOTGUN
Similar to Model AL-390 Sport Skeet. Gauges: 12 or 20 ga., 28- or 30-inch bbls. Weight: 6.8 to 8 lbs. Imported 1997 to date.
Model AL390 Sport Sporting . . . . NiB $667 Ex $534 Gd $363
Model AL390 Sport Sporting Collection . . . . . . NiB $614 Ex $570 Gd $387
Mdl. AL390 Sport Sporting
Yth. (20 ga. only) . . . . NiB $637 Ex $510 Gd $346
Model AL390 Sport Gold Sporting . . . . NiB $892 Ex $714 Gd $486
Mdl. AL390 EELL Sport
Diamond Sporting. . . . . NiB $3292 Ex $2634 Gd $1791
W/Ported bbl., add $75

AL390 SPORT SKEET SHOTGUN
Gauges: 12 ga. only. 26- or 28-inch bbl. w/3-shot chamber. Weight: 7.6 to 8 lbs. Matte finish wood and metal. Imported 1997 to date.
Model AL390 Sport Skeet . . . . NiB $680 Ex $543 Gd $370
Mdl. AL390 Sport Super Skeet (Semi-Auto) . . . . NiB $930 Ex $743 Gd $506
W/ported bbl., add $95

BERETTA AL390 SPORT TRAP SHOTGUN
Gauges: 12 ga. only. 30- or 32-inch bbl. w/3-shot chamber. Weight: 7.8 to 8.25 lbs. Matte finish wood and metal. Black recoil rubber pad. Imported 1997 to date.
Model AL390 Sport Trap . . . . NiB $680 Ex $543 Gd $370
Model AL390 Sport Super Trap . . . . NiB $976 Ex $781 Gd $531
Multi-choke bbl. (30" only), add $40
Ported bbl., add $95

AL391 URIKA AUTOLOADING SHOTGUN
Gauge: 12 and 20 ga. w/3-inch chambers. 28- 30- or 32-inch bbl. Weight: 6.6 to 7.7 lbs. Self-compensating gas valve. Adjustable synthetic and walnut stocks w/ five interchangeable chokes. Imported 2000 to date.
Model AL391 Urika. . . . . NiB $784 Ex $627 Gd $426
Model AL391 Urika synthetic . . . . NiB $801 Ex $641 Gd $436
Model AL391 Urika camo
w/Realtree Hardwoods . . . . NiB $885 Ex $708 Gd $481
Model AL391 Urika
Gold w/black receiver . . . . NiB $928 Ex $742 Gd $504
Model AL391 Urika Gold
w/silver receiver, lightweight . . . . NiB $1004 Ex $803 Gd $546
Model AL391 Urika Youth. . . . . NiB $793 Ex $634 Gd $432
Model AL391 Urika Sporting . . . . NiB $903 Ex $722 Gd $491
Model AL391 Urika Gold
Sporting w/black receiver. . . . . NiB $970 Ex $776 Gd $527
Model AL391 Urika
Gold Sporting w/silver receiver . . . . NiB $1038 Ex $830 Gd $564
Model AL391 Urika Trap. . . . . NiB $911 Ex $729 Gd $495
Model AL391 Gold Trap . . . . NiB $1004 Ex $803 Gd $546

SHOTGUNS

Beretta Model BL-1

Beretta Model BL3

Beretta Model BL-6

Beretta Model ASEL

MODEL ASE 90 O/U SHOTGUN
Competition-style receiver w/coin-silver finish and gold inlay featuring drop-out trigger group. Gauge: 12; 2.75-inch chamber. Bbls.: 28- or 30-inch w/fixed or Mobilchoke tubes; vent rib. Weight: 8.5 lbs. (30-inch bbl.). Checkered high-grade walnut stock. Imported 1992 to date.
Pigeon, Skeet, Trap models .... NiB $7313 Ex $5850 Gd $3978
Sporting Clays model......... NiB $7494 Ex $5995 Gd $4077
Trap Combo model......... NiB $11,563 Ex $9250 Gd $6290
Deluxe (introduced 1996)........ NiB $13,438 Ex $10,750 Gd $7310

MODEL ASE SERIES O/U SHOTGUN
Boxlock. Single non-selective trigger. Selective automatic ejectors. gauges: 12 and 20. Bbls. 26-, 28-, 30-inch; IC and M choke or M and F choke. Weight: about 5.75-7 lbs. Checkered pistol-grip stock and forearm. Receiver w/various grades of engraving. Imported 1947-64.
Model ASE (light scroll engraving)........ NiB $2055 Ex $1644 Gd $1118
Model ASEL (half coverage engraving) .... NiB $2956 Ex $2365 Gd $1608
Model ASEELL (full coverage engraving) ... NiB $4530 Ex $3624 Gd $2465
For 20 ga. models, add 95%

MODEL BL-1/BL-2 O/U
Boxlock. Plain extractors. Double triggers.12 gauge, 2.75-inch chambers only. Bbls.: 30-and 28-inch M/F choke, 26-inch IC/M choke. Weight: 6.75-7 lbs., depending on bbl. length. Checkered pistol-grip stock and forearm. Imported 1968-73.
Model BL-1............. NiB $375 Ex $300 Gd $204
Model BL-2 (single selective trigger)........ NiB $469 Ex $375 Gd $255

MODEL BL-2/S .... NiB $481 Ex $385 Gd $262
Similar to Model BL-1, except has selective "Speed-Trigger," vent-rib bbls., 2.75- or 3-inch chambers. Weight: 7-7.5 lbs. Imported 1974-76.

MODEL BL-3 .... NiB $694 Ex $555 Gd $377
Same as Model BL-1, except has deluxe engraved receiver, selective single trigger, vent-rib bbls., 12 or 20 ga., 2.75-inch or 3-inch chambers in former, 3-inch in latter. Weight: 6-7.5 lbs. depending on ga. and bbl. length. Imported 1968-76.

MODELS BL-4, BL-5 AND BL-6
Higher grade versions of Model BL-3 w/more elaborate engraving and fancier wood; Model BL-6 has sideplates. Selective automatic ejectors standard. Imported 1968-76.
Model BL-4 .... NiB $844 Ex $675 Gd $459
Model BL-5 .... NiB $1119 Ex $895 Gd $609
Model BL-6 (1973-76)........ NiB $1406 Ex $1125 Gd $765

SERIES BL SKEET GUNS
Models BL-3, BL-4, BL-5 and BL-6 w/standard features of their respective grades plus wider rib and skeet-style stock, 26-inch bbls. SK choked. Weight: 6-7.25 lbs. depending on ga.
Model BL-3 skeet gun .... NiB $750 Ex $600 Gd $408
Model BL-4 skeet gun .... NiB $869 Ex $695 Gd $473
Model BL-5 skeet gun .... NiB $1156 Ex $925 Gd $629
Model BL-6 skeet gun .... NiB $1569 Ex $1255 Gd $853

SERIES BL TRAP GUNS
Models BL-3, BL-4, BL-5 and BL-6 w/standard features of their respective grades plus wider rib and Monte Carlo stock w/recoil pad; 30-inch bbls., improved M/F or both F choke. Weight: About 7.5 lbs.
Model BL-3 trap gun .... NiB $669 Ex $535 Gd $364
Model BL-4 trap gun .... NiB $744 Ex $595 Gd $405
Model BL-5 trap gun .... NiB $1156 Ex $925 Gd $629
Model BL-6 trap gun .... NiB $1494 Ex $1195 Gd $813

MODEL FS-1 FOLDING SINGLE .... NiB $225 Ex $150 Gd $100
Formerly "Companion." Folds to length of bbl. Hammerless. Underlever. Gauge: 12, 16, 20, 28 or .410. Bbl.: 30-inch in 12 ga., 28-inch in 16 and 20 ga.; 26-inch in 28 and .410 ga.; all F choke. Checkered semipistol-grip stock/forearm. Weight: 4.5-5.5 lbs. depending on ga. Disc. 1971.

GOLDEN SNIPE O/U
Same as Silver Snipe (see page 430) except has automatic ejectors, vent rib is standard feature. Imported 1959-67.
W/non-selective single trigger .... NiB $995 Ex $850 Gd $450
W/selective single trigger, add $100

Beretta Model GR-2

Beretta FS-1 Folding

Beretta Mark II Trap

Beretta S58 Trap

MODEL GR-2 HAMMERLESS DOUBLE . . . NiB $930 Ex $743 Gd $506
Boxlock. Plain extractors. Double triggers. Gauges: 12, 20; 2.75-inch chambers in former, 3-inch in latter. Bbls.: Vent rib; 30-inch M/F choke (12 ga. only); 28-inch M/F choke, 26-inch IC/M choke. Weight: 6.5 to 7.5 lbs. depending on ga. and bbl. length. Checkered pistol-grip stock and forearm. Imported 1968-76.

MODEL GR-3 . . . . NiB $1055 Ex $843 Gd $573
Same as Model GR-2 except has selective single trigger chambered for 12-ga. Three inch or 2.75-inch shells. Magnum model has 30-inch M/F choke bbl., recoil pad. Weight: about 8 lbs. Imported 1968-76.

MODEL GR-4 . . . . NiB $1445 Ex $1156 Gd $786
Same as Model GR-2 except has automatic ejectors and selective single trigger, higher grade engraving and wood. 12 ga., 2.75-inch chambers only. Imported 1968-76.

GRADE 100 O/U
SHOTGUN . . . . NiB $1869 Ex $1495 Gd $1017
Sidelock. Double triggers. Automatic ejectors. 12 ga. only. Bbls.: 26-, 28-, 30-inch, any standard boring. Weight: About 7.5 lbs. Checkered stock and forend, straight or pistol grip. Disc.

GRADE 200 . . . . NiB $2438 Ex $1950 Gd $1326
Same general specifications as Grade 100 except higher quality; bores and action parts hard chrome plated. Disc.

MARK II SINGLE-BARREL TRAP GUN . . . . NiB $563 Ex $450 Gd $306
Boxlock action similar to that of Series "BL" over-and-unders. Engraved receiver. Automatic ejector. 12 ga. only. 32- or 34-inch bbl. w/wide vent rib. Weight: About 8.5 lbs. Monte Carlo stock w/pistol grip and recoil pad, beavertail forearm. Imported 1972-76.

MODEL S55B O/U
SHOTGUN . . . . NiB $600 Ex $550 Gd $425
Boxlock. Plain extractors. Selective single trigger. Gauges: 12, 20; 2.75- or 3-inch chambers in former, 3-inch in latter. Bbls. vent rib; 30-inch M/F choke or both F choke in 12-ga. Three inch Magnum only; 28-inch M/F choke; 26 inch IC/M choke. Weight: 6.5 to 7.5 lbs. depending on ga. and bbl. length. Checkered pistol-grip stock and forearm. Introduced in 1977. Disc.

MODEL S56E . . . . NiB $850 Ex $600 Gd $400
Same as Model S55B except has scroll-engraved receiver selective automatic ejectors. Introduced in 1977. Disc.

MODEL S58 SKEET GUN . . . . NiB $800 Ex $550 Gd $400
Same as Model S56E except has 26-inch bbls. of Boehler Antinit Anticorro steel, SK choked, w/wide vent rib; skeet-style stock and forearm. Weight: 7.5 lbs. Introduced in 1977.

MODEL S58 TRAP GUN . . . . NiB $795 Ex $425 Gd $400
Same as Model S58 Skeet Gun except has 30-inch bbls. bored IM/F Trap, Monte Carlo stock w/recoil pad. Weight: 7 lbs. 10 oz. Introduced in 1977. Disc.

SILVER HAWK FEATHERWEIGHT
HAMMERLESS DOUBLE-BARREL SHOTGUN
Boxlock. Double triggers or non-selective single trigger. Plain extractor. Gauges: 12, 16, 20, 28, 12 Mag. Bbls.: 26- to 32-inch w/high matted rib, all standard choke combinations. Weight: 7 lbs. (12 ga. w/26-inch bbls.). Checkered walnut stock w/beavertail forearm. Disc. 1967.
W/double triggers . . . . NiB $650 Ex $475 Gd $300
For non-selective single trigger, add $65

SHOTGUNS

Beretta S682 Gold E Trap

Beretta S682 Gold E Double Trap

Beretta S682 Gold E X Trap

SILVER SNIPE O/U SHOTGUN
Boxlock. Non-selective or selective single trigger. Plain extractor. Gauges: 12, 20, 12 Mag., 20 Mag. Bbls.: 26-, 28-, 30-inch; plain or vent rib; chokes IC/M, M/F, SK number 1 and number 2, F/F. Weight: From about 6 lbs. in 20 ga. to 8.5 lbs. in 12 ga. (Trap gun). Checkered walnut pistol-grip stock and forearm. Imported 1955-67.

W/plain bbl., non-selective trigger . . . . NiB $725 Ex $650 Gd $325
W/vent rib bbl., non-selective
single trigger . . . . NiB $750 Ex $675 Gd $350
For selective single trigger, add $65

MODEL SL-2 PIGEON SERIES PUMP GUN
Hammerless. Takedown.12 ga. only. Three shot magazine. Bbls.: Vent rib; 30-inch F choke, 28-inch M, 26-inch IC. Weight: 7-7.25 lbs., depending on bbl. length. Receiver w/various grades of engraving. Checkered pistol-grip stock and forearm. Imported 1968-71.

Model SL-2 . . . . NiB $395 Ex $316 Gd $215
Silver Pigeon . . . . NiB $323 Ex $258 Gd $175
Gold Pigeon. . . . . NiB $503 Ex $402 Gd $273
Ruby Pigeon. . . . . NiB $647 Ex $517 Gd $351

SERIES "SO" SERIES SHOTGUNS
Jubilee Series introduced in 1998. The Beretta Boxlock is made with mechanical works from a single block of hot forged, high- resistance steel. The gun is richly engraved in scroll and game scenes. All engraving is signed by master engravers. High-quality finishing on the inside with high polishing of all internal points. Sidelock. Selective automatic ejectors. Selective single trigger or double triggers. 12 ga. only, 2.75- or 3-inch chambers. Bbls.: Vent rib (wide type on skeet and trap guns); 26-, 27-, 29-, 30-inch; any combination of standard chokes. Weight: 7 to 7.75 lbs., depending on bbl. length, style of stock and density of wood. Stock and forearm of select walnut, finely checkered; straight or pistol-grip, field, skeet and trap guns have appropriate styles of stock and forearm. Models differ chiefly in quality of wood and grade of engraving. Models SO-3EL, SO-3EELL, SO4 and SO-5 have hand-detachable locks. "SO-4" is used to designate skeet and trap models derived from Model SO-3EL, but with less elaborate engraving. Models SO3EL and SO-3EELL are similar to the earlier SO-4 and SO-5, respectively. Imported 1933 to date.

(cont'd.) SERIES "SO" SERIES SHOTGUNS
Jubilee O/U 410-28-20-12 . . . .
. . . . NiB $7812 to 17,243 Ex $6250 to 13,795 Gd $4250 to 9381
Jubilee II Side-by-side
. . . . NiB $8146 to 18,693 Ex $6517 to 14,074 Gd $4431 to 9571
Mdl. SO-2 . . . NiB $3884 to 8243 Ex $3107 to 4394 Gd $2113 to 2988
Mdl. SO-3 . . . NiB $5431 to 6868 Ex $4345 to 6374 Gd $2954 to 4335
Mdl. SO-3EL . . . . NiB $6497 to 8793 Ex $5197 to 7474 Gd $3534 to 5083
Mdl. SO-3EELL. . . NiB $9281 to 10,443 Ex $7425 to 10,994 Gd $5049 to 7476
Mdl. SO-4 Field, Skeet or Trap gun
. . . . NiB $5907 to 7994 Ex $4725 to 8795 Gd $3213 to 5981
Model SO-5 Sporting, Skt. or Trp.
. . . . NiB $10,377 to 11,375 Ex $8301 to 9500 Gd $5645 to 7260
W/extra bbl. set, add 25%

MODELS SO-6 AND SO-9 PREMIUM GRADE SHOTGUNS
High-grade over/unders in the SO series. Gauges: 12 ga. only (SO-6); 12, 20, 28 and .410 (SO-9). Fixed or Mobilchoke (12 ga. only). Sidelock action. Silver or casehardened receiver (SO-6); English custom hand-engraved scroll or game scenes (SO-9). Supplied w/leather case and accessories. Imported from about 1990 to date.

SO-6 O/U . . . . . . NiB $6657 to 7688 Ex $5325 to 6550 Gd $3621 to 4454
SO-6 EELL O/U . . . . . NiB $8188 to 5494 Ex $6550 to 8395 Gd $4454 to 5709
SO-9 O/U . . . . $21,950 to 46,795
SO-9 EELL special engraver . . . . $50,000 to 90,000
W/extra bbl. set, add 25%

MODEL SO6/SO-7 S/S DOUBLES
Side-by-side shotgun w/same general specifications as SO Series over/unders except higher grade w/more elaborate engraving, fancier wood.

SO-6 SxS (imported 1948-82) . . . . $5,325 to 6,550
SO-7 SxS (imported 1948-90) . . . . 6,550 to 8,395

MODEL TR-1 SINGLE-SHOT TRAP GUN. . . . . . NiB $336 Ex $269 Gd $183
Hammerless. Underlever action. Engraved frame.12 ga. only. 32-inch bbl. w/vent rib. Weight: About 8.25 lbs. Monte Carlo stock w/pistol grip and recoil pad, beavertail forearm. Imported 1968-71.

MODEL TR-2 . . . . NiB $378 Ex $302 Gd $205
Same as Model TR-1 except has extended ventilated rib. Imported 1969-73.

Beretta Model SO-2

Beretta Model SO-3

Beretta Model SO-4

Beretta Model SO-5

Beretta Model SO-7

VICTORIA PINTAIL (ES100) SEMIAUTOLOADER
Short Montefeltro-type recoil action. Gauge: 12 w/3-inch chamber. Bbl.: 24-inch slug, 24-, 26- or 28-inch vent rib w/Mobilchoke tubes. Weight: 7 lbs. to 7 lbs., 5 oz. Checkered synthetic or walnut buttstock and forend. Matte finish on both metal and stock. Imported 1993 to date.
Field model w/synthetic
stock (intro. 1998) . . . . NiB $584 Ex $467 Gd $317
Field model w/walnut stock (disc. 1998) . . . . . . NiB $543 Ex $434 Gd $295
Rifled slug model w/synthetic
stock (intro. 1998) . . . . NiB $721 Ex $577 Gd $392
Standard slug model
w/walnut stock (disc. 1998) . . . . NiB $515 Ex $412 Gd $280
Wetland Camo model (intro. 2000) . . . . . . NiB $680 Ex $544 Gd $370

VINCENZO BERNARDELLI —
Gardone V.T. (Brescia), Italy

Previously imported by Armsport, Miami, FL (formerly by Magnum Research, Inc., Quality Arms, Stoeger Industries, Inc. & Action Arms, LTD).

115 SERIES O/U SHOTGUNS
Boxlock w/single trigger and ejectors. 12 ga. only. 25.5-, 26.75-, and 29.5-inch bbls. Concave top and vented middle rib. Anatomical grip stock. Blued or coin-silver finish w/various grades of engraving. Imported 1985-97.

(cont'd.) 115 SERIES O/U SHOTGUNS
Hunting Model 115 (disc. 1990) . . . . . . NiB $1780 Ex $1424 Gd $969
Hunting Model 115E (disc. 1990) . . . . . NiB $5355 Ex $4284 Gd $2913
Hunting Model 115L (disc. 1990) . . . . . NiB $2956 Ex $2365 Gd $1608
Hunting Model 115S (disc. 1990) . . . . NiB $2509 Ex $2007 Gd $1365
Target Model 115 (disc. 1992) . . . . NiB $1994 Ex $1595 Gd $1084
Target Model 115E (disc. 1992) . . . . . . NiB $6043 Ex $4834 Gd $3287
Target Model 115L (disc. 1992) . . . . . . NiB $3746 Ex $2997 Gd $2038
Target Model 115S (disc. 1992) . . . . . . NiB $2681 Ex $2145 Gd $1458
Trap/Skeet Model 115S
(imported 1996-97) . . . . NiB $2743 Ex $2194 Gd $1492
Sporting Clays Model 115S
(imported 1995-97). . . . . NiB $4056 Ex $3245 Gd $2206

BRESCIA
HAMMER DOUBLE . . . . NiB $938 Ex $750 Gd $510
Back-action sidelock. Plain extractors. Double triggers. Gauges: 12, 20. Bbls.: 27.5 or 29.5-inch M/F choke in 12 ga. 25.5-inch IC/M choke in 20 ga.. Weight: From 5.75 to 7 lbs., depending on ga. and bbl. length. English-style stock and forearm, checkered. No longer imported.

ELIO . . . . NiB $1119 Ex $895 Gd $609
Lightweight game gun, 12 ga. only, w/same general specifications as Standard Gamecock (S. Uberto 1) except weight: About 6 to 6.25 lbs.; has automatic ejectors, fine English-pattern scroll engraving. No longer imported. See illustration next page.

Bernardelli Gamecock

Bernardelli Standard Gamecock

Bernardelli Gardone

Bernardelli Italia

Bernardelli Roma 6

Bernardelli Elio

GAMECOCK, PREMIER
(ROME 3)
Same general specifications as Standard Gamecock (S. Uberto 1) except has sideplates, auto ejectors, single trigger. No longer imported.

Roma 3 (disc. 1989,
Reintroduced 1993-97) . . . . NiB $1563 Ex $1250 Gd $850
Roma 3E (disc. 1950) Roma 3M
w/single trigger (disc. 1997) . . . . NiB $1744 Ex $1395 Gd $949

GAMECOCK, STANDARD
(S. UBERTO 1) HAMMERLESS
DOUBLE-BARREL SHOTGUN . . . . NiB $1082 Ex $866 Gd $589
Boxlock. Plain extractors. Double triggers. Gauges: 12, 16, 20; 2.75-inch chambers in 12 and 16, 3-inch in 20 ga. Bbls. 25.5-inch IC/M choke; 27.5-inch M/F choke. Weight: 5.75-6.5 lbs., depending on ga. and bbl. length. English-style straight-grip stock and forearm, checkered. No longer imported.

GARDONE HAMMER DOUBLE . . . NiB $2428 Ex $1942 Gd $1320
Same general specifications as Brescia except for higher grade engraving and wood, but not as high as the Italia. Half-cock safety. Disc. 1956.

HEMINGWAY HAMMERLESS DOUBLE
Boxlock. Single or double triggers w/hinged front. Selective automatic ejectors. Gauges: 12 and 20 w/2.75- or 3-inch chambers, 16 and 28 w/2.75-inch. Bbls.: 23.5- to 28-inch w/fixed chokes. Weight: 6.25 lbs. Checkered English-style European walnut stock. Silvered and engraved receiver.

Standard model . . . . NiB $1942 Ex $1553 Gd $1056
Deluxe model
w/sideplates (disc. 1993) . . . . . . NiB $2267 Ex $1813 Gd $1233
For single trigger, add $100

ITALIA . . . . NiB $3293 Ex $2634 Gd $1791
Same general specifications as Brescia except higher grade engraving and wood. Disc. 1986.

ROMA 4 AND ROMA 6
Same as Premier Gamecock (Rome 3) except higher grade engraving and wood, double triggers. Disc. 1997.

Roma 4 (disc. 1989) . . . . NiB $1244 Ex $995 Gd $677
Roma 4E (disc. 1997) . . . . NiB $1563 Ex $1250 Gd $850
Roma 6 (disc. 1989) . . . . NiB $1281 Ex $1025 Gd $697
Roma 6E (disc. 1997) . . . . NiB $1938 Ex $1550 Gd $1054

ROMA 7, 8, AND 9
Side-by-side. Anson & Deeley boxlock; hammerless. Ejectors; double triggers. 12 ga. Barrels: 27.5-or 29.5-inch. M/F chokes. Fancy hand-checkered European walnut straight or pistol-grip stock, forearm. Elaborately engraved, silver-finished sideplates. Imported 1994-97.

Roma 7 . . . . NiB $2313 Ex $1850 Gd $1258
Roma 8 . . . . NiB $2813 Ex $2250 Gd $1530
Roma 9 . . . . NiB $3494 Ex $2795 Gd $1901

S. UBERTO 2 . . . . **NiB $1368 Ex $1094 Gd $744**
Same as Standard Gamecock (S. Uberto 1) except higher grade engraving and wood. Currently imported.

S. UBERTO F.S.
Same as Standard Gamecock except w/higher grade engraving, wood and has auto-ejectors. Disc. 1989, reintroduced 1993-97.
Model FS . . . . **NiB $1719 Ex $1375 Gd $935**
Model V.B. Incisio . . . . **NiB $1959 Ex $1567 Gd $1065**
W/single trigger, add **$75**

HOLLAND V.B. SERIES SHOTGUNS
Holland & Holland-type sidelock action. Auto-ejectors. Double triggers. 12 ga. only. Bbl. length or choke to custom specification. Silver-finish receiver (Liscio) or engraved coin finish receiver (Incisio). Extra-select wood and game scene engraving (Lusso). Checkered stock (straight or pistol-grip). Imported 1992-97.
Model V.B. Liscio . . . . **NiB $5994 Ex $4795 Gd $3261**
Model V.B. Incisio . . . . **NiB $7438 Ex $5950 Gd $4046**
Model V.B. Lusso . . . . **NiB $8869 Ex $7095 Gd $4825**
Model V.B. Extra . . . . **NiB $10313 Ex $8250 Gd $5610**
Model V.B. Gold . . . . **NiB $36188 Ex $28950 Gd $19686**
Engraving Pattern
No. 4, add **$950**
Engraving Pattern
No. 12, add **$4450**
Engraving Pattern No. 20, add **$8750**
Single trigger, add **$595**

Bernardelli Uberto 2

Bernardelli Uberto F.S.

BOSS & COMPANY — London, England

HAMMERLESS DOUBLE-BARREL
SHOTGUN . . . . **NiB $62,676 Ex $50,000 Gd $32,800**
Sidelock. Automatic ejectors. Double triggers, non-selective or selective single trigger. Made in all gauges, bbl. lengths and chokes. Checkered stock and forend, straight or pistol-grip.

HAMMERLESS O/U
SHOTGUN . . . . **NiB $109,683 Ex $80,500 Gd $40,000**
Sidelock. Automatic ejectors. Selective single trigger. Made in all gauges, bbl. lengths and chokes. Checkered stock and forend, straight or pistol-grip. Disc.

Bernardelli V.B. Holland Liscio

BREDA MECCANICA BRESCIANA — Brescia, Italy, *formerly* ERNESTO BREDA, Milan, Italy

AUTOLOADING SHOTGUN
Recoil-operated.12 ga, 2.75-inch chamber. Four shell tubular magazine. Bbls.: 25.5- and 27.5-inch, plain, matted or vent rib, IC, M or F choke; current model has 26-inch vent-rib bbl. w/interchangeable choke tubes. Weight: About 7.25 lbs. Checkered straight or pistol-grip stock and forearm. Disc. 1988.
W/plain bbl. . . . . **NiB $444 Ex $355 Gd $241**
W/raised matted rib bbl. . . . . **NiB $494 Ex $395 Gd $269**
W/vent rib bbl. . . . . **NiB $519 Ex $415 Gd $282**
W/vent rib,
interchangeable choke tubes. . . . . **NiB $538 Ex $430 Gd $292**

MAGNUM
Same general specifications as standard model except chambered for 12-ga. 3-inch Magnum, 3-shot magazine; latest model has 29-inch vent-rib bbl. Disc. 1988.
W/plain bbl. . . . . **NiB $581 Ex $465 Gd $316**
W/vent rib bbl. . . . . **NiB $594 Ex $475 Gd $323**

Boss Hammerless
Double-Barrel

American Browning Grade I
(see page 435)

American Browning Special
(see page 435)

BRETTON SHOTGUNS — St. Etienne (Cedex1), France

BABY STANDARD SPRINT O/U . . . . NiB $995 Ex $890 Gd $550
Inline sliding breech action. 12 or 20 gauge w/2.75-inch chambers. 27.5-inch separated bbls. w/vent rib and choke tubes. Weight: 4.8 to 5 lbs. Engraved alloy receiver. Checkered walnut buttstock and forearm w/satin oil finish. Imported 1992 to date.

SPRINT DELUXE O/U . . . . NiB $895 Ex $775 Gd $495
Similar to the Standard Model except w/engraved coin-finished receiver and chambered 12, 16 and 20 ga. Discontinued 1994.

FAIR PLAY O/U . . . . NiB $950 Ex $795 Gd $475
Lightweight action similar to the Sprint Model except w/hinged action that pivots open and is chambered 12 or 20 gauge only.

BRNO SHOTGUNS — Brno and Uherski Brod, Czech Republic, (formerly Czechoslovakia)

500 O/U SHOTGUN . . . . NiB $850 Ex $725 Gd $425
Hammerless boxlock w/double triggers and ejectors.12 ga. w/2.75-inch chambers. 27.5-inch bbls.. choked M/F. 44 inches overall. Weight: 7 lbs. Etched receiver. Checkered walnut stock w/classic style cheekplece. Imported 1987-91.

500 SERIES O/U COMBINATION GUNS
Similar to the 500 Series over/under shotgun, except w/lower . bbl. chambered in rifle calibers and set trigger option. Imported 1987-95.
Model 502 12/222, 12/243 (disc. 1991) . . . . . NiB $1042 Ex $834 Gd $567
Model 502 12/308, 12/30.06 (disc. 1991) . . . NiB $1087 Ex $870 Gd $591
Model 571 12/6x65R (disc. 1993) . . . . NiB $937 Ex $750 Gd $510
Model 572 12/7x65R (imported since 1992) . . . . . NiB $1012 Ex $810 Gd $550
Model 584 12/7x57R (imported since 1992) . . . . . NiB $1042 Ex $834 Gd $567
Sport Series 4-bbl. set (disc. 1991) . . . . NiB $2775 Ex $2220 Gd $1509

CZ 581 SOLO O/U SHOTGUN. . . . . NiB $790 Ex $632 Gd $430
Hammerless boxlock w/double triggers, ejectors and automatic safety. 12 ga. w/2.75- or 3-inch chambers. 28-inch bbls. choked M/F. Weight: 7.5 lbs. Checkered walnut stock. Disc. 1996.

SUPER SERIES O/U SHOTGUN
Hammerless sidelock w/selective single or double triggers and ejectors. 12 ga. w/2.75- or 3-inch chambers. 27.5-inch bbls. choked M/F. 44.5 inches overall. Weight: 7.25 lbs. Etched or engraved side

(cont'd.) **SUPER SERIES O/U SHOTGUN**
plates. Checkered European walnut stock w/classic-style cheekpiece. Imported 1987-91.
Super Series Shotgun (disc. 1992). . . . . NiB $996 Ex $797 Gd $542
Super Series Combo (disc. 1992) . . . . NiB $1169 Ex $935 Gd $635
Super Ser. 3-bbl. set (disc. 1990). . . . . NiB $2330 Ex $1864 Gd $1268
Super Series engraving, add $1250

ZH 300 SERIES O/U SHOTGUNS
Hammerless boxlock w/double triggers. Gauge: 12 or 16 w/2.75- or 3-inch chambers. Bbls.: 26, 27.5 or 30 inches; choked M/F. Weight: 7 lbs. Skip-line checkered walnut stock w/classic-style cheekpiece. Imported 1986-93.
Model 300 (disc. 1993) . . . . NiB $570 Ex $456 Gd $310
Model 301 Field (disc. 1991) . . . . NiB $584 Ex $467 Gd $317
Model 302 Skeet (disc. 1992) . . . . NiB $653 Ex $522 Gd $355
Model 303 Trap (disc. 1992) . . . . NiB $680 Ex $544 Gd $370

ZH 300 SERIES O/U COMBINATION GUNS
Similar to the 300 Series over/under shotgun except lower bbl. chambered in rifle calibers.
Model 300 Combo
8-bbl. Set (disc. 1991) . . . . NiB $3244 Ex $2595 Gd $1765
Model 304 12 ga./7x57R (disc. 1995) . . . . NiB $656 Ex $525 Gd $357
Model 305 12 ga./5.6x52R (disc. 1993) . . . . . . NiB $744 Ex $595 Gd $405
Model 306 12 ga./5.6x50R (disc. 1993) . . . . . . NiB $781 Ex $625 Gd $425
Model 307 12 ga./.22 Hornet
(Imported since 1995) . . . . NiB $688 Ex $550 Gd $374
Model 324 16 ga./7x57R (disc. 1987 . . . . NiB $719 Ex $575 Gd $391

ZP 149 HAMMERLESS DOUBLE
Sidelock action w/double triggers, automatic ejectors and automatic safety.12 ga. w/2.75- or 3-inch chambers. 28.5-inch bbls. choked M/F. Weight: 7.25 lbs. Checkered walnut buttstock w/cheekpiece.
Standard model . . . . NiB $594 Ex $475 Gd $323
Engraved model . . . . NiB $650 Ex $520 Gd $354

BROLIN ARMS, INC. — Pomona, California

ARMS HAWK PUMP SHOTGUN, FIELD SERIES
Slide-action. Gauge: 12 ga. w/3-inch chamber. 24-, 26-, 28- or 30-inch bbl. 44 and 50 inches overall. Weight: 7.3 to 7.6 lbs. Cross-bolt safety. Vent rib bbl. w/screw-in choke tube and bead sights. Non-reflective metal finish. Synthetic or oil-finished wood stock w/swivel studs. Made 1997-98.
Synthetic stock model . . . . NiB $219 Ex $175 Gd $119
Wood stock model. . . . . NiB $206 Ex $165 Gd $112

ARMS HAWK PUMP SHOTGUN COMBO MODEL
Similar to the Field Model except w/extra 18.5- or 22-inch bbl. w/bead or rifle sight. Made 1997-98.
Synthetic stock model .... **NiB $244 Ex $195 Gd $133**
Wood stock model............. **NiB $231 Ex $185 Gd $126**

ARMS HAWK PUMP SHOTGUN LAWMAN MODEL
Similar to the Field Model except has 18.5-inch bbl. w/cylinder bore fixed choke. Weight: 7 lbs. Dual operating bars. Bead, rifle or ghost ring sights. Black synthetic or wood stock. Matte chrome or satin nickel finish. Made 1997-99.
Synthetic stock model .... **NiB $206 Ex $165 Gd $112**
Wood stock model .... **NiB $194 Ex $155 Gd $105**
Rifle sights, add................................**$20**
Ghost ring sights, add **$35**
Satin nickel finish (disc. 1997), add **$25**

ARMS HAWK SLUG MODEL
Similar to the Field Model except has 18.5- or 22-inch bbl. w/IC fixed choke or 4-inch extended rifled choke. Rifle or ghost ring sights or optional cantilevered scope mount. Black synthetic or wood stock. Matte blued finish. Made 1998-99.
Synthetic stock model .... **NiB $206 Ex $165 Gd $112**
Wood stock model .... **NiB $194 Ex $155 Gd $105**
W/rifled bbl., add **$20**
W/cantilevered scope mount, add **$35**

ARMS HAWK TURKEY SPECIAL
Similar to the Field Model except has 22-inch vent-rib bbl. w/extended extra-full choke. Rifle or ghost ring sights or optional cantilevered scope mount. Black synthetic or wood stock. Matte blued finish. Made 1998-99.
Synthetic stock model .... **NiB $200 Ex $160 Gd $109**
Wood stock model .... **NiB $188 Ex $150 Gd $102**
W/cantilevered
scope mount, add **$25**

BROWNING SHOTGUNS —
Morgan (formerly Ogden), Utah
AMERICAN BROWNING SHOTGUNS

Designated "American" Browning because they were produced in Ilion, New York, the following Remington-made Brownings are almost identical to the Remington Model 11A and Sportsman and the Browning Auto-5. They are the only Browning shotguns manufactured in the U.S. during the 20th century and were made for Browning Arms when production was suspended in Belgium because of WW II.

NOTE: *Fabrique Nationale Herstal (formerly Fabrique Nationale d'Armes de Guerre) of Herstal, Belgium, is the longtime manufacturer of Browning shotguns dating back to 1900. Miroku Firearms Mfg. Co. of Tokyo, Japan, bought into the Browning company and has, since the early 1970s, undertaken some of the production. The following shotguns were manufactured for Browning by these two firms.*

GRADE I AUTOLOADER (AUTO-5)
Recoil-operated autoloader. Similar to the Remington Model 11A except w/different style engraving and identified w/the Browning logo. Gauges: 12, 16 or 20. Plain 26- to 32-inch bbl. w/any standard boring. Two or four shell tubular magazine w/magazine cut-off. Weight: About 6.88 lbs. (20 ga.) to 8 lbs. (12 ga.). Checkered pistol-grip stock and forearm. Made 1940-49.

(cont'd.) GRADE I AUTOLOADER (AUTO-5)
American Browning Grade I
Auto-5, 12 or 16 ga................... **NiB $675 Ex $575 Gd $250**
20 ga., add...................................**20%**

SPECIAL 441
Same general specifications as Grade I except supplied w/raised matted rib or vent rib. Disc. 1949.
W/raised matted rib .... **NiB $750 Ex $650 Gd $325**
W/vent rib .... **NiB $775 Ex $675 Gd $325**
20 ga., add...................................**20%**

SPECIAL SKEET MODEL .... **NiB $656 Ex $525 Gd $357**
Same general specifications as Grade I except has 26-inch bbl. w/vent rib and Cutts Compensator. Disc. 1949.

UTILITY FIELD GUN............ **NiB $500 Ex $300 Gd $200**
Same general specifications as Grade I except has 28-inch plain bbl. w/Poly Choke. Disc. 1949.

MODEL 12 PUMP SHOTGUN
Special limited edition Winchester Model 12. Gauge: 20 or 28. Five-shot tubular magazine. 26-inch bbl., M choke. 45 inches overall. Weight: about 7 lbs. Grade I has blued receiver, checkered walnut stock w/matte finish. Grade V has engraved receiver, checkered deluxe walnut stock w/high-gloss finish. Made 1988-92. See illustration next page.
Grade I,
20 ga. (8600) .... **NiB $563 Ex $450 Gd $306**
Grade I, 28 ga. .... **NiB $594 Ex $475 Gd $323**
Grade V,
20 ga (4000) .... **NiB $994 Ex $795 Gd $541**
Grade V, 28 ga .... **NiB $969 Ex $775 Gd $527**

MODEL 42 LIMITED EDITION SHOTGUN
Special limited edition Winchester Model 42 pump shotgun. Same general specifications as Model 12 except w/smaller frame in .410 ga. and 3-inch chamber. Made 1991-93.
Grade I
(6000 produced) .... **NiB $619 Ex $495 Gd $337**
Grade V
(6000 produced) .... **NiB $994 Ex $795 Gd $541**

2000 BUCK SPECIAL............ **NiB $394 Ex $315 Gd $214**
Same as Field Model except has 24-inch plain bbl. Bored for rifled slug and buck shot, fitted w/rifle sights (open rear, ramp front). 12 ga., 2.75-inch or 3-inch chamber; 20 ga., 2.75-inch chamber. Weight: 12 ga., 7 lbs., 8 oz.; 20 ga., 6 lbs., 10 oz. Made 1974-81 by FN.

2000 GAS AUTOMATIC SHOTGUN, FIELD MODEL
Gas-operated. Gauge: 12 or 20. 2.75-inch chamber. Four-shot magazine. Bbl.: 26-, 28-, 30-inch, any standard choke plain matted bbl. (12 ga. only) or vent rib. Weight: 6 lbs. 11 oz.-7 lbs. 12 oz. depending on ga. and bbl. length. Checkered pistol-grip stock/forearm. Made 1974-81 by FN; Assembled in Port gal.
W/plain
matted bbl. .... **NiB $550 Ex $325 Gd $225**
W/vent rib bbl. .... **NiB $560 Ex $350 Gd $230**

2000 MAGNUM MODEL .... **NiB $560 Ex $350 Gd $230**
Same as Field Model except chambered for 3-inch shells, three-shot magazine. Bbl.: 26- (20 ga. only), 28-, 30- or 32-inch (latter two 12 ga. only); any standard choke; vent rib. Weight: 6 lbs., 11 oz.-7 lbs., 13 oz. depending on ga. and bbl. Made 1974-81 by FN.

SHOTGUNS

Browning Model 12 Limited Editon Grade I

Browning Model 12 Limited Editon Grade V

Browning Model 42 Limited Editon Grade V

Browning 2000 Field Model

Browning Model A-500

2000 SKEET MODEL . . . . **NiB $431 Ex $345 Gd $235**
Same as Field Model except has skeet-style stock w/recoil pad, 26-inch
vent-rib bbl., SK choke. 12 or 20 ga., 2.75-inch chamber. Weight: 8
lbs., 1 oz. (12 ga.); 6 lbs., 12 oz. (20 ga.) Made 1974-81 by FN.

2000 TRAP MODEL . . . . **NiB $431 Ex $345 Gd $235**
Same as Field Model except has Monte Carlo stock w/recoil pad,
30- or 32-inch bbl. w/high-post vent rib and receiver extension,
M/I/F chokes. 12 ga., 2.75-inch chamber. Weight: About 8 lbs., 5 oz.
Made 1974-81 by FN.

A-500G GAS-OPERATED SEMIAUTOMATIC
Same general specifications as Browning Model A-500R except gas-
operated. Made 1990-93.
Buck Special . . . . **NiB $551 Ex $445 Gd $309**
Hunting model . . . . **NiB $564 Ex $455 Gd $316**

A-500G SPORTING CLAYS . . . . **NiB $564 Ex $455 Gd $316**
Same general specifications as Model A-500G except has matte
blued receiver w/"Sporting Clays" logo. 28- or 30-inch bbl.
w/Invector choke tubes. Made 1992-93.

A-500R SEMIAUTOMATIC
Recoil-operated. Gauge: 12. 26- to 30-inch vent-rib bbls. 24-inch
Buck Special. Invector choke tube system. 2.75- or 3-inch Magnum
cartridges. Weight: 7 lbs., 3 oz.-8 lbs., 2 oz. Cross-bolt safety. Gold-
plated trigger. Scroll-engraved receiver. Gloss-finished walnut stock

(cont'd.) A-500R SEMIAUTOMATIC
and forend. Made by FN from 1987-93.
Hunting model . . . . **NiB $556 Ex $445 Gd $303**
Buck Special . . . . **NiB $594 Ex $475 Gd $323**

A-BOLT SERIES SHOTGUN
Bolt-action repeating single-barrel shotgun. 12 ga. only w/3-inch
chambers, 2-shot magazine. 22- or 23-inch rifled bbl., w/or w/o a
rifled invector tube. Receiver drilled and tapped for scope mounts.
Bbl. w/ or w/o open sights. Checkered walnut or graphite/fiberglass
composite stock. Matte black metal finish. Imported 1995-98.
Stalker model w/
composite stock . . . . **NiB $394 Ex $315 Gd $214**
Hunter model w/walnut stock . . . . **NiB $375 Ex $300 Gd $204**
W/rifled bbl., add **$95**
W/open sights, add **$25**

AUTOLOADING SHOTGUNS, GRADES II, III AND IV
These higher grade models differ from the Standard or Grade I in
general quality, grade of wood, checkering, engraving, etc., other-
wise specifications are the same. Grade IV guns, sometimes called
Midas Grade, are inlaid w/yellow and green gold. Disc. in 1940.
Grade II, plan bbl. . . . . **NiB $1350 Ex $1150 Gd $782**
Grade III, plain bbl. . . . . **NiB $2650 Ex $2300 Gd $1564**
Grade IV, plain bbl. . . . . **NiB $3975 Ex $3700 Gd $3564**
For raised matte rib bbl., add **15%**
For vent rib bbl., add **30%**

Browning Model A-Bolt Hunter

Browning Model A-Bolt Stalker

Browning Automatic-5
Gold Classic

Browning Automatic-5 Buck Special

Browning Automatic-5 Classic

SHOTGUNS

AUTOMATIC-5, LIGHT 20

Same general specifications as Standard Model except lightweight and 20 ga. Bbl.: 26- or 28-inch; plain or vent rib. Weight: About 6.25-6.5 lbs. depending on bbl. Made 1958-76 by FN, since then by Miroku.

FN manuf., plain bbl.. . . . . NiB $644 Ex $515 Gd $350
FN manuf., vent-rib bbl. . . . . NiB $850 Ex $750 Gd $450
Miroku manuf., vent rib,fixed choke . . NiB $775 Ex $595 Gd $300
Miroku manuf., vent rib, invectors . . . NiB $825 Ex $650 Gd $350

AUTOMATIC-5, BUCK SPECIAL MODELS

Same as Light 12, Magnum 12, Light 20, Magnum 20, in respective gauges, except 24-inch plain bbl. bored for rifled slug and buckshot, fitted w/rifle sights (open rear, ramp front). Weight: 6.13-8.25 lbs. depending on ga. Made 1964-76 by FN, since then by Miroku.

FN manuf., w/plain bbl. . . . . NiB $850 Ex $595 Gd $340
Miroku manuf., ... NiB $725 Ex $550 Gd $325
W/3-inch mag. rec., add 10%

AUTOMATIC-5 CLASSIC . . . . NiB $1095 Ex $850 Gd $750

Gauge: 12. 5-shot capacity. 28-inch vent rib bbl./M choke. 2.75-

(cont'd.) AUTOMATIC-5 CLASSIC

inch chamber. Engraved silver-gray receiver. Gold-plated trigger. Crossbolt safety. High-grade, hand-checkered select American walnut stock w/rounded pistol grip. 5,000 issued; made in Japan in 1984, engraved in Belgium.

AUTOMATIC-5 GOLD CLASSIC . . . . . NiB $3800 Ex $3150 Gd $2300

Same general specifications as Automatic-5 Classic except engraved receiver inlaid w/gold. Pearl border on stock and forend plus fine-line hand-checkering. Each gun numbered "1 of Five Hundred," etc. 500 issued in 1984; made in Belgium.

AUTOMATIC-5, LIGHT 12

12 ga. only. Same general specifications as Standard Model except lightweight (about 7.25 lbs.), has gold-plated trigger. Guns w/rib have striped matting on top of bbl. Fixed chokes or Invector tubes. Made 1948-76 by FN, since then by Miroku.

FN manuf., plain bbl. . . . . NiB $563 Ex $450 Gd $306
FN manuf., raised matte rib . . . . . . NiB $650 Ex $550 Gd $425
FN manuf., ventilated rib . . . . NiB $850 Ex $725 Gd $450
Miroku manuf., vent rib, fixed choke . . NiB $563 Ex $450 Gd $306
Miroku manuf., vent rib, invectors . . . NiB $775 Ex $595 Gd $350

Browning Auto-5 Sweet Sixteen (New Model)

Browning Model B-80 Upland Special

Browning BPS Hunter

Browning BPS Youth & Ladies Model

AUTOMATIC-5, MAGNUM 12 GAUGE
Same general specifications as Standard Model. Chambered for 3-inch Magnum 12-ga. shells. Bbl.: 28-inch M/F, 30- or 32-inch F/F, plain or vent rib. Weight: 8.5-9 lbs. depending on bbl. Buttstock has recoil pad. Made 1958-76 by FN, since then by Miroku. Fixed chokes or Invector tubes.
FN manuf., plain bbl. . . . . NiB $769 Ex $615 Gd $418
FN manuf., vent rib bbl. . . . . NiB $833 Ex $667 Gd $453
Miroku manuf., vent rib, fixed chokes . . NiB $625 Ex $500 Gd $340
Miroku manuf., vent rib, invectors . . . . NiB $711 Ex $569 Gd $387

AUTOMATIC-5, MAGNUM 20 GAUGE
Same general specifications as Standard Model except chambered for 3-inch Magnum 20-ga. shell. Bbl.: 26- or 28-inch, plain or vent rib. Weight: 7 lbs., 5 oz.-7 lbs., 7 oz. depending on bbl. Made 1967-76 by FN, since then by Miroku.
FN manuf., plain bbl. . . . . NiB $762 Ex $610 Gd $415
FN manuf., vent rib bbl. . . . . NiB $805 Ex $644 Gd $437
Miroku manuf., vent rib, invectors . NiB $630 Ex $504 Gd $342

AUTOMATIC-5, SKEET MODEL
12 ga. only. Same general specifications as Light 12. Bbl.: 26-or 28-inch, plain or vent rib, SK choke. Weight: 7 lbs., 5 oz.-7 lbs., 10 oz. depending on bbl. Made by FN prior to 1976, since then by Miroku.
FN manuf., plain bbl. . . . . NiB $711 Ex $569 Gd $387
FN manuf., vent rib bbl. . . . . NiB $754 Ex $603 Gd $410
Miroku manuf., vent rib bbl. . . . . NiB $568 Ex $454 Gd $309

AUTOMATIC-5 STALKER
Same general specifications as Automatic-5 Light and Magnum models except w/matte blue finish and black graphite fiberglass

(cont'd.) AUTOMATIC-5 STALKER
stock and forearm. Made 1992 to date.
Light model . . . . NiB $773 Ex $618 Gd $421
Magnum model . . . . NiB $820 Ex $656 Gd $446

AUTOMATIC-5, STANDARD (GRADE I)
Recoil-operated. Gauge: 12 or 16 (16-gauge guns made prior to WW II were chambered for 2-inch shells; standard 16 disc. 1964). Four shell magazine in 5-shot model, prewar guns were also available in 3-shot model. Bbls.: 26- to 32-inch; plain, raised matted or vent rib; choice of standard chokes. Weight: About 8 lbs., in 12 ga., 7.5 lbs., in 16 ga. Checkered pistol-grip stock and forearm. (Note: Browning Special, disc. about 1940.) Made 1900-73 by FN.
Grade I, plain bbl. . . . . NiB $617 Ex $493 Gd $336
Grade I or Browning Special,
Raised matted rib . . . . NiB $788 Ex $631 Gd $428
Grade I or Browning Special, vent rib . . . . NiB $812 Ex $650 Gd $442

AUTOMATIC-5, SWEET 16
16 ga. Same general specifications as Standard Model except lightweight (about 6.75 lbs.), has gold plated trigger. Guns w/rib have striped matting on top of bbl. Made 1937-76 by FN.
W/plain bbl. . . . . $NiB $703 Ex $562 Gd $382
W/raised matted or ventilated rib . . . . NiB $773 Ex $618 Gd $421

AUTO-5,
SWEET SIXTEEN NEW MODEL . . . . NiB $866 Ex $693 Gd $471
Reissue of popular 16-gauge Hunting Model w/5-shot capacity, 2.75-inch chamber, scroll-engraved blued receiver, high-gloss French walnut stock w/rounded pistol grip. 26- or 28-inch vent-rib bbl. F choke tube. Weight: 7 lbs., 5 oz. Reintro. 1987-93.

Browning BPS
Waterfowl – Mossy Oak Shadow Grass

Browning BPS Stalker

AUTOMATIC-5, TRAP MODEL . . . . NiB $850 Ex $650 Gd $400
12 ga. only. Same general specifications as Standard Model except has trap-style stock, 30-inch vent-rib bbl. F choke. Weight: 8.5 lbs. Disc. 1971.

MODEL B-80 GAS-OPERATED
AUTOMATIC . . . . NiB $494 Ex $395 Gd $269
Gauge: 12 or 20; 2.75-inch chamber. Four shot magazine. Bbl.: 26-, 28- or 30-inch, any standard choke, vent-rib bbl. w/fixed chokes or Invector tubes. Weight: 6 lbs., 12 oz.-8 lbs., 1 oz. depending on ga. and bbl. Checkered pistol-grip stock and forearm. Made 1981-87.

MODEL B-80 PLUS . . . . NiB $544 Ex $435 Gd $296
Same general specifications as Browning Model B-80 except chambered for 3-inch shotshells. Made in 1988 only.

MODEL B-80 SUPERLIGHT . . . . NiB $494 Ex $395 Gd $269
Same as Standard Model except weighs 1 lb. less.

MODEL B-80 UPLAND SPECIAL . . NiB $506 Ex $405 Gd $275
Gauge: 12 or 20. 22-inch vent-rib bbl. Invector choke tube system. 2.75-inch chambers. 42 inches overall. Weight: 5 lbs., 7 oz. (20 ga.); 6 lbs., 10 oz. (12 ga.). German nickel silver sight bead. Crossbolt safety. Checkered walnut straight-grip stock and forend. Disc. 1988.

BPS GAME GUN DEER SPECIAL . . . NiB $438 Ex $350 Gd $238
Same general specifications as Standard BPS model except has 20.5-inch bbl. w/adj. rifle-style sights. Solid scope mounting system. Checkered walnut stock w/sling swivel studs. Made from 1992 to date.

BPS GAME GUN TURKEY SPECIAL . . . . . . NiB $450 Ex $360 Gd $245
Same general specifications as Standard BPS model except w/matte blue metal finish and satin-finished stock. Chambered for 12 ga. 3-inch only. 20.5-inch bbl. w/extra full invector choke system. Receiver drilled and tapped for scope. Made 1992 to date.

BPS PIGEON GRADE . . . . NiB $594 Ex $475 Gd $323
Same general specifications as Standard BPS model except w/select grade walnut stock and gold-trimmed receiver. Available in 12 ga. only w/26- or 28-inch vent-rib bbl. Made 1992 to date.

BPS PUMP INVECTOR STALKER
Same general specifications as BPS Pump Shotgun except in 10 and 12 ga. w/Invector choke system, 22-, 26-, 28- or 30-inch bbls.; matte blue metal finish w/matte black stock. Made 1987 to date.
12 ga. model (3-inch) . . . . NiB $419 Ex $335 Gd $228
10- & 12 ga. model (3.5-inch) . . . . NiB $581 Ex $465 Gd $316

BPS PUMP SHOTGUN
Takedown. Gauges: 10, 12 (3.5-inch chamber); 12, 20 and .410 (3-inch) and 28 ga. chambered 2.75-inch. Bbls.: 22-, 24-, 26-, 28-, 30-, or 32-inch; fixed choke or Invector tubes. Weight: 7.5 lbs. (w/28-inch bbl.). Checkered select walnut pistol-grip stock and semi-beavertail forearm, recoil pad. Introduced in 1977. Made by Miroku.

Model BPS Magnum Hunter	NiB $594	Ex $475	Gd $323
Model BPS Magnum Stalker	NiB $575	Ex $460	Gd $313
Model BPS Magnum Camo	NiB $650	Ex $520	Gd $354
Model BPS Hunter	NiB $494	Ex $395	Gd $269
Model BPS Upland	NiB $494	Ex $395	Gd $269
Model BPS Stalker (26- 28- or 30-inch bbl.) . . .	NiB $475	Ex $380	Gd $258
Model BPS Stalker 24-inch bbl	NiB $500	Ex $400	Gd $272
Model BPS Game Gun—Turkey Special	NiB $531	Ex $425	Gd $289
Model BPS Game Gun—fully rifled bbl.	NiB $600	Ex $480	Gd $326
Model BPS Hunter 20 ga.	NiB $494	Ex $395	Gd $269
Model BPS Upland 20 ga.	NiB $494	Ex $395	Gd $269
Model BPS Micro	NiB $494	Ex $395	Gd $269
Model BPS Hunter 28 ga.	NiB $525	Ex $420	Gd $286
Model BPS Bore Hunter .410	NiB $525	Ex $420	Gd $286
Model BPS Buck Spec. (10 or 12 ga., 3.5-inch)	NiB $563	Ex $450	Gd $306
Model BPS Buck Spec. (12 or 20 ga.)	NiB $394	Ex $315	Gd $214
Model BPS Waterfowl			
(10 or 12 ga., 3.5-inch)	NiB $619	Ex $495	Gd $337
W/fixed choke, deduct $50			

BPS YOUTH AND LADIES' MODEL
Lightweight (6 lbs., 11 oz.) version of BPS Pump Shotgun in 20 ga. w/22-inch bbl. and floating vent rib, F choke (invector) tube. Made 1986 to date.
Standard Invector model (disc. 1994) . . . . NiB $369 Ex $295 Gd $201
Invector Plus model . . . . NiB $406 Ex $325 Gd $221

BSA 10 SEMIAUTOMATIC SHOTGUN
Gas-operated short-stroke action. 10 ga.; 3.5-inch chamber. Five shot magazine. Bbls.: 26-, 28-or 30-inch w/Invector tubes and vent rib. Weight: 10.5 lbs. Checkered select walnut buttstock and forend. Blued finish. Made 1993 to date. Note: Although intro. as the BSA 10, this model is now marketed as the Gold Series. See separate listing for pricing.

B-SS SIDE-BY-SIDE
Boxlock. Automatic ejectors. Non-selective single trigger (early production) or selective-single trigger (late production). Gauges: 12 or 20 w/3-inch chambers. Bbls. 26-, 28-, or 30-inch; IC/M, M/F, or F/F chokes; matte solid rib. Weight: 7 to 7.5 lbs. Checkered straight-grip stock and beavertail forearm. Made 1972-88 by Miroku.
Standard model (early/NSST) . . . . NiB $531 Ex $425 Gd $289
Standard model (late/SST) . . . . NiB $619 Ex $495 Gd $337
Grade II (antique silver receiver) . . . . NiB $1063 Ex $850 Gd $578
20 ga. models, add $100

SHOTGUNS

Browning B-SS 20 Gauge Sporter

Browning BT-99 Competition Trap

B-SS SIDE-BY-SIDE SIDELOCK
Same general specifications as B-SS boxlock models except sidelock version available in 26- or 28-inch bbl. lengths. 26-inch choked IC/M; 28-inch, M/F. Double triggers. Satin-grayed receiver engraved w/rosettes and scrolls. German nickel-silver sight bead. Weight: 6.25 lbs. to 6 lbs., 11 oz. 12 ga. made in 1983; 20 ga. Made in 1984. Disc. 1988.

12 ga. model	NiB $895	Ex $675	Gd $949
20 ga. model	NiB $2392	Ex $1914	Gd $1302

B-SS S/S 20 GAUGE SPORTER .... NiB $721 Ex $577 Gd $392
Same as standard B-SS 20 ga. except has selective single trigger, straight-grip stock. Introduced 1977. Disc. 1987.

BT-99 COMPETITION TRAP SPECIAL
Same as BT-99 except has super-high wide rib and standard Monte Carlo or fully adj. stock. Available w/adj. choke or Invector Plus tubes w/optional porting. Made 1976-94.

Grade I w/fixed			
choke (disc. 1992)	NiB $856	Ex $685	Gd $466
Grade I w/Invectors	NiB $1063	Ex $850	Gd $578
Grade I stainless (disc. 1994)	NiB $1119	Ex $895	Gd $609
Grade I Pigeon Grade (disc. 1994)	NiB $1031	Ex $825	Gd $561

BT-99 GRADE I SINGLE BBL. TRAP ...... NiB $776 Ex $621 Gd $422
Boxlock. Automatic ejector. 12 ga. only. 32- or 34-inch vent rib bbl., M, IM or F choke. Weight: About 8 lbs. Checkered pistol-grip stock and beavertail forearm, recoil pad. Made 1971-76 by Miroku.

BT-99 MAX
Boxlock. 12 ga. only w/ejector selector and no safety. 32- or 34-inch ported bbl. w/high post vent rib. Checkered select walnut buttstock and finger-grooved forend w/high luster finish. Engraved receiver w/blued or stainless metal finish. Made 1995-96.

Blued	NiB $1143	Ex $914	Gd $622
Stainless	NiB $1718	Ex $1374	Gd $934

BT-99 PLUS
Similar to the BT-99 Competition except w/Browning Recoil Reduction System. Made 1989-95.

Grade I	NiB $1119	Ex $895	Gd $609
Pigeon grade	NiB $1281	Ex $1025	Gd $697
Signature grade	NiB $1244	Ex $995	Gd $677
Stainless model	NiB $1369	Ex $1095	Gd $745
Golden Clays	NiB $2369	Ex $2195	Gd $1945

BT-99 PLUS MICRO .... NiB $1156 Ex $925 Gd $629
Same general specifications as BT-99 Plus except scaled down for smaller shooters. 30-inch bbl. w/adj. rib and Browning's recoil reducer system. Made 1991 to date.

BT-100 SINGLE-SHOT TRAP
Similar to the BT-99 Max, except w/additional stock options and removable trigger group. Made 1995 to date.

Model BT-100 Grade I blued	NiB $1375	Ex $1100	Gd $748
Model BT-100 stainless	NiB $1594	Ex $1275	Gd $867
Model BT-100 satin	NiB $1281	Ex $1025	Gd $697
Model BT-100 w/adj. comb, add			$250
Thumbhole stock, add			$295
Replacement trigger assembly, add			$495
Fixed choke, deduct			$65

CITORI HUNTING O/U MODELS
Boxlock. Gauges: 12, 16 (disc. 1989), 20, 28 (disc. 1992) and .410 bore (disc. 1989). Bbl. lengths: 24-, 26-, 28-, or 30-inch w/vent rib. Chambered 2.75-, 3- or 3.5-inch mag. Chokes: IC/M, M/F (Fixed Chokes); Standard Invector, or Invector plus choke systems. Overall length ranges from 41-47 inches. 2.75-, 3- or 3-inch Mag. loads, depending on ga. Weight: 5.75 lbs. to 7 lbs. 13 oz. Single selective, gold-plated trigger. Medium raised German nickel-silver sight bead. Checkered, rounded pistol-grip walnut stock w/beavertail forend. Invector Chokes and Invector Plus became standard in 1988 and 1995, respectively. Made from 1973 to date by Miroku.

Grade I (disc. 1994)	NiB $781	Ex $625	Gd $425
Grade I - 3.5-inch Mag.(1989 to date)	NiB $1056	Ex $845	Gd $575
Grade II (disc. 1983)	NiB $969	Ex $775	Gd $527
Grade III (1985-95)	NiB $1119	Ex $895	Gd $609
Grade V (disc. 1984)	NiB $1563	Ex $1250	Gd $850
Grade VI (1985-95)	NiB $1744	Ex $1395	Gd $949
Model Sporting Hunter			
(12 and 20 ga.; 1998 to date)	NiB $938	Ex $750	Gd $510
Model Satin Hunter			
(12 ga. only; 1998 to date)	NiB $844	Ex $675	Gd $459
Mdls. w/o Inv. choke syst., deduct			$120
For 3.5-inch Mag., add			$90
For disc. ga 16, 28 and .410, add			15%

CITORI LIGHTNING O/U MODELS
Same general specifications as the Citori Hunting models except w/classic Browning rounded pistol-grip stock. Made from 1988 to date by Miroku.

Grade I	NiB $800	Ex $640	Gd $435
Grade III	NiB $1206	Ex $965	Gd $656
Grade VI	NiB $1744	Ex $1395	Gd $949
Gran Lightning model	NiB $1281	Ex $1025	Gd $697
Feather Model (alloy receiver)	NiB $969	Ex $775	Gd $527
Feather Combo model (2-bbl. set)	NiB $2313	Ex $1850	Gd $1258
Privilege Mdl. (engraved w/sideplates)	NiB $4494	Ex $3595	Gd $2445
Micro model, add			10%
Models w/o Invector			
choke system, deduct			$120
28 and .410 ga., add			15%

Browning BT-100 Monte Carlo Stock

Browning BT-99 Competition Trap

Browning Citori Lightning

Browning Citori Gran Lightning

Browning Citori Skeet Gun

CITORI SKEET GUN

Same as Hunting model except has skeet-style stock and forearm, 26- or 28-inch bbls., both bored SK choke. Available w/either standard vent rib or special target-type, high-post, wide vent rib. Weight (w/26-inch bbls.): 12 ga., 8 lbs., 20 ga., 7 lbs. Made 1974 to date by Miroku.

Grade I . . . . NiB $1395 Ex $950 Gd $550
Grade II . . . . NiB $1063 Ex $850 Gd $578
Grade III . . . . NiB $1244 Ex $995 Gd $677
Grade VI (disc. 1995) . . . . NiB $1869 Ex $1495 Gd $1017
Golden Clays . . . . NiB $2063 Ex $1650 Gd $1122
28 and .410 ga., add 15%
3-bbl. Set, Grade I (disc. 1996) . . . . . . NiB $2188 Ex $1750 Gd $1190
3-bbl. Set, Grade III (disc. 1996) . . . . . NiB $2369 Ex $1895 Gd $128
3-bbl. Set, Grade VI (disc. 1994) . . . . . NiB $2688 Ex $2150 Gd $1462
3-bbl. Set, Golden Clays (disc. 1995) . . . . . NiB $3494 Ex $2795 Gd $1901
4-bbl. Set, Grade I . . . . NiB $3199 Ex $2559 Gd $1740
4-bbl. Set, Grade III . . . . NiB $3563 Ex $2850 Gd $1938
4-bbl. Set, Grade VI (disc. 1994) . . . . . NiB $3494 Ex $2995 Gd $2077
4-bbl. Set, Golden Clays (disc. 1995) . . NiB $4438 Ex $3550 Gd $2414

CITORI SPORTING CLAYS

Similar to the standard Citori Lightning model except Classic-style stock with rounded pistol-grip. 30-inch back-bored bbls. with Invector Plus tubes. Receiver with "Lightning Sporting Clays Edition" logo. Made 1989 to date.

(cont'd.) CITORI SPORTING CLAYS

GTI model (disc. 1995) . . . . NiB $1225 Ex $850 Gd $525
GTI Golden Clays model (1993-94) . . . NiB $1869 Ex $1495 Gd $1017
Lightning model (intro. 1989) . . . . NiB $1081 Ex $865 Gd $588
Lightning Golden Clays (1993-98) . . . . NiB $1938 Ex $1550 Gd $1054
Lightning Pigeon Grade (1993-94) . . . . . . NiB $1156 Ex $925 Gd $629
Micro Citori Lightning model
(w/low rib) . . . . NiB $1288 Ex $850 Gd $54
Special Sporting model (intro. 1989) . . . . NiB $1319 Ex $875 Gd $563
Special Sporting
Golden Clays (1993-98) . . . . NiB $2219 Ex $1775 Gd $1207
Special Sporting Pigeon Gr. (1993-94) . . . NiB $1188 Ex $950 Gd $646
Ultra mdl. (intro. 1995-previously GTI) . . NiB $1219 Ex $975 Gd $663
Ultra Golden Clays (intro. 1995) . . . . . NiB $2244 Ex $1795 Gd $1221
Model 325 (1993-94) . . . . NiB $1156 Ex $925 Gd $629
Model 325 Golden Clays (1993-94) . . . NiB $1906 Ex $1525 Gd $1037
Model 425 Grade I (intro. 1995) . . . . . NiB $1244 Ex $995 Gd $677
Model 425 Golden Clays (intro. 1995) . . . . NiB $2244 Ex $1795 Gd $1221
Model 425 WSSF (intro. 1995) . . . . NiB $1188 Ex $950 Gd $646
Model 802 Sporter (ES)
Extended Swing (intro. 1996 . . . . NiB $1313 Ex $1050 Gd $714
For 2 bbl. set add $850
For adjustable stock, add $200
For high rib, add $85
For ported barrels, add $65

Browning Citori Superlight Field Shotgun

Browning Citori Trap

Browning Citori White Lightning Over/Under

Browning Citori Sporting Hunter Over/Under

Browning Gold Hunter

Browning Liége Over/Under Shotgun

CITORI SUPERLIGHT O/U FIELD SHOTGUNS
Similar to the Citori Hunting model except w/straight-grip stock and Schnabel forend tip. Made by Miroku 1982 to date.

Grade I . . . . NiB $1219 Ex $975 Gd $663
Grade III . . . . NiB $1617 Ex $1293 Gd $880
Grade V (disc. 1985) . . . . NiB $2104 Ex $1683 Gd $1145
Grade VI . . . . NiB $2429 Ex $1943 Gd $1324
Models w/o Invector choke system, deduct $120
28 and .410 ga., add 15%

CITORI TRAP GUN
Same as Hunting model except 12 ga. only, has Monte Carlo or fully adjustable stock and beavertail forend, trap-style recoil pad; 20- or 32-inch bbls.; M/F, IM/F, or F/F. Available with either standard vent rib or special target-type, high-post, wide vent rib. Weight: 8 lbs. Made from 1974 to date by Miroku.

(cont'd.) CITORI TRAP GUN
Grade I Trap . . . . NiB $1340 Ex $1072 Gd $729
Grade I Trap Pigeon grade (disc. 1994) . . NiB $1617 Ex $1293 Gd $880
Grade I Trap Signature grade (disc. 1994) . . . NiB $1584 Ex $1267 Gd $861
Grade I Plus Trap (disc. 1994) . . . NiB $1665 Ex $1332 Gd $906
Grade I Plus Trap
w/ported bbls. (disc. 1994) . . . . . NiB $1779 Ex $1423 Gd $968
Grade I Plus Trap
Combo (disc. 1994) . . . . NiB $3859 Ex $3087 Gd $2099
Grade I Plus Trap
Golden Clays (disc. 1994) . . . . . NiB $1665 Ex $1332 Gd $906
Grade II w/HP rib (disc. 1984) . . NiB $1454 Ex $1163 Gd $791
Grade III Trap . . . . NiB $1779 Ex $1423 Gd $968
Grade V Trap (disc. 1984) . . . . . NiB $1942 Ex $1553 Gd $1056
Grade VI Trap (disc. 1994) . . . . . NiB $2267 Ex $1813 Gd $1233
Grade VI Trap
Golden Clays (disc. 1994) . . . . NiB $2754 Ex $2203 Gd $1498

CITORI UPLAND SPECIAL O/U SHOTGUN
A shortened version of the Hunting model fitted with 24-inch bbls. and straight-grip stock.

Upland Special 12, 20 ga. models...... NiB $1097 Ex $877 Gd $596
Upland Spec. 16 ga. mdl. (disc. 1989) .. NiB $1292 Ex $1033 Gd $703
Models w/o Inv. choke sys., deduct $120

CITORI WHITE LIGHTNING O/U SHOTGUN
Similar to the standard Citori Lightning model except w/silver nitride receiver w/scroll and rosette engraving. Satin wood finish w/round pistol grip. Made 1998 to date.

12, 20 ga. models................ NiB $1292   Ex $1033   Gd $703
28, .410 ga. models (Intro. 2000)...... NiB $1405 Ex $1124 Gd $764

CITORI WHITE UPLAND SPECIAL...... NiB $1129 Ex $903 Gd $614
Similar to the standard Citori Upland model except w/silver nitride receiver w/scroll and rosette engraving. Satin wood finish w/round pistol grip. Made 2000 to date.

DOUBLE AUTOMATIC (STEEL RECEIVER)
Short recoil system. Takedown. 12 ga. only. Two shots. Bbls.: 26-, 28-, 30-inch; any standard choke. Checkered pistol-grip stock and forend. Weight: About 7.75 lbs. Made 1955-1961.

With plain bbl. .... NiB $581 Ex $465 Gd $316
With recessed-rib bbl........... NiB $738 Ex $590 Gd $401

GOLD DEER HUNTER AUTOLOADING SHOTGUN
Similar to the Standard Gold Hunter model except chambered 12 ga. only. 22-inch bbl. W/rifled bore or smooth bore w/5-inch rifled invector tube. Cantilevered scope mount. Made 1997 to date.

Gold Deer Hunter (w/standard finish) .... NiB $738 Ex $590 Gd $401
Field model (w/Mossy Oak finish) .... NiB $619 Ex $495 Gd $337

GOLD HUNTER SERIES
Self-cleaning, gas-operated, short-stroke action. Gauges: 10 or 12 (3.5-inch chamber); 12 or 20 (3-inch chamber). 26-, 28-, or 30-inch bbl. w/Invector or Invector Plus choke tubes. Checkered walnut stock. Polished or matte black metal finish. Made 1994 to date.

Gold Hunter (Light 10 ga. 3.5-inch w/wal. St.) .... NiB $831 Ex $665 Gd $452
Gold Hunter (12 ga. 3.5-inch)........... NiB $781 Ex $625 Gd $425
Gold Hunter (12 or 20 ga. 3-inch) .... NiB $500 Ex $400 Gd $272
Gld. Hunter Clas. Mdl. (12 or 20 Ga. 3-inch) ..... NiB $531 Ex $425 Gd $289
Gld. Hunter High Gr.
Classic (12 or 20 ga. 3-inch)........... NiB $1094 Ex $875 Gd $595
Gold Deer Hunter
(12 ga. w/22-inch bbl.)............. NiB $563 Ex $450 Gd $306
Gold Turkey Hunter Camo
(12 ga. w/24-inch bbl.)............. NiB $519 Ex $415 Gd $282
Gold Waterfowl Hunter
Camo (12 ga. w/24-inch bbl.).......... NiB $500 Ex $400 Gd $272

GOLD STALKER SERIES
Self-cleaning, gas-operated, short-stroke action. Gauges: 10 or 12 (3.5-inch chamber); 12 or 20 (3-inch chamber). 26-, 28-, or 30-inch bbl. w/Invector or Invector Plus choke tubes. Graphite/fiberglass composite stock. Polished or matte black metal finish. Made 1998 to date.

Gold Stalker (Light 10 ga.
3.5-inch w/composite stock)........... NiB $813 Ex $650 Gd $442
Gold Stalker (12 ga. 3.5-inch).......... NiB $744 Ex $595 Gd $405
Gold Stalker (12 or 20 ga. 3-inch) .... NiB $494 Ex $395 Gd $269
Gold Stalker Classic
Model (12 or 20 ga. 3-inch)......... NiB $500 Ex $400 Gd $272
Gold Deer Stalker
(12 ga. w/22-inch bbl.)............. NiB $563 Ex $450 Gd $306
Gold Turkey Stalker Camo
(12 ga. w/24-inch bbl.)............. NiB $519 Ex $415 Gd $282

Browning Over/Under Gold Classic

(cont'd.) GOLD STALKER SERIES
Gold Waterfowl Stalker
Camo (12 Ga. w/24-inch bbl.) .... NiB $875 Ex $460 Gd $400

GOLD SPORTING SERIES
Similar to Gold Hunter Series except w/2.75-inch chamber and 28- or 30-inch ported bbl. w/Invector Plus chokes. Made 1999 to date.

Gold Sporting Clays (standard).......... NiB $763 Ex $650 Gd $506
Gold Sporting Clays (youth or ladies)..... NiB $781 Ex $665 Gd $516
Gold Sporting Clays w/Eng. nick. rec..... NiB $1194 Ex $995 Gd $741

LIEGE O/U SHOTGUN (B26/27)
Boxlock. Automatic ejectors. Non-selective single trigger. 12 ga. only. Bbls.: 26.5-, 28-, or 30-inch; 2.75-inch chambers in 26.5- and 28-inch, 3-inch in 30-inch, IC/M, M/F, or F/F chokes; vent rib. Weight: 7 lbs., 4 oz.to 7 lbs., 14 oz., depending on bbls. Checkered pistol-grip stock and forearm. Made 1973-75 by FN.

Liège (B-26 BAC production) .... NiB $855 Ex $684 Gd $465
Liège (B-27 FN prod.) Stand. Game Mdl. .. NiB $826 Ex $661 Gd $449
Deluxe Game model................... NiB $934 Ex $747 Gd $508
Grand Delux Game model .... NiB $1143 Ex $914 Gd $622
Deluxe Skeet model .... NiB $970 Ex $776 Gd $527
Deluxe Trap model .... NiB $955 Ex $764 Gd $519
COL Commemorative model .... NiB $1366 Ex $1092 Gd $742

LIGHT SPORTING 802ES .... NiB $1244 Ex $995 Gd $677
Over/under. Invector-plus choke tubes. 12 ga. only with 28-inch bbl. Weight: 7 lbs., 5 oz.

LIGHTNING SPORTING CLAYS
Similar to the standard Citori Lightning model except Classic-style stock with rounded pistol grip. 30-inch back-bored bbls. with Invector Plus tubes. Receiver with "Lightning Sporting Clays Edition" logo. Made 1989 to date.

Standard model .... NiB $1096 Ex $850 Gd $573
Pigeon grade .... NiB $1156 Ex $925 Gd $629

O/U CLASSIC .... NiB $2063 Ex $1650 Gd $1122
Gauge: 20, 2.75-inch chambers. 26-inch blued bbls. choked IC/M. Gold-plated, single selective trigger. Manual, top-tang-mounted safety. Engraved receiver. High grade, select American walnut straight-grip stock with Schnabel forend. Fine-line checkering with pearl borders. High-gloss finish. 5,000 issued in 1986; made in Japan, engraved in Belgium.

O/U GOLD CLASSIC.............. NiB $4994 Ex $3995 Gd $2717
Same general specifications as Over/Under Classic except more elaborate engravings, enhanced in gold, including profile of John M. Browning. Fine oil finish. 500 issued; made in 1986 in Belgium.

RECOILLESS TRAP SHOTGUN
The action and bbl. are driven forward when firing to achieve 72 percent less recoil. 12 ga, 2.75-inch chamber. 30-inch bbl. with Invector Plus tubes; adjustable vent rib. 51.63 inches overall. Weight: 9 lbs. Adj. checkered walnut buttstock and forend. Blued finish. Made from 1993-96.

SHOTGUNS

Browning Superposed Broadway 12 Trap

Browning Superposed Grade I Lightning

Left Side

Right Side

Browning Superposed Bicentennial

Browning Superposed Grade IV Diana (Postwar)

Browning Superposed Grade V Midas (Postwar)

(cont'd.) RECOILLESS TRAP SHOTGUN
Standard model . . . . NiB $844 Ex $675 Gd $459
Micro model (27-inch bbl.) . . . . NiB $869 Ex $695 Gd $473
Signature model (27-inch bbl.) . . . . NiB $1271 Ex $1017 Gd $723

SUPERPOSED BICENTENNIAL
COMMEMORATIVE . . . . NiB $12813 Ex $10250 Gd $6970
Special limited edition issued to commemorate U.S. Bicentennial. 51 guns, one for each state in the Union plus one for Washington, D.C. Receiver with sideplates has engraved and gold-inlaid hunter and wild turkey on right side, U.S. flag and bald eagle on left side, together with state markings inlaid in gold, on blued background. Checkered straight-grip stock and Schnabel-style forearm of highly-figured American walnut. Velvet-lined wood presentation case. Made in 1976 by FN. Value shown is for gun in new, unfired condition. See illustration next page.

SUPERPOSED
BROADWAY 12 TRAP . . . . NiB $1906 Ex $1525 Gd $1037
Same as Standard Trap Gun except has 30- or 32-inch bbls. with wider Broadway rib. Disc. 1976.

SUPERPOSED SHOTGUNS, HUNTING MODELS
Over/under boxlock. Selective automatic ejectors. Selective single trigger; earlier models (worth 25% less) supplied w/double triggers, twin selective triggers or non-selective single trigger. Gauges: 12, 20 (intro. 1949, 3-inch chambers in later production), 28, .410 (latter two ga. intro. 1960). Bbls.: 26.5-, 28-, 30-, 32-inch, raised matted or vent rib, prewar Lightning Model made w/ribbed bbl., postwar version supplied only w/vent rib; any combination of standard chokes. Weight (w/26.5-inch vent-rib bbls.): Standard 12, 7 lbs., 11 oz., Lightning 12, 7 lbs., 6 oz.; Standard 20, 6 lbs., 8 oz.; Lightning 20, 6 lbs., 4 oz.; Lightning 28, 6 lbs., 7 oz.; Lightning .410, 6 lbs., 10 oz. Checkered pistol-grip stock/forearm.
Higher grades (Pigeon, Pointer, Diana, Midas, Grade VI) differ from standard Grade I models in overall quality, engraving, wood and checkering; otherwise, specifications are the same. Midas Grade and Grade VI guns are richly gold inlaid. Made by FN 1928-1976. Prewar models may be considered as disc. in 1940 when Belgium was occupied by Germany. Grade VI offered 1955-1960. Pointer Grade disc. in 1966, Grade I Standard in 1973, Pigeon Grade in 1974. Lightning Grade I, Diana and Midas Grades were not offered after 1976.
Grade I standard weight . . . . NiB $1643 Ex $1314 Gd $894
Grade I Lightning . . . . NiB $1994 Ex $1595 Gd $1084
Grade I Lightning, prewar,
matted bbl., no rib . . . . NiB $2880 Ex $2304 Gd $1567
Grade II—Pigeon. . . . . NiB $3018 Ex $2414 Gd $1642

Browning Superposed Ltd.
Pintail Duck Issue

(cont'd.) SUPERPOSED SHOTGUNS

Grade III—Pointer	NiB $2938	Ex $2350	Gd $1598
Grade IV—Diana	NiB $3619	Ex $2895	Gd $1969
Grade V—Midas	NiB $9063	Ex $7250	Gd $4930
Grade VI	NiB $6119	Ex $4895	Gd $3329

Add for 20 ga. 20%
Add for 28 ga. 75%
Add for .410. .... 45%
Values shown are for models w/ventilated rib.
If gun has raised matted rib, deduct 10%

SUPERPOSED LIGHTNING AND SUPERLIGHT MODELS (REISSUE B-25)
Reissue of popular 12-and 20-ga. Superposed shotguns. Lightning models available in 26.5- and 28-inch bbl. lengths w/2.75- or 3-inch chambering, full pistol grip. Superlight models available in 26.5-inch bbl. lengths w/2.75-inch chambering only, and straight-grip stock w/Schnabel forend. Both have hand-engraved receivers, fine-line checkering, gold-plated single selective trigger, automatic selective ejectors, manual safety. Weight: 6 to 7.5 lbs. Reintroduced 1985.

Grade I, Standard	NiB $1619	Ex $1295	Gd $881
Grade II, Pigeon	NiB $2994	Ex $2395	Gd $1629
Grade III, Pointer	NiB $3744	Ex $2995	Gd $2037
Grade IV, Diana	NiB $4119	Ex $3295	Gd $2241
Grade V, Midas	NiB $5369	Ex $4295	Gd $2921

W/extra bbls., add 45%

SUPERPOSED MAGNUM ...... NiB $1563 Ex $1250 Gd $850
Same as Grade I except chambered for 12-ga. 3-inch shells, 30-inch vent-rib bbls., stock w/recoil pad. Weight: About 8.25 lbs. Disc. 1976.

SUPERPOSED LTD.
BLACK DUCK ISSUE .... NiB $7000 Ex $5600 Gd $3808
Gauge: 12. Superposed Lightning action. 28-inch vent-rib bbls. Choked M/F. 2.75-inch chambers. Weight: 7 lbs., 6 oz. Gold-inlaid receiver and trigger guard engraved w/black duck scenes. Gold-plated, single selective trigger. Top-tang mounted manual safety. Automatic, selective ejectors. Front and center ivory sights. High-grade, hand-checkered, hand-oiled select walnut stock and forend. 500 issued in 1983.

SUPERPOSED LTD.
MALLARD DUCK ISSUE ...... NiB $7188 Ex $5750 Gd $3910
Same general specifications as Ltd. Black Duck issue except mallard duck scenes engraved on receiver and trigger guard, dark French walnut stock w/rounded pistol-grip. 500 issued in 1981.

SUPERPOSED LTD.
PINTAIL DUCK ISSUE .... NiB $7369 Ex $5895 Gd $4009
Same general specifications as Ltd. Black Duck issue except pintail duck scenes engraved on receiver and trigger guard. Stock is of dark French walnut w/rounded pistol-grip. 500 issued in 1982.

SUPERPOSED, PRESENTATION GRADES
Custom versions of Super-Light, Lightning Hunting, Trap and Skeet

(cont'd.) SUPERPOSED, PRESENTATION GRADES
Models, w/same general specifications as those of standard guns, but of higher overall quality. The four Presentation grades differ in receiver finish (grayed or blued), engraving gold inlays, wood and checkering. Presentation 4 has sideplates. Made by FN, these models were Intro. in 1977.

Presentation 1	NiB $2994	Ex $2395	Gd $1629
Presentation 1, gold-inlaid	NiB $3438	Ex $2750	Gd $1870
Presentation 2	NiB $3869	Ex $3095	Gd $2105
Presentation 2, gold-inlaid	NiB $4563	Ex $3650	Gd $2482
Presentation 3, gold-inlaid	NiB $5906	Ex $4725	Gd $3213
Presentation 4	NiB $6619	Ex $5295	Gd $3601
Presentation 4, gold-inlaid	NiB $8563	Ex $6850	Gd $4658

SUPERPOSED SKEET GUNS, GRADE I
Same as standard Lightning 12, 20, 28 and .410 Hunting models, except has skeet-style stock and forearm, 26.5- or 28-inch vent-rib bbls. w/SK choke. Available also in All Gauge Skeet Set: Lightning 12 w/one removable forearm and three extra sets of bbls. in 20, 28 and .410 ga. in fitted luggage case. Disc. 1976. (For higher grades see listings for comparable Hunting models)

12 or 20 ga.	NiB $1813	Ex $1450	Gd $986
28 or .410 ga.	NiB $2244	Ex $1795	Gd $1221
All ga. skeet set	NiB $5744	Ex $4595	Gd $3125

SUPERPOSED SUPER
LIGHT MODEL .... NiB $1781 Ex $1425 Gd $969
Ultralight field gun version of Standard Lightning Model has classic straight-grip stock and slimmer forearm. Available only in 12 and 20 gauges (2.75-inch chambers), w/26.5-inch vent-rib bbls. Weight: 6.5 lbs., (12 ga.); 6 lbs., (20 ga.). Made 1967-76.

SUPERPOSED TRAP GUN ..... NiB $1844 Ex $1475 Gd $1003
Same as Grade I except has trap-style stock, beavertail forearm, 30-inch vent-rib bbls., 12 ga. only. Disc. 1976. (For higher grades see listings for comparable hunting models)

TWELVETTE DOUBLE AUTOMATIC
Lightweight version of Double Automatic w/same general specifications except aluminum receiver. Bbl. w/plain matted top or vent rib. Weight: 6.75 to 7 lbs., depending on bbl. Receiver is finished in black w/gold engraving; 1956-1961 receivers were also anodized in gray, brown and green w/silver engraving. Made 1955-71.

W/plain bbl.	NiB $531	Ex $425	Gd $289
W/vent rib bbl.	NiB $656	Ex $525	Gd $357

CENTURY INTERNATIONAL ARMS INC. — St. Albans, VT

CENTURION .... NiB $331 Ex $265 Gd $180
O/U boxlock action with double triggers and extractors. 12 ga. w/2.75-inch chamber. Bbls: 28-inch choked modified/full with ventilated rib. Weight: 7-1/4 lbs. Checkered European walnut buttstock and forend. Polished blue finish. Imported 1993 to date.

SHOTGUNS

Churchill Automatic Shotgun

Churchill Windsor Grade Side-by-Side Shotgun

Churchill Windsor Grade Flyweight Shotgun

CHURCHILL SHOTGUNS — Italy and Spain Imported by Ellett Brothers, Inc., Chapin, SC; previously by Kassnar Imports, Inc., Harrisburg, PA

AUTOMATIC SHOTGUN
Gas-operated. Gauge: 12, 2.75- or 3-inch chambers. Five shot magazine w/cutoff. Bbl.: 24-, 25-, 26-, 28-inch w/ICT choke tubes. Checkered walnut stock w/satin finish. Imported from Italy 1990-94.
Standard model . . . . NiB $494 Ex $395 Gd $269
Turkey model . . . . NiB $519 Ex $415 Gd $282

MONARCH O/U SHOTGUN
Hammerless, takedown w/engraved receiver. Selective single or double triggers. Gauges: 12, 20, 28, .410; 3-inch chambers. Bbls.: 25- or 26-inch (IC/M); 28-inch (M/F). Weight: 6.5-7.5 lbs. Checkered European walnut buttstock and forend. Made in Italy 1986-93.
W/double triggers . . . . NiB $460 Ex $368 Gd $250
W/single trigger. . . . . NiB $515 Ex $412 Gd $280

REGENT O/U SHOTGUNS
Gauges: 12 or 20; 2.75-inch chambers. 27-inch bbls. w/interchangeable choke tubes and wide vent rib. Single selective trigger, selective automatic ejectors. Checkered pistol-grip stock in fancy walnut. Imported from Italy 1984-88 and 1990-94.
Regent V(disc. 1988). . . . . NiB $938 Ex $750 Gd $510
Regent VII w/
sideplates (disc. 1994) . . . . NiB $1063 Ex $850 Gd $578

REGENT SKEET . . . . NiB $781 Ex $625 Gd $425
12 or 20 ga. w/2.75-inch chambers. Selective automatic ejectors, single-selective trigger. 26-inch over/under bbls. w/vent rib. Weight: 7 lbs. Made in Italy 1984-88.

REGENT TRAP . . . . NiB $794 Ex $635 Gd $432
12-ga. competition shotgun w/2.75-inch chambers. 30-inch over/under bbls. choked IM/F, vent side ribs. Weight: 8 lbs. Selective automatic ejectors, single selective trigger. Checkered Monte Carlo stock w/Supercushion recoil pad. Made in Italy 1984-88.

SPORTING CLAYS O/U . . . . NiB $831 Ex $665 Gd $452
Same general specifications as Windsor IV except in 12 ga. only w/28-inch ported bbls. and choke tubes. Selective automatic ejectors. Weight: 7.5 lbs. Made from 1992-94.

WINDSOR O/U SHOTGUNS
Hammerless, boxlock w/engraved receiver, selective single trigger. Extractors or ejectors. Gauges: 12, 20, 28 or .410; 3-inch chambers. Bbls.: 24 to 30 inches w/fixed chokes or choke tubes. Weight: 6 lbs., 3 oz. (Flyweight) to 7 lbs., 10 oz. (12 ga.). Checkered straight (Flyweight) or pistol-grip stock and forend of European walnut. Imported from Italy 1984-93.
Windsor III w/fixed chokes. . . . . NiB $623 Ex $498 Gd $339
Windsor III w/choke tubes . . . . NiB $781 Ex $624 Gd $425
Windsor IV w/fixed
chokes (disc. 1993) . . . . NiB $728 Ex $582 Gd $395
Windsor IV w/choke tubes . . . . NiB $728 Ex $519 Gd $253

WINDSOR SIDE-BY-SIDE SHOTGUNS
Boxlock action w/double triggers, ejectors or extractors and automatic safety. Gauges: 10, (3.5-inch chambers); 12, 20, 28, .410 (3-inch chambers), 16 (2.75-inch chambers). Bbls.: 23 to 32 inches w/various fixed choke or choke tube combinations. Weight: 5 lbs., 12 oz. (Flyweight) to 11.5 lbs. (10 ga.). European walnut buttstock and forend. Imported from Spain 1984-90.
Windsor I 10 ga. . . . . NiB $702 Ex $562 Gd $382
Windsor I 12 thru .410 ga. . . . . NiB $534 Ex $427 Gd $290
Windsor II 12 or 20 ga.. . . . . NiB $500 Ex $400 Gd $272
Windsor VI 12 or 20 ga. . . . . NiB $731 Ex $585 Gd $397

E.J. CHURCHILL, LTD. —
Surrey (previously London), England

The E.J. Churchill shotguns listed below are no longer imported.

PREMIERE QUALITY HAMMERLESS DOUBLE
Sidelock. Automatic ejectors. Double triggers or selective single trigger. Gauges: 12, 16, 20, 28. Bbls.: 25-, 28- 30-, 32-inch; any degree of boring. Weight: 5-8 lbs. depending on ga. and bbl. length. Checkered stock and forend, straight or pistol-grip.
W/double triggers . . . . NiB $17,210 Ex $13,950 Gd $10,000
W/selective single trigger, add. 10%

FIELD MODEL HAMMERLESS DOUBLE
Sidelock Hammerless ejector gun w/same general specifications as Premiere Model but of lower quality.
W/double triggers . . . . NiB $9500 Ex $7500 Gd $6500
W/selective single trigger, add 10%

PREMIERE QUALITY O/U SHOTGUN
Sidelock. Automatic ejectors. Double triggers or selective single trigger. Gauges: 12, 16, 20, 28. Bbls.: 25-, 28-, 30-, 32-inch, any degree of boring. Weight: 5-8 lbs. depending on ga. and bbl. length. Checkered stock and forend, straight or pistol-grip.
W/double triggers. . . . . NiB $19,375 Ex $15,500 Gd $10,540
W/selective single trigger, add. 10%
Raised vent rib, add. 15%

UTILITY MODEL HAMMERLESS DOUBLE-BARREL
Anson & Deeley boxlock action. Double triggers or single trigger. Gauges: 12, 16, 20, 28, .410. Bbls.: 25-, 28-, 30-, 32-inch, any degree of boring. Weight: 4.5-8 lbs. depending on ga. and bbl. length. Checkered stock and forend, straight or pistol-grip.
W/double triggers . . . . NiB $6250 Ex $4500 Gd $3250
W/selective single trigger, add 10%

XXV PREMIERE
HAMMERLESS DOUBLE . . . NiB $16,563 Ex $13,250 Gd $9010
Sidelock. Assisted opening. Automatic ejectors. Double triggers. Gauges: 12, 20. 25-inch bbls. w/narrow, quick-sighting rib; any standard choke combination. English-style straight-grip stock and forearm, checkered.

XXV IMPERIAL . . . . NiB $13,781 Ex $11,025 Gd $7497
Similar to XXV Premiere but no assisted opening feature.

XXV HERCULES. . . . . NiB $9619 Ex $7695 Gd $5233
Boxlock, otherwise specifications same as for XXV Premiere.

XXV REGAL . . . . NiB $5313 Ex $4250 Gd $2890
Similar to XXV Hercules but w/o assisted opening feature. Gauges: 12, 20, 28, .410.

CLASSIC DOUBLES — Tochigi, Japan

Imported by Classic Doubles International, St. Louis, MO, and previously by Olin as Winchester Models 101 and 23.

MODEL 101 O/U SHOTGUN
Boxlock. Engraved receiver w/single selective trigger, auto ejectors and combination bbl. selector and safety. Gauges: 12, 20, 28 or .410, 2.75-, 3-inch chambers, 25.5- 28- or 30-inch vent-rib bbls. Weight: 6.25 – 7.75 lbs. Checkered French walnut stock. Imported 1987-90.

E.J. Churchill Premiere

(cont'd.) MODEL 101 O/U SHOTGUN
Classic I Field . . . . NiB $1494 Ex $1195 Gd $813
Classic II Field. NiB $1688 Ex $1350 Gd $918
Classic Sporter . . . . NiB $1813 Ex $1450 Gd $986
Classic Sporter combo . . . . NiB $2938 Ex $2350 Gd $1598
Classic Trap. . . . . NiB $1469 Ex $1175 Gd $799
Classic Trap Single. . . . . NiB $1494 Ex $1195 Gd $813
Classic Trap combo . . . . NiB $2188 Ex $1750 Gd $1190
Classic Skeet . . . . NiB $1563 Ex $1250 Gd $850
Classic Skeet
2-bbl. set . . . . NiB $2369 Ex $1895 Gd $1289
Classic Skeet
4-bbl. set . . . . NiB $4063 Ex $3250 Gd $2210
ClassicWaterfowler . . . . NiB $1244 Ex $995 Gd $677
For Grade II (28 ga.), add $750
For Grade II (.410 ga.), add $250

MODEL 201 SIDE-BY-SIDE SHOTGUN
Boxlock. Single selective trigger, automatic safety and selective ejectors. Gauges: 12 or 20; 3-inch chambers. 26- or 28-inch vent-rib bbl., fixed chokes or internal tubes. Weight: 6 to 7 lbs. Checkered French walnut stock and forearm. Imported 1987-90.
Field model . . . . NiB $1505 Ex $1204 Gd $819
Skeet model . . . . NiB $1780 Ex $1424 Gd $969
With internal choke tubes, add. $100

MODEL 201
SMALL BORE SET . . . . NiB $4494 Ex $3595 Gd $2445
Same general specifications as the Classic Model 201 except w/smaller frame, in 28 ga. (IC/M) and .410 (F/M). Weight: 6-6.5 lbs. Imported 1987-90.

COGSWELL & HARRISON, LTD. —
London, England

AMBASSADOR HAMMERLESS
DOUBLE-BARREL SHOTGUN . . . . NiB $5500 Ex $4925 Gd $3100
Boxlock. Sideplates w/game scene or rose scroll engraving. Automatic ejectors. Double triggers. Gauges: 12, 16, 20. Bbls.: 26- 28-, 30-inch; any choke combination. Checkered straight-grip stock and forearm. Disc.

SHOTGUNS

Colt Auto Shotgun
Ultra Light Standard

Colt Custom
Hammerless Double

Colt Standard Pump

Cogswell & Harrison
Best Quality
Hammerless Sidelock

Colt-Sauer
Drilling

AVANT TOUT SERIES HAMMERLESS DOUBLE-BARREL SHOTGUNS

Boxlock. Sideplates (except Avant Tout III Grade). Automatic ejectors. Double triggers or single trigger (selective or non-selective). Gauges: 12, 16, 20. Bbls.: 25-, 27.5-, 30-inch, any choke combination. Checkered stock and forend, straight grip standard. Made in three models (Avant Tout I or Konor, Avant Tout II or Sandhurst, Avant Tout III or Rex) which differ chiefly in overall quality of engraving, grade of wood, checkering, etc. General specifications are the same. Disc.

Avant Tout I	NiB $3369	Ex $2695	Gd $1833
Avant Tout II	NiB $2938	Ex $2350	Gd $1598
Avant Tout III	NiB $2244	Ex $1795	Gd $1221
Single trigger, non-selective, add			$225
Single trigger, selective, add			$395

BEST QUALITY HAMMERLESS SIDELOCK DOUBLE-BARREL SHOTGUN

Hand-detachable locks. Automatic ejectors. Double triggers or single trigger (selective or non-selective). Gauges: 12, 16, 20. Bbls.: 25-, 26-, 28-, 30-inch, any choke combination. Checkered stock and forend, straight grip standard.

Victor model	NiB $9532	Ex $7626	Gd $5185
Primic model (disc.)	NiB $6592	Ex $5274	Gd $3586
Single trigger, non-selective, add			$225
Single trigger, selective, add			$395

HUNTIC MODEL HAMMERLESS DOUBLE

Sidelock. Automatic ejectors. Double triggers or single trigger (selective or non-selective). Gauges: 12, 16, 20. Bbls.: 25-, 27.5-, 30-inch; any choke combination. Checkered stock and forend, straight grip standard. Disc.

(cont'd.) HUNTIC MODEL HAMMERLESS DOUBLE

W/double triggers	NiB $4060	Ex $3250	Gd $2210
Single trigger, non-selective, add			$225
Single trigger, selective, add			$350

MARKOR HAMMERLESS DOUBLE

Boxlock. Non-ejector or ejector. Double triggers. Gauges: 12, 16, 20. Bbls.: 27.5 or 30-inch; any choke combination. Checkered stock and forend, straight grip standard. Disc.

Non-ejector	NiB $1688	Ex $1350	Gd $918
Ejector model	NiB $2063	Ex $1650	Gd $1122

REGENCY HAMMERLESS DOUBLE ...... NiB $2869 Ex $2295 Gd $1560

Anson & Deeley boxlock action. Automatic ejectors. Double triggers. Gauges: 12, 16, 20. Bbls.: 26-, 28-, 30-inch, any choke combination. Checkered straight-grip stock and forearm. Introduced in 1970 to commemorate the firm's bicentennial, this model has deep scroll engraving and the name "Regency" inlaid in gold on the rib. Disc.

COLT INDUSTRIES — Hartford, Connecticut

Auto Shotguns were made by Franchi and are similar to corresponding models of that manufacturer.

AUTO SHOTGUN — ULTRA LIGHT STANDARD

Recoil-operated. Takedown. Alloy receiver. Gauges: 12, 20. Mag. holds 4 shells. Bbls.: plain, solid or vent rib, chrome-lined; 26-inch IC or M choke, 28-inch M or F choke, 30-inch F choke, 32-inch F choke. Weight: 12 ga., about 6.25 lbs. Checkered pistol-grip stock and forearm. Made 1964-66.

W/plain bbl.	NiB $469	Ex $375	Gd $255
W/solid rib bbl.	NiB $344	Ex $275	Gd $187
W/vent rib bbl.	NiB $369	Ex $295	Gd $201

Charles Daly Over/Under
Field Grade (Postwar)

AUTO SHOTGUN — MAGNUM CUSTOM
Same as Magnum except has engraved receiver, select walnut stock and forearm. Made 1964-66.
W/Solid-rib bbl. . . . . NiB $531 Ex $425 Gd $289
W/ventilated rib bbl. . . . . NiB $594 Ex $475 Gd $323

AUTO SHOTGUN — ULTRA LIGHT CUSTOM
Same as Standard Auto except has engraved receiver, select walnut stock and forearm. Made 1964-66.
W/solid-rib bbl. . . . . NiB $438 Ex $350 Gd $238
W/ventilated-rib bbl. . . . . NiB $469 Ex $375 Gd $255

AUTO SHOTGUN — MAGNUM
Same as Standard Auto except steel receiver, 3-inch Magnum shells, 30- and 32-inch bbls. in 12 ga., 28-inch in 20 ga. Weight: 12 ga., about 8.25 lbs. Made 1964-66.
W/plain bbl. . . . . NiB $419 Ex $335 Gd $228
W/solid-rib bbl. . . . . NiB $469 Ex $375 Gd $255
W/ventilated rib bbl. . . . . NiB $494 Ex $395 Gd $269

CUSTOM HAMMERLESS DOUBLE . . . . NiB $744 Ex $595 Gd $405
Boxlock. Double triggers. Auto ejectors. Gauges: 12 Mag., 16. Bbls.: 26-inch IC/M; 28-inch M/F; 30-inch F/F. Weight: 12 ga., about 7.5 lbs. Checkered pistol-grip stock and beavertail forearm. Made in 1961.

STANDARD PUMP SHOTGUN . . . . NiB $332 Ex $265 Gd $180
Takedown. Gauges: 12, 16, 20. Magazine holds 4 shells. Bbls.: 26-inch IC; 28-inch M or F choke; 30-inch F choke. Weight: About 6 lbs. Plain pistol-grip stock and forearm. Made 1961-65 by Manufrance.

CUSTOM PUMP . . . . NiB $365 Ex $292 Gd $198
Same as Standard Pump shotgun except has checkered stock, vent-rib bbl. Weight: About 6.5 lbs. Made 1961-63 by Manufrance.

SAUER DRILLING . . . . NiB $2919 Ex $2335 Gd $1588
Three-bbl. combination gun. Boxlock. Set rifle trigger. Tang bbl. selector, automatic rear sight positioner. 12 ga. over .30-06 or .243 rifle bbl. 25-inch bbls., F and M choke. Weight: About 8 lbs. Folding leaf rear sight, blade front w/brass bead. Checkered pistol-grip stock and beavertail forearm, recoil pad. Made 1974 to date by J. P. Sauer & Sohn, Eckernförde, Germany.

CONNECTICUT VALLEY CLASSICS — Westport, Connecticut

SPORTER O/U
Gauge: 12; 3-inch chamber. Bbls.: 28-, 30- or 32-inch w/ screw-in tubes. Weight: 7.75 lbs. Engraved stainless or nitrided receiver; blued bbls. Checkered American black walnut buttstock and forend w/low-luster satin finish. Made from 1993 to date.
Classic Sporter. . . . . NiB $1994 Ex $1595 Gd $1085
Stainless Classic Sporter . . . . . . NiB $2369 Ex $1895 Gd $1289

FIELD O/U
Similar to the standard Classic Sporter over/under model except w/30-inch bbls. only and non-reflective matte blued finish on both bbls. and receiver for Waterfowler; other grades w/different degrees of embellishment; Grade I the lowest and Grade III the highest. Made 1993 to date.
Grade I . . . . NiB $2240 Ex $1952 Gd $1327
Grade II . . . . NiB $2605 Ex $2084 Gd $1417
Grade III . . . . NiB $2956 Ex $2365 Gd $1608
Waterfowler . . . . NiB $2330 Ex $1864 Gd $1268

CHARLES DALY, INC. — New York, New York

The pre-WWII Charles Daly shotguns, w/the exception of the Commander, were manufactured by various firms in Suhl, Germany. The postwar guns, except for the Novamatic series, were produced by Miroku Firearms Mfg. Co., Tokyo. Miroku ceased production in 1976 and the Daly trademark was acquired by Outdoor Sports Headquarters, in Dayton, Ohio. OSHI continued to market O/U shotguns from both Italy and Spain under the Daly logo. Automatic models were produced in Japan for distribution in the USA. In 1996, KBI, Inc. in Harrisburg, PA acquired the Daly trademark and currently imports firearms under that logo.

COMMANDER O/U SHOTGUN
Daly-pattern Anson & Deeley system boxlock action. Automatic ejectors. Double triggers or Miller selective single trigger. Gauges: 12, 16, 20, 28, .410. Bbls.: 26- to 30-inch, IC/M or M/F choke. Weight: 5.25 to 7.25 lbs. depending on ga. and bbl. length. Checkered stock and forend, straight or pistol grip. The two models, 100 and 200, differ in general quality, grade of wood, checkering, engraving, etc.; otherwise specs are the same. Made in Belgium c. 1939.
Model 100 . . . . NiB $495 Ex $395 Gd $275
Model 200 . . . . NiB $656 Ex $525 Gd $357
Miller single trigger, add $100

HAMMERLESS DOUBLE-BARREL SHOTGUN
Daly-pattern Anson & Deeley system boxlock action. Automatic ejectors except "Superior Quality" is non-ejector. Double triggers. Gauges: 10, 12, 16, 20, 28, .410. Bbls.: 26- to 32-inch, any combination of chokes. Weight: from 4 to 8.5 lbs. depending on ga. and bbl. length. Checkered pistol-grip stock and forend. The four grades—Regent Diamond, Diamond, Empire, Superior—differ in general quality, grade of wood, checkering, engraving, etc.; otherwise specifications are the same. Disc. about 1933.
Diamond quality . . . . NiB $10,938 Ex $8750 Gd $5950
Empire quality . . . . NiB $5313 Ex $4250 Gd $2890
Regent Diamond quality . . . . NiB $13,125 Ex $10,500 Gd $7140
Superior quality . . . . NiB $1188 Ex $950 Gd $646

**Charles Daly Diamond
GTX DL Hunter**

**Charles Daly Empire
EDL Hunter**

HAMMERLESS DRILLING
Daly pattern Anson & Deeley system boxlock action. Plain extractors. Double triggers, front single set for rifle bbl. Gauges: 12, 16, 20, .25-20, .25-35, .30-30 rifle bbl. Supplied in various bbl. lengths and weights. Checkered pistol-grip stock and forend. Auto rear sight operated by rifle bbl. selector. The three grades — Regent Diamond, Diamond, Superior—differ in general quality, grade of wood, checkering, engraving, etc.; otherwise, specifications are the same. Disc. about 1933.
Diamond quality . . . . NiB $5938 Ex $4750 Gd $3230
Regent Diamond quality . . . NiB $12,813 Ex $10,250 Gd $6970
Superior quality . . . . NiB $3244 Ex $2595 Gd $1765

HAMMERLESS DOUBLE
EMPIRE GRADE . . . . NiB $882 Ex $742 Gd $561
Boxlock. Plain extractors. Non-selective single trigger. Gauges: 12, 16, 20; 3-inch chambers in 12 and 20, 2.75-inch in 16 ga. Bbls.: vent rib; 26-, 28-, 30-inch (latter in 12 ga. only); IC/M, M/F, F/F. Weight: 6 to 7.75 lbs., depending on ga. and bbls. Checkered pistol-grip stock and beavertail forearm. Made 1968-71.

1974 WILDLIFE COMMEMORATIVE . . . . NiB $2119 Ex $1695 Gd $1153
Limited issue of 500 guns. Similar to Diamond Grade over/under. 12-ga. trap and skeet models only. Duck scene engraved on right side of receiver, fine scroll on left side. Made in 1974.

NOVAMATIC LIGHTWEIGHT AUTOLOADER
Same as Breda. Recoil-operated. Takedown.12 ga., 2.75-inch chamber. Four shell tubular magazine. Bbls.: Plain vent rib; 26-inch IC or Quick-Choke w/three interchangeable tubes, 28-inch M or F choke. Weight (w/26-inch vent-rib bbl.): 7 lbs., 6 oz. Checkered pistol-grip stock and forearm. Made 1968 by Ernesto Breda, Milan, Italy.
W/plain bbl. . . . . NiB $406 Ex $325 Gd $221
W/vent rib bbl. . . . . NiB $438 Ex $350 Gd $238
W/Quick-Choke, add $20

NOVAMATIC SUPER LIGHTWEIGHT
Lighter version of Novamatic Lightweight. Gauges: 12, 20. Weight (w/26-inch vent-rib bbl.): 12 ga., 6 lbs., 10 oz., 20 ga., 6 lbs. SK choke available in 26-inch vent-rib bbl. 28-inch bbls. in 12 ga. only. Quick-Choke in 20 ga. w/plain bbl. Made 1968 by Ernesto Breda, Milan, Italy.
12 ga., plain bbl. . . . . NiB $369 Ex $295 Gd $201
12 ga., vent rib bbl. . . . . NiB $406 Ex $325 Gd $221
20 ga., plain bbl. . . . . NiB $375 Ex $300 Gd $204
20 ga., plain bbl. w/Quick-Choke . . . . NiB $406 Ex $325 Gd $221
20 ga., vent rib bbl. . . . . NiB $431 Ex $345 Gd $235

NOVAMATIC SUPER LIGHTWEIGHT
20 GA. MAGNUM . . . . NiB $431 Ex $345 Gd $235
Same as Novamatic Super Lightweight 2, except 3-inch chamber, has 3-shell magazine, 28-inch vent-rib bbl., F choke.

NOVAMATIC
12 GA. MAGNUM . . . . NiB $438 Ex $350 Gd $238
Same as Novamatic Lightweight, except chambered for 12-ga. Magnum 3-inch shell. Has 3-shell magazine, 30-inch vent rib bbl., F choke, and stock w/recoil pad. Weight: 7.75 lbs.

Post-War Charles Daly shotguns were imported by Sloan's Sporting Goods trading as Charles Daly in New York. In 1976, Outdoor Sports Headquarters acquired the Daly trademark and continued to import European-made shotguns under that logo. In 1996, KBI, Inc., in Harrisburg, PA, acquired the Daly trademark and currently imports firearms under that logo.

NOVAMATIC TRAP GUN
. . . . NiB $469 Ex $375 Gd $255
Same as Novamatic Lightweight except has 30-inch vent rib bbl., F choke and Monte Carlo stock w/recoil pad. Weight: 7.75 lbs.

O/U SHOTGUNS (PREWAR)
Daly-pattern Anson & Deeley-system boxlock action. Sideplates. Auto ejectors. Double triggers. Gauges: 12, 16, 20. Supplied in various bbl. lengths and weights. Checkered pistol-grip stock and forend. The two grades — Diamond and Empire — differ in general quality, grade of wood, checkering, engraving, etc.; otherwise specifications are the same. Disc. about 1933.
Diamond
Quality . . . . NiB $5494 Ex $4395 Gd $2989
Empire
Quality . . . . NiB $4188 Ex $3350 Gd $2278

O/U SHOTGUNS (POSTWAR)
Boxlock. Auto ejectors or selective auto/manual ejection. Selective single trigger. Gauges: 12, 12 Magnum (3-inch chambers), 20 (3-inch chambers), 28, .410. Bbls.: Vent rib; 26-, 28-, 30-inch; standard choke combinations. Weight: 6 to 8 lbs. depending on ga. and bbls. Select walnut stock w/pistol grip, fluted forearm checkered; Monte Carlo comb on trap guns; recoil pad on 12-ga. mag. and trap models. The various grades differ in quality of engraving and wood. Made 1963-76.
Diamond grade . . . . NiB $1244 Ex $995 Gd $677
Field grade . . . . NiB $688 Ex $550 Gd $374
Superior grade . . . . NiB $906 Ex $725 Gd $493
Venture grade . . . . NiB $656 Ex $525 Gd $357

Charles Daly
Field Semiauto

Charles Daly Field III
Over/Under

SEXTUPLE MODEL SINGLE-BARREL TRAP GUN

Daly-pattern Anson & Deeley system boxlock action. Six locking bolts. Auto ejector. 12 ga. only. Bbls.: 30-, 32-, 34-inch, vent rib. Weight: 7.5 to 8.25 lbs. Checkered pistol-grip stock and forend. The two models made Empire and Regent Diamond differ in general quality, grade of wood, checkering, engraving, etc., otherwise specifications are the same. Disc. about 1933.

Regent Diamond quality (Linder)	NiB $531	Ex $425	Gd $289
Empire quality (Linder)	NiB $4744	Ex $3795	Gd $2581
Regent Diamond quality (Sauer)	NiB $3369	Ex $2695	Gd $1833
Empire quality (Sauer)	NiB $2494	Ex $1995	Gd $1357

SINGLE-SHOT TRAP GUN

Daly-pattern Anson & Deeley system boxlock action. Auto ejector. 12 ga. only. Bbls.: 30-, 32-, 34-inch, vent rib. Weight: 7.5 to 8.25 lbs. Checkered pistol-grip stock and forend. This model was made in Empire Quality only. Disc. about 1933.

Empire grade (Linder)	NiB $4188	Ex $3350	Gd $2278
Empire grade (Sauer)	NiB $2063	Ex $1650	Gd $1122

SUPERIOR GRADE SINGLE-SHOT TRAP .. NiB $744 Ex $595 Gd $405

Boxlock. Automatic ejector. 12 ga. only. 32- or 34-inch vent-rib bbl., F choke. Weight: About 8 lbs. Monte Carlo stock w/pistol grip and recoil pad, beavertail forearm, checkered. Made 1968-76.

DIAMOND GRADE O/U

Boxlock. Single selective trigger. Selective automatic ejectors. Gauges: 12 and 20, 3-inch chambers (2.75 target grade). Bbls.: 26, 27- or 30-inch w/fixed chokes or screw-in tubes. Weight: 7 lbs. Checkered European walnut stock and forearm w/oil finish. Engraved antique silver receiver and blued bbls. Made 1984-90.

Standard model	NiB $781	Ex $624	Gd $425
Skeet model	NiB $853	Ex $682	Gd $464
Trap model	NiB $912	Ex $729	Gd $496

DIAMOND GTX DL HUNTER O/U SERIES

Sidelock. Single selective trigger and selective auto ejectors. Gauges: 12, 20, 28 ga. or .410 bore. 26-, 28- and 30-inch bbls w/3-inch chambers (2.75-inch 28 ga.). Choke tubes (12 and 20 ga.), Fixed chokes (28 and 410). Weight: 5-8 lbs. Checkered European walnut stock w/hand-rubbed oil finish and recoil pad. Made 1997 to date.

Diamond GTX DL Hunter	NiB $9438	Ex $7550	Gd $5134
Diamond GTX EDL Hunter	NiB $11656	Ex $9325	Gd $6341
Diamond GTX Sporting (12 or 20 ga.)	NiB $5244	Ex $4195	Gd $2853
Diamond GTX Skeet (12 or 20 ga.)	NiB $4869	Ex $3895	Gd $2649
Diamond GTX Trap (12 ga. only)	NiB $5063	Ex $4050	Gd $2754

EMPIRE DL HUNTER O/U ...... NiB $1150 Ex $975 Gd $600

Boxlock. Ejectors. Single selective trigger. Gauges:12, 20, 28 ga. and .410 bore. 26- or 28- inch bbls. w/3-inch chambers (2.75-inch 28 ga.). Choke tubes (12 and 20 ga.), Fixed chokes (28 and .410). Engraved coin-silver receiver w/game scene. Imported 1997 to date.

EMPIRE EDL HUNTER SERIES

Similar to Empire DL Hunter except engraved sideplates. Made 1998 to date.

Empire EDL Hunter	NiB $1156	Ex $925	Gd $629
Empire Sporting	NiB $1125	Ex $900	Gd $612
Empire Skeet	NiB $1094	Ex $875	Gd $595
Empire Trap	NiB $1156	Ex $925	Gd $629
28 ga., add			$95
.410 ga., add			$120
Multi-chokes w/Monte			
Carlo stock, add			$125

DSS HAMMERLESS DOUBLE ..... NiB $656 Ex $525 Gd $357

Boxlock. Single selective trigger. Selective automatic ejectors. Gauges: 12 and 20; 3-inch chambers. 26-inch bbls. w/screw-in choke tubes. Weight: 6.75 lbs. Checkered walnut pistol-grip stock and semi-beavertail forearm w/recoil pad. Engraved antique silver receiver and blued bbls. Made from 1990 to date.

FIELD GRADE O/U .... NiB $481 Ex $385 Gd $262

Boxlock. Single selective trigger. Extractors. Gauges: 12 and 20; 3-inch chambers. Bbls.: 26-inch, IC/M; 28-inch, M/F. Weight: 6.75 lbs. (12 ga.). Checkered walnut stock and forearm w/semi-gloss finish and recoil pad. Engraved color-casehardened receiver and blued bbls. Made from 1989 to date.

FIELD SEMIAUTO SHOTGUN..... NiB $369 Ex $295 Gd $201

Recoil-operated. Takedown. 12-ga. and 12-ga. Magnum. Bbls.: 27- and 30-inch; vent rib. Made 1982-88.

FIELD III O/U SHOTGUN .... NiB $494 Ex $395 Gd $269

Boxlock. Plain extractors. Non-selective single trigger. Gauges: 12 or 20. Bbls.: vent rib; 26- and 28-inch; IC/M, M/F. Weight: 6 to 7.75 lbs. depending on ga. and bbls. Chrome-molybdenum steel bbls. Checkered pistol-grip stock and forearm. Made from 1982 to date.

LUX O/U .... NiB $719 Ex $575 Gd $391

Similar to the Field Grade except w/selective automatic ejectors and choke tubes. Gauges: 12, 20, 28 and .410. Receiver w/antique silver finish and blued bbls. Made from 1989 to date.

Charles Daly Over/Under Presentation Grade

Charles Daly Over/Under Superior II

Davidson Model 63B Double-Barrel Shotgun

MULTI-XII SELF-LOADING SHOTGUN . . . . . . NiB $494 Ex $395 Gd $269
Similar to the gas-operated field semiauto except w/new Multi-Action gas system designed to shoot all loads w/o adjustment. 12 ga. w/3-inch chamber. 27-inch bbl. w/Invector choke tubes, vent rib. Made in Japan from 1987 to date.

O/U
PRESENTATION GRADE . . . . .NiB $1056 Ex $845 Gd $575
Purdey boxlock w/double cross-bolt. Gauges: 12 or 20. Engraved receiver w/single selective trigger and auto-ejectors. 27-inch chrome-molybdenum steel, rectified, honed and internally chromed, vent-rib bbls. Hand-checkered deluxe European walnut stock. Made 1982-86.

O/U
Superior II Shotgun . . . . NiB $898 Ex $718 Gd $488
Boxlock. Plain extractors. Non-selective single trigger. Gauges: 12 or 20. Bbls.: chrome-molybdenum vent rib 26-, 28-, 30-inch, latter in magnum only, assorted chokes. Silver engraved receiver. Checkered pistol-grip stock and forearm. Made from 1982 to date.

SPORTING CLAYS O/U . . . . NiB $782 Ex $625 Gd $425
Similar to the Field Grade except in 12 ga. only w/ported bbls. and internal choke tubes. Made from 1990 to date.

DAKOTA ARMS, INC. — Sturgis, South Dakota

CLASSIC FIELD GRADE
S/S SHOTGUN . . . . NiB $7469 Ex $5895 Gd $3881
Boxlock. Gauge: 20 ga. 27-inch bbl. w/fixed chokes. Double triggers. Selective ejectors. Color-casehardened receiver. Weight: 6 lbs. Checkered English walnut stock and splinter forearm w/hand-rubbed oil finish. Made 1996 to date.

PREMIUM GRADE
S/S SHOTGUN . . . . NiB $13,900 Ex $10,200 Gd $6500
Similar to Classic Field Grade model except w/50% engraving coverage. Exhibition grade English walnut stock. Made 1996 to date.

AMERICAN LEGEND
S/S SHOTGUN . . . . NiB $16,625 Ex $13,500 Gd $9500
Limited edition built to customer's specifications. Gauge: 20 ga. 27-inch bbl. Double triggers. Selective ejectors. Fully engraved, coin-silver finished receiver w/gold inlays. Weight: 6 lbs. Hand checkered special-selection English walnut stock and forearm. Made 1996 to date.

DARNE S.A. — Saint-Etienne, France

HAMMERLESS DOUBLE-BARREL SHOTGUNS
Sliding-breech action w/fixed bbls. Auto ejectors. Double triggers. Gauges: 12, 16, 20, 28; also 12 and 20 Magnum w/3-inch chambers. Bbls.: 27.5-inch standard, 25.5- to 31.5-inch lengths available; any standard choke combination. Weight: 5.5 to 7 lbs. depending on ga. and bbl. length. Checkered straight-grip or pistol-grip stock and forearm. The various models differ in grade of engraving and wood. Manufactured 1881-1979.

Model R11
(Bird Hunter) . . . . NiB $1500 Ex $1350 Gd $700
Model R15
(Pheasant Hunter). . . . . NiB $2238 Ex $1759 Gd $1126
Model R16
(Magnum) . . . . NiB $3500 Ex $2900 Gd $1800
Model V19
(Quail Hunter) . . . . NiB $4500 Ex $4000 Gd $3500
Model V22 . . . . NiB $5063 Ex $4250 Gd $2310
Model V Hors Série No. 1. . . . . NiB $6375 Ex $5500 Gd $4380

Exel Model 101

Exel Model 200
Side-by-Side Shotgun

DAVIDSON GUNS — Mfd. by Fabrica de Armas ILJA, Eibar, Spain; distributed by Davidson Firearms Co., Greensboro, North Carolina

MODEL 63B DOUBLE-BARREL
SHOTGUN . . . . NiB $359 Ex $287 Gd $195
Anson & Deeley boxlock action. Frame engraved and nickel plated. Plain extractors. Auto safety. Double triggers. Gauges: 12, 16, 20, 28, .410. Bbl. lengths: 25 (.410 only), 26, 28, 30 inches (latter 12 ga. only). Chokes: IC/ M, M/F, F/F. Weight: 5 lbs., 11 oz. (.410) to 7 lbs. (12 ga.). Checkered pistol-grip stock and forearm of European walnut. Made 1963. Disc.

MODEL 63B MAGNUM
Similar to standard Model 63B except chambered for 10 ga. 3.5-inch, 12 and 20 ga. 3-inch Magnum shells; 10 ga. has 32-inch bbls., choked F/F. Weight: 10 lb., 10 oz. Made from 1963. Disc.
12-and 20 ga. magnum . . . . NiB $419 Ex $335 Gd $228
10 ga. magnum. . . . . NiB $494 Ex $395 Gd $269

MODEL 69SL DOUBLE-BARREL
SHOTGUN. . . . . NiB $619 Ex $515 Gd $382
Sidelock action w/detachable sideplates, engraved and nickel plated. Plain extractors. Auto safety. Double triggers. 12 and 20 ga. Bbls.: 26-inch IC/M, 28-inch M/F. Weight: 12 ga., 7 lbs., 20 ga., 6.5 lbs. Pistol-grip stock and forearm of European walnut, checkered. Made 1963-76.

MODEL 73 STAGECOACH
HAMMER DOUBLE . . . . NiB $331 Ex $265 Gd $180
Sidelock action w/detachable sideplates and exposed hammers. Plain extractors. Double triggers. Gauges: 12, 20, 3-inch chambers. 20-inch bbls, M/F chokes. Weight: 7 lbs., 12 ga.; 6.5 lbs., 20 ga. Checkered pistol-grip stock and forearm. Made from 1976. Disc.

EXEL ARMS OF AMERICA — Gardner, Massachusetts

SERIES 100 O/U SHOTGUN
Gauge: 12. Single selective trigger. Selective auto ejectors. Hand-checkered European walnut stock w/full pistol grip, tulip forend. Black metal finish. Chambered for 2.75-inch shells (Model 103 for 3-inch). Weight: 6. 88 to 7.88 lbs. Disc 1988.
Model 101, 26-inch bbl., IC/M . . . . NiB $469 Ex $375 Gd $255
Model 102, 28-inch bbl., IC/IM . . . . NiB $475 Ex $380 Gd $258
Model 103, 30-inch bbl., M/F . . . . NiB $494 Ex $395 Gd $269
Model 104, 28-inch bbl., IC/IM . . . . NiB $544 Ex $435 Gd $296
Model 105, 28-inch bbl., 5 choke tubes . . . . . . NiB $688 Ex $550 Gd $374
Model 106, 28-inch bbl., 5 choke tubes . . . . . . NiB $831 Ex $660 Gd $45
Model 107 Trap, 30-inch bbl., Full or 5 tubes . . . . . NiB $894 Ex $695 Gd $569

SERIES 200 SIDE-BY-SIDE
SHOTGUN . . . . NiB $494 Ex $395 Gd $269
Gauges: 12, 20, 28 and .410. Bbls.: 26-, 27- and 28-inch; various choke combinations. Weight: 7 lbs. average. American or European-style stock and forend. Made 1985 to 87.

SERIES 300 O/U
SHOTGUN . . . . NiB $563 Ex $450 Gd $306
Gauge: 12. Bbls.: 26-, 28- and 29-inch. Non-glare black-chrome matte finish. Weight: 7 lbs. average. Selective auto ejectors, engraved receiver. Hand-checkered European walnut stock and forend. Made 1985-86.

FABARM SHOTGUNS — Brescia, Italy

Currently imported by Heckler & Koch, Inc., of Sterling, VA (previously by Ithaca Acquisition Corp., St. Lawrence Sales, Inc. and Beeman Precision Arms, Inc.)

See Current listings under "Heckler & Koch."

FIAS — Fabrica Italiana Armi Sabatti Gardone Val Trompia, Italy

GRADE I O/U
Boxlock. Single selective trigger. Gauges: 12, 20, 28, .410; 3-inch chambers. Bbls.: 26-inch IC/M; 28-inch M/F; screw-in choke tubes. Weight: 6.5 to 7.5 lbs. Checkered European walnut stock and forearm. Engraved receiver and blued finish.
12 ga. model . . . . NiB $469 Ex $375 Gd $255
20 ga. model . . . . NiB $531 Ex $425 Gd $289
28 and .410 ga. models . . . . NiB $688 Ex $550 Gd $374

FOX SHOTGUNS — Made by A. H. Fox Gun Co., Philadelphia, PA, 1903 to 1930, and since then by Savage Arms, originally of Utica, NY, now of Westfield, MA. In 1993, Connecticut Manufacturing Co. of New Britain, CT, reintroduced selected models.

Values shown are for 12 and 16 ga. doubles made by A. H. Fox. Twenty gauge guns often are valued up to 75% higher. Savage-made Fox models generally bring prices 25% lower. With the exception of Model B, production of Fox shotguns was discontinued about 1942.

Fox Model B

Fox Sterlingworth

Fox Grade AE

Fox Grade CE

MODEL B-SE................. NiB $703 Ex $562 Gd $382
Same as Model B except has selective ejectors and single trigger. Made 1966-89.

HAMMERLESS DOUBLE-BARREL SHOTGUNS
The higher grades have the same general specifications as the standard Sterlingworth model, w/differences chiefly in workmanship and materials. Higher grade models are stocked in fine select walnut; quantity and quality of engraving increases w/grade and price. Except for Grade A, all other grades have auto ejectors.

Grade A .... NiB $2803 Ex $2242 Gd $1525
Grade AE .... NiB $3238 Ex $2590 Gd $1761
Grade BE .... NiB $4494 Ex $3595 Gd $2445
Grade CE .... NiB $5706 Ex $4565 Gd $3104
Grade DE .... NiB $11,171 Ex $10,224 Gd $10,591
Grade FE .... NiB $20,938 Ex $16,750 Gd $11,390
Grade XE .... NiB $7281 Ex $5825 Gd $3961
Kautzky selective single trigger, add.........................$350
Ventilated rib, add $450
Beavertail forearm, add $275
20 ga., add...60%

SINGLE-BARREL TRAP GUNS
Boxlock. Auto ejector.12 ga. only. 30- or 32-inch vent-rib bbl. Weight: 7.5 to 8 lbs. Trap-style stock and forearm of select walnut, checkered, recoil pad optional. The four grades differ chiefly in quality of wood and engraving; Grade M guns, built to order, have finest Circassian walnut. Stock and receiver are elaborately engraved and inlaid w/gold. Disc. 1942. Note: In 1932, the Fox Trap Gun was redesigned and those manufactured after that date have a stock w/full pistol grip and Monte Carlo comb; at the same time frame was changed to permit the rib line to extend across it to the rear.

Grade JE .... NiB $4943 Ex $3954 Gd $2689
Grade KE .... NiB $5625 Ex $4500 Gd $3060
Grade LE .... NiB $7792 Ex $6234 Gd $4239
Grade ME .... NiB $14,325 Ex $11,460 Gd $7792

"SKEETER" DOUBLE-BARREL SHOTGUN
.... NiB $4494 Ex $3595 Gd $2445
Boxlock. Gauge: 12 or 20. Bbls.: 28 inches w/full-length vent rib. Weight: Approx. 7 lbs. Buttstock and beavertail forend of select American walnut, finely checkered. Soft rubber recoil pad and ivory bead sights. Made in early 1930s.

STERLINGWORTH DELUXE
Same general specifications as Sterlingworth except 32-inch bbl. also available, recoil pad, ivory bead sights.
W/plain extractors............. NiB $1619 Ex $1295 Gd $881
W/automatic ejectors .... NiB $1994 Ex $1595 Gd $1085
20 ga., add......................................45%

STERLINGWORTH HAMMERLESS DOUBLE
Boxlock. Double triggers (Fox-Kautzky selective single trigger extra). Plain extractors (auto ejectors extra). Gauges: 12,16, 20. Bbl. lengths: 26-, 28-, 30-inch; chokes F/F, M/F, C/M (any combination of C to F choke borings was available at no extra cost). Weight: 12 ga., 6.88 to 8.25 lbs.; 16 ga., 6 to 7 lbs.; 20 ga., 5.75 to 6.75 lbs. Checkered pistol-grip stock and forearm.
W/plain extractors .... NiB $1494 Ex $1195 Gd $813
W/automatic ejectors .... NiB $1906 Ex $1525 Gd $1037
Selective single trigger, add 25%

MODEL B HAMMERLESS DOUBLE ...... NiB $294 Ex $235 Gd $160
Boxlock. Double triggers. Plain extractor. Gauges: 12, 16, 20, .410. 24- to 30-inch bbls., vent rib on current production; chokes: M/F, C/M, F/F (.410 only). Weight: About 7.5 lbs., 12 ga. Checkered pistol-grip stock and forend. Made about 1940-85.

MODEL B-ST................. NiB $469 Ex $375 Gd $255
Same as Model B except has non-selective single trigger. Made 1955-66.

MODEL B-DE .... NiB $496 Ex $397 Gd $270
Same as Model B-ST except frame finished in satin chrome, select walnut buttstock w/checkered pistol grip and beavertail forearm. Made 1965-66.

MODEL B-DL .... NiB $553 Ex $442 Gd $301
Same as Model B-ST except frame finished in satin chrome, select walnut buttstock w/checkered pistol grip side panels, beavertail forearm. Made 1962-66.

Franchi Model 500
Standard Autoloader

Franchi Model 520 Deluxe

Franchi Model 520
Eldorado Gold

SHOTGUNS

STERLINGWORTH SKEET AND UPLAND GAME GUN
Same general specifications as the standard Sterlingworth except
has 26- or 28-inch bbls. w/skeet boring only, straight-grip stock.
Weight: 7 lbs. (12 ga.).
W/plain extractors. . . . . NiB $2234 Ex $1787 Gd $1215
W/automatic ejectors . . . . NiB $2681 Ex $2145 Gd $1458
20 ga., add 45%

SUPER HE GRADE. . . . . NiB $5218 Ex $4174 Gd $2839
Long-range gun made in 12 ga. only (chambered for 3-inch shells on
order), 30- or 32-inch full choke bbls., auto ejectors standard. Weight:
8.75 to 9.75 lbs. General specifications same as standard Sterlingworth.

CMC HAMMERLESS DOUBLE-BARREL SHOTGUNS
High-grade doubles similar to the original Fox models. 20 ga. only. 26-
28- or 30-inch bbls. Double triggers automatic safety and ejectors.
Weight: 5.5 to 7 lbs. Custom Circassian walnut stock w/hand-rubbed
oil finish. Custom stock configuration: straight, semi- or full pistol-grip
stock w/traditional pad, hard rubber plate checkered or skeleton butt;
Schnabel, splinter or beavertail forend. Made 1993 to date.
CE grade . . . . NiB $7994 Ex $6395 Gd $4349
XE grade . . . . NiB $8438 Ex $6750 Gd $4590
DE grade . . . . NiB $12,344 Ex $9875 Gd $6715
FE grade . . . . NiB $16,563 Ex $13,250 Gd $9010
Exhibition grade . . . . NiB $23,744 Ex $18,995 Gd $12,917

LUIGI FRANCHI S.P.A. — Brescia, Italy

MODEL 48/AL ULTRA LIGHT SHOTGUN
Recoil-operated, takedown, hammerless shotgun w/tubular magazine. Gauges:
12 or 20 (2.75-inch); 12-ga. Magnum (3-inch chamber). Bbls.: 24- to 32-inch
w/various choke combinations. Weight: 5 lbs., 2 oz. (20 ga.) to 6.25 lbs. (12
ga.). Checkered pistol-grip walnut stock and forend w/high-gloss finish.
Standard model . . . . NiB $486 Ex $395 Gd $278
Hunter or magnum models . . . . . . NiB $524 Ex $425 Gd $299

MODEL 500 STANDARD AUTOLOADER . . . . NiB $394 Ex $315 Gd $214
Gas-operated. 12 gauge. Four shot magazine. Bbls.: 26-, 28-inch;
vent rib; IC, M, IM, F chokes. Weight: About 7 lbs. Checkered pistol-grip stock and forearm. Made 1976-80.

MODEL 520 DELUXE . . . . NiB $438 Ex $350 Gd $238
Same as Model 500 except higher grade w/engraved receiver. Made
1975-79.

MODEL 520 ELDORADO GOLD . . . . NiB $935 Ex $745 Gd $505
Same as Model 520 except custom grade w/engraved and gold-
inlaid receiver, finer quality wood. Intro. 1977.

MODEL 610VS SEMIAUTOMATIC SHOTGUN
Gas-operated Variopress system adjustable to function w/2.75- or 3-
inch shells. 12 gauge. Four shot magazine. 26- or 28-inch vent rib
bbls. w/Franchoke tubes. Weight: 7 lbs., 2 oz. 47.5 inches overall.
Alloy receiver w/four-lug rotating bolt and loaded chamber indicator. Checkered European walnut buttstock and forearm w/satin finish. Imported 1997-98.
Standard SV model . . . . NiB $563 Ex $450 Gd $306
Engraved SVL model . . . . NiB $619 Ex $495 Gd $337

MODEL 612 VARIOPRESS AUTOLOADING SHOTGUN
Gauge: 12 ga. Only. 24- to 28-inch bbl. 45 to 49-inches overall.
Weight: 6.8 to 7 lbs. Five shot magazine. Bead type sights with C,
IC, M chokes. Blued, matte or Advantage camo finish. Imported
1999 to date.
Model 612 satin walnut
stock w/blued finish. . . . . NiB $438 Ex $350 Gd $238
Model 612 synthetic
stock w/matte finish. . . . . NiB $469 Ex $375 Gd $255
Model 612 Advantage stock and finish . . . . . . NiB $531 Ex $425 Gd $289
Model 612 Defense . . . . NiB $406 Ex $325 Gd $221
Model 612 Sporting . . . . NiB $744 Ex $595 Gd $405

MODEL 620 VARIOPRESS AUTOLOADING SHOTGUN
Gauge: 20 ga. Only. 24- 26- or 28-inch bbl. 45 to 49-inches over-
all. Weight: 5.9 to 6.1 lbs. Five shot magazine. Bead type sights with
C, IC, M chokes. Satin walnut or Advantage camo stock. Imported
1999 to date.
Model 620 satin walnut
stock w/matte finish . . . . NiB $438 Ex $350 Gd $238
Model 620 Advantage
camo stock and finish . . . . NiB $531 Ex $425 Gd $289
Model 620 Youth (short stock). . . . . NiB $444 Ex $355 Gd $241

Franchi 612 Variopress Advantage

Franchi 612 Variopress Sporting

Franchi 612 Variopress

Franchi 620 Variopress Advantage

Franchi 620 Variopress

**Franchi Model 2004
Trap Single Barrel**

MODEL 2003 TRAP O/U . . . . NiB $1200 Ex $1095 Gd $800
Boxlock. Auto ejectors. Selective single trigger. 12 ga. Bbls.: 30-, 32-inch
IM/F, F/F, high-vent rib. Weight (w/30-inch bbl.): 8.25 lbs. Checkered walnut beavertail forearm and stock w/straight or Monte Carlo comb, recoil
pad. Luggage-type carrying case. Introduced 1976. Disc.

MODEL 2004 TRAP SINGLE BARREL . . . . NiB $1232 Ex $985 Gd $670
Same as Model 2003 except single bbl., 32- or 34-inch. Full choke.
Weight (w/32-inch bbl.): 8.25 lbs. Introduced 1976. Disc.

MODEL 2005 COMBINATION TRAP . . . NiB $1794 Ex $1435 Gd $976
Model 2004/2005 type gun w/two sets of bbls., single and
over/under. Introduced 1976. Disc.

MODEL 2005/3 COMBINATION TRAP . . . . . NiB $2494 Ex $1995 Gd $1357
Model 2004/2005 type gun w/three sets of bbls., any combination
of single and over/under. Introduced 1976. Disc.

MODEL 3000/2 COMBINATION TRAP . . . . . NiB $2807 Ex $2245 Gd $1527
Boxlock. Automatic ejectors. Selective single trigger. 12 ga. only.
Bbls.: 32-inch over/under choked F/IM, 34-inch underbarrel M
choke; high vent rib. Weight (w/32-inch bbls.): 8 lbs., 6 oz. Choice
of six different castoff buttstocks. Introduced 1979. Disc.

AIRONE HAMMERLESS DOUBLE . . . . . . NiB $1152 Ex $922 Gd $627
Boxlock. Anson & Deeley system action. Auto ejectors. Double triggers. 12 ga. Various bbl. lengths, chokes, weights. Checkered
straight-grip stock and forearm. Made 1940-50.

ALCIONE O/U SHOTGUN
Hammerless, takedown shotgun w/engraved receiver. Selective sin-
gle trigger and ejectors. 12 ga. w/3-inch chambers. Bbls.: 26-inch
(IC/M, 28-inch (M/F). Weight: 6.75 lbs. Checkered French walnut
buttstock and forend. Imported from Italy 1982-89.
Standard model . . . . NiB $656 Ex $525 Gd $357
SL model
(disc. 1986) . . . . NiB $1119 Ex $895 Gd $609

ALCIONE FIELD (97-12 IBS) O/U
Similar to the Standard Alcione model except w/nickel-finished receiv-
er. 26- or 28-inch bbls. w/Franchoke tubes. Imported 1998 to date.
Standard Field model . . . . NiB $844 Ex $675 Gd $459
SL Field model
(w/sideplates, disc.) . . . . NiB $1031 Ex $825 Gd $561

ALCIONE SPORT (SL IBS) O/U . . . . NiB $994 Ex $795 Gd $541
Similar to the Alcione Field model except chambered for 2.75 or 3-inch shells. Ported 29-inch bbls. w/target vent rib and Franchoke tubes.

ALCIONE 2000 SX O/U SHOTGUN . . . . NiB $1457 Ex $1165 Gd $792
Similar to the Standard Alcione model except w/silver finished receiver and gold inlays. 28-inch bbls. w/Franchoke tubes. Weight: 7.25 lbs. Imported 1996-97.

**ARISTOCRAT FIELD
MODEL O/U** . . . . NiB $581 Ex $465 Gd $316
Boxlock. Selective auto ejectors. Selective single trigger. 12 ga. Bbls.: 26-inch IC/M; 28- and 30-inch M/F choke, vent rib. Weight (w/26-inch bbls.): 7 lbs. Checkered pistol-grip stock and forearm. Made 1960-69.

ARISTOCRAT DELUXE AND SUPREME GRADES
Available in Field, Skeet and Trap models w/the same general specifications as standard guns of these types. Deluxe and Supreme Grades are of higher quality, w/stock and forearm of select walnut, elaborate relief engraving on receiver, trigger guard, tang and top lever. Supreme game birds inlaid in gold. Made 1960-66.
Deluxe grade . . . . NiB $1039 Ex $831 Gd $565
Supreme grade . . . . NiB $1494 Ex $1195 Gd $813

ARISTOCRAT IMPERIAL AND MONTE CARLO GRADES
Custom guns made in Field, Skeet and Trap models w/the same general specifications as standard for these types. Imperial and Monte Carlo grades are of highest quality w/stock and forearm of select walnut, fine engraving — elaborate on the latter grade. Made 1967-69.
Imperial grade . . . . NiB $2744 Ex $2195 Gd $1493
Monte Carlo grade . . . . NiB $3869 Ex $3095 Gd $2105

ARISTOCRAT MAGNUM MODEL . . . . NiB $653 Ex $522 Gd $355
Same as Field Model except chambered for 3-inch shells, has 32-inch bbls. choked F/F; stock has recoil pad. Weight: About 8 lbs. Made 1962-65.

ARISTOCRAT SILVER KING . . . . NiB $754 Ex $603 Gd $410
Available in Field, Magnum, Meet and Trap models w/the same general specifications as standard guns of these types. Silver King has stock and forearm of select walnut more elaborately engraved silver-finished receiver. Made 1962-69.

ARISTOCRAT SKEET MODEL . . . . . NiB $715 Ex $572 Gd $389
Same general specifications as Field Model except made only w/26-inch vent-rib bbls. w/SK chokes No. 1 and No. 2, skeet-style stock and forearm. Weight: About 7.5 lbs. Later production had wider (10mm) rib. Made 1960-69.

ARISTOCRAT TRAP MODEL . . . . . . NiB $722 Ex $577 Gd $392
Same general specifications as Field Model except made only w/30-inch vent-rib bbls., M/F choke, trap-style stock w/recoil pad, beaver-tail forearm. Later production had Monte Carlo comb, 10mm rib. Made 1960-69.

ASTORE HAMMERLESS DOUBLE . . . . NiB $994 Ex $795 Gd $541
Boxlock. Anson & Deeley system action. Plain extractors. Double triggers. 12 ga. Various bbl. lengths, chokes, weights. Checkered straight-grip stock and forearm. Made 1937-60.

ASTORE II . . . . NiB $1244 Ex $995 Gd $677
Similar to Astore S but not as high grade. Furnished w/either plain extractors or auto ejectors, double triggers, pistol-grip stock. Bbls.: 27-inch IC/IM; 28-inch M/F chokes. Currently manufactured for Franchi in Spain.

Franchi Astore 5

ASTORE 5 . . . . NiB $2019 Ex $1615 Gd $1098
Same as Astore except has higher grade wood, fine engraving. automatic ejectors, single trigger, 28-inch bbl. M/F or IM/F chokes are standard on current production. Disc.

STANDARD MODEL AUTOLOADER
Recoil operated. Light alloy receiver. Gauges: 12, 20. Four shot magazine. Bbls.: 26-, 28-, 30-inch; plain, solid or vent rib, IC/ M, F chokes. Weight: 12 ga., about 6.25 lbs. 20 ga., 5.13 lbs. Checkered pistol-grip stock and forearm. Made 1950 to date.
W/plain bbl. . . . . NiB $469 Ex $315 Gd $246
W/solid rib . . . . NiB $419 Ex $335 Gd $228
W/vent rib . . . . NiB $450 Ex $360 Gd $245

CROWN, DIAMOND AND IMPERIAL GRADE
Same general specifications as Standard Model except these are custom guns of the highest quality. Crown Grade has hunting scene engraving, Diamond Grade has silver-inlaid scroll engraving; Imperial Grade has elaborately engraved hunting scenes w/figures inlaid in gold. Stock and forearm of fancy walnut. Made 1954-75.
Crown grade . . . . NiB $1619 Ex $1295 Gd $881
Diamond grade . . . . NiB $2119 Ex $1695 Gd $1153
Imperial grade . . . . NiB $2688 Ex $2150 Gd $1462

STANDARD MODEL MAGNUM
Same general specifications as Standard model except has 3-inch chamber, 32-inch (12 ga.) or 28-inch (20 ga.) F choke bbl., recoil pad. Weight: 12 ga., 8.25 lbs.; 20 ga., 6 lbs. Formerly designated "Superange Model." Made 1954-88.
W/plain bbl. . . . . NiB $466 Ex $372 Gd $253
W/vent rib . . . . NiB $491 Ex $393 Gd $267

DYNAMIC-12
Same general specifications and appearance as Standard Model, except 12 ga. only, has heavier steel receiver. Weight: About 7.25 lbs. Made 1965-72.
W/plain bbl. . . . . NiB $369 Ex $295 Gd $201
W/vent rib . . . . NiB $406 Ex $325 Gd $221

DYNAMIC-12 SLUG GUN . . . . NiB $419 Ex $335 Gd $228
Same as standard gun except 12 ga. only, has heavier steel receiver. Made 1965-72.

DYNAMIC-12 SKEET GUN . . . . NiB $518 Ex $414 Gd $282
Same general specifications and appearance as Standard model except has heavier steel receiver, made only in 12 ga. w/26-inch vent-rib bbl., SK choke, stock and forearm of extra fancy walnut. Made 1965-72.

ELDORADO MODEL . . . . NiB $544 Ex $435 Gd $296
Same general specifications as Standard model except highest grade w/gold-filled engraving, stock and forearm of select walnut, furnished w/vent-rib bbl. only. Made 1954-75.

SHOTGUNS

Franchi Falconet Over/Under Buckskin

Franchi Crown Grade

Franchi Diamond Grade

Franchi Eldorado

FALCONET INTERNATIONAL SKEET MODEL... NiB $1098 Ex $878 Gd $597
Similar to Standard Skeet model but higher grade. Made 1970-74.

**FALCONET INTERNATIONAL
TRAP MODEL** .... NiB $1121 Ex $897 Gd $610
Similar to Standard model but higher grade; w/straight or Monte Carlo comb stock. Made 1970-74.

FALCONET O/U FIELD MODELS
Boxlock. Auto ejectors. Selective single trigger. Gauges: 12, 16, 20, 28, .410. Bbls.: 24-, 26-, 28-, 30-inch; vent rib. Chokes: C/IC, IC/M, M/F. Weight: from about 6 lbs. Engraved lightweight alloy receiver, light-colored in Buckskin model, blued in Ebony model, pickled silver in Silver model. Checkered walnut stock and forearm. Made 1968-75.
Buckskin or Ebony model .... NiB $680 Ex $544 Gd $370
Silver model .... NiB $756 Ex $605 Gd $411

FALCONET STANDARD SKEET MODEL ..... NiB $950 Ex $760 Gd $517
Same general specifications as Field models except made only w/26-inch bbls. w/SK chokes No. 1 and No. 2, wide vent rib, color-casehardened receiver skeet-style stock and forearm. Weight: 12 ga., about 7.75 lbs. Made 1970-74.

FALCONET STANDARD TRAP MODEL ...... NiB $939 Ex $751 Gd $511
Same general specifications as Field models except made only in 12 ga. w/30-inch bbls., choked M/F, wide vent rib, color-casehardened receiver, Monte Carlo trap style stock and forearm, recoil pad. Weight: About 8 lbs. Made 1970-74.

HAMMERLESS SIDELOCK DOUBLES
Hand-detachable locks. Self-opening action. Auto ejectors. Double triggers or single trigger. Gauges: 12,16, 20. Bbl. lengths, chokes, weights according to customer's specifications. Checkered stock and forend, straight or pistol grip. Made in six grades — Condor, Imperiale, Imperiale S, Imperiale Montecarlo No. 5, Imperiale Montecarlo No.11, Imperiale Montecarlo Extra — which differ chiefly in overall quality, engraving, grade of wood, checkering, etc.; general specifications are the same. Only the Imperiale Montecarlo Extra Grade is currently manufactured.
Condor grade. .... NiB $8262 Ex $6609 Gd $4495
Imperiale, Imperiale S grades .... NiB $11,747 Ex $9397 Gd $6390
**Imperiale Monte Carlo
grades No. 5, 11** .... NiB $16,531 Ex $13,224 Gd $8993
Imperiale Monte Carlo Extra grade ..... NiB $19,228 Ex $15,382 Gd $10,460

HUNTER MODEL
Same general specifications as Standard Model except higher grade w/engraved receiver; furnished w/ribbed bbl. only. Made 1950 to 90.
W/solid rib .... NiB $426 Ex $341 Gd $232
W/vent rib .... NiB $459 Ex $367 Gd $249

HUNTER MODEL MAGNUM .... NiB $518 Ex $414 Gd $282
Same as Standard Model Magnum except higher grade w/engraved receiver, vent rib bbl. only. Formerly designated "Wildfowler Model." Made 1954-73.

PEREGRINE MODEL 400 .... NiB $706 Ex $565 Gd $384
Same general specifications as Model 451 except has steel receiver. Weight (w/26.5-inch bbl.): 6 lbs., 15 oz. Made 1975-78.

PEREGRINE MODEL 451 O/U .... NiB $635 Ex $508 Gd $345
Boxlock. Lightweight alloy receiver. Automatic ejectors. Selective single trigger. 12 ga. Bbls.: 26.5-, 28-inch; choked C/IC, IC/M, M/F; vent rib. Weight (w/26.5-inch bbls.): 6 lbs., 1 oz. Checkered pistol-grip stock and forearm. Made 1975-78.

PG-80 GAS-OPERATED SEMIAUTOMATIC SHOTGUN
Gas-operated, takedown, hammerless shotgun w/tubular magazine. 12 ga. w/2.75-inch chamber. Five shot magazine. Bbls.: 24 to 30 inches w/vent rib. Weight: 7.5 lbs. Gold-plated trigger. Checkered pistol-grip stock and forend of European walnut. Imported from Italy 1985-90.
Prestige model .... NiB $557 Ex $446 Gd $303
Elite model .... NiB $623 Ex $498 Gd $339

SKEET GUN .... NiB $501 Ex $401 Gd $272
Same general specifications and appearance as Standard Model except made only w/26-inch vent-rib bbl., SK choke. Stock and forearm of extra fancy walnut. Made 1972-74.

SLUG GUN .... NiB $385 Ex $308 Gd $209
Same as Standard Model except has 22-inch plain bbl., Cyl. bore, folding leaf open rear sight, gold bead front sight. Made 1960 to date.

Franchi Hunter Model
w/Ventilated Rib

Franchi Black Magic
48/AL Semiautomatic

Francotte Model 8446

Francotte Model 6886

TURKEY GUN . . . . **NiB $469 Ex $375 Gd $255**
Same as Standard Model Magnum except higher grade w/turkey
scene engraved receiver, 12 ga. only, 36-inch matted-rib bbl., Extra
Full choke. Made 1963-65.

BLACK MAGIC 48/AL SEMIAUTOMATIC
Similar to the Franchi Model 48/AL except w/Franchoke screw-in
tubes and matte black receiver w/Black Magic logo. Gauge: 12 or
20, 2.75-inch chamber. Bbls.: 24-, 26-, 28-inch w/vent rib; 24-inch
rifled slug w/sights. Weight: 5.2 lbs. (20 ga.). Checkered walnut
buttstock and forend. Blued finish.
Standard model . . . . **NiB $543 Ex $434 Gd $295**
Slug bbl. model . . . . **NiB $584 Ex $467 Gd $317**

FALCONET 2000 O/U . . . . **NiB $1271 Ex $1017 Gd $691**
Boxlock. Single selective trigger. Selective automatic ejectors. Gauge:
12, 2.75-inch chambers. Bbls.: 26-inch w/Franchoke tubes; IC/M/F.
Weight: 6 lbs. Checkered walnut stock and forearm. Engraved silver
receiver w/gold-plated game scene. Imported from 1992-93.

LAW-12 SHOTGUN. . . . . **NiB $564 Ex $451 Gd $306**
Similar to the SPAS-12 Model except gas-operated semiautomatic
action only, ambidextrous safety, decocking lever and adj. sights.
Made 1983-94.

SPAS-12 SHOTGUN
Selective operating system functions as a gas-operated semi-automatic or pump action. Gauge: 12, 2.75-inch chamber. Seven shot
magazine. Bbl.: 21.5 inches w/cylinder bore and muzzle protector
or optional screw-in choke tubes, matte finish. 41 inches overall
w/fixed stock. Weight: 8.75 lbs. Blade front sight, aperture rear sight.
Folding or black nylon buttstock w/pistol grip and forend, non-
reflective anodized finish. Made 1983-94.
Fixed stock model . . . . **NiB $869 Ex $695 Gd $473**
Folding stock model . . . . **NiB $994 Ex $795 Gd $541**
Optional choke tubes, add **$125**

SPORTING 2000
O/U . . . . **NiB $1306 Ex $1045 Gd $710**
Similar to the Franchi Falconet 2000. Boxlock. Single selective trigger. Selective automatic ejectors. Gauge: 12; 2.75-inch chambers.
Ported (1992-93) or unported 28-inch bbls., w/vent rib. Weight:
7.75 lbs. Blued receiver. Bead front sight. Checkered walnut stock
and forearm; plastic composition buttplate. Imported from 1992-93
and 1997 to date.

AUGUSTE FRANCOTTE & CIE., S.A. —
Liège, Belgium

*Francotte shotguns for many years were distributed in the U.S. by
Abercrombie & Fitch of New York City. This firm has used a series
of model designations for Francotte guns which do not correspond
to those of the manufacturer. Because so many Francotte owners
refer to their guns by the A & F model names and numbers, the A
& F series is included in a listing separate from that of the standard
Francotte numbers.*

BOXLOCK HAMMERLESS DOUBLES
Anson & Deeley system. Side clips. Greener crossbolt on models
6886, 8446, 4996 and 9261; square crossbolt on Model 6930,
Greener-Scott crossbolt on Model 8457, Purdey bolt on Models
11/18E and 10/18E/628. Auto ejectors. Double triggers. Made in all
standard gauges, barrel lengths, chokes, weights. Checkered stock
and forend, straight or pistol-grip. The eight models listed vary
chiefly in fastenings as described above, finish and engraving, etc.;
general specifications are the same. Disc.
Model 6886 . . . . **NiB $3313 Ex $2650 Gd $1802**
Model 8446 (Francotte Special),
6930, 4996 . . . . **NiB $3744 Ex $2995 Gd $2037**
Model 8457,
9261 (Francotte Original), 11/18E . . . . **NiB $4813 Ex $3850 Gd $2618**
Model 10/18E/628 . . . . **NiB $6119 Ex $4895 Gd $3329**

SHOTGUNS

Franchi LAW-12

Franchi SPAS-12

Franchi Sporting 2000

Francotte Model 10/18E628

Francotte Model 9261

BOXLOCK HAMMERLESS DOUBLES — A & F SERIES
Boxlock, Anson & Deeley type. Crossbolt. Sideplate on all except Knockabout Model. Side clips. Auto ejectors. Double triggers. Gauges: 12, 16, 20, 28, .410. Bbls.: 26- to 32-inch in 12 ga., 26- and 28-inch in other ga.; any boring. Weight: 4.75 to 8 lbs. depending on ga. and bbl. length. Checkered stock and forend; straight, half or full pistol grip. The seven grades (No. 45 Eagle Grade, No. 30, No. 25, No. 20, No. 14, Jubilee Model, Knockabout Model) differ chiefly in overall quality, engraving, grade of wood, checkering, etc.; general specifications are the same. Disc.
Jubilee model
No. 14 . . . . NiB $2050 Ex $1640 Gd $1115
Jubilee model
No. 18 . . . . NiB $2694 Ex $2155 Gd $1466
Jubilee model
No. 20 . . . . NiB $3438 Ex $2750 Gd $1870
Jubilee model
No. 25 . . . . NiB $3707 Ex $2965 Gd $2016

(cont'd.) **BOXLOCK HAMMERLESS DOUBLES — A & F SERIES**
Jubilee model
No. 30 . . . . NiB $5641 Ex $4512 Gd $3068
Eagle grade
No. 45 . . . . NiB $7868 Ex $6294 Gd $4280
Knockabout model . . . . NiB $2406 Ex $1925 Gd $1309

BOXLOCK HAMMERLESS DOUBLES (SIDEPLATES)
Anson & Deeley system. Reinforced frame w/side clips. Purdey-type bolt except on Model 8455, which has Greener crossbolt. Auto ejectors. Double triggers. Made in all standard gauges, bbl. lengths, chokes, weights. Checkered stock and forend, straight or pistol grip. Models 10594, 8455 and 6982 are of equal quality, differing chiefly in style of engraving; Model 9/40E/38321 is a higher grade gun in all details and has fine English-style engraving. Present models quoted and built to customer specifications.
Models 10594, 8455, 6982 . . . . NiB $4869 Ex $3895 Gd $2649
Model 9/40E/38321 . . . . NiB $5938 Ex $4750 Gd $3230

Galef Silver Snipe Over/Under Shotgun

Galef Companion Folding Single-Barrel Shotgun

Galef Zabala Hammerless Double-Barrel Shotgun

FINE O/U SHOTGUN **$9000**
Model 9/40.SE. Boxlock, Anson & Deeley system. Auto ejectors. Double triggers. Made in all standard gauges; bbl. length, boring to order. Weight: About 6.75 lbs. 12 ga. Checkered stock and forend, straight or pistol grip. Currently manufactured to customer specifications.

FINE SIDELOCK
HAMMERLESS DOUBLE . . . . **NiB $24,063 Ex $19,250 Gd $13,090**
Model 120.HE/328. Automatic ejectors. Double triggers. Made in all standard ga.; bbl. length, boring, weight to order. Checkered stock and forend, straight or pistol-grip. Currently manufactured to customer specifications.

HALF-FINE O/U SHOTGUN . . . . **NiB $9906 Ex $7925 Gd $5389**
Model SOB.E/11082. Boxlock, Anson & Deeley system. Auto ejectors. Double triggers. Made in all standard gauges; barrel length, boring to order. Checkered stock and forend, straight or pistol grip. Note: This model is similar to No. 9/40.SE except general quality lower. Disc.

GALEF SHOTGUNS — Manufactured for J. L. Galef & Son, Inc., New York, New York, by M. A. V. I., Gardone F. T., Italy, by Zabala Hermanos, Eiquetta, Spain, and by Antonio Zoli, Gardone V. T., Italy

SILVER SNIPE OVER/UNDER SHOTGUN . . . . **NiB $506 Ex $405 Gd $275**
Boxlock. Plain extractors. Single trigger. Gauges: 12, 20; 3-inch chambers. Bbls: 26-, 28-, 30-inch (latter in 12 ga. only); IC/M, M/F chokes; vent rib. Weight: 12 ga. w/28-inch bbls., 6.5 lbs. Checkered walnut pistol-grip stock and forearm. Introduced by Antonio Zoli in 1968. Disc. See illustration previous page.

GOLDEN SNIPE . . . . **NiB $583 Ex $467 Gd $318**
Same as Silver Snipe, except has selective automatic ejectors. Made by Antonio Zoli 1968 to date.

MONTE CARLO TRAP
SINGLE-BARREL SHOTGUN. . . . . **NiB $244 Ex $195 Gd $133**
Hammerless. Underlever. Plain extractor. 12 ga. 32-inch bbl., F choke, vent rib.

(cont'd.) MONTE CARLO TRAP SINGLE-BARREL SHOTGUN
Weight: About 8.25 lbs. Checkered pistol-grip stock w/Monte Carlo comb and recoil pad, beavertail forearm. Introduced by M. A. V. I. in 1968. Disc.

SILVER HAWK HAMMERLESS DOUBLE. . . . . . **NiB $492 Ex $393 Gd $267**
Boxlock. Plain extractors. Double triggers. Gauges: 12, 20; 3-inch chambers. Bbls.: 26-, 28-, 30-inch (latter in 12 ga. only); IC/M, M/F chokes. Weight: 12 ga. w/26-inch bbls., 6 lbs. 6 oz. Checkered walnut pistol-grip stock and beavertail forearm. Made by Antonio Zoli 1968-72.

COMPANION FOLDING SINGLE-BARREL SHOTGUN
Hammerless. Underlever. Gauges: 12 Mag., 16, 20 Mag., 28, .410. Bbls.: 26-inch (.410 only), 28-inch (12, 16, 20, 28), 30-inch (12-ga. only); F choke; plain or vent rib. Weight: 4.5 lbs. for .410 to 5 lbs., 9 oz. for 12 ga. Checkered pistol-grip stock and forearm. Made by M. A. V. I. from 1968 to date.
W/plain bbl. . . . . **NiB $124 Ex $99 Gd $68**
W/ventilated rib . . . . **NiB $163 Ex $131 Gd $89**

ZABALA HAMMERLESS DOUBLE-BARREL SHOTGUN
Boxlock. Plain extractors. Double triggers. Gauges: 10 Mag., 12 Mag., 16, 20 Mag., 28, .410. Bbls.: 22-, 26-, 28-, 30-, 32-inch; IC/IC, IC/M, M/F chokes. Weight: 12 ga. w/28-inch bbls., 7.75 lbs. Checkered walnut pistol-grip stock and beavertail forearm, recoil pad. Made by Zabala from 1972 to date. See illustration previous page.
10 ga. . . . . **NiB $281 Ex $225 Gd $153**
Other ga.. . . . . **NiB $206 Ex $165 Gd $112**

GAMBA — Gardone V. T. (Brescia), Italy

DAYTONA COMPETITION O/U
Boxlock w/Boss-style locking system. Anatomical single trigger; optional adj., single-selective release trigger. Selective automatic ejectors. Gauge: 12 or 20; 2.75- or 3-inch chambers. Bbls.: 26.75-, 28-, 30- or 32-inch choked SK/SK, IM/F or M/F. Weight: 7.5 to 8.5 lbs. Black or chrome receiver w/blued bbls. Checkered select walnut stock and forearm w/oil finish. Imported by Heckler & Koch until 1992.
American Trap model. . . . . **NiB $5313 Ex $4250 Gd $2890**
Pigeon, Skeet, Trap models . . . . **NiB $6119 Ex $4895 Gd $3329**

Garbi Model 200

Golden Eagle
Model 5000 Grade II Field

(cont'd.) DAYTONA COMPETITION O/U
Sporting model . . . . NiB $5063 Ex $4050 Gd $2754
Sideplate model . . . . NiB $10,406 Ex $8325 Gd $5661
Engraved models
 . . NiB $9375 to 12,500 Ex $7500 to 10,000 Gd $5100 to 6800
Sidelock model . . . . NiB $26,875 Ex $21,500 Gd $14,620

GARBI SHOTGUNS — Eibar, Spain

MODEL 100
SIDELOCK SHOTGUN . . . . NiB $3730 Ex $2984 Gd $2029
Gauges: 12, 16, 20 and 28. Bbls.: 25-, 28-, 30-inch. Action: Holland
& Holland pattern sidelock; automatic ejectors and double trigger.
Weight: 5 lbs., 6 oz. to 7 lbs. 7 oz. English-style straight grip stock
w/fine-line hand-checkered butt; classic forend. Made 1985 to date.

MODEL 101
SIDELOCK SHOTGUN . . . . NiB $4744 Ex $3795 Gd $2580
Same general specifications as Model 100 except the sidelocks
are handcrafted w/hand-engraved receiver; select walnut straight-
grip stock.

MODEL 102
SIDELOCK SHOTGUN . . . . NiB $5080 Ex $4064 Gd $2764
Similar to the Model 101 except w/large scroll engraving. Made
1985-93.

MODEL 103 HAMMERLESS DOUBLE
Similar to Model 100 except w/Purdey-type, higher grade engraving.
Model 103A Standard . . . . NiB $5156 Ex $4125 Gd $2805
Model 103A Royal Deluxe. . . . . NiB $9618 Ex $7694 Gd $5232
Model 103B. . . . . NiB $7769 Ex $6215 Gd $4226
Model 103B Royal Deluxe . . . . NiB $13,743 Ex $10,994 Gd $7476

MODEL 200
HAMMERLESS DOUBLE . . . . . . NiB $7693 Ex $6154 Gd $4185
Similar to Model 100 except w/double heavy-duty locks. Continental-style
floral and scroll engraving. Checkered deluxe walnut stock and forearm.

GARCIA CORPORATION —
Teaneck, New Jersey

BRONCO 22/.410 O/U COMBO . . . . NiB $119 Ex $95 Gd $65
Swing-out action. Takedown. 18.5-inch bbls.; .22 LR over, .410 ga.
under. Weight: 4.5 lbs. One-piece stock and receiver, crackle finish.
Intro. 1976. Disc.

BRONCO .410 SINGLE SHOT. . . . . . . NiB $94 Ex $75 Gd $51
Swing-out action. Takedown. .410 ga. 18.5-inch bbl. Weight: 3.5 lbs.
One-piece stock and receiver, crackle finish. Intro. In 1967. Disc.

GOLDEN EAGLE FIREARMS INC. —
Houston, Texas, Mfd. By Nikko Firearms
Ltd., Tochigi, Japan

EAGLE MODEL 5000
GRADE I FIELD O/U . . . . NiB $850 Ex $775 Gd $510
Receiver engraved and inlaid w/gold eagle head. Boxlock. Auto
ejectors. Selective single trigger. 12, 20 ga.; 2.75- or 3-inch chambers, 12 ga., 3-inch, 20 ga. Bbls.: 26-, 28-, 30-inch (latter only in 12-
ga. 3-inch Mag.); IC/M, M/F chokes; vent rib. Weight: 6.25 lbs., 20
ga.; 7.25 lbs., 12 ga.; 8 lbs., 12-ga. Mag. Checkered pistol-grip stock
and semi-beavertail forearm. Imported 1975-82. Note: Guns marketed 1975-76 under the Nikko brand name have white receivers;
since 1976 are blued.

EAGLE MODEL 5000
GRADE I SKEET . . . . NiB $938 Ex $750 Gd $510
Same as Field model except has 26- or 28-inch bbls. w/wide (11
mm) vent rib, SK choked. Imported 1975-82.

EAGLE MODEL 5000
GRADE I TRAP . . . . NiB $896 Ex $717 Gd $487
Same as Field model except has 30-, or 32-inch bbls. w/wide (11
mm) vent rib (M/F, IM/F, F/F chokes), trap-style stock w/recoil pad.
Imported 1975-82.

EAGLE MODEL 5000
GRADE II FIELD . . . . NiB $979 Ex $783 Gd $532
Same as Grade I Field model except higher grade w/fancier wood,
more elaborate engraving and "screaming eagle" inlaid in gold.
Imported 1975-82.

EAGLE MODEL 5000
GRADE II SKEET . . . . NiB $1009 Ex $807 Gd $549
Same as Grade I Skeet model except higher grade w/fancier wood,
more elaborate engraving and "screaming eagle" inlaid in gold;
inertia trigger, vent side ribs. Imported 1975-82.

EAGLE MODEL 5000
GRADE II TRAP . . . . NiB $1026 Ex $821 Gd $558
Same as Grade I Trap model except higher grade w/fancier wood,
more elaborate engraving and "screaming eagle" inlaid in gold;
inertia trigger, vent side ribs. Imported 1975-82.

EAGLE MODEL 5000
GRADE III GRANDEE . . . . NiB $2688 Ex $2150 Gd $1462
Best grade, available in Field, Skeet and Trap models w/same
general specifications as lower grades. Has sideplates w/game
scene engraving, scroll on frame and bbls., fancy wood (Monte
Carlo comb, full pistol-grip and recoil pad on Trap model). Made
1976-82.

Gorosabel
Model 504 Shotgun

Greener Empire Model
Hammerless

GOROSABEL SHOTGUNS — Spain

MODEL 503 SHOTGUN . . . . **NiB $869 Ex $695 Gd $473**
Gauges: 12, 16, 20 and .410. Action: Anson & Deely-style boxlock. Bbls.: 26-, 27-, and 28-inch. Select European walnut, English or pistol grip, sliver or beavertail forend, hand-checkering. Scalloped frame and scroll engraving. Intro. 1985; disc..

MODEL 504 SHOTGUN . . . . **NiB $938 Ex $750 Gd $510**
Gauge: 12 or 20. Action: Holland & Holland-style sidelock. Bbl.: 26-, 27-, or 28-inch. Select European walnut, English or pistol grip, sliver or beavertail forend, hand-checkering. Holland-style large scroll engraving. Inro. 1985; disc..

MODEL 505 SHOTGUN . . . . **NiB $1306 Ex $1044 Gd $710**
Gauge: 12 or 20. Action: Holland & Holland-style sidelock. Bbls.: 26-, 27-, or 28-inch. Select European walnut, English or pistol grip, silver or beavertail forend, hand-checkering. Purdey-style fine scroll and rose engraving. Intro. 1985; disc..

STEPHEN GRANT — London, England

BEST QUALITY SELF-OPENER DOUBLE-BARREL SHOTGUN . . . . **NiB $15,313 Ex $12,250 Gd $8330**
Sidelock, self-opener. Gauges: 12, 16 and 20. Bbls.: 25 to 30 inches standard. Highest-grade English or European walnut straight-grip buttstock and forearm w/Greener type lever. Imported by Stoeger in the 1950s.

BEST QUALITY SIDE-LEVER DOUBLE-BARREL SHOTGUN . . . . **NiB $13,125 Ex $10,500 Gd $7140**
Sidelock, self-lever. Gauges: 12, 16 and 20. Bbls.: 25 to 30 inches standard. Highest-grade English or European walnut straight-grip buttstock and forearm w/Greener type lever. Imported by Stoeger in the 1950s.

W. W. GREENER, LTD. — Birmingham, England

EMPIRE MODEL HAMMERLESS DOUBLES
Boxlock. Non-ejector or w/automatic ejectors. Double triggers. 12 ga. only (2.75-inch or 3-inch chamber). Bbls.: 28- to 32-inch; any choke combination. Weight: from 7.25 to 7.75 lbs. depending on bbl. length. Checkered stock and forend, straight- or half-pistol grip. Also furnished in "Empire Deluxe Grade," this model has same general specs, but deluxe finish.
Empire model, non-ejector . . . . **NiB $1938 Ex $1550 Gd $1054**
Empire model, ejector . . . . **NiB $2119 Ex $1695 Gd $1153**
Empire Deluxe model, non-ejector . . . **NiB $1969 Ex $1575 Gd $1071**
Empire Deluxe model, ejector . . . . **NiB $2244 Ex $1795 Gd $1221**

FAR-KILLER MODEL GRADE FH35
HAMMERLESS DOUBLE-BARREL SHOTGUN
Boxlock. Non-ejector or w/automatic ejectors. Double triggers. Gauges: 12 (2.75-inch or 3-inch), 10, 8. Bbls.: 28-, 30- or 32-inch. Weight: 7.5 to 9 lbs. in 12 ga. Checkered stock, forend; straight or half-pistol grip. See illustration next page.
Non-ejector, 12 ga. . . . . **NiB $2744 Ex $2195 Gd $1493**
Ejector, 12 ga. . . . . **NiB $3319 Ex $2655 Gd $1805**
Non-ejector, 10 or 8 ga. . . . . . . **NiB $2807 Ex $2245 Gd $1527**
Ejector, 10 or 8 ga. . . . . **NiB $3707 Ex $2965 Gd $2016**

G. P. (GENERAL PURPOSE)
SINGLE BARREL . . . . **NiB $438 Ex $350 Gd $238**
Greener Improved Martini Lever Action. Takedown. Ejector. 12 ga. only. Bbl. lengths: 26-, 30-, 32-inch. M or F choke. Weight: 6.25 to 6.75 lbs. depending on bbl. length. Checkered straight-grip stock and forearm.

HAMMERLESS EJECTOR
DOUBLE-BARREL SHOTGUNS
Boxlock. Auto ejectors. Double triggers, non-selective or selective single trigger. Gauges: 12, 16, 20, 28, .410 (two latter gauges not supplied in Grades DH40 and DH35). Bbls.: 26-, 28-, 30-inch; any choke combination. Weight: From 4.75 to 8 lbs. Depending on ga. and bbl. length. Checkered stock and forend, straight- or half-pistol grip. The Royal, Crown, Sovereign and Jubilee Models differ in quality, engraving, grade of wood, checkering, etc. General specifications are the same.
Royal Model Grade DH75 . . . . . **NiB $4494 Ex $3595 Gd $2445**
Crown Model Grade DH55 . . . . **NiB $3319 Ex $2655 Gd $1805**
Sovereign Model Grade DH40 . . . . **NiB $2919 Ex $2335 Gd $1588**
Jubilee Model Grade DH35 . . . . **NiB $2419 Ex $1935 Gd $1315**
W/selective single trigger, add $330
W/non-selective single trigger, add $250

GREIFELT & COMPANY — Suhl, Germany

GRADE NO. 1 O/U SHOTGUN
Anson & Deeley boxlock, Kersten fastening. Auto ejectors. Double triggers or single trigger. Elaborately engraved. Gauges: 12, 16, 20, 28, .410. Bbls.: 26- to 32-inch, any combination of chokes, vent or solid matted rib. Weight: 4.25 to 8.25 lbs. depending on ga. and bbl. length. Straight- or pistol-grip stock, Purdey-type forend, both checkered. Manufactured prior to World War II.
W/solid matted-rib bbl.,
except .410 & 28 ga. . . . . **NiB $3369 Ex $2695 Gd $1833**
W/solid matted-rib bbl., .410 & 28 ga
. . . . **NiB $4219 Ex $3375 Gd $2295**
W/ventilated rib, add $395
W/single trigger, add $425

SHOTGUNS

**Francotte Model
10/18E628**

**Greifelt Grade No. 1
Over-and-Under Shotgun**

**Greener Hammerless Ejector Double-Barrel
Shotguns: Jubilee, Royal and Sovereign**

GRADE NO. 3 O/U SHOTGUN
Same general specifications as Grade No. 1 except less fancy engraving. Manufactured prior to World War II.
W/solid matted-rib bbl.,
except .410 & 28 ga. .... NiB $2694 Ex $2155 Gd $1466
W/solid matted-rib bbl.,
.410 & 28 ga. .... NiB $3206 Ex $2565 Gd $1744
W/ventilated rib, add $395
W/single trigger, add $425

MODEL 22 HAMMERLESS DOUBLE... NiB $1856 Ex $1485 Gd $1009
Anson & Deeley boxlock. Plain extractors. Double triggers. Gauges: 12 and 16. Bbls.: 28- or 30-inch, M/F choke. Checkered stock and forend, pistol grip and cheekpiece standard, English-style stock also supplied. Manufactured since World War II.

MODEL 22E
HAMMERLESS DOUBLE ...... NiB $2469 Ex $1975 Gd $1343
Same as Model 22 except has automatic ejectors.

MODEL 103
HAMMLERLESS DOUBLE ...... NiB $1794 Ex $1435 Gd $976
Anson & Deeley boxlock. Plain extractors. Double triggers. Gauges: 12 and 16. Bbls.: 28- or 30-inch, M and F choke. Checkered stock and forend, pistol grip and cheekpiece standard, English-style stock also supplied. Manufactured since World War II.

MODEL 103E
HAMMERLESS DOUBLE ...... NiB $1907 Ex $1525 Gd $1037
Same as Model 103 except has automatic ejectors.

MODEL 143E O/U SHOTGUN
General specifications same as pre-war Grade No. 1 Over-and-Under, except this model is not supplied in 28 and .410 ga. or w/32-inch bbls. Model 143E is not as high quality as the Grade No. 1 gun. Mfd. Since World War II.
W/raised matted rib,
double triggers .... NiB $2194 Ex $1755 Gd $1193
W/ventilated rib,
selective single trigger .... NiB $2694 Ex $2155 Gd $1466

HAMMERLESS DRILLING (THREE-BARREL
COMBINATION GUN) .... NiB $3503 Ex $2802 Gd $1905
Boxlock. Plain extractors. Double triggers, front single set for rifle bbl. Gauges: 12, 16, 20; rifle bbl. in any caliber adapted to this type of gun. 26-inch bbls. Weight: About 7.5 lbs. Auto rear sight operated by rifle bbl. selector. Checkered stock and forearm, pistol-grip and cheekpiece standard. Manufactured prior to WW II. Note: Value shown is for guns chambered for cartridges readily obtainable. If

O/U COMBINATION GUN

Similar in design to this maker's over-and-under shotguns. Gauges: 12, 16, 20, 28, .410; rifle bbl. in any caliber adapted to this type of gun. Bbls.: 24- or 26-inch, solid matted rib. Weight: From 4.75 to 7.25 lbs. Folding rear sight. Manufactured prior to WWII. Note: Values shown are for gauges other than .410 w/rifle bbl. Chambered for a cartridge readily obtainable; if in an odd foreign caliber, value will be considerably less. .410 ga. increases in value by about 50%.

W/non-automatic ejector . . . . . **NiB $5744 Ex $4595 Gd $3125**
W/automatic ejector . . . . **NiB $6563 Ex $5250 Gd $3570**

HARRINGTON & RICHARDSON ARMS COMPANY — Gardner, Massachusetts, Now H&R 1871, Inc.

Formerly Harrington & Richardson Arms Co. of Worcester, Mass. One of the oldest and most distinguished manufacturers of handguns, rifles and shotguns, H&R suspended operations on January 24, 1986. In 1987, New England Firearms was established as an independent company producing selected H&R models under the NEF logo. In 1991, H&R 1871, Inc. was formed from the residual of the parent company and then took over the New England Firearms facility. H&R 1871 produced firearms under both their logo and the NEF brand name until 1999, when the Marlin Firearms Company acquired the assets of H&R 1871.

NO. 3 HAMMERLESS
SINGLE-SHOT SHOTGUN . . . . **NiB $110 Ex $75 Gd $50**
Takedown. Automatic ejector. Gauges: 12, 16, 20, .410. Bbls.: plain, 26- to 32-inch, F choke. Weight: 6.5 to 7.25 lbs. depending on ga. and bbl. length. Plain pistol-grip stock and forend. Disc. 1942.

NO. 5 STANDARD LIGHTWEIGHT
HAMMER SINGLE . . . . **NiB $130 Ex $80 Gd $55**
Takedown. Auto ejector. Gauges: 24, 28, .410. Bbls.: 26- or 28-inch, F choke. Weight: About 4 to 4.75 lbs. Plain pistol-grip stock/forend. Disc. 1942.

NO. 6 HEAVY BREECH SINGLE-SHOT
HAMMER SHOTGUN . . . . **NiB $130 Ex $80 Gd $55**
Takedown. Automatic ejector. Gauges: 10, 12, 16, 20. Bbls.: Plain, 28- to 36-inch, F choke. Weight: About 7 to 7.25 lbs. Plain stock and forend. Disc. 1942.

NO. 7 OR 9 BAY STATE SINGLE-SHOT
HAMMER SHOTGUN . . . . **NiB $130 Ex $80 Gd $55**
Takedown. Automatic ejector. Gauges: 12, 16, 20, .410. Bbls.: Plain 26- to 32-inch, F choke. Weight: 5.5 to 6.5 lbs. depending on ga. and bbl. length. Plain pistol-grip stock and forend. Disc. 1942.

NO. 8 STANDARD SINGLE-SHOT
HAMMER SHOTGUN . . . . **NiB $150 Ex $90 Gd $60**
Takedown. Automatic ejector. Gauges: 12, 16, 20, 24, 28, .410. Bbl.: plain, 26- to 32-inch, F choke. Weight: 5.5 to 6.5 lbs. depending on ga. and bbl. length. Plain pistol-grip stock and forend. Made 1908-42.

MODEL 348 GAMESTER
BOLT-ACTION SHOTGUN . . . . **NiB $110 Ex $75 Gd $50**
Takedown. 12 and 16 ga. Two shot tubular magazine, 28-inch bbl, F choke. Plain pistol-grip stock. Weight: About 7.5 lbs. Made 1949-54.

**Harrington & Richardson
No. 3, 5, 6, 7 and 8 Shotguns**

MODEL 349 GAMESTER DELUXE . . . . **NiB $150 Ex $80 Gd $55**
Same as Model 348 except has 26-inch bbl. W/adj. choke device, recoil pad. Made 1953-55.

MODEL 351 HUNTSMAN
BOLT-ACTION SHOTGUN . . . . **NiB $156 Ex $125 Gd $85**
Takedown. 12 and 16 ga. Two shot tubular magazine. Pushbutton safety. 26-inch bbl. w/H&R variable choke. Weight: About 6.75 lbs. Monte Carlo stock w/recoil pad. Made 1956-58.

MODEL 400 PUMP . . . . **NiB $219 Ex $175 Gd $119**
Hammerless. Gauges: 12, 16, 20. Tubular magazine holds 4 shells. 28-inch bbl., F choke. Weight: About 7.25 lbs. Plain pistol-grip stock (recoil pad in 12 and 16 ga.), grooved slide handle. Made 1955-67.

SHOTGUNS

Harrington & Richardson
Model 400 Pump

Harrington & Richardson
Model 403 Autoloading

Harrington & Richardson
Model 404C

Harrington & Richardson
Model 440

Harrington & Richardson
Model 442

MODEL 401 . . . . **NiB $219 Ex $175 Gd $119**
Same as Model 400 except has H&R variable choke. Made 1956-63.

MODEL 402 . . . . **NiB $231 Ex $185 Gd $126**
Similar to Model 400 except .410 ga., weight: About 5.5 lbs. Made 1959-67.

MODEL 403 AUTOLOADING
SHOTGUN . . . . **NiB $237 Ex $190 Gd $129**
Takedown. .410 ga. Tubular magazine holds four shells. 26-inch bbl., F choke. Weight: About 5.75 lbs. Plain pistol-grip stock and forearm. Made in 1964.

MODEL 404/404C. . . . . **NiB $281 Ex $225 Gd $153**
Boxlock. Plain extractors. Double triggers. Gauges: 12, 20, .410. Bbls.: 28-inch in 12 ga. (M/F choke), 26-inch in 20 ga. (IC/M and .410 (F/F). Weight: 5.5 to 7.25 lbs. Plain walnut-finished hardwood stock and forend on Model 404; 404C checkered. Made in Brazil by Amadeo Rossi 1969-1972.

MODEL 440 PUMP . . . . **NiB $181 Ex $145 Gd $99**
Hammerless. Gauges: 12, 16, 20. 2.75-inch chamber in 16 ga., 3-inch in 12 and 20 ga. Three shot magazine. Bbls.: 26-, 28-, 30-inch; IC, M, F choke. Weight: 6.25 lbs. Plain pistol-grip stock and slide handle, recoil pad. Made 1968-73.

MODEL 442 . . . . **NiB $231 Ex $185 Gd $126**
Same as Model 440 except has vent rib bbl., checkered stock and forearm, weight: 6.75 lbs. Made 1969-73.

ULTRA SLUG SERIES . . . . **NiB $194 Ex $155 Gd $105**
Singel shot 12 or 20 ga w/3-inch chamber w/heavy-wall 24-inch fully rifled bbl. w/scope . Weight: 9 lbs. Walnut-stained Monte Carlo stock, sling swivels, black nylon sling. Made 1995 to date.

MODEL 1212 FIELD . . . . **NiB $332 Ex $265 Gd $180**
Boxlock. Plain extractors. Selective single trigger. 12 ga., 2.75-inch chambers. 28-inch bbls., IC/IM, vent rib. Weight: 7 lbs. Checkered walnut pistol-gip stock and fluted forearm. Made 1976-80 by Lanber Arms S. A., Zaldibar (Vizcaya), Spain.

Harrington & Richardson
Model 1212 Field

Harrington & Richardson
Model 1212 Waterfowl

Harrington & Richardson
Golden Squire — Model 159

Harrington & Richardson
Harrich No. 1

MODEL 1212
WATERFOWL GUN. . . . . **NiB $365 Ex $292 Gd $198**
Same as Field Gun except chambered for 12-ga, 3-inch mag. shells, has 30-inch bbls., M/F chokes, stock and recoil pad, weight: 7.5 lbs. Made 1976-1980.

MODEL 1908
SINGLE-SHOT SHOTGUN . . . . **NiB $150 Ex $95 Gd $60**
Takedown. Automatic ejector. Gauges: 12, 16, 24 and 28. Bbls.: 26- to 32-inch, F choke. Weight: 5.25 to 6.5 lbs. depending on ga. and bbl. length. Casehardened receiver. Plain pistol-grip stock. Bead front sight. Made 1908-1934.

MODEL 1908 .410 (12MM)
SINGLE-SHOT SHOTGUN . . . . **NiB $140 Ex $112 Gd $76**
Same general specifications as standard Model 1908 except chambered for .410 or 12mm shot cartridge w/bbl. milled down at receiver to give a more pleasing contour.

MODEL 1915 SINGLE-SHOT SHOTGUN
Takedown. Both non-auto and auto-ejectors available. Gauges: 24, 28, .410, 14mm and 12mm. Bbls.: 26- or 28-inch, F choke. Weight: 4 to 4.75 lbs. depending on ga. and bbl. length. Plain black walnut stock w/semi pistol-grip.
24 ga. . . . . **NiB $206 Ex $165 Gd $112**
28, .410 ga. **NiB $169 Ex $135 Gd $92**

FOLDING GUN . . . . **NiB $169 Ex $135 Gd $92**
Single bbl. hammer shotgun hinged at the front of the frame, the bbl. folds down against the stock. Light Frame model: gauges — 28, 14mm, .410; 22-inch bbl.; weighs about 4.5 lbs. Heavy Frame model: gauges — 12, 16, 20, 28, .410; 26-inch bbl.; weighs from 5.75 to 6.5 lbs. Plain pistol-grip stock and forend. Disc. 1942.

GOLDEN SQUIRE MODEL 159
SINGLE-BARREL
HAMMER SHOTGUN . . . . **NiB $125 Ex $100 Gd $68**
Hammerless. Side lever. Automatic ejection. Gauges: 12, 20. Bbls: 30-inch in 12 ga., 28-inch in 20 ga., both F choke. Weight: About 6.5 lbs. Straight-grip stock w/recoil pad, forearm w/Schnabel. Made 1964-66.

GOLDEN SQUIRE JR. MODEL 459 . . **NiB $144 Ex $115 Gd $78**
Same as Model 159 except gauges 20 and .410, 26-inch bbl., youth stock. Made in 1964.

HARRICH NO. 1 SINGLE-BARREL
TRAP GUN . . . . **NiB $1495 Ex $1196 Gd $813**
Anson & Deeley-type locking system w/Kersten top locks and double underlocking lugs. Sideplates engraved w/hunting scenes. 12 ga. Bbls.: 32-, 34-inch; F choke; high vent rib. Weight: 8.5 lbs. Checkered Monte Carlo stock w/pistol-grip and recoil pad, beaver-tail forearm, of select walnut. Made in Ferlach, Austria, 1971-75.

**Harrington & Richardson
Topper No. 48**

**Harrington & Richardson
Topper No. 099**

**Harrington & Richardson
Topper No. 162 — Slug Gun**

**Harrington & Richardson
Topper Model 198 (098)**

**Harrington & Richardson
Topper Model 490 — Greenwing**

**"TOP RIB"
SINGLE-BARREL SHOTGUN . . . . NiB $208 Ex $173 Gd $128**
Takedown. Auto ejector. Gauges: 12, 16 and 20. Bbls.: 28- to 30-inch, F choke w/full-length matted top rib. Weight: 6.5 to 7 lbs. depending on ga. and bbl. length. Black walnut pistol-grip stock (capped) and forend; both checkered. Flexible rubber buttplate. Made during 1930s.

**TOPPER NO. 48 SINGLE-BARREL
HAMMER SHOTGUN . . . . NiB $163 Ex $131 Gd $89**
Similar to old Model 8 Standard. Takedown. Top lever. Auto ejector. Gauges: 12, 16, 20, .410. Bbls.: plain; 26- to 30-inch; M or F choke. Weight: 5.5 to 6.5 lbs. depending on ga. and bbl. length. Plain pistol-grip stock and forend. Made 1946-57.

TOPPER MODEL 099 DELUXE . . . . . NiB $131 Ex $105 Gd $71
Same as Model 158 except has matte nickel finish, semipistol grip walnut-finished American hardwood stock; semibeavertail forearm; 12, 16, 20, and .410 ga. Made 1982-86.

**TOPPER MODEL 148 SINGLE-SHOT
HAMMER SHOTGUN . . . . NiB $138 Ex $110 Gd $75**
Takedown. Side lever. Auto-ejection. Gauges: 12, 16, 20, .410.

(cont'd.) TOPPER MODEL 148
Bbls.: 12 ga.,30-, 32- and 36-inch; 16 ga., 28- and 30-inch; 20 and .410 ga., 28-inch; F choke. Weight: 5 to 6.5 lbs. Plain pistol-grip stock and forend, recoil pad. Made 1958-61.

**TOPPER MODEL 158 (058) SINGLE-SHOT
HAMMER SHOTGUN . . . . NiB $144 Ex $115 Gd $78**
Takedown. Side lever. Automatic ejection. Gauges: 12, 20, .410 (2.75-inch and 3-inch shells); 16 (2.75-inch). bbl. length and choke combinations: 12 ga., 36-inch/F, 32-inch/F, 30-inch/F, 28-inch/F or M; .410, 28-inch/F. Weight: about 5.5 lbs. Plain pistol-grip stock and forend, recoil pad. Made 1962-81. Note: Designation changed to 058 in 1974.

TOPPER MODEL 162 SLUG GUN. . NiB $189 Ex $151 Gd $103
Same as Topper Model 158 except has 24-inch bbl., Cyl. bore, w/rifle sights. Made 1968-86.

**TOPPER MODEL 176 10 GA.
MAGNUM. . . . . NiB $181 Ex $145 Gd $99**
Similar to Model 158, but has 36-inch heavy bbl. chambered for 3.5-inch 10- ga. Mag. shells, weight: 10 lbs.; stock w/Monte Carlo comb and recoil pad, longer and fuller forearm. Made 1977-86.

Harrington & Richardson
Topper — Classic Youth

Harrington & Richardson
Topper — Deluxe

TOPPER MODEL 188 DELUXE . . . . . NiB $156 Ex $125 Gd $85
Same as standard Topper Model 148 except has chromed frame, stock and forend in black, red, yellow, blue, green, pink, or purple colored finish. .410 ga. only. Made 1958-61.

TOPPER MODEL 198 (098) DELUXE . . . . . . NiB $163 Ex $130 Gd $88
Same as Model 158 except has chrome-plated frame, black finished stock and forend; 12, 20 and .410 ga. Made 1962-81. Note: Designation changed to 098 in 1974.

TOPPER JR. MODEL 480 . . . . NiB $150 Ex $95 Gd $70
Similar to No. 48 Topper except has youth-size stock, 26-inch bbl, .410 ga. only. Made 1958-61.

TOPPER NO. 488 DELUXE . . . . NiB $151 Ex $121 Gd $82
Same as standard No. 48 Topper except chrome-plated frame, black lacquered stock and forend, recoil pad. Disc. 1957.

TOPPER MODEL 490 . . . . NiB $144 Ex $115 Gd $78
Same as Model 158 except has youth-size stock (3 inches shorter), 26-inch bbl.; 20 and 28 ga. (M choke), .410 (F). Made 1962-86.

TOPPER MODEL 490 GREENWING . . . . NiB $163 Ex $130 Gd $88
Same as the Model 490 except has a special high-polished finish. Made 1981-86.

TOPPER JR. MODEL 580 . . . . NiB $125 Ex $100 Gd $68
Same as Model 480 except has colored stocks as on Model 188. Made 1958-61.

TOPPER MODEL 590 . . . . NiB $131 Ex $105 Gd $71
Same as Model 490 except has chrome-plated frame, black finished stock and forend. Made 1962-63.

The following models are manufactured and distributed by the reorganized company of H&R 1871, Inc.

MODEL 098 TOPPER CLASSIC YOUTH . . . . . NiB $119 Ex $95 Gd $65
Same as Topper Junior except also available in 28 ga. and has checkered American black walnut stock/forend w/satin finish and recoil pad. Made 1991 to date.

MODEL 098 TOPPER DELUXE . . . . . . NiB $119 Ex $95 Gd $65
Same as Model 098 Single Shot Hammer except in 12 ga., 3-inch chamber only. 28-inch bbl.; Mod. choke tube. Made 1992 to date.

MODEL 098 TOPPER
DELUXE RIFLED SLUG GUN . . . . . . NiB $150 Ex $120 Gd $81
Same as Topper Deluxe Shotgun except has compensated 24-inch rifled slug bbl. Nickel plated receiver and blued bbl. Black finished hardwood stock. Made 1996 to date.

MODEL 098 TOPPER HAMMER
SINGLE-SHOT SHOTGUN . . . . NiB $100 Ex $80 Gd $54
Side lever. Automatic ejector. Gauges: 12, 20 and .410; 3-inch chamber. Bbls.: 28-inch, (12 ga./M); 26-inch, (20 ga./M); 26-inch (.410/F). Weight: 5 to 6 lbs. Satin nickel receiver, blued bbl. Plain pistol-grip stock and semibeavertail forend w/black finish. Re-Intro. 1992.

MODEL 098 TOPPER JUNIOR . . . . . . NiB $106 Ex $85 Gd $58
Same as Model 098 except has youth-size stock and 22-inch bbl. 20 or .410 ga. only. Made 1991 to date.

MODEL .410 TAMER SHOTGUN . . . . NiB $119 Ex $95 Gd $65
Takedown. Topper-style single-shot, side lever action w/auto ejector. Gauge: .410; 3-inch chamber. 19.5-inch bbl. 33 inches overall. Weight: 5.75 lbs. Black polymer thumbhole stock designed to hold 4 extra shotshells. Matte nickel finish. Made 1994 to date.

MODEL N. W. T. F. TURKEY MAG
Same as Model 098 Single-Shot Hammer except has 24-inch bbl. chambered 10 or 12 ga. w/3.5-inch chamber w/screw-in choke tube. Weight: 6 lbs. American hardwood stock, Mossy Oak camo finish. Made 1991-96.
NWTF 10 ga. Turkey Mag (Made 1996) . . . . NiB $140 Ex $112 Gd $76
NWTF 12 ga. Turkey Mag (Made 1991-95) . . . NiB $124 Ex $99 Gd $67

MODEL N. W. T. F.
YOUTH TURKEY GUN . . . . NiB $137 Ex $110 Gd $74
Same as Model N.W.T.F. Turkey Mag except has 22-inch bbl. chambered in 20 ga. w/3-inch chamber and fixed full choke. Realtree camo finish. Made 1994-95.

MODEL SB1-920
ULTRA SLUG HUNTER . . . . NiB $185 Ex $148 Gd $101
Special 12 ga. action w/12 ga. bbl. blank underbored to 20 ga. to form a fully rifled slug bbl. Gauge: 20 w/3 inch chamber. 24-inch bbl. Weight: 8.5 lbs. Satin nickel receiver, blued bbl. Walnut finished hardwood Monte Carlo stock. Made 1996-98.

Heckler & Koch Red Lion Mark II

Heckler & Koch Classic Lion Grade I

MODEL ULTRA SLUG HUNTER $135
12 or 20 ga. w/3-inch chamber. 22- or 24-inch rifled bbl. Weight: 9 lbs. Matte black receiver and bbl. Walnut finished hardwood Monte Carlo stock. Made 1997 to date.

MODEL ULTRA SLUG HUNTER DELUXE . . . . . NiB $194 Ex $155 Gd $105
Similar to Ultra Slug Hunter model except with compensated bbl. Made 1997 to date.

HECKLER & KOCH FABARM SHOTGUNS — Oberndorf/Neckar, West Germany, and Sterling, Virginia

CLASSIC LION SIDE-BY-SIDE SHOTGUN
12 ga. only. 28- or 30-inch non-ported Tribor bbl. w/3-inch chamber. 46.5 to 48.5-inches overall. Weight: 7 to 7.2 lbs. Five choke tubes; C, IC, M, IM, F. Traditional boxlock design. Oil-finished walnut forearms and stocks w/diamond-cut checkering. Imported 1999 to date.
Classic Lion Grade I . . . . NiB $1286 Ex $1029 Gd $700
Classic Lion Grade II . . . . NiB $1941 Ex $1552 Gd $1055

CAMO LION SEMI-AUTO SHOTGUN . . . . NiB $850 Ex $725 Gd $450
12 ga. Only. 24 to 28-inches Tribor bbl. 44.25-48.25-inches overall. Weight: 7-7.2 lbs. 3 inch chamber w/5 choke tubes - C, IC, M, IM, F. 2-shot mag. Camo covered walnut stock w/rear front bar sights. Imp. 1999 to date.

MAX LION O/U SHOTGUN . . . . NiB $1695 Ex $1450 Gd $800
12 or 20 ga. 26- 28- or 30-inch TriBore system bbls. 42.5-47.25-inches overall. Weight: 6.8-7.8 lbs. 3-inch chamber w/5 choke tubes - C, IC, M, IM, F. Single selective adj. trigger and auto ejectors. Side plates w/high-grade stock and rubber recoil pad. Made 1999 to date.

RED LION MARK II SEMI-AUTO
SHOTGUN . . . . NiB $744 Ex $595 Gd $405
12 ga. Only. 24- 26- or 28-inch TriBore system bbls. 44.25 to 48.25-inches overall. Weight: 7 to 7.2 lbs. 3-inch chamber w/five choke tubes- C, IC, M, IM, F. Two shot magazine. Matte finish w/walnut wood stock. Rubber vented recoil pad w/leather cover. Made 1999 to date.

SILVER LION O/U SHOTGUN . . . . NiB $1129 Ex $905 Gd $619
12 or 20 ga. 26- 28- or 30-inch TriBore system bbls. 43.25-47.25 inchesoverall. 3-inch chamber w/5 choke tubes - C, IC, M, IM, F. Single selective trig. and auto ejectors. Wal. stock w/rubber recoil pad. Made 1999 to date.

SPORTING CLAY LION
SEMI-AUTO SHOTGUN . . . . NiB $869 Ex $695 Gd $473
12 ga. only. 28- or 30-inch bbl. w/3-inch chamber and ported Tribore system barrel. Matte finish w/gold plated trigger and carrier release button. Made 1999 to date.

HERCULES SHOTGUNS

See Listings under "W" for Montgomery Ward.

HEYM SHOTGUNS — Münnerstadt, Germany

MODEL 22S
"SAFETY" SHOTGUN/
RIFLE COMBINATION . . . . NiB $3200 Ex $2560 Gd $1741
16 and 20 ga. Cal: .22 Mag., .22 Hornet, .222 Rem., .222 Rem. Mag., 5.6x50R Mag., 6.5x57R, 7x57R, .243 Win. 24-inch bbls. 40 inches overall. Weight: About 5.5 lbs. Single-set trigger. Left-side bbl. selector. Integral dovetail base for scope mounting. Arabesque engraving. Walnut stock. Disc. 1993.

MODEL 55 BF SHOTGUN/
RIFLE COMBO . . . . NiB $6947 Ex $5557 Gd $3779
12, 16 and 20 ga. Calibers: 5.6x50R Mag., 6.5x57R, 7x57R, 7x65R, .243 Win., .308 Win., .30-06. 25-inch bbls. 42-inches overall. Weight: About 6.75 lbs. Black satin-finished, corrosion-resistant bbls. of Krupp special steel. Hand-checkered walnut stock w/long pistol-grip. Hand-engraved leaf scroll. German cheekpiece. Disc. 1988.

J. C. HIGGINS SHOTGUNS

See Sears, Roebuck & Company.

HUGLU HUNTING FIREARMS — Huglu, Turkey, Imported by Turkish Firearms Corp.

MODEL 101 B 12 AT-DT
COMBO O/U TRAP . . . . NiB $1994 Ex $1595 Gd $1085
Over/Under boxlock. 12 ga. w/3-inch chambers. Combination 30- or 32-inch top single & O/U bbls. w/fixed chokes or choke tubes. Weight: 8 lbs. Automatic ejectors or extractors. Single selective trigger. Manual safety. Circassian walnut Monte Carlo trap stock w/palm-swell grip and recoil pad. Silvered frame w/engraving. Imported 1993-97.

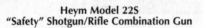

Heym Model 22S
"Safety" Shotgun/Rifle Combination Gun

Heym Model 55
BF Shotgun/Rifle

MODEL 101 B 12 ST O/U TRAP. . . . NiB $1345 Ex $1076 Gd $731
Same as Model 101 AT-DT except in 32-inch O/U configuration only. Imported 1994-96.

MODEL 103 B 12 ST O/U
Boxlock. Gauges: 12, 16, 20, 28 or .410. 28-inch bbls. w/fixed chokes. Engraved action w/inlaid game scene and dummy sideplates. Double triggers, extractors and manual safety. Weight: 7.5 lbs. Circassian walnut stock. Imported 1995-96.
Model 103B w/extractors . . . . NiB $984 Ex $787 Gd $535
28 and .410, add $100

MODEL 103 C 12 ST O/U
Same general specs as Model 103 B 12 S except w/extractors or ejectors. 12 or 20 ga. w/3-inch chambers. Black receiver w/50% engraving coverage. Imported 1995-97.
Model 103C w/extractors . . . . NiB $994 Ex $795 Gd $541
Model 103C w/ejectors. . . . . NiB $1244 Ex $995 Gd $677

MODEL 103 D 12 ST O/U
Same gen. specs as Mdl. 103 B 12 ST except stand. boxlock. Ext. or eject. 12 or 20 ga. w/3-inch chambers. 80% engraving coverage. Imp. 1995-97.
Model 103D w/extractors . . . . NiB $969 Ex $775 Gd $527
Model 103D w/ejectors. . . . . NiB $1219 Ex $975 Gd $663

MODEL 103 F 12 ST O/U
Same as Model 103 B except extractors or ejectors. 12 or 20 ga. only. 100% engraving coverage. Imported 1996-97.
Model 103F w/extractors . . . . NiB $1063 Ex $850 Gd $578
Model 103F w/ejectors . . . . NiB $1313 Ex $1050 Gd $714

MODEL 104 A 12 ST O/U
Boxlock. Gauges: 12, 20, 28 or .410. 28-inch bbls. w/fixed chokes or choke tubes. Silvered, engraved receiver w/15% engraving coverage. Double triggers, manual safety and extractors or ejectors. Weight: 7.5 lbs. Circassian walnut stock w/field dimensions. Imported 1995-97.
Model 104A w/extractors . . . . . . .NiB $938 Ex $750 Gd $510
Model 104A w/ejectors. . . . . NiB $1188 Ex $950 Gd $646

(cont'd.) MODEL 104 A 12 ST O/U
28 and .410, add $100
W/Choke Tubes, add $50

MODEL 200 SERIES DOUBLE
Boxlock. Gauges: 12, 20, 28, or .410 w/3-inch chambers. 28-inch bbls. w/fixed chokes. Silvered, engraved receiver. Extractors, manual safety, single selective trigger or double triggers. Weight: 7.5 lbs. Circassian walnut stock. Imported 1995-97.
Model 200 (w/15%
engraving coverage, SST) . . . . NiB $969 Ex $775 Gd $527
Model 201 (w/30%
engraving coverage, SST). . . . . NiB $1244 Ex $995 Gd $677
Model 202 (w/Greener
cross bolt, DT). . . . . NiB $1031 Ex $825 Gd $561
28 and .410, add $100

HIGH STANDARD SPORTING ARMS — East Hartford, Connecticut, Formerly High Standard Mfg. Corp. of Hamden, Conn.

In 1966, High Standard introduced new series of Flite-King Pumps and Supermatic autoloaders, both readily identifiable by the damascened bolt and restyled checkering. To avoid confusion, these models are designated "Series II" in this text. This is not an official factory designation. Operation of this firm was discontinued in 1984.

FLITE-KING FIELD
PUMP—12 GA. . . . . NiB $269 Ex $215 Gd $146
Hammerless. Magazine holds 5 shells. Bbls.: 26-inch IC, 28-inch M or F, 30-inch F choke. Weight: 7.25 lbs. Plain pistol-grip stock and slide handle. Made 1960-66.

FLITE-KING BRUSH—12 GA. . . . . . NiB $200 Ex $180 Gd $150
Same as Flite-King Field 12 except has 18- or 20-inch bbl. (cylinder bore) w/rifle sights. Made 1962-64.

High Standard Flite-King Brush

High Standard Flite-King Deluxe Rib — 12 Gauge

High Standard Flite-King Deluxe Rib — 12 Gauge (Adjustable Choke)

FLITE-KING BRUSH DELUXE . . . . . NiB $265 Ex $230 Gd $150
Same as Flite-King Brush except has adj. peep rear sight, checkered pistol grip, recoil pad, fluted slide handle, swivels and sling. Not available w/18-inch bbl. Made 1964-66.

FLITE-KING BRUSH (SERIES II). . . . NiB $255 Ex $204 Gd $138
Same as Flite-King Deluxe 12 (II) except has 20-inch bbl., cylinder bore, w/rifle sights. Weight: 7 lbs. Made 1966-75.

FLITE-KING BRUSH DELUXE (II) . . NiB $297 Ex $237 Gd $161
Same as Flite-King Brush (II) except has adj. peep rear sight, swivels and sling. Made 1966-75.

FLITE-KING DELUXE 12 GA. (SERIES II)
Hammerless. 5-shot magazine. 27-inch plain bbls.w/adj. choke. 26-inch IC, 28-inch M or F. 30-inch F choke. Weight: About 7.25 lbs. Checkered pistol-grip stock and forearm, recoil pad. Made 1966-75.
W/adj. choke . . . . NiB $297 Ex $238 Gd $162
W/O adj. choke . . . . NiB $270 Ex $216 Gd $146

FLITE-KING DELUXE
20, 28, .410 GA. (SERIES II) . . . . . . NiB $266 Ex $213 Gd $145
Same as Flite-King Deluxe 12 (II) except chambered for 20 and .410 ga. 3-inch shell, 28 ga. 2.75-inch shell w/20- or 28-inch plain bbl. Weight: About 6 lbs. Made 1966-75.

FLITE-KING DELUXE RIB 12 GA. . . . . . NiB $326 Ex $261 Gd $177
Same as Flite-King Field 12 except vent rib bbl. (28-inch M or F. 30-inch F). Checkered stock and forearm. Made 1961-66.

FLITE-KING DELUXE RIB 12 GA. (II)
Same as Flite-King Deluxe 12 (II) except has vent rib bbl., available in 27-inch w/adj. choke, 28-inch M or F, 30-inch F choke. Made 1966-75.
W/adj. choke . . . . NiB $350 Ex $280 Gd $190
W/O adj. choke. . . . . NiB $326 Ex $261 Gd $177

FLITE-KING DELUXE RIB 20 GA. . . . . NiB $314 EX $251 GD $171
Same as Flite-King Field 20 except vent-rib bbl. (28 inch M or F), checkered stock and slide handle. Made 1962-66.

FLITE-KING DELUXE RIB 20, 28, .410 GA. (SERIES II)
Same as Flite-King Deluxe 20, 28, .410 (II) except 20 ga. available w/27-inch adj. choke, 28-inch M or F choke. Weight: about 6.25 lbs. Made 1966-75.
W/adj. choke. . . . . NiB $369 Ex $295 Gd $201
W/O adj. choke. . . . . NiB $344 Ex $275 Gd $187

FLITE-KING DELUXE SKEET GUN
12 GA. (SERIES II) . . . . NiB $319 Ex $255 Gd $173
Same as Flite-King Deluxe Rib 12 (II) except available only w/26-inch vent rib bbl., SK choke, recoil pad optional. Made 1966-75.

FLITE-KING DELUXE SKEET GUN
20, 28, .410 GA. (SERIES II). . . . . . NIB $369 EX $295 GD $201
Same as Flite-King Deluxe Rib 20, 28, .410 (II) except available only w/26-inch vent-rib bbl., SK choke. Made 1966-75.

FLITE-KING DELUXE
TRAP GUN (II) . . . . NIB $303 EX $242 GD $164
Same as Flite-King Deluxe Rib 12 (II) except available only w/30-inch vent-rib bbl., F choke; trap-style stock. Made 1966-75.

FLITE-KING FIELD PUMP 20 GA. . . . . NIB $244 EX $195 GD $133
Hammerless. Chambered for 3-inch Magnum shells, also handles 2.75-inch. Magazine holds four shells. Bbls.: 26-inch IC, 28-inch M or F choke. Weight: About 6 lbs. Plain pistol-grip stock and slide handle. Made 1961-66.

FLITE-KING PUMP SHOTGUNS 16 GA.
Same general specifications as Flite-King 12 except not available in Brush, Skeet and Trap Models or 30-inch bbl. Values same as for 12-ga. guns. Made 1961-65.

High Standard Flite-King Field
12 Gauge

High Standard Flite-King Field
20 Gauge

High Standard Flite-King Field Trophy
20 Gauge

High Standard Supermatic Deluxe
12 Gauge (II)

High Standard Supermatic Deluxe
12 Gauge (II) (Adjustable Choke)

FLITE-KING PUMP SHOTGUNS (.410 GA.)
Same general specifications as Flite-King 20 except not available in Special and Trophy Models, or w/other than 26-inch choke bbl. Values same as for 20 ga. guns. Made 1962-66.

FLITE-KING SKEET
12 GA.. . . . . **NiB $350 Ex $280 Gd $190**
Same as Flite-King Deluxe Rib except 26-inch vent rib bbl., w/SK choke. Made 1962-66.

FLITE-KING SPECIAL 12 GA. . . . . . **NiB $255 Ex $204 Gd $138**
Same as Flite-King Field 12 except has 27-inch bbl. w/adj. choke. Made 1960-66.

FLITE-KING SPECIAL 20 GA. . . . . . **NiB $261 Ex $209 Gd $142**
Same as Flite-King Field 20 except has 27-inch bbl. w/adj. choke. Made 1961-66.

FLITE-KING TRAP 12 GA. . . . . **NiB $350 Ex $280 Gd $190**
Same as Flite-King Deluxe Rib 12 except 30-inch vent rib bbl., F choke, special trap stock w/recoil pad. Made 1962-66.

FLITE-KING TROPHY 12 GA. . . . . . **NiB $326 Ex $261 Gd $177**
Same as Flite-King Deluxe Rib 12 except has 27-inch vent rib bbl. w/adj. choke. Made 1960-66.

FLITE-KING TROPHY
20 GA.. . . . . **NiB $350 Ex $280 Gd $190**
Same as Flite-King Deluxe Rib 20 except has 27-inch vent rib bbl. w/adj. choke. Made 1962-66.

SUPERMATIC DEER GUN . . . . **NiB $344 Ex $275 Gd $187**
Same as Supermatic Field 12 except has 22-inch bbl. (cylinder bore) w/rifle sights, checkered stock and forearm, recoil pad. Weight: 7.75 lbs. Made in 1965.

SUPERMATIC DELUXE 12 GA. (SERIES II)
Gas-operated autoloader. Four shot magazine. Bbls.: Plain; 27-inch w/adj. choke (disc. about 1970); 26-inch IC, 28-inch M or F. 30-inch F choke. Weight: About 7.5 lbs. Checkered pistol-grip stock and forearm, recoil pad. Made 1966-75.
W/adj. choke . . . . **NiB $369 Ex $295 Gd $201**
W/O adj. choke . . . . **NiB $299 Ex $245 Gd $176**

SUPERMATIC DELUXE 20 GA. (SERIES II)
Same as Supermatic Deluxe 12 (II) except chambered for 20 ga. Three inch shell; bbls. available in 27-inch w/adj. choke (disc. about 1970), 26-inch IC, 28-inch M or F choke. Weight: About 7 lbs. Made 1966-75.
W/adj. choke . . . . **NiB $269 Ex $215 Gd $146**
W/O adj. choke . . . . **NiB $319 Ex $255 Gd $173**

SUPERMATIC DELUXE DEER GUN (II) NiB $406 Ex $325 Gd $221
Same as Supermatic Deluxe 12 (II) except has 22-inch bbl., cylinder bore, w/rifle sights. Weight: 7.75 lbs. Made 1966-74.

SUPERMATIC DELUXE DUCK
12 GA. MAGNUM (SERIES II) . . . . . **NiB $279 Ex $225 Gd $156**
Same as Supermatic Deluxe 12 (II) except chambered for 3-inch magnum shells, 3-shot magazine, 30-inch plain bbl., F choke. Weight: 8 lbs. Made 1966-74.

High Standard Supermatic Deluxe Deer II

High Standard Supermatic Deluxe Duck Rib

High Standard Supermatic Deluxe Rib

High Standard Supermatic Duck —12 Gauge Magnum

SUPERMATIC DELUXE RIB
12 GA. . . . . NiB $266 Ex $213 Gd $145
Same as Supermatic Field 12 except vent rib bbl. (28-inch M or F, 30-inch F), checkered stock and forearm. Made 1961-66.

SUPERMATIC DELUXE RIB 12 GA. (II)
Same as Supermatic Deluxe 12 (II) except has vent rib bbl.; available in 27-inch w/adj. choke, 28-inch M or F, 30-inch F choke. Made 1966-75.
W/adj. choke . . . . NiB $331 Ex $265 Gd $180
W/O adj. choke . . . . NiB $300 Ex $240 Gd $163

SUPERMATIC DELUXE RIB
20 GA. . . . . NiB $331 Ex $265 Gd $180
Same as Supermatic Field 20 except vent rib bbl. (28-inch M or F), checkered stock and forearm. Made 1963-66.

SUPERMATIC DELUXE RIB 20 GA. (II)
Same as Supermatic Deluxe 20 (II) except has vent rib bbl. Made 1966-75.
W/adj. choke . . . . NiB $303 Ex $242 Gd $164
W/O adj. choke . . . . NiB $279 Ex $223 Gd $152

SUPERMATIC DELUXE
SKEET GUN
12 GA. (SERIES II) . . . . NiB $303 Ex $242 Gd $164
Same as Supermatic Deluxe Rib 12 (II) except available only w/26-inch vent rib bbl., SK choke. Made 1966-75.

SUPERMATIC DELUXE SKEET GUN
20 GA. (SERIES II) . . . . NiB $314 Ex $251 Gd $171
Same as Supermatic Deluxe Rib 20 (II) except available only w/26-inch vent rib bbl., SK choke. Made 1966-75.

SUPERMATIC DELUXE
TRAP GUN (SERIES II) . . . . NiB $326 Ex $261 Gd $177
Same as Supermatic Deluxe Rib 12 (II) except available only w/30-inch vent rib bbl., full choke; trap-style stock. Made 1966-75.

SUPERMATIC DELUXE DUCK RIB
12 GA. MAG. (SERIES II) . . . . NiB $303 Ex $242 Gd $164
Same as Supermatic Deluxe Rib 12 (II) except chambered for 3-inch magnum shells, 3-shot magazine; 30-inch vent rib bbl., F choke. Weight: 8 lbs. Made 1966-75.

SUPERMATIC DUCK 12 GA. MAG. . . . . NiB $303 Ex $242 Gd $164
Same as Supermatic Field 12 except chambered for 3-inch Magnum shell, 30-inch F choke bbl., recoil pad. Made 1961-66.

SUPERMATIC TROPHY 12 GA. . . . . NiB $255 Ex $204 Gd $138
Same as Supermatic Deluxe Rib 12 except has 27-inch vent-rib bbl. w/adj. choke. Made 1961-66.

SUPERMATIC DUCK RIB 12 GA. MAG.. . . . . NiB $326 Ex $261 Gd $177
Same as Supermatic Duck 12 Magnum except has vent rib bbl., checkered stock and forearm. Made 1961-66.

SUPERMATIC FIELD AUTOLOADING
SHOTGUN 12 GA. . . . . NiB $350 Ex $280 Gd $190
Gas-operated. Magazine holds four shells. Bbls.: 26-inch IC, 28-inch M or F choke, 30-inch F choke. Weight: About 7.5 lbs. Plain pistol-grip stock and forearm. Made 1960-66.

SUPERMATIC FIELD AUTOLOADING
SHOTGUN 20 GA.. . . . . NiB $269 Ex $215 Gd $146
Gas-operated. Chambered for 3-inch mag. shells, also handles 2.75-inch. Magazine holds three shells. Bbls.: 26-inch IC, 28-inch M or F choke. Weight: About 7 lbs. Plain pistol-grip stock and forearm. Made 1963-66.

SUPERMATIC SHADOW AUTOMATIC . . . NiB $394 Ex $315 Gd $214
Gas-operated. Ga.: 12, 20, 2.75- or 3-inch chamber in 12 ga., 3-inch in 20 ga. Mag. holds four 2.75-inch shells, three 3-inch. Bbls.: Full-size airflow rib; 26-inch (IC or SK choke), 28-inch (M, IM or F), 30-inch (trap or F choke), 12-ga. 3-inch Mag. available only in 30-inch F choke; 20 ga. not available in 30-inch. Weight: 12 ga., 7 lbs. Checkered walnut stock and forearm. Made 1974-75 by Caspoll Int'l., Inc., Tokyo.

High Standard Supermatic Duck Rib — 12 Gauge

High Standard Supermatic Shadow Automatic

High Standard Supermatic Shadow Indy

High Standard Supermatic Shadow Seven

SUPERMATIC SHADOW
INDY O/U . . . . NiB $994 Ex $795 Gd $541
Boxlock. Fully engraved receiver. Selective auto ejectors. Selective single trigger. 12 ga. 2.75-inch chambers. Bbls.: Full-size airflow rib; 27.5 inch both SK choke, 29.75-inch IM/F or F/F. Weight: W/29.75-inch bbls., 8 lbs. 2 oz. Pistol-grip stock w/recoil pad, ventilated forearm, skip checkering. Made 1974-75 by Caspoll Int'l., Inc., Tokyo.

SUPERMATIC SHADOW SEVEN . . . NiB $844 Ex $675 Gd $459
Same general specifications as Shadow Indy except has conventional vent rib, less elaborate engraving, standard checkering forearm is not vented, no recoil pad. 27.5-inch bbls.; also available in IC/M, M/F choke. Made 1974-75.

SUPERMATIC SKEET 12 GA. . . . . . . NiB $269 Ex $215 Gd $146
Same as Supermatic Deluxe Rib 12 except 26-inch vent-rib bbl. w/SK choke. Made 1962-66.

SUPERMATIC SKEET 20 GA. . . . . . . NiB $288 Ex $230 Gd $156
Same as Supermatic Deluxe Rib 20 except 26-inch vent-rib bbl. w/SK choke. Made 1964-66.

SUPERMATIC SPECIAL 12 GA. . . . . NiB $238 Ex $190 Gd $129
Same as Supermatic Field 12 except has 27-inch bbl. w/adj. choke. Made 1960-66.

SUPERMATIC SPECIAL 20 GA. . . . . NiB $263 Ex $210 Gd $143
Same as Supermatic Field 20 except has 27-inch bbl. w/adj. choke. Made 1963-66.

SUPERMATIC TRAP 12 GA. . . . . . . NiB $269 Ex $215 Gd $146
Same as Supermatic Deluxe Rib 12 except 30-inch vent rib bbl., F choke, special trap stock w/recoil pad. Made 1962-66.

SUPERMATIC TROPHY 20 GA. . . . . NiB $281 Ex $225 Gd $153
Same as Supermatic Deluxe Rib 20 except has 27-inch vent rib bbl. w/adj. choke. Made 1963-66.

HOLLAND & HOLLAND, LTD. —
London England

BADMINTON MODEL HAMMERLESS DOUBLE-BARREL SHOTGUN. ORIGINALLY NO. 2 GRADE
General specifications same as Royal Model except without self-opening action. Made as a game gun or pigeon and wildfowl gun. Introduced in 1902. Disc.
W/double triggers . . . . NiB $10,438 Ex $8350 Gd $5678		
W/single trigger . . . . NiB $11,938 Ex $9550 Gd $6494		
20 ga., add 25%		
28 ga., add 40%		
.410, add 65%		

CENTENARY MODEL HAMMERLESS DOUBLE-BARREL SHOTGUN
Lightweight (5.5 lbs.). 12 ga. game gun designed for 2-inch shell. Made in four grades—Model Deluxe, Royal, Badminton, Dominion — values same as shown for standard guns in those grades. Disc. 1962.

High Standard Supermatic Special

High Standard Supermatic Trophy

Holland & Holland
Royal Model

Holland & Holland Badminton

Holland & Holland Dominion

**DOMINION MODEL HAMMERLESS
DOUBLE-BBL. SHOTGUN .... NiB $6162 Ex $4929 Gd $3352**
Game Gun. Sidelock. Auto ejectors. Double triggers. Gauges: 12,
16, 20. bbls. 25- to 30-inch, any standard boring. Checkered stock
and forend, straight grip standard. Disc. 1967.

MODEL DELUXE HAMMERLESS DOUBLE
Same as Royal Model except has special engraving and exhibition
grade stock and forearm. Currently manufactured.
**W/double triggers ...... NiB $56,875 Ex $45,500 Gd $30,940
W/single trigger .... NiB $62,188 Ex $49,750 Gd $33,830**

**NORTHWOOD MODEL HAMMERLESS
DOUBLE-BARREL SHOTGUN.. NiB $6619 Ex $5295 Gd $3601**
Anson & Deeley system boxlock. Auto ejectors. Double triggers.
Gauges: 12, 16, 20, 28 in Game Model; 28 ga. not offered in Pigeon
Model; Wildfowl Model in 12 ga. only (3-inch chambers available).
Bbls.: 28-inch standard in Game and Pigeon Models, 30-inch in
Wildfowl Model; other lengths, any standard choke combination

(cont'd) **NORTHWOOD MODEL
HAMMERLESS DOUBLE-BARREL SHOTGUN**
available. Weight: From 5 to 7.75 lbs. depending on ga. and bbls.
Checkered straight-grip or pistol-grip stock and forearm. Disc.

**RIVIERA MODEL
PIGEON GUN .... NiB $14,437 Ex $11,550 Gd $7854**
Same as Badminton Model but supplied w/two sets of bbls., double
triggers. Disc. 1967.

ROYAL MODEL HAMMERLESS DOUBLE
Self-opening. Sidelocks hand-detachable. Auto ejectors. Double
triggers or single trigger. Gauges: 12, 16, 20, 28 .410. Built to customer's specifications as to bbl. length, chokes, etc. Made as a
Game Gun or Pigeon and Wildfowl Gun, the latter having treble-
grip action and side clips. Checkered stock and forend, straight grip
standard. Made from 1885 to date.
**W/double triggers ...... NiB $56,563 Ex $45,250 Gd $30,770
W/single trigger .... NiB $60,938 Ex $48,750 Gd $33,150**

Holland & Holland
Royal Double-Barrel Shotgun

IGA Coach Gun

ROYAL MODEL O/U

Sidelocks, hand-detachable. Auto-ejectors. Double triggers or single trigger. 12 ga. Built to customer's specifications as to bbl. length, chokes, etc. Made as a Game Gun or Pigeon and Wildfowl Gun. Checkered stock and forend, straight grip standard. Note: In 1951 Holland & Holland introduced its New Model Under/Over w/an improved, narrower action body. Disc. 1960.

**New model
(double triggers)** .... NiB $36,563 Ex $29,250 Gd $19,890
**New model
(single trigger)** .... NiB $38,125 Ex $30,500 Gd $20,740
**Old model
(double triggers)** .... NiB $31,188 Ex $24,950 Gd $16,966
**Old model
(single trigger)** .... NiB $33,125 Ex $26,500 Gd $18,020

SINGLE-SHOT SUPER TRAP GUN

Anson & Deeley system boxlock. Auto-ejector. No safety. 12 ga. Bbls.: Wide vent rib, 30- or 32-inch, w/Extra Full choke. Weight: About 8.75 lbs. Monte Carlo stock w/pistol grip and recoil pad, full beavertail forearm. Models differ in grade of engraving and wood. Disc.

**Standard
grade** .... NiB $5313 Ex $4250 Gd $2890
**Deluxe
grade** .... NiB $8438 Ex $6750 Gd $4590
**Exhibition
grade** .... NiB $10,313 Ex $8250 Gd $5610

SPORTING O/U .... NiB $26,875 Ex $21,500 Gd $14,620
Blitz action. Auto ejectors; single selective trigger. Gauges: 12 or 20 w/2.75-inch chambers. Barrels: 28- to 32-inch w/screw-in choke tubes. Hand-checkered European walnut straight-grip or pistol grip stock, forearm. Made 1993 to date.

HOLLAND & HOLLAND SPORTING

O/U DELUXE .... NiB $34,938 Ex $27,950 Gd $19,006
Same general specs as Sporting O/U except better engraving and select wood. Made 1993 to date.

HUNTER ARMS COMPANY —
Fulton, New York

HUNFULTON HAMMERLESS DOUBLE-BARREL. SHOTGUN

Boxlock. Plain extractors. Double triggers or non-selective single trigger. Gauges: 12 16, 20. Bbls.: 26- to 32-inch various choke combinations. Weight: about 7 lbs. Checkered pistol-grip stock and forearm. Disc. 1948.

W/double triggers .... NiB $385 Ex $308 Gd $209
W/single trigger .... NiB $653 Ex $470 Gd $355

SPECIAL HAMMERLESS DOUBLE-BARREL. SHOTGUN

Boxlock. Plain extractors. Double triggers or non-selective single trigger. Gauges: 12,16, 20. Bbls.: 26- to 30-inch various choke combinations. Weight: 6.5 to 7.25 lbs. depending on bbl. length and ga. Checkered full pistol-grip stock and forearm. Disc. 1948.

W/double triggers .... NiB $590 Ex $472 Gd $321
W/single trigger .... NiB $731 Ex $585 Gd $397

IGA SHOTGUNS — Veranopolis, Brazil
Imported by Stoeger Industries, Inc.
Accokeek, Maryland

COACH GUN

Side-by-side double. Gauges: 12, 20 and .410. 20-inch bbls. w/3-inch chambers. Fixed chokes (standard model) or screw-in tubes (deluxe model). Weight: 6.5 lbs. Double triggers. Ejector and automatic safety. Blued or nickel finish. Hand-rubbed oil-finished pistol grip stock and forend w/hand checkering (hardwood on standard model or Brazilian walnut (deluxe). Imported 1983 to date.

Standard Coach Gun (blued finish) .... NiB $266 Ex $213 Gd $145
Standard Coach Gun (nickel finish) ... NiB $326 Ex $261 Gd $177
**Standard Coach Gun
(engraved stock)** .... NiB $350 Ex $280 Gd $190
Deluxe Coach Gun (intro. 1997) ... NiB $385 Ex $308 Gd $209
Choke tubes, add $20

IGA Turkey S/S Shotgun

IGA Condor Turkey O/U Shotgun

IGA Condor Waterfowl O/U Shotgun

CONDOR I O/U SINGLE-TRIGGER SHOTGUN
Gauges: 12 or 20. 26- or 28-inch bbls. of chrome-molybdenum steel. Chokes: Fixed — M/F or IC/M; screw-in choke tubes (12 and 20 ga.). Three inch chambers. Weight: 6.75 to 7 lbs. Sighting rib w/anti-glare surface. Hand-checkered hardwood pistol-grip stock and forend. Imported 1983 to date.
W/fixed chokes . . . . NiB $350 Ex $280 Gd $190
W/screw-in tubes . . . . NiB $398 Ex $318 Gd $216

CONDOR II O/U DOUBLE-TRIGGER
SHOTGUN . . . . NiB $344 Ex $275 Gd $187
Same general specifications as the Condor I O/U except w/double triggers and fixed chokes only; 26-inch bbls., IC/M; 28-inch bbls., M/F.

CONDOR SUPREME . . . . NiB $534 Ex $427 Gd $291
Same general specifications as Condor I except upgraded w/fine-checkered Brazilian walnut buttstock and forend, a matte-laquered finish, and a massive monoblock that joins the bbls. in a solid one-piece assembly at the breech end. Bbls. w/recessed interchangeable choke tubes formulated for use w/steel shot. Automatic ejectors. Imported 1996 to date.

CONDOR TURKEY MODEL
O/U SHOTGUN . . . . NiB $623 Ex $498 Gd $339
12 gauge only. 26-inch vent-rib bbls. w/3-inch chambers fitted w/recessed interchangeable choke tubes. Weight: 8 lbs. Mechanical single trigger. Ejectors and automatic safety. Advantage camouflage on stock and bbls. Made 1997 to date.

CONDOR WATERFOWL MODEL. . . . . NiB $636 Ex $509 Gd $346
Similar to Condor Turkey-Advantage camo model except w/30-inch bbls. Made 1998 to date.

DELUXE HUNTER CLAY SHOTGUN
Same general specifications and values as IGA Condor Supreme. Imported 1997 to date.

ERA 2000 O/U SHOTGUN . . . . NiB $459 Ex $367 Gd $249
Gauge: 12 w/3-inch chambers. 26- or 28-inch bbls. of chrome-molybdenum steel w/screw-in choke tubes. Extractors. Manual safety. (Mechanical triggers.) Weight: 7 lbs. Checkered Brazilian hardwood stock w/oil finish. Imported 1992-95.

REUNA SINGLE-SHOT SHOTGUN
Visible hammer. Under-lever release. Gauges: 12, 20 and .410; 3-inch chambers. 26- or 28-inch bbls. w/fixed chokes or screw-in choke tubes (12 ga. only). Extractors. Weight: 5.25 to 6.5 lbs. Plain Brazilian hardwood stock and semi-beavertail forend. Imported 1992 to date.
W/fixed choke. . . . . NiB $106 Ex $85 Gd $58
W/choke tubes . . . . NiB $181 Ex $145 Gd $99

UPLANDER SIDE-BY-SIDE SHOTGUN
Gauges: 12, 20, 28 and .410. 26- or 28-inch bbls. of chrome-molybdenum steel. Various fixed-choke combinations; screw-in choke tubes (12 and 20 ga.). Three inch chambers (2.75-inch in 28 ga.). Weight: 6.25 to 7 lbs. Double triggers. Automatic safety. Matte-finished solid sighting rib. Hand checkered pistol-grip or straight stock and forend w/hand-rubbed, oil-finish. Imported 1983 to date.
Upland w/fixed chokes . . . . NiB $290 Ex $232 Gd $158
Upland w/screw-in tubes . . . . NiB $350 Ex $280 Gd $190
English model (straight grip) . . . . . . NiB $338 Ex $270 Gd $184
Ladies model . . . . NiB $350 Ex $280 Gd $190
Supreme model . . . . NiB $469 Ex $375 Gd $255
Youth model . . . . NiB $314 Ex $251 Gd $171

UPLANDER TURKEY
MODEL S/S DOUBLE . . . . NiB $460 Ex $368 Gd $250
12 gauge only. 24-inch solid rib bbls. w/3-inch chambers choked F&F. Weight: 6.75 lbs. Double triggers. Automatic safety. Advantage camouflage on stock and bbls. Made 1997 to date.

ITHACA GUN COMPANY — King Ferry (formerly Ithaca), New York. Now Ithaca Acquisition Corp./Ithaca Gun Co.

MODEL 37 BICENTENNIAL
COMMEMORATIVE. . . . . NiB $650 Ex $425 Gd $289
Limited to issue of 1976. Similar to Model 37 Supreme except has special Bicentennial design etched on receiver, full-fancy walnut stock and slide handle. Serial numbers U.S.A. 0001 to U.S.A. 1976. Originally issued w/presentation case w/cast-pewter belt buckle. Made in 1976. Best value is for gun in new, unfired condition.

IGA Deluxe Hunter Clay Shotgun

IGA Uplander Side-by-Side Shotgun

Ithaca Model 37 English Ultra

Ithaca Model 37 Featherlight Standard

Ithaca Model 37 Deerslayer Super Deluxe

Ithaca Model 37 Supreme Grade

SHOTGUNS

MODEL 37 DEERSLAYER DELUXE
Formerly "Model 87 Deerslayer Deluxe" reintroduced under the original Model 37 designation w/the same specifications. Available w/smooth bore or rifled bbl. Reintroduced 1996.
Deluxe model (smoothbore) . . . . . . NiB $439 Ex $351 Gd $239
Deluxe model (rifled bbl.) . . . . NiB $492 Ex $393 Gd $267

MODEL 37 DEERSLAYER II . . . . NiB $525 Ex $420 Gd $286
Gauges: 12 or 20 ga. Five shot capacity. 20- or 25-inch rifled bbl. Weight: 7 lbs. Monte Carlo checkered walnut stock and forearm. Receiver drilled and tapped for scope mount. Made 1996 to date.

MODEL 37 DEERSLAYER STANDARD . . . . NiB $313 Ex $250 Gd $170
Same as Model 37 Standard except has 20- or 26-inch bbl. bored for rifled slugs, rifle-type open rear sight and ramp front sight. Weight: 5.75 to 6.5 lbs. depending on ga. and bbl. length. Made 1959-86.

MODEL 37 DEERSLAYER
SUPER DELUXE . . . . NiB $406 Ex $325 Gd $221
Formerly "Deluxe Deerslayer." Same as Model 37 Standard Deerslayer except has stock and slide handle of fancy walnut. Made from 1962-86.

MODEL 37 ENGLISH ULTRA . . . . . NiB $466 Ex $372 Gd $253
Same general specifications as Model 37 Ultralite except straight buttstock, 25-inch Hot Forged vent-rib bbl. Made 1984-87.

MODEL 37 FEATHERLIGHT STANDARD GRADE
SLIDE-ACTION REPEATING SHOTGUN
Adaptation of the earlier Remington Model 17, a Browning design patented in 1915. Hammerless. Takedown. Gauges: 12, 16 (disc. 1973), 20. Four shell magazine. Bbl. lengths: 26-, 28-, 30-inch (the latter in 12 ga. only); standard chokes. Weight: From 5.75 to 7.5 lbs. depending on ga. and bbl. length. Checkered pistol-grip stock and slide handle. Some guns made in the 1950s and 1960s have grooved slide handle; plain or checkered pistol-grip. Made 1937-84.
Standard w/checkered pistol-grip . . NiB $281 Ex $225 Gd $153
W/plain stock . . . . NiB $250 Ex $200 Gd $136
Mdl 37D Deluxe (1954-77) . . . . NiB $356 Ex $285 Gd $194
Mdl 37DV Deluxe vent rib (1962-84) . . . NiB $406 Ex $325 Gd $221
Mdl 37R Deluxe
solid rib (1955-61) . . . . NiB $344 Ex $275 Gd $187
Mdl 37V Standard
vent rib (1962-84) . . . . NiB $331 Ex $265 Gd $180

Ithaca Model 51
Deluxe Trap

MODEL 37 FIELD GRADE
MAG. W/TUBES . . . . **NiB $328 Ex $262 Gd $178**
Same general specifications as Model 37 Featherlight except 32-inch bbl. and detachable choke tubes. Vent rib bbl. Made 1984-87.

MODEL 37 NEW CLASSIC . . . . **NiB $591 Ex $472 Gd $321**
Ggs: 12 or 20 ga. 20- or 28-inch vent rib bbl. w/choke tubes. Knuckle-cut receiver and orig. style "ring-tail" forend. Lim. prod. 1998 to date.

MODEL 37 THOUSAND DOLLAR GRADE
Custom built, elaborately engraved and inlaid w/gold, hand-finished working parts, stock and forend of select figured walnut. General specifications same as standard Model 37. Note: The same gun was designated the $1000 Grade prior to World War II. Made 1937-67.
$1000 grade . . . . **NiB $6550 Ex $5240 Gd $3563**
$5000 grade . . . . **NiB $6250 Ex $5000 Gd $3400**

MODEL 37 SUPREME GRADE . . . . . **NiB $656 Ex $525 Gd $357**
Available in Skeet or Trap Gun, similar to Model 37T. Made 1967-86 and 1996-97.

MODEL 37 ULTRALITE
Same general specifications as Model 37 Featherlight except streamlined forend, gold trigger, Sid Bell grip cap and vent rib. Weight: 5 to 5.75 lbs. Made 1984-87.
Standard . . . . **NiB $456 Ex $365 Gd $248**
W/choke tubes . . . . **NiB $494 Ex $395 Gd $269**

MODEL 37R SOLID RIB GRADE
Same general specifications as the Model 37 Featherlight except has a raised solid rib, adding about .25 pounds of weight. Made 1937-67.
W/checkered grip
and slide handle . . . . **NiB $375 Ex $300 Gd $204**
W/plain stock . . . . **NiB $369 Ex $295 Gd $201**

MODEL 37S SKEET GRADE . . . . **NiB $531 Ex $425 Gd $289**
Same general specifications as the Model 37 Featherlight except has vent rib and large extension-type forend; weight: About .5 lb. more. Made 1937-55.

MODEL 37T TARGET GRADE . . . . . **NiB $493 Ex $394 Gd $267**
Same general specifications as Model 37 Featherlight except has vent-rib bbl., checkered stock and slide handle of fancy walnut (choice of skeet- or trap-style stock). Note: This model replaced Model 37S Skeet and Model 37T Trap. Made 1955-61.

MODEL 37T TRAP GRADE . . . . **NiB $531 Ex $425 Gd $289**
Same gen. specs. as Mdl. 37S except has straighter trap-style stock of select walnut, recoil pad; weight: About .5 lb. more. Made 1937-55.

MODEL 37 TURKEYSLAYER
Gauges: 12 ga. (Standard) or 20 ga. (youth). Slide action. 22-inch bbl. Extended choke tube. Weight: 7 lbs. Advantage camouflage or Realtree pattern. Made 1996 to date.
Standard model . . . . **NiB $459 Ex $367 Gd $249**
Youth model(intro. 1998) . . . . **NiB $492 Ex $393 Gd $267**

MODEL 37 WATERFOWLER . . . . . . **NiB $478 Ex $383 Gd $260**
12 ga. only w/28-inch bbl. Wetlands camouflage. Made 1998 to date.

MODEL 51 DEERSLAYER . . . . **NiB $361 Ex $288 Gd $196**
Same as Model 51 Standard except has 24-inch plain bbl. w/slug boring, rifle sights, recoil pad. Weight: About 7.25 lbs. Made 1972-84.

MODEL 51 DELUXE SKEET GRADE . . . **NiB $494 Ex $395 Gd $269**
Same as Model 51 Standard except 26-inch vent-rib bbl. only, SK choke, skeet-style stock, semi-fancy wood. Weight: About 8 lbs. Made 1970-87.

MODEL 51 DELUXE TRAP GRADE
Same as Model 51 Standard except 12 ga. only, 30-inch bbl. w/broad floating rib, F choke, trap-style stock w/straight or Monte Carlo comb, semifancy wood, recoil pad. Weight: About 8 lbs. Made 1970-87.
W/straight stock . . . . **NiB $426 Ex $341 Gd $232**
W/Monte Carlo stock . . . . **NiB $452 Ex $362 Gd $246**

MODEL 51 STANDARD AUTOMATIC SHOTGUN
Gas-operated. Gauges: 12, 20. 3-shot. Bbls.: Plain or vent rib, 30-inch F choke (12 ga. only), 28-inch F or M, 26-inch IC. Weight: 7.25-7.75 lbs. depending on ga. and bbl. Checkered pistol-grip stock, forearm. Made 1970-80. Still avail. in 12 and 20 ga., 28-inch M choke only.
W/plain barrel . . . . **NiB $288 Ex $230 Gd $156**
W/ventilated rib . . . . **NiB $344 Ex $275 Gd $187**

MODEL 51 STANDARD MAGNUM
Same as Model 51 Standard except has 3-inch chamber, handles Magnum shells only; 30-inch bbl. in 12 ga., 28-inch in 20 ga., F or M choke, stock w/recoil pad. Weight: 7.75-8 lbs. Made 1972 to date.
W/plain bbl. (disc. 1976) . . . . **NiB $279 Ex $223 Gd $152**
W/ventilated rib . . . . **NiB $326 Ex $261 Gd $177**

MODEL 51A TURKEY GUN . . . . **NiB $350 Ex $280 Gd $190**
Same general specifications as standard Model 51 Magnum except 26-inch bbl. and matte finish. Disc. 1986.

MODEL 66 LONG TOM . . . . **NiB $125 Ex $100 Gd $68**
Same as Model 66 Standard except has 36-inch F choke bbl., 12 ga. only, checkered stock and recoil pad standard. Made 1969-74.

MODEL 66 STANDARD SUPER SINGLE LEVER
Single shot. Hand-cocked hammer. Gauges: 12 (disc. 1974), 20, .410, 3-inch chambers. Bbls.: 12 ga., 30-inch F choke, 28-inch F or M; 20 ga., 28-inch F or M; .410, 26-inch F. Weight: About 7 lbs. Plain or checkered straight-grip stock, plain forend. Made 1963-78.
Standard model . . . . **NiB $156 Ex $125 Gd $85**
Vent rib model (20 ga., checkered
stock, recoil pad, 1969-74) . . . . **NiB $181 Ex $145 Gd $99**
Youth model (20 & .410 ga., 26-inch bbl.,
shorter stock, recoil pad, 1965-78) . . . . . **NiB $156 Ex $125 Gd $85**

MODEL 66RS BUCKBUSTER . . . . . . **NiB $188 Ex $150 Gd $102**
Same as Model 66 Standard except has 22-inch bbl. cylinder bore w/rifle sights, later version has recoil pad. Originally offered in 12 and 20 ga.; the former was disc. in 1970. Made 1967-78.

Ithaca Model
66RS Buckbuster

Previously issued as the Ithaca Model 37, the Model 87 guns list-ed below were made available through the Ithaca Acquisition Corp. From 1986-95. Production of the Model 37 resumed under the original logo in 1996.

MODEL 87 DEERSLAYER SHOTGUN

Gauges: 12 or 20, 3-inch chamber. Bbls.: 18.5-, 20- or 25-inch (w/special or rifled bore). Weight: 6 to 6.75 lbs. Ramp blade front sight, adj. rear. Receiver grooved for scope. Checkered American walnut pistol-grip stock and forearm. Made 1988-96.

Basic model	NiB $344	Ex $275	Gd $187
Basic Field Combo (w/extra 28-inch bbl.)			
	NiB $394	Ex $315	Gd $214
Deluxe model	NiB $369	Ex $295	Gd $201
Deluxe Combo (w/extra 28-inch bbl.)			
	NiB $469	Ex $375	Gd $255
DSPS model (8-shot)	NiB $350	Ex $280	Gd $190
Field model	NiB $300	Ex $240	Gd $160
Monte Carlo model	NiB $319	Ex $255	Gd $173
Ultra model (disc. 1991)	NiB $438	Ex $350	Gd $238

MODEL 87 DEERSLAYER II

RIFLED SHOTGUN . . . . NiB $406 Ex $325 Gd $221
Similar to Standard Deerslayer except w/solid frame construction and 25-inch rifled bbl. Monte Carlo stock. Made 1988-96.

MODEL 87 ULTRALITE

FIELD PUMP SHOTGUN. . . . . NiB $387 Ex $309 Gd $211
Gauges: 12 and 20; 2.75-inch chambers. 25-inch bbl. w/choke tube. Weight: 5 to 6 lbs. Made 1988-90.

MODEL 87 FIELD GRADE

Gauge: 12 or 20.; 3-inch chamber. Five shot magazine. Fixed chokes or screw-in choke tubes (IC, M, F). Bbls.: 18.5-inch (M&P); 20- and 25-inch (Combo); 26-, 28-, 30-inch vent rib. Weight: 5 to 7 lbs. Made from 1988-96.

Basic field model (disc. 1993)	NiB $363	Ex $290	Gd $197
Camo model	NiB $394	Ex $315	Gd $214
Deluxe model	NiB $425	Ex $340	Gd $231
Deluxe Combo model	NiB $431	Ex $345	Gd $235
English model	NiB $369	Ex $295	Gd $201
Hand grip model			
(w/polymer pistol-grip)	NiB $406	Ex $325	Gd $221
M&P model (disc. 1995)	NiB $350	Ex $280	Gd $190
Supreme model	NiB $563	Ex $450	Gd $306
Turkey model	NiB $369	Ex $295	Gd $201
Ultra Deluxe model (disc. 1992)	NiB $456	Ex $365	Gd $248

HAMMERLESS DOUBLE-BARREL SHOTGUNS

Boxlock. Plain extractors, auto ejectors standard on the "E" grades. Double triggers, non-selective or selective single trigger extra. Gauges: Magnum 10, 12; 12, 16, 20, 28, .410. Bbls.: 26- to 32-inch, any standard boring. Weight: 5.75 (.410) to 10.5 lbs. (Magnum 10).

(cont'd.) HAMMERLESS DOUBLE-BARREL SHOTGUNS
Checkered pistol-grip stock and forearm standard. Higher grades differ from Field Grade in quality of workmanship, grade of wood, checkering, engraving, etc.; general specifications are the same. Ithaca doubles made before 1925 (serial number 425,000) the rotary bolt and a stronger frame were adopted. Values shown are for this latter type; earlier models valued about 50% lower. Smaller gauge guns may command up to 75% higher. Disc. 1948.

Field grade	NiB $853	Ex $682	Gd $464
No. 1 grade	NiB $912	Ex $729	Gd $596
No. 2 grade	NiB $1369	Ex $1095	Gd $745
No. 3 grade	NiB $1744	Ex $1395	Gd $949
No. 4E grade (ejector)	NiB $3119	Ex $2395	Gd $1697
No. 5E grade (ejector)	NiB $7438	Ex $3350	Gd $4046
No. 7E grade (ejector)			$12,500
$2000 (pre-war $1000) grade			
ejector and selective single trigger standard			$8,950

Extras:
Magnum 10 or 12 ga.
(in other than the four highest grades), add. 20%
Automatic ejectors (grades No. 1, 2, 3, w/ejectors designated
No. 1E, 2E, 3E), add. $200
Selective single trigger, add. $250
Non-selective single trigger, add $175
Beavertail forend (Field No. 1 or 2), add. $150
Beavertail forend (No. 3 or 4), add $175
Beavertail forend (No. 5, 7 or $2000 grade), add $250
Ventilated rib (No. 4, 5, 7 or $2000 grade), add. $250
Ventilated rib (lower grades), add $175

LSA-55 TURKEY GUN . . . . NiB $656 Ex $525 Gd $357
Over/under shotgun/rifle combination. Boxlock. Exposed hammer. Plain extractor. Single trigger. 12 ga./222 Rem. 24.5-inch ribbed bbls. (rifle bbl. has muzzle brake). Weight: About 7 lbs. Folding leaf rear sight, bead front sight. Checkered Monte Carlo stock and forearm. Made 1970-77 by Oy Tikkakoski AB, Finland.

MAG-10 AUTOMATIC SHOTGUN

Gas-operated. 10 ga. 3.5-inch Magnum. Three shot. 32-inch plain (Standard Grade only) or vent-rib bbl. F choke. Weight: 11 lbs., plain bbl.; 11.5 lbs., vent rib. Standard grade has plain stock and forearm. Deluxe and Supreme Grades have checkering, semi-fancy and fancy wood respectively, and stud swivel. All have recoil pad. Deluxe and Supreme grades made 1974-1982. Standard Grade intro. in 1977. All grades disc. 1986.

Camo model	NiB $706	Ex $565	Gd $384
Deluxe grade	NiB $741	Ex $593	Gd $403
Roadblocker	NiB $765	Ex $612	Gd $417
Standard grade, plain barrel	NiB $623	Ex $498	Gd $339
Standard grade, ventilated rib	NiB $653	Ex $522	Gd $355
Standard grade, w/tubes	NiB $741	Ex $593	Gd $403
Supreme grade	NiB $860	Ex $688	Gd $468

SHOTGUNS

**Ithaca Hammerless
Field Grade**

**Ithaca Hammerless
No. 2**

**Ithaca Hammerless
No. 4**

**Ithaca Mag-10
Standard**

Ithaca Model 5-E

**Ithaca Single-Shot Trap
"Dollar Grade"**

SINGLE-SHOT TRAP, FLUES AND KNICK MODELS

Boxlock. Hammerless. Ejector. 12 ga. only. Bbl. lengths: 30-, 32-, 34-inch (32-inch only in Victory grade). Vent rib. Weight: About 8 lbs. Checkered pistol-grip stock and forend. Grades differ only in quality of workmanship, engraving, checkering, wood, etc. Flues Model, serial numbers under 400,000, made 1908-1921. Triple-bolted Knick Model, serial numbers above 400,000, made since 1921. Victory Model disc. in 1938, No. 7-E in 1964, No. 4-E in 1976, No. 5-E in 1986, Dollar Grade in 1991. Values shown are for Knick Model; Flues models about 50% lower.

Victory grade	NiB $1119	Ex $895	Gd $609
No. 4-E	NiB $2688	Ex $2150	Gd $1462
No. 5-E	NiB $3119	Ex $2495	Gd $1697
No. 6-E	NiB $15,000+	Ex $12,000+	Gd $8160+
No. 7-E	NiB $5994	Ex $4795	Gd $3261
$5000 grade (prewar $1000 grade)	NiB $11,063	Ex $8850	Gd $6018
Sousa grade	NiB $12,500+	Ex $10,000+	Gd $6800+

NOTE: *The following Ithaca-Perazzi shotguns were manufactured by Manifattura Armi Perazzi, Brescia, Italy. See also separate Perazzi listings.*

PERAZZI COMPETITION I SKEET . . . . NiB $3313 Ex $2650 Gd $1802
Boxlock. Auto ejectors. Single trigger. 12 ga. 26.75-inch vent-rib bbls. SK choke w/integral muzzle brake. Weight: About 7.75 lbs. Checkered skeet-style pistol-grip buttstock and forearm; recoil pad. Made 1969-74.

PERAZZI COMPETITION TRAP I O/U . . . . NiB $3438 Ex $2650 Gd $1870
Boxlock. Auto ejectors. Single trigger. 12 ga. 30- or 32-inch vent-rib bbls. IM/F choke. Weight: About 8.5 lbs. Checkered pistol-grip stock, forearm; recoil pad. Made 1969-74.

**PERAZZI COMPETITION I
TRAP SINGLE BARREL** . . . . NiB $2438 Ex $1950 Gd $1326
Boxlock. Auto ejection. 12 ga. 32- or 34-inch bbl., vent rib, F choke. Weight: 8.5 lbs. Checkered Monte Carlo stock and beavertail forearm, recoil pad. Made 1973-78.

**PERAZZI COMPETITION IV
TRAP GUN** . . . . NiB $2994 Ex $2395 Gd $1629
Boxlock. Auto ejection. 12 ga. 32- or 34-inch bbl. With high, wide vent rib, four interchangeable choke tubes (Extra Full, F, IM, M). Weight: About 8.75 lbs. Checkered Monte Carlo stock and beavertail forearm, recoil pad. Fitted case. Made 1977-78.

Ithaca-Perazzi
Competition I Skeet

Ithaca-Perazzi
Competition I Trap

Ithaca-Perazzi
Light Game

Ithaca-Perazzi
Mirage Trap

PERAZZI LIGHT GAME O/U FIELD
. . . . NiB $3799 Ex $3039 Gd $2067
Boxlock. Auto ejectors. Single trigger. 12 ga. 27.5-inch vent rib
bbls., M/F or IC/M choke. Weight: 6.75 lbs. Checkered field-style
stock and forearm. Made 1972-74.

PERAZZI MIRAGE LIVE BIRD . . NiB $4266 Ex $3412 Gd $2320
Same as Mirage Trap except has 28-inch bbls., M and Extra Full
choke, special stock and forearm for live bird shooting. Weight:
About 8 lbs. Made 1973-78.

PERAZZI MIRAGE SKEET. . . . . . NiB $3609 Ex $2887 Gd $1963
Same as Mirage Trap except has 28-inch bbls. w/integral muzzle
brakes, SK choke, skeet-stype stock and forearm. Weight: About 8
lbs. Made 1973-78.

PERAZZI MIRAGE TRAP . . . . . . NiB $3741 Ex $2992 Gd $2034
Same general specifications as MX-8 Trap except has tapered rib.
Made 1973-78.

PERAZZI MT-6 SKEET . . . . NiB $3668 Ex $2934 Gd $1996
Same as MT-6 Trap except has 28-inch bbls. w/two skeet choke
tubes instead of Extra Full and F, skeet-style stock and forearm.
Weight: About 8 lbs. Made 1976-78.

PERAZZI MT-6 TRAP COMBO . . . . NiB $4718 Ex $3774 Gd $2567
MT-6 w/extra single under bbl. w/high-rise aluminum vent rib, 32-
or 34-inch; seven interchanageable choke tubes (IC through Extra
Full). Fitted case. Made 1977-78.

PERAZZI MT-6
TRAP O/U . . . . NiB $3274 Ex $2619 Gd $1781
Boxlock. Auto selective ejectors. Non-selective single trigger. 12 ga.
Barrels separated, wide vent rib, 30-or 32-inch, five interchangeable
choke tubes (Extra full, F, IM, M, IC). Weight: About 8.5 lbs.
Checkered pistol-grip stock/forearm, recoil pad. Fitted case. Made
1976-78.

PERAZZI MX
8 TRAP COMBO . . . . NiB $5184 Ex $4147 Gd $2820
MX-8 w/extra single bbl., vent rib, 32- or 34-inch, F choke, forearm;
two trigger groups included. Made 1973-78.

PERAZZI MX-8 TRAP
O/U . . . . NiB $3799 Ex $3039 Gd $2067
Boxlock. Auto selective ejectors. Non-selective single trigger. 12 ga.
Bbls.: High vent rib; 30- or 32-inch, IM/F choke. Weight: 8.25 to 8.5
lbs. Checkered Monte Carlo stock and forearm, recoil pad. Made
1969-78.

PERAZZI SINGLE-BARREL
TRAP GUN . . . . NiB $2526 Ex $2021 Gd $1374
Boxlock. Auto ejection. 12 ga. 34-inch vent rib bbl., F choke.
Weight: Abaout 8.5 lbs. Checkered pistol-grip stock, forearm; recoil
pad. Made 1971-72.

*The following Ithaca-SKB shotguns, manufactured by SKB Arms
Company, Tokyo, Japan, were distributed in the U.S. by Ithaca Gun
Company from 1966-1976. See also listings under SKB.*

Ithaca-SKB
Model 100

Ithaca-SKB
Model 280 English

Ithaca-SKB
Model 700 Skeet Grade

Ithaca-SKB
Model 900 Deluxe

SKB MODEL 100 SIDE-BY-SIDE.... NiB $504 Ex $403 Gd $274
Boxlock. Plain extractors. Selective single trigger. Auto safety. Gauges: 12 and 20; 2.75-inch and 3-inch chambers respectively. Bbls.: 30-inch, F/F (12 ga. only); 28-inch, F/M; 26-inch, IC/M (12 ga. only); 25-inch, IC/M (20 ga. only). Weight: 12 ga., about 7 lbs.; 20 ga., about 6 lbs. Checkered stock and forend. Made 1966-76.

SKB MODEL 150 FIELD GRADE ... NiB $534 Ex $427 Gd $290
Same as Model 100 except has fancier scroll engraving, beavertail forearm. Made 1972-74.

SKB 200E FIELD GRADE S/S ...... NiB $756 Ex $605 Gd $411
Same as Model 100 except auto selective ejectors, engraved and silver-plated frame, gold-plated nameplate and trigger, beavertail forearm. Made 1966-76.

SKB MODEL 200E SKEET GUN.... NiB $818 Ex $654 Gd $445
Same as Model 200E Field Grade except 26-inch (12 ga.) and 25-inch (20 ga./2.75-inch chambers) bbls., SK choke; nonautomatic safety and recoil pad. Made 1966-76.

SKB MODEL 280 ENGLISH....... NiB $955 Ex $764 Gd $520
Same as Model 200E except has scrolled game scene engraving on frame, English-style straight-grip stock; 30-inch bbls. not available; special quail gun in 20 ga. has 25-inch bbls., both bored IC. Made 1971-76.

**SKB MODEL 300 STANDARD
AUTOMATIC SHOTGUN**
Recoil-operated. Gauges: 12, 20 (3-inch). Five shot. Bbls.: plain or vent rib; 30-inch F choke (12 ga. only), 28-inch F or M, 26-inch IC. Weight: about 7 lbs. Checkered pistol-grip stock and forearm. Made 1968-72.
W/plain barrel.................. NiB $294 Ex $235 Gd $160
W/ventilated rib .... NiB $331 Ex $265 Gd $180

**SKB MODEL 500
FIELD GRADE O/U .... NiB $531 Ex $425 Gd $289**
Boxlock. Auto selective ejectors. Selective single trigger. Non-automatic safety. Gauges: 12 and 20; 2.75-inch and 3-inch chambers respectively. Vent-rib bbls.: 30-inch M/F (12 ga. only); 28-inch M/F; 26-inch IC/M. Weight: 12 ga., about 7.5 lbs; 20 ga., about 6.5 lbs. Checkered stock and forearm. Made 1966-76.

SKB MODEL 500 MAGNUM...... NiB $623 Ex $498 Gd $339
Same as Model 500 Field Grade except chambered for 3-inch 12 ga. shells, has 30-inch bbls., IM/F choke. Weight: About 8 lbs. Made 1973-76.

SKB MODEL 600 DOUBLES GUN .... NiB $731 Ex $585 Gd $398
Same as Model 600 Trap Grade except specially choked for 21-yard first target, 30-yard second. Made 1973-75.

SKB MODEL 600 FIELD GRADE ... NiB $688 Ex $551 Gd $374
Same as Model 500 except has silver-plated frame, higher grade wood. Made 1969-76.

SKB MODEL 600 MAGNUM...... NiB $715 Ex $572 Gd $389
Same as Model 600 Field Grade except chambered for 3-inch 12 ga. shells; has 30-inch bbls., IM/F choke. Weight: 8.5 lbs. Made 1969-72.

SKB MODEL 600 SKEET GRADE
Same as Model 500 except also available in 28 and .410 ga., has silver-plated frame, higher grade wood, recoil pad, 26- or 28-inch bbls. (28-inch only in 28 and .410), SK choke. Weight: 7 to 7.75 lbs. depending on ga. and bbl. length. Made 1966-76.
12 or 20 ga.................... NiB $838 Ex $700 Gd $524
28 or .410 ga. .... NiB $931 Ex $775 Gd $575

SKB MODEL 600 SKEET COMBO SET NiB $1994 Ex $1595 Gd $1085
Model 600 Skeet Grade w/matched set of 20, 28 and .410 ga. bbls., 28-inch, fitted case. Made 1970-76.

Ithaca-SKB
Century Trap

Ithaca-SKB
Century II Trap

Ithaca-SKB
Model XL300

SHOTGUNS

SKB MODEL 600

TRAP GRADE O/U . . . . **NiB $670 Ex $536 Gd $364**
Same as Model 500 except 12 ga. only, has silver-plated frame, 30- or 32-inch bbls. choked F/F or F/IM, choice of Monte Carlo or straight stock of higher grade wood, recoil pad. Weight: About 8 lbs. Made 1966-76.

SKB MODEL 680 ENGLISH . . . . **NiB $706 Ex $565 Gd $384**
Same as Model 600 Field Grade except has intricate scroll engraving, English-style straight-grip stock and forearm of extra-fine walnut; 30-inch bbls. not available. Made 1973-76.

SKB MODEL 700

SKEET COMBO SET . . . . **NiB $3169 Ex $2535 Gd $1723**
Model 700 Skeet Grade w/matched set of 20, 28 and .410 ga. bbls., 28-inch fitted case. Made 1970-71.

SKB MODEL 700 SKEET GRADE . . . **NiB $917 Ex $715 Gd $416**
Same as Model 600 Skeet Grade except not available in 28 and .410 ga., has more elaborate scroll engraving, extra-wide rib, higher grade wood. Made 1969-75.

SKB MODEL 700 TRAP GRADE. . . . **NiB $882 Ex $706 Gd $480**
Same as Model 600 Trap Grade except has more elaborate scroll engraving, extra-wide rib, higher grade wood. Made 1969-75.

SKB MODEL 700

DOUBLES GUN . . . . **NiB $1017 Ex $813 Gd $553**
Same as Model 700 Trap Grade except choked for 21-yard first target, 30-yard second target. Made 1973-75.

SKB MODEL 900

DELUXE AUTOMATIC . . . . **NiB $394 Ex $315 Gd $214**
Same as Model 30 except has game scene etched and gold-filled on receiver, vent rib standard. Made 1968-72.

SKB MODEL 900 SLUG GUN . . . . . **NiB $356 Ex $285 Gd $194**
Same as Model 900 Deluxe except has 24-inch plain bbl. w/slug boring, rifle sights. Weight: About 6.5 lbs. Made 1970-72.

SKB CENTURY SINGLE-SHOT

TRAP GUN . . . . **NiB $787 Ex $630 Gd $428**
Boxlock. Auto ejector. 12 ga. Bbls.: 32- or 34-inch, vent rib, F choke.

(cont'd) SKB CENTURY SINGLE-SHOT
Weight: About 8 lbs. Checkered walnut stock w/pistol grip, straight or Monte Carlo comb, recoil pad, beavertail forearm. Made 1973-74.

SKB CENTURY II . . . . **NiB $719 Ex $575 Gd $391**
Boxlock. Auto ejector. 12 ga. Bbls: 32- or 34-inch, vent rib, F choke. Weight: 8.25 lbs. Improved version of Century. Same general specifications except has higher comb on checkered stock stock, reverse-taper beavertail forearm w/redesigned locking iron. Made 1975-76.

SKB MODEL XL300 STANDARD AUTOMATIC
Gas-operated. Gauges: 12, 20 (3-inch). Five shot. Bbls.: Plain or vent rib; 30-inch F choke (12 ga. only), 28-inch F or M, 26-inch IC. Weight: 6 to 7.5 lbs. depending on ga. and bbl. Checkered pistol-grip stock, forearm. Made 1972-76.
W/plain barrel . . . . **NiB $269 Ex $215 Gd $146**
W/ventilated rib . . . . **NiB $294 Ex $235 Gd $160**

SKB MODEL XL900

DELUXE AUTOMATIC . . . . **NiB $344 Ex $275 Gd $187**
Same as Model XL300 except has game scene finished in silver on receiver, vent rib standard. Made 1972-76. See illustration previous page.

SKB MODEL XL

900 SKEET GRADE . . . . **NiB $419 Ex $335 Gd $228**
Gas-operated. Gauges: 12, 20 (3-inch). Five shot tubular magazine. Same as Model XL900 Deluxe except has scrolled receiver finished in black chrome, 26-inch bbl. only, SK choke, skeet-style stock. Weight: 7 or 7.5 lbs. depending on ga. Made 1972-76.

SKB MODEL XL

900 SLUG GUN . . . . **NiB $369 Ex $295 Gd $201**
Same as Model XL900 Deluxe except has 24-inch plain bbl. w/slug boring, rifle sights. Weight: 6.5 or 7 lbs. depending on ga. Made 1972-76.

SKB MODEL

XL900 TRAP GRADE . . . . **NiB $409 Ex $327 Gd $223**
Same as Model XL900 Deluxe except 12 ga. only, has scrolled receiver finished in black chrome, 30-inch bbl. only, IM or F choke, trap style w/straight or Monte Carlo comb, recoil pad. Weight: About 7.75 lbs. Made 1972-76.

Krieghoff Model 32
Standard Field Gun

Krieghoff Model 32
Single-Shot Trap

IVER JOHNSON ARMS & CYCLE WORKS — Fitchburg, Massachusetts. Currently a division of the American Military Arms Corp., Jacksonville, Arkansas

CHAMPION GRADE SINGLE-SHOT HAMMER SHOTGUN
Auto ejector. Gauges: 12,16, 20, 28 and .410. Bbls.: 26- to 36-inch, F choke. Weight: 5.75 to 7.5 lbs. depending on ga. and bbl.length. Plain pistol-grip stock and forend. Extras include checkered stock and forend, pistol-grip cap and knob forend. Known as Model 36. Also made in a Semi-Octagon Breech, Top Matted and Jacketed Breech (extra heavy) models. Made in Champion Lightweight as Model 39 in gauges 24, 28, 32 and .410, .44 and .45 caliber, 12 and 14mm w/same extras. $200; add $100 in the smaller and obsolete gauges. Made 1909-73.
Standard model . . . . NiB $178 Ex $142 Gd $96
Semi-octagon breech . . . . NiB $290 Ex $232 Gd $158
Top matted rib (disc. 1948) . . . . . . NiB $273 Ex $218 Gd $148

HERCULES GRADE HAMMERLESS DOUBLE
Boxlock. (Some made w/false sideplates.) Plain extractors and auto ejectors. Double or Miller single triggers (both selective or non-selective). Gauges: 12, 16, 20 and .410. Bbl. lengths: 26- to 32-inch, all chokes. Weight: 5.75 to 7.75 lbs. depending on ga. and bbl. length. Checkered stock and forend. Straight grip in .410 ga. w/both 2.5- and 3-inch chambers. Extras include Miller single trigger, Jostam Anti-Flinch recoil pad and Lyman ivory sights at extra cost. Disc. 1946.
W/double triggers, extractors . . . . . NiB $680 Ex $544 Gd $370
W/double triggers, auto. ejectors . . . . . NiB $818 Ex $654 Gd $445
W/non-selective single trigger, add $100
W/selective single trigger, add $135
.410 ga., add $185

MATTED RIB SINGLE-SHOT HAMMER SHOTGUN
IN SMALLER GAUGES. . . . . NiB $344 Ex $275 Gd $187
Same general specifications as Champion Grade except has solid matted top rib, checkered stock and forend. Weight: 6 to 6.75 lbs. Disc. 1948.

SILVER SHADOW O/U SHOTGUN
Boxlock. Plain extractors. Double triggers or non-selective single trigger. 12 ga., 3-inch chambers. Bbls.: 26-inch IC/M; 28-inch IC/M, 28-inch M/F; 30-inch both F choke; vent rib. Weight: w/28-inch bbls., 7.5 lbs. Checkered pistol-grip stock/forearm. Made by F. Marocchi, Brescia, Italy 1973-78.
Model 412 w/double triggers . . . . . NiB $469 Ex $375 Gd $255
Model 422 w/single trigger . . . . . . NiB $588 Ex $470 Gd $320

SKEETER MODEL HAMMERLESS DOUBLE
Boxlock. Plain extractors or selective auto ejectors. Double triggers or Miller single trigger (selective or non-selective). Gauges: 12, 16, 20, 28 and .410. 26- or 28-inch bbls., skeet boring standard. Weight: About 7.5 lbs.; less in smaller gauges. Pistol- or straight-grip stock and beavertail forend, both checkered, of select fancy-figured black walnut. Extras include Miller single trigger, selective or non-selective, Jostam Anti-Flinch recoil pad and Lyman ivory rear sight at additional cost. Disc. 1942.
W/double triggers,
plain extractors . . . . NiB $1342 Ex $1074 Gd $730
W/double triggers,
automatic ejectors . . . . NiB $1642 Ex $1314 Gd $894
W/non-selective
single trigger, add $150
W/selective single
trigger, add $200
20 ga., add 25%
28 ga., add 75%
.410 ga., add 90%

SPECIAL TRAP SINGLE-SHOT
HAMMER SHOTGUN . . . . NiB $387 Ex $309 Gd $211
Auto ejector. 12 ga. only. 32-inch bbl. w/vent rib, F choke. Checkered pistol-grip stock and forend. Weight: about 7.5 lbs. Disc. 1942.

SUPER TRAP HAMMERLESS DOUBLE
Boxlock. Plain extractors. Double trigger or Miller single trigger (slective or non-selective), 12 ga. only, F choke 32-inch bbl., vent rib. Weight: 8.5 lbs. Checkered pistol-grip stock and beavertail forend, recoil pad, Disc. 1942.
W/double triggers . . . . NiB $1100 Ex $750 Gd $400
W/non-selective
single trigger, add $100
W/selective single trigger, add. $100

KBI INC. SHOTGUNS

See listings under Armscor, Baikal, Charles Daly, Fias, & Omega

KESSLER ARMS CORP. — Silver Creek, New York

LEVER-MATIC REPEATING SHOTGUN
. . . . NiB $177 Ex $141 Gd $96
Lever action. Takedown. Gauges: 12, 16, 20; three-shot magazine. Bbls.: 26-, 28-, 30-inch; F choke. Plain pistol-grip stock, recoil pad. Weight: 7 to 7.75 lbs. Disc. 1953.

Krieghoff K-80
w/Screw-in Choke Tubes

Krieghoff K-80
Trap Unsingle

THREE SHOT BOLT-ACTION REPEATER . . . NiB $94 Ex $75 Gd $51
Takedown. Gauges: 12, 16, 20. Two-shell detachable box magazine. Bbls.: 28-inch in 12 and 16 ga.; 26-inch in 20 ga.; F choke.
Weight: 6.25 to 7.25 lbs. depending on ga. and bbl. length. Plain
one-piece pistol-grip stock recoil pad. Made 1951-53.

H. KRIEGHOFF JAGD UND SPORTWAFFEN-
FABRIK — Ulm (Donau), West Germany
MODEL 32 FOUR-BARREL SKEET SET
Over/under w/four sets of matched bbls.: 12, 20, 28 and .410 ga.,
in fitted case. Available in six grades that differ in quality of engrav-
ing and wood. Disc. 1979.
Standard grade . . . . NiB $11,188 Ex $8950 Gd $6086
München grade. . . . . NiB $12,438 Ex $9950 Gd $6766
San Remo grade. . . . . NiB $15,313 Ex $12,250 Gd $8330
Monte Carlo grade . . . . . . NiB $19,938 Ex $15,950 Gd $10,846
Crown grade. . . . . NiB $24,688 Ex $19,750 Gd $13,430
Super Crown grade. . . . . . NiB $26,875 Ex $21,500 Gd $14,620
Exhibition grade . . . . NiB $37,438 Ex $29,950 Gd $20,366

MODEL 32 STANDARD GRADE O/U
Similar to prewar Remington Model 23. Boxlock. Auto ejector.
Single trigger. Gauges: 12, 20, 28, .410. Bbls.: Vent rib, 26.5- to 32-
inch, any chokes. Weight: 12 ga. Field gun w/28-inch bbls., about
7.5 lbs. Checkered pistol-grip stock and forearm of select walnut;
available in field, skeet and trap styles. Made 1958-1981.
W/one set of bbls. . . . . NiB $3503 Ex $2802 Gd $1905
Low-rib two-bbl. trap combo . . NiB $4506 Ex $3605 Gd $2451
Vandalia (high-rib) two- bbl. trap combo . . NiB $4744 Ex $3795 Gd $2581

MODEL 32 STANDARD GRADE
SINGLE-SHOT TRAP GUN . . . . . NiB $1744 Ex $1395 Gd $949
Same action as over/under. 12 ga. 32- or 34-inch bbl. w/high vent
rib on bbl.; M, IM, or F choke. Checkered Monte Carlo buttstock
w/thick cushioned recoil pad, beavertail forearm. Disc. 1979.

MODEL K-80
Refined and enhanced version of the Mdl. 32. Single selective
mech. trig., adj. for position; release trigger optional. Fixed chokes
or screw-in choke tubes. Interchangeable front bbl. Hangers to
adjust point of impact. Quick-removable stock. Color casehardened
or satin grey fin. rec.; alum. alloy rec.r on lightweight models. Avail.
in stand. plus 5 engraved grades. Made 1980 to date. Stand. gr.
shown except where noted.

SKEET MODELS
Skeet International . . . . NiB $5878 Ex $4702 Gd $3197
Skeet Special . . . . NiB $5169 Ex $4135 Gd $2812

(cont'd.) MODEL K-80
Skeet standard model . . . . .NiB $4938 Ex $3950 Gd $2686
Skeet w/choke tubes . . . . NiB $5938 Ex $4750 Gd $3230
SKEET SETS
Standard grade 2-bbl. set. . . . . NiB $9416 Ex $7532 Gd $5122
Standard grade 4-bbl. set. . . NiB $12,892 Ex $10,314 Gd $7014
Bavaria grade 4-bbl. set. . . . NiB $18,375 Ex $14,700 Gd $9996
Danube grade 4-bbl. set. . . . . NiB $23,925 Ex $19,140 Gd $13,015
Gold Target grade 4-bbl. set. . . . NiB $28,125 Ex $22,500 Gd $15,300
SPORTING MODELS
Pigeon . . . . NiB $6455 Ex $5164 Gd $3512
Sporting Clays . . . . NiB $6497 Ex $5197 Gd $3534
TRAP MODELS
Trap Combo. . . . . NiB $8744 Ex $6995 Gd $4757
Trap Single. . . . . NiB $6188 Ex $4950 Gd $3366
Trap Standard . . . . NiB $5744 Ex $4595 Gd $3125
Trap Unsingle . . . . NiB $6431 Ex $5145 Gd $3499
RT models (removable trigger) add $1385

KRIEGHOFF MODEL KS-5 SINGLE-BARREL TRAP
Boxlock w/no sliding top-latch. Adjustable or optional release trig-
ger. Gauge: 12; 2.75-inch chamber. Bbl.: 32-, 34-inch w/fixed
choke or screw-in tubes. Weight: 8.5 lbs. Adjustable or Monte Carlo
European walnut stock. Blued or nickel receiver. Made from 1980
to date. Redesigned and streamlined in 1993.
Standard model w/fixed chokes . . . NiB $3188 Ex $2550 Gd $1734
Standard model w/tubes . . . . . . NiB $3744 Ex $2995 Gd $2037
Special model w/adj. rib & stock
. . . . . NiB $3994 Ex $3195 Gd $2173
Special model w/adj. rib
& stock, choke tubes . . . . NiB $4563 Ex $3650 Gd $2482

TRUMPF DRILLING . . . . NiB $8994 Ex $7595 Gd $5805
Boxlock. Steel or Dural receiver. Split extractor or ejector for shotgun bbls. Double triggers. Gauges: 12, 16, 20; latter w/either 2.75-
or 3-inch chambers. Calibers: .243, 6.5x57r5, 7x57r5, 7x65r5, .30-
06; other calibers available. 25-inch bbls. w/solid rib, folding leaf
rear sight, post or bead front sight; rifle bbl. soldered or free floating. Weight: 6.6 to 7.5 lbs. depending on type of receiver, ga. and
caliber. Checkered pistol-grip stock w/cheekpiece and forearm of
figured walnut, sling swivels. Made 1953 to date.

NEPTUN DRILLING . . . . NiB $11,938 Ex $9550 Gd $6494
Same general specifications as Trumpf model except has sidelocks
w/hunting scene engraving. Currently manufactured.

NEPTUN-PRIMUS DRILLING
. . . . . NiB $13,688 Ex $10,950 Gd $7446
Deluxe version of Neptun model; has detachable sidelocks, higher
grade engraving and fancier wood. Currently manufactured.

SHOTGUNS

**Krieghoff
Neptun Drilling**

**Krieghoff ULM
Over/Under**

TECK O/U

RIFLE-SHOTGUN . . . . **NiB $6688 Ex $5350 Gd $3638**
Boxlock. Kersten dble. crossbolt system. Steel or Dural receiver. Split extractor or eject. for shotgun bbl. Single or double triggers. Gauges: 12, 16, 20; latter w/either 2.75- or 3-inch chamber. Cal: .22 Hornet, .222 Rem., .222 Rem. Mag., 7x57r5, 7x64, 7x65r5, .30-30, .300 Win. Mag., .30-06, .308, 9.3x74R. 25-inch bbls. With solid rib, folding leaf rear sight, post or bead front sight; over bbl. is shotgun, under bbl. rifle (later fixed or interchangeable; ext. rifle bbl., $175). Wt: 7.9-9.5 lbs. depending on type of rec. and caliber. Checkered pistol-grip stock w/cheekpiece and semi-beavertail forearm of fig. walnut, sling swivels. Made 1967 to date. Note: This comb. gun is similar in appearance to the same model shotgun.

TECK O/U SHOTGUN . . . . NiB $6256 Ex $5005 Gd $3403
Boxlock. Kersten double crossbolt system. Auto ejector. Single or double triggers. Gauges: 12, 16, 20; latter w/either 2.75- or 3-inch chambers. 28-inch vent-rib bbl., M/F choke. Weight: About 7 lbs. Checkered walnut pistol-grip stock and forearm. Made 1967-89.

ULM O/U
RIFLE-SHOTGUN . . . . **NiB $15,938 Ex $13,750 Gd $10,950**
Same general specifications as Teck model except has sidelocks w/leaf Arabesque engraving. Made from 1963 to date. Note: This combination gun is similar in appearance to the same model shotgun.

ULM O/U SHOTGUN . . . . . . NiB $11,869 Ex $9895 Gd $7369
Same general specifications as Teck model except has sidelocks w/leaf Arabesque engraving. Made 1958 to date.

ULM-P LIVE PIGEON GUN
Sidelock. Gauge: 12. 28- and 30-inch bbls. Chokes: F/IM. Weight: 8 lbs. Oil-finished, fancy English walnut stock w/semi-beavertail forearm. Light scrollwork engraving. Tapered, vent rib. Made from 1983 to date.
Bavaria . . . . NiB $17,625 Ex $14,500 Gd $10,500
Standard . . . . NiB $13,688 Ex $11,350 Gd $8358

ULM-PRIMUS O/U . . . . NiB $11,281 Ex $9025 Gd $6137
Deluxe version of Ulm model; detachable sidelocks, higher grade engraving and fancier wood. Made 1958 to date.

ULM-PRIMUS O/U
RIFLE-SHOTGUN . . . . **NiB $18,119 Ex $15,795 Gd $12,821**
Deluxe version of Ulm model; has detachable sidelocks, higher grade engraving and fancier wood. Made 1963 to date. Note: This combination gun is similar in appearance to the same model shotgun.

ULM-S SKEET GUN
Sidelock. Gauge: 12. Bbl.: 28-inch. Chokes: Skeet/skeet. Other specifications similar to the Model ULM-P. Made 1983-86.
Bavaria . . . . NiB $11,494 Ex $9595 Gd $7165
Standard . . . . NiB $9494 Ex $7995 Gd $6077

ULM-P O/U LIVE TRAP GUN
Over/under sidelock. Gauge: 12. 30-inch bbl. Tapered vent rib. Chokes: IM/F; optional screw-in choke. Custom grade versions command a higher price. Disc. 1986.
Bavaria . . . . NiB $17,313 Ex $14,250 Gd $10,330
Standard . . . . NiB $13,688 Ex $11,350 Gd $8358

ULTRA O/U RIFLE-SHOTGUN
Deluxe Over/Under combination w/25-inch vent-rib bbls. Chambered 12 ga. only and various rifle calibers for lower bbl. Kickspanner design permits cocking w/thumb safety. Satin receiver. Weight: 6 lbs. Made from 1985 to date.
Ultra O/U combination . . . . . . NiB $4744 Ex $4095 Gd $3265
Ultra B w/selective front trigger . . . NiB $4994 Ex $4295 Gd $3401

LANBER SHOTGUNS — Spain

MODEL 82 O/U SHOTGUN . . . . . . NiB $500 Ex $400 Gd $272
Boxlock. Gauge: 12 or 20; 3-inch chambers. 26- or 28-inch vent-rib bbls. w/ejectors and fixed chokes. Weight: 7 lbs., 2 oz. Double or single-selective trigger. Engraved silvered receiver. Checkered European walnut stock and forearm. Imported 1994.

MODEL 87 DELUXE . . . . NiB $781 Ex $625 Gd $425
Over/Under; boxlock. Single selective trigger. 12 or 20 gauge w/3-inch chambers. Barrels: 26- or 28-inch w/choke tubes. Silvered engraved receiver. Imported 1994 only.

MODEL 97 SPORTING CLAYS . . . . NiB $813 Ex $650 Gd $442
Over/Under; boxlock. Single selective trigger. 12 ga. w/2.75-inch chambers. Bbls: 28-inch w/choke tubes. European walnut stock, forend. Engraved receiver. Imported 1994 only.

MODEL 844 MST MAGNUM O/U . . . . NiB $419 Ex $335 Gd $228
Field grade. Gauge: 12. 3-inch Mag. chambers. 30-inch flat vent-rib bbls. Chokes: M/F. Weight: 7 lbs., 7 oz. Single selective trigger. Blued bbls. and engraved receiver. European walnut stock w/hand-checkered pistol grip and forend. Imported 1984-86.

MODEL 2004 LCH O/U . . . . NiB $594 Ex $475 Gd $323
Field grade. Gauge: 12. 2.75-inch chambers. 28-inch flat vent-rib bbls. 5 interchangeable choke tubes: Cyl, IC, M, IM, F. Weight: About 7 lbs. Single selective trigger. Engraved silver receiver w/fineline scroll. Walnut stock w/checkered pistol-grip and forend. Rubber recoil pad. Imported 1984-86.

MODEL 2004 LCH O/U SKEET . . . . NiB $744 Ex $595 Gd $405
Same as Model 2004 LCH except 28-inch bbls. w/5 interchangeable choke tubes. Imported 1984-86.

Lamber Model
82 Field Grade

Laurona Grand
Trap — GTO

MODEL 2004
LCH O/U TRAP . . . . NiB $731 Ex $585 Gd $398
Gauge: 12. 30-inch vent-rib bbls. Three interchangeable choke
tubes: M, IM, F. Manual safety. Other specifications same as Model
2004 LCH O/U. Imported 1984-86.

CHARLES LANCASTER — London, England

"TWELVE-TWENTY" DOUBLE-BARREL
SHOTGUN . . . . NiB $15,313 Ex $12,250 Gd $8330
Sidelock, self-opener. Gauge: 12. Bbls.: 24 to 30 inches standard.
Weight: About 5.75 lbs. Elaborate metal engraving. Highest quality
English or French walnut buttstock and forearm. Imported by
Stoeger in the 1950s.

JOSEPH LANG & SONS — London, England

HIGHEST QUALITY
O/U SHOTGUN . . . . NiB $27,000 Ex $21,600 Gd $14,688
Sidelock. Gauges: 12, 16, 20, 28 and .410. Bbls.: 25 to 30 inches standard. Highest grade English or French walnut buttstock and
forearm. Selective single trigger. Imported by Stoeger in 1950s.

LAURONA SHOTGUNS — Eibar, Spain

GRAND TRAP COMBO
Same general specifications as Model 300 except supplied w/29-
inch over/under bbls., screw-in choke tubes and 34-inch single bar-
rel. Disc. 1992.
Model GTO (top single) . . . . NiB $2224 Ex $1779 Gd $1210
Model GTU (bottom single) . . . NiB $2356 Ex $1884 Gd $1282
Extra Field O/U bbls.
(12 or 20 ga.), ... NiB $820 Ex $656 Gd $446

SILHOUETTE 300 O/U
Boxlock. Single selective trigger. Selective automatic ejectors. Gauge:
12; 2.75-, 3- or 3.5-inch chambers. 28- or 29-inch vent-rib bbls.
w/flush or knurled choke tubes. Weight: 7.75 to 8 lbs. Checkered pis-
tol-grip European walnut stock and beavertail forend. Engraved
receiver w/silvered finish and black chrome bbls. Made 1988-92.
Model 300 Sporting Clays . . . . NiB $1250 Ex $975 Gd $650
Model 300 Trap . . . . NiB $1250 Ex $975 Gd $650
Model 300 Trap, single . . . . NiB $1250 Ex $975 Gd $650
Model 300 Ultra-Magnum . . . . . . NiB $1300 Ex $1025 Gd $650

SUPER MODEL O/U SHOTGUNS
Boxlock. Single selective or twin single triggers. Selective automat-
ic ejectors. Gauges: 12 or 20; 2.75- or 3-inch chambers. 26-, 28- or
29-inch vent-rib bbls. w/fixed chokes or screw-in choke tubes.
Weight: 7 to 7.25 lbs. Checkered pistol-grip European walnut stock.
Engraved receiver w/silvered finish and black chrome bbls. Made
from 1985 to date.
Model 82 Super Game (disc.) . . . . . NiB $651 Ex $521 Gd $354
Model 83 MG Super Game . . . . NiB $996 Ex $797 Gd $542
Model 84 S Super Trap . . . . NiB $1306 Ex $1045 Gd $710
Model 85 MG Super Game . . . . . . NiB $1010 Ex $808 Gd $550
Model 85 MG 2-bbl. set . . . . . . NiB $1856 Ex $1457 Gd $1009
Model 85 MS Special Sporting (disc.) . . . NiB $1271 Ex $1017 Gd $691
Model 85 MS Super Trap . . . . NiB $1279 Ex $1023 Gd $696
Model 85 MS Pigeon . . . . NiB $1244 Ex $995 Gd $677
Model 85 S Super Skeet . . . . NiB $1313 Ex $1050 Gd $713

LEBEAU-COURALLY SHOTGUNS — Belgium

BOXLOCK SIDE
BY-SIDE SHOTGUNS . . . . . . NiB $17,438 Ex $13,950 Gd $9486
Gauges: 12, 16, 20 and 28. 26- to 30-inch bbls. Weight: 6.5 lbs.
average. Checkered, hand-rubbed, oil-finished, straight-grip stock of
French walnut. Classic forend. Made from 1986 to date.

**Lefever A Grade
Hammerless Double-Barrel Shotgun**

LEFEVER ARMS COMPANY — Syracuse and Ithaca, N.Y.

Lefever sidelock hammerless double-barrel shotguns were made by Lefever Arms Company of Syracuse, New York from about 1885-1915 (serial numbers 1 to 70,000) when the firm was sold to Ithaca Gun Company of Ithaca, New York. Production of these models was continued at the Ithaca plant until 1919 (serial numbers 70,001 to 72,000). Grades listed are those that appear in the last catalog of the Lefever Gun Company, Syracuse. In 1921, Ithaca introduced the boxlock Lefever Nitro Special double, followed in 1934 by the Lefever Grade A; there also were two single-barrel Lefevers made from 1927-42. Manufacture of Lefever brand shotguns was disc. in 1948. Note: "New Lefever" boxlock shotguns made circa 1904-06 by D. M. Lefever Company, Bowling Green, Ohio, are included in a separate listing.

GRADE HAMMERLESS DOUBLE-BARREL SHOTGUN
Boxlock. Plain extractors or auto ejector. Single or double triggers. Gauges: 12, 16, 20, .410. Bbls.: 26-32 inches, standard chokes. Weight: About 7 lbs. in 12 ga. Checkered pistol-grip stock and forearm. Made 1934-42.

W/plain extractors, double triggers..	NiB $969 Ex $775 Gd $527
W/automatic ejector, add	$250
W/single trigger, add	$100
W/Beavertail Forearm, add	$75
16 ga., add	25%
20 ga., add	45%
.410 ga., add	200%

GRADE SKEET MODEL
Same as A Grade except standard features include auto ejector, single trigger, beavertail forearm; 26-inch bbls., skeet boring. Disc. 1942.

A grade skeet model, 12 ga.	NiB $1165 Ex $930 Gd $633
16 ga., add	45%
20 ga., add	90%
.410 ga., add	200%

HAMMERLESS SINGLE-SHOT
TRAP GUN . . . . NiB $564 Ex $451 Gd $306
Boxlock. Ejector. 12 ga. only. 30- or 32-inch bbl.; vent rib. Weight: About 8 lbs. Checkered pistol-grip stock and forend, recoil pad. Made 1927-42.

LONG RANGE HAMMERLESS
SINGLE-BARREL FIELD GUN . . . . . NiB $344 Ex $275 Gd $187
Boxlock. Plain extractor. Gauges: 12, 16, 20, .410. Bbl. lengths: 26-32 inches. Weight: 5.5 to 7 lbs. depending on ga. and bbl. length. Checkered pistol-grip stock and forend. Made 1927-42.

NITRO SPECIAL HAMMERLESS DOUBLE
Boxlock. Plain extractors. Single or double triggers. Gauges: 12, 16, 20, .410. Bbls.: 26- to 32-inch, standard chokes. Weight: about 7 lbs. in 12 ga. Checkered pistol-grip stock and forend. Made 1921-48.

Nitro Special W/ double triggers	NiB $519 Ex $395 Gd $237
Nitro Special W/ single trigger	NiB $619 Ex $495 Gd $337
16 ga., add	25%
20 ga., add	50%
.410 ga., add	200%

SIDELOCK HAMMERLESS DOUBLES
Plain extractors or auto ejectors. Double triggers or selective single trigger. Gauges: 10, 12, 16, 20. Bbls.: 26-32 inches; standard choke combinations. Weight: 5.75 to 10.5 lbs. depending on ga. and bbl. length. Checkered walnut straight-grip or pistol-grip stock and forearm. Grades differ chiefly in quality of workmanship, engraving, wood, checkering, etc.; general specifications are the same. DS and DSE Grade guns lack the cocking indicators found on all other models. Suffix "E" means model has auto ejector; also standard on A, AA, Optimus, and Thousand Dollar Grade guns.

H grade	NiB $1813 Ex $1450 Gd $986
HE grade	NiB $2406 Ex $1925 Gd $1309
G grade	NiB $2119 Ex $1695 Gd $1153
GE grade	NiB $2844 Ex $2275 Gd $1547
F grade.	NiB $1895 Ex $1516 Gd $1031
FE grade.	NiB $2897 Ex $2317 Gd $1575
E grade.	NiB $2756 Ex $2205 Gd $1499
EE grade.	NiB $4244 Ex $3395 Gd $2309
D grade .	NiB $3406 Ex $2725 Gd $1853
DE grade .	NiB $5313 Ex $4250 Gd $2890
DS grade .	NiB $1476 Ex $1181 Gd $803
DSE grade .	NiB $1831 Ex $1464 Gd $996
C grade .	NiB $4669 Ex $3735 Gd $2539
CE grade .	NiB $8744 Ex $6995 Gd $4757
B grade .	NiB $5619 Ex $4495 Gd $3057
BE grade .	NiB $10,153 Ex $8122 Gd $5523
A grade.	NiB $17,634 Ex $15,437 Gd $14,259
AA grade.	NiB $26,125 Ex $20,900 Gd $14,212
Optimus grade	NiB $35,625 Ex $28,500 Gd $19,380
Thousand Dollar grade . . .	NiB $53,125 Ex $42,500 Gd $28,900
W/single trigger, add	10%
10 ga., add	15%
16 ga., add	45%
20 ga., add	90%

D. M. LEFEVER COMPANY — Bowling Green, Ohio

In 1901, D. M. "Uncle Dan" Lefever, founder of the Lefever Arms Company, withdrew from that firm to organize D. M. Lefever, Sons & Company (later D. M. Lefever Company) to manufacture the "New Lefever" boxlock double- and single-barrel shotguns. These were produced at Bowling Green, Ohio, from about 1904-1906, when Dan Lefever died and the factory closed permanently. Grades listed are those that appear in the last catalog of D. M. Lefever Co.

HAMMERLESS DOUBLE-BARREL SHOTGUNS

"New Lefever." Boxlock. Auto ejector standard on all grades except O Excelsior, which was regularly supplied w/plain extractors (auto ejector offered as an extra). Double triggers or selective single trigger (latter standard on Uncle Dan Grade, extra on all others). Gauges: 12, 16, 20. Bbls.: Any length and choke combination. Weight: 5.5 to 8 lbs. depending on ga. and bbl. length. Checkered walnut straight-grip or pistol-grip stock and forearm. Grades differ chiefly in quality of workmanship, engraving, wood, checkering, etc. General specifications are the same.

O Excelsior grade
w/plain extractors . . . . NiB $3188 Ex $2550 Gd $1734
O Excelsior grade
w/automatic ejectors. . . . . NiB $3619 Ex $2895 Gd $1969
No. 9, F grade . . . . NiB $4494 Ex $3595 Gd $2445
No. 8, E grade . . . . NiB $5313 Ex $4250 Gd $2890
No. 7, D grade. . . . . NiB $5719 Ex $4575 Gd $3111
No. 6, C grade . . . . NiB $6494 Ex $5195 Gd $3533
No. 5, B grade . . . . NiB $8619 Ex $6895 Gd $4689
No. 4, AA grade. . . . . NiB $12,500 Ex $10,000 Gd $6800
Uncle Dan grade . . . . NiB $18,750 Ex $15,000 Gd $10,200
W/single trigger, add 10%
16 ga., add 45%
20 ga., add 15%

D. M. LEFEVER SINGLE-BARREL

TRAP GUN. . . . . NiB $6244 Ex $4995 Gd $3397
Boxlock. Auto ejector. 12 ga. only. Bbls.: 26- to 32 inches, F choke. Weight: 6.5 to 8 lbs. depending on bbl. length. Checkered walnut pistol-grip stock and forearm.

MAGTECH SHOTGUNS — San Antonio, Texas
Mfd. By CBC in Brazil
MODEL 586.2 SLIDE-ACTION SHOTGUN

Gauge: 12; 3-inch chamber. 19-, 26- or 28-inch bbl.; fixed chokes or integral tubes. 46.5 inches overall. Weight: 8.5 lbs. Double-action slide bars. Brazilian hardwood stock. Polished blued finish. Imported 1992 to date.

Model 586.2 F
(28-inch bbl., fixed choke) . . . . NiB $219 Ex $175 Gd $119
Model 586.2 P
(19-inch plain bbl., cyl. bore) . . . . . NiB $219 Ex $175 Gd $119
Model 586.2 S
(24-inch bbl., rifle sights, cyl. bore) . . . NiB $225 Ex $180 Gd $122
Model 586.2 VR
(vent rib w/tubes) . . . . NiB $219 Ex $175 Gd $119

MARLIN FIREARMS CO. — North Haven
(formerly New Haven), Conn.
MODEL 16 VISIBLE HAMMER SLIDE-ACTION REPEATER

Takedown. 16 ga. Five shell tubular magazine. Bbls.: 26- or 28-inch, standard chokes. Weight: About 6.25 lbs. Pistol-grip stock, grooved slide handle; checkering on higher grades. Difference among grades is in quality of wood, engraving on Grades C and D. Made 1904-10.

Grade A . . . . NiB $406 Ex $325 Gd $221
Grade B . . . . NiB $563 Ex $450 Gd $306
Grade C . . . . NiB $688 Ex $550 Gd $374
Grade D. . . . . NiB $1406 Ex $1125 Gd $765

Lefever Sidelock AA Grade

Lefever Sidelock DE Grade

Lefever Sidelock Sideplate BE Grade

Lefever Sidelock Sideplate CE Grade

Lefever Sidelock Optimus Grade

SHOTGUNS

Magtech Model 586.2
Slide-Action

Marlin Model 17
Standard

Marlin Model 28B
Hammerless Slide-Action Repeater

Marlin Model 30
Visible Hammer Slide-Action Repeater

Marlin Model 43A
Hammerless Slide-Action Repeater

MODEL 17 BRUSH GUN . . . . **NiB $350 Ex $280 Gd $190**
Same as Model 17 Standard except has 26-inch bbl., cylinder bore.
Weight: About 7 lbs. Made 1906-08.

MODEL 17 RIOT GUN . . . . **NiB $374 Ex $299 Gd $203**
Same as Model 17 Standard except has 20-inch bbl., cylinder bore.
Weight: About 6.88 lbs. Made 1906-08.

**MODEL 17 STANDARD VISIBLE HAMMER
SLIDE-ACTION REPEATER** . . . . **NiB $350 Ex $280 Gd $190**
Solid frame.12 ga. 5-shot tubular magazine. Bbls.: 30- or 32-inch, F
choke. Weight: About 7.5 lbs. Straight-grip stock, grooved slide handle. Made 1906-08.

MODEL 19 VISIBLE HAMMER SLIDE-ACTION REPEATER
Similar to Model 1898 but improved, lighter weight, w/two extrac-
tors, matted sighting groove on receiver top. Weight: About 7 lbs.
Made 1906-07.
Grade A . . . . NiB $356 Ex $285 Gd $194
Grade B . . . . NiB $617 Ex $493 Gd $336
Grade C . . . . NiB $669 Ex $535 Gd $364
Grade D . . . . NiB $1369 Ex $1095 Gd $745

**MODEL 21 TRAP VISIBLE HAMMER
SLIDE-ACTION REPEATER**
Similar to Model 19 w/same general specifications except has
straight-grip stock. Made 1907-09.
Grade A . . . . NiB $350 Ex $280 Gd $190
Grade B . . . . NiB $516 Ex $413 Gd $281
Grade C . . . . NiB $653 Ex $522 Gd $355
Grade D . . . . NiB $1313 Ex $1050 Gd $714

MODEL 24 VISIBLE HAMMER SLIDE-ACTION REPEATER
Similar to Model 19 but has improved takedown system and auto
recoil safety lock, solid matted rib on frame. Weight: About 7.5 lbs.
Made 1908-15.
Grade A . . . . NiB $326 Ex $261 Gd $177
Grade B . . . . NiB $540 Ex $432 Gd $293
Grade C . . . . NiB $683 Ex $546 Gd $371
Grade D. . . . . NiB $1419 Ex $1135 Gd $772

**MODEL 26
BRUSH GUN** . . . . **NiB $297 Ex $237 Gd $161**
Same as Model 26 Standard except has 26-inch bbl., cylinder bore.
Weight: About 7 lbs. Made 1909-15.

Marlin Model 43T
Hammerless Slide-Action Repeater

Marlin Model 53
Hammerless Slide-Action

Marlin Model 55
Goose Gun

Marlin Model 55
Humter Bolt-Action Repeater

Marlin Model 55
Swap Gun

MODEL 26 RIOT GUN . . . . **NiB $266 Ex $213 Gd $145**
Same as Model 26 Standard except has 20-inch bbl., cylinder bore.
Weight: About 6.88 lbs. Made 1909-15.

MODEL 26 STANDARD VISIBLE HAMMER
SLIDE-ACTION REPEATER. . . . . **NiB $279 Ex $223 Gd $152**
Similar to Model 24 Grade A except solid frame and straight-grip
stock. 30- or 32-inch full choke bbl. Weight: About 7.13 lbs. Made
from 1909-15.

MODEL 28 HAMMERLESS SLIDE-ACTION REPEATER
Takedown. 12 ga. Five shot tubular magazine. Bbls.: 26-, 28-, 30-,
32-inch, standard chokes; matted-top bbl. except on Model 28D,
which has solid matted rib. Weight: About 8 lbs. Pistol-grip stock,
grooved slide handle; checkering on higher grades. Grades differ in
quality of wood, engraving on Models 28C and 28D. Made 1913-
22; all but Model 28A disc. in 1915. See illustration previous page.
Model 28A . . . . **NiB $332 Ex $265 Gd $180**
Model 28B . . . . **NiB $477 Ex $382 Gd $260**
Model 28C . . . . **NiB $619 Ex $495 Gd $336**
Model 28D . . . . **NiB $1300 Ex $1040 Gd $707**

MODEL 28T TRAP GUN . . . . **NiB $590 Ex $472 Gd $321**
Same as Model 28 except has 30-inch matted-rib bbl., F choke,
straight-grip stock w/high-fluted comb of fancy walnut, checkered.
Made in 1915.

MODEL 28TS
TRAP GUN . . . . **NiB $426 Ex $341 Gd $232**
Same as Model 28T except has matted-top bbl., plainer stock. Made
in 1915.

MODEL 30 FIELD GUN . . . . **NiB $328 Ex $262 Gd $178**
Same as Model 30 Grade B except has 25-inch bbl., M choke,
straight-grip stock. Made 1913-14.

MODEL 30 VISIBLE HAMMER SLIDE-ACTION REPEATER
Similar to Model 16 but w/Model 24 improvements. Made 1910-14.
See illustration previous page.
Grade A . . . . **NiB $361 Ex $288 Gd $196**
Grade B . . . . **NiB $557 Ex $446 Gd $303**
Grade C . . . . **NiB $715 Ex $572 Gd $389**
Grade D . . . . **NiB $1531 Ex $1225 Gd $833**

MODELS 30A, 30B, 30C, 30D
Same as Model 30; designations were changed in 1915. Also avail-
able in 20 ga. w/25- or 28-inch bbl., matted-top bbl. on all grades.
Suffixes "A," "B," "C" and "D" correspond to former grades. Made
in 1915.
Model 30A . . . . **NiB $420 Ex $336 Gd $228**
Model 30B . . . . **NiB $525 Ex $440 Gd $285**
Model 30C . . . . **NiB $781 Ex $624 Gd $425**
Model 30D . . . . **NiB $1344 Ex $1075 Gd $731**

**Marlin Model 59
Bolt-Action Single**

**Marlin Model 60
Single Shot**

MODEL 31 HAMMERLESS SLIDE-ACTION REPEATER
Similar to Model 28 except scaled down for 16 and 20 ga. Bbls.: 25-inch (20 ga. only), 26-inch (16 ga. only), 28-inch, all w/matted top, standard chokes. Weight: 16 ga., about 6.75 lbs.; 20 ga., about 6 lbs. Pistol-grip stock, grooved slide handle; checkering on higher grades; straight-grip stock optional on Model 31D. Made 1915-17; Model 31A until 1922.
Model 31A .... NiB $374 Ex $299 Gd $203
Model 31B .... NiB $504 Ex $403 Gd $274
Model 31C .... NiB $653 Ex $722 Gd $355
Model 31D .... NiB $1425 Ex $1140 Gd $775

MODEL 31F FIELD GUN........ NiB $400 Ex $350 Gd $250
Same as Model 31B except has 25-inch bbl., M choke, straight- or pistol-grip stock. Made 1915-17.

MODEL 42A VISIBLE HAMMER
SLIDE-ACTION REPEATER........ NiB $250 Ex $225 Gd $150
Similar to pre-World War I Model 24 Grade A w/same general specifications but not as high quality. Made from 1922-34.

MODEL 43 HAMMERLESS SLIDE-ACTION REPEATER
Similar to pre-World War I Models 28A, 28T and 28TS, w/same general specifications but not as high quality. Made 1923-30.
Model 43A .... NiB $281 Ex $225 Gd $153
Model 43T .... NiB $557 Ex $445 Gd $303
Model 43TS .... NiB $590 Ex $472 Gd $321

MODEL 44 HAMMERLESS SLIDE-ACTION REPEATER
Similar to pre-World War I Model 31A w/same general specifications but not as high quality. 20 ga. only. Model 44A is a standard-grade field gun. Model 44S Special Grade has checkered stock and slide handle of fancy walnut. Made 1923-35.
Model 44A .... NiB $365 Ex $292 Gd $198
Model 44S .... NiB $444 Ex $355 Gd $242

MODEL 49 VISIBLE HAMMER SLIDE-
ACTION REPEATING SHOTGUN .. NiB $445 Ex $356 Gd $242
Economy version of Model 42A, offered as a bonus on the purchase of four shares of Marlin stock. About 3000 were made 1925-28.

MODEL 50DL BOLT
ACTION SHOTGUN .... NiB $266 Ex $213 Gd $145
Gauge: 12 w/3-inch chamber. Two shot magazine. 28-inch bbl. w/modified choke. 48.75 inches overall. Weight: 7.5 lbs. Checkered black synthetic stocks w/ventilated rubber recoil pad. Made 1997 to date.

MODEL 53 HAMMERLESS
SLIDE-ACTION REPEATER....... NiB $350 Ex $280 Gd $190
Similar to Model 43A w/same general specifications. Made 1929-30.

MODEL 55 GOOSE GUN
Same as Model 55 Hunter except chambered for 12-ga. 3-inch Magnum shell, has 36-inch bbl., F choke, swivels and sling. Weight: About 8 lbs. Walnut stock (standard model) or checkered black synthetic stock w/ventilated rubber recoil pad (GDL model). Made 1962 to date.
Model 55 Goose Gun .... NiB $216 Ex $173 Gd $117
Model 55GDL Goose Gun
(intro. 1997) .... NiB $321 Ex $257 Gd $175

MODEL 55 HUNTER BOLT-ACTION REPEATER
Takedown. Gauges: 12, 16, 20. Two shot clip magazine. 28-inch bbl. (26-inch in 20 ga.), F or adj. choke. Plain pistol-grip stock; 12 ga. has recoil pad. Weight: About 7.25 lbs.; 20 ga., 6.5 lbs. Made 1954-65.
W/plain bbl. .... NiB $81 Ex $65 Gd $44
W/adj. choke .... NiB $103 Ex $82 Gd $56

MODEL 55 SWAMP GUN......... NiB $106 Ex $85 Gd $58
Same as Model 55 Hunter except chambered for 12-ga. 3-inch Magnum shell, has shorter 20.5-inch bbl. w/adj. choke, sling swivels and slightly better-quality stock. Weight: About 6.5 lbs. Made 1963-65.

MODEL 55S SLUG GUN......... NiB $144 Ex $115 Gd $78
Same as Model 55 Goose Gun except has 24-inch bbl., cylinder bore, rifle sights. Weight: About 7.5 lbs. Made 1974-79.

MODEL 59 AUTO-SAFE
BOLT-ACTION SINGLE .... NiB $106 Ex $85 Gd $58
Takedown. Auto thumb safety, .410 ga. 24-inch bbl., F choke. Weight: About 5 lbs. Plain pistol-grip stock. Made 1959-61.

MODEL 60 SINGLE-SHOT
SHOTGUN .... NiB $197 Ex $157 Gd $107
Visible hammer. Takedown. Boxlock. Automatic ejector. 12 ga. 30- or 32-inch bbl., F choke. Weight: About 6.5 lbs. Pistol-grip stock, beavertail forearm. Note: Only about 600 were produced in 1923.

MODEL 63 HAMMERLESS SLIDE-ACTION REPEATER
Similar to Models 43A and 43T w/same general specifications. Model 63TS Trap Special is same as Model 63T Trap Gun except stock style and dimensions to order. Made 1931-35.
Model 63A .... NiB $326 Ex $261 Gd $177
Model 63T or 63TS .... NiB $416 Ex $332 Gd $226

Marlin Model 90
Standard Over-and-Under

Marlin Model 120
Magnum Slide-Action Repeater

Marlin Model 410
Lever-Action Repeater

Marlin Model 512
Slugmaster

Marlin Model 55-10
Super Goose 10

Marlin Premier Mark I
Slide-Action Repeater

Marlin Premier Mark IV

Marlin-Glenfield
Model 50 Bolt-Action Repeater

SHOTGUNS

**Marocchi Conquista
Sporting Clays**

MODEL 90 STANDARD O/U SHOTGUN

Hammerless. Boxlock. Double triggers; non-selective single trigger was available as an extra on pre-war guns except .410. Gauges: 12, 16, 20, .410. Bbls.: Plain; 26-, 28- or 30-inch; chokes IC/M or M/F; bbl. design changed in 1949, eliminating full-length rib between bbls. Weight: 12 ga., about 7.5 lbs.; 16 and 20 ga., about 6.25 lbs. Checkered pistol-grip stock and forearm, recoil pad standard on prewar guns. Postwar production: Model 90-DT (double trigger), Model 90-ST (single trigger). Made 1937-58.

W/double triggers	NiB $469	Ex $375	Gd $255
W/single trigger	NiB $588	Ex $470	Gd $320
Combination model	NiB $706	Ex $565	Gd $384
16 ga., deduct			10%
20 ga., add			15%
.410, add			30%

MODEL 120 MAGNUM

SLIDE-ACTION REPEATER . . . . **NiB $294   Ex $235   Gd $160**
Hammerless. Takedown. 12 ga. (3-inch). Four shot tubular magazine. Bbls.: 26-inch vent rib, IC; 28-inch vent rib M choke; 30-inch vent rib, F choke; 38-inch plain, F choke; 40-inch plain, F choke; 26-inch slug bbl. w/rifle sights, IC. Weight: About 7.75 lbs. Checkered pistol-grip stock and forearm, recoil pad. Made 1971-85.

MODEL 120 SLUG GUN . . . . **NiB $281   Ex $225   Gd $153**

Same general specifications as Model 120 Magnum except w/20-inch bbl. and about .5 lb. lighter in weight. No vent rib. Adj. rear rifle sights; hooded front sight. Disc. 1990.

MODEL 410 LEVER-ACTION REPEATER

Action similar to that of Marlin Model 93 rifle. Visible hammer. Solid frame. .410 ga. (2.5-inch shell). Five shot tubular magazine. 22- or 26-inch bbl., F choke. Weight: About 6 lbs. Plain pistol-grip stock and grooved beavertail forearm. Made 1929-32.

Model 410 w/22-inch bbl.	NiB $1419	Ex $1135	Gd $772
Model 410 w/26-inch bbl.	NiB $1181	Ex $945	Gd $643
Deluxe model, add			30%

MODEL 512 SLUGMASTER SHOTGUN

Bolt-action repeater. Gauge: 12; 3-inch chamber, 2-shot magazine. 21-inch rifled bbl. w/adj. open sight. Weight: 8 lbs. Walnut-finished birch stock (standard model) or checkered black synthetic stock w/ventilated rubber recoil pad (GDL model). Made 1994 to date.

Model 512 Slugmaster	NiB $295	Ex $236	Gd $160
Model 512DL Slugmaster (intro. 1998)	NiB $321	Ex $257	Gd $175
Model 512P Slugmaster w/ported bbl. (intro. 1999)	NiB $328	Ex $262	Gd $178

MODEL 1898 VISIBLE HAMMER SLIDE-ACTION REPEATER

Takedown. 12 ga. Five shell tubular magazine. Bbls.: 26-, 28-, 30-, 32-inch; standard chokes. Weight: About 7.25 lbs. Pistol-grip stock, grooved slide handle; checkering on higher grades. Difference among grades is in quality of wood, engraving on Grades C and D. Made 1898-05. Note: This was the first Marlin shotgun.

Grade A (Field)	NiB $350	Ex $275	Gd $200
Grade B	NiB $575	Ex $495	Gd $300
Grade C	NiB $875	Ex $700	Gd $500

(cont'd.) MODEL 1898 VISIBLE HAMMER

Grade D	NiB $1800	Ex $1550	Gd $700

MODEL 55-10 SUPER GOOSE 10 . . **NiB $216   Ex $173   Gd $117**
Similar to Model 55 Goose Gun except chambered for 10 ga. 3.5-inch Magnum shell, has 34-inch heavy bbl., F choke. Weight: About 10.5 lbs. Made 1976-85. See illustration on page 495.

PREMIER MARK I

SLIDE-ACTION REPEATER . . . . **NiB $206   Ex $165   Gd $112**
Hammerless. Takedown. 12 ga. Magazine holds 3 shells. Bbls.: 30-inch F choke, 28-inch M, 26-inch IC or SK choke. Weight: About 6 lbs. Plain pistol-grip stock and forearm. Made in France 1960-63.

PREMIER MARK II AND IV

Same action and mechanism as Premier Mark except engraved receiver (Mark IV is more elaborate), checkered stock and forearm, fancier wood, vent rib and similar refinements. Made 1960-63.

Premier Mark II	NiB $281	Ex $225	Gd $153
Premier Mark IV (plain barrel)	NiB $313	Ex $250	Gd $170
Premier Mark IV (vent rib barrel)	NiB $369	Ex $295	Gd $201

GLENFIELD MODEL 50

BOLT-ACTION REPEATER . . . . **NiB $81   Ex $65   Gd $44**
Similar to Model 55 Hunter except chambered for 12-or 20-ga., 3-inch Magnum shell; has 28-inch bbl. in 12 ga., 26-inch in 20 ga., F choke. Made 1966-74.

GLENFIELD 778 SLIDE-ACTION

REPEATER . . . . **NiB $231   Ex $185   Gd $126**
Hammerless. 12 ga. 2.75-inch or 3-inch. Four shot tubular magazine. Bbls.: 26-inch IC, 28-inch M, 30-inch F, 38-inch MXR, 20-inch slug bbl. Weight: 7.75 lbs. Checkered pistol-grip. Made from 1979-84.

MAROCCHI SHOTGUNS — Brescia, Italy Imported by Precision Sales International of Westfield, MA

CONQUISTA MODEL O/U SHOTGUN

Boxlock. Gauge: 12; 2.75-inch chambers. 28-, 30- or 32-inch vent rib bbl. Fixed choke or internal tubes. 44.38 to 48 inches overall. Weight: 7.5 to 8.25 lbs. Adj. single-selective trigger. Checkered American walnut stock w/recoil pad. Imported since 1994.

Lady Sport Grade I	NiB $1861	Ex $1489	Gd $1013
Lady Sport Grade II	NiB $2228	Ex $1782	Gd $1212
Lady Sport Grade III	NiB $4018	Ex $3214	Gd $2186
Skeet Model Grade I	NiB $1594	Ex $1275	Gd $867
Skeet Model Grade II	NiB $1994	Ex $1595	Gd $1085
Skeet Model Grade III	NiB $3216	Ex $2572	Gd $1749
Sporting Clays Grade I	NiB $1753	Ex $1402	Gd $953
Sporting Clays Grade II	NiB $2055	Ex $1644	Gd $1118
Sporting Clays Grade III	NiB $3155	Ex $2524	Gd $1717
Trap Model Grade I	NiB $1821	Ex $1457	Gd $991
Trap Model Grade II	NiB $2165	Ex $1732	Gd $1178
Trap Model Grade III	NiB $3069	Ex $2695	Gd $1832

Maverick Model 60
Autoloading Shotgun

Maverick Model 88
Pump Shotgun (Vent Rib)

Merkel Model
47E Side-by-Side

MAVERICK ARMS, INC. — Eagle Pass, Texas

MODEL 60 AUTOLOADING SHOTGUN
Gauge: 12, 2.75- or 3-inch chamber. Five round capacity. Bbls.: Magnum or non-Magnum; 24- or 28-inch w/fixed choke or screw-in tubes, plain or vent rib; blued. Weight: 7.25 lbs. Black synthetic buttstock and forend. Announced in 1993, but not produced.
Standard model . . . . NiB $349 Ex $279 Gd $190
Combo model
w/extra 18.5 inch bbl. . . . . NiB $390 Ex $312 Gd $212
Turkey/Deer model
(w/ghost ring sights) . . . . NiB $405 Ex $324 Gd $220

MODEL 88 BULLPUP . . . . NiB $281 Ex $225 Gd $153
Gauge: 12; 3-inch chamber. Bbl.: 18.5-inch w/fixed choke, blued. Weight: 9.5 lbs. Dual safeties: Grip style and crossbolt. Fixed sights in carrying handle. High-impact black synthetic stock; trigger-forward bullpup configuration w/twin pistol-grip design. Made 1991-94.

MODEL 88 DEER GUN . . . . NiB $190 Ex $152 Gd $103
Crossbolt safety and dual slide bars. Cylinder bore choke. Gauge: 12 only w/3-inch chamber. Bbl.: 24-inch. Weight: 7 lbs. Synthetic stock and forearm.

MODEL 88 PUMP SHOTGUN
Gauge: 12; 2.75- or 3-inch chamber. Bbl.: 28 inches/M or 30 inches/F w/fixed choke or screw-in integral tubes; plain or vent rib, blued. Weight: 7.25 lbs. Bead front sight. Black synthetic or wood buttstock and forend; forend grooved. Made from 1989 to date.
Synthetic stock
w/plain bbl. . . . . NiB $169 Ex $135 Gd $92
Synthetic stock
w/vent-rib bbl. . . . . NiB $188 Ex $150 Gd $102
Synthetic Combo
w/18.5 inch bbl. . . . . NiB $213 Ex $170 Gd $116
Wood stock
w/vent-rib bbl./tubes. . . . . NiB $206 Ex $165 Gd $112
Wood Combo w/vent-rib bbl./tubes . . . . NiB $244 Ex $195 Gd $133

MODEL 88 SECURITY . . . . NiB $177 Ex $141 Gd $96
Crossbolt safety and dual slide bars. Optional heat shield. Cylinder bore choke. Gauge: 12 only w/3-inch chamber. Bbl.: 18.5-inches. Weight: 6 lbs., 8 ozs. Synthetic stock and forearm. Made 1993 to date.

MODEL 91 PUMP SHOTGUN
Same as Model 88, except w/2.75-, 3- or 3.5-inch chamber, 28-inch bbl. W/ACCU-F choke, crossbolt safety and synthetic stock only. Made 1991-95.
Synthetic stock w/plain bbl. . . . . . . NiB $225 Ex $180 Gd $122
Synthetic stock w/vent-rib bbl. . . . . NiB $238 Ex $190 Gd $129

MODEL 95 BOLT-ACTION . . . . NiB $156 Ex $125 Gd $85
Modified, fixed choke. Built-in 2-round magazine. Gauge: 12 only. Bbl.: 25-inch. Weight: 6.75 lbs. Bead sight. Synthetic stock and rubber recoil pad. Made 1995 to date.

GEBRÜDER MERKEL — Suhl, Germany
Mfd. by Suhler Jagd-und Sportwaffen GmbH, *Imported by GSI, Inc., Trussville, AL, (Previously by Armes de Chasse)*

MODEL 8 HAMMERLESS DOUBLE. . . NiB $1169 Ex $935 Gd $635
Anson & Deeley boxlock action w/Greener double-bbl. hook lock. Double triggers. Extractors. Automatic safety. Gauges: 12, 16, 20; 2.75- or 3-inch chambers. 26-or 28-inch bbls. w/fixed standard chokes. Checkered European walnut stock, pistol-grip or English-style w/or w/o cheekpiece. Scroll-engraved receiver w/tinted marble finish.

SIDE-BY-SIDE MODEL 47E . . . . NiB $2291 Ex $2233 Gd $1519
Hammerless boxlock similar to Model 8 except w/automatic ejectors and cocking indicators. Double hook bolting. Single selective or double triggers. 12, 16 or 20 ga. w/2.75-inch chambers. Standard bbl lengths, choke combos. Hand-checkered European walnut stock, forearm; pistol-grip and cheekpiece or straight English style; sling swivels.

SHOTGUNS

**Merkel Model 47LSC
Sporting Clay**

**Merkel Model 47S
Hammerless Sidelock**

**Merkel Model 247S
Hammerless Sidelock**

**Merkel Model 347S
Hammerless Sidelock**

**Merkel Model 122
Hammerless Double**

MODEL 47LSC
SPORTING CLAYS S/S . . . . . NiB $2744 Ex $2195 Gd $1493
Anson & Deeley boxlock action w/single-selective adj. trigger, cocking indicators and manual safety. Gauge: 12; 3-inch chambers. 28-inch bbls.w/Briley choke tubes and H&H-style ejectors. Weight: 7.25 lbs. Color case-hardened receiver w/Arabesque engraving. Checkered select-grade walnut stock, beavertail forearm. Imported 1993-94.

MODELS 47SL, 147SL, 247SL, 347SL, 447SL
HAMMERLESS SIDELOCKS
Same general specifications as Model 147E except has sidelocks engraved w/Arabesques, borders, scrolls or game scenes in varying degrees of elaborateness.

Model 47SL . . . . NiB $4943 Ex $3954 Gd $2689
Model 147SL . . . . NiB $5431 Ex $4345 Gd $2954
Model 147SSL. . . . . NiB $5905 Ex $4724 Gd $3213
Model 247SL . . . . NiB $5493 Ex $4394 Gd $2988
Model 347SL . . . . NiB $5844 Ex $4675 Gd $3179
Model 447SL . . . . NiB $6318 Ex $5054 Gd $3437
28 ga. .410, add 20%

NOTE: Merkel over/under guns were often supplied with accessory barrels, interchangeable to convert the gun into an arm of another type; for example, a set might consist of one pair each of shotgun, rifle and combination gun barrels. Each pair of interchangeable barrels has a value of approximately one-third that of the gun with which they are supplied.

MODEL 100 O/U SHOTGUN
Hammerless. Boxlock. Greener crossbolt. Plain extractor. Double triggers. Gauges: 12, 16, 20. Made w/plain or ribbed bbls. in various lengths and chokes. Plain finish, no engraving. Checkered forend and stock w/pistol grip and cheekpiece or English-style. Made prior to WWII.
W/plain bbl. . . . . NiB $1894 Ex $1515 Gd $1030
W/ribbed bbl. . . . . NiB $1959 Ex $1567 Gd $1065

MODELS 101 AND 101E O/U
Same as Model 100 except ribbed bbl. standard, has separate extractors (ejectors on Model 101E), English engraving. Made prior to World War II.
Model 101 . . . . NiB $2013 Ex $1610 Gd $1095
Model 101E . . . . NiB $2166 Ex $1733 Gd $1178

MODEL 122
HAMMERLESS DOUBLE . . . . NiB $3710 Ex $2968 Gd $2018
Similar to the Model 147S except w/nonremovable sidelocks in gauges 12, 16 or 20. Imported since 1993.

MODEL 122E
HAMMERLESS SIDELOCK. . . . . NiB $4119 Ex $3295 Gd $2241
Similar to the Model 122 except w/removable sidelocks and cocking indicators. Importation disc. 1992.

MODEL 126E
HAMMERLESS SIDELOCK . . . . NiB $28,125 Ex $22,500 Gd $15,300
Holland & Holland system, hand-detachable locks. Auto ejectors. Double triggers. 12, 16 or 20 gauge w/standard bbl. lengths and chokes. Checkered forend and pistol-grip stock; available w/cheekpiece or English-style buttstock. Elaborate game scenes and engraving. Made prior to WW II.

MODEL 127E
HAMMERLESS SIDELOCK . . . . NiB $28,688 Ex $22,950 Gd $15,606
Similar to the Model 126E except w/elaborate scroll engraving on removable sidelocks w/cocking indicators. Made prior to WW II.

MODEL 128E
HAMMERLESS BOXLOCK DOUBLE . . . . NiB $12,188 Ex $9750 Gd $6630
Scalloped Anson & Deeley action w/hinged floorplate and removable sideplates. Auto-ejectors. Double triggers. Elaborate hunting scene or Arabesque engraving. 12, 16 or 20 gauge w/various bbl. lengths and chokes. Checkered forend and stock w/pistol grip and cheekpiece or English-style. Made prior to WW II.

MODEL 130
HAMMERLESS BOXLOCK DOUBLE . . . . NiB $12,188 Ex $9750 Gd $6630
Similar to Model 128E except w/fixed sideplates. Auto ejectors. Double triggers. Elaborate hunting scene or Arabesque engraving. Made prior to WW II.

MODESL 147 & 147E HAMMERLESS BOXLOCK DOUBLE-BARREL SHOTGUN
Anson & Deeley system w/extractors or auto ejectors. Single selective or double triggers. Gauges: 12, 16, 20 or 28 ga. (Three inch chambers available in 12 and 20 ga.). Bbls.: 26-inch standard, other lengths available w/any standard choke combination. Weight: 6.5 lbs. Checkered straight-grip stock and forearm. Disc. 1998.
Model 147 w/extractors . . . . . . NiB $2494 Ex $1995 Gd $1357
Model 147E w/ejectors . . . . NiB $2938 Ex $2350 Gd $1598

Merkel Model 147E
Hammerless Boxlock Double-Barrel Shotgun

Merkel Model 200E
O/U Shotgun

MODELS 200, 200E, 201, 201E, 202 AND 202E O/U SHOTGUNS
Hammerless. Boxlock. Kersten double crossbolt. Scalloped frame. Sideplates on Models 202 and 202E. Arabesque or hunting engraving supplied on all except Models 200 and 200E. "E" models have ejectors, others have separate extractors, signal pins, double triggers. Gauges: 12, 16, 20, 24, 28, 32 (last three not available in postwar guns). Ribbed bbls. in various lengths and chokes. Weight: 5.75 to 7.5 lbs. depending on bbl. length and gauge. Checkered forend and stock w/pistol grip and cheekpiece or English-style. The 200, 201, and 202 differ in overall quality, engraving, wood, checkering, etc.; aside from the faux sideplates on Models 202 and 202E, general specifications are the same. Models 200, 201, 202, and 202E, all made before WW II, are disc. Models 201E &202E in production w/revised 2000 series nomenclature.
Model 200 . . . . NiB $2224 Ex $1779 Gd $1210
Model 200E . . . . NiB $3119 Ex $2495 Gd $1697
Model 200 ES Skeet. . . . . NiB $4619 Ex $3695 Gd $2513
Model 200ET Trap . . . . NiB $4438 Ex $3550 Gd $2414
Model 200 SC Sporting Clays . . . . NiB $4994 Ex $3995 Gd $2717
Model 201 (disc.). . . . . NiB $2688 Ex $2150 Gd $1462
Model 201E (Pre-WW II) . . . . NiB $3081 Ex $2465 Gd $1676
Model 201E (Post-WW II) . . . . NiB $4388 Ex $3510 Gd $2387
Model 201 ES Skeet. . . . . NiB $6994 Ex $5595 Gd $3805
Model 201 ET Trap. . . . . NiB $6938 Ex $5550 Gd $3774
Model 202 (disc.). . . . . NiB $3556 Ex $2845 Gd $1935
Model 202E (Pre-WW II) . . . . NiB $4188 Ex $3350 Gd $2278
Model 202 E (Post-WW II & 2002EL). . . . . NiB $6525 Ex $5220 Gd $3550

Merkel Model 203E
Sidelock O/U Shotgun

Merkel Model 303E
O/U Shotgun

MODEL 203E SIDELOCK O/U SHOTGUNS
Hammerless action w/hand-detachable sidelocks. Kersten double cross bolt, auto ejectors and double triggers. Gauges: 12 or 20 (16, 24, 28 and 32 disc.). 26.75- or 28-inch vent rib bbls. Arabesque engraving standard or hunting engraving optional on coin-finished receiver. Checkered English or pistol-grip stock and forend. See illustration previous page.

Model 203E sidelock (disc. 1998) . . NiB $5957 Ex $4765 Gd $3240
Model 203ES skeet
(imported 1993-97) . . . . NiB $8494 Ex $6795 Gd $4620
Model 203ET trap (disc. 1997) . . . . NiB $8544 Ex $6835 Gd $4648

MODEL 204E
O/U SHOTGUN . . . . NiB $7188 Ex $5750 Gd $3910
Similar to Model 203E; has Merkel sidelocks, fine English engraving. Made prior to World War II.

MODEL 210E
SIDE-LOCK O/U SHOTGUN . . . NiB $5806 Ex $4645 Gd $3159
Kersten double cross-bolt, scroll-engraved, casehardened receiver. 12, 16 or 20 ga. Double-triggers; pistol-grip stock w/cheekpiece.

MODEL 211E
SIDE-LOCK O/U SHOTGUN . . . NiB $7025 Ex $5620 Gd $3822
Same specifications as Model 210E except w/engraved hunting scenes on silver-gray receiver.

MODELS 300, 300E, 301, 301E AND 302 O/U
Merkel-Anson system boxlock. Kersten double crossbolt, two underlugs, scalloped frame, sideplates on Model 302. Arabesque or hunting engraving. "E" models and Model 302 have auto ejectors, others have separate extractors. Signal pins. Double triggers. Gauges: 12, 16, 20, 24, 28, 32. Ribbed bbls. in various lengths and chokes. Checkered forend and stock w/pistol grip and cheekpiece or English-style. Grades 300, 301 and 302 differ in overall quality, engraving, wood, checkering, etc.; aside from the dummy sideplates on Model 302, general specifications are the same. Manufactured prior to World War II.

Model 300 . . . . NiB $2606 Ex $2085 Gd $1418
Model 300E . . . . NiB $3188 Ex $2550 Gd $1734
Model 301 . . . . NiB $6744 Ex $5395 Gd $3669
Model 301E . . . . NiB $8063 Ex $6450 Gd $4386
Model 302 . . . . NiB $14,372 Ex $11,497 Gd $7818

MODEL 303EL O/U
SHOTGUN . . . . NiB $16,844 Ex $13,475 Gd $9163
Similar to Model 203E. Has Kersten crossbolt, double underlugs, Holland & Holland-type hand-detachable sidelocks, auto-ejectors. This is a finer gun than Model 203E. Currently manufactured.

MODEL 304E O/U
SHOTGUN . . . . NiB $21,656 Ex $17,325 Gd $11,781
Special version of the Model 303E-type, but higher quality throughout. This is the top grade Merkel over/under. Currently manufactured.

MODELS 400, 400E, 401, 401E O/U
Similar to Model 101 except have Kersten double crossbolt, Arabesque engraving on Models 400 and 400E, hunting engraving on Models 401 and 401E, finer general quality. "E" models have Merkel ejectors, others have separate extractors. Made prior to World War II.

Model 400 . . . . NiB $2131 Ex $1705 Gd $1159
Model 400E . . . . NiB $2715 Ex $2172 Gd $1477
Model 401 . . . . NiB $2269 Ex $1815 Gd $1234
Model 401E . . . . NiB $3746 Ex $2997 Gd $2038

O/U COMBINATION GUNS ("BOCKBÜCHSFLINTEN")
Shotgun bbl. over, rifle bbl. under. Gauges: 12, 16, 20; calibers: 5.6x35 Vierling, 7x57r5, 8x57JR, 8x60R Mag., 9.3x53r5, 9.3x72r5, 9.3x74R and others including domestic calibers from .22 Hornet to .375 H&H. Various bbl. lengths, chokes and weights. Other specifications and values correspond to those of Merkel over/under shotguns listed below. Currently manufactured. Model 210 & 211 series disc. 1992.

Models 410, 410E, 411E
(see shotgun models 400, 400E, 401, 401E)
Models 210, 210E, 211, 211E, 212, 212E
(see shotgun models 200, 200E, 201, 201E, 202, 202E)

MODEL 2000EL O/U SHOTGUNS
Kersten double cross-bolt. Gauges: 12 and 20. 26.75- or 28-inch bbls. Weight: 6.4 to 7.28 lbs. Scroll engraved silver-gray receiver. Automatic ejectors and single selective or double triggers. Checkered forend and stock w/pistol grip and cheekpiece or English-style stock w/luxury grade wood. Imported 1998 to date.

Model 2000EL Standard . . . . . NiB $4881 Ex $3905 Gd $2655
Model 2000EL Sporter . . . . NiB $5080 Ex $4064 Gd $2764

MODEL 2001EL O/U SHOTGUNS
Gauges: 12, 16, 20 and 28; Kersten double cross-bolt lock receiver. 26.75- or 28-inch IC/mod, mod/full bbls. Weight: 6.4 to 7.28 lbs. Three-piece forearm, automatic ejectors and single selective or double triggers. Imported 1993 to date.

Model 2001EL 12 ga. . . . . NiB $5801 Ex $4641 Gd $3156
Model 2001EL 16 ga. (disc. 1997)
. . . . NiB $5801 Ex $4641 Gd $3156
Model 2001EL 20 ga. . . . . NiB $5801 Ex $4641 Gd $3156
Model 2001EL 28 ga.
(made 1995) . . . . NiB $6392 Ex $5113 Gd $3477

MODEL 2002EL . . . . NiB $6525 Ex $5220 Gd $3550
Same specifications as Model 2000EL except hunting scenes w/Arabesque engraving.

ANSON DRILLINGS
Three-bbl. combination guns; usually made w/double shotgun bbls., over rifle bbl., although "Doppelbüchsdrillingen" were made w/two rifle bbls. over and shotgun bbl. under. Hammerless.

Miida Model 612
Field Grade O/U

(cont'd.) ANSON DRILLINGS
Boxlock. Anson & Deeley system. Side clips. Plain extractors. Double triggers. Gauges: 12, 16, 20; rifle calibers: 7X57r5, 8X57JR and 9.3X74R are most common, but other calibers from 5.6mm to 10.75mm available. Bbls.: standard drilling 25.6 inches; short drilling, 21.6 inches. Checkered pistol-grip stock and forend. The three models listed differ chiefly in overall quality, grade of wood, etc.; general specifications are the same. Made prior to WW II.
Model 142 Engraved . . . . NiB $5184 Ex $4147 Gd $2820
Model 142 Standard . . . . NiB $3913 Ex $3130 Gd $2128
Model 145 Field . . . . NiB $3266 Ex $2612 Gd $1776

MIIDA SHOTGUNS — Manufactured for Marubeni America Corp., New York, N.Y., by Olin-Kodensha Co., Tochigi, Japan

MODEL 612 FIELD GRADE O/U . . . NiB $801 Ex $641 Gd $436
Boxlock. Auto ejectors. Selective single trigger. 12 ga. Bbls.: Vent rib; 26-inch, IC/M; 28-inch, M/F choke. Weight: W/26-inch bbl., 6 lbs., 11 oz. Checkered pistol-grip stock and forearm. Made 1972-74.

MODEL 2100 SKEET GUN . . . . NiB $906 Ex $725 Gd $493
Similar to Model 612 except has more elaborate engraving on frame (50 percent coverage), skeet-style stock and forearm of select grade wood; 27-inch vent-rib bbls., SK choke. Weight: 7 lbs., 11 oz. Made 1972-74.

**MODEL 2200T TRAP GUN,
MODEL 2200S SKEET GUN . . . . . . NiB $944 Ex $755 Gd $513**
Similar to Model 612 except more elaborate engraving on frame (60 percent coverage), trap- or skeet-style stock and semi-beavertail forearm of fancy walnut, recoil pad on trap stock. Bbls.: Wide vent rib; 29.75-inch, IM/F choke on Trap Gun; 27-inch, SK choke on Skeet Gun. Weight: Trap, 7 lbs., 14 oz.; Skeet, 7 lbs., 11 oz. Made 1972-74.

**MODEL 2300T TRAP GUN,
MODEL 2300S SKEET GUN . . . . . NiB $1009 Ex $807 Gd $549**
Same as models 2200T and 2200S except more elaborate engraving on frame (70% coverage). Made 1972-74.

**GRANDEE MODEL GRT/IRS
TRAP/SKEET GUN . . . . NiB $2488 Ex $1990 Gd $1353**
Boxlock w/sideplates. Frame, breech ends of bbls., trigger guard and locking lever fully engraved and gold inlaid. Auto ejectors. Selective single trigger. 12 ga. Bbls.: Wide vent rib; 29-inch, F choke on Trap Gun; 27-inch, SK choke on Skeet Gun. Weight: Trap, 7 lbs., 14 oz.; Skeet, 7 lbs., 11 oz. Trap- or skeet-style stock and semi-beavertail forearm of extra fancy wood, recoil pad on trap stock. Made 1972-74.

MITCHELL ARMS — Santa Ana, California

MODEL 9104/9105 PUMP SHOTGUNS
Slide action in Field/Riot configuration. Gauge: 12; 5-shot tubular magazine. 20-inch bbl.; fixed choke or screw-in tubes. Weight: 6.5 lbs. Plain walnut stock. Made 1994 to date.

(cont'd.) MODEL 9104/9105 PUMP SHOTGUNS
Model 9104 (w/plain bbl.) . . . . NiB $231 Ex $185 Gd $125
Model 9105 (w/rifle sight) . . . . NiB $494 Ex $195 Gd $933
W/choke tubes, add $20

MODEL 9108/9109 PUMP SHOTGUN
Slide action in Military/Police/Riot configuration. Gauge: 12, 7-shot tubular magazine. 20-inch bbl.; fixed choke or screw-in tubes. Weight: 6.5 lbs. Plain walnut stock and grooved slide handle w/brown, green or black finish. Blued metal. Made 1994 to date.
Model 9108 (w/plain bbl.) . . . . NiB $238 Ex $190 Gd $129
Model 9109 (w/rifle sights) . . . . NiB $256 Ex $205 Gd $139
W/choke tubes, add $20

MODEL 9111/9113 PUMP SHOTGUN
Slide action in Military/Police/Riot configuration. Gauge: 12; 6-shot tubular magazine. 18.5-inch bbl.; fixed choke or screw-in tubes. Weight: 6.5 lbs. Synthetic or plain walnut stock and grooved slide handle w/brown, green or black finish. Blued metal. Made 1994 to date.
Model 9111 (w/plain bbl.) . . . . NiB $231 Ex $185 Gd $126
Model 9113 (w/rifle sights) . . . . NiB $256 Ex $205 Gd $139
W/choke tubes, add $20

MODEL 9114/9114FS
Slide action in Military/Police/Riot configuration. Gauge: 12; 7-shot tubular magazine. 20-inch bbl.; fixed choke or screw-in tubes. Weight: 6.5-7 lbs. Synthetic pistol-grip or folding stock. Blued metal. Made 1994 to date.
Model 9114 . . . . NiB $281 Ex $225 Gd $153
Model 9114FS . . . . NiB $313 Ex $250 Gd $170

**MODEL 9115/9115FS
PUMP SHOTGUN . . . . NiB $313 Ex $250 Gd $170**
Slide action in Military/Police/Riot configuration. Gauge: 12; 6-shot tubular magazine. 18.5-inch bbl. w/heat-shield handguard. Weight: 7 lbs. Gray synthetic stock and slide handle. Parkerized metal. Made 1994 to date.

MONTGOMERY WARD

See shotgun listings under "W"

MORRONE SHOTGUN — Manufactured by Rhode Island Arms Company, Hope Valley, RI

STANDARD MODEL 46 O/U . . . . . NiB $951 Ex $761 Gd $517
Boxlock. Plain extractors. Non-selective single trigger. Gauges: 12, 20. Bbls.: Plain, vent rib; 26-inch IC/M; 28-inch M/F choke. Weight: About 7 lbs., 12 ga.; 6 lbs., 20 ga. Checkered straight- or pistol-grip stock and forearm. Made 1949-53. Note: Less than 500 of these guns were produced, about 50 in 20 ga., a few had vent-rib bbls. Value shown is for 12 ga. w/plain bbls.; the rare 20 ga. and vent-rib types should bring considerably more.

SHOTGUNS

Mossberg Model 83D

Mossberg Model 85D
Bolt-Action Repeating Shotgun

Mossberg Model 183K

Mossberg Model 185K

Mossberg Model 200K
Slide-Action Repeater

Mossberg Model 395K
Bolt-Action Repeater

O. F. MOSSBERG & SONS, INC. —
North Haven, Connecticut,
Formerly New Haven, Conn.

MODEL 83D OR 183D . . . . **NiB $131 Ex $105 Gd $71**
3-shot. Takedown. .410 ga. only. Two shell fixed top-loading magazine. 23-inch bbl. w/two interchangeable choke tubes (M/F). Later
production had 24-inch bbl. Plain one-piece pistol-grip stock.
Weight: about 5.5 lbs. Originally designated Model 83D, changed
in 1947 to Model 183D. Made 1940-71.

MODEL 85D OR 185D BOLT-ACTION
REPEATING SHOTGUN . . . . **NiB $111 Ex $89 Gd $60**
Takedown. Three-shot. 20 ga. only. Two-shell detachable box mag-
azine. 25-inch bbl., three interchangeable choke tubes (F, M, IC).

(cont'd.) MODEL 85D OR 185D
Later production had 26-inch bbl. w/F/IC choke tubes. Weight:
About 6.25 lbs. Plain one-piece, pistol-grip stock. Originally desig-
nated Model 85D, changed in 1947 to Model 185D. Made 1940-71.

MODEL 183K . . . . **NiB $124 Ex $99 Gd $68**
Same as Model 183D except has 25-inch bbl. w/variable C-Lect-
Choke instead of interchangeable choke tubes. Made 1953-86.

MODEL 185K . . . . **NiB $131 Ex $105 Gd $71**
Same as Model 185D except has variable C-Lect-Choke instead of
interchangeable choke tubes. Made 1950-63.

MODEL 190D . . . . **NiB $124 Ex $99 Gd $68**
Same as Model 185D except in 16 ga. Weight: About 6 lbs. Made
1955-71.

Mossberg Mode 500
Accu-Choke

Mossberg Model 500
Camo Pump

Mossberg Model 500
Bullpup Shotgun

Mossberg Model 500
Camper

SHOTGUNS

MODEL 190K . . . . **NiB $131 Ex $105 Gd $71**
Same as Model 185K except in 16 ga. Takedown. Three shot; 2-shell magazine. Weight: About 6.75 lbs. Made 1956-63.

MODEL 195D . . . . **NiB $131 Ex $104 Gd $71**
Same as Model 185D except in 12 ga. Takedown. Three shot; 2-shell magazine. Weight: About 6.75 lbs. Made 1955-71.

MODEL 195K . . . . **NiB $131 Ex $105 Gd $71**
Same as Model 185K except in 12 ga. Takedown. Three shot; 2-shell magazine. Weight: About 7.5 lbs. Made 1956-63.

MODEL 200D . . . . **NiB $136 Ex $109 Gd $74**
Same as Model 200K except w/two interchangeable choke tubes instead of C-Lect choke. Made 1955-59.

MODEL 200K
SLIDE-ACTION REPEATER . . . . **NiB $151 Ex $120 Gd $81**
12 ga. 3-shot detachable box magazine. 28-inch bbl. C-Lect choke. Plain pistol-grip stock. Black nylon slide handle. Weight: About 7.5 lbs. Made 1955-59.

MODEL 395K BOLT-ACTION REPEATER . . . . . . **NiB $125 Ex $100 Gd $68**
Takedown. Three shot (detachable-clip magazine holds two shells).12 ga. (3-inch chamber). 28-inch bbl. w/C-Lect-Choke. Weight: About 7.5 lbs. Monte Carlo stock w/recoil pad. Made 1963-83.

MODEL 385K . . . . **NiB $125 Ex $100 Gd $68**
Same as Model 395K except 20 ga. (3-inch), 26-inch bbl. w/C-Lect-Choke. Weight: About 6.25 lbs.

MODEL 390K . . . . **NiB $136 Ex $109 Gd $74**
Same as Model 395K except 16 ga. (2.75-inch). Made 1963-74.

MODEL 395S SLUGSTER . . . . **NiB $163 Ex $130 Gd $88**
Same as Model 395K except has 24-inch bbl., cylinder bore, rifle sights, swivels and web sling. Weight: About 7 lbs. Made 1968-81.

MODEL 500 ACCU-CHOKE SHOTGUN . . . . . **NiB $266 Ex $213 Gd $145**
Pump-action. Gauge: 12. 24- or 28-inch bbl. Weight: 7.25 lbs. Checkered walnut-finished wood stock w/ventilated recoil pad. Available w/synthetic field or Speed-Feed stocks. Drilled and tapped receivers, swivels and camo sling on camo models. Made from 1987 to date.

Mossberg Model 500
Persuader Law Enforcement

Mossberg Model 500
Mariner

MODEL 500 BANTAM SHOTGUN
Same as Model 500 Sporting Pump except 20 or .410 ga. only. 22-inch w/ACCU-Choke tubes or 24-inch w/F choke; vent rib. Scaled-down checkered hardwood or synthetic stock w/standard or Realtree camo finish. Made from 1990-96 and 1998-99.
Bantam Model (hardwood stock) . . . . NiB $229 Ex $183 Gd $124
Bantam Model (synthetic stock) . . . . NiB $216 Ex $173 Gd $117
Bantam Model (Realtree camo), add. $50

MODEL 500 BULLPUP SHOTGUN . . . . . . NiB $469 Ex $375 Gd $255
Pump. Gauge: 12. 6- or 8-shot capacity. Bbl.: 18.5 to 20 inches. 26.5 and 28.5 inches overall. Weight: About 9.5 lbs. Multiple independent safety systems. Dual pistol grips, rubber recoil pad. Fully enclosed rifle-type sights. Synthetic stock. Ventilated bbl. heat shield. Made 1987-90.

MODEL 500 CAMO PUMP
Same as Model 500 Sporting Pump except 12 ga. only. Receiver drilled and tapped. QD swivels and camo sling. Special camouflage finish.
Standard model . . . . NiB $231 Ex $185 Gd $126
Combo model (w/ext. Slugster bbl.) . . . NiB $297 Ex $237 Gd $161

MODEL 500 CAMPER . . . . NiB $239 Ex $191 Gd $130
Same general specifications as Model 500 Field Grade except .410 bore, 6-shot magazine, 18.5-inch plain cylinder bore bbl. Synthetic pistol grip and camo carrying case. Made 1986-90.

MODEL 500 FIELD GRADE
HAMMERLESS SLIDE-ACTION REPEATER
Pre-1977 type. Takedown. Gauges: 12, 16, 20, .410. Three inch chamber (2.75-inch in 16 ga.). Tubular magazine holds five 2.75-inch shells or four three-inch. Bbls.: Plain- 30-inch regular or heavy Magnum, F choke (12 ga. only); 28-inch, M or F; 26-inch, IC or adj. C-Lect-Choke; 24-inch Slugster, cylinder bore, w/rifle sights. Weight: 5.75 to lbs. Plain pistol-grip stock w/recoil pad, grooved slide handle. After 1973, these guns have checkered stock and slide handles; Models 500AM and 500AS have receivers etched w/game scenes. The latter has swivels and sling. Made 1962-76.
Model 500A, 12 ga., ... NiB $242 Ex $194 Gd $132
Model 500AM, 12 ga., hvy. Mag. bbl. . . . . NiB $250 Ex $200 Gd $136
Model 500AK, 12 ga., C-Lect-Choke . . . . NiB $281 Ex $225 Gd $153
Model 500AS, 12 ga., Slugster . . . . NiB $288 Ex $231 Gd $157
Model 500B 16 ga., ... NiB $242 Ex $194 Gd $132
Model 500BK, 16 ga., C-Lect-Choke . . . . . NiB $294 Ex $235 Gd $160
Model 500BS, 16 ga., Slugster . . . . NiB $281 Ex $225 Gd $153
Model 500C 20 ga., ... NiB $244 Ex $195 Gd $133
Model 500CK, 20 ga., C-Lect-Choke . . . . . NiB $313 Ex $250 Gd $170
Model 500CS, 20 ga., Slugster . . . . NiB $281 Ex $225 Gd $153
Model 500E, .410 ga., ... NiB $306 Ex $245 Gd $167
Model 500EK, .410 ga., C-Lect-Choke . . . . NiB $344 Ex $275 Gd $187

MODEL 500 "L" SERIES
"L" in model designation. Same as pre-1977 Model 500 Field Grade except not available in 16 ga., has receiver etched w/different game scenes; Accu-Choke w/three interchangeable tubes (IC, M, F) standard, restyled stock and

(cont'd.) MODEL 500 "L" SERIES
slide handle. Bbls.: plain or vent rib; 30- or 32-inch, heavy, F choke (12 ga. Magnum and vent rib only); 28-inch, Accu-Choke (12 and 20 ga.); 26-inch F choke (.410 bore only); 18.5-inch (12 ga. only), 24-inch (12 and 20 ga.) Slugster w/rifle sights, cylinder bore. Weight: 6 to 8.5 lbs. Intro. 1977.
Model 500ALD, 12 ga.,
plain bbl. (disc. 1980) . . . . NiB $273 Ex $220 Gd $153
Model 500ALDR, 12 ga., vent rib . . . . NiB $313 Ex $250 Gd $170
Model 500ALMR, 12 ga.,
Heavy Duck Gun (disc. 1980) . . . . NiB $313 Ex $250 Gd $170
Model 500ALS, 12 ga., Slugster (disc. 1981) . . . NiB $250 Ex $200 Gd $136
Model 500CLD, 20 ga.,
plain bbl. (disc. 1980) . . . . NiB $244 Ex $195 Gd $133
Model 500CLDR, 20 ga., vent rib . . . . NiB $281 Ex $225 Gd $153
Model 500CLS, 20 ga.,
Slugster (disc. 1980) . . . . NiB $313 Ex $250 Gd $170
Model 500EL, .410 ga.,
plain bbl. (disc. 1980) . . . . NiB $269 Ex $215 Gd $146
Model 500ELR, .410 ga., vent rib . . . . NiB $313 Ex $250 Gd $170

MODEL 500 MARINER SHOTGUN . . . . . . NiB $400 Ex $300 Gd $150
Slide action. Gauge: 12. 18.5 or 20-inch bbl. Six shot and 8-shot respectively. Weight: 7.25 lbs. High-strength synthetic buttstock and forend. Available in extra round-carrying Speed Feed synthetic butt-stock. All metal treated for protection against saltwater corrosion. Intro. 1987.

MODEL 500 MUZZLE LOADER COMBO . . NiB $326 Ex $261 Gd $177
Same as Model 500 Sporting Pump except w/extra 24-inch rifled .50-caliber muzzleloading bbl. w/ramrod. Made from 1992 to date.

MODEL 500 PERSUADER LAW ENFORCEMENT
Similar to pre-1977 Model 500 Field Grade except 12 ga. only, 6- or 8-shot, has 18.5- or 20-inch plain bbl., cylinder bore, either shotgun or rifle sights, plain pistol-grip stock and grooved slide handle, sling swivels. Special Model 500ATP8-SP has bayonet lug, Parkerized finish. Currently manufactured.
Model 500ATP6, 6-shot, 18.5-inch
bbl., shotgun sights . . . . NiB $242 Ex $194 Gd $132
Model 500ATP6CN, 6-shot,
nickle finish "Cruiser" pistol-grip. . . . . . . NiB $256 Ex $204 Gd $139
Model 500ATP6N, 6-shot, nickel
finish, 2.75- or 3-inch Mag. shells . . . . . . NiB $249 Ex $199 Gd $135
Model 500ATP6S, 6-shot,
18.5-inch bbl., rifle sights . . . . NiB $242 Ex $194 Gd $132
Model 500ATP8, 8-shot,
20-inch bbl., shotgun sights . . . . NiB $268 Ex $215 Gd $145
Model 500ATP8S, 8-shot,
20-inch bbl., rifle sights . . . . NiB $282 Ex $225 Gd $153
Model 500ATP8-SP Spec. Enforcement . . . NiB $328 Ex $262 Gd $178
Model 500 Bullpup . . . . NiB $518 Ex $414 Gd $282
Model 500 Intimidator w/laser sight, blued . . . NiB $478 Ex $383 Gd $260
Model 500 Intimidator w/laser sight,
parkerized . . . . NiB $492 Ex $393 Gd $267
Model 500 Security combo pack . . . . NiB $197 Ex $157 Gd $107

Mossberg Model 500
Turkey/Deer Combo

Mossberg Model 590
Military

Mossberg Model 595
Bolt-Action Repeater

MODEL 500 PIGEON GRADE

Same as Model 500 Super Grade except higher quality w/fancy wood, floating vent rib; field gun hunting dog etching, trap and skeet guns have scroll etching. Bbls.: 30-inch, F choke (12 ga. only); 28-inch, M choke; 26-inch, SK choke or C-Lect-Choke. Made 1971-75.

Model 500APR, 12 ga., field, trap or skeet ... NiB $438 Ex $350 Gd $238
Model 500APKR, 12 ga.
field gun, C-Lect-Choke .... NiB $450 Ex $360 Gd $245
Model 500 APTR, 12 ga.,
Trap gun, Monte Carlo stock .... NiB $531 Ex $425 Gd $289
Model 500CPR, 20 ga., field or skeet gun .... NiB $456 Ex $365 Gd $248
Model 500EPR, .410 ga.
field or skeet gun .... NiB $469 Ex $375 Gd $255

MODEL 500 PUMP COMBO SHOTGUN .... NiB $306 Ex $245 Gd $167

Gauges: 12 and 20. 24- and 28-inch bbl. w/adj. rifle sights. Weight: 7 to 7.25 lbs. Available w/blued or camo finish. Drilled and tapped receiver w/sling swivels and camo web sling. Made from 1987 to date.

MODEL 500 PUMP SLUGSTER SHOTGUN

Gauges: 12 or 20 w/3-inch chamber. 24-inch smoothbore or rifled bbl. w/adj. rifle sights or integral scope mount and optional muzzle break (1997 porting became standard). Weight: 7 to 7.25 lbs. Wood or synthetic stock w/standard or Woodland Camo finish. Blued, matte black or Marinecote metal finish. Drilled and tapped receiver w/camo sling and swivels. Made 1987 to date.

Slugster (w/cyl. bore, rifle sights) .... NiB $240 Ex $192 Gd $130
Slugster (w/rifled bore, ported) .... NiB $302 Ex $242 Gd $165
Slugster (w/rifled bore, unported) .... NiB $268 Ex $214 Gd $146
Slugster (w/rifled bore, ported,
integral scope mount) .... NiB $336 Ex $269 Gd $183
Slugster (w/Marinecote and
synthetic stock), add $60
Slugster (w/Truglo fiber optics), add........................... $30

MODEL 500 REGAL SLIDE-ACTION REPEATER

Similar to regular Model 500 except higher quality workmanship throughout. Gauges: 12 and 20. Bbls.: 26- and 28-inch w/various chokes, or Accu-Choke. Weight: 6.75 to 7.5 lbs. Checkered walnut stock and forearm. Made 1985 to date.

Model 500 w/Accu-Choke .... NiB $242 Ex $194 Gd $132
Model 500 w/fixed choke .... NiB $223 Ex $178 Gd $121

MODEL 500 SPORTING PUMP

Gauges: 12, 20 or .410, 2.75- or 3-inch chamber. Bbls.: 22 to 28 inches w/fixed choke or screw-in tubes; plain or vent rib. Weight: 6.25 to 7.25 lbs. White bead front sight, brass mid-bead. Checkered hardwood buttstock and forend w/walnut finish.

Standard model .... NiB $244 Ex $195 Gd $133
Field combo (w/extra Slugster bbl.) .... NiB $306 Ex $245 Gd $167

MODEL 500 SUPER GRADE

Same as pre-1977 Model 500 Field Grade except not made in 16 ga., has vent rib bbl., checkered pistol grip and slide handle. Made 1965-76.

Model 500AR, 12 ga. .... NiB $256 Ex $204 Gd $139
Model 500AMR, 12 ga.,
heavy magnum bbl. .... NiB $288 Ex $231 Gd $157
Model 500AKR, 12 ga., C-Lect-Choke .... NiB $295 Ex $236 Gd $160
Model 500CR 20 ga. .... NiB $276 Ex $220 Gd $150
Model 500CKk, 20 ga., C-Lect-Choke........ NiB $361 Ex $309 Gd $244
Model 500ER, .410 ga..................... NiB $249 Ex $199 Gd $135
Model 500EKR, .410 ga., C-Lect-Choke ...... NiB $315 Ex $252 Gd $171

MODEL 500 TURKEY/DEER COMBO........ NiB $334 Ex $267 Gd $181

Pump (slide action). Gauge: 12. 20- and 24-inch bbls. Weight: 7.25 lbs. Drilled and tapped receiver, camo sling and swivels. Adj. rifle sights and camo finish. Vent rib. Made from 1987 to date.

**Mossberg Model 1000
Junior Autoloading**

**Mossberg Model 5500
Guardian**

MODEL 500 TURKEY GUN . . . . NiB $308 Ex $247 Gd $168
Same as Model 500 Camo Pump except w/24-inch ACCU-Choke bbl. w/extra full choke tube and ghost ring sights. Made from 1992 to date.

MODEL 500 VIKING PUMP SHOTGUN
Gauges: 12 or 20 w/3-inch chamber. 24-, 26- or 28-inch bbls. available in smoothbore w/Accu-Choke and vent rib or rifled bore w/iron sights and optional muzzle break (1997 porting became standard). Optional optics: Slug Shooting System (SSS). Weight: 6.9 to 7.2 lbs. Moss-green synthetic stock. Matte black metal finish. Made 1996-98.
Mdl. 500 Viking
(w/VR & choke tubes, unported) . . . . NiB $216 Ex $173 Gd $117
Mdl. 500 Viking (w/rifled bore, ported) . . . NiB $268 Ex $205 Gd $139
Mdl. 500 Viking
(w/rifled bore, SSS & ported) . . . . NiB $344 Ex $275 Gd $187
Mdl. 500 Viking
(w/rifled bore, unported) . . . . NiB $244 Ex $195 Gd $133
Mdl. 500 Viking Turkey
(w/VR, tubes, ported) . . . . NiB $219 Ex $175 Gd $119

MODEL 500
WATERFOWL/DEER COMBO . . . . NiB $331 Ex $265 Gd $180
Same general specifications as the Turkey/Deer combo except w/either 28- or 30-inch bbl. along w/the 24-inch bbl. Made from 1987 to date.

MODEL 500 ATR SUPER
GRADE TRAP . . . . NiB $417 Ex $333 Gd $226
Same as pre-1977 Model 500 Field Grade except 12 ga. only w/vent-rib bbl.; 30-inch F choke, checkered Monte Carlo stock w/recoil pad, beavertail slide handle. Made 1968-71.

MODEL 500DSPR DUCK STAMP
COMMEMORATIVE . . . . NiB $669 Ex $535 Gd $364
Limited edition of 1000 to commemorate the Migratory Bird Hunting Stamp program. Same as Model 500DSPR Pigeon Grade 12-Gauge Magnum Heavy Duck Gun w/heavy 30-inch vent-rib bbl., F choke; receiver has special wood duck etching. Gun accompanied by a special wall plaque. Made in 1975.

MODEL 590 BULLPUP . . . . NiB $438 Ex $350 Gd $238
Same general specifications as the Model 500 Bullpup except 20-inch bbl. and 9-shot magazine. Made 1989-90.

MODEL 590 MARINER PUMP
Same general specifications as the Model 590 Military Security except has Marinecote metal finish and field configuration synthetic stock w/pistiol-grip conversion included. Made from 1989 to date.
Model 590 Mariner (w/18.5-inch bbl.) . . . . . . NiB $309 Ex $247 Gd $167
Model 590 Mariner (w/20-inch bbl.) . . . . NiB $323 Ex $258 Gd $175
Model 590 Mariner (w/grip conversion), add $20
Model 590 Mariner (w/ghost ring sight), add $50

MODEL 590 MILITARY SECURITY . . . . NiB $378 Ex $302 Gd $205
Same general specifications as the Model 590 Military except there is no heat shield and gun has short pistol-grip style instead of buttstock. Weight: About 6.75 lbs. Made from 1987 to date.

MODEL 590 MILITARY SHOTGUN
Slide-action. Gauge: 12. 9-shot capacity. 20-inch bbl. Weight: about 7 lbs. Synthetic or hardwood buttstock and forend. Ventilated bbl. heat shields. Equipped w/bayonet lug. Blued or Parkerized finish. Made from 1987 to date. See illustration Previous Page.
Synthetic model, blued . . . . NiB $331 Ex $265 Gd $180
Synthetic model Parkerized . . . . . . NiB $356 Ex $285 Gd $194
Speedfeed model, blued . . . . NiB $350 Ex $280 Gd $190
Speedfeed model, Parkerized . . . . . NiB $350 Ex $280 Gd $190
Intimidator model
w/laser sight, blued . . . . NiB $456 Ex $365 Gd $248
Intimidator model
w/laser sight, Parkerized . . . . NiB $469 Ex $375 Gd $255
For ghost ring sight, add $75

MODEL 595/595K
BOLT-ACTION REPEATER . . . . NiB $177 Ex $141 Gd $96
12 ga. only. Four shot detachable magazine. 18.5-inch bbl. Weight: About 7 lbs. Walnut finished stock w/recoil pad and sling swivels. Made 1985-86.

MODEL 695 BOLT-ACTION SLUGSTER
Gauge: 12 w/3-inch chamber. Two round detachable magazine. 22-inch fully rifled and ported bbl. w/blade front and folding leaf rear sights. Receiver drilled and tapped for Weaver style scope bases. Also available w/1.5x-4.5x scope or fiber optics installed. Weight: 7.5 lbs. Black synthetic stock w/swivel studs and recoil pad. Made 1996 to date.
Model 695 (w/ACCU-choke bbl.) . . NiB $206 Ex $165 Gd $112
Model 695
(w/open sights) . . . . NiB $268 Ex $214 Gd $146
Model 695
(w/1.5x-4.5x Bushnell scope) . . . . . NiB $378 Ex $302 Gd $205
Model 695 (w/Truglo fiber optics) . . . . NiB $295 Ex $236 Gd $160
Model 695 OFM Camo . . . . NiB $254 Ex $203 Gd $138

MODEL 695 BOLT-ACTION TURKEY GUN NiB $256 Ex $204 Gd $139
Similar to 695 Slugster Model except has smoothbore 22-inch bbl. w/extra-full turkey Accu-choke tube. Bead front and U-notch rear sights. Full OFM camo finish. Made 1996 to date.

MODEL 712 AUTOLOADING SHOTGUN
Gas-operated, takedown, hammerless shotgun w/5-shot (4-shot w/3-inch chamber) tubular magazine. 12 ga. Bbls.: 28-inch vent rib or 24-inch plain bbl. Slugster w/rifle sights. Fixed choke or ACCU-choke tube system. Weight: 7.5 lbs. Plain alloy receiver w/top-mounted ambidextrous safety. Checkered

(cont'd.) MODEL 712 AUTOLOADING SHOTGUN
Mdl. 712 w/fixed chokes .... NiB $262 Ex $210 Gd $142
Mdl. 712 w/ACCU-Choke tube system ..... NiB $295 Ex $236 Gd $160
Mdl. 712 Regal w/ACCU-Choke tube system . NiB $328 Ex $262 Gd $178
Mdl. 712 Regal w/ACCU-Choke II tube sys... NiB $361 Ex $288 Gd $196

MODEL 835 FIELD PUMP SHOTGUN
Similar to the Model 9600 Regal except has walnut-stained hard-wood stock and one ACCU-Choke tube only.
Standard model .... NiB $269 Ex $215 Gd $146
Turkey model .... NiB $281 Ex $225 Gd $153
Combo model (24- & 28-inch bbls.) NiB $306 Ex $245 Gd $167

MODEL 835 "NWTF" ULTI-MA SHOTGUN
National Wild Turkey Federation pump-action. Gauge: 12, 3.5-inch chamber. 24-inch vent-rib bbl. w/four ACCU-MAG chokes. Realtree camo finish. QD swivel and post. Made 1989-93.
Limited Edition model .... NiB $438 Ex $350 Gd $238
Special Edition model .... NiB $369 Ex $295 Gd $201

MODEL 835 REGAL ULTI-MAG PUMP
Gauge: 12, 3.5-inch chamber. Bbls.: 24- or 28-inch vent-rib w/ACCU-Choke screw-in tubes. Weight: 7.75 lbs. White bead front, brass mid-bead. Checkered hardwood or synthetic stock w/camo finish. Made 1991-96.
Special model .... NiB $281 Ex $225 Gd $153
Standard model .... NiB $350 Ex $280 Gd $190
Camo Synthetic model .... NiB $375 Ex $300 Gd $204
Combo model .... NiB $406 Ex $325 Gd $221

MODEL 835 VIKING PUMP SHOTGUN
Gauge: 12 w/3-inch chamber. 28-inch smoothbore bbl. w/Accu-Choke, vent rib and optional muzzle brake (in 1997 porting became standard). Weight: 7.7 lbs. Green synthetic stock. Matte black metal finish. Made 1996-98.
Model 835 Viking (w/VR and
choke tubes, ported) .... NiB $268 Ex $215 Gd $145
Model 835 Viking (w/VR
and choke tubes, unported)....... NiB $256 Ex $204 Gd $139

MODEL 1000 AUTOLOADING SHOTGUN
Gas-operated, takedown, hammerless shotgun w/tubular magazine. Gauges: 12, 20; 2.75- or 3-inch chamber. Bbls.: 22- to 30-inch vent rib w/fixed choke or ACCU-Choke tubes; or 22-inch plain bbl, Slugster w/rifle sights. Weight: 6.5 to 7.5 lbs. Scroll-engraved alloy receiver, crossbolt-type safety. Checkered walnut buttstock and forend. Imported from Japan 1986-87.
Junior model, 20 ga., 22-inch bbl... NiB $409 Ex $327 Gd $223
Standard model w/fixed choke .... NiB $421 Ex $337 Gd $228
Standard model w/choke tubes ... NiB $445 Ex $356 Gd $242

MODEL 1000 SUPER AUTOLOADING SHOTGUN
Similar to Model 1000, but in 12 ga. only w/3-inch chamber and new gas metering system. Bbls.: 26-, 28- or 30-inch vent rib w/ACCU-Choke tubes.
Standard model w/choke tubes ... NiB $494 Ex $395 Gd $269
Waterfowler model (Parkerized) .. NiB $531 Ex $425 Gd $289

MODEL 1000S SUPER SKEET ..... NiB $588 Ex $470 Gd $320
Similar to Model 1000 in 12 or 20 ga., except w/all-steel receiver and vented jug-type choke for reduced muzzle jump. Bright-point front sight and brass mid-bead. 1 and 2 oz. forend cap weights.

MODEL 5500 AUTOLOADING SHOTGUN
Gas-operated. Takedown. 12 ga. only. Four shot magazine (3-shot w/3-inch shells). Bbls.: 18.5- to 30-inch; various chokes. Checkered walnut finished hardwood. Made 1985-86.
Model 5500 w/ACCU-Choke ..... NiB $281 Ex $225 Gd $153
Model 5500 modified junior ..... NiB $287 Ex $229 Gd $155

(cont'd.) MODEL 5500 AUTOLOADING SHOTGUN
Model 5500 Slugster .... NiB $297 Ex $238 Gd $162
Model 5500 12 ga. .... NiB $252 Ex $202 Gd $137
Model 5500 Guardian .... NiB $242 Ex $193 Gd $131

MODEL 5500 MKII AUTOLOADING SHOTGUN
Same as Model 5500 except equipped w/two Accu-Choke bbls.: 26-inch ported for non-Magnum 2.75-inch shells; 28-inch for magnum loads. Made 1988-93.
Standard model .... NiB $266 Ex $213 Gd $145
Camo model .... NiB $297 Ex $237 Gd $161
NWTF Mossy Oak model .... NiB $326 Ex $261 Gd $177
USST model (Made 1991-92) ..... NiB $279 Ex $223 Gd $152

MODEL 6000 AUTO SHOTGUN. . . NiB $279 Ex $223 Gd $152
Similar to the Model 9200 Regal except has 28-inch vent-rib bbl. w/mod. ACCU-Choke tube only. Made from 1993 to date.

MODEL 9200 CAMO SHOTGUN
Similar to the Model 9200 Regal except has synthetic stock and forend and is completely finished in camouflage pattern (incl. bbl.). Made from 1993 to date.
Standard model (OFM camo) ..... NiB $391 Ex $313 Gd $213
Turkey model (Mossy Oak camo) ..... NiB $433 Ex $346 Gd $235
Turkey model (Shadow Branch camo)... NiB $515 Ex $412 Gd $280
Comb. model (24 & 28-inch bbls.
w/OFM camo).................. NiB $481 Ex $385 Gd $261

MODEL 9200 CROWN (REGAL) AUTOLOADER
Gauge: 12; 3-inch chamber. Bbls.: 18.5- to 28-inch w/ACCU-Choke tubes; plain or vent rib. Weight: 7.25 to 7.5 lbs. Checkered hardwood buttstock and forend w/walnut finish. Made from 1992 to date.
Model 9200 Bantam (w/1-inch shorter stock) .... NiB $378 Ex $302 Gd $205
Model 9200 w/ACCU-Choke .... NiB $391 Ex $313 Gd $213
Model 9200 w/rifled bbl.............. NiB $405 Ex $324 Gd $221
Model 9200 Combo (w/extra Slugster bbl.).... NiB $454 Ex $363 Gd $246
Model 9200 SP (w/matte blue finish,
18.5-inch bbl.) .... NiB $309 Ex $247 Gd $168

MODEL 9200 PERSUADER .... NiB $331 Ex $265 Gd $180
Similar to the Model 9200 Regal except has 18.5-inch plain bbl. w/fixed mod. choke. Parkerized finish. Black synthetic stock w/sling swivels. Made 1996 to date.

MODEL 9200 A1 JUNGLE GUN . . . NiB $600 Ex $500 Gd $225
Similar to the Model 9200 Persuader except has mil-spec heavy wall 18.5-inch plain bbl. w/cyl. bore designed for 00 Buck shot. 12 ga. w/2.75-inch chamber. 5-shot magazine. 38.5 inches overall. Weight: 7 lbs. Black synthetic stock. Parkerized finish. Made 1998 to date.

MODEL 9200 SPECIAL HUNTER . . NiB $391 Ex $313 Gd $213
Similar to the Model 9200 Regal except has 28-inch vent-rib bbl. w/ACCU-Choke tubes. Parkerized finish. Black synthetic stock. Made from 1998 to date.

MODEL 9200 TROPHY
Similar to the Model 9200 Regal except w/24-inch rifled bbl. or 24- or 28-inch vent-rib bbl. w/ACCU-Choke tubes. Checkered walnut stock w/sling swivels. Made from 1992-98.
Trophy (w/vent rib bbl.) $288
Trophy (w/rifled bbl. & cantilever scope mount) 309
Trophy (w/rifled bbl. & rifle sights) 278

MODEL 9200 USST AUTOLOADER $302
Similar to the Model 9200 Regal except has 26-inch vent-rib bbl. w/ACCU-Choke tubes. "United States Shooting Team" engraved on receiver. Made from 1993 to date.

SHOTGUNS

Navy Arms Model 83
Bird Hunter O/U

Navy Arms Model 100
Field Hunter Double-Barrel Shotgun

MODEL 9200
VIKING AUTOLOADER..........NiB $361 Ex $288 Gd $196
Gauge: 12 w/3-inch chamber. 28-inch smoothbore bbl. W/Accu-Choke and vent rib. Weight: 7.7 lbs. Green synthetic stock. Matte black metal finish. Made 1996-98.

MODEL HS410
HOME SECURITY PUMP SHOTGUN
Gauge: .410; 3-inch chamber. Bbl.: 18.5-inch w/muzzle brake; blued. Weight: 6.25 lbs. Synthetic stock and pistol-grip slide. Optional laser sight. Made from 1990 to date. A similar version of this gun is marketed by Maverick Arms under the same model designation.
Standard model ....NiB $231 Ex $185 Gd $126
Laser model ....NiB $406 Ex $325 Gd $221

LINE LAUNCHER...............NiB $844 Ex $675 Gd $459
Gauge: 12 w/blank cartridge. Projectile travels from 250 to 275 feet.

"NEW HAVEN BRAND" SHOTGUNS
Promotional models, similar to their standard guns but plainer in finish, are marketed by Mossberg under the "New Haven" brand name. Values generally are about 20 percent lower than for corresponding standard models.

NAVY ARMS SHOTGUNS —
Ridgefield, New Jersey

MODEL 83/93 BIRD HUNTER O/U
Hammerless. Boxlock, engraved receiver. Gauges: 12 and 20; 3-inch chambers. Bbls.: 28-inch chrome lined w/double vent-rib construction. Checkered European walnut stock and forearm. Gold plated triggers. Imported 1984-90.
Model 83 w/extractors ....NiB $281 Ex $225 Gd $153
Model 93 w/ejectors ....NiB $331 Ex $265 Gd $180

MODEL 95/96 O/U SHOTGUN
Same as the Model 83/93 except w/five interchangeable choke tubes. Imported 1984-90.
Model 95 w/extractors ....NiB $369 Ex $295 Gd $201
Model 96 w/ejectors ....NiB $493 Ex $394 Gd $267

MODEL 100/150 FIELD HUNTER
DOUBLE-BARREL SHOTGUN
Boxlock. Gauges: 12 and 20. Bbls.: 28-inch chrome lined. Checkered European walnut stock and forearm. Imported 1984-90.
Model 100 ....NiB $350 Ex $280 Gd $190
Model 150 (auto ejectors) ....NiB $456 Ex $365 Gd $248

MODEL 100 O/U SHOTGUN.....NiB $231 Ex $185 Gd $126
Hammerless, takedown shotgun w/engraved chrome receiver. Single trigger. 12, 20, 28, or .410 ga. w/3-inch chambers. Bbls.: 26-inch (F/F or SK/SK); vent rib. Weight: 6.25 lbs. Checkered European walnut buttstock and forend. Imported 1986-90.

NEW ENGLAND FIREARMS —
Gardner, Massachusetts

In 1987, New England Firearms was established as an independent company producing selected H&R models under the NEF logo after Harrington & Richardson suspended operations on January 24, 1986. In 1991, H&R 1871, Inc. was formed from the residual of the parent H&R company and then took over the New England Firearms facility. H&R 1871 produced firearms under both their logo and the NEF brand name until 1999, when the Marlin Firearms Company acquired the assets of H&R 1871.

NEW ENGLAND FIREARMS NWTF TURKEY SPECIAL
Similar to Turkey and Goose models except 10 or 20 gauge w/22- or 24-inch plain bbl. w/screw-in full-choke tube. Mossy Oak camo finish on entire gun. Made from 1992-96.
Turkey Special 10 ga. ....NiB $190 Ex $160 Gd $145
Turkey Special 20 ga. ....NiB $110 Ex $90 Gd $60

NRA FOUNDATION YOUTH ......NiB $171 Ex $137 Gd $94
Smaller scale version of Pardner Model chambered for 20, 28 or .410 w/22- inch plain bbl. High luster blue finish. NRA Foundation logo laser etched on stock. Made 1999 to date.

PARDNER SHOTGUN
Takedown. Side lever. Single bbl. Gauges: 12, 20 and .410 w/3-inch chamber; 16 and 28 w/2.75-inch chamber. 26-, 28- or 32-inch, plain bbl. w/fixed choke. Weight: 5-6 lbs. Bead front sight. Pistol grip-style hardwood stock w/walnut finish. Made from 1988 to date.
Standard model ....NiB $98 Ex $78 Gd $53
Youth model ....NiB $105 Ex $84 Gd $56
Youth Turkey model ....NiB $118 Ex $94 Gd $64
W/32-inch bbl., add $15

PARDNER SPECIAL PURPOSE 10 GA. SHOTGUN
Similar to the standard Pardner model except chambered 10 ga. only w/3.5-inch chamber. 24- or 28-inch, plain bbl. w/full choke tube or fixed choke. Weight: 9.5 lbs. Bead front sight. Pistol-grip-style hardwood stock w/camo or matte black finish. Made from 1989 to date.
Special Purpose model w/fixed choke ...NiB $124 Ex $99 Gd $68
W/camo finish, add $15
W/choke tube, add $20
W/24-inch bbl. turkey option, add $30

Noble Model 65

Noble Model 66RCLP
Hammerless Slide-Action Repeating Shotgun

Noble Key Lock Fire Control Mechanism
Supplied with models 66, 166L, and 602

PARDNER SPECIAL PURPOSE
WATERFOWL SINGLE-SHOT ...... NiB $156 Ex $125 Gd $85
Similar to Special Purpose 10 Ga. model except w/32-inch bbl. Mossy Oak camo stock w/swivel and sling. Made 1988 to date.

PARDNER TURKEY GUN
Similar to Pardner model except chambered in 12 ga. w/3.0- or 3.5-inch chamber. 24-inch plain bbl. W/turkey full-choke tube or fixed choke. Weight: 9.5 lbs. American hardwood stock w/camo or matte black finish. Made from 1999 to date.
Standard Turkey model .... NiB $138 Ex $110 Gd $75
Camo Turkey model .... NiB $150 Ex $120 Gd $82

SURVIVOR SERIES
Takedown single bbl. shotgun w/side lever release, Automatic ejector and patented transfer-bar safety. Gauges: 12, 20, and .410/.45 ACP w/3-inch chamber. 22-inch bbl. w/modified choke and bead sight. Weight: 6 lbs. Polymer stock and forend w/hollow cavity for storage. Made 1992-93 and 1995 to date.
12 or 20 ga.
w/blued finish .... NiB $117 Ex $93 Gd $63
12 or 20 ga.
w/nickel finish .... NiB $148 Ex $118 Gd $81
.410/.45 ACP, add .... NiB $38 Ex $add30 Gd $20

TRACKER SLUG GUN
Similar to Pardner model except in 10, 12 or 20 ga. w/24-inch w/cylinder choke or rifled slug bbl. (Tracker II). Weight: 6 lbs. American hardwood stock w/walnut or camo finish, Schnabel forend, sling swivel studs. Made from 1992 to date.
Tracker Slug
(10 ga.) .... NiB $119 Ex $95 Gd $65
Tracker Slug
(12 or 20 ga.) .... NiB $120 Ex $90 Gd $50
Tracker II (rifled bore) .... NiB $150 Ex $120 Gd $60

NIKKO FIREARMS LTD. — Tochigi, Japan
See listings under Golden Eagle Firearms, Inc.

NOBLE MANUFACTURING COMPANY — Haydenville, Massachusetts

Series 602 and 70 are similar in appearance to the corresponding Model 66 guns.

MODEL 40 HAMMERLESS SLIDE-ACTION
REPEATING SHOTGUN .... NiB $144 Ex $115 Gd $78
Solid frame. 12 ga. only. Five shell tubular magazine. 28-inch bbl. w/ventilated Multi-Choke. Weight: About 7.5 lbs. Plain pistol-grip stock, grooved slide handle. Made 1950-55.

MODEL 50
SLIDE-ACTION .... NiB $144 Ex $115 Gd $78
Same as Model 40 except w/o Multi-Choke. M or F choke bbl. Made 1953-55.

MODEL 60 HAMMERLESS SLIDE-ACTION
REPEATING SHOTGUN .... NiB $203 Ex $162 Gd $110
Solid frame. 12 and 16 ga. Five shot tubular magazine. 28-inch bbl. w/adj. choke. Plain pistol-grip stock w/recoil pad, grooved slide handle. Weight: About 7.5 lbs. Made 1955-66.

MODEL 65 .... NiB $169 Ex $135 Gd $92
Same as Model 60 except without adj. choke and recoil pad. M or F choke bbl. Made 1955-66.

MODEL 66CLP .... NiB $156 Ex $125 Gd $85
Same as Model 66RCLP except has plain bbl. Introduced in 1967. Disc.

MODEL 66RCLP HAMMERLESS SLIDE-ACTION
REPEATING SHOTGUN .... NiB $197 Ex $157 Gd $107
Solid frame. Key lock fire control mechanism. Gauges: 12, 16. 3-inch chamber in 12 ga. Five shot tubular magazine. 28-inch bbl., vent rib, adj. choke. Weight: About 7.5 lbs. Checkered pistol-grip stock and slide handle, recoil pad. Made 1967-70.

MODEL 66RLP .... NiB $181 Ex $145 Gd $99
Same as Model 66RCLP except w/F or M choke. Made 1967-1970.

Noble Model 66XL

Noble Model 80
Autoloading Shotgun

Noble Model 166L
Deer Gun

Noble Model 420
Hammerless Double

MODEL 66XL . . . . NiB $156 Ex $125 Gd $85
Same as Model 66RCL except has plain bbl., F or M choke, slide
handle only checkered, no recoil pad. Made 1967-70.

MODEL 70CLP HAMMERLESS SLIDE-ACTION
REPEATING SHOTGUN . . . . NiB $181 Ex $145 Gd $99
Solid frame. .410 gauge. Magazine holds 5 shells. 26-inch bbl.
w/adj. choke. Weight: About 6 lbs. Checkered buttstock and forearm, recoil pad. Made 1958-70.

MODEL 70RCLP . . . . NiB $188 Ex $150 Gd $102
Same as Model 70CLP except has vent rib. Made 1967-70.

MODEL 70RLP . . . . NiB $175 Ex $140 Gd $95
Same as Model 70CLP except has vent rib and no adj. choke. Made
1967-70.

MODEL 70XL . . . . NiB $131 Ex $105 Gd $71
Same as Model 70CLP except without adj. choke and checkering on
buttstock. Made 1958-70.

MODEL 80
AUTOLOADING SHOTGUN. . . . . . NiB $229 Ex $183 Gd $124
Recoil-operated. .410 ga. Magazine holds three 3-inch shells, four
2.5-inch shells. 26-inch bbl., full choke. Weight: About 6 lbs. Plain
pistol-grip stock and fluted forearm. Made 1964-66.

MODEL 166L DEER GUN . . . . NiB $256 Ex $204 Gd $139
Solid frame. Key lock fire control mechanism. 12 ga. 2.75-inch
chamber. Five shot tubular magazine. 24-inch plain bbl., specially
bored for rifled slug. Lyman peep rear sight, post ramp front sight.

(cont'd.) **MODEL 166L DEER GUN**
Receiver dovetailed for scope mounting. Weight: About 7.25 lbs.
Checkered pistol-grip stock and slide handle, swivels and carrying
strap. Made 1967-70.

MODEL 420
HAMMERLESS DOUBLE . . . . NiB $332 Ex $265 Gd $180
Boxlock. Plain extractors. Double triggers. Gauges: 12 ga. 3-
inch mag.; 16 ga.; 20 ga. 3-inch mag.; .410 ga. Bbls.: 28-inch,
except .410 in 26-inch, M/F choke. Weight: About 6.75 lbs.
Engraved frame. Checkered walnut stock and forearm. Made
1958-70.

MODEL 450E
HAMMERLESS DOUBLE . . . . NiB $372 Ex $297 Gd $202
Boxlock. Engraved frame. Selective auto ejectors. Double trig-
gers. Gauges: 12, 16, 20. 3-inch chambers in 12 and 20 ga. 28-
inch bbls., M/F choke. Weight: About 6 lbs., 14 oz., 12 ga.
Checkered pistol-grip stock and beavertail forearm, recoil pad.
Made 1967-70.

MODEL 602CLP . . . . NiB $194 Ex $155 Gd $105
Same as Model 602RCLP except has plain bbl. Made 1958-70.

MODEL 602RCLP
HAMMERLESS SLIDE-ACTION
REPEATING SHOTGUN . . . . NiB $206 Ex $165 Gd $112
Solid frame. Key lock fire control mechanism. 20 ga. 3-inch
chamber. Five shot tubular magazine. 28-inch bbl., vent rib, adj.
choke. Weight: About 6.5 lbs. Checkered pistol-grip stock/slide
handle, recoil pad. Made 1967-70.

Omega Deluxe Side-by-Side Shotgun

Parker B.H. Grade

Noble Model 450E Hammerless Double

Parker C.H. Grade

MODEL 602RLP . . . . NiB $188 Ex $150 Gd $102
Same as Model 602RCLP except without adj. choke, bored F or M choke. Made 1967-70.

MODEL 602XL . . . . NiB $156 Ex $125 Gd $85
Same as Model 602RCL except has plain bbl., F or M choke, slide handle only checkered, no recoil pad. Made 1958-70.

MODEL 662 . . . . NiB $194 Ex $155 Gd $105
Same as Model 602CLP except has aluminum receiver and bbl. Weight: About 4.5 lbs. Made 1966-70.

OMEGA SHOTGUNS — Brescia, Italy, and Korea

FOLDING OVER/UNDER SHOTGUN, STANDARD
Hammerless Boxlock. Gauges: 12, 20, 28 w/2.75-inch chambers or .410 w/3-inch chambers. Bbls.: 26- or 28-inch vent-rib w/fixed chokes (IC/M, M/F or F/F (.410). Automatic safety. Single trigger. 40.5 inches overall (42.5 inches, 20 ga., 28-inch bbl.). Weight: 6 to 7.5 lbs. Checkered European walnut stock and forearm. Imported 1984-94.
Standard model (12 ga.) . . . . NiB $425 Ex $330 Gd $200
Standard model (20 ga.) . . . . NiB $425 Ex $330 Gd $200
Standard model (28 ga. & .410) . . . . NiB $494 Ex $395 Gd $269

O/U SHOTGUN, DELUXE . . . . NiB $416 Ex $332 Gd $226
Gauges: 20, 28 and .410. 26- or 28-inch vent-rib bbls. 40.5 inches overall (42.5 inches, 20 ga., 28-inch bbl.). Chokes: IC/M, M/F or F/F (.410). Weight: About 5.5-6 lbs. Single trigger. Automatic safety. European walnut stock w/checkered pistol grip and tulip forend. Imported from Italy 1984-90.

OMEGA DELUXE
SIDE-BY-SIDE SHOTGUN . . . . NiB $207 Ex $166 Gd $113
Same general specifications as the Standard Side-by-Side except has checkered European walnut stock and low bbl. rib. Made in Italy from 1984-89.

STANDARD SIDE-BY-SIDE SHOTGUN, ...NiB $206 Ex $165 Gd $112
Gauge: .410. 26-inch bbl. 40.5 inches overall. Choked F/F. Weight: 5.5 lbs. Double trigger. Manual safety. Checkered beechwood stock and semi-pistol grip. Imported from Italy 1984-89.

DELUXE SINGLE-SHOT SHOTGUN . . . . NiB $103 Ex $82 Gd $56
Same general specifications as the Standard single bbl. except has checkered walnut stock, top lever break, fully-blued receiver, vent rib. Imported from Korea 1984-87.

STANDARD SINGLE-SHOT SHOTGUN
Gauges: 12, 16, 20, 28 and .410. Bbl. lengths: 26-,28- or 30-inch. Weight: 5 lbs., 4 oz. to 5 lbs., 11 oz. Indonesian walnut stock. Matte-chromed receiver and top lever break. Imported from Korea 1984-87.
Standard fixed . . . . NiB $81 Ex $65 Gd $44
Standard folding . . . . NiB $156 Ex $125 Gd $85
Deluxe folding . . . . NiB $194 Ex $155 Gd $105

PARKER BROTHERS — Meriden, Connecticut

This firm was taken over by Remington Arms Company in 1934 and its production facilities moved to Remington's Ilion, New York, plant.

HAMMERLESS DOUBLE-BARREL SHOTGUNS
Grades V.H. through A-1 Special. Boxlock. Auto ejectors. Double triggers or selective single trigger. Gauges: 10, 12, 16, 20, 28, .410. Bbls.: 26- to 32-inch, any standard boring. Weight: 6.88-8.5 lbs.,12 ga. Stock and forearm of select walnut, checkered; straight, half-or full-pistol grip. Grades differ only in quality of workmanship, grade of wood, engraving, checkering, etc. General specifications are the same for all. Disc. about 1940.
V.H. grade, 12 or 16 ga. . . . . NiB $3119 Ex $2495 Gd $1697
V.H. grade, 20 ga. . . . . NiB $4563 Ex $3650 Gd $2482
V.H. grade, 28 ga. . . . . NiB $7438 Ex $5950 Gd $4046
V.H. grade, .410 ga. . . . . NiB $18,688 Ex $14,950 Gd $10,166
G.H. grade, 12 ga. . . . . NiB $4244 Ex $3395 Gd $2309
G.H. grade, 16 ga. . . . . NiB $4438 Ex $3550 Gd $2414

Parker A-1 Special Grade

Parker A.H. Grade

Parker S.C. Grade

Parker D.H. Grade

Parker G.H. Grade

(cont'd.) HAMMERLESS DOUBLE-BARREL SHOTGUNS
G.H. grade, 20 ga. . . . . NiB $5992 Ex $4794 Gd $3260
G.H. grade, 28 ga. . . . . NiB $9375 Ex $7500 Gd $5100
G.H. grade, .410 ga. . . . . NiB $23,925 Ex $19,140 Gd $13,015
D.H. grade, 12 or 16 ga. . . . . NiB $6825 Ex $5460 Gd $3712
D.H. grade, 20 ga. . . . . NiB $8775 Ex $7020 Gd $4773
D.H. grade, 28 ga. . . . . NiB $13,192 Ex $10,554 Gd $7177
D.H. grade, .410 ga. . . . . NiB $44,250 Ex $35,400 Gd $24,072
C.H. grade, 12 or 16 ga. . . . . NiB $7575 Ex $6060 Gd $4120
C.H. grade, 20 ga. . . . . NiB $9892 Ex $7914 Gd $5382
C.H. grade, 28 ga. . . . . NiB $1875 Ex $1500 Gd $1020
B.H. grade, 12 or 16 ga. . . . . NiB $11,325 Ex $9060 Gd $6160
B.H. grade, 20 ga. . . . . NiB $19,875 Ex $15,900 Gd $10,812
B.H. grade, 28 ga. . . . . NiB $37,125 Ex $29,700 Gd $20,196
A.H. grade, 12 or 16 ga. . . . . NiB $26,250 Ex $21,000 Gd $14,280
A.H. grade, 20 ga. . . . . NiB $32,625 Ex $26,100 Gd $17,748
A.H. grade, 28 ga. . . . . NiB $57,750 Ex $46,200 Gd $31,416
A.A.H. grade, 12 or 16 ga. . . . . NiB $59,925 Ex $47,940 Gd $32,599
A.A.H. grade, 12 or 16 ga. . . . . NiB $49,875 Ex $39,900 Gd $27,132
A.A.H. grade, 20 ga. . . . . NiB $72,750 Ex $58,200 Gd $39,576
A.A.H. grade, 28 ga. . . . . NiB $108,375 Ex $86,700 Gd $58,956
A-1 Special grade, 12 or 16 ga. . . . . . NiB $93,750 Ex $75,000 Gd $51,000
A-1 Special grade, 20 ga. . . . . NiB $138,000 Ex $110,400 Gd $75,072
A-1 Special grade, 28 ga. . . . . NiB $184,500 Ex $147,600 Gd $100,368
W/selective-single trigger, add 20%
W/ventilated rib, add 35%
For non-ejector guns, deduct 30%

SINGLE-SHOT TRAP GUNS
Hammerless. Boxlock. Ejector. 12 ga. only. Bbl. lengths: 30-, 32-, 34-inch, any boring, vent rib. Weight: 7.5-8.5 lbs. Stock and forearm of select walnut, checkered; straight, half-or full-pistol grip. The five grades differ only in quality of workmanship, grade of wood, checkering, engraving, etc. General specifications same for all. Disc. about 1940.
S.C. grade . . . . NiB $4875 Ex $3900 Gd $2652
S.B. grade . . . . NiB $5962 Ex $4770 Gd $3242
S.A. grade . . . . NiB $6675 Ex $5340 Gd $3631
S.A.A. grade . . . . NiB $8542 Ex $6834 Gd $4647
S.A.1 Special . . . . NiB $26,250 Ex $21,000 Gd $14,280

SKEET GUN
Same as other Parker doubles from Grade V.H.E. up except selective single trigger and beavertail forearm are standard on this model, as are 26-inch bbls., SK choke. Discontinued about 1940. Values are 35 percent higher.

TROJAN HAMMERLESS DOUBLE-BARREL SHOTGUN
Boxlock. Plain extractors. Double trigger or single trigger. Gauges: 12, 16, 20. Bbls.: 30-inch both F choke (12 ga. only), 26- or 28-inch M and F choke. Weight: 6.25-7.75 lbs. Checkered pistol-grip stock and forearm. Disc. 1939.
12 ga. . . . . NiB $2269 Ex $1815 Gd $1234
16 ga. . . . . NiB $3018 Ex $2414 Gd $1642
20 ga. . . . . NiB $3919 Ex $3135 Gd $2131

Parker-Hale Model 545A

Parker-Hale Model 645E

Parker Trojan Hammerless
Double-Barrel Shotgun

PARKER REPRODUCTIONS — Middlesex, New Jersey

HAMMERLESS DOUBLE-BARREL SHOTGUNS

Reproduction of the original Parker boxlock. Single selective trigger or double triggers. Selective automatic ejectors. Automatic safety. Gauges: 12, 16, 20, 28 or .410 w/2.75- or 3-inch chambers. Bbls.: 26- or 28-inch w/fixed or internal screw choke tubes SK/SK, IC/M, M/F. Weight: 5.5-7 lbs. Checkered English-style or pistol-grip American walnut stock w/beavertail or splinter forend and checkered skeleton buttplate. Color casehardened receiver with game scenes and scroll engraving. Produced in Japan by Olin Kodensha 1984-88.

DHE grade, 12 ga.	NiB $3313	Ex $2650	Gd $1802
DHE grade, 12 ga Sporting Clays.	NiB $4156	Ex $3325	Gd $2261
DHE grade, 20 ga.	NiB $2744	Ex $2195	Gd $1493
DHE grade, 28 ga.	NiB $3063	Ex $2450	Gd $1666
DHE grade 2-barrel set (16 & 20 ga.)	NiB $5313	Ex $4250	Gd $2890
DHE grade 2-barrel set (28 & .410)	NiB $5938	Ex $4750	Gd $3230
DHE grade 3-barrel set	NiB $7369	Ex $5895	Gd $4009
B grade Bank Note Lim. Ed., 12 ga.	NiB $5244	Ex $4195	Gd $2853
B grade Bank Note Lim. Ed., 20 ga.	NiB $6563	Ex $5250	Gd $3570
B grade Bank Note Lim. Ed., 28 ga.	NiB $10,244	Ex $8195	Gd $5573
B grade Bank Note Lim. Ed., .410 ga.	NiB $9688	Ex $8350	Gd $5614
A-1 Special grade, 12 ga.	NiB $9494	Ex $7595	Gd $5165
A-1 Special grade, 16 ga.	NiB $11,188	Ex $8950	Gd $6086
A-1 Special grade, 20 ga.	NiB $9119	Ex $7295	Gd $4961
A-1 Special grade, 28 ga.	NiB $13,688	Ex $10,950	Gd $7446
A-1 Special gr. 2-barrel set	NiB $10,688	Ex $8550	Gd $5814
A-1 Special gr. 3-barrel set	NiB $25,625+	Ex $20,500+	Gd $13,940+
A-1 Special gr. custom engraved	NiB $15,625	Ex $12,500	Gd $8500
A-1 Special gr. custom 2-barrel set	NiB $11,938	Ex $9550	Gd $6494
Extra barrel set, add			$250

PARKER-HALE SHOTGUNS — Mfd. by Ignacio Ugartechea, Spain

MODEL 645A (AMERICAN)
SIDE-BY-SIDE SHOTGUN . . . . NiB $1031 Ex $825 Gd $561
Gauges: 12, 16 and 20. Boxlock action. 26- and 28-inch bbls. Chokes: IC/M, M/F. Weight: 6 lbs. average. Single non-selective trigger. Automatic safety. Hand-checkered pistol grip walnut stock w/beavertail forend. Raised matted rib. English scroll-design engraved receiver. Discontinued 1990.

MODEL 645E (ENGLISH) SIDE-BY-SIDE SHOTGUN
Same general specifications as the Model 645A except double triggers, straight grip, splinter forend, checkered butt and concave rib. Disc. 1990.

(cont'd.) **MODEL 645E (ENGLISH) SIDE-BY-SIDE SHOTGUN**
MODEL 645E

12, 16, 20 ga. with 26- or 28-inch bbl.	NiB $1093	Ex $874	Gd $595
28, .410 ga. with 27-inch bbl.	NiB $1485	Ex $1187	Gd $807

MODEL 645E-XXV

12, 16, 20 ga. with 25-inch bbl.	NiB $1031	Ex $825	Gd $561
28, .410 ga. with 25-inch bbl.	NiB $1398	Ex $1118	Gd $761

PEDERSEN CUSTOM GUNS — North Haven, Connecticut, Div. of O. F. Mossberg & Sons, Inc.

MODEL 1000 O/U HUNTING SHOTGUN
Boxlock. Auto ejectors. Selective single trigger. Gauges: 12, 20. 2.75-inch chambers in 12 ga., 3-inch in 20 ga. Bbls.: Vent rib; 30-inch M/F (12 ga. only); 28-inch IC/M (12 ga. only), M/F; 26-inch IC/M. Checkered pistol-grip stock and forearm. Grade I is the higher quality gun with custom stock dimensions, fancier wood, more elaborate engraving, silver inlays. Made 1973-75.

Grade I	NiB $2250	Ex $1800	Gd $1224
Grade II	NiB $1810	Ex $1448	Gd $985

MODEL 1000 MAGNUM
Same as Model 1000 Hunting Gun except chambered for 12-ga. Magnum 3-inch shells, 30-inch bbls., IM/F choke. Made 1973-75.

Grade I	NiB $2438	Ex $1950	Gd $1326
Grade II	NiB $1994	Ex $1595	Gd $1085

MODEL 1000 SKEET GUN
Same as Model 1000 Hunting Gun except has skeet-style stock; 26- and 28-inch bbls. (12 ga. only), SK choke. Made 1973-75.

Grade I	NiB $2095	Ex $1676	Gd $353
Grade II	NiB $1695	Ex $1356	Gd $922

MODEL 1000 TRAP GUN
Same as Model 1000 Hunting Gun except 12 ga. only, has Monte Carlo trap-style stock, 30- or 32-inch bbls., M/F or IM/F choke. Made 1973-75.

Grade I	NiB $1850	Ex $1480	Gd $1006
Grade II	NiB $1495	Ex $1196	Gd $813

SHOTGUNS

Pedersen Model 1000 Grade I

Pedersen Model 1000 Grade II

MODEL 1500 O/U
HUNTING SHOTGUN . . . . **NiB $758 Ex $605 Gd $411**
Boxlock. Auto ejectors. Selective single trigger. 12 ga. 2.75- or 3-inch chambers. Bbls.: vent rib; 26-inch IC/M; 28- and 30-inch M/F; Magnum has 30-inch, IM/F choke. Weight: 7-7.5 lbs., depending on bbl. length. Checkered pistol-grip stock and forearm. Made 1973-75.

MODEL 1500 SKEET GUN . . . . NiB $781 Ex $624 Gd $425
Same as Model 1500 Hunting Gun except has skeet-style stock, 27-inch bbls., SK choke. Made 1973-75.

MODEL 1500 TRAP GUN . . . . NiB $647 Ex $517 Gd $351
Same as Model 1500 Hunting Gun except has Monte Carlo trap-style stock, 30- or 32-inch bbls., M/F or IM/F chokes. Made 1973-75.

MODEL 2000 HAMMERLESS DOUBLE
Boxlock. Auto ejectors. Selective single trigger. Gauges: 12, 20. 2.75-inch chambers in 12 ga., 3-inch in 20 ga. Bbls.: Vent rib; 30-inch M/F (12 ga. only); 28-inch M/F, 26-inch IC/M choke. Checkered pistol-grip stock and forearm. Grade I is the higher quality gun w/custom dimensions, fancier wood, more elaborate engraving, silver inlays. Made 1973-74.
Grade I . . . . NiB $2438 Ex $1950 Gd $1326
Grade II . . . . NiB $2244 Ex $1795 Gd $1221

MODEL 2500
HAMMERLESS DOUBLE . . . . **NiB $456 Ex $365 Gd $248**
Boxlock. Auto ejectors. Selective single trigger. Gauges: 12, 20. 2.75-inch chambers in 12 ga., 3-inch in 20 ga. Bbls.: Vent rib; 28-inch M/F; 26-inch IC/M choke. Checkered pistol-grip stock and forearm. Made 1973-74.

MODEL 4000 HAMMERLESS SLIDE-ACTION
REPEATING SHOTGUN . . . . **NiB $469 Ex $375 Gd $255**
Custom version of Mossberg Model 500. Full-coverage floral engraving on receiver. Gauges: 12, 20, .410. Three inch chamber. Bbls.: Vent rib; 26-inch IC or SK choke; 28-inch F or M; 30-inch F. Weight: 6-8 lbs. depending on ga. and bbl. Checkered stock and slide handle of select wood. Made in 1975.

MODEL 4000 TRAP GUN . . . . NiB $478 Ex $383 Gd $260
Same as standard Model 4000 except 12 ga. only, has 30-inch F choke bbl., Monte Carlo trap-style stock w/recoil pad. Made in 1975.

MODEL 4500 . . . . NiB $426 Ex $341 Gd $232
Same as Model 4000 except has simpler scroll engraving. Made in 1975.

MODEL 4500 TRAP GUN . . . . NiB $438 Ex $350 Gd $238
Same as Model 4000 Trap Gun except has simpler scroll engraving. Made in 1975.

J. C. PENNEY CO., INC. — Dallas, Texas

MODEL 4011
AUTOLOADING SHOTGUN. . . . . . **NiB $219 Ex $175 Gd $119**
Hammerless. Five shot magazine. Bbls.: 26-inch IC; 28-inch M or F; 30-inch F choke. Weight: 7.25 lbs. Plain pistol-grip stock and slide handle.

MODEL 6610
SINGLE-SHOT SHOTGUN . . . . **NiB $100 Ex $80 Gd $54**
Hammerless. Takedown. Auto ejector. Gauges: 12, 16, 20 and .410. Bbl. length: 28-36 inches. Weight: About 6 lbs. Plain pistol-grip stock and forearm.

MODEL 6630
BOLT-ACTION SHOTGUN . . . . **NiB $138 Ex $110 Gd $75**
Takedown. Gauges: 12, 16, 20. Two shot clip magazine. 26- and 28-inch bbl. lengths; with or without adj. choke. Plain pistol-grip stock. Weight: About 7.25 lbs.

MODEL 6670
SLIDE-ACTION SHOTGUN. . . . . **NiB $163 Ex $130 Gd**
Hammerless. Gauges: 12, 16, 20, and .410. Three shot tubular magazine. Bbls.: 26- to 30-inch; various chokes. Weight: 6.25-7.25 lbs. Walnut finished hardwood stock.

MODEL 6870 SLIDE-ACTION
SHOTGUN . . . . **NiB $231 Ex $182 Gd $126**
Hammerless. Gauges: 12, 16, 20, .410. Four shot magazine. Bbls.: Vent rib; 26- to 30-inch, various chokes. Weight: Average 6.5 lbs. Plain pistol-grip stock.

PERAZZI SHOTGUNS — Manufactured by Manifattura Armi Perazzi, Brescia, Italy

See also listings under Ithaca-Perazzi.

DB81 O/U TRAP . . . . **NiB $4781 Ex $3825 Gd $2601**
Gauge: 12; 2.75-inch chambers. 29.5- or 31.5-inch bbls. w/wide vent rib; M/F chokes. Weight: 8 lbs., 6 oz. Detachable and interchangeable trigger with flat V-springs. Bead front sight. Interchangeable and custom-made checkered stock; beavertail forend. Imported 1988 to date.

DB81 SINGLE-SHOT TRAP . . . . **NiB $4781 Ex $3825 Gd $2601**
Same general specifications as the DB81 over/under except in single bbl. version w/32- or 34-inch wide vent-rib bbl., F choke. Imported 1988 to date.

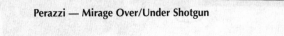

Perazzi — DB81 Over/Under Trap

Perazzi — Mirage Over/Under Shotgun

Perazzi — MX3 Over/Under Shotgun

Perazzi — MX8 Over/Under Shotgun

SHOTGUNS

GRAND AMERICAN 88 SPECIAL SINGLE TRAP
Same general specifications as MX8 Special Single Trap except w/high ramped rib. Fixed choke or screw-in choke tubes.
Model 88 standard . . . . NiB $4219 Ex $3375 Gd $2295
Model 88 w/interchangeable
choke tubes . . . . NiB $4494 Ex $3595 Gd $2445

MIRAGE O/U SHOTGUN
Gauge: 12; 2.75-inch chambers. Bbls.: 27.63-, 29.5- or 31.5-inch vent-rib w/fixed chokes or screw-in choke tubes. Single selective trigger. Weight: 7 to 7.75 lbs. Interchangeable and custom-made checkered buttstock and forend.
Competition Trap,
Skeet, Pigeon, Sporting . . . . NiB $6037 Ex $4830 Gd $3284
Skeet 4-barrel sets . . . . NiB $12,813 Ex $10,250 Gd $6970
Competition Special (w/adj.
4-position trigger) add. $350

MX1 O/U SHOTGUN
Similar to Model MX8 except w/ramp-style, tapered rib and modified stock configuration.
Competition Trap, Skeet,
Pigeon & Sporting . . . . NiB $3150 Ex $2520 Gd $1713
MXlC (w/choke tubes) . . . . . . NiB $3324 Ex $2660 Gd $1808
MXlB (w/flat low rib) . . . . NiB $3024 Ex $2420 Gd $1645

MX2 O/U SHOTGUN
Similar to Model MX8 except w/broad high-ramped competition rib.
Competition-Trap, Skeet,
Pigeon & Sporting . . . . NiB $3813 Ex $3050 Gd $2074
MX2C (w/choke tubes) . . . . . . NiB $4344 Ex $3475 Gd $2363

MX3 O/U SHOTGUN
Similar to Model MX8 except w/ramp-style, tapered rib and modified stock configuration.

(cont'd.) MX3 O/U SHOTGUN
Competition Trap, Skeet,
Pigeon & Sporting . . . . NiB $44941 Ex $35953 Gd $24448
Competition Special (w/adj. 4-position trigger) add $300
Game models . . . . NiB $3994 Ex $3195 Gd $2173
Combo O/U plus SB . . . . NiB $4938 Ex $3950 Gd $2686
SB Trap 32- or 34-inch . . . . NiB $3369 Ex $2695 Gd $1833
Skeet 4-bbl. sets . . . . . . NiB $10,688 Ex $8550 Gd $5814
Skeet Special 4-bbl. sets . . . . NiB $10,906 Ex $8725 Gd $5933

MX3 SPECIAL PIGEON SHOTGUN. . . NiB $4781 Ex $3825 Gd $2601
Gauge: 12; 2.75-inch chambers. 29.5- or 31.5-inch vent rib bbl.; IC/M and extra full chokes. Weight: 8 lbs., 6 oz. Detachable and interchangeable trigger group w/flat V-springs. Bead front sight. Interchangeable and custom-made checkered stock for live pigeon shoots; splinter forend. Imported 1991 to date.

MX4 O/U SHOTGUN
Similar to Model MX3 in appearance and shares the MX8 locking system. Detachable, adj. 4-position trigger standard. Interchangeable choke tubes optional.
Competition Trap, Skeet, Pigeon & Sporting
. . . . NiB $4563 Ex $3650 Gd $2482
MX4C (w/choke tubes) . . . . NiB $4869 Ex $3895 Gd $2649

MX5 O/U GAME GUN
Similar to Model MX8 except in hunting configuration, chambered in 12 or 20 ga. Non-detachable single selective trigger.
MX5 Standard . . . . NiB $3119 Ex $2495 Gd $1697
MX5C (w/choke tubes) . . . . NiB $3438 Ex $2750 Gd $1870

MX6 AMER. TRAP SINGLE-BARREL . . NiB $2875 Ex $2300 Gd $1564
Single shot. Removable trigger group. 12 ga. Barrels: 32- or 34-inch with fixed or choke tubes. Raised vent rib. Checkered European walnut Monte Carlo stock, beavertail forend. Imported 1995 to date.

Perazzi — MX20 Over/Under Game Gun

Perazzi — TMX Single Shot Trap

MX6 SKEET O/U . . . . NiB $3250 Ex $2600 Gd $1768
Same general specs as MX6 American Trap single barrel except over/under; boxlock. Barrels: 26.75- or 27.50-inch. Imported 1995 to date.

MX6 SPORTING O/U . . . . NiB $3412 Ex $2730 Gd $1856
Same specs as MX6 American Trap single barrel except over/under; boxlock. Single selective trigger; external selector. Barrels: 28.38-, 29.50-, or 31.50-inch. Imported 1995 to date.

MX6 TRAP O/U . . . . NiB $2865 Ex $2292 Gd $1558
Same general specs as MX6 American Trap single barrel except over/under; boxlock. Barrels: 29.50-, 30.75-, or 31.50-inch. Imported 1995 to date.

MX7 O/U SHOTGUN . . . . NiB $4063 Ex $3250 Gd $2210
Similar to Model MX12 except w/MX3-style receiver and top-mounted trigger selector. Bbls.: 28.73-, 2.5-, 31.5-inch w/vent rib; screw-in choke tubes. Imported 1992 to date.

MX8 O/U SHOTGUN
Gauge: 12, 2.75-inch chambers. Bbls.: 27.63-, 29.5- or 31.5-inch vent-rib w/fixed chokes or screw-in choke tubes. Weight: 7 to 8.5 lbs. Interchangeable and custom-made checkered stock; beavertail forend. Special models have detachable and interchangeable 4-position trigger group w/flat V-springs. Imported 1988 to date.
MX8 Standard . . . . NiB $3695 Ex $2956 Gd $2010
MX8 Special (adj. 4-pos. trigger) . . . . . . NiB $3795 Ex $3036 Gd $2064
MX8 Special single
(32-or 34-inch bbl.) . . . . NiB $3595 Ex $2876 Gd $1956
MX8 Special combo . . . . NiB $7390 Ex $5912 Gd $4020

MX8/20 O/U SHOTGUN . . . . . NiB $3750 Ex $3000 Gd $2040
Similar to the Model MX8 except w/smaller frame and custom stock. Available in sporting or game configurations with fixed chokes or screw-in tubes. Imported 1993 to date.

MX9 O/U SHOTGUN . . . . NiB $6744 Ex $5395 Gd $3669
Gauge: 12; 2.75-inch chambers. Bbls.: 29.5- or 30.5-inch w/choke tubes and vent side rib. Selective trigger. Checkered walnut stock w/adj. cheekpiece. Available in single bbl., combo, O/U trap, skeet, pigeon and sporting models. Imported 1993 to date.

MX10 O/U SHOTGUN . . . . NiB $6595 Ex $5276 Gd $3588
Similar to the Model MX9 except w/fixed chokes and different rib configuration. Imported 1993 to date.

MX10 PIGEON-ELECTROCIBLES O/U . . . . NiB $6422 Ex $5137 Gd $3493
Over/Under; boxlock. Removable trigger group; external selector. 12 gauge. Barrels: 27.50- or 29.50-inch. Checkered European walnut adjustable stock, beavertail forend. Imported 1995 to date.

MX11 AMERICAN TRAP COMBO . . NiB $5212 Ex $4170 Gd $2835
Over/Under; boxlock. External selector. Removable trigger group; single selective trigger. 12 ga. Bbls: 29-1/2- to 34-inch with fixed or choke tubes; vent rib. European walnut Monte Carlo adjustable stock, beavertail forend. Imported 1995 to date.

**MX11 AMERICAN TRAP
SINGLE BARREL** . . . . NiB $4619 Ex $3695 Gd $2513
Same general specs as MX11 American Trap combo except 32- or 34-inch single bbl. Imported 1995 to date.

MX11 PIGEON-ELECTROCIBLES O/U . NiB $4813 Ex $3850 Gd $2618
Same specs as MX11 American Trap combo except 27.50 O/U bbls. Checkered European walnut pistol grip adjustable stock, beavertail forend. Imported 1995 to date.

MX11 SKEET O/U . . . . NiB $4869 Ex $3895 Gd $2649
Same general specs as MX11 American Trap combo except 26.75 or 27.50-inch O/U bbls. Checkered European walnut pistol-grip adjustable stock, beavertail forend. Imported 1995 to date.

MX11 SPORTING O/U . . . . NiB $5313 Ex $4250 Gd $2890
Same general specs as MX11 American Trap combo except 28.38, 29.50-, or 31.50-inch O/U bbls. Checkered European walnut pistol-grip adjustable stock, beavertail forend. Imported 1995 to date.

MX11 TRAP O/U . . . . NiB $4813 Ex $3850 Gd $2618
Same general specs as MX11 American Trap combo except 29.50,-30.75, or 31.50-inch O/U bbls. Checkered European walnut pistol-grip adjustable stock, beavertail forend. Imported 1995 to date.

MX12 O/U GAME GUN
Gauge: 12, 2.75-inch chambers. Bbls.: 26-, 27.63-, 28.38- or 29.5-inch, vent rib, fixed chokes or screw-in choke tubes. Non-detachable single selective trigger group w/coil springs. Weight: 7.25 lbs. Interchangeable and custom-made checkered stock; Schnabel forend.
MX12 Standard . . . . NiB $4813 Ex $3850 Gd $2618
MX12C (w/choke tubes) . . . . . . NiB $5313 Ex $4250 Gd $2890

**MX14 AMERICAN TRAP
SINGLE-BARREL** . . . . NiB $4044 Ex $3235 Gd $2200
Single shot. Removable trigger group; unsingle configuration. 12 ga. Bbl: 34-inch with fixed or choke tubes; vent rib. Checkered European walnut Monte Carlo adjustable stock, beavertail forend. Imported 1995 to date.

**MX15 AMERICAN TRAP
SINGLE-BARREL** . . . . NiB $4506 Ex $3605 Gd $2451
Full choke. Detachable trigger group. Gauge: 12 only with 2.75-inch chamber. Bbls: 32 and 34-inch. Weight: 8 lbs., 6 oz. .

Piotti
Piuma Boxlock Side-by-Side Shotgun

**Powell No. 7
Aristocrat Grade Double**

MX20 O/U GAME GUN
Gauges: 20, 28 and .410; 2.75- or 3-inch chambers. 26-inch vent-rib bbls., M/F chokes or screw-in chokes. Auto selective ejectors. Selective single trigger. Weight: 6 lbs., 6 oz. Non-detachable coil-spring trigger. Bead front sight. Interchangeable and custom-made checkered stock w/Schnabel forend. Imported from 1988 to date.

Standard grade	NiB $4744	Ex $3795	Gd $2581
Standard grade			
w/gold outline	NiB $8253	Ex $6602	Gd $4489
MX20C w/choke tubes	NiB $5100	Ex $4080	Gd $2774
SC3 grade	NiB $8906	Ex $7125	Gd $4845
SCO grade	NiB $12,291	Ex $9832	Gd $6686

MX28 O/U GAME GUN . . . NiB $13,688 Ex $10,950 Gd $7446
Similar to the Model MX12 except chambered in 28 ga. w/26-inch bbls. fitted to smaller frame. Imported 1993 to date.

MX410 O/U GAME GUN . . . . . NiB $13,688 Ex $10,950 Gd $7446
Similar to the Model MX12 except in .410 bore w/3-inch chambers, 26-inch bbls. fitted to smaller frame. Imported 1993 to date.

TM1 SPECIAL
SINGLE-SHOT TRAP . . . . NiB $4103 Ex $3282 Gd $2231
Gauge: 12- 2.75-inch chambers. 32- or 34-inch bbl. w/wide vent rib; full choke. Weight: 8 lbs., 6 oz. Detachable and interchangeable trigger group with coil springs. Bead front sight. Interchangeable and custom-made stock w/checkered pistol grip and beavertail forend. Imported 1988 to date.

TMX SPECIAL
SINGLE-SHOT TRAP . . . . NiB $4263 Ex $3410 Gd $2318
Same general specifications as Model TM1 Special except w/ultra-high rib. Interchangeable choke tubes optional.

PIOTTI SHOTGUNS — Italy

BOSS O/U . . . . NiB $34,000 Ex $28,000 Gd $13,000
Over/Under; sidelock. Gauges: 12 or 20. Barrels: 26- to 32-inch. Standard chokes. Best quality walnut. Custom-made to customer's specifications. Imported 1993 to date.

KING NO. 1 SIDELOCK . . . NiB $20,900 Ex $17,000 Gd $7000
Gauges: 10, 12, 16, 20, 28 and .410. 25- to 30-inch bbls. (12 ga.), 25- to 28-inch (other ga.). Weight: About 5 lbs. (.410) to 8 lbs. (12 ga.) Holland & Holland pattern sidelock. Double triggers standard. Coin finish or color casehardened. Level file-cut rib. Full-coverage scroll engraving, gold inlays. Hand-rubbed, oil-finished, straight-grip stock with checkered butt, splinter forend.

KING EXTRA SIDE-BY-SIDE
SHOTGUN . . . . NiB $21,125 Ex $17,000 Gd $10,000
Same general specifications as the Piotti King No. 1 except has choice of engraving, gold inlays, plus stock is of exhibition-grade wood.

LUNIK SIDE-LOCK
SHOTGUN
. . . . NiB $21,438 Ex $17,950 Gd $13,486
Same general specifications as the Monte Carlo model except has level, file-cut rib. Renaissance-style, large scroll engraving in relief, gold crown in top lever, gold name, and gold crest in forearm, finely figured wood.

MONTE CARLO
SIDE-LOCK SHOTGUN . . . . . NiB $10,938 Ex $8750 Gd $5950
Gauges: 10, 12, 16, 20, 28 or .410. Bbls.: 25- to 30-inch. Holland & Holland pattern sidelock. Weight: 5-8 lbs. Automatic ejectors. Double triggers. Hand-rubbed oil-finished straight-grip stock with checkered butt. Choice of Purdey-style scroll and rosette or Holland & Holland-style large scroll engraving.

PIUMA BOXLOCK
SIDE-BY-SIDE SHOTGUN . . . . NiB $10,494 Ex $8395 Gd $5709
Same general specifications as the Monte Carlo model except has Anson & Deeley boxlock action w/demi-bloc bbls., scalloped frame. Standard scroll and rosette engraving. Hand-rubbed, oil-finished straight-grip stock.

WILLIAM POWELL & SON LTD. — Birmingham, England

NO. 1 BEST GRADE
DOUBLE-BARREL
SHOTGUN . . . . NiB $50,112 Ex $39,000 Gd $18,000
Sidelock. Gauges: Made to order with 12, 16 and 20 the most common. Bbls.: Made to order in any length but 28 inches was recommended. Highest grade French walnut buttstock and forearm with fine checkering. Metal elaborately engraved. Imported by Stoeger about 1938-51.

NO. 2 BEST GRADE
DOUBLE-BARREL . . . . . . NiB $27,500 Ex $22,000 Gd $14,960
Same general specifications as the Powell No. 1 except plain finish without engraving. Imported by Stoeger about 1938-51.

NO. 6 CROWN GRADE
DOUBLE-BARREL . . . . NiB $13,750 Ex $11,000 Gd $7480
Boxlock. Gauges: Made to order with 12, 16 and 20 the most common. Bbls.: Made to order, but 28 inches was recommended. Highest grade French walnut buttstock and forearm w/fine checkering. Metal elaborately engraved. Uses Anson & Deeley locks. Imported by Stoeger about 1938-51.

NO. 7 ARISTOCRAT GRADE
DOUBLE-BARREL
SHOTGUN . . . . NiB $6875 Ex $5500 Gd $740
Same general specifications as the Powell No. 6 except w/lower quality wood and metal engraving.

SHOTGUNS

Premier Ambassador
Field Grade

Premier Continental
Field Grade

PRECISION SPORTS SHOTGUNS —
Cortland, New York, Manufactured by
Ignacio Ugartechea, Spain

600 SERIES AMERICAN HAMMERLESS DOUBLES

Boxlock. Single selective trigger. Selective automatic ejectors. Automatic safety. Gauges: 12, 16, 20, 28, .410; 2.75- or 3-inch chambers. Bbls.: 26-,27- or 28-inch w/raised matte rib; choked IC/M or M/F. Weight: 5.75-7 lbs. Checkered pistol-grip walnut buttstock with beavertail forend. Engraved silvered receiver with blued bbls. Imported from Spain 1986-94.

640A (12, 16, 20 ga. w/extractors) ...... NiB $846 Ex $677 Gd $460
640A (28, .410 ga. w/extractors) .... NiB $984 Ex $787 Gd $535
640 Slug Gun (12 ga. w/extractors) ..... NiB $964 Ex $771 Gd $525
645A (12, 16, 20 ga. w/ejectors) .... NiB $912 Ex $729 Gd $496
645A (28, .410 ga. w/ejectors) .... NiB $1116 Ex $892 Gd $606
645A (20/28 ga. two-bbl. set) .... NiB $1306 Ex $1044 Gd $710
650A (12 ga. w/extractors, choke tubes) ... NiB $859 Ex $687 Gd $467
655A (12 ga. w/ejectors, choke tubes) ... NiB $951 Ex $761 Gd $517

600 SERIES ENGLISH HAMMERLESS DOUBLES

Boxlock. Same general specifications as American 600 series except w/double triggers and concave rib. Checkered English-style walnut stock w/splinter forend, straight grip and oil finish.

640E (12, 16, 20 ga. w/extractors) ...... NiB $728 Ex $582 Gd $395
640E (28, .410 ga. w/extractors) .... NiB $820 Ex $656 Gd $446
640 Slug Gun (12 ga. w/extractors) ...... NiB $964 Ex $771 Gd $525
645E (12, 16, 20 ga. w/ejectors) .... NiB $984 Ex $787 Gd $535
645E (28, .410 ga. w/ejectors) .... NiB $938 Ex $750 Gd $510
645E (20/28 ga. two-bbl. set) .... NiB $1240 Ex $992 Gd $675
650E (12 ga. w/extractors, choke tubes) .... NiB $853 Ex $682 Gd $464
655E (12 ga. w/ejectors, choke tubes) .... NiB $912 Ex $729 Gd $496

MODEL 640M MAGNUM 10 HAMMERLESS DOUBLE

Similar to Model 640E except in 10 ga. w/3.5-inch Mag. chambers. Bbls.: 26-, 30-, 32-inch choked F/F.

Model 640M Big Ten, Turkey ..... NiB $844 Ex $675 Gd $459
Model 640M Goose Gun........ NiB $869 Ex $695 Gd $473

MODEL 645E-XXV HAMMERLESS DOUBLE

Similar to Model 645E except w/25-inch bbl. and Churchill-style rib.

645E-XXV (12, 16, 20 ga. w/ejectors) ...... NiB $912 Ex $729 Gd $496
645E-XXV (28, .410 ga. w/ejectors) ...... NiB $1043 Ex $834 Gd $568

PREMIER SHOTGUNS

Premier shotguns have been produced by various gunmakers in Europe.

AMBASSADOR MODEL
FIELD GRADE HAMMERLESS
DOUBLE-BARREL SHOTGUN..... NiB $416 Ex $332 Gd $226

Sidelock. Plain extractors. Double triggers. Gauges: 12, 16, 20, .410. 3-inch chambers in 20 and .410 ga., 2.75- inch in 12 and 16 ga. Bbls.: 26-inch in .410 ga., 28 inch in other ga.; choked M/F. Weight: 6 lbs., 3 oz.-7 lbs., 3 oz. depending on gauge. Checkered pistol-grip stock and beavertail forearm. Intro. in 1957; disc.

BRUSH KING .... NiB $297 Ex $237 Gd $161

Same as standard Regent model except chambered for 12 (2.75-inch) and 20 ga. (3-inch) only; has 22-inch bbls., IC/M choke, straight-grip stock. Weight: 6 lbs., 3 oz. in 12 ga.; 5 lbs., 12 oz. in 20 ga. Introduced in 1959; disc.

CONTINENTAL MODEL
FIELD GRADE HAMMER
DOUBLE-BARREL SHOTGUN..... NiB $416 Ex $332 Gd $226

Sidelock. Exposed hammers. Plain extractors. Double triggers. Gauges: 12, 16, 20, .410. Three inch chambers in 20 and .410 ga., 2.75-inch in 12 and 16 ga. Bbls.: 26-inch in .410 ga.; 28-inch in other ga.; choked M/F. Weight: 6 lbs., 3 oz.-7 lbs., 3 oz. depending on gauge. Checkered pistol-grip stock and English-style forearm. Introduced in 1957; disc.

MONARCH SUPREME GRADE HAMMERLESS
DOUBLE-BARREL SHOTGUN..... NiB $445 Ex $356 Gd $242

Boxlock. Auto ejectors. Double triggers. Gauges: 12, 20. 2.75-inch chambers in 12 ga., 3-inch in 20 ga. Bbls.: 28-inch M/F; 26-inch IC/M choke. Weight: 6 lbs., 6 oz., 7 lbs., 2 oz. depending on gauge and bbl. Checkered pistol-grip stock and beavertail forearm of fancy walnut. Introduced in 1959; disc.

PRESENTATION
CUSTOM GRADE .... NiB $1128 Ex $902 Gd $613

Similar to Monarch model but made to order of higher quality with hunting scene engraving, gold and silver inlay, fancier wood. Introduced in 1959; disc.

REGENT 10 GA.
MAGNUM EXPRESS .... NiB $350 Ex $280 Gd $190

Same as standard Regent model except chambered for 10-ga. Magnum 3.5-inch shells, has heavier construction, 32-inch bbls. choked F/F, stock with recoil pad. Weight: 11.25 lbs. Introduced in 1957; disc.

REGENT 12 GA.
MAGNUM EXPRESS .... NiB $314 Ex $251 Gd $171

Same as standard Regent model except chambered for 12-ga. Magnum 3-inch shells, has 30-inch bbls. choked F and F, stock with recoil pad. Weight: 7.25 lbs. Introduced in 1957; disc.

Purdey Hammerless
Double-Barrel Shotgun

Purdey Over and Under

Purdey Single-Shot Trap

SHOTGUNS

REGENT FIELD GRADE
HAMMERLESS
DOUBLE-BARREL SHOTGUN. . . . . NiB $281 Ex $225 Gd $153
Boxlock. Plain extractors. Double triggers. Gauges: 12,16, 20, 28, .410. Three inch chambers in 20 and .410 ga., 2.75-inch in other gauges. Bbls.: 26-inch IC/M, M/F (28 and .410 ga. only); 28-inch M/F; 30-inch M/F (12 ga. only). Weight: 6 lbs., 2 oz.-7 lbs., 4 oz. depending on gauge and bbl. Checkered pistol-grip stock and beavertail forearm. Introduced in 1955; disc.

JAMES PURDEY & SONS, LTD. —
London, England

HAMMERLESS DOUBLE-BARREL SHOTGUN
Sidelock. Auto ejectors. Single or double triggers. Gauges: 12, 16, 20. Bbls.: 26-, 27-, 28-, 30-inch (latter in 12 ga. only);any boring, any shape or style of rib. Weight: 5.25-5.5 lbs. depending on model, gauge and bbl length. Checkered stock and forearm, straight grip standard, pistol-grip also available. Purdey guns of this type have been made from about 1880 to date. Models include: Game Gun, Featherweight Game Gun, Two-Inch Gun (chambered for 12 ga. 2-inch shells), Pigeon Gun (w/3rd fastening and side clips), values of all models are the same.
With double triggers. . . . . NiB $40,625 Ex $32,500 Gd $22,100
With single trigger . . . . . . NiB $43,438 Ex $34,750 Gd $23,630

OVER/UNDER SHOTGUN
Sidelock. Auto ejectors. Single or double triggers. Gauges: 12 16, 20. Bbls.: 26-, 27-, 28-, 30-inch (latter in 12 ga. only); any boring, any style rib. Weight: 6-7.5 pounds depending on gauge and bbl. length. Checkered stock and forend, straight or pistol grip. Prior to WW II, the Purdey Over/Under Gun was made with a Purdey action; since the war James Purdey & Sons have acquired the business of James Woodward & Sons and all Purdey over/under guns are now built on the Woodward principle. General specifications of both types are the same.
With Purdey act., double triggers . . . NiB $80,000 Ex $50,000 Gd $22,000
With Woodward action,
double triggers . . . . NiB $55,750 Ex $45,000 Gd $31,240
W/single trigger, add . . . . NiB $1875 Ex $1500 Gd $1020

Purdey Hammerless
Double-Barrel Shotgun

Purdey Hammerless
Double-Barrel Shotgun
w/Single Trigger

SINGLE-BARREL TRAP GUN . NiB $11,625 Ex $9300 Gd $6324
Sidelock. Mechanical features similar to those of the over/under model with Purdey action. 12 ga. only. Built to customer's specifications. Made prior to World War II.

REMINGTON ARMS CO. — Ilion, New York

Eliphalet Remington Jr. began making long arms with his father in 1816. In 1828 they moved their facility to Ilion, N.Y., where it remained a family-run business for decades. As the family began to diminish, other people bought controlling interests and today, still a successful gunmaking company, it is a subsidiary of the DuPont Corporation.

**Remington Model 11-87
Premier Autoloader**

MODEL 10A STANDARD GRADE
SLIDE-ACTION REPEATING SHOTGUN . . . . . NiB $361 Ex $288 Gd $196
Hammerless. Takedown. 6-shot. 12 ga. only. Five shell tubular magazine. Bbls.: Plain; 26- to 32-inch; choked F, M or Cyl. Weight: About 7.5 lbs. Plain pistol-grip stock, grooved slide handle. Made 1907-29.

MODEL 11 SPECIAL, TOURNAMENT, EXPERT AND PREMIER GRADE GUNS
These higher grade models differ from the Model 11A in general quality, grade of wood, checkering, engraving, etc. General specifications are the same.
Model 11B Special grade . . . . NiB $557 Ex $446 Gd $303
Model 11D Tournament grade . . . NiB $1116 Ex $892 Gd $606
Model 11E Expert grade . . . . . . NiB $1568 Ex $1254 Gd $853
Model 11F Premier grade . . . . . NiB $2526 Ex $2021 Gd $1374

MODEL 11A STANDARD GRADE AUTOLOADER
Hammerless Browning type. 5-shot. Takedown. Gauges: 12, 16, 20. Tubular magazine holds four shells. Bbls.: Plain, solid or vent rib, lengths from 26-32 inches, F, M, IC, Cyl., SK chokes. Weight: About 8 lbs., 12 ga.; 7.5 lbs., 16 ga.; 7.25 lbs., 20 ga. Checkered pistol grip and forend. Made 1905-49.
With plain barrel . . . . NiB $313 Ex $250 Gd $170
With solid-rib barrel . . . . NiB $406 Ex $325 Gd $221
With ventilated-rib barrel . . . . NiB $456 Ex $365 Gd $248

MODEL 11R RIOT GUN . . . . NiB $361 Ex $288 Gd $196
Same as Model 11A Standard grade except has 20-inch plain barrel, 12 ga. only. Remington Model 11-48. (See Remington Sportsman-48 Series.)

MODEL 11-87 PREMIER AUTOLOADER
Gas-operated. Hammerless. Gauge: 12; 3-inch chamber. Bbl.: 26-, 28- or 30-inch with REMChoke. Weight: 8.13- 8.38 lbs., depending on bbl. length. Checkered walnut stock and forend in satin finish. Made 1987 to date.
Premier Deer Gun . . . . NiB $529 Ex $423 Gd $288
Premier Deer Gun w/cant-
ilever scope mount . . . . NiB $670 Ex $480 Gd $292
Premier Skeet . . . . NiB $543 Ex $434 Gd $295
Premier Sporting Clays . . . . NiB $650 Ex $520 Gd $354
Premier Sporting Clays SCNP (nickel plated) . . . . . NiB $688 Ex $550 Gd $374
Premier Standard Autoloader . . . . NiB $543 Ex $434 Gd $295
Premier Trap. . . . . NiB $639 Ex $511 Gd $347
Left-hand models, add. $55

MODEL 11-87 SPECIAL PURPOSE MAGNUM
Same general specifications as Model 11-87 Premier except with non-reflective wood finish and Parkerized metal. 21-, 26- or 28-inch vent-rib bbl. with REMChoke tubes. Made 1987-93.
Model 11-87 SP Field Magnum . . . . NiB $637 Ex $510 Gd $346
Model 11-87 SP Deer Gun (w/21-inch bbl.). . . NiB $577 Ex $462 Gd $314
Model 11-87 SP Deer Gun
w/cantilever scope mount. . . . . NiB $625 Ex $500 Gd $340

MODEL 11-87 SPS MAGNUM
Same general specifications as Model 11-87 Special Purpose Magnum except with synthetic buttstock and forend. 21-, 26- or 28-inch vent-rib bbl. with REMChoke tubes. Matte black or Mossy Oak camo finish (except NWTF turkey gun). Made 1990 to date.
Model 11-87 SPS Magnum (matte black) . . . . . NiB $570 Ex $456 Gd $310
Model 11-87 SPS Camo (Mossy Oak camo) . . NiB $598 Ex $478 Gd $325
Model 11-87 SPS Deer Gun (w/21 inch bbl.). . NiB $515 Ex $412 Gd $280
Model 11-87 SPS Deer Gun w/cant. scope mt. . . . . NiB $584 Ex $467 Gd $317
Model 11-87 NWTF Turkey Gun
(Brown Trebark) disc. 1993. . . . . NiB $680 Ex $544 Gd $370
Model 11-87 NWTF Turkey Gun
(Greenleaf) disc. 1996. . . . . NiB $653 Ex $522 Gd $355
Model 11-87 NWTF Turkey
Gun (Mossy Oak) disc. 1996. . . . . NiB $666 Ex $533 Gd $363
Model 11-87 NWTF Turkey Gun
(Mossy Oak Breakup) introduced 1999 . . . . . NiB $680 Ex $544 Gd $370
Model 11-87 NWTF 20 ga. Turkey Gun
(Mossy Oak Breakup) Produced 1998 only . . . NiB $639 Ex $511 Gd $347
Model 11-87 SPST Turkey Gun (matte bl.) . . . NiB $584 Ex $467 Gd $317

MODEL 11-96 EURO LIGHTWEIGHT
AUTOLOADING SHOTGUN . . . . NiB $635 Ex $508 Gd $345
Lightweight version of Model 11-87 w/reprofiled receiver. 12 ga. only w/3-inch chamber. 26- or 28-inch bbl. w/6mm vent rib and REM Choke tubes. Semi-fancy Monte Carlo walnut buttstock and forearm. Weight: 6.8 lbs. w/26-inch bbl. Made 1996 to date.

MODEL 17A STANDARD GRADE SLIDE-ACTION REPEATING SHOTGUN
Hammerless. Takedown. Five shot. 20 ga. only. Four shell tubular magazine. Bbls.: plain; 26- to 32-inch; choked F, M or Cyl. Weight: About 5.75 lbs. Plain pistol-grip stock, grooved slide handle. Made 1921-33. Note: The present Ithaca Model 37 is an adaptation of this Browning design.
Plain barrel . . . . NiB $387 Ex $309 Gd $211
Solid rib. . . . . NiB $518 Ex $414 Gd $282

MODEL 29A STANDARD GRADE
SLIDE-ACTION REPEATING SHOTGUN . . . . . NiB $416 Ex $332 Gd $226
Hammerless. Takedown. Six shot. 12 ga. only. Five shell tubular magazine. Bbls.: plain- 26- to 32-inch, choked F, M or Cyl. Weight: About 7.5 lbs. Checkered pistol-grip stock and slide handle. Made 1929-33.

MODEL 29T TARGET GRADE . . . . . NiB $478 Ex $383 Gd $260
Same general specifications as Model 29A except has trap-style stock with straight grip, extension slide handle, vent rib bbl. Disc. 1933.

MODEL 31 AND 31L SKEET GRADE
Same general specifications as Model 31A except has 26-inch bbl. with raised solid or vent rib, SK choke, checkered pistol-grip stock and beavertail forend. Weight: About 8 lbs., 12 ga. Made 1932-1939.
Model 31 Standard w/raised solid rib . . . . NiB $742 Ex $594 Gd $404
Model 31 Standard w/ventilated rib . . . . . NiB $892 Ex $714 Gd $486
Model 31L Lightweight w/raised solid rib . . . . NiB $675 Ex $540 Gd $367
Model 31L Lightweight w/ventilated rib . . NiB $817 Ex $654 Gd $445

Remington Model 11-87 SPS

Remington Model 11-87 SPS Camo

Remington Model 11-87 SP Walnut Stock

Remington Model SP-10 Magnum Camo

MODEL 31 SPECIAL, TOURNAMENT, EXPERT AND PREMIER GRADE GUNS
These higher grade models differ from the Model 31A in general quality, grade of wood, checkering, engraving, etc. General specifications are the same.
Model 31B Special grade . . . . NiB $653 Ex $522 Gd $355
Model 31D Tournament grade . . . . NiB $944 Ex $755 Gd $513
Model 31E Expert grade . . . . NiB $1300 Ex $1040 Gd $707
Model 31F Premier grade . . . . . NiB $2119 Ex $1695 Gd $1153

MODEL 31A SLIDE-ACTION REPEATER
Hammerless. Takedown. 3- or 5-shot. Gauges: 12, 16, 20. Tubular magazine. Bbls.: Plain, solid or vent rib; lengths from 26 -32 inches; F, M, IC, C or SK choke. Weight: About 7.5 lbs., 12 ga.; 6.75 lbs., 16 ga.; 6.5 lbs., 20 ga. Earlier models have checkered pistol-grip stock and slide handle; later models have plain stock and grooved slide handle. Made 1931-49.
Model 31A with plain barrel . . . . . NiB $385 Ex $308 Gd $209
Model 31A with solid rib barrel . . . NiB $469 Ex $375 Gd $255
Model 31A with vent rib barrel . . . NiB $504 Ex $403 Gd $274
Model 31H Hunters' Special
w/sporting-style stock . . . . NiB $469 Ex $375 Gd $255
Model 31R Riot Gun w/20-
inch plain bbl., 12 ga. . . . . NiB $328 Ex $262 Gd $178

MODEL 31S TRAP SPECIAL/31TC TRAP GRADE
Same general specifications as Model 31A except 12 ga. only, has 30- or 32-inch vent-rib bbl., F choke, checkered trap stock with full pistol grip and recoil pad, checkered extension beavertail forend. Weight: About 8 lbs. (Trap Special has solid-rib bbl., half pistol-grip stock with standard walnut forend).
Model 31S Trap Special . . . . NiB $504 Ex $403 Gd $274
Model 31TC Trap grade . . . . NiB $669 Ex $535 Gd $364

MODEL 32 SKEET GRADE
Same general specifications as Model 32A except 26- or 28-inch bbl., SK choke, beavertail forend, selective single trigger only. Weight: About 7.5 lbs. Made 1932-42.

MODEL 32 TOURNAMENT, EXPERT AND PREMIER GRADE GUNS
These higher-grade models differ from the Model 32A in general quality, grade of wood, checkering, engraving, etc. General specifications are the same. Made 1932-42.
Model 32D Tournament grade . . . . NiB $3744 Ex $2995 Gd $2037
Model 32E Expert grade . . . . . . NiB $4691 Ex $3752 Gd $2551
Model 32F Premier grade . . . . NiB $6375 Ex $5100 Gd $3468

MODEL 32A STANDARD GRADE O/U
Hammerless. Takedown. Auto ejectors. Early model had double triggers, later built with selective single trigger only. 12 ga. only. Bbls.: Plain, raised matted solid or vent rib; 26-, 28-, 30-, 32-inch; F/M choke standard, option of any combination of F, M, IC, C, SK choke. Weight: About 7.75 lbs. Checkered pistol-grip stock and forend. Made 1932-42.
With double triggers . . . . NiB $1938 Ex $1550 Gd $1054
With selective single trigger . . . NiB $2188 Ex $1750 Gd $1190
With raised solid rib, add $200
With ventilated rib, add $300

MODEL 32TC
TARGET (TRAP) GRADE . . . . . . NiB $3032 Ex $2425 Gd $1649
Same general specifications as Model 32A except 30- or 32-inch vent-rib bbl., F choke, trap-style stock with checkered pistol-grip and beavertail forend. Weight: About 8 lbs. Made 1932-42.

MODEL 89 (1889) . . . . NiB $1188 Ex $950 Gd $646
Hammers. Circular action. Gauges: 10, 12, 16, 28- to 32-inch bls.; steel or Damascus twist. Weight 7-10 lbs. Made 1889-1908.

MODEL 90-T SINGLE-SHOT TRAP . . . . . NiB $1995 Ex $1596 Gd $1085
Gauge: 12; 2.75-inch chambers. 30-, 32- or 34-inch vent-rib bbl. with fixed chokes or screw-in REMChokes; ported or non-ported. Weight: 8.25 lbs. Checkered American walnut standard or Monte Carlo stock with low-luster finish. Engraved sideplates and drop-out trigger group optional. Made 1990-97.

SHOTGUNS

Remington Model 870
Competition Trap

Remington Model 870
Brushmaster

Remington Model 870
Express Super Magnum

Remington Model 870
Marine Magnum

Remington Model 870
Special Field

MODEL 396 O/U
Boxlock. 12 ga. only w/2.75-inch chamber. 28- and 30-inch blued bbls. w/Rem chokes. Weight: 7.50 lbs. Nitride-grayed, engraved receiver, trigger guard, tang, hinge pins and forend metal. Engraved sideplates. Checkered satin-finished American walnut stock w/target style forend. Made 1996 to date.

396 Sporting
Clays . . . . NiB $1875 Ex $1500 Gd $1020
396 Skeet. . . . . NiB $1942 Ex $1554 Gd $1057

MODEL 870
"ALL AMERICAN" TRAP GUN . . . . NiB $996 Ex $797 Gd $542
Same as Model 870TB except custom grade with engraved receiver, trigger guard and bbl.; Monte Carlo or straight-comb stock and forend of fancy walnut; available only with 30-inch F choke bbl. Made 1972-77.

MODEL 870 COMPETITION TRAP
. . . . NiB $563 Ex $450 Gd $306
Based on standard Model 870 receiver except is single-shot with gas-assisted recoil-reducing system, new choke design, a high step-up vent rib and redesigned stock, forend with cut checkering and satin finish. Weight: 8.5 lbs. Made 1981-87.

MODEL 870 STANDARD. . . . . NiB $369 Ex $295 Gd $201
Same as Model 870 Wingmaster Riot Gun except has rifle-type sights.

MODEL 870 BRUSHMASTER DELUXE
Same as Model 870 Standard except available in 20 ga. as well as 12, has cut-checkered, satin-finished American walnut stock and forend, recoil pad.
Right-hand model . . . . NiB $405 Ex $324 Gd $221
Left-hand model . . . . NiB $474 Ex $379 Gd $258

MODEL 870 EXPRESS
Same general specifications Model 870 Wingmaster except has low-luster walnut-finished hardwood stock with pressed checkering and black recoil pad. Gauges: 12, 20 or .410, 3-inch chambers. Bbls.: 26- or 28-inch vent-rib with REMChoke; 25-inch vent-rib with fixed choke (.410 only). Black oxide metal finish. Made 1987 to date.
Model 870 Express (12 or
20 ga., REMChoke) . . . . NiB $244 Ex $195 Gd $133
Model 870 Express
(.410 w/fixed choke) . . . . NiB $276 Ex $220 Gd $150
Express Combo (w/extra
20-inch deer bbl.) . . . . NiB $331 Ex $265 Gd $180

Remington Model 870
Special Purpose Deer Gun

Remington Model 870
Wingmaster Field Gun

MODEL 870 EXPRESS DEER GUN
Same general specifications as Model 870 Express except in 12 ga. only, 20-inch bbl. with fixed IC choke, adj. rifle sights and Monte Carlo stock. Made 1991 to date.
Express Deer Gun
w/standard barrel . . . . NiB $268 Ex $215 Gd $145
Express Deer Gun
w/rifled barrel . . . . NiB $302 Ex $241 Gd $163

MODEL 870 EXPRESS SUPER MAGNUM
Similar to Model 870 Express except chambered for 12 ga. mag. w/3.5-inch chamber. Bbls.: 23-, 26- or 28-inch vent rib w/REM Choke. Checkered low-luster walnut-finished hardwood, black synthetic or camo buttstock and forearm. Matte black oxide metal finish or full camo finish. Made 1998 to date.
Model 870 ESM
(w/hardwood stock) . . . . NiB $254 Ex $203 Gd $138
Model 870 ESM
(w/black synthetic stock) . . . . NiB $268 Ex $214 Gd $146
Model 870 ESM
(w/camo synthetic stock) . . . . NiB $364 Ex $291 Gd $198
Model 870 ESM Synthetic
Turkey (w/synthetic stock) . . . . NiB $268 Ex $214 Gd $146
Model 870 ESM como
Turkey (w/full camo) . . . . NiB $344 Ex $275 Gd $187
Model 870 ESM combo
(w/full camo, extra bbl.) . . . . NiB $405 Ex $324 Gd $221

MODEL 870 EXPRESS
SYNTHETIC HOME DEFENSE . . . . . NiB $242 Ex $194 Gd $132
Slide action, hammerless, takedown. 12 ga. only. 18-inch bbl. w/cylinder choke and bead front sight. Positive checkered synthetic stock and forend with non-reflective black finish. Made 1995 to date.

MODEL 870EXPRESS TURKEY GUN . . . NiB $268 Ex $203 Gd $214
Same general specifications as Model 870 Express except has 21-inch vent-rib bbl. and Turkey Extra-Full REMChoke. Made 1991 to date.

MODEL 870 EXPRESS YOUTH GUN . . NiB $254 Ex $203 Gd $138
Same general specifications as Model 870 Express except has scaled-down stock with 12.5-inch pull and 21-inch vent rib bbl. with REMChoke. Made 1991 to date.

MODEL 870 LIGHTWEIGHT
Same as standard Model 870 but with scaled-down receiver and lightweight mahogany stock; 20 ga. only. 2.75-inch chamber. Bbls.: plain or vent rib; 26-inch, IC; 28-inch, M or F choke. REMChoke available from 1987. Weight 5.75 lbs. w/26-inch plain bbl. American walnut stock and forend with satin or Hi-gloss finish. Made 1972-94.
With plain barrel . . . . NiB $279 Ex $223 Gd $152
With ventilated rib barrel . . . . NiB $308 Ex $247 Gd $168
With REMChoke barrel . . . . NiB $350 Ex $280 Gd $190

MODEL 870 LIGHTWEIGHT MAGNUM
Same as Model 870 Lightweight but chambered for 20 ga. Magnum 3-inch shell; 28-inch bbl., plain or vent rib, F choke. Weight: 6 lbs. with plain bbl. Made 1972-94.
With plain barrel . . . . NiB $338 Ex $270 Gd $184
With ventilated rib barrel . . . . NiB $385 Ex $308 Gd $209

MODEL 870 MAGNUM DUCK GUN
Same as Model 870 Field Gun except has 3-inch chamber 12 and 20 gauge Magnum only. 28- or 30-inch bbl., plain or vent rib, M or F choke, recoil pad. Weight: About 7 or 6.75 lbs. Made 1964 to date.
With plain barrel . . . . NiB $405 Ex $324 Gd $221
With ventilated rib barrel . . . . NiB $446 Ex $357 Gd $243

MODEL 870
MARINE MAGNUM . . . . NiB $424 Ex $339 Gd $251
Same general specifications as Model 870 Wingmaster except with 7-shot magazine, 18-inch plain bbl. with fixed IC choke, bead front sight and nickel finish. Made 1992 to date.

MODEL 870
SA SKEET GUN, SMALLBORE. . . . . NiB $406 Ex $325 Gd $221
Similar to Wingmaster Model 870SA except chambered for 28 and .410 ga. (2.5-inch chamber for latter); 25-inch vent rib bbl., SK choke. Weight: 6 lbs., 28 ga.; 6.5 lbs., .410. Made 1969-82.

MODEL 870 MISSISSIPPI
MAGNUM DUCK GUN . . . . NiB $416 Ex $332 Gd $226
Same as Remington Model 870 Magnum duck gun except has 32-inch bbl. "Ducks Unlimited" engraved receiver, Made in 1983.

MODEL 870
SPECIAL FIELD SHOTGUN . . . . NiB $405 Ex $324 Gd $221
Pump action. Hammerless. Gauge: 12 or 20. 21-inch vent-rib bbl. with REMChoke. 41.5 inches overall. Weight: 6-7 lbs. Straight-grip checkered walnut stock and forend. Made 1987-95.

MODEL 870 SPECIAL PURPOSE DEER GUN
Similar to Special Purpose Magnum except with 20-inch IC choke, rifle sights. Matte black oxide and Parkerized finish. Oil-finished, checkered buttstock and forend with recoil pad. Made 1986 to date.
Model 870 SP Deer Gun . . . . NiB $344 Ex $275 Gd $187
Model 870 SP Deer Gun,
cant. scope mt. . . . . NiB $406 Ex $325 Gd $221

MODEL 870 SPECIAL
PURPOSE MAGNUM . . . . NiB $405 Ex $324 Gd $221
Similar to the 870 Magnum duck gun except with 26-, 28- or 30-inch vent rib REMChoke bbl.12 ga. only; 3-inch chamber. Oil-finished field-grade stock with recoil pad, QD swivels and Cordura sling. Made 1985 to date.

**Remington Model 870TC
Wingmaster Trap**

MODEL 870SPS MAGNUM
Same general specifications Model 870 Special Purpose Magnum except with synthetic stock and forend. 26- or 28-inch vent-rib bbl. with REMChoke tubes. Matte black or Mossy Oak camo finish. Made 1991 to date.
70 SPS Mag. (black syn. stock) .... NiB $388 Ex $310 Gd $211
870 SPS-T Camo (Mossy Oak camo)...... NiB $402 Ex $322 Gd $218

MODEL 870 WINGMASTER FIELD GUN
Same general specifications as Model 870AP except checkered stock and forend. Later models have REMChoke systems in 12 ga. Made 1964 to date.
With plain barrel .... NiB $266 Ex $212 Gd $144
With ventilated rib barrel .... NiB $313 Ex $250 Gd $170

MODEL 870 WINGMASTER FIELD GUN, SMALL BORE
Same as standard Model 870 except w/scaled-down lightweight receivers. Gauges: 28 and .410. Plain or vent rib 25-inch bbl. choked IC, M or F. Weight: 5.5-6.25 lbs. depending on gauge and bbl. Made 1969-94.
With plain barrel .... NiB $503 Ex $402 Gd $273
With ventilated-rib barrel .... NiB $579 Ex $454 Gd $309

MODEL 870 WINGMASTER
MAGNUM DELUXE GRADE ...... NiB $507 Ex $406 Gd $276
Same as Model 870 Magnum standard grade except has checkered stock and extension beavertail forearm, bbl. with matted top surface. Disc. in 1963.

MODEL 870 WINGMASTER
MAGNUM STANDARD GRADE ... NiB $445 Ex $356 Gd $242
Same as Model 870AP except chambered for 12 ga. 3-inch Magnum, 30-inch F choke bbl., recoil pad. Weight: About 8.25 lbs. Made 1955-63.

MODEL 870 WINGMASTER REMCHOKE SERIES
Slide action, hammerless, takedown with blued all-steel receiver. Gauges: 12, 20; 3-inch chamber. Tubular magazine. Bbls.: 21-, 26-, 28-inch vent-rib with REM Choke. Weight: 7.5 lbs. (12 ga.). Satin-finished, checkered walnut buttstock and forend with recoil pad. Right- or left-hand models. Made 1986 to date.
Standard model, 12 ga. .... NiB $332 Ex $265 Gd $180
Standard model, 20 ga. .... NiB $354 Ex $283 Gd $192
Youth model, 21-inch barrel ...... NiB $349 Ex $279 Gd $189

MODEL 870ADL WINGMASTER DELUXE GRADE
Same general specifications as Wingmaster Model 870AP except has pistol-grip stock and extension beavertail forend, both finely checkered; matted top surface or vent-rib bbl. Made 1950-63.
With matted top-surface barrel.... NiB $338 Ex $270 Gd $184
With ventilated-rib barrel .... NiB $380 Ex $304 Gd $207

MODEL 870AP WINGMASTER STANDARD GRADE
Hammerless. Takedown. Gauges: 12, 16, 20. Tubular magazine holds four shells. Bbls.: Plain, matted top surface or vent rib; 26-inch IC, 28-inch M or F choke, 30-inch F choke (12 ga. only). Weight: About 7 lbs., 12 ga.; 6.75 lbs., 16 ga.; 6.5 lbs., 20 ga. Plain pistol-grip stock, grooved forend. Made 1950-63.
With plain barrel .... NiB $250 Ex $200 Gd $136
With matted surface barrel .... NiB $263 Ex $210 Gd $143
With ventilated rib barrel .... NiB $288 Ex $230 Gd $156
Left-hand model .... NiB $300 Ex $240 Gd $163

MODEL 870BDL WINGMASTER DELUXE SPECIAL
Same as Model 870ADL except select American walnut stock and forend. Made 1950-63.
With matted surface barrel .... NiB $361 Ex $288 Gd $196
With ventilated-rib barrel .... NiB $400 Ex $320 Gd $217

REMINGTON MODEL 870D, 870F WINGMASTER TOURNAMENT AND PREMIER GRADE GUNS
These higher-grade models differ from the Model 870AP in general quality, grade of wood, checkering, engraving, etc. General operating specifications are essentially the same. Made 1950 to date.
Model 870D Tournament grade ...... NiB $2468 Ex $1974 Gd $1343
Model 870F Premier grade .... NiB $5431 Ex $4345 Gd $2954
Model 870F Premier gr. w/gold inlay ..... NiB $8618 Ex $6894 Gd $4688

REMINGTON MODEL 870R
WINGMASTER RIOT GUN .... NiB $350 Ex $280 Gd $190
Same as Model 870AP except 20-inch bbl., IC choke, 12 ga. only.

REMINGTON MODEL 870SA WINGMASTER SKEET GUN
Same general specifications as Model 870AP except has 26-inch vent-rib bbl., SK choke, ivory bead front sight, metal bead rear sight, pistol-grip stock and extension beavertail forend. Weight: 6.75 to 7.5 lbs. depending on gauge. Made 1950-82.
Model 870SA Skeet grade (disc. 1982) ...... NiB $361 Ex $288 Gd $196
Model 870SC Skeet Target
grade (disc. 1980) .... NiB $518 Ex $414 Gd $282

REMINGTON MODEL 870TB
WINGMASTER TRAP SPECIAL .... NiB $438 Ex $350 Gd $238
Same general specifications as Model 870AP Wingmaster except has 28- or 30-inch vent rib bbl., F choke, metal bead front sight, no rear sight. "Special" grade trap-style stock and forend, both checkered, recoil pad. Weight: About 8 lbs. Made 1950-81.

REMINGTON MODEL
870TC TRAP GRADE............ NiB $588 Ex $470 Gd $320
Same as Model 870 Wingmaster TC except has tournament-grade walnut in stock and forend w/satin finish. Over-bored 30-inch vent rib bbl. w/ 2.75-inch chamber and RemChoke tubes. Reissued in 1996. See separate listing for earlier model.

REMINGTON MODEL 870TC WINGMASTER TRAP GRADE
Same as Model 870TB except higher-grade walnut in stock and forend, has both front and rear sights. Made 1950-79. Model 870 TC reissued in 1996. See separate listing for later model.
Model 870 TC Trap (Standard)..... NiB $594 Ex $475 Gd $323
Model 870 TC Trap (Monte Carlo) .. NiB $619 Ex $495 Gd $337

REMINGTON MODEL
878A AUTOMASTER............ NiB $269 Ex $213 Gd $142
Gas-operated Autoloader. 12 ga., 3-shot magazine. Bbls.: 26-inch IC, 28-inch M choke, 30-inch F choke. Weight: About 7 lbs. Plain pistol-grip stock and forearm. Made 1959-62.

NOTE: *New stock checkering patterns and receiver scroll markings were incorporated on all standard Model 1100 field, magnum, skeet and trap models in 1979.*

Remington Model 1100
Field w/Ventilated Rib

Remington Model 1100
Deer Gun

Remington Model 1100
SA Skeet Gun

MODEL 1100 AUTOMATIC FIELD GUN

Gas-operated. Hammerless. Takedown. Gauges: 12, 16, 20. Bbls.: plain or vent. rib; 30-inch F, 28-inch M or F, 26-inch IC; or REMChoke tubes. Weight: Average 7.25-7.5 lbs. depending on ga. and bbl. length. Checkered walnut pistol-grip stock and forearm in high-gloss finish. Made 1963 to date. 16 ga. discontinued.

With plain barrel . . . . NiB $331 Ex $265 Gd $180
With ventilated-rib barrel . . . . NiB $381 Ex $305 Gd $207
REMChoke model . . . . NiB $419 Ex $335 Gd $228
REMChoke, Left-hand action . . . . . NiB $456 Ex $365 Gd $248

MODEL 1100 DEER GUN . . . . NiB $426 Ex $341 Gd $232

Same as Model 1100 Field Gun except has 22-inch barrel, IC, with rifle-type sights; 12 and 20 ga. only; recoil pad. Weight: About 7.25 lbs. Made 1963-96.

MODEL 1100 DUCKS UNLIMITED
ATLANTIC COMMEMORATIVE. . . . NiB $955 Ex $764 Gd $520

Limited production for one year. Similar specifications to Model 1100 Field except with 32-inch F choke, vent rib bbl. 12-ga. Magnum only. Made in 1982.

MODEL 1100 DUCKS UNLIMITED "THE
CHESAPEAKE" COMMEMORATIVE NiB $688 Ex $551 Gd $374

Limited edition 1 to 2400. Same general specifications as Model 1100 Field except sequentially numbered with markings, "The Chesapeake." 12-ga. Magnum with 30-inch F choke, vent rib bbl. Made in 1981.

REMINGTON MODEL 1100 FIELD GRADE, SMALL BORE

Same as standard Model 1100 but scaled down. Gauges: 28, .410. 25-inch bbl., plain or vent rib; IC, M or F choke. Weight: 6.25-7 lbs. depending on gauge and bbl. Made 1969-94.

With plain barrel . . . . NiB $529 Ex $423 Gd $288
With ventilated rib . . . . NiB $625 Ex $500 Gd $339

MODEL 1100 LIGHTWEIGHT

Same as standard Model 1100 but scaled-down receiver and lightweight mahogany stock; 20 ga. only, 2.75-inch chamber. Bbls.: Plain or vent rib; 26-inch IC; 28-inch M and F choke. Weight: 6.25 lbs. Made 1971 to date.

With plain barrel . . . . NiB $459 Ex $367 Gd $249
With ventilated rib . . . . NiB $518 Ex $414 Gd $282

MODEL 1100 LIGHTWEIGHT MAGNUM

Same as Model 1100 Lightweight but chambered for 20 gauge Magnum 3-inch shell; 28-inch bbl., plain or vent rib, F choke. Weight: 6.5 lbs. Made 1971 to date.

With plain barrel . . . . NiB $492 Ex $393 Gd $267
With ventilated rib . . . . NiB $551 Ex $441 Gd $300
With choke tubes . . . . NiB $591 Ex $472 Gd $321

MODEL 1100 LT-20
DUCKS UNLIMITED
SPECIAL COMMEMORATIVE . . . . . NiB $619 Ex $495 Gd $337

Limited edition 1 to 2400. Same general specifications as Model 1100 Field except sequentially numbered with markings, "The Chesapeake." 20 ga. only. 26-inch IC, vent-rib bbl. Made in 1981.

MODEL 1100 LT-20 SERIES

Same as Model 1100 Field Gun except in 20 ga. with shorter 23-inch vent rib bbl., straight-grip stock. REMChoke series has 21-inch vent rib bbl., choke tubes. Weight: 6.25 lbs. Checkered grip and forearm. Made 1983 to date.

Model 1100
LT-20 Special . . . . NiB $505 Ex $404 Gd $275
Model 1100
LT-20 Deer Gun. . . . . NiB $478 Ex $383 Gd $260
Model 1100
LT-20 Youth . . . . NiB $492 Ex $393 Gd $267

REMINGTON MODEL
1100 MAGNUM . . . . NiB $438 Ex $350 Gd $238

Limited production. Similar to the Model 1100 Field except with 26-inch F choke, vent rib bbl. and 3-inch chamber. Made in 1981.

MODEL 1100 MAGNUM DUCK GUN

Same as Model 1100 Field Gun except has 3-inch chamber, 12 and 20 ga. Mag. only. 30-inch plain or vent rib bbl. in 12 ga., 28-inch in 20 ga.; M or F choke. Recoil pad. Weight: About 7.75 lbs. Made 1963-88.

With plain barrel . . . . NiB $387 Ex $309 Gd $211
With ventilated
rib barrel . . . . NiB $439 Ex $351 Gd $239

Remington Model 1100
Special Field

Remington Model 1100
Tournament Trap

Remington Model 3200
"One of 1000" Skeet

MODEL 1100
ONE OF 3000 FIELD . . . . **NiB $1181 Ex $945 Gd $643**
Limited edition, numbered 1 to 3000. Similar to Model 1100 Field except with fancy wood and gold-trimmed etched hunting scenes on receiver. 12 gauge with 28-inch Mod., vent rib bbl. Made in 1980.

MODEL 1100 SA SKEET GUN
Same as Model 1100 Field Gun, 12 and 20 ga. except has 26-inch vent-rib bbl., SK choke or with Cutts Compensator. Weight: 7.25-7.5 lbs. Made 1963-94.
**With skeet-
choked barrel** . . . . **NiB $494 Ex $395 Gd $269**
With Cutts Comp. . . . . **NiB $513 Ex $410 Gd $279**
Left-hand action . . . . **NiB $531 Ex $425 Gd $289**

MODEL 1100 SA
LIGHTWEIGHT SKEET . . . . **NiB $469 Ex $375 Gd $255**
Same as Model 1100 Lightweight except has skeet-style stock and forearm, 26-inch vent-rib bbl., SK choke. Made 1971-97.

MODEL 1100 SA
SKEET SMALL BORE . . . . **NiB $531 Ex $425 Gd $289**
Similar to standard Model 1100SA except chambered for 28 and .410 ga. (2.5-inch chamber for latter); 25-inch vent-rib bbl., SK choke. Weight: 6.75 lbs., 28 ga.; 7.25 lbs., .410. Made 1969 to date.

MODEL 1100 SB
LIGHTWEIGHT SKEET . . . . **NiB $518 Ex $414 Gd $282**
Same as Model 1100SA Lightweight except has select wood. Introduced in 1977.

MODEL 1100
SB SKEET GUN . . . . **NiB $492 Ex $393 Gd $267**
Same specifications as Model 1100SA except has select wood. Made 1963-97.

MODEL 1100
SPECIAL FIELD SHOTGUN . . . . **NiB $518 Ex $414 Gd $282**
Gas-operated. Five shot. Hammerless. Gauges: 12 and 20. 21-inch vent-rib bbl. with REMChoke. Weight: 6.5-7.25 lbs. Straight-grip checkered walnut stock and forend. Made 1987 to date.

MODEL 1100 SP MAGNUM
Same as Model 1100 Field except 12 ga. only with 3-inch chambers. Bbls.: 26- or 30-inch F choke; or 26-inch with REM Choke tubes; vent rib. Non-reflective matte black, Parkerized bbl. and receiver. Satin-finished stock and forend. Made 1981 to date.
With fixed choke . . . . **NiB $406 Ex $325 Gd $221**
With REMChoke . . . . **NiB $456 Ex $365 Gd $248**

MODEL 1100 TOURNAMENT AND PREMIER
These higher grade guns differ from standard models in overall quality, grade of wood, checkering, engraving, gold inlays, etc. General specifications are the same. Made 1963 to date.
**Model 1100D
Tournament** . . . . **NiB $2600 Ex $1850 Gd $1300**
**Model 1100F
Premier** . . . . **NiB $5700 Ex $4200 Gd $2757**
**Model 1100F Premier
with gold inlay** . . . . **NiB $8700 Ex $4950 Gd $3325**

MODEL 1100
TOURNAMENT SKEET . . . . **NiB $623 Ex $498 Gd $339**
Similar to Model 1100 Field except with 26-inch bbl. SK choke. Gauges: 12, LT-20, 28, and .410. Features select walnut stocks and new cut-checkering patterns. Made 1979-89.

MODEL 1100TA TRAP GUN . . . . . . **NiB $426 Ex $341 Gd $232**
Similar to Model 1100TB Trap Gun except with regular-grade stocks. Available in both left- and right-hand versions. Made 1979-86.

MODEL 1100TB TRAP GUN
Same as Model 1100 Field Gun except has special trap stock, straight or Monte Carlo comb, recoil pad; 30-inch vent-rib bbl., F or M trap choke; 12 ga. only. Weight: 8.25 lbs. Made 1963-79.
With straight stock . . . . **NiB $469 Ex $375 Gd $255**
With Monte Carlo stock . . . . **NiB $493 Ex $394 Gd $267**

MODEL 1900
HAMMERLESS DOUBLE . . . . **NiB $1063 Ex $850 Gd $578**
Improved version of Model 1894. Boxlock. Auto ejector. Double triggers. Gauges: 10, 12, 16. Bbls.: 28 to 32 inches. Value shown is for standard grade with ordnance steel bbls. Made 1900-10.

Remington Rider No. 9 Single-Shot Shotgun

Remington Sportsman Autoloader

Remington Sportsman — 48A

MODEL 3200
COMPETITION SKEET GUN . . . . NiB $1631 Ex $1305 Gd $887
Same as Model 3200 Skeet Gun except has gilded scrollwork on frame, engraved forend, latch plate and trigger guard, select fancy wood. Made 1973-84.

MODEL 3200
COMPETITION SKEET SET . . . . NiB $5195 Ex $4156 Gd $2826
Similar specifications to Model 3200 Field. 12-ga. O/U with additional, interchangeable bbls. in 20, 28, and .410 ga. Cased. Made 1980-84.

MODEL 3200
COMPETITION TRAP GUN. . . . NiB $2005 Ex $1604 Gd $1091
Same as Model 3200 Trap Gun except has gilded scrollwork on frame, engraved forend, latch plate and trigger guard, select fancy wood. Made 1973-84.

MODEL 3200
FIELD GRADE MAGNUM . . . . . . NiB $1694 Ex $1355 Gd $922
Same as Model 3200 Field except chambered for 12 ga. mag. 3-inch shells 30-inch bbls., M and F or both F choke. Made 1975-84.

MODEL 3200 FIELD GRADE O/U . . . NiB $1119 Ex $896 Gd $609
Boxlock. Auto ejectors. Selective single trigger. 12 ga. 2.75-inch chambers. Bbls.: Vent rib, 26- and 28-inch M/F; 30-inch IC/M. Weight: About 7.75 lbs. with 26-inch bbls. Checkered pistol-grip stock/forearm. Made 1973-78.

MODEL 3200
"ONE OF 1000" SKEET . . . . NiB $1859 Ex $1487 Gd $1011
Same as Model 3200 "One of 1000" Trap except has 26- or 28-inch bbls., SK choke, skeet-style stock and forearm. Made in 1974.

MODEL 3200
"ONE OF 1000" TRAP . . . . NiB $2019 Ex $1615 Gd $1098
Limited edition numbered 1 to 1000. Same general specifications as Model 3200 Trap Gun but has frame, trigger guard and forend latch elaborately engraved (designation "One of 1,000" on frame side), stock and forearm of high grade walnut. Supplied in carrying case. Made in 1973.

MODEL 3200 SKEET GUN . . . . . NiB $1473 Ex $1178 Gd $801
Same as Model 3200 Field Grade except skeet-style stock and full beavertail forearm, 26- or 28-inch bbls., SK choke. Made 1973-80.

MODEL 3200
SPECIAL TRAP GUN . . . . NiB $1328 Ex $1062 Gd $722
Same as Model 3200 Trap Gun except has select fancy-grade wood and other minor refinements. Made 1973-84.

MODEL 3200 TRAP GUN . . . . NiB $1222 Ex $977 Gd $664
Same as Model 3200 Field Grade except trap-style stock w/Monte Carlo or straight comb, select wood, beavertail forearm, 30- or 32-inch bbls. w/ventilated rib, IM/F or F/F chokes. Made 1973-77.

RIDER NO. 9
SINGLE-SHOT SHOTGUN . . . . NiB $406 Ex $325 Gd $221
Improved version of No. 3 Single Barrel Shotgun made in the late 1800s. Semi-hammerless. Gauges 10, 12, 16, 20, 24, 28. 30- to 32-inch plain bbl. Weight: About 6 lbs. Plain pistol-grip stock and forearm. Auto ejector. Made 1902-10.

SP-10
MAGNUM AUTOLOADER . . . . NiB $996 Ex $797 Gd $539
Takedown. Gas-operated with stainless steel piston. 10 ga., 3.5-inch chamber. Bbls.: 26- or 30-inch vent-rib with REMChoke screw-in tubes. Weight: 11 to 11.25 lbs. Metal bead front. Checkered walnut stock with satin finish. Made 1989 to date.

SP-10
MAGNUM TURKEY COMBO . . . . NiB $1007 Ex $805 Gd $548
Same general specifications as Model SP-10 Magnum except has extra 22-inch REMChoke bbl. with M, F and Turkey extra-full tubes. Rifle sights. QD swivels and camo sling. Made 1991 to date.

PEERLESS O/U . . . . NiB $1039 Ex $831 Gd $565
Boxlock action and removable, engraved sideplates. Gauge: 12 only with 3-inch chambers. Barrels: 26-, 28-, or 30-inch with vent rib and REMChoke system. Automatic safety and single selective trigger. Weight: 7.25 lbs. to 7.5 lbs. Blued receiver and bbls. Checkered American walnut stock. Made 1993-98.

SPORTSMAN A STANDARD GRADE AUTOLOADER
Same general specifications as Model 11A except magazine holds two shells. Also available in "B" Special Grade, "D" Tournament Grade, "E" Expert Grade, "F" Premier Grade. Made 1931-48. Same values as for Model 11A.
48D . . . . NiB $1100 Ex $825 Gd $450

Remington Sportsman
48SC Skeet Target Grade

Remington Sportsman
48A Standard

Remington Sportsman
48A Small Gauge

SPORTSMAN SKEET GUN
Same general specifications as the Sportsman A except has 26-inch bbl. (plain, solid or vent rib), SK choke, beavertail forend. Disc. 1949.

With plain barrel . . . . NiB $385 Ex $208 Gd $209
With solid-rib barrel . . . . NiB $469 Ex $375 Gd $255
With ventilated rib barrel . . . . . . NiB $516 Ex $413 Gd $281

SPORTSMAN-48A STANDARD GRADE 3-SHOT AUTOLOADER
Streamlined receiver. Hammerless. Takedown. Gauges: 12, 16, 20. Tubular magazine holds two shells. Bbls.: Plain, matted top surface or vent rib; 26-inch IC, 28-inch M or F choke, 30-inch F choke (12 ga. only). Weight: About 7.5 lbs., 12 ga.; 6.25 lbs., 16 ga.; 6.5 lbs., 20 ga. Pistol-grip stock, grooved forend, both checkered. Made 1949-59.

With plain bbl. . . . . NiB $350 Ex $295 Gd $190
With matted top-surface bbl. . . . . NiB $385 Ex $308 Gd $209
With ventilated rib bbl. . . . . NiB $409 Ex $327 Gd $223

SPORTSMAN-48 B, D, F SPECIAL, TOURNAMENT AND PREMIER GRADE GUNS
These higher grade models differ from the Sportsman-48A in general quality, grade of wood, checkering, engraving, etc. General specifications are the same. Made 1949-59.

Sportsman-48B Special grade . . . . . NiB $421 Ex $337 Gd $228
Sportsman-48D Tournament grade . . . NiB $920 Ex $736 Gd $500
Sportsman-48F Premier grade . . . . NiB $2013 Ex $1610 Gd $1095

SPORTSMAN-48SA SKEET GUN
Same general specifications as Sportsman-48A except has 26-inch bbl. with matted top surface or vent rib, SK choke, ivory bead front sight, metal bead rear sight. Made 1949-60.

With matted top-surface barrel . . . NiB $344 Ex $275 Gd $187
With ventilated rib barrel . . . . NiB $406 Ex $325 Gd $221
Sportsman-48SC Skeet
Target grade . . . . NiB $500 Ex $400 Gd $272
Sportsman-48SD Skeet
Tournament grade . . . . NiB $900 Ex $720 Gd $490
Sportsman-48SF Skeet
Premier grade . . . . NiB $2119 Ex $1695 Gd $1153

MODEL 11-48A RIOT GUN . . . . . . NiB $237 Ex $242 Gd $164
Same as Model 11-48A except 20-inch plain barrel and 12 ga. only. Disc. in 1969.

MODEL 11-48A STANDARD GRADE 4-SHOT AUTOLOADER .410 & 28 GAUGE
Same general specifications as Sportsman-48A except gauge, 3-shell magazine, 25-inch bbl. Weight: About 6.25 lbs. 28 ga. introduced 1952, .410 in 1954. Disc. in 1969. Values same as shown for Sportsman-48A.

MODEL 11-48A STANDARD GRADE 5-SHOT AUTOLOADER
Same general specifications as Sportsman-48A except magazine holds four shells, forend not grooved. Also available in Special Grade (11-48B), Tournament Grade (11-48D) and Premier Grade (11-48F). Made 1949-69. Values same as shown for Sportsman-48A.

MODEL 11-48SA
.410 AND 28 GA. SKEET . . . . NiB $385 Ex $308 Gd $209
Same general specifications as Model 11-48A 28 gauge except has 25-inch vent rib bbl., SK choke. 28 ga. introduced 1952, .410 in 1954.

SPORTSMAN-58 SKEET, TARGET, TOURNAMENT AND PREMIER GRADES
These higher grade models differ from the Sportsman-58SA in general quality, grade of wood, checkering, engraving, and other refinements. General operating and physical specifications are the same.

Sportsman-58C Skeet Target . . . . . . NiB $563 Ex $450 Gd $306
Sportsman-58D Skeet Tournament . . . NiB $825 Ex $660 Gd $449
Sportsman-58SF Skeet Premier . . NiB $1619 Ex $1295 Gd $881

SPORTSMAN-58 TOURNAMENT AND PREMIER
These higher grade models differ from the Sportsman-58ADL with vent-rib bbl. in general quality, grade of wood, checkering, engraving, etc. General specifications are the same.

Sportsman-58D Tournament . . . . . . NiB $891 Ex $712 Gd $484
Sportsman-58F Premier . . . . NiB $1656 Ex $1325 Gd $901

SPORTSMAN-58ADL AUTOLOADER
Deluxe grade. Gas-operated. 12 ga. Three shot magazine. Bbls.: plain or vent rib, 26-, 28- or 30-inch; IC, M or F choke, or Remington Special Skeet choke. Weight: About 7 lbs. Checkered pistol-grip stock and forearm. Made 1956-64.

With plain barrel . . . . NiB $332 Ex $265 Gd $180
With ventilated rib barrel . . . . NiB $385 Ex $308 Gd $209

Richland Model 200

Richland Model 202

Richland Model 707 Deluxe

Richland Model 711
Long Range Waterfowl Magnum

SHOTGUNS

SPORTSMAN-58BDL DELUXE SPECIAL GRADE
Same as Model 58ADL except select grade wood.
With plain barrel . . . . **NiB $350 Ex $280 Gd $190**
With ventilated rib barrel . . . . **NiB $409 Ex $327 Gd $223**

SPORTSMAN-58SA
SKEET GRADE . . . . **NiB $398 Ex $318 Gd $216**
Same general specifications as Model 58ADL with vent-rib bbl.
except special skeet stock and forearm.

REVELATION SHOTGUNS
See Western Auto listings.

RICHLAND ARMS COMPANY — Blissfield, Michigan; Manufactured in Italy and Spain

MODEL 200
FIELD GRADE DOUBLE . . . . **NiB $320 Ex $285 Gd $175**
Hammerless, boxlock, Anson & Deeley-type. Plain extractors.
Double triggers. Gauges: 12, 16, 20, 28, .410 (3-inch chambers in
20 and .410; others have 2.75-inch). Bbls.: 28-inch M/F choke, 26-
inch IC/M; .410 with 26-inch M/F only; 22-inch IC/M in 20 ga. only.
Weight: 6 lbs., 2 oz. to 7 lbs., 4 oz. Checkered walnut stock with
cheekpiece, pistol grip, recoil pad; beavertail forend. Made in Spain
1963 to date.

MODEL 202
ALL PURPOSE FIELD GUN . . . . **NiB $306 Ex $245 Gd $167**
Hammerless, boxlock, Anson & Deeley-type. Same as Model 200

(cont'd.) **MODEL 202 ALL-PURPOSE FIELD GUN**
except has two sets of barrels same gauge. 12 ga.: 30-inch bbls. F/F,
3-inch chambers; 26-inch bbls. IC/M, 2.75-inch chambers. 20
gauge: 28-inch bbls. M/F; 22-inch bbls. IC/M, 3-inch chambers.
Made 1963 to date.

MODEL 707
DELUXE FIELD GUN . . . . **NiB $337 Ex $270 Gd $183**
Hammerless, boxlock, triple bolting system. Plain extractors.
Double triggers. Gauges: 12, 2.75-inch chambers; 20, 3-inch
chambers. Bbls.: 12 ga., 28-inch M/F, 26-inch IC/M; 20 ga., 30-
inch F/F, 28-inch M/F, 26-inch IC/M. Weight: 6 lbs., 4 oz. to 6
lbs., 15 oz. Checkered walnut stock and forend, recoil pad.
Made 1963-72.

MODEL 711 LONG-RANGE WATERFOWL
MAGNUM DOUBLE-BARREL SHOTGUN
Hammerless, boxlock, Anson & Deeley-type, Purdey triple lock.
Plain extractors. Double triggers. Auto safety. Gauges: 10, 3.5-inch
chambers; 12, 3-inch chambers. Bbls.: 10 ga., 32-inch; 12 ga., 30-
inch; F/F. Weight: 10 ga., 11 pounds; 12 ga., 7.75 lbs. Checkered
walnut stock and beavertail forend; recoil pad. Made in Spain
1963 to date.
10 ga. magnum . . . . **NiB $406 Ex $325 Gd $221**
12 ga. magnum . . . . **NiB $344 Ex $275 Gd $187**

MODEL 808
O/U SHOTGUN . . . . **NiB $409 Ex $327 Gd $223**
Boxlock. Plain extractors. Non-selective single trigger. 12 ga. only.
Bbls. (Vickers steel): 30-inch F/F; 28-inch M/F; 26-inch IC/M.
Weight: 6 lbs., 12 oz. to 7 lbs., 3 oz. Checkered walnut
stock/forend. Made in Italy 1963-68.

Richland Model 808
Over/Under

Rossi
Hammerless Double-Barrel Shotgun

Rossi
Overland Hammer Double

Rigby Regal
Side Lock

JOHN RIGBY & COMPANY — London, England

HAMMERLESS BOX LOCK DOUBLE-BARREL SHOTGUNS
Auto ejectors. Double triggers. Made in all gauges, barrel lengths and chokes. Checkered stock and forend, straight grip standard. Made in two grades: Sackville and Chatsworth. These guns differ in general quality, engraving, etc.; specifications are the same.
Sackville grade . . . . NiB $5938 Ex $4750 Gd $3230
Chatsworth grade . . . . NiB $4456 Ex $3564 Gd $2424

HAMMERLESS SIDE LOCK DOUBLE-BARREL SHOTGUNS
Auto ejectors. Double triggers. Made in all gauges, barrel lengths and chokes. Checkered stock and forend, straight grip standard. Made in two grades: Regal (best quality) and Sandringham; these guns differ in general quality, engraving, etc., specifications are the same.
Regal grade . . . . NiB $12,500 Ex $10,000 Gd $6000
Sandringham grade . . . . NiB $9500 Ex $7500 Gd $3775

AMADEO ROSSI, S.A. — Sao Leopoldo, Brazil

HAMMERLESS DOUBLE-
BARREL SHOTGUN. NiB $331 Ex $265 Gd $180
Boxlock. Plain extractors. Double triggers. 12 ga. Three inch chambers. Bbls.: 26-inch IC/M; 28-inch M/F choke. Weight: 7 to 7.5 lbs. Pistol-grip stock and beavertail forearm, uncheckered. Made 1974 to date. Note: H&R Model 404 (1969-72) is same gun.

OVERLAND
HAMMER DOUBLE . . . . NiB $266 Ex $213 Gd $145
Sidelock. Plain extractors. Double triggers. Gauges: 12, .410; 3-inch chambers. Bbls.: 20-inch, IC/M in 12 g.; 26-inch, F/F choke in .410. Weight: 7 lbs. (12 ga.); 6 lbs. (.410). Pistol-grip stock and beavertail forearm, uncheckered. Note: Because of its resemblance to the short-barreled doubles carried by guards riding shotgun on 19th-century stagecoaches, the 12 ga. version originally was called the "Coach Gun." Made 1968-89.

ROTTWEIL SHOTGUNS — West Germany

MODEL 72 O/U
SHOTGUN. . . . . NiB $1894 Ex $1515 Gd $1030
Hammerless, takedown with engraved receiver. 12 ga.; 2.75-inch chambers. 26.75-inch bbls. with SK/SK chokes. Weight: 7.5 lbs. Interchangeable trigger groups and buttstocks. Checkered French walnut buttstock and forend. Imported from West Germany.

MODEL 650 FIELD
O/U SHOTGUN . . . . NiB $741 Ex $593 Gd $403
Breech action. Gauge: 12. 28-inch bbls. Six screw-in choke tubes. Automatic ejectors. Engraved receiver. Checkered pistol grip stock. Made 1984-86.

AMERICAN SKEET . . . . NiB $1841 Ex $1472 Gd $1001
Boxlock action. Gauge: 12. 27-inch vent-rib bbls. 44.5 inches overall. SK chokes. Weight: 7.5 lbs. Designed for tube sets. Hand-checkered European walnut stock with modified forend. Made 1984-87.

INTERNATIONAL
TRAP SHOTGUN. NiB $1894 Ex $1515 Gd $1030
Box lock action. Gauge: 12. 30-inch bbls. 48.5 inches overall. Weight: 8 lbs. Choked IM/F. Selective single trigger. Metal bead front sight. Checkered European walnut stock w/pistol grip. Engraved action. Made 1984-87.

Rottweil American Skeet

Ruger Red Label — 20 Gauge (1982)

Ruger Red Label Over and Under (Stainless)

Sarasqueta Model 3
Hammerless Boxlock

STURM, RUGER & COMPANY, INC. — Southport, Connecticut

PLAIN GRADE RED LABEL O/U

Boxlock. Auto ejectors. Selective single trigger. 12, 20 or 28 ga. w/2.75- or 3-inch chambers. 26-inch vent-rib bbl., IC/M or SK choke. Single selective trigger. Selective automatic ejectors. Automatic top safety. Standard gold bead front sight. Pistol-grip or English-style American walnut stock and forearm w/hand-cut checkering. The 20 ga. Model was introduced in 1977; 12 ga. version in 1982 and the stainless receiver became standard in 1985. Choke tubes were optional in 1988 and standard in 1990. Weight: 7.0 to 7.5 lbs.

Red Label w/fixed chokes . . . . NiB $813 Ex $650 Gd $442
Red Label w/screw-in tubes . . . . . NiB $1041 Ex $833 Gd $566
Red Label w/grade 1 engraving. . . . NiB $2119 Ex $1695 Gd $1153
Red Label w/grade 2 engraving . . . NiB $2450 Ex $1960 Gd $1332
Red Label w/grade 3 engraving . . . NiB $2795 Ex $2236 Gd $1520

RED LABEL O/U ALL-WEATHER STAINLESS

Gauges: 12 ga. Only. Bbls.: 26- 28- or 30-inch w/various chokes, fixed or screw-in tubes. Stainless receiver and barrel. Checkered black synthetic stock and forearm. Weight: 7.5 lbs. Made 1999 to date.
All-weather stainless model . . . . . NiB $1125 Ex $900 Gd $612
W/30-inch bbl., add $56

RED LABEL "WOODSIDE" O/U

Similar to the Red Label O/U Stainless except in 12 ga. only with wood sideplate extensions. Made 1995 to date.
Standard Woodside . . . . NiB $1473 Ex $1178 Gd $801
Engraved Woodside . . . . NiB $2081 Ex $1665 Gd $1132

RED LABEL SPORTING CLAYS O/U

Similar to the standard Red Label model except chambered 12 or 20 ga. only w/30-inch vent-rib bbls., no side ribs; back-bored w/screw-in choke tubes (not interchangeable w/other Red Label O/U models). Brass front and mid-rib beads. Made 1992 to date.
Standard Sporting Clays. . . . . NiB $1288 Ex $1031 Gd $701
Engraved Sporting Clays . . . . . . NiB $2284 Ex $1827 Gd $1242

RED LABEL SPECIAL EDITION - WILDLIFE FOREVER

Limited edition commemorating the 50th Wildlife Forever anniversary. Similar to the standard Red Label model except chambered 12 ga. only w/engraved receiver enhanced w/gold mallard and pheasant inlays. 300 produced in 1993.
Special edition . . . . NiB $1650 Ex $1320 Gd $897
Special edition w/hard case . . . . NiB $1795 Ex $1436 Gd $976

VICTOR SARASQUETA, S. A. — Eibar, Spain

SARASQUETA MODEL 3 HAMMERLESS BOXLOCK DOUBLE-BARREL SHOTGUN

Plain extractors or auto ejectors. Double triggers. Gauges: 12, 16, 20. Made in various bbl. lengths, chokes and weights. Checkered stock and forend, straight grip standard. Imported 1985-87.
Model 3, plain extractors . . . . NiB $444 Ex $355 Gd $242
Model 3E, automatic ejectors . . . . . NiB $557 Ex $445 Gd $303

HAMMERLESS SIDELOCK DOUBLES

Automatic ejectors (except on Models 4 and 203 which have plain extractors). Double triggers. Gauges: 12, 16, 20. Barrel lengths, chokes and weights made to order. Checkered stock and forend, straight grip standard. Models differ chiefly in overall quality, engraving, grade of wood, checkering, etc.; general specifications are the same. Imported 1985-87.

Sarasqueta Models 6E, 11E and 12E

Sauer Model 66 Field Grade II

(cont'd.) HAMMERLESS SIDELOCK DOUBLES

Model 4	NiB $619	Ex $495	Gd $336
Model 4E	NiB $669	Ex $535	Gd $364
Model 203	NiB $647	Ex $517	Gd $351
Model 203E	NiB $702	Ex $562	Gd $382
Model 6E	NiB $815	Ex $652	Gd $443
Model 7E	NiB $872	Ex $697	Gd $474

Sauer Model 66 Field Grade III

(cont'd.) HAMMERLESS SIDELOCK DOUBLES

Model 10E	NiB $1595	Ex $1276	Gd $868
Model 11E	NiB $1650	Ex $1320	Gd $897
Model 12E	NiB $1895	Ex $1516	Gd $1031

J. P. SAUER & SOHN — Eckernförde, Germany, Formerly located in Suhl, Germany

MODEL 66 O/U FIELD GUN
Purdey-system action with Holland & Holland-type sidelocks. Selective single trigger. Selective auto ejectors. Automatic safety. Available in three grades of engraving. 12 ga. only. Krupp special steel bbls. w/vent rib 28-inch, M/F choke. Weight: About 7.25 lbs. Checkered walnut stock and forend; recoil pad. Made 1966-75.

Grade I	NiB $2330	Ex $1864	Gd $1268
Grade II	NiB $3091	Ex $2472	Gd $1681
Grade III	NiB $4118	Ex $3294	Gd $2240

MODEL 66 O/U SKEET GUN
Same as Model 66 Field Gun except 26-inch bbls. with wide vent rib, SK choked- skeet-style stock and ventilated beavertail forearm; non-automatic safety. Made 1966-75.

Grade I	NiB $2263	Ex $1811	Gd $1231
Grade II	NiB $3094	Ex $2475	Gd $1683
Grade III	NiB $4393	Ex $3514	Gd $2390

MODEL 66 O/U TRAP GUN
Same as Model 66 Skeet Gun except has 30-inch bbls. choked F/F or M/F; trap-style stock. Values same as for Skeet model. Made 1966-75.

MODEL 3000E DRILLING
Combination rifle and double barrel shotgun. Blitz action with Greener crossbolt, double underlugs, separate rifle cartridge extractor, front set trigger, firing pin indicators, Greener side safety, sear slide selector locks right shotgun bbl. for firing rifle bbl. Gauge/calibers12 ga. (2.75-inch chambers); .222, .243, .30-06, 7x65R. 25-inch Krupp-Special steel bbls.; M/F choke automatic folding leaf rear rifle sight. Weight: 6.5 to 7.25 lbs. depending on rifle caliber. Checkered walnut stock and forend; pistol grip, Monte Carlo comb and cheekpiece, sling swivels. Standard model with Arabesque engraving; Deluxe model with hunting scenes engraved on action. Currently manufactured. Note: Also see listing under Colt.

Standard model	NiB $4266	Ex $3412	Gd $2320
Deluxe model	NiB $5169	Ex $4135	Gd $2812

ARTEMIS DOUBLE-BARREL SHOTGUN
Holland & Holland-type sidelock with Greener crossbolt double underlugs, double sear safeties, selective single trigger, selective auto ejectors. Grade I with fine-line engraving, Grade II with full English Arabesque engraving. 12 ga. (2.75-inch chambers). Krupp special steel bbls., 28-inch, M/F choke. Weight: About 6.5 lbs. Checkered walnut pistol-grip stock and beavertail forend; recoil pad. Made 1966-77.
Grade I . . . . NiB $5493 Ex $4394 Gd $2988
Grade II . . . . NiB $6806 Ex $5445 Gd $3702

BBF 54 O/U COMBINATION RIFLE/SHOTGUN
Blitz action with Kersten lock, front set trigger fires rifle bbl., slide-operated sear safety. Gauge/calibers: 16 ga.; .30-30, .30-06, 7x65R, 25-inch Krupp special steel bbls.; shotgun bbl. F choke, folding-leaf rear sight. Weight: About 6 lbs. Checkered walnut stock and forend; pistol grip, mod. Monte Carlo comb and cheekpiece, sling swivels. Standard model with Arabesque engraving; Deluxe model with hunting scenes engraved on action. Currently manufactured.
Standard model . . . . NiB $2605 Ex $2084 Gd $1417
Deluxe model . . . . NiB $3018 Ex $2414 Gd $1642

ROYAL DOUBLE-BARREL SHOTGUNS
Anson & Deeley action (boxlock) with Greener crossbolt, double underlugs, signal pins, selective single trigger, selective auto ejectors, auto safety. Scalloped frame with Arabesque engraving. Krupp special steel bbls. Gauges: 12, 2.75-inch chambers, 20, 3-inch chambers. Bbls.: 30-inch (12 ga. only) and 28-inch, M/F- 26-inch (20 ga. only), IC/M. Weight: 12 ga., about 6.5 lbs.; 20 ga., 6 lbs. Checkered walnut pistol-grip stock and beavertail forend; recoil pad. Made 1955-77.
Standard model . . . . NiB $1538 Ex $1230 Gd $836
20 ga. . . . . NiB $2019 Ex $1615 Gd $1098

SAVAGE ARMS — Westfield, Massachusetts
Formerly located in Utica, New York

MODEL 24 22-.410
O/U COMBINATION . . . . NiB $163 Ex $130 Gd $88
Same as Stevens No. 22-.410 with walnut stock and forearm. Made 1950-65.

MODEL 24C
CAMPER'S COMPANION . . . . NiB $166 Ex $133 Gd $91
Same as Model 24FG except made in .22 Magnum/20 ga. only; has 20-inch bbls., shotgun tube Cyl. bore. Weight: 5.75 lbs. Trap in butt provides ammunition storage; comes with carrying case. Made 1972-89.

MODEL 24 . . . . NiB $231 Ex $185 Gd $126
Same as Models 24DL and 24MDL except frame has black or case-hardened finish. Game scene decoration of frame eliminated in 1974; forearm uncheckered after 1976. Made 1970-88.

MODEL 24DL . . . . NiB $171 Ex $137 Gd $94
Same general specifications as Model 24S except top-lever opening; satin-chrome-finished frame decorated with game scenes, checkered Monte Carlo stock and forearm. Made 1965-69.

MODEL 24F-12T TURKEY GUN . . . NiB $442 Ex $354 Gd $241
12- or 20-ga. shotgun bbl./.22 Hornet, .223 or .30-30 caliber rifle. 24-inch blued bbls., 3-inch chambers, extra removable F choke tube. Hammer block safety. Color casehardened frame. DuPont Rynite camo stock. Swivel studs. Made 1989 to date.

Sauer Model 3000E Drilling

Sauer BBF 54 Combination Rifle/Shotgun

Sauer Royal Double-Barrel Shotgun

SHOTGUNS

MODEL 24FG FIELD GRADE . . . . . . NiB $163 Ex $131 Gd $89
Same general specifications as Model 24S except top lever opening. Made 1972 to date.

MODEL 24MDL. . . . . NiB $175 Ex $140 Gd $95
Same as Model 24DL except rifle bbl. chambered for 22 WMR. Made 1965-69.

MODEL 24MS . . . . NiB $163 Ex $131 Gd $89
Same as Model 24S except rifle bbl. chambered for 22 WMR. Made 1965-71.

Savage Model 24
.22-/.410 O/U Combination

Savage Model 24-VS
Camper/Survival/Centerfire Rifle/Shotgun

MODEL 24S O/U COMBINATION . . NiB $181 Ex $145 Gd $99
Boxlock. Visible hammer. Side lever opening. Plain extractors. Single trigger. 20 ga. or .410 bore shotgun bbl. under 22 LR bbl., 24-inch. Open rear sight, ramp front, dovetail for scope mounting. Weight: About 6.75 lbs. Plain pistol-grip stock and forearm. Made 1965-71.

MODEL 24V . . . . NiB $306 Ex $245 Gd $167
Similar to Model 24D except 20 ga. under .222 Rem., .22 Rem., .357 Mag., .22 Hornet or .30-30 rifle bbl. Made 1971-89.

MODEL 24-VS CAMPER/SURVIVAL/
CENTERFIRE RIFLE/SHOTGUN . . . . NiB $256 Ex $204 Gd $139
Similar to Model 24V except .357 Rem. Mag. over 20 ga. Nickel finish full-length stock and accessory pistol-grip stock. Overall length: 36 inches with full stock; 26 inches w/pistol grip. Weight: About 6.5 lbs. Made 1983-88.

MODEL 28A STANDARD GRADE
SLIDE-ACTION REPEATING SHOTGUN . . . . NiB $313 Ex $250 Gd $170
Hammerless. Takedown. 12 ga. Five shell tubular magazine. Plain bbl., lengths: 26-,28-, 30-, 32-inches, choked C/M/F. Weight: About 7.5 lbs. with 30-inch bbl. Plain pistol-grip stock, grooved slide handle. Made 1928-31.

MODEL 28B . . . . NiB $331 Ex $265 Gd $180
Raised matted rib; otherwise the same as Model 28A.

MODEL 28D TRAP GRADE . . . . . . NiB $356 Ex $285 Gd $194
Same general specifications as Model 28A except has 30-inch F choke bbl. w/matted rib, trap-style stock w/checkered pistol grip, checkered slide handle of select walnut.

MODEL 30 SOLID FRAME HAMMERLESS
SLIDE-ACTION SHOTGUN . . . . . . NiB $225 Ex $180 Gd $122
Gauges: 12, 16, 20, .410. 2.75-inch chamber in 16 ga., 3- inch in other ga. Magazine holds four 2.75-inch shells or three 3-inch shells. Bbls.: Vent rib; 26-, 28-, 30-inch; IC, M, F choke. Weight: Average 6.25 to 6.75 lbs. depending on ga. Plain pistol-grip stock (checkered on later production), grooved slide handle. Made 1958-70.

MODEL 30 TAKEDOWN SLUG GUN . . NiB $208 Ex $166 Gd $113
Same as Model 30FG except 21-inch cyl. bore bbl. with rifle sights. Made 1971-79.

MODEL 30AC SOLID FRAME . . . . . NiB $231 Ex $185 Gd $126
Same as Model 30 Solid Frame except has 26-inch bbl. with adj. choke; 12 ga. only. Made 1959-70.

MODEL 30AC TAKEDOWN . . . . . . NiB $229 Ex $183 Gd $124
Same as Model 30FG except has 26-inch bbl. with adj. choke; 12 and 20 ga. only. Made 1971-72.

MODEL 30ACL SOLID FRAME . . . . NiB $244 Ex $195 Gd $133
Same as Model 30AC Solid Frame except left-hand model with ejection port and safety on left side; 12 ga. only. Made 1960-64.

MODEL 30D TAKEDOWN . . . . NiB $208 Ex $166 Gd $113
Deluxe Grade. Same as Model 30FG except has receiver engraved with game scene, vent rib bbl., recoil pad. Made 1971 to date.

MODEL 30FG TAKEDOWN HAMMERLESS
SLIDE-ACTION SHOTGUN . . . . NiB $171 Ex $137 Gd $94
Field Grade. Gauges: 12, 20, .410. Three inch chamber. Magazine holds four 2.75-inch shells or three 3-inch shells. Bbls.: plain; 26-inch F choke (.410 ga. only); 28-inch M/F choke; 30-inch F choke (12 ga. only). Weight: Average 7 to 7.75 lbs. depending on gauge. Checkered pistol-grip stock, fluted slide handle. Made 1970-79.

MODEL 30L SOLID FRAME . . . . . . NiB $202 Ex $161 Gd $110
Same as Model 30 Solid Frame except left-handed model with ejection port and safety on left side; 12 ga. only. Made 1959-70.

MODEL 30T SOLID FRAME
TRAP AND DUCK . . . . NiB $231 Ex $185 Gd $126
Same as Model 30 Solid Frame except only in 12 ga. w/30-inch F choke bbl.; has Monte Carlo stock with recoil pad, weight: About 8 lbs. Made 1963-70.

MODEL 30T TAKE DOWN
TRAP GUN . . . . NiB $208 Ex $166 Gd $113
Same as Model 30D except only in 12 ga. w/30-inch F choke bbl. Monte Carlo stock with recoil pad. Made 1970-73.

MODEL 69-RXL SLIDE-ACTION
SHOTGUN . . . . NiB $195 Ex $156 Gd $106
Similar to Model 67 (law enforcement configuration). Hammerless, side ejection top tang safe for left- or right-hand use. 12 ga. chambered for 2.75- and 3-inch bbl. Tubular magazine holds 6 rounds (one less for 3-inch mag). Walnut finish hardwood stock with recoil pad and grooved operating handle. Weight: About 6.5 lbs. Made 1982-89.

MODEL 210F BOLT-ACTION
SLUG GUN . . . . NiB $344 Ex $275 Gd $187
Built on Savage 110 action. Gauge: 12 w/3-inch chamber. Two round detachable magazine. 24-inch fully rifled bbl. Receiver drilled and tapped for scope mounts w/no sights. Weight: 7.5 lbs. Checkered black synthetic stock w/swivel studs and recoil pad. Made 1997 to date.

MODEL 210FT BOLT-ACTION SHOTGUN . . . NiB $413 Ex $330 Gd $224
Similar to Model 210F except has smoothbore 24-inch bbl. w/choke tubes. Bead front and U-notch rear sights. Advantage Camo finish. Made 1997 to date.

Savage 24-C

Savage 24-D

Savage Model 24-F -12T

Savage Model 24-V

Savage Model 30

Savage Model 30 Slug Gun

Savage Model 30-FG

MODEL 220 SINGLE-BARREL SHOTGUN. . . NiB $124 Ex $99 Gd $68
Hammerless. Takedown. Auto ejector. Gauges: 12,16, 20 .410. Single shot. Bbl. lengths: 12 ga., 28- to 36-inch, 16 ga., 28- to 32-inch; 20 ga., 26- to 32-inch; .410 bore, 26-and 28-inch. F choke. Weight: about 6 lbs. Plain pistol-grip stock and wide forearm. Made 1938-65.

MODEL 220AC . . . . NiB $148 Ex $118 Gd $80
Same as Model 220 except has Savage adj. choke.

MODEL 220L. . . . . NiB $106 Ex $85 Gd $58
Same general specifications as Model 220 except has side lever opening instead of top lever. Made 1965-72.

MODEL 220P . . . . NiB $124 Ex $99 Gd $67
Same as Model 220 except has PolyChoke bbl., made in 12 ga. with 30-inch bbl., 16 and 20 ga. with 28-inch bbl., no .410 bore; recoil pad.

Savage Model 69-RXL

Savage Model 220

Savage Model 242

MODEL 242 O/U SHOTGUN . . . . . NiB $356 Ex $285 Gd $194
Similar to Model 24D except both bbls. .410 bore, F choke. Weight: About 7 lbs. Made 1977-80.

MODEL 312 FIELD GRADE O/U. . . NiB $526 Ex $420 Gd $286
Gauge: 12; 2.75- or 3-inch chambers. 26- or 28-inch bbls. w/vent rib; F/M/IC chokes. 43 or 45 inches overall. Weight: 7 lbs. Internal hammers. Top tang safety. American walnut stock with checkered pistol grip and recoil pad. Made 1990-93.

MODEL 312 SPORTING CLAYS O/U . . . . . NiB $557 Ex $446 Gd $303
Same as Model 312 Field Grade except furnished with number 1 and number 2 Skeet tubes and 28-inch bbls. only. Made 1990-93.

MODEL 312 TRAP O/U . . . . NiB $596 Ex $477 Gd $324
Same as Model 312 Field Grade except with 30-inch bbls. only, Monte Carlo buttstock, weight: 7.5 lbs. Made 1990-93.

MODEL 330 O/U SHOTGUN . . . . . NiB $557 Ex $446 Gd $303
Boxlock. Plain extractors. Selective single trigger. Gauges: 12, 20. 2.75-inch chambers in 12 ga., 3-inch in 20 gauge. Bbls.: 26-inch IC/M; 28-inch M/F; 30-inch M/F choke (12 ga. only). Weight: 6.25 to 7.25 lbs., depending on gauge. Checkered pistol-grip stock and forearm. Made 1969-78.

MODEL 333 O/U SHOTGUN
Boxlock. Auto ejectors. Selective single trigger. Gauges: 12, 20. 2.75-inch chambers in 12 ga., 3-inch in 20 ga. Bbls.: vent rib; 26-inch SK choke, IC/M; 28-inch M/F; 30-inch M/F choke (12 ga. only). Weight: Average 6.25 to 7.25 lbs. Checkered pistol-grip stock and forearm. Made 1973-79.
Model 333 12 ga. . . . . NiB $635 Ex $508 Gd $345
Model 333 20 ga. . . . . NiB $772 Ex $617 Gd $419

MODEL 333T TRAP GUN . . . . NiB $563 Ex $450 Gd $306
Similar to Model 330 except only in 12 ga. with 30-inch vent-rib bbls., IM/F choke; Monte Carlo stock w/recoil pad. Weight: 7.75 lbs. Made 1972-79.

MODEL 420
O/U SHOTGUN
Boxlock. Hammerless. Takedown. Automatic safety. Double triggers or non-selective single trigger. Gauges: 12, 16, 20. Bbls.: Plain, 26- to 30-inch (the latter in 12 ga. only); choked M/F, C/IC. Weight with 28-inch bbls.: 12 ga., 7.75 lbs.; 16 ga., 7.5 lbs.; 20 ga., 6.75 lbs. Plain pistol-grip stock and forearm. Made 1938-42.
With double triggers . . . . NiB $419 Ex $335 Gd $228
With single trigger . . . . NiB $478 Ex $382 Gd $260

MODEL 430
Same as Model 420 except has matted top bbl., checkered stock of select walnut with recoil pad, checkered forearm. Made 1938-42.
With double triggers . . . . NiB $478 Ex $382 Gd $260
With single trigger . . . . NiB $526 Ex $420 Gd $286

MODEL 440
O/U SHOTGUN . . . . NiB $504 Ex $403 Gd $306
Boxlock. Plain extractors. Selective single trigger. Gauges: 12, 20. 2.75-inch chambers in 12 ga., 3-inch in 20 ga. Bbls.: Vent rib; 26-inch SK choke, IC/M; 28-inch M/F; 30-inch M/F choke (12 ga. only). Weight: Average 6 to 6.5 lbs. depending on ga. Made 1968-72.

MODEL 440T
TRAP GUN . . . . NiB $522 Ex $418 Gd $284
Similar to Model 440 except only in 12 ga. with 30-inch bbls., extra-wide vent rib, IM/F choke. Trap-style Monte Carlo stock and semibeavertail forearm of select walnut, recoil pad. Weight: 7.5 lbs. Made 1969-72.

MODEL 444 DELUXE
O/U SHOTGUN . . . . NiB $526 Ex $420 Gd $286
Similar to Model 440 except has auto ejectors, select walnut stock and semi-beavertail forearm. Made 1969-72.

Savage Model 312
Field Grade O/U

Savage Model 312
Trap O/U

Savage Model 330

Savage Model 333Y

Savage Model 333
20 Gauge

SHOTGUNS

MODEL 550
HAMMERLESS DOUBLE .... **NiB $264 Ex $211 Gd $144**
Boxlock. Auto ejectors. Non-selective single trigger. Gauges: 12, 20. 2.75-inch chamber in 12 ga., 3-inch in 20 ga. Bbls.: Vent rib; 26-inch IC/M; 28-inch M/F; 30-inch M/F choke (12 ga. only). Weight: 7 to 8 lbs. Checkered pistol-grip stock and semi-beavertail forearm. Made 1971-73. See illustration page 516.

MODEL 720 STANDARD GRADE
5 SHOT AUTOLOADING
SHOTGUN .... **NiB $266 Ex $213 Gd $145**
Browning type. Takedown. 12 and 16 ga. Four shell tubular magazine. Bbl.: plain; 26- to 32-inch (the latter in 12 ga. only); choked IC, M, F. Weight: About 8.25 lbs., 12 ga. with 30-inch bbl.; 16 ga., about .5 lb. lighter. Checkered pistol-grip stock and forearm. Made 1930-49.

MODEL 726 UPLAND SPORTER GRADE
3-SHOT AUTOLOADING
SHOTGUN .... **NiB $270 Ex $216 Gd $146**
Same as Model 720 except has 2-shell magazine capacity. Made 1931-49.

MODEL 740C
SKEET GUN .... **NiB $342 Ex $265 Gd $227**
Same as Model 726 except has special skeet stock and full beavertail forearm, equipped with Cutts Compensator. Bbl. length overall with spreader tube is about 24.5 inches. Made 1936-49.

MODEL 745 LIGHT-WEIGHT
AUTOLOADER .... **NiB $266 Ex $213 Gd $145**
Three- or five-shot models. Same general specifications as Model 720 except has lightweight alloy receiver, 12 ga.only, 28-inch plain bbl. Weight: About 6.75 lbs. Made 1940-49.

MODEL 750
AUTOMATIC SHOTGUN .... **NiB $275 Ex $220 Gd $150**
Browning-type autoloader. Takedown. 12 ga. Four shot tubular magazine. Bbls.: 28-inch F or M choke; 26-inch IC. Weight: About 7.25 lbs. Checkered walnut pistol-grip stock and grooved forearm. Made 1960-67.

MODEL 750-AC .... **NiB $309 Ex $247 Gd $168**
Same as Model 750 except has 26-inch bbl. with adj. choke. Made 1964-67.

Savage Model 440

Savage Model 440T

Savage Model 550

Savage Model 750

Savage Model 775

Savage Model 775-SC

MODEL 750-SC . . . . NiB $281 Ex $225 Gd $153
Same as Model 750 except has 26-inch bbl. with Savage Super
Choke. Made 1962-63.

**MODEL 755 STANDARD
GRADE AUTOLOADER** . . . . NiB $266 Ex $213 Gd $145
Streamlined receiver. Takedown.12 and 16 ga. Four shell tubular
magazine (a three-shot model with magazine capacity of two
shells was also produced until 1951). Bbl.: Plain, 30-inch F
choke (12 ga. only), 28-inch F or M, 26-inch IC. Weight: About
8.25 lbs., 12 ga. Checkered pistol-grip stock and forearm. Made
1949-58.

MODEL 755-SC . . . . NiB $262 Ex $210 Gd $142
Same as Model 755 except has 26-inch bbl. w/recoil-reducing, adj.
Savage Super Choke.

MODEL 775 LIGHTWEIGHT . . . . . . NiB $269 Ex $215 Gd $146
Same general specifications as Model 755 except has lightweight
alloy receiver, weight: About 6.73 lbs. Made 1950-65.

MODEL 775-SC . . . . NiB $281 Ex $225 Gd $153
Same as Model 775 except has 26-inch bbl. with Savage Super
Choke.

**MODEL 2400 O/U
COMBINATION** . . . . NiB $619 Ex $575 Gd $519
Boxlock action similar to that of Model 330. Plain extractors. Selective
single trigger. 12-ga. (2.75-inch chamber) shotgun bbl., F choke over
.308 Win. or .222 Rem. rifle bbl.; 23.5-inch; solid matted rib with
blade front sight and folding leaf rear, dovetail for scope mounting.
Weight: About 7.5 lbs. Monte Carlo stock w/pistol grip and recoil pad,
semibeavertail forearm, checkered. Made 1975-79 by Valmet.

Savage Model 2400
O/U Combination Gun

SEARS, ROEBUCK & COMPANY — Chicago, Illinois. (J. C. Higgins and Ted Williams Models)

Although they do not correspond to specific models below, the names Ted Williams and J. C. Higgins have been used to designate various Sears shotguns at various times.

MODEL 18
BOLT-ACTION REPEATER . . . . NiB $106 Ex $85 Gd $58
Takedown. 3-shot top-loading magazine. Gauge: .410 only. Bbl.: 25-inch w/variable choke. Weight: About 5.75 lbs.

MODEL 20 SLIDE-ACTION REPEATER . . NiB $210 Ex $168 Gd $114
Hammerless. 5-shot magazine. Bbls.: 26- to 30-inch w/various chokes. Weight: 7.25 lbs. Plain pistol-grip stock and slide handle.

MODEL 21 SLIDE-ACTION REPEATER . . . . . NiB $231 Ex $185 Gd $126
Same general specifications as the Model 20 except vent rib and adj. choke.

MODEL 30 SLIDE-ACTION REPEATER . . . NiB $219 Ex $175 Gd $119
Hammerless. Gauges: 12, 16, 20 and .410. Four shot magazine. Bbls.: 26- to 30-inch, various chokes. Weight: 6.5 lbs. Plain pistol-grip stock, grooved slide handle.

MODEL 97 SINGLE-SHOT SHOTGUN . . . . NiB $81 Ex $65 Gd $44
Takedown. Visible hammer. Automatic ejector. Gauges: 12, 16, 20 and .410. Bbls.: 26- to 36-inch, F choke. Weight: Average 6 lbs. Plain pistol-grip stock and forearm.

MODEL 97-AC SINGLE-SHOT SHOTGUN . . . . . NiB $100 Ex $80 Gd $54
Same general specifications as Model 97 except fancier stock and forearm.

MODEL 101.7 DOUBLE-BARREL
SHOTGUN . . . . NiB $210 Ex $168 Gd $114
Boxlock. Double triggers. Gauges: 12, 16, 20, .410. Bbls.: 26- to 32-inch, choked M and F. Weight: From 6 to 7.5 lbs. Plain stock and forend.

MODEL 101.7C DOUBLE-BARREL
SHOTGUN . . . . NiB $225 Ex $170 Gd $90
Same general specifications as Model 101.7 except checkered stock and forearm.

MODEL 101.25 BOLT-ACTION SHOTGUN . . . . NiB $100 Ex $80 Gd $54
Takedown. .410 gauge. Five shell tubular magazine. 24-inch bbl., F choke. Weight: About 6 lbs. Plain, one-piece pistol-grip stock.

MODEL 101.40 SINGLE-SHOT SHOTGUN . . NiB $85 Ex $68 Gd $46
Takedown. Visible hammer. Automatic ejector. Gauges: 12, 16, 20 and .410. Bbls.: 26- to 36-inch, F choke. Weight: Average 6 lbs. Plain pistol-grip stock and forearm.

MODEL 101.1120 BOLT-ACTION REPEATER . . . . . NiB $100 Ex $80 Gd $54
Takedown. .410 ga. 24-inch bbl., F choke. Weight: About 5 lbs. Plain one-piece pistol-grip stock.

MODEL 101.1380 BOLT-ACTION REPEATER . . . NiB $113 Ex $90 Gd $61
Takedown. Gauges: 12, 16, 20. Two shell detachable box magazine. 26-inch bbl., F choke. Weight: About 7 lbs. Plain one-piece pistol-grip stock.

MODEL 101.1610 DOUBLE-BARREL
SHOTGUN . . . . NiB $308 Ex $246 Gd $168
Boxlock. Double triggers. Plain extractors. Gauges: 12, 16, 20 and .410. Bbls.: 24- to 30-inch. Various chokes, but mostly M and F. Weight: About 7.5 lbs, 12 ga. Checkered pistol-grip stock and forearm.

MODEL 101.1701 DOUBLE-BARREL
SHOTGUN . . . . NiB $306 Ex $245 Gd $167
Same general specifications as Model 101.1610 except satin chrome frame and select walnut stock and forearm.

MODEL 101.5350-D
BOLT-ACTION REPEATER . . . . NiB $95 Ex $76 Gd $51
Takedown. Gauges: 12, 16, 20. 2-shell detachable box magazine. 26-inch bbl., F choke. Weight: About 7.25 lbs. Plain one piece pistol-grip stock.

MODEL 101.5410
BOLT-ACTION REPEATER . . . . NiB $100 Ex $80 Gd $54
Same general specifications as Model 101.5350-D.

SKB ARMS COMPANY — Tokyo, Japan
Imported by G.U. Inc., Omaha, Nebraska

MODEL 385 SIDE-BY-SIDE . . . . . NiB $1619 Ex $1295 Gd $881
Boxlock action w/double locking lugs. Gauges: 12, 20 and 28 w/2.75- and 3-inch chambers. 26- or 28-inch bbls. w/Inter-Choke tube system. Single selective trigger. Selective automatic ejectors and automatic safety. Weight: 6 lbs., 10 oz. Silver nitride receiver w/engraved scroll and game scene. Solid rib w/flat matte finish and metal front bead sight. Checkered American walnut English or pistol-grip stock. Imported 1992 to date.

MODELS 300 AND 400 SIDE-BY-SIDE DOUBLES
Similar to Model 200E except higher grade. Models 300 and 400 differ in that the latter has more elaborate engraving and fancier wood.
Model 300 . . . . NiB $898 Ex $718 Gd $488
Model 400 . . . . NiB $1093 Ex $874 Gd $595

MODEL 400 SKEET . . . . NiB $1031 Ex $825 Gd $561
Similar to Model 200E Skeet except higher grade with more elaborate engraving and full fancy wood.

MODEL 480 ENGLISH . . . . NiB $1342 Ex $1074 Gd $73
Similar to Model 280 English except higher grade with more elaborate engraving and full fancy wood.

SHOTGUNS

SKB Model 585 Field

SKB Model 605 Trap

SKB Model 885 Trap

MODEL 500 SERIES O/U SHOTGUN
Boxlock. Gauges: 12 and 20 w/2.75-or 3-inch chambers. Bbls.: 26-, 28- or 30-inch with vent rib; fixed chokes. Weight: 7.5 to 8.5 lbs. Single selective trigger. Selective automatic ejectors. Manual safety. Checkered walnut stock. Blue finish with scroll engraving. Imported 1967-80.
500 Field, 12 ga. . . . . NiB $525 Ex $420 Gd $285
500 Field, 20 ga. . . . . NiB $623 Ex $498 Gd $339
500 Magnum, 12 ga.
3-inch chambers . . . . NiB $591 Ex $472 Gd $321

MODEL 500 SMALL
GAUGE O/U SHOTGUN . . . . NiB $653 Ex $522 Gd $355
Similar to Model 500 except gauges 28 and .410; has 28-inch vent-rib bbls., M/F chokes. Weight: About 6.5 lbs.

MODEL 505 O/U SHOTGUN
Blued boxlock action. Gauge: 12, 20, 28 and .410. Bbls.: 26-, 28, 30-inch; IC/M, M/F or inner choke tubes. 45.19 inches overall. Weight: 6.6 to 7.4 lbs. Hand checkered walnut stock. Metal bead front sight, ejectors, single selective trigger and ejectors. Introduced 1988.
Standard Field, Skeet or Trap grade. . . . . . . NiB $872 Ex $697 Gd $474
Standard Two-bbl. Field set . . . . . NiB $1328 Ex $1062 Gd $722
Skeet grade, three-bbl. set . . . . NiB $1894 Ex $1515 Gd $1030
Sporting Clays . . . . NiB $931 Ex $745 Gd $507
Trap grade two-bbl. set . . . . NiB $1603 Ex $1282 Gd $872

MODEL 585 DELUXE O/U SHOTGUN
Boxlock. Gauges: 12, 20, 28 and .410; 2.75-or 3-inch chambers. Bbls.: 26-, 28-, 30-, 32- or 34-inch with vent rib; fixed chokes or Inter-choke tubes. Weight: 6.5 to 8.5 lbs. Single selective trigger. Selective automatic ejectors. Manual safety. Checkered walnut stock in standard or Monte Carlo style. Silver nitride finish with engraved game scenes. Made 1987 to date.
Field, Skeet, Trap grades . . . . NiB $1185 Ex $948 Gd $644
Field grade, two-bbl. set . . . . . . NiB $2092 Ex $1674 Gd $1138
Skeet set (20, 28, .410 ga.) . . . . NiB $2542 Ex $2034 Gd $1383
Sporting Clays . . . . NiB $1443 Ex $1155 Gd $785
Trap Combo (two-bbl.) . . . . NiB $2092 Ex $1674 Gd $1138

MODEL 600 SERIES O/U SHOTGUN
Similar to 500 Series except w/silver nitride receiver. Checkered deluxe walnut stock in both Field and Target Grade configurations . Imported 1969-80.
600 Field, 12 ga. . . . . NiB $653 Ex $522 Gd $355
600 Field, 20 ga. . . . . NiB $840 Ex $650 Gd $500
600 Magnum, 12 ga.
3-inch chambers . . . . NiB $720 Ex $500 Gd $325
600 Skeet or Trap grade . . . . NiB $700 Ex $550 Gd $400
600 Trap Doubles Gun. . . . . NiB $653 Ex $522 Gd $355

MODEL 600 SMALL GA. . . . . NiB $850 Ex $750 Gd $454
Same as Model 500 Small Gauge except higher grade with more elaborate engraving and fancier wood.

MODEL 605 SERIES O/U SHOTGUN
Similar to the Model 505 except w/engraved silver nitride receiver and deluxe wood. Introduced 1988.
Field, Skeet, Trap grade . . . . NiB $894 Ex $715 Gd $486
Skeet three-bbl. set . . . . NiB $1940 Ex $1552 Gd $1055
Sporting Clays . . . . NiB $905 Ex $724 Gd $492

MODEL 680 ENGLISH O/U SHOTGUN
Similar to 600 Series except w/English style select walnut stock and fine scroll engraving. Imported 1973-77.
680 English, 12 ga. . . . . NiB $754 Ex $603 Gd $410
680 English, 20 ga. . . . . NiB $860 Ex $764 Gd $468

MODEL 685 DELUXE O/U
Similar to the 585 Deluxe except with semi-fancy American walnut stock. Gold trigger and jeweled barrel block. Silvered receiver with fine engraving.
Field, Skeet, Trap grade . . . . NiB $1230 Ex $984 Gd $669
Field grade, two-bbl. set . . . . . . NiB $1918 Ex $1534 Gd $1043
Skeet set . . . . NiB $2618 Ex $2094 Gd $1424
Sporting Clays . . . . NiB $1271 Ex $1017 Gd $691
Trap Combo. two bbl. . . . . NiB $1894 Ex $1515 Gd $1030

Sile Field Master II

MODEL 800 SKEET/TRAP O/U
Similar to Model 700 Skeet and Trap except higher grade with more elaborate engraving and fancier wood.

Model 800 Skeet . . . . NiB $1275 Ex $1020 Gd $693
Model 800 Trap . . . . NiB $1156 Ex $925 Gd $629

MODEL 880 SKEET/TRAP
Similar to Model 800 Skeet except has sideplates.

Model 880 Skeet . . . . NiB $1494 Ex $1195 Gd $813
Model 880 Trap . . . . NiB $1531 Ex $1225 Gd $833

MODEL 885 DELUXE O/U
Similar to the 685 Deluxe except with engraved sideplates.

Field, Skeet, Trap grade . . . . NiB $1216 Ex $973 Gd $662
Field grade, two-bbl. set . . . . . . NiB $1918 Ex $1534 Gd $1043
Skeet Set . . . . NiB $3081 Ex $2465 Gd $1676
Sporting Clays . . . . NiB $1567 Ex $1254 Gd $853
Trap Combo . . . . NiB $2542 Ex $2034 Gd $1383

The following SKB shotguns were distributed by Ithaca Gun Co. from 1966-76. For specific data, see corresponding listings under Ithaca.

CENTURY SINGLE-BARREL TRAP GUN
The SKB catalog does not differentiate between Century and Century II; however, specifications of current Century are those of Ithaca-SKB Century II.

Century (505) . . . . NiB $898 Ex $718 Gd $488
Century II (605) . . . . NiB $1041 Ex $833 Gd $566

GAS-OPERATED AUTOMATIC SHOTGUNS
Model XL300 with plain barrel . . . . NiB $331 Ex $265 Gd $180
Model XL300 with vent rib . . . . NiB $369 Ex $295 Gd $201
Model XL900 . . . . NiB $326 Ex $261 Gd $177
Model XL900 Trap . . . . NiB $387 Ex $310 Gd $211
Model XL900 Skeet . . . . NiB $398 Ex $318 Gd $216
Model XL900 Slug . . . . NiB $350 Ex $280 Gd $190
Model 1300 Upland, Slug . . . . NiB $445 Ex $356 Gd $242
Model 1900 Field, Trap, Slug . . . . . . NiB $500 Ex $400 Gd $272

SKB OVER/UNDER SHOTGUNS
Model 500 Field . . . . NiB $531 Ex $425 Gd $289
Model 500 Magnum . . . . NiB $623 Ex $498 Gd $339
Model 600 Field . . . . NiB $721 Ex $577 Gd $392
Model 600 Magnum . . . . NiB $749 Ex $599 Gd $408
Model 600 Trap . . . . NiB $714 Ex $536 Gd $364
Model 600 Doubles . . . . NiB $694 Ex $555 Gd $378
Model 600 Skeet—12 or 20 ga. . . . . . . NiB $756 Ex $605 Gd $411
Model 600 Skeet—28 or .410 . . . . NiB $820 Ex $656 Gd $446
Model 600 Skeet Combo . . . . NiB $1994 Ex $1595 Gd $1085
Model 600 English . . . . NiB $706 Ex $565 Gd $384
Model 700 Trap . . . . NiB $882 Ex $706 Gd $480
Model 700 Doubles . . . . NiB $775 Ex $620 Gd $421
Model 700 Skeet . . . . NiB $844 Ex $675 Gd $459
Model 700 Skeet Combo . . . . NiB $2194 Ex $1755 Gd $1193

SKB RECOIL-OPERATED AUTOMATIC SHOTGUNS
Model 300—with plain barrel . . . . NiB $294 Ex $235 Gd $160
Model 300—with vent rib . . . . NiB $331 Ex $265 Gd $180
Model 900 . . . . NiB $374 Ex $299 Gd $203
Model 900 Slug . . . . NiB $356 Ex $285 Gd $194

SKB SIDE-BY-SIDE DOUBLE-BARREL SHOTGUNS
Model 100 . . . . NiB $477 Ex $382 Gd $260
Model 150 . . . . NiB $534 Ex $427 Gd $290
Model 200E . . . . NiB $791 Ex $632 Gd $430
Model 200E Skeet . . . . NiB $781 Ex $624 Gd $425
Model 280 English . . . . NiB $1086 Ex $868 Gd $591

SIG SAUER — (SIG) Schweizerische Industrie-Gesellschaft, Neuhausen, Switzerland

MODEL SA3 O/U SHOTGUN
Monobloc boxlock action. Single selective trigger. Automatic ejectors. Gauges: 12 or 20 w/3- inch chambers. 26-, 28- or 30-inch vent rib bbls. w/choke tubes. Weight: 6.8 to 7.1 lbs. Checkered select walnut stock and forearm. Satin nickel-finished receiver w/game scene and blued bbls. Imported 1997-98.

Field model . . . . NiB $1185 Ex $948 Gd $645
Sporting Clays model . . . . NiB $1286 Ex $1029 Gd $700

MODEL SA5 O/U SHOTGUN
Similar to SA3 Model except w/detachable sideplates. Gauges: 12 or 20 w/3- inch chambers. 26.5-, 28- or 30-inch vent rib bbls. w/choke tubes. Imported 1997-99.

Field model . . . . NiB $2191 Ex $1753 Gd $1192
Sporting Clays model . . . . NiB $2372 Ex $1897 Gd $1290

SILE SHOTGUNS — Sile Distributors, New York, NY

FIELD MASTER II O/U SHOTGUN . . . . NiB $563 Ex $450 Gd $306
Gauge: 12, 3-inch chambers. 28-inch bbl., IC, M, IM, F choke tubes. 45.25 inches overall. Weight: 7.25 lbs. Satin-finished walnut, checkered stock and forend. Introduced 1989.

L. C. SMITH SHOTGUNS — Made 1890-1945 by Hunter Arms Company, Fulton, N.Y.; 1946-51 and 1968-73 by Marlin Firearms Company, New Haven, Conn.

L. C. SMITH DOUBLE-BARREL SHOTGUNS
Values shown are for L. C. Smith doubles made by Hunter. Those of 1946-51 Marlin manufacture generally bring prices about 1/3 lower. Smaller gauge models, especially in the higher grades, command premium prices: Up to 50 percent more for 20 gauge, up to 400 percent for .410 gauge.

SHOTGUNS

L.C. Smith Crown

L.C. Smith Field

(cont'd.) L. C. SMITH DOUBLE-BARREL SHOTGUNS

Crown grade, double triggers,
automatic ejectors . . . . NiB $6162 Ex $4929 Gd $3352
Crown grade, selective single trigger,
automatic ejectors . . . . NiB $7212 Ex $4824 Gd $3923
Deluxe grade, selective single trigger,
automatic ejectors . . . NiB $21,875+ Ex $17,500+ Gd $11,900+
Eagle grade, double triggers,
automatic ejectors . . . . NiB $5019 Ex $4015 Gd $2730
Eagle grade, selective
single trigger . . . . NiB $5355 Ex $4284 Gd $2913
Field grade, double triggers,
plain extractors . . . . NiB $1174 Ex $939 Gd $639
Field grade, double triggers
auto. ej. . . . . NiB $1568 Ex $1254 Gd $853
Field grade, non-selective single trigger,
plain extractors . . . . NiB $1476 Ex $1181 Gd $803
Field grade, selective single trigger,
automatic ejectors . . . . NiB $1568 Ex $1254 Gd $853
Ideal grade, double triggers,
plain extractors . . . . NiB $1641 Ex $1312 Gd $892
Ideal grade, double triggers,
auto. ej. . . . . NiB $2224 Ex $1779 Gd $1210
Ideal grade, selective single trigger,
automatic ejectors . . . . NiB $2559 Ex $2047 Gd $1392
Monogram grade, selective single trigger,
automatic ejectors . . . . NiB $12,593 Ex $10,074 Gd $6851
Olympic grade, selective single trigger,
automatic ejectors . . . . NiB $2349 Ex $1879 Gd $1277
Premier grade, selective single trigger
automatic ejectors . . . NiB $17,187+ Ex $13,750+ Gd $9350+
Skeet Special, non-selective single trigger,
automatic ejectors . . . . NiB $2263 Ex $1811 Gd $1231
Skeet Special, selective single trigger,
auto ejectors . . . . NiB $2953 Ex $2362 Gd $1606
.410 ga. . . . . NiB $13,125 Ex $10,500 Gd $7140
Specialty grade, double triggers,
auto ejectors . . . . NiB $3799 Ex $3039 Gd $2067
Specialty grade, selective single trigger,
automatic ejectors. . . . . NiB $4062 Ex $3249 Gd $2210
Trap grade, sel. single trigger,
auto ej. . . . . NiB $1699 Ex $1359 Gd $925

L C. SMITH HAMMERLESS DOUBLE-BARREL SHOTGUNS

Sidelock. Auto ejectors standard on higher grades, extra on Field and Ideal Grades. Double triggers or Hunter single trigger (non-selective or selective). Gauges: 12, 16, 20, .410. Bbls.: 26- to 32-inch, any standard boring. Weight: 6.5 to 8.25 lbs., 12 ga. Checkered stock and forend; choice of straight, half or full pistol grip, beavertail or standard-type forend. Grades differ only in quality of workmanship, wood, checkering, engraving, etc. Same general specifications apply to all. Manufacture of these L. C. Smith guns

(cont'd.) L. C. SMITH HAMMERLESS DOUBLE-BARREL SHOTGUNS

was discontinued in 1951. Production of Field Grade 12 ga. was resumed 1968-73. Note: L. C. Smith Shotguns manufactured by the Hunter Arms Co. 1890-13 were designated by numerals to indicate grade with the exception of Pigeon and Monogram.

00 grade . . . . NiB $1473 Ex $1178 Gd $801
0 grade . . . . NiB $1797 Ex $1437 Gd $977
1 grade . . . . NiB $1994 Ex $1595 Gd $1085
2 grade . . . . NiB $2197 Ex $1757 Gd $1195
3 grade . . . . NiB $3125 Ex $2500 Gd $1700
Pigeon . . . . NiB $3919 Ex $3135 Gd $2131
4 grade . . . . NiB $8250 Ex $6600 Gd $4488
5 grade . . . . NiB $8925 Ex $7140 Gd $4855
Monogram . . . . NiB $10,794 Ex $8635 Gd $5871
A1 . . . . NiB $6562 Ex $3675 Gd $2499
A2. NiB $11,156 Ex $8925 Gd $6069
A3 . . . . NiB $25,000+ Ex $20,000+ Gd $13,600+

L. C. SMITH HAMMERLESS DOUBLE

MODEL 1968 FIELD GRADE. . . . . . NiB $706 Ex $565 Gd $384
Re-creation of the original L. C. Smith double. Sidelock. Plain extractors. Double triggers. 12 ga. 28-inch vent-rib bbls., M/F choke. Weight: About 6.75 lbs. Checkered pistol-grip stock and forearm. Made 1968-73.

L. C. SMITH HAMMERLESS DOUBLE

MODEL 1968 DELUXE . . . . NiB $1017 Ex $813 Gd $553
Same as 1968 Field Grade except has Simmons floating vent rib, beavertail forearm. Made 1971-73.

L. C. SMITH SINGLE-SHOT TRAP GUNS

Boxlock. Hammerless. Auto ejector.12 gauge only. Bbl. lengths: 32- or 34-inch. Vent rib. Weight: 8 to 8.25 lbs. Checkered pistol-grip stock and forend, recoil pad. Grades vary in quality of workmanship, wood, engraving, etc.; general specifications are the same. Disc. 1951. Note: Values shown are for L. C. Smith single-barrel trap guns made by Hunter. Those of Marlin manufacture generally bring prices about one-third lower.

Olympic grade. . . . . NiB $1772 Ex $1417 Gd $963
Specialty grade . . . . NiB $2224 Ex $1779 Gd $1210
Crown grade . . . . NiB $3872 Ex $3097 Gd $2106
Monogram grade . . . . NiB $5768 Ex $4614 Gd $3138
Premier grade . . . . NiB $8918 Ex $7134 Gd $4852
Deluxe grade. . . . . NiB $13,781 Ex $11,025 Gd $7497

SMITH & WESSON SHOTGUNS —
Springfield, Massachusetts, Mfd. by Howa Machinery, Ltd., Nagoya, Japan
In 1985, Smith and Wesson sold its shotgun operation to O. F. Mossberg & Sons, Inc.

L.C. Smith 1968 Field Grade

L.C. Smith 1968 Deluxe

L.C. Smith Single-Shot Trap Gun

Smith & Wesson Model 1000 Magnum

Smith & Wesson Model 3000 Slide Action

MODEL 916 SLIDE-ACTION REPEATER
Hammerless. Solid frame. Gauges: 12, 16, 20. Three inch chamber in 12 and 20 ga. Five shot tubular magazine. Bbls.: plain or vent rib; 20-inch C (12 ga., plain only); 26-inch IC- 28-inch M or F; 30-inch F choke (12 ga. only). Weight: With 28-inch plain bbl., 7.25 lbs. Plain pistol-grip stock, fluted slide handle. Made 1972-81.
With plain bbl. . . . . NiB $171 Ex $137 Gd $94
With ventilated rib bbl. . . . . NiB $219 Ex $175 Gd $119

MODEL 916T
Same as Model 916 except takedown, 12 ga. only. Not available with 20-inch bbl. Made 1976-81.
With plain bbl. . . . . NiB $185 Ex $148 Gd $100
With ventilated rib bbl. . . . . NiB $219 Ex $175 Gd $119

MODEL 1000 AUTOLOADER . . . . . NiB $324 Ex $260 Gd $176
Gas-operated. Takedown. Gauges: 12, 20. 2.75-inch chamber in 12 ga., 3-inch in 20 ga. Four shot magazine. Bbls.: Vent rib, 26-inch SK choke, IC; 28-inch M or F; 30-inch F choke (12 ga. only). Weight: With 28-inch bbl., 6.5 lbs. in 20 ga.,7.5 lbs. in 12 ga. Checkered pistol-grip stock and forearm. Made 1972 to date.

MODEL 1000 MAGNUM . . . . NiB $398 Ex $318 Gd $216
Same as standard Model 1000 except chambered for 12 ga. magnum, 3-inch shells; 30-inch bbl. only, M or F choke; stock with recoil pad. Weight: About 8 lbs. Introduced in 1977.

MODEL 1000P . . . . NiB $345 Ex $276 Gd $187
Same general specifications as Model C 3000 Slide Action, but an earlier version.

MODEL 3000
SLIDE ACTION . . . . NiB $350 Ex $280 Gd $190
Hammerless. 20-ga. Bbls.: 26-inch IC; 28-inch M or F. Chambered for 3-inch magnum and 2.75-inch loads. American walnut stock and forearm. Checkered pistol grip and forearm. Introduced 1982.

SPRINGFIELD ARMS — Built by Savage Arms Company, Utica, New York

SPRINGFIELD DOUBLE-BARREL
HAMMER SHOTGUN . . . . NiB $406 Ex $325 Gd $221
Gauges: 12 and 16. Bbls.: 28 to 32 inches. In 12 ga., 32-inch model, both bbls. have F choke. All other gauges and barrel lengths are left barrel, Full; right barrel, Mod. Weight: 7.25 to 8.25 lbs., depending on gauge and barrel length. Black walnut checkered buttstock and forend. Disc. 1934.

SQUIRES BINGHAM CO., INC. — Makati, Rizal, Philippines

MODEL 30
PUMP SHOTGUN . . . . NiB $200 Ex $160 Gd $109
Hammerless. 12 ga. Five shot magazine. Bbl.: 20-inch Cyl.; 28-inch M; 30-inch F choke. Weight: About 7 lbs. Pulong Dalaga stock and slide handle. Currently manufactured.

Squires Bingham Model 30 Pump Shotgun

J. STEVENS ARMS COMPANY — Chicopee Falls, Massachusetts, Division of Savage Arms Corporation

NO. 20 "FAVORITE" SHOTGUN . . NiB $328 Ex $262 Gd $178
Calibers: .22 and .32 Shot. Smoothbore bbl. Blade front sight; no rear. Made 1893-1939.

**NO. 39 NEW MODEL
POCKET SHOTGUN** . . . . NiB $632 Ex $505 Gd $344
Gauge: .410. Calibers: .38-40 Shot, .44-40 Shot. Bbls.: 10, 12, 15 or 18 inches, half-octagonal smoothbore. Shotgun sights. Made 1895-1906.

NO. 22-.410 O/U COMBINATION GUN
.22 caliber rifle barrel over .410 ga. shotgun barrel. Visible hammer. Takedown. Single trigger. 24-inch bbls., shotgun bbl. F choke. Weight: About 6 lbs. Open rear sight and ramp front sight of sporting rifle type. Plain pistol-grip stock and forearm; originally supplied with walnut stock and forearm. "Tenite" (plastic) was used in later production. Made 1938-50. Note: This gun is now manufactured as the Savage Model 24.
With wood stock and forearm . . . . NiB $219 Ex $175 Gd $119
With Tenite stock and forearm . . . . . NiB $162 Ex $130 Gd $89

**MODEL 51 BOLT-ACTION
SHOTGUN** . . . . NiB $106 Ex $85 Gd $58
Single shot. Takedown. .410 ga. 24-inch bbl., F choke. Weight: About 4.75 lbs. Plain one-piece pistol-grip stock. checkered on later models. Made 1962-71.

**MODEL 58 BOLT-ACTION
REPEATER** . . . . NiB $131 Ex $105 Gd $71
Takedown. Gauges: 12, 16, 20. Two shell detachable box magazine. 26-inch bbl., F choke. Weight: About 7.25 lbs. Plain one piece pistol-grip stock on early models w/takedown screw on bottom of forend. Made 1933-81. Note: Later production models have 3-inch chamber in 20 ga., checkered stock with recoil pad.

**MODEL 58-.410 BOLT-ACTION
REPEATER** . . . . NiB $124 Ex $99 Gd $68
Takedown. .410 ga. Three shell detachable box magazine. 24-inch bbl., F choke. Weight: About 5.5 lbs. Plain one piece pistol-grip stock, checkered on later production. Made 1937-81.

**MODEL 59 BOLT-ACTION
REPEATER** . . . . NiB $169 Ex $135 Gd $92
Takedown. .410 ga. Five shell tubular magazine. 24-inch bbl., F choke. Weight: About 6 lbs. Plain, one piece pistol-grip stock, checkered on later production. Made 1934-73.

MODEL 67 PUMP SHOTGUN
Hammerless, side-ejection solid-steel receiver. Gauges: 12, 20 and .410, 2.75- or 3-inch shells. Bbls.: 21-, 26-, 28- 30-inch with fixed chokes or interchangeable choke tubes, plain or vent rib. Weight: 6.25 to 7.5 lbs. Optional rifle sights. Walnut-finished hardwood stock with corncob-style forend.

(cont'd.) MODEL 67 PUMP SHOTGUN
Standard model, plain bbl. . . . . NiB $219 Ex $175 Gd $119
Standard model, vent rib . . . . NiB $231 Ex $185 Gd $126
Standard model, w/choke tubes . . . NiB $244 Ex $195 Gd $133
Slug model w/rifle sights . . . . NiB $206 Ex $165 Gd $112
Lobo model, matte finish . . . . NiB $269 Ex $215 Gd $146
Youth model, 20 ga. . . . . NiB $231 Ex $185 Gd $126
Camo model. w/choke tubes . . . . . NiB $281 Ex $225 Gd $153

MODEL 67 WATERFOWL SHOTGUN . . . . NiB $256 Ex $204 Gd $139
Hammerless. Gauge: 12. Three shot tubular magazine. Walnut finished hardwood stock. Weight: About 7.5 lbs. Made 1972-89.

MODEL 77 SLIDE-ACTION REPEATER . . . . NiB $197 Ex $157 Gd $107
Solid frame. Gauges: 12, 16, 20. Five shot tubular magazine. Bbls.: 26-inch IC, 28-inch M or F choke. Weight: About 7.5 lbs. Plain pistol-grip stock with recoil pad, grooved slide handle. Made 1954-71.

MODEL 77-AC. . . . . NiB $231 Ex $185 Gd $126
Same as Model 77 except has Savage Super Choke.

MODEL 79-VR SUPER VALUE . . . . . NiB $219 Ex $175 Gd $119
Hammerless, side ejection. Bbl.: Chambered for 2.75-inch and 3-inch mag. shells. 12, 20, and .410 ga. vent rib. Walnut finished hardwood stock with checkering on grip. Weight: 6.75-7 lbs. Made 1979-90.

MODEL 94 SINGLE-SHOT SHOTGUN . . . NiB $113 Ex $90 Gd $61
Takedown. Visible hammer. Auto ejector. Gauges: 12, 16, 20, 28, .410. Bbls.: 26-, 28-, 30-, 32-, 36-inch, F choke. Weight: About 6 lbs. depending on gauge and barrel. Plain pistol-grip stock and forearm. Made 1939-61.

MODEL 94C . . . . NiB $156 Ex $125 Gd $85
Same as Model 94 except has checkered stock, fluted forearm on late production. Made 1965-90.

MODEL 94Y YOUTH GUN . . . . NiB $154 Ex $123 Gd $83
Same as Model 94 except made in 20 and .410 ga. only; has 26-inch F choke bbl., 12.5-inch buttstock with recoil pad; checkered pistol grip and fluted forend on late production. Made 1959-90.

MODEL 95 SINGLE-SHOT SHOTGUN . . . NiB $113 Ex $90 Gd $61
Solid frame. Visible hammer. Plain extractor. 12 ga. Three inch chamber. Bbls.: 28-inch M- 30-inch F choke. Weight: About 7.25 lbs. Plain pistol-grip stock, grooved forearm. Made 1965-69.

**MODEL 107 SINGLE-SHOT
HAMMER SHOTGUN** . . . . NiB $106 Ex $85 Gd $58
Takedown. Auto ejector. Gauges: 12, 16, 20, .410. Bbl. lengths: 28- and 30-inch (12 and 16 ga.), 28-inch (20 ga.), 26-inch (.410); F choke only. Weight: About 6 lbs., 12 bore ga. Plain pistol-grip stock and forearm. Made about 1937-53.

MODEL 124 CROSS-BOLTREPEATER . . . NiB $166 Ex $133 Gd $90
Hammerless. Solid frame. 12 ga. only. Two shot tubular magazine. 28-inch bbl.; IC, M or F choke. Weight: About 7 lbs. Tenite stock and forearm. Made 1947-52.

Stevens Model 51

Stevens Model 58

Stevens Model 58-410

Stevens Model 67 Pump Shotgun

Stevens Model 67 Waterfowl Shotgun

Stevens Model 77

Stevens Model 94C

Stevens Model 95

SHOTGUNS

Stevens Model
94 Youth

Stevens Model 124
Cross-Bolt Repeater

MODEL 240 O/U SHOTGUN . . . . . NiB $309 Ex $247 Gd $168
Visible hammer. Takedown. Double triggers. .410 ga. 26-inch bbls.,
F choke. Weight: 6 lbs. Tenite (plastic) pistol-grip stock and forearm.
Made 1940-49.

MODEL 258 BOLT-ACTION
REPEATER . . . . NiB $119 Ex $95 Gd $65
Takedown. 20-gauge. Two shell detachable box magazine. 26-inch
barrel, Full choke. Weight: About 6.25 lbs. Plain, one piece pistol-
grip stock. Made 1937-65.

MODEL 311 SPRINGFIELD
HAMMERLESS DOUBLE
Same general specifications as Stevens Model 530 except earlier
production has plain stock and forearm; checkered on current guns.
Originally produced as a "Springfield" gun, this model became a
part of the Stevens line in 1948 when the Springfield brand name
was discontinued. Made 1931-89.
Pre-WW II . . . . NiB $377 Ex $301 Gd $205
Post-WW II . . . . NiB $332 Ex $265 Gd $180

MODEL 311-R
HAMMERLESS DOUBLE . . . . NiB $271 Ex $216 Gd $147
Same general specifications as Stevens Model 311 except compact
design for law enforcement use. Bbls.: 18.25-inch 12 gauge with
solid rib, chambered for 2.75 and 3-inch Mag. shells. Double triggers and auto top tang safety. Walnut finished hardwood stock with
recoil pad and semi-beavertail forend. Weight: About 6.75 lbs.
Made 1982-89.

MODEL 530
HAMMERLESS DOUBLE . . . . NiB $331 Ex $265 Gd $180
Boxlock. Double triggers. Gauges: 12, 16, 20, .410. Bbl. lengths:
26- to 32-inch; choked M/F, C/M, F/F. Weight: 6 to 7.5 pounds
depending on gauge and barrel length. Checkered pistol-grip stock
and forearm; some early models with recoil pad. Made 1936-54.

MODEL 530M . . . . NiB $240 Ex $192 Gd $130
Same as Model 530 except has Tenite (plastic) stock and forearm.
Disc. about 1947.

MODEL 530ST
DOUBLE GUN . . . . NiB $303 Ex $242 Gd $164
Same as Model 530 except has non-selective single trigger. Disc.

MODEL 620 HAMMERLESS
SLIDE-ACTION
REPEATING SHOTGUN . . . . NiB $309 Ex $247 Gd $168
Takedown. Gauges: 12, 16, 20. Five shell tubular magazine. Bbl.
lengths: 26-, 28-, 30-, 32-inch; choked F, M IC, C. Weight: About
7.75 lbs., 12 ga.; 7.25 lbs., 16 ga.- 6 lbs., 20 ga. Checkered pistol-
grip stock and slide handle. Made 1927-53.

MODEL 620-C . . . . NiB $309 Ex $247 Gd $168
Same specifications as Model 620 except equipped with Cutts
Compensator and two choke tubes.

MODEL 620-P . . . . NiB $323 Ex $258 Gd $176
Same specifications as Model 620 equipped with Aero-Dyne
PolyChoke and 27-inch bbl.

MODEL 620-PV . . . . NiB $323 Ex $258 Gd $176
Same specifications as Model 620 except equipped with ventilated
PolyChoke and 27-inch bbl.

MODEL 621 . . . . NiB $378 Ex $302 Gd $205
Same as Model 620 except has raised solid matted-rib barrel. Disc.

MODEL 820 HAMMERLESS
SLIDE-ACTION
REPEATING SHOTGUN . . . . NiB $244 Ex $195 Gd $133
Solid frame. 12 gauge only. Five shell tubular magazine. 28-inch
barrel; IC, M or F choke. Weight: About 7.5 lbs. Plain pistol-grip
stock, grooved slide handle. Early models furnished w/Tenite buttstock and forend. Made 1949-54.

MODEL
820-SC. . . . . NiB $269 Ex $215 Gd $146
Same as Model 820 except has Savage Super Choke.

MODEL 940 SINGLE-
SHOT SHOTGUN . . . . NiB $101 Ex $81 Gd $54
Same general specifications as Model 94 except has side lever
opening instead of top lever. Made 1961-70.

MODEL 940Y
YOUTH GUN . . . . NiB $124 Ex $99 Gd $67
Same general specifications as Model 94Y except has side lever
opening instead of top lever. Made 1961-70.

Stevens Model 258

Stevens Model 311

Stevens Model 530

Stevens Model 620

Stevens Model 620-P

Stevens Model 820

MODEL 9478 . . . . **NiB $107 Ex $85 Gd $58**
Takedown. Visible hammer. Automatic ejector. Gauges: 12, 20, .410. Bbls.: 26-, 28-, 30-, 36-inch; Full choke. Weight: Average 6 pounds depending on gauge and barrel. Plain pistol-grip stock and forearm. Made 1978-85.

MODEL 5151 SPRINGFIELD . . . . . . **NiB $385 Ex $308 Gd $209**
Same specifications as the Stevens Model 311 except with checkered grip and forend; equipped with recoil pad and two ivory sights.

STOEGER SHOTGUNS

See IGA and Tikka Shotguns

TAR-HUNT CUSTOM RIFLES, INC. — Bloomsburg, PA

MODEL RSG-12 MATCHLESS
BOLT-ACTION SLUG GUN . . . . . **NiB $1699 Ex $1359 Gd $925**
Similar to Professional model except has McMillan Fibergrain stock and deluxe blue finish. Made 1995 to date.

MODEL RSG-12 PEERLESS
BOLT-ACTION SLUG GUN . . . . . **NiB $1772 Ex $1417 Gd $963**
Similar to Professional model except has McMillan Fibergrain stock and deluxe NP-3 (Nickel/Teflon) metal finish. Made 1995 to date.

MODEL RSG-12 PROFESSIONAL
BOLT-ACTION SLUG GUN
Bolt action 12 ga. w/2.75-inch chamber, 2-round detachable magazine, 21.5-inch fully rifled bbl. w/ or w/o muzzle brake. Receiver drilled and tapped for scope mounts w/no sights. Weight: 7.75 lbs. 41.5 inches overall. Checkered black McMillan fiberglass stock w/swivel studs and Pachmayr Deacelerator pad. Made 1991 to date.
RSG-12 model
W/O muzzle brake (disc. 1993) . . . . NiB $1368 Ex $1094 Gd $744
RSG-12 model
W/muzzle brake . . . . NiB $1505 Ex $1204 Gd $819

MODEL RSG-20 MOUNTAINEER
BOLT ACTION SLUG GUN . . . . . . NiB $1230 Ex $984 Gd $669
Similar to Professional model except 20 ga. w/2.75 inch chamber. Black McMillan synthetic stock w/blind magazine. Weight: 6.5 lbs. Made 1997 to date.

TECNI-MEC SHOTGUNS — Italy, Imported by RAHN Gun Work, Inc., Hastings, MI

MODEL SPL 640
FOLDING SHOTGUN
Gauges: 12, 16, 20, 24, 28, 32 and .410 bore. 26-inch bbl. Chokes: IC/IM. Weight: 6.5 lbs. Checkered walnut pistol-grip stock and forend. Engraved receiver. Available with single or double triggers. Imported 1988-94.
640 w/single trigger . . . . NiB $438 Ex $350 Gd $238
640 w/double trigger . . . . NiB $494 Ex $395 Gd $269

THOMPSON/CENTER ARMS — Rochester, New Hampshire

CONTENDER
.410 GA. CARBINE . . . . NiB $350 Ex $280 Gd $190
Gauge: .410 smoothbore. 21-inch vent rib bbl. 34.75 inches overall. Weight: About 5.25 lbs. Bead front sight. Rynite stock and forend. Made 1991 to date.

ENCORE
20 GA. SHOTGUN
Gauge: 20 smoothbore w/rifled slug bbl. or 26-inch vent-rib bbl. w/three internal screw choke tubes, 38 to 40.5 inches overall. Weight: About 5.25 to 6 lbs. Bead or fiber optic sights. Walnut stock and forend. Made 2000 to date.
Encore 20 ga.
W/vent rib . . . . NiB $518 Ex $414 Gd $282
Encore 20 ga.
w/rifled slug bbl. . . . . NiB $478 Ex $383 Gd $260
W/extra
bbl., add $262

MODEL '87
HUNTER SHOTGUN . . . . NiB $456 Ex $365 Gd $248
Single shot. Gauge: 10 or 12, 3.5-inch chamber, 25-inch field bbl. with F choke. Weight: 8 lbs. Bead front sight. American black walnut stock with recoil pad. Made 1987 to 1992.

MODEL '87
HUNTER SLUG . . . . NiB $469 Ex $375 Gd $255
Gauge: 10 (3.5-inch chamber) or 12 (3-inch chamber). Same general specifications as Model '87 Hunter Shotgun except with 22-inch slug (rifled) bbl. and rifle sights. Made 1987 to 1992.

TIKKA SHOTGUNS — Manufactured by: Armi Marocchi, Italy, (formerly by Valmet), Riihimaki, Finland

M 07 SHOTGUN/
RIFLE COMBINATION . . . . NiB $994 Ex $795 Gd $541
Gauge/caliber: 12/.222 Rem. Shotgun bbl.: About 25 inches; rifled bbl.: About 22.75 inches. 40.66 inches overall. Weight: About 7 lbs. Dovetailed for telescopic sight mounts Single trigger with selector between the bbls. Vent rib. Monte Carlo-style walnut stock with checkered pistol grip and forend. Made 1965-87.

M 77 O/U SHOTGUN. . . . . NiB $119 Ex $95 Gd $65
Gauge: 12. 27-inch vent-rib bbls., approx. 44 inches overall, weight: About 7.25 lbs. Bbl. selector. Ejectors. Monte Carlo-style walnut stock with checkered pistol grip and forend; rollover cheek-piece. Made 1977-87.

M 77K SHOTGUN/ RIFLE
COMBINATION . . . . NiB $1313 Ex $1050 Gd $714
Gauge: 12/70. Calibers: .222 Rem., 5.6x52r5, 6.5x55, 7x57r5, 7x65r5, .308 Win. Vent-rib bbls.: About 25 inches (shotgun); 23 inches (rifle), 42.3 inches overall. Weight: About 7.5 lbs. Double triggers. Monte Carlo-style walnut stock with checkered pistol grip and forend; rollover cheekpiece. Made 1977-86.

412S/512S SHOOTING SYSTEM
Boxlock action with both under lug and sliding top latch locking mechanism designed to accept interchangeable monobloc barrels, including O/U shotgun, combination and double rifle configurations. Blued or satin nickel receiver w/cocking indicators. Selective single trigger design w/barrel selector incorporated into the trigger (double triggers available). Blued barrels assemblies w/extractors or auto ejectors as required. Select American walnut stock with checkered pistol grip and forend. Previously produced in Finland (same as the former Valmet Model 412) but currently manufactured in Italy by joint venture arrangement with Armi Marocchi. From 1990-93, Stoeger Industries imported this model as the 412/S. In 1993 the nomenclature of this shooting system was changed to 512/S and is now imported under that designation. Note: For double rifle values, see Tikka Rifles.

MODEL 412S/512S O/U SHOTGUN
Gauge: 12 w/3-inch chambers. 24-, 26-, 28- or 30-inch chrome-lined bbls. w/blued finish and integral stainless steel choke tubes. Weight: 7.25 to 7.5 lbs. Blue or matte nickel receiver. Select American walnut stock with checkered pistol grip and forend. Imported 1990 to date.
Standard Field model . . . . NiB $781 Ex $625 Gd $425
Standard Trap model . . . . NiB $931 Ex $745 Gd $507
Premium Field model . . . . NiB $844 Ex $675 Gd $459
Premium Trap model . . . . NiB $1119 Ex $895 Gd $609
Sporting Clays model . . . . NiB $944 Ex $755 Gd $513
Standard Trap model . . . . NiB $1119 Ex $895 Gd $609
W/Extra O/U shotgun bbl., add $575
W/Extra O/U combination bbl., add $695
W/Extra O/U rifle bbl., add $995

MODEL 412S/512S OVER/UNDER COMBINATION
Gauge: 12 w/3-inch chamber. Calibers: .222 Rem., .30-06 or .308 Win. Blue or matte nickel receiver, 24-inch chrome-lined bbls. w/extractors and blued finish. Weight: 7.25 to 7.5 lbs. Select American walnut stock with checkered pistol grip and forend. Imported 1990 to date.
Standard Combination model . . . . NiB $938 Ex $750 Gd $510
Premium Combination model . . . . NiB $994 Ex $795 Gd $541
Extra barrel options . . . . NiB $994 Ex $795 Gd $541

TRADITIONS PERFORMANCE FIREARMS — Importers of shotguns produced by Fausti Stefano of Brescia, Italy and ATA Firearms, Turkey.

CLASSIC SERIES, FIELD I O/U
Available in 12, 20, 28 (2 3/4-inch chamber) and .410 gauge, 26- or 28-inch vent rib bbls. W/fixed chokes and extractors. Weight: 6 3/4 to 7 1/4 lbs. Blued finish, silver receiver engraved with game birds. Single, selective trigger. Brass bead front sight. European walnut stock. Overall length 43 to 45 inches. Intro. 2000. . . . . **$619**

FIELD HUNTER MODEL
Same as Field I except 12 and 20 gauge, 3-inch chambers, screw-in chokes and extractors. **$669**

FIELD II MODEL
Same as Field I except with screw-in chokes and automatic ejectors. **$789**

FIELD III GOLD MODEL
Same as Field I model except 12 gauge only, high-grade, oil-finish walnut, coin-finish receiver with engraved pheasants and woodcock, deep blue finish on barrels, automatic ejectors and non-slip recoil pad. **$999**

CLASSIC SERIES O/U SPORTING CLAY III
Available in 12 and 20 gauge, 3-inch chambers, high grade walnut stock, oil-satin finish, palm swell Schnabel forend. 28- and 30-inch bbls. with 3/8-inch top and middle vent rib, red target front bead sight. Automatic ejectors, extended choke tubes. Weight: 8 1/4 lbs. Intro. 2000. . . . . **$1189**

SPORTING CLAY II MODEL
Same as Sporting Clay III model but with European walnut stocks, cut checkering and extended choke tubes. Overall length: 47 inches. Weight: 7 3/4 lbs. **$959**

UPLAND III MODEL
Same as Sporting Clay III model but round pistol grip and Schnabel forend, blued receiver with engraved upland scene, weight: 7 1/2 lbs **$1059**

UPLAND II MODEL
Same as Upland III model except with English walnut straight-grip stock and Schnabel forend, 24- and 26-inch vent rib bbls., floral engraving on blued receiver, automatic ejectors. **$839**

MAG 350 SERIES
TURKEY II O/U
Magnum 3 1/2-inch chambers in 12 gauge only, 24- and 26-inch bbls., screw-in flush fitting chokes: F and XF. Matte finish, engraved receiver, Mossy Oak or Realtree camo. Intro. 2000. . . . . **$889**

WATERFOWL II MODEL
Same as Turkey II model except with Advantage Wetlands camo stock and barrels, weight: 8 lbs., overall length 45 inches. Waterfowl model has 28-inch bbls. **$889**

MAG HUNTER II
Same as Turkey II model except blued engraved receiver and matte finish walnut stocks, 3 1/2-inch chambers, 28-inch bbls. with screw-in chokes. **$799**

ELITE SERIES DOUBLE-BARREL SHOTGUNS
ELITE FIELD III ST
Checkered English walnut straight stock, splinter forend, fixed chokes. Available in 28 and .410 gauge, 26-inch chrome-lined bbls., Cylinder and Modified chokes. Silver trigger guard and receiver with hand-finished engraving of upland game scenes with gold inlays. Automatic ejectors. Brass front sight bead. Weight: About 6 1/2 lbs. Intro. 2000. . . . . **$2099**

ELITE HUNTER ST
Same as Elite Field model except 12 and 20 gauge, European walnut stock, beavertail forend, screw-in choke tubes, extractors, three-inch chambers. Blued finish. Vent-rib, tang safety. Weight: 6 1/2 pounds **$999**

ELITE FIELD I ST
Same as Elite Field III except single trigger, fixed chokes, extractors; European walnut stock. Available in 12, 20, 28 (2 3/4-inch chambers) and .410 gauge; fixed IC/M chokes. Weight: 5 3/4 to 6 1/2 lbs. **$919**

ELITE FIELD I DT
Same as Elite Field I except with double triggers, fixed chokes, extractors. Available in 12, 20, 28 (2 3/4-inch chambers) and .410. Bbls: 26 inches, fixed IC/M chokes. Weight: 5 1/2 to 6 1/4 lbs **$869**

ALS 2100 SEMI-AUTOMATIC SHOTGUNS
FIELD SERIES, WALNUT MODEL
Gas-operated, 12 and 20 gauge, 3-inch chambers, cut-checkered Turkish walnut stock and forend, blued 26- and 28-inch vent rib bbls., multi-choke system, chrome bore lining. Weight: About 6 lbs. Rifled barrel with cantilever mount available Intro. 2001. . . . **$479**

SYNTHETIC STOCK MODEL
Same as the ALS 2100 Walnut model except with synthetic stock, matted finish on receiver and bbl., weight: About 6 lbs **$459**

YOUTH MODEL
Same as ALS 2100 Walnut model except with a shorter walnut stock (length of pull: 13 1/2 inches). Available in 12 or 20 gauge with 24-inch vent rib barrel, weight: 5 1/2 to 6lbs **$479**

HUNTER COMBO MODEL
Same as ALS 2100 Walnut model except comes with two bbls. (28-inch vent rib and 24-inch slug), TruGlo adjustable sights and cantilever mount. Available with Turkish walnut or synthetic stock with matte barrel finish. Weight: 6 1/2 lbs.
(Walnut) **$629**
(Synthetic) **$579**

SLUG HUNTER MODEL
Same as ALS 2100 Walnut except with fully-rifled barrel, choice of walnut or synthetic stocks, matte or blue finish; rifle or TruGlo adjustable sights. Weight: About 6 1/4 lbs. **$549**

TURKEY HUNTER/WATERFOWL MODEL
Same as ALS 2100 Walnut except with synthetic stock, 3-inch chambers, 26-inch vent rib bbl., screw-in chokes, Mossy Oak or Realtree camo stocks. **$519**

HOME SECURITY MODEL
Same as ALS 2100 Walnut but with 20-inch cylinder-bore bbl., synthetic stock, 3-inch chambers, six-shot capacity with 2 3/4-inch shells. Weight: About 6 lbs. **$399**

SHOTGUNS

Valmet Model 412 K O/U Field Shotgun

Ward Western Field Model 50

Ward Western Field Model 52

TRISTAR SPORTING ARMS — North Kansas City, MO

MODEL 1887 LEVER-ACTION REPEATER .... NiB $563 Ex $450 Gd $306
Copy of John Browning's Winchester Model 1887 lever-action shotgun. 12 ga. only. 30-inch bbl. which may be cut down to any desired length of 18 inches or more. Version shown has 20-inch bbl. Imported 1997-98.

MODEL 300 O/U SHOTGUN ..... NiB $406 Ex $325 Gd $221
Similar to the Model 333 except 12 ga. only w/3-inch chambers, 26- or 28-inch vent rib bbls. w/extractors and fixed chokes. Etched receiver w/double triggers and standard walnut stock. Imported 1994-98.

MODEL 311 SIDE-BY-SIDE SHOTGUN
Boxlock action w/underlug and Greener cross bolt. 12 or 20 ga. w/3-inch chambers, 20, 28- or 30-inch bbls. w/choke tubes or fixed chokes (311R). Double triggers. Extractors. Black chrome finish. Checkered Turkish walnut buttstock and forend. Weight: 6.9 to 7.2 lbs. Imported 1994-97.
311 Model (w/extractors and choke tubes) ... NiB $563 Ex $450 Gd $306
311R Model
(w/20-inch bbls. and fixed chokes) .... NiB $406 Ex $325 Gd $221

MODEL 330 O/U SHOTGUN
Similar to the Model 333 except 12 ga. only w/3-inch chambers. 26-, 28- or 30-inch vent rib bbls w/extractors or ejectors and fixed chokes or choke tubes. Etched receiver and standard walnut stock. Imported 1994 to date.
330 model (w/ extractor and fixed chokes) ... NiB $494 Ex $395 Gd $269
330 D model (w/ejectors and choke tubes) ... NiB $656 Ex $525 Gd $357

MODEL 333 O/U SHOTGUN
Boxlock action. 12 or 20 ga. w/3-inch chambers. 26-, 28- or 30-inch vent rib bbls. w/choke tubes. Single selective trigger. Selective automatic ejectors. Engraved receiver w/satin nickel finish. Checkered Turkish fancy walnut buttstock and forend. Weight: 7.5 to 7.75 lbs. Imported 1994 to date..
333 Field model .... NiB $754 Ex $603 Gd $410
333 Sporting Clays model (1994-97) ..... NiB $853 Ex $682 Gd $464
333 TRL Ladies Field model .... NiB $767 Ex $614 Gd $417
333 SCL Ladies Sporting Clays model
(1994-97) .... NiB $872 Ex $698 Gd $474

SHOTGUNS OF ULM — Ulm, West Germany

See listings under Krieghoff.

U.S. REPEATING ARMS CO. — New Haven, Connecticut

See Winchester Shotgun listings.

VALMET OY — Jyväskylä, Finland

NOTE: In 1987, Valmet and Sako merged and the Valmet production facilities were moved to Riihimaki, Finland. In 1989 a joint venture agreement was made with Armi Marocchi, and when production began in Italy, the Valmet name was changed to Tikka (Oy Tikkakoski Ab).

See also Savage Models 330, 333T, 333 and 2400, which were produced by Valmet.

VALMET LION O/U SHOTGUN ... NiB $478 Ex $383 Gd $260
Boxlock. Selective single trigger. Plain extractors. 12 ga. only. Bbls.: 26-inch IC/M; 28-inch M/F, 30-inch M/F, F/F. Weight: About 7 lbs. Checkered pistol-grip stock and forearm. Imported 1947-68.

MODEL 412 K O/U FIELD SHOTGUN .... NiB $806 Ex $645 Gd $439
Hammerless. 12-ga., 3-inch chamber, 36-inch bbl., F/F chokes. American walnut Monte Carlo stock. Made 1982-87.

MODEL 412 K SHOTGUN RIFLE
COMBINATION .... NiB $969 Ex $775 Gd $527
Similar to model 412 K except bottom bbl. chambered for .222 Rem., .223 Rem., .243 Win., .308 Win. or .30-06. 12-ga. shotgun bbl. with IM choke. Monte Carlo American walnut stock, recoil pad.

MODEL 412 KE O/U
FIELD SHOTGUN .... NiB $781 Ex $625 Gd $425
12-ga. chambered for 2.75-inch shells. 26-inch bbl., IC/M chokes; 28-inch bbl., M/F chokes; 12-ga. chambered for 3-inch shells, 30-inch bbl., M/F chokes. 20-ga. (3-inch shells); 26-inch bbl., IC/M chokes; 28-inch bbl., M/ F chokes. American walnut Monte Carlo stock.

Weatherby Model 82
Autoloading Shotgun

MODEL 412 KE SKEET . . . . NiB $912 Ex $729 Gd $496
Similar to Model 412 K except skeet stock and chokes. 12 and 20 ga. Disc. 1989.

MODEL 412 KE TRAP . . . . NiB $951 Ex $761 Gd $517
Similar to Model 412 K Field except trap stock, recoil pad. 30-inch bbls., IM/F chokes. Disc.1989.

MODEL 412 3-BARREL SET . . . . . . .NIB $2494 EX $1995 GD $1357

MONTGOMERY WARD — Chicago, Illinois
Western Field and Hercules Models

Although they do not correspond to specific models below, the names Western Field and Hercules have been used to designate various Montgomery Ward shotguns at various times.

MODEL 25 SLIDE-ACTION REPEATER . . . . . . NiB $200 Ex $160 Gd $109
Solid frame. 12 ga. only. Two or 5-shot tubular magazine. 28-inch bbl., various chokes. Weight: About 7.5 lbs. Plain pistol-grip stock, grooved slide handle.

MODEL 40 O/U SHOTGUN . . . . . . NiB $688 Ex $551 Gd $374
Hammerless. Boxlock. Double triggers. Gauges: 12, l6, 20, .410. Bbls.: Plain; 26- to 30-inch, various chokes. Checkered pistol-grip stock and forearm.

MODEL 40N
SLIDE-ACTION REPEATER . . . . NiB $206 Ex $165 Gd $112
Same general specifications as Model 25.

(WESTERN FIELD) MODEL 50 PUMPGUN . . . NiB $213 Ex $170 Gd $116
Solid frame. Gauges: 12 and 16. Two and 5-shot magazine. 26-, 28- or 30-inch bbl., 48 inches overall w/28-inch bbl. Weight: 7.25 - 7.75 lbs. Metal bead front sight. Walnut stock and grooved forend.

(WESTERN FIELD) MODEL 52
DOUBLE-BARREL SHOTGUN . . . . . NiB $242 Ex $194 Gd $132
Hammerless coil-spring action. Gauges: 12, 16, 20 and .410. 26-, 28-, or 30-inch bbls., 42 to 46 inches overall, depending upon bbl. length. Weight: 6 (.410 ga. w/26-inch bbl.) to 7.25 lbs. (12 ga. w/30-inch bbls.), depending upon gauge and bbl. length. Casehardened receiver; blued bbls. Plain buttstock and forend. Made circa 1954.

MODEL 172 BOLT-ACTION SHOTGUN . . . . NiB $106 Ex $85 Gd $58
Takedown. Two shot detachable clip magazine.12 ga. 28-inch bbl. with variable choke. Weight: About 7.5 lbs. Monte Carlo stock with recoil pad.

MODEL 550A SLIDE-ACTION REPEATER . . . . NiB $244 Ex $195 Gd $133
Takedown. Gauges: 12, 16, 20, .410. Five shot tubular magazine. Bbls.: Plain, 26- to 30-inch, various chokes. Weight: 6 (.410 ga. w/26-inch bbl.) to 8 lbs. (12 ga. w/30-inch bbls.). Plain pistol-grip stock and grooved slide handle.

MODEL SB300 DOUBLE-BARREL
SHOTGUN . . . . NiB $262 Ex $210 Gd $142
Same general specifications as Model SD52A.

MODEL SB312 DOUBLE-BARREL SHOTGUN . . . NiB $295 Ex $236 Gd $160
Boxlock. Double triggers. Plain extractors. Gauges: 12, 16, 20, .410. Bbls.: 24- to 30-inch. Various chokes. Weight: About 7.5 lbs. in 12 ga.; 6.5 lbs in .410 ga. Checkered pistol-grip stock and forearm.

MODEL SD52A DOUBLE-BARREL SHOTGUN . . . . NiB $219 Ex $175 Gd $119
Boxlock. Double triggers. Plain extractors. Gauges: 12, 16, 20, .410. Bbls.: 26- to 32-inch, various chokes. Plain forend and pistol-grip buttstock. Weight: 6 (.410 ga., 26-inch bbls.) to 7.5 lbs. (12 ga., 32-inch bbls.).

WEATHERBY, INC. — Atascadero, California
(previously South Gate, California)

MODEL 82 AUTOLOADING SHOTGUN
Hammerless, gas-operated. 12 ga. only. Bbls.: 22- to 30-inch, various integral or fixed chokes. Weight: 7.5 lbs. Checkered walnut stock and forearm. Imported 1982-89.

Standard Autoloading Shotgun . . . . NiB $409 Ex $327 Gd $223
BuckMaster Auto Slug
w/rifle sights (1986-90) . . . . NiB $416 Ex $332 Gd $226
W/fixed chokes, deduct. $40

MODEL 92 SLIDE-ACTION SHOTGUN
Hammerless, short-stroke action. 12 ga.; 3-inch chamber. Tubular magazine. Bbls.: 22-, 26-, 28-, 30-inch with fixed choke or IMC choke tubes; plain or vent rib with rifle sights. Weight: 7.5 lbs. Engraved, matte black receiver and blued barrel. Checkered high-gloss buttstock and forend. Imported from Japan since 1982.

Standard Model 92 . . . . NiB $326 Ex $261 Gd $177
BuckMaster Pump Slug
w/rifle sights (intro. 1986) . . . . NiB $350 Ex $280 Gd $190
W/fixed chokes, deduct. $25

ATHENA O/U SHOTGUN
Engraved boxlock action with Greener crossbolt and sideplates. Gauges: 12, 20, 28 and .410; 2.75- or 3.5-inch chambers. Bbls.: 26-, 28-, 30- or 32-inch with fixed or IMC Multi-choke tubes. Weight: 6.75 to 7.38 lbs. Single selective trigger. Selective auto ejectors. Top tang safety. Checkered Claro walnut stock and forearm with high-luster finish. Imported 1982 to date.
Field Model w/IMC multi-choke
(12 or 20 ga.) . . . . NiB $2092 Ex $1674 Gd $1138
Field Model w/fixed chokes (28 or .410 ga.) . . . NiB $1942 Ex $1554 Gd $1057
Skeet Model w/fixed chokes (12 or 20 ga.) . . . . . NiB $1753 Ex $1402 Gd $953
Skeet Model w/fixed chokes
(28 or .410 ga.) . . . . NiB $1959 Ex $1567 Gd $1065
Master skeet tube set . . . . NiB $3378 Ex $2702 Gd $1837
Trap Model w/IC tubes . . . . NiB $1792 Ex $1434 Gd $975
Grade V (1993 to date) . . . . NiB $2193 Ex $1754 Gd $1193

SHOTGUNS

Weatherby Model 92
Slide-Action Shotgun

Weatherby Athena
O/U Shotgun

Weatherby Centurion
Automatic Shotgun

Weatherby Olympian Trap
O/U Shotgun

Weatherby Orion
O/U Shotgun

Weatherby Patrician
Deluxe Grade

Weatherby Regency
Trap Gun

CENTURION AUTOMATIC SHOTGUN
Gas-operated. Takedown. 12 ga. 2.75-inch chamber. Three shot magazine. Bbls.: Vent ribs; 26-inch SK, IC or M 28-inch M or F; 30-inch Full choke. Weight: With 28-inch bbl., 7 lbs. 10.5 oz. Checkered pistol-grip stock and forearm, recoil pad. Made in Japan 1972-81.
Centurion Field grade . . . . NiB $332 Ex $265 Gd $180
Centurion Trap Gun
(30-inch full choke bbl.) . . . . NiB $385 Ex $308 Gd $209
Centurion Deluxe (etched
receiver, fancy wood) . . . . NiB $503 Ex $402 Gd $273

OLYMPIAN O/U SHOTGUN
Gauges: 12 and 20. 2.75- (12 ga.) and 3-inch (20 ga.) chambers. Bbls.: 26-, 28-, 30, and 32-inch. Weight: 6.75 - 8.75 lbs. American walnut stock and forend.
Field
Model . . . . NiB $884 Ex $707 Gd $481
Skeet
Model . . . . NiB $908 Ex $726 Gd $494
Trap
Model . . . . NiB $891 Ex $712 Gd $484

ORION O/U SHOTGUN

Boxlock with Greener crossbolt. Gauges: 12, 20, 28 and .410; 2.75- or 3-inch chambers. Bbls.: 26-, 28, 30-, 32- or 34-inch with fixed or IMC Multi-Choke tubes. Weight: 6.5 to 9 lbs. Single selective trigger. Selective auto ejectors. Top tang safety. Checkered, high-gloss pistol-grip Claro walnut stock and forearm. Finish: Grade I, plain blued receive; Grade II, engraved blued receiver; Grade III, silver gray receiver. Imported 1982 to date.

Orion I Field w/IC (12 or 20 ga.)	NiB $1065	Ex $852	Gd $579
Orion II Field w/IC (12 or 20 ga.)	NiB $1108	Ex $887	Gd $603
Orion II Classic w/IC (12, 20 or 28 ga.)	NiB $1093	Ex $874	Gd $595
Orion II Sporting Clays w/IC (12 ga.)	NiB $1275	Ex $1020	Gd $693
Orion III Field w/IC (12 or 20 ga.)	NiB $1148	Ex $918	Gd $624
Orion III Classic w/IC (12 or 20 ga.)	NiB $1382	Ex $1106	Gd $752
Orion III English Field w/IC (12 or 20 ga.)	NiB $1342	Ex $1074	Gd $730
Orion Upland w/IC (12 or 20 ga.)	NiB $1237	Ex $990	Gd $673
Skeet II w/fixed chokes	NiB $1342	Ex $1074	Gd $730
Super Sporting Clays	NiB $1642	Ex $1314	Gd $894

PATRICIAN SLIDE-ACTION SHOTGUN

Hammerless. Takedown. 12 ga. 2.75-inch chamber. Four shot tubular magazine. Bbls.: Vent rib; 26-inch, SK, IC M; 28-inch, M F; 30-inch, F choke. Weight: With 28-inch bbl., 7 lbs., 7 oz. Checkered pistol-grip stock and slide handle, recoil pad. Made in Japan 1972-82.

Patrician Field grade	NiB $279	Ex $223	Gd $152
Patrician Deluxe (etched receiver, fancy grade wood)	NiB $326	Ex $261	Gd $177
Patrician Trap Gun (30-inch F choke bbl.)	NiB $297	Ex $237	Gd $161

REGENCY FIELD GRADE O/U SHOTGUN.... NiB $1211 Ex $968 Gd $658

Boxlock with sideplates, elaborately engraved. Auto ejectors. Selective single trigger. Gauges: 12, 20. 2.75-inch chamber in 12 ga., 3-inch in 20 ga. Bbls.: Vent rib; 26-inch SK, IC/M, M/F (20 ga. only); 28-inch SK, IC/M, M/F; 30-inch M/F (12 ga only). Weight with 28-inch bbls.: 7 lbs., 6 oz., 12 ga.; 6 lbs., 14 oz., 20 ga. Checkered pistol-grip stock and forearm of fancy walnut. Made in Italy 1965-82.

REGENCY TRAP GUN .... NiB $1242 Ex $993 Gd $676

Similar to Regency Field Grade except has trap-style stock with straight or Monte Carlo comb. Bbls. have vent side ribs and high, wide vent top rib; 30- or 32-inch, M/F, IM/F or F/F chokes. Weight: With 32-inch bbls., 8 lbs. Made in Italy 1965-1982.

WESTERN ARMS CORP. — Ithaca, New York
Division of Ithaca Gun Company

LONG RANGE HAMMERLESS DOUBLE

Boxlock. Plain extractors. Single or double triggers. Gauges: 12, 16, 20, .410. Bbls.: 26- to 32-inch, M/F choke standard. Weight: 7.5 lbs., 12 ga. Plain pistol-grip stock and forend. Made 1929-46.

With double triggers	NiB $309	Ex $247	Gd $168
With single trigger	NiB $394	Ex $315	Gd $214

WESTERN AUTO SHOTGUNS — Kansas City, Missouri

MODEL 300H SLIDE-ACTION REPEATER .... NiB $244 Ex $195 Gd $133

Gauges: 12,16, 20, .410. Four shot tubular magazine. Bbls.: 26- to 30-inch, various chokes. Weight: About 7 lbs. Plain pistol-grip stock, grooved slide handle.

MODEL 310A SLIDE-ACTION REPEATER .... NiB $231 Ex $185 Gd $126

Takedown. 12 ga. Five shot tubular magazine. Bbls.: 28- and 30-inch. Weight: About 7.5 lbs. Plain pistol-grip stock.

**Westley Richards
Deluxe Sidelock**

MODEL 310B SLIDE-ACTION REPEATER..... NiB $219 Ex $175 Gd $119

Same general specifications as Model 310A except chambered for 16 ga.

MODEL 310C SLIDE-ACTION REPEATER .... NiB $244 Ex $195 Gd $133

Same general specifications as Model 310A except chambered for 20 ga.

MODEL 310E SLIDE-ACTION REPEATER..... NiB $281 Ex $225 Gd $153

Same general specifications as Model 310A except chambered for .410 bore.

MODEL 325BK BOLT-ACTION REPEATER ...... NiB $111 Ex $89 Gd $60

Takedown. Two shot detachable clip magazine. 20 ga. 26-inch bbl. with variable choke. Weight: 6.25 lbs.

WESTERN FIELD SHOTGUNS

See "W" for listings under Montgomery Ward.

WESTLEY RICHARDS & CO., LTD. — Birmingham, England

The Pigeon and Wildfowl gun, available in all of the Westley Richards models except the Ovundo, has the same general specifications as the corresponding standard field gun except has magnum action of extra strength and treble bolting, chambered for 12 gauge only (2.75- or 3-inch); 30-inch full choke barrels standard. Weight: About 8 lbs. The manufacturer warns that 12-gauge magnum shells should not be used in their standard weight double-barrel shotguns.

BEST QUALITY BOXLOCK HAMMERLESS
DOUBLE-BARREL SHOTGUN

Boxlock. Hand-detachable locks and hinged cover plate. Selective ejectors. Double triggers or selective single trigger. Gauges: 12, 16, 20. Barrel lengths and boring to order. Weight: 5.5 to 6.25 lbs. depending on ga. and bbl. length. Checkered stock and forend, straight or half-pistol grip. Also supplied in Pigeon and Wildfowl models with same values. Made from 1899 to date.

With double triggers	NiB $21,312	Ex $17,050	Gd $11,594
With selective single trigger	NiB $24,062	Ex $19,250	Gd $13,090

BEST QUALITY SIDELOCK HAMMERLESS
DOUBLE-BARREL SHOTGUN

Hand-detachable sidelocks. Selective ejectors. Double triggers or selective single trigger. Gauges: 12, 16, 20, 28, .410. Bbl. lengths and boring to order. Weight: 4.75 to 6.75 lbs., depending on ga. and bbl. length. Checkered stock and forend, straight or half-pistol grip. Also supplied in Pigeon and Wildfowl models with same values. Currently manufactured.

With double triggers	NiB $25,031	Ex $20,225	Gd $14,073
With selective single trigger	NiB $27,250	Ex $22,000	Gd $15,280

SHOTGUNS

**Westley Richards
Best Quality Sidelock**

**Westley Richards
Deluxe Boxlock**

**Westley Richards
Model E**

**Winchester Model 12 Classic
Limited Edition Grade I**

**Winchester Model 12
Field Gun — 1972 Type**

MODEL DELUXE BOX LOCK
HAMMERLESS DOUBLE-BARREL SHOTGUN
Same general specifications as standard Best Quality gun except higher quality throughout. Has Westley Richards top-projection and treble-bite lever-work, hand-detachable locks. Also supplied in Pigeon and Wildfowl models with same values. Currently manufactured.
With double triggers .... NiB $11,188 Ex $8950 Gd $6086
With selective
single trigger .... NiB $30,000 Ex $28,000 Gd $12,000

MODEL DELUXE SIDELOCK
Same as Best Quality Sidelock except higher grade engraving and wood. Currently manufactured.
With double triggers .... NiB $25,000 Ex $20,000 Gd $13,600
With single trigger ...... NiB $30,000 Ex $24,000 Gd $16,320

MODEL E HAMMERLESS DOUBLE
Anson & Deeley-type boxlock action. Selective ejector or non-ejector. Double triggers. Gauges: 12, 16, 20. Barrel lengths and boring to order. Weight: 5.5 to 7.25 lbs. depending on type, ga. and bbl. length. Checkered stock and forend, straight or half-pistol grip. Also supplied in Pigeon and Wildfowl models with same values. Currently manufactured.
Ejector model .... NiB $4744 Ex $3795 Gd $2581
Non-ejector model .... NiB $4125 Ex $3300 Gd $2244

OVUNDO (O/U) .... NiB $18,744 Ex $14,995 Gd $10,197
Hammerless. Boxlock. Hand-detachable locks. Dummy sideplates. Selective ejectors. Selective single trigger. 12 ga. Barrel lengths and boring to order. Checkered stock/forend, straight or half-pistol grip. Mfd. before WW II.

TED WILLIAMS SHOTGUNS
See Sears shotguns.

WINCHESTER SHOTGUNS —
New Haven, Connecticut
Formerly Winchester Repeating Arms Co., now mfd. by Winchester-Western Div., Olin Corp., and by U.S. Repeating Arms Company. In 1999, production rights were acquired by Browning Arms.

MODEL 12 CLASSIC LIMITED EDITION
Gauge: 20; 2.75-inch chamber. Bbl.: 26-inch vent rib; IC. Weight: 7 lbs. Checkered walnut buttstock and forend. Polished blue finish (Grade I) or engraved with gold inlays (Grade IV). Made 1993 to 1995.
Grade I (4000) .... NiB $869 Ex $695 Gd $473
Grade IV (1000) .... NiB $1369 Ex $1095 Gd $745

Winchester Model 12
Pigeon Grade

Winchester Model 12
Standard

Winchester Model 12
Trap w/Monte Carlo Stock

Winchester Model 12
12-4 Engraving

MODEL 12 FEATHERWEIGHT..... NiB $506 Ex $405 Gd $275
Same as Model 12 Standard w/plain barrel except has alloy trigger guard. Modified takedown w/redesigned magazine tube, cap and slide handle. 12 ga. only. Bbls.: 26-inch IC; 28-inch M or F; 30-inch F choke. Serial numbers with "F" prefix. Weight: About 6.75 lbs. Made 1959-62.

MODEL 12 FIELD GUN, 1972 TYPE...... NiB $619 Ex $495 Gd $336
Same general specifications as Standard Model 12 but 12 ga. only, 26- 28- or 30-inch vent rib bbl., standard chokes. Engine-turned bolt and carrier. Hand-checkered stock/slide handle of semifancy walnut. Made 1972-75.

MODEL 12 HEAVY DUCK GUN
Same general specifications as Standard Grade except 12 ga. only chambered for 3-inch shells. 30- or 32-inch plain, solid or vent rib bbl. w/full choke only. Three shot magazine. Checkered slide handle and pistol-grip walnut buttstock w/recoil pad. Weight: 8.5 to 8.75 lbs. Made 1935-63.
Heavy Duck Gun, plain bbl. .... NiB $825 Ex $660 Gd $449
Heavy Duck Gun, solid
rib (disc. 1959)..................... NiB $1244 Ex $995 Gd $677
Heavy Duck Gun, vent rib
(Special order only) .... NiB $1619 Ex $1295 Gd $881

MODEL 12 PIGEON GRADE
Deluxe versions of the regular Model 12 Standard or Field Gun, Duck Gun, Skeet Gun and Trap Gun made on special order. This grade has finer finish throughout, hand-smoothed action, engine-

(cont'd.) MODEL 12 PIGEON GRADE
turned breech bolt and carrier, stock and extension slide handle of high grade walnut, fancy checkering, stock dimensions to individual specifications. Engraving and carving available at extra cost ranging from about $135 to over $1000. Disc. 1965.
Field Gun, plain bbl. .... NiB $1719 Ex $1375 Gd $935
Field Gun, vent rib.................... NiB $2096 Ex $1677 Gd $1140
Skeet Gun, matted rib .... NiB $1918 Ex $1534 Gd $1043
Skeet Gun, vent rib .... NiB $2406 Ex $1925 Gd $1309
Skeet Gun, Cutts Compensator .... NiB $1409 Ex $1127 Gd $766
Trap Gun, matted rib.................. NiB $2055 Ex $1644 Gd $1118
Trap Gun, vent rib .... NiB $2269 Ex $1815 Gd $1234
16 ga. (Field), add 20%
16 ga. (Skeet), add 90%
20 ga. (Field), add 25%
20 ga. (Skeet), add 45%
28 ga. (Skeet), add 350%

MODEL 12 RIOT GUN .... NiB $781 Ex $625 Gd $425
Same general specifications as plain barrel Model 12 Standard except has 20-inch cylinder bore bbl.,12 gauge only. Made 1918-1963.

MODEL 12 SKEET GUN .... NiB $1063 Ex $850 Gd $578
Gauges: 12, 16, 20, 28. Five shot tubular magazine. 26-inch matted rib bbl., SK choke. Weight: About 7.75 lbs., 12 ga.; 6.75 lbs., other gauges. Bradley red or ivory bead front sight. Winchester 94B middle sight. Checkered pistol-grip stock and extension slide handle. Disc. after WWII.

Winchester Model 21
Custom Grade

Winchester Model 21
Pigeon Grade

**MODEL 12 SKEET GUN,
CUTTS COMPENSATOR** . . . . NiB $891 Ex $712 Gd $484
Same general specifications as standard Model 12 Skeet Gun except has plain bbl. fitted with Cutts Compensator, 26 inches overall. Disc. 1954.

MODEL 12 SKEET GUN, PLAIN-BARREL . . . . . NiB $825 Ex $660 Gd $449
Same general specifications as standard Model 12 Skeet except w/no rib.

MODEL 12 SKEET GUN, VENT RIB . . . . NiB $1438 Ex $1150 Gd $782
Same general specifications as standard Model 12 Skeet Gun except has 26-inch bbl. with vent rib, 12 and 20 ga. Disc. in 1965.

MODEL 12 SKEET GUN, 1972 TYPE. . . . . NiB $906 Ex $725 Gd $493
Same gen. specifications as Standard Model 12 but 12 ga. only. 26-inch vent rib bbl., SK choke. Engine-turned bolt and carrier. Hand-checkered skeet-style stock and slide handle of choice walnut, recoil pad. Made 1972-75.

MODEL 12 STANDARD GR., MATTED RIB. . . . . . NiB $1140 Ex $912 Gd $637
Same general specifications as plain bbl. Model 12 Standard except has solid raised matted rib. Disc. after World War II.

MODEL 12 STANDARD GR., VENT RIB. . . . . NiB $1288 Ex $1031 Gd $703
Same general specifications as plain barrel Model 12 Standard except has vent rib. 26.75- or 30-inch bbl.,12 ga. only. Disc. after World War II.

MODEL 12 STANDARD SLIDE-ACTION REPEATER
Hammerless. Takedown. Gauges: 12, 16, 20, 28. Six shell tubular magazine. Plain bbl. Lengths: 26- to 32-inches; choked F to Cyl. Weight: About 7.5 lbs., 12 ga. 30-inch, 6.5 lbs. in other ga. with 28-inch bbl. Plain pistol-grip stock, grooved slide handle. Made 1912-64.
12 ga., 28-inch bbl. (full choke) . . . . NiB $744 Ex $595 Gd $405
16 ga. . . . . NiB $656 Ex $525 Gd $357
20 ga. . . . . NiB $869 Ex $695 Gd $473
28 ga. . . . . NiB $3744 Ex $2995 Gd $2037

MODEL 12 SUPER PIGEON GRADE . NiB $2994 Ex $2395 Gd $1629
Custom version of Model 12 with same general specifications as standard models. 12 ga. only. 26-, 28- or 30-inch vent-rib bbl., any standard choke. Engraved receiver. Hand-smoothed and fitted action. Full fancy walnut stock and forearm made to individual order. Made 1965-72.

MODEL 12 TRAP GUN
Same general specifications as Standard Model 12 except has straighter stock, checkered pistol grip and extension slide handle, recoil pad, 30-inch matted-rib bbl., F choke, 12 ga. only. Disc. after World War II; vent rib model disc. 1965.
Matted rib bbl. . . . . NiB $956 Ex $765 Gd $520
With straight stock, vent rib . . . . . . NiB $950 Ex $760 Gd $516
With Monte Carlo stock, vent rib . . . . . NiB $1244 Ex $995 Gd $677

MODEL 12 TRAP GUN, 1972 TYPE . . . . NiB $869 Ex $695 Gd $473

(cont'd.) **MODEL 12 TRAP GUN, 1972 TYPE**
Same general specifications as Standard Model 12 but 12 gauge only. 30-inch vent-rib bbl., F choke. Engine-turned bolt and carrier. Hand-checkered trap-style stock (straight or Monte Carlo comb) and slide handle of select walnut, recoil pad. Intro. in 1972. Disc.

MODEL 20 SINGLE-SHOT HAMMER GUN . . . . NiB $702 Ex $562 Gd $382
Takedown. .410 bore. 2.5-inch chamber. 26-inch bbl., F choke. Checkered pistol-grip stock and forearm. Weight: About 6 lbs. Made 1919-24.

**ORIGINAL MODEL 21 DOUBLE-BARREL SHOTGUNS
(ORIGINAL PRODUCTION SERIES - 1930 TO 1959)**
Hammerless. Boxlock. Automatic safety. Double triggers or selective single trigger, selective or non-selective ejection (all postwar Model 21 shotguns have selective single trigger and selective ejection). Gauges: 12, 16, 20, 28 and .410 bore. Bbls.: Raised matted rib or vent rib; 26-, 28-, 30-, 32-inch, the latter in 12 ga. only; F, IM, M, IC, SK chokes. Weight: 7.5 lbs., 12 ga. w/30-inch bbl.; about 6.5 lbs. 16 or 20 ga. w/28-inch bbl. Checkered pistol- or straight-grip stock, regular or beavertail forend. Made 1930-59.
Standard grade, 12 ga. . . . . NiB $4744 Ex $3795 Gd $2581
Standard grade, 16 ga. . . . . NiB $5972 Ex $4777 Gd $3248
Standard grade, 20 ga. . . . . NiB $6182 Ex $4945 Gd $3363
**Tournament grade, 12 ga.
(1933-34)** . . . . NiB $4994 Ex $3995 Gd $2717
**Tournament grade, 16 ga.
(1933-34)** . . . . NiB $6188 Ex $4950 Gd $3366
**Tournament grade, 20 ga.
(1933-34)** . . . . NiB $7369 Ex $5895 Gd $4009
Trap grade, 12 ga. (1940-59) . . . . . NiB $4813 Ex $3850 Gd $2618
Trap grade, 16 ga. (1940-59) . . . . . NiB $5394 Ex $4315 Gd $2934
Trap grade, 20 ga. (1940-59) . . . . . NiB $6694 Ex $5355 Gd $3641
Skeet grade, 12 ga. (1936-59) . . . . . NiB $4744 Ex $3795 Gd $2581
Skeet grade, 16 ga. (1936-59) . . . . . NiB $5456 Ex $4365 Gd $2968
Skeet grade, 20 ga. (1936-59) . . . . . NiB $6356 Ex $5085 Gd $3457
Duck Gun, 12 ga. 3-inch (1940-52) . . . NiB $5244 Ex $4195 Gd $2853
**Magnum Gun, 12 ga. 3-inch
(1953-59)** . . . . NiB $5063 Ex $4050 Gd $2754
**Magnum Gun, 20 ga. 3-inch
(1953-59)** . . . . NiB $6188 Ex $4950 Gd $3366
**Cust. built/deluxe gr.,
12 ga.(1933-59)** . . . . NiB $7494 Ex $5995 Gd $4077
**Cust. built/deluxe gr.,
16 ga. (1933-59)** . . . . NiB $8688 Ex $6950 Gd $4726
**Cust. built/deluxe gr.,
20 ga. (1933-59)** . . . . NiB $9563 Ex $7650 Gd $5202
Custom built/deluxe grade, 28 ga.(1933-59) . . . . Very Rare*
Custom built/deluxe grade, .410 1933-59) . . . . Very Rare*
*Fewer than 100 sm. bore models (28 ga. and .410) were built, which precludes accurate pricing, but projected values could exceed $30,000. Such rare specimens should be authenticated by factory letter and/or independent appraisals.

Winchester Model 23

Winchester Model 24

Winchester Model 25

Winchester Model 36

Winchester Model 37

Winchester Model 37A

Winchester Model 37A Youth

(cont'd) ORIGINAL MODEL 21

W/vent rib on 12 ga. models, add	$650
W/vent rib on 16 ga. models, add	$1500
W/vent rib on 20 ga. models, add	$1000
W/double triggers ans extractors, deduct	30%
W/double trigger, selective ejection, deduct	20%

For Custom Engraving from this period:

No. 1 Pattern, add	25%
No. 2 Pattern, add	35%
No. 3 Pattern, add	50%
No. 4 Pattern, add	35%
No. 5 Pattern, add	65%

(cont'd) ORIGINAL MODEL 21

No. 6 Pattern, add	75%

MODEL 21 CUSTOM, PIGEON, GRAND AMERICAN (CUSTOM SHOP SERIES - PRODUCTION 1959 TO 1981)
Since 1959 the Model 21 has been offered through the Custom Shop in deluxe models. (Custom, Pigeon, Grand American) on special order. General specifications same as for Model 21 standard models except these custom guns have full fancy American walnut stock and forearm with fancy checkering, finely polished and hand-smoothed working parts, etc.; engraving inlays, carved stocks and other extras are available at additional cost. Made 1959-81.

Winchester
Model 40 Skeet

Winchester
Model 41 Deluxe

(cont'd) **MODEL 21 CUSTOM, PIGEON,**

Custom grade, 12 ga.	NiB $9438 Ex $7550 Gd $5134
Custom grade, 16 ga.	NiB $14,375 Ex $11,500 Gd $7820
Custom grade, 20 ga.	NiB $12,813 Ex $10,250 Gd $6970
Pigeon grade, 12 ga.	NiB $14,688 Ex $11,750 Gd $7990
Pigeon grade, 16 ga.	NiB $20,625 Ex $16,500 Gd $11,220
Pigeon grade, 20 ga.	NiB $19,063 Ex $15,250 Gd $10,370
Grand American, 12 ga.	NiB $22,438 Ex $17,950 Gd $12,206
Grand American, 16 ga.	NiB $35,625 Ex $28,500 Gd $19,380
Grand American, 20 ga.	NiB $26,563 Ex $21,250 Gd $14,450
Grand American 3-barrel Set	22,500 to 38,000
Small Bore Models	
(28 ga. And .410)	Very Rare*

*Fewer than 20 Small Bore models (28 ga. and .410) were built during this period, which precludes accurate pricing, but projected values could exceed $35,000. Such rare specimens should be authenticated by factory letter and/or independent appraisals.
For Custom Shop Engraving from this period:

#1 Pattern, add	10%
#2 Pattern, add	15%
#3 Pattern, add	25%
#4 Pattern, add	35%
#5 Pattern, add	45%
#6 Pattern, add	50%

MODEL 21 - U.S.R.A. CUSTOM-BUILT SERIES (CUSTOM SHOP PRODUCTION 1982 TO DATE)

In 1982, the individual model designations for the Model 21 were changed again when U. S. Repeating Arms Company assumed production. The new model nomenclature for the Custom/Built catagory, includes: Standard Custom, Special Custom and Grand American — all of which are available on special order through the Custom Shop. General specifications remained the same on these consolidated model variations and included the addition of a Small Bore 2-Barrel Set (28/.410) and a 3-Barrel Set (20/28/.410). Made 1982 to date.

Custom Built -	
Standard Custom.	NiB $6063 Ex $4850* Gd $3298
Custom Built -	
Special Custom.	NiB $7188 Ex $5750* Gd $3910
Custom Built - Grand American	NiB $13,125 Ex $10,500* Gd $7140
Custom Built - Grand	
American 2-barrel set	NiB $43,688 Ex $34,950* Gd $23,766
Custom Built - Grand	
American 3-barrel set	NiB $65,625 Ex $52,500* Gd $35,700

*The values shown above represent the basic model in each catagory. Since many customers took advantage of the custom built options, individual gun appointments vary and values will need to be adjusted accordingly. For this reason, individual appraisals should be obtained on all subject firearms.

MODEL 23 SIDE-BY-SIDE SHOTGUN

Boxlock. Single trigger. Automatic safety. Gauges: 12, 20, 28, .410. Bbls.: 25.5-, 26-, 28-inch with fixed chokes or Winchoke tubes. Weight: 5.88 to 7 lbs. Checkered American walnut buttstock and forend. Made in 1979 for Olin at its Olin-Kodensha facility, Japan.

Classic 23 — Gold inlay, engraved	NiB $1894 Ex $1515 Gd $1030
Custom 23 — Plain receiver,	
Winchoke system	NiB $1119 Ex $895 Gd $609
Heavy Duck 23 — Standard	NiB $1832 Ex $1470 Gd $999
Lightweight 23 — Classic	NiB $1822 Ex $1458 Gd $991
Light Duck 23 — Standard	NiB $1725 Ex $1380 Gd $938
Light Duck 23 — 12 ga. Golden Quail	NiB $2025 Ex $1620 Gd $1101
Light Duck 23 — .410 Golden Quail	NiB $3525 Ex $2820 Gd $1917
Custom Set 23 — 20 & 28 ga.	NiB $5542 Ex $4434 Gd $3015

MODEL 24 HAMMERLESS DOUBLE

Boxlock. Double triggers. Plain extractors. Auto safety. Gauges: 12, 16, 20. Bbls.: 26-inch IC/M; 28-inch M/F (also IC/M in 12 ga. only); 30-inch M and F in 12 ga. only. Weight: About 7.5 lbs., 12 ga. Metal bead front sight. Plain pistol-grip stock, semi-beavertail forearm. Made 1939-57.

Model 24, 12 ga.	NiB $649 Ex $519 Gd $353
Model 24, 16 ga.	NiB $722 Ex $577 Gd $392
Model 24, 20 ga.	NiB $1050 Ex $625 Gd $425

MODEL 25 RIOT GUN . . . . NiB $515 Ex $412 Gd $280
Same as Model 25 Standard except has 20-inch cylinder bore bbl., 12 ga. only. Made 1949-55.

MODEL 25 SLIDE-ACTION REPEATER . . . . NiB $469 Ex $375 Gd $255
Hammerless. Solid frame. 12 ga. only. Four shell tubular magazine. 28-in. Plain bbl.; IC, M or F choke. Weight: About 7.5 lbs. Metal bead front sight. Plain pistol-grip stock, grooved slide handle. Made 1949-55.

MODEL 36 SINGLE-SHOT BOLT ACTION . . . . NiB $563 Ex $450 Gd $306
Takedown. Uses 9mm Short or Long shot or ball cartridges interchangeably. 18-inch bbl. Plain stock. Weight: About 3 lbs. Made 1920-27.

MODEL 37 SINGLE-SHOT SHOTGUN

Semi-hammerless. Auto ejection. Takedown. Gauges: 12, 16, 20, 28, .410. Bbl. lengths: 28-, 30-, 32-inch in all gauges except .410; 26- or 28-inch in .410; all barrels plain with F choke. Weight: About 6.5 pounds, 12 ga. Made 1937-63.

12 ga.	NiB $304 Ex $243 Gd $165
16 ga.	NiB $244 Ex $195 Gd $133
20 ga.	NiB $350 Ex $280 Gd $190
20 ga. (Youth w/red dot indicator)	NiB $422 Ex $356 Gd $242
28 ga. (red letter only)	NiB $1450 Ex $1160 Gd $788
410 ga.	NiB $416 Ex $332 Gd $226
Other "Red Letter" models, add	20%
W/32-inch bbl., add	15%

Winchester Model 42
Classic Limited Edition

Winchester Model 42
Standard

MODEL 37A SINGLE SHOT SHOTGUN
Similar to Model 370 except has engraved receiver and gold trigger, checkered pistol-grip stock, fluted forearm; 16 ga. available with 30-inch bbl. only. Made 1973-80.
Model 37A, 12, 16, or 20 ga. . . . . . . NiB $156 Ex $125 Gd $85
Model 37A, 28 ga. . . . . NiB $231 Ex $185 Gd $126
Model 37A, .410 ga. . . . . NiB $281 Ex $225 Gd $153
W/32-inch bbl., add $20

MODEL 37A YOUTH. . . . . NiB $169 Ex $135 Gd $92
Similar to Model 370 Youth except has engraved receiver and gold trigger, checkered pistol-grip stock, fluted forearm. Made 1973-80.

MODEL 40 STANDARD AUTOLOADER. . NiB $721 Ex $577 Gd $392
Streamlined receiver. Hammerless. Takedown. 12 ga. only. Four shot tubular magazine. 28- or 30-inch bbl.; M or F choke. Weight: About 8 lbs. Bead sight on ramp. Plain pistol-grip stock, semi-beavertail forearm. Made 1940-41.

MODEL 40 SKEET GUN . . . . NiB $938 Ex $750 Gd $510
Same general specifications as Model 40 Standard except has 24-inch plain bbl. w/Cutts Compensator and screw-in choke tube, checkered forearm and pistol grip, grip cap. Made 1940-1941.

MODEL 41 SINGLE-SHOT BOLT ACTION
Takedown. .410 bore. 2.5-inch chamber (chambered for 3-inch shells after 1932). 24-inch bbl., F choke. Plain straight stock standard. Also made in deluxe version. Made 1920-34.
Standard model . . . . NiB $623 Ex $498 Gd $339
Deluxe model. . . . . NiB $750 Ex $600 Gd $4087

MODEL 42 CLASSIC LTD. EDITION. NiB $1563 Ex $1250 Gd $850
Gauge: .410 with 2.75-inch chamber. Bbl.: 26-inch vent rib; F choke. Weight: 7 lbs. Checkered walnut buttstock and forend. Engraved blue with gold inlays. Limited production of 850. Made 1993.

MODEL 42 DELUXE . . . . NiB $5599 Ex $4479 Gd $3046
Same general specifications as the Model 42 Trap Grade except available w/vent rib after 1955. Finer finish throughout w/hand-smoothed action, engine-turned breech bolt and carrier, stock and extension slide handle of high grade walnut, fancy checkering, stock dimensions to individual specifications. Engraving and carving were offered at extra cost. Made 1940-63. Note: Exercise caution on VR models not marked "DELUXE" on the bottom of the receiver. A factory letter will insure that the rib was installed during the initial manufacturing process. Unfortunately, factory authentication is not always possible due to missing or destroyed records. To further complicate this matter, not all VR ribs were installed by Winchester. From 1955-63, both Deluxe and Skeet Grade models were available with Simmons style ribs. After-market rib installations are common.

MODEL 42 PIGEON GRADE
This higher-grade designation is similar to the Deluxe grade and is available in all configurations. May be identified by engraved Pigeon located at the base of the magazine tube. Most production occurred in the late 1940's. *NOTE: To determine the value of any Model 42 Pigeon Grade, add 50 % to value listed under the specified Model 42 configuration.*

MODEL 42 SKEET GUN
Same general specifications as Model 42 Standard except has checkered straight or pistol-grip stock and extension slide handle, 26- or 28-inch plain, solid-rib or vent-rib bbl. May be choked F., Mod., Imp. Cyl. or Skeet. Note: Some Model 42 Skeet Guns are chambered for 2.5-inch shells only. Made 1933-63.
Model 42 Skeet
w/plain bbl. . . . . NiB $2369 Ex $1895 Gd $1289
Model 42 Skeet
w/solid rib . . . . NiB $3119 Ex $2495 Gd $1697
Model 42 Skeet
w/vent rib . . . . NiB $4188 Ex $3350 Gd $2278
W/2.5-inch
chamber, add 35%

MODEL 42 TRAP GRADE
This higher grade designation was available in both field and skeet configurations and is fitted w/deluxe wood w/trap grade checkering pattern and marked "TRAP" on bottom of receiver. Made 1934-39. Superseded by the Deluxe model in 1940.
Model 42 Trap grade
w/plain bbl. . . . . NiB $8500 Ex $7000 Gd $3500
Model 42 Trap grade
w/solid rib . . . . NiB $5500 Ex $4500 Gd $2000
Model 42 Trap grade
w/vent rib . . . . NiB $6500 Ex $5000 Gd $2250

MODEL 42 STANDARD GRADE
Hammerless. Takedown. .410 bore (3- or 2.5-inch shell). Tubular magazine holds five 3-inch or six 2.5-inch shells. 26- or 28-inch plain or solid-rib bbl.; cylinder bore, M or F choke. Weight: 5.8 to 6.5 lbs. Plain pistol-grip stock; grooved slide handle. Made 1933-63.
Model 42 Standard w/plain bbl. . . NiB $1244 Ex $995 Gd $677
Model 42 Standard w/solid rib . . . . NiB $1950 Ex $1800 Gd $1400

MODEL 50 FIELD GUN, VENT RIB . . . NiB $494 Ex $395 Gd $269
Same as Model 50 Standard except has vent rib.

MODEL 50 SKEET GUN . . . . NiB $564 Ex $451 Gd $306
Same as Model 50 Standard except has 26-inch vent-rib bbl. with SK choke, skeet-style stock of select walnut.

SHOTGUNS

Winchester Model 50 Skeet

Winchester Model 97 Riot Gun

Winchester Model 101

MODEL 50 STANDARD GRADE . . . NiB $439 Ex $351 Gd $239
Non-recoiling bbl. and independent chamber. Gauges: 12 and 20.
Two shot tubular magazine. Bbl.: 12 ga. — 26-, 28-, 30-inch; 20 ga.
— 26-, 28-inch; IC, SK, M, F choke. Checkered pistol-grip stock and
forearm. Weight: About 7.75 lbs. Made 1954-61.

MODEL 50 TRAP GUN . . . . NiB $750 Ex $575 Gd $350
Same as Model 50 Standard except 12 ga. only, has 30-inch vent-
rib bbl. with F choke, Monte Carlo stock of select walnut.

MODEL 59 AUTO-LOADING SHOTGUN . . . NiB $591 Ex $472 Gd $321
Gauge: 12. Magazine holds two shells. Alloy receiver. Win-Lite steel
and fiberglass bbl.: 26-inch IC, 28-inch M or F choke, 30-inch F
choke; also furnished with 26-inch bbl. with Versalite choke (interchangeable F, M, IC tubes; one supplied with gun). Weight: About
6.5 lbs. Checkered pistol-grip stock and forearm. Made 1959-65.

MODEL 97 BUSH GUN
Takedown or solid frame. Same general specifications as standard
Model 97 except w/26-inch cylinder bore bbl. Made 1897-1931.
Model 97 Riot Gun w/solid frame . . . NiB $119 Ex $95 Gd $65
Model 97 Riot Gun takedown . . . . NiB $1031 Ex $825 Gd $561

MODEL 97 RIOT GUN
Takedown or solid frame. Same general specifications as standard
Model 97 except 12 ga. only, 20-inch cylinder bore bbl. Made
1898-1935.
Model 97 Riot Gun w/solid frame . . . NiB $1188 Ex $950 Gd $646
Model 97 Riot Gun takedown . . . . NiB $1031 Ex $825 Gd $561

MODEL 97 TRAP, TOURNAMENT AND PIGEON
These higher grade models offer higher overall quality than the stan-
dard grade. Made 1897-39.
Standard Trap grade . . . . NiB $1407 Ex $1125 Gd $765
Special Trap grade . . . . NiB $1594 Ex $1275 Gd $867
Tournament grade (Black Diamond) . . . . NiB $2484 Ex $1987 Gd $1351
Pigeon grade . . . . NiB $4813 Ex $3850 Gd $2618

MODEL 97 TRENCH GUN . . . . NiB $1994 Ex $1595 Gd $1085
Solid frame. Same as Model 97 Riot Gun except has handguard and

(cont'd.) **MODEL 97 TRENCH GUN**
is equipped with a bayonet. World War I government issue,
1917-18.
Model 97 Trench Gun
w/solid frame . . . . NiB $2925 Ex $2340 Gd $1591
Model 97 Trench Gun takedown . . . . . NiB $1237 Ex $990 Gd $673

MODEL 97 SLIDE-ACTION REPEATER
Standard Grade. Takedown or solid frame. Gauges: 12 and 16. 5-
shell tubular magazine. Bbl.: Plain; 26 to 32 inches, the latter in 12
ga. only; choked F to Cyl. Weight: About 7.75 lbs. (12 ga. w/28-
inch barrel). Plain pistol-grip stock, grooved slide handle. Made
1897-1957.
Model 97, 12 ga. w/solid frame . . . NiB $826 Ex $661 Gd $449
Model 97, 16 ga. w/solid frame . . NiB $1078 Ex $862 Gd $586
Model 97, 12 ga. takedown . . . . . . NiB $855 Ex $684 Gd $465
Model 97, 16 ga. takedown . . . . . . NiB $1114 Ex $891 Gd $606

*NOTE: All Winchester Model 101s are mfd. for Olin Corp. at its
Olin-Kodensha facility in Tochigi, Japan. Production for Olin Corp.
stopped in Nov. 1987. Importation of Model 101s was continued
by Classic Doubles under that logo until 1990. See separate head-
ing for additional data.*

MODEL 101 DIAMOND
GRADE TARGET . . . . NiB $1656 Ex $1325 Gd $901
Similar to Model 101 Standard except silvered frame and Winchoke
interchangeable choke tubes. Made 1981-90.

MODEL 101 FIELD GUN O/U
Boxlock. Engraved receiver. Auto ejectors. Single selective trigger.
Combination bbl. selector and safety. Gauges: 12 and 28, 2.75-
inch chambers; 20 and .410, 3-inch chambers. Vent rib bbls.: 30-
(12 ga. only) and 26.5-inch, IC/M. Weight: 6.25 to 7.75 lbs.
depending on gauge and bbl. length. Hand-checkered French
walnut and forearm. Made 1963-81. Gauges other than 12 introduced 1966.
12 and 20 ga. . . . . NiB $938 Ex $750 Gd $510
28 and .410 ga. . . . . NiB $1156 Ex $925 Gd $629
12 and 20 ga. mag. . . . . NiB $994 Ex $795 Gd $541

Winchester Model 370

Winchester Model 1001
Sporting Clays

Winchester Model 1200
Field Gun

Winchester Model 1200
Field Gun w/Vent Rib

MODEL 101 QUAIL SPECIAL O/U
Same specifications as small-frame Model 101 except in 28 and
.410 ga. with 3-inch chambers. 25.5-inch bbls. with choke tubes
(28 ga.) or M/F chokes (.410). Imported from Japan in 1984-87.

12 ga.	NiB $2093	Ex $1674	Gd $1139
20 ga.	NiB $2487	Ex $1989	Gd $1353
28 ga.	NiB $3084	Ex $2467	Gd $1677
.410 ga.	NiB $2166	Ex $1732	Gd $1178

MODEL 101 SHOTGUN/RIFLE
COMBINATION GUN. . . . . NiB $2224 Ex $1779 Gd $1210
12-ga. Winchoke bbl. on top and rifle bbl. chambered for .30-06 on
bottom (over/under). 25-inch bbls. Engraved receiver. Hand checkered walnut stock and forend. Weight: 8.5 lbs. Mfd. for Olin Corp.
in Japan.

MODEL 370
SINGLE-SHOT SHOTGUN . . . . NiB $119 Ex $95 Gd $65
Visible hammer. Auto ejector. Takedown. Gauges: 12, 16, 20, 28,
.410. 2.75-inch chambers in 16 and 28 ga., 3-inch in other ga.
Bbls.: 12 ga., 30-, 32- or 36-inch,16 ga; 30- or 32-inch; 20 and 28
ga., 28-inch; .410 bore, 26-inch, all F choke. Weight: 5.5-6.25 lbs.
Plain pistol-grip stock and forearm. Made 1968-73.

MODEL 370 YOUTH
Same as standard Model 370 except has 26-inch bbl. and 12.5-inch
stock with recoil pad; 20 gauge with IM choke, .410 bore with F
choke. Made 1968-73.
Model 370, 12,

16, or 20 ga.	NiB $137	Ex $110	Gd $74
Model 37A, 28 ga.	NiB $197	Ex $157	Gd $107
Model 37A, .410 ga.	NiB $163	Ex $131	Gd $89

MODEL 1001 O/U SHOTGUN
Boxlock. 12 ga., 2.75- or 3-inch chambers. Bbls.: 28- or 30-inch
vent rib; WinPlus choke tubes. Weight: 7-7.75 lbs. Checkered wal-
nut buttstock and forend. Blued finish with scroll engraved receiver.
Made 1993 to date.
Field model
(28-inch bbl., 3-inch) . . . . NiB $944 Ex $755 Gd $513
Sporting
Clays . . . . NiB $1063 Ex $850 Gd $578
Sporting
Clays Lite . . . . NiB $979 Ex $783 Gd $532

MODEL 1200
DEER GUN . . . . NiB $244 Ex $195 Gd $133
Same as standard Model 1200, except has special 22-inch bbl. with
rifle-type sights, for rifled slug or buckshot; 12 ga. only. Weight: 6.5
lbs. Made 1965-74.

MODEL 1200 DEFENDER SERIES
SLIDE-ACTION SECURITY SHOTGUNS
Hammerless. 12 ga. w/3-inch chamber. 18-inch bbl. w/cylin-
der bore and metal front bead or rifle sights. Four or 7-shot
magazine. Weight: 5.5 to 6.75 lbs. 25.6 inches (PG Model) or
38.6 inches overall. Matte blue finish. Synthetic pistol grip or
walnut finished hardwood buttstock w/grooved synthetic or
hardwood slide handle. NOTE: Even though the 1200 series
was introduced in 1964 and was supplanted by the Model
1300 in 1978, the Security series (including the Defender
model) was marketed under 1200 series alpha-numeric product codes (G1200DM2R) until 1989. In 1990, the same
Defender model was marketed under a 4-digit code (7715) and
was then advertised in the 1300 series.

Winchester Model 1300
Deer Series — Black Shadow
Synthetic Stock

Winchester Model 1300
Deer Series — Advantage
Full Camo Pattern

Winchester Model 1300
Defender Series — Stainless
Marine Synthetic Stock

(cont'd) MODEL 1200 DEFENDER SERIES
Defender
w/hardwood stock,bead sight . . . . . NiB $206 Ex $165 Gd $112
Defender
W/hardwood stock, rifle sights . . . . NiB $219 Ex $175 Gd $119
Defender model w/pistol-grip stock . . . NiB $225 Ex $180 Gd $122
Defender Combo model
W/extra 28-inch plain bbl. . . . . NiB $256 Ex $205 Gd $139
Defender Combo model
W/extra 28-inch vent rib bbl. . . . . . NiB $275 Ex $220 Gd $150

MODEL 1200 FIELD GUN — MAGNUM
Same as standard Model 1200 except chambered for 3-inch 12 and 20 ga. magnum shells; plain or vent-rib bbl., 28- or 30-inch, F choke. Weight: 7.38 to 7.88 lbs. Made 1964-83.
With plain bbl. . . . . NiB $237 Ex $180 Gd $122
With vent rib bbl. . . . . NiB $252 Ex $202 Gd $137
Add for Winchester recoil reduction system $65

MODEL 1200 RANGER
SLIDE-ACTION SHOTGUN . . . . . . NiB $225 Ex $180 Gd $122
Hammerless. 12 and 20 ga.; 3-inch chambers. Walnut finished hardwood stock, ribbed forearm. 28-inch vent-rib bbl.; Winchoke system. Weight: 7.25 lbs. Made 1982 to 1990 by U. S. Repeating Arms.

MODEL 1200 RANGER YOUTH
SLIDE-ACTION SHOTGUN . . . . NiB $219 Ex $175 Gd $119
Same general specifications as standard Ranger Slide-Action except chambered for 20 ga. only, has Four shot magazine, recoil pad on buttstock, weight: 6.5 lbs. Mfd. by U. S. Repeating Arms.

MODEL 1200 SLIDE-ACTION FIELD GUN
Front-locking rotary bolt. Takedown. 4-shot magazine. Gauges: 12, 16, 20 (2.75-inch chamber). Bbl.: Plain or vent rib; 26-, 28-, 30-inch; IC, M, F choke or with Winchoke (interchangeable tubes IC-M-F). Weight: 6.5 to 7.25 lbs. Checkered pistol-grip stock and fore

(cont'd.) MODEL 1200 SLIDE-ACTION FIELD GUN
arm (slide handle), recoil pad; also avail. 1966-70 w/Winchester recoil reduction system (Cycolac stock). Made 1964-83.
With plain bbl. . . . . NiB $219 Ex $175 Gd $119
With vent rib bbl. . . . . NiB $230 Ex $184 Gd $125
Add for Winchester recoil reduction ystem $65
Add for Winchoke $25

MODEL 1200 STAINLESS
MARINE SERIES SLIDE-ACTION SECURITY SHOTGUN
Similar to Model 1200 Defender except w/6-shot magazine. 18-inch bbl. of ordnance stainless steel w/cylinder bore and rifle sights. Weight: 7 lbs. Bright chrome finish. Synthetic pistol grip or walnut finished hardwood buttstock w/grooved synthetic or hardwood slide handle.Made 1984-90.
Marine model w/hardwood stock . . . NiB $250 Ex $190 Gd $85
Marine model w/pistol-grip stock . . NiB $250 Ex $190 Gd $85

MODEL 1200 STAINLESS POLICE
SERIES SLIDE-ACTION SECURITY SHOTGUN
Similar to Model 1200 Defender except w/6-shot magazine. 18-inch bbl. of ordnance stainless steel w/cylinder bore and rifle sights. Weight: 7 lbs. Matte chrome finish. Synthetic pistol grip or walnut-finished hardwood buttstock w/grooved synthetic or hardwood slide handle.Made 1984-90.
Police model w/hardwood stock . . . NiB $266 Ex $213 Gd $145
Police model w/pistol grip stock . . . NiB $326 Ex $261 Gd $177

MODEL 1200 TRAP GUN
Same as standard Model 1200 except 12 gauge only. Has 2-shot magazine, 30-inch vent-rib bbl., Full choke or 28-inch with Winchoke. Semi-fancy walnut stock, straight Made 1965-73. Also available 1966-70 with Winchester recoil reduction system.
With straight-trap stock. . . . . NiB $314 Ex $251 Gd $171
With Monte Carlo stock . . . . NiB $392 Ex $313 Gd $212
Add for Winchester recoil reduction system $75
Add for Winchoke $30

Winchester Model 1300
Lady Defender — Synthetic Full Stock

Winchester Model 1300
Lady Defender — Synthetic Pistol Grip Stock

Winchester Model 1300
Defender 5-Shot Combo

Winchester Model 1300
Turkey Gun

Winchester Model 1300
XTR w/Winchoke

Winchester Model 1300
Magnum Waterfowl

SHOTGUNS

MODEL 1200 RANGER
COMBINATION SHOTGUN......NiB $266 Ex $213 Gd $145
Same as Ranger Deer combination except has one 28-inch vent-rib bbl. with M choke and one 18-inch Police Cyl. bore bbl. Made 1987-90.

MODEL 1200 SKEET GUN ....NiB $334 Ex $267 Gd $181
Same as standard Model 1200 except 12 and 20 ga. only; has 2-shot magazine, specially tuned trigger, 26-inch vent-rib bbl. SK choke, semi-fancy walnut stock and forearm. Weight: 7.25 to 7.5 lbs. Made 1965-73. Also avail. 1966-70 with Winchester recoil reduction system (add $50 to value).

MODEL 1300 CAMOPACK ....NiB $374 Ex $299 Gd $203
Gauge: 12.3-inch Magnum. Four shot magazine. Bbls.: 30-and 22-inch with Winchoke system. Weight: 7 lbs. Laminated stock with Win-Cam camouflage green, cut checkering, recoil pad, swivels and sling. Made 1987-88.

MODEL 1300 DEER SERIES
Similar to standard Model 1300 except 12 or 20 ga. only w/special 22-inch cyl. bore or rifled bbl. and rifle-type sights. Weight: 6.5 lbs. Checkered walnut or synthetic stock w/satin walnut, black or Advantage Full Camo Pattern finish. Matte blue or full-camo metal finish. Made 1994 to date.
Deer model
w/walnut stock (intro. 1994)......NiB $347 Ex $278 Gd $189
Black Shadow Deer
w/synthetic stock (intro. 1994)....NiB $236 Ex $189 Gd $128
Advantage Full Camo
Pattern (1995-98) ....NiB $334 Ex $267 Gd $181
Deer Combo
w/22- and 28-inch bbls. (1994-98)....NiB $295 Ex $236 Gd $160
W/rifled bbl. (intro. 1996), add........................$25

MODEL 1300 DEFENDER SERIES
Gauges: 12 or 20 ga. 18- 24- 28-inch vent rib bbl. w/3-inch chamber. Four 7- or 8- shot magazine. Weight: 5.6 to 7.4 lbs. Blued, chrome or matte stainless finish. Wood or synthetic stock. Made 1985 to date.
Combo model ....NiB $424 Ex $339 Gd $231
Hardwood stock model..........NiB $242 Ex $194 Gd $132
Synthetic pistol-grip model ....NiB $268 Ex $215 Gd $145
Synthetic stock ....NiB $256 Ex $204 Gd $139
Lady Defender synthetic
Stock (made 1996) ....NiB $275 Ex $220 Gd $149
Lady Defender synthetic
Pistol-grip (made 1996)..........NiB $244 Ex $195 Gd $133
Stainless marine synthetic stock ...NiB $406 Ex $325 Gd $221

MODEL 1300 DELUXE SLIDE-ACTION
Gauges: 12 and 20 w/3-inch chamber. Four shot magazine. Bbl.:22, 26 or 28 inch vent rib bbl. w/Winchoke tubes. Weight: 6.5 lbs. Checkered walnut buttstock and forend w/high luster finish. Polished blue metal finish with roll-engraved receiver. Made 1984 to date.
Model 1300 Deluxe
w/high gloss finish.............NiB $350 Ex $280 Gd $190
Model 1300 Ladies/Youth
w/22-inch bbl.(disc. 1992) ....NiB $308 Ex $246 Gd $168

MODEL 1300 FEATHERWEIGHT SLIDE-ACTION SHOTGUN
Hammerless. Takedown. Four shot magazine. Gauges: 12 and 20 (3-inch chambers). Bbls.: 22, 26 or 28 inches w/plain or vent rib w/Winchoke tubes. Weight: 6.38 to 7 lbs. Checkered walnut buttstock, grooved slide handle. Made 1978-94.
Model 1300 FW (plain bbl.) ......NiB $275 Ex $220 Gd $149
Model 1300 FW (vent rib) ....NiB $323 Ex $258 Gd $176
Model 1300 FW XTR ....NiB $336 Ex $269 Gd $183

MODEL 1300 RANGER SERIES
Gauges: 12 or 20 ga. w/3-inch chamber. Five shot magazine. 22-(Rifled), 26- or 28-inch vent-rib bbl. w/Winchoke tubes. Weight: 7.25 lbs. Blued finish. Walnut-finished hardwood buttstock and forend. Made 1984 to date.
Standard model ....NiB $281 Ex $225 Gd $153
Combo model ....NiB $344 Ex $275 Gd $187
Ranger Deer combo
(D&T w/rings & bases) ....NiB $363 Ex $290 Gd $197
Ranger Ladies/Youth ....NiB $288 Ex $230 Gd $156

MODEL 1300 SLIDE-ACTION FIELD GUN
Takedown w/front-locking rotary bolt. Gauges: 12, 20 w/3-inch chamber. Four shot magazine. Bbl.: Vent rib; 26-, 28-, 30-inch w/Win-choke tubes IC-M-F). Weight: 7.25 lbs. Checkered walnut or synthetic stock w/standard, black or Advantage Full Camo Pattern finish. Matte blue or full-camo metal finish. Made 1994 to date.
Model 1300 Standard Field
(w/walnut stock) ....NiB $254 Ex $203 Gd $138
Model 1300 Black Shadow
(w/black synthetic stock).........NiB $216 Ex $173 Gd $117
Model 1300 Advantage Camo .....NiB $315 Ex $252 Gd $171

MODEL 1300 SLUG HUNTER SERIES
Similar to standard Model 1300 except chambered 12 ga. only w/special 22-inch smoothbore w/Sabot-rifled choke tube or fully rifled bbl. w/rifle-type sights. Weight: 6.5 lbs. Checkered walnut, hardwood or laminated stock w/satin walnut or WinTuff finish. Matte blue metal finish. Made 1988-94.
Slug Hunter w/hardwood stock ...NiB $295 Ex $236 Gd $160
Slug Hunter w/laminated stock....NiB $347 Ex $278 Gd $189
Slug Hunter w/walnut stock ......NiB $321 Ex $257 Gd $175
Whitetails Unlimited
w/beavertail forend ....NiB $328 Ex $262 Gd $178
W/sabot-rifled choke tubes, add $15

MODEL 1300 TURKEY SERIES
Gauges: 12 or 20 ga. 22-inch bbl. w/3-inch chamber. Four shot magazine. 43 inches overall. Weight: 6.4 to 6.75 lbs. Buttstock and magazine cap, sling studs w/Cordura sling. Drilled and tapped to accept scope base. Checkered walnut, synthetic or laminated wood stock w/low luster finish. Matte blue or full camo finish. Made 1985 to date.
Turkey Advantage Full Camo.........NiB $309 Ex $247 Gd $168
Turkey Realtree All-Purpose Full Camo....NiB $338 Ex $270 Gd $184
Turkey Realtree Gray
All-Purpose Full Camo ....NiB $350 Ex $280 Gd $190
Turkey Realtree All-Purpose
Camo (matte metal) ....NiB $295 Ex $236 Gd $160
Turkey Black Shadow
(black synthetic stock) ....NiB $203 Ex $162 Gd $110
Turkey Win-Cam (green laminated wood)...NiB $314 Ex $251 Gd $171
Turkey Win-Cam Combo
(22- and 30-inch bbls.) ....NiB $350 Ex $280 Gd $190
Turkey Win-Cam NWTF
(22- and 30-inch bbls.) ....NiB $328 Ex $262 Gd $178
Turkey Win-Cam Youth/
Ladies model (20 ga.) ....NiB $387 Ex $309 Gd $211
Turkey Win-Tuf (br. laminated wood) ..NiB $321 Ex $257 Gd $175

MODEL 1300 WATERFOWL SLIDE-ACTION SHOTGUN
Similar to 1300 Standard model except has 28- or 30-inch vent rib bbl. w/Winchoke tubes. Weight: 7 lbs. Matte blue metal finish. Checkered walnut finished hardwood or brown laminated Win-Tuffwood stock w/camo sling, swivels and recoil pad. Made 1984-92.
Model 1300 Waterfowl w/hardwood stock ...NiB $295 Ex $236 Gd $160
Model 1300 Waterfowl w/laminated stock....NiB $321 Ex $257 Gd $175

Winchester Model 1400 Field

Winchester Model 1500 w/Plain Barrel

Winchester Model 1500 w/Vent Rib Barrel

MODEL 1300 XTR SLIDE-ACTION . NiB $387 Ex $309 Gd $211
Hammerless. Takedown. Four shot magazine. Gauges: 12 and 20 (3-inch chambers). Bbl.: Plain or vent rib; 28-inch bbls.; Winchoke (interchangeable tubes IC-M-F). Weight: About 7 lbs.

MODEL 1400 AUTOMATIC FIELD GUN
Gas-operated. Front-locking rotary bolt. Takedown. Two shot magazine. Gauges: 12, 16, 20 (2.75-inch chamber). Bbl.: Plain or vent rib; 26-, 28-, 30-inch; IC, M, F choke, or with Winchoke (interchangeable tubes IC-M-F). Weight: 6.5 to 7.25 lbs. Checkered pistol-grip stock and forearm, recoil pad, also available with Winchester recoil reduction system (Cycolac stock). Made 1964-68.
With plain bbl. . . . . NiB $297 Ex $237 Gd $161
With vent rib bbl. . . . . NiB $326 Ex $261 Gd $177
Add for Winchester recoil reduction system $100
Add for Winchoke $25

MODEL 1400 DEER GUN . . . . NiB $295 Ex $236 Gd $160
Same as standard Model 1400 except has special 22-inch bbl. with rifle-type sights, for rifle slug or buckshot; 12 ga. only. Weight: 6.25 lbs. Made 1965-68.

MODEL 1400 MARK II DEER GUN. NiB $344 Ex $275 Gd $187
Same general specifications as Model 1400 Deer Gun. Made 1968-73.

MODEL 1400 MARK II FIELD GUN
Same general specifications as Model 1400 Field Gun, except not chambered for 16 gauge; Winchester Recoil Reduction System not available after 1970- only 28-inch barrels w/Winchoke offered after 1973. Made 1968-78.
With plain bbl. . . . . NiB $315 Ex $252 Gd $171
With plain bbl. and Winchoke. . . . . NiB $341 Ex $273 Gd $185
With vent-rib bbl. . . . . NiB $361 Ex $288 Gd $196
With vent-rib bbl. and Winchoke . . NiB $387 Ex $309 Gd $211
Add for Winchester recoil reduction system $100

MODEL 1400 MARK II
SKEET GUN . . . . NiB $406 Ex $325 Gd $221
Same general specifications as Model 1400 Skeet Gun. Made 1968-73.

MODEL 1400 MARK II TRAP GUN
Same general specifications as Model 1400 Trap Gun except also

(cont'd) **MODEL 1400 MARK II TRAP GUN**
furnished with 28-inch bbl. and Winchoke. Winchester recoil reduction system not available after 1970. Made 1968-73.
With straight stock . . . . NiB $440 Ex $352 Gd $239
With Monte Carlo stock . . . . NiB $481 Ex $385 Gd $261
With Winchester recoil reduction system, add $100
With Winchoke, add $25

MODEL 1400 MARK II UTILITY SKEET NiB $336 Ex $269 Gd $183
Same general specifications as Model 1400 Mark II Skeet Gun except has stock and forearm of field grade walnut. Made 1970-73.

MODEL 1400 MARK II UTILITY TRAP . NiB $364 Ex $291 Gd $198
Same as Model 1400 Mark II Trap Gun except has Monte Carlo stock/forearm of field grade walnut. Made 1970-73.

MODEL 1400 RANGER
SEMIAUTOMATIC SHOTGUN . . . . NiB $256 Ex $204 Gd $139
Gauges: 12, 20. Two shot magazine. 28-inch vent rib bbl. with F choke. Overall length: 48.63 inches. Weight: 7 to 7.25 lbs. Walnut finish, hardwood stock and forearm with cut checkering. Made 1984 to 1990 by U. S. Repeating Arms.

MODEL 1400 RANGER SEMIAUTOMATIC
DEER SHOTGUN. . . . . NiB $269 Ex $215 Gd $146
Same general specifications as Ranger Semiautomatic except 24.13-inch plain bbl. with rifle sights. Mfd. by U.S. Repeating Arms.

MODEL 1400 SKEET GUN . . . . NiB $378 Ex $302 Gd $205
Same as standard Model 1400 except 12 and 20 ga. only, 26-inch vent-rib bbl., SK choke, semi-fancy walnut stock and forearm. Weight: 7.25 to 7.5 lbs. Made 1965-68. Also available with Winchester recoil reduction system (add $50 to value).

MODEL 1400 TRAP GUN
Same as standard Model 1400 except 12 ga. only with 30-inch vent-rib bbl., F choke. Semi-fancy walnut stock, straight or Monte Carlo trap style. Also available with Winchester recoil reduction system. Weight: About 8.25 lbs. Made 1965-68.
With straight stock . . . . NiB $426 Ex $341 Gd $232
With Monte Carlo stock . . . . NiB $459 Ex $367 Gd $249
Add for Winchester recoil red. system. $100

SHOTGUNS

Winchester Ranger Deer

Winchester Ranger Slide-Action

Winchester Model 1885
Single-Shot

Winchester Model 1
Field Super-X

Winchester Xpert
96 Field

Winchester Xpert
96 Trap

MODEL 1500 XTR SEMIAUTOMATIC . . NiB $313 Ex $250 Gd $170
Gas-operated. Gauges: 12 and 20 (2.75-inch chambers). Bbl.: Plain
or vent rib; 28-inch; WinChoke (interchangeable tubes IC-M-F).
American walnut stock and forend; checkered grip and forend.
Weight: 7.25 lbs. Made 1978-82.

MODEL 1885
SINGLE-SHOT SHOTGUN . . . . NiB $3744 Ex $2995 Gd $2037
Falling-block action, same as Model 1885 Rifle. Highwall receiver.
Solid frame or takedown. 20 ga. 3-inch chamber. 26-inch bbl.;
plain, matted or matted rib; Cyl. bore, M or F choke. Weight: About
5.5 lbs. Straight-grip stock and forearm. Made 1914-16.

MODEL 1887 LEVER-ACTION SHOTGUN
First of John Browning's patent shotgun designs produced by
Winchester. 10 or 12 ga. on casehardened frame fitted w/20-inch
blued, cylinder bore or full choke 30- or 32-inch bbl. Plain or
checkered walnut stock and forend. Made 1887 to 1901.
Model 1887 10 or 12 ga. standard . . . . NiB $2330 Ex $1864 Gd $1268
Model 1887 10 or 12 ga. deluxe. . . NiB $4875 Ex $3900 Gd $2652
Model 1887 10 or 12 ga. riot gun . . . . NiB $2219 Ex $1775 Gd $1207

(cont'd.) MODEL 1887 LEVER-ACTION SHOTGUN
W/.70-150 Ratchet rifled bbl.
.70 cal. rifle/87 produced) . . . . NiB $3188 Ex $2550 Gd $1734
W/3 or 4 blade Del. Damascus bbl., add 20%

MODEL 1901 LEVER-ACTION SHOTGUN
Same general specifications as Model 1887, of which this is a
redesigned version. 10 ga. only. Made 1901-20.
Model 1901 Standard. . . . . . . NiB $1942 Ex $1554 Gd $1057
Model 1901 Deluxe . . . . NiB $2475 Ex $1980 Gd $1346

MODEL 1911 AUTO-
LOADING SHOTGUN. . . . . NiB $594 Ex $475 Gd $323
Hammerless. Takedown. 12 gauge only. Four shell tubular magazine.
Bbl.: plain, 26- to 32-inch, standard borings. Weight: About 8.5 lbs.
Plain or checkered pistol-grip stock and forearm. Made 1911-25.

RANGER DEER COMBINATION . . . NiB $285 Ex $228 Gd $154
Gauge: 12, 3-inch Magnum. Three shot magazine. Bbl.: 24-inch
Cyl. bore deer bbl. and 28-inch vent rib bbl. with WinChoke sys-
tem. Weight: 7.25 lbs. Made 1987-90.

Woodward
Single-Shot Trap

Woodward O/U
Special Trap Grade

SUPER-X MODEL I AUTO FIELD GUN.... NiB $469 Ex $375 Gd $255
Gas-operated. Takedown.12 ga. 2.75-inch chamber Four shot magazine. Bbl.: Vent rib 26-inch IC; 28-inch M or F; 30-inch F choke. Weight: About 7 lbs. Checkered pistol-grip stock. Made 1974-84.

SUPER-X MODEL I SKEET GUN ... NiB $706 Ex $565 Gd $384
Same as Super-X Field Gun except has 26-inch bbl., SK choke, skeet-style stock and forearm of select walnut. Made 1974-84.

SUPER-X MODEL I TRAP GUN
Same as Super-X Field Gun except has 30-inch bbl., IM or F choke, trap-style stock (straight or Monte Carlo comb) and forearm of select walnut, recoil pad. Made 1974-84.
With straight stock .... NiB $557 Ex $446 Gd $303
With Monte Carlo stock .... NiB $649 Ex $519 Gd $353

XPERT MODEL 96 O/U FIELD GUN ..... NiB $886 Ex $708 Gd $481
Boxlock action similar to Model 101. Plain receiver. Auto ejectors. Selective single trigger. Gauges: 12, 20. 3-inch chambers. Bbl.: Vent rib; 26-inch IC/M; 28-inch M/F, 30-inch F/F choke (12 ga. only). Weight: 6.25 to 8.25 lbs. depending on ga. and bbls. Checkered pistol-grip stock and forearm. Made 1976-81 for Olin Corp. at its Olin-Kodensha facility in Japan.

XPERT MODEL 96 SKEET GUN.... NiB $938 Ex $750 Gd $510
Same as Xpert Field Gun except has 2.75-inch chambers, 27-inch bbls., SK choke, skeet-style stock and forearm. Made 1976-1981.

XPERT MODEL 96 TRAP GUN
Same as Xpert Field Gun except 12 ga. only, 2.75-inch chambers, has 30-inch bbls., IM/F or F/F choke, trap-style stock (straight or Monte Carlo comb) with recoil pad. Made 1976-81.
With straight stock .... NiB $860 Ex $688 Gd $468
With Monte Carlo stock .... NiB $884 Ex $707 Gd $481

JAMES WOODWARD & SONS — London, England

James Woodward & Sons was acquired by James Purdey & Sons after World War II.

BEST QUALITY HAMMERLESS DOUBLE
Sidelock. Automatic ejectors. Double triggers or single trigger. Built to order in all standard gauges, bbl. lengths, boring and other specifications. Made as a field gun, pigeon and wildfowl gun, skeet gun or trap gun. Manufactured prior to World War II.
12 ga.
w/double triggers ...... NiB $26,906 Ex $21,525 Gd $14,637
20 ga.
w/double triggers ...... NiB $30,516 Ex $24,412 Gd $16,600

(cont'd.) BEST QUALITY HAMMERLESS DOUBLE
28 ga.
w/double triggers ...... NiB $37,731 Ex $30,187 Gd $20,527
.410 ga.
w/double triggers ...... NiB $42,656 Ex $34,125 Gd $23,205
W/selective single trigger, add 5%

BEST QUALITY O/U SHOTGUN
Sidelock. Automatic ejectors. Double triggers or single trigger. Built to order in all standard gauges, bbl. lengths, boring and other specifications, including Special Trap Grade with vent rib. Woodward introduced this type of gun in 1908. Made until World War II.
12 ga.
w/double triggers ...... NiB $29,531 Ex $23,425 Gd $16,065
20 ga.
w/double triggers ...... NiB $39,703 Ex $31,762 Gd $21,598
28 ga.
w/double triggers ...... NiB $52,172 Ex $41,737 Gd $28,381
.410 ga.
w/double triggers .... NiB $59,062 Ex $47,250+ Gd $32,130
W/single trigger, add 5%

BEST QUALITY SINGLE-SHOT TRAP........ NiB $12,406 Ex $9925 Gd $6749
Sidelock. Mechanical features of the O/U gun. Vent rib bbl. 12 ga. only. Built to customer's specifications and measurements, including type and amount of checkering, carving and engraving. Made prior to World War II.

ZEPHYR SHOTGUNS — Manufactured by Victor Sarasqueta Company, Eibar, Spain

MODEL 1 O/U
SHOTGUN .... NiB $1156 Ex $925 Gd $629
Same general specifications as Field Model O/U except with more elaborate engraving, finer wood and checkering. Imported by Stoeger 1930s-51.

MODEL 2 O/U
SHOTGUN .... NiB $1516 Ex $1212 Gd $824
Sidelock. Auto ejectors. Gauges: 12, 16, 20, 28 and .410. Bbls.: 25 to 30 inches most common. Modest scroll engraving on receiver and sideplates. Checkered, straight-grain select walnut buttstock and forend. Imported by Stoeger 1930s-51.

MODEL 3 O/U SHOTGUN .... NiB $2093 Ex $1674 Gd $1139
Same general specifications as Zephyr Model 2 O/U except with more elaborate engraving, finer wood and checkering. Imported by Stoeger 1930s-51.

SHOTGUNS

Zephyr Crown, Premier and Royal Grades

MODEL 400E FIELD GRADE DOUBLE-BARREL SHOTGUN
Anson & Deeley boxlock system. Gauges: 12 16, 20, 28 and .410. Bbls.: 25 to 30 inches. Weight: 4.5 lbs. (.410) to 6.25 lbs. (12 ga.). Checkered French walnut buttstock and forearm. Modest scroll engraving on bbls., receiver and trigger guard. Imported by Stoeger 1930s-50s.

12, 16 or 20 ga.	NiB $1366 Ex $1092 Gd $742
28 or .410 ga.	NiB $1538 Ex $1230 Gd $836
W/selective single trigger, add	$200

MODEL 401 E SKEET GRADE DOUBLE-BARREL SHOTGUN
Same general specifications as Field Grade except with beavertail forearm. Bbls.: 25 to 28 inches. Imported by Stoeger 1930s-50s.

12, 16 or 20 ga.	NiB $1631 Ex $1305 Gd $887
28 or .410 ga.	NiB $1794 Ex $1435 Gd $976
W/selective single trigger, add	$350
W/nonselective single trigger, add	$250

MODEL 402E DELUXE
DOUBLE-BARREL SHOTGUN . . NiB $2078 Ex $1662 Gd $1130
Same general specifications as Model 400E Field Grade except for custom refinements. The action was carefully hand-honed for smoother operation; finer, elaborate engraving throughout, plus higher quality wood in stock and forearm. Imported by Stoeger 1930s-50s.

CROWN GRADE . . . . NiB $1484 Ex $1187 Gd $807
Boxlock. Gauges: 12, 16, 20, 28 and .410. Bbls.: 25 to 30 inches standard but any lengths could be ordered. Weight: 6 lbs., 4 oz. (.410) to 7 lbs., 4 oz. (12 ga.). Checkered Spanish walnut stock and beavertail forearm. Receiver engraved with scroll patterns. Imported by Stoeger 1938-51.

FIELD MODEL
O/U SHOTGUN . . . . NiB $725 Ex $580 Gd $395
Anson & Deeley boxlock. Auto ejectors. Gauges: 12, 16 and 20. Bbls.: 25 to 30 inches standard- full-length matt rib. Double triggers. Checkered buttstock and forend. Light scroll engraving on receiver. Imported by Stoeger 1930s-51.

HONKER SINGLE-SHOT SHOTGUN . . . . . NiB $495 Ex $396 Gd $269
Sidelock. Gauge: 10; 3.5-inch magnum. 36-inch vent rib barrel w/F choke. Weight: 10.5 lbs. Checkered select Spanish walnut buttstock and beavertail forend; recoil pad. Imported by Stoeger 1950s-72.

PINEHURST
DOUBLE-BARREL SHOTGUN . . . . NiB $1063 Ex $850 Gd $578
Boxlock. Gauges: 12, 16, 20, 28 and .410. Bbls.: 25 to 28 inches most common. Checkered, select walnut buttstock and forend. Selective single trigger and auto ejectors. Imported by Stoeger 1950s-72.

PREMIER GRADE
DOUBLE-BARREL SHOTGUN . . . . NiB $2306 Ex $1845 Gd $1254
Sidelock. Gauges: 12, 16, 20, 28 and .410. Bbls.: Any length, but 25 to 30 inches most popular. Weight: 4.5 lbs. (.410) to 7 lbs. (12 ga.). Checkered high-grade French walnut buttstock and forend. Imported by Stoeger 1930s-51.

ROYAL GRADE
DOUBLE-BARREL SHOTGUN . . . . NiB $3556 Ex $2845 Gd $1935
Same general specifications as the Premier Grade except with more elaborate engraving, finer checkering and wood. Imported by Stoeger 1930s-51.

STERLINGWORTH II
DOUBLE-BARREL SHOTGUN . . . . . NiB $894 Ex $715 Gd $486
Genuine sidelocks with color-casehardened sideplates. Gauges: 12, 16, 20 and .410. Bbls.: 25 to 30 inches. Weight: 6 lbs., 4 oz. (.410) to 7 lbs., 4 oz. (12 ga.). Select Spanish walnut buttstock and beavertail forearm. Light scroll engraving on receiver and sideplates. Automatic, sliding-tang safety. Imported by Stoeger 1950s-72.

THUNDERBIRD
DOUBLE-BARREL SHOTGUN . . . . NiB $895 Ex $716 Gd $487
Sidelock. Gauges: 12 and 10 Magnum. Bbls.: 32-inch, both F choke. Weight: 8 lbs., 8 oz. (12 ga.), 12 lbs. (10 ga.). Receiver elaborately engraved with waterfowl scenes. Checkered select Spanish walnut buttstock and beavertail forend. Plain extractors, double triggers. Imported by Stoeger 1950-72.

UPLAND KING
DOUBLE-BARREL SHOTGUN . . . NiB $1040 Ex $832 Gd $566
Sidelock. Gauges: 12, 16, 20, 28 and .410. Bbls.: 25 to 28 inches most popular. Checkered buttstock and forend of select walnut. Selective single trigger and auto ejectors. Imported by Stoeger 1950-72.

UPLANDER 4E
DOUBLE-BARREL SHOTGUN . . . . NiB $844 Ex $675 Gd $459
Same general specifications as the Zephyr Sterlingworth II except with selective auto ejectors and highly polished sideplates. Imported by Stoeger 1951-72.

WOODLANDER II
DOUBLE-BARREL SHOTGUN . . . . NiB $591 Ex $472 Gd $321
Boxlock. Gauges: 12, 20 and .410. Bbls.: 25 to 30 inches. Weight: 6 lbs., 4 oz. (.410) to 7 lbs., 4 oz. (12 ga.). Checkered Spanish walnut stock and beavertail forearm. Engraved receiver. Imported by Stoeger 1950-72.

Angelo Zoli — Patricia Side-by Side

ANGELO ZOLI —
Mississauga, Ontario, Canada

ALLEY CLEANER
S/S SHOTGUN . . . . **NiB $619 Ex $495 Gd $336**
Gauges: 12 and 20. 20-inch bbl. 26.5 inches overall. Weight: 7 lbs. average. Chokes: F/M, F, IM, M, IC, SK. Chrome-lined barrels. Walnut stock and engraved action. Made 1986-87.

APACHE O/U FIELD SHOTGUN
Gauge: 12. Chokes: F/M, F, IM, M, IC and stock fixed or tubes. 20-inch bbl. Short vent rib. Weight: 7.5 lbs. Checkered walnut stock and forearm. Lever action. Pistol grip. Made 1986-88.
Apache w/fixed chokes . . . . **NiB $416 Ex $332 Gd $226**
Apache w/choke tubes . . . . **NiB $504 Ex $403 Gd $274**

DAINO I AND II
FOLDING SINGLE SHOT
Gauges: 12, 20 and .410. 28- or 30-inch bbl. Weight: 6 lbs. average. Choke: Full. Chrome-lined barrel, vent rib. Pistol-grip walnut stock. Engraved action. Made 1986-88.
Daino I w/top lever . . . . **NiB $148 Ex $118 Gd $80**
Daino II w/bottom lever . . . . **NiB $160 Ex $128 Gd $87**

HK 2000 SEMIAUTO-
MATIC SHOTGUN . . . . **NiB $656 Ex $525 Gd $357**
Gauge: 12. Five shot capacity. Bbls.: 24-, 26-, 28- and 30-inch; vent rib. Weight: 6.5 to 7.5 lbs. Checkered walnut stock and forearm. Glossy finish. Pistol grip. Engraved receiver. Made 1988.

PATRICIA
SIDE-BY-SIDE SHOTGUNS . . . . . **NiB $1300 Ex $1040 Gd $707**
Gauge: .410 only. 28-inch bbl. Choke: F/M. Weight: 5.5 lbs. Automatic ejectors; Zoli single selective trigger, box lock. Hand-checkered walnut stock with English straight grip, splinter forearm. Made 1986-88.

SAINT GEORGE
O/U COMPETITION . . . . **NiB $1907 Ex $1525 Gd $1037**
Gauge: 12. 30- and 32-inch vent rib barrels. Weight: 8 lbs. Single selective trigger. Oil-finished, pistol-grip walnut stock. Made 1986-88.

SILVER SNIPE
O/U SHOTGUN . . . . **NiB $585 Ex $468 Gd $318**
Purdey-type box lock with crossbolt. Selective single trigger. Gauges: 12, 20; 3-inch chambers. Bbls.: 26-, 28- or 30-inch with a variety of choke combinations. Weight: 5.75 to 6.75 lbs. Checkered European walnut buttstock and forend. Made in Italy.

Z43 STANDARD
O/U SHOTGUN . . . . **NiB $398 Ex $318 Gd $216**
Gauge: 12 or 20. 26-, 28- or 30-inch bbls. Chokes: F/M, M/IC Weight: 6.75 to 8 lbs. vent lateral ribs, standard extractors, single non-selective trigger. Glossy-finished walnut stock and forearm. Automatic safety. Made 1986-88.

ANTONIO ZOLI, U.S.A., INC. — Fort Wayne, Indiana, Manufactured in Italy

SILVER FALCON
O/U . . . . **NiB $1132 Ex $906 Gd $616**
Gauges: 12 and 20; 3-inch chambers. 26- or 28-inch blued barrels. Weight: 6.25 to 7.25 lbs. Antiqued silver finish on receiver. Pistol-grip stock of Turkish Circassian walnut with polyurethane-type finish. Imported 1989-1990.

UPLANDER
SIDE/SIDE SHOTGUN . . . . **NiB $744 Ex $595 Gd $405**
Gauges: 12 and 20. Casehardened receiver. Checkered oil-finished, hand-rubbed stock of Turkish Circassian walnut; splinter forend. Imported 1989-90.

Index

INDEX

INDEX

INDEX

INDEX

SHOTGUNS

INDEX

REVELATION SHOTGUNS — *See Western Auto listings*

RG REVOLVERS
Model 23, 136
Model 38S, 136

RICHLAND ARMS COMPANY
Model 200 Field Grade Double, 529
Model 202 All-Purpose Field Gun, 529
Model 707 Deluxe Field Gun, 529
Model 711 Long Range Waterfowl Magnum, 529
Model 808 Over/Under Gun, 529

RIGBY, John & Company
RIFLES
Model 275 Lightweight Magazine Rifle, 331
Model 275 Magazine Sporting Rifle, 331
Model 350 Magnum Magazine Sporting Rifle, 331
Model 416 Big Game Magazine Sporting Rifle, 331
Best Quality Hammerless Ejector, 331
Second Quality Hammerless Ejector, 331
Third Quality Hammerless Ejector, 331
SHOTGUNS
Hammerless Box Lock Double Barrel Shotguns, 530
Hammerless Side Lock Double-Barrel Shotguns, 530

ROSS RIFLE CO
Model 1910 Bolt-Action Sporting Rifle , 331

ROSSI, Amadeo, S.A.
REVOLVERS
Model 31 DA, 136
Model 51 DA, 136
Model 68, 136
Model 84 DA, 136
Model 85, 136
Model 88 DA, 136
Model 88/2 DA, 136
Model 89 DA, 136
Model 94 DA, 137
Model 95 (951), 137
Models 351/352 Revolvers, 137
Models 461/462 Revolvers, 137
Model 511 DA, 137
Model 515 DA, 137
Model 518 DA, 137
Model 677 DA, 137
Model 720 DA, 137
Model 841 DA, 137
Model 851 DA, 137
Model 877 DA, 137
Model 941 DA, 137
Model 951 DA, 137
Model 971 DA, 137
Model 971 VRC DA, 137
Cyclops DA, 137
DA Revolver, 137
Sportsman's 22, 137
RIFLES
62 Gallery Model SAC Carbine, 331
62 Gallery Model Magnum, 331
62 Gallery Model Slide-Action Repeater, 332
Lever-Action 65/92 Carbine, 332
SHOTGUNS
Hammerless Double-Barrel Shotgun, 530
Overland Hammer Double, 530

ROTTWEIL SHOTGUNS
Model 72 Over/Under Shotgun, 530
Model 650 Field Over/Under Shotgun, 530
American Skeet, 530
International Trap Shotgun, 530

RUBY PISTOL
7.65mm Automatic Pistol, 137

RUGER
AUTOMATIC/SINGLE-SHOT PISTOLS
Hawkeye Single-Shot Pistol, 138
Mark I Target Model, 138
Mark II Automatic Pistol, 138
Mark II 22/45 Automatic Pistol, 138
Mark II Bull Barrel Model, 138
Mark II Government Model, 138
Mark II Target Model, 138
Model P-85 Automatic Pistol, 139
Model P-89 Automatic Pistol, 139
Model P-89 DAC/DAO Auto Pistols, 139
Model P-90, KP90 DA, 139
Model P-91 DA Automatic Pistol, 139
Model P-93 Compact Auto Pistol, 139
Model P-94 Automatic Pistol, 139
Model P-95 Automatic Pistol, 140
Model P-97 Automatic Pistol, 140
Standard Model Automatic Pistol, 140

REVOLVERS
Bearcat SA (Old Model), 140
Bearcat, Super, 141
Bisley SA Revolver, Large Frame, 141
Bisley Single-Six Revolver, Small Frame, 141
Blackhawk SA Flat-Top (Old Model) Revolver, 141
Blackhawk SA Convertible, 141
Blackhawk SA Revolver, 141
GP-100 DA, 141
New Model Bearcat, 141
New Model Blackhawk Convertible, 141
New Model Blackhawk SA, 141
New Model Single-Six SSM, 142
New Model Super Blackhawk SA, 142
New Model Super Single-Six Convertible, 142
Police Service-Six, 142
Redhawk DA Revolver, 143
Super Redhawk Stainless DA Scope-Ring Revolver, 143
Security-Six DA Revolver, 143
Single-Six SA Revolver (Old Model), 143
Single-Six Lightweight, 143
SP101 DA, 143
Speed-Six DA, 143
Super Blackhawk SA 44 Mag. Revolver (Old Model), 144
Vaquero SA, 144
RIFLES
Number One (1) Light Sporter, 332
Number One (1) Medium Sporter, 332
Number One (1) "North Americans" Presentation Rifle, 332
Number One (1) RSI International Single-Shot Rifle, 332
Number One (1) Special Varminter, 332
Number One (1) Standard Rifle, 332
Number One (1) Tropical Rifle, 332
Number Three (3) Single-Shot Carbine, 332
Model 10/22 Autoloading Carbine, 334
Model 44 Autoloading Carbine, 334
Model 77 Bolt-Action Rifle, 334
Model 77 Mark II All-Weather Rifle, 334
Model 77 Mark II Bolt-Action Rifle, 335
Model 77/22 Hornet Bolt-Action Rifle, 335
Model 77/22 Rimfire Bolt-Action Rifle, 335
Model 77/44 Bolt-Action, 336
Model 96 Lever Action Carbine, 336
Mini-14 Semiautomatic Rifle, 336
Mini-Thirty (30) Autoloader, 336
PC Series Semiautomatic Carbines, 336
SHOTGUNS
Red Label Plain Grade Over/Under, 531
Red Label Over/Under All Weather Stainless, 531
Red Label "Woodside" Over/Under, 531
Red Label Sporting Clays Over/Under Stainless, 531
Red Label Special Edition - Wildlife Forever, 531

RUSSIAN
SERVICE PISTOLS
Model 30 Tokarev Service, 144
Model PM Makarov, 144
MILITARY RIFLES
Model 1891 Mosin Military Rifle, 338
Tokarev Model 40 Semiautomatic Military Rifle, 338

SAKO
HANDGUNS
22-32 Olympic Pistol, 144
RIFLES
Model 72, 338
Model 73 Lever-Action Rifle, 338
Model 74 Carbine, 338
Model 74 Heavy Barrel Rifle, Long Action, 338
Model 74 Heavy Barrel Rifle, Medium Action, 338
Model 74 Heavy Barrel Rifle, Short Action, 338
Model 74 Super Sporter, Long Action, 338
Model 74 Super Sporter, Medium Action, 338
Model 74 Super Sporter, Short Action, 338
Model 75 Deluxe, 338
Model 75 Hunter, 338
Model 75 Stainless Synthetic, 338
Model 75 Varmint Rifle, 338
Model 78 Super Hornet Sporter, 338
Model 78 Super Rimfire Sporter, 338
Classic Bolt-Action Rifle, 338
Deluxe Grade AI, 340
Deluxe Grade AII, 340
Deluxe Grade AIII, 340
Deluxe Lightweight Bolt-Action Rifle, 340
Fiberclass Bolt-Action Rifle, 340
Finnbear Carbine, 340
Finnbear Sporter, 340
Finnfire Bolt-Action Rifle, 340

Finnwolf Lever-Action Rifle, 340
Finsport 2700, 341
Forester Carbine, 341
Forester Heavy Barrel, 341
Forester Sporter, 341
Golden Anniversary Model, 341
High-Power Mauser Sporting Rifle, 341
Hunter Lightweight Bolt-Action Rifle, 341
Laminated Stock Bolt-Action Rifles, 341
Magnum Mauser, 341
Mannlicher-Style Carbine, 341
Safari Grade, 341
Sporter Deluxe, 341
Standard Grade AI, 342
Standard Grade AII, 342
Standard Grade AIII, 342
Super Deluxe Rifle, 342
TRG Bolt-Action Target Rifle, 342
TRG-S Bolt-Action Rifle, 342
Vixen Carbine, 342
Vixen Heavy Barrel, 342
Vixen Sporter, 342

SARASQUETA, S. A.
Model 3 Hammerless Boxlock Double-Barrel SG, 531
Hammerless Sidelock Doubles, 532
Model 4 & 4E, 532
Model 6E, 532
Model 7E, 532
Model 10E, 532
Model 11E, 532
Model 12E, 532
Model 203 & 203E, 532

SAUER HANDGUNS — *See listings under Hawes and Sig Sauer*
1913 Pocket, 145
1930 Pocket, 145
Model 38H DA, 145
Pocket 25, 145
Single-Action Revolvers — *See Listings under Hawes*

SAUER, J.P., & Sohn
RIFLES
Mauser Bolt-Action Sporting Rifle, 343
Model S-90 Bolt-Action Rifles, 343
Model 200 Bolt-Action Rifles, 343
Model 202 Bolt-Action Rifles, 343
SHOTGUNS
Model 66 Over/Under Field Gun, 532
Model 66 Over/Under Skeet Gun, 532
Model 66 Over/Under Trap Gun, 532
Model 3000E Drilling, 532
Artemis Double-Barrel Shotgun, 533
BBF 54 Over/Under Combination Rifle/Shotgun, 533
Royal Double-Barrel Shotguns, 533

SAVAGE ARMS
PISTOLS
Model 101 SA, 145
Model 501/502 "Striker" Series Pistols, 145
Model 510/516 "Striker" Series Pistols, 145
Model 1907, 145
Model 1910, 146
Model 1915, 146
Model 1917, 146
U.S. Army Test Model 1910, 146
RIFLES
Model 3 Bolt-Action Single-Shot Rifle, 343
Model 3S, 343
Model 3ST, 343
Model 4 Bolt-Action Repeater, 344
Model 4M, 344
Model 4S, 344
Model 5 Bolt-Action Repeater, 344
Model 5S, 344
Model 6 Autoloading Rifle, 344
Model 6S, 344
Model 7 Autoloading Rifle, 344
Model 7S, 344
Model 19 Bolt-Action Target Rifle, 344
Model 19 NRA Bolt-Action Match Rifle, 345
Model 19H, 345
Model 19L, 345
Model 19M, 345
Model 20-1926 Hi-Power, 345
Model 23A Bolt-Action Sporting Rifle, 345
Model 23AA, 345
Model 23B, 345
Model 23C, 345
Model 23D, 345
Model 25 Slide-Action Repeater, 345

INDEX